EMERGING MARKET OF RUSSIA

SOURCEBOOK FOR INVESTMENT
AND TRADE

SUBSCRIPTION NOTICE

This Wiley product is updated on a periodic basis with supplements to reflect important changes in the subject matter. If you purchased this product directly from John Wiley & Sons, Inc., we have already recorded your subscription for this update service.

If, however, you purchased this product from a bookstore and wish to receive (1) the current update at no additional charge, and (2) future updates and revised or related volumes billed separately with a 30-day examination review, please send your name, company name (if applicable), address, and the title of the product to:

Supplement Department
John Wiley & Sons, Inc.
One Wiley Drive
Somerset, NJ 08875
1-800-225-5945

For customers outside the United States, please contact the Wiley office nearest you:

Professional & Reference Division
John Wiley & Sons Canada, Ltd.
22 Worcester Road
Rexdale, Ontario M9W 1L1
CANADA
(416) 675-3580
1-800-567-4797
FAX (416) 675-6599

John Wiley & Sons, Ltd.
Baffins Lane
Chichester
West Sussex, PO19 1UD
UNITED KINGDOM
(44) (243) 779777

Jacaranda Wiley Ltd.
PRT Division
P.O. Box 174
North Ryde, NSW 2113
AUSTRALIA
(02) 805-1100
FAX (02) 805-1597

John Wiley & Sons (SEA) Pte. Ltd.
37 Jalan Pemimpin
Block B # 05-04
Union Industrial Building
SINGAPORE 2057
(65) 258-1157

EMERGING MARKET OF RUSSIA

SOURCEBOOK FOR INVESTMENT AND TRADE

VLADIMIR L. KVINT

Editor

JACQUELINE GALLUS

Associate Editor

JOHN WILEY & SONS, INC.

New York • Chichester • Weinheim • Brisbane • Singapore • Toronto

ADVISORY BOARD

Dr. Oleg D. Davydov
Former Vice Prime Minister and Minister of Foreign
Economic Relations of Russia

Dr. Viktor I. Danilov-Danilian
Chairman of the State Committee for the Protection of the Environment of Russia

Dr. Alexander G. Granberg
Chairman, Council for Location of Productive Forces and
Economic Cooperation with Ministry of Economics of Russia
Chairman, Russian National Committee for Pacific Rim Economic Cooperation

J. Donald Hanson
Andersen Worldwide

James R.S. Hatt
Chairman, President, CEO
PLD Telekom, Inc.

Hans J. Horn
Arthur Andersen

Gordon J. Humphrey
United States Senator (1979–1991)

Dr. Vladimir L. Kvint
Editor-in-Chief
Arthur Andersen
Professor, Fordham University

Ambassador Sergey V. Lavrov
Permanent Representative of the Russian Federation to the United Nations

Richard L. Measelle
Arthur Andersen

Dr. J. Mark Mobius
President of Templeton Emerging Markets Fund

Dr. Ernest J. Scalberg
Dean of Graduate School of Business
Fordham University

Manuel Soto
Arthur Andersen

Lawrence A. Weinbach
Andersen Worldwide

Jacqueline E. Gallus
Assistant Editor
Executive Secretary to the Advisory Board

ABOUT THE EDITOR

Dr. Vladimir L. Kvint is Director of Economic Consulting For Emerging Markets, with Arthur Andersen. Dr. Kvint is a Professor of Management Systems and International Business at Fordham University's Graduate School of Business, and sits on boards for several companies in emerging markets. He is a specialist on worldwide emerging markets and has helped start a number of successful international ventures with leading global investment and industrial companies. He conducts market and feasibility studies in a wide variety of industries, provides strategic investment analysis, develops economic and political forecasts, and provides operational support.

A frequent contributor to *Forbes* and *Harvard Business Review,* Dr. Kvint has authored seven award-winning books, coauthored six others, and written over 250 articles. His most recent books include *The Barefoot Shoemaker: Capitalizing on the New Russia,* and *Creating and Managing International Joint Ventures.* He holds a lifetime membership in the Russian Academy of Natural Sciences and The Bretton Woods Committee. Dr. Kvint is an Honorary Fellow of the New England Center for International and Regional Studies, and holds a Doctorate of Science in Economics, Ph.D. in Managerial Economics, Doctorate of Humane Letters, honoris causa, and a Masters of Science in Mining Electrical Engineering.

CONTRIBUTORS

Dr. Aleko A. Adamescu is a member of the Russian Academy of Economics and Business and Deputy Chairman of the Council for the Location of Productive Forces and Economic Cooperation.

Parry Aftab is a partner with Aftab & Savitt, New York and New Jersey, and the representative of the Moscow Legal Center of the Moscow City government.

Yuri V. Akhremenko is the trade representative of the Russian Federation in the United States.

Dr. Sergey S. Alekseev is the Director of the Institute of Civil Law and a corresponding member of the Russian Academy of Sciences.

Natasha Alexeeva is an associate with Patterson, Belknap, Webb & Tyler LLP.

Sergey N. Almasov is the Director of Federal Tax Police Service of Russia.

Scott C. Antel is with Arthur Andersen.

Dr. Andrei A. Auzan is the President of the Confederation of the Consumers Associations of Russia.

Vladimir S. Babichev is Federal Minister and the Chief of Staff for the Prime Minister.

Baker & McKenzie is an internationally recognized law firm.

Eugene A. Baranov is the Deputy Trade Representative, Commercial Counsul of the Consultate General of the Russian Federation in the United States.

Konstantin V. Bazarkin is with Most-Bank, Moscow.

Rita Berlin is an associate at the law office of Sandra G. Levitt in New York City, a firm specializing in all areas of immigration and nationality.

Sergiy Bezsmertny is the Chairman of the Moscow Investment Corporation of the Moscow City Government.

Leonid A. Bochin is the former Chairman of the State Anti-Monopoly Committee.

Dr. Mikhail M. Boguslavskiy is the leading fellow, and researcher at the Institute of State and Law of the Russian Academy of Sciences.

Boris S. Bolotsky is with the Ministry of the Interior.

Dr. Vladimir B. Bulgak is the Deputy Prime Minister of Russia.

Yuri S. Bugaev is the former Chairman of the Federal Service for Surveillance of Insurance Activity.

Andrei E. Bugrov is the Russian Executive Director for the World Bank.

Eileen Cassidy is the Acting Assistant Administrator and Director for the Office of International Trade, U.S. Small Business Administration.

Dr. Viktor I. Danilov-Danilian is the Chairman of the State Committee for the Protection of the Environment of Russia.

Dr. Oleg D. Davydov is a former Deputy Prime Minister of Russia.

Dr. Sergey K. Dubinin is the Chairman of the Central Bank of the Russian Federation.

Pavel Efremkin is the Chairman and CEO of Supco Corporation.

Dr. Vladimir E. Fortov is Federal Minister of Science and Technologies.

Jacqueline E. Gallus is Executive Secretary to the Editorial Board at Arthur Andersen.

Dr. Gadji G. Gamzatov is a member of the Russian Academy of Science.

Dr. Stoyan D. Ganev is the President of the 47th General Assembly of the UN and Former Minister of Foreign Affairs, Bulgaria.

Dr. Jeffery L. Geller is with Independent Research Associates.

Dr. Arkadiy S. Golubkov is the former Chairman of the Committee on Information Policy under the president of Russia.

Aleksey A. Goroholinsky is the head of the Department of Ministry of Economics.

Dr. Alexander G. Granberg is a member of the Russian Academy of Sciences, Chairman of the Council for the Location of Productive Forces and Economic Cooperation (CDPFEC) with the Ministry of Economics, and a former state advisor to President Boris Yeltsin.

Joseph J. Grandmaison is the Director for the U.S. Trade and Development Agency in Russia.

Anne Grey is the Director of BISNIS, U.S. Department of Commerce.

Alexei S. Gumilevski

Vladimir V. Gusev is the former Chairman of the State Taxation Services.

Ruth Harkin is the former President and CEO of the Overseas Private Investment Corporation.

Viktor N. Hklystun is the Federal Minister of Agriculture and Food of Russia.

Hans J. Horn is a managing partner with Arthur Andersen, Commonwealth of Independent States.

Sergey V. Ivanenko is Deputy Chairman of the State Committee on State Property Management.

Jan H. Kalicki is counselor for the U.S. Department of Commerce and the U.S. Ombudsman for energy and commercial cooperation with Russia and the New Independent States.

Dr. Alexander P. Kalinin is with the Ministry of the Interior.

Alfred R. Kokh is former Deputy Prime Minister and Chairman of the State Committee on State Property Management.

Alexander S. Kolesnikov is Deputy Chairman of the Federal Commission on Securities and Capital Market.

Andrey A. Konoplianik is an advisor to the Ministry of Fuel and Energy, consultant to the Ministry of Finance and Committee on Economic Policy of the Duma.

Mikhail U. Kopeykin is the head of the Department of Economics of Prime Minister Chernomyrdin's office.

Dr. Vladimir V. Kossov is Deputy Minister of Economics of Russia.

Andrei L. Kostin is a Chairman of Vnesheconombank.

Dr. Yuri A. Kotlyar is the former First Deputy Chairman of the Committee of Precious Metals and Stones.

Dr. Valentin A. Kovalev, J.D., is a professor and former Minister of Justice of Russia.

Dr. Yuri A. Kovalev is the Sector Head of the Council for the Location of Productive Forces and Economic Cooperation.

Vladimir Krouglyak is the President of the Ingosstrakh Joint Stock Insurance Company.

Dr. Y. A. Kudimov

Gennadiy O. Kuranov is the Chief of the Macroeconomics Forecasting Department in the Ministry of Economics.

Ambassador Sergey V. Lavrov is the Permanent Representative of the Russian Federation to the United Nations.

Oleg N. Lobov is the former Deputy Prime Minister and a former Executive Secretary of the Security Council of Russia.

Igor Lojevsky is the Director of Finance, Yukos, America, Inc.

Vladimir P. Lukin is a member of the Duma and Chairman of the Committee for International Affairs.

Elena Lytkina is with Arthur Andersen.

Dr. Mogamed Magomedhanov is a researcher at the Daghestan branch of the Russian Academy of Sciences.

Vitaliy B. Malkin is the President of Rossiyskiy Kredit Bank, Moscow.

Dr. Yevgeni N. Malyshev is the President of the Academy of Mining Sciences, corresponding member of the Russian Academy of Sciences, and General Director of Rossugol (state company for production of coal).

Dr. Gennadiy G. Melikian is Federal Minister of Labor and Social Development.

Viktor N. Mihaylov is Federal Minister of Nuclear Power.

Dennis Montz is a specialist with the Office of International Trade, U.S. Small Business Administration.

Dr. Sergey L. Morozov is the CEO and Chairman of the Board of ELBIM Bank, Moscow.

Dmitri L. Mozgin is the head of the Custody Department at Vneshtorgbank, Moscow.

Dr. Andrei A. Nechaev is the President of the Russian State Financial Corporation and the former Minister of Economics.

Yuri A. Nisnevich is a member of the Duma.

Tatiana Orobeiko is with Arthur Andersen.

Dr. Valeriy Oreshkin is the Director of the Russian International Market Research Institute (Vniki).

Dr. Vladimir S. Ovchinsky is Head of the Department, Ministry of the Interior.

Dr. Deborah A. Palmieri is President and CEO of the Russian-American Chamber of Commerce.

Vladimir G. Panskov is the former Minister of Finance and First Deputy Minister of Economics.

Peter Pettibone is a partner with Patterson, Belknap, Webb & Tyler LLP, New York.

Yuri D. Poroykov is the First Deputy Director General of ITAR-TASS News Agency.

Yevgeni M. Primakov is the Federal Minister of Foreign Affairs of Russia.

Tatiana M. Regent is the Head of the Department of Migration, Ministry of Labor and Social Development.

Vladimir I. Resin is the First Deputy Prime Minister of Moscow City Government.

Barbara Ristau is a staff member of BISNIS, U.S. Department of Commerce.

S.B. Romazin is a member of the State Counsel of Justice, Ministry of Justice.

Thomas D. Sanford is Vice President of The Bank of New York.

Dr. Mikhail Sarafanov is Deputy Minister of the Foreign Economic Relations and Trade of Russia.

Valeriy M. Serov is Deputy Prime Minister of Russia.

Dr. E. Serova is a member of the Duma.

Nikolai V. Sevrugin is the former Governor of the Tula Oblast.

Emilia Sherifova is with the University of Bridgeport.

Dr. Irina Shin is with Independent Research Associates.

Dr. Vyacheslav F. Shumeyko is the former Chairman of the Council of Federation of the Russian Parliament.

Dr. Sergey A. Smirnov is the President of the Chamber of Commerce and Industry of the Russian Federation.

Sergey S. Sobynin is the Speaker of the Duma of the Autonomous Okrug of Khanty-Mansi.

Vadim Solovyov is the Investment Officer of the Europe Department, International Finance Corporation.

E. Vivian Spathopoulos is Deputy Director for Europe for the American Business Centers, U.S. Department of Commerce, International Trade Administration.

Michael A. Tappan is the Chairman of Ward Howell Russia, Inc., and serves on the board of the Advisory Council of the International Executive Service Corps.

Dr. Alexander N. Troshin is former Deputy Executive Secretary of the Security Council of Russia.

Dr. Dmitri V. Tulin is Chairman of the Board Vneshtorgbank.

Dr. Kapitolina E. Turbina is former Deputy Chairman of the Federal Service for Surveillance of Insurance Activity.

Georgy Urjuzhnikov is the Managing Director of Ingo, Inc., New York.

Arkadiy I. Volskiy is the President of the Russian Union of Industrialists and Entrepreneurs.

Vitali B. Yefimov is the former Minister of Transportation.

Dr. I. A. Zakharchenkov

Dr. Bella Zlatkis is the head of the Department of Ministry of Finance.

PREFACE

Since December 1991, the map of the global business world has changed. This period has been marked by the dissolution of the Soviet Union, which resulted in the appearance of 15 independent countries. Russia, one of the newly emerged states, is currently the largest country by territory in the world, is ranked sixth in terms of population (which is highly educated), and has tremendous natural resources. Russia, however, is short of capital and its outstanding production facilities lack of market-oriented management, marketing, and twenty-first-century technology.

Over the past five years, Russia has made some significant progress, adopting a democratically oriented political system, a mostly market-oriented economy, and all the major capitalist institutions. Furthermore, Russia's postcommunist laws and regulations differ substantially from those of the *communist* Soviet Union.

The global business world faces tremendous difficulties in understanding all the changes taking place in Russia. This problem is mainly due to the lack of objective and accurate information about the similarities and differences between modern Russia on one side, and the United States and other developed countries on the other. Numerous publications on this subject make it difficult for readers to get *correct* information and first-hand opinions about the subject. As you are reading this, thousands of entrepreneurs, executives, economists, and politicians are trying to contact decision makers, top-level analysts, and consultants in Russia, in order to get advice and guidance on conducting business with and within Russia. Business executives are vitally interested in learning with whom they should meet, and whom to consult on investment and trade transactions. All of these issues brought us to the conclusion that this unusual encyclopedic sourcebook is needed to encourage and facilitate the internationalization of Russia.

This book is unique, primarily because of its authors and contributors. It provides first-hand information directly from the actual decision makers, including current and former members of the Russian government, representatives of multilateral institutions, and authorities from the U.S. government and quasi-governmental institutions. These authors have years of experience in the preservation and promotion of the U.S.-Russian cooperation. Furthermore, the book gives opinions of top-level experts and analysts from Russia, the United States, and some European countries, on the internationalization of Russian business. The second part of the book provides a detailed analysis of political, economic, and business systems in modern Russia, and answers questions regarding the political and economic risks of investment in and the problems of international trade with this country. Finally, this book contains a specific description of Russian macro-and microeconomics, and describes the levels of development of all capitalist domestic and foreign institutions cooperating with or established in Russia.

We have divided this book into the following sections:

1. General Information, which contains an economic history of Russia, its geographical, cultural, language, and religious characteristics, and the technological and industrial structure of the Russian economy
2. Political Structure, Government, and Administration
3. Economic Structure
4. Financial System
5. Business Environment
6. Legal System
7. Foreign Trade and Investment
8. Tax System
9. Regional Economies
10. Infrastructure

This book is especially designed for business executives and entrepreneurs that are already doing business with Russia or who are seriously considering opportunities within this market. Furthermore, this book is of extreme importance to decision makers and analysts with financial and banking institutions, as well as those involved in various service and industrial companies. As this book covers the Russian political system and contains analyses of the country's political and economic environments, it gives an insight into the Russian Federation, useful not only for business people, but also for political leaders, political scientists, and students majoring in international business, international economics, or political science. Furthermore, the economic and business relationships of European Union and Pacific Rim countries with Russia described in this book should attract the attention of leaders and entrepreneurs from these areas of the world, and of U.S. investors.

To our readers: My ultimate goal for this book has been to collect opinions from top-level experts, government leaders, and business executives and to share their knowledge under a single cover so as to give the reader a richer portrayal of Russian business. Though their points of view sometimes conflict, their incongruities only mirror the contradictions inherent in Russian business life. I am happy with the results, even if they took longer than expected, but as always, the readers are the final judges.

Dr. Vladimir L. Kvint
Editor-in-Chief

ACKNOWLEDGMENTS

I wish to thank our advisors for their support and the individuals who helped collect and edit the articles in this book, especially Dr. Olga I. Blinkova, Dr. Oleg Davydov, Ambassador Sergey V. Lavrov, Dr. Alexander G. Granberg, Igor A. Korotin and Dr. Alexander N. Shohin. I am thankful to our research assistants Roman Arzhintar, Christopher B. Cox, Olga Drobinina, Vigen Ghazarian, Elena Lytkina, Tatiana Orobeiko, Averki Savostianov, Emilia Sherifova, Ivana Taborosi, Noriko Tsukada, and Vicki Weiner. Thanks go to Theresa King for her invaluable support, and Jeffery Geller, Irina Shin, and Vicki M. Weiner for their help in translating and editing some of the articles. I am also deeply grateful to the group of authors contributing articles on these important subjects. Finally, I give my warmest personal gratitude to my daughters Liza and Valery, and my dearest friends Dina Rosenberg, Arthur Taylor, and Stoyan Ganev. You comfort my soul and enable me to distance myself from New York's mayhem and daily business problems.

CONTENTS

PART I

GENERAL INFORMATION

CHAPTER 1

RUSSIAN FEDERATION OPPORTUNITIES AND RISKS FOR FOREIGN INVESTORS

Vladimir L. Kvint and Jacqueline E. Gallus

1.1 OVERVIEW. The Soviet Union was established on December 30, 1922, with five republics: Zakavkazskaya (Transcaucasus), Russia, Ukraine, Belarus, and Turkestan. Between 1956 and 1991, the Soviet Union was comprised of 15 republics (prior to 1956, there had been 16, including the Karel-Fin Republic). At the time of its dissolution in 1991, the Soviet Union covered an area of approximately 22.4 million square kilometers, and had a population of approximately 302 million. It was the world's largest country by territory, and the third largest by population.

In December 1991, three of the former Soviet Republics (Russia, Ukraine, and Belarus) signed an agreement to form the Commonwealth of Independent States (CIS). During 1992 and 1993, the number of CIS members increased to 12 (the three Baltic states are not members.) Of the 15 former USSR republics, Russia has the largest territory.

Both *Russia* and the *Russian Federation* are official names for this land, according to its Constitution. Russia accounts for about 76% of the territory of the former Soviet Union and has 11 time zones. At 6.6 million square miles, it covers about one-eight of the world's land surface, making it by far the largest single country in the world. Just the European part of Russia is larger than all of western Europe. Even Siberia, a part of Russia, has more territory and population than the world's second largest country by territory, Canada.

Russia's population is approximately 148 million, the sixth largest in the world. Twelve Russian cities have populations of over one million. Although the European part of Russia makes up 25% of Russia's territory, it accounts for 78% of its population. The Asian part of Russia has a population of 32 million. Russians (119.9 million) constitute the largest ethnic group in the country and make up 81.5% of the country's permanent population. Tatars (5.5 million) are the next largest ethnic group.

Illiteracy is almost nonexistent, and the educational level of Russia's population is one of the highest in the world. This foundation gave Russia the capability to develop many scientific and technological achievements, such as nuclear icebreakers, laser technology (for which Russian scientists won the Nobel Prize in 1965), modern nuclear, space, and membrane technologies, and continuous-casting technology for steel production (which is now the standard used throughout the Japanese and American steel industries). Twenty-one percent of the world's scientists are in Russia.

(a) Reserves and Production. Russia has the world's largest registered reserves of natural gas and the second largest reserves of oil and gold. It also has the world's largest geological reserves of diamonds, nickel, cobalt, copper, platinum, palladium, iridium, lead, uranium, osmium, and potassium salt, as well as the world's largest combined forest area (one-quarter of the earth's total) and freshwater reserves.

Even in this very difficult transitional time, Russia is currently the world's number-one producer of natural gas (exports of Russia's natural gas comprise 35% of world exports) and is the world's leading producer of raw diamonds, gold, platinum, palladium, iridium, nickel, cobalt, aluminum (the world's four largest aluminum plants are in Russia), osmium, steel, iron, mineral fertilizers, brown coal, timber, steel-cutting equipment, tractors (2.5 times more than the United States), and electric trolleys. In addition, Russia has the world's longest network (in miles) of electrified railroads. It is the second largest producer in the world of electricity (after the United States), copper (after Chile), cement (after China), and tin, and is the number-three producer of coal (after the United States and China), fish (after Japan and China), and grain.

1.2 POLITICAL ENVIRONMENT. When evaluating the political environment of Russia, indeed, of any country, several factors must be considered, including the four that follow.

(a) Government Institutions. A primary consideration is the enforcement of Russia's Constitution and the stability of political structures, including the office of the president, Parliament, and cabinet, as well as regularly scheduled democratic elections.

Adopted in 1993, the Russian Constitution is in operation and enforced. In 1991, for the first time in Russia's 1000-year history, the Russian people democratically elected their leader, President Boris Nikolaevich Yeltsin. The president has strong executive power, with the Cabinet of Ministers and prime minister who work under the president's direct guidance. It is crucial to understand that President Yeltsin has held power for seven years, and although his popularity has fallen, his executive powers have effectively increased. Yeltsin has far greater control of the government's daily activities and strategic economic decisions than Parliament does. He and the Cabinet of Ministers have complete control over all foreign policy, the army, and the secret services. Although some believe that Yeltsin has some of the characteristics of a dictator, he and the government have maintained their strong orientation and commitment toward a market economy.

Since 1991, presidential elections, in spite of friction among various parties and factions, subsequent elections have *not* been postponed or canceled, as they have been in some other former Soviet Republics. Yeltsin won democratic elections in 1991 and 1996 in a very competitive environment and after tough political battles. In 1990, 1993, and 1995, Russia also democratically elected representatives to the Parliament. The results of the December 1995 elections were mixed. On one hand, the "new" Communists took the majority of votes (22%), but several results were positive as well. Only one of the parties that won seats, that of Mr. Zhirinovsky, is against cooperation with the West. In addition, the 1993 elections gave Zhirinovsky's party 25% of the votes, but only 11% in the 1995 elections, a decrease of more than half. The party of pro-market Prime Minister Viktor S. Chernomyrdin, whose Cabinet of Ministers works under the direct guidance of President Yeltsin, has more Parliament seats than Zhirinovsky's party. Not one Nationalist party member obtained the minimum 5% vote necessary to be elected to the Parliament. But because the opposition parties have more parliamentary seats than the party in power, a struggle developed between the executive and legislative branches.

Russia has an independent Supreme Court and Constitutional Court. Beginning in 1991, the year of Russia's declaration of independence, elections to regional executive offices and regional legislatures have been held according to the Constitution and on schedule.

The Russian military has never played a political role, nor has any military leader until after retirement, as General Makashov did in 1991 and General Alexander Lebed in 1995 and 1996. The role of Russia's army should not be confused with that of the military in Latin America or Africa. While the USSR was alive, its army was under the strong control of the Communist Party. Thereafter, the Russian army came under the leadership of President Yeltsin.

(b) Nonproliferation Treaties and Export Restrictions.   Russia follows nuclear nonproliferation treaties and has shown a willingness to exceed its obligations. Since 1992, at Yeltsin's initiative, Russia has voluntarily halted all nuclear testing. Russia strictly abides by restrictions on exports of weapons and dual-use, high-technology products, except for its deal to send Iran such products, which has greatly displeased the United States and many other countries. In general, Russia adheres to international agreements and is much more in accordance with these agreements than many other countries.

(c) Crime, Corruption, and Nepotism.   In Russia, crime, corruption, and nepotism have created substantial political, economic, and commercial risks. These problems are more serious in Russia than in most other countries, and are so severe that they were noted in a joint statement released following the March 1997 Helsinki summit of Presidents Clinton and Yeltsin. However, it is important to understand that Russia has made efforts to fight crime. It has been a member of Interpol since 1992, and in 1995, Louis J. Freeh, the Director of the U.S. Federal Bureau of Investigation, visited Moscow for the opening of the FBI's office there.

(d) Decentralization and Regionalization.   Russia has 20 autonomous republics and 69 administrative regions, including oblasts and krais, and two metropolitan cities, Moscow and St. Petersburg. Regional governments and private companies have greater control over their own destiny and a stronger say in how business is conducted within their areas than previously. The increase in authority and power of the autonomous republics and regions is an important reflection of the democratization of Russia's business life. All regions have democratically elected executive and legislative bodies.

During the Soviet period, the government included 68 industrial ministries, which had direct executive power and total control over industrial production and distribution. But since 1995, the ministries have no direct control over such operations. Rather, their role is one of coordination and regulation, and they are responsible for the issue of licenses and for a few major federal procurement contracts. The Russian government, in general, continues to control industry through its issue of various licenses. However, while 87% of products manufactured in Russia were regulated and controlled by license in 1992, only 5% of products are now federally regulated.

1.3 DEVELOPMENT OF CAPITALISM AND ECONOMIC REFORM.   The speed of Russia's transition from a command to a market-oriented economy is unprecedented. Until recently, the Russian economy was administered by the central authorities of the former Soviet Union. In 1988, Russia did not have a single private bank, private insurance company, private accounting firm, or private law firm. Following the collapse of the central authorities and the command economy they managed, the government tried to implement policies to introduce free-market economies. These policies involved freeing prices from central control, reducing defense expenditures and subsidies for state-owned enterprises, privatizing state-owned enterprises, reforming the tax system, introducing legal structures designed to facilitate private, market-based activities, and encouraging foreign trade and investment.

The speed of the privatization process in Russia has no analogy in modern history. In 1990, less than 3% of Russian business was in private hands. In 1992, all Russian citizens born prior to September 1, 1992, were issued vouchers entitling them to buy shares in enterprises or to be deposited in private investment funds. By January 1994, voucher auctions resulted in the privatization of 11,000 (out of 14,500) medium and large enterprises.

These reform policies have met with some success. Beginning in 1992, the national currency, the ruble, became convertible on a limited basis in Russia. By January 1, 1997, 78% of Russia's economy was in private hands, and all of the major capitalist institutions were in place.

(a) Economic Progress. Russia passed through the worst of its economic hardships in 1992, when inflation reached, according to official statistics, 1,600% per year; according to other statistics, it rose as high 2,100% or even 2,300%. Russian industrial production decreased, which was easily foreseeable as the structure of the Soviet industrial economy had been based on command decisions and not on market forces and economic needs. Since its independence, Russia has downsized its military-industrial complex, affecting virtually all its industrial suppliers.

One must remember that these economic shifts are part of the transition to a market economy. The changes were essential, and while one can argue with the methods by which the market economy was developed, in the end the changes have all been positive. The process of privatization, decentralization, and intense internationalization of the Russian economy has ultimately benefited Russia. This does not mean, however, that the Russian economy is without problems. Russia now has high government debt relative to gross domestic product (60% of GDP, as announced in April 1997 by the Auditor of the Accounting Chamber); weak currencies; and the possibility of widespread bankruptcies, high unemployment, and the decline of certain sectors of the economy. Moreover, there is, in 1997, a lack of political consensus.

(b) Economic Indicators. Economic indicators show that Russia is beginning to rebound from its decline. The standard of living hit its lowest point in 1994, stayed level for most of 1995, and by September 1995 began to increase. From 1991 through 1994, both GDP and industrial production decreased substantially. The decrease in GDP in 1994 was 13%, and 4% in 1995. Statistics showed, indeed, that by the second half of 1995 the drop in GDP had halted, and secondary indicators offered some evidence that the economy might have begun to rebound, with electricity output somewhat increased. In fact, 1995 closed with industrial production having decreased only 3% from 1994. Some areas, such as ferrous and non-ferrous metals, building materials, petrochemicals, and segments of the paper industry grew rather substantially. In addition, for the first time since 1991, some light industries also showed growth. Production of consumer durables, including electronics, and agriculture, however, continued to decline throughout 1995. And in 1996, industrial production again fell 5%, with real GDP falling 6%.

To understand this trend, it is important to consider that the structure of GDP has also changed over the years. In 1993, industrial production accounted for 50% of GDP and services accounted for only 43%. In contrast, by 1995, industrial production made up only 41% of GDP and services 51.5%. This is an indication of Russia's progress to a postindustrial society. In addition, because many firms underreported activities and earnings, it is likely that the contribution from the service sector was even greater.

As mentioned earlier, inflation, in annual terms, was between 1,600 and 2,300% in 1992, 840% in 1993, and 215% in 1994. However, the growth in the ruble money supply decreased from 195% in 1994 to 110% in 1995. In January, inflation was at its 1995 peak, (18% per month), but near the end of the year it fell to about 4% per month, and in December, fell to 3.2%, its lowest point since the collapse of the Soviet Union. This was due, in part, to a tight monetary policy. During 1995, monthly inflation averaged about 7.3%, and for the year was 131%. During 1995, interest rates stayed high, in keeping with the tight monetary situation. In addition, the discount rate, although high, remained stable; and commercial banks did not often turn to the Russian Central Bank for short-term liquidity needs. Inflation during 1996 totaled only 21.8%. In April 1997, however, the Central Bank cut its rates on short-term (Lombard) loans that provide liquidity to banks, and reduced the refinancing rate (which is often used for contract transactions establishing commercial-bank rates) from 42 to 36%.

(c) Reserves.   As of April 1, 1997, Russia's gold and currency reserves were at $16.5 billion, an increase from March of more than $1 billion. Of this $16.5 billion, only $4.08 billion was held in gold, with the rest in currency.

(d) Government Deficit.   The Russian government promised to keep the 1995 federal budget deficit to 4.1% of GDP, and to finance this deficit without having to borrow from the Central Bank. The actual deficit was close to the estimate, with virtually no lending from the Central Bank. The Russian Ministry of Economy reported that the government deficit was 3% of GDP in 1995, down from approximately 10% in 1994, and from 12% in 1992. Other sources, however, say the deficit was more like 4.9%. In 1996, the government stated it would lower the deficit to 3.85% of GDP by maintaining revenues at 1995 rates and decreasing expenditures. The 1996 deficit was, in fact, reported at 3.3%. Projections for 1997 are similar—3.5% of GDP.

1.4 INTERNATIONAL AND MULTILATERAL INSTITUTIONS.   When the Russian Federation became an independent sovereign country in 1991, it inherited the USSR's permanent seat on the United Nations Security Council (the other permanent members are the United States, Great Britain, France, and China), exerting a strong influence on all Security Council decisions. Russia participates in several of the UN peacekeeping activities in the former Yugoslavia, including the UN mission in Bosnia-Herzegovina. Furthermore, Russia has only a very small outstanding debt to the UN and has been making most of its contributions on schedule.

In 1992, Russia became a full member of the World Bank and all of the World Bank Group institutions, including the International Bank for Reconstruction and Development (IBRD), the International Finance Corp. (IFC), the International Development Association (IDA), the International Centre for Settlement of Investment Disputes, and the Multilateral Investment Guarantee Agency (MIGA). During 1995, the World Bank granted loans worth $1.74 billion for projects in Russia, and, in 1996, committed $1.81 billion in lending.

Russia is also a member of the International Monetary Fund (IMF). In 1995, Russia was granted a $6.3 billion standby credit from the IMF, and reached an agreement in March 1996 for an extended fund facility of about $10 billion over three years. In February 1997, the IMF executive board, after reviewing the fiscal and monetary achievements of Russia for December 1996, distributed two monthly tranches of about $647 million.

Russia is not only a founding member and a recipient, but also a donor member of the European Bank for Reconstruction and Development (EBRD). In 1996, EBRD approved financing of 918 million European Currency Units (ECU) for 30 projects. As of December 1996, EBRD had approved about 2.5 billion ECU for 84 projects in Russia.

In 1992, Russia was granted GATT observer status, and has retained observer status with GATT's successor, the World Trade Organization, and works according to WTO guidelines. Russia has requested that its status be elevated to a member country, but this has not yet been approved.

1.5 POLITICAL RELATIONSHIPS WITH NEIGHBORING COUNTRIES AND BI-LATERAL AND INTERNATIONAL AGREEMENTS AND COOPERATION.

Russia has stable diplomatic relations and many regional multilateral agreements with neighboring countries. These include the Black Sea Agreement of Cooperation, to which Russia was a key signatory, and the Caspian Sea Agreement. Russia is bound by the CIS agreement as an equal partner. It has a guaranteed 50% of the votes in the CIS Executive Economic Committee, with the remaining 50% divided among the other 11 members. Russia has duty-free border agreements, invisible border agreements, and nontariff barrier agreements with many members of the CIS.

Russia has treaties governing bilateral trade and bilateral investments, and banning double taxation, with most countries, including the United States, Canada, and most Western European counties, although some of the agreements have not yet been ratified. For example, the Russian Parliament has not yet ratified the Bilateral Investment Treaty (guarantees nondiscriminatory treatment of investors, hard-currency repatriation rights, expropriation compensation, and the right to third-party arbitration in disputes between U.S. firms and the Russian government) signed by Presidents Clinton and Yeltsin. Russia has negotiated and signed several other important agreements with the United States, including a bilateral trade agreement, which grants both countries most-favored-nation (MFN) status and nondiscriminatory market access, as well as strong property rights protection. In October 1993, the United States granted Russia generalized-system-of-preferences (GSP) status. These privileges, however, were suspended by the U.S. Congress in August 1995. The provisions have since been reinstated. Since January 1994, the United States and Russia have had an agreement protecting firms against double taxation. With Canada, Russia has a foreign trade treaty granting MFN status, a double-taxation treaty, and an agreement granting GSP status (or GPT, as it is referred to in Canada). Russia has bilateral agreements with China, a strategically important neighbor. In addition, it has agreements with major regional and multilateral institutions, such as the European Union.

In recognition of Russia's maintaining its obligations to and responsibilities within multilateral institutions, President Yeltsin was invited to participate in all the economic meetings of the G7. Moreover, in 1996, Russia was asked to participate in the G7's political meetings as well. In 1997, Russia became the eighth member-country.

Russia, having inherited all of the Soviet debt, has established relationships with the London Club of commercial creditors and the Paris Club of government creditors.

Russia's membership in the Council of Europe, which obligates its members to ban capital punishment and to provide the highest level of human-rights protection, is very important. The aim of the Council of Europe, an international organization headquartered in Strasbourg comprised of European democratic countries, is "to defend democracy." On February 28, 1996, Russia was accepted as a full member of the council.

Russia has established relations with the Overseas Private Investment Corporation (OPIC), the U.S. Export-Import Bank, the Export Development Corporation of Canada, the Export Credits Guarantee Department of the United Kingdom, the Export-Import Bank of Japan, and other financial institutions.

The U.S. Export-Import Bank is very active in Russia. In 1995, for example, it approved over $521 million in guarantees for U.S. firms exporting to Russia. Russia has never defaulted on a single Ex-Im Bank payment. For a few years, Ex-Im had been providing guarantees on U.S. exports with a short-term (less than one year) payback and a medium-term (one to seven years) payback. Then, in what could be seen as a strong vote of confidence in Russia's long-term stability, Ex-Im decided to also guarantee exports with long-term (over seven years) repayment schedules. Ex-Im will consider applications from Russian commercial banks on a case-by-case basis, with the decision on whether to back a transaction based on the capital of the applying bank (based on accounts audited to international standards). This is a change from previous policy, which specified only a few preapproved Russian banks as acceptable applicants. As of the end of 1996, Ex-Im's activity in Russia totaled almost $2.2 billion, covering 43 cases. Ex-Im estimates the 1997 potential at $2.1 billion.

1.6 FOREIGN INVESTMENT.   In 1987, foreign investment in Russia became legal, and the first 23 joint-venture companies with foreign capital were established in the former Soviet Union; only two of them with American capital. On January 1, 1997, nine years later, more than 33,000 companies with foreign capital were registered in Russia. Over the last 10 years, more than $80 billion of foreign investment has been committed to Russia. In the last five years alone, $8.5 billion of direct private investments (not including portfolio investments or state and multilateral-agency loans and investments) went to Russia. The countries most active in investing in Russia are, in order, the United States, Germany, Switzerland, Italy, Great Britain, and South Korea.

(a) Risk of Investment.   There are several risks that investors in Russia need to be aware of.

(i) Expropriation and Nationalization.   Russia has laws regarding the protection of foreign investment and private property, as well as antimonopoly laws. All these laws strongly protect foreign and private property against expropriation and nationalization. Bilateral agreements with many countries guarantee compensation in case of legal (according to a court decision) nationalization. In addition, the risks of property nationalization are low, as evidenced by the fact that only two incidents have occurred where a government official suggested the possibility. In January 1995, the newly appointed chairman of the State Property Committee, which conducted the state privatization process, mentioned the possible renationalization of some companies. Within one week he was fired. In March 1997, the deputy prime minister and head of the Ministry of Interior mentioned the possible renationalization of the aluminum industry. These are minor incidents, and for the last four years,

there has not been one claim made to OPIC or MIGA regarding the nationalization or expropriation of property in Russia.

(ii) Civil Disobedience and Vandalism. In general, Russia is politically stable and sound in spite of the activity of the Chechen Republic, which became part of Russia in 1859 and accounts for less than 0.2% of its territory. In contrast to this situation, Russia's relationship with the Tatar Republic is quite good. In trying to gain a measure of independence, the Tatar Republic did not try to secede from the Russian Federation. Instead, it used constitutional methods whereby the president of the republic signed an agreement with under which the republic received more power over foreign economic activity and the development of its budget. As it now stands, the relationship between Russia and the Tatar Republic is similar to that between Belgium and the semiautonomous region of Flanders.

During its first six years of independence, there has not been a single case of vandalism for political reasons in Russia. However, there *is* risk of civil disobedience in about 4% of Russia's territory, which includes the Chechen Republic. One vector of civilian disobedience in Russia' runs east and west, with the risk lower in the east and higher in the west, the European part of Russia. Another vector runs north and south, with a higher risk in the south. Thus, the greatest risk of civil disobedience lies in the southwest portion of Russia, with a small enclave in the Asian part of Russia (Tuva Autonomous Republic in eastern Siberia). Even in these regions, however, any vandalism would not be directed specifically against Western property. Disputes among various ethnic and social groups might lead to Western property being vandalized, but only coincidentally.

(iii) Risk Rating and Mitigation. The International Banking Credit Analysis Agency (IBCA) gave Russia a rating of B for the short term, and BB+ for the long term (as of October 1996). Russia's sovereign risk rating from Moody's is BA2, and BB− from Standard and Poor's. Russia's first Eurobond issue was considered by many to be a success, with the five-year issue raising over $1 billion.

The risk of investment by foreign firms in Russia can be mitigated through the use of various national, multilateral-agency, or private-insurance facilities. Two of these are the U.S. government's OPIC and the World Bank's MIGA. By 1997, over 300 projects were registered for OPIC support, totaling about $30 billion. Of 16 projects in Russia for which OPIC provided either investment guarantees or direct project finance in 1995, six were in the communications sector. OPIC backed more than 40 investments in 1996, with over $1 billion in support.[1] The projects it supported were in industries that included telecommunications, financial/brokerage/securities services, oil and gas, soft drinks, fishing and forestry, and others.

One indication that investors perceive the risk in Russia to be lower is that the Templeton Russia mutual fund has grown from $65 million since it began trading on the New York Stock Exchange in September 1995 to $ 168 million. Several Russian companies, including GUM, Gazprom, Mosenergo, and others recently issued American depository receipts (ADRs); and Vimpelcom became the first Russian firm, in November 1996, to be listed on the New York Stock Exchange.

1.7 FOREIGN TRADE. Even at the time of the Russia's most severe economic adjustments, foreign trade and economic cooperation increased. Russia experienced a $16 billion trade surplus in 1993, while 1994's was $12 billion, and 1995's was over $30 billion.

---

[1]"News from OPIC," January 1997, p. 1.

About half of Russia's exports were of energy and fuel products, coal, iron ore, and timber. Russia's 1996 surplus was almost $40 billion (exports of $86.5 billion, imports of $46.6 billion). Overall, Russia exports grew 8.7%, spurred on by energy exports. Reflecting a boost in relations with the former Soviet republics, Russia's trade with CIS members grew to $34.2 billion. Russia's largest export markets are, in order, Germany, China, Italy, the United Kingdom, Hungary, Japan, the United States, and South Korea.

Russia also liberalized some of its trade policies. In 1995, for example, the oil export quota was abolished by President Yeltsin, and the government began to abolish many tax and duty exemptions, including the special exporter regime for oil. While 1995 also saw the top tariff rate reduced to 30%, however, some products that previously had no tariff were taxed, causing an increase in the average tariff rate from 11 to 15%. Moreover, a law on foreign economic activity was established in 1995 that had some defensive trade measures, and the government began to further investigate antidumping safeguards.

In 1993, the United States had a trade surplus with Russia, exporting almost $2.97 billion of products (including agricultural products, civil-engineering and builders' facilities equipment, telecommunications equipment, automobiles, tobacco, mechanical-handling equipment, etc.), while importing from Russia about $1.74 billion of product (including iron, precious stones, aluminum, platinum and other metals, art, etc.). By 1994, however, Russia had the trade surplus, exporting $3.23 billion of goods to the United States, and importing only $2.56 billion of goods. Although Russia still has the surplus, U.S. exports to Russia increased by 18% in 1996, to $3.34 billion. The exports included meat, machinery, tobacco, aluminum, silver, other base metals, diamonds, raw steel, crude oil, chemicals, fish and seafood, and fertilizer. The U.S. Department of Commerce has listed the products with the best potential for export to Russia as general consumer goods, building products, computers and peripherals, telecommunications equipment, aircraft and aircraft parts, and food products, among others.

In November 1995, Great Britain also showed a trade deficit with Russia for the year. As of January 1, 1996, Canada's trade deficit with Russia was $309.1 million (Canadian dollars). Canada's exports to Russia totaled C$189.1 million (including radio transmission equipment, electrical apparatus for telephone lines, food products, consumer products such as clothing and cosmetics, engines, bakery machinery, etc.), while Russia's exports to Canada were valued at C$489.2 million (including petroleum, silver, uranium, frozen fish, steel, and tractors).

1.8 FOREIGN DEBT.   When the USSR collapsed, Russia accepted the responsibility of $104 billion of foreign debt (of all 15 former Soviet Republics), and its total foreign debt by late 1996 was a reported $125 billion. It is difficult to accurately estimate the debt, however, because of different exchange rates over the years. Before 1961, one ruble was equal to 68¢; but in the 1970s, the Soviets set an artificial exchange rate of $1 equaling .6 rubles. It is estimated that the Russian debt to international and national entities is really about $172–180 billion. One should also note, however, that Russia has $184 billion owed to it by foreign countries, such as Iraq ($11 billion), Cuba ($24 billion), India, Ukraine, Mongolia, Brazil, and others.

Russia has successfully negotiated with both the London Club of commercial banks and the Paris Club of government creditors on rescheduling of its debt payments. In 1994, an agreement was reached with the Paris Club to reschedule $7 billion in payments on debt inherited from the USSR. In June 1995, the Paris Club agreed to reschedule $6.3 billion in payments on inherited debt. On an individual country basis, the U.S. and Russian governments agreed in October 1995 to reschedule payments of $64 million. In November 1995,

Russia reached a preliminary agreement (with a final agreement expected in August 1997) with the London Club to reschedule payments of almost $35 billion, with principal to be repaid over 25 years (with a seven-year grace period).

1.9 CURRENCY.   Prior to 1992, the Russian ruble was inconvertible; and in 1992, it became convertible on a limited basis. Throughout early 1995, the depreciation of the ruble against the dollar corresponded with inflation, until April 29, when it fell to its lowest point, $1/5,130 rubles. In May and June 1995, it appreciated, until in July the Russian Central Bank intervened to slow the rise. In July 1995, the government pledged to keep the dollar/ruble rate within a band between $1/4,3000–4,9000 rubles. After August 1995, the ruble became far more stable, and by December had depreciated slowly to $1/4,650 rubles. This was immediately noted by OPIC, which in 1995, for the first time, began to issue insurance against currency inconvertibility for U.S. businesses in Russia. This move reflects the belief that the ruble has become relatively convertible.

However, if one takes inflation into account, by December 1995 the ruble appreciated in real terms over December 1994. In January 1996, the band was expanded for six months to allow the dollar/ruble rate to range from $1/4,550–5,150 rubles. Even through March 1, 1996, the rate did not fluctuate significantly. Then the Central Bank and the government announced on May 17, 1996, that the band would be replaced with a crawling bank mechanism. In July, the band moved to $1/5,000–5,600 rubles. The rate was $1/5,570 rubles by the end of 1996, which represented a 20% nominal decrease; but with inflation factored in, it was a 1.9% real increase over 1995.

In April 1997, the first deputy chairman of the Central Bank announced that he was concerned about the appreciation of the ruble, and said the Central Bank would raise its dollar-sell rate, which would, he hoped, encourage organizations not to postpone dollar purchases, resulting in less demand for rubles. The Central Bank bought $1.5 billion during the end of March and April 1997.

(a) Tax and Currency Regulation.   Russia's tax system is quite unstable and very complicated. According to provisions enacted by the Duma, Russians will have new taxes imposed in 1997. These include a tax on interest income if higher than the Central Bank's refinancing rate, a 15% tax on profits from T-bill trading, an excise tax of 12,000 rubles per liter of spirits and 700 rubles per liter of beer, and a 1.5% tax on foreign currency purchases.

1.10 UNEMPLOYMENT AND WAGES.   Unemployment is a problem new to Russia. Under the Soviet's terribly inefficient command economy, employment was almost 100%. Unemployment in 1995 rose to 8.5% of the labor force (based on UN International Labor Organization statistical methods), was reported by Russian official statistics as 5%, and was as high as 10%, according to our estimate. Unemployment in January 1997 was 9.5%, up 0.2% from December 1996, according to Russian official statistics based on the UN's methods. Actual unemployment may indeed be higher. While this condition is new to Russia, its rate is still lower than in many areas of central and eastern Europe, and even lower than in areas of western Europe.

In 1995, average wages went up to 710,000 rubles per month. In the first three months of 1995, however, *real* wages fell to their lowest level since 1991. Statistics show that real wages, in fact, fell 13% in 1995 from 1994. This may be somewhat distorted, however, as companies tried to reduce their wage reporting to avoid the excess-wage tax (which was terminated in January 1996) and because most analysts used real-consumption figures instead of distorted real-income figures. Real consumption, however, also declined in 1995, by 5.3%. By mid-1996, the average wage was 835,000 rubles per month, and by January 1997, it increased to 870,000 rubles. The increase, however, is not sufficient to allow people to keep up with the higher cost of living. In addition, the gap between rich and poor has increased substantially.

After the breakup of the Soviet Union, the Russian Constitution, for the first time in 74 years, permitted workers to strike; and the strikes have been widely publicized. Nevertheless, by 1997, there were fewer strikes than there had been in 1991 and 1992.

1.11 LEGAL FRAMEWORK. Russia's first Parliament (1990–1993) created laws guaranteeing protection of private property and foreign investment, creating free economic zones, and allowing concessions (including foreign concessions). Russia passed a bankruptcy law, an antimonopoly law (1992), the Civil Code (1996), and a law on privatization of state and municipal companies, as well as numerous treaties with other countries that guarantee protection of foreign investment. At present, the legal framework governing foreign investment is based on the law On Foreign Investment in the RSFSR, from July 4, 1991, No. 1545–1, amended by presidential edict, dated December 24, 1993, No. 2288, and Federal Law No. 89–FZ, of June 19, 1995. The Duma voted overwhelmingly in favor of a new law on foreign economic zones on April 23, 1997. The law, if passed by the higher house of Parliament and President Yeltsin, would permit the government to set up several different kinds of free economic zones (FEZs), which provide special tax incentives and exemption from customs duties. There are 19 FEZs in Russia, but only two are currently operational (Yantar, in Kaliningrad Oblast, and Nakhodka, in Primorsky Krai). The law would also allow South Korean companies in Nakhodka an eight-year tax holiday.

The laws regarding repatriation of profits in hard currency have also changed. Now there are no legal obstacles to full repatriation of profits.

Russia recognizes intellectual property rights, including copyrights, trademarks, and patents. There has, however, been some controversy about enforcement of the protection.

Russia recognizes the rights of foreign investors to bring disputes with the government in front of third-party arbitration, including international courts. Russia has agreed to recognize the decisions of the International Court of Justice (the World Court) in The Hague, whose judges are elected by the UN General Assembly and the Security Council, as well as decisions of the Court of First Instance in Geneva (which follows the United Nations Commission on International Trade Law's Convention on the International Sales of Goods) and the Arbitration Institute of the Stockholm Chamber of Commerce.

(a) Legal Risks. It is apparent that the Russian government has introduced laws, regulations, and legal structures intended to support the effort to transform its command economy into a market economy. The lack of consensus about the scope, content, and speed of economic and political reform, however, has resulted in legislation that in many instances has left key issues unresolved. In many areas where legislation has been enacted, the government has contemplated implementing regulations that have not yet been promulgated. Furthermore, the language of the legislation is sometimes vague, or leaves room for substantial interpretation. There are, therefore, inconsistent interpretations and enforcement of laws that have been passed. But, as the legislative process matures, the actual language of the laws should become much clearer and more specific.

According to the Russian Constitution, the hierarchy of legislation is constitutional law, federal and nonfederal law, presidential decree, government resolutions, and administrative acts of ministries and other federal bodies.[2] In reality, the hierarchy is often ignored. A rather unsettling element has been the Russian government's resorting to rule by presidential decree, brought about by the deadlock between the government and Parliament. Parliament retains the power to reverse decisions made by decree.

Because Russian laws are changing so quickly, investors have some difficulty in analyzing the legal issues affecting their current or potential investment. These factors have led to conflicts and inconsistencies, as well as to substantive gaps in the applicable laws and uncertainties as to where jurisdiction to administer the laws resides. The result has been considerable legal confusion, particularly in areas such as company law, commercial and contract law, property law, securities law, foreign-trade and investment law, and tax law.

Furthermore, the absence of a tradition of a judiciary insulated from the political considerations of the moment, as well as the judiciary system's relative inexperience with market-oriented contract and commercial law, adds a further element of inconsistency in the application of these new laws.

Finally, the existing business culture continues to be influenced by attitudes formed in the former Soviet Union, during which time laws and legal commitments were often regarded as arbitrary impositions by the state and thus matters to be avoided rather than observed. As a result, the commitment of local businesspeople, government officials and agencies, and the judicial system to honor legal rights granted and agreements entered into, and generally to uphold the rule of law, is still uncertain.

1.12 DEVELOPMENT OF CAPITALIST INSTITUTIONS.   Russia has established all the major capital-market institutions necessary for the full development of a free-market economy, including the availability of international law firms, insurers, the Big Six auditing and accounting firms (as well as thousands of Russian auditing companies), commercial and investment banks, and other capital- and financial-market institutions. In 1997, there are five stock exchanges, international-currency exchanges, and about 20 commodity exchanges in operation. A Federal Commission on Securities and Exchanges has been established to regulate the securities industry, and clearing systems are being improved.

(a) Insurance.   While in 1990 not a single private insurance company existed in Russia, by 1996 there were about 3,000 such firms. In 1996, the Government revoked licenses of 10% of the insurance firms, and others closed or dissolved due to commercial or other reasons. There were, as of April 1997, 2500 private insurance companies, including AIG, which has a joint venture. Foreign insurance firms face substantial operational barriers in Russia, including laws that require foreign insurers to partner with a Russian firm to form a joint-stock company and that forbid them from owning more than 49% of the company. Nonetheless, AIG, Munich Reinsurance, and Zurich Reinsurance have all set up operations with Russian partners.

(b) Banking.   By March 1997, there were 152 banks with foreign capital in Russia; of these, only two were totally foreign-owned. In three years, however, there has been a decline in the number of new banks. In 1994, 500 new banks were created, in 1995, 85 were set up, and in 1996, only 26 were established. By April 1, 1997, the number of banks dropped to 1936, after 282 bank licenses were revoked in 1996, and only three new licenses were issued. The banks have over 5,000 branches. This does not include Sberbank, with its 34,000 branches.

---

[2]White Paper, American Chamber of Commerce in Russia, January 1996.

Foreign banks face fewer barriers than foreign insurance firms, and enjoy much greater freedom of operations. Twenty-eight major foreign banks (including Credit Suisse First Boston, Credit Lyonnais, Deutsche Bank, Dresdner Bank, Creditanstalt, Chase Manhattan, Bank of New York, Bank of America, Citibank, Barclay's Bank, and Bank of China) are now fully operational in Russia. The majority of these are authorized to have ruble and foreign-currency accounts, and can service nonresident and resident companies and individuals. Many of these banks have already received auditing consultation from a Big Six accounting firm, and several have been audited to International Accounting Standards by a Big Six firm.

(c) Legal Firms.   Many major international law firms (including Baker & McKenzie; White & Case; Patterson, Belknap, Webb & Tyler; and Debevoise & Plimpton) have operating offices in Russia.

(d) Accounting and Auditing.   All of the Big Six accounting and auditing firms have a strong presence in Russia, with a combined total of over 3,500 employees. By March 1996, Russian accounting regulations were reoriented to allow conversion to the International Accounting Standards.

(e) Financial Markets.   Since 1992, thousands of retail currency-exchange kiosks and stands have appeared in Russia. The largest exchange is the Moscow Interbank Currency Exchange, which holds trading sessions five days a week, with minimum trades of $10,000. In addition, the Moscow Central Stock and Currency Exchange trades hard-currency contracts. Other currency exchanges are in St. Petersburg, Ekaterinburg, Omsk, Novosibirsk, and Vladivostok.

Five stock exchanges have been opened in Russia: in Moscow, St. Petersburg, Ekaterinburg (the Ural region), Novosibirsk (western Siberia) and Vladivostok (Pacific region). The smallest of these, in Vladivostok, has about 200 stocks traded on it. There are also currently only about 20 commodity exchanges in Russia, consolidated from approximately 450 in 1992.

The stock exchange systems are modeled after the U.S. NASDAQ system, and a brokers' organization similar to the NASD has been created. With Western assistance, clearing and settlement systems, and a group similar to the U.S. Depository Trust Company are being established in Russia.

The Templeton Russia Fund, Inc., a member of the $190 billion Franklin Templeton Group, is the first mutual fund dedicated solely to investing in Russia to trade on the New York Stock Exchange. Other foreign funds have also entered the market. In 1996, Russia was rated as the top performer of emerging markets by the IFC.

With the trading of stocks also came the need for supervision. Thus, by presidential decree in November 1994, Russia created the Presidential Commission on Securities and Exchanges. The commission was actually a ministry, but it had representatives of 10 governmental regulatory agencies, such as the Ministry of Finance, the Central Bank, the Anti-Monopoly Committee, the Russian Fund for Federal Property, and other institutions on its board, which also included a member of Parliament. Each of the regional stock exchanges has a commission authorized to investigate problems, thereafter referring them to the Federal Commission on Securities and Exchanges. This body was established on July 1, 1996, to monitor and control the capital markets, and to enforce state policy. The Central Bank, however, regulates the foreign exchange markets and the T-bill market in Russia.

Securities law is still a new area, and many parts of it have yet to be perfected. Laws and regulations that are intended to protect the rights of shareholders remain unenforced; shareholders can be, and are, refused access to company books, and can be excluded from shareholder meetings. In addition, there have been substantial problems with registration, in some cases resulting in shareholders' names being deleted from the registers.

Although part of the solution to the problem could possibly be found with investors, most of them do not know how, or whether, they can affect legislation. The imprecision with which fiscal legislation has been drafted, coupled with the desperate need of the government for tax revenues, can lead to very subjective interpretations of such legislation on the part of taxing authorities. In addition, the authorities can occasionally resort to extralegal measures to ensure taxpayer compliance.

(f) Chambers of Commerce and Other Not-for-Profit Organizations.   The Russian Chamber of Commerce and Industry is independent of the government; and within its structure is the International Arbitration Court. It is important to note that hundreds of organizations dedicated to improving relationships between Russia and other countries have been established. In the United States, for example, there is the Russian-American Chamber of Commerce, and the U.S.-Russia Business Council; and in Moscow, there is the American Chamber of Commerce in Russia, which has about 350 member firms. Russia is also a focus of many internationally recognized institutions, like the Bretton Woods Committee, the Institute for East-West Studies, the Council on Foreign Relations, and the newly-established International Academy of Emerging Markets. Other groups, like the Pennsylvania-Russia Business Council, have a more regional focus.

1.13 INFRASTRUCTURE.   The following discussion provides details of the Russian infrastructure:

(a) Transportation.   Russia is aware of and has given special priority to its need for telecommunications and transportation systems development. Its transportation system is extremely undeveloped, particularly ground transportation, which, while improving in metropolitan areas, is terribly inadequate in rural areas.

The Russian transportation system requires substantial investment in modern technology and more financial expertise from the West, if activities in other sectors of the economy are to be supported. A modern transportation system is crucial to the growth of Russia, to the development of its vast stores of natural resources, and to its assumption of a larger role in international business. At present, Russia's crumbling aviation infrastructure presents real and growing problems. In 1994, the air transportation industry suffered 45 accidents, involving 14 crashes in which a total of 299 people were killed. This compares with 53 fatalities in 1993. The condition of Russia's ground transportation system is also atrocious. The number of road accidents jumped by 17% in the first four months of 1995, with at least 25% of these caused by bad road conditions. Trucks in Russia do not meet international safety standards.

The transportation of exported goods improved somewhat, with more on-time deliveries occuring in 1994 than in 1993.

The Russian merchant-marine fleet has not yet recovered from communist-era mismanagement. The shipment of goods declined by 17% in 1994, even though much of the fleet was rented by foreigners for export-import operations. Another problem for Russia has been its loss of its Black Sea ports, except for Novorossisk; but it, like other Russian ports, badly needs upgrading. Fully 60% of Russia's ports are too shallow for modern tankers.

Gas and oil pipelines in Russia play an enormous role in its economy. In 1995, they were used to deliver 405 million tons of natural gas, 265 million tons of crude oil, and 17 million tons of oil products. The pipelines, however, are also in need of major repair and renovation.

Transportation to and within Russia is being revolutionized. Hundreds of new flights have been added since 1991, and there are now several direct flights each week between Moscow and New York, Los Angeles, San Francisco, Seattle, Chicago, Miami, and Anchorage. There are also several flights per week between the city of Krasnoyarsk (in eastern Siberia) and London and Tel Aviv. The former Soviet republics are trying to renovate airports and air-traffic-control systems, and are seeking foreign investment, which unfortunately is coming in slowly.

About $60 billion will be needed over the next 15 years to improve Russia's transportation system. Even then, the system will only be brought to the level at which the United States was in the 1950s.

(b) Telecommunications. According to virtually all Western standards, Russia's telecommunications system desperately needs upgrading, and some progress is being made in this direction. Russia added approximately 1,025,000 new telecommunications lines in 1994, another 1,100,000 in 1995, and 1,200,000 in 1996. It is now possible to dial directly to most Russian cities and even to small towns. Three fiber-optic links have been set up: one from Palermo, Italy, through Istanbul, Turkey, to the Russian seaport of Novorossisk; another runs from Copenhagen, Denmark to Russia's Baltic Sea coast; and the third runs from Japan, through South Korea, to the Russian seaport of Nakhodka on the Pacific coast. Information systems have also proliferated in Russia. E-mail and Internet use is experiencing rapid growth, and information service providers such as Lexis-Nexis, Dun and Bradstreet, Reuters, and others are offering on-line data services.

More than 400 Western telecommunications service and equipment providers have been licensed to operate in Russia. All major Western telecommunications companies, and even small ones, have entered this market and have been granted licenses to operate. In fact, stocks of Russia's telecommunications companies are doing quite well, often better than firms in other sectors of the economy. One index of telecommunications stocks increased by 52% over the winter of 1996–97. By some estimates, telephone ownership has increased to 18 per 100 people. In spite of this activity, however, only about 6% of Russia's telecommunications systems are digital.

(c) Other Infrastructure Elements. Medical, hotel, and hospitality services are now widely available in major cities, but in rural areas and Siberia are severely lacking.

1.14 CONCLUSION. For the first time in its history, Russia has experienced six years of democracy with a stable political structure. The economic crisis that began in 1991 reached its nadir in 1994. In 1995, the economy stabilized; only the agricultural sector continued to fall, but the rate of decline substantially decreased. Russia's standard of living also reached its lowest level in 1994, but by the fourth quarter of 1995 began to slowly rise. Inflation gradually decreased from 2,100% in 1992 to approximately 131% in 1995, with the monthly rate staying at only 4% from December 1995 through February 1997. Inflation during 1996 totaled 21.8%. From August 1, 1995, the dollar/ruble rate stabilized and stayed within the band set by the Central Bank. By the end of September 1997, the rate was $1/5,880 rubles, which represented a 22% nominal decrease; but when taking into account inflation, it was actually a 1.9% real increase over 1995. Finally, the legal framework saw sustainable development from 1991 to 1997 in regard to privatization and internationalization of the Russian economy, but legislation continues to lack detail and still requires substantial development. Many experts have concluded that by all political, economic, and commercial indicators, Russia is an emerging market[3] with positive conditions for foreign investment activity. This analysis illustrates that after considering all political and economic factors and legal risks, one can definitely conclude that Russia is an emerging market on the world scene.

---

[3]Four major publications focusing on emerging markets have evaluated Russia as an emerging market, including *The Economist, Emerging Market Investor, JP Morgan Emerging Markets Economic Outlook,* and *The Emerging Markets Monitor.*

CHAPTER 2

GEOGRAPHY, CULTURE, AND HISTORY

Vladimir L. Kvint, Emilia Sherifova, Gadji G. Gamzatov, Mogamed Magomedhanov, Jeffery L. Geller, Irina Shin, Gennadiy G. Melikian, and Andrei A. Auzan

2.1 ECONOMIC HISTORY.* Nothing determines business culture within Russia more than its history. To attempt to predict Russia's business future, its economic past must be examined. It is extremely important to analyze the very factors that have played such an important role in determining both Russia's history and economy. The history of this great country is defined by its geographical location, ethnic composition, religions, relations with surrounding countries and territories, and, in later years, by its productive forces. The role of these factors can be quantified through the use of some basic economic parameters:

- Natural resources (including land)
- Labor resources (including cultural and educational level of the population)
- Capital resources (domestic and foreign)
- Production facilities
- Technological development (from the nineteenth century)

(a) Development as a Nation. The history of Russia can be divided into seven major periods from both an economic and political point of view:

1. The prestate period, prior to the ninth century, characterized by communal and patrimonial relations.
2. The origin of undivided authority and the development of statehood (the ninth through the sixteenth centuries), personified by characters such as the invited Scandinavian, Prince Ruerich; Ivan the Terrible; and the last representative of that dynasty, Fyodor Ioannovich.
3. The transition period during which the seeds of the empire were planted in Russia (the sixteenth to the seventeenth centuries), personified by figures such as Boris Godunov and the father of Peter the Great, Alexei Romanov the Meek.

---

*This section was written by Vladimir L. Kvint.

4. The Russian empire and late Renaissance period, represented by the Romanovs from Peter the Great to Alexander II the Liberator (the eighteenth to the nineteenth centuries).

5. The degradation of the empire and the miscarriage of capitalism (Alexander III the Peacemaker and Nikolai II) (the nineteenth to the beginning of twentieth centuries).

6. The period of communist despotism and the death of the empire (1917 to 1990).

7. The period of emerging modern capitalism and introduction of Western values.

When Christianity had a thousand years of history behind it in western Europe, when the Western Roman Empire emerged and collapsed, and when the Eastern Roman Empire was nearing its end, a huge country was coming to life on the vast terrain to their north and east; it was larger than any country already known, stretching from the Baltic to the Black Sea and from the Danube to the Urals. The first settlements in that territory became the cornerstone of that society, similar to the western ones and a challenge to the combative tribes of the steppe.

The fertile soils and woods attracted not only the steppe nomads but also Western conquerors. In the process of migration, through periods of peace and war, a new nation was brought to life. It was a melting pot for Scandinavian tribes, Ugro-Finnic populations, southern and western Slavs, and Turks that crossed the Caucasus and came in waves from the Black Sea steppe and Central Asia.

Having passed the stage of hunting and gathering, these people took advantage of the rich soils between the Danube and the Dniepr Rivers. Every settlement consisted of a clan with an elder as its head. Clan leadership was typically transferred from father to oldest son; however, occasionally a talented younger son would be chosen as leader. Kins continually subdivided, and the population spread into the northeast and onto the shores of the Black Sea.

Life in this early society flowed in accordance with its own harsh laws and is difficult to assess from a modern standpoint. Typically, a father was faced with the harsh duty of killing his invalid offspring because it was useless to society; likewise, it was the son's duty to free the family from the burden of infirm elderly parents.

The subdivisions of the kins brought about the first Russian cities in the eighth and ninth centuries. These new subdivisions resulted in multiple conflicts between rival kins. To settle these conflicts, a system of undivided authority was instituted. The main form of decision making, at that time, was through a gathering of people (assembly). Nevertheless, conflicting economic interests, a growing population, ever-increasing competition, and pressures from foreign neighbors soon produced a situation in which the people felt they must invite a foreigner to be their leader and judge. The first Prince of Rus (as Russia was referred to at the time) was a Scandinavian by the name of Prince Ruerich. This was a good choice, as Ruerich, his brothers, and their armed forces created the groundwork for one of the most powerful nations in the world.

Initially, Ruerich and his volunteers governed the majority of developed Russian cities (namely, Novgorod, Pskov, and Ostrov), all near the modern borders of Poland, Finland, and Germany. But increasing economic interests spurred the development of river and ground transportation between the Baltic and Black Seas. The southern end of this route, for centuries earlier, had been managed by the economically talented Greeks and Byzantines. But the Russians needed this land to increase their trade routes, so that, through Christian Armenia and Georgia, they could gain access to the markets of Persia and surrounding countries.

In the ninth and tenth centuries, under the leadership of Prince Oleg and later his daughter-in-law Olga, the city of Kiev was founded and became the dominant city in Russia. From this base camp, the Russian armed forces made multiple, violent, conquering onslaughts on their neighbors, reaching out as far as Constantinople. Byzantium was pressed into a very concessive and humiliating treaty, under which it was made to pay tribute, protect Russian property in Byzantium, and accept the Higher Embassies. These agreements were repeatedly signed and consistently neglected by Byzantium, but nonetheless, the relationship remained intact until the decline of the Eastern Roman Empire. These relations were no less important for Rus, as hordes of nomad tribes of Polovts, Khazars, Bolgars, Bulgars, and the armies of Scandinavian and German rulers were a constant threat to the Russian lands. The Russians needed both land and troops to stave off the invading tribes.

(b) Orthodox Christianity. In the tenth century, the strongest and youngest son of Prince Sviatoslav, Vladimir the Red Sun, developed and unified the territories of Rus. He initially settled in Novgorod and had some success in establishing relations with the assembly. After his father's death and multiple victories over his brothers, Vladimir managed to vigorously increase the nation's power. Because Vladimir had grown so strong, the Eastern Roman emperor tried to keep peace and proposed his sister as Vladimir's wife.

As a condition to the marriage, Vladimir was required to convert to Orthodox Christianity. Vladimir's grandmother, Olga, had been converted to Christianity years earlier, during her visit to Byzantium, but still Christianity was not prevalent among the Russian people. The earlier Russian religion had been pagan, with a pantheistic idea of the gods, among whom the figure known as Perun was preeminent. With Vladimir's conversion, the balance of religions shifted, as he ordered that numerous churches be constructed. The pagan religion survived secretly, though, through many centuries after that.

The conversion to Orthodox Christianity was a key event in Russian history. Rus rapidly Christianized its culture, and although this shift proved to be positive at the time, it became controversial later.

However, after the Byzantine Empire collapsed, Orthodox Christianity separated Russia from the Catholic world. This, in turn, created an economic and cultural gap between Russia and the rest of the Western world. The gap became evident in the thirteenth and fourteenth centuries as the great prince of Lithuania, Yageilo, united his country with Poland and introduced Lithuania to Catholicism.

A major development in Russian statehood came when Vladimir Monomakh offered the country the first comprehensive law of the land, the Russkaya Pravda. This written codification of law was one indication that Russia was not ruled only by a dictatorship, and was continuing its positive development into statehood.

(c) Invasions from the East and West. The twelfth and thirteenth centuries were a gloomy period in Russian history. Civil wars were common. The economy of the different princedoms, as well as the princes' well-being, was directly dependent on the size of their territory's population, which, in turn, depended on how often and how successfully the prince was engaged in wars to acquire land. The birth of Moscow in 1147 resulted from one such war, which is when the city is believed to have been founded by Yuri Dolgorukiy. The hostile relationships between related princes finally caused a total division of Rus and the independence of various princedoms.

During this period, Genghis Khan, one of history's greatest warriors, came to power in the East. He united the Tatars, the multiple tribes living on the Asian steppe, an event that allowed him to conquer China and middle Asia. Genghis Khan immediately made use of the advanced cultures of these regions in his war campaigns against Rus. Eventually only Russia was able to repulse Genghis Khan and his successor. Although the Russian princes were fighting among themselves, together they succeeded in throwing back the Tatars. Thus, the Tatars did not conquer Europe; if they did occasionally gain a foothold in Europe, they could not sustain it for long. By inflicting that severe blow against the Tatars, Russia saved Europe. That sacrifice, however, held back Russia's own development.

At the same time, Russia's northwestern borders were under constant threat from the Germans and Scandinavians. In response, the military and diplomatic talents of Alexander Nevsky (a name given to him for his victory at the Neva River) soon surfaced. He delivered a crushing blow to the Teutons in the West and, at the same time, made a temporary peace with the Tatars in the East. These developments made the situation for Novgorod, where Alexander was a prince, extremely advantageous. However, one can only speculate about their possible effects on Russia's cultural development, which was not progressing at the same speed as Europe's. The centuries of Tatar invasions, however, stimulated the economic and political unification of the Russian territories. The conquering Tatars did not want to get involved with how the princes governed their territories as long as the Tatars were getting their tribute. This hands-off attitude was amenable to the Russian nobles.

During this time, Moscow started its growth as a territory containing a large but poor population. Moscow's location in the center of the country triggered its role as "the gatherer of the Russian lands." Located at the intersection of several trade routes, Moscow became a trade center. Because the prince of Moscow at the time, Ivan Kalita, paid the largest monetary tribute to the Tatars, he was later permitted to gather tributes from the other territories and was granted additional privileges by the Tatars. He persuaded the patriarch (metropolitan) to move from Kiev to Moscow, a seemingly insignificant step that signaled the end of Kiev as Russia's most important city and the beginning of Moscow's rise to national prominence. Another of Ivan Kalita's achievements was his creation of *one* currency for use throughout all the territories of Russia. In addition, the national emblem of the two-headed eagle facing the West and the East dates back to Ivan Kalita; this emblem clearly shows the influence of the Byzantine Empire.

(d)   Ivan the Terrible.   Russia ended its slavery to the Tatars during the fourteenth century, when it stopped paying tribute to the Khan. At about this time, the title "czar" was first applied to Ivan III and his son, Vassiliy III, who finally brought the country to a state of unity not observed for centuries. It was not until the 50-year rule of Ivan IV (the Terrible), however, that Russia became a totally unified and centrally governed state. Ivan IV's first step was to increase the power Russia's western borders and strengthen its presence on the Baltic and Caspian Seas with the establishment of the cities of Narva and Astrakhan.

Ivan IV's greatest achievement, however, is still not recognized by historians. In terms of its importance, this achievement can be compared only with the "Christening" of Russia in 988. In 1581, Ivan IV organized an expedition through the Ural Mountains into Siberia, under the leadership of Ermak Timofeevich. Thanks to his tactical talent, this disgraced military officer and a small group of soldiers managed to win many small but important battles, and added Siberia to Russia. Because Siberia was larger than all the known Russian territory at that time, this expansion permitted Russia to enter the ranks of the superpowers in centuries to come. Siberia contains enormous amounts of natural resources, rivers, and forests; and it is larger in size than every country on earth, including the United States and Canada.

To illustrate the power of Russia at that time, note Ivan IV's nickname, the Terrible. His conceit and suspiciousness made him one of the most ruthless rulers of this country. Probably the only Russian ruler who surpassed him in terms of repression and deceit was Stalin. But, unlike Stalin, Ivan the Terrible eliminated many of his enemies with his own hands.

Under Ivan IV, the economic center of Russia moved eastward toward the Pacific. He gained access to the Baltic, White, and Caspian Seas, which enabled Russia later to become a sea superpower under Peter the Great. Under Ivan IV, the taxation system was crushing the economic interests of the people. His despotism provoked widescale migrations to Siberia, as thousands left their homes to escape the oppressive system. This economic situation forced Fyodor, Ivan's son, to establish the serf system, which tied peasants to their land, and the land to the boyars (highest nobles). This measure, usually considered regressive, was probably progressive for that time. It helped stabilize the economy and the country as a whole. Fyodor redefined both the military service procedure for the nobility and the tax system. Taxes were reduced drastically if the payer served in the army.

(e)   Boris Godunov.   Fyodor left no heirs—some say on purpose, so as to let the people decide on his replacement. After Fyodor's death, the throne was seized in 1598 by one of the cleverest and most active czars, Boris Godunov, who ruled until 1605. Godunov came from a moderately noble family, with Tatar roots and worked his way to the top of the army. Although he was officially crowned, he was never popular with the people, and failed to see his son placed in power.

Despite the complexity of the situations on the European and Turkish borders, and the unrest in Siberia, Godunov managed to deal with Russia's angry factions by engaging in a complex, geopolitical struggle. The Polish royal family, under Sigismund, was fighting the Swedish crown. Taking advantage of this dispute, Godunov persuaded Sigismund to sign a treaty with Russia, which put pressure on Sweden. The treaty was very advantageous for Russia; under its terms, Poland became totally dependent on Russia—a situation that lasted until 1918. Godunov continued Ivan's push to gain access to the Baltic Sea and talked Poland into giving up part of its shore to Russia. Trying to strengthen his position in the region and gain its population's loyalty to Moscow, he exempted Novgorod of most taxes.

Godunov feared that he would be unable to protect his lands from both the West and the invading Muslims of the North Caucasus and the Volga regions'. He strengthened his positions in the Crimea and Astrakhan, making the local khans his vassals. With only small armies, he managed to crush the Tatars in Siberia and built fortresses there.

Godunov pushed to bring Russian culture closer to that of Europe. He was the first Russian ruler to send people to study in countries such as Britain and Austria, and in the Hanseatic Cities. His economic policies were based mainly on tax reduction and increased efforts to stimulate the nobility's involvement in production. Godunov even implemented a two-year tax holiday for merchants and a one-year tax holiday for landlords. He actually created some protective measures for serfs, and is credited with setting time limits on work hours. But his most important step was to motivate skilled foreigners to work in Russia, and to share their experience and knowledge with the people. He exempted all foreigners from taxes. He devoted tremendous attention to fighting corruption, a task that was destined to fail because of the opposition of the nobility. It was the nobility who, after Godunov's death, resisted installing his son on the throne. Godunov's fight against corruption, as well as other factors, led to the beginning of the so-called Time of Troubles after his death.

This period can be characterized as one of the most dangerous to the stability of Russia's statehood. Several princes laid claim to the Russian crown. In addition, two commoners, who also competed with the nobles, succeeded in mounting the throne with the help of Poland, who was more than happy to turn Russia's weakness against itself. Poland was joined by other prospective adversaries, who pushed Russia from the Baltic and Caspian

Seas and prevented it from securing its position on the Black Sea. At one point, there was no czar in power, and seven boyars ruled the country.

Finally, after a long fight between noble families, a new young czar and, with him, a new dynasty was elected to the throne. Mikhail Romanov was from an ancient family and could trace his ancestors to Ivan IV. On February 21, 1613, the Romanovs began their 300-year rule with Mikhail's ascendency to the throne. The teenage czar managed to stay in power because of his father's influence. Having been made a monk by Godunov, his father rose to the nation's top secular position of Metropolitan Filaret. Many of Mikhail's rulings were in both his and the Filaret's name. During the first years of rule, his powers were restricted harshly by the boyars.

(f)   Peter the Great.   Mikhail's son, Alexei, ascended the throne of a Russia that was much diminished in size since Ivan IV had left it to his son. Many treaties with neighboring countries helped Russia survive, but it was a nation stripped of major territories. This period ushered in a regular mail system that connected Russia's far-flung regions. Although brilliant at stabilizing situations on Russia's borders, Alexei could not keep unrest at bay within the country, a problem faced by each czar before and after him. Alexei's son, Peter the Great, grew up influenced by this constant. Peter the Great and Ivan the Terrible, both rulers since childhood, grew up in fear of losing something they truly believed was given to them by God—the throne of Russia.

As Peter I mounted the throne, the greatest period in Russian history began. As were Vladimir the Red Sun and Ivan the Terrible, Peter was born to be a person of state. Showing extreme steadfastness peppered with a hint of brutality, Peter centralized numerous governmental powers while decentralizing many functions. He created Russia's first structured system for managing the territories. At the lowest district level, appointed officers ruled in combination with elected bodies. This system allowed Peter the freedom to establish a harmonious tax-collection system. Being well-educated, Peter promptly realized that the progress of the nation hinged on orienting it towards the Western world. Until the very end of his life, he followed this vision: on one hand gaining new territories in the West, and on the other cooperating and trading with Europe, tapping into its scientific potential. For example, Peter worked under an alias at the Dutch wharves to learn the basics of ship-building. It is in these years that he learned the ways and means of the West.

Peter invited the most educated and skilled people to join him in developing the country. Highly tolerant of other religions and cultures, Peter was the first czar to let foreigners approach the throne and be eligible for noble titles. He founded the Russian Academy of Sciences in 1724, and made a German mathematician its first president.

However, Peter's first priority was to make Russia a naval power. Nothing stopped him from building his fleet, even if it meant melting down church bells into cannons. Having created the fleet, Peter proceeded to deliver crushing sea and land defeats to Sweden.

In the early 1700s, he restored Russia's presence on the Caspian Sea, delivering a successful blow to the Ottomans. For his entire life, Peter worried about Russia's western and northern borders. He invited Vitus Bering to head an expedition to explore the Arctic, which disproved the age-old myth of a ground passage to America. Victorious over Sweden, Peter added the Baltic regions to his vast empire, though the Protestant influence was still too strong there to fully integrate them into Russia.

In 1703, Peter started building St. Petersburg, calling it a "window to Europe." This proved to be a very challenging ordeal. Realizing that volunteer labor would not be sufficient for the task of building the future capital on a swamp, he compelled serfs to work, often under brutal conditions. The city, bearing the name of Peter's guardian angel, reflected all of the most wonderful things he had seen in the West. During his lifetime, the city became astonishingly beautiful, yet it was not completed until long after his death.

Peter is quite a contradictory and controversial figure. He strove for absolute power, but also created a Senate with wide powers. No other leader ever gave so much attention to the scientific life of the nation. By creating the Academy of Science, along with the Cabinet of Curiosities, he led Russia into the mainstream of European scientific life for ages to come. Peter proclaimed himself the first Russian Emperor, stressing the greatness of his country. But he also created a political system that was very different from that of other autocratic regimes. Peter was a dictator, but he tried to develop a framework for authority and established democratic institutions, such as a legal system and various methods for its implementation.

Because Peter left neither a son nor a will, his wife, Catherine I, became the first Empress of Russia and the first woman to rule the country. In general, she maintained his policies, but under pressure from advisors, she practically destroyed the system of regional government Peter had created. As a result, the regional rulers regained their former power and stayed above the law. Corruption increased drastically, especially on the part of Prince Menshikov.

After only a few years on the throne, Catherine I unexpectedly died, and the grandson of Peter I, Peter II (then only 12-years old) was proclaimed the next Emperor of Russia. But the real power returned to the hands of Menshikov. Trying to concentrate his power, Menshikov married his daughter to Peter II and created the Secret Council, which had greater authority and power than the Senate. Russia's western borders became vulnerable. Poland, Austria, and Sweden began ignoring Russia's influence in Europe, which had fallen drastically. At this time, the first diplomatic border treaty was signed with China.

Peter II's brief rule ended abruptly in 1730 with his death. A new group of behind-the-throne schemers emerged and brought to power one of Peter's nieces, Anna Ioannovna. The power of the schemers was limited, though, by their promise to follow the decisions of the Secret Council. Of Prussian origin, Anna brought to Russia her compatriot Biron (who actually ruled the country with her). One of Anna's successes was the stabilization of the monetary system. She also strengthened the regional powers and increased her own power by exiling some of Peter's appointees from the capital. She also liquidated the Secret Council and established the Cabinet of Ministers. Anna introduced the first cadet corps, in which not only military, but also civil-service disciplines were taught.

After Anna's death, Peter the Great's daughter, Elizaveta, ascended the throne, ruling from 1741 to 1761. Elizaveta's major successes included the stabilization of relations with Turkey and of Russian positions in the Baltic. She sent the infant Ivan VI to jail. Under her rule, German influence suffered a strong blow. As her father had done before her, Elizaveta defeated Sweden on the battlefield, thereby gaining control over part of Finland in 1743. She started Russia's banking business by founding two major institutions, one to serve nobles and the other to serve merchants. She increased tariffs on imported goods. She also made interregional ties far less complicated.

Under her reign, Moscow State University became the first Russian university in 1755. She also opened two gymnasiums, one for the nobles and another for the children of *raznochintsy* (nongentry intellectuals). In 1757, the Academy of Arts was founded. As the Academy of Science was the nucleus of Russia's scientific life, the Academy of Arts formed the center of artistic life during the Russian Renaissance. During this time, the level of fine arts, theater (originating back to Alexei Mikhailovich,) and music rose rapidly, laying the groundwork for the future geniuses of Tchaikovsky, Glinka, Rimsky-Korsakov, Borodin, Repin, Surikov, Levitan and Serov, among others.

Russian culture underwent constant changes, being influenced by various regions within the country, as well as by other countries, especially those its rulers came from. Originally, Russia was under the influence of Scandinavia. As Russia became Christian, Byzantium was the major source of outside culture. Starting with Peter I, Europe became the chief influence, with Germany and then Holland leading the way. Elizaveta was the first ruler to sow the seeds of French cultural development.

At the very beginning of her rule, Elizaveta brought her nephew, Peter (later known as Peter III), from Holstein in Prussia and proclaimed him to be her heir. Because of his background and affection for everything originating in Germany, Peter III is harshly remembered by Russian historians. Under him, infantry soldiers were especially unhappy because they were forced to drill in the Prussian style. During the one year he held power, however, he made a few very important decisions. The State Bank was founded, the Secret Police eliminated, the gentry was waived of compulsory military service, and people were no longer persecuted because of their religious beliefs.

(g)   Catherine the Great.   Using the army's well known hostility toward Peter III, his wife, Catherine the Great, staged a coup proclaimed herself the new empress, and seized power for the next 34 years. Under her reign, the role and influence of Russia in the world grew enormously. She expanded Russia's access to the Black and Baltic Seas by building ports on both. Russia was victorious in its war with Turkey, which finally and forever ceded the Crimea to Russia. During the Turkish campaign, the military genius of Generalissimo Suvorov surfaced. Suvorov is one of Russia's greatest military commanders, having never lost a single battle.

Under Catherine, Russia continued to push its way into Central Asia. The western Ukraine and a major piece of Poland were added to Russia. For the first time, cities were built according to a unified plan. A new impetus was given to the postal service, with new roads being constructed to link the far-flung regions of the country. The empress was the first ruler since Peter the Great to travel extensively and inspect the country.

Catherine the Great favored the rapid development of Russian science and culture, using France as an example. (She was actually engaged in personal correspondence with Voltaire.) Under her reign, the Russian monetary system was given a new boost. In addition to a new mint in St. Petersburg, one was opened in the Urals, where special Siberian coins made of Urals copper, which had a higher gold content, were produced. This fostered the industrial development of eastern Russia, which was spearheaded by Demidov, a mining tycoon, noted for his never-ending energy and promotional talent.

Under Catherine the Great, a systematization of property was undertaken, and merchants were separated into three guilds. At the same time, the bureaucracy and expenses of the Court were increasing beyond reason. Trying to solve this pressing problem, Catherine introduced the first state loan, borrowing an amount equal to three times the country's budget by the time of her death. Considering her successful venture into industrial development, victorious military activities, and three-fold expansion of the army, this investment was a positive factor in developing the national economy.

For the first time since the reforms of Peter the Great, attention was given to the structure of the empire, which Catherine divided into 20 provinces in 1775. She developed a public education system in 1782 and saw the foundation of the Russian Academy. Under Catherine's rule, Russian science advanced rapidly: the first native Russian, Mikhail Lomonosov, was elected as an academician of the Imperial Academy and the first chemistry library was created.

After Catherine died, her son Pavel held the throne for five years, beginning in 1796. He strongly promoted democratic change, though he is usually viewed by Russian historians as being on a par with Peter III. Under Pavel's rule, the rights of landowners were restricted. Serfs who had been treated as slaves were now obligated to work for their respective landlords only three days a week. Pavel also made efforts to systematize and even limit the powers of the czar in financial spheres. At the same time, he drastically increased press censorship, and banned young people from traveling abroad to get an education. It was, and even now is, a little-known fact that he took an active part in European politics; he was, among other things, the Head of the Malthusian Order. Pavel also contributed to the independence of Luxembourg. Under Pavel, Generalissimo Suvorov's troops crushed the French army in several encounters, particularly during the Italian campaign, when the Russians stormed over the icy peaks of the Alps to attack the French from the rear. This battle was probably the peak of Suvorov's military career.

(h)   The Renaissance and the Degradation.   Pavel was murdered in his sleep by supporters of his son, Alexander I (the Blessed). Like most Russian rulers, Alexander I was educated at home, with his grandmother, Catherine the Great, a strong influence. In his efforts to democratize Russia, Alexander freed entire villages of serfs. He paid special attention to education, instituting a system of engineering education, and creating universities in Kharkiv and Kazan. Alexander was strongly influenced by Speransky, who greatly contributed to Russia's legislation. Under Speransky, political power was achieved only through legal means, via appointment or election. A system of ministries was created for this purpose. Even after he was banished from Moscow, Speransky undertook major developments in Siberia and was appointed its general-governor.

Alexander ruled during hard times, which were marked by the global influence of Napoleon. Russia's wars with Napoleon were characterized by numerous victories as well as losses. In 1808, Russia finished a successful military campaign against Sweden, which brought it most of the Finnish territory. The war with Turkey resulted in the territories today known as Moldova and southeastern Ukraine. In its wars with Napoleon, however, Russia was initially unsuccessful, but the French invasion of Russia proved to be Napoleon's downfall. The Russian army won numerous battles and eventually entered Paris in 1814. Victories over Napoleon were followed by a union with Prussia and, later, with Austria. One of the reasons for the Russian triumph was Commander-in-Chief Kutuzov. During the war against Napoleon, Russia, for the first time, played an integral part in shaping European politics. The next time that was to occur was between 1941 and 1945.

Victory in Europe, a new political role in Europe, the reforms of Speransky, and the cumulative effect of Russian reforms from Alexei Romanov to Catherine the Great—these formed the basis on which Russian science and history, as well as the renaissance of Russian culture in the beginning of the century, were built. The great Russian poets Pushkin, Baratynsky, and Tutchev were born, and the genius of Gogol was in full bloom. The victory over Napoleon has been noted as the beginning of Russia's integration into European life.

Revolutionary ideas spread from France into Russia during the Napoleonic Wars. The coronation of Russia's next czar, Nikolai I, was marked by the revolt of progressive military officers, who were trying to put an end to autocracy and serfdom. The era of Nikolai I can be described as one in which the Russian cultural renaissance continued to flourish. Under Nikolai's rule, the first system of pensions for the civil service was introduced. The czar, however, was careful to avoid democracy taking root. At the same time, Russia was successful in the Balkans, freeing Moldova and Serbia of the Turkish yoke, and helping Greece in its fight against Turkey. The empire, however, fiercely opposed the liberation of Poland, then part of Russia, and crushed the famous revolt. The Russian government was able to strengthen its positions in the Caucasus, on the east shore of the Black Sea, while at the same time further developing Crimea, Siberia, and the bigger part of Central Asia. Because of the presence of the rich, fertile Crimea, which was joined to the empire during Catherine the Great's reign, the secondary role accorded to the development of eastern Russia becomes more apparent.

Alexander II, succeeding Nikolai I on the throne, undertook the most ambitious efforts to date to carry out democratic reform. In 1861, serfdom was abolished, the non-nobility obtained access to universities (with the addition of new universities in Odessa and Warsaw), and economic ties to Europe and America flourished. After Bulgaria finally became free from the Ottoman Empire, it became strongly dependent on Russia. Armenia and Moldova also became part of the Russian Empire. In a succession of reforms during the 1860s and the 1870s, the courts became more open, the justice system was based upon a completely new and civilized set of rules, and the cities obtained newly elected governing bodies.

The next czar, Alexander III carefully restrained Russia's movement toward western democracy. He went on with his predecessors' reforms of the national economy and the court system, but avoided democratic reforms. At the same time, the vigorous growth of the country's railway system was a result of his efforts. At this time, the financial skill and diplomatic genius of Count S.Y. Vitte threw him into the Russian spotlight as one of the most outstanding statesmen of the nineteenth century.

Nikolai II, the last Russian czar, introduced the institution of the State Duma. Russia was defeated in its war with Japan in 1905, the nation's political system was unprepared for multipartisanship, and the bureaucracy was overwhelmingly heavy. These factors combined to lead to a drastic social conflict. Prime Minister Peter Stolypin's many efforts to conduct democratic reform within the economy were unsuccessful. The czar held too much power and, not being a talented statesman, he was destined for failure. Nicholai attempted to head both the army and the state, a situation that led to the tragic crisis of 1917, when he was forced to abdicate. The monarchy was finally abolished in Russia.

Eight months of what some consider the most democratic period in Russia's history prior to 1992 followed Nikolai's abdication. The interim government of A.F. Kerensky had a very flexible foreign policy and very tolerant internal policy. As a result, the Bolsheviks carried out a successful coup d'etat on October 25, 1917 (November 7, according to the new calendar), under the leadership of Lenin and Trotsky.

(i)   Lenin.   The economic history of Soviet Russia began with the total devastation of a capitalist economy caused by political crisis and the consequences of war. The Bolsheviks came to power as result of a coup, liquidated the briefly proclaimed sovereignty of the people, and dismissed the Duma. Thereafter, the only way for them to keep power and defend against internal and foreign enemies was with military force. Under the strains of a collapsing economy and ongoing civil war, Russia was forced to immediately accept the independence of Poland and Finland. The Bolsheviks also lost part of the Ukraine and Moldova to Romania.

Lenin's attempt to implement Karl Marx's economic theories decimated Russia's entire economic system. This resulted in a colossal decline in industrial output, an enormous food deficit, and the starvation of hundreds of thousands of Russians, particularly in rural areas where foodstuffs were confiscated to feed the city proletarian masses. Realizing the absurdity of Marx's theories, Lenin instituted the New Economic Policy (NEP) and re-established a monetary system. When Lenin died in 1924, Stalin, his successor, quickly put an end to the capitalist practices and concentrated his efforts on converting the country's industrial output to a military track. By that time, only the army could keep the enslaved country from revolting; and so the majority of Russia's budget was allocated to the military machine. Because the production of military equipment required not only educated engineers, but also workers, the country started a program of comprehensive education, which later on led to military success over Germany and a race with the United States in space, technology, military efforts, and scientific research.

(j)   Stalin.   Russia's military industry required the increased production of raw materials, including coal, oil, steel, and cast iron. For that purpose, Stalin completed the work started by Lenin on the five-year plans for the development of the economy. It was during the development of the First Five-Year Plan that the elements of an *input/output* balance system were introduced. The young economist Vassiliy Leontief studied, developed, and promoted this system. He later brought it to Germany, Japan, and America, a feat that brought him the Nobel Prize in economics in 1973.

To strengthen his absolute and centralized power in a multinational country, Stalin developed a plan for structuring the various nations of Soviet Russia. Four Union Soviet republics were formed and, as the official propaganda said, based "on the free will of the people" the Union of Soviet Socialist Republics was created on December 30, 1922. At that time, the USSR consisted of Russia, Ukraine, Belarussia, and the ZSFSR (between 1922 and 1936, it included Azerbaijan, Armenia and Georgia). Stalin divided the country with the purpose of causing tension among the regions. Their leaders had to continually report their problems to the central government and, therefore, were completely dependent on it. The territorial structure of the Soviet Union changed many more times, having a maximum of 16 republics right after World War II (including the Karelo-Finnish Republic) and 15 republics between 1956 and 1991.

The implementation of the first three Five-Year Plans led to the formation of Russia's military-industrial complex. Huge enterprises were built to extract coal, and produce steel and cast iron on the borders of the Ukraine and Russia, in Western Siberia, and in the Moscow coalfields. The Volga region and Azerbaijan were rapidly developing their own oilfields. By the end of the 1930s, at a great cost to human life, production of nickel, copper, and platinum was established above the arctic circle in the city of Norilsk in Eastern Siberia. Gold started to be mined on the Pacific coast as well. During the 1930s, however, Russia did not yet have the need or the means for wide-ranging exploitation of Siberian resources. At the same time, the aluminum industry was established on the Volga and in the Urals. Metal works were developed in Komsomolsk-on-Amur in the far eastern portion of the country. As paradoxical as it may seem, creation of a huge military industry at this time, in an unstable and warlike country, proved to be fortuitous. It was this vehicle that helped Russia defeat a much larger danger to humanity, Nazi Germany. Entering into an agreement with Hitler, through the Molotov-Ribbentrop Pact, Russia gained time to produce heavy and light weaponry, and planes, as well as the industry essential for their production: metallurgy, heavy engineering, electromechanical engineering, and oil refining.

The German offensive began in June 1941 killed millions of Russians and brought devastation, atrocities, hunger, and the death of a social infrastructure in western Russia. The war also precipitated the full or partial evacuation of Russia's industrial facilities to the Urals, Siberia, and the far eastern region. These facilities became the core industries in these regions. By 1943, Russia had not only successfully restructured its industrial production, but had also managed to develop its military industries so quickly that the nation soon surpassed all the German bloc countries' production of such items as planes, tanks, and high-tech armaments like the "Katyushas." The dedication of huge human resources and the development of the military complex made victory against Germany inevitable. By opening up

Second Front, the western allies cut short German resistance, helping to save hundreds of thousands of Russian people. In addition, the lend-lease program, which brought American technology and food supplies after World War II to Russia, helped many Russians to survive.

Russia attained its victory over Germany through marvelously developed military production, but this intense focus ruined the production of consumer goods. During the war, the standard of living was reduced to the grim days of the 1921 and 1923 famine. By the end of the 1940s, the conversion of about 30% of the military industry to consumer production was started. One means of rebuilding the civil industries was to use German facilities seized during and after the war. Using these facilities, modern auto and ship-building industries were formed. In the mid-1950s, production of other goods, such as refrigerators, was started, based on American examples such as General Electric.

The realization of these successful economic programs boosted the average Russian's standard of living, to say nothing of the national sense of pride. This centralized control over production, distribution, and prices on one hand provided for people's basic needs, such as food, supplies, and clothing. On the other hand, even centralized planning could not suppress the inflation that was a residual effect of the war years. Stalin's solution to the problem was confiscatory devaluation of the currency; he shaved the zeros off the currency and printed new bank notes accordingly. People were not allowed to exchange the bank notes in their wallets or under their mattresses for new notes, and all currency in circulation and not held in bank accounts became worthless. Purchase of long-term government bonds was compulsory from the end of the 1940s until the early 1950s; after the bonds were issued, the government frequently changed the repayment terms, so that people were repaid many years later at dramatically reduced rates.

(k) Khrushchev.   After Stalin's death in 1953 and after a two-year, behind-the-scenes struggle, power was firmly seized by Nikita Khrushchev, a controversial figure in the history of modern-day Russia. He participated in all of Stalin's crimes against humanity and was seen as a ruthless leader in his own right. But unwillingly and unwittingly, many of the steps taken during his regime would, 35 years later, help lead to the collapse of communism.

In 1956, from the podium of the 20th Party Congress, Khrushchev openly denounced Stalin and his policies. A short political thaw settled over the land. The lessening of the dictatorial reigns led to brisk development of culture and to the transformation and application of the highest technological developments for civil purposes. It was in these years that Russia showed itself as the true technological leader of the world. To support this assertion, one need only look at the development of the world's first nuclear power station (1954), the first nuclear icebreaker *Lenin* (1956), the launching of the first Sputnik (1957), and the first manned space flight (April 1961). These achievements shocked the West so much that the U.S. Congress set up a special commission to investigate the reasons for Russia's sudden achievements. At the same time, however, the Russians continued to neglect natural economic rules and the market's effect upon production. These led to complications in supplying the nation with, among others things, bread. As a result, Russia became an importer of grain for the first time and continued to do so for many years until now.

Social tensions rose in the 1960s and Khrushchev, abandoning the course he proclaimed originally, returned to the harsh noneconomic methods of directly governing the economy. By this time, the country could not provide for its people. The economic decisions made then eventually led to the crash of communism at the end of the 1980s.

(l) Brezhnev.   This economic destabilization happened to prove lucky for Leonid Brezhnev. He came to power when he headed a successful coup d'etat in October 1964 while Khrushchev was on vacation. As is often the case when a dictator comes to power in a centralized country, the economy soon took a turn for the better. For example, from 1966 to 1970, the average annual growth of the gross domestic product (GDP) was 7.2%.

In large part, that growth can be attributed to the 1965 program, Methods of Economic Motivation in Managing Industrial Enterprises, under the supervision of Prime Minister Alexei Kosygin. Introducing these methods gave the management of industrial enterprises some freedom to implement the so-called *khozraschet* system. At the same time, though, the country was still extensively developing, which meant that 75% of the GDP was based on additional new labor and natural or financial resources. This led to the construction of new facilities rather than the renovation or modernization of existing ones. New and old products alike were sold to the consumer. Sales did not soar, though, because of shortages of everything and because distribution was also centralized. Enterprises received funds only until the end of each year, and only to purchase products in the market. Because money was not being spent on development, it was plowed back into the budget. The system for motivating workers was also severely handicapped by red tape. Multiple regulations stifled the remuneration of employees, and no worker's salary could be 35 to 50% more or less than of the average national salary for each category of employees. All these conditions hampered the efforts of the production managers at the microeconomic level.

These factors, along with extensive industrial growth, ushered in the need for the development of natural resources in Russia's eastern and northern regions, the least developed and populated territories. This, in turn, led to an increase in per-unit production costs, higher transportation costs, and the need for a more developed social infrastructure. Together, these factors resulted in severe economic problems and slowed the GDP average annual growth to 5.3% in 1971 through 1975. At the same time, the positive effects of the geological discoveries of the 1950s were becoming evident, such as the unique oil reserves of Tyumen and Tomsk, and the new nickel and copper reserves near Norilsk at Talnakh. In the 15 years after 1965, production of oil in western Siberia rose from one million tons per year to one million tons per day, with production of natural gas reaching one billion cubic meters per day. Until that time, this kind of growth had been unprecedented.

This sudden growth in production was soon hampered by a sudden shortage of labor resources, which was caused by several factors. City workers did not want to leave their jobs to work in the Siberian mines. The labor force was depleted due to the major loss of life during World War II. In addition, centralized methods of management had created a surplus of jobs, so competition for available workers was increased. Moreover, enterprises wanted to increase their labor force because the more workers they employed, the larger the amount of financing they received from the state.

From 1976 through 1980, the average GDP annual growth decreased to a mere 3.5%. This depleted economy, coupled with the need to develop a stronger military complex, led to a Soviet Russia that could no longer maintain its high postwar levels of construction, education, science, and cultural development. The terribly low standard of living in rural areas led to a massive exodus of people from these regions, which in turn, resulted in a decrease in agricultural production. Stagnation of the whole economic system followed. From 1981 through 1985, the annual GDP growth did not exceed 3.1%. As early as the end of the 1970s, Siberian economic scholars concluded that the economy of communist Russia would face tremendous difficulty. The measures proposed by these economists were rather soft, suggesting that it would be possible to implement an intensive economy, but still maintain socialist principles and ideology.

(m)   Gorbachev.   The route suggested by the economists seemed impossible, though. Their intensive method of economy (as opposed to an extensive method) and employees' direct interest in the results of their work would result in an inequality in the distribution of goods and services, which was contradictory to the very idea of communist labor. In the early 1980s, the theory of *perestroika* was introduced by the Siberian economists. Later, under the influence of intellectuals like A. Yakovlev, this theory was supplemented by *glasnost,* a movement that millions of people attribute to Mikhail Gorbachev, who headed the country from March 1985.

In April 1985, Gorbachev stepped forward with the idea of simultaneously restructuring and implementing intensive methods of economy. It is, virtually impossible, however, to accelerate economic development while some enterprises are being closed and others are being restructured or are only newly opened. Another element of Gorbachev's economic plan was the channeling of investments from energy production and heavy industry to consumer goods production. No doubt it was necessary to increase production of consumer goods, but the inability to maintain the stable development of the energy sector would only hasten the collapse of the whole economy. Such investments could only be diverted from the military budget, but that idea directly conflicted with the idea of achieving military parity with the United States. This seemingly unresolvable situation was further complicated by the Reagan administration's decision to increase U.S. military spending. As a result, the Russian economy could not compete. In the mid-1980s, the gap between the U.S. and Soviet economies, and the U.S. technological dominance, made the end of the cold war inevitable and brought both sides to the negotiating table. In addition, slower investment in the fuel-energy complex led to faster decreases (up to 4% annually) in the production of oil. Such declines were previously unheard of in Russia.

At the same time, Russia's foreign economic relations saw some positive changes. In January 1987, unprecedented decisions were made that allowed Soviet entities to enter into joint ventures with foreign partners. The first 21 joint ventures were created that same year, two of them with U.S. capital. On December 2, 1988, the Council of Ministers passed a very important decree regarding the further liberalization of foreign investment activity. This decree removed the 49% limit on foreign ownership of enterprises in most industries and regions. Thus began the process of developing cooperative entities and other forms of ownership. The process developed slowly, however, as relevant legislation had not yet been passed. Because no structure was in place to support the process, decisions were not made in any standard way, but solely according to the whim of various bureaucrats. This lack of procedure limited officials at all levels, and corruption reached a record high. Cooperatives, which were operating in a more capitalistic, entrepreneurial manner, were performing adequately; but state workers, and especially blue-collar workers, were hard hit by the economic decline and restructuring, and their standard of living suffered.

Gorbachev was a progressive figure; early in his regime, he limited the role of the Communist Party in the country's politics. Sensing the party's waning prestige, he supported the first semidemocratic elections in 1989, which led to the election of the first and only Soviet president. As with everything else Gorbachev did, however, this was only a temporary measure. He was walking on thin ice, with no idea of the realities of the day. When organizing elections for Parliament, for example, he included himself in the 100 deputies that were appointed by the party, not elected.

Gorbachev could have organized the USSR into a confederation, but chose instead to try to hold onto the old structures. He spoke of democracy, but did not conduct the necessary reforms of decentralization, demilitarization, and demonopolization of the economy.

As a result, the collapse of the economy continued; and the leaders of the republics, who could not take control of their own resources under Gorbachev's plan, abandoned his rule.

(n)   The Disintegration of the USSR.   On March 11, 1990, Lithuania was the first USSR nation to declare independence. The rebellious Russian Parliament, with Boris Yeltsin at its helm, was one of the first nations in the world to recognize Lithuania as an independent entity. After this initial step, Russia paved the way for its own sovereignty. At the beginning of that year, the first free elections to the Russian Parliament took place. They ended with Yeltsin being elected as its head, despite Gorbachev's efforts. In the summer of 1991, Yeltsin and other Russian leaders declared their departure from the Communist Party. In June, Yeltsin became the first democratically-elected Russian president, with Russia remaining a part of the USSR. Gorbachev's struggle to maintain the empire and its central bodies, his misunderstanding of the new political realities, and his unwillingness to denounce the old Soviet Union Treaty (dating back to December 1922) and restructure the country into a looser federation/confederation cost him his job. The Parliaments of most of the union republics announced their sovereignty, as well as the primacy of the republican legislation over the union. Land and national resources were grabbed by the republics, and federal taxes were forgotten. A coup d'etat, staged by hard-core apparatchiks and KGB leaders in August 1991, could not save the USSR; and it only served to hasten the collapse of the empire.

The Soviet Union Treaty was legally denounced by the leaders of Russia, the Ukraine, and Belarussia (the founding members) in December 1991. In that same month, they were joined by the Central Asian republics and Kazakstan. The USSR was no more.

One has to realize that the former USSR was not a typical empire. Usually, the center of power robs its colonies, with major states succeeding at the expense of smaller ones. In this case, however, it was the other way around. Mother Russia was the indulgent parent, while the republics were the insatiable children, and she soon ran out of everything. By the start of the new year in 1992, the Soviet Union was at an end, giving way to present-day Russia.

2.2   CLIMATE.*   Russia's climate is mostly continental in type. It has long and bitter winters, brief summers, and short autumn and spring seasons. There is a wide variation in average temperatures between summer and winter, with low precipitation (most of which occurs in the summers). The country's severe climate helped stop various invaders during its history, including the large armies of Napoleon in 1812 and of Nazi Germany in 1941–42. This central fact of the Russian climate, which greatly affects the national life, can be explained by realizing that so much of the country extends so far north and is so far from the open sea. Economically, the Russian winter has two major consequences. In most parts of the country, the rivers freeze over for prolonged periods in winter, and inland water transport comes to a halt. Road transportation also slows, and therefore the railways and air services become essential for the country's economic survival.

(a)   Temperatures.   January temperatures range from 6°C (45°F) on the southeastern shore of the Black Sea to as low as −71°C (−96°F) in northeastern Siberia. Northeastern Siberia is one of the coldest regions in the world. No other part of the world registers such a wide range of temperatures. Most of the Siberian land has a phenomenon called permafrost whereby subsoil remains frozen all year.

---

*This section was written by Emilia Sherifova.

(b) Precipitation.   Precipitation (rain, melted snow, and other forms of moisture) is light to moderate. Annual precipitation decreases from about 64–76 cm (25–30 in) in the European region to less than 5 cm (2 in) a year in parts of central Asia. The European plain and parts of the east Siberian uplands receive the most rain. July and August, the warmest months, are also the wettest months in most places, with as much as one rainy day in three. But only the Caucasus receives really serious precipitation. The area between Moscow and St. Petersburg, which receives about 53 cm (21 in), is marginally wetter than most of the rest of European Russia, but still gets only half as much rain in a year as New York City.

(c) Moscow and St. Petersburg.   The two main cities, Moscow and St. Petersburg, are both warm from mid-May to early September. Summer days in these northern latitudes are long—so long that at midsummer St. Petersburg experiences the so-called white nights phenomenon, when there is no real darkness. The increasing length of daylight is an important influence on both warmth and sunshine. Autumn is very brief in the region, and by the end of November, Moscow is frozen most of the time. Heavy snow arrives in December and stays until late March or early April. St. Petersburg, located beside an arm of the Baltic Sea, is a few degrees milder than Moscow in winter, but in midwinter is reduced to about five hours of murky light a day.

2.3 LANGUAGE.*   Historically, Russia has developed as a country of many ethnic communities. The people in this country are classified according to a number of different criteria defined by their genetic and historical origins, their geographical and territorial identities, and their economic and cultural backgrounds. The most evident, however, is the classification according to ethnic and linguistic criteria.

(a) Language Families.   According to the last general census of the population in 1989, 129 different ethnic groups live in contemporary Russia. On the so-called additional list, there are another 54. All of these 183 groups belong to different language families. The sociolinguistic map of Russia contains a fixed traditional classification of language families, groups, and subgroups based on genealogical principles. The major languages are Slavic, Turkic, Finno-Ugric, Mongolian, and Caucasian. About 87.4% of the Russian population belong to the Indo-European family of languages. The Altaic family of languages is divided into three branches: Turkic-Mongolian with the group of Turkic and Mongolian languages, Manchu-Tungusic, and Japanese-Korean. The North Caucasian language family includes the Abkhaz-Adygeic and *Nakhsk*-Dagestanic groups of languages, which consist of about 30 languages. The Uralic family of languages contains the subdivisions of Finno-Ugric and Samodic languages.

The density of the major linguistic groups is summarized in Exhibit 2.1.

The modern practice in the field of ethnosociolinguistics is to classify the people of Russia according to a quantitative criterion—the number of people speaking each language. According to this principle, the 183 groups in the country are classified into three categories: multiplex nationalities, which comprise more than a million people; median nationalities, whose quantity ranges from hundreds of thousands to fifty thousand; and minorities, which are represented by from fifty thousand to a single person. According to the official data, minorities in Russia compose 63 ethnic units. Those that are in the zone of ethnic disaster are a priority for ethnic, linguistic, and ecological protection and are included in *The Red Book of Protection of the Peoples of Russia.*

---

*This section was written by Gadji G. Gamzatov.

Exhibit 2.1.   Major Linguistic Groups in Russia (Census of 1989)

Slavic group of Indo-European Family	85.4%
Turkic group of Altaic family	7.6%
Finno-Ugric group of Uralic family	2.2%
Nakhsk-Dagestanic group of North Caucasian family	1.7%
Other language groups	3.0%

National identity does not always determine knowledge of a native language. According to the 1989 census, 94% of the population spoke the language of their nationality as their native language. A change in native language is rather characteristic of the urban population and national groups living outside their republics, and also of minorities. Preference is usually given to speak their native language in the densely populated rural areas. The strongest adherence to their native language is shown by the groups living within the boundaries of their republics. This can be seen in Exhibit 2.2.

(b)   Languages of Minorities.   The languages of minorities belong to different genetic families, groups, and subgroups. Only several languages, like Ukaric, Nivkh, and Yug, are isolated. The Avar-Andi-Cezs group of minor Dagestanian languages particularly stands out. The Finno-Ugric language family has two minority groups—Obsko-Ugric (Khanty and Mansi languages) and Finno-Baltic. The Samodic family of languages includes the Nenets, Enets, Nganasanian, and Selkupsk languages. The Manchu-Tungusic family includes Nanaian, Negidalian, Oroks, Orochs, Udegei, Even, and Evenk. The Chukchi-Kamchatka family includes Chukchi, Koryak, Kerek, and Alutor. The Eskimo-Aleutian family is represented by the Eskimo and Aleutian languages.

Some of these languages were not listed in the official census until recently. According to linguistic specialists, virtually half of the minority languages are in a danger of extinction, including for instance, Kereks and Yugs (spoken by two or three groups) and Aleutians (10 to 15 groups). These and other dying languages demand urgent measures and special programs for their revitalization, preservation, and development.

Work is currently being directed at overcoming the assimilation of minorities and their languages and strengthening conditions for their free functioning and development. This policy is similar to the "orientation toward assimilation" principle established at the International Labor Organization Convention, "About Indigenous Peoples and Tribes in Independent States," in 1959. In 1991, Russia issued legislation entitled, "About the Languages

Exhibit 2.2.   Percentage of Ethnic Group Members Speaking Their Native Language

Chechens	99.8	Tatars	96.6
Ingushes	99.5	Kalmyks	96.1
Karachais	99.2	Buryats	89.4
Tuvinians	99.0	Altaians	98.1
Kabardinians	98.9	Mordvinians	88.5
Dagestanians	98.4	Maris	88.4
Balkars	98.4	Chuvashes	85.0
Adygeis	98.4	Khakases	83.1
Ossetes	98.2	Udmurts	75.7
Chircessians	98.0	Bashkirs	74.7
Yakuts	95.1	Komis	74.4
		Karelians	51.5

of the Russian Federation," which declares all the languages of the people of the Russian Federation to be its national property and its historical and cultural inheritance, protected by the state. The law provides for state guarantees supporting child rearing and education in the native language, regardless of how many people speak the language. It also says that "all people . . . with no written language of their own have the right to establish their written language in the native language. The state provides all the necessary conditions."

During the past few years, written languages have been developed for a number of people with no written language of their own. A system of primary education, the publication of books and newspapers, and regular television and radio broadcasting were introduced in the native languages. For the first time, Dagestan minorities such as the Aguls, Rutuls, and Tsukhurs (some of which have no more than 20,000 people) established a national written language and literary norms. They also achieved equal rights with other peoples for representation in the highest bodies of government.

(c) Organization of Society. The diverse ethnic and linguistic nature of Russia determines the complex political and state organization of its society. Russia has different kinds of political entities, such as national and state, national and territorial, and territorial and administrative. All this gives a unique picture of the national life and determines the development of the different national cultures. The diversity in the Russian Federation's structure is determined by its Constitution of 1993 and is characterized by the presence of 89 political entities, including 21 national republics. The republics experience the most complex effects of the language situation.

The official language of the Russian Federation is Russian. Russian enjoys the status of being a universally recognized means of international communication. In some republics, the principal languages (the so-called title languages) are Turkic (Altaic, Bashkir, Tatar, Tuvinian, Karachai, Khakass, Chuvash, and Yakut); Finno-Ugric (Karelian, Komi, Mari, and Mordovinian); North Caucasian (Adygei, Ingush, Chechen, and Kabardian), Mongolic (Buryat and Kalmyk), and Iranian (Ossetic). The languages of many of the title nationalities have been declared official languages. An exception is the republic of Dagestan, where there is no title nationality among more than 30 nationalities. As a corollary, there is no title language that lends its name to the republic. Here every functioning native written language has an official status that is equal to Russian.

According to the 1989 census, 88% of the non-Russian peoples of Russia speak Russian well (27.6% consider it native, and 60.4% have a good command of Russian).

(d) Functional Development of Languages. Languages in the Russian Federation can also be classified functionally. For example, there are regional international languages, such as Avar among the *Avar-Andi-Cezs* group of languages in Dagestan. In addition, some written languages were established during the Soviet times, and others were established recently. There are also quite a few unwritten languages that still function among the people.

The most significant of the social criteria that determine the level of functional development of languages is the number of native speakers of the language and their settlement patterns. Thus, for instance, different republics have far from equal objective possibilities regarding the functional development of the title language. In some of them, the title nationality comprises the majority of the population (e.g., Tuva—64.3%, Chuvash—68%). In other regions, the title nationality comprises less than 50% (Kalmyk—47%, Udmurt—33%, Karelia—10%). The language situation in Russia is such that political, social, economic, and cultural life is impossible without bilingualism, and in a number of regions, without polylingualism. The state provides its citizens with all the necessary conditions for using any language of Russia in public and political life.

Development and implementation of the proper language policy in a multinational country like Russia is impossible without an overall understanding and assessment of all the sociolinguistic factors of national and language life. Russian democracy has only one way to build a proper linguistic environment—through the stable and democratic development of interethnic, international, and interlingual relations.

2.4   RELIGION AND ETHNIC GROUPS.*   Russia's ethnic and religious background is colorful and unique. It contains a great number of nationalities and ethnic groups practicing different religions and beliefs. The majority are Orthodox Christians. Christianity first came to Russia in the sixth century, spreading among the Adygei tribes. Later, it was adopted by the Ossetes, the people of Chechnya and Dagestan. In the seven to eight centuries under Arabic conquerors, however, Christianity yielded to Islam in these areas.

(a)   Spread of Christianity.   The beginning of the intensive spread of Christianity in Russia occurred at the end of the tenth century from Byzantium. For many centuries thereafter, Russians were converted to Christianity, a process that rose to a large scale after the Russian liberation from Mongol-Tatar conquerors and the permanent expansion of Russian boundaries by conquests and annexations of neighboring countries.

By the end of the nineteenth century, the Russian Empire covered a territory of almost 22.5 million square kilometers. Its 125.7 million inhabitants comprised, apart from Russians, 200 ethnic groups whose members spoke about 150 languages, all of whom were followers of different religions and beliefs. According to the first general census in 1887, Orthodox Christians constituted 69.4% of the total population, Roman Catholics 9.1%, Muslims 11.1%, Jews 4.2%, Lutherans 2.8%, Old-Believers 1.8%, and Buddhists, Lamaists, and other non-Christian faiths 0.5%.

The official policy of the czar toward subjects of the empire was conversion to Christianity and Russification (i.e., assimilation into Russian culture). Missionary work rose to a great scale that was directed to pagans, as well as against Roman Catholicism, Judaism, and Islam. In 1870, an Office of Baptism Affairs was established in Kazan that conducted conversion efforts directed at the peoples living along the Volga river. By the beginning of the nineteenth century, the New Testament was translated into Tatar, Persian, Chuvash, Kalmyk, and other languages. In 1860, the Society of Restoration of Orthodox Christianity in the Caucasus was established. The society was "called up to struggle against Islam." Similar missionary organizations and societies worked in virtually all national regions. Apart from eastern Slavic peoples, a lot of other peoples joined Orthodox Christianity. Among them were baptized Tatars; a large group of the Siberian Tatars; a faction of Ossetes; the Finno-Ugric people; people of the north and Siberia; and some others. However, the Orthodox Christianity of the newly converted was often superficial and formal. Pagan rites, shamanism, and other religious traditions still remained popular.

Side by side with Christianity, there existed at various times dissident societies of Old-Believers, Dukhobors, Molokans, Christ-Believers, Protestant sects of Adventists, Baptists, Evangelists, and others. These groups still exist.

Monastic life, with its asceticism and refusal of all temporal joys, was widespread. By 1917, the Russian Orthodox Church had about 50,000 actively functioning churches. Four academies (at Saint Petersburg, Moscow, Kiev, and Kazan), 57 theological seminaries, and

---

*This section was written by Gadji G. Gamzatov and Mogamed Magomedhanov.

184 theological colleges trained ecclesiastics. About 100,000 nuns, monks, lay sisters, and lay brothers lived in 1,256 monasteries and nunneries.

(b) Nationalization of Church Property. In 1918–1925, Soviet power nationalized the property of the Russian Orthodox Church, which owned 8,275,000 hectares of land, 424,476 million roubles, 84 factories, 1,816 businesses and hotels, 277 hospitals and shelters, 436 milk farms, 603 kettle farms, and 311 apiaries. The property of other faiths was treated in a similar manner. Shamans and ecclesiastics of other religions were subject to severe repression. Many temples were turned into storehouses and eventually destroyed. The spread of atheism through Russian society became one of the major goals of the Soviet ideology.

(c) Revival. The last two decades have been marked by revival of the religious life in Russia. In 1988, the thousandth anniversary of the adoption of Christianity in Russia was widely celebrated. Religious establishments are being restored and built, and numerous religious publications are being published. The Russian Orthodox Church has about 7,000 parishes that constitute 70 eparchies. The former are governed by bishops, archbishops, and metropolitans. Supreme church power belongs to the Landed Synod, which elects the Holy Synod and the All-Russia Patriarch. There are two theological seminaries and academies in Moscow and Saint Petersburg, along with 269 monasteries.

About 90% of Russian worshippers are Orthodox Christians. Orthodox Christianity is the main religion of Russians, who constitute 80% of the population, and also of many other peoples, such as the Karels, Vepses, Saams, Udmurts, Yakuts, Maris, Chuvashes, Ossetes, Khakases, the majority of the groups living in the north, and many others. The Russian Orthodox Church is one of the independent organizations of worldwide Orthodox Christianity.

(d) Spread of Islam. The second most popular religion in Russia is Islam. Its spread among the people of Russia began in the seventh century and continued for centuries. By 1913, Bashkortostan and Tatarstan had more than 6,000 mosques and 7,000 theological schools; and there were about 2,060 mosques and 1,000 theological schools in Dagestan that had a population of no more than a million people. Many mosques and theological schools also existed in the Crimea, Chechnya, and other regions of the North Caucasus.

According to the census of 1989, the number of Islam believers was under 12 million people, which is 6% of the entire population. These included Tatars (5.5 million), Bashkirs (1.4 million), Chechens (0.9 million), Kazakhs (0.6 million), Avars (0.5 million), Kabardinians (0.4 million), Dargins (0.4 million), Lezgins (0.3 million), Karachais (0.7 million), Uzbeks (0.1 million), and other nationalities.

The majority of Russian Muslims are followers of Orthodox Islam, that is, Sunnism. Sunnism is represented by two schools—Khanafism and Shafiism. Russian Sunnites are primarily Tatars, Kabardinians, Bashkirs, Adygei, Chirkassians, Abazins, Karachais, and Dagestanians. Kazakhs, Uzbeks, Kirgizes, Turkmens, Tadjiks, Crimean Tatars, and others follow the school of Khanafits. The adherents of Shaffiism are Avars, Chechens, Ingushes, many Ossetes, and others.

There is no unified organizational structure of Russian Muslims. The All-Russian Center of Ecclesiastic Affairs was established in 1993, and the All-Russia Islamic Cultural Center in 1992. Both are situated in Moscow. The Administration of the North Caucasus Muslims functioned until 1988, when it subsequently divided into twelve Islamic administrations according to the nationality principle. The same happened to the former Muslim administration of the European part of Russia and Siberia. A noticeable revival of Muslim religion and culture has recently occured in the country.

(e)   Judaism.   The followers of Judaism number two million in Russia, with most of them living in the big cities. Their religious life is relatively active in Moscow, Saint Petersburg, Ekaterinburg, Nijniy Novgorod, Saratov, Samara, and Irkutsk where there are synagogues and theological schools. About 20,000 Mountain Jews live in Dagestan and some other parts of the North Caucasus and Russia. Synagogues are located in cities such as Derbent, Buinaks, and Makhachkala.

(f)   Buddhism.   Presently, there are two million followers of Lamaist Buddhism. They are Buryats, Tuvinians, and Kalmyks. Buddhism was spread by Mongolian and Tibetan lamas in the sixteenth and seventeenth centuries. The Religious Administration of Buddhists and official representation of the Dalai Lama exist in Russia.

(g)   Other Religions.   During recent years, Russia has seen a small increase in Bahaism. In addition, some members of the population adhere to traditional belief systems, such as shamanism. These traditional systems are popular among the minority people of Siberia, the Urals, and those living along the Volga river.

2.5   RECENT SOCIAL, POLITICAL, AND ECONOMIC DEVELOPMENTS.*   With a conventional military force and a nuclear arsenal commensurate with the status of a superpower, the Soviet Union exercised sovereignty over a vast geographic territory. Institutions associated with Soviet rule included a well-funded and prestigious scientific community, an influential diplomatic corps, an extensive social-welfare program, a cumbersome bureaucratic administration, and the hegemony of the Communist Party. Even before the USSR was dissolved on December 25, 1991, these institutions were in various states of disarray. Because their degeneration is so conspicuous, change in Russia has been defined and measured primarily in retrospective terms. While reference to the past is a legitimate way to track change, plans for the future are also significant in any effort to understand purposive human affairs. The question is not only, or primarily, about the fall of the old, but about the rise of the new: what institutions will fill the void?

A standard answer is *democracy* and *capitalism.* When Presidents Reagan and Bush declared that the West had won the Cold War, their rhetoric suggested that the "winning" ideology would replace the institutions represented by the "losing" ideology. As events have unfolded, the reliability of this rhetoric has become increasingly open to question. Predictions in international politics require a stronger foundation than patriotic rhetoric.

The foundation necessary to support such predictions consists of *policy statements* and *observations of actual trends.* The search for areas that exhibit convergence between policy and enforcement and in which there is a clearly observable trend, does not yield positive results. In the following section, 14 key areas will be summarized.

1. One area to consider is the effort made by the current Russian government and by such agencies as the Chamber of Commerce and Industry (CCI) to create an environment conducive to entrepreneurship. The CCI releases subscribed electronic publications to keep entrepreneurs apprised of the latest news on legislation, domestic real estate, financial markets, and currency markets. Its publications include the

---

*This section was written by Jeffery L. Geller and Irina Shin.

newspaper, *Torgovo-Promyshlennye Novosti.* The CCI provides news on import and export services through Zlaki, the International Center for Business Information. Quality inspections are provided by Sojuzexpertiza, which has branches in Russian ports, major trade centers, and border posts. The Moscow Center for International Trade and Scientific Ties with Foreign Countries (CMT) is one of the largest business centers in the world. The CCI's efforts are complemented by such programs as the tender system, whereby, under certain conditions, promising investment projects receive between 20% and 50% of their funding from the government. Despite these efforts, entrepreneurs in Russia face a dilemma. The probability of their success is much greater in major urban centers, particularly Moscow, than outside those centers. In major urban centers, however, the monetary profits have been an irresistible attraction to organized crime. Despite the efforts mentioned, investment has steadily declined, reaching its lowest level yet in 1996.

2. As indicated, Russia has made an effort to stimulate the private economic sector. Somewhat paradoxically, much of the formal initiative for this effort comes from a governmental planning commission that has formulated national goals, including the technological modernization of the Russian economy, the strengthening of the national industrial infrastructure, and a policy for export development (particularly for the export of high-tech products). Though not an obvious contradiction, the fact that the development of private enterprise is supervised by government agencies, a phenomenon known as state stimulation, shows that the administrative command system that dominated the Soviet Union is still part of Russian life.

3. Another area to consider is the effect of the business environment on foreign investment. The law entitled Property in the Russian Federation, enacted January 1, 1991, secures the right of foreign persons to own enterprises, buildings, and other property for business purposes. This and similar legislation provide guarantees against forced confiscation and "illegal actions" on the part of state bodies and officials. Any exception is to be compensated in the amount of the damage, including lost profit. The law, Foreign Investments in the Russian Federation, stipulates that "foreign investments in the Russian Federation are not subject to nationalization and cannot be requisitioned or confiscated." However, exceptions are allowed "when these measures are necessary due to social interests." As to compensation, the current legislation does not outline a mechanism to estimate the actual value of damages, nor does it delegate responsibility for implementing procedures for repayment. The vagueness of these measures has motivated the formation of bilateral interstate agreements for "the encouragement and mutual protection of investments." The total number of such agreements exceeds 25, including 14 that were inherited from the USSR. A bilateral agreement between the Russian Federation and the United States was signed in Washington in 1993. The agreement contains, among other provisions, guarantees on the convertibility of currency and on market exchange rates. As part of the agreement, the Russian government legally recognizes the authority of the Overseas Private Investment Corporation (OPIC), which oversees any insurance claims that might arise. Since international law is granted priority over national legislation, such bilateral agreements help shore up the inadequacies of national legislation. But such agreements cannot go into effect until they are ratified by the Federal Assembly of the Russian Federation. The agreements with the United States and several others cases are awaiting ratification.

4. Another important area is privatization. Since 1992, when the first of three stages of privatization got underway, over 50% of the formerly state-owned enterprises have changed their form of ownership. Presently, approximately 122,000 privatized enterprises account for over half of Russia's gross national product. As in several aspects of Russian life, there are significant inconsistencies between conditions in Moscow, which in many ways is a separate social, political, and economic entity, and other cities, including St. Petersburg. More than half of the 6,000 enterprises initially privatized were in Moscow. Today, 20% of all privatized enterprises are in Moscow, despite the fact that only 7% of Russia's population live in the capital city.

   The main problems affecting privatization, however, are not so much a matter of *where* as of *who*. Because of the way in which ownership changed hands, economic power still belongs to those who had it before, namely the *nomenklatura,* the old administrative elite. Only 10% to 15% of the new managers are equipped to work efficiently under market conditions. Because of the domination of the *nomenklatura,* only paltry leftovers remain for the new private sector. The owners of new corporations that evolved from former state enterprises include not only their ex-managers, but also government officials, gangsters, security guards, suppliers, and clients. Such owners have a much greater interest in maintaining control, which was the major objective of the old system, than they have in increasing profitability and dividends, which is the major objective of the new system. Finally, many of Russia's remaining enterprises have become the property of their employees. This mixture between collective property and the market system, which some commentators have called market socialism, has proved so far to be inefficient.

5. Explicit policy statements dealing with the development of Russia's consumer market are codified in the Consumers' Rights Defense, the law on Certification, and the law on Competition and Restrictions of Conduct in the Market, all of which are designed to protect the rights of consumers. For this same purpose, there are approximately 200 regional and four national consumer organizations. They have been active, as illustrated by the 1991 case involving inauthentic Levi's jeans and the 1995 campaign against Sony, Matsushita, and Samsung. Despite these gestures, contemporary Russia is hardly a haven for consumers. One problem is that the cost of corruption is reflected in higher prices. Each person who shares the profit, whether a factory worker, supervisor, truck driver, wholesaler, delivery person, retail clerk, government official, or bodyguard, raises the price consumers must pay. Another problem is that the poor management of most enterprises obliges consumers to pay a portion of every purchase to subsidize inefficiency. Third, the rate of inflation and the instability of the ruble do not inspire consumer confidence. Finally, the government's chronic nonpayment of salaries, pensions, and social benefits dramatically reduces the population's disposable income.

6. The task assigned to the State Committee of the Russian Federation for Anti-Monopoly and Support for New Economic Structures (GKAP), a federal organ of executive power with 2,700 personnel, is the "prevention, restriction, and cessation of monopolistic activity." The decision to treat a variety of industries (including oil and gas by pipelines, transmission of electrical and thermal power, railroad transportation, services at transportation terminals, ports and airports, services of general electrical utilities, and the postal service) as natural monopolies, that is, as exempt from GKAP regulation, is consistent with international standards. A practice that is not in line with international standards is the state ownership of 25 to 51% of the

shares of over 3,000 enterprises whose products and services are deemed "strategically important for the national security."

In a related problem, Article 10 of the law on competition charges the GKAP with the task of combatting "piracy." It is responsible for preventing violations that involve obtaining, using, or disclosing scientific, technical, production or trade information (including trade secrets) without the consent of the owner. It is also responsible for preventing the illegal use of labels, brand names, and marking of goods. These are admirable objectives, given that copyright infringements and violations of intellectual property rights undermine the economic incentive to do creative work. Experts estimate, however, that 60 to 95% of the records, CDs, videotapes, software, and books sold in Russia are produced without the consent of their copyright owners.

7. The "transitional economy" has been mired in a protracted crisis. While there are some relatively positive trends, for example, the relatively dramatic increase in fuel and energy industries from 12% of total industrial output in 1990 to 31% in 1995, there has been no net gain because general production has declined in every sector by an average of 50%. A detailed list of the declines in different industries (for example, metallurgy by 45%, light industries by 70%, and so on) is less important than the general decline of every major economic indicator from gross domestic product to the population's real income. The various stages of "financial stabilization" have had little positive effect on gross domestic product, which declined by 38% from 1990 to 1995, or on industrial output, which declined by 55% during the same period.

8. Some indication of a trend is occurring in international trade. From 1991 to 1996, Russia moved dramatically from a state monopoly of foreign trade to a "liberal foreign trade regime." At present, any Russian national who has the status of a "private entrepreneur" can participate in foreign trade. As of 1996, 440,000 out of 2.6 million individual private entrepreneurs were engaged in foreign economic activities. These figures stand in sharp contrast to 1991, when only about 60 governmental organizations were allowed to participate in foreign trade.

In the Far East, the rate of growth in trade between the Russian Federation and the United States increased threefold in 1995 alone, making the United States Russia's second leading trading partner after Japan in the region. The joint ventures in mineral production, oil development, and fish processing are promising. Up to the present, however, the American-Russian Investment Fund has invested a paltry $15 million in the region, far below the expected level. On a nationwide basis, two of the greatest impediments to profitable foreign trade have been the inflation rate and the consequent instability of the ruble. Until these problems are brought under control, Russia will not be competitive in the international market.

9. The Federal Tax Service was established by a presidential decree on December 21, 1991. Also by presidential decree, a centralized system of federal treasury agencies, consisting of the Federal Treasury and the Ministry of Finance, was established on December 8, 1992. Despite the elaborate laws governing taxation, noncompliance was so high that a tax police was created in 1993. Though there is a consistent trend reflected by the policy statements, the fact that tax evasion remains rampant and mechanisms for the apprehension and prosecution of offenders are poorly defined and ineffective, betrays a failure of resolve on the part of policy makers.

10. The authority of the Russian Parliament appears to be rising. However, under the constitution adopted on December 12, 1993, the powers of Parliament, which consists of a Lower House (the Duma) and an Upper House (the Council of Federation) are unclear. Under the old constitution (which dates to 1977), the Communist Party and powerful elements of the national bureaucracy were allowed to exercise de facto power. Whether this can be avoided under the new constitution remains to be seen. At present, the Communist Party has a firm grip on the Parliament and a battle is taking place over the relative power of the legislative and executive branches of government.

11. Another battle is being waged over the federal structure of the new Russia. According to Article 11 of the Constitution, the Council of Federation of Russia's Parliament is one of the supreme bodies of state power. A decidedly lowly supreme power, the Council of Federation is limited in many legislative actions to "suggest, make proposals, and persuade." Its actual impact on the country has been minimal. In 1992 and 1993, a number of subjects of the Federation stopped making payments to the federal budget in protest against the budget system. This so-called war ended, at least temporarily, when the subjects of the Federation gained more independence to conduct their own taxation and formulate their own budget policies. The 1994 reform of interbudget relations set up a commission to develop a transfer mechanism to decentralize financial resources. Ironically, to support this reform effort, a unified budget fund, financed by consolidated budget revenues, was established. Financial matters aside, in order for the Council of Federation to play any significant role in national affairs, or even to provide adequate representation for the various regions, its power must be augmented by constitutional amendment.

12. With regard to demilitarization, the defense industry and the civilian industries that fill military orders are being "structurally reshaped." In 1992 and 1993, fourteen conversion programs, including the Rebirth of the Russian fleet and conversions of civilian aviation, the agro-industrial sector, medicine, and the energy complex got underway. Demilitarization has obvious implications for foreign policy. In the new role that Russia envisages for itself in international politics, the decisive renunciation of superpower status will come only with the dismantling of nuclear weapons. Russia has been reluctant to take decisive steps, however, preferring to retain enough of its nuclear capabilities to preserve its status as a superpower. Although the first steps have been taken, including consent to the reunification of Germany, an agreement on conventional weapons that undermined Soviet superiority in that field, and the agreement on "Europe without blocs" contained in the 1990 Paris Charter, attitudes have recently begun to shift to a more militant stance. Some accuse the former foreign minister of the Russian Federation, Andrei Kozyrev, of having blindly followed the United States and call for a more assertive policy in pursuit of Russia's own interests.

13. Supported by national legislation, presidential decrees, and governmental provisions, the mass media have expanded their range of operation under the new regime. Ironically, the sensitive area of mass media is now protected from censorship by the government. There are three federal television companies that broadcast nationwide and 90 regional television companies in Russia. The former receive 47% of their operating budget from the state. The print media have also expanded, at least in the number of different publications available. They have been mired in a deep financial

crisis for the last five years, however, and have only managed to survive because of state subsidies. Currently, there are approximately 600 publications receiving subsidies, including such governmental publications as *Rossijskaya Gazeta, Rossijskiye Vesti, Rossijskaya Federatsiya,* and *Rodina.* In 1994, governmental publications received approximately 40 billion rubles. Nongovernmental publications, including *Pravda* and *Sovetskaya Rossija,* also received subsidies. The 4,526 newspapers published in Russia have a combined annual circulation of 8 billion copies.

As impressive as these statistics sound, freedom of the press in Russia remains a questionable proposition. With government subsidies keeping the industry afloat, the mass media lack the independence their counterparts enjoy in Western countries. To make matters worse, a law was enacted in 1995 that makes it illegal for advertising to exceed 40% of the total space in any publication, whether subsidized or not. Such a law favors publications that are subsidized and makes it difficult for others to compete. Also, censorship can take many forms. Russia is one of three countries in the world where the profession of journalism is considered highly dangerous. Between January 1994 and April 1995, fourteen Russian journalists died while practicing their profession.

14. One final issue to consider is the change occurring in Russia's scientific community. Notable recent achievements have come in the fields of theoretical physics, solid-state physics, energy technologies of steam and gas cycles, catalysis, and genetic engineering. The space program, which is currently involved in several collaborative projects with NASA, has also been very successful. Official support for scientific advancement is expressed in the law entitled Science and State Policy on Science and Technology and in the Doctrine on the Development of Russian Science. These documents seek to secure a respectable place for science among the public, reform the management and organization of scientific research, insure the continued link between science and national security, and secure the international prominence of Russian science and technology. To accomplish these goals, legislation mandated a specific level of funding, namely, not less that 4% of federal expenditures. In addition, several technologies were designated as crucial. Among the 70 to be granted this status were, for example, microsystem equipment, microsensorics, electrostatic plasma technologies, and biotechnologies. These 70 technologies were earmarked to receive additional financial support from the government. Further demonstrations of the Federation's commitment to science are the network of 60 technoparks, which employ over 10,000 workers, and the financial support granted to over 500 projects reflecting international scientific cooperation and exchange of technologies.

Despite the ongoing efforts to maintain a viable scientific community, economic circumstances make this goal extremely challenging. For example, the 4% of the federal budget allocated to the Russian fund for fundamental research has not materialized. Instead, the figure has varied between 1.9% and 2.65% from 1992 to 1996. Considering that the federal budget has suffered along with the general economy, this amounts to a substantially smaller piece of a substantially smaller pie. Adjusted for inflation and the resulting currency devaluation, the federal budget allocation for research and development between 1991 and 1995 decreased by a staggering 80%. During this period, budget expenditures represented by research and development decreased by approximately 30%. In terms of personnel, over 600,000 jobs were lost, representing nearly 40% of the workforce in research and development. These adverse conditions have resulted in an inevitable braindrain.

As this survey indicates, the current situation is not promising. Various factions have neutralized each other, rendering each party, branch, and interest group powerless. This paralyzing balance arose when Russia emerged from the collapse of the USSR. The initial success of the Soviet model was due to an enormous concentration of power in a small number of hands. Centralization of power, consolidation of society, rigid planning, and vast mineral and labor resources made it possible for the USSR to accomplish an economic breakthrough and join the powerful nations of the world, a situation that the Soviet Union enjoyed for several decades.

The success of the socialist model was crucial to the survival of the USSR. When the model started to show signs of serious weakness in the early 1980s, the Soviet leadership made minor changes in order to keep it functioning. Economically, the Soviet model depended on the use of such resources as minerals and labor, which had been vital in an industrial age but which were becoming less so in the new age of technology and information. The revolution in computerization and information processing introduced factors that were crucial to societal development in western Europe and America, but that were incompatible with the ideological orientation and political operation of the USSR. This revolution brought about the proliferation of easily accessible information throughout the world, but it ran counter to the Soviet practice of dispensing information only for political objectives.

To avoid being isolated in a qualitatively different historical age, a new Soviet leadership relaxed its central control and let some fresh air into Russian society. Whether voluntarily or involuntarily, the leaders awakened the country's population. The first to react to the changes were Western-oriented intellectuals who initiated a movement for democratization and market reform. The awakened Soviet society, through self-examination, began to realize its identity or, to be more precise, identities. This growing nationalist consciousness led to the spread of nationalism among ethnic groups that had once embraced, to varying degrees, proletarian internationalism. This trend brought the disintegration of the USSR.

In place of the rigid structure that had been forcibly maintained by a consolidated ideology, the concentration of political power in the hands of the ruling party, and economic centralization, a new living organism was born. That the new organism would be diffuse, as indicated by the fact that 56 languages are spoken in Russia, was expected. This organism, however, turned out to be more complex, unpredictable, and demanding than anticipated. Its cells developed into self-contained entities determined to lead their own independent lives. This meant a further disintegration—but this time, of Russia. As a result, the task of elaborating new principles of interaction and integration among the entities is vital to Russia's survival. This task should either replace or supplement military efforts in holding the Russian Federation together.

In the midst of this increasing nationalism, the new generation of leaders have come into office. In terms of their political background and experience, they belong to the younger, reform-minded generation of the Soviet leadership. At the same time, these new leaders have been influenced by Western-oriented intellectuals who demand democracy and market reforms, that is, changes toward the values that comprise the dominant political and economic model found in the contemporary world. Their leadership on behalf of this model, however, resembles a meandering drift more than a purposeful march.

Russia's ethnic, social, political, and economic identity is highly disintegrated. There are Russians who enjoy their new situation, and there are those who cannot adjust to it. The part of the general population that is interested in the political and economic life of the country is divided into three camps: democratic, communist, and nationalist. Recently, a new political force, the military opposition, has emerged. Young and inexperienced in political struggles, but strongly desirous to put the country in order, the military opposition lacks a clear sense of economic and ideological destination. Because of its inexperience in theoretical and ideological matters, however, it is likely to provide the impetus for a different group's push for power.

The last decade has witnessed the steady erosion of the central power structure and its control over the country. The legislature is paralyzed by endless debates between the communist majority and other factions. Despite the loss of control, the relative power of executive authority is growing, as is the strength of the military opposition. With these factors in the background, there is a strong probability that leadership will strengthen, perhaps even to the extent that it is transformed into authoritarian rule.

2.6   STANDARD OF LIVING.*   Standard of living is defined as the degree of development and satisfaction of the needs of a group of people. It is measured by a system of indices based on the level of income, basic needs (including diet and housing), education, cultural development, and social support.

(a)   Diet and Russian Health.   The estimate used to determine the standard and quality of a country's diet is based on the average daily consumption of protein per person measured in kilocalories and grams. Statistical data indicate that before 1990, the diet of the Russian population gradually improved and the calorie consumption of protein including animal protein, was 92% of the worldwide level—equal to that of the developed countries of America and Europe.

In recent years, though, the Russian diet has gotten worse, both in calorie content and in the composition of food. Whereas in 1990, an average family member consumed 3,085 calories per day, and protein consumption averaged 82.5 grams, in 1995, the figures dropped to 2,293 calories per day and 61 grams of protein. Consumption of meat, per person, per year, decreased from 65 kilograms in 1991 to 52 kilograms in 1995. Milk and milk products dropped from 349 kilograms to 247 kilograms, eggs from 229 kilograms to 196 kilograms, and fish from 14 kilograms to 9 kilograms.

Levels of food consumption differ between city and country. Between 1990 and 1995, urban Russians increased their consumption of bread products, potatoes, vegetable oil, but decreased consumption of vegetables, meat, milk, eggs, sugar, and fish. People living in rural areas consumed more potatoes, vegetables, and melons, but fewer bread products, meat, milk, vegetable oil, sugar, eggs, and fish.

These dietary trends are determined by the population's financial condition. Most expenditure for food remains more than the rest of the family budget, in most cases. In 1995, food comprised 52% of most family's total household budget. Of this food budget, 27% was for meat and meat products, 17% for bread products, 15% for milk and dairy products, and 12% for confectionery items.

The consumption level of these products is determined, first of all, by the volume of agricultural production. From 1994 to 1995, the production of meat, milk, and eggs in all categories of industries dropped by 10 to 15%, while potato and vegetable production increased by 17 to 18%. In recent years the increase in volume of agricultural production in private subsized farming caused a decrease in the supply of food products. The following represent the portions of agricultural production from private farming; meat and meat products 26%, milk and dairy products 35%, eggs 28%, potatoes 78%, and vegetables 49%.

---

*This section was written by Gennadiy G. Melikian.

In recent years, a decrease has occurred in the industrial production of food products as well. In 1995, the output from meat-processing enterprises was down by 33%, all milk products by 25%, animal oil, bakery items, vegetable oil, and flour by 35 to 53%. This lowered output was caused by a decrease in the production of agricultural raw material and a failure of the standard obligatory sale of agricultural products to the state. Two other problems were the nonpayment of products purchased and the lack of development of the market infrastructure in villages.

The drop in industrial production of food products, to a certain degree, is related to an increase in the development of products by small industries, special reprocessing of agricultural products, and an increase in permissible conditions for processing.

The state of the food products market, at the present time, is determined, to a significant degree, by the import revenue. In 1995, imported food products comprised 54% of the country's food market, as opposed to 48% in 1994. In 1995, imported food products and raw materials for their production (such as seeds or feed) totaled 13.2 billion dollars, or 25% more than in 1994. The portion of food imports comprised 28% of the total market.

Of the imported foodstuffs and raw material for food production, 20% were meat and meat products, 13% vegetables and fruits, and 12% sugar and confectionery goods. In 1995, 736,000 tons of freshly frozen meat, 826,000 tons of poultry meat, 298,000 tons of canned meat, 80,200 tons of dried and condensed milk, 244,000 tons of butter, 284,000 tons of sunflower oil, 1,253,000 tons of sugar syrup, 1,794,000 tons of white sugar, 533,000 tons of rye flour, and 35,800 tons of groats were imported.

In the consumer market, there is a high degree of saturation among nearly all the food groups and even a decrease in the turnover for various food products. This is in distinct contrast to the trend toward increased turnover that occurred between 1992 and 1993.

There is more trading activity in the local markets than in commercial enterprises. In the local markets, the population accounts for 30 to 34% of the total purchases of meat, vegetable oil, vegetables, and potatoes; 14 to 21% of meat and eggs; and 6 to 9% of sausage items, sugar, and confectionery goods.

(b) Housing in Russia. The most important factor in creating good living conditions is providing the population with decent housing. At the present time in Russia, on average, one dweller occupies about 18 square meters of common living area. According to this index, Russia is two to three times behind the developed countries of Europe, the United States, and Japan. Russia differs from these countries in the amount and quality of the services, utilities, and apartments provided. In Russia, there are significant differences between the amount of utilities in the homes in the city and the country. Eighty-four percent of the city dwellers have some sort of water supply, 81% have drainage, 85% have central heating, and 71% have a hot-water supply. By contrast, 53%, 42%, 44%, and 24% of people in rural areas enjoyed these services.

The limited number of dwellings in Russia does not allow every family to have its own apartment; and the number of dwellings being constructed has proved to be inadequate. In the 1990s, housing construction was cut back so that by 1995 new construction in the Russian Federation was less than 66% of the 1990 volume. After 1991, a new housing policy was enacted. It called for housing reform that protected the needy and guaranteed citizens decent housing standards and living conditions.

During the years of housing reform, significant changes were made. In a majority of the regions of the Russian Federation, housing securities were issued and funds were formed for the development of housing; efforts to attract foreign investment into this sphere grew, offering needy families subsidies for construction. Free privatization of dwellings continues, a situation that creates conditions for the normal functioning of the housing market. All in all, reform of communal housing has begun.

The acuteness of the housing problem, however, has not been reduced. In a number of regions, the volume of new construction has decreased, which can be primarily explained by the decrease in investment activity, the interruption of financing, and increased construction costs.

New approaches are needed to solve the problems associated with housing reform, to accelerate it, and to improve the social well-being of the citizenry. The purpose of the current housing policy is to guarantee access to improved housing conditions for families with modest-to-average income, as well as to retain a free supply of housing to the needy and other groups of citizens. This policy will be realized only through the following steps:

- Renewal of efforts to increase new housing
- Expansion of sources and a guarantee of stable financing for housing, with an increase in the extra-budget investment
- Implementation of a progressive technical policy in capital construction and reconstruction, modern architecture, and city-planning decisions
- Improvement in the structure of housing funds based on to property type, with an emphasis on personal dwellings, and the development of a housing market
- A gradual transition to communal housing on a nonprofit basis, with the guaranteed protection of needy groups of the population
- Guaranteed standards in maintaining the quality of living conditions

(c)   Public Health.   At the present time, the Russian public-health system contains than 12,000 hospitals, and institutions with 1.9 million beds, and 20,000 ambulatory polyclinics with more than 3 million beds. More than 600,000 doctors and about 1.6 million midlevel medical personnel work in public-health institutions. On average, for every 10,000 persons there are 45 doctors, 107 midlevel medical personnel, 127 hospital beds, and 235 available openings for outpatients in polyclinics.

In recent years, the Russian Federation has successfully maintained a network of public-health institutions. Concurrently there has been a deterioration in the medical-demography situation, an improvement in the medical demographic situation. One can note the negative dynamics of the most important indices of the health of the population. In the past 10 years, the life expectancy of the average Russian has decreased from 69.3 to 65 years, and the mortality rate has increased by 11.3 persons per 1,000. Since the beginning of the 1990s, the general health of the people has declined.

There has also been an increase in the disease rate of the adult population and in the rate of teenagers suffering from tuberculosis, venereal disease, drug addiction, and alcoholism. The threat of epidemics and diseases caused by declining living conditions remains. The present condition of the state finance departments prevents an adequate amount of free medical assistance from reaching the population, and sharply reduces the preventive programs.

For the general population, expensive hospital stays are the norm and inadequate resources exist for public-health institutions. The conditions under which people can obtain medical aid are confusing and continually changing.

The observation of strict constitutional guarantees for providing medical care and creating sanitary living conditions for the population has led to a movement for structural and functional redevelopment. Under this redevelopment, the public-health system must guarantee:

- The stability of public-health institutions based on changes and reforms in the state of finance departments
- Priority public-health preventive measures in government and municipal systems to decrease disease and mortality rates from basic causes, alleviate the threat of epidemics, and provide training for a healthy way of life
- A more effective system for using financial, material, and team resources in public health
- The protection of the rights of the patient to receive timely, high-quality medical care

Public-health reform must be carried out through multistructural training while retaining the government's basic position on health-care, creating competitive means for setting up therapeutic and preventative institutions independent of the form of ownership, and adopting mechanisms for regulating and running the institution.

The gradual introduction and development of both obligatory and voluntary medical insurance by insurance organizations will be an effective economic tool for reforming the system.

(d)   Education.   The Russian Federation has one of the most developed systems of education in the world, with more than 163,600 institutions of various types and kinds. About 5.9 million persons work in Russia's educational institutions; this comprises more than 8% of the working population. Also, methods other than public education (e.g., of family education, self-education, and external studies) are practiced by more than 50 million persons.

At the present time, more than 68,000 daytime general education schools run by the government are operating, populated by 21.5 million students. The number of nontraditional institutions—lycees, gymnasiums, colleges, professional lycees, preschools, kindergartens, and others—has reached 3,237. There are also 525 nongovernmental general education schools, attended by 45,800 students.

There has been a massive expansion of a program for the professionalization of the population, primarily of young people, whose most important objectives are professional training and the beginning of a professional education. In 1994–95, 566 state institutions of higher professional education trained 2.6 million students; and 2,603 institutions for mid-level professional education trained 2 million students.

Russia's modern educational system is characterized by contradictory tendencies. On the whole, the reform years have successfully guaranteed the constitutional rights of citizens to obtain an education, including midlevel and higher professional training on a competitive basis; established a network of governmental and municipal educational institutions, and of students and collectives of students and instructors; and developed a network of nongovernmental educational institutions. In this way, education has retained its potential as a determining factor in the socioeconomic development of Russia. At the same time these reforms are taking place, however, the portion of the budget and actual budget allocated for education have decreased.

The main purposes of further progress in education is to satisfy the educational needs of Russian citizens, develop the personality and creative capabilities of every citizen, person, and increase the intellectual, creative, and cultural potential of the country, while observing the principles of equal opportunity and minimal governmental interference. The following tasks have been defined for achieving this goal:

- Guaranteeing general access to free education, but within the limits of the government's educational standards

- Developing a system of educational institutions representing various legal organizations, including nongovernmental ones
- Creating a governmental system for evaluating the curriculum and standards of educational institutions of all types (including their licensing, certification, and government and public accreditation)
- Implementing government standards for education norms of material-technical guarantee and financing of institutions and organization of the educational system, and also educational-professional programs
- Guaranteeing a single educational, cultural and information platform, and creating a system of laws and rules governing education
- Developing a mechanism for administrating the financing of educational goals and activities
- Supporting regional programs for education development, but also increasing coordination of regional and federal programs
- Increasing the independence of educational institutions and organizations, and in determining strategies for the development and the content of their training and educational programs, including professional education of a scientific, business, financial and industrial nature

(e)   Culture.   At the present time in the Russian Federation, 61,300 clubs are in operation, along with 1,547 museums, 470 theaters, and 54,800 libraries. Every year, an average of 30,400 books are published, selling 594 million copies; 2,307 journals and other periodicals are published, selling 306 million copies; and 4,526 newspapers are published, with an annual circulation of 8.1 billion copies.

In recent years, there has been a trend toward development of a government network of cultural institutions. Since 1992, this network is composed of museums, libraries, theaters, and all types of educational institutions. One hundred and forty-seven new children's music and art schools have opened that currently enroll 1.2 million children.

Establishing the status of especially valuable objects of Russia's cultural heritage has become a top priority of the government. The goal is to protect unique historical memorials, museum and library collections, noteworthy architectural works, and creative collections, all of which have value on a worldwide scale.

The strategic purpose of the government policy in regard to culture is to create conditions for the cultural development of the citizens and society, guarantee the continuity of Russia's cultural traditions, and fulfill the country's cultural potential. The government's priorities are to maintain the historical and cultural inheritance of the country and establish cultural continuity as a basis for a stable development of society. The most important goal is providing broad access to domestic and worldwide culture and art to all segments of society. In addition, the system of aesthetic and artistic training in general educational institutions must be further developed.

(f)   Consumer Market and the Standard of Living.   During the prereform period, there was a steady increase in the volume of goods and services produced for the Russian consumer market, which was the result of an increased demand by the population for higher wages. From 1986 to 1990, retail sales increased by 27%, and the volume of paid services grew by 62%.

The recent transition to a market economy has sharply changed the level of actual money available to the population. This level of liquidity has caused a decrease in capacity of the internal market, and has proven to be one of the main causes for the decrease in the sales of retail goods. In 1992–93, the cash level stayed at 90%. The manufacturing of consumer goods has doubled, yet the average citizen's pay has dropped by 70%.

The Russian economy has changed in fundamental ways. The most characteristic trait of the planned distribution economy had been a deficit of goods, a situation that was typical in prereform years. The present state of the consumer market is characterized by a high saturation of goods and a stable level of reserve goods. More than 85% of these goods are used in the private sector, 15% in the government. About 27% of the total sales of goods is comprised of goods for consumer and food markets.

The country's commercial resources, to a significant degree, are complemented by imports from abroad. The specific amount of the import purchases in total resources comprises about 54%. It should be noted that the objective of the Russian enterprise system in buying goods abroad is to acquire items with high profitability without taking into consideration the interests of the mass buyer. In the sales of retail goods, food products comprise 42%, alcoholic beverages 6%, and nonfood goods 52%.

The basic problem of commerce remains inadequate working capital in commercial organizations. Their instability forces them to buy goods for a quick sale and does not permit the creation of standard commercial reserves.

2.7 CONSUMER MARKET.*   The market reforms in Russia in the early 1990s have led to a revolution in the Russian consumer market, which has been developing faster and more significantly than other sectors of the national economy. The Russian consumer market of the mid-1990s has virtually nothing in common with the relatively weak consumer market of the early 1990s. Crucial changes have taken place in the consumer's earnings and spending, the organization and forms of trade, and the supply side of the consumer market.

It is very difficult to describe all these processes by relying on government statistics. The dominance of cash exchange, high taxation rates that lead to mass tax evasion, and the widespread practice by individuals of multiple employment have resulted in official statistics inaccurately reflecting reality. A more accurate picture can be obtained by using qualitative characteristics.

The main qualitative change in the population's personal income is the sharp stratification that has taken place within the last few years. The most visible manifestation of this is the formation of a superrich class (nouveaux riches), while the majority of the population has become poorer. Another less visible trend, but one no less important for consumer market development, is the emergence of a diversified middle class. Though it is still difficult to estimate its size and level of income, the middle class has become the primary determinant of consumer market behavior.

The stratification of the Russian population in the course of recent market reforms affects the consumer's spending habits. An income decrease for a large part of the population caused a relative increase in spending for food and the rapid development of this market sector in 1993–94. The spending pattern of the "nouveaux riches" evolved as a luxury consumption model and stimulated demand for expensive and state-of-the-art goods from all over the world. Middle-class spending stimulated the continuous growth of imported goods and of the service market (travel, health, finances, and construction industries).

The differences in income and needs of various population groups resulted in diversified forms of trade, a system vastly different from the pre-existing government trade structure. On one hand, there have appeared elite stores resembling expensive supermarkets and

---

*This section was written by Andrei A. Auzan.

world famous designer stores. On the other hand, extensive chains of *kiosks,* small stores, and flea markets became widespread. Today's consumer in Russia has a broad selection of prices, items, and terms of purchase. Despite the fact that this trade system differs from the standard European and American model, it provides goods from virtually all world famous manufacturers. The dominance of imported goods over domestic goods is characteristic of the Russian market of the mid-1990s in general and is especially noticeable in the big cities.

In this way, foreign business is aggressively conquering the Russian consumer market. This foreign presence, however, is represented more by the quality of imports than by the quality of investments. Whereas in 1992, foreign businesses were entering the Russian market in a vacuum characterized by a deficit economy, today the market is significantly different. It is different not only because the Russian consumer has forgotten shortages and long lines, but also because competition has become a reality in the Russian consumer market. Certain rules and regulations—both formal and informal—have appeared in the market, rules that regulate business conduct. The Russian market no longer can be labeled as wild and uncontrollable. These rules are not created by state legislation alone. They are also formed by public institutions that put laws into practice, by consumer behavior shaping common norms, and, by an ethical code regulating business practices, although this is in a formative stage.

Recently, there were a number of laws adopted to regulate the consumer market. First of all, there are laws on consumers' rights defense, certification, competition and restrictions of conduct in the market, and advertising. These laws set stricter demands for businesses than is generally accepted in many developed countries. The primary reason for enacting these laws has been the lack of tradition dictating civilized and ethical relations between businesses and their clients. Evolving from these laws, regulations were created by the local executive authorities setting more specific rules for activities on the consumer market.

A number of laws adopted in the 1990s by the Russian legislature have not worked. For the consumer market, however, the situation is very different. All four of the laws mentioned, particularly the consumers' rights defense, were supported by a well-developed mechanism for their application, were popular with the public, and were heavily used for the defense of consumers' rights. The successful application of the law relies on three factors: active consumer organizations (there are approximately 200 regional and four national consumer organizations); positive attention of mass media to the consumers' problems; and the active use of judicial defense in cases of consumers' rights violation.

Legal cases in which the consumers' rights defense is involved are characterized by frequent award of compensation for moral harm. (It is important to note that amounts awarded by the court are constantly increasing.) Recently this legal defense has been applied not only in cases involving shoddy goods, but also in cases of violations in the service industry. More and more often, courts impose liens on the property and assets of the guilty party. The number of legal cases involving the consumers' rights defense has risen so strikingly that in the fall of 1994, the Supreme Court of Russia held a meeting about issues surrounding the legal defense of consumers' rights.

This aggressive shift of Russian consumers toward the use of legal defense, historically an unpopular method, demonstrates serious changes in the consumer's mentality. The new attitude prompted the organization of class-action lawsuits by consumer associations against large firms. Among these actions were group lawsuits, actions on behalf of an "indefinite group of people," and mass anti-advertising campaigns in the media. For instance, in 1991 the Confederation of the Consumers Associations took legal action on behalf of an "indefinite group of people" against one of Moscow's largest trading firms, which was selling inauthentic Levi's jeans. The court ordered the firm either to refund money to consumers or exchange the inauthentic goods. In 1995, lawyers of the same association organized a campaign against Sony, Matsushita and Samsung, demanding that they adjust their guarantees to the Russian laws. During negotiations, these firms not only reviewed their guarantees, but also compensated consumers for damages. Today, practically all leading foreign companies adjust their guarantees to comply with Russian regulations. As a result of that action, Russian consumers have become more careful about purchase terms, the specific contents of agreements, and guarantees.

New informal rules of business conduct and consumer behavior are continually being formed, influenced by the efforts of the press, as well as by government and nongovernment consumer associations. Special consumer sections appear now in practically all newspapers, radio and television programs. A new consumers' magazine *Spros (Demand)* is now published in Russia. The goals of magazine are very similar to those of publications in other countries, and its circulation equals that of most popular commercial magazines. This information network has taught consumers to be very cautious of advertising, to demand additional information about what they are buying, and to rely on independent analysis of goods and services when making their choices.

The change in consumers behavior has brought about drastic changes in the business community, which has not only become more aware of legal requirements, but has also initiated self-regulation in relations with customers and established new business practices. Of course, this characterization applies to those companies that want to obey the law, maintain higher moral standards, and to expel unprincipled competitors from the market.

In 1995, the Public Council for Advertisement, which consists of the country's most influential advertisers, advertising agencies, state officials, and public figures, was established. The Council is in charge of reviewing improper advertising practices and of creating an ethical code of conduct. Better Business Bureaus have started to develop in Russia, established by business people seeking to promote precourt regulation of disputes with consumers. This new ethical conduct toward the consumer has been applied by a relatively small number of companies. There are strong expectations, however, that under pressure from tough legislation, strong consumer organizations, and an active press, this practice will spread very quickly.

The conditions and norms of the Russian consumer market should be considered by companies planning to enter the Russian market. A realistic picture of the Russian consumer market has another aspect, however. Since the conditions and norms of business conduct in the big cities differ from those in the rest of the country, and since the entire scope of the Russian consumer market is just being formed, companies entering the Russian market other than in the large business centers may face distinctly different conditions. Such a gap in the conditions for doing business has been present in Russia at various stages of her history. The business conduct and living standards of large cities influence those of other parts of the country, but this process can take several years. This is one of the reasons why businesspeople entering the Russian market should be psychologically prepared for gigantic variety in the forms of business conduct.

CHAPTER 3

ENERGY RESOURCES

Viktor N. Mihaylov, Yevgeni N. Malyshev, and Igor Lojevsky

3.1 NUCLEAR POWER AND ITS FUEL CYCLE.* Nuclear-power plants generate 12% of the total power produced in Russia, and in certain regions, this contribution is substantially greater, for example, about 48% in the northwest, nearly 24% in the center, and in excess of 16% in the Volga region.

Twenty-nine reactors with an installed capacity of 21.2 GWt are operating at nine nuclear plants in Russia: six reactors of the VVER–440 type, seven VVER–1000 reactors, 11 RBMK reactors, one fast-neutron BN–600 reactor, and four EGP–6 reactors at the Bilibinsk nuclear-power plant. The nuclear reactors at the Rostov, Kalinin, and Kursk plants, as well as at the Yuzhno-Uralsk and Byeloyarsk plants are currently at different stages of construction and preconstruction.

Technological and organizational measures have been implemented to drastically enhance safety at all the nuclear-power plants in Russia following the Chernobyl accident. Safety is a high priority at the plants that have been constructed under the former norms and regulations; these plants provide a considerable share of the regional power needs. The most obsolete reactors at the Byeloyarsk and Novo-Voronezh plants have been taken out of service.

The safe operation of the nuclear reactors is maintained by the following measures:

- Implementing fundamental procedures to eliminate critical factors of danger
- Implementing programs to enhance the safety and reliability features
- Reviewing and toughening the operating procedures
- Enhancing the requirements of the staff, creating training centers and simulators, conducting training sessions, particularly under emergency conditions

Plants of the first generation are operated under specific conditions. Their safety is ensured by a comprehensive checkup and annual diagnosis of the equipment. These power plants must secure annual permits for operation. In addition, international experts are invited to examine the safety features.

If safety is maintained at an acceptable level, the nuclear-power plants can operate throughout the entire life of the main equipment. If ensuring an acceptable level of safety for individual reactors becomes impossible, they will be taken out of service before the end of their normal life. This approach has been used in countries that operate large numbers of

---

*This section was written by Viktor N. Mihaylov.

obsolete reactors. New nuclear reactors, on the other hand, are designed in conformity with modern safety requirements and international recommendations.

The construction of a new generation of pressurized-water reactors will be initiated in the current decade. The VVER–640 and VVER–1000 reactors will be the first to be constructed, and their design and specifications will consider domestic and international experience.

Pressurized-water reactors with an integral design and a capacity of 640 MWt, and a loop design with a capacity of 1100–1200 MWt will be developed. All the designs incorporate modern principles and measures that will ensure their safety. These designs, dependent on the timely completion of all research and development and testing, will fulfill the basic needs of the nuclear-power industry for a long period of time.

Nevertheless, there are proposals to continue work on a graphite water-cooled reactor, to transfer to 800 MWt, and to develop a reactor with safety features that are as good as those of a VVER reactor. This development could eventually lead to a replacement of the RBMK reactors at the operating plants.

The nuclear power industry of Russia is ready to start construction of the modern, safe, and fast BN–800 reactors with sodium cooling. These reactors conform to all modern requirements and may be instrumental in the fuel cycle for the production of electric power and weapon-grade plutonium, the implementation of the actinoid incineration cycle, and the resolution of specific environmental problems in the southern Urals.

Safe nuclear-power plants, thermal-power plants, and boiler facilities have been designed for remote regions in the north and northeast regions. The competitiveness of nuclear power has increased due to rising prices for organic fuel and an increase in the expenditures for environmental protection measures near plants operating on organic fuel. The main areas for the development of the nuclear-power industry are located in the northwest and central regions, Northern Caucasus, the Urals, and the Far East.

The development of the nuclear-power industry in the next 15 years will depend greatly on the rates of introducing and mastering new reactors. The Ministry of Nuclear Energy anticipates such extreme possibilities as stagnation, including only approximately doubling the capacity of the nuclear-power industry by the year 2010. Intensive commissioning of the new generation of reactors will begin after 2000. After 2010, the nuclear-power industry will expand greatly because of the anticipated shortage of organic fuel.

The Russian nuclear industry owns sufficient supplies of uranium to cover the expansion of nuclear reactors to the year 2010. No difficulties are anticipated in the enrichment of uranium and the production of fuel for the VVER and RBMK reactors.

Russia owns a plant that reprocesses spent fuel from VVER–440 reactors, transport and research reactors, and fuel from the fast reactors BN–350 and BN–600 at the Mayak facility. Following conditioning, the regenerated uranium is used to produce fuel for RBMK reactors. The plutonium that is produced is placed in storage; the inventory amounts to about 30 metric tons.

The VVER–1000 spent-fuel assemblies are still stored in a facility at RT–2 (Krasnoyarsk GXK) currently under construction, and their reprocessing will commence following the commissioning of this plant at the end of the next decade. Plans call for spent RBMK fuel to be stored for a long time.

Utilization of plutonium, particularly considering the release of weapon-grade plutonium, will commence in the next decade, first in fast BN–800 reactors, which will be constructed at the Yuzhno-Uralsk and Byeloyarsk plants. A plant needs to be built at the Production Association's Mayak facility for the production of plutonium-based fuel. Experimental work on the utilization of plutonium in VVER reactors will be conducted in the next five to seven years.

A Federal program exists for handling radioactive waste and spent nuclear fuel from nuclear-power plants and their fuel cycle (another larger section of the program deals with problems associated with the waste in the defense industry). In the near future, all the operating nuclear-power plants will be equipped with hardware to reprocess, solidify, and compact waste of low and medium activity. This waste will be stored at the power plants until the construction of disposal sites is completed. Small quantities of highly radioactive waste will be transported to specialized sites for reprocessing and storage.

The waste from the radiochemical reprocessing of the nuclear fuel will be vitrified for long-term storage. Vitrification technology is being successfully implemented at the Mayak facility, and the volume of vitrification will be increased until it fully meets the capacity of the fuel facility. Plans also exist to solidify waste at the PT–2 facility, which is currently under construction.

Specialized research and development is being conducted on the technology of incinerating in reactors the hazardous and long half-life transuranic isotopes of plutonium, neptunium, and americium. This technology, naturally included in the fuel cycle of fast reactors, makes it possible to reduce radically the potential danger of the long-term existence of actinoids. The actinoids are transformed into fragments of fission and buried for several hundred years until they are no longer dangerous.

On the whole, the Ministry of Nuclear Energy promotes the concept of a closed fuel loop in the nuclear-power industry, including thermal and fast reactors, reprocessing of fuel, utilization of released weapon-grade plutonium, the incineration of actinoids, solidification, compaction, and burial of radioactive wastes.

The Ministry of Nuclear Energy and its research institutions, designing bureaus, and nuclear power-plants participate in wide-scale international cooperation. Russian nuclear power plants, via an international organization on nuclear-power plants, regularly and comprehensively exchange information about operating procedures. There is scientific and technological cooperation with different countries and international organizations regarding safety issues, reactor, the utilization of plutonium, the transmutation of actinoids, the technology of the fuel cycle, and in particular, the handling of wastes. Russian nuclear-power plants also receive technological assistance from the Commission of European Cooperation to enhance their safety.

The design of nuclear-power plants developed in Russia, is of great interest to countries that are preparing to construct several VVER–1000 reactors.

The ties that Russia is developing with the International Atomic Energy Agency (IAEA), its bilateral and multilateral ties, with other international organizations, and participation in international discussions of problems in the nuclear-power industry indicate Russia's commitment to the successful and safe development of nuclear energy.

3.2 COAL INDUSTRY: CONDITIONS AND PROSPECTS.*

The coal industry is one of the pillars of the Russian economy. It was formed in the years preceding World War II. In the mid-1950s, coal became the core of the country's fuel structure, comprising 59% of its total output. The 1960s brought about a discovery of large oil and natural gas reserves and the development of nuclear energy, trends that decreased the importance of coal in the Russian fuel structure. By the early 1980s, its share had decreased to 20%, before declining still further to 14% in the 1990s.

In eastern Siberia and Russian far east where oil and gas resources are minimal, however, coal's share of the regional fuel structure is still 90%. The largest coal-mining output

*This section was written by Yevgeni N. Malyshev.

(425.4 million tons, including 228.6 million tons extracted from open-cut mines) was reached in 1988. In the late 1980s and early 1990s, the continuous growth of the coal-mining industry declined dramatically. This resulted in decreasing coal-mining output in all major coal regions of Russia.

The long-term prospects for coal demand vary by region and depend on a number of factors. Among these are Russia's ability to quickly resolve the current economic crisis, the dynamics of power consumption, the Russian coal industry's competitiveness, governmental support for the coal industry, governmental regulation of gas prices, and railway transportation rates.

As of early 1995, the Russian coal-mining industry had a total of 261 subterranean mines. There were 90 open-cut mines, 68 coal-concentrating plants, one briquette factory, 260 construction organizations, 19 mechanical engineering plants for coal mining, a chain of trading and food related organizations, and over 370 agricultural farms. The total number of employees in the coal industry was 841,000, including 418,000 in subterranean mines and open-cut mines. Today, there are 547 joint-stock public companies and 12 closed corporations encompassing these various enterprises. The industrial capacity of coal mining is 374 million tons, including 163 million tons extracted from subterranean mines and 211 million tons from open-cut mines.

Most of the joint-stock coal companies are incorporated into Rossugol—the company that, according to the presidential decree of December 1992, is responsible for the commercial management of the controlling block of shares owned by the federal government. Other enterprises in the coal industry are included either in Rosstopprom or Oblkemerovugol. There are also a few coal-mining enterprises not incorporated into these conglomerates.

In accordance with a decree of the Cabinet of Ministers of July 27, 1993, the coal-mining industry receives financial recourses from the federal budget with no obligation to pay the money back.

The major coal-mining regions in Russia are located in Siberia (63.6% of the country's output), the Far East (12.3%), the Urals (6.7%) and in the European part of the country. The main coal-consuming regions are Siberia (44%), the European part (23%), the Far East (16%), and the Urals (17%).

Russia possesses approximately one-fifth of the world's coal reserves. The situation in the Russian coal industry, however, cannot be considered satisfactory because 57% of these reserves do not meet world standards for quality, capacity, bedding, conditions, and safety. This situation is especially true in the Podmoskov, Kizelov, and Donet coalfields, and in the Prokopievsko-Kiseliov region of Kuzbass and Sakhalin, where difficult mining and geological conditions lead to frequent injuries and high costs.

For a long time, the financing of the development and reconstruction of the coal industry was insufficient, resulting in a substantial reduction in the industry's potential. Recently, even maintaining the same level of investment in the industry's capital assets could not be accomplished.

Mines have undergone natural aging. Whereas more than 50% of the mines have been active for over 40 years, only 8% of them are relatively new. Almost half of all mines have not been modernized for a substantial period of time. Basic mining equipment has become obsolete. Also, coal-processing plants are lagging behind modern standards. Due to the low technical level of coal-enrichment equipment, only 73 million tons of coal are properly enriched to acceptable levels. Unenriched coal has an ash content up to 35%, creating difficulties in marketing it. Most of the coal-concentrating plants are obsolete and need major renovation and modernization of equipment.

To stabilize the deterioration of the coal industry and to overcome current negative trends, the only possible and efficient measure is a large-scale restructuring of the industry. The restructuring is to be introduced incrementally.

Urgent measures have been designed to reconstruct the industry and adapt it to market requirements. To accomplish this goal, governmental subsidies need to enhance the efficiency of internationally competitive and open-cut mines and to close unprofitable ones.

Legislative and economic mechanisms need to adapt the industry to international economic standards and to create conditions for the qualitative renovation of the industry based on targeted investment programs.

Production capacities and coal consumption need to increase. The use of economically efficient and ecologically safe coal-mining technologies is important. The most important development should be the industry's improvement of product quality and competitiveness.

In the course of restructuring the coal industry in 1993-94, the old rigid system of centralized planning and management was virtually abolished. Also, the system of fixed prices and of federal subsidies covering 100% of all production losses was canceled. A new economic mechanism is being formed that is based on the liberal pricing of coal, selective governmental support for mines and open-cut mines, the transformation of forms of property, and the evolution of new organizational and economic structures.

A more selective approach to the distribution of governmental subsidies has resulted in positive changes in their structure. For the first time in four years, signs of qualitative improvements in the industry have become evident. Ash content in coal has decreased, and labor productivity has started to increase. Governmental financing for the improvement of economic conditions at the mines, as well as for shutting down the worst and the most outdated ones, has helped to improve the prospects for mining. As a result, coal mining has ceased at 34 of the most unprofitable mines. Over 120,000 mine workers (about 15% of the industry) have been laid off. The reduction of coal-mining operations has occurred primarily at those mines where labor conditions are especially dangerous. It is still necessary to cease operations at approximately 90 additional mines.

At the same time, productivity needs to be increased by one-third. During the past two years, mines with strong potential have been reequipped with the latest technical innovations. The new equipment is produced not only at mechanical engineering plants specializing in the coal industry, but also, as part of the conversion process, at plants belonging to the military-industrial complex. Thirty-six different kinds of equipment and tools are made at those converted plants. The involvement of military enterprises in manufacturing mining equipment has resulted in an increase in its sophistication and reliability, and has helped satisfy the demand for refining equipment that was previously imported. The participation of the leading military enterprises is crucial in providing potentially strong mines with equipment that meets world standards.

Russia is interested in purchasing the best products, technologies, and manufacturing licenses from the leading mining companies of Europe and America. Russia can offer these companies mutually beneficial joint agreements in the manufacture of tunneling combines, complexes, and graders. For its open-cut mines, Russia needs conveyers, bulldozers, drills, and coal-concentrating equipment. The country already has about a dozen efficient coal-concentrating systems imported from the West. Presently, a front-operated excavator surface miner is being installed at the Taldinskoye open-cut mine in Kuzbass. The Western partner participating in this project is the German company Krupp. Also, joint production of DonWestphalia graders has been started by Russian and German partners in Russian part of Donbass.

Recently, a contract with the German firm Westphalia Alpine was signed to manufacture a tunneling combine. Negotiations with two other Western companies, Joy and Long-woll, are in a progress, with the goal of producing combines for the chamber system of mining, face conveyers, and automotive carts. Such cooperation is mutually beneficial. Jobs are provided both for the foreign companies and Russian enterprises. Also, Russia's production capabilities can be used to satisfy the virtually unlimited demand in Vietnam, India, and China.

According to the governmental program Russia's Strategy in the Energy Industry, by the year 2000 the annual output of Russian coal mining probably will not exceed 260–290 million tons. Approximately 25 million tons are estimated to be exported annually. In the meantime, the demand for Kansko-Achinsky coal may significantly grow and stabilize because of its increased use as a low-cost source of electric power in the production of aluminum. This power is generated by burning brown coal at an electric power plant. Another potential way to increase the demand for Kansko-Achinsky coal is the mass introduction of small boilers using the technology of fluidized beds.

There is a possibility of not only maintaining the current level of export of Kuznetsk coal, but also of increasing it. This can be achieved by the integration of coal mining with the by-product coke industries of Kuzbass. Growth in the exports of Kuznetsk coal can also be achieved by exporting coke itself, which is always in high demand in countries experiencing fuel shortages.

The program for development elaborated by Rossugol' is intended to provide competitive and high-quality coal products: for example, the percentage of sulfur is 0.7–1% and that of ash is 7–8% in coal intended for general service; the percentage of ash in commercially used coal does not exceed 12–15%. These figures meet world standards.

Also, the classification of coal and coal products will be implemented in order that the general population will be provided with high-quality fuel. Heat and electric power plants will use siftings. If there are enough investments from both domestic and international sources, Russian coal mining will be capable of sustaining a high level of production. This can be accomplished primarily by the use of Siberian coal mines, particularly the Kuzbass mines. But an increase in coal-mining production should be complemented by governmental regulation of the railroad tariffs, which at present are growing faster than the inflation rate. This is especially important for the Russian Far East, where coal is the only source of energy and power. All potential foreign partners are invited to participate in an exploration of Russia's unique coalfields, such as Yerunakovskoye in Kuzbass or Obukhovskoye in Donbass.

Presently, a coal mine is under construction near the Don River that will be one of the most technologically advanced in the world. Its planned annual capacity is two million tons of a high-quality anthracite containing less than 0.7% of sulfur. The production costs are expected not to exceed $15–$16 per ton. This anthracite will be transported via water (the least expensive mode) to the Ust'-Donetsk port and, from there, to a number of European countries to be used as smokeless fuel. The expected profit is $10–$15 per ton.

Another modern mine is being constructed in the Sokolovsky coal field in Yerunakovsky district, Kuzbass, which will have equipment imported from Eikgoff, Chemscheidt, and other firms. The annual capacity is expected to be 2.8 million tons, and production costs are estimated not to exceed $9 per ton. If the price is about $16 per ton, the earning capacity of the mine will be approximately 47%. The open-cut mines in Taldinskoye, Kuzbass, present another example of such a mine.

All prospective foreign partners are invited to participate in:

- Joint exploration of the coalfields mentioned and others, which are similar and which are expected to be equally profitable; the forms of participation involving leasing loans, and supplies of equipment may vary
- Construction of railroads to improve export routes
- Reconstruction of ports and the building of new coal terminals in the Baltic Sea (at St. Petersburg) and the Black Sea (at Novorossisk and Tuapsse)

These projects need investments to be developed. Unfortunately, the world community remains unduly cautious about financing the Russian coal industry, and thereby misses a mutually profitable venture for all parties involved. Along with participation in Russian coal projects, European and American companies would get a chance to continue their international activities because most of the mines in western Europe either have been closed or will be closed within the next few years. Also, demand for mining equipment in those countries is decreasing while Russian demand is on the rise. In addition, second-hand mining equipment can be purchased at 20–50% of its original price. There are already a few instances of such purchases.

The industry is certain that combining the best resources of the Russian coal industry with foreign investments and advanced technology will result in sufficient supplies of ecologically pure solid fuel for Russia and the entire world community.

3.3 YUKOS: THE RUSSIAN OIL COMPANY.* A series of decrees of the Russian government and the presidential decree of August and September 1995 set the pace for the privatization process and helped establish a new structure for the Russian petroleum industry. International Monetary Fund experts called this "the engine of democratic reform policy." The process of uniting dozens of widely separated petroleum-extracting associations and petroleum-processing plants, and thirteen nonstate vertically integrated petroleum joint-stock companies into a single system, did not coincide with the stabilization process in the oil industry. Yet this unlikely union would be necessary for the extraction, processing, and marketing of petroleum products. Achieved in the second half of 1995, the stabilization of oil production, after a four-year decline, was a remarkable event noted by numerous independent experts. The Russian Ministry of Economics' 1996 forecast predicted growth in oil output, in sharp contrast to the previous estimates predicting the further decline of the industry until the year 2000. The liberalization of prices for oil and petroleum products introduced by the Russian government last year has stimulated petroleum companies to increase sales both in domestic and foreign markets. The establishment of vertically integrated oil companies, combined with conditions favorable for industry stabilization, significantly increases the probability of realizing one of the largest and most important projects in the Russian oil industry. Of course, this project also involves the participation of strategically important Western partners.

Despite the present difficulties in the Russian economy, Yukos (which began to operate in both domestic and foreign markets in April 1993) enjoys a high reputation in the world business community. British experts, for example, have included Yukos on a list of the ten largest petroleum companies in the world.

Founded by a decree of the Russian Cabinet of Ministers on April 4, 1993, and based on the presidential decree of November 17, 1992, Yukos consists today of:

---

*This section was written by Igor Lojevsky.

- The petroleum-extracting associations Yugaskneftegaz (in western Siberia) and Samaraneftegaz (in central Russia)
- One of the most promising oil-processing complexes, Povolzhsky, which has three plants in Samara, Syzran', and Novo-Kuybyshev
- Regional oil-marketing associations in Oryol, Lipetsk, Voronezh, Penza, Tambov, Briansk, Ulyanovsk, Samara, Belgorod, Khanty-Mansi and Nefteyugansk

Also, Yukos has a number of research and development institutions: the Research and Development Institute for Oil Processing, Srednevolzhsky; Voronezhnefteproduktavtomatika; Samaranefteproduktavtomatika; Samaraneftekhimavtomatika; the specialized machinery set-up department, Nefteyuganskoye.

Yukos has significant resource, production, and marketing potential characterized by the following facts:

- Total geological resources of crude oil—over 65 billion barrels (13% of Russia's oil resources)
- Extractable resources of oil—over 17 billion barrels (15% of Russia's oil resources)
- Crude oil output—about 700,000 barrels a day (12% of Russia's total crude oil output)
- Petroleum processing—about 500,000 barrels a day (10% of Russia's total oil processing)
- A virtual monopoly on petroleum products in 11 regions of Russia, with a population exceeding 15 million (10% of Russia's population)

Today, Yukos is the leader among Russian oil companies in its reserves of hydrocarbon raw materials. Yukos is also the only Russian company whose resource availability increases at a greater rate than its output of crude oil. Another advantage of Yukos is its partnership with Amoco in developing Priobskoye, one of the largest oil sites in the world. The exploration of Priobskoye has not been completed yet, and the possibility for the discovery of more resources there remains.

The goal of Yukos is to develop into a competitive and leading company in the world's petroleum market, a company capable of guaranteeing increasing profits for its shareholders and acting in the strategic interests of Russia. Seeking to accelerate the integration of Yukos into the world economy, the company is consistently implementing its program for strategic development. One of the main pillars of the program is "information transparency," the communication of information on the company to both Russian and foreign investors. Information transparency embraces:

- Following world standards in reporting information
- Implementing financial and legal audits
- Estimating resources and technical conditions
- Preparing presentations on the initial distribution of blocks of shares
- Providing all other necessary information according to world standards

Currently, Yukos is being audited by Coopers & Lybrand L.L.P. The issuing of depository certificates is being handled by the Bank of New York. The company's legal consultant is Cleary, Gottlieb, Steen & Hamilton, and financial consulting is provided by Lazard Freres & Company. Cooperation with such established and respected companies allows

Yukos not only to overcome problems of the transitional period, but also to promote its proper entrance into the world petroleum community.

Yukos has a modernization program that allocates $60 billion to develop the Priobskoye oil site and dozens of other, smaller sites. The program also includes a plan for a multibillion-dollar investment in the development of oil-processing plants and a chain of Yukos gas stations in central Russia. To fund these ventures, in 1994 Yukos spent more than $200 million of its profits and significant amounts of credit resources provided by the World Bank for Reconstruction and Development and other financial institutions. Yukos pays significant attention to the introduction of ecologically pure technologies and measures to ensure the safety of the environment.

One of the main goals of the program for strategic development is developing the company's international policy. The president of Yukos, Sergei Mouravlenko, commented that by relying on the enormous potential of this company and striving to protect the interests of the Russian shareholders (and in the future, foreign shareholders and prospective investors too), Yukos consistently fulfills the strategic program of diversification all over the world. Intensive research on the European markets led to the establishment of a joint venture with Turkey in oil processing and oil products marketing, and the acquisition of production facilities in Hungary.

Yukos has projects for oil exploration and crude-oil extraction in South America. The joint venture YuganskPetroandes in Peru is working on these. Seventy percent of the YuganskPetroandes personnel are Russians who have petroleum industry experience.

Such an aggressive approach helps the company obtain the experience necessary for working in the international markets and prepare the next generation of executives for accomplishing the company's goals.

CHAPTER 4

SCIENTIFIC RESOURCES AND POLICY

Vladimir E. Fortov

4.1 SCIENTIFIC COMPLEX IN TRANSITION. Prior to *perestroika,* Russian science was a unique phenomenon. The Russian scientific complex was one of the leading institutions of its type in the world in terms of its scope, the qualifications of its scientists, and the significance of its achievements. The high prestige of Russian fundamental and defense sciences is still unquestionable today. Russia's most recent scientific achievements have been in theoretical physics, solid-state physics, energy technologies regarding steam and gas cycles, catalysis, genetic engineering, and other fields.

Despite its substantial reduction (see Exhibit 4.1), Russia's scientific complex is still an important resource for economic development and a source that will assist in postindustrial development. In the course of the reform, the nucleus of scientific potential—the scientific divisions of the Russian Academy of Sciences, and research and development leading institutes in the industrial sector—has been preserved. The number of Ph.D.s and graduate students has increased. Foundations for corporate research and development programs have been laid. The level of education and personnel training is still as high as before. More applicants are striving to get into major universities.

4.2 MAJOR DIRECTIONS OF SCIENTIFIC POLICY. The status of Russian science and its place on the priority list for governmental support are judicially secured by the law on Science and the State Policy in Science and Technology and by the doctrine on development of Russian science. These documents state that Russia's position as a great power is due mainly to the achievements of its scientists. The law and doctrine outline the major aims of the government's policy on science:

- Creating conditions to preserve and develop national scientific potential, to increase its contribution to the economy, and to provide a respectable place for science within the system of public interests
- Reforming the system of management and organization of scientific research
- Strengthening national security
- Securing the international positions of Russia in the field of science and technology

In order to achieve these aims, a new model of science is needed, one that will be adequate to Russia's status as a scientific power. Such legislation confirms the state's

Exhibit 4.1.   Major Indicators of Russian R & D

Dimensions of scientific potential[a]	1991	1995
Federal budget allocations for research and development (in constant prices 1991)	25.84	4.94
Percentage of federal budget expenditures	3.87	2.65
Number of persons involved in research and development (1,000)	1,677.8	1,061
Number of organizations involved in research and development	4,564	4,059

[a]According to data provided by the State Committee for Statistics.

obligations to support science, including guaranteed financing amounting to at least 4% of federal expenditures.[1]

The law and doctrine are complemented by a package of legislative regulations concerning intellectual property. These regulations provide security for state interests and strengthen the rights of scientists and scientific groups in the use of their achievements, particularly in the field of international exchange. The state policy on science and technology is aimed at financing high-priority projects and programs and giving selective support to research projects and leading scientific organizations.

Within the framework of these priorities, there are 70 crucial technologies on the federal level that will determine the technological future of the country. These include: microsystem equipment, microsensorics, electrostatic-plasma technologies, systems of human survival and protection under extreme conditions, biotechnology, transportation vehicles powered by alternative fuels, technologies for the processing of oil and gas, and technologies for environmental monitoring.

The technologies deemed crucial were selected on the basis of several criteria. Determining crucial technologies by means of legislation provides a direction for Russia's technological development within the framework of state priorities. To participate in developing crucial technologies, any type of scientific organization is eligible. The selection of applicants for a project of state priority is based on the granting of a state contract and on other organizational mechanisms new to Russia. The contract system provides fair competition among scientists for state funding and balances the need for new ideas with the state's demand for innovations.

An important ingredient of the present Russian scientific policy is the set of conditions for sponsoring the development of science. Russian budgetary and nonbudgetary funds will be used for this purpose. The funds were established as a system of alternative sources of financing (vs. direct budgetary allocations). Among budgetary funds, there is the Russian Fund for Fundamental Research (which enjoys 4% of federal expenditures for research and development); the Russian Scientific Fund for Humanities (1%); and the fund for the Promotion of Small Business in Science and Technology (1%). Nonbudgetary funds include the Russian Fund for the Development of Technology and the fund for Industrial Innovations.[2] Budgetary and nonbudgetary funds are targeted for both projects and programs. Funding is conducted on a competitive basis.

---

[1]Unfortunately, the real situation is far from the original goal. In 1992–96, this amount varied between 1.9 and 2.65%.

[2]These funds are based on deductions from the profit of enterprises and on expenditures for investment programs; they are tax-exempt.

Second, the increased openness of Russia's political and economic systems created favorable conditions for the granting of funds by international organizations. The most famous and effective among them is the International Scientific Fund. This fund has provided over 27,000 individual grants and financed more than 3,000 long-term projects. It has also financed programs for telecommunications, support for libraries, and the participation of Russian scientists in international conferences. The fund's provides financing primarily for fundamental science and allocates funds for additional activities (in 1994, $12.5 million).

A number of commercial and noncommercial funds promote innovation among a variety of Russian enterprises. These innovation funds have developed through a complex governmental program for the state support and development of innovative entrepreneurship. The goal of the program is to create a climate conducive to innovation in Russia and create conditions for the development of entrepreneurship. Innovation funds support the infrastructure of science-intensive businesses. They are also used to train personnel and provide financing for the completion of projects. The regional fund for the scientific and technological development of St. Petersburg and others that foster innovation concentrate on the preparation and realization of projects that will help Russia gain experience in a market economy. The innovation funds finance important projects in new ecologically safe and resource-saving technologies, medical equipment, and new technologies in food-processing and light industries. In the future, these funds will finance large-scale projects and provide support for applied research and high-tech products.

Russia is continually searching for new forms of support in the development of science and technology. As a result, the country is financing programs for the development of State Scientific Centers (SSCs), for the maintenance of unique testing units and installations, for the support of leading scientists and scientific schools, and for creating a computerized database in fundamental sciences and education.

The State Scientific Centers are based at elite research and development institutes, most of which are a part of the defense complex. The special state funding for the development of 61 centers is intended to support the maintenance of a unique scientific equipment, which allow SSCs to hold their leading position in many crucial areas of fundamental research. The program also supports the development of applied sciences and research.

The government, on both federal and regional levels, promotes scientific and technological activities by funding industrial/scientific parks and business innovation centers. At present, there are about 60 parks hosting over 700 small enterprises that provide jobs for more than 10,000 workers. They are engaged in developing and manufacturing high-tech products in information technology, biotechnology, and new materials science.

4.3 SUPPORT OF INTERNATIONAL TIES FOR SCIENTIFIC COOPERATION AND EXCHANGE OF TECHNOLOGIES.

Russia is interested in attracting foreign investments in the scientific and technological complex as well as improving the integration of Russia into the international scientific community, increasing its participation in solving global problems in science and technology, and maintaining its specialized role in the world technological market.

International contacts involving Russian science are emerging in several areas. Intergovernmental and interministerial agreements in scientific and technological cooperation are being forged. Russia is expanding its participation in international organizations and programs like the United Nations Industrial Development Organization (UNIDO) and others. More than 500 international projects involving Russian scientific organizations are supported financially by the Russian government (e.g., a project for the protection of the environment from oil and hydrocarbon pollution).

The area in which Russia has traditionally maintained international contacts is fundamental research. Such cooperation is reflected, for example, in the establishment of international institutes or and laboratories for joint research based on inter-institute agreements. Also, foreign investors have been attracted to participate in unique scientific projects.

Russia has substantial resources for the organization of joint institutions in higher education. Such schools were founded at Moscow State University, Moscow Bauman High Technical College, and New University in Pushchino. In the field of applied science, a center for training and upgrading the skills of personnel was established by the Russian association for technology in the auto industry. This center also works closely with German firms.

Significant efforts have been made to promote Russian science-intensive technologies in the world market by attracting foreign technical and financial resources to implement governmental programs. The existing joint research and development organizations are conducting an examination of Russian technologies in applied physics, microelectronics, medicine, and the petrochemical industry. Foreign organizations, funds, and private business are also taking part in the conversion of the defense industry. International cooperation in these ventures has developed through joint research and the use of scientific knowledge in defense industries. Such cooperation is also displayed in the use of Western technologies, licenses, and know-how. The results of Russia's policy on science and technology demonstrate that this policy has established a basis for the consistent reform of the future organization and management of science.

PART II

POLITICAL STRUCTURE, GOVERNMENT, AND ADMINISTRATION

CHAPTER 5

NATIONAL GOVERNMENT

Sergey S. Alekseev, Oleg N. Lobov, Vladimir S. Babichev, and Vyacheslav F. Shumeyko

5.1 RUSSIAN CONSTITUTION: PAST, PRESENT, AND FUTURE.* For the first time in Russian history, a democratic Constitution is in effect. The process of instituting a constitutional government has not yet been completed, however. One of the significant factors affecting the constitutional process is the long and complex heritage weighing on Russia while it builds its democratic constitution. Here, two circumstances are significant: (1) Russia does not have a historic constitutional tradition; and (2) unlike other countries, Russia did not experience a significant desire for freedom or the limitation of power, which could have become the core for its constitutional development.

The first steps in the direction of constitutional development, made in the second half of nineteenth century and early twentieth century, were not driven by a desire for constitutional reform. Sociopolitical transformations under Czar Alexander II (including the peasants' liberation, introduction of *zemstvo*—the county council system—and judicial reform), Nicholas II's Manifesto in 1917, and the rise of the *Duma* evolved under authoritarian rule, unrestricted by any law.

Various abnormalities in the development of the Constitution followed these first "child's" steps, further complicating that development without giving it a chance to find any solid support.

At their inception, the Bolsheviks wanted to fulfill the Russian dream of a constitution. In 1918, the Russian Socialist Federation of the Soviet Republics (RSFSR) Constitution was adopted. Later, three Soviet all-Union Constitutions followed in 1924, 1936, and 1977. None of these, however, added any significant rights or privileges to the first weak attempt at constitutional development. In fact, they worsened the situation and actually contributed to an anticonstitutional spirit. All the Soviet Constitutions were insignificant because none of them:

- was a strict judicial document, but existed as a statement of ideology for the Communist Party;
- regulated or restricted the political power of the state; on the contrary, they constitutionally legalized the system of all-powerful Soviets and the so-called directing and guiding role of the Communist Party;
- prioritized the individual; on the contrary, they gave priority to "public beginnings," and "state property"; as for individuals' rights, the most significant among them were

---

*This section was written by Sergey S. Alekseev.

declared "socio-political rights," which were heavily dependent on the mercy of the state and the arbitrariness of the bureaucracy.

Under this burden, Russia decided the time was right for a genuinely democratic constitution. The country, however, could not find any appropriate model for a new constitution either in its own past or in the history of other nations.

The first attempt to write a democratic constitution occurred in 1990–92 under the continuing rule of the Soviet regime. That attempt was based on an inquiry by the constitutional commission selected by the RSFSR People's Deputies Congress and moved in two directions. On one side, there were amendments and corrections made to improve the existing RSFSR Constitution of 1977. On the other, work was carried out on what was referred to as The New Word in constitutional development. That work brought certain positive results. Basic Communist Party ideological theses were removed from the constitution draft. Foreign constitutions were considered (particularly, the American constitutional principle of division of power), new democratic institutions (e.g., the presidency and constitutional court) were established, and internationally recognized rights and freedoms were summarized and included in the new text.

On the whole, however, the attempt to create any satisfactory draft of the Russian Constitution failed. The resulting document remained deeply pro-Soviet in all its inherent features. The governmental power structure on all levels was still controlled by the Soviets, and the introductory section of the Constitution still contained declarations propagating the idea of Soviet authority.

The pro-Soviet character of the official constitutional draft made it necessary to prepare an alternative document. In March 1992, the Movement for Democratic Reforms engaged several lawyers, including the author of this section, to accomplish that task. Work on the alternative draft (with contributions by A. Sobchak, S. Khokhlov, and Y. Kalmykov) was completed within a short period of time. Based on the chain principle, the process started with a general concept, moved to the issue of setting judicial structure, and ended with a technically thorough judicial elaboration of the text.

Generally, the alternative draft has been considered successful. A year after it appeared, by the end of April 1993, another version—the "presidential" draft—was prepared, based on ideas borrowed from the alternative draft. Incorporation of the alternative draft's main ideas into the presidential draft, and especially into the final text of the Constitution, however, warrants a different evaluation. From the beginning, the alternative draft was conceived and developed as a single concept. Even before the work on the draft was begun, several ideas were thoroughly elaborated to define the project and were consistently implemented throughout document.

Taking into consideration the latest interpretations of the division of power, the increased role of the courts, and, more generally, the range of experience in the developed democracies, the framers of the draft elaborated four main ideas:

1. Separation of the functions of the head of the state (the president) and those of the head of the Cabinet of Ministers (the prime minister), with the purpose that the president would represent the state as a whole and provide unity for the country, while all the divisions of the state machine and the government (the Cabinet of Ministers) would perform administrative and managerial functions.

2. Formation of a responsible government that would work as a united team and be equally controlled by the president and the Parliament.

3. Establishment of a strong judicial system as an autonomous entity (not just one division like, for example, the constitutional court); it would become the "third authority," capable of withstanding the arbitrariness of the administrative and managerial apparatus and the legislative institutions, and able to curb the bureaucracy.

4. Distinct separation of local municipal authority from state authority, including the significant augmentation of administrative territories that were originally introduced for detailed supervision by the Communist Party and later became *gubernias*—counties subject of the federation; the separation is intended to prevent their development into "local governments" or sovereign lands on one side, and to allow the use of the authentic Russian principles of *zemstvo* on the other.

The alternative draft presented all these ideas explicitly, but in the presidential draft, the ideas became vague. The most harm to the original ideas, however, was done at the constitutional meeting in June 1993. The purpose of that meeting was to bring the constitutional draft "to the people" for "public approval." Among the participants were a number of adherents to the Soviet constitutional traditions. So, the final draft of the document, influenced by these judicial bureaucrats, did not differ much from the old Soviet Constitutions. Russia's chance to establish, via a constitution, one of the basic principles of civil society—the absolute rights of individuals—and to move on to the difficult task of reform was missed. The Constitution was adopted on December 12, 1993.

Today we have, despite all its shortcomings, including elements of authoritarian presidential power and a lack of the democratic spirit present in the original drafts, a democratic Constitution—the first one in Russia's history. Generally, the democratic nature of the current Russian Constitution is expressed in the following issues.

First, the Constitution managed to overcome the disastrous Soviet organization of power. Under the Soviet system, representative bodies that were not officially and institutionally sanctioned assumed absolute power. Behind the people's backs—actually outside of the law—nonconstitutional bodies such as the Communist Party and the bureaucracy were actually exercising de facto power.

The current Constitution has strictly outlined the general administrative and judicial structure of the country, following the best and most advanced models on the principles of separation of power and federalism. The primary exception is the transformation of federal bodies into *gubernias*. The fact that the constitutional chapters on the presidency and the Cabinet of Ministers were written separately allows room for additional amendments that deal with principles concerning the head of state and responsible government. Also, there are numerous statements throughout the text that deserve high praise. Among them is the thesis that human rights are inherent and that they constrain—in a positive way—both legislative and executive activities.

At the same time, we have to regretfully recognize that the present Constitution is not final. It is not the basic law that will exist and rule for ages, and is therefore disappointing to the authors of the alternative draft. The principle of constitutional invariability, along with some very complicated procedures for making amendments and revisions, were present in the alternative draft, but are absent from the final version.

Very soon it will be necessary to adopt amendments concerning the functions of the Federal Assembly and government. The functions of the Parliament need to be strengthened. The Parliament, interacting with the head of state, has the right and responsibility to exert some degree of control over the government. Future amendments concerning the designation of ministers need to be introduced by the prime minister in coordination with the appropriate committees of the *Duma* and the Council of Federation.

A more thorough revision of the Constitution, particularly its first chapters and the chapter on the judicial system, may be necessary in the near future. The goal is not just to eliminate pro-Soviet elements, but to again attempt to imbue the Constitution—and through it the entire government and its law—with the principles of basic human rights and freedoms. Thus the Russian Constitution would be more in line with the world's best and most progressive constitutional models.

5.2   FEDERAL SECURITY COUNCIL.*

The birth of a new Russia on June 12, 1991, confronted the nation's leaders with the task, unprecedented in Russian history, of effecting radical economic reforms in all areas of society. The magnitude of the problems facing the country stemmed not only from the significance of the historic choice made by Russians and the scale of the reforms, but also from the difficulties of the transitional period, when uncompromising political battles were fought and the state was making its first unsure steps.

The management system Russia inherited from the USSR was utterly incompetent to take up the tasks facing the country; moreover, the system posed a tangible political threat to the incipient reforms and provided the defeated conservative forces with a real opportunity to take revenge. The tense political situation in the country ruled out gradual evolution as the chief means for the emergence of a new state structure.

The problems of the transitional period and the entirely new geopolitical environment throughout the country were largely instrumental in lowering the security threshold from the level it had been under the USSR. The state's constitutional commitment to recognizing, respecting, and protecting human rights and civil liberties, however, expanded immeasurably the idea of security.

(a)   Formation.   President Yeltsin realized that the sole forces that could pull the country out of its unstable position and launch it firmly toward democracy were the pragmatic interaction between all the power branches and, simultaneously, strict adherence to the principle of separation of powers. Under these uncommon conditions, it was urgently necessary to give the head of state an appropriate mechanism that could offer a comprehensive solution to the problems at hand and to make adequate decisions.

The Security Council of the Russian Federation became, in fact, one of the leading consultative and coordinating mechanisms of this kind. It was instituted in June 1992 by a presidential decree, pursuant to the Russian Constitution and the Federal Law on Security. Its principal functions include:

- Helping the president govern the country
- Formulating security-related domestic, foreign, and defense policies
- Safeguarding Russia's state sovereignty
- Maintaining sociopolitical stability
- Protecting human rights and civil liberties

The Security Council deals with various security-related aspects of Russia's domestic and foreign policies; examines the strategic issues of state, economic, social, defense, information, and ecological security, among others; addresses public-health concerns by

---

*This section was written by Oleg N. Lobov.

forecasting and preventing emergency situations and addressing their aftereffects; and maintains stability and law and order. The Security Council is responsible for protection of the vital interests of the individual, society, and the state against external and internal threats.

The Security Council is comprised of a chairperson, secretary, permanent members, and nonpermanent members. By virtue of his office, the country's president is the Security Council chairperson. The permanent members include ex officio the chairperson of the government, secretary of the Security Council, chairperson of the Federal Assembly's State Duma, and the chairperson of the Federal Assembly's Council of Federation. Members of the Security Council may include heads of the federal ministries and departments and any other persons appointed by a presidential decree. At present, the Security Council members include the defense minister, interior minister, minister of justice, foreign minister, director of the Federal Borderguard Service, finance minister, director of the External Intelligence Service, director of the Federal Security Service, deputy government chairperson, and minister for Civil Defense, Emergencies, and Natural Disaster Control. Depending on the issue that comes under examination, the Security Council may ask any other civil-service officials to attend its sessions as consultants.

The permanent Security Council members have equal decision-making rights, whereas members sit on the Security Council's sessions in a nonvoting capacity. The Security Council holds it sessions at least once a month; if needed, extra sessions are convened. Security Council resolutions are adopted by a simple majority of the permanent members and take effect immediately upon approval by the Security Council chairperson. They are made public in the form of presidential decrees, directives, or session minutes. From time to time, the president may ask all Security Council members to vote on a particular issue and to endorse a ready resolution draft.

(b) Basic Tasks. The Security Council's basic tasks are outlined in the Law on Security and include:

- Specifying the vital interests of the individual, society, and the state and identifying internal and external threats to security.
- Developing guidelines for a strategy of security maintenance in the Russian Federation and providing for federal programs to be drawn up to implement it.
- Preparing recommendations that the president can follow to make decisions on domestic and foreign-policy issues relating to the maintenance of security of the individual, society, and the state.
- Preparing resolutions on ways to prevent emergencies that entail serious sociopolitical, economic, military, ecological, or other consequences, and to device measures for dealing with their aftereffects.
- Drafting proposals for the president to introduce, extend, or lift a state of emergency.
- Developing proposals on ways to coordinate the operation of executive bodies in carrying out the resolutions dealing with security and assessing their effectiveness.
- Improving the system of maintaining the security of the individual, society, and the state by developing proposals on ways to either reform the existing measures or set up new ones.

(c) Intersectional Coordination. The role of the Security Council in preparing and adopting resolutions consists of developing an integrated state policy of maintaining the country's security and of avoiding narrow institutional approaches by, among others, the power structure and special services. The Security Council's key objective, however, is working out an intersectional coordination system that allows, at the decision-making level on a countrywide scale, a unified approach to national issues. In so doing, the Security Council does not insist on an automatic integration of ministerial and departmental functions, but seeks to formulate an integrated state policy in which the interests of the individuals, society, and the state are carefully balanced. In fact, the previous system was supplemented with a political-control unit made up of all the executive and legislative bodies responsible for security maintenance.

The Security Council's intersectional commissions are the principal working bodies responsible for the implementation of this approach. They have been formed according to the key strategic objectives relating to the protection of the country's vital interests. The Security Council has within its framework the following permanent intersectional commissions: foreign policy, interregional defense security, borderguard policy, economic security, environmental security, public-health protection, social security, crime and corruption control, information security, science and technology, and the defense industry. Whenever required, the Security Council may set up intersectional commissions on a *temporary* basis to prepare recommendations on (1) the prevention of emergencies and the resolution of their aftereffects; (2) on individual issues of stability and law and order in society and the state; and (3) on protection of the constitutional system, sovereignty, and territorial integrity of the country. As a general rule, commissions are chaired by heads of the respective ministries and departments, their deputies, or experts authorized by the Russian president.

Along with their routine work on basic issues, the intersectional commissions draft recommendations on current aspects of national security. Despite being mere recommendations, the resolutions adopted by the commissions have great organizational and political weight because they embody the coordinated position of the departments that drafted them. If needed, their recommendations serve as a basis for executive action to be taken by the president. Intersectional commissions hold their sessions at least once a month, but are convened whenever the need arises.

All work, therefore, is done on a comprehensive basis, with the result that the joint security policy is used in formulating and adjusting the practical activities of the individual ministries and departments through the Security Council. The president can exercise his right to control legal state policy in maintaining national security.

(d)   Cooperation with Other Security Bodies.   The Security Council places great emphasis on cooperating with similar bodies in other states for the purpose of jointly tackling problems and exchanging ideas related to national security maintenance. One example is the signing of a protocol on cooperation between the Security Council and the National Security Council of Mongolia. This protocol provides for holding consultations, when needed, on specific aspects of security; exchanging information on issues of interest to the respective staffs and working teams of both councils; and holding round tables, familiarization trips, and other functions relating to the maintenance of national and international security.

(e)   Public Information.   One important task of the Security Council is informing the public of state policies on security and comprehensive measures regarding political, socioeconomic, military, ecological, and internal or external threats. Although the current mass media appear to effectively communicate the Council's activities to the people, the

Council is searching for new ways of expanding the coverage. The issues examined at intersectional commission sessions and the manner in which the Council arrives at its findings are undoubtedly of considerable interest to relevant ministries and departments, as well as to a wide range of other organizations and individuals. To satisfy this interest, the Security Council has begun publication of scientific and engineering materials to give the public as much detail as possible regarding the key security issues. Law Literature has published *Russia's Ecological Security,* a collection of articles that provides information about the nation's environmental problems and the proposals adopted to correct them. A similar publication on health protection in Russia has been prepared.

(f) Staff. All technical, organizational, and informational services are provided for the Security Council by its staff, at the core of which are qualified experts with a broad range of knowledge and vast practical experience. The role of the Security Council's staff is to provide a productive environment for work on joint resolutions by intersectional commissions and working groups. Additionally, the staff prepares Security Council sessions and current analytical information on national security issues and drafts initial documents and proposals to be considered by the head of state. The Security Council generates resolutions, written inquiries, and proposals to improve the performance of the tasks defined by the President. Based on the results of its sessions, including current issues in national security the Security Council sends these materials to various ministries and departments. The Security Council's staff is the center of all efforts to prepare comprehensive programs when they involve various ministries and departments.

The Security Council devotes considerable attention to cooperating with the legislative power structure. This cooperation takes the form of council representatives participating in Federal Assembly committees and commissions, holding round tables, and involving Duma and Federation Council legislators in the preparation of Security Council resolutions.

The staff is led by the Security Council secretary. As a permanent Security Council member, he is directly involved in resolving problems examined at Security Council sessions. In addition, he is chiefly responsible for planning Security Council work, preparing materials and draft documents on matters to be dealt with by the Security Council, and monitoring their implementation. He informs the president of key current and long-range issues of the country's security and submits for the president's consideration any initiatives and regulations relating to Russia's domestic and foreign policies. At the Security Council level, the secretary is the chief coordinator of efforts by the executive and legislative bodies represented on the Council.

Another important activity of the Security Council's secretary is informing the general public about the work of this body and about the progress achieved in security maintenance for the individual, society, and the state. The secretary is required to hold press conferences on the more important decisions adopted by the Security Council and to publish articles and give interviews to explain the goals of the president's policies. The secretary's other tasks extend to some aspects of international activities, which he handles based on the president's instructions. The secretary has three deputies in charge of the chief areas of the Council's activities: international and military security; public security; and economic, social, and other aspects of the country's security.

The Scientific Council plays a prominent role in ensuring the smooth operation of the Security Council. The Scientific Council is charged with identifying the main priorities of scientific research, coordinating the activities of research enterprises, and commissioning work on projects in the theory and practice of security maintenance.

Pursuant to the law, the intersectional commissions and staff of the Security Council perform the following general tasks:

- Assessing the internal and external threats to national security and identifying the sources of such threats.
- Preparing science-based forecasts of changes in the internal and external conditions and factors affecting the country's security standards.
- Developing and coordinating federal programs to maintain the country's security and assessing their effectiveness.
- Accumulating, analyzing, and processing information about the operation of Russia's security maintenance system and drafting recommendations to improve its performance.
- Informing the Security Council regarding progress in implementation of its resolutions.
- Organizing scientific research in security maintenance.
- Drafting Security Council resolutions and presidential decrees on security issues.
- Preparing materials for an annual report to be submitted by the President to Russia's Federal Assembly on the maintenance of the country's security.

The information and analysis base on which the Security Council and its structural divisions build their work is formed by analytical and informational materials prepared by various ministries and departments, as well as research projects commissioned by the Security Council's staff from scientific and research centers and institutes within the Russian Academy of Sciences. By law, the Security Council may request from federal agencies any routine or analytical information it needs to deal with matters of state security. As a way to improve the decision-making process, the Security Council staff has set up, within its framework, a situation center charged with monitoring various situations and examining possible scenarios that may develop from these situations.

By long-established tradition, some ministries and departments refer their materials to the president and to higher state authorities entirely on their own. This decentralized procedure has its merits, as it obviates the monopolization of information. Yet, the establishment of the Security Council's Situation Center has created a common database for storing information from various sources. By cross-checking this information, verifying the available data, and obtaining missing details, the Center has created a system that provides a more comprehensive and objective analysis of events and that generates adequate decisions.

(g) Reporting Relationship with the President. The Security Council secretary reports every week to the President on state problems that require immediate attention. Generally, these are five or six issues relating, for example, to rising social tensions in some regions or manufacturing industries, pressing international developments, or the likelihood of increased ethnic tensions. The principal purpose of these reports is to prevent the situations from degenerating into a crisis and to inform the president of the status of key aspects of the current national security policy. In addition, the Security Council staff receives specific assignments from the president. For example, the Security Council was, by a presidential decision, involved in preparing a federal budget plan for 1996. Accordingly, it set up a working group that studied the budgetary policy guidelines prepared by the Russian Finance Ministry and approved by the government. The analysts focused their attention on the feasibility of the budget revenues and the adequacy of funds to finance high-priority economic targets. They also identified financing priorities from the perspective of national security and the maintenance of Russia's economic independence and safety.

Despite the very short time the Security Council has been in operation, it is already clear that this federal body is capable of giving an objective assessment of both underlying and current problems of the transitional period through which the country is passing.

(h) Federal Programs.   Another effective tool in maintaining democratic reforms is a system of comprehensive federal programs, which are developed within the Security Council. The Security Council is able to take a broad and all-encompassing approach to the country's major problems, examine them in combination, and formulate an integrated and interlinked national-security policy.

One of these is the federal program to improve crime control, which accurately mirrors the problems of the transitional period and, in particular, the change of ownership patterns in the country. The program offers a wide range of measures, from improvements in law-enforcement equipment, to the adoption of new laws reflecting the changes that have occurred in Russian society.

(i) Environmental Issues.   The Security Council is closely involved in environmental issues, which are vital to the security of the individual and society. Environmental problems are particularly acute in Russia. Living by the rules of a closed society, the former Soviet administration ruled without adequate public and government control for a long time, a practice that threw Russia into a deep environmental crisis.

The Security Council and its divisions are active in environmental legislation. Proceeding from the basic ideas and principles adopted by the United Nations Conference on the Environment and Development held in Rio de Janeiro in 1992, the Council has drafted a presidential decree that assigns specific environmental tasks to the ministries and departments; these tasks are to be started when the country begins a steady recovery. The Security Council staff has also been involved in drafting plans for the country's transition to a sustainable development model. The Council's environmentalists are widely known for their uncompromising stand in favor of the destruction of chemical and nuclear weapons and the disposal of their wastes.

(j) Foreign Policy.   Foreign policy occupies much of the Security Council's attention. Problems in this regard are addressed by a new system of stable international ties and by efforts to maintain a favorable international climate for ensuring the success of domestic reforms. At present, Russia is engaged in laying a solid foundation for its integration into the world community.

In June 1995, the Security Council sponsored an international conference in Moscow entitled Russia-Europe: A Strategy for Energy Security. In addition, the Security Council is working to establish friendly working relationships with similar bodies in other countries, with the aim of reaching an understanding of common global problems and of creating systems for maintaining stability and security to meet the challenges of our time

(k) Military Security.   Much of the Security Council's time is spent on the military aspects of security. There are several pressing issues that need to be addressed: the need for radical reforms in the armed forces; the country's efforts to bring its military in line with the international climate; the partnerships Russia is establishing with Western countries; and the economic reforms underway in Russia. Currently, both the armed forces and the defense industry are undergoing comprehensive reforms. The Security Council has made a major contribution to cutting back on the supermilitarization of the country's economy, especially to the issue of converting arms production to civilian output.

5.3   GOVERNMENT STRUCTURE.* The government of the Russian Federation Council of Ministers, according to the Constitution that came into existence in 1993, has executive power over the country. The structure of the Russian Federation calls for a president, a federal conference (a Parliament consisting of two bodies, the Council of Federation and the Duma), a government (Council of Ministers), and a legal system. Unlike the previous Constitution that gave all executive power to the president, the current Constitution established legislative, executive, and judicial branches, each with its own power. (This structure is similar to that in the United States.)

The president is the head of state. He has the functions and means to influence the government and be in control of its activities. The president makes, with the agreement of the Duma, personnel appointments by recommendation of the prime minister (the official head of government) and has the right to accept resignations. The president appoints federal ministers and other members of the government. Additionally, he can serve as chairperson of meetings of the Council of Ministers. He has the right to veto decisions of the government if they are not in accordance with the Constitution, federal laws, or his decrees. With the appointment of a new president, the members of the Council of Ministers can resign, and the new president can accept or reject these resignations.

(a)   Council of Ministers. The government consisted of the Prime Minister, two first deputy prime ministers, deputy prime ministers, ministers and heads of state committees, and Federal commissions.

(b)   Division of the Ministers. The ministers of the current government are as follows: finance, economics, foreign affairs, defense, interior, civil engineering, social protection of the population, communication, ecology and natural resources, transportation, justice, labor, national affairs and regional policy, atomic energy, agriculture and food, health and pharmaceutical industry, science and technical policy, cooperation with the commonwealth of independent states, culture, education, railroads, fuel and energy, and the civil defense of extraordinary situations and natural disasters. See Exhibit 5.1 for a complete list of the federal ministries and other federal bodies.

(c)   Presidium. A permanent arm of the government is the Presidium. The Presidium consists of the chairperson of the government (prime minister), the first deputy prime ministers, a deputy prime minister, the minister of the Russian Federation, the chief of staff, the minister of finance, the minister of economics, the minister of foreign affairs, the minister of defense, and the minister of the interior (who is in charge of the police force).

(d)   Government Operation. The major functions of the prime minister are to assign responsibilities and to conduct meetings between his deputies, and to prepare proposals for the president on the structure of the federal government. The Council of Ministers prepares and proposes the state budget to the Duma. Parliament has a strong influence on the

---

*This section was written by Vladimir S. Babichev.

Exhibit 5.1.   The List of Ministries, the Russian Federation (as of March 26, 1997)

1. Federal Ministries

Ministry of Finance
The Ministry of the Interior
Ministry of Economics
Ministry of Nuclear Power
Ministry of Foreign Economic Relations and Trade
Ministry of the Civic Defense, Extreme Situations and Liquidation
   of the Consequences Due to Disasters
Ministry of Nationalities and Federal Relations
Ministry of Health
Ministry of Foreign Affairs
Ministry of Culture
Ministry of Science and Technologies
Ministry of Defense
Ministry of General and Vocational Education
Ministry of Natural Resources
Ministry of Railroads
Ministry of Agriculture and Food
Ministry for Cooperation with the CIS Members
Ministry of Fuel and Energy
Ministry of Transportation
Ministry of Labor and Social Development
Ministry of Justice

2. State Committees

The State Anti-Monopoly Committee
The State Committee for the North Development
The State Supreme Attestation Committee
The State Committee on State Reserves
The State Committee on Youth Affairs
The State Committee on Housing and Construction Policies
The State Committee on Land Resources and Land Development
The State Committee on Cinematography
The State Committee for Support and Promotion of Small Business
The State Committee for the Protection of the Environment
The State Committee on Publishing
The State Committee on Communication and Information Development
The State Committee on Standardization, Metrology and Certification
The State Committee on Statistics
The State Committee on State Property Management
The State Customs Committee
The State Committee for Physical Education and Tourism

3. Federal Commissions

Federal Commission on Securities and the Capital Market
Federal Commission on Real Estate and Appraisal
Federal Energy Commission
Federal Transportation Service

4. Federal Services

Federal Tax Police Service
Federal Service of Russia on Providing State Monopoly on Alcoholic Products
Federal Service of Guarding
Federal Border Service
Federal Service of Russia on Regulation of Natural Monopolies in Communication
Federal Service of Russia on Regulation of Natural Monopolies in Transportation

Exhibit 5.1.   The List of Ministries, the Russian Federation (*Cont'd.*)

4. Federal Services (*Cont'd.*)

Federal Service of Russia on Television and Radio Broadcasting
The Federal Aviation Service
The Federal Archive Service
The Foreign Intelligence Service
The Federal Transportation Service
The Federal Service on Geodesy and Cartography
The Federal Service on Hydrometeorology and Environmental Monitoring
The Federal Service on Bankruptcies and Financial Reorganization
The Federal Service on the Railroad Military Forces
The Federal Forestry Service
The Federal Security Service
The Federal Migration Service
The State Tax Service

5. Federal Monitoring Agencies

The Federal Agency for Mining and Industrial Monitoring
Russian Space Agency
Russian Agency for Patent and Trademark
Russian Agency on Government Communication and Information on the President
   of the Russian Federation
Federal Monetary Agency
Federal Monitoring Agency on Nuclear and Radiation Security

government through the budget. Also, the Duma has the special right to appoint the prime minister, and it can also take a vote of no confidence.

The government's power extends to all of Russia. It implements the laws, reports progress, issues decrees and decisions, and has the right to propose laws to the Duma. The government is required to meet at least once every three months, at which time there needs to be a quorum of two-thirds present to transact business. Voting is done by a simple majority.

(e)   State and Local Responsibilities.   The federal structure of government can create territorial branches and appoint executives. The system of the executive structure of the Russian Federation is the responsibility of the autonomous republics, oblasts, krais, and major cities. They have the right to create their own system of executive power according to the Constitution and general rules of federal power.

On the local level, according to the Constitution, the unified system of executive power consists of the federal arm of executive power and the executive arm of the subjects of the federation (composed of the autonomous republics, oblasts, and krais). The current structure of the federal executive arm includes 76 entities, including 11 state committees, 16 committees, 15 federal services, two federal agencies, one federal inspection agency, one department (with rights of the state committee), three supervisors, one federal commission, one main executive department, and one executive department.

5.4   FEDERATION AND SUBJECTS OF FEDERATION.*   In accordance with the Constitution (Article 11), the Council of Federation of Russia's Federal Assembly is one of the supreme bodies of state power. The Council of Federation includes two representatives from each subject of the Federation (see chapter appendix for a list of members), and one

---

*This section was written by Vyacheslav F. Shumeyko.

from each of the executive bodies of state power. The Council of Federation is distinctive among Russian state institutions because of its steadfast expression of the principles of federalism. Representatives include not only those from the subjects of the Federation, but also the leaders of most of the autonomous republics, oblasts and krais are members as well. There are 13 presidents of the autonomous republics, 45 prime ministers, and 45 heads of legislative power.

One of the main concerns of the Council is to study and attempt to solve problems of regional and ethnic policies. The Council takes responsibility for settling ethnic conflicts in Russia, stabilizing ethnic relations, and harmonizing regional and federal interests. The most important result of its activity is the Council's evolution into a "chamber of regions." A structure of representative power has been formed, which provides each subject of the Federation with equal representation, an equal vote, and equal rights in the decision-making process. None of the autonomous republics, regions, or districts is deprived of any rights in comparison with others.

The members of the Council of Federation are elected and have been entrusted by the population with a mandate to represent their regional interests and to protect these interests on the federal level. The Council uses this right in approving top officials for offices and presidential decrees.

Between January 1994 and June 1995, the Council held 22 meetings, during which over 500 issues were considered, including 152 bills. In June 1994, a Coordinating Committee was established. It is in charge of regulating relationships between the Chamber of the Federal Assembly on one hand, and legislative bodies of the subjects of the Federation on the other. The Coordinating Committee:

- Promotes unified legislative power in the Russian Federation and its subjects
- Coordinates legislative activities of the subjects
- Helps legislative bodies of the subjects draft laws on issues relating to both the Federation and its subjects

Along with the Coordinating Committee, the agreement on cooperation between the Federal Assembly and interregional associations for economic interaction is also very important for developing relationships with regions. As a result of the agreement, the Council of Federation has softened militant separatist movements in various regions that arose from economic and financial hardships. This action was possible because Russia has been following a principle of budget federalism. This principle embodies the idea that a federal structure should maintain effective budgetary relations between various levels of power. By using this new approach to relations between federal power and the regions, the Council has managed to avoid a fiscal war inside the Russian Federation.

Actually, such a war was close to starting in 1992–93, when a number of subjects of the Federation stopped making payments to the federal budget and demanded a one-way budgetary system. Any further delay of the federalization of the budget system would have lead to serious consequences. As a result, the Council of Federation put forth serious efforts that led to the establishment of a new type of budgetary system. The powers of the Ministry of Finance were restricted. The subjects of the Federation gained more independence to conduct their own taxation and budget policies.

The influence of the Council of Federation on the situation in the country has been limited. The Council has not yet become the sort of institution in which a consensus of opinion on an issue can be reached by all regions and made public. Also, the powers of the Council of Federation are limited constitutionally. In those legislative areas where the

Constitution does not outline the Council's powers, the Council is limited only to suggest, make, and *pursue proposals.*

To increase the Council's role in state affairs, it is necessary not only to improve its effectiveness but also to delegate much more power and rights to the Council. This means adding the necessary amendments to the Constitution. Without them, the Council could not represent, protect, and fulfill the interests of the regions.

To build a new Russian state, the government must rely on a national concept of democratic statehood. Today, there are different points of view on what a Russian state should look like. All the political groups in today's Russia, however, have a common opinion on two important aspects concerning the concept of a Russian state.

1. It should be a state reflecting Russia's specific history, traditions, culture and spirit. It is evident that attempts to impose Western economic and political models on Russia have not produced good results. There is no universal recipe to renew a society that works in all countries. Even the idea of basic human values is different in various countries; truth and human rights have different meanings in the United States, Japan, Great Britain, and Italy.

2. The efforts to establish a federation have become more and more important. The efficiency and strength of a Russian state depend on how flexible and skillful the establishment of a new relationship between the federal center and the subjects of the Federation will be. This relationship will determine the redistribution of power.

The Council of Federation has extensive work to do in this regard. According to the Constitution, all subjects of the Federation are equal. In real life, however, they have different responsibilities to the state and its citizens. Thus, the fundamental constitutional provision on equality of all subjects of the Federation has not yet been fully implemented.

Another issue that remains to be resolved involves imposing sanctions against legislative and executive bodies of the subjects of the Federation when their decisions oppose the interests of the Federation as a whole. A number of autonomous Russian republics have adopted constitutions and individual laws that contradict Russia's Constitution. The Constitution has not outlined any limits or acceptable forms of control by the federal power regarding the responsibility of the subjects of the Federation in cases of mutual conflict. The lack of such a provision has resulted in the Federation's imposition of socioeconomic models on some regions that had disregarded their unique needs.

The institution of local self-government within a framework of executive and legislative power has not been clearly enough defined. This has made it possible for some regions to restore the old system of power in which a local self-government is a part of a state political structure. In some other regions, local self-government is being ignored and suppressed.

There is an urgent need for complete constitutional regulation of the basic economic relations in accordance with a principle of federalism. Particularly, the mechanism of budgetary federalism should be improved significantly.

APPENDIX: THE SUBJECTS OF THE RUSSIAN FEDERATION

Republics:

Adyghei Republic, Altai Republic, Bashkortostan Republic, Buriatian Republic, Daghestan Republic, Republic of Ingush, Kabardino-Balkarian Republic, Republic of Kalmykia (Khalm Tangch), Karachaevo-Circassian Republic, Republic of Karelia, Komi Republic,

Mari El Republic, Mordovian Republic, Republic of Sakha (Yakutia), Northern Osetian Republic, Tatarstan Republic, Tuva Republic, Republic of Udmurtia, Khakassian Republic, Chechen Republic, Republic of Chuvashia;

Krais:
Altai Krai, Krasnodar Krai, Krasnoyarsk Krai, Primorsky Krai, Stavropol Krai, Khabarovsk Krai;

Oblasts:
Amur, Arkhangelsk, Astrakhan, Belgorod, Bryansk Oblast, Vladimir, Volgograd, Vologda Oblast, Voronezh, Ivanovo, Irkutsk, Kaliningrad, Kaluga, Kamchatka, Kemerovo, Kostroma, Kurgan, Kursk, Leningrad Oblast, Lipetsk, Magadan, Moscow Oblast, Murmansk Oblast, Nizhny Novgorod Oblast, Novgorod Oblast, Novosibirsk, Omsk, Orenburg, Orel, Penza, Perm, Pskov Oblast, Rostov, Ryazan, Samara, Saratov, Sakhalin, Sverdlovsk, Smolensk, Tambov, Tver, Tomsk, Tula, Tyumen, Ulyanovsk, Vyatka, Chelyabinsk Oblast, Chita, Yaroslavl; Moscow and St. Petersburg (cities of federal significance); Yevreiskaya (Jewish) Autonomous Oblast;

Okrugs:
Aghinsky-Buryatsky Autonomous Okrug, Komi-Permyatsk Autonomous Okrug, Koryaksky Autonomous Okrug, Nenets Autonomous Okrug, Taymyrsky (Dolgano-Nenets) Autonomous Okrug, Ust-Ordynsky Autonomous Okrug, Khanty-Mansi Autonomous Okrug, Chukotsky Autonomous Okrug, Evenkisky Autonomous Okrug, Yamal-Nenets Autonomous Okrug.

CHAPTER 6

REGIONAL GOVERNMENT

Nikolai V. Sevrugin and Sergey S. Sobynin

6.1 TULA OBLAST: EXECUTIVE BODIES.* According to the Constitution of the Russian Federation and the common principles guiding the structure of executive and legislative powers, the regional administrations independently determine their system of government. Such factors as the size of the region and its natural resources, its scientific and industrial potential, demography, infrastructure, environment, and social situation influence the composition of government bodies, their functions, and the number of their subdivisions.

Located in the most populated European part of Russia and possessing developed transportation systems, Tula Oblast is a good example of the regional authority structure in the central region. With a territory of 26,000 square kilometers and the population close to two million people, Tula Oblast has a powerful scientific and industrial foundation, with significant agriculture, food, and processing industries, a developed infrastructure, and sufficient amounts of mineral resources and raw materials.

(a) Resources. Rich in minerals, Tula Oblast produces brown coal, phosphates, celestite, rock salt, gypsum, limestone, unique clays, and carbonic minerals—all of which create desirable conditions for the development of various industries. These natural resources, as well as those obtained from the surrounding regions, allowed Tula Oblast to foster the growth of mining, metallurgical, chemical, petrochemical, electrical, and timber industries. Machine-building and metal-working, as well as traditional crafts, such as small-arms and samovar manufacturing, play a significant role in Tula's economy. Over 50 scientific and research institutes and design offices, as well as about 200 private scientific organizations, help maintain a high level of manufacturing and the creation of new, highly competitive products.

The State Technological University of Tula provides large scientific and educational base in the region. The State Pedagogical University of Tula, (named after Leo N. Tolstoy), the branches of the State University of Chemistry and Technology, the branches of the Institute of Law, the Institute of Commerce, and the Institute of Economics and Finance graduate trained people needed in the local economy.

(b) Administrative Bodies. According to the concept of territorial management, two management groups were established in the administrative structure of Tula, based on the industrial orientation principle:

---

*This section was written by Nikolai V. Sevrugin.

1. The first group deals with production, services, and distribution. It is comprised of the departments for fuel and energy industries, construction, housing, communal services, transportation and communication, agriculture, and retail and consumer service industries. The main goal of this group is to provide conditions for the growth of production and the consumer market, and to maintain the oblast's budget for the government's social programs.

2. The second group deals with social issues. It is comprised of the departments for the health and education industries, the social-security system, culture, physical education and sports, and tourism. The main task of this group is to create a system of social well-being and to maintain an adequate standard of living based on judicious budget spending.

To coordinate the economic and financial activities of these departments, and to enable the administration to function as an entity, management departments were created for economics, international economic relations, finances, state legislation, and other areas.

To find solutions for the new economic problems, the administration had to create a new approach in forming its bodies. For this purpose, specialized Centers for Problem Solving were created. These centers deal with issues relating to:

- Privatization and management of state property
- Innovation and investment
- Leasing
- Ecology and environmental safety
- Employment and work relations
- General policies, analysis, and strategies
- Personnel policies

For the purposes of handling the issues related to both production and social issues, a joint administrative body was formed, headed by the oblast's first vice-governor. With this body, the first vice-governor can effectively manage the complex development of the oblast's economy, plan and realize industrial programs, and implement social and political reforms. Simultaneously, the first vice-governor can coordinate structural reforms in the oblast's economy, reform scientific, technological, and investment policies, encourage creation of production facilities, and promote reciprocity with the credit and financial system.

The harmonious efforts of the administration's members are important to ensure the professional and organizational performance of the top administrators and the bodies of executive authority. The goals of the administrative body include the preparation of forecasting and analytical materials for strategic development and general policies, and sociological research and dissemination of information about the reforms. The administrative body facilitates interaction with legislative and judicial bodies, social organizations, cultural movements, religious organizations, the mass media, and bodies of local governments. Selecting and training state employees is also a responsibility of the administrative body.

(c) Leadership. The actual leadership of the oblast's administration and the reigns of executive power are assumed by the governor of Tula Oblast. The governor's authority extends to having strategic decision-making power over social and economic development of the oblast, implementation of the reforms, maintenance of political stability, and the interaction among all the branches of authority, governmental agencies, and presidential structures. The governor recommends legislative proposals to the oblast's Duma, exercises the right of veto, and drafts the oblast's budget proposals. To fulfill these responsibilities, the governor coordinates the activities of the tax, credit, and financial systems and various power structures within the territory of the oblast. The governor also manages the actions of the government council and the council of the heads of administrations of cities and regions.

6.2   KHANTY-MANSI AUTONOMOUS OKRUG: ORGANIZATIONAL STRUCTURE.*

The Khanty-Mansi Autonomous Okrug was established on December 10, 1930. It is located in Tyumen Oblast and has been under its administration since 1944. The okrug's total population in 1996 was 1,300,100, of which 1,212,600 are city dwellers, while 89,500 live in the country. The okrug's population consists of 123 different nationalities, among which Russians account for 66.3%, Ukrainians 11.6%, Khanty 0.9%, Mansi 0.5%, and others 20.7%.

The largest cities in the okrug are Nizhnevartovsk (population 244,600), Surgut (261,200), Nefteyugansk (95,800), and Niagan (62,300). Its harsh continental climate is characterized by long, severe, snowy winters and short summers. The average temperatures are –19 to –23 °C in January, and 16 to 19 °C in July.

Because of high precipitation in the region and the flat landscape, river floods are a constant nuisance. They cause the formation of marshlands, which spread over half the okrug's territory. The two largest rivers of the West Siberian Plain—the Ob and the Irtysh—flow from south to north into the Karskoye Sea across the territory. The watery meadows provide a rich food source for farm cattle.

(a)   Structure of Governmental Bodies.   The government of the okrug consists of legislative, executive, and judicial bodies. The structure of its governmental authority is determined from within the okrug independently and in compliance with the constitution of the Russian Federation.

The Duma is the legislative branch of the okrug's authority. The governor and the administration of Khanty-Mansi Okrug represent the executive branch. The judicial system is regulated by the code of the federal laws and is carried out through federal and local courts of law.

Khanty-Mansi Okrug recognizes and supports self-management and self-regulation of the local authorities. Self-regulated local authorities are not part of the governmental authority system of the okrug.

All forms of private ownership are recognized. Khanty-Mansi Okrug accepts and protects free enterprise and the union of economic territories of the Russian Federation. The government of the okrug, in coordination with the federal government, supports international business relationships in the autonomous okrug, signs agreements, subscribes to the international agreements of the Russian Federation, and abides by the Federation's foreign policy.

(b)   Economics.   The okrug's main industries are oil (78.7%), electric energy (13%), natural gas (5.2%), lumber (1%), and fishing (less than 1%). The leading industry of the okrug, oil production, constitutes 60% of all the oil produced in the country. Twenty-three joint-stock enterprises and eight joint-ventures are involved in the okrug's oil production.

---

*This section was written by Sergey S. Sobynin.

Five geological and one geophysical enterprises are responsible for exploration of natural resources in the region. Natural gas, a by-product of oil production, is processed by eight gas-refining factories. It feeds the three largest electric gas plants (EGP) in the country—Surgut EGP #1 and #2, and Nizhnevartovsk EGP. Together they produce a total of 50 billion kilowatt-hours of electricity annually.

The lumber industry is comprised of 46 joint-stock tree-felling enterprises, the largest of which are Torsk TFE (tree-felling enterprise), Yukon, and Balykles. The level of timber production has been decreasing—from 11,267,000 cubic meters in 1990 to 3,000,000 in 1994. Lumber processing constitutes 25% of the lumber production volume in the region.

The total fish harvest in the okrug from 1990 to 1996 decreased by half. Fish canning went down fourfold in the same period.

In addition to the fur-hunting industry, the okrug has 22 fur-breeding farms that raise valuable types of fur animals, such as the silver, red, and blue fox. The sale of fur amounts to 50,000 skins annually.

The okrug's farming satisfies about 10 to 15% of its agricultural needs. The main farming industries are cattle raising, reindeer breeding, fur breeding and hunting, and fishing. Altogether, the okrug has 17 agricultural, 11 fishing, and three poultry farms, as well as 235 subsidiary farms. Areas under cultivation cover 7,884 hectares, which is approximately 0.006 hectares per capita.

Five house-building plants, three brickyards, and five building materials plants provide for the construction industry of the okrug.

Transportation in the region can be outlined as follows:

- Trunk pipelines—over 9,000 km
- Paved roads—10620 km
- Railroad tracks—1804 km
- Airline routes—2800 km
- River routes—612 km

The okrug has four main railroad junctions—Nizhnevartovsk, Surgut, Kogalym, and Niagan—five river ports, and 14 airports. Flights are available to 78 cities in Russia. Most of the freight is carried by water and rail—29% by road and 2% by air. Long-distance telephone communication has been established with all the regions of Russia, as well as numerous foreign countries. There are 84 hotels, which can accommodate 4,476 guests at a time.

The okrug has a number of modern resorts suited for skiing. In 2002, the okrug will host the world's biathlon championship, for which facilities are currently being created.

So far, tourism has not developed as an industry. With some investment, however, the okrug's picturesque landscape could become a great attraction for domestic and foreign tourists.

The okrug has had a history of trading with foreign countries. The main exports are oil, lumber, and saw-timber. Imports are predominantly raw materials and consumer goods, including produce, medicine, machinery, heavy equipment, and construction services.

In Khanty-Mansi Okrug, there are 91 branches of 22 commercial banks based in Russia, as well as 23 local independent commercial banks. Among the largest banks are Khanty-Mansi Bank of North Nations, Yugorsk Joint-Stock Bank, Surgutneftegasbank, Langepas, Kogalymneftekombank, and Nizhnevartovsk KIB-Bank. The founders of these are large-scale enterprises of western Siberia's fuel and energy complex. The banks are licensed by the Central Bank of Russia to provide all types of transactions. The banks negotiate with a number of foreign financial institutions about their participation in investment programs for the economic development of the okrug.

Insurance services in the okrug are provided by two subsidiaries of the insurance companies ASKO and Finno-Ugriya, as well as the local insurance companies NASKO and VITA, which offer 40 different types of insurance services to the public and business community.

(c)   Potential Development.   A number of potential projects are awaiting foreign investment and partnership in the okrug, the construction of:

- The petrochemical complex Obpolimer, with an annual production capacity of 120,000 tons, located in the city of Niagan
- A plastics plant, with 600,000 tons of annual production capacity in the city of Surgut
- Construction of Cable communications networks
- An engine fuel plant, with 3,000,000 tons of annual production capacity in the city of Nizhnevartovsk
- The Niagam EGP, with a capacity of 600 megawatts
- A transportation bridge over the Ob river near Surgut city
- Facilities for fine lumber processing at several existing lumber mills
- Plants and facilities for the storage and processing of fish and pelts on the lands of the native peoples

Due to the lack of developed production and an adequate social infrastructure in the region, the okrug's policy for attracting foreign investment includes offering favorable conditions for foreign enterprises, such as tax breaks.

CHAPTER 7

FOREIGN ECONOMIC POLICY

Yevgeni M. Primakov, Vladimir P. Lukin, Valeriy M. Serov, Stoyan D. Ganev, Alexander G. Granberg, Sergey V. Lavrov, and Eugene A. Baranov

7.1 ECONOMIC DIPLOMACY.* The role played by economic issues in modern foreign policy is growing steadily. This trend is caused by three factors: (1) increasingly vigorous development processes in the world economy; (2) the globalization of trade, investment, and finance; and (3) an increasingly close intertwining of the economies of separate countries and whole geographic regions. Not only has the economic constituent in Russia's foreign policy been growing, but radical economic reform and the opening of the domestic market have also assigned Russian diplomacy a large number of tactical tasks and strategic goals, including:

- Creating external conditions favorable to the development of the Russian economy
- Implementing market reforms in Russia
- Protecting the rights and interests of the subjects of the federation and Russian entrepreneurs
- Promoting integration with the Commonwealth of Independent States (CIS)

(a) Development of a Market Economy. Since the early 1990s, Russia has been pursuing an irreversible and firm policy designed to abandon the centralized economic system and establish a market economy. Russia has made great progress along this path. The system of centralized planning and distribution of production has been completely dismantled. Any state interference with the economy is accomplished mainly through indirect methods. Freedom of manufacturers of goods—no matter what their form of property—is guaranteed. The share of the nonstate sector in the economy is already about 70%. The structure of Russia's gross domestic product (GDP) has started to resemble that of the other industrially developed nations in that its service sector now exceeds 50% of the total.

The elimination of the foreign-trade monopoly has been completed. Russia has no restrictions on external economic activities, regardless of the forms of property (except for those activities related to maintaining security and the public's well-being). The newly established private businesses and the remaining state-owned foreign-trade companies (the

---

*This section was written by Yevgeni M. Primakov.

latter are declining steadily) carry out their external economic activity based on market principles and strictly commercial considerations.

Over the last few years, a free cost-factor pricing system has been in effect in the country, except for state-regulated prices on the goods and services of natural monopolies. The scale of state subsidizing has become notably more restricted; at present, it focuses mainly on strategically crucial projects. The Russian government has been pursuing an aggressive policy of combating monopolies and encouraging free competition.

A fairly solid normative and legal basis has been established for important reform activities. The ruble has grown stronger and become, in fact, convertible. Inflation has been finally curtailed. There has been a notable improvement in the federal budget: its deficit in 1995 was 2.9% of GDP, compared to 10.7% in 1994. It is noteworthy that its financing was accomplished mainly through noninflationary methods. There remains a steady positive trade balance ($ 9.8 billion in 1994, and $ 15.9 billion in 1995).

(b)   Federalism.   A new phenomenon in Russia's national life is a shift from a nominally proclaimed federalism (the USSR was in fact a unitary state) to a genuine federal system. This change has resulted in a high level of self-dependency among the subjects of the Federation—entities that have gained not only a constitutional right, but also a material basis for direct, external economic relations. Transborder trade has also picked up considerably.

Russian diplomacy is making efforts to broaden and deepen the external economic activity of the country's various regions while guiding and monitoring the expansion of independent regional ties from the federal level. The Consultative Council of the Ministry of Foreign Affairs of the Russian Federation helps to address numerous issues relating to the foreign economic activity of the Federation's subjects. Consequently, the quality of documentation, as well as the level of information and interregional coordination, has improved remarkably. In fact, the international economic activities of the various regions have become an additional means of economic cooperation with other countries.

(c)   Bilateral and Multilateral Relations.   Russia's foreign policy uses both bilateral and multilateral connections. Bilateral relations emphasize the consolidation of a normative and legal basis for cooperation in the economic sphere, the establishment or re-establishment of cooperative business mechanisms, promotion of a wide exchange of delegations and trade missions, and a direct diplomatic guardianship over the most significant joint projects.

The Russian Federation, which is currently undergoing serious economic hardships, is extremely interested in an influx of foreign investments, mainly into the production sphere. In this connection, Russia's attempts to reach bilateral agreements to encourage and mutually protect investments have become extremely important. Six such agreements were signed in 1995–96, with about 20 more in the final stage of development.

Over the last few years, Russian economic diplomacy has been very active at the regional and subregional levels, especially in relation to the Commonwealth of Independent States, Central and Eastern Europe, Asia and the Pacific, the Group of Seven, and the European Union. Priority has been given to strengthening the integration processes within the Commonwealth of Independent States. Russia is openly interested in transforming the Commonwealth into a politically and economically integrated body of sovereign states that would achieve a respected position in the world community.

Economic measures are playing a leading role in reaching this goal. Such measures include the implementation of the Treaty on Economic Union, a gradual expansion of the

Customs Union of interested countries, and an acceleration of activities for the establishment of a Payment Union (a treaty aimed at closer cooperation in monetary issues) among the CIS. Related tasks include establishing closer national, legal, and economic mechanisms and abolishing barriers that prevent the development of free enterprise among the Commonwealth countries. Among additional measures considered especially important are the establishment of financial and industrial groups, including manufacturers and banks from the CIS, and the development of transnational, production, research and development, and other structures.

Russia is also working to reinvigorate economic relationships with traditional partners in Central and Eastern Europe. During the existence of the Council for Mutual Economic Assistance (CMEA), the share of its member states in the foreign trade of the USSR was about 50%, whereas the same share for Russia in 1995 was only 8%. Hindsight shows that the dismantling of the CMEA not only ended paternalistic relationships, but also destroyed the spirit of cooperation accumulated over the years. New possibilities are emerging for an efficient articulation of economic complexes along market-oriented lines: the Central and Eastern Europe and countries that had abandoned a unilateral economic relationship are coming to see the usefulness of developing economic ties with the new Russia.

Other regions of the world that are especially important for Russian economic diplomacy include Asia and the Pacific, a region that has been steadily gaining global stature. Russia intends to expand its participation as a member of the Pacific Economic Cooperation Council and the Pacific Basin Economic Council. Russia is also interested in full membership in the Asian-Pacific Economic Cooperation intergovernmental forum, as well as serving on its committees and working groups.

With regard to the Group of Seven, Russia is pursuing a gradual—not artificially accelerated—transformation of an established "political" G–8 into a full-fledged G–8. That actually is already the case with the Denver summit.

The current goal in relation to the European Union is a gradual increase in business cooperation according to the wide range of topics stipulated in the Agreement on Partnership and Cooperation. At the same time, Russia intends to pursue a dynamic policy to overcome remaining overt and covert trade discrimination against Russia, to abolish unfair practices of the dumping of Russian goods, to remove the ban on Russia's access to the high-tech market. All of these measures are a part of the country's long-term policy to establish a free-trade zone with the EU.

The Ministry of Foreign Affairs is well aware of the importance of multilateral mechanisms for achieving worldwide economic relationships. Russia already is a full and equal member of influential institutions such as the International Monetary Fund, the World Bank Group, and the European Bank of Reconstruction and Development. Russia also is striving for a closer relationship with the Organization for Economic Cooperation and Development; the purpose of this policy is to achieve full membership in this body.

(d) World Trade Organization. Joining the World Trade Organization (WTO) is another high priority for Russia. It is clear, however, that full-fledged participation would require numerous amendments to Russian legislation in the areas of economics, investment and finance, trade, taxation, customs, and others, as well as a whole series of new legislative and regulatory acts. This constitutes the introduction into Russia's economic life of experiences accumulated over decades by the world community in market economy regulation. Serious and difficult negotiations will be required to define a balance of rights and obligations that would take into account the current delicate situation in the Russian economy and the need to provide selective protection to domestic manufacturers. At the same time, these rights and obligations would need to provide Russia with the trade and political status enjoyed by the developed member states of the WTO.

(e)   Abolishment of Discriminatory Restrictions.   Another important goal of Russian economic diplomacy is the abolishment of direct and covert discriminatory restrictions and limitations on trade stipulated in the legislation of a number of Russia's Western partners; many of these practices have existed since the cold war. Unfortunately, multilateral and bilateral efforts to this end have been fruitless. So far, Russia has not been granted the status of a country with market economy by some industrialized nations. They still regulate their economic relationships with Russia as if dealing with a country with a centrally planned economy and still apply legal measures that had been developed mainly during the cold war and that discriminate against Russia's interests rather strongly.

Russia's economy now follows market rules and has a structure fairly close to that of the industrialized nations. An agreement with the EU to jointly review the issue of Russia's economic status is, therefore, a positive development. Also, the topic of acknowledging Russia as a country with a market economy was broached in earnest at the Lyons G–8 Summit and at a number of other international forums.

7.2   THE UNITED STATES.*   The relationship between Russia and the United States is characterized by the following three features:

1. Similar experiences of the people; for example, early pioneers of both countries crossed their mainlands and almost met at Fort Ross, near San Francisco;
2. Absence of military action against each other, which is very rare for such powerful countries with differing idealogies;
3. They were allies during both world wars when they saved Europe and eastern Asia from militarism and fascism.

During the eighteenth and nineteenth centuries, relations between Russia and the United States were very friendly. Relations became tense during the Communist rule (1917–1991) and started improving again in the 1990s.

When the 13 original North American colonies declared their independence, Russia provided them substantial support. Under the rule of Catherine the Great, who had close ties with the philosophers of the French Enlightenment, Russia regarded the colonies' quest for independence with consideration and sympathy. This attitude resulted in Russia's establishment of the League of Military Neutrality in 1780. Despite declaring itself neutral, the league aided the colonies struggling for their independence. The league, for example, blocked the movement of the British fleet, the most powerful navy in the world.

The United States was deeply gratified that St. Petersburg declared its military neutrality and gathered under its flag all neutral European countries. The United States also appreciated Catherine the Great's refusal of the British request to send Russian mercenaries to fight against the Americans. The beginning of Russian-American relations was characterized by mutual sympathy and American gratitude to Russia for holding back the British Empire.

When the United States purchased Louisiana and thus doubled its territory, Alexander I established diplomatic relations with the emerging nation. This promoted close cooperation between the two nations. For example, between 1842 and 1851, a road connecting

*This section was written by Vladimir P. Lukin.

St. Petersburg and Moscow was constructed under the direction of an American; at the time, it was the most ambitious project of its kind.

The following two episodes further illustrate the warm friendship between the two countries in the nineteenth century. During the American Civil War. Britain and France were aiding the South in its struggle against the North. In 1868, two Russian navy squadrons left Kronstadt and Vladivostok for New York and San Francisco. They had received the order that, in case of a conflict involving Britain and France on one side, and Russia and America on the other, to establish bases at several North American ports.

The second episode is related to Russia's sale of Alaska, to the United States for a very low, purely symbolic price. This was done so that the United States would have Alaska and to prevent Britain from making a claim to that region.

Another example of the close ties between the United States and Russia was the proposal on cooperation between Russia and Japan that was made by President Theodore Roosevelt in 1905. In addition, Russia and the United States became military allies during World War I.

The relationship between the two countries cooled from 1918 to 1941, and from 1946 to 1991. The beginning of the first period was marked by the Brest peace agreement and by U.S. military intervention when American troops landed in Vladivostok. Although, Moscow realized that the Americans were there to hold back the Japanese, the intervention left a long-standing scar on relations between the two countries.

In President Wilson's famous Fourteen Points, he proclaimed Russia "single and indivisible." Wilson supported Russia until almost mid-1918 when the Russian civil war forced Washington to make a choice. The United States, however, provided enormous humanitarian help to Russia during the famine of 1921.

In the 1920s, American entrepreneurs such as Armand Hammer, Averill Harriman Sr., and Henry Ford, managed to establish business connections with Russia, despite the absence of diplomatic relations, American engineers took part in completing many important projects (Dneproges, the Gorky automobile plant, and others).

Changes in the world's geopolitical situation, specifically the militant rise of Japan and Germany, brought about the diplomatic recognition of the Soviet Union by the United States in 1933. After World War II began, the United States and Russia found themselves in the same military alliance. Together with Britain, they established a powerful anti-Hitler coalition. The summit conferences in Tehran (1943), Yalta, and Potsdam (1945) were mutually beneficial to both countries. In accordance with the policy of lend-lease, the United States supplied Russia with approximately 10% of the tanks and aircraft it used in the war. Russia's human losses in that conflict were about one-hundred times higher than those of the United States.

Following World War II, the period later called the cold war was marked by mutual misunderstanding, ignorance of mutual interests, the brutality of Stalin, and the rise of U.S. nuclear might. After the USSR developed its own nuclear weaponry in 1949, the situation between the two nations reached a strategic stalemate, a condition they both recognized when they started talks on limiting strategic weapons in 1968. Eventually agreements on limiting such weapons were signed in 1972, 1979, 1991, and 1993. These created a system of guarantees against a nuclear holocaust arising between the two superpowers of the contemporary world.

In the late 1980s and early 1990s, both nations arrived at the conclusion that the cold war was irrelevant. They recognized the necessity of integrating Russia into the world community lead by the United States. To get closer to the United States, the USSR (and later, new Russia) took important steps. First, the USSR agreed on the unification of Germany. Second, it signed an agreement on limiting conventional arms that undermined its superiority in such weapons. Third, the USSR approved an agreement on the mutual disso-lution of military blocs, as contained in the Paris Charter signed in 1990.

After the Russian Federation was created in 1991, a new chapter began in the develop-ment of Russian-American relations. For now, only two pages of this chapter have been written. The first deals with the period when Kozyrev was the foreign minister and Russia was blindly following the United States. That period brought Russia few benefits. The sec-ond page is still being written: Russia, which finds itself in a complex economic and social situation, has begun to clearly pursue its own interests. At this historical crossroad, friendly relations with the United States are one of Russia's most important assets in for-eign policy, a guarantee of her peaceful and successful entrance into the new world of in-formation and technology.

7.3   CIS COUNTRIES: STARTING POINT FOR A NEW SYSTEM OF RELATIONS.*
In the wake of the spontaneous disintegration of the USSR and proclamations of national and state sovereignty by its former members, an organizational and legal vacuum devel-oped in the relations between the new states. Unlike Czechoslovakia, for example, where the emergence of two states was preceded by a long preparatory stage, the division of the USSR into independent entities was almost an overnight happening. No rules or proce-dures had been thrashed out in advance to divide up the Soviet Union's assets and foreign debts, or to organize the flow of commodities between the different states, or to introduce tariffs and nontariff regulations to control it, or to settle mutual liabilities, etc.

Now, everyone acutely feels the need to minimize, as far as possible, the considerable economic losses caused by the rupture of the traditional economic links between the re-publics. At the time they declared state sovereignty, all the union republics remained, in economic terms, the components of an integrated economic complex.

The economic links within the borders of the former USSR were much closer than those between the nations of the European Economic Community, with more than 20% of the gross domestic product involved in the interrepublic exchange, against 14% for the EEC. The intersectoral balance sheet composed of 104 industries shows that Russia imported the output of 102 industries and exported products manufactured in all the 104 industries.

Russia met 23% of its needs in engineering products by getting them from other former union republics, more than 33% of its requirements in ferrous and nonferrous metal prod-ucts, and about 25% in chemicals, textiles, and leather. Russia depended on other republics for all of its requirements in ferrous and nonferrous metal products, and about 25% in chemicals, textiles and leather. Russia depended on other republics for all of its mainline diesel locomotives, electric railroad cars, corn and beet harvesters, cotton, and many other finished products and components that were produced in other republics.

In turn, the latter relied heavily on deliveries from Russia. At the end of the 1980s, the republics obtained almost all of their oil and natural gas in this way, and 40% of their tim-ber. The share of products from Russia in the total consumption of some small republics reached 25% or even 30%. Russia's share in the products from the present Commonwealth countries equaled 79% for Ukraine, 69% for Belarus, more than 50% for Uzbekistan, and 68% for Kazakhstan. Generally, about three-quarters of all economic ties maintained by the former union republics are with Russia.

With the breakup of the totalitarian regime and proclamation of independence, the newly emergent states were free to opt for an open economy and to join the world commu-nity by combining, within reasonable limits, bilateral and multilateral relations.

---

*This section was written by Valeriy M. Serov.

For over three years, the president and government of the Russian Federation have been pursuing a consistent policy of normalizing the full range of relations with the former USSR republics and forming a new system of economic cooperation based on the principles of sovereignty, market economy, and mutual benefit.

The organizational groundwork for multilateral relations between the republics was laid with the formation of the Commonwealth of Independent States (CIS). It is an association based on the free will of the sovereign countries enjoying the advantages of independence and equality under international law for the purpose of regulating political, economic, humanitarian, cultural, ecological, military, and any other types of cooperation among the member states by instruments of international law. The CIS does not posses authority that can override national laws.

The Commonwealth was formed under an agreement signed by Belarus, the Russian Federation, and Ukraine on December 8, 1991, in Minsk. These three countries, which were co-founders of the USSR in 1922, assumed the right to announce the end of the union as an international legal entity and a geopolitical reality, and proclaimed the formation of the CIS. The protocol to this agreement was signed in Alma Ata on December 21, 1991. The protocol was initially signed by Azerbaijan, Armenia, Kazakhstan, Kyrgyzstan, Moldova, Tajikistan, Uzbekistan, and Turkmenistan; they were joined by Georgia in December 1993.

In January 1993, the CIS members adopted that organization's charter specifying the principles, realm, legal basis, and organizational forms of the CIS. It was based on the practical experience the organization had built up from its initiation.

The relations within the CIS are based on principles consonant with such norms of international law as respect for state sovereignty, equality of all Commonwealth participants, the inalienable right to self-determination, recognition of the territorial integrity of states and inviolability of state borders, noninterferences in each other's internal and external affairs, the renunciation of the use of force, respect for human rights and basic freedoms for all, and the bona fide discharge of commitments assumed under any Commonwealth documents.

The CIS is open to other states and subject to endorsement by all its current members, which share the goals and principles of the Commonwealth and assume upon themselves commitments under the charter. The Commonwealth functions on the basis of very democratic rules: the participants have equal rights in their interactions with one another; decisions are made by a consensus; any state is free to announce its lack of interest in a particular issue and withdraw from involvement (and responsibility) in it. The CIS charter provides for an associate-membership status for states wishing to participate in particular cooperative projects and for an observer status on the CIS governing bodies. The charter does not anticipate any specific sanctions for breach of agreements, except very general measures allowed under international law.

The Commonwealth's highest governing body is the Council of Heads of State, which was created to discuss and take decisions on strategic issues of concern to the member states. The interaction between the member-states' bodies of executive power is coordinated by the Council of Heads of Government. A CIS executive secretariat, with an appropriate staff, has been formed to provide organizational and technical support for both councils and to discharge other organizational and representative functions.

Meetings of the heads of relevant state bodies are called to deal with issues of concern and to draft recommendations for these councils. The CIS Charter provides for the operation of a Council of Foreign Ministers, a Council of Defense Ministers, a Council of Border Troops Commanders, and a Human Rights Commission.

The CIS has committed itself to a search for equitable solutions to the following problems at the interstate level:

- Completing separation of the economy and the state, including the (division of assets and liabilities of the former USSR, its property, including military hardware and facilities; the establishment of state borders; and a mutually acceptable border regime);
- Developing a mechanism for mutual trade and economic relations on a new-market and sovereign basis;
- Restoring, within economically justified levels, the interrepublic economic, manufacturing, and technological links that were severed with the disintegration of the USSR;
- Finding a solutions to humanitarian issues (e.g., guarantees of human rights, labor rights, migration);
- Maintaining regular interstate contacts on economic, political, strategic military, and humanitarian matters.

The CIS institutions have been instrumental in avoiding any serious conflicts over the division of the former USSR's property. The process has been largely completed. Essentially, it has been carried out on the zero-option principle, which provides for the appropriation of property by those in whose territory it is located. In addition, Russia has inherited the former USSR's international commitments and, by implication, any property on foreign soil.

It was particularly important to repair the severed interrepublic links in trade and cooperation. Their rupture has had an extremely negative impact on the economies of the CIS countries and severely aggravated the structural crisis in each of them. According to conservative estimates, this factor is responsible for at least a third of Russia's slump in manufacturing. A still greater harm was done to Russia's CIS partners, whose economies are much less self-sufficient than Russia's. The formation of new integrational mechanisms has, therefore, become vital for the CIS countries.

The most significant of them are the agreements that recommend:

1. The General conditions and mechanisms of support for developing cooperation between enterprises and industries of the CIS member states.
2. Assistance in the establishment and development of manufacturing, financial, lending, insurance, and mixed transnational associations.
3. Operation in the field of investments.
4. Establishment of an interstate Eurasian coal and metal association.
5. Cooperation in engineering.
6. Commodity turnover and production cooperation in engineering on a reciprocal basis.
7. Cooperation in the chemical and petrochemical industries, construction operations, and others.

One measure that has played an exceptionally major role in improving relations between Russia and its CIS partners is the Treaty on the Formation of an Economic Union, signed on September 24, 1993. It is, in effect, a long-term program for the worldwide development and expansion of cooperation in regard to promising economic opportunities.

At present, a significant move has been made toward implementation of the treaty's key objective: the formation of a Customs and Payments Unions, which are intended to resolve the most controversial problems between the republics, in particular tariff and nontariff restrictions and nonpayments between economic agents.

The Customs Union was initiated as an association composed of Russia, Belarus, and Kazakhstan, countries that were best prepared to honor its rules. As of today, unified customs regulations between Russia and Belarus has been restored, and some major strides have been made in this direction with Kazakhstan. Intensive talks have been conducted with other countries interested in joining the Customs Union.

Significantly, the formation of the Customs and Payments Unions is speeding systemic reforms in the CIS countries. These efforts are aimed at unifying the national economic mechanisms on market principles.

Many issues can best be resolved through bilateral negotiations. This approach allows the debt problem of countries and economic entities to be settled more routinely, and trade and manufacturing links to be improved. The bilateral format also facilitates implementation of multilateral agreements, such as the one on the formation of the Customs Union.

Cooperation in trade and economic development is, by and large, based on treaties that are signed annually. These are, in fact, clear examples of bilateral cooperation between Russia and other CIS states, actually dictated by the ongoing reformation of the national economic systems. Such interstate arrangements, which guarantee mutual deliveries of a very limited number of critical commodities, are essential.

As the market surges ahead, the level of interdependent output has steadily declined, so that today it only includes fuels, primary materials, and equivalent commodities, all of which accounted for a mere 11.5% of the total turnover in 1994.

Purposeful efforts to create a new cooperative mechanism among the Commonwealth states has drastically altered its institutional and legal basis. Trade has been extensively liberalized, especially in 1995, and is now conducted on the same principles as it is in third countries. The principle of contractual market prices has taken firm root.

In the view of the Russian Federation, the most reliable basis for cooperation can be assured by integration at the micro level and the development of horizontal ties between market participants, with businesses of all forms of ownership as the most dynamic and constructive driving force of these processes. Indeed, such businesses are not constrained by any political or national preferences, and relations between partners are based on economic expedience and mutual gain.

The importance of horizontal links between enterprises and commercial entities is steadily growing. Today, their share in trade with the CIS countries has reached almost 90%, with twice as many payments being made through Russia's commercial banks as through its Central Bank.

In foreign-trade operations a free-trade zone, without duties and nontariff regulations, has been adopted on a multilateral basis by the CIS. Today, only a few tariff restrictions have been retained, primarily because the domestic prices of fuel, power, and some primary materials are significantly below world prices. In Russia beginning in 1995, presidential decrees have removed quotas, licenses, special exports, and privileges for individual enterprises and organizations engaged in external economic activities. Under the latest rules, qualitative restrictions can be imposed on exports and imports of goods and services only if this helps Russia meet its international commitments. No restrictions are allowed on the export of goods and services, such as requiring that a specific proportion of either be delivered to the domestic market. Exports for federal needs can only be used to meet the country's international economic obligations, including those related to currency loans.

Great advantages are derived from the exchange of goods by various types of enterprises, which sign agreements on cooperative production with partners in the CIS countries.

In particular, this activity is stipulated in the multilateral agreement on the general conditions and support mechanisms for developing cooperation in manufacturing among CIS-member enterprises and industries. Under this agreement, import and export quotas, taxes and excises, or any quantitative restrictions cannot be imposed on goods supplied under cooperative arrangements and within the framework of customs regulations.

In the Russian Federation, sectoral agreements with CIS countries are signed by the relevant ministries. These agreements specify information about the deliveries of primary materials, semifinished products, components, spare parts and units needed in the manufacture of finished goods under the cooperative programs. The agreements are carried out as contracts signed by enterprises.

Broad opportunities to develop horizontal links between enterprises and to promote integrational trends at the microlevel have been opened by a network of interstate structures that unite various types of businesses. Today, more than 50 coordinating councils operate in key industries of the Commonwealth economies, including the Electric Power Council, the Intergovernmental Council on Oil and Natural Gas, and those concerned with aviation and the uses of air space, railroad transport, communications, and space research. The councils coordinate mutual deliveries of products, draw up restructuring programs, develop projects in science and engineering, and deal with investment matters. Under the Interstate Economic Committee, the organizational structure of cooperation in manufacturing has been streamlined and made more efficient.

Russia has taken steps to create a suitable legal basis for setting up transnational commercial and manufacturing entities. Legislative support for the establishment of financial-industrial groups has been passed. Agreements based on the organizational principles of these groups have been signed, for example, with Kazakhstan and Belarus. Typically, transnational associations are set up on the initiative of economic agents.

A key role in mutual relations has been played by cooperation between bordering territories in the Russian Federation and other Commonwealth countries. Cross-border trade is acquiring growing importance, especially in Russia's relations with Ukraine and Kazakhstan. This activity involves goods and services produced from local resources and intended for consumption in neighboring territories. Such trade stimulates the growth of small- and medium-sized businesses.

Neither Russia nor any of its partners have ever viewed the Commonwealth as an independent and self-sufficient entity. On the contrary, its members are eager to cooperate with any interested countries, firms, and organizations. The political, economic, organizational, and legal climate for this cooperation is growing ever more favorable.

All matters pertaining to economic cooperation with CIS countries are dealt with in Russia by the Ministry for Cooperation with Member States of the Commonwealth of Independent States (Russian Ministry for Commonwealth Affairs). The Ministry is a federal body of executive power charged with the development and implementation of Russia's state policy in cooperating with Commonwealth members and the Baltic republics. Its functions include preparing state cooperation programs, coordinating the operation of federal executive bodies concerned with the signing and implementation of Russia's international treaties and agreements with these states with the aim of pursuing a unified policy. In addition, the Ministry arranges negotiations with Commonwealth and Baltic countries.

The Ministry's functions includes developing trade, economic, financial, and monetary relations; promoting the establishment and operation of joint financial-industrial groups and other transnational economic structures; and expanding cooperation in production and economic activities. It also is closely involved in cooperative programs in such areas as transportation, communications, power generation, environmental protection, and many more.

The Ministry's work follows two key guidelines—preparing a legal framework and developing specific cooperative projects in manufacturing industries, infrastructures, investments, and technologies, including those involving third countries, firms, and organizations.

The majority of the treaties, agreements and projects under way in the CIS today have been drawn up by the Ministry itself or with its direct participation. In addition, the Ministry maintains the contacts established by the Russian executive power bodies with the CIS countries.

7.4 THE FORMER SOVIET BLOC IN EUROPE.* During the communist era, the USSR and six European countries (Bulgaria, Czechoslovakia, the German Democratic Republic, Hungary, Poland and Romania) had formed the so-called Soviet Bloc in Europe domination. It had been bound politically and militarily by the Warsaw Treaty Organization (WTO), as well as economically by the Council for Mutual Economic Assistance (CMEA or Comecon). The revolutions of 1989 and 1990 in Eastern Europe (including the uprising in what was formerly known as Yugoslavia) overthrew the communist regimes and brought about the demise of the alliance. The WTO and CMEA were broken up, and Germany was unified. The USSR was dissolved. The geopolitical and geoeconomic framework within which Russia operated had been changed dramatically.

(a) Economic and Trade Relations with Eastern Europe. Economic self-sufficiency was the main feature of the foreign-trade behavior of these Soviet-type socialist economies. Relations with other socialist countries accounted for 60 to 75% of the overall foreign trade of each of their countries by the end of the 1980s. The share was 62% for the USSR.[1] The framework for these mutual relations was the CMEA.

The CMEA was established in January 1949, with the USSR, Bulgaria, Czechoslovakia, Hungary, Poland, and Romania as its original members. Albania and the German Democratic Republic (GDR) joined soon after. (Albania left the organization in 1961.) The CMEA was created by Stalin in response to the Marshall Plan and the Organization for European Economic Cooperation (OEEC). Its only purpose at that time was to ensure that the east European satellite states followed the USSR's trade embargo of Yugoslavia, which had an earlier falling-out with Stalin. During the 1960s, the CMEA was given additional functions. In 1963, the International Bank for Economic Cooperation was established and the transferable ruble was introduced for the purposes of the preferential trade system and the system of payments outlined by the CMEA. An international bank for investment was also set up.

The CMEA had gradually become the major formal means through which the USSR conducted trade with its Eastern European partners, the mechanism by which the Soviets exercised economic and trade leverage over these countries' policies, as well as the instrument through which the Soviets had to pay an economic price for their political dominion over Eastern Europe, which had terms-of-trade advantages from trading with the USSR under the CMEA rules. Eastern European members of the CMEA were subsidized by the USSR through overpricing (compared to international pricing) of low-quality goods, which were predominant in Eastern European exports; and the underpricing of energy and raw materials, which were predominant in Soviet exports. Of course, the CMEA-oriented economic policy that was the basis for such advantages in trade with the USSR, was the reason for the weak export potential of eastern Europe in international markets.

---

*This section was written by Stoyan D. Ganev.
[1]Marie Lavigne, *The Economics of Transition* (New York: St. Martin's Press, 1995), 65.

The political transformation in Eastern Europe was the major cause of the sharp turn in the USSR's (and, since 1991, Russia's) economic and trade relationships with its former allies. The latter considered their detachment from the Soviet Union, the discontinuation of CMEA-type relations, and an integration with Western Europe as crucial for their post-communist political and economic transformation. The collapse of communism in Eastern Europe almost immediately led to a fundamental questioning of the CMEA. At its January 1991 meeting in Moscow, the CMEA Executive Committee was agreed to disband the CMEA and to replace it with the Organization for International Economic Cooperation (OIEC), based in Budapest and designed primarily to resolve the ownership dispute over the Bank for Investment and the Bank for Economic Cooperation. This decision was followed by the introduction of compulsory hard-currency trading and the application of world-market prices in mutual trade, which eventually caused the end of the CMEA and the failure of the plan to replace it. The Soviet Union, Bulgaria, Cuba, Czechoslovakia, Hungary, Mongolia, Poland, Romania, and Vietnam officially dissolved the CMEA at a ministerial meeting held in Budapest on June 26, 1991.

The breakup of the CMEA was not opposed by the USSR and, later, Russia. The switch to hard-currency (i.e., dollar) payments was considered by Russia as a way to substantially improve its terms of trade and balance of payments regarding Eastern Europe and its overall foreign trade. As it turned out, the first of those expectations proved to be true. The terms of trade of the Soviet Union/Russia are estimated to have improved 40 to 50% with respect to the other former CMEA members. This corresponds to roughly a 30% deterioration in the terms of trade of the Eastern European countries with the Soviet Union/Russia.[2]

The effects of the improvement were insignificant, however, compared to the other consequences of the CMEA breakup and the switch to dollar trading. The impact on trade volumes was much more substantial, but because of the simultaneous change in prices and currency of trade, it is difficult to estimate the effect. According to some estimates, the volume of the Eastern European exports to Russia declined by about 50 to 55%, and imports from Russia declined 35 to 40%.[3] The UN Economic Commission for Europe (ECE) attempted to measure the change in U.S. dollar terms. For 1991, these estimates indicate a 25% fall in Eastern European exports to the USSR, and a 52% decline in Soviet imports to this region. Similarly, there is a large difference in the estimate for imports: a 9.5% fall in Eastern European imports from the Soviet Union, but a 40% decrease in Soviet exports from these countries.[4] According to another estimate, in 1980, 49% of Soviet exports went to CMEA partners, while 48.2% of Soviet imports came from them. The respective figures for 1989 were 55.2% and 56.3%. In the first half of 1992, however, only 21.2% of Russian exports went to its former CMEA partners, and a mere 15.4% of imports were from these countries. In the first half of 1993, the figures had dropped even further, to 18.6% and 12.9% respectively.[5]

The sudden disintegration of Russian-Eastern Europe trade connections has removed not only so-called unjustifiable trade, but also has negatively affected economic relations that in market conditions would be effective. The decision to disband the CMEA and to move trade relations toward market principles was based on an overly optimistic progno-

---

[2]Andras Koves and Gabor Oblath, "The Regional Role of the Former Soviet Union and the CMEA: A Net Assessment," in *East-Central European Economics in Transition.* (Armonk, New York; London, England: M.E. Sharpe, 1995), 360.

[3]Ibid., p. 360.

[4]*Economic Survey of Europe in 1992–93* (New York: UN ECE, 1993), 112.

[5]Leslie Holmes, "Russia's Relations with the Former External Empire," in *Russia In Search of Its Future,* eds. Amin Saikal and William Maley, (Cambridge: Cambridge University Press, 1995), 134.

sis regarding the pace at which the former communist countries would adapt to new trade conditions.

Despite the political and economic drift of Eastern European countries toward Western Europe, there has been a tendency to restorate some economic ties with Russia. One of the major causes for this attitude are the restrictions placed on Eastern European goods in the European Union market, especially for such important ones as textiles, ferrous metals, and agricultural products. The European Union's restrictive policy has stimulated eastern Europe to seek new markets and, in particular, the Russian market.

In addition to these strategic trade concerns, there are some interest groups in Eastern Europe behind the efforts to restore trade connections with Russia. For a significant group, the Soviet market had been the only one they could deal with based on their personal ties, language, and know-how. For some of these, their presence in the former Soviet Union market means not only the survival of their firms, but also large and rapid profits.

It seems that Russia will also try to restore some effective economic ties with its former allies. One of the possible reasons is the European Union's policy of isolationism. Another, is that foreign trade has become one of the most profitable economic activities in Russia. Tradition and geographical proximity are two of the factors behind the attempt of many Russian companies to develop trade relations with Eastern Europe. Gradually, Russia has grown to appreciate the importance of the Eastern Europe market. Subsequent Russian estimates indicate that a large part of the economic decline in Russia was due to the collapse of intra-CMEA trade. Some estimates showed that the collapse in intra-CMEA trade was responsible for about 30% of the decline in Russia's output in 1991 to 1992, and for a 70% fall of manufactured goods exported from the country.[6]

Russia has already signed new treaties with most of its former allies. Some barter and clearing agreements have been adopted. Russia and Hungary agreed that the Russian debt to Hungary will be covered by air-force supplies. In Russia, approximately 400 joint-venture companies have been set up with Eastern European participation. The cooperation in the natural-gas industry has been motivated by the prospect that gas supplies will be increased substantially. For instance, Poland has signed an agreement with Russia to participate in the construction and operation of a Russian-German gas pipeline, which will pass through Polish territory and have a capacity of 67 billion cubic meters (75% of the Russian export of gas in 1992). Recently, a holding company for supplying natural gas to Bulgaria and the region was established by that country and Russia.

Despite the tendency toward the activation of Russian-Eastern European trade, Russia will remain a limited market for Eastern Europe. First of all, trade will continue to be limited by the Russian capacity to export competitive goods to Eastern Europe. Russia will also be a restricted market for food and other agricultural products from the former CMEA countries. This is because the dominant Eastern European exports (e.g., meat, grain) are much more expensive than the highly subsidized and low-cost foods of Western Europe and North America.

(b) Strategic Military Relations with Eastern Europe. Until the death of Stalin, the USSR's political and military control over its Eastern European satellite states had been based on the loyalty of their leaders to Stalin. His death and the acceleration of the integration of West Germany into the Western military structure had changed Soviet military tactics in Europe, including Eastern Europe.

---

[6]I. Faminski and V. Vinogradov, "Vneshneekonomitsheskie sviazi Rossii so Stranami Vostotshnoi Evropi" (Foreign Trade Relations of Russia with the Countries of Eastern Europe), *Vneshnaija Torgovlia (Foreign Trade)* 2–3 (1994): 41.

On May 14, 1955 (a few days after West Germany's inclusion in NATO and the Western European Union), the USSR, Albania, Bulgaria, Czechoslovakia, the German Democratic Republic, Hungary, Poland, and Romania signed a treaty of friendship, cooperation, and mutual assistance, which resulted in the Warsaw Treaty Organization (WTO). As the preamble states, the organization was prompted by the rearmament of West Germany and its inclusion in NATO. Gradually, the WTO became the principal formal mechanism through which the USSR exercised its military strategic dominion over Eastern Europe and through which the military interests of the latter were subordinated to those of the USSR. In 1961, Eastern European military forces replaced some of those of the Soviet Union in the region. The WTO became the counterweight to NATO in the European balance of power. Soviet military dominance of the region was reaffirmed, however, in the 1968 invasion of Czechoslovakia and articulated by the Brezhnev Doctrine, suggesting that the needs of the Soviet Bloc were to be placed above the territorial integrity of the WTO countries.

Perestroika had driven the new Soviet leadership to reconsider the security dilemma in Europe and in the world, an idea that was reflected in the doctrine stressing that each communist state should find its own way, without external interference. The USSR thus recognized that the WTO could no longer be a tool of its military dominion in Eastern Europe. This factor played a crucial role in the demise of the Soviet Bloc and its military framework, and in the beginning of the dissolution of the WTO. In November 1990, at the Conference on Security and Cooperation in Europe (CSCE), the WTO and NATO declared that they no longer regarded each other as enemies. In January 1991, Czechoslovakia, Hungary, and Poland agreed to cease cooperating with the WTO by July 1991 at the latest. At the same time, the Hungarian Parliament almost unanimously voted to accept a NATO offer of associate membership in the North Atlantic Assembly. In early 1991, the Romanian and Bulgarian presidents declared the WTO to be an anachronism. All members of the WTO (excluding the GDR, which had ceased to exist in October 1990), signed a protocol in February 1991 canceling the validity of all military agreements and structures of the WTO, to take effect on March 31. The political structure of the WTO was temporarily transformed into a voluntary consultative organization. It was finally disbanded at a meeting of the political consultative committee in Prague in July 1991. The signed protocol recommended a gradual shift toward all European security structures on the basis of agreements reached at the November 1990 CSCE summit.

The breakup of the WTO did not automatically solve the question of Soviet troops in Eastern Europe. (This did not pertain to Bulgaria and Romania, since there had been no permanent Soviet troops in those countries.) The problem was eventually worked out, and the last Soviet troops withdrew from Hungary and Czechoslovakia in June 1991. The Polish situation was far more complicated, but it was finally resolved in October 1993.

Yet there remained a number of other issues to resolve concerning Russia's strategic military relationship with its former WTO allies. The most important was the issue of compensation. Hungary, for example, claimed the equivalent of nearly two billion dollars from the USSR or its successor for environmental damage caused by Soviet troops since the 1956 uprising and for other aspects of its military presence. This issue has been resolved, in principle, through an agreement to cancel approximately $800 million of the debt in return for 28 MIG–29 fighter jets. In September 1993, Russia agreed to transfer all of its property in Poland to the state in return for Poland's agreement to drop all claims for compensation for environmental clean-ups.

With the collapse of communism in Eastern Europe and the dissolution of the USSR, Russia had begun its transition from an imperial to a postimperial state. Russia's self-perception as a major European power with legitimate interests both in the countries of the former Soviet Union and Eastern Europe, is still very much alive.[7]

Despite this self-perception, Russia's strategic attitude toward Eastern Europe after the breakup of the WTO was one of considerable neglect (as evidenced in its economic relations). After a period of relative inactivity, Russia has initiated a more assertive foreign policy in Eastern Europe, more actively stressing its legitimate security interests in that region. As a result of the disintegration of the Soviet Bloc and the USSR, Russia has become geographically separated from Europe by two regions—Eastern Europe and the former Soviet republics. Since then, one of Russia's major diplomatic concerns has been preventing these zones from becoming an impenetrable shield isolating Russia from Europe. In regard to countries beyond the borders of the former Soviet Union, Russia's strategic policy is aimed at ensuring that Eastern Europe does not threaten Russian territorial and economic security by joining an alliance that could be directed against Russia.[8] The final goal of such a policy seems to be to minimize opportunities for eastern Europe's involvement in Western power structures. This policy is clearly evident in Russia's attitude toward NATO's eastward expansion.

(c)   Relations with the West Regarding Eastern Europe.   In November 1991, the former members of the WTO and the NATO countries created the North Atlantic Cooperation Council (NACC). The creation of the NACC was an important move toward an all-European approach to defense and military issues in the region. It was a symbol of the end of the cold war and a clear sign that the NATO countries were trying to integrate the former USSR and Eastern Europe into a common European security structure, eliminating the military division of Europe. The NACC set up a high-level working group, which met in the beginning of 1992 to discuss the ratification and implementation of the Conventional Forces in Europe Treaty (CFE).

The prevailing tendency in security relations following the breakup of the WTO was demonstrated once again by the March 1992 signing by 51 states-members of the CSCE Open Skies Agreement. The idea, originally expressed by President Eisenhower in 1955, was raised again by President Bush at a NATO summit held in May 1989. The negotiations on the Open Skies concept began immediately after the establishment of the NACC under the auspices of the CSCE. In July 1993, Hungary permitted the United States to run test flights over its territory.

The official NATO position regarding post-WTO eastern Europe was expressed in March 1992 by its Secretary General Manfred Woerner during his visit to Poland and the Baltic states. Stressing NATO commitment to ensuring that no security vacuums would emerge in Eastern Europe, he left no doubt that NATO would be willing to offer formal security guarantees and membership to the countries of the region in the foreseeable future.

By 1993, it was clear that the Visegrad Four (the Czech Republic, Hungary, Poland, and Slovakia) had firm intentions to join NATO. In August 1993, President Yeltsin indicated that he had no objection to Poland, the Czech Republic or Hungary doing so. A month later, the Russian Parliament strongly opposed any eastern expansion of NATO. The major reason for the shift was the developments in Russia in the fall of 1993. These, along with the emergence and success of Zhirinovskii in December 1993 elections forced the Eastern European leaders to strengthen their appeals for admission to NATO. The leading force in

---

[7]Angela Stent, *Between Moscow and Bonn: East-Central Europe in Transition.* p. 451.

[8]Allen Lynch, "After Empire: Russia and its Western Neighbors," *RFE/RL Research Report,* Vol. 3, no. 12, (25 March 1994).

these efforts was the president of Poland. In January 1994, the president of Lithuania made the first formal request for NATO membership from a former Soviet republic.

Meanwhile the NATO countries continued to be cautious and apprehensive about eastern NATO expansion. Their strategic relations with Russia were a bigger concern. The west was trying to consistently follow the policy demonstrated immediately after the breakup of the WTO and aimed at the creation of an all-European security structure. This policy was further developed by Partnership for Peace, a program introduced by the United States and endorsed at the NATO summit in January 1994. Partnership for Peace was designed to enhance security throughout Europe by proposing security relationships among all European countries. The program does not extend Article V protection (the NATO Treaty's mutual-defense commitment in case of attack) to members, but NATO regards it as a stepping-stone to NATO membership. Partnership for peace gives its members an opportunity to intensify relations with NATO, including participation in some NATO exercises and the formal expression of security concerns to NATO. The offer was taken up wholesale by the former WTO states. After some hesitation, Russia joined the Partnership in June 1994. Thus the Partnership for Peace has become the first real mechanism that established concrete military ties between former enemies as well as between former allies in post-WTO Europe.

At the summit in January 1994, NATO members also created the Combined Joint Task Force (CJTF), by which the NATO command can designate forces for contingencies outside the NATO treaty area. Forces from non-NATO states could join NATO in peacekeeping operations, crisis-management efforts, and humanitarian missions. The implementation force in Bosnia became the first peacekeeping operation of NATO with Russian participation. NATO-Russia cooperation has been extended in a new U.S.-led CJTF in Bosnia, consisting of 31,000 soldiers from more than 20 countries inside and outside NATO.

Despite NATO efforts to ensure that no security vacuum would emerge in Eastern Europe and a genuine partnership for peace would be created, the security structure of post-WTO Europe continues to be an open and moot question. The end of the WTO resulted in eliminating the division of Europe into mutually threatening military blocs. Although the NATO countries and other western institutions have tried, as shown above, to involve Russia and the other former WTO allies in new all-European security relations, Pan-European unity has not been achieved. What is more, the very definition of post-WTO security in Europe continues to evolve, challenging existing norms and institutions such as NATO.

After the collapse of the WTO and the USSR, the possibility of a surprise attack, sustained invasion, or nuclear assault against Western Europe has become so improbable as to lack all credibility.[9] Russia cannot, and should not, be considered a potential threat to NATO. At the same time, the dissolution of the Soviet Bloc has left a security vacuum in Eastern Europe that has bred instability in the region. The growing security concerns of the Eastern European states and the lack of substantial success in the West's efforts to build a new strategic relationship with Russia, have forced the former Soviet allies to seek urgent security solutions to NATO's eastward expansion. NATO's growth has already become the top item on its agenda; propelled by American leadership, NATO has committed itself to that policy. NATO expansion would move the alliance's boundaries considerably closer to Russia as well as commit American conventional and nuclear forces to the defense of newly independent European nations. The United States and its allies will have to grapple with these issues as well as the consolidation of reform in Russia and its inclusion in the

---

[9]Karl Kaiser, "Reforming NATO," *Foreign Policy* 103 (Summer 1996): p. 129.

democratic system of Europe as an established power. Despite the fact that it has not removed fundamental differences between NATO and Russia, The Founding Act on Mutual Relations, Cooperation, and Security, signed on May 27, 1997, in Paris by NATO leaders and the Russian president, is an essential step toward a new European order.

(d) Relations with the Balkans.   After the disintegration of Yugoslavia and other changes in southeastern Europe, Russia faced the need of establishing a new policy on the Balkans. Historically, this region has been one of the focal points of Russia's European policy, mainly for its security and the stability of its borders. Moreover, Russia has traditionally shown a strong interest to the fate of the Balkan Slavs and Christians.

Following its vested interests after the collapse of Yugoslavia, Russia gradually established a close relationship with Serbia and active participation in Bosnian peacekeeping efforts. Russia's goals in the region are to secure a leading role in the Balkan political game, to discourage NATO from making decisions on the Balkans without Russia, to play a central role in the crisis at the UN Security Council (where Russia has the right of veto), and, last but not least, to prevent the spread of the conflict. From a strategic point of view, keeping close relations with Serbia is advantageous for Russia. Because Serbia has the potential to become the most powerful country in southeastern Europe, Russia would be well served to not only keep its strong presence there, but also to play much a more important role in this part of Europe in the near future. A serious set-back for Russian plans, however, would result from its support for Mr. Milosevic's regime, regardless of its political orientation.

The pro-Serbian policy of Russia has been combined with its efforts to hasten its relations with Bulgaria. The initial crisis in mutual relations after the 1989 changes in Bulgaria has been overcome. In 1992, a new political treaty was signed. Russia will try to use Bulgaria's economic and military dependence on the former Soviet Union to maintain special connections with Sofia despite Bulgaria's recent pro-Western orientation. The chance of such an occurrence has increased since Bulgaria's former Communist Party came back to power after parliamentary elections in 1994. At the same time, such a rapprochement between Bulgaria and Russia could place long-term Russian-Serbian relations in a delicate situation because of long-standing dissension between Bulgaria and Serbia, especially over the Macedonia issue. A short-term favorable circumstance for Russia could be the fact that the former communist government has already shown clear signs of closer relations with Serbia.

Russia is a member of the Black Sea Economic Cooperation Council (BSECC), established in 1990 on the initiative of Turkey. In addition to Turkey and Russia, its nine other members include Albania, Bulgaria, Romania, Greece, the Ukraine, Moldova, Georgia, Armenia, and Azerbaijan. The intention of its founders was to create a new free economic association similar to the European Union. Russia's involvement in such a long-term economic association will probably grant it an important role in this region.

7.5 THE PACIFIC RIM.*   More than half the territory of Russia is directly adjacent to or economically linked to the Pacific Ocean (the region known as the Far East encompasses 6,215,900 square kilometers, while eastern Siberia encompasses 4,215,800 square kilometers). The length of Russia's Pacific coastline (including the shore of the Bering and the Okhotsk seas and the Sea of Japan) comprises more than 12,000 kilometers. The immediate and Pacific Ocean neighbors of Russia are China, Japan, North and South Korea, and the United States. Russia's interest in the Pacific Ocean region and its rich potential

---

*This section was written by Alexander G. Granberg.

was reinforced after the fall of the USSR, when the basic outlets to the Atlantic Ocean and the Black and Baltic Seas became controlled by the new independent states of Ukraine, Georgia, Lithuania, Latvia, and Estonia.

The Pacific Ocean region (also known as the Pacific Rim) joins more than 30 countries of eastern Asia, Oceania, and the western parts of North and South America. This macroregion boasts about 60% of the worldwide gross product and about 50% of the volume of world trade. In the past 10 years, it has sustained a high rate of economic growth. Impressive economic progress, besides that of the United States and Japan, was achieved by the new industrial countries (Republic of Korea, Taiwan, Hong Kong, and Singapore). Malaysia, Thailand, and Indonesia have also seen impressive economic growth. The economic development of China has been turbulent; Vietnam and the Latin American countries are gathering speed. The dynamic development of the majority of Pacific Ocean countries has combined with an increase in international tendencies in the region.

The closeness of eastern Russia, which contains rich natural resources and enormous industrial and scientific potential, to the countries of the Pacific Rim creates favorable circumstances for developing mutual trade, technological exchange, and foreign-investment opportunities. For many years, however, Russia (within the framework of the USSR) had been separated from the turbulent economic growth and economic integration in the region. Until the mid-1980s, the USSR did not make noticeable efforts to be included in the multicountry cooperative efforts of the Pacific Rim the countries, giving its European foreign policy higher priority.

It should be noted that serious political, institutional, and economic obstacles have stood in the way of Russia's active participation in Pacific Rim cooperative activities.

The only way that Russia could emerge as a full participant was the reformation of political and economic systems in the USSR in the second half of the 1980s and in independent Russia since 1992, along with changes of priorities in governmental foreign policy. Some of the necessary economic reforms include the demonopolization and liberation of extraeconomic activity, formation of the market infrastructure, creation of legal bases for foreign business, and expansion of economic rights of regional administrations.

In the new extrapolitical doctrines of Russia, the necessity for the increase of policy and diplomacy in the Pacific Ocean region, especially from the point of view of national economic interests, is most evident. In reality, Russia has recently made progress in its relations with Japan, China, and South Korea. (In particular, visits by President Yeltsin to these countries have resulted in international agreements.) The Pacific Ocean aspect in Russian-U.S. relations has also been recognized.

In its efforts to increase its political and economic ties in the region, Russia has sought membership in various international Pacific Ocean organizations. In 1992, it became a fully recognized member of the Pacific Economic Cooperation Council (PECC); and in 1994, it became a member of the Pacific Basin Economic Council (PBEC). Russia also became a regional member of the Economic and Social Commission for Asia and the Pacific (ESCAP). Participation of Russian politicians, businesspeople, and specialists in such organizations exposes them to a useful variety of business practices and experiences; and it puts them into direct contact with the largest and most successful financial and commercial businesses in the world. In March 1995, Russia applied to join the intergovernmental forum of the Asia-Pacific Economic Cooperation (APEC), and announced its intention to participate in the formation of the Pacific Ocean Economic Society.

As a member of these and other Pacific Ocean organizations, Russia can contribute in at least four ways to increased international economic cooperation:

1. Participation in strategic decision making for the continued development of the region and the economic mechanism of Pacific Ocean integration.
2. Elimination of restrictions to trade, thereby increasing the movement of capital and technology in separate countries that affect the interests of Russia.
3. The use of international organizations as collective ministers in the economics of Russia (directly and in different forms of cooperation).
4. Progress in the actual projects of cooperation.

Within the framework of regional and subregional cooperation in Russia's Pacific Ocean approach, problems such as the development of ocean transportation, an international railroad system, air transportation, and the creation of a telecommunications system are being solved. It is important then for the Pacific Ocean partners to maintain a competitive atmosphere, thereby preventing monopolies by individual countries (e.g., Japan and China) in certain Russian regions and sectors of the economy. At the same time, measures are required for preventing unnecessary competition both among Russian exporters in the markets of the Pacific Rim and among individual regions of Russia in attracting foreign investors.

While the Russian share of international trade in the Pacific Ocean region comprises just 1% of Russia's total foreign trade, Russia's share for the Pacific Rim totals 12 to 14% of the region's total trade. Consequently, Russia proposes following a broad path in order to become an influential participant in the Pacific Ocean economic society.

The benefits of economic cooperation with the countries and international organizations of the Pacific Rim will affect primarily the eastern regions of Russia. In April 1996, President Yeltsin expressed a great desire for adoption of federal programs of development in the far eastern region and the Baikal Region. The strategies of the program are based on two main assumptions:

1. The far eastern region and the Baikal Region make up the largest natural raw material base, capable of meeting the demands of the internal market and deriving significant income from the foreign market.
2. The location of this area near the ocean will favor development of extraeconomic bonds with countries of the Pacific Rim and, to a significant degree, can compensate for its distance from the main Russian markets.

The financial reserves for realization of such a program from 1996 to 2005 would cost 371 trillion rubles (approximately $75 billion, an average of $7 to $8 billion per year). It is proposed that 20 to 25% of this sum comprises foreign investment and credit.

A major objective, of the program, in conjunction with investors from the United States and Japan is the extraction of petroleum deposits in the shelf of Sakhalin Island (the volume of investment for 20 to 25 years could be as high as $60 billion). Petroleum and gas deposits in Yakutia are also being tapped. By the year 2005, the yield of petroleum is expected to increase to 21 million tons and gas to 22 billion cubic meters. Construction of gas lines in China and South Korea is planned to alleviate the exporting of petroleum and liquefied gas by sea. There other attractive opportunities for foreign investors in the region:

- Diamond mines in Yakutia
- Gold deposits in Kamchatka
- Tin in Khabarovsk and the Primorsky Krai
- Rich timber reserves in the Khabarovsk Krai

- Fishing resources of the eastern seas
- Recreation opportunities in Kamchatka
- Conservation of military factories
- Construction of transportation-warehouse and port complexes
- Construction of bridges across the Amur River
- Creation of modern telecommunications systems

The result of these investment projects will be the expansion of exports, including electrical power, nonferrous metals, woodworking products, seafood, and products from converted military enterprises.

Because the weak infrastructure of the Russian's Far East is one of the obstacles to trade and investment cooperation, the program includes construction and reconstruction of 12 maritime ports, expansion of the Trans-Siberian Railway, and completion of construction of the Baikal-Amur and Amur-Irkutsk railway lines.

Stimulation of foreign investment in the far eastern region and the Baikal area requires the creation of an investment climate as attractive as that in neighboring regions of Asia Pacific Rim countries. Work in this direction must be carried out through appropriate changes in federal, as well as regional legislation. For example, regional deposit funds and other guaranteed funds for foreign investors are being created. The program supports the development of free economic zones, technical fleets, and technical policy. In recent years, development of various forms of border and shore economic cooperation among countries of the Far East and regions of the United States, Japan, and China has taken place.

Within the framework of the Gore-Chernomyrdin Intergovernmental Commission, a working group is promoting incentives for commercial cooperation between the Russia's far eastern region and four U.S. states bordering the Pacific Ocean. On the Russian side, 11 eastern territories are participating; on the U.S. side, California, Oregon, Washington, and Alaska are participating. This working group has facilitated the successful investment mission of the Overseas Private Investment Corporation (OPIC) in Russia's far eastern regions, and the mission of the U.S. Department of Commerce in developing business cooperation in the fields of medicine and health and strengthening business contacts between Russian and American enterprises and companies.

Cooperation has been apparent in the activity of the American business centers in Khabarovsk, Vladivostok, and South Sakhalin in serving the workers of American companies in the Russian market and in receiving commercial delegations. The United States (BISNIS) Department of Commerce Business Information Service for the Newly Independent States has presented working proposals to Russian Far East enterprises; they are among more than 20,000 American companies interested in the Russian market. A large contribution to the work of training Russian enterprises has been made by a joint Russian-American scientific-research center created in Magadan. Increasingly, more enterprises and companies in the far eastern regions are using the services of American consultants available to the Body of Citizens for Democracy and the International Body of Experts.

An investment fund of the United States and Russia, financed by the U.S. Agency for International Development in the summer of 1996, approved direct investments totaling $14.5 million for Russia's far eastern enterprises. Another important activity of the working group is the project called CLEAR-PAC, which promotes the accelerated development of goods through various services on the region's borders. This project is especially important for Russia's far eastern seaports, which, up until now, have been inadequate for supporting a customs infrastructure and tracking the movement of exported and imported goods via telecommunications and computer.

At a meeting of the working group in September 1996 in Khabarovsk, about 20 projects for cooperation were selected. The group proposed that an American-Russian investment fund be created with capital up to $100 million; its activities will be concentrated in Russia's far eastern regions. A strategy was devised for development of cooperation among representatives of Russia's 15 regions, the federal government, and the United States. The primary purpose will be to develop a strategy for obtaining key initiatives and bringing them to realization. In Russian-Japanese economic relations, regular contact between the administrative regions of the Baikal and the Japanese prefectures (especially Tokaido and Niigata), has been established. Economic communication along the borders of Russia and China has played a large role in revitalizing mutual trade between the two countries. Right now, the ground is being laid for accomplishing a number of joint investment projects and solving the problems of joint use of natural resources and labor migration.

The process of economic activity and the degree of Russian integration into the economics of the Pacific Rim undoubtedly will become a priority in the extraeconomic and regional policy of Russia. The success of this plan depends on creation of favorable conditions for the international movement of goods, services, capital, and information in Russia, especially in its eastern regions. This process must be accomplished in three organized steps:

1. Increased activity in the Pacific Ocean unions
2. Maintaining two-sided intergovernmental relationships
3. Providing more intense interaction between border and shoreline regions

7.6 UNITED NATIONS: SUPPORT FOR ECONOMIC REFORM.* Russia's policy of reform to establish a market-oriented economy and a democratic society is now well established. Considerable progress has been achieved in building a market infrastructure; in the establishment of a viable private sector in the national economy; in the liberalization of foreign trade and external economic activity; in financial stabilization; and in the development of a legal basis to support the needs of the market, Russia's integration into the world economy, foreign investment, and social welfare.

Although these tasks are primarily the responsibility of Russia, bilateral and multilateral international cooperation also plays a role. Participation in international economic and financial institutions furthers Russia's integration into the world economy and contributes to its receipt of financial support and expert technical assistance. In this context, cooperation with the United Nations is significant.

(a) Economic Reform. One of Russia's major goals in participating in UN economic organizations is to create—on a multilateral level—conditions that provide practical support for economic reform in Russia, a transition to a market economy at the lowest social cost possible, and an effective integration into the world economy. Russia also attaches great importance to the search by UN members for practical ways of addressing global issues, such as promotion of sustainable development (including such components as economic growth, population, environment, and social justice), energy supply, foreign debt, globalization of world commodities, service and capital markets, and the development of information systems. Russia wants to make a constructive contribution to attaining a consensus on a new

---

*This section was written by Sergey V. Lavrov.

partnership of states in the post-bloc era and to promoting multilateralism in economic, social, and environmental spheres. Also Russia seeks to hammer out the UN's cooperative principles in these areas with other partners, including Bretton Woods institutions, the World Trade Organization (WTO), and the nongovernmental community.

Since the early 1990s, the socioeconomic activities of the United Nations have gradually turned toward addressing the interests of all countries, including those that are creating market economies, referred to as "economies in transition." This reflects the increasing interdependency in the world economy and the role that worldwide balanced development plays in the successful economic reforms in these countries.

UN resolutions and decisions regarding economies in transition over the last few years have motivated the UN system to provide comprehensive support to reforms underway and to the integration of these countries into the world economy. The documents and programs of action adopted by international UN conferences on development issues—the Conference on Environment and Development in Rio de Janeiro, the Population Conference in Cairo, the Social Summit in Copenhagen, the Women's Conference in Beijing—contain provisions consolidating specific needs of the countries with economies in transition. In addition, a wide range of resolutions regarding issues of international trade, privatization, entrepreneurship, public administration, operational activities, population, and science and technology have been adopted by the United Nations. The resolutions stress the significance of improving access to world markets for exports from these countries, abolishing discriminatory tariff and nontariff measures, providing assistance to countries in the process of joining the WTO, carrying out privatization, fostering small and medium-sized businesses, demonopolizing the economy, and providing technical assistance to these countries in high-priority matters. Taken together, the resolutions constitute a necessary legal basis for UN activities in the interests of countries with economies in transition, including Russia.

(b) Priorities for Cooperation.   The following areas are among the priorities for cooperation between Russia and UN agencies and institutions:

- Development of a modern market infrastructure (e.g., exchange trade, stock markets, banking)
- Support for small- and medium-sized businesses, encouragement of national entrepreneurship, and consumer protection
- Development of exports and new forms of international economic cooperation (special economic zones, technological parks)
- Attraction of foreign investments
- Carrying out military conversion
- Enhancement of social protection of the population in the course of reform
- Adaptation and capacity-building of public institutions in the period of reform

Russia's cooperation with the UN Development Program (UNDP) has improved notably. The UNDP Country Program for Russia, adopted in September 1995, reflected a more comprehensive and integral approach to this cooperation. Included in the program are the priority directives of the National Governmental Program for Socio-Economic Development for the Years 1995–97. Currently underway in Russia are UNDP projects for assisting the country in joining the WTO, encouraging foreign investments, improving financial management, speeding up military conversion, developing small- and medium-size businesses (the creation of so-called business incubators), streamlining the Moscow public-transportation infrastructure, promoting environmentally sustainable development of the Barents Sea region, and supporting the activity of the Federal Assembly of the Russian Federation. Projects are underway for the establishment at the Russian Ministry of Economics of an information system for economic decision-making; support for democracy and governance; development of traditional economies in the Republic of Sakha (Yakutia); industrial capacity-building of the Vologda region; development of a program for encouraging foreign investment in the Primorsk territory; and providing various kinds of technical assistance to Bashkiria and the Republic of Ingush.

As a result of the implementation of the UNDP Tumen River Project in northeast Asia with the Russian Federation, the People's Republic of China, Democratic North Korea, Mongolia, and South Korea as its participants, two intergovernmental agreements have been signed providing for the establishment of a coordination committee and a consultative commission for the development of northeast Asia. Cooperation between these countries includes specific interaction in the areas of trade, industrial development, transportation, communications, and the environment.

Investment forums for Bashkiria, Kalmykia, Komi, Tatarstan, Yakutia, the Volgograd, Perm, Saratov, the Orenburg regions, and Krasnodar Krai were held under the auspices of the UN Industrial Development Organization (UNIDO). Preparations for similar forums, intended to promote and encourage foreign investments for a number of regions of the far eastern regions, southern Siberia, the Urals, and southern Russia are currently underway. UNIDO participates in the Kaliningrad–2000 Project designed to overhaul the region's industry and infrastructure. Assisted by UNIDO, a conference entitled East-West: Investments, Military Conversion, High Technologies was held in St. Petersburg and Novgorod.

Russia's cooperation with the UN Economic Commission for Europe (ECE) has progressively developed. Numerous standards regulating trade relations between eastern and western countries have been established at the ECE, as well as international environmental conventions, guidelines, and methodologies for cooperation in industry, scientific research, and technology. The activities of the ECE have led to decisions regarding the structural adjustment of industries, introduction of new technologies, development of a transportation infrastructure, identification of key sectors of the economy, and social protection of the population. A number of key projects (e.g., transportation networks and electronic bookkeeping in international trade) are directly linked to relevant goals defined in the governmental programs of the Russian Federation.

Russia has been active in employing the analytical capacity and expertise of the UN Conference on Trade and Development (UNCTAD). In particular, it has worked with the associated Commission on Investment, Technology, and Related Financial Issues (the former UN Commission on TNCs); the UN Population Commission (on demographic analysis issues); the UN Statistical Commission (on improving statistical methodologies and introducing a unified system for national accounts); the Expert Group on International Cooperation in Tax Matters; the Expert Group on International Standards of Accounting and Reporting; the Expert Group on Public Administration and Finance; and the UN Expert Group on Macroeconomic Forecasting (the so-called LINK Project).

(c) Social Issues. Social issues are the focus of Russia's cooperation with the International Labor Organization for assistance in developing employment policies and labor-relations strategies, promoting concepts of social partnership, and providing training and extension courses. Russia has also worked with the UN Children's Fund for the protection of the interests of children and mothers during the transition to a market economy and for safeguarding the rights of children, with the UN Population Fund in the area of reproductive health, and with the World Health Organization.

(d)   Environmental Issues.   Russia's cooperation with the United Nations regarding environmental concerns is intended to address specific ecological problems faced by the country. In particular, cooperation with the UN Environment Program (UNEP) and participation in various environmental conventions sponsored by the UN pursue the goal of restraining "unreasonable" and wasteful activity affecting the environment. Russia's cooperative stance is also meant to recruit qualified experts and use available international expertise to combat drought, deforestation, and water and air pollution; and to enhance efforts for soil restoration, improvement of the drinking water, and the safe transportation of dangerous goods and waste materials.

(e)   Foreign Investment.   Many of these projects not only aim at promoting a search for solutions to Russia's current crucial problems, but also are likely to contribute to the creation of conditions that would increase the interest of foreign investors. The business world's increasing knowledge about these opportunities is likely to renew their energy in searching for new forms of cooperation in the trilateral partnership composed of Russia, the UN system, and business. Additional private capital in the Russian projects implemented with UN assistance may turn out to be a promising endeavor that is beneficial to all three participants.

7.7   COOPERATION BETWEEN THE RUSSIAN FAR EAST AND THE U.S. WEST COAST.*   Russian-American economic cooperation in Russia's far eastern region has consistently grown over the last few years. It can be illustrated by the rate of growth in trade between the Russian Federation and the United States; that rate increased threefold in 1995 alone. As a result, the United States has become Russia's second leading trade partner (after Japan) in this region. Available data indicate that this growth is likely to continue.

Some American companies have been active in the investments in the Russian far eastern region. Several hundred companies have established joint ventures. Among them are well-known enterprises in gold-mining in Magadan Oblast (Cyprus Amax Minerals), enterprises in oil development on the Sakhalin shelf (McDermott; Marathon), and fish-processing in Primorsk Krai (All Alaskan Seafoods). In early 1996, however, the total number of joint ventures involving U.S. partners was less than the number involving the Chinese. Also, American joint ventures were trailing their Japanese counterparts in terms of currency contribution. Thus, despite the current progress in trade and economic relations between Russia and the United States, full cooperation is yet to be achieved.

Among the projects likely to accelerate Russian-American cooperation are those related to developing natural resources, primarily oil fields on the Sakhalin shelf (Sakhalin–1 and Sakhalin–2). The major partner participating in the Sakhalin–1 project is Exxon. The seismic research and trial drilling have been done, and in 1997 work on the project will expand substantially. An additional $140 million will be invested in the project.

The Sakhalin–2 project, which is similar to Sakhalin–1, involves two American companies, McDermott and Marathon. The project is expected to receive $130 million in 1997.

These projects, whose total cost is estimated in the tens of millions of dollars, will spawn the establishment of a wide range of related production. This will revive the econ-

---

*This section was written by Eugene A. Baranov.

omy of Sakhalin and the entire region. The first steps in this direction have already been taken. The Amur shipyards in Komsomolsk-on-Amur and Khabarovsk Krai have gotten a large order for the construction of drilling platforms to extract the Sakhalin oil. Another project involving the construction of a plant to manufacture insulators for future pipelines is under consideration. In addition, substantial investments are expected to be made in environmental and infrastructural projects. Among them are the modernization of the South-Sakhalin airport and the construction of a new power plant there. All these projects are based on exploiting one sector of the economy—drilling for oil. But the region also has enormous resources in gold, diamonds, coal, and timber.

The potential for cooperation in the far eastern region goes beyond the projects involving only natural resources. This is especially true if the opportunities for conversion of defense industries are taken into consideration. For example, the Amur shipyards, which previously manufactured submarines, are currently building oil platforms.

Major opportunities for cooperation are available in the free economic zone in Nakhodka, Primorsky Krai. This site has been selected for an industrial complex that will contain about 200 electronics, machinery, and chemical plants. As soon as the law on free economic zones is adopted, the enterprises in the complex will be exempt from both customs duties and federal taxes on profit. Also, they will enjoy a number of additional federal and local benefits.

One of the important conditions for successful cooperation with foreign partners in Russia's far eastern region is the realization by local authorities of the need to implement measures to create favorable conditions for investors. Such economic policies have been consistently adopted, for example, by the administration in Khabarovsk Krai and Sakhalin Oblast.

To stimulate investments, the administration in Khabarovsk Krai granted an exemption from the local portion of the profit tax to newly established enterprises during the first three years after they begin to operate at a profit. Land rent and other local fees have also been reduced. The communications system has been significantly improved. According to estimates of the U.S. Chamber of Commerce in Moscow, Khabarovsk Krai has become the safest place in the region in terms of personal security.

On Sakhalin, the administration supports large projects as well as small- and medium-sized businesses. An insurance fund for financial risk factors has been established. Also, a method for making accurate estimates on investment projects was introduced to reduce financial risks for small and medium-sized enterprises. The long-term character of this eminently practical policy was secured by the 1996 reelection of the heads of the administrations in Khabarovsk Krai and Sakhalin Oblast.

Local initiatives are combined with the support of the federal government. One of the main agencies for such support is the working group for promoting business cooperation between the Russian Far East and the U.S. West Coast. This working group was established in mid-1995 according to the initiative of President Yeltsin and the Gore-Chernomyrdin Commission. The priorities set by the working group were fishing, timber, mining, telecommunications, energy industries, ecology, conversion of defense industries, transportation, agribusiness, and the services sector (primarily, trade and finance). Among the factors that have hindered cooperation in the fields of trade and investment are difficulties in the preparation of cargo for shipping at Russian ports and the lack of financial resources to fulfill existing investment opportunities.

In order to simplify and accelerate customs-processing, the working group is considering a project called CLEAR-PAC (Customs Link Entry / Exit American-Russian Pacific). The project, once realized, will provide an electronic information system connecting computer terminals in Seattle and Vladivostok to inform customs offices of both countries about cargoes that are being shipped. Successful realization of the CLEAR-PAC project would substantially accelerate preparing documents, reduce demurrage of ships, and, in the final analysis, meet the needs of consumers. At the same time, CLEAR-PAC would be a good model for cooperation between customs and other offices of the two countries in other regions.

Despite the fact that over a dozen different investment funds specifically designed for Russia exist, their role in the Russian Far East is insufficient. During the several years of its existence, the American-Russian Investment Fund invested less than $15 million in the region. In this connection, the Russian consulate general in San Francisco (at a meeting of the working group in Khabarovsk in September 1996) proposed to establish a regional investment fund for the area. The idea was supported by V. Ishaev, the head of administration in Khabarovsk Krai, and by several American participants. To promote the proposal, the Russian consulate general and the trade mission, together with the American law firm Baker & McKenzie, are seeking potential investors among American and Russian corporations and banks.

At the same time, it should be noted that an existing intergovernmental mechanism of support for Russian-American cooperation cannot itself guarantee priority access to the Russian Far East for American entrepreneurs. Competition in the region is becoming stronger, especially in fields where projects can bring fast profits. The main competitors for those projects are neighboring countries such as China, South Korea, Canada, and Japan as well as Western European countries. Therefore, the success of American business will depend primarily on its own initiative and activity.

PART III

ECONOMIC STRUCTURE

CHAPTER 8

RUSSIAN ECONOMIC STRATEGY: 1997–2002

Alexander N. Troshin and Gennadiy O. Kuranov

8.1 THE ECONOMY AS AN INTEGRAL PART OF NATIONAL SECURITY. [*]
Unrecognizably reformed, the Russian economy has acquired a character that is full of new driving forces and motivations. The heavily centralized planned-distribution principle has given way to market mechanisms, economic incentives, and consumer demand. The new structure is guided by the principles of profit and cost effectiveness.

With its enormous regulatory powers over the economy, the state must be an active force because of the peculiar conditions of the transitional period and the specific features of the Russian economy. Also, only the state can give Russia economic security and protect its vital interests. In fact, this is the role played by the state in all market-economy countries.

(a) Production Structure and Economic Independence. The slump in output that has occurred during the economic reforms is frequently referred to as the greatest threat to Russia's economic security. Indeed, output has reached a dangerously low point. In 1994, it was just about half of the 1991 level, a record low for Eastern Europe. Reversing this trend is certainly the key objective in preserving the country's economic security.

This formidable slide in manufacturing is not, however, a cause for panic. To some extent, the fall can be explained by the reduced production of armaments and of noncompetitive, low-quality, or unnecessary products. The period of industrial decline seems to be ending, and a period of stability is starting, which should be followed by a complete recovery.

From the start of the reforms, structural changes in manufacturing were proclaimed the main objective of the market-oriented economic policy. The election platforms of many of the candidates some of whom are now in positions of power or the heads of parties and movements, contained reform promises to make the country's economy less dependent on fuels and raw materials, and to place more emphasis on the consumer and human needs in general.

The specific nature of the market mechanisms in Russia has led to changes in the industrial structure that may provoke serious threats to the country's economic security. In particular, as part of the average 50% decline in the country's industrial output, the textile industry plunged 360%, engineering 230%, the metal industry 180%, and the fuel industry 150%. Thanks to exports, the fuel and metal fabrication industries have avoided a deeper recession. By contrast, the other industries, which were not competitive in the world market, and

---

[*]This section was written by Alexander N. Troshin.

catered only to the domestic consumer, slashed output as the demand for their products waned. The intensity of this trend differed from industry to industry.

Today, the reform process must receive a critical assessment. The continuing dismantling of the country's industrial structure may pose a real threat to its economic security. This threat may grow immeasurably within a few years, when an investment boom materializes and conditions are ripe for the nation to fall into a heavy dependence on foreign countries. At about that time, the demand for engineering and other industrial products is likely to rise. Whether the threat to the country's security is transformed into a real danger will depend on: (1) how much of the former production and labor potential has been retained in individual industries; and (2) their ability to revive production to meet the rising demand. Unless a measure of control is imposed, the domestic industry may fail in its objectives, allowing the emerging domestic demand to be met by imports. This eventuality has become a full reality in the consumer market, where imports are approaching the 50% watershed in domestic sales. (Their share stood at 23% in 1992.)

We are, therefore, witnessing the emergence of an economic-development model based essentially on the export of fuels and raw materials and the import of machinery, equipment, and consumer goods purchased with the money earned from exports. The country's existence will largely depend on the whims of the world market and the economic decisions and steps taken by other countries and foreign communities. Russia certainly needs a state policy that can protect its national economic interests.

(b) Living Standards and Social Stability.   Over the last three years of reforms, the sociopolitical situation in Russia has been, and will increasingly be, dictated by developments in the economy, the population's living standards and conditions, and the scope and dependability of the democratic freedoms the population has obtained. The attitudes of segments of the population to government authorities and political parties will be heavily influenced by the extent to which their expectations have been fulfilled and by the real results of the reforms.

For all the drawbacks and hardships of these first three years, for all the heavy economic burden that Russians have had to shoulder, the nation has remained stable. Social conflicts such as strikes were locally significant and never spilled over into Russia as a whole. This relative political stability is responsible for some headway in the economic reform. However, the country has reached a period when the huge antireform sentiment may worsen social tensions to the extent that political stability can no longer be maintained.

The growing income gap between different segments of the population and the instability of everyday life caused by delays in wage payments and plant closings, are breeding uncertainty and discontent among the people. Opposition parties and movements are capitalizing on these conditions, loudly drumming the figures that confirm the impoverishment of a significant proportion of the nation. The population is beginning to heed these messages, which puts the reformists' victory in the elections in jeopardy.

New promises or half-hearted attempts to sharpen the social edge of the reforms appear to be insufficient to make the prospects of economic reforms more attractive. These developments have created a breeding ground for social tensions and criminal activities that are entirely new to Russia (drug addiction, organized crime, prostitution, etc.). The split of the nation into the rich few and the poor multitudes, many of whom are unemployed, will create two classes standing poles apart and entertaining different perceptions about social justice.

A persistent threat to social peace is posed by the instability of the financial market and money supply. Recurring peaks of inflation, ruble exchange-rate fluctuations, wide swings in the interest rates of citizens' deposits, bankruptcies of financial companies, and similar developments have combined to create an atmosphere of uncertainty and an environment in which the population is likely to lose whatever savings it has amassed. In many aspects, financial stabilization is turning from a purely economic issue into a sociopolitical objective.

(c)   Strategy for Economic Security.   Averting and removing threats to Russia's economic security is a major goal of the federal executive authorities and influential bodies in the Federation. As a result, the government has adopted a resolution to draw up a state strategy to ensure the country's economic security.

The basic principles of the strategy have already been drafted. They contain definitions of the key concepts and structure of the problem. The principles also identify determinants of economic security, provide a list of major threats to economic security, and map ways to establish a mechanism to maintain it.

According to the strategy, economic security may be interpreted as the ability and preparedness of the economy to create adequate living conditions for the people, to maintain social, economic, military, and political stability in society and the state, and to resist the pressure of internal and external threats.

Implementation of the strategy should provide conditions that support national security, guarantee protection of the country's vital interests, and, in the long run, allow Russia to:

- Effectively influence world developments that have a bearing on Russia's national interests, forestalling those that conflict with the country's interests;
- Deal with domestic political, economic, and social problems within the context of national interests and allowing no interference from the outside;
- Provide living standards and a quality of life that guarantee social peace;

Russia has enormous resources to further itself, such as its skilled work force, varied and plentiful natural resources, and a strong, productive scientific and engineering base in manufacturing.

Implicitly, the strategy for economic security must contain the following:

- A characterization of external and internal challenges to economic security as a combination of conditions and factors creating a threat to the vital economic interests of the individual, society, and the state. In other words, the characterization of these threats to security has to provide a specific analysis of the situation from the sectorial and regional viewpoints.
- A definition of the criteria and parameters of the economic conditions that meet the security requirements and ensure protection of vital interests. This requires the development of quantitative parameters—"threshold values" of key economic, social, and production determinants that shed light on the health of those sectors of the economy on which economic security depends.
- A mechanism to maintain the country's economic security and to protect its vital interests through the use of legal, economic, and administrative levers by all levels of state authority.

In a multimodal market economy, when the state cannot control businesses by directives, the government must be able to provide steady economic regulation. The government's efforts to ensure the country's economic security must tentatively include the following components:

- Creation of an information base to provide an unbiased and comprehensive monitoring of the economy and society. This monitoring must seek to identify and predict internal and external threats to the vital interests of economic security objectives.
- Development of a set of current and longer-term measures to forestall and neutralize internal and external threats. A procedure should be in place to assess the results of these measures.
- Launching efforts to implement a set of statewide measures to maintain economic security.

The economic-security strategy will be carried out through a security system that is formed by legislative, executive, and judicial branches, public organizations, and individuals involved in maintaining security in accordance with Russia's federal law on security. This function must be regulated by laws governing the field of security. The strategy must be developed and implemented within the framework of current economic policy. For the strategy to be effective, the state must have a comprehensive system for influencing the economy to minimumize any losses incurred through the regulation of economic reforms. Limits and conditions must be set for state intervention in the economy, especially in regard to those of the state.

8.2   MACROECONOMIC PROPORTIONS, TRENDS, AND FORECAST OF THE ECONOMY*

(a)   The Russian Economy from 1992 to 1995.   From 1992 to 1995, the Russian economy developed under the influence of three factors. The first is the economy inherited by Russia from the former USSR; the previous system had a bad effect on the current one and created an inefficient production structure. The second is the series of political and economic transformations that took place in the early 1990s (the dissolution of the USSR, the break-up of traditional economic ties between former Soviet republics, and the break-up of ties within the Council for Mutual Economic Assistance). Third, there is the implementation of radical economic reform since 1992.

The development of economic reform was uneven, primarily because monetary and credit policies were not carried out consistently. Periods of strict policy alternated with periods of loosening measures, which resulted in slowing economic changes and weakened attempts to get over the deep crisis that struck the Russian economy in the late 1980s.

The first steps toward radical economic reform occurred from late 1991 to early 1992. They included the liberalization of economic and foreign trade policies, the liberalization of most prices, the abolition of the administrative system in production and supplies, tax reform, the liberalization of currency regulations, and the rejection of beneficial financing. This approach brought a major change in the macroeconomic situation during the first months of 1992.

The skyrocketing increase (350%) in consumer prices in January 1992 was gradually replaced by a more moderate pace of inflation, which approached 10% per month by late July and August. Simultaneously, industrial production dropped. This was the result of the break-up of economic ties; the reduction of governmental contracts, especially in the defense and construction industries; the reduction of consumer demand; an increase in mutual nonpayments by various enterprises; and the lack of circulating assets. In August, production fell by 27% over the same period of the previous year. The fall in the gross

---

*This section was written by Gennadiy O. Kuranov.

domestic product (GDP), which had already been evident in 1991, accelerated within the first six months of 1992. Following the liberalization of prices, the real income of the population dropped approximately in half. In June 1992, however, it began to increase (the salary index equaled 50–70% of the growth of consumer prices) and approached 70% of the 1990 level during the second half of 1992.

Rigid monetary and credit policies at a time when industries were not prepared to operate under the new conditions, resulted in a sharp increase in mutual nonpayments. In the summer 1992, the government had to introduce the mutual cancellation of debts with part of them by credit emission, which resulted in substantial changes in the economy in the second half of 1992. Inflation continued to increase, approaching 23–27% a month. The fall in industrial production stopped, however, and occasionally showed signs of growth.

In early 1993, the threat of hyperinflation forced the government and Central Bank of Russia to return to moderately rigid monetary and credit policies and to set the limits for credit paid to the Central bank. The technical loans that had usually been provided to former Soviet republics were stopped. Rules and norms of regulation in the foreign economic realm were revised.

In 1993, particularly in the second half of the year, a new period of financial stabilization began in Russia. In late 1993, however, the industrial decline resumed, especially in investment and manufacturing industries; by March 1994, the industrial production output declined by 25%. As industrial production began to adjust to the new level of demand in the consumer market later in the year, the decline in output virtually stopped. Inflation rates gradually slowed to 4.6% in August, and savings rates started to grow. Between 1993 and early 1994, the ruble's exchange rate steadily increased.

Despite all positive external signs, however, financial instability remained. Loans provided to the economy in the spring and summer of 1994 exceeded the set limits. An increase in monetary circulation began in April. The structure of savings did not appear to be sound: the general population made many investments into financial firms of suspicious origin, and purchases of foreign currency increased. Mutual debts of enterprises resumed, although not at the rate of 1992.

In the summer of 1994, a number of funds based on the principle of financial pyramids ceased their activities. The Central Bank refused further interventions, which in the past had usually been made to support the ruble's exchange rate. In September alone, the ruble's rate fell by 12%. On October 11 (known as Black Tuesday), the ruble devalued by 20%. In the autumn inflation began to grow, reaching 18% a month by the end of the year. As a result, the real income of the population substantially dropped.

In October 1994, the government declared the beginning of a new stage of financial stabilization. The goal for the new stage was set at 2% by 1995, reducing the federal budget deficit to 4% of GDP, and setting up conditions for the revival of investment activities and further economic growth. The government refused to use loans of the Central Bank for financing deficit spending, but instead chose to rely on external and internal borrowing. Simultaneously, by the fall 1994, the situation in the foreign economic field became generally favorable for Russian exporters because of the gap between world and domestic prices. Russian enterprises began to successfully enter the world market of primary materials.

As a result of this combination of factors, the first half of 1995 saw inflation rates steadily decline. After July they did not exceed 5%. During the same period, the export of primary materials, especially ferrous and nonferrous metals, chemicals, and lumber, began to grow. Industrial production started to increase. The pace of the reduction in the GDP slowed substantially. Real incomes of the population began to show signs of relative growth.

The potential for stabilization, however, has not been used to its full extent. By the middle of 1995, foreign-trade conditions worsened for Russian exporters. Enterprises were restructuring too slowly and were unable to adjust to the substantial reduction of inflation rates and the diminishing gap between prices in domestic and world markets. The growth of export-oriented industries slowed down and the shrinkage of manufacturing industries resumed.

(b)   The Russian Economy in 1996.   In 1996, some tangible steps were taken toward further liberalization and openness of the Russian economy. All benefits relating to the foreign economics realm (e.g., the reduction of export duties) were canceled. Measures to continue the liberalization of currency regulation were taken, as were measures to achieve the full convertibility of the ruble.

The inflation rate steadily dropped and reached zero in August. In October, the increase in consumer prices was 1.2%, which reflected the impact of the seasonal factor and an increase in prices in the service sector. Debts in terms of payroll and social benefits, as well as debts of enterprises to budgetary and nonbudgetary funds, are growing. This trend is determined primarily by the increasing use of barter and cash substitutes, for example, bills, mutual cancellation of payments, etc.

The use of tax exemptions and loans of commercial banks to cover budget expenses has had a serious negative impact on the economy. Also, the difficult financial state of numerous enterprises has had the same effect. The lack of circulating assets and the unavailability of loans have forced a number of enterprises to default on their payments and to reduce production. The general political situation, including the uncertain results of the 1996 presidential elections, also had an impact.

The need for urgent borrowing raised the profitability of state stocks and securities. On the eve of the presidential elections, interest rates jumped to 170–200% as an annual yield. By mid-November, however, they fell to 45%. As a result, the interest rates for loans did not decrease for a long time and investments continued to drop. The total amount of investments in fixed assets declined during the first 10 months of 1996 by 18%. The internal-revenue rates for the federal budget remain at a low level—about 11% of GDP, which falls short of the 15% anticipated by the program and the 14.2% in 1995.

To improve the situation in tax collecting, the government has taken measures designed to attract additional sources of revenue and prevent tax evasion. Negotiations are taking place with the largest debtors to the federal budget, and tax exemptions have been halted.

Despite the drop in production, the population's standard of living has stabilized. Large differences in personal income are gradually diminishing. The difference in income of the top 10% of the Russian population compared to the income of the bottom 10% was reduced from 15-fold in early 1995 to 13-fold in the fall of 1996. Fewer people are below the poverty line: in early 1995, they constituted 33% of the population, and in October 1996, they comprised 20%.

Fortunately, the Russian Government managed to avoid a sharp aggravation of the situation in the labor market. The total number of unemployed workers in 1996 averaged about 2.6 million (3.6% of the economically active population). The percentage of persons seeking jobs is much higher—9.2%.

(c)   Major Macroeconomic Indicators and Proportions.   As a result of the economic trends from 1992 to 1996, there has been a drastic change in the basic indicators and proportions in the Russian economy (see Exhibit 8.1).

Exhibit 8.1. Dynamics of Macroeconomic Indicators in Russia, 1992–96

Indicators	% to the previous year				
	1992	1993	1994	1995	1996
Gross domestic product	85.5	91.3	87.3	96	95
Inflation (December of current year/ December of previous year)	2510	840	220	131	22
Total industrial output	82	85.9	79.1	96.7	95
Total agricultural output	91	96	88	92	93
Investments in fixed assets	60	88	76	90	92
Real income	52	116	113	87	99
Unemployment rate at the end of the year (percent of economically active population)	0.8	1.1	2.2	3.2	3.4

Compared with that of 1990 the 1995 gross domestic product declined by 38%, and industrial output was cut in half. The most substantial changes took place in the field of fixed-capital investments—in 1995 they constituted only 37% of the 1990 level. Total foreign investments in the Russian economy in 1996 are estimated to be approximately $3 billion (4.5% of all investments).

As for the structure of the consumed GDP, the share of final consumption (including consumption by households) has increased because of significant decrease in gross accumulation (from 33–36% in early 1990s to 24% in 1996) and a reduction of net export (see Exhibit 8.2).

During the period of reform, the structure of material production has undergone significant changes: the share of industry and construction has decreased while the share of money circulation and agriculture has grown (see Exhibit 8.3).

Regarding the structure of industrial production, the share of fuel, energy, and metallurgical industries has increased. Shares of all other industries have decreased, especially mechanical engineering, food processing, and light industry.

(d) Potential for the Development of the Russian Economy. The medium-term forecast for the development of the Russian economy is based on the estimates of Russia's economic potential, the foreign economic situation, general economic limits, and the goals of the new stage of economic reform.

Exhibit 8.2. Structure of Consumption of GDP, in Percent

	1992	1993	1994	1995	1996
Gross domestic product	**100**	**100**	**100**	**100**	**100**
Final consumption	48.4	60.2	69.1	67.5	70.9
Consumption by households	—	38.0	43.7	46.1	48.3
Gross accumulation	**33.7**	**31.0**	**25.5**	**25.5**	**23.9**
Fixed capital	—	22.5	21.8	20.0	19.1
Net export of goods and services	**14.1**	**7.7**	**4.6**	**4.1**	**3.6**

Exhibit 8.3.   Structure of Material Production, in Percent

	1989	1996
Total material production	**100**	**100**
Industry	53.0	44.9
Fuel and energy industries	9.6	12.2
Metallurgy	6.0	6.8
Chemical and petrochemical	4.9	4.1
Mechanical engineering	12.3	8.2
Timber, paper and pulp	3.6	2.6
Construction materials	3.2	2.5
Light industry	3.6	1.2
Food processing	8.5	6.1
Agriculture	9.8	13.2
Construction	12.8	10.2
Transportation and communications	14.8	13.1
Money circulation	9.6	18.6

Russia has some competitive advantages that it can utilize to accelerate the growth of its economy, including these six:

1. Population and labor resources. One of Russia's competitive advantages is a skilled and relatively low-cost labor supply. Within the next few years, the size of the economically active population is going to increase, which will create the preconditions for the growth of Russia's labor potential. This will necessitate the creation of new jobs. The shortcomings of the labor supply include the wide gap between the skill level demanded by industry and the skill level of the workers. Another shortcoming is the poor quality of management. The most serious problem is the polarization the people caused by the wide gulf in personal income levels and the lack of a middle class.

2. Natural and primary resources. Russia possesses basic mineral and primary resources in quantities that can meet the current and future needs of domestic production and export. In terms of mineral resources, fuel and energy reserves (gas, coal, and oil) constitute 71%; nonferrous-metal resources 15%; ferrous, nonferrous, and rare metals 13%. The major problem of these resources is that the exploration of reserves has failed to keep pace with mining. Another problem is the lack of an infrastructure for primary processing and transportation at new mining sites.

3. Financial potential. Russia has an established basis for economic growth resulting from a large accumulation of savings especially of the nongovernmental variety. This potential can be efficiently used while improving the structure of savings, maintaining optimum level of their dynamics, methods for their utilization in the economy, and converting savings into an effective investment. An additional financial burden on the national economy is the payment of external debts.

4. Production potential. Low levels of investment activity and efficiency resulted in great amounts of deteriorating and obsolete fixed capital. The average length of service of major equipment and buildings is approximately 25 years. The degree of de-

terioration of fixed capital has increased to 45%. The cost of maintaining large numbers of out-of-service production facilities (about 50–60%), demand, lays a heavy burden on manufacturers' finances.

The economy needs a large-scale and fast withdrawal of obsolete production capacity. At present, the mass removal of noncompetitive, obsolete equipment and machinery has become more active, a process that is expected to expand as investments increase.

5. Scientific and technical potential. In this regard, Russia's competitive advantages lie in the developed fundamental sciences and many technologically advanced fields.

6. Potential for integration processes. Russia's location as a bridge between East and West creates preconditions for the full realization of economic growth. At the same time, as Russia is integrated into the world economy, it will have to face competition with foreign manufacturers both in domestic and world markets.

This situation sets high standards for the dynamics of Russia's socioeconomic development. The estimated rate of growth of the world economy by the end of this century is 2.5–3% annually. To take a respected place in the world economy and fulfill its potential, Russia has to increase its level of economic development. Taking into account the possibilities for economic growth, Russia needs to increase its average annual economic growth rate to twice the average rate of the world economy. Such acceleration should be based on the intensive use of the six competitive advantage mentioned.

(e)   New Stage of Reform—the Structural Transformation of the Russian Economy.
Along with the enormous difficulties the Russian economy is experiencing, there have been other serious qualitative changes. The liberalization of prices and the establishment of economic ties have been basically accomplished. There are virtually no restrictions applied to the exchange of goods between enterprises and regions. Mass privatization has been conducted; today, over 70% of the GDP is from the nonstate sector. The inflation rate has been lowered. All these developments lead to the conclusion that the major goals of the first stage of reform have been accomplished—the Russian economy has become predominantly a market economy.

Thus, the important preconditions have been laid for a transition to the next stage of reform, a structural transformation that will lead to the resumption of economic growth. These aims, outlined in the governmental program for 1997–2000, are based on the estimates of what can be achieved during 1997–2000. Here are the four aims.

1. By the year 2000, it can be realistically expected that there will be a stable economic growth rate of 5% annually and high investment growth rates for the dynamic development of the economy and for structural transformation.

2. Institutional transformations are necessary for the efficient functioning of the market economy. These measures should secure property rights, competition, and the regulation of natural monopolies, as well as strengthen law and judicial order.

3. Positive structural shifts in production and export are necessary, which should strengthen the efficiency and competitiveness of the enterprises. This reduces the share of noncompetitive production.

4. The real income and consumption of the population will increase, making additional inroads in the struggle against poverty.

To achieve these goals, this reform is expected to accomplish the following tasks:

1. Provide macroeconomic conditions for structural transformation and economic growth: inflation rates should not exceed 10% annually, and the budget deficit by the end of fiscal year 2000 should not exceed 2% of the GDP;

2. Implement reform among enterprises in order to substantially improve the level of their management to compete in a market economy;

3. Implement reform of the social sphere in order to increase its efficiency, including the cessation of price subsidies for goods and services and the replacement of these subsidies with targeted benefits to the needy to provide a minimum standard of living;

4. Implement tax reform by simplifying the tax system, increasing the level of tax collecting, lowering the tax burden on enterprises; and provide stabilized tax revenues for the governmental budget (including pension funds and nonbudgetary social funds) at a level of 35–40% of GDP; and put into effect a tax code that would meet these requirements;

5. Form a competitive financial sector, reduce governmental borrowing, lower the interest rate for state stocks and securities to 2–3% above the inflation rate, and lower the average interest rate to 3–5% above the inflation rate;

6. Solve the problem of nonpayments on a noninflationary basis, and reduce the use of barter and money substitutes in economic activities;

7. Maintain a level of savings at 28–30% of the GDP and create conditions for the conversion of savings into investments, increase the share of investments into fixed capital to 20–30% of the GDP, stimulate investments in high-tech, science-intensive industries, and create a favorable climate for foreign investments, in order to attract $10–12 billion annually by the year 2000;

8. Establish a policy of fair competition in the domestic market and increase the competitiveness of domestic producers;

9. Strengthen the national currency and increase the profitability of saving in rubles, and to stop capital flight;

10. Provide a set of minimum social standards in the areas of market consumption, education, health, and culture;

11. Implement reform in the military, and change the structure of budget expenses for defense purposes;

12. Continue strengthening the economic and financial positions of the subjects of the Federation and of bodies of local self-administration in order to provide independence in solving socioeconomic problems within their competence.

(f) Industrial Policy.   During the next few years, Russia's industrial strategy will be aimed at achieving a new technological edge, and increasing the efficiency and competitiveness of Russian industry in domestic and foreign markets. The likelihood of achieving these goals based on initial possibilities will differ depending on the group of industries.

1. Export-capable mining industries, especially oil, gas, and timber industries. Policies toward these industries will be oriented primarily to their independent development on the basis of self-financing and natural diversification. This will be carried out by means of investments in adjacent processing industries and industries producing

corresponding equipment and materials. In these industries, it is expedient to attract strategic investors (both domestic and foreign) and to create a stable judicial and tax regime. As a tool for providing such a regime, agreements on production sharing will be used.

2. Industries with scientific and technical potential that have the short-term capability of creating competitive products for the world and domestic markets, but that need governmental support. Taking into account the shortage of financial resources, direct state financing will be limited to priority projects such as the production of civil-aviation equipment, space-exploration activities, nuclear-power projects, and mechanical engineering for the energy industry. These high-priority industries promote the entrance of highly competitive Russian goods, works, and services, into the world market and help strengthen Russia's previously established positions.

   The main tools for realizing favorable policies in these industries will be the financing of activities in patenting, standardization, and certification of exported goods. These tools will provide financing for export contracts and provide governmental contracts for conducting individual research and development projects. A central role in supporting these industries may belong to state investments and the development of leasing.

3. Some industries are characterized by a significant technical lag and therefore are unable to enter the foreign market in the short term. They should nevertheless hold a significant share of the domestic market, including various parts of the electronics industry, automobile industry, transportation, roads, agricultural machine building, food processing, and light industry.

   The main policy tools in these industries will be protecting import tariffs within the limits allowed by international norms. These tariffs will consequently be lowered to reach acceptable standards of quality and expenses. Another tool will be the standard methods of regulation accepted by the industries.

In certain industries, especially favorable conditions should be created for foreign investments. Such industries include those that bring with them new technologies and management experience.

(g)   Major Indicators of Economic Development, 1997–2000.   If the goals of the program are met, beginning in 1998 stable positive growth rates of the GDP will be achieved; by 2000, they are expected to be 5–6%.

The proportions between consumption and accumulation in the GDP will shift toward accumulation, whose share will increase to 28–30%. The growth of the economy will spur an increase in consumption, especially in 1999–2000. During 1997–2000, consumption will grow by 14–15%. Relatively low growth rates will be determined by the increasing demand for investment resources, as well as by the incremental withdrawal of subsidies and the cessation of cross-financing in the housing, municipal, and passenger transportation fields.

In addition, the termination of major sources of inflation will promote a stable, low-inflationary environment.

There will be changes in the proportions between the manufacturing and financial sectors of the economy as well. This will lead to the growth of industrial production outpacing the GDP growth in 1998–2000. The increase in industrial production will be 21–23%, including 17% at medium and large enterprises. The acceleration of industrial development will be determined to an increasing extent by small and medium enterprises.

Exhibit 8.4.   Major Macroeconomic Indicators of the Forecast for Socioeconomic Development of the Russian Federation, 1996–2000

Indicators	1996	Forecast			
		1997	1998	1999	2000
Gross domestic product	95	100	103	105	105
Inflation (December of current year/ December of previous year)	23	12	8	7	6
Industrial output	95	100	105	107	108
Gross output of agriculture	93	98	101	104	104
Investments in fixed capital	82	99	107	112	114
Foreign investments, in US$ billion	3	5–6	7–8	9–10	10–12
Unemployment rate (percent of the economically active population)	3.6	4.7	5.2	5.4	5.6

The share of fuel and energy industries, as part of industrial production, will decrease to 47%, and the share of gas will increase.

In the mechanical engineering industry, priority will be given to the development of aviation and space technology, nuclear and other energy equipment, quantum electronics, the production of ultrahigh-frequency equipment, electron-optical converters, and powerful semiconductor instruments. Domestic aircraft construction will be integrated into the world aircraft market through the creation of a new generation of aircraft.

The most dynamic sector will be in the development of light industry, construction materials, chemicals, and petroleum-chemical industries.

The growth of real income and institutional reform in the agro-industrial complex will cause an increase in agricultural production, especially plant growing, poultry farming, and swine breeding. An increase in meat and milk production will start at the end of this period. The introduction of new technologies and cultures will reduce the amount of land used for crops. The overall productivity of agriculture will increase.

The volume of trade with foreign countries is expected to increase by 25–30%. Imports will develop at a high rate. A positive balance in foreign trade is related to more active investment and an increase in the demand for equipment and tools.

The process of replacing aging production factories and equipment will speed up the use of new technologies. Investments in fixed capital are expected to grow by approximately 40%. The removal of obsolete and inefficient fixed capital will increase from 2% to 5.5%. The processes for reviving the economy and balancing the development of different sectors will increase the share of payroll in the income structure and motivate more effective labor activity.

As a result of changing conditions, by the year 2000 the economy will be based on new production indicators that will provide balanced development and high growth rates (see Exhibit 8.4).

CHAPTER 9

EXTERNAL DEBT*

Andrei L. Kostin

9.1   PARAMETERS OF INHERITANCE.   As of November 1991, the external debt of
the former USSR was $81 billion, as noted in the agreement entitled On the Succession of
the External State Debt of the USSR. For purposes of this discussion, this sum is the
amount of the external debt inherited by the Commonwealth of Independent States.

In October 1991, the agreement entitled Memorandum of Understanding on the Debt to
the Foreign Creditors of the Union of Soviet Socialist Republics and its Successors (MOU)
was signed between the states of the former USSR (except for three Baltic states) and the
Soviet Union as a whole, being the predecessor state. This document recognized the joint
and individual responsibility of the CIS member states toward external creditors. In December 1991, however, the successor states of the former Soviet Union signed an agreement
entitled On the Succession of the External Debt of the USSR, confirming their joint and individual liabilities for the debt of the former Soviet Union to foreign creditors and determining their shares in the debt. They also agreed upon the order of debt repayment. When
the CIS member states failed to meet their commitments under this agreement, the Russian
Federation assumed all the responsibilities for the external debt of the former USSR.

From 1992 to 1994, Russia signed the so-called zero-option agreements to settle the
former USSR's external debt and declare its assets with each of the CIS member states.
These agreements stipulated that the Russian Federation will assume responsibility for all
of the former USSR's external debt. In exchange, the CIS member states had to relinquish
their shares of the former USSR's foreign assets.

Russia has been recognized as the rightful successor of the former USSR's external
debt by all Western creditors. At the Paris Club session in April 1993, the Participating
Creditor Countries (PCC) confirmed that the other successor states who had entered into
zero-option agreements with the Russian Federation would not be held liable to pay the
former Soviet Union's debt.

As of January 1, 1992 (when the zero-option agreements had not yet been signed), the
external debt of the former USSR roughly amounted to $96.6 billion and exceeded almost
by twice the CIS annual exports. At the beginning of 1992, the foreign assets of the former
USSR (*overdue payments* included) were more than $140 billion (at the current official
Gosbank ruble-U.S. dollar exchange rate). More than 50 foreign countries owe this
amount under the interstate credits. A part of these credits was expressed in rubles, and
repayment should have been affected through deliveries of goods and services. Hard-
currency external assets of the former USSR are nominally 1.5 times as much as its foreign

---

*For the period between January 1, 1991, to January 1, 1997, according to Vnesheconombank
and the other official sources.

debt; but, taking into account a number of factors, they are considerably less than its liabilities and do not exceed 15% of their value.

The dynamic of growth of the Russian Federation's total external indebtedness, including the former USSR's external debt and credits granted by international financial organizations, are as follows:

Year	Total External Indebtedness (in $ billions)
1992	96.6
1993	106.7
1994	112.7
1995	119.9
1996	120.4
1997*	124.1
1998*	136.2

*The limit and the forecast of the external debt for 1997 is borrowed from the Law on the Russian Federation Budget for 1996. The forecast for 1998 is based on the draft of the Russian Federation Budget for 1997.

The pure Russian indebtedness after January 1992 comprises 10 to 12% of the total Russian Federation's external debt. A significant part of this indebtedness falls on the borrowings from international financial institutions, including those allocated for financing the state budget deficit. Since 1993, Russia has dramatically increased its loan volume from International Monetary Fund, the International Bank for Reconstruction and Development, and the European Bank for Reconstruction and Development. By mid-1996, Russia owed these institutions over $12.5 billion. This amount keeps growing due to:

1. The new loans received through the extended credit facility from the International Monetary Fund.
2. The loans received from the International Bank for Reconstruction and Development, including such loans as the Coal Loan, the Humanitary Loan, and several others.

Debts owed to the international financial institutions are never restructured. As of January 1, 1996, out of the total amount of Russian external debt of $120.4 billion (including the former USSR's debt of $103 billion and the Russian Federation's debt of $17.4 billion), $48 billion fell on the Paris Club (state and guaranteed credits). Of the latter amount, the former USSR's indebtedness eligible for the restructure was $42 billion. A total of $20.7 billion fell on the other official creditors (non-Paris Club members), with $16.6 billion falling on the former socialist countries.

A total of $32.3 billion fell on the London Club, including $7 billion of overdue interest indebtedness. Commercial indebtedness to Western exporters was estimated at $4.5 billion, and Russia's debt to the international financial institutions at $11.4 billion.

9.2   SETTLEMENT OF DEBT.   By the end of 1991, the main portion of the former USSR's external debt consisted of debts under medium- and long-term credits (80%). Most of the payments were expected between 1992 and 1995. If the former USSR's external debt had not been rescheduled, the Russian Federation would have had to pay $3.5 billion by December 1991. Western creditors alone were due interest and principal debt of approximately $90 billion (i.e., 1.5 times as much as the amount of Russian principal debt at the beginning of 1991). By 1991, however, the Russian Federation began negotiating with international financial institutions—the Paris and London Clubs, and other creditors—regarding other ways of settling the former USSR's and Russia's external debt.

In January 1992, the Paris Club members agreed to defer payments of the former USSR's principal debt of $3.2 billion. Foreign commercial banks have also consented to deferred payments. In both cases, these deferrals related to debts incurred prior to January 1991 and falling due in December 1991. In 1993, Russia signed its first agreement with the Paris Club member countries on debt rescheduling. In 1994 and 1995, two more agreements were signed. In all these instances, the purpose was to reschedule payments falling due in those years only. In April 1996, a multiyear rescheduling agreement on the former USSR's debt was signed with the Paris Club. The agreement specified debt rescheduling conditions. The following debts were considered eligible for rescheduling:

1. The principal debt and interest under credits received by the former USSR prior to January 1991, with original payments prior to the first quarter of 1991. The rescheduled part of the debt under the agreements of 1993, 1994, and 1995 were also included with a total rescheduled period of 20 years.

2. The principal debt under credits received by the former USSR in the period from January to December 1991, with original payments originally due through the end of 1998. This agreement also rescheduled part of the debt under the agreements of 1993, 1994, and 1995, with a total rescheduled period of 20 years.

Repayment should begin in the year 2002, since a seven-year grace period was stipulated. Only interest will be paid during this period. The total amount of the former USSR's external debt to be rescheduled under this agreement is $42 billion. This agreement provides for necessary bilateral interstate agreements to be signed with all the Paris Club member countries. The agreement also provides for a number of serious commitments and obligations for the Russians. Russia must comply with the terms of the extended financing facility agreed upon with the International Monetary Fund. Russia also has no right to enter into agreements with any other creditors on conditions more favorable than those stated in the agreement.

Between 1993 and 1995, Russian indebtedness towards some of the non-Paris Club member official creditors was settled on conditions similar to those of the Paris Club. The principal intention of these agreements was that, after the year 2000, agreement on the existing debt repayment (amounting to 6.3 billion transferable rubles) would be reached with Germany (with respect to the former German Democratic Republic). On January 1, 1996, the volume of rescheduled indebtedness towards this group of creditors reached $8.2 billion. As the rescheduling conditions of the indebtedness towards the Paris Club changed, similar negotiations were held with official creditors, in particular, with Czech Republic.

Along with the Paris Club, Russia conducted negotiations with foreign banks that were united into the London Club. Its Banking Advisory Committee is headed by Deutsche Bank. In November 1995 (prior to the Paris Club Agreement), a memorandum was signed in Frankfurt on the agreed principles of a comprehensive rescheduling of a certain part of the former USSR's external debt towards this club. This amount totaled $32.3 billion, interest included, for a period of 25 years with a seven-year grace period. The rescheduling conditions, in general, were similar to those of the Paris Club. This agreement, however, comes into force only when the majority of the bank's creditors accept its conditions and, respectively, upon verification of the indebtedness with each of the creditor banks or their agents.

As of this writing, Vnesheconombank continues to verify the indebtedness claimed by debt holders for settlement within the framework of the London Club agreement. Commercial indebtedness of the former USSR rose when Russian importers failed to comply with their payment obligations for the goods supplied from abroad under contracts. As of January 1, 1996, commercial indebtness was estimated at $4.5 billion.

A statement made in October 1994 by the Russian government entitled On Settlement of Commercial Indebtedness of the Former USSR towards Foreign Creditors is considered a cornerstone document for settlement of commercial indebtedness. The statement defines the general principles and the order of settlement for this category of Russia's external debt. To execute the statement's principles, Vnesheconombank, together with the Ministry of Foreign Economic Affairs, carry out commercial indebtedness verification procedures, priority being given to the firms and suppliers united into regional clubs.

In December 1996, at the Forum of Commercial Creditors of the former USSR in London, financial conditions for the rescheduling of commercial indebtedness, similar to those of the London Club, were agreed upon with 12 regional creditor clubs. They agreed that Vnesheconombank would act as the "debtor" under agreements with leading clubs and commercial creditors. It also acts as the issuer of registered bonds.

CHAPTER **10**

INVESTMENT POLICY

Vladimir V. Kossov

Nineteen ninety-six is the first year in which a sharp decrease in the inflation rate occurred—it dropped from three to two figures. A substantial decrease in inflation is a prerequisite to stimulating investment. In 1997, Russia is expected to approach its lowest level of inflation ever. For the first time since 1992, an industrial decline will occur that will not accompany a global decline. This decline will be felt on the local level, particularly by industries. If the 1989 level is taken as the highest in the Soviet period, the volume of the gross domestic product is anticipated to decline by 50%, and the volume of capital investment by 75%. Even if the fact that the Soviet economy was subject to overaccumulation is taken into account, today's volume of capital investment in the economy, which is approximately $50 billion, is one-third the level needed for the normal development of Russia's current potential. The total volume of capital investment necessary to guarantee the functioning of a normal economy can be estimated at $130–$150 billion.[1]

Not less than $115–$135 billion should be generated by sources inside Russia, as determined by the following factor. The world investment total in 1995 was $315 billion. Considering the sharp competition between countries in the world capital market, it could be assumed that Russia's share will barely exceed 10%, or about $35 billion.

10.1 SOURCES OF INTERNAL INVESTMENTS. The Russian economy is shifting the investment focus from state-sector to private-sector investing. To mobilize additional financial resources, the Russian government adopted a program for attracting domestic and foreign investments. Along with macroeconomic stabilization, the program envisions restoring trust in national financial institutions by such measures as establishing mutual funds.

Among internal sources of investment, amortization and personal savings are the main ones. To protect amortization from inflation, the government has elaborated a system of indexation. Enterprises are given the right to accelerate their tax deductions on capital invested in the most modern types of equipment. As a result, the share of amortization in financing direct investments in 1995 was 45%. Economic entities, however, use only about half of the available depreciation charges for such investments. The second half is used primarily as a source to replenish circulating assets. The draft of the Tax Code outlines norms of amortization that can be used by groups with fixed assets. Profit that is reinvested in production is exempt from taxes if depreciation charges are used to their fullest extent for those purposes. The share of this source in the total volume of investments is approximately 15%.

---

[1]These figures are intended to illustrate the scale of the problem, and should not be considered a forecast in the strict sense.

Personal savings in Russia now exceed 20% of nominal income (before taxes). Only a small portion of savings, however, is used for investment and accounts for less than 10% of total investment capital. The problem is that a large portion of savings is spent on the purchase of hard currency. The program mentioned earlier includes specific measures to convince the population to keep their savings in rubles.

10.2 RATIONAL USE OF INVESTMENTS. The degree of rationalization of an investment process is determined by several factors. The first is related to the conversion of investment resources (primarily, the savings of the population) into real investments, that is, direct investment into concrete projects.

One of the important directions of the current structural transformation of the Russian economy is the normalization of the structure of material production. The normal structure of industry in a market economy resembles a seashore on which there are more small pebbles than large boulders. In the case of Soviet industry, the picture is completely different. Soviet industry is more like a seashore on which there are many large stones and very few small pebbles.

In this connection, the most important task involved in restructuring the Russian economy is to promote in every possible way the establishment of small and medium-sized enterprises. This will help fill the void within the material structure of production. To stimulate this process, incentives will be granted to small enterprises.

The practice of leasing is gaining more attention in regard to creating better conditions for the development of small business. The use of a limited portion of state resources to attract private investments helps entrepreneurs develop their businesses while being supported by the government. The tender system of support for highly promising investment projects (the term for recouping the cash outlay for these projects is not to exceed two years) allows entrepreneurs who invest not less than 20% of their own resources to receive from the government 20 to 50% of the necessary funding. These funds are granted on a basis determined by the character of the project: 20% is usually provided for regular commercial projects and up to 50% for "Russian" projects. Terms that will be beneficial under the circumstances of high inflation were established by reducing interest rates for state loans by 75%.

In accordance with the tender terms, the entrepreneur chooses a form of support: either a loan with a favorable interest rate or the sale of shares to the state. (In the latter case, the shares should be sold by the state two years later on the open market.) Despite the fact that the practice of making loans is one of the most expensive means of support, only one participant has heretofore chosen the sale of shares. This may be a sign that entrepreneurs have full confidence in their businesses and a corresponding reluctance to share their property.

CHAPTER 11

PRIVATIZATION

Alfred R. Kokh and Sergey V. Ivanenko

11.1 HISTORY.* The privatization of state enterprises is one of the necessary conditions for the formation of a market economy in Russia. The monopoly of state ownership in the Soviet Union, under which the state was considered the only owner, excluded the possibility of building production facilities on private property. The only personal property of citizens in regard to the state (and to other forms of socialist property) was secondary (derivative) and reserved for consumer items.

The law on property adopted by the Russian Federation in December 1990 stipulated for the first time the equality of different types of property. The law also regulates the possibility of transfer of state and municipal property to private property held by citizens and judicial persons.

The beginning of legitimate privatization regulated by laws occurred in 1991 when the government led by Yegor Gaidar came into office. In mid-1991, a law on privatization was prepared that outlined the procedures and terms of state property transfer. In 1992, the government program for privatization and the decree on vouchers were adopted.

The privatization of state property in Russia is a unique process that is unprecedented in the world. The creation of a broad stratum of free proprietors required mass privatization of state property and its transfer to private ownership. Since the short-term privatization of tens of thousands of enterprises was so demanding, it was impossible to take an individual approach to each case. The process that had begun in early 1992 reached the point by early 1996 at which 120,000 enterprises had been privatized. About 31% of them were privatized by becoming joint-stock companies, and 69% by being sold (see Exhibit 11.1). With the rapid pace of the privatization, there was no hope of getting the full price for the properties sold because domestic demand was very limited. Also, foreign investors had neither the opportunity nor the confidence to invest in the Russian market.

This can explain two specific features of the early stages of Russian privatization—its being implemented on a mass basis and the free, unregulated manner in which it had taken place. The Russian government has been repeatly blamed for these tactics.

In actuality, these features were clearly outlined in the "universal" procedures contained in the agreements on privatization, and in creating demand by distributing privatization coupons (vouchers) among the entire population.

Public opinion of the so-called voucher privatization is still not unanimous. The political and economic situation of that period should be kept in mind, however. The idea of using only public property for the production of goods was still strong among the people. The sale of "the people's property" to individuals for cash did not receive support and

---

*This section was written by Alfred R. Kokh.

Exhibit 11.1.   Major Indicators of the Process of Privatization

Years	Number of privatized units	Cost of privatized enterprises (in million rubles)	Sales price of privatized enterprises (in million rubles)	Ratio of total number of privatized enterprises to total number of enterprises (%)
1991–1992	48,295	20,799	164,678	19.2
1993	40,519	631,763	595,415	36.3
1994	23,811	439,193	851,499	47.0
1995	6,172	526,262	893,403	56.7
Total:	118,797	1,618,017	2,504,995	56.7

could not be used at that time as a strategy for privatization (even though, as the eastern European experience confirms, it is the most effective method for the economy). Also, it should be kept in mind that the so called directors corps was very influential in the privatization process. A lack of support for it would have significantly complicated privatization.

These circumstances resulted in a "people's privatization," which contained three different methods of transferring shares, and accompanying benefits, to an enterprise's employees and administration. The first stipulates the transfer of 35% of the shares to employees and 5% to the administration. The second grants employees the right to purchase 51%. According to the third, 30% of the shares are delegated to a group of managers who pledge to carry out privatization and to prevent the bankruptcy of the enterprise; 20% are to be given to the employees.

The world practice of corporate management demonstrates that such a large participation of employees in joint-stock capital diminishes the efficiency of management and its attractiveness to outside investors. This problem is urgent for Russian privatized enterprises, most of which (72.5%) were privatized in accordance with the second method of transfer. Nevertheless, vouchers became the first "stock" in Russia. Millions of ordinary people thus were introduced to the principles of stock-exchange trading and the market for stocks and securities. Vouchers became a kind of engine for the development of a share market without which the mechanism of attracting investments cannot function.

The voucher program was intended not only to distribute vouchers among the entire population, some of which was skeptical about the program, but also to find an effective mechanism for transforming vouchers into shares of privatized enterprises through specialized voucher auctions.

Another mechanism of mass participation in voucher privatization was the institution of voucher investment funds. These funds accumulated vouchers and then began actively seeking state property that was for sale. This activity created pressures among the people that influenced the power structure.

In 1992–93, mass privatization took place in small businesses, mostly in the trade, restaurant, and service industries. Also, privatization began of nonresidential properties where businesses were located. The first results were favorable—namely, an increase in production efficiency. Western experts do not consider the process here as successful as that in Eastern Europe, due to the Russian tradition of delegating control to employees. Nevertheless, a substantial improvement in service became evident after a few months of privatization. These results were achieved where enterprises were privatized on a tender basis. This restricted the possibilities for respecializing after privatization and for maintaining jobs over a certain period of time. The main buyers of privatized small businesses were their employees, who purchased from 70 to 100% of these enterprises.

The second stage of privatization took place between late 1993 and mid-1994. The beginning of this stage coincided with the adoption of the Russian Constitution on December 12, 1993. The Constitution secured the equality of all types of property, including private, in Russia. On December 24, the State Program for the Privatization of State and Municipal Enterprises was adopted. The program, which was adopted as law, outlined the main directions of voucher privatization. The major provisions of the program are still in effect.

The third stage of privatization began in mid-1994. That was the so-called cash privatization, which followed the completion of the voucher stage. Beginning in July 1994, vouchers were not in circulation. To purchase privatized objects, it became necessary to offer money rather than vouchers. The new stage was intended to ease the burden on the budget and increase the state's revenues. However, despite the fact that many countries, including Russia, considered this goal a top priority, it is a consequence of the myth that privatization will yield profitability. Of course, privatization will aid in accomplishing that goal, but not via gains generated by the sale of state property. The only way is through the growth of the gross national product (GNP) and the increase of tax revenues.

The analysis of the dynamics of privatization demonstrates that in 1995 privatization reached the saturation point. There was no longer any need for a rush of mass privatization. Governmental policies could be directed toward more specific targets, and the government began to show signs of tighter control over the management of state property. The result of these new trends was the beginning of the next stage of privatization—the transition to effective management of state property. At the same time, local authorities received more power in managing the property on their territories that was not considered federal property.

Among the first individual projects realized were mortgage auctions and the issuance of convertible bonds, such as those by the petroleum company LUKOIL. The necessity for undertaking these projects was dictated by the fact that a significant number of enterprises were owned by the state. The state owned 25–51% of the shares of 3,000 enterprises producing products and services strategically important for the national security. Such enterprises bring no profit to the federal budget. Since selling these shares is currently prohibited by the government, there is a movement afoot to change their status. If these enterprises are sold, the government receives money immediately. But shares can be transferred to their new owners only after the ban on their sale has been lifted. In the case of convertible bonds, their owners receive the shares after the redemption of the bonds. In the case of mortgage auctions, mortgage holders fulfill their rights as shareholders before the term of the mortgage has expired. After that they can sell their shares on a commission basis.

The realization of individual projects presupposes the following:

- The preparation of joint-stock companies that should complete consolidation of blocks of shares in the authorized capital; this measure is intended to strengthen vertical integration and improve the structure of shares management;
- The sale of shares by commercial tender after consulting a professional financial advisor; the advisor should be selected on a competitive basis and be responsible for organizing the tender, attracting prospective investors to participate in it, and preparing the necessary information.

The privatization of land has begun to occur on a cash basis. At present, enterprises are being privatized without the land on which they are located. This substantially diminishes an investment's attractiveness because the enterprise has less value. According to a presidential decree, privatized enterprises in which the state's share is less than 25% are allowed to buy the land on which they are located at a reasonable price. This is very important for establishing a property complex that includes the land and buildings.

The issue of land privatization, however, is still a subject of political dispute. Land privatization is regulated by the Duma as well as local authorities. It should be noted that according to the law entitled General Principles of Local Self-Administration, the privatization of municipal property is to be regulated entirely by local authorities.

The judicial basis for privatization in Russia is the set of laws entitled Privatization in the Russian Federation and The State Program for Privatization in the Russian Federation whose drafts by the State Duma are now pending.

It is evident that privatization in Russia continues to develop, and that its mechanisms are improving. These developments give hope that an effective market economy will be built in Russia.

11.2   PROBLEMS AND PROSPECTS.*   When the strategy for privatization was selected, its authors believed that a rapid implementation was more important than a thoroughly planned doctrine. The so-called first stage of privatization (1992–94) focused on quantitative factors and resulted in ambiguous outcomes. Since the goal was speed, little attention was paid to the negative consequences of giving away state property for free or at a purely symbolic price. In that sense, the goal was achieved.

Though we must give credit to the authors of reform for their efforts, especially considering the political difficulties of large-scale privatization, we should nevertheless take into account the serious problems that arose from this model of privatization.

First, privatization has been administrative, meaning that economic power still belongs to those who had it before, namely the *nomenklatura,* or the old administrative elite. The current condition of property in Russia is basically the result of the abrupt removal of state control over all aspects of economic life after August 1991. Only 10–15% of new managers are capable of working efficiently under market conditions. The dominance of the *nomenklatura* results in the new private sector having very limited access to resources. Therefore, new entrepreneurs have to adjust to what remains of the old state (or semistate) economy and operate in an environment that is actually criminal.

Second, the owners of the new corporations that evolved from former state enterprises are not only their ex-managers, but also government officials, gangsters, security guards, suppliers, and clients. These owners control the general environment of the enterprise, including its profits and expenses, and strive more for control (the chief objective of the old system) than to increase profitability and dividends. Under the current conditions of a legislative vacuum and a weak state, such a situation leads to a rapid decapitalization of these enterprises.

Third, 75% of Russia's enterprises have become the property of their employees. We have built and continue to build a mixture of collective property and a market system, a mixture that might be called market socialism. Although this practice is extremely inefficient and should be abandoned as soon as possible, it is very difficult to terminate, especially for large enterprises.

Fourth, in the course of privatization, the government cannot stop supporting big enterprises. The opposite side of the "big leap" policy in privatization is that it is very difficult to deny numerous enterprises (which are formally no longer state enterprises) subsidies and overt protectionism.

Fifth, there are no signs of substantial growth in the economic freedom of Russian business enterprises. Actually, their dependence on the state has merely changed from direct

---

*This section was written by Sergey V. Ivanenko.

administration to a diversified system of indirect administration reflected in the tax system, land and realty leases, and issuance of licenses. Under conditions where the power of the state is still justified, control over enterprises has become more decentralized.

Sixth, during the process of systematic transformation, the monopolization of the economy has been preserved and, in some cases, even strengthened. The consolidation of the present production structures in basic industries (fuel, energy, defense, and primary materials production) has been secured by huge holding companies. Public control of such super monopolies faces more obstacles than overt state monopolies.

The first (voucher) stage of privatization ended. The obvious result of this stage is the birth of a new sector of the economy. This new sector consists of enterprises that hold a large block of state shares and are dominated by former top managers supported by Mafia-like corporate groups. The economic activity of these semistate—semiprivate enterprises is very low because control over their management belongs not to investors, but to a few so-called accidental stockholders. These stockholders are those who received sufficient blocks of shares during the first stage of privatization, when state property was virtually free.

Today, a situation exists in which the state's ownership of any significant portion of its former holdings (especially blocks of shares and the property right of land on which privatized enterprises are located) has been lost. Control over the economic activity of new stock companies and over their profits has also been relinquished. Profit is usually taken by the actual owners, who have control over the management of the enterprise.

Regardless of how one feels about privatization, it is necessary to solve the problem concerning state shareholdings. There are three possible solutions that are currently being explored by various political groups:

1. *Cash privatization.* This is the method chosen by the present government. Cash privatization requires the prompt disposal of state property through sale to the highest bidder. The same approach is being applied to the privatization of land.

2. *Management of state property.* This is the alternative proposed by the so-called left opposition. It would terminate the sale of state shares and establish a system under which the state representatives of stock corporations would maximize revenues for the state treasury. Several members of the left opposition also oppose private ownership of land lots. They believe that for the efficient economic activity of stock companies, a long-term land lease is enough.

3. *Efficient privatization.* This alternative is preferred by the democratic opposition, particularly the association Yabloko. The essence of this approach is the sale of remnants of state property under the condition that the new owner accepts the obligation to increase the efficiency of the enterprise, either by restructuring it or investing in it. These measures would presumably result in increasing revenues. Accordingly, the privatization of land would be carried out only after proper legislation was created.

It is important to reject any top-down approach to system transformation. Instead, a policy should be created to pursue individual projects on the level of regions and enterprises, an activity that would promote the necessary transformation. Privatization would thus change from being a package of extreme measures to a set of regular management steps. The policy would also help eliminate the excessive politicization of this process.

The program carried out by executive authorities should be based on specified projects of privatization for each individual enterprise. The government should choose one of three approaches:

1. Selling of an enterprise or gaining control of a block of shares either at a high price or under the condition that a large investment will remain in its name.
2. Creating contracts with executives concerning the trustee management of blocks of shares.
3. Bankruptcy.

The essence of this approach is that a procedure for economically efficient privatization has been elaborated.

This approach involves three steps. In the first step, an investment tender auctions enterprises (or blocks of shares) and thus investments. In such cases, it is possible to sell real estate at a high price and the enterprise's assets at a low price, which is the most reasonable way to proceed with the privatization of a number of enterprises. Offers for tender will include only those enterprises that are subject to privatization and are in demand.

In addition it is necessary to single out those projects that are in high demand because of their high profitability (like fuel, energy, primary materials, processing, trade, hotel, and food industries) and to sell them at a higher price. It should be noted here that the initial bid offered at an auction should be high. The major political task of the authorities in this situation is to make a list of enterprises scheduled for privatization and schedule their auction dates.

In case an investment tender or auction failed due to the lack of an interested buyer, the second step should be taken. This involves a contract with a manager concerning the so-called trustee management of the property. According to the contract, the manager obtains all the owner's formal rights for a specified time in order to prepare the enterprise for an investment tender. It is possible to sign such a contract not only with an individual manager or with the management of an enterprise, but also with large commercial firms, including banks. Such cases, however, call for a great deal of caution. First, it is necessary to consider the consulting services offered by banks when a list of shares has been turned over to them for trustee management. An estimate of their basic rates should also be secured. Second, it is necessary to obtain the largest list of brokers possible and to negotiate with a number of investment consortia, including foreign companies. Third, it is very important to use the resources of Russian commercial institutions (including banks) for solving the most difficult problems of privatization, that is, the formation of investment tenders and the restructuring of enterprises. Such resources should not be employed, however, for the relatively simple task of completing a discount sale.

The third step consists of launching a bankruptcy system. If the situation of the enterprise is not improving, then the contract with the manager should be terminated and a new contract be signed with another manager to recommence the process. Changing the property structure through bankruptcy may be advisable in some formally privatized enterprises. Federal and local budgets should be considered because there will be substantial expenses in restructuring these enterprises and supporting priority industries. One of the conditions for state support should be the formation of a reasonable internal structure of the property held by these enterprises.

The final goal of the proposed model of privatization is to attract investments and to revive the economy. Only when there are investment tenders, efficient management, and policy decisions that protect private property, will investments begin to flow into the economy.

CHAPTER 12

INDUSTRY AND AGRICULTURE

Arkadiy I. Volskiy, Viktor N. Hklystun, and E. Serova

12.1 INDUSTRY: PROBLEMS AND FORECAST.* Diversified Russian industries achieved a level of production in 1995 that provided approximately one-third of the gross domestic product (GDP).

The protracted crisis during the transitional economy has affected industrial production the most. The structure of industrial production has changed drastically with the growth of the raw-materials sector. The share of fuel and energy industries increased from 12% in 1990 to 31% in mid-1995. Over 19% of the production volume comes from metallurgy, along with 15% from chemicals, forestry, and construction materials. At the same time, the share of the investment sector (particularly in mechanical engineering and the metalworking industry) in industrial production comprises 16%, and the share of consumer goods and food-processing industries comprises another 15%.

These structural shifts are especially unpleasant because they are taking place while production volume on the whole is shrinking. By 1995, industrial production had decreased by 48%; metallurgy had decreased by 45%, mechanical engineering and metalworking industries by 56%, and light industries by 70%.

The problems inherited from the administrative command system have been compounded. The command system is a weak mechanism for the production of consumer goods. It has resulted in available products that are insufficiently competitive and a high degree of militarization of the economy. This or the latter effect has produced a broad gap between civilian and defense sectors. Other results include an obsolescence rate of equipment approaching 50 or 60% in some industries, the autarchy of the national industrial complex, inadequate participation in the world division of labor, and isolation from the global processes of economic, technological, and scientific developments. Other hindrances to integration into the world market include the low technological level of many industries, and the inability of many industries to adopt scientific and technological methods that would facilitate innovation and production. Related issues include the improvement of the production apparatus, more efficient processing of raw materials, and the reduction of material and energy consumption input per unit of final industrial production.

The situation has worsened because of the break up of economic ties during the reform. The situation has been further aggravated by a sharp decrease in demand, mistakes in fiscal and credit policy, increase in the price of energy and raw materials, and the failure to convert the economy from one based on defense industries.

In order to solve these problems of economic reform, government and nongovernment industrial and business associations are trying to put a two-part plan into effect. First, they

---

*This section was written by Arkadiy I. Volskiy.

are implementing a rational and structural policy that would meet the specific needs of Russia. Second, they are soliciting investments of Russian private capital as well as of foreign capital, an effort that should be strongly supported by the government.

The new structural policy is aimed at a revival of the country's scientific and technical potential, based on advanced technologies and other new scientific achievements. The goal of the policy is directed at reducing the share of the raw-materials sector by increasing the share of manufacturing industries, especially science-intensive industries, the service sector, and intellectual activity.

To support long-term federal and interstate industrial growth, government resources have been redirected from supporting nonproductive industries to stimulating the growth of the more efficient private sector, including privatized enterprises and private capital investments. It is hoped that this will stop the drop in production of the older industries, in particular, by the acquisition and reconstruction of the most viable of them.

There are three main tactics of the structural policy:

1. *The technological modernization of the Russian economy* that is intended to recoup qualitative losses of fixed capital that occurred during the current crisis, and to establish the preconditions for stable economic growth in late 1990s.

2. *The strengthening of the national industrial infrastructure* that involves the accumulation of resources, including budgetary resources for financing federal roads, ports, airports, and communication systems. This will contribute to stable economic growth and help solve the unemployment problem.

3. *By the development of exports, particularly high-tech products,* domestic demand will increase. Priority should be given to the sectors with unique advanced technology and competitive potential in the world market. There are a number of such industries in Russia.

One of the main directions of Russian economic policy is state stimulation of such new institutions as strong national and transnational corporations, and industrial and financial groups. These new corporations need to be capable of modernizing their facilities and equipment, and creating organizational and managerial structures, and channeling needed capital into production by merging financial capital and industry. These corporations proved they can overcome production downturns and a nonpayment crisis, and promote the reasonable conversion and modernization of out-of-date technologies.

Also, it is very important to form a new system of contract relations between large and small businesses. Through such relations, the competitive potential of small companies will be in demand by large industrial, trading, and even financial corporations.

The essence of the new stage of structural transformation is the goal of increasing production efficiency by individual enterprises. Now is the time for an internal stimulus that will motivate enterprises to reduce costs and prices, to increase labor productivity, and to master new production techniques.

An analysis of developments at manufacturing plants demonstrates their extensive adaptation to new conditions dictated by their entrance into a market economy. The strategic vision of top management, a thorough integration of the industries' administrative teams, an ongoing concern about technology and product quality, and most important, a higher level of economic performance, should yield excellent chances for success in the market place. In the first six months of 1995, a variety of innovations were introduced by more than 50% of the country's manufacturing enterprises, while in 1994, similar innovations were introduced by only 40%.

The reduction in the total industrial output had some positive consequences because it forced the industrial sector to eliminate unnecessary production and reduce excessive capacities. This phenomenon was particularly evident in mechanical engineering and defense industries where 15–25% of the slower industries were eliminated.

In the first quarter of 1995, the nonstate sector produced 84% of the total output, including 12% by private enterprises. Thus the nonstate sector finally became dominant in Russian industry.

Demilitarization of the economy, use of accumulated production, and mobilization of the military's potential (encompassing the defense industry, as well as civilian industries filling military orders) are other important trends in the structural reshaping of the economy. In 1992–93, 14 government conversion programs were started. Among them were the rebirth of the Russian fleet, and conversions of civilian aviation, forestry, the industrial complex, the agro-industrial sector, medicine, and the energy complex.

The ultimate result of these must be the establishment of modern production techniques and facilities, with new technologies, strong engineering, and a research and development foundation. This production system must be capable of designing and creating the military equipment necessary for maintaining current military programs, and also of supplying durable consumer goods and mass-investment products. While maintaining the military portion of their production, these enterprises should become economically independent and form a basis for the long-term growth of an emerging market economy.

Market reform mechanisms that were supposed to lead Russia out of the crisis have been irrevocably neglected.

What can be expected in the near future for Russian industry? Considering the economic conditions and potential investment volume of late 1996, it is reasonable to expect that in 1997 industrial stagnation will cease. In the energy, metallurgy, and food-processing industries, there is some likelihood that production will increase. And 1997 will probably bring an increase in industrial output on the whole. The period of 1995–97 should see significant changes in the industrial structure. By 1997, it is expected that manufacturing industries, as part of the total volume of industrial output, will stop declining.

This trend is related to a reorientation of the external market for raw materials, demand for which is limited by the relatively low growth rate of developed economies. The trend is also related to the fact that Russian manufacturing industries, which are not competitive because of their high consumption of resources, will have to reduce costs.

A noninflationary increase in the demand for industrial products and steadily growing sales in domestic and foreign markets are possible only when production efficiency is high. As mentioned, creating this condition will require a decrease in the use of resources, a turn toward resource-efficient technologies, and an increase in returns on investment. This leads to the crucial issue of industrial strategy which will require production methods that effectively use resource-maximizing technologies and equipment, while producing better quality products.

The most significant corrective measures are being implemented in the investment sphere, particularly in mechanical engineering and metalworking. Among these measures are the following:

- Expanded production of modern equipment for mining and manufacturing, including for increased oil extraction and processing, mechanization, and safety in coal mines;

- Improvement in the production of commercial vehicles in terms of a fuel type, load capacity, diesel fuel consumption, small tonnage sizes, and specialized types of vehicles;
- Development of competitive machine equipment and tools;
- Increased production of modern transportation, construction, and road vehicles, including those for low-story building and cottage production;
- Adequate supply of modern printing equipment, including machines for processing textual and visual information;
- Development of modern cash register production;
- Cost reduction in the production and expansion of a wide range of agricultural equipment and equipment for the agro-industrial complex.

An analysis of the economic situation demonstrates that in the short-run, such products as tractors, trucks, dredges, forklifts, graders, wristwatches, as well as other types of equipment, machines, and tools will be competitive in the domestic market. Active support for the aviation industry, nuclear and mechanical engineering, and the space program could make them competitive in the international market. In 1997, the expected stabilization of production should lead to the beginning of growth for some mechanical engineering products.

12.2   MAJOR RESULTS OF AGRARIAN REFORMS: 1992–96.* Agrarian reforms in Russia were initiated by general economic reform. That is why the reforms were directed toward economic issues from the beginning (i.e., to make the agrarian sector efficient and less dependent on the state budget). The general economic reforms in Russia were aimed at the transition from a totalitarian, centrally planned economy to a market economy. Therefore, it became necessary to create productive units in the agrarian sector able to operate on their own under new conditions, which collective (*kolkhoz*) and soviet (*sovkhoz*) economic units were largely unable to manage in their existing forms.

Above all, conditions were created for the development of family-operated farms. The first people who rented land in sovkhozes and kolkhozes were strongly dependent on their leasors. Later, it became possible to obtain land with the right-of-lifetime ownership and the right to bequeath it by heritage, but with no right of sale or leasing. However, the kolkhozes and sovkhozes were slow in distributing the land. In many areas, numerous social conflicts arose due to land disputes.

(a)   Defining the Terms of Land Ownership through Legislation and Reorganization. During the initial reform period, polls showed that only 10 to 15% of peasants wanted to leave kolkhozes and sovkhozes and act on their own land. So it was necessary to develop a means of reorganizing the existing large kolkhozes and sovkhozes, which were the main producers of agricultural products, and transforming them into market entities.

At the end of 1991, key resolutions were passed that marked the beginning of the present stage of agrarian reform. All kolkhozes and sovkhozes had to be reorganized in one year. During this rather formal procedure, collectives of enterprises received practically all the land cultivated by them up to that time, and all funds as collective property. These were free of charge and with no conditions. All the funds received had to be divided among workers and pensioners on the basis of conditional shares; land was divided equally, while

---

*This section was written by Viktor N. Hklystun and E. Serova.

other property was divided based on its value and the number of days worked at the collective enterprise. Owners of shares were further given the right to fully and independently determine their fate. It was possible, for example, to take one's share in products and leave the enterprise to organize one's own business. It was also possible to put these shares into the collective enterprise and keep working there.

Land shares were not very large by Russian standards (six to ten hectares per person). To avoid fragmentation, the state allowed the selling and leasing of shares within kolkhozes and sovkhozes. Hence, peasants wanting to set up their own farms could enlarge their land by buying or leasing shares from their neighbors.

(b)   Three Alternatives for Farmers.   As a result of these decisions, the number of farmers rose sharply; at the beginning of 1992, there were fewer than 50,000 farmers in Russia, while there are now 280,000. Acquiring land is no longer a key issue. During a two-year period, nearly all the kolkhozes and sovkhozes in Russia were reorganized. According to the conditions for reorganization, these enterprises had three main alternatives.

First, they could become joint-stock companies or productive cooperatives, an option that most enterprises in agriculture chose. The variety of names of the reorganized kolkhozes and sovkhozes is not an indication of the reality of the situation, however. Most of them, independent of their names, were transformed into productive cooperatives where the main funds belong to the collective with the rights of shared property and a management based on electoral cooperative principles (e.g., "one member, one vote"; distribution of profits mainly based on work and not on shares; elected president and management, etc.). There were also real joint-stock companies, but they were few.

The second alternative was motivated by the fact that, in the beginning of the reforms, a group opposed to reorganization emerged. Primarily because of badly implemented preparatory work, these opponents began to interpret the measures taken to reorganize enterprises as a forced process, although in fact all procedures were voluntary. Facing certain resistance from peasants in the spring of 1992, the government permitted those enterprises that did not want to reorganize themselves to retain their status. Presently, about one-third of the enterprises have done so. But they also have taken land and funds as their property and, as a rule, have divided it into shares. Keeping the previous status of an enterprise is, thus, essentially the same as keeping its previous name.

Finally, the most radical and difficult alternative regarding reorganization was the full liquidation of old enterprises and their division into small, technologically advanced productive units—farms, agricultural cooperatives, and private or cooperative enterprises of service. As a rule, these subentities use and keep the productive infrastructure of the previous enterprise. There are about 1,000 such enterprises (out of 27,000 kolkhozes and sovkhozes), including well-known enterprises in the Nizhnegorodsk region.

(c)   Changes in the Structure of Agrarian Producers.   During the last several years, the number of private farms has risen sharply. Undoubtedly, they serve as a catalyst for the real market in the agrarian sector. The process of farm formation has slowed recently, which is explained first by the fact that the 10 to 15% of peasants who wanted to set up farms have left their kolkhozes and sovkhozes; and second, they work under difficult conditions and lack the promised government aid. It is also necessary to note that most peasants are not skilled enough to operate a somewhat commercial economic entity.

The second change in the structure of producers in the agrarian sector was the transformation of agricultural enterprises. Of course, it would be naive to expect that the name change from kolkhozes to joint-stock companies could create a new motivational mechanism for employees and farms in general. This did not and could not happen. The real task for agricultural enterprises is attaining formal, legal separation from the state systems of financing, marketing, distribution and supply, with the hope that, under the influence of market environment, they would begin to adapt economically, and to change their structure and behavior accordingly. These changes are intended for the long term and will not be realized in the immediate future. Certain social and economic consequences of the first stage of reorganization are already apparent, however.

(d) Three Methods for Setting Up New Farms. Three main types of transformations of the former kolkhozes and sovkhozes have already appeared. The first is the division of enterprises into small, independent productive subentities—family-operated farms, partnerships, cooperatives, etc. Some enterprises do this very quickly. Although the division usually goes more smoothly if it has been preceded by painstaking preparation, it is often carried out spontaneously, without any groundwork. In many cases, the preparation occurs in stages. In many enterprises, leases and other similar forms of economic self-sufficiency are applied. In today's economic conditions, such forms inevitably lead to the next step, legal formalization of the division.

The second method of economic transformation of large enterprises is common in regions with high grain production. These are efficient enterprises with highly industrial technologies to handle the output, and usually with well-educated, energetic employees capable of and wanting to make production more efficient. In these enterprises, concentration of property in the hands of a small group of co-owners occurs by means of buying, exchanging, and renting shares. Such agricultural and industrial enterprises, especially natural monopolies, are being actively bought, for example, the oil complex GaspromYu, Rosenergo, several railroads, etc. In the future, these and other enterprises, probably in a somewhat diminished form, will become big commercial farms controlled by a small group or even by a single efficient proprietor, renting land from local inhabitants and hiring a considerable number of people, mainly for seasonal work. There is no well-written legislation concerning land ownership in these cases.

Finally, the third and least desirable, but probably inevitable method in today's situation, is clearly evident in many of Russia's nonblack-soil regions, which face a serious economic crisis in the agrarian sector. Most of these farms are likely to retain their collective form no matter what (their names—a kolkhoz or joint-stock company); but in fact many peasants will leave for their private auxiliary farms (PAF). The collective parts of funds will only be used for serving the PAFs. Production will be cut to the level necessary for the survival of peasants' families, and their stock of two or three cows, pigs, birds, etc. With a rise in demand for agricultural products, the most competitive PAFs will become the basis for the quick establishment of farms in these regions.

During the agrarian reform, the importance of PAFs rose sharply. All the restrictions imposed on this sector were lifted, and peasants received rather large pieces of land for auxiliary farming. The lifting of the restriction obligating farmers to supply agricultural products to the state allowed them to distribute the increasing quantity of agricultural products among their employees in the form of either free or very low-priced products. This also created a favorable basis for the development of PAFs. In addition, the weakening of discipline in farms led to a rise in the theft of collective property, a situation that enhances the potential of PAFs.

Thus, the rapid development of PAFs is entirely due to the structural changes in collective farming. A widespread transformation of PAFs into farms is possible only with a strong and unfavorable external economic influence, and with a certain economic obligation. Working in a PAF also psychologically prepares one for full separation from the collective-farm system and for setting up one's own farm.

(e) Creating an Adequate Market Infrastructure and Policy.   In today's agrarian reform, the emphasis is being shifted to the creation of an adequate market infrastructure for producers of agricultural products and formation of an effective state agrarian policy. Private farms reorganized into large agricultural enterprises will be able to succeed as real market entities only with the presence of an adequate distribution system for products, supplies, services, and loans. The state regulation of the agro-industrial complex has to correspond to the principles of a market-oriented economy, in order to support the commercialization of this sector of economy and protect the interests of both domestic producers and consumers.

These problems were addressed from 1992 to 1994. Together with the institutional reform of the agrarian sector, land relations were developed: private ownership of land became well established, renting and pawning began to develop, and in several regions a land market was born. Land is increasing in value, and it is becoming capital, which is very important in this process. The legal basis of the land market, however, is not sufficiently developed yet. There remains political misunderstanding among governmental institutions about the land market. Nevertheless, a "gray" land market has begun to form in the regions with high demand.

Several steps have been taken to liberalize the markets for agricultural products: government purchases and the distribution of resources by the center have been sharply cut, the prices for foodstuffs and agricultural raw materials have been almost fully liberalized, and international trade markets for these products have opened up. It can be claimed that 1994 was the last year of government purchases of agricultural products: government purchases of grain with existing federal and regional funds are subject to a formal definition, while the funds for other products are nonexistent.

The traditional system of government purchases has almost fully ceased, but the replacement of this system with market structures is proceeding rather slowly. The producers of agricultural products are often faced with difficulties in distributing their products, while periodic shortages of products occur in the market. In this situation, the fight against the so called monopolists of the processing industry is continuing. The situation has lead to the further underfinancing of the industry and a corresponding decrease in the opportunities to enlarge distribution channels for the entire foodstuffs industry. This situation accounts for the financial crisis in the agricultural sector and, the necessity for prolonging debts.

(f) Subsidies and the Future of the Market.   The level of subsidies for the agrarian sector is still high. Expenditures for agriculture constitute almost one-fourth of the federal budget, while the agrarian sector share of gross domestic product is about 18%. The largest share of these expenses goes to subsidies for livestock production and, until 1994, to subsidies for privileged loans to producers of agricultural products. The expense of maintaining the productivity of land is also considerable.

The principal problem today is not only the reduction of the agrarian sector's share of the national budget, which is actually a political, noneconomic problem, but also the more important issue of the effective use of subsidies. The subsidies established during the reform period not only have failed to support the sector, but also have played a depressing and harmful role. Shining examples of such subsidies are those for livestock production and so-called state-leasing operations.

In 1992, the introduction of direct subsidies to livestock producers, in response to a decreased demand for these products, led to a fall in purchase prices and a corresponding deterioration of the financial situation of agricultural producers. Similarly, in 1994 the introduction of leasing operations for agricultural equipment, which were intended to facilitate its purchase by producers, resulted in 20 to 30% increase in prices. Many forms of subsidies simply do not reach producers or reach them so late that they lose their real value.

In today's conditions, state subsidies for agriculture cannot be a source of real investment for the sector because it is small relative to the demand, a fact that is not understood by most agrarian lobbyists. The national budget can only support certain aspects of the restructuring or act as a buffer for the most negative social consequences of the reconstruction. As the experience of the last few years shows, all efforts to increase the agrarian budget result in a rise in the inflation rate, which, due to the specifics of the agrarian sector, negatively influences it. Nineteen ninety-five was a breakthrough year for the agro-industrial complex in its adaptation to the market. The problems that accumulated during the last years in the agrarian sector do not give much hope that production will increase in the near future, but there are some processes that may give rise market changes. For example, relative prices in the agro-industrial complex have moved closer to world prices, have become more stable, and have even been regarded as being favorable to agriculture. Together with the positive changes in the federal government's financial policy in regard to the agro-industrial complex, these price trends somewhat reduced the financial tensions of the last year.

With further reduction of the state's interference with the agro-industrial sector, the dealer sector has become more active, and the market infrastructure is being formed. Producers of agricultural products do not rely on state assistance as much as before, and private business has become more attractive to them. Despite all the unsolved problems, the current changes in the sector show that it is moving in the direction of a market-oriented economy and, hence, closer to possible regulation by the methods appropriate to the market.

CHAPTER 13

RUSSIAN FINANCIAL CORPORATION: A STATE ENTERPRISE

Andrei A. Nechaev

13.1 OVERVIEW. A key economic task facing the Russian government is altering its role in the investment process by moving from direct investment to the commitment of public funds to stimulate private investment. To meet this objective, the government has established specialized financial investment institutions that lend public funds on preferential terms. These loans include a charge and are repayable at maturity. The purpose of the loans is to provide funds for investment projects that are high-yielding undertakings and are financed largely from nonpublic capital sources.

Among the earliest of these specialized financial investment institutions is the state-owned Russian Financial Corporation (RFC), created pursuant to a presidential decree in March 1993. In it the RFC was given the status of a government agency for working with domestic and foreign investors.

The RFC is fully owned by the state, but it is financially self-sufficient, operating on commercial principles. The RFCs bylaws have been endorsed by the government and approved by the State Property Committee. The RFC holds a license from the Russian Finance Ministry to operate on the securities market as an investment company, a financial broker, and an investment consultant, with the right to deal with private individuals. It also holds a license from Russia's Central Bank to conduct selected banking operations in rubles and foreign exchange.

The RFC is also an authorized agent commissioned by the Russian State Property Committee, the Russian Federal Property Foundation, and the Moscow government to manage privatization programs and to examine investment programs drawn up by enterprises slated for privatization.

13.2 OBJECTIVES AND AREAS OF OPERATION. The following are the RFC's key objectives:

- Selecting, examining, and financing investment projects, using public and private funds
- Providing supervision over efficient use of the invested funds
- Recruiting investors, including foreign capital, on a commercial basis
- Issuing, on the government's instructions, state guarantees to foreign investors and creditors

- Using, on the government's instructions, foreign loans, including allocation of funds on a competitive basis
- Conducting securities market operations

The RFC's main areas of operations include the following:

- Examining and developing business plans and investment projects to meet Western requirements. The RFC uses modern Western and domestic programming tools to evaluate the financial standing of enterprise and the extent of investment risk exposure, adapted to Russian statistical, accounting, and economic practices;
- Financing investment projects and programs by attracting public and private funds, including foreign investors' capital;
- Providing services to Russian and foreign companies that are looking for partners and investment targets.

The RFC cooperates with a number of well-known banks, investment and consulting firms, and manufacturing companies in Austria, the Czech Republic, Germany, Great Britain, Greece, Italy, the Netherlands, and the United States. It also has a working relationship with leading Russian banks, investment companies, and stock exchanges.

The RFC maintains vigorous relations with renowned international and national investment promotion institutions, including the American Overseas Private Investment Corporation (OPIC), the Italian Promotion Organization (SIMEST), the German bank Kreditanstalt fur Wiederaufbau, the European Bank for Reconstruction and Development (EBRD), the International Financial Corporation, and the United Nations Industrial Development Organization (UNIDO), headquartered in Vienna.

13.3   INVESTMENT ACTIVITIES.   The RFC assists government-owned enterprises that wish to become privatized. The RFC provides guidance for developing privatization plans and investment programs. It also helps Russian and foreign investors to acquire stakes in promising Russian enterprises.

The RFC is licensed by the Russian Finance Ministry as an investment company, a financial broker, and an investment consultant, with the right to deal with private individuals. It provides high-yielding outlets for customers' funds in the financial and stock markets and invests them in fast-payback and high-yielding projects. The RFC deals actively with the Finance Ministry's foreign exchange bonds and other government and corporate securities, including government bonds, corporate short- and long-term bonds, and treasury notes. The RFC issues its own bonds in rubles and U.S. dollars, and its bond-issue prospectus is registered with the Finance Ministry.

13.4   BANKING SERVICES.   The RFC holds a license from the Russian Central Bank to conduct some banking operations, including lending, trust, and depository services and financial management. The banking network of the daughter bank of RFC named "Investcredit" covers about 50 Russian regions. Working both on its own and through its subsidiary banks RFC provides its customers with modern banking services in roubles and hard currencies.

The RFC is authorized dealer of the Central Bank of Russia to operate with all types of Russian state bonds and securities.

13.5 INFORMATION AND EDUCATION. The RFC is active in presenting investment projects and opportunities offered by the Russian financial market, and in offering training courses to financial market participants. To this end, the RFC arranges regular conferences and seminars, and sponsors training courses on investments and on financial and stock-market operations. The RFC maintains a database of investment projects, issues methodological and information materials, and publishes thematic journals and monographs.

13.6 SUBSIDIARIES. The RFC has established several subsidiaries to provide services in various investment fields in Russia. These include the following:

- The Interbank Investment Union—Bank of Regions "Investcredit"
- The United National Insurance Company
- The National Insurance Brokerage Group
- The Trade House of RFC
- Security agency "Investment security"
- An international business journal, *Investments,* and a business journal, *Financier*

The RFC is a cofounder of several investment-oriented banks, including the Russian Bank for Reconstruction and Development, the Investcredit Interbank Association, Crossinvestbank, and Creditsojuzcombank. The RFC is closely cooperating with the Russian Association of Private and Privatized Enterprises and is a member of the Russian Business Round Table, which is the country's association of labor unions and organizations.

The RFC is headed by the well-known economist and politician, former Minister of Economy in the first post-communist government, Dr. Andrei Netchaev.

13.7 REGIONAL CENTERS AND HEADQUARTERS. The RFC has worked with local authorities and business communities to create regional branches in key industrial areas across Russia, in particular, the Northwest (based in St. Petersburg), the South Urals (Chelyabinsk), Central Black Earth (Belgorod), South Russia and Northern Caucasus (Rostov), and Far East (Nakhodka). In addition, the RFC has co-sponsored the establishment of several regional investment units, including the Mordovian Economic Investment Center and the Daghestan Financial Corporation.

The RFC is headquartered in downtown Moscow, close to the Duma, at the following address: Russian Financial Corporation, 1 Georgievsky Pereulok, Moscow 103009, Russia, tel. 0070952929107.

PART IV

FINANCIAL SYSTEM

CHAPTER 14

OVERVIEW OF THE FINANCIAL SYSTEM

Vladimir G. Panskov

14.1 RESTRUCTURING. The Russian financial system is undergoing restructuring as a result of the current economic and political conditions. The process will be nearly completed in 1995–96 with the adoption of a number of very important laws. These laws will define judicial and organizational mechanisms of various financial institutions, their interaction, and the combination of efficient governmental control and the free and independent functioning of economic units. The laws will secure the positive changes that recently occurred in the financial sector. They will help overcome the mistakes and contradictions of inefficient government regulation by stimulating Russian socioeconomic and political development.

The transition to a market economy, while based on examples from the world, also takes into consideration Russia's peculiarities. The transition is expressed in the gradual formation of optimum macroeconomic relationships involving the accumulation and redistribution of the nation's financial resources via a budget system, other financial institutions, and state-owned and private enterprises.

14.2 BUDGET SYSTEM. The political structure of Russia as a federal state is based on the 1993 Constitution. The Constitution requires consistent implementation of budget federalism, the optimal distribution of the budget's resources, judicial independence, and income stabilization.

The budget system of the Russian Federation consists of:

- A federal (national) budget
- Budgets of the 89 subjects of the Federation, that is, the republics; budgets of other autonomous territories, regions and districts; and regional budgets for cities of federal significance such as Moscow and St. Petersburg
- 30,000 local budgets (cities, towns, and villages)

Aggregate budget revenues from all three levels, which comprise the consolidated budget, amounted in 1993 to 30.5% of the gross domestic product, and in 1994 to 27.9%. The federal budget share in the 1994 consolidated budget was revenues 48.9%, expenditures 50.6%. The fact that expenditures exceeded revenues caused a deficit in the federal budget. The regional and local budgets show greater revenues than expenditures.

During recent years, some decrease of the federal budget deficit has been achieved: in 1994 the deficit was 9.5% of GDP; for 1995 its limit was set at 7.3%. In 1997, the federal budget deficit is planned as approximately 3% of GDP. Beginning in 1995, the deficit of the federal budget finally decreased. This allowed the government to cover the deficit by distributions of government stocks (securities) among Russian banks and commercial institutions, instead of issuing new money. Foreign loans also played an important role in reducing the deficit. As of 1998, borrowing from international financial institutions is expected to decrease significantly.

In 1994, a reform in interbudget relations was instituted between the federal government and subjects of the Federation. Instead of the old system whereby the region's revenues and expenditures were strictly controlled and regulated by the top levels of government, a new system was introduced, which entrusted planning to regional levels based on their financial security. A unified budget fund was established, financed by the consolidated budget revenues. This fund is intended to provide the subjects of the Federation with financial support on the basis of the principle of equality. In practice, there were many advantages to this approach. It became evident, however, that improvement of the transfer mechanism is required in order to continue decentralization of financial resources. This improvement will also stimulate local government authorities to develop their own revenue sources, attract investors, and carry structural economic transformations into outlying regions.

The new law on budget structure and budget processes in Russia replaces the 1991 law. The new law defines the basic concept of the federal budget and helps define financial and taxation policies. The new law also delineates principles of budget structure for Russia as a federal state, and guarantees the equality of all subjects of the Federation in terms of budget relations with federal authorities. The law regulates all levels of state authorities regarding budget creation, approval, and implementation, and spells out rules for budget regulation and partial redistribution of financial resources among regions.

Another task is the improvement of the links between subjects of the Federation and local budgets in order to develop unified regulatory and legal norms in the entire country.

14.3 TAXES.   The majority of revenues for both federal and consolidated budgets comes from taxes. The current fiscal system began with the Law on Fundamental Principles of the Taxation System in the Russian Federation adopted in December 1991. The main features of the taxation system are:

- Combination of direct and indirect taxes
- Differentiation of taxation power between federal and other bodies of power
- Coordination of treasury interests and the market interests of manufacturers
- Single taxation regime for enterprises and organizations irrespective of the type of ownership
- Differentiation of taxation levels based on income and property

These principal fundamentals are elaborated and secured in the new law, which was passed by the Russian Parliament.

Federal taxes include a value-added tax, indirect taxes on some goods and some mineral raw materials, a federal tax on profits, taxes related to the use of natural resources, a personal income tax, customs duty, a tax on sales of combustibles, tolls, licenses and registration fees. Regional and local taxes include a regional tax on profits, a business property tax, a land tax, a personal property tax, an inheritance tax, municipal taxes, regional and local license and registration fees, and hotel and resort fees. Also, subjects of the Federation have the right to add other taxes to these. General rules for imposing certain taxes are described by federal laws. Primarily, they involve limitations on taxation and the granting of tax exemptions to various organizations, particularly, the budget organizations.

Among the most important changes to be rendered by the new law are tax reduction, simplification of the tax system, and the regulation of relations between taxpayers and tax collectors. The legal tax cut is supposed to be compensated by more efficient tax collection.

14.4 NONBUDGET FUNDS.   Along with the budget system, a significant role is performed by state nonbudget funds. Mostly they have a social purpose: pension funds, social insurance funds, compulsory medical-insurance funds, and the state fund of employment. All these funds have the same primary source, a set percentage of deductions from employee-payroll funds made by enterprises and organizations. These deductions are included in the production and service cost. In 1995, the majority of enterprises and organizations contributed 39% to those funds: 27% to the Pension Fund, 5.4% to the Social Insurance Fund, 3.6% to the Compulsory Medical Insurance Fund, and 2% to the Employment Fund.

The Pension Fund of the Russian Federation was established as an independent financial institution in 1991, the decision of the Parliament in December 1990. It is a federal fund with branches in all regions. The fund's resources are being used for retirement payments, premature retirement payments to the unemployed, retirement payments to the military and their dependents, and social-security checks. It is also being used for benefits to children, as well as financial support and funerals for the Chernobyl victims and victims of other disasters. The majority of employers deduct 28% of payroll funds for the Pension Fund, farmers and professionals who own private practices pay 5%, and 1% is deducted from the employees payroll.

The Social Insurance Fund operates as a specialized federal financial and credit institution, according to a presidential decree in August 1992. The Fund has regional branches. Its resources are used to pay benefits for temporary disability, pregnancy and maternity leave, and sanitariums for the employed population, among other benefits.

The State Employment Foundation, was established by a parliamentary decree in June 1993. Its fund has federal and regional levels. The foundation's resources are designated for professional training and/or retraining of the unemployed, unemployment benefits, compensation for income loss and expenses for moving to another city to take a new job. The Fund also has resources for creating jobs both public and private.

Federal and regional funds for compulsory medical insurance are administered by independent state financial and credit institutions founded in accordance with a parliamentary decree of February 1993. These funds are intended to provide medical insurance for the general population, that is, to ensure that all Russian citizens have equal access to medical services.

Since the so-called financial legislature is still underdeveloped, numerous other federal and regional funds have recently mushroomed. The Ministry of Finance strives to incorporate all of the these funds into a budget system while maintaining its main mission and goals.

14.5 ADMINISTRATIVE BRANCHES.   The administrative organs of the financial system are being improved. A government decree in August 1994 confirmed and adopted the provision of the Ministry of Finance. According to the decree, the ministry is a federal organ with executive authority designated to implement a unified government financial policy and guide the Russian financial system. The Ministry of Finance of the Russian

Federation, comparable ministries in the autonomous republics, and other financial institutions in the regions comprise the whole system of state control over finances in Russia.

The main tasks of the Russian Ministry of Finance are:

- Setting and following strategic directives of state financial policy;
- Drafting and implementing a federal budget;
- Providing stability for the state financial system and ensuring its contribution to the social and economic development of the country;
- Implementing measures to develop the financial market;
- Concentrating financial resources for priorities in the social and economic development of the country and regions;
- Attracting foreign-credit capital and designing methods for repaying debts;
- Improving methods of finance, budget planning, and reporting;
- Controlling rational expenditures of both budget and federal nonbudget resources.

In conjunction with the Federal Tax Service and other concerned federal agencies, the Ministry of Finance:

- Works to improve taxation policies and the taxation system;
- Participates, along with the Ministry of Economics and the Central Bank, in elaborating and implementing measures to establish commodity-money proportions, stabilize monetary circulation, and strengthen the purchasing power of the ruble;
- Is responsible for improving monetary and credit relations with foreign countries, increasing the country's currency resources, and ensuring effective spending;
- Takes part in elaborating the financial terms of agreements with foreign countries;
- Performs other duties delegated by the government.

To improve management of the financial system and in accordance with a presidential decree in December 1992, a centralized system of federal treasury agencies was established. This system consists of the main agency of the Federal Treasury of the Ministry of Finance and subordinate territorial branches.

The main tasks of the treasury system are:

- Organization, implementation, and control of the federal budget performance;
- Control of the budget's revenues and expenditures on the treasury banks' accounts;
- Regulation of financial relations between the federal budget and state (federal) nonbudget funds, financial performances of those funds, control of incoming resources, and expenditures of nonbudget (federal) resources;
- Short-term forecasts for state financial resources and the operative management of these resources;
- Submission of information on the government's financial transactions within the federal budget, and of information on the current status of the financial system and state nonbudget funds; this information is supplied to the supreme legislative and executive bodies of the state;
- Providing management and consulting services, in cooperation with the Central Bank and other authorized banks, concerning Russia's internal and external debt.

The Ministry of Finance is working on the issue of the further transfer of regional and local budgets in the treasury system.

The formation of a modern taxation system has led to an evolution of the Federal Tax Service of the Russian Federation, which embraces a central (federal) body as well as state tax inspections for the various regions. The main task of the Federal Tax Service is to control the implementation of laws on taxation, make proper calculations of taxes, and determine whether taxes are paid in full and on time. Together with the Ministry of Finance, the Federal Tax Service also participates in developing taxation policy and laws. (The responsibilities collecting taxes and fees on the transportation of commodities to the customs territories of the Russian Federation fall to customs officers.)

In 1993, an autonomous system of federal branches of so-called tax police was established, with offices in each subject of the Federation. The tasks of these federal tax policing bodies are:

- Overseeing and preventing tax crimes
- Providing safety for the activities of the state tax inspections and their staff
- Preventing and uncovering corruption in tax agencies

In accordance a law passed in January 1995, the Counting Chamber of the Russian Federation was founded as a permanent organ of state financial control; and it is under the direction of the Parliament. The scope of tasks assigned to this branch is very broad:

- Organization and implementation of a system to insure the timely performance of "revenues and expenditures" articles of federal budget and federal nonbudget funds;
- Judgment concerning the efficiency and worthiness of expenditures of state resources and use of federal property;
- Evaluation of the basis for "revenues and expenditures" articles of federal budget and nonbudget funds' drafts;
- Financial evaluation of drafts of federal laws and law provisions made by the federal organs of the state, and of provisions concerning costs charged to the federal budget;
- Financial evaluation of factors affecting the formation and performance of federal budget and federal nonbudget funds.

The transition to a market economy stimulated the creation of a network of nonstate financial institutions, particularly investment and pension funds. Originally, the scope of responsibilities of the investment funds was limited to transactions in stocks and securities markets, to issues of publicly held enterprises, and to the privatization of state property. Currently, the funds' resources can be invested not only in stocks and securities, but also in real estate, bank certificates of deposit, and other kinds of property. As the legislation defined it, the purpose of nonstate funds is to improve the country's pension and retirement system and to protect people's savings from inflation.

To provide the efficient operation of nonstate investment and pension funds, an entire package of normative and legislative documents was prepared and passed in 1997. Finances of enterprises, organizations, and institutions of state, private, and mixed ownership are considered part of Russia's financial system.

Legally, the same tax regime, the same relations with state nonbudget funds, and the same norms and standards for depreciation expenses apply to all enterprises and profit organizations regardless of their ownership type. Internal financial relations are determined according to the order set for different types of businesses—public and private stock corporations, production cooperatives, state and municipal enterprises, etc.

The most important task of Russia's financial, budget, and tax policies is to stimulate investment activities in the economy for improving the production structure. The ultimate goal is technological renovation, which will increase production output and make the whole economy more competitive in terms of quality and costs.

CHAPTER **15**

BANKING SYSTEM

Y.A. Kudimov, Vitaliy B. Malkin, Sergey L. Morozov, Vneshtorgbank Staff, and Dmitri L. Mozgin

15.1 NATIONAL RESERVE BANK.* The National Reserve Bank (NRB) is one of the largest and most dynamically developing financial institutions in Russia. This co-op share bank is a limited liability partnership and is a large investment bank.

The National Reserve Bank was founded in May 1994. Its current top management came to NRB from the Russian Investment Financial Company (RIFC) in 1993. RIFC specializes in the commercial debts of the USSR and Russian Federation. Due to the effective management of RIFC, the external debt of Russia was reduced by almost one-half of a billion dollars in 1993–94, and tens of millions of dollars in budget funds were also saved.

At present, according to the Interfax rating, the National Reserve Bank is on the list of top 10 Russian banks in terms of its assets; it holds third place, trailing Sberbank and Vneshtorgbank in terms of resources. This amount exceeds five trillion rubles, or approximately one billion dollars. The main reason for the substantial growth of NRB resources is the more than tenfold increase (from 187 billion rubles to 1,987 billion rubles) of share capital resulting from a proportionate increase of shares.

In the third quarter of 1996, the NRB gained approximately 900 billion rubles in profit, which is 75% of its total profit since the beginning of that year. The main portion of profit was generated by operations involving the state short-term bonds (GKOs). As of January 1, 1997, the balance of currency of the NRB was 11.2 trillion rubles. As for the bank's structure of assets, investments in state bonds dominate, reaching 3.9 trillion rubles, or 47% of total assets. Issued credits were 0.9 trillion rubles, or 11%, one-third of which were interbank credits.

The NRB does not serve individuals. Among the Bank's shareholders are Russian joint-stock companies, Gazprom and its subsidiary Gazexport (56.9%); a joint-stock company Almastrust (14.9%); a holding company Bratsky Timber Industrial complex (6%); and Coopvneshtorg, Mashinoimport, Zarubezhtsvetmet, Sudoexport, Mashinoexport, Aviaexport, and Technosnabexport.

The leadership of the NRB has sought to widen its clientele while paying special attention to selecting reliable new partners and to satisfying the needs of current customers. Among the clients and partners of the bank are only those international financial institutions that have the highest business reputation along with the strongest and most promising companies and banks of Russia.

---

*This section was written by Y.A. Kudimov

The major partners of the NRB in the Russian market are the largest Russian banks: SBS-Agro, Inkombank, Menatep, and Imperial. Among the foreign partners of the NRB are such Western banks as Chase Manhattan, Credit Suisse First Boston, J.P. Morgan, Morgan Stanley, Warburg, Chemical, Bank of America, Morgan Grenfell, Indosuez, and Paris Bank.

The NRB pays very close attention to maintaining efficient management practices as well as upgrading the professional level of the bank's personnel. The bank has been successful because of the skillful work of NRB employees and modern methods of handling clients. Other factors in this success include the use of efficient tools in the financial markets and the improvement of technical support for banking operations. The NRB is equipped with high-tech systems such as Reuters and Bloomberg, and it is connected to the Portal system.

The NRB is a specialized bank. Its main sphere of interest is directed at operations related to the Russian external debt and to servicing the international financial transactions of Gazprom. The NRB works with state stocks and securities, including state short-term bonds, treasury bonds, and bonds of the government foreign exchange debt. After Sberbank, the NRB is the second largest proprietor of Russian securities.

The NRB is an authorized bank for the governmental commission on the state external debt and financial reserves of the Russian Federation. It conducts operations involving external assets and liabilities of the Federation. The NRB is one of the main operators of a bank consortium that handles issues of Russia's external debt.

Together with creditors from former socialist countries, the NRB offered the Russian government original proposals for the settlement of debt via export delivery. These include projects for the capitalization of debt (conversion of debt into stocks of Russian enterprises), debt-swap currency operations, set-off schemes, and others. As a result of implementing these plans, Russian products have been promoted in a variety of foreign markets, and new jobs have been created in Russia, thereby decreasing social tensions.

The NRB was involved with the settlement of Russia's debt with Hungary, the Czech Republic, Slovakia, Bulgaria, and South Korea. The bank's activities in the settlement of Russia's external debt should not, however, be taken as an indication that this is the only sphere of its activities. The NRB has been authorized to operate as the government bank for transferring the commercial debt of the former USSR to firms and suppliers in the form of promissory notes issued by the Ministry of Finance to holders of bonds. The National Reserve Bank has a strong position in a number of Commonwealth of Independent States countries, especially Ukraine, Belarus, and Moldova.

The NRB participates in implementing the agreement On the settlement of the Debt of Ukrainian Consumers for Supplies of Russian Gas in 1994–95, which was signed between the Ukrainian government and Gazprom. Gazprom, a major shareholder of NRB, has entrusted the bank to be its depositary and has given bonds to the NRB as collateral. These bonds were issued in the amount of $1.4 billion by the Ministry of Finance of Ukraine in 1995 to settle a $700 million debt to Gazprom.

The strategic task of the NRB regarding the Ukrainian bonds is to establish a primary market. Together with the Ukrainian investment and credit corporation, the NRB is currently working on plans for settling Ukraine's debt to Russia via mutual settlements with the Czech Republic and Hungary, whose debtor is Russia.

In the summer of 1996, the NRB signed an agreement with J.P. Morgan Bank, aimed at putting the Ukrainian bonds on the world market. In particular, the NRB plans to create a special system of clearing and custody, introducing new securities to the SEDEL and Euroclear systems. In order to do that, the NRB intends to establish, on the basis of the bonds, a special purpose vehicle. Simultaneously, this problem is being resolved on the intergovernmental level, where a discussion regarding amendments to Ukrainian legislation on securities is currently taking place.

In August 1996, the NRB issued a credit in the amount of 1.5 trillion rubles to Gazprom in order to pay taxes. Credit was arranged as a soft loan based on a 20% annual interest rate to be paid within one to six months. This credit was of political origin because it allowed the government to substantially increase federal revenues in a very short period. As a result, Russia could receive another tranche in the amount of $340 million from the International Monetary Fund.

In December 1996, the NRB proposed to establish an investment consortium of the largest Russian banks and corporations. In addition to the NRB, other banks expressing an interest in participating in the consortium included Vnesheconombank, Savings Bank Stolichny, Sberbank, Imperial, Avtobank, Gazprombank, Mezhkombank, Mosbusinessbank, Promstroybank, and Ingosstrakh. Among the companies expressing an interest were Gazprom, LUKOIL, KomiTEK, Sibneft', Rossvooruzhenije, Sovkomflot, Mashinoexport, Aviaexport, and others.

The consortium's goal is based on the policy that makes it possible to defer the bad debts of enterprises for several years, by converting them to bonds and transferring them to the Federal Tax Service. With the help of banks, these securities will be put into circulation in the financial market, and part of the earnings will be used to satisfy the payroll debt. The rest of the money will go to investment projects.

At present, the consortium has prepared about 50 projects that, if strongly supported by the government of the Federation, capable of adding $15–20 billion to the budget in 1997–98. During the next few years, the implementation of this program may bring, in addition to budget allocations and foreign credits, $50–$60 billion in investments into the Russian economy.

The investment program of the consortium is aimed at creating new jobs, increasing efficiency, improving the competitiveness of the Russian economy, and easing social tensions. The consortium is expected to involve large foreign financial institutions. The coordinating body will be comprised of representatives of executive and legislative power.

The first practical step in the consortium's activities is the purchase of 8.5% of the shares of the Russian joint stock company EES in order to prevent their purchase by foreign investors. If the purchase cannot be made, foreign investors will have a block of shares big enough to give them strategic decision-making power.

Among the projects that are financed by the consortium are the design of the IL–96 aircraft for Aeroflot, the construction of tankers and drilling platforms, and Morskoj Start, which is the largest known international project involving a sea-floating rocket launching site.

As a specialized bank, the NRB prefers not to issue credits to industrial enterprises if they cannot provide guarantees: also, it avoids working in the market of interbank operations and purchasing real estate. At the same time, the NRB issued substantial credits to the Ministry of Nuclear Energy, the administration of the Omsk region, and to a number of plants in the defense industry. These loans were expected to support domestic manufacturers, help resolve payroll shortfalls, and improve the social climate in several regions of Russia.

The NRB is one of the largest operations in the world dealing with Russian currency transactions, state securities, and external debt. The external debt includes the group of London Club creditors and so called nonguaranteed commercial debts. According to Russian and foreign experts, the NRB is a well-controlled organization with many profitable and successful operations. This characterization attests to NRB's excellent management and justifies describing it as one of Russia's most reliable and promising financial institutions in the long run.

15.2 COMMERCIAL BANKING SERVICES ROSSIYSKIY KREDIT BANK.* Russia is in the midst of a vigorous process in which a money market is growing along with a capital market. The Russian banking system is fluid. Only a few of the more than 2,500 banks that have appeared since the start of the reforms have survived and achieved stable growth rates. Customers, therefore, must be very discriminating in choosing a bank that is stable and reliable.

As a rule, banks with total assets in excess of 10 trillion rubles (2.2 million) have a stable financial position and tend to provide across-the-board banking services. One of the largest in Russia is Rossiyskiy Kredit Bank, with an authorized capital of 234 billion rubles ($5.2 million) and current assets exceeding 11 trillion rubles ($24.2 million).

Credit banks are rapidly introducing automated information-processing and transfer systems. Their customers can use the remote access system, which allows them to manage their accounts right from their office desks. All these financial institutions are members of the international SWIFT system and have a far-flung network both in the CIS countries and around the world. For example, the Rossiyskiy Kredit Bank has correspondent relations with over 300 foreign banks. The bank has a subsidiary in Switzerland and will open branch offices in Hungary and Vietnam. Approval has been received from the Bank of England to open a branch office in London; others will be opened in the near future in Israel and Bahrain. Also, the bank is actively developing the CIS markets, with a subsidiary bank recently opened in Turkmenistan. The Rossiyskiy Kredit Bank has plans to open similar banks in Azerbaijan, Kazakstan, and Kyrgyzstan. All the new banks will be able to make payments both within and outside Russia within one or two business days.

(a) Customer Service. The majority of Russian banks do not accept orders by fax or telephone. Some banks, including Rossiyskiy Kredit Bank, are exploring the possibility of soon communicating with their customers by fax.

Personalized service to customers with heavy account activity is not yet widespread in Russia. The service has been pioneered by several banks, including Rossiyskiy Kredit Bank, which has opened a specialized division in Smolenskaya Square to deal with major customers. Each of them has been assigned a personal account manager and a consultant, who can supply information on any financial or legal problem the customer may encounter.

Today, the biggest commercial banks open and provide services for all types of accounts held by artificial and natural persons, both residents and nonresidents.

(b) Banking Rules. Accounts are opened without restrictions for legal entities and natural persons who are nonresidents. A specific procedure must be followed. Legal persons can open two types of accounts with a Russian bank. These are the investment-ruble account (I-account) and the current foreign-exchange account (T-account). Investment accounts can be used to conduct business and make investments. These accounts can be credited with dividends paid on shares or earnings from the sale of shares, interest on stock and equity deposits, or receipts from the sale of foreign exchange. Funds kept in an investment account can be used to finance production or can be transferred to the current account.

---

*This section was written by Vitaliy B. Malkin.

Characteristically, foreign exchange can be purchased on the domestic market only with funds kept in this account.

To open a current foreign-exchange account, a foreign firm must have an officially registered representative office in the Russian Federation. The office is considered accredited following registration with the Russian Chamber of Commerce and Industry. As a rule, representative offices of foreign firms are opened for a term not exceeding three years, with the right to seek an extension of accreditation. To start operation, a representative office must obtain a permit from the registration chamber in its local area, and must register with the Federal Tax Service, the Pension Fund, the Employment Fund, the Social Insurance Fund, and the Medical Insurance Fund.

(c) Trust Management Services.   The biggest Russian banks offer their customers another unique service, trust management of their funds. This service is provided to foreign natural and legal persons, regardless of whether they are registered in the Russian territory.

(d) Securities Investment.   To have a T-account foreign firms must have an office in Russia that is officially registered with the Chamber of Commerce and Industry of Russia. Banks are active in the Russian stock market, where they offer their customers investment portfolios, which are formed from I-accounts. Russia's developing market characteristically offers high risks and high yields. High yields attract many players. Nonresidents wishing to invest their money in securities need to find a reliable partner, a role multipurpose banks can fill because they manage their portfolio investments in a vigorous and professional manner.

Foreign investors who want to place Russian government securities in their portfolios should deal only with a bank that has an authorized status. This status gives the bank the right to participate in primary auctions trading short-term government bonds or any other government securities.

Corporate securities are growing in popularity. Their yields are rising by the day because of the undervaluation of the fixed assets of most Russian enterprises. Investments in corporate securities should be handled by major banks instead of investment companies. These banks have sufficient assets to promptly arrange registration of securities in their capacity as nominal holders. Banks can also improve the reliability of investments in corporate securities by hedging against foreign exchange risk.

A bank is likely to request that investors in the Russian financial market who want to conduct transactions based on credit provide reliable security, such as the pledge or guarantee of a large domestic or foreign bank. The cost of credit is high in Russia. This is due to macroeconomic conditions, especially the shortage of hard currency.

The role of the new banking facilities in the Russian financial market is coming into greater prominence. The major Russian banks offer services that differ very little from those a Western customer is used to receiving. Foreign investors can identify reliable banks based on their assets, customer services, and financial services.

15.3 PAYMENT SYSTEM: FREELY CONVERTIBLE INTERNATIONAL MULTI-CURRENCY DEBIT (IMD) CHEQUES.*   The single European currency, the Euro, is scheduled to appear in circulation on January 1, 1999. This is the currency that, in accordance with the Maastricht Treaty, will replace the national currencies of the member states

---

*This section was written by Sergey L. Morozov.

in the European Monetary Union (or EMU) by July 1, 2002. If this happens, the Euro and U.S. dollar may come into conflict on international financial markets, and disturb the existing balance of the national currencies of most of the non-EMU countries. Therefore, it is necessary to begin preparations for adapting the payment systems of the United States, Russia, the other countries of the former Soviet Union, and other nonmember EMU countries. This is an important undertaking because the impending crisis is not only Russia's problem, it also affects the world payment system as a whole.

The interdependence of the U.S. dollar and the Russian ruble is a widely accepted fact. Indeed, the financial system of Russia today is divided into two parts: ruble and dollar. Only rubles can be used for payments, while the dollar is used for savings, exchange-rate hedging, and as the unit of account, or measure of value. This two-pronged approach results from the different levels of real inflation and from changes in purchasing power between the ruble and the dollar. The ruble's inflation rate is at least 20–30% per year, while the dollar's is not more than 3%. Russian citizens hedge the ruble exchange-rate risk, and preserve their salarys' purchasing power by up to 17–27% per year by buying U.S. dollars. Therefore, nearly the entire population of Russia buys U.S. dollars, even though the dollar cannot officially be used for payments.

In reality, prices in Russia are set in rubles and at the same time in so-called relative units or, if a special license is available, in dollars. This causes huge losses and artificially accelerates inflation. This acceleration is caused by the increased ruble-dollar (or ruble-deutsche mark) conversion rates at the shops that want reimbursement for fluctuations of the exchange rates within the currency corridor set by the Central Bank of Russia. Surely, no one in the United States could imagine a situation where goods are purchased with dollars while savings are held in, for example, French francs. Unfortunately, this paradox is the norm in Russia.

There were between 290–295 trillion rubles in circulation in Russia by the end of 1996, and twice as many U.S. dollars—the equivalent of 540–600 trillion rubles. The dollar is actively forcing the ruble out and is becoming the *surrogate* currency for Russia. Flooding Russia with U.S. cash is moving Russia's financial system toward crisis and collapse. Russia's financial system is completely dependent on the Central Bank's reserves of gold and hard currency in liquid form, namely, U.S. dollars (and to a lesser degree, deutsche marks). These gold and hard-currency reserves have dropped below the critical level.

In reality, the structure of Russia's state debt is similar to that of a pyramid scheme, where the government's payments of high interest rates on bonds is covered by issuing other bonds. For instance, issues of state short-Term bonds (GKOs) have led to the growth of the internal state debt to about 70 billion U.S. dollars. It seems that the internal reserves to pay the GKOs have already been exhausted. The Ministry of Finance has recently begun to use external reserves by issuing Eurobonds. The possibilities of increasing foreign debt, however, limited by the natural resources of Russia, which are finite and irreplaceable. As soon as all the resources have been pledged, there will be nothing left to support these GKO securities pyramids. If workers are unable to convert their ruble-based paychecks into dollars, there will be a financial collapse in Russia; and the social situation will get considerably worse, especially because more than 50% of the wage debt is to the army.

It is not too late to cure Russia's financial system, however. The cure should start with the introduction of a single universal payment means, which would be freely convertible into any national currency, and which could be used for payments and savings, exchange-rate hedging, and as the unit of account or measure of value. This tool has already been created and patented in the Republic of Ireland, Germany, Spain, Japan, and Russia. In Russia, it would take the form of the ELBIM Bank's freely convertible international Multicurrency Debit Cheques. These checks should, in our opinion, be effected throughout Russia by a central reserve commercial bank. The proposal to establish such a bank has been recently submitted to the government of Russia, and endorsed by the Association of Russian Banks and its president.

The circulation of freely convertible international Multicurrency Debit Cheques, denominated in the equivalent of the world's reserve currency, which is now exclusively the U.S. dollar, will make it possible to accumulate funds in the accounts of the proposed central reserve commercial bank, instead of keeping dollars in private homes. Today, the population keeps up to $90 billion and up to 140 trillion rubles in banknotes. This is enough to pay off the internal state debt of Russia, with enough left over to put into low-interest international funds that invest in the development of domestic industry and agriculture. Issuing freely convertible international Multicurrency Debit Cheques would make it possible to attract not only the dollars held in Russia, but also part of the estimated $180 billion in international markets.

Here are several advantages of ELBIM checks:

- Can be denominated in any currency, which avoids two commissions on foreign exchange if traveling internationally (when compared with dollar-denominated traveler's checks);
- Do not require countersigning, which can be time-consuming, especially if they are for large amounts;
- Can be traded freely as quasi-currency. Traveler's checks can be used only once, as payment to a vendor. ELBIM checks could be used as payment to participating vendors or to other private citizens;
- Are more attractive to vendors because the commission vendors pay is lower;
- Used widely by the Russian market, especially in Moscow;
- Can be used for international business in place of wire transfers, which are costly, or cash transactions, which provide no record;
- A traveler may have one nonbearer, ELBIM Bank check cut in the quantity and currency desired. This allows the user to have one check, even in an odd amount, instead of many traveler's checks. In this way, the check is similar to a bank draft, but again the user does not pay a commission for the foreign-exchange transaction.

We suggest that the universal noncash payment system be implemented in Russia. This system would be based on four basic principles: international processing centers, international electronic cash machines, international plastic cards, and freely convertible international Multicurrency Debit Cheques with which all cash dispensers would be stocked, instead of with national currencies.

Such a payment system would normalize the financial market in Russia, simplify all types of settlements, make the Russian financial market compatible with those of all the other developed countries, and serve as a model for a unified international mechanism of payments.

15.4 VNESHTORGBANK: ACTIVITIES AND SERVICES FOR FOREIGN INVESTORS.* Since its inception in 1990, the Bank for Foreign Trade (Vneshtorgbank) has been a leader in the fast-growing banking market in Russia. In terms of its capital,

---

*This section was written by the Staff of Vneshtorgbank.

assets, and profit, Vneshtorgbank ranks second after the Bank for Savings (Sberbank). As of early 1997, the total holdings of Vneshtorgbank were 24.4 trillion rubles and its own capital was more than six trillion rubles. *The Banker* magazine ranks Vneshtorgbank as the 390th, largest bank in the world.

A young bank, Vneshtorgbank is the same age as the new Russia. It was especially designed to serve the needs of the Russian economy in foreign trade. Also, Vneshtorgbank inherited the best traditions and expertise of the previous banking system. Today there is a large number of highly qualified specialists at the bank who have substantial banking experience, including experience with foreign banks. Also, Vneshtorgbank has specialists who are intimately familiar with the financing of import and export projects, international clearing and currency transactions, organization of crediting, and project financing. Starting in 1993, the official auditor of Vneshtorgbank is Price Waterhouse. Vneshtorgbank deals primarily with wholesale operations and specializes in servicing currency transactions of their clients who engage in foreign trade.

With a wide network of 12 branches including six subsidiary banks in Russia's major regions, and three overseas banks, Vneshtorgbank provides extensive services for various clients. This network has become the basis of the financial group of Vneshtorgbank. As opposed to many other Russian commercial banks that seek to form diversified groups on an industrial basis, Vneshtorgbank is aimed first and foremost at establishing and developing purely financial subsidiaries that promote the bank's interests in the banking sector. The investments of the bank in the authorized capitals of other banking institutions exceed 500 billion rubles.

Currently, the financial structure of the bank includes over a dozen banks and financial organizations in Moscow, Ulyanovsk, Novosibirsk, Nizhny Novgorod, Ryazan, and Krasnodar. It also includes banks and financial organizations in Zurich, New York, Berlin, Vienna, Milan, and Limassol, Cyprus. Many Vneshtorgbank subsidiaries have established their own network of affiliated offices. Most of these are leaders in their regions in servicing operations in foreign trade and they have been authorized by local administrations to serve regional budgets. Vneshtorgbank branches operate in Vyborg, St. Petersburg, Nakhodka, Irkutsk, Blagoveshchensk, Krasnoyarsk, Magadan, Sochi, Khabarovsk, Stavropol, Novorossisk. It also has representative offices in Italy and China.

Along with these, Vneshtorgbank is a large shareholder in a wide range of successful financial firms. The network of subsidiaries and associated financial institutions may be used by the bank's clients. Vneshtorgbank pays special attention to automated banking services. All regional branches have switched to SWIFT, an automated system that allows the bank and its clients to conduct all operations in real time.

Vneshtorgbank's reliability is confirmed by Russian as well as international rating agencies. According to various Russian agencies, the bank is considered one of the country's most dependable and stable; and, according to the international rating agency Thomson BankWatch, it has the highest credit rating among Russian commercial banks.

Since its inception, Vneshtorgbank has exceeded the economic standards set by the Central Bank of Russia. Vneshtorgbank also performs up to international standards—and with a large amount of reliability. For example, regarding the two basic requirements introduced by the Basel Agreement, the bank has maintained the necessary level of fixed capital and the minimum allowable volume of aggregate capital. This success is brought about by the bank's goal of integration into the world financial market, as well as by the need to efficiently serve clients, including authorized state organs and institutions.

In January 1997, Vneshtorgbank was among the 13 largest Russian banks to be included by the government in a group of universal bank-agents of the government. These banks have been authorized to implement all governmental programs. Performing as an authorized bank means that Vneshtorgbank will participate in operations on:

- Servicing domestic currency loans;
- Withdrawal of precious metals as collateral;
- Performing agent operations by selling precious metals in accordance with an order of the president and government of the Russian Federation;
- Regulating foreign debt;
- Placing and servicing externally funded loans;
- Servicing credits of international financial organizations;
- Conducting individual operations and clearing at the order of the federal government.

The bank is also an official dealer of GKOs and bonds of the internal state currency loan (OVGVZs). It is also a major depository, depositary and clearing center for OVGVZs, and an authorized bank for implementing state investment programs.

Vneshtorgbank is one of a few Russian commercial banks whose guarantees of credit, letters of credit, and other financial obligations are accepted by major Western banks and national institutes of the world's largest countries for export insurance, such as Coface (France), Serg (Switzerland), Cesce (Spain), Hermes (Germany), Ex-Im Bank (United States) and Ex-Im Bank (Japan). A number of Swiss, Austrian, Spanish, and German banks have issued credit lines to Vneshtorgbank in order to finance the national export of their respective countries. These banks also accept guarantees of Vneshtorgbank. Among Russian commercial banks, Vneshtorgbank has the largest limits for credit, conversion, and deposit operations, a policy that confirms its solid business reputation in the world financial market.

Vneshtorgbank has actively cooperated with the European Bank for Reconstruction and Development on a number of joint-investment projects. In 1996, Vneshtorgbank signed an agreement with EBRD that granted it a revolving credit line up to $100,000 for a five-year term.

Having credit lines also strengthens the position of Vneshtorgbank in the field of long-term crediting. This allows the bank to attract foreign creditors to participate in investment projects in Russia. For example, in accordance with agreements on supplying equipment for the Russian natural-gas industry, Vneshtorgbank gave guarantees and met obligations of the Russian joint-stock company Gazprom toward Ex-Im Bank (United States), as well as Japanese, German, and Argentinean firms for more than $850 billion.

Vneshtorgbank takes part in programs that are financed by state and international organizations. The bank is particularly involved in programs related to an agreement on Russian oil and gas industries that was signed between the Ex-Im Bank (USA) on one side, and the Russian Ministries of Fuel and Energy, and of Finance, and the Central Bank on the other. According to the agreement, Vneshtorgbank, as a part of international consortia led by Chase Manhattan Bank, is participating in granting credit for a large investment project in Russia.

An important direction in Vneshtorgbank activities is promoting and servicing direct foreign loans and investments in the Russian economy, including those that are stipulated within a framework of project financing. The bank carries out these tasks by fulfilling its powers as a government agent in attracting foreign interest in investment projects. The bank also completes these tasks on a commercial basis. In particular, Vneshtorgbank acts as a financial consultant and agent for Gazprom in attracting foreign credit to finance the supplies of machines and equipment for modernizing the Russian gas industry. Recently, three loan agreements were signed. One of them, in the amount of $1.6 billion, was granted by an international consortium of banks against the guarantee of SACE, an Italian agency for the insurance of export credits. According to two other agreements, 936 million and 1 billion deutsche marks will be provided by consortia of German banks-creditors against guarantees of Hermes, a German agency for the insurance of export credits.

Seventy-five percent of the credit portfolio of Vneshtorgbank is used for financing operations in foreign trade, including import and export. This confirms the evident foreign-trade orientation of the bank's credit investments and strengthens its position as a foreign-trade bank of national scope.

As of early 1997, the credit portfolio of Vneshtorgbank was 7.8 trillion rubles. The share of medium- and long-term credits in the total amount of its credit investments is substantial. Sixty percent of all the bank's loans are to industry, including mechanical engineering, oil, gas, chemical, defense, textile, and ship-building industries. The average amount of a loan is more than $10 million, and approximately half of all loans are those of over $20 million each.

The largest credit partners of Vneshtorgbank are the Russian joint-stock companies Norilsk Nickel, Yuganskneftegas, Energomashexport, Rosvooruzheniye, other foreign-trade organizations, and enterprises in metallurgy, petrochemicals, and the mechanical-engineering industry. Over 90% of its credit portfolio is in currency credits.

Vneshtorgbank uses strict criteria in its crediting policy and its control over the targeted use of credits and their payment. This approach is aimed at minimizing credit risks and at maintaining a balanced structure of credit investments (in terms of the correlation between risk and profitability). One of the top priorities of the bank is developing cooperation with other financial institutions in order to create optimum conditions for clearing, for increased efficiency in using funds at correspondent accounts, and for the maximum satisfaction of clients' needs.

Vneshtorgbank continues to improve its international correspondent network, which is one of the widest among Russian banks. Covering all of the largest financial institutions in the world, the network of correspondent accounts allows Vneshtorgbank's clients to make payments to any region of the world and in any major currency.

Another priority of the bank is the development of ties with other Russian banks. Vneshtorgbank's stable financial position, stellar business reputation, and high quality of service have made it one of the largest clearing banks in Russia. As of early 1997, it had more than 600 correspondent banks, in Russia as well as outside it.

At present, more than 300 Russian banks have set up currency and ruble accounts with Vneshtorgbank. In addition, more than 20 banks of the Commonwealth of Independent States and the Baltics use their correspondent accounts at the bank to make their import-export payments.

Over 40 major banks of Western Europe opened LORO accounts in hard currency at Vneshtorgbank in order to speed up bilateral payments. It also offers its foreign correspondent banks ruble T-accounts, which help them make payments in rubles to their Russian partners.

Vneshtorgbank has been active in developing a share market, particularly in the state securities market. As of early 1997, the bank invested 3.7 trillion rubles in state securities. Clients are offered a wide variety of services related to securities, including the following:

- Purchase of securities in the primary market
- Operations with all types of state, municipal, and corporate bonds as well as securities issued by subjects of the Federation

- Options and futures contracts
- Management of clients' money through securities portfolios
- Reaper-chase crediting
- Repo operations

Starting in August 1996, Vneshtorgbank was authorized to open C-accounts to service the investments of nonresidents in the state securities market. At present, a number of the largest foreign financial institutions have such accounts with the bank. Also, it offers nonresidents E-accounts, which are designed for operations with Russian corporate securities.

Its custody service is one of the most important tools used by Vneshtorgbank in the activities of foreign investors in Russia. The bank has created a system of depositary trustee service to service Russian and foreign investors. Vneshtorgbank is one of the few Russian banks that meet the requirement of the U.S. Securities and Exchange Commission for the minimum amount of authorized capital a foreign-custody bank can have, which is not less than $200 billion. Vneshtorgbank's custody services are primarily intended to meet the needs of foreign investors who are shareholders in Russian enterprises; these services are:

- Responsible custody and accounting on transactions involving securities;
- Registration of corporate securities;
- Clearing;
- Servicing dividends and interest payments on securities;
- Gathering information on corporate activities;
- Participating in a shareholders' meeting by proxy for a client;
- Consulting on taxing transactions involving securities in Russia and on the procedure for income repatriation.

Custody services provided by Vneshtorgbank to its foreign clients enable them to work directly in the primary and secondary securities markets in Russia, a situation that creates new opportunities to attract investments to the Russian economy.

15.5 DEVELOPMENT OF CUSTODY SERVICES AT THE BANK FOR FOREIGN TRADE (VNESHTORGBANK)*

(a) **Seven Reasons to Invest in Russia.**   Everyone is aware that Russia, which is recognized as a country with enormous economic potential, is now of considerable interest to foreign investors. This interest is primarily due to:

- The existence of a vast domestic market;
- High yields on government securities coupled with low risk;
- The potentially high capital gains on shares of Russian companies, many of which were initially undervalued;
- Low labor costs due to the low average salary in Russia;
- The availability of a highly educated and qualified workforce;
- Russia's proximity to the markets of Western Europe;
- Its wealth of natural resources, especially oil and gas.

---

*This section was written by Dmitri L. Mozgin.

(b) Brief History of Foreign Investments in Russia.   At the beginning of the 1990s, Western investors avoided the Russian stock market and focused instead on emerging markets in Southeast Asia and Latin America. Beginning in 1994, however, because of changes in economic policy, in particular the privatization of large state corporations like Rostelekom and the demand from Russian businesspeople for a well-developed domestic stock market, the views of Western investors about the Russian securities market underwent a gradual shift.

Thus, while the value of portfolio investments in Russia for 1993 amounted to less than $300 million, the same indicator for 1994 grew significantly to $1.5 billion, and is currently estimated at $5 billion.

Needless to say, these figures are still disproportionately low compared to the real demands of the Russian stock market. Until recently, the significant growth in the volume of foreign investments, long foreseen by Western analysis, was hampered by numerous factors, with the key obstacle being political instability in Russia. After the presidential elections, which were closely followed by the international community, the general attitude radically changed. It became obvious that the reforms, once started, would continue.

(c) Investment Today.   Today, the most important task is the promotion of a favorable investment climate. On July 1, 1996, President Yeltsin signed Presidential Decree No. 1008, which states, "It is necessary to pursue a vigorous government policy of promoting the development of an independent Russian capital market that is responsive to the national interests of Russia, integrated into the international capital market, and capable of ensuring a flow of investment into the Russian economy." In order to achieve this goal, the Russian government realizes that it is necessary to establish safeguards protecting foreign investors' rights. The presidential decree, also states that, "Promoting and protecting private property, using all means available to the State, is the cornerstone of the government's policy with respect to capital market development."

Such safeguards have taken a long time to create, and, in many respects, 1996 was a watershed year in the creation of a legislative framework for the Russian stock market. In particular, two crucial documents defining the relationships between market participants and clients have become law: the first statute is the Joint Stock Company Law, which came into effect on January 1, 1996, and is the first step toward the establishment of a sound legal basis for the operations of joint stock companies; the second critical piece of legislation is the Securities Market Law, which became effective on April 22, 1996. In addition, there have been a large number of other decrees, regulations and laws passed since December 1991 that have established a comprehensive legal framework for the regulation and operation of the securities industry in Russia.

As the Russian securities industry develops, new services are being introduced to assist Russian and foreign investors. One of the new services for foreign investors operating in Russia is the provision of custodial services. This is a new sector of the Russian securities industry, and Vneshtorgbank is among the key providers.

(d) Bank for Foreign Trade and the Russian Securities Market.   The Bank for Foreign Trade (Vneshtorgbank) was reorganized in October 1990 in its present form, but it was originally established in 1922 and, therefore, has a long and impressive record of working with foreign financial institutions. Vneshtorgbank is now one of the largest Russian banks, with a shareholder capital of $844 million as of the end of 1995. *The Banker* magazine rated the bank as the 390th largest bank in the world in 1995, the highest rating of any Russian commercial bank.

In 1993, five tranches of Government Domestic Hard-Currency Denominated Bonds (OVGVZ or MinFins) were issued, laying the foundation of the market for these securities. From the moment these bonds were issued, Vneshtorgbank became the principal depository, thus effectively embarking on custody operations.

(e) Privatization and the Development of the Corporate Securities Market. The first wave of Russian privatization in 1994 was followed by the development of the market for corporate securities, and above all, equities. This market continues to grow. In November 1996, Prime Minister Victor Chernomyrdin was quoted in *The Financial Times* as saying that investor interest in Russian bonds exceeded expectations and reflected the trust international investors had in Russia. Mr. Chernomyrdin also said, "The market is ready to take our bonds in greater numbers than we had initially planned. This means that we are joining the most demanding ranks of the international financial markets."

The issue of $1 billion of Russian bonds in November 1996, the recent Gazprom equity placement of $429 million in October, and its plans for a $500 million Eurobond issue highlight the dynamic state of the Russian market.

In 1995, Vneshtorgbank launched its custody operations, focusing mainly on providing services to foreign investors who owned shares in Russian companies. This decision was based on the following six considerations:

1. Vneshtorgbank is one of the largest banks in Russia. It's shareholder's equity of $844 million substantially exceeds the $200 million requirement of the United States for eligibility as a foreign custodian for mutual funds (and therefore all U.S. investors). Vneshtorgbank is, therefore, an eligible foreign custodian, by virtue of its compliance with Rule 17f–5, made under the U.S. Investment Company Act of 1940. This status has been confirmed by the law firm of Baker & MacKenzie on the basis of the bank's 1995 annual report and of the audit statement prepared by Price Waterhouse L.L.P. and was subsequently recognized by the U.S. Securities and Exchange Commission.

2. It has a significant international presence, with a network of branches and offices in Russia and abroad, in cities such as New York and Milan;

3. It is a major depository for MinFin bonds;

4. Its experienced and English-speaking employees guarantee first-class standards;

5. Its professional integrity and knowledge of the Russian market;

6. Its long-term relationships, built up over many years, with a network of more than 600 correspondent banks worldwide, including a number of leading U.K. and U.S. custody providers.

Vneshtorgbank provides custodial services to the holders of government securities, such as MinFin bonds, short-term treasury bills, and medium-term variable coupon treasury bonds, and also to holders of corporate securities. At present, Vneshtorgbank offers the following types of custodial services:

- Securities safekeeping
- Trade processing and settlement
- Registration of corporate securities
- Income collection

- Corporate actions
- Proxy voting
- Consulting on the taxation of securities transactions and income repatriation procedures
- Foreign-exchange transactions

As a provider of custody services, Vneshtorgbank complies with the international standards set by global custodians. Vneshtorgbank provides its clients with complete information for assessing the accuracy of its accounting records, asset safekeeping standards, custody department operating procedures, auditors' reports, and other procedures.

Vneshtorgbank intends to further diversify its range of services, which will enable it to take on the role of a pro-active custodian, helping clients make informed choices in strategic and tactical decision making and managing their investments. Its prospective services include securities lending, and analysis of portfolio investments from an economic, political, and structural standpoint to evaluate the associated risk and return.

Vneshtorgbank is the principal depository and clearing center for MinFin bonds in Russia. The bank continuously strives to maximize the efficiency of settlements while minimizing their time frame, which is particularly important in Russia. The best scenario is for both parties to the transaction to have both cash and deposit accounts with Vneshtorgbank. It should be noted that a growing number of MinFin bond market participants are becoming aware of the advantages of working through Vneshtorgbank.

Another key component of Vneshtorgbank's custody operations is servicing GKO and OFZ transactions for its resident and nonresident clients. The market procedures for GKO and OFZ trading regarding foreign investors were changed in August 1996. The provisional restrictive procedures for allowing access to the GKO and OFZ market to nonresidents, enforced since February 1996, were liberalized significantly by the Central Bank. Whereas nonresidents could not previously buy GKOs at auctions via former foreign banks with Soviet participation, now, having obtained a permit for opening a special (S-type) nonresident's account with an authorized Russian bank, a foreign investor can participate in trading sessions and has effectively the same rights as any Russian resident in the market. In addition, following the regulations established by the Russian Federal Commission on Securities, Vneshtorgbank also services unit-investment funds.

Vneshtorgbank has installed Sungard's Omni IC global custody program. This is a comprehensive client-server, Windows-based, real-time software package that runs on the UNIX platform and integrates with the bank's other systems. This international multicurrency, multilanguage system has been customized to meet Vneshtorgbank's specific requirements and has the flexibility to support Russian securities market practices and to enable the bank to maximize settlement and safekeeping efficiencies. Omni IC allows for automated generation and transmission of transaction confirmations, SWIFT messages, and reconciliation; provides a comprehensive management information system; and undertakes commission calculations and other client communications. The bank also plans to introduce additional functionality, as the requirements of the Russian market develop.

In Russia, there is a certain amount of risk inherent in the registration and reregistration of equity ownership. This risk is fairly low, however, due to the substantial efforts to improve the situation made by the Federal Commission on Securities over the last few years. Minimizing this risk, as well as increasing liquidity in the Russian stock market, is facilitated by the use of remote-access systems, signature-verification packages, and cooperation agreements signed with registrars. The risk in using registrars is further controlled by the new and stringent registrar licensing requirements, imposed by the Federal Commission on Securities, and by the legal liability of registrars for losses (including unrealized gains) arising from an investor's inability to exercise rights inherent in the securities, where the registrar fails in its duty to ensure that securities are free of encumbrances. Vneshtorgbank has agreements with a number of registrars.

It has to be noted that the Federal Commission on Securities has not yet established a definition of custody. Instead, Russia only has depositories, and there is no mention of custody operations in the Federal Commission on Securities Provisions for Depository Operations and Licensing. Hence, the concept and status of custody operations in Russia are currently unclear. Often a custodian is called a depository, which is the term sometimes used in the West to define custodians offering only core custodial services.

Despite these difficulties, Vneshtorgbank continues to implement the idea of promoting custody operations in Russia. The bank has made a major investment in developing its custody operations, basing the development of this service on the best international practices, on an understanding of the requirements of U.S. and other foreign investors, and on the acquisition of state-of-the-art software and hardware systems equal to those in any bank in the world. In the fast-moving and sometimes chaotic environment of the Russian securities industry, Vneshtorgbank offers professional integrity, knowledge, and experience, which will guide its clients to success.

CHAPTER 16

EMERGENCE OF A COMMERCIAL FINANCIAL SYSTEM

Sergey K. Dubinin, I. A. Zakharchenkov, and Vitaliy B. Malkin

16.1 COMMERCIAL FINANCING SYSTEM.* A developed commercial financial system would be a prime indication of the health of the Russian economy. Neither the bank-lending industry nor the stock market, however, can fully meet the needs of the economy. Bank credits have boomed over recent years. According to figures from the Central Bank, Russia now has more than 1,800 commercial banks and 5,500 branches operating around the nation. A majority of the banks, however, operate within their hometown's boundaries, are rigidly specialized, and bow to the interests of their stockholders. The only banks that maintain a national network of branches serving their customers nationwide are the Savings Bank (Sberbank), the Agro-Industrial Bank (Agroprombank), and the Construction Industrial Bank (Promstroybank), which are all former state-run institutions. Some commercial banks are little more than settlement centers for large enterprises.

Despite the abundance of banks, the lending industry cannot satisfy the growing business-loan needs of Russia's industrial enterprises. High lending and investment risks are forcing commercial banks to restrict the growth of lending to manufacturing and agricultural businesses. Instead of long-term loans, the banks focus primarily on short-term money markets and high-yielding investments (with a payback period of 1 to 1.5 years). In the current macroeconomic environment, a considerable decline in inflation rates in the next few years will enable manufacturers to earn enough profits to form a capital base of their own, whereas banks will hardly provide them with long-term development loans. Therefore the only hope for long-term financing is in the Russian stock market.

(a) Stock Market Evolution. The Russian stock market remains in a formative phase because of the current laws and its inability to register transactions and transfer ownership rights. It is not yet ready to play a major role in the economy. The mass-scale privatization of state-owned and municipal enterprises provided a strong boost to the growth of stock markets. Thousands of companies have been converted into joint-stock companies with huge packages of shares issued by privatized enterprises.

A broad-based class of stockholders, totaling 30 to 40 million people by some estimates, has materialized in Russia. Yet the securities movement in the market tends to be a one-way street: from the stock-issuing enterprise (or a securities-dealing firm) to the end-investor. As

---

*This section was written by Sergey K. Dubinin and I. A. Zakharchenkov.

a general rule, these end-investors are interested in acquiring a controlling stake or share that would enable them to dictate their policy to the enterprise. Therefore, stocks frequently end up in the hands of enterprise executives who hold the securities in their own name or in the name of investment companies that are under their control. The suppliers and customers of such enterprises are other major stockholders. This group of investors does not have a stake in the continued movement of securities because of their fear that large blocks might be grabbed by outsiders. One of the top priorities is to make the secondary corporate-securities market liquid.

The institutional structure of the stock market is just beginning to form. Although Russia has stock exchanges that hold securities-trading licenses, nearly 90% of the total stock of privatized enterprises is traded over the counter. The highly commissioned fees and un-justified delays in the delivery of securities compel both buyers and sellers to seek direct contacts, bypassing the intermediaries. In this case, however, the burden of delivery, storage, and verification of securities is shouldered by the buyer.

The situation is further compounded by the shortage of operators such as stock-market registrars, depositories, custodians, and transfer-clearing agents that are capable of performing to international standards. Many banks opt to set up their own depositories, but these deal primarily with treasury bonds and stockholders' securities. There is a need for depositories for the securities of large companies that are most active in the market, such as oil and metal companies. These depositories would provide a full range of services, including keeping a register of stockholders. This register is especially relevant because many large companies refuse to recognize the validity of transactions involving their stocks (particularly share certificates that have multiplied during the privatization campaign) unless they are entered in the stockholder register. An example of this occurred during the privatization of the Gazprom Joint Stock Company. These problems will be resolved, in part, if a number of major projects are implemented to develop deposit-clearing systems in Russia.

Several commercial banks such as Chase Manhattan and The Bank of New York have announced their readiness to serve as global custodians on behalf of the Russian market for the purpose of American depository receipts (ADRs) and global depository receipts (GDRs) on the stock market. Another initiative calls for several large banks to set up a deposit-clearing union.

(b) Broadening the Financial Base to Individuals.   A further problem is the reliability of financial institutions and the services they provide, a condition that applies to both commercial banks and financial companies built on the pyramid principle (e.g., dividends are paid from new investments). Russia's Central Bank registers the charters of new commercial banks per month. Lack of experience in evaluating credit risks and collateral, over-lending to single-stockholder enterprises and investment in high-risk assets are major threats to the banks' solvency. Adopting a general-purpose bank model poses problems to adequate security-trading operations. The notorious scandals involving the Chara bank and financial companies like MMM, Tibet, and Technology Progress, strikingly illustrate these operational deficiencies.

The efforts to stimulate financial markets should not overlook the needs of the general population. Creating a system of reliable and low-par instruments for private individuals may become an effective way to transform public savings into investments. In the almost complete absence of consumer credit, the people are forced to hoard needed amounts of uncalled funds, and they urgently need financial services to protect their savings from inflation.

The high-par values of a number of instruments, such as bankers' bills, make them beyond the reach of most of the population. Furthermore, many banks are unwilling to handle public savings because of high operating costs. Although these instruments are available on the corporate-securities market, the numberless encroachments on stockholders' interests, the flawed dividend policies of many companies, and poor law-enforcement practices generate little incentive for mass-scale investment.

(c) Demand for Financial Instruments.   The following plan will lead to a new phase in the development of the corporate-securities market: the transition to a cash privatization stage of state-owned enterprises replacing the voucher-based distribution of public property with sales of government and local authority-owned share packages at cash auctions and by investment bidding.

Commercial banks have been active in state-owned blocks of stock by sponsoring tenders at the request of the Russian Federal Property Fund. Banks have procured a plan to extend loans to the government that are based on the security of the stocks of privatized enterprises. Preparations are under way to float convertible bonds, whose owners will have access to government-held stock portfolios in oil-producing and refining enterprises, on the Russian and international markets. One possibility to attract broad-based investments is to create low-par, high-yielding derivatives of reliable issuers and to develop a municipal securities market.

As health care, housing, utilities, and education are taken over by local governments from the central authorities, there is a sustained, long-term demand for funds to finance these services. Considering the ordinary Russian's preference for nonbank savings instruments, the rapid growth of the municipal bond market, especially in housing, is expected. Provided the issuer furnishes adequate security and reliable guarantees, this type of lending may become a key, fast-growing segment of the stock market.

(d) Meeting International Standards.   Even though the Russian financial market is attracting a number of foreign institutional investors, it falls short of international requirements in many respects. There are a number of ways to improve its performance, including refining the banking and stock market laws (especially with regard to title transfers), expanding the set of available financial instruments (particularly the issue of low-par securities), upgrading the operators' professional skills and know-how, and streamlining the institutional structure of the stock market in order to deal in securities on the secondary market. These improvements are expected to lower the general risk of investing in the Russian economy by stabilizing its performance. A low exposure to risk may help foreign investors shift their priorities from venture operations to long-term financing of production. This shift would promote trust in the Russian financial system and improve the overall general investment climate.

Leading international investment institutions have either opened up branches or established country-oriented funds to trade in Russian securities. The operation of many foreign investment banks and companies in Russia is clear evidence of the high-yielding potential and long-term attractiveness of the Russian financial market.

16.2 CAPITAL MARKET: THE NEED FOR INTERNATIONAL COOPERATION*

(a) Assessment of the Current Investment Climate in Russia.   Current economic reforms in Russia are being carried out in accordance with formulas suggested by international financial organizations. Russian market relations have been firmly established and

---

*This section was written by Vitaliy B. Malkin.

the private sector has already become more powerful than the state. Enterprises are already being regulated by the market and, in this regard, privatization should undoubtedly be considered a success. Although it does not produce large budget revenues, privatization eliminates the principal bottleneck of Russian enterprises—inefficient bureaucratic management. The state financial policy is also satisfactory: the abandonment of the emission practice to cover budget deficits and the move toward allocation of government securities are especially encouraging.

At the present stage of Russian economic development, one can conclude that resources of foreign investors are the only major source of investment available to Russia that can overcome the protracted period of stagnation. And the potential of this source, as regards both its economic impact and the investments volume, is far from being exhausted.

The consultative Council on Foreign Investments has been created in order to enhance the investment process in Russia. Among its members are such prominent firms as ABB, Coca-Cola, United Technologies, Mars, Thomson, and British Petroleum. Members of the Council have defined their priorities and have proceeded to develop practical solutions. As a result, investment offices of Russian banks will be established in many parts of the world with the assistance of the Russian government.

Until recently, portfolio investments were directed primarily to the market for state short-term bonds (SDBs), which proved to be a very attractive investment. In the past year these bonds provided the basis for a mature state-securities market (T-market). This market plays an important role in lowering Russia's budget deficit and inflation rate, a benefit that piques the interest of Western investors.

Moreover, foreign portfolio investments have found another attractive source in the equity of privatized enterprises. Privatization has lead to the conversion of the country's largest enterprises into open joint stock companies enabling them to realize secondary emissions of equity and to increase their authorized capital while attracting outside investors. This market segment became available for foreign investors in the second half of 1993, when Russian brokerage firms received their initial orders for shares from foreign companies. By summer 1994, the interest shown in these types of equities was almost equal to that shown in the SDB market. Unlike the SDB market, however, this line of portfolio investments is subject to greater risks.

The activities of major investors aimed at acquiring major share holdings of enterprises and participating in their joint modernization are important. In this connection, the experience gained during the establishment of venture funds in various Russian regions, under the auspices of the European Bank for Reconstruction and Development, is of great importance. An essential goal of these funds was to develop a mechanism for the selection of investment projects that would be attractive to Western investors, including investment lines as well as their expected return on the investments.

The stock market has experienced a significant recovery. Because the equity of Russian privatized enterprises had been underestimated, they became attractive to Western investors who are returning to the market after a long interval. The principal Russian equity-market indices (AKM, ACII, CSFB, and ROS Indices) have tended to grow, an indication of a sufficiently meaningful stabilization of the Russian equity market. There is growing attention being paid to the utilities sector, which is considered to be the most secure sector in a steady or falling market. It is worth noting here that a great deal of interest has been shown not only to the equities of the Single Energy System Joint Stock Company (RAO ES) and the Mossenergo Joint Stock Company, investments that would be rather traditional for a typical Western investor's portfolio, but also to the equities of regional energy-producing companies.

This burst of interest in Russian equity is very different from what happened a while ago under similar conditions in certain emerging markets outside Russia. Because growing speculative interest in these led to the increase of local indices, Western investors' demand for equity had increased, which in turn initiated the second cycle of demand growth. Eventually, when the first signs of the problem began to emerge, a wave of investors decided to dispose of their shareholdings, which led to a sudden collapse of the whole market. This scenario is not possible in Russia because the capacity of the Russian market is much greater and new investment instruments that are not yet available to Western investors continue to emerge, which can lead to a change in the demand pattern. Under the present conditions, heads of Russian enterprises, realizing the benefits of attracting strategic investors and ordinary Western purchasers of their equity, are moving towards a purposeful marketing policy aimed at promoting further investment.

(b) Investment Attractiveness. Here are some of the principal reasons for investing money in the Russian economy.

1. Russia constitutes an internal market with enormous capacity. Its potential has gone unfulfilled because its industrial base is obsolete, most of its domestically manufactured goods are not competitive at present, and that it lacks many types of goods and services. Sales volumes and profit rates for various categories of goods have the potential to exceed those in the developed and even "mature" developing countries. At the same time, the government is pursuing a protectionist policy aimed at protecting domestic production. In this situation, importing capital is more profitable than importing goods. Therefore, the manufacturing of goods must be initiated in order to lessen the need for imported goods and decrease the costs of satisfying demand. This applies first of all to high-quality consumer goods and pharmaceuticals. Among the interesting examples of such production lines are the Lenvest joint venture created by the Salamander footwear company, a Mars confectionery concern, under construction near Moscow, Coca-Cola soft-drink factories, and an IBM joint venture assembly plant in Zelenograd.

2. Russia has a great deal of relatively low-cost land, buildings, and facilities.

3. Russia has enormous natural resources. After the collapse of the centralized state economic system, the production of many types of raw materials was reduced by more than half. Under these circumstances, it is necessary not only to develop new mineral and metal deposits, for example, but also to regenerate idle ones and to use technology to provide high output. The expected improvement in the world's principal markets for Russian export goods provides an additional impetus for investments.

4. Despite the fact that most of the staff of Russian enterprises not meet Western standards, few problems arise in connection with retraining. This is due to the fact that the majority of those employed in the production sphere have a secondary education. Russian scientific and technical personnel are college educated and are thus similar, for example, to American technicians. Russian workers also have extensive on-the-job experience, the level of pay, however, for highly qualified workers and the staff of research institutions is very low.

5. A number of industries have significant scientific and technological potential and have established a bank of innovative ideas and projects for the creation of high-tech products aimed at both the domestic market and the export market. In this

respect, it is worth noting some defense enteprises being converted to manufacture nonmilitary goods. The production of such goods will be based on domestic technology while foreign investors will introduce modern marketing techniques.

6. In instances where the production of goods at Russian enterprises is based on Western technologies, their potential as exports would be enhanced by the utilization of the established marketing networks of foreign partners. In these instances, their success would be guaranteed by relatively low production costs and cheap labor.

7. In Russia, there exist high-technology islands with science-intensive production facilities, qualified personnel, and an established reputation in the world labor market. The space industry is the most notable example, with its large infrastructure in the form of research bases, pilot and serial production lines, and launching complexes. Russia's numerous scientific and industrial complexes specializing in physics and chemistry also deserve attention.

8. The equity of Russian privatized enterprises has been underestimated as a result of large-scale privatization and the large number of shares of former state enterprises that have been put on the market in a short period of time.

(c) Special Features of the Capital Market and Prospects for Its Development. There are several factors that have hindered and slowed the investment process in Russia, including the following.

1. The instability and vagueness of the legislation governing taxes, tariffs, and the registration of enterprises with foreign participation are probably the factors that have produced the most unfavorable effects for potential investors. Effective measures aimed at promoting the inflow of foreign capital to Russia, however, are being planned. Among these are the coordination of activities between federal authorities and the subjects of the federation on issues regarding foreign investors, including the establishment of free economic zones.

   Other measures include the organization and holding of international investment tenders, preparation of concession production-sharing contracts, "filling" of loans received from international financial institutions and foreign states with specific investment projects, as well as finalizing Russian draft laws regulating the attraction of foreign investments and terms of foreign investors' economic activities. In addition, the measure regarding negotiations on agreements providing for mutual protection and promotion of investments is also important. At the same time, consideration should be given to the establishment of a system of insurance and guarantees for direct foreign investments, as well as to the development of a mechanism for use of mortgage forms to attract investments.

   A presidential decree providing for the introduction of up to 50% reduction in customs duties on individual goods for a period of up to five years has been implemented. This rate applies to goods produced and imported into the country by foreign companies that are implementing projects in Russia with capital costs of over $100 million.

   The government has adopted the resolution calling for preferential tariffs regarding of exports of crude oil and oil products from the Russian Federation that have been produced by enterprises with foreign investments. The regulation establishing the scope and application periods of these preferential tariffs has been approved. In addition, an interdepartmental commission composed of representatives from the Ministry of Fuel and Energy, Ministry of Economics, Ministry of Foreign Economic Relations, and Ministry of Finance has been created to prepare proposals regarding the tariffs.

2. Financial and economic instability has been aggravated by a sizable foreign debt and budget deficit. The external debt Russia inherited from the former USSR grew at an accelerated rate between 1985 and 1992 (i.e., the period of drastic economic and political reforms). Being the most developed country of those remaining from the Soviet Union and its successor, Russia has undertaken to repay the entire inherited debt, with the agreement of most states, that in exchange for repayment of the debt, Russia will acquire the rights to the other states' debts to the USSR and their property abroad. Currently, work is under way to recover loans provided to developing countries, the greatest progress being made with regard to the debts of India. The governmental policy aimed at minimizing and financing the budget deficit is satisfactory. The government declared that the practice of financing the deficit with emissions has been abandoned, and that a deficit-free budget was one of the government's strategic goals.

3. Uncertainty regarding the ownership of natural resources was another hindrance to the optimism of potential investors. Two laws were adopted recently, however, that help clarify and regulate the rights of ownership of mineral resources. These are the laws on concession contracts and production-sharing agreements. A major step has been taken towards establishment of a legislative base providing not only for temporary benefits, but also for necessary long-term guarantees of the repatriation of capital investments into the Russian economy. The law on production-sharing agreements permits certain adjustments to the investment mechanism in mining industries by the introduction of contractual relations between investors and the state. The law carries special importance due to the high capital intensity of investment projects in these industries and the resulting higher cost of investment risks. At the same time, the mining industry is the most attractive sector for today's potential investors because of the "convertible" character of, and stable demand for, its products.

4. The poor infrastructure outside metropolitan regions is another reason for the slow pace of foreign investments in the country. There are however, signs of change for the better. New regions are now served by eight currency exchanges, a development that opens broad opportunities for diverse arbitration operations based on the development of derivative instruments. The leading metropolitan banks are also creating a network of branches in the regions.

Helped in part by the cooperation of leading foreign firms, major improvements have been made in communication systems of the regions. The promising entrepreneurial opportunities make this sector attractive for foreign investment. In addition, the lack of hotels meeting international standards in the regional centers suggests that investing in the construction of new hotels would be a profitable venture.

5. Foreign investors are especially concerned about taxation in Russia. For instance, when enterprises with foreign investments import equipment, it is subject to a value-added tax that considerably increases its cost. Moreover, foreign investors, as well as domestic businesspeople, are concerned about the excess payroll tax that increases labor costs.

One should take into account the fact that the Russian power structure realizes the defects in its legislation and takes consistent measures to improve it. For instance, the rate of the value-added tax has recently decreased from 28 to 20%, the property tax base was drastically narrowed, and the maximum rate of income tax paid by individuals has dropped from 60 to 30%. Enterprises with foreign investments established after January 1, 1994, are exempt from the profit tax paid to the federal budget if the investment of a foreign partner exceeds $10 million.

6. There is an acute shortage of information that foreign investors need for establishing operations in Russia. Guidelines on the operation of the Russian stock market that meet international standards are badly needed. There are no standard accounting formats and, moreover, the management of some business enterprises conceals accounting data. In spite of the presence of the "Big Six" accounting firms, only the leading Russian firms and banks are audited according to international standards.

7. One of the most important problems impeding the increase of investments is the lack of adequate training and project-feasibility studies in the country. The overwhelming majority of proposals presented to potential investors contain only a definition of the project or a very sketchy general description with few economic calculations. Some projects, however, are built on a solid economic and marketing basis and undergo thorough examination by experts; but even then the project is usually far from meeting Western standards. Therefore, Russian banks have to be very selective about which projects should be implemented. Only the biggest Russian banks are able to examine all relevant facets of an enterprise that needs direct investment and to conduct an expert evaluation of a project. What the system needs are new approaches to project design and an accounting system that meets western standards.

In spite of all these shortcomings, it would be unrealistic and probably foolish to risk waiting for an improvement in investment legislation before entering the Russian market; smarter competitors simply may not wait. Immediate investing in the market makes sense. As the environment for Russian investments improves, it will be easier to add to them by using the channels and lines that have already been established. One cannot wait for market stability as the idea is understood in the west. In Russia, it should be viewed exclusively in the context of the Russian economic experience. Moreover, the fact cannot be ignored that a delay in investing may result in missed profits that will never be recovered.

(d) Russian Banks as the Driving Force in the Investment Process.   Banking is the most market-oriented sector of Russian business. In fact, commercial banks are the focal point of business activities; they develop new methods of investment and activity in the securities market. In recent years, rapidly growing Russian banks have influenced the market by buying up shareholdings of the privatized enterprises and investing in them. Within the framework of the second stage of privatization, the merger of bank and industrial capitals, including financial and industrial groups, is under way. The largest Russian banks are interested in constructive and long-term cooperation with Western investors. In turn, cooperation with Russian banks would be beneficial for Western investors because only Russian banks possess detailed and accurate information about the market and can forecast its fluctuations.

(e) The Role of Banks in the Development of the Russian Securities Market.   The continued development of the securities market in Russia is dependent on its integration with Western stock markets. For Western investors this means, in particular, guarantees for their investments in the Russian economy; for Russian investors, it means the expansion of their investment portfolios by acquiring Western securities. Such a process is possible only with the participation of stock-market professionals, one of which is the Rossiyskiy Kredit Bank because it is experienced and has a General License of the Russian Central Bank, which allows it to conduct operations with foreign securities. The Rossiyskiy Kredit Bank ranks fifth in the country in the volume of its assets, controls 20 enterprises, has subsidiary structures abroad, has gained authority in Russia and abroad, and can act as a guarantor. Its notable position in the stock market, extensive experience, close cooperation with enterprises, and knowledge of the legislation for developing investment projects allow the bank to provide legal, investment, and information services. Foreign investors can receive advice concerning the stock market, buy and sell equity, and acquire depositary services. Rossiyskiy Kredit Bank was the first in the country to adopt the CEDEL international-clearing system.

Potential investors often find there is a problem of providing a legal basis for the investment process. According to Russian legislation, foreign investors can make investments only from specific accounts designed for that purpose and in rubles. Since there are few foreign banks in the domestic market, and the majority of registered banks with foreign capital participation are not allowed to deal with Russian residents, a special plan involving the participation of a Russian bank is used. A foreign investor opens two accounts in an authorized Russian bank (which has a license for foreign exchange operations) through its office in Russia; these are an investment account and a foreign currency account. The funds are converted and transferred, as appropriate, from one account to the other and are freely repatriated to the donor county. (See Exhibit 16.1.)

Exhibit 16.1.   Investment in Equity of Russian Enterprises

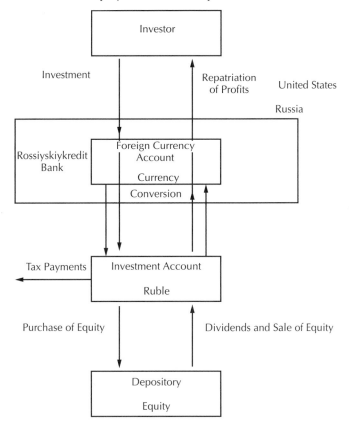

In reference to conservative portfolios, it is thought that the government securities market will receive an impetus for development in the near future. Future sales of SDBs, as well as U.S. dollars are being arranged at the Moscow Interbank Currency Exchange, which will attract additional investors by investment hedging. The MICE is developing a network of official dealers needed to manage these operations, including the Rossiyskiy Kredit Bank. Due to the introduction of new securities such as gold certificates, federal bonds, and foreign-exchange bonds, the market of government securities is constantly expanding.

A portfolio that includes equity of Russian privatized enterprises would increase the profits of its owner. Western investors are familiar only with the equity of a limited number of enterprises with low-risk investment potential. Within the framework of cash privatization, however, a lot of equities that would be of interest to foreign investors have emerged on the market. The introduction of the equity of Russian enterprises in the international market is an expensive and protracted process. Therefore, foreign investors might be interested in taking advantage of a number of Russian investment funds currently being formed; these will be registered in accordance with Russian legislation where maximum benefits are provided for operations with securities. The promoters of these funds include state bodies and authorized banks, and there are plans to invite foreign financial institutions to participate. The equity of Russian enterprises from the state share will be contributed as unauthorized capital. After they are established, these investments funds will issue their own securities, which will be quoted on the world's largest stock exchanges. Another avenue of cooperation between the financial institutions of Russia and the United States is the idea of establishing a joint financial company, the activities of which would include all kinds of stock services on the Russian and world markets.

CHAPTER 17

GOVERNMENT DEBT MARKET

Bella Zlatkis

17.1 OVERVIEW. In 1992, a term reappeared in Russian that had been forgotten for many years: internal state debt of the Russian Federation. The term is illogical because 96% of Russian property was held by the state. A special Russian law describes what is included in the internal state department. The law also covers the rights, obligations, and the government's legislative and executive powers to increase internal borrowing. According to Russian law, the government can impose, concurrent with the adoption of the federal budget, a ceiling for increasing internal debt. The government has the power to create the form and method of such borrowing. The responsibility of circulation and service of state treasury bills lies with the executive branch.

17.2 STATE TREASURY BILLS ISSUED. The Ministry of Finance of the Russian Federation made a decision to become, in a short period of time, a highly rated borrower. Its strategy was described in a program for the creation of state treasury bonds, whose quality was to be on par with bonds issued on Western markets. To reach this goal, it was necessary for Russia to create a very reliable trade, payment, and depository system. Treasury bonds must not only be reliable and highly liquid, but they must also offer a competitive return to investors.

Winning the trust of investors in Russia has not been an easy task. Russia was saddled with the internal debt inherited from the former USSR (almost equal to the state's annual budget), with no means of repayment. The situation was exacerbated by the high inflation that shook the Russian economy in 1992 and 1993. Nevertheless, in the past few years Russia has solved the problem and, in large measure, regained the trust of investors. Russia is gradually repaying the unconditional obligations of the former USSR, and has recognized the remainder of its obligations, which will be repaid in the future.

The government is also trying to build trust within the internal market. A relationship has been established with the Central Bank of the Russian Federation, for example. The Supreme Soviet of Russia and the Duma passed federal laws regarding banks and banking activities, and another law regarding the Central Bank. These laws unconditionally prohibit both the government from obtaining credit from the Central Bank, and the bank from buying treasury bonds during their initial offering.

The remaining government debt owed to the Central Bank (from the Soviet period and the first year of perestroika) was serviced by the government according to schedule. Gradually, the credit situation stabilized, allowing the Ministry of Finance to issue the first substantial tranche of short-term state bonds.

The main goal of issuing government debt in Russia was to cover the annual budget deficit and refinance previous debt obligations. Traditionally, to achieve these goals, governments sell long- and medium-term obligations. Due to the relatively high inflation, however, the Russian government is issuing predominantly short-term bonds. Occasionally, midterm obligations are issued with one- to three-year maturity rates.

Debt securities in Russia are primarily structured for the wholesale market of large banks and financial institutions by the Ministry of Finance. Individual companies and small institutional investors, however, can also participate in these issues.

The bonds, called GKOs (government short-term noncoupon bonds), mature within three months, six months, or one year. These bonds are issued at discount; in other words, the income on the GKOs is the difference between the face value (nominal) and price of the investment held to maturity. The capital gains are tax free. The bonds take the form of global certificates, issued from the Central Bank and are kept on account in a special depository. Because of its trustworthiness and liquidity, the Central Bank was chosen as the agent; and the Moscow Interbank Currency Exchange (MICE) was selected for its trading system.

During the last two and a half years of GKO sales, the Ministry of Finance held 70 auctions. Bonds sold at these auctions have been paid off from special accounts at the MICE. Due to the success and security of these issues, the market has gained a fair amount of trust in them. The Moscow Interbank Currency Exchange, the most modern trading and depository system in the country, makes it possible to organize daily secondary trades of GKOs; money to buy the GKOs is deposited by primary dealers. Cash payments and bonds are delivered within the day.

In 1995, the total market for short-term GKO obligations was 60 trillion rubles. Daily turnover was approximately one trillion rubles. Their high liquidity and safety in the market have paved the way for raising additional funds that allow the Ministry of Finance to cover, from the internal market, approximately half of the budget deficit. Non-Russian residents are also permitted to buy GKO's, but with some limitations. They cannot buy more than 10% of the common market value and only from current special accounts. The capital-gains tax benefits also apply to nonresidents.

The limits on foreign investors are based on a projectionist financial-market policy and a domestic policy that favors the interest of national capital. Russia is facing a problem in that the foreign capital invested in the country is sought after by other emerging markets. There is a constant threat that the foreign invested funds could flow out of Russia and into other emerging markets. If this happens, it could cause major problems for Russia's economy, which is the reason for the foreign participation limit.

Midterm state bonds (OFZs) were issued with maturities from one to 15 years. The gains on the bonds are paid quarterly and are tax free; all calculations are made on an interday basis. The interest rate on both short- and medium-term bonds provides a good return against inflation. As inflation decreases, however, the paper profit also decreases, providing safety to the government exchange system.

17.3 FUTURE SIGNIFICANT WORK.   In addition to the achievements in the financial market, solving the problem of financing Russia's deficit budget will require a good relationship with the main players in the market, including the Ministry of Finance and the Central Bank. It will require the trust of all the government ministries and agencies, as well as the creation of financial instruments that allow people to hold first-class debt. Funds that are put aside for financing the budget do not represent all available resources; the remaining free money can find its place in other safe, liquid markets. The main financial problem facing the government is not the lack of funds or the competition for them, but the ability to create a market in which Russia can issue secure and liquid treasury paper.

In 1995, faith in Russia's national currency increased over the prior year; however, relatively high inflation persists. The main factor in stabilizing the ruble will be to change Russian institutional investor's preference for foreign currency. With this goal in mind, the government has issued interest-bearing treasury bills in order to gradually attract dollars to be invested in ruble-denominated instruments. One of the main problems that must be solved is the creation of viable agent-banks that can work with the population as well as with the current trade system.

Another significant problem for the government is its inability to protect pension funds from inflation. To address this issue, the government has issued special obligations for individual investors. Moreover, the government plans to issue medium-term obligations with interest that not only keeps pace with inflation but also could exceed it.

The government treasury-bill market has made significant progress and gained international recognition. With economic and political stabilization, Russia could become, in the near future, one of the most important financial centers in the world.

CHAPTER 18

FUTURE OF THE DEBT MARKET FOR FOREIGN INVESTORS

Konstantin V. Bazarkin

18.1 TYPES OF SECURITIES IN CIRCULATION: QUANTITATIVE AND QUALITATIVE INDICES OF THE MARKETS. In the Russian stock market, the following types of government securities are currently in circulation:

- Government short-term noncoupon bonds (GKOs)
- Government savings-and-loan bonds (OGSZs)
- Government internal hard-currency denominated bonds (OGVVZs)
- Federal loan bonds with variable coupons (OFZ-PKs)
- Republican government internal bonds of 1991 (OGRVZs)

The portion of each type of bond in the total structure of government borrowing can be seen in Exhibit 18.1.

(a) Government Internal Noncoupon Bonds (GKOs). Borrowing through the use of republican government internal bonds for internal loans is conducted on a long-term basis only. In accordance with conditions for issuing bonds, they are issued for a period of 30 years. The announced nominal volume is equal to 80 billion rubles (about $50 million at the exchange rate of 5,450 rubles per dollar), divided into 16 subsections of five billion rubles each. Actually, on the current market, bonds are being circulated with total nominal volume on the order of 30 billion rubles (about $5.5 million at the rate of exchange of 5,450 rubles/dollar). Income is paid once a year according to a floating interest rate.

Bonds are sold by the institutions governed by the Central Bank of Russia and only by legal persons. At the present time, loans are not liquid and are low income; there is no demand for them from participants in the market.

(b) Government Savings-and-Loan Bonds (OGSZs). Government savings-and-loan bonds are issued, at present, in separate series for an average period of one year. There are four coupons made out to actual persons. Interest income for the coupon is determined separately for each coupon period and equals the last officially announced coupon rate for federal bonds with variable coupon income (OFZ-PKs). The bonds have different nominal costs (100,000 and 500,000 rubles).

On November 1, 1996, the nominal cost of all issues in circulation was nine trillion rubles ($1.65 billion at the exchange rate of 5,450 rubles/dollar). The duration of the market

Exhibit 18.1. Government Bond Market Structure

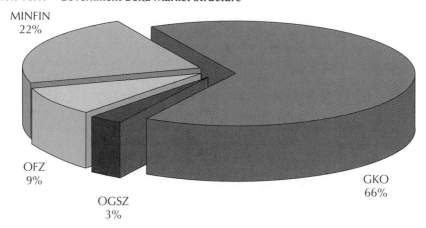

is 368 days. The distribution of volumes according to time period can be seen in Exhibits 18.2 and 18.3.

(c) Government Internal Hard-Currency Denominated Bonds (OGVVZs). These bonds were issued in 1993 for adjusting the internal currency debt of the former USSR. The following basic conditions for issuance exist:

Issuer	Ministry of Finances
Currency of loan	U.S. dollars
Coupon interest rate	3% annual (May 14 of each year)
Current time period until full payment	3–15 years (3–7 minimum)

The current nominal cost of all issues in circulation is 29 billion rubles ($5.327 million at the current exchange rate of 5,450 rubles/dollar). Exhibit 18.4 shows the distribution of volumes according to time period.

Exhibit 18.2. Capitalization of 26 Trillion Rubles ($4.77 Billion)

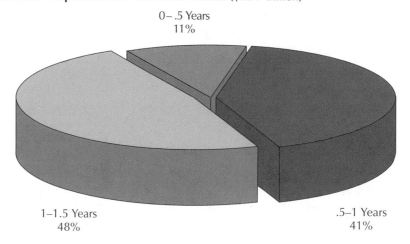

Exhibit 18.3.   Total Face Amount of Issued Debt 9 Trillion Rubles ($1.65 Billion)

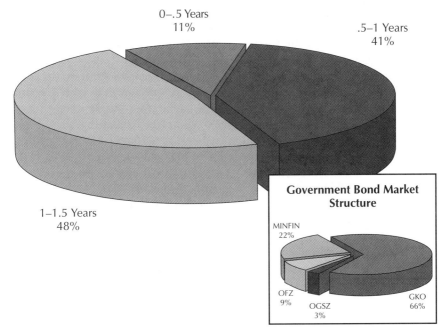

0–.5 Years
11%

.5–1 Years
41%

1–1.5 Years
48%

Government Bond Market Structure

MINFIN
22%

OFZ
9%

OGSZ
3%

GKO
66%

**Exhibit 18.4.   MinFin Bonds
Total Face Amount of Issued Debt $11.12 Billion
Total Market Value of Issued Debt $5.37 Billion**

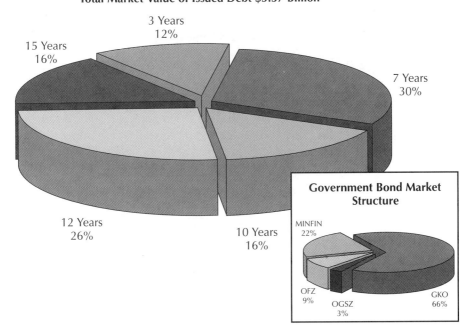

3 Years
12%

15 Years
16%

7 Years
30%

12 Years
26%

10 Years
16%

Government Bond Market Structure

MINFIN
22%

OFZ
9%

OGSZ
3%

GKO
66%

The duration of the market is 9.5 years. The average interest rate for this time period is 12% per year in dollars.

(d) Federal Loan Bonds with Variable Coupons (OFZ-PKs or T-notes).   Medium-term borrowing has been offered since June 1995 (from one to five years). The issuer is the Ministry of Finance, and the Central Bank is the general agent for servicing. Income from the bonds comprises quarterly payments. The value of the coupon income is determined separately for each coupon period and is divided into average-weight income for paying off GKO issues equal to the time period of the coupon. (See Exhibit 18.4.)

Data on the existing coupon payments are reported seven days before paying the previous coupon (date for beginning distribution). The first and second circulation is accomplished at the Moscow Interbank Currency Exchange (MICE) jointly with GKO.

According to conditions on November 1, 1996, the nominal cost of all issues put into circulation was 26 trillion rubles ($4.77 billion at the exchange rate of 5,450 rubles/dollar) with the distribution of volumes according to the time period shown in Exhibits 18.5 and 18.6.

The duration of the market is 375 days.

18.2 SPECIAL POSITION OF THE GKO/OFZ-PK MARKET

(a) Exchange Technology as a Guarantee of the Absence of Credit and Operational Risks.   The modern GKO/OFZ-PK market is being developed on the basis of very forward-looking currency technologies, which have shown their effectiveness in practice. There are

Exhibit 18.5.   OFZ
Total Face Amount of Issued Debt 26 Trillion Rubles ($4.77 Billion)
Total Market Value of Issued Debt 27 Trillion Rubles ($4.95 Billion)

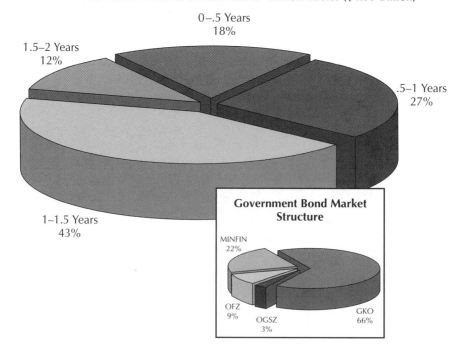

Exhibit 18.6.   Capitalization 26 Trillion Rubles ($4.77 Billion)

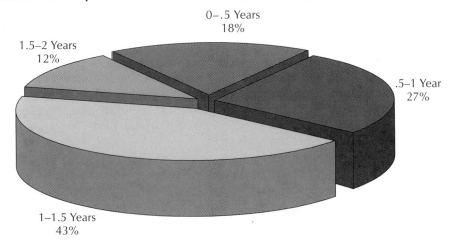

several basic procedures that guarantee interaction between the exchange and other sections of the market:

- Permission of GKO/OFZ-PK circulation
- Permission for participants in commerce
- Output of application and completion of transaction
- Accounts of transactions

(b) Admittance for GKO/OFZ-PKs into Circulation.   GKO/OFZ-PKs are issued only in noncash form, and each of the issuances is formulated by a general certificate retained at the Central Bank. The right of ownership to GKO/OFZ-PK begins the moment they are recorded in the books of the Central Bank. Issuance is accomplished, as a rule, once a week for a time period of three and/or six months. Repayment is made in noncash form by recalculating the nominal cost of the GKO/OFZ-PKs to their owners at the moment of full payment.

Circulation of GKO/OFZ-PKs is accomplished only after completion of the buying and selling transactions through the commercial system. Calculations, according to transaction, are accomplished for securities through the depository and through the accounting system for money. The functions of the commercial system, the depository, and the accounting system are carried out by the Moscow Interbank Currency Exchange on the basis of the appropriate agreement with the Central Bank of Russia. A commercial deposit system and a system of electronic interbank payments have been developed and adopted for the marketing of these functions at MICE.

(c) Participants in the GKO/OFZ-PK Market.   The participants in the GKO/OFZ-PK market include:

- The issuer, the Ministry of Finance
- The general agent for servicing issues, the Central Bank
- The owners of the GKOs, investors including citizens and naturalized residents, non-residents, and dealers. See Exhibits 18.7 and 18.8

Exhibit 18.7.   GKO
Total Face Amount of Issued Debt 183 Trillion Rubles ($34 Billion)
Total Market Value of Issued Debt 160 Trillion Rubles ($29 Billion)

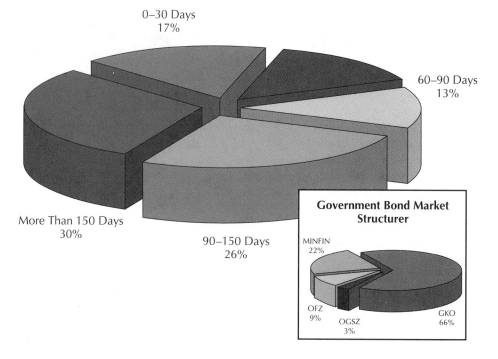

Exhibit 18.8.   Average Annual GKO Yield

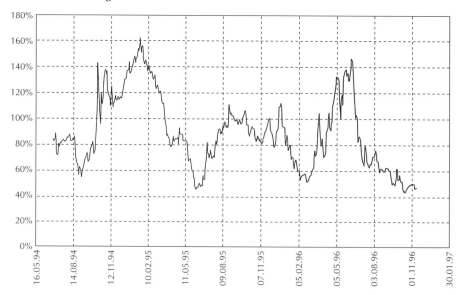

A total of 310 dealers of GKO/OFZ-PKs were legally listed according to specified conditions as of November 1, 1996. The dealers were divided into two categories: 42 primary and 268 secondary. The primary dealers were involved with functions of market makers. Most-Bank, one of Russia's leading financial institutions, received the honor of being one of the first primary dealers.

(d) Taking Applications and Completion of Transactions. Taking applications and completing transactions are accomplished with the help of the commerce system. The commerce system organizes the:

- Conduct of commerce;
- Recording of transactions;
- Compilation of various documents according to the transaction made. (The rights for this are given by the dealer, in accordance with the agreement on participation in the system of electronic commerce issued by the MICE regarding GKO/OFZ-PK transactions.)
- Presentation of accounting documents in the accounting system and deposition system. (These functions are carried out by the commerce-deposition system of the MICE.)

GKO/OFZ-PK operations are accomplished using the following methods:

- Primary placement (public sale)
- Circulation of GKO/OFZ-PKs in the secondary market (commerce)
- Payment of GKO/OFZ-PKs

(e) Payment for Transactions. The Payment for GKO/OFZ-PKs is accomplished after:

- Delivery according to specifications;
- Full reservation of monetary means and bonds guaranteeing unconditional fulfillment of debt has been established.

Relying on these principles, the calculation per day $(T + O)$ fully eliminates all risks for default of obligations and presents participants with the possibility of:

- Using monetary means obtained from sale of GKO/OFZ-PKs in the course of a commercial session for reverse buying of GKO/OFZ-PKs during bidding;
- Selling all GKO/OFZ-PKs purchased earlier during an exchange session for the period of this same session.

Considering all the information that is available about the exchange technology, one can conclude that there is almost no operational and credit risks in the GKO/OFZ-PK market.

18.3 ORDER OF ADMITTANCE OF NONRESIDENTS IN THE GKO/OFZ-PK MARKETS. At the present time, a special system for investment by nonresidents in the GKO/OFZ-PK market has been established. For investment in GKO/OFZ-PKs, according to this system, it is necessary for a nonresident to:

Exhibit 18.9.   Principal Mechanism of Exchange Operations from Special C-Type Accounts

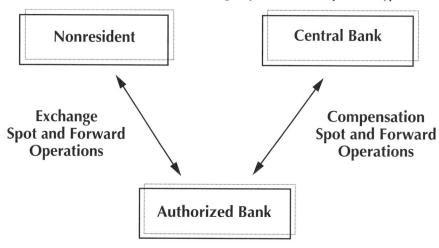

- In an authorized Russian bank, open a C-type bank account in the currency of the Russian Federation. (Exhibit 18.9 outlines the exchange operations regarding these types of accounts.) At the present time, the Central Bank has identified 22 authorized banks that have the right to open and operate C-type accounts. (Exhibit 18.10 shows the cities in which regional trading floors of the GKO/OFZ-PKs are located.) Most-Bank was one of the country's first banks to receive this authorization.

Exhibit 18.10.   Regional Trading Floors of the GKO/OFZ-PK Markets

- Make an agreement with an official GKO market dealer for servicing.
- Through an authorized bank, sell, foreign currency for Russian Federation rubles. Money from the sale is put into a nonresident C-type account. The rubles from the account must acquire GKO/OFZ-PKs.
- Prepare a timely conversion transaction with an authorized bank. The minimum time period for conversion transactions is three months. The exchange rate of the transaction is set by the Central Bank depending on the current currency rate and the income from issues of GKOs established during the redemption period. In this way, the purchase of the GKOs, with subsequent forward execution guarantees an income of 16% annually in foreign currency.

The transaction time period is calculated to include the possibility of rejecting the execution (option). After the transaction is concluded, the nonresident pays the bank a fee (option premium) of 1.0 to 1.5% of the total future transaction.

The simplest strategy is to purchase a forward conclusion simultaneously with the GKOs for the corresponding time period before full payment, which guarantees a profit, including the commission expense, of at least 15% annually in hard currency. (Exhibit 18.11 provides an example of the effectiveness of using forward and option strategies.)

Exhibit 18.11. Example of the Effectiveness of Investments Using Forward and Option Strategies

1. Conversion cash transaction

Volume of investment	$10 000 000
Rate of TSB rubles/$	5,456
Rate of Most-Bank rubles/$	5,451
Losses in conversion, %	0.09
Commission for investment in GKO	
Commission of MICE, %	0.05
Commission of Most-Bank, %	0.005

2. Conversion short-term transaction

2.1. Transaction in forward conditions

Time period—6 months	
Rate, % annual	16
Commission Most-Bank, %	0.09
Effectiveness of the entire operation, %	~15

2.2 Transaction in option conditions

Premium offered by TSB, %	1.0
Premium offered by Most-Bank, %	0.3
Profitability of the GKO market for a three month period (taking into consideration the predicted dynamics of the rate of the dollar), % annual in $	29
Profitability obtained in a time period of 3 months in case of refusal of the option, % annual in $	24
Total profitability obtained in a 6-month period with forward conclusion for a rate of 16% for the succeeding 3 months	20

18.4 CONCLUSION.   Several basic elements of the Russian GKO/OFZ-PK market have caught the attention of Western investors:

- The great interest of the government in attracting external investment and the creation of a positive precedent that involves governmental trusteeship of the project;
- Full hedging of the risk of currency using the option issued by the Central Bank;
- The fairly high current profit in currency, undoubtedly larger than that proposed for Eurobonds, whose issuance is planned for the near future;
- Government control of all stages of commerce and calculations.

CHAPTER 19

INVESTING

Thomas D. Sanford

19.1 FUNDAMENTAL FACTS.   The most popular and fastest-growing way to buy Russian stocks and bonds today is through depository receipts (American depository receipts—ADRs, or global depository receipts—GDRs.) Today only The Bank of New York issues Russian ADRs and GDRs, but more depositories are expected to enter the field once some of the political and business uncertainties are reduced.

Depository receipts (including depository shares) are securities issued by a depository bank evidencing local, home-market shares, which the depository either holds in a local custodian bank or, as registrant, on the books of the company that issued the home-market shares. In Russia, The Bank of New York uses two custodian banks: ING Bank Eurasia facilitates reregistrations of equity shares into and out of BNY's name and receives a copy of the share extract (page in the Share Register) each time a reregistration occurs; RosVneshtorgbank custodizes physical MinFin bonds, providing BNY with complete records of bond series, par values, serial numbers, and deposit dates.

Depository receipts are exchangeable for the shares and vice versa, so the price of either should be about identical. Depository receipts trade in U.S. dollars, but their underlying values are local shares; so if the local currency appreciates against the dollar, the depository receipt price rises and vice versa, all other things equal. Depository receipts trade over-the-counter and are listed on many exchanges throughout the world, including the NYSE, AMEX, NASDAQ, London, Singapore, Australia, Luxembourg, Berlin, Frankfurt, Munich, Johannesburg, and most recently, Budapest (see Exhibit 19.1). The trend toward regional listings will grow as more exchanges and local settlement systems link up with the New York Depository Trust Company, Euroclear, and CEDEL. These major central depository systems, as well as most regional stock exchanges, all accept depository receipts as eligible securities, giving them a major advantage over local shares, which may not be eligible for either deposit into these depositories or listing on regional exchanges.

Depository receipts are usually called ADRs when they are sold or pitched towards the U.S. market, and GDRs when they are sold or pitched towards worldwide institutional investors. In fact, most ADRs are registered, to some extent, with the U.S. Securities and Exchange Commission for trading in the U.S. public markets, while most GDR issues are sold privately to institutional investors without going through the registration process. GDR issuers usually rely on Rule 144A and Regulation S to avoid registration.

Companies use depository receipts to sell equity and enhance liquidity. Depository receipts repackage a company's shares so they can be sold to international investors who want the convenience and safety of a security that is eligible for deposit and settlement in the major depositories such as DTC and Euroclear. Depository receipts enhance liquidity

Exhibit 19.1.   Depository Receipts

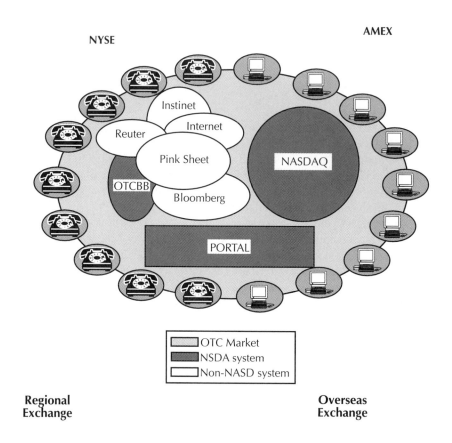

Regional
Exchange

Overseas
Exchange

by moving the locus of share trading to the larger, more liquid markets in the Americas, Europe, and Asia without sacrificing any home-market liquidity. Investors prefer investing in depository receipts because they are easy to buy and sell through a broker, they enjoy the dual liquidity of both the depository-receipt market and the home market, dividends and other distributions are conveniently paid in U.S. dollars and all the problems and concerns of share transfer and custody are left to the depository, the issuing company, and their agents. (See Exhibit 19.2.)

19.2 TYPES OF PROGRAMS.   Companies have a choice of three types of *unrestricted* sponsored ADR programs that all trade publicly in the United States, and *restricted* depository-receipts programs (sponsored Rule 144A ADRs and GDRs), which trade privately in the United States.

(a) Sponsored Level-I ADRs.   The DR program that is the easiest to set up is the Level-I program because it requires the least level or degree of SEC reporting and disclosure.

Exhibit 19.2.   Total Number of Depository Receipt Programs

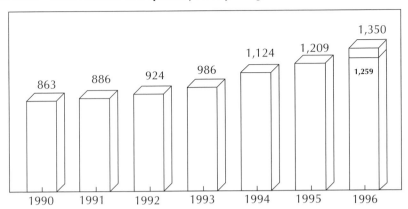

First, the company complies with the 1934 Exchange Act by applying for a reporting exemption known as Rule 12g3–2(b). The exemption simply requires the company to furnish the SEC the same information it makes public in its home market, with no requirement to conform its financial statements to U.S. Generally Accepted Accounting Principles (GAAP). Next, the company and the depository sign a deposit agreement and register the ADRs, which will be issued by the depository on the simple Form F–6, thus complying with the 1933 Securities Act. Once Form F–6 is declared effective by the SEC, the depository may issue unrestricted ADRs in response to deposits of home-market shares that are bought in secondary market transactions. Level-I ADRs cannot be used by the company to raise new capital, and they trade only on the U.S. unlisted, over-the-counter market, not over NASDAQ, or on an exchange such as the New York or the American.

Level-I ADRs are the fastest growing type. Of the 866 sponsored programs, 531 are Level-I. Most companies begin by sponsoring a Level-I program before they upgrade to a higher level.

(b) Sponsored Level-II and III ADRs.   Companies that choose to list their securities on a U.S. exchange or raise capital use Level-II or III ADRs, respectively. Companies that wish to list on a U.S. exchange must register under the 1934 Exchange Act on Form 20–F, which requires U.S. GAAP, and meet the listing requirements of the exchange or NASDAQ. Companies that raise capital must do what is required for a listing as well as register the offering under the 1933 Securities Act on Form F–1 or prospectus, which also requires U.S. GAAP disclosures. (See Exhibit 19.3 for total number of depository receipt programs.)

(c) Restricted DRs.   Companies that wish to raise capital overseas without registering a U.S. public offer with the SEC generally make global offerings of unregistered, restricted securities. (See Exhibit 19.4 for total capital raised in public depository receipt offering.) The most common global offering structures include a share offering in the home-country market, a U.S. private placement of Rule 144A DRs (GDRs or ADRs) to very large institutional investors known as QIBs (Qualified Institutional Buyers), and a Euro-placement of either more shares or Regulation S DRs to other non-U.S. investors. Rule 144A DRs carry resale restrictions for at least two years before they may be sold to U.S. public investors, whereas Regulation S DRs carry shorter resale restrictions. After the statutory 40-day seasoning period following the completion of the global offering, most companies that

Exhibit 19.3. **Total Number of Listed Depository Receipt Programs (NYSE, AMEX, and NASDAQ)**

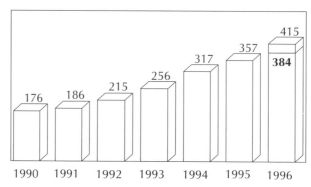

offer restricted DRs set up side-by-side Level-I DR programs, creating U.S. public-market demand for their securities, which may counter the postoffering flow back into securities of the home market.

Additionally, companies that offered restricted DRs in the past are now registering public offerings of DRs that may be exchanged for the restricted ones. These registered exchange offers give institutional investors a far more liquid investment and the company an opportunity to raise additional capital and/or list on a U.S. exchange. The SEC encourages this process and coined the phrase *stepping stone* to describe companies that raise private capital first and then register an exchange offer later. (See Exhibit 19.5 for a comparison of ADR Facilities.)

19.3 HOW DEPOSITORY RECEIPTS WORK. DRs are issued or created by the depository when an investor or its broker purchases home-market securities and deposits them with the depository's local custodian along with instructions to issue and deliver DRs. Conversely, DRs are canceled and home-market securities are released from custody when an investor or its broker surrenders DRs to the depository along with instructions to deliver securities in the home market. Once DRs are issued by the depository, they trade and settle as DRs, just like any security that trades and settles in that particular market-

Exhibit 19.4. **Total Capital Raised in Public Depository Receipt Offerings (Millions of U.S. Dollars)**

Exhibit 19.5.   ADR Facility Comparison

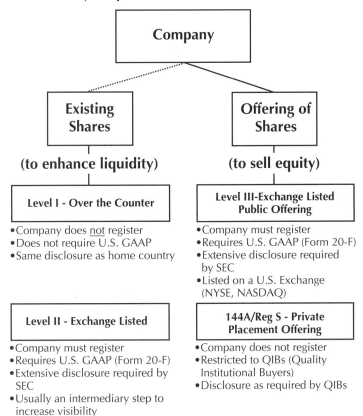

place, be it the United States, Europe, or Asia. (See Exhibit 19.6 for an illustration of the settlement process for depository receipts.)

19.4 RUSSIAN REALITY.   Depository receipts are ideal for Russian stocks and bonds because they deal effectively with all the widely publicized risks relating to registration, settlement, custody, and ownership that are the aftermath of Russia's economic revolution. We all know that the voucher privatization program resulted in thousands of share registries being set up all over Russia. Many of these registries were poorly managed and were captive operations of the companies issuing the stock. Not surprisingly, some abuses occurred. Names of some investors were not properly added to the share register or, in some instances, names were removed from the register for no apparent reason. International investors and regulatory bodies became concerned about reported abuses and the lack of reliable independent registries.

The other side of voucher privatization was that thousands of new securities flooded brand new markets with little or no infrastructure. Obviously, a great deal of chaos would have occurred while securities laws were written, stock exchanges organized, creditable institutions created, and market practices evolved. So while the largest remaining economy privatized, there were few opportunities for foreign investors to participate with any safety, until The Bank of New York adapted its depository receipts programs to the special concerns of investing in Russia and began offering Russian DRs.

Exhibit 19.6.   Depository Receipts Settlement (DRs are created by crossborder transactions and then trade intramarket)

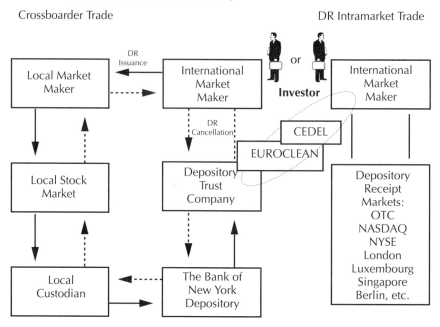

Crossboarder Trade   DR Intramarket Trade

3 Business Days (New York)

(a) Deposit Agreements.   The legal basis for a DR program is the deposit agreement, a three-party contract among the company, the depository, and owners and holders of depository receipts. The deposit agreement sets forth in detail how the program operates and all duties, responsibilities, liabilities, and exonerations of each of the three parties. While all deposit agreements are largely the same, it is not unusual to find *country specific* provisions in deposit agreements for all companies from a certain country.

Russian deposit agreements include unusually thorough details about local market practice, share registration, and dispute resolution. These provisions were largely mandated by the U.S. SEC, which not only demanded full disclosure of risks, but also insisted on certain procedures and undertakings that would presumably reduce investor risk. In fact, the Russian deposit agreements are excellent for both the companies that want to sell their stock in the global markets and for investors who want to minimize operational or systemic risk. Now, many of the special features in Russian deposit agreements have found their way into agreements signed by companies from other emerging markets.

(b) Registry Risk.   The Bank of New York's Russian deposit agreement all but eliminate Russian registry risk by (1) pre-qualifying the depository as a registrant on the company's books and (2) placing the responsibility of the registrar's performance squarely with the issuer company that appoints its registrar. This legal concept of a principal's responsibility for its agent is part of all depository receipts, but is highlighted in Russian programs. Finally, if the company becomes disenchanted with its depository receipts program, it need not erase the depository from its share register. The company simply and legally terminates the program, and share ownership will return to Russia.

(c) Settling Disputes.   Russian deposit agreements include a provision to settle disputes through arbitration in New York or London because the Russian courts will not necessarily uphold a U.S. court decision. In addition to the arbitration provision, the Russian company appoints an agent for service of process and agrees to submit to the U.S. courts under certain circumstances, including matters involving U.S. securities law.

(d) Settlement Risk.   The settlement of Russian securities purchases and sales requires numerous documents, physical presentation among custodians, registrars, buyers and sellers, and attorneys-in-fact. The Depository receipts mechanism shifts the responsibility away from the investor to the depository and its agent. Once Russian depository receipts are issued, they become either book-entry securities within the global system of central depositories or paper certificates that can be kept in any safe-deposit box or vault. Depository receipts, no matter their country of origin, settle as reliably as AT&T or IBM.

(e) Custody Risk.   Russian custody risk (or the risk of holding and servicing shares) is a bit of a myth because there are usually no physical securities to hold. Equity ownership is typically evidenced by the shareholder's name on the share register with no paper certificates to back it up. While this system has its efficiencies, it does not eliminate the need for custodians to facilitate transfers at the registry, collect dividends, and vote shares at shareholder meetings. Fortunately, there is a growing number of capable custodian banks in Russia to perform these tasks, though few, if any, qualify under Rule 17f-5 of the Investment Company Act of 1940 to act on behalf of U.S. institutional investors. Nevertheless, these same U.S. institutions may purchase Russian depository receipts, which they can hold with their qualified non-Russian custodian banks because, for purposes of this statute, depository receipts are viewed as separate securities. Without depository receipts, most U.S. funds would be precluded from investing in Russian securities.

(f) Ownership Risk.   Ownership is not always clear cut, particularly in Russia, where these rights are now only evolving into laws that remain unclear, untested, and sometimes contradictory. Depository receipts do not eliminate the risk of ownership (or confiscation by a previous owner), but they do highlight the risk and prorate the loss. Russian deposit agreements highlight the risk by containing a legend that appears on the face of receipts, alerting investors to some of the legal risks and vagaries of purchasing Russian securities. Furthermore, if some of the securities deposited in good faith into the program prove to be stolen and are seized by the courts, depository receipt investors, owning an undivided interest in a pool of securities, will share equally in the loss. Here again, depository receipts address features unique to Russia's evolving legal system.

(g) Russian Depository Receipt Update.   The Bank of New York's 17 Russian depository receipts programs have been very successful. The market capitalization of Russian equity depository receipts outstanding is $3.5 billion and $1 billion face value for Russian MinFin bond depository receipts. In terms of the entire depository receipt market value of $280 billion, Russia's 1.5% is small, but growing rapidly and results from very few issues having traded for less than one year. Within two years, Russia's share of the entire depository receipts market could exceed 5%.

Here is a list of Russian depository receipts issued by The Bank of New York:

Equity Depository Receipts	**Debt Depository Receipts**
Chernogorneft	MINFIN Series 3—5/14/99
Gazprom	MINFIN Series 4—5/14/03
GUM	MINFIN Series 5—5/14/08
Inkombank	MINFIN Series 6—5/14/06
LUKOIL	MINFIN Series 7—5/14/11
Menatep Bank	
Mosenergo	
Seversky Tube Works	
Sun Brewing	
Tatneft	
VimpelCom	
Vozrozhdeniye Bank	

CHAPTER 20

ESTABLISHING A SECURITIES MARKET IN MOSCOW

Sergiy Bezsmertny

20.1 OVERVIEW. Two 1991 federal documents serve as the legislative cornerstone of the Moscow securities market: Council of Ministers of the USSR Resolution No. 601, In Affirmation of the Joint Stock Company Statute; and Resolution No. 78, In Affirmation of the Statute on Issuing and Turnover of Securities and Stock Exchanges in Russia. The privatization legislation of 1992 through 1994, which effectively started the corporate stock market, has played a giant role in the formation and development of a securities market. In addition, two major Moscow government acts regulate securities market transactions: Major's Ruling No. 477–RM, September 29, 1994, On Creation of the Moscow Securities Board; and the Moscow Government Resolution No. 915, November 14, 1995, On Incoming Funds from Privatization and Leasing City Property and Recommendations on Raising the Profits on the City Share of Privatized Enterprises. In addition, several pieces of legislation, which are expected to be affirmed or adopted, will considerably improve the climate of the market. They are the

- Joint Stock Companies Act
- Securities Market Act
- Commercial Banks Act
- Promissory Notes Turnover Act

20.2 CREATION OF THE SECURITIES MARKET. A specialty of the Russian financial market is concentration of banks in the Moscow region. By mid-1996, about 1,000 banks and 500 branches existed in Moscow, as well as 1,000 savings-bank branches. Such a concentration has contributed to the economic crisis, but is also responsible for the structure of the Moscow securities market—the first stock exchanges appeared in the capital in 1991. The first Russian depositories were created in Moscow, and the Moscow trade-depository system still serves as a model for regional systems. The Moscow Investment Corporation was founded by a Moscow government decree in June 1994, with the Moscow committee for property and the Moscow fund for property acting as co-founders. Moscow is the home of the first association of professional participants of the securities market, uniting more than 100 investment and financial companies and banks.

Since 1993, the Moscow Interbank Currency Exchange (MICE) has been the leading Russian exchange for trading state short-term bonds. The same can be said of bank and privatized-enterprise stocks. The only types of securities that were slow in coming to Moscow and remain undeveloped are municipal bonds.

20.3 STATE SHORT-TERM BONDS.   The first state securities—state short-term bonds (GKOs)—appeared in Moscow in 1993. The main documents governing the formation of these are Government Resolution No. 107 of February 8, 1993, On Release of State Coupon-less Short-Term Bonds; Supreme Soviet Resolution No. 4526–1 of February 19, 1993, On Release of State Couponless Short-Term Bonds; and Central Bank order of May 6, 1993, The Affirmation of the Provisions on Serving and Turnover of State Short-Term Bond Issues.

The GKO market is not limited to Moscow and trades in six other cities, including St. Petersburg, Novosibirsk, and Rostov-on-Don. The market, which includes the funds of Moscow dealers, regional dealers, and their clients, determines the investment climate of the whole country. Active regional trade accounts for not more than 5% of the total volume, and Moscow banks and financial companies comprise the majority of dealers.

The highly technological trading system is an evident advantage of the market: the system meets Western standards and unites all stages of the trading process—from custodial keeping to registration. Currently, the MICE trading system is the most developed securities market in Russia.

20.4 OTHER GOVERNMENT SECURITIES.   The following are also circulated on the Moscow market:

- State savings bonds according to the Presidential Decree, On State Savings Loans. The Ministry of Finance has a right to distribute a total of 10 series of the papers (OGSZs) of one trillion rubles each;
- Internal hard-currency bonds (also called Taiga bonds) issued at the end of 1993 to liquidate the Vnesheconombank debt of approximately $7.9 billion;
- Treasury bonds.

20.5 CORPORATE SECURITIES.   The privatized-enterprise (corporate) stock market started to grow vigorously in mid-1994, as the first stage of privatization was completed and a large supply of shares appeared on the market. A massive inflow of foreign capital played a crucial role in establishing the corporate stock market. In 1994 alone, foreign investment in Russian stocks totaled about $2 billion. Like most other segments of the securities market, this one started in Moscow; and these securities are traded primarily on the Moscow over-the-counter market.

Although corporate stocks are growing rapidly, many problems persist, especially concerning the infrastructure and the legislative structure. These problems include the system for reregistering stocks and a system of payments. Because these systems are not currently reliable, many operators require predelivery of stocks, which considerably reduces the liquidity of the market.

The Federal Securities Commission (FSC) has issued a number of depository activity regulations, which can sharply reduce the risks involved in the transition of property rights. Nonetheless, the issue of depository services for trading participants is still unresolved. This situation will improve when the clearing company (central depository) and Interbank Creditor's Union (clearing center) are united.

The corporate stock market depends on Western venture capital and therefore lags behind those of developed countries in terms of capitalization. According to some estimates, the market value of Russian companies is not more than $20 billion. Nevertheless, the internal investment potential is immense. Because of the strong centralization of capital and the presence of major trade systems in Moscow, a market rise is likely.

20.6 FOREIGN MARKET. Trading the stock of Moscow enterprises on the foreign market indirectly fosters higher stock liquidity, as well as raises the market value inside the country. The easiest corporate stocks on the foreign market from Moscow are sponsored first-level ADRs (American depository receipts) and restricted ADRs.

20.7 MUNICIPAL SECURITIES. The municipal-loan market is comparable to those in other developed countries. It offers the following benefits:

- Acquiring additional funds for the local budget and financing the current budget deficit;
- Financing social and investment programs for the region;
- Paying loans due;
- Serving as a guarantee for municipal debentures;
- Providing companies with liquid and highly reliable secondary assets;
- Preventing export of funds from the region.

The active use of the municipal bonds in Russia started in 1992 and has led to the circulation of a large number of securities with difference parameters (volume periods, income, taxation, guarantees, and settlement). The issuance of bonds by local authorities is regulated by Government Regulation No. 78 of December 1991 and a few Ministry of Finance instructions.

In spite of all numerous methods of circulation, most existing municipal securities can be divided into two types: general-coverage (security) bonds and income-generating bonds. The first are issued as papers with a short term of circulation secured by the budget funds or local authority property and are mostly used to finance the budget deficit. In that light, they do not circulate differently from the federal securities. The other main type is special-purpose loans. These bonds are issued for both short and medium terms for a specific investment project or group of projects. The most popular purpose for municipal bonds of this type is housing construction, which make up more than a half of the issues in this category.

Moscow is still very much behind the regions regarding municipal bonds. So far, the only paper issued by the Moscow government are housing bonds, which are paid off either in cash or as apartments in newly built projects. Incombank, a commercial institution, is the general agent. According to FSC experts, the Moscow bond project can be considered one of the few successful programs of its type.

Because of the developed state banking market in Moscow, the local government will likely increase bond issues. The main effort should probably be directed to individual investors, not financial institutions, because competition with the state for funds from financial institutions would raise interest rates.

20.8 BANKS. Banks were one of the first joint stock companies. The first, other than the Menatep Bank, which started trading its stock in 1990, appeared in 1991, and its stock immediately became popular. At that time, banks were viewed as a reliable investment, and banking operations were among the most profitable, allowing banks to pay high dividends on their stocks.

The peak of the bank stock market occurred in 1993 and 1994, a period that was characterized by high inflation and by a rise in popularity of hard-currency stocks. In 1994, the popularity of bank stocks started to decrease and many companies switched to the privatized-enterprise market.

In 1996, the market showed little interest in bank stocks. This was due to several reasons. One was the bank crisis, which led to the collapse of some large, stable banks. In addition, harsh competition between banks took its toll. Banks also experienced considerable decreases in revenue from operations in the securities and finance markets. Therefore, dividends are expected to fall sharply. In spite of these conditions, owners of bank stocks are in no hurry to part with them. Because the banking infrastructure serves the current economic process adequately, forecasts in this market are optimistic.

20.9 PROMISSORY NOTES.   When the first industrial-enterprise promissory notes were issued, most financial companies showed interest, although trading in these securities was not adequately regulated. In fact, issuing entities decided on their policies according to their own wishes.

Railway notes managed to provide the highest liquidity, which they sometimes do even today. The energy sector is more complicated. Energy systems originally restricted buyers. For example, Mosenergo and Lemenergo accepted promissory notes as payment for electricity only from budget organizations that had restricted access to notes and did not participate in the market. The bank promissory note is a more complex and flexible vehicle, and it inspires greater trust.

The government strategy regarding promissory notes will depend on what is the highest priority at the moment—the nonpayment crisis or the need to decrease inflation. Nonpayment needs to be addressed through strict legal regulations. If the priority is curbing inflation, however, the government is not likely to show interest in promissory notes, which currently function much like surrogate money.

20.10 MAJOR PARTICIPANTS.   Banks are the main participants in the state-bond market, and they are less active in the corporate-securities market. This applies to both dealer banks and investor banks. Financial companies trade corporate and bank securities. Their main problem is lack of cash, which keeps them from operating on their own and places them in the mediator position. Multiple-partner projects of broker companies and foreign-investment banks primarily sell to foreign partners.

Insurance companies and nonstate pension funds cannot be considered large-market participants, but there is growth potential in that segment of the market. At present, insurers primarily invest in state short-term papers. The government law on insuring dictates that insurance reserves must be diversified into a broader spectrum of securities with various maturity periods, a situation that will occur in the near future.

A separate group of securities-market participants is represented by share investment funds (SIFs), which was established in 1996. Created with Western collective investment funds in mind, the SIFs can find their place in the market and provide for necessary capital mobilization. Twenty companies, mostly located in Moscow, plan to participate in SIFs.

CHAPTER 21

SECURITIES MARKET: CURRENT SITUATION, PROBLEMS, GOALS, AND THE FUTURE

Alexander S. Kolesnikov

21.1 OVERVIEW. More than three years have passed since the birth of the Russian securities market. In this period, however, global changes have occurred that have affected its development. As one of the events that occurred during the political and economic reform, the development of the Russian stock market that began in the early 1990's is characterized by turbulent growth. This is apparent both in the development of its quantitative capitalization, for example, the volume of issues, difference in instruments, number of professional participants; and in the improvement in its qualitative characteristics such as the presence of exchange and extra-exchange commerce and improvement in its regulation.

At the present time, there are 52 exchanges in operation in Russia holding licenses from the Ministry of Finance. Of these, 18 are stock exchanges specializing exclusively in securities, and 34 are universal exchanges (commodity-stock, currency, etc.) that have stock sections. The largest development was achieved by the currency markets, including an interregional system of commerce with government securities (GKO/OFZ-PKs), whose exchange transactions comprise 98% of the total exchange turnover of securities in Russia. Second place in volume of trade is occupied by transactions with long-term bonds (GKOs) of regional and local government bodies, (primarily from St. Petersburg MKO). Corporate securities on the exchange market comprise only 1 to 2% of the transactions.

21.2 STRUCTURE OF THE SECURITIES MARKET. The structure of the Russian exchange and extra-exchange securities market includes:

- Government securities, making up 67.4% of all new issues;
- Securities issued by government agencies of the Russian Federation and by local self-government bodies (2.2% of new issues), called *subfederal* securities;
- Corporate securities, making up 30.4% of all new issues.

(a) Government Securities. The volume and role of the government-securities market have reached such a high level that they have become the regulator of the entire financial market and the barometer for interest rates in the economy. Because of this, in spite of the large number of corporate issuers on the stock market (on a level with the governmental securities) only shares of 100 to 120 of the most active issuers are circulated. This situation is unavoidable because the issuance of government securities involves the urgent necessity to solve budgetary problems.

(b) Subfederal Securities.   In all, more than 130 issues totaling more than 12 trillion rubles were recorded, including issuances by government executive agencies of the Russian Federation (93%) and by local self-government bodies (7%). On the whole, the issuances of subfederal securities do not have a specific character or nature. Of those that are specific, the most widespread are in housing and telephone markets.

Subfederal borrowing has had a reciprocal and comparatively stable development and has an experimental character because of its relatively small volume. Statistics also show a large investment in housing loans (50%) and in GKO-like securities (50%).

(c) Corporate Securities.   The total volume of corporate securities nominally comprises more than 140 trillion rubles, of which:

59% are stocks of share-holding companies
36% are corporate promissory notes
1% are bonds
4% are securities of commercial banks

There is a great internal potential for the growth of corporate securities' long-term rates because they are significantly undervalued compared with Western securities.

21.3   CHANGES IN THE STOCK MARKET.   Since September 1996, a new stage of development has begun in the Russian stock market. A number of positive economic and political changes have occurred that have affected the stock market, including:

- The end of the two election campaigns
- Macroeconomic stabilization
- The beginning of a period of intense profitability of government securities
- Russia's receipt of an IFC credit rating
- The affiliation of Russia's commission on securities with the International Organization of Securities Commissions (IOSCO), an organization of market regulators of the developed countries

After several long battles, a legislative base governing the securities market has emerged in Russia. The legislation is not in the form of edicts from the president, resolutions of the government, or instructions of the majority of ministers and departments as in the former USSR, but in the form of basic laws. A civil code and two federal laws on joint-stock companies and on the securities market have emerged.

Since January 1997, a new criminal code has been put into effect under which it is possible to receive a three-year prison term for unlicensed activity on the stock market. Thus, the time has ended for pyramid schemes, unlicensed dealers, and thieves. For the first time, a legal document exists in Russia that outlines and defines the regulations for the development of the stock market. It was approved in the summer of 1996 by order of the president of the Russian Federation. In particular, this document defines governmental policy on the securities market, laying out both a model for the market and for its regulation. In particular it defines six basic principles.

1. The principle of government regulation of the stock market, based on the fact that the government, fulfilling the universal function of protecting its citizens as well as their legal rights and interests, takes measures for safeguarding the rights of participants in the securities market by licensing and regulating of all types of professional activity. The implementation of this principle will be based on the necessity for minimizing the possible of conflicts of interest regarding the dual functions of direct participation in market operations and regulation of the market.

2. The principle of unity of a standard legal base, regime, and methods for adjustment of the market in the entire Russian Federation.

3. The principle of minimum state interference and maximum self-regulation, which means that the government regulates market activity only in those cases where it is absolutely necessary and delegates part of its normal creative and control functions to a professional operator of the securities market, organized in self-regulated groups. To realize this principle, the government must begin with some necessary steps:

   a. Minimize expenditures from the federal budget for creating a market infrastructure;

   b. Refuse to get involved with centralized decisions when creating the infrastructure of the market;

   c. Guarantee creative openness and the rights of all professional participants in establishing the standardized legal basis for the market.

4. The principle of equal opportunity, meaning:

   a. Government stimulation of competition in the securities market by avoiding preferencial treatment of individual participants;

   b. Equal treatment of all market participants by the bodies that regulate it;

   c. Open and competitive government support of all projects in the market;

   d. Absence of favoritism for governmental enterprises over commercial ones functioning in the market;

   e. Prohibiting government bodies from giving public evaluations of professional participants in the market;

   f. Refusal of governmental regulation of prices for the services of unlicensed professional participants.

   Simply stated, the principle of equal opportunity means that the government will control the level of competition in the market so tightly that it could declare one of the market participants a monopolist if circumstances warranted it. If this occurred, the monopolist could only become a government enterprise. This principle also recognizes that different groups of participants in the securities market have different goals, policies, and methods and that these groups can provide benefits to the market as a result of these differences. The principle also states that the government will take measures to equalize the opportunities of different groups of participants, if the need arises.

5. The principle of promoting a state policy in the securities market recognizes the continuity of government policy and its adherence to the Russian model for the securities market.

6. The principle of orientation into the worldwide market takes into consideration the tendencies of global financial markets toward new markets and recognizes the

recommendations of Group 30 for creating a civilized and competitive securities market. The principle also includes the development of an external policy regarding investors and foreign participants in the Russian securities market.

In order to realize these principles and to carry out government policy in the market, certain concepts had to be defined as basic principles of government regulation. They include these four.

1. Functional regulation combined with instructional regulation regarding questions of organization of control and supervision of the activities of professional participants in the market;

2. The use of self-regulating mechanisms created with the help of the government and under its control;

3. Distribution of authority for regulating the market between the Russian Federation, its subjects, and various government bodies;

4. Making the protection of small investors a high priority, including all forms of collective investments, through the development of a regulatory system for the market. Such a system of regulation would ensure:

   a. Priority in developing infrastructure organizations;

   b. A maximum decrease and division of risks;

   c. Competition in the market;

   d. Preliminary or partial removal of conflicts of interest by regulating professional activity.

These concepts were defined in a basic model of the securities market. Formation and implementation of this model will only be accomplished if it is based on the following two assumptions.

1. Russia, as a self-sufficient economic system, will not have a preference for dealing with only one of the world's basic financial centers, but will interact with and utilize the results of the interaction with all financial centers;

2. Russia will develop its own model of the securities market on the basis of its national interests and traditions.

This model can be applied to any system of trade used in the various exchanges and segments of the markets; however, it must be constructed on the basis of a unified system of information distribution and disclosure. A model created during the development of the securities market must guarantee:

- Maximum liquidity of securities handled in the market;
- Distribution of responsibilities and an effective system for controlling risks;
- An open exchange of information about the market;
- The possibility of increasing turnover without making significant structural changes in the model;
- The possibility of technological compatibility of the Russian securities market with foreign markets.

Russia is now in a new situation, never seen before in its history. It is on the edge of a new financial frontier. If it can implement and manage sound economic practices and policies for its securities market, it can become a leader in the world's financial markets. The following section contains a brief history of the Russian stock market and its regulations and an insight into its complex structure and participants, which shed more light on the vast potential of this emerging market.

21.4 BRIEF HISTORY.   Until 1993, before mass privatization began, there was no real securities market and, correspondingly, there was no demand for its regulation. No one talked about the inadequacies of the infrastructure, the standardization documents, and a host of other issues. In fall 1994, a critical period began in the development of the market. Unexpectedly, Russia found itself in a situation where a colossal number of shares of privatized enterprises appeared on the market. At the same time, it appeared that the population had substantial savings in various pyramid systems. A stiff battle began for the redistribution of control over enterprises and, consequently, an immediate disturbance arose among stockholders. As a result, after six months, Russian legislation and infrastructures significantly lagged behind the level of market development.

In 1994 and 1995, Russian macroeconomic stimulation began in a very interesting form. The deficit of the federal budget was transferred into the form of government securities. Consequently, the market for government securities became tremendously profitable, while the market for corporation securities dropped significantly. This situation caused Western investors to withdraw their money from the risky markets.

(a) The First Commission.   At the end of 1994, the Commission on Stocks and the Stock Market Under the Government (the first commission) was created. To some degree, it was the answer to the problem, but the answer was received halfheartedly. Although the commission was successful, it was still a body composed of representatives of different government agencies, each of whom lobbied for the interests of his or her own department or agency. As a result, of their activities, however, solutions to many of the problems were reached. The commission successfully created a large section of the standard foundation for the stock market. Plans for legislative acts were developed, some of which have already been adopted, in particular, the federal laws on joint-stock companies and the securities market. Corrections were made in the Criminal and Civil Procedural Codes, and plans for laws on investment funds, nongovernmental pension funds, the protection of investors' rights were laid out. All of these efforts were the result of the work of the commission.

It was also involved in the extremely complex and undesirable job of dealing with deceitful contributions and joint-stock companies. Another positive outcome of the commission was the beginning of licensing and the compilation of records. A significant decrease in investment risk has been achieved because of the work of the commission.

At the beginning of 1995, a project was undertaken for creating and developing the Russian Trade System (RTS), which is, in some ways, similar to the U.S. NASDAQ. Championed by market regulators, this system has been extremely successful, and the volume of shares traded has grown dramatically. Today, it trades about $50 million per day—several times larger than the volume of turnover in the largest Russian exchanges per month.

The RTS is a working system recognized by regulators and by the market participants. The organizers of the RTS recently have introduced a second echelon of shares (less liquid than blue chips) an effort that has been supported by the commission in every possible way.

(b) The Second Commission and the Expert Council.   The first commission, for all its achievements, did not successfully solve a number of basic problems that were controversial or unique. It could not establish standards for issuance or obligations for disclosing information, solve questions of brokers and dealers, or define exchange and deposit activity.

In summer 1996, in accordance with the federal law on the securities market, a second commission was created—the Federal Commission on the Securities Market, The focus of the second commission has been clearly defined. It is directed toward the regulation of professional participants in the corporate and government-securities markets, collective investors with legislative initiatives, and territorial departments of the Russian Parliament.

Each of the six member of the commission was named by the Russian president and is responsible for a very clearly defined aspect of the project. Members and participants in the commission support individual views, not those of corporations. They are responsible for the securities market, not for the communication, transportation, or fuel industries, for example. The people on the commission make decisions in the interest of developing the market. The commission has top-quality experts and jurists, who have proven capable of processing documents in the shortest period of time and at the world-market level.

The second commission is composed of six managing members. The Expert Council has also been created, which includes practical professionals (not bureaucrats), representing almost all the largest regions of the country and all groups of professionals engaging in market activity. These members were selected by the professionals themselves in October 1996 at the All-Russian Conference of Professional Participants in the Market.

The federal law on the securities market initiated a basic system of weights and counterweights. On one hand is the second commission with its six members named by the president of Russia. On the other hand is the Expert Council, which not only votes on all the commission documents of a general character, but also has the right of a delayed veto. In this way, the Expert Council forces members of the commission and officials to serve as the voice of the market participants. It does not permit making independent or unfounded decisions.

21.5 LICENSING AND REGISTRATION.   The process of licensing registrars is practically complete; more than 150 licenses for registration activity have been issued. The creation of share-investment fund (mutual funds) has begun for the first time in Russia. The first licenses for special deposits, directed by mutual fund companies, have recorded their first prospects and have started to distribute their shares.

New standards for issuance also have been adopted, which is a primary step in solving the problem of disclosure of information. A proposal has been adopted about general licensing that guarantees interaction with the Ministry of Finance, the Central Bank, and other government bodies for creation of a regulation system. Consideration will be given to the division of duties among the different government bodies and delineation of their obligations. Under consideration are:

- A guarantee of unity and compatibility in the government regulation of the securities market through a mechanism based on an obligatory agreement related to the regulation of standard legal acts of government bodies by the commission;
- Transfer of power for the regulation of the securities market solely on the basis of responsibility for results;
- A broad use of all forms of interaction of government bodies regarding the development and adoption of standard legal acts (including their operation and agreement),

and the involvement of specialists from different departments for preparing standard legal acts for solving questions about the development of the securities market;

- Functional and effective regulation and specialization of government bodies regarding questions of securities-market regulation.

In agreement with the directors of the largest regions of Russia, a decision was made and work has begun on creating a network of territorial departments of the commission. In the first stage, 12 departments were created, encompassing practically the entire territory of Russia. Documents were approved outlining deposit activity regulations for those who already have licenses and for the introduction of back-office brokerage firms, an important factor in making Russian participants competitive in the stock market.

In a meeting November 1996, the commission created a central depository for corporate securities, and the first step was also taken for creating a centralized storage and accounts model. In addition, work is being completed on several projects, including the following:

- Establishment of self-regulating organizations (SROs) of professional participants in the market;
- Licensing of broker-dealer activities;
- Exchange activity;
- Organizers of commercial activity;
- Regulations regarding output, recording, and exchange of opinions, whose active basis is issued securities.

The president of Russia gave the commission a global purpose—to convert Russia into an independent financial and trade center a task that will take a fairly long time. The commission has outlined the following steps that need to be taken in order to achieve such a goal.

1. Change the tax system in order to guarantee the profitability of operations with Russian securities and not through foreign activity.

2. Guarantee the inflow of brand new investors to Russia. Russia needs to attract western institutional investors because they increase the liquidity of the market and do not try to control the enterprises. For the most part, they are portfolio investors who buy 1 to 2% of an enterprise and expect an increase in long-term rates; they play these indices. The main conditions for their participation are the maximum disclosure of information and high-quality custodial servicing.

    Strengthen the competitive capability of Russian negotiators in the securities market in relation to their Western competitors. The commission will not imitate Western companies by restricting the rights of investors. There is only one possible course of action—improving the training of Russian firms in order to strengthen their competitiveness in catching up with their Western counterparts and working with them effectively.

These tasks represent only the tip of the iceberg of what the commission must accomplish. The most important one is to create a system to regulate the market, and it is already beginning to be built. The system will include a powerful set of legal controls consisting of a central apparatus and territorial departments of the commission. The task of monitoring the market for compliance with legislation will be taken on by people in territorial departments and by inspectors of the commission in those regions that lack departments or complaint officers within the market structures themselves. This is in keeping with the practices of other countries, where firms have workers who are constantly in touch with regulatory bodies. Solving regulation problems will lead to the achievement of two basic goals:

1. The protection of the rights of issuers through the establishment of the limits of responsibility of issuers over investors and professional participants in the securities markets; regulation of processes for buying large and controlled packets of shares and/or merging and absorbing companies; and full disclosure of information about investors.

2. The protection of the rights of investors (including protection of private, government, and other types of property that will be developed), and consideration of the special features of individual groups of investors, their preparation, and social significance. Government policy toward protecting investors' rights will be applied differentially to each of the following types of investors: inhabitants, collective investors, commercial banks, insurance companies, government, foreign investors (nonresidents) and other investors.

Self-regulated organizations have played a tremendous role in the market structure. Once only a dream, self-regulation in Russia is now a reality. Professional associations are being created literally every week. One example is a professional association of participants of the stock market, which includes only representatives of brokers and dealers. The association has the potential to be converted quickly and efficiently into an actual working SRO with its own rules, sanctions, and disciplinary committees.

The main task of the commission is not licensing, but guaranteeing the normal activity of the license holders. Here lies, however, a very serious judicial, socioeconomic, and political problem: bankrupt and inefficient institutions that have ceased operations. Conscientious financial companies in Russia confirm that it is difficult to eliminate a dead company from the registrar. Overseeing this registration and clearance operation is another task for the commission.

Now and in the future, the commission intends to strengthen requirements for operators in the market. This tighter control however, must come from individual companies practicing self-regulation.

The commission considers it extremely important, especially in the interests of national safety, to transform the largest Russian dealer-broker houses, firms, and investment banks. This work primarily requires solving two problems—guaranteeing adequate in-house and raising the necessary capitalization. Capitalization is one of the central points that makes it possible for the Russian market to exist as an independent stock market.

21.6 ENSURING DISCLOSURE.   An increase in the exchange of information is one of the key tasks of the government for ensuring the proper development of the securities market. The Commission therefore, must take the necessary steps for the realization of an effective disclosure policy. These steps should include:

• Creation of a generally accepted system of indices for analyzing the positions of the securities market;

- Precise delineation of public information and information that is considered a commercial secret;

- Obligatory publication of any facts about the activity of issuers that has the potential of significantly influencing the market;

- Support of independent rating agents and the introduction of recognized rate evaluations of company issuers and securities;

- Support of specialized publications that treat separate branches of the economy as objects of investment;

- Formation of centers for disclosing information;

- Reinforcement of liability for communicating unverified information; and

- Disclosure of information about prices and the volume of operation in securities and goods.

21.7 FUTURE OF THE SECURITIES MARKET.   The commission must objectively evaluate what can be achieved in Russia in the next five years. It must not present unattainable goals, such as reaching a level of disclosure of information equal to the west's in that period. This would be impossible because some enterprises will battle against disclosing information in the next five years. In a recent study, however, significant number of Russian enterprises (40%) are fully prepared for disclosure. The commission, with the Central Bank, is working on a large project for creating a center for disclosing information.

As has already been indicated, a large group of enterprises are just beginning to understand that if they enter the market with their own securities, they must disclose information about these instruments to potential investors. Also, there are lawbreakers who do not wish to disclose any information. Therefore, a mechanism must be developed that will allow a regulatory procedure for registering industrial enterprises that have increased the flow of information about these companies.

In order to increase the development of the infrastructure of the Russian stock market, a number of primary problems must be solved. The first is increasing the number of registrars. The commission's basic position is that, in the future, registration requirements must be raised and recording activity become essential.

The second problem is the creation of an infrastructure for collective investment. Its absence caused the delay in development of mutual funds in Russia. Through the World Bank, financial centers for collective investment will be created that not only trade shares of different stocks, but will also provide investment consultants, who are badly needed in Russia.

The third problem is the improvement in deposit servicing, accounts, and clearing. The commission has already initiated regulations on deposit activities, licenses, and depositories; and a central depository has been established.

The fourth problem deals with organized commerce. At the present time, conditions in the Russian stock market are restricting the development of organized commerce. Overliquidation of existing currencies and organized commercial systems require collective investors. These investors have to approve reconstruction of the commercial systems, which are needed for liquid shares. If this does not occur, many investors will trade abroad rather than in Russia.

There remains the urgent problem of tax avoidance—one of the basic causes for the Russian market slipping into offshore activity. The problem involves not only the development of business for the Russian participants, but also the national security.

No less important are the problems of budgetary calculation and financial accounting. Most Western investors do not speak Russian and therefore cannot understand Russian budgetary accounts, financial statements, or prospectuses. Therefore, Russian enterprises wishing to attract Western capital carry tremendous expenditures for double bookkeeping. Unfortunately, this problem cannot be solved by the commission.

The Russian stock market, on one hand, depends on political and social stability in the country; but, on the other, development is necessary and important for raising the national economy and, consequently, a guarantee of political and social stability. Therefore, all government bodies should make every possible effort to ensure stability. Professional participants too must help create and develop a sophisticated, effective, and stable market for securities in Russia.

PART V

BUSINESS ENVIRONMENT

CHAPTER 22

THE LABOR MARKET
AND WORK FORCE

Gennadiy G. Melikian, Michael A. Tappan, Tatiana M. Regent, and Rita Berlin

22.1 OVERVIEW.* For decades, the centralized management of labor resources had been used to maintain labor and economic requirements in Russia. Until the late 1980s, when the current reforms were initiated, the state was the bona fide sole owner and manager of the country's productive potential and virtually its sole employer.

State authorities achieved balance between the available labor and jobs through productive forces distribution programs, investment programs, and direct-pay regulation at state-fixed rates. Centrally legalized privileges in work remuneration and benefits, in the form of housing and services, helped the authorities recruit labor for key industries, areas, and enterprises. In addition, state authorities and management bodies developed student admission and graduation plans for vocational training and higher and specialized secondary education, and also developed personalized job assignment plans.

The labor-management system in prereform Russia was backed by the constitutional right to work combined with the duty of all able-bodied persons to work in public production. Unemployment was viewed as a social evil incompatible with the socioeconomic system prevailing in the country at the time; it was beyond the law and was not registered until mid-1991.

The system that operated in the prereform period helped maintain virtual full employment of the able-bodied population (excluding some labor-surplus areas) and provided labor for full-time operation of enterprises and construction projects in priority regions and industries. The efficiency of labor utilization was low, however. Despite full employment on a countrywide scale, many enterprises built up considerable labor surpluses. The lack of competition on the labor market quenched employees' natural desire to increase their skills and advance their professional careers. This was a significant drag on industrial productivity and hampered adoption of intensive work techniques.

Russia's transition to market-type methods of economic regulation and the burgeoning of various ownership patterns in the country have led to an overhaul of the labor-management mechanism. As in other developed market economies, adjusting labor supply to demand has called into existence a labor market that takes care of labor allocation and distribution according to industries and jobs by matching the hired labor demand and supply.

(a) Employment Law. The legal foundations for the operation of a labor market in Russia were laid in the nation's new Constitution and in legislation. Adopted in 1993, the

---

*This section was written by Gennadiy G. Melikian.

Russian Constitution proclaims the freedom of work, with everyone free to apply his or her abilities in seeking employment and choosing an occupation or profession. Forced labor was banned. Passed in 1991, the Law on Population Employment, legalized unemployment for the first time in decades, codified in law the right to voluntary unemployment, and provided social guarantees in the event of redundancy.

Job seekers now have much stronger guarantees of employment and safeguards against dismissal. The Code of Labor Laws prohibits unjustified refusal of employment. Any direct or indirect restriction of rights is not allowed, nor can any direct or indirect privileges be extended in employment for any reason or under any circumstances unrelated to the professional skills of the applicants. Generally, employment agreements or contracts are not limited to any particular time period. The possibility of an employment contract being signed for a specified time exists only in situations where industrial relations cannot be established for a specific term in view of the nature of the work to be done, the work environment, or the employee's interests. In signing an employment agreement, the parties may, by mutual agreement, fix a probation period to test the employee's ability to do the assigned work.

The employment agreement may be terminated at the employer's initiative only in instances expressly specified in the laws, such as the closing of an enterprise, workforce or staff reductions, an employee's inadequate performance because of low skills or poor health, repeated neglect of duties or in-house rules without reasonable excuses, absenteeism, or reporting for work under the influence of alcohol. When employees are dismissed because of enterprise liquidation or workforce or staff reductions, the affected employees must receive at least a two months' warning.

In general, the basic laws relating to labor regulation, employment, and unemployment have been brought in line with the norms prescribed by the International Labor Organization and international law.

(b) Employment Patterns.   Changes in employment law, along with the government's renunciation of direct interference in the economic activities of business, the liberalization of wages, and the expansion of contract forms to regulate industrial relations, have laid the groundwork for a labor market. The process has set off major changes in employment patterns. The number of redundant workers has increased, and the affected employees are encouraged to seek employment in industries and businesses that have labor shortages. The employment structure is changing as well, so that employment in the private sector is now 44% of total employment. Workforce numbers are growing particularly rapidly in industries and businesses related to the emerging market infrastructure, such as banks, insurance institutions, tax-collection and legal services, and notary offices. Small businesses are multiplying fairly rapidly, as are many other self-employed entities. Contact relationships established within the social partnership system are playing a growing part in regulating the labor market and employment levels.

The nation is gradually developing a novel system of state regulation of labor and employment. The Russian Labor Ministry conducts studies in and offers forecasts for the labor market; it is closely involved in formulating the state's economic and financial policies in the field of employment and drafts bills on these matters. The implementation of the employment policy and of social guarantees for the population has been assigned to the state employment service, which forecasts labor demand and supply; keeps records of job openings and job applicants; notifies and advises job seekers about employment opportunities; organizes vocational training, retraining, and skill upgrading programs; keeps a jobless register; and pays unemployment benefits to those qualified under the law.

(c) Labor Resources.   In spite of these changes, the labor market in Russia has not yet developed into an effective tool to manage labor resources. The complex socioeconomic situation and fading investment activities have reduced the number of job openings in growth industries and regions. In turn, layoffs have been restrained by the low labor mobility and the rooted mentality of business managers who want to retain their labor potential in the expectation of an imminent stabilization and industrial recovery.

The absence of a housing market severely curtails opportunities for labor flow between regions and, not infrequently, between cities and administrative districts within the same region. In practical terms, this means that labor is firmly tied to permanent places of residence, a factor that delays still further the emergence of a labor market on a countrywide scale. Actually, the current labor market is an aggregate of the regional and local markets, each left face to face with its specific problems arising from the labor-pool structure, unemployment level, economic opportunities for new job openings, and some other local specifics.

The labor resources consist of a portion of the population that has the physical and mental capacities for work. The labor pool includes both the population at work and the idle segments capable of taking up economic activities. In Russia, the labor resources embrace the able-bodied population (men 16 to 59 years of age and women 16 to 54 years of age). The resources do not include nonworking handicapped persons and those who have retired with pensions earlier than the norm because of heavy or unhealthy working conditions. The labor resources also include people above or below the employment age who work in social production or are full-time students. The bulk of the labor resources (95%) are within the employment age. The country, however, has a high proportion of people working beyond their retirement age, which is explained by the low age threshold for pension qualification and the relatively low pensions compared to those of most other countries.

Today, the total labor pool in Russia is about 86 million, including nearly 75 million economically active people, that is, jobholders and job seekers of working age, including the officially registered unemployed. In early 1995, the share of the economically active segment in Russia was equal to almost 50% of the country's total population. Some 93% of the economically active people were actually employed, and the remaining 7% were seeking jobs and, in accordance with the International Labor Organization classification, were listed as jobless. At present, 2.7% of the working-age population are officially registered as unemployed.

As in most other countries, employment is defined in Russia as socially useful activity pursued to satisfy personal and public wants, and, as a rule, to derive gains (earned income). Under the current Russian laws, the employed population includes persons working for hire, which also implies full- or part-time work done for pay, those performing any other paying work, and individuals taking time away from work because of temporary disability, vacation, skill-upgrading courses, or work suspension caused by industrial action. Also listed as employed are persons providing themselves with work, including self-employed entrepreneurs such as private farmers and producer-cooperative members, able-bodied persons studying at general education schools or taking full-time courses at higher, specialized secondary and other educational institutions, and armed-forces personnel.

The situation now emerging on the labor market can be said to exhibit several firm trends. The most important of them are the growing redundant workers, a considerable increase in part-time employment, intensified movement of labor between economic sectors and industries, and longer unemployment periods.

(d) Unemployment.   The unemployed are able-bodied persons who are out of work and without pay, registered with the employment service as seeking a job and ready to take a job, provided it is adequate to the job seeker's professional training, experience, and health, and is accessible via available transportation.

In 1994, the number of dismissals rose nearly 50% over those in 1993. About half of the dismissals occurred in manufacturing enterprises. The dismissal rate is particularly high in the textile industry and in engineering. The highest rate of layoffs occur in industries with relatively low pay levels and those with diminishing orders. By contrast, activities such as financial mediation, realty operations, and tax management are registering a steady growth in employment. The regional disparities in unemployment levels are intensifying. In some areas, the level of officially registered unemployment is more than 4.5 times the countrywide average. Employment is at a dangerously low point in many cities with single dominant industry, especially textile, leather, coal, or defense. A particularly alarming fact is that frequently the dismissals include a large number of skilled workers and professionals.

Within the next few years, employment problems may, for a number of natural reasons, acquire a high urgency. According to current forecasts, even if production stabilizes and sets on a recovery course, it would hardly be possible to provide jobs to all the able-bodied population. As the economic reforms go deeper, as competition among producers intensifies, and as the market is glutted with goods and services, enterprises will be forced to take drastic steps to cut production costs and improve performance in real terms, and, therefore, to trim their payrolls. The process will gather speed, especially at enterprises in the state sector, under the impact of measures that will be introduced to tighten fiscal policies in a bid to arrest inflation and to balance the budget.

Over the last few years, the unemployment problem has been mitigated by a portion of the work-age population going into the so-called informal sector—street peddling, consumer services, and intermediary activities—without registering their employment officially. Today, nearly all possibilities for expanding informal employment have been exhausted, so pressure will build in the labor market.

(e) Labor Policy.   Because the situation in the labor market is taking a turn for the worse, the top priorities for Russia's labor policy will be creating conditions conducive to relative stability in employment and taking steps to forestall mass-scale unemployment. The authorities are considering amendments to the general economic, budget, and credit policies that would boost investments sharply to create new jobs and modernize existing jobs so they can be filled by laid-off employees and young people entering the work force. Work is underway on measures to stimulate private investment and attract foreign investors. Employment will be regarded as a major factor affecting the general objectives and priorities of the country's economic policy, including the budget and lending policies. From this angle, it will be vital to determine the maximum tolerable unemployment level.

Plans have been prepared to improve the job-seeking assistance provided by state employment services, create additional jobs with allocations from the State Employment Fund, establish job quotas for hiring persons in need of special attention, and enhance the standards of vocational training and job counseling. Other initiatives include increasing incentives to employees to improve their skills and improving the sensitivity of vocational training to changes in the employment field.

The government intends to increase support to small- and medium-sized businesses and to employers who create jobs for persons who are otherwise unemployable. The government also plans to expand the scale of public works and temporary job programs for the unemployed.

Additional measures are planned to soften the impact of unemployment in regions notorious for high labor-market tensions, including a social program to extend financial assistance to employers in creating new jobs and expanding employment.

Particular attention will be focused on steps to increase social support to the unemployed, including partial compensation of the shortfalls in pay for employees compelled by circumstances to work part time (or short weeks), and for those forced to take vacations without pay. Targets for such support will include employees of single-industry cities, former defense industry enterprises engaged in conversion programs, and enterprises located in areas with high unemployment levels.

22.2 NEW CHALLENGES IN STAFFING RUSSIAN OPERATIONS.* At the present time in Russia, demand is set to explode for both foreign and national executives with the experience and skills to succeed in companies determined to compete on a national and international scale. Russian and Western companies alike will face a critical shortage of qualified executives for at least the next five years.

During the past four years, there has been steady growth in the demand for qualified managers. But this growth has taken place in a period when foreign direct investment in Russia has been only a trickle compared to many other emerging markets, and when Russian companies have not yet been ready to build organizations up to international standards. Both of these conditions will soon change radically.

Although many problems remain, the signs are that Russian economic and political conditions are stabilizing and are about to improve. The dam holding back foreign investment in Russia will soon burst, and both Russian and foreign companies will have access to the financing they need to dramatically expand their operations in Russia. Money will not be a problem, but management talent will. Demand for this talent will skyrocket.

Furthermore, many major Russian companies now recognize that they need managers from the West to make their companies viable on a global scale. There are already unmistakable signs that these companies are beginning to take the steps necessary to build management teams that can compare with those in the rest of the world. To do so, they will compete aggressively with Western companies in the international market for executives. These trends can only mean that the competition for a relatively small and slow-growing pool of qualified candidates for senior-management positions in Russia will greatly intensify.

In this context of rapidly increasing demand, the supply side of the equation is not encouraging. The required qualifications for positions in Russia have been very exacting. In almost all executive searches, candidates from the West must demonstrate a demanding array of qualifications: strong functional expertise, an excellent career track record, a significant international business background, exposure to the emerging markets if not to Russia itself, some fluency in the Russian language, and the willingness to live and work in what can often be a very difficult environment. Likewise, Russian candidates must speak fluent English, have Western company experience, be able, with proper training, to function effectively in a Western profit-motivated organization, and generally hold their own with Western colleagues who have usually had much more business experience. Clearly, candidates in both categories are relatively rare and difficult to find.

Relief for this situation will be a long time coming, especially on the part of expatriate candidates whose numbers, up to now, have been limited to executives meeting these criteria largely based on the circumstance of Russian ancestry or of Russian language studies long before any but a very few considered doing business in Russia.

---

*This section was written by Michael A. Tappan.

The positions at Western industrial companies in Russia most often filled by expatriates are country manager, regional manager, business-unit general manager, and chief financial officer. The demand from Russian companies for expatriates has been primarily at the departmental head level, including board positions. To date, the vast majority of these positions have been based in Moscow and, to a much lesser extent, in St. Petersburg; but as foreign companies extend their geographical reach in Russia, there is a definite trend toward more and more positions in regional cities and, not infrequently, in exceedingly remote locations.

Living conditions in Moscow, though costly, have improved in the last several years to the point that it can no longer be considered a true hardship post. However, serious concerns remain about crime, personal safety, health care, educational opportunities for children, and recreational outlets. Nonetheless, Moscow has, without question, resumed its status as an exciting modern and cosmopolitan city.

In the regions, of course, the story is entirely different; and it takes a special breed to succeed there. Past experience in Russia, very strong Russian-language skills, good understanding of Russian culture, and an unencumbered family situation (maybe even a Russian spouse) are highly desirable, if not essential. The number of candidates with these attributes, plus a willingness to live in Russia and the essential business qualifications, is quite limited; and there is no reason to expect the situation will improve.

There are, however, some current changes in the job environment for expatriates in Russia that may make it possible to expand the candidate universe to include executives who up to recently would not have been qualified. As foreign operations in Russia become larger and more established, business qualifications become more important than they were when foreign companies were just putting their toe in the water with small representative offices. Further, the growing second tier of increasingly competent Russian managers gives the general manager more support than was available to the early Western pioneers in Russia. These changes make it possible in assessing candidates to gradually shift emphasis from language ability and cultural knowledge, and to put more weight on business and leadership skills, thus expanding the pool of qualified candidates. This also means that internal candidates can now be considered more often than in the past. However, it should be kept in mind that past educational or career experience in Russia often makes it easier to attract Western executives to positions there.

Four years ago, viable Russian candidates were few, even in the concentrated Moscow market. The Soviet command-economy system promoted volume at the expense of quality and utility, and the managers that developed in it tended to be bureaucratic and risk-averse, having had little appreciation for market needs and product quality. The unfortunate result has been a large number of seasoned enterprise managers who cannot adjust to the demands of the market and competition. As more and more foreign corporations entered the Russian market after 1991, the demand for Russians with Western-company experience, or at least exposure to Western business through Soviet trade organizations and the like, set off a free-for-all during which Russians routinely changed jobs every 12 months or so, and compensation for highly qualified Russians at the departmental management level increased tenfold in about three years.

Today, however, although the pool of Russian candidates qualified to work successfully in a Western company is still quite small, the situation has improved a great deal and conditions have settled down. In the last four years, Russians have been joining Western companies and gaining essential business experience, and an increasing number of these have earned MBAs and other graduate degrees in Western schools. These young executives are now well prepared to succeed in multinational corporations and especially in the increasing number of Russian companies that need their talents to restructure, build competitive capacity, and achieve profitability. The prevalence of job-hopping abated, and the rate of escalation in compensation levels has modified. However, the supply of these managers will not keep up with the explosive demand that is likely to develop, and the rampant seller's market of the recent past may well return with a vengeance.

Foreign companies are hiring Russians for virtually the full spectrum of managerial functions, including most often chief financial officer, chief accountant, regional general manager, head of sales and marketing, chief counsel, and head of human resources. During the past year, a new and highly significant trend has begun: a few major multinationals are placing Russians in the country manager position, either through internal promotion or by external recruitment. These companies perceive advantages in sacrificing years of experience for a knowledge of the Russian marketplace and the ability to connect effectively with Russian customers, employees, the local community, and local and national government agencies. This new phenomenon was nearly inconceivable two or three years ago, but today there exists a small cadre of Russian managers with the experience and ability to handle country manager responsibilities for multinationals. In this complex and challenging market for executive talent, it is clear that companies intending to compete successfully will need to acquire and manage their human resources with extraordinary skill.

In efforts to recruit Westerners to Russia, success will not only depend on demanding the necessary business qualifications, but also on the necessary flexibility to compromise on qualifications such as language and cultural skills, which are becoming less important in a rapidly changing environment. Expatriates can be attracted to positions in Russia by the challenge and adventure; but career opportunity, higher compensation, wealth-building opportunities, steady support from headquarters, and an appropriate exit strategy will ultimately make the difference between the success and failure of attractive executives.

Because Russia will remain a seller's market, it is essential to be sure that Russian employees are paid at the current market rate and have the best career opportunity that can be offered. A few years ago, it was possible to treat Russian employees as second-class citizens, but those days are long gone. It is very important to avoid underestimating how quickly and thoroughly Russians can absorb and put to effective use Western business principles and methods. Experienced Russian managers have earned their place in the process, hierarchy, and rewards of management responsibility.

The high stakes in the huge Russian market promise ample reward for the company that makes the effort to understand, respond to, and keep current on the changing conditions of recruitment and management in that dynamic and challenging environment.

22.3 INTERNAL AND EXTERNAL MIGRATION.* The population dispersion throughout the Russian Federation is extremely uneven, with an average density of fewer than nine persons per square kilometer. A large portion (78%) of the population is concentrated in the European part of the country (27 persons per square kilometer). Yet this European section makes up only 25% of the total landmass. The eastern zone (Siberia and the far eastern region) comprises the remaining 75% of the total area, yet only 22% of the total population (2.5 persons per square kilometer). So the highest concentration of population occurs in the central and southern regions of the European part of Russia. In the eastern part of the country, the population is concentrated in a narrow band along the southern border.

Since 1991, the territory of the Russian Federation as a whole has experienced a natural decrease in population. Migration from one region to another has also played an important

---

*This section was written by Tatiana M. Regent.

role in the resettlement of the Russian people. This movement has primarily been toward the regions that were already populated.

(a) Changing Migration Patterns.   *Intra-Russian migration* is the exchange of population among individual territories within the country. Migration flows, which had been stable for decades, with the population moving from the middle and southern regions of the European part to the eastern and northern territories, have recently undergone a powerful reverse movement. The decisive factors causing the outflow of population include:

A decrease in the production or outright termination of basic mining operations employing the majority of the labor force in the north and east;

Limited possibilities for specialized redistribution of labor in various branches;

The collapse of the social sphere and system for supplying basic food and industrial goods;

The end of previous policies offering wage incentives for working under difficult climatic conditions in many of the territories.

Many complex social and economic problems have arisen in the areas settled in by migrants from the north. These include inadequate housing and limited job prospects based on their limited existing specialties and qualifications.

(b) Emigration from Former USSR Republics.   External migration or emigration is the movement of people to foreign countries. This includes population migration from states that were former republics of the USSR. Russia's population increase due to migration from the Commonwealth of Independent States and the Baltic countries in the past few years has grown severalfold (in 1994, it comprised 915,000 people). Between 1991 and 1994, this figure was 3.7 million people. According to predictions by the State Committee on Statistics and the Center for Economic Conditions, this figure will exceed 1.6 million people from 1995 to 2005.

Migratory population exchanges in the Russian Federation from states of the "old border" have occurred in two basic flows. The first is the ethnic emigration of Russians into Germany, Israel, and the United States, comprising 94% of the total number of emigrants. This emigration resulted from both ethnic and economic conditions. The emigration from Russia in 1991 was 145,100 persons—a substantial number.

The second basic flow is immigration into Russia, which involves the migration of illegal immigrants through easily transgressed borders with the CIS countries. A large portion of these immigrants consider Russia a temporary stop on their way to resettlement in developed countries of the West. At the present time, there are up to 500,000 illegal immigrants of this nature in the Russian Federation.

(c) Problems of a Migrant Population.   The recent increase in the volume of migration into Russia has caused international and interreligious friction among the resident population, resulting in numerous armed conflicts. As a result, an increased external migration has been forced, namely to the CIS and Baltic countries. With the collapse of the USSR, the former nonindigenous people of these regions now have legal status. In accordance with the laws of the Federation on refugees and on forced resettlers in the territories of Russia, in July 1995 more than 850,000 persons were registered with legal status.

With the breakup of the USSR, the area that is attracting migrants from countries of the "new border" are middle and southern regions of the European part of Russia. Migrants have moved here from the eastern and northern Russian territories and southwest Siberia. The basic burden for taking care of the now defunct military units arriving from eastern Europe falls on these regions.

The organization of housing and adaptation of the forced immigrants to their new surroundings is now one of the most important and serious problems faced by the Russian Federation. The problem is manifested by the high cost of housing and glutted labor markets in the majority of regions with mass inflows of immigrants.

Many of these immigrants were forced from troubled regions. Many have lost practically all of their possessions. This situation places an added burden on the state and seriously complicates their attempt at a new life in Russia.

(d) Federal Migration Service.   During the forced migration, it is common to redistribute immigrants in order to benefit everyone affected. This policy almost unavoidably complicates the process of arranging housing for forced immigrants, who, before arriving in Russia lived mainly in cities. They possess specific urban specialties, have high professional and educational levels, which are comparable to, and often exceed the corresponding levels of the population occupying the territory. Thus, the majority of forced immigrants in Russia need assistance from various governmental and nongovernmental institutions for their normal housing arrangements.

The basic duties of offering material, financial, legal, and organizational support for the forced immigrants is directed by the Federal Migration Service (FMS), founded in 1992. In 1995 alone, the FMS organized construction of dwellings in 56 locations in the Russian Federation for forced immigrants. Most of this construction is occurring in Belgorod, Bryansk, Kostrom, Novgorod, Novosibirsk, Orenburg, Ryazan, Saratov, and Tambov Oblasts and in the republic of Tatarstan. In addition, there is also a program underway to help house indigent families at 27 locations throughout the Federation. The largest number of such families was recorded in the Tartar, Bashkir, Northern Oset, Altay, and Stavropol Krais and in the Astrakhan, Lipetsk, Novgorod, Orenburg, Rostov, Samara, Saratov, Sverdlovsk, and Tambov Oblasts.

In 1994, the government developed a program of financial assistance in creating jobs for forced emigrants, including financial support for production enterprises created and operated by immigrants. The need for this type of financing was caused by growing pressure on the labor market on one hand, and the need for smoothing adaptation process of the immigrants on the other. The mechanism for distributing resources proposes a decrease of the budget burden, and is instead based on returns from investments of construction and purchases of dwellings.

In the second half of 1994, 82 agreements were signed with 80 production collectives in 27 Russian territories, including:

The Republic of Chuvash	Kaluga
Altay Krai	Kursk
Stavropol Krai	Leningrad
Belgorod	Lipetsk
Vladimir	Nizhny Novgorod
Volgograd	Novgorod
Voronezh	Novosibirsk

Omsk	Smolensk
Orenburg	Tambov
Orlov	Tver
Pskov	Tomsk
Rostov	Tula
Ryazan	Yaroslav
Saratov	

The agreements led to the creation of 4,430 jobs and about 40,000 square meters of housing for indigent forced immigrants. In the second half of 1994 and the first half of 1995, 2,850 jobs were made available and, more than 2,000 square meters of housing were created.

Since 1995, projects for the creation of jobs are being financed from the State Fund on Employment of the Population of the Russian Federation, starting with the Agreement on Joint Activity for Guaranteeing Employment in the Russian Federation to Unemployed Refugees and Forced Immigrants. Implementation of these measures is limited to the employment service and migration service through the appropriate regional and local bodies.

Many immigrants resettling in Russia have not lost touch with their fellow nationals but, on the contrary, are united with them in constructing housing and creating small production units. These groups of immigrants are often put into working collectives.

Due to the scarcity of housing and prices that are well beyond the means of the majority of immigrants, obtaining apartments or existing houses has become nearly impossible. The only alternative to this situation is to build an individual dwelling. However, in a number of territories, such as Krasnodar Krai, increased demand for housing has caused a sharp rise in prices. Also, the efforts of many immigrants to obtain land for construction has led to a shortage of land. The total area available in 1994 for individual dwellings in the Krasnodar Krai is 718,000 square meters, compared to the 1,027,000 square meters of housing made available in western Siberia, eastern Siberia, and the far eastern regions. The total cost of construction of individual dwellings in Krasnodar Krai was 352 billion rubles, compared to the 250 billion rubles spent for the same purpose in all of the eastern zones.

In 1994, refugees and forced immigrants had available to them 568,000 square meters of individual dwellings (1,157 dwellings and apartments). Of these, 37% were in the Northern Caucasus and 20% in the central Chernozem regions. This construction was mainly in rural areas (84% of the total area). Thus, even in a territory with a high immigrant population, there is a concentration of capital spent on individual housing construction.

22.4 HIRING OF RUSSIAN CITIZENS BY U.S. ENTITIES AND OTHER RELATED ISSUES.*   The increase in investment and trade opportunities in the republics of the former Soviet Union is having a widespread effect on the U.S. business community. Issues that would ordinarily play a role only in the large-scale corporate world, are now found on the planning agendas of U.S. entities engaging in virtually every type of commercial activity. The issue at hand is one of immersing Russian citizens into the U.S. workforce by employing such individuals in U.S. entities.

For companies conducting business with Russia or any other country, it is important to consider whether to employ or transfer individuals from abroad who can offer specialized knowledge (i.e. expertise in the foreign market, computers, economics, etc.) for which it may be difficult to locate a qualified individual in the United States. These decisions need

---

*This section was written by Rita Berlin.

to be analyzed in light of the immigration and nationality law as it is exercised at the time. This article will provide a general introduction to the options available to U.S. entities and the kinds of commitments and responsibilities such entities undertake when they decide to utilize the services of foreign workers.

On September 30, 1996, President Clinton enacted into law the Illegal Immigration Reform and Immigrant Responsibility Act of 1996. Although this act contains many restrictive provisions with regard to immigration in general, fortunately, several proposed provisions dramatically reducing employment-based immigration were struck out of the final bill. Accordingly, a U.S. employer maintains several options with respect to employing foreign nationals.

There are various nonimmigrant, employment-based visas an employer (also known as the petitioner for Immigration and Naturalization Service's purposes) can obtain on behalf of an alien that will allow him or her to enter the United States in order to temporarily engage in employment. The most prevalent nonimmigrant visas are H–1B (professional/specialty occupation visas); L–1A/L–1B (intracompany transferee visas for managers/executives or specialized knowledge); E–1/E–2 (treaty trader/investor visas); F–1 (student visas); J–1 (scholar and exchange visas); O and P (artist/athlete visas); and R (religious-worker visas).

It should be noted that nonimmigrants, unlike immigrants, enter the United States for a limited period of time and are restricted to the activity consistent with their visas. Unlike immigrants, however, they are less subject to numerical restrictions. The only nonimmigrant visa categories that are numerically limited are H–1B and H–2B, restricted to 65,000 and 66,000 visas respectively per fiscal year. It is interesting to note that for the first time since the enactment of the Immigration Act of 1990, the Immigration and Naturalization Service in 1996 temporarily suspended adjudication of H–1B nonimmigrant visa applications over concern that the 65,000 ceiling had been reached. While the Immigration Service's count proved to be erroneous, the H–1B is the most widely used visa, and concern about the ceiling being reached in the future still exists.

The H–1B nonimmigrant visa category is set aside for foreign workers in specialty occupations. The Immigration & Nationality Act of 1952, as amended, defines *specialty occupation* as one that requires the theoretical and practical application of a body of highly specialized knowledge, and attainment of a bachelor's or higher degree in the specific specialty (or its equivalent), as a minimum for entry into the occupation in the United States. Many U.S. employers, including banking and financial institutions, health-care research facilities, and large multinational corporations, utilize the H–1B visa category to employ a variety of professionals.

Prior to the filing of an H–1B nonimmigrant visa petition, the employer must submit a Labor Condition Application to the Department of Labor for certification, asserting that the conditions being offered to the alien are prevailing in the industry and that the hiring of the H–1B worker will not adversely affect the wages and working conditions of any U.S. worker. An H–1B visa authorizes the individual to work only for the petitioning company for a maximum initial validity period of three years. After that time, a three-year extension may be granted for a maximum stay of six years. The individual is not authorized to work until the application is approved by the Immigration and Naturalization Service, which takes approximately two to four weeks to obtain.

The L–1A/L–1B visa category is designed for multinational corporations that have offices in the United States and abroad to facilitate the transfer of foreign nationals with management, executive, and specialized skills to the United States, to continue employment with an office of the same employer, its parent, subsidiary or affiliate. L–1A/L–1B visas are available to persons who have worked abroad for one continuous year within the preceding three years in an executive, managerial or specialized knowledge capacity for a qualifying, related business entity, and who are being transferred temporarily to the United States to work in an executive, managerial or specialized knowledge capacity for a qualifying business entity.

The L–1 visas are issued for an initial period of one to three years, renewable for up to seven years for managers or executives, and up to five years for specialized knowledge transferees. In contrast to the H–1B visa category, a bachelor's degree equivalent is not required. Furthermore, the L–1 visa category does not require a Labor Condition Application to be filed with the Department of Labor.

The E–1/E–2 visa category is a treaty-trader and investor category and is based on a Treaty of Friendship, Commerce and Navigation between the United States and the country of the alien's nationality. Under this category, a person is entering the country solely to carry on substantial trade between the United States and the foreign state of which he or she is a national (E–1 treaty trader); or solely to develop and direct the operations of an enterprise in which the alien has invested or is actively in the process of investing a substantial amount of capital (E–2 treaty investor). There are no time limitations on this E visa category, the focus being on the volume of trade in dollars and the number of transactions. The nationality of a corporation is determined by the nationality of the individual who owns at least 50% of its stock.

Bilateral Investment Treaties are a modern, investment-oriented version of Friendship, Commerce and Navigation Treaties. As with the latter, Bilateral Investment Treaties often include provisions allowing nationals of other countries to enter the United States in E status. The United States has entered into such treaties with numerous countries, Kazakstan, Kyrgyzstan, Armenia, Romania, and Russia. As of the date of this writing, the treaty with Russia has not yet entered into force.

Each of the nonimmigrant visa categories mentioned authorizes an individual to work only for the petitioning company for the authorized period of stay. A foreign worker who is not sponsored by a company may otherwise be authorized to work if he or she possesses valid employment authorization pursuant to a student visa practical-training program (F–1 or J–1 visa), the filing of an asylum application, or by virtue of being a U.S. permanent resident.

A U.S. employer can also petition a foreign national for lawful permanent residence status (also known as the green card process) pursuant to the employment-based immigration visa allowance. Employment visas are divided into several categories, including persons of extraordinary ability, outstanding professors and researchers, certain multinational executives and managers, professionals holding advanced degrees, professionals holding baccalaureate degrees, skilled workers in short supply, religious workers, and investors. Employment-related immigrant visas are subject to per-country numerical caps and, therefore, for certain categories it may take a few years before a visa number becomes available for a particular country.

It is critical that a foreign worker be authorized to work in the United States. Unauthorized work can result in deportation of the alien for failure to maintain lawful nonimmigrant status. Whether or not a U.S. business employs foreign workers, it is still greatly affected by immigration legislation in the form of employment verification. To determine which employment applicants are authorized to work in the United States, employers are required to complete Form I–9 for each new hire after November 6, 1996, which obligates the employer to verify the identity and work authorization of the employee. At the same time, employers cannot ask for more information than is required by law, as they may be in danger of violating antidiscrimination provisions. A company in violation of such rules can be subject to employer sanctions. Accordingly, it is extremely important for a U.S. employer to be in compliance with employer sanctions and antidiscrimination provisions of the immigration law and be familiar with issues pertaining to the withholding of social security and other related taxation matters.

By September 1997, the Attorney General will implement three employment-eligibility confirmation pilot programs of limited duration. These programs will create databases designed to confirm an individual's eligibility to work in the United States. Job applicants denied employment due to database errors will not be protected, and those seeking to prove job discrimination based on immigration status will have to prove intent to discriminate by the employer.

It is important to recognize that a person entering the United States on a B–1 (visitor-for-business visa) or B–2 (visitor-for-pleasure visa) is generally not entitled to work in the country until such time when a nonimmigrant visa petition and change of status, if applicable, are approved. Furthermore, it is essential to emphasize that, particularly with Russia, the Immigration and Naturalization Service, as well as U.S. consular posts, carefully scrutinize every application in an effort to avoid misrepresentation or fraudulent conduct. Bearing that in mind, the company and/or the foreign national may be required to provide extensive documentation in support of a nonimmigrant visa application.

In conclusion, every U.S. entity inclined to employ a foreign national needs to evaluate its needs carefully in light of the immigration restrictions and the entity's short- and long-term goals and objectives. This article is solely a prelude to the options available and the types of considerations a U.S. entity confronts when determining how to best fulfill its staffing needs. For individual assessment, it is always recommended that one contact a professional in order to thoroughly review all the options before making any decisions.

PART VI

LEGAL SYSTEM

CHAPTER 23

LEGAL STATUS OF FOREIGN ENTITIES (CORPORATIONS)

Valentin A. Kovalev

23.1 OVERVIEW.   The legal position of foreign corporate bodies in the Russian Federation is defined both by the rules of legislation of the Federation and by its international agreements with other governments. In accordance with Point 6, Article 1, of the law of the Russian Federation On Currency Regulation and Currency Control, foreign corporate bodies can be participants in legal currency relations in the Federation as nonresidents.

In accordance with Article 161 of the law The Basis of Civil Legislation of the USSR and its Republics, foreign corporate bodies are legally recognized under the law of the country where the corporate body is established. During any transactions, a firm must register properly in Russia to be legally recognized under Russian law. Foreign legal entities have the rights, according to law of country where this legal entity was established. During performance of any transaction, foreign legal entities cannot use limits of its authority branch or representative, if these authorities are not known in the country where the legal entities branch or representative is transacting business.

In accordance with Article 22 of the law dealing with the customs code, diplomatic representatives of foreign governments in Russia, in observing the established procedures for passing through the customs border of the Russian Federation, can bring into and take out of the country goods intended for the official use of the representatives, free of customs payment except for storage, payment, and the customs registration of goods outside locations defined for this location or outside work time of the customs bodies of the Russian Federation or a similar type of service. According to the Civil Code of the Russian Federation (Point 1, Article 2), the rules established by civil legislation regarding foreign corporate bodies are in effect if a legal issue is not covered by the federal law.

23.2 TAXES ON PROFITS.   Taxes on profits are paid by (1) enterprises and organizations considered corporate bodies under the legislation of the Federation, and (2) by companies, firms, and other organizations formed in accordance with the legislation of foreign governments that conduct business in the Federation through a permanent representative (Point 3 of Article 1 of the law On Tax on Profit of Enterprises and Organizations). All enterprises, independent of the results their activity or the presence of exemptions from taxes on profits, pay an excess wage tax on total excess wages paid, i.e., the amount exceeding the standard value of wages as set by the government (Point 13, Article 2).

Tax exemptions apply to (1) the profits of foreign corporate bodies made from carrying out social and economic programs regarding the construction of housing facilities for military personnel and veterans of military service (Point 6, Article 6); and (2) the excess of expenditure on workers' pay (Point 13, Article 2).

Value-added tax is paid by foreign corporate bodies conducting any commercial activity in the Federation (Paragraph d, Article 2 of the law On Value-Added Tax).

Customs duties are waived for (1) goods intended for official use by foreign diplomats and those attached to the government (Paragraph b, Article 5); and (2) work done while carrying out social and economic programs regarding the construction of housing for military personnel and veterans of military service (Paragraph t, Article 5). The indicated tax is paid by the foreign corporate bodies and comprises an account in the taxing body (Point 5 of Article 7).

23.3 OTHER TAXES.   All foreign corporate bodies are considered taxpayers in accordance with the law On Valuable Funds in the Russian Federation. These taxes include those for the use of roads; owners of transport vehicles; acquisition of automobiles or other transportation.

Foreign corporate bodies are exempt from paying the indicated taxes for the period of their work on social and economic programs involved in the construction of housing facilities for military personnel and veterans of military service. The corporate bodies exempt from paying taxes are determined by the government of the Federation.

Property taxes on foreign corporate bodies are determined by law of the Russian Federation. These include companies, firms, and other organizations formed in accordance with the legislation of foreign governments that have property in the Federation, on its continental shelf, or in an exclusive trading zone of the Federation (Article 1 of the law On Taxes on Property of Enterprises). This tax does not affect the property of foreign corporate bodies used during the implementation of social and economic programs regarding the construction of housing facilities for military personnel and veterans of military service (Paragraph p of Article 4).

Governmental duty is paid by corporate bodies and naturalized persons in whose interest specially authorized bodies have taken action and issued documents that have legal significance (Article 1 of the law On Government Duty).

The Russian Federation law On the Federal Budget for 1995 established that borrowers against the federal budget (on a returnable basis) cannot be enterprises with foreign investments (Article 36).

CHAPTER 24

LEGAL STATUS
OF FOREIGN CITIZENS

Valentin A. Kovalev

24.1 OVERVIEW. The legal position of foreign citizens in the Russian Federation is regulated by the Constitution. The laws are founded on those of the former USSR enacted on June 24, 1981, entitled On the Legal Position of Foreign Citizens in the USSR. These laws are effective in sections not contradicting the Constitution of the Russian Federation, the standard legal acts of the Russian Federation, and the international agreements of the Russian Federation.

A foreign citizen in the Federation is a person who is not a citizen of the Federation and who has proof of citizenship of a foreign state.

The legal position of foreign citizens in the Federation, is confirmed in the Constitution, which states that foreign citizens can enjoy the same rights and have the same obligations as the citizens of the Federation, except for cases established by federal law or international agreements of the Federation. The Constitution outlines the rights given to each person and exclusively to its citizens.

24.2 CITIZEN AND POLITICAL RIGHTS. With a legal standing equal to that of Russian citizens in the Federation, foreign citizens who are legally in the territory of Russia, are granted the following rights and freedom.

- The right to life (Article 20 of the Constitution). The death penalty was established as the ultimate punishment for especially horrible crimes against life; the death penalty can be requested by the prosecution for consideration and is determined by a judge with the participation of civilian advisers.
- Preservation of the dignity of the individual (Article 21). No one may be subjected to any severe punishment that degrades human dignity. No one can, without voluntary agreement, be subjected to medical, scientific, or other experiments.
- Freedom and personal inviolability (Article 22). Arrest, detention, or being held under guard can be approved only by judicial decision. Prior to the judicial order, a person cannot be held for a period of more than 48 hours.
- Inviolability of one's private life, personal and family secrets, and protection of one's honor and good name, including secrecy of letters, telephone conversations, the mail, and other types of communications (Article 23).
- Equality before a judge and the law (Article 19). The Federation guarantees the equality of human rights and freedom of its citizens independent of their sex, race,

nationality, language, origin, property ownership, job position, place of living, religious beliefs, personal convictions, membership in social organizations, and other circumstances.

- Freedom of movement and the ability to choose a place of living (Article 27).
- Freedom of conscience, self-expression, freedom to select, have, and promote religious and other beliefs (Article 28).
- Freedom of thought and words (Article 29).
- In spite of the fact that the law on gatherings, meetings, demonstrations, and picketing in the Constitution (Article 31) is mentioned only in relation to Russian citizens, according to Section 4, Article 15, of the Constitution on the priority of international standards over Russian legislation, the rule of Article 20 of the General Declaration of the Rights of Man is used—namely, "each person has the right to freedom of peaceful meetings and associations."
- Right of association (Article 30).

24.3 ECONOMIC, SOCIAL, AND CULTURAL RIGHTS.   Foreign citizens in the territory of Russia, as well as Russian citizens, enjoy the following economic, social, and cultural rights equally under Russian law.

- The right to free use of one's capacities and property for business undertakings and other economic activities not forbidden by law (Article 34). In accordance with Article 160 of the Basis of Civilian Legislation of the USSR, foreign citizens in Russia have the same rights as Russian citizens.
- The right to hold goods and property (Article 35);
- The right to work in conditions meeting safety and hygiene standards, to be rewarded for work without discrimination, at a wage level that meets the federal law on minimum wages, and the right of protection from being jobless and the right to a vacation (Article 37);
- Guarantee of health and social care because of old age, sickness, invalidism, lack of food, as well as a guarantee of an education for children (Article 39);
- In accordance with the laws on governmental pensions, foreign citizens have the right to a work pension in cases where two-thirds of the length of time necessary for getting a pension has been completed in the USSR or Russia;
- Right to housing (Article 40);
- Right to health and medical care (Article 41);
- Right to education (Article 43);
- Right to decide one's national affiliation and use of the native language (Article 26).

24.4 POLITICAL ASYLUM.   A special constitutional guarantee (Article 63) covers persons seeking political asylum. The Russian Federation offers political asylum to foreign citizens and persons without citizenship in accordance with the generally accepted standards of international law. The Federation is not permitted to return persons to other countries who are seeking political asylum or persons whose actions (or nonactions) have not been recognized in the Federation as a crime. The extradition of persons who are guilty of crimes and those who have been sentenced to punishment in other countries, is based on federal law or the international law of the Federation.

24.5 RIGHTS OF REFUGEES.   In accordance with the duties undertaken by Russia when joining the Convention of 1951 and the Protocol of 1976, the law On Refugees was adopted on February 19, 1993. The appropriate government and local self-regulation bodies are obligated to follow certain procedures concerning the rights of refugees:

- To present to refugees a list of settlements recommended for permanent dwelling and information about living conditions and work opportunities in these settlements;
- To provide refugees who have been residing in permanent living quarters, under the direction of an authorized body, a dwelling from the special housing fund designated for refugees;
- To cooperate with refugees on entry into a living cooperative or an individual dwelling;
- To offer to refugees assistance in finding work in accordance with their profession and qualifications;
- A refugees cannot be returned to the country from which they came against their will.

24.6 RIGHTS OF FOREIGN CITIZENS REGARDING INVESTMENTS, BUSINESS ACTIVITY, AND OBLIGATIONS TO PAY TAXES.   Foreign citizens, under the law of the Russian Federation of September 9, 1992, On Currency Regulation and Currency Control, can be considered residents or nonresidents. Also in accordance with the law, foreign nationals can carry out currency operations.

In accordance with sections of the first Article 20 and Article 42 of the law of the RSFSR of July 4, 1991, foreign investors can conduct any type of business activity except for those forbidden by federal legislation, and conduct business activity in free economic zones. Besides the rights and guarantees established by legislation of the Federation, foreign citizens have additional privileges, including a simplified means of entry and exit (this privilege does not extend to refugees).

Just as for Russian citizens, foreign nationals have obligations to pay taxes on goods and to pay government duties in cases where, in the interests of the foreign citizen, special assistance is needed for activities and the issuance of legal documentation relating to the transaction. Both of these obligations are based on laws of the Federation.

24.7 LIMITATION OF RIGHTS OF FOREIGN CITIZENS IN THE RUSSIAN FEDERATION.   Foreign citizens in the Russian Federation do not have the right:

- To participate in the controlling activities of the government, to vote, to participate in the administration of justice, to access government services (Article 32 of the Constitution), or to belong to governmental bodies and local self-governing bodies (Article 33);
- To carry out military obligations (Article 59);
- To enjoy protection and patronage abroad, and to be immune from extradition or expulsion to another country (Article 61).

Certain special limitations apply to labor rights, particularly the hiring of foreign citizens. By order of the president in December 1993, (no. 2146) it was established that foreigners working or carrying out other professional activities in Russia who break the rules for attracting and using foreign workers, should be deported at the expense of the employer.

According to a position confirmed by this order, foreign citizens engaging in professional activities in Russia can work for hire only when permission has been granted to the employer by the appropriate bodies of the Federation.

Foreign citizens cannot enter the air force or navy (Article 23 of the Air Code of the USSR and Article 41 of the Commercial Fleet Code of the USSR).

In marriage and family relations, limitations exist for foreign citizens in adopting children who are citizens of the Russian Federation. The adoption of such children by foreign citizens is permitted only in cases where it is not possible for these children to be adopted under the guardianship (trusteeship) of a Russian citizen, brought up in a family of citizens, or be adopted by relatives of the child independent of their dwelling place and citizenship (Article 98 of the Code on Marriage and Family).

When a child who is a Russian citizen is adopted by persons who are not citizens, the child retains his or her Russian citizenship. If one or both of the adopters has foreign citizenship, then they can apply to have the child's Russian Federation citizenship terminated if he or she is to be given the citizenship of another country.

CHAPTER 25

LEGAL RESPONSIBILITY FOR ECONOMIC CRIMES

Valentin A. Kovalev

25.1 CRIMINAL CODE. Criminal responsibility for business- and commerce-related offenses has always existed in Russia. In recent years, however with the formation of new economic, political, and social relations, and with the creation of a civilian society and a new government based on the Constitution of 1993, there is an acute need for the basic reform of legislation regarding offenses in the area of economics. This reform was outlined in the new Criminal Code of the Russian Federation, adopted in July 1995 by the Duma and went into effect in 1996.

The new Criminal Code of Russia, distinct from the Criminal Code of the Russian Soviet Federal Socialist Republic, contains a special section on responsibility for economics-based offenses, which, in turn, is subdivided into two independent parts: offenses in economic activity and offenses against property. The practice of establishing and developing market-economy relations in Russia and the laws established by other countries regarding business- and commerce-related offenses, have resulted in the introduction of numerous regulations covering such crimes into the Criminal Code. These include the following:

(a) Prevention of activity of the legal owner. This includes the responsibility for the following actions:

Unlawful failure to register an individual owner or commercial organization, or evasion of registration;

Illegal refusal to get special permission (license) for the right to conduct certain activities, or evasion in getting it;

Restriction of rights and legal interests of an individual owner or commercial organization in relation to organizational legal forms or forms of responsibility; and restriction of independence or any illegal interference in the activity of an individual owner or commercial organization. Responsibility for the indicated actions takes effect when the persons using their service position complete their actions.

(b) Registering illegal land transactions. This standard includes the responsibility not only for knowingly registering illegal transactions involving land, but also for distorting records for the Government Land Survey and for intentionally misrepresenting the dimensions of plots of land. Responsibility for these actions occurs when, for profit or any personal interest, the responsible person completes these actions using his or her service position.

(c) Illegal bank activity. This covers conducting banking operations without registration or specific permission (license), if such permission is obligatory and causes great harm. This covers pseudo-ownership, that is, creation of a commercial organization without the intent of carrying out business or banking activities, but only for the purposes of obtaining loans, credits, and avoiding taxes; removing goods to cover up illegal activity; or causing great harm.

(d) Legalization (laundering) of money obtained by an illegal method. This standard establishes responsibility for conducting financial operations and other transactions with money or goods obtained in any knowingly illegal way and equally for the use of these means to conduct legal business or any other economic activity.

(e) Obtaining credit by fraud. This is obtaining, for an individual business or head of an organization, credit or preferential conditions for getting credit by knowingly presenting to the bank or any creditor false information about the business or financial status of an individual businessperson or organization if these actions cause great harm.

(f) Fraudulent evasion of repayment of credit. This deals with the intentional failure by the head of an organization or individual to pay a legal judgment for a large-scale credit obligation. Creditor-debt judgments cover debts that total in excess of 500 times pay for individuals and total more than 2,500 times revenue for organizations.

(g) Restriction of competition. This is created by an agreement among enterprises that limits the entrance of other firms into or limits access to the market or that fixes prices.

(h) Forcing a transaction to completion or refusal to complete it. Responsibility for these actions begins when they are carried out by a threat to use force, to destroy or damage property, and, equally, to spread information that can cause significant damage to the rights and legal interests of the other party or related parties, without the signs of interference.

(i) Knowingly false advertisement. This covers the use of advertisements containing deliberately false information about goods, works, or services including manufacturers (executives, salespeople, etc.), that have caused significant damage to the rights and legal interests of citizens or organizations, or damage to the legal interests of society or the government.

(j) Illegal procurement and dissemination of information containing commercial or banking secrets. Responsibility for this standard begins with the following activities:

Collection of information containing commercial or bank secrets by stealing documents, by bribes or threats and, equally, by any other illegal methods in order to disclose or illegally use this information;

Illegal disclosure or use of commercial secrets, without the agreement of the owner, for a base motive or any personal interests that cause great harm.

(k) Bribery of participants and organizers of professional sports contests and places of entertainment for commercial competitions. This standard is intended to cover the following activities:

Bribery of athletes, judges, trainers, coaches, and other participants or organizers of professional sports contests, and of organizers or members of a jury at commercial or entertainment events involving competition in order to influence the results of these events;

Illegal acceptance of money or any material goods or services by athletes or performers in order to influence the results of competitions or entertainments;

Illegal acceptance of money or material goods or services by judges, trainers, coaches, and other participants or organizers of professional sporting competitions and, equally, organizers or members of the jury for entertainment and commercial competitions.

(l) Misuse of the issuance of securities. This deals with issuing securities with knowingly inaccurate information and supporting a prospectus for issuance with knowingly inaccurate information, or confirmation of the knowingly inaccurate results of an issuance, if these actions result in causing significant harm to the investor;

(m) Illegal actions during bankruptcy. This standard covers two different types of activities:

Hiding goods or goods' obligations; concealing information about belongings, their scale, location or any information about goods; transferring goods to another owner; alienation or destruction of goods; and concealment, destruction, or falsification of bookkeeping and other accounting documents that reflect the economic activity, if these actions were conducted by the director or owner of the debtor-organization or individual enterprise during bankruptcy or when foreseeing bankruptcy that caused great harm;

Illegal satisfaction of the debt obligations of particular creditors by the director or owner of an debtor-enterprise or citizen-owner; knowledge of the actual bankruptcy that is damaging to other creditors and equally taken for satisfaction of the creditor familiar with the preference shown to him by a bankrupt debtor to the detriment of other creditors, if these actions cause great harm.

(n) Malicious bankruptcy. This is intentionally creating or increasing one's inability to pay by the director or owner of a commercial organization, and also by an individual employer in the interest of other persons, causing great harm or any serious consequences.

(o) Fictional bankruptcy. This deals with issuing knowingly false statements to the director or owner of a commercial organization and, equally, to an individual employer about its insolvency in order to cause alarm to creditors trying to obtain the postponement or installment payment of what is due them or a reduction and nonpayment of debts, causing great harm.

The methods of punishment for these offenses that do not include the limitation of freedom are:

Fines up to 800 times the payment due or obligatory work for a certain time period;

Deprivation of the right to work on certain tasks or carry out certain activities;

Deprivation of work for a time period not to exceed two years.

In addition, if these crimes are first-time offenses or there are other extenuating circumstances, the punishment also includes such measures as:

Limiting freedom for a time period up to three years

Arrest for a period up to six months

Deprivation of freedom for a certain time period without time limit.

In individual cases, the limitation of freedom can represent a period up to 10 years (e.g., for laundering money by illegal means). Forcing completion of transactions or failure to do so can earn the offender up to 12 years.

In the new Criminal Code of Russia, the business- and commerce-related crimes that were carried over from the Criminal Code of the RSFSR are:

- Illegal business undertakings;
- Knowingly acquiring or selling goods obtained illegally;
- Illegal use of a trademark;
- Manufacture or sale of counterfeit money or securities;
- Dealing in contraband;
- Illegal export of scientific and technical information and services relating to weapons of mass destruction, armament, and military technology;
- Failure to return to the Russian Federation artistic, historic, and archeological objects valued by the people of the Federation and foreign countries;
- Illegal transactions with currency values;
- Illegal transfers of valuable metals and stones;
- Evasion of custom duties;
- Tax evasion;
- Deception of customers.

The new code contains a few other minor changes.

The chapter of the new Criminal Code of Russia outlining punishment for crimes against society basically repeats the corresponding chapter of the Criminal Code of the RSFSR. The major changes in the new Criminal Code cover some new measures of punishment, including obligatory work, arrest, and an increase in the parameters for monetary fines.

CHAPTER 26

JUDICIAL SYSTEM

S.B. Romazin

26.1 OVERVIEW. In accordance with Part III, Article 118, of the Constitution of the Russian Federation, courts in Russia were established under federal constitutional law. The Constitution does not contain a full list of the courts comprising the Russian judicial system. In the Constitution, the legislature has formulated only the provisions related to the structure of judicial power. Articles 125, 126, and 127 contain provisions for the Constitutional Court, the Supreme Court, and the Supreme Arbitration Court of the Russian Federation. Also, some other federal courts are mentioned in the Constitution (Point E, Article 83; Part II, Article 128).

In accordance with Article 4 of the federal constitutional law The Judicial System of the Russian Federation adopted on December 31, 1996, there are in effect in Russia federal courts, constitutional courts, and justices of the peace, which comprise the national judicial system. The unity of the judicial system in Russia is achieved by:

Abiding by the judicial rules and regulations that were established as federal laws by federal courts and justices of the peace;

Applying the Constitution, federal constitutional laws, federal laws, widely recognized principles and norms of international law, and international agreements of the Russian Federation; also, all courts recognizing the Constitutions (Charters) and other laws of the subjects of the Federation;

Accepting court decisions as binding for the entire Russian territory;

Legally securing the status of judges;

Financing federal courts and justices of the peace by means of funds supplied by the federal budget.

Federal courts include the Constitutional Court and the Supreme Court of the Russian Federation, the Supreme Courts of the republics, regional and district courts, courts of Moscow and St. Petersburg as cities of federal subordination, courts of autonomous districts and counties, martial courts, and specialized courts. All these comprise a system of federal courts of general jurisdiction. The category of federal court also includes the Supreme Arbitration court of the Russian Federation, federal arbitration courts of districts, and arbitration courts of subjects of the Federation, which make up a system of federal arbitration courts. As for the courts of subjects of the Federation, there are constitutional courts of subjects of the Federation and justices of the peace, who are judges of general jurisdiction of subjects of the Federation.

Thus, the judicial power of Russia consists of three branches:

1. The Constitutional Court (following the initial establishment of the Constitution, this became a system of constitutional courts of subjects of the Federation);
2. The Supreme Court and a system of general courts;
3. The Supreme Arbitration Court and a system of commercial courts.

The Constitutional Court of the Russian Federation is a judicial organ of constitutional control that autonomously and independently exercises judicial power via constitutional judicial proceedings. The Constitutional Court deals with cases concerning the constitutional nature of laws and other legal norms, which have been adopted by the Russian Federal Assembly, Russia's president, and legislative and executive bodies of the subjects of the Federation. The Constitutional Court of the Russian Federation is a specialized body for the judicial protection of the Constitution. Activity of the Constitutional Court is regulated by the federal constitutional law The Constitutional Court of the Russian Federation enacted July 21, 1994.

26.2 SUPREME COURT.   According to Article 126 of the Constitution and Article 19 of the law The Judicial System, the Supreme Court is the highest judicial organ concerning civil, criminal, administrative and other cases of general jurisdiction.

The Supreme Court performs judicial supervision over courts of general jurisdiction, including martial and specialized courts. Within the limits of its competence, the Supreme Court examines cases as a court of second instance, as a supervising body, and in the event that there are newly discovered circumstances in a case. In some cases, the Supreme Court can act as the court of first instance. It is a superior judicial body in regard to the Supreme Courts of the republics, district courts, the courts of Moscow and St. Petersburg, courts of the autonomous regions and districts, and martial courts.

The Supreme Court provides explanations concerning issues of judicial practice to the lower courts. Its powers, as well as procedures for establishing and defining its functions, are set by federal constitutional laws.

The Supreme Courts of republics, regions, districts, cities of federal subordination, courts of autonomous regions, or of autonomous districts, within their competence limits, examine cases as courts of the first and second instance, as supervising bodies, and if there are new circumstances in a case. Their powers, including procedures for establishing and defining their functions, are set by federal constitutional law.

26.3 DISTRICT COURT.   District courts, within the limits of their competence, deal with cases as a court of first and second instance and perform other duties outlined by federal constitutional law. District court is a superior judicial instance vis-à-vis judges who perform their duties in the territory of that judicial district. Their powers, including procedures for establishing and defining their functions, are set by federal constitutional law.

26.4 MARTIAL COURT.   The martial courts that are included in the federal judicial system are based on the location of the armed forces. These courts implement judicial power over military matters, as federal law stipulates. Within the limits of their competence, martial courts deal with cases as courts of first and second instances, as supervising bodies, and if there are new circumstances in a case. Their powers, including procedures for establishing and defining their functions, are set by federal constitutional law. At present, martial courts act on the basis of the federal law Issues of Organization and Activity of Martial Courts and Courts of Military Justice, enacted in December 1994.

26.5 ARBITRATION COURTS.   Disputes that arise in the course of business activities and are related either to civil relations or violations of the law by management, are dealt with by a system of arbitration courts of the Russian Federation. According to Article 3 of the federal constitutional law on arbitration courts enacted in April 1995, the system of arbitration courts in Russia is comprised of the Supreme Arbitration Court, federal arbitration courts of districts, arbitration courts of the republics, regions, districts, cities of federal subordination, autonomous regions and districts, and arbitration courts of subjects of the Federation.

The Supreme Arbitration Court is the highest judicial organ for resolving economic disputes and other cases that are examined by lower arbitration courts. The Supreme Arbitration Court is a superior judicial instance vis-à-vis the federal arbitration courts of the regions and arbitration courts of subjects of the Federation. The Supreme Arbitration Court deals with cases as a court of first instance, as a supervising organ, and in the event that there are new circumstances in a case.

The federal arbitration court of a region, within the limits of its competence, deals with cases that might require reversal or have new circumstances revealed. The federal arbitration court of a region is superior to arbitration courts of subjects of the Federation in the territory of the corresponding judicial district. The arbitration courts of the subjects of the Federation, within the limits of their competence, deal with cases as courts of first instance, and with cases that might require reversals or in which new circumstances have surfaced.

26.6 SPECIALIZED COURTS.   Specialized federal courts dealing with civil and administrative cases are established by amendments to the federal constitutional law the judicial System of the Federation. Their powers, including procedures for establishing and defining their functions, are set by federal constitutional law. At present, there are no specialized federal courts in Russia's territory.

The Constitutional Court of a subject of the Federation can be established by a subject of the Federation to examine issues involving how the subject's laws and legal provisions issued by a state organ or by local authorities conform to the subject's Constitution. The Constitutional Court of a subject of the Federation deals with issues referred to it in an order that is outlined by a law of the subject of the Federation. Decisions of this court that have been made within the limits of its power cannot be revised by any other court.

The justice of the peace, within the limits of his or her competence, deals with civil, administrative, and criminal cases as a court of first instance. Justices of the peace are judges of general jurisdiction of the subjects of the Federation. The powers, procedures, and activities of the justice of the peace are set by federal law and by a law of the subject of the Federation. At present, however, justices of the peace have not yet assumed their duties in Russian.

Activities of the Constitutional Court, the Supreme Court, and the Supreme Arbitration Court of the Russian Federation are provided by the apparatus of these courts. The activities of other courts of general jurisdiction are provided by the Justice Department of the Supreme Court, while the activities of other arbitration courts are provided by the Supreme Arbitration Court.

CHAPTER 27

FOREIGN INVESTMENT: REGULATION, STIMULATION, AND REGISTRATION

Aleksey A. Goroholinsky

27.1 OVERVIEW.   Russia's vast natural resources, highly skilled labor, established production facilities, and intellectual potential can be of significant interest to foreign investors. The Russian government has been practicing a goodwill policy toward foreign investment in recent years, and a number of crucial decisions have been made to stimulate foreign investment in the Russian economy.

Various decrees of the president of the Russian Federation have lightened the tax burden. For example, the property tax on technological equipment and spare parts imported to Russia was dropped. Customs duties have been reduced by half for a period of five years on goods imported by foreign enterprises that invested at least $100,000. In the wake of this decision, an agreement was signed with Mars Incorporated, and another with United Technologies is currently in the process of negotiation. The limit on the number of current and budgetary accounts that enterprises and organizations can obtain from banks and other credit institutions has been abolished. The fluctuations of the Russian currency in relation to hard currencies are now considered when determining the taxable income of an enterprise. On January 1, 1996, the tax on overtime pay was removed.

A bill entitled Alterations and Amendments to the Law on Foreign Investment in Russia is being prepared for consideration in the Duma, as well as some corresponding amendments to the income-tax and customs bill, Concession Agreements with Domestic and Foreign Investors. In addition, a bill supporting economic free zones, passed by the Duma, has been submitted for floor discussion in the Council of Federation.

27.2 PROGRAM TO STIMULATE INVESTMENT.   A composite program to stimulate domestic and foreign investment in the Russian economy has been adopted. It encompasses a wide variety of economic, legal, credit, financial, informational, and organizational measures to foster domestic and foreign investment. This program extends the already existing government-sponsored program entitled Reforms and Development of Russian Economy for 1995–97, as well as some other investment programs. In essence, the goals of this new program are:

- To increase investment activity to prevent any further slide into a long-term depression;
- To emphasize the development of certain procedures to implement major legislative decisions, which have already been or will be made in the near future, to form a legal

foundation for investment. This is why a significant portion of the program is dedicated to such methods and procedures.

The overall logic behind this program can be defined as follows:

- To continue improving the investment climate in Russia. A necessary condition for this is a further reduction of inflation, followed by refinancing by the Central Bank of Russia. One of the pivotal issues will be to guarantee various protective measures, including the personal security of investors and the security of their investments in the Russian market.
- To implement measures to increase the volume of investments. One of the most important tasks in this regard will be to establish conditions for converting the immobile savings of the population and enterprises into dynamic investments.
- To increase profits on capital investment by increasing efficiency;
- To attract foreign investments to help develop international economic relations, as well as utilize the most advanced scientific and technological achievements—although foreign investment alone cannot compensate for the lack of domestic investment. Active foreign investment can be made possible only by active domestic investment, provided that foreign investors have the same regulations and benefits as domestic investors, in accordance with the legislation on foreign investment.

These programs and actions are essential in creating a favorable investment environment in Russia through purposeful application of debt amortization; stimulation of profit capitalization by proper taxation; development of the secondary market, consisting of bonds, securities, and mobile capital; insurance; methods to discourage capital from leaving Russia, and to promote the return of Russian capital from abroad; and active foreign investment. In the upcoming years, Russian leaders expect to adjust the levels of taxes, tariffs, and benefits to correspond with investment conditions found in the countries competing with Russia for capital investment.

A blueprint of the federal law Amending and Adding to the Law of Russia on Investment Activity is being prepared. This law is expected to change and expand the legislative and normative acts that regulate the relationship between taxpayers and the state, and to establish the order of granting appeals to protect taxpayers.

The question of land ownership and long-term leases for foreign investors will be resolved in the Land Code of the Russian Federation. Normative documents will be created outlining the criteria for estimating land values, particularly land currently possessed by factories, including those with foreign investments.

27.3 INSURANCE.   Insurance protection for Russian investments owned by domestic and foreign investors has not been resolved yet. The general principles of insuring investments are:

- Enumeration of the instances of loss and the causes that establish the impossibility of their return, thus obligating the insurer to compensate the investor for the losses;
- The amounts of insurance payments;
- The procedures for signing an insurance agreement.

Adoption is anticipated for the resolution that will define the mechanism of putting the law on collateral into practice, particularly the provisions that establish procedures for estimating the real value of property and its transference to a new owner, domestic or foreign, in case the defendant has not fulfilled his or her obligations.

Negotiations regarding the mutual insurance of investments is well under way. So far, about 30 agreements have been reached, the majority of which are with major countries. The agreements are an important element in the legal prerequisites for Russian participation in international investment cooperation. They provide indispensable guarantees to foreign investors in the Russian market, as well as to domestic investors abroad.

27.4 INVESTMENT COLLABORATION.

The Consulting Council on International Investments in Russia, comprised of the 25 largest global corporations, is actively working in the field of international investment collaboration, as well as preparing recommendations to the Russian government. This work is characterized as extremely useful and effective.

The image of Russia as a country ripe for investment is being actively promoted. With this in mind, the Russian Center of Assistance to Foreign Investors has been founded at the Ministry of Economics. Arrangements have been made to open investment bureaus in Washington, Chicago, Paris, London, Frankfurt, and Milan. Their main goal is to provide foreign investors with the necessary economic information on the market conditions and legal requirements for foreign investment in Russia.

27.5 REGISTRATION.

The system of state registration of enterprises with foreign investment plays an important role in regulating foreign investment. The system consists of the State Registration Chamber (SRC) and registration agencies which are members of the executive power of the Federation.

The state registration of all enterprises—except for those in the crude-oil, oil-refining, and coal industries—that have a total volume of foreign-held shares under of 100 million rubles, is carried out by the Councils of Ministers of the republics—members of the Russian Federation, the administrative powers of regions, and the cities of Moscow and St. Petersburg. An enterprise whose legal address is in the city of Moscow city is registered by the Moscow Registration Chamber, and one whose legal address is in Moscow Oblast is registered by the Administration of the Moscow Oblast.

The following entities may engage in the creation of an enterprise with foreign investment:

- Foreign legal entities, in particular any companies, firms, organizations, or associations registered and competent to invest abroad in accordance with the legislation of the country of their registration;
- Foreign citizens or Russian citizens permanently residing abroad, on the condition that they are registered in the country of their citizenship or place of permanent residence;
- Foreign states;
- International organizations.

The following are considered to be investments in the fixed capital of an enterprise with foreign investment:

- Newly founded and modernized basic funds and circulating assets in all branches and areas of national economy;
- Investments in rubles and foreign currency;

- Securities;
- Patents for intellectual property backed up by proper documents;
- Scientific and technical products.

The state registration of enterprises with foreign investments is carried out in accord with the code defined in the law On Foreign Investments.

The registration of enterprises with foreign investments takes 21 days from the time of submitting the application. All changes and additions to the original documents of registered enterprises must be registered with the state. These include all changes in the founding membership (i.e., adding and dropping members), the amount of the fixed capital, the redistribution of shares, the legal address, and the area of activities. These changes and additions will come into effect only after registration.

Registration will be denied if violations of the code governing establishment of an enterprise occur, or if the establishing documents do not meet the legislative requirements of the Russian Federation. Any activity by an unregistered enterprise is prohibited. The revenues received by an unregistered enterprise are recovered through a court of law and redirected into the budget of a local government.

A registered enterprise with foreign investment is granted a standardized certificate of registration. An enterprise with foreign investments acquires the status of a legal entity from the time of its registration.

The state register of enterprises, a bank of information about all enterprises founded in Russia, is maintained by the SRC. The procedure of entering enterprises into the state register takes 21 days from the time of submitting the application.

All enterprises established on the national soil of Russia, regardless of their organizational and legal status, must be entered into the state register immediately following their official registration. All enterprises in the state register are granted a standardized certificate authenticated with the official stamp of the SRC.

27.6 ACCREDITATION OF SUBSIDIARIES. Accreditation of a foreign company's subsidiary in Russia is granted in conformity with the following: the resolution by the Council of Ministers entitled the Affirmation of Code of Establishing and Activities of Subsidiaries of Foreign Firms, Banks and Organizations; the resolution of the president of the Supreme Soviet of the Russian Federation, Certain Issues of Trade and Production Chamber of the Russian Federation; and Order No. 25 of February 1993, Accreditation of Subsidiaries of Foreign Firms on the National Soil of the Russian Federation at the Russian Agency of International Cooperation and Development. A resolution of the Russian Federation regarding the State Registration Chamber at the Ministry of Economics gives the SRC the authority not only to accredit foreign firms, but also to enter them into the state register.

Permission to establish a subsidiary of a foreign company in Russia is based on the nature of the firm's activities. Acceptable activities include assisting in extending cooperation in the areas of trade, production, science, transportation, tourism, finance and other areas, as well as supporting and extending international relations and developing international cooperation.

A subsidiary of a foreign firm established in Russia is considered a separate subdivision of that firm. The subsidiary is not a separate legal entity and can act only on behalf of the represented firm whose name is incorporated in the name of the subsidiary. Over 500 foreign firms and more than 700 subsidiaries have already acquired accreditation and have been entered into the state register.

27.7 ENTERPRISES WITH FOREIGN INVESTMENT.   About 20,000 enterprises with foreign investments have already been entered into the state register. Initially, these ventures were small and mid-sized businesses, primarily in those emerging sectors of the economy where returns on investments were quick and could be obtained in the form of hard currency. In recent years, however, there has been a tendency toward a decreasing foreign currency as part of the fixed capital of a joint venture. This tendency indicates a general propensity to use imported equipment and technology to form the fixed capital of an enterprise.

In the Russian market, companies with foreign investments sell goods and services worth 500 billion rubles annually. The number of employees in these companies has reached 400,000 people, having doubled in the last two years.

The SRC is taking an active part in the privatization of state-owned ventures and municipal property. Commissioned by the Ministry of Finance, the SRC keeps track of acquisitions of companies' shares by foreign investors.

As a result of the efforts of the state system to attract foreign investments, a surge of foreign investors in Russia was evident in 1995. According to the State Committee of Statistics of Russia, by January 1, 1995, commercial organizations had accumulated $4.64 billion and 374.8 billion rubles of foreign investment.

The volume of foreign investments during a nine-month period in 1995 amounted to $1.57 billion and 567.9 billion rubles, as shown in Exhibit 27.1. Compared with the second quarter of 1995 ($472.2 million), the volume of investments in the third quarter of 1995 rose 184% ($870 million). Altogether, by September 3, 1995, foreign investments had climbed to $6.21 billion and 947.7 billion rubles. Of these amounts, direct investment totaled $3.03 billion and 714 billion rubles.

The most attractive industries for foreign investors in a nine-month period in 1995 are shown in Exhibit 27.2. Most foreign investments came from the United States (27.6%),

Exhibit 27.1.   Foreign Investment During Nine-Month Period in 1995

	US $ (billions)	Rubles (billions)
Direct investments	1.04	382.1
Portfolio investments	0.01	37.9
Other investments (trade credits, credits from international financial organizations, bank deposits)	0.52	147.9

Exhibit 27.2.   Areas of Foreign Investment During a Nine-Month Period in 1995

	US $ (millions)	%
Retail and catering industries	231.7	14.8
Financial, credit, insurance, and pension services	205.8	13.1
Fuel industry	162.5	10.4
Science and research	127.5	8.1
Chemical and petrochemical industry	127.3	8.1
Commercial industry	102.6	6.5
Timber, pulp, and paper industries	102.0	6.5
Food industry	101.1	6.4
State purchases	70.2	4.4
Machine-building and metallurgical industries	59.7	3.8

Germany (13%), Switzerland (9%), Liechtenstein (8.9%), Belgium (6.3%), Japan (4.2%), and France (4.1%). During the same period, foreign investments occurred primarily in Moscow (56.6%), Tyumen Oblast (4.6%), Tver Oblast (4.3%), the Republic of Tartastan (4.0%), Nizhny Novgorod Oblast (2.9%), Novosibirsk Oblast (2.8%), Samara Oblast (2.6%), and St. Petersburg (2.4%). In addition, the following oblasts are characterized by a low level of foreign investment: Rostov, Astrakhan, Tambov, Penza, Kostroma, Orlov, and Ivanovo. During this period, the gross volume of products and services involving foreign investments amounted to 34.67 trillion rubles. Exports totaled $4.1 billion, and imports were $2.28 billion.

The average monthly wage per officially employed worker during the same nine months of 1995 was 635,000 rubles, compared to 315,000 rubles in 1994.

CHAPTER 28

CORPORATE LAW AND ITS EFFECT ON AMERICAN INVESTMENT

Peter Pettibone and Natasha Alexeeva

28.1 OVERVIEW. In the beginning of the twentieth century, czarist Russia had a developed system of corporate and commercial legislation, including laws regulating trade, company formation, securities and exchanges. The Russian Civil Code of 1917 is sometimes referred to by scholars as the most advanced civil code of its time. After the Bolshevik revolution, however, most business-related legislation was abolished, and an article that made making a profit a criminal activity was introduced into the Soviet Criminal Code and survived many of its subsequent editions.

Modern Russian corporate legislation is only about eight years old. Such laws were first adopted in the late 1980s by the USSR and were intended to allow the people to create small family-type businesses—*cooperatives*—income from which was intended to supplement their state-paid salaries. At that time, no one could imagine that by the mid-1990s, Russia's private sector would account for nearly half the gross domestic product and that corporate legislation would reach a level comparable to that of similar legislation of some of most developed countries.

28.2 CORPORATE LAW: ITS SOURCES AND PLACE IN THE RUSSIAN LEGAL SYSTEM

(a) Constitution, Laws, and Other Normative Acts. The Constitution of the Russian Federation of 1993, adopted on December 12, 1993, established that the most significant laws in Russia are passed by the *Duma,* the lower house of the Russian Parliament. These laws must also be approved by the upper house of Parliament, the Council of Federation. The majority of the laws adopted by the Duma usually go through two or three readings. After it is adopted by both houses, a draft becomes law if it is signed by the president within 14 days after it is presented for signature. The president can refuse to sign the draft and send it back to the Parliament with recommendations for amendments. President Yeltsin recently exercised his veto right several times after the election of the current Parliament.

In the hierarchy of Russian legislation, laws adopted by the Duma are the most important ones after the Constitution. All other legislation, including decrees of the government, edicts of the president, and regulations, instructions, and normative acts issued by various branches of the government and the Central Bank, are subordinate to the laws passed by the Parliament and should be in conformity with them.

This system has its pluses and minuses. Because of the long list of items on its agenda, the Duma cannot react quickly to the changing needs of the Russian business environment, thereby giving the government and the president an opportunity to fill the legislative vacuum. Interestingly enough, some governmental decrees and presidential edicts were initially drafted as laws to be adopted by the Duma but, due to the long delays and political uncertainty associated with the Parliament, were then passed by either the government or the president.

Among the drawbacks of this system is the fact that very often several governmental bodies are issuing legislation on the same subject. For instance, securities legislation is issued by the Duma, the government, the president, and by several governmental agencies: the Ministry of Finance, the State Privatization Agency, and by the recently created Federal Commission on the Securities Market.

(b) Sources of Corporate Law.   Russian law on corporations is not contained in a single document and its provisions are spread through several laws and normative acts. Legislation on company formation is primarily contained in Part I of the Civil Code of the Federation, enacted on January 1, 1995; in the federal law On Joint Stock Companies (herein referred to the Joint Stock Company Law), effective January 1, 1996; and in the federal law On the Securities Market, effective April 22, 1996. The adoption of these laws created the second wave of Russian corporate legislation and replaced corporate and privatization laws that governed the creation of companies in Russia in the early through mid-1990s.

28.3 TYPES OF BUSINESS ENTERPRISES

(a) Legal Entities.   Chapter 4 of the Civil Code separates various legal entities available in Russia into two major categories: for-profit and not-for-profit. The for-profit legal entities are described in the Code as "organizations pursuing the deriving of profit as the principal purpose of their activity," while the not-for-profit ones "do not have the derival of profit as such a goal," and profits received by them may not be distributed among the founders. This distinction is important since certain types of business vehicles that are available for the for-profit organizations may not be available for the not-for-profits: they can be organized only in a limited number of ways, such as, for instance, social and religious associations, organizations financed by their founder and charitable foundations.

The for-profit organizations may be set up in many different forms, which under the Code fall into one of the following four categories: commercial partnerships; commercial companies, production cooperatives, and state and municipal enterprises.

(i) Commercial Partnerships.   Partnerships are not often used as vehicles of foreign investment in Russia, but the new Civil Code, which is more sophisticated and consistent in its treatment of partnerships than previous corporate legislation, may make them more attractive to foreign investors.

The Civil Code provides that a partnership can exist in two forms: *full* (or general) partnership and *limited* (*kommandit*) partnership. All members of a full partnership are equal with respect to their unlimited liability for the debts of the partnership: their personal assets may be reached by the partnership's creditors and any agreements limiting such liability are void. A kommandit partnership, on the other hand, has two types of members: full partners whose liability is unlimited, and one or more kommandit partners whose liability extends only to the assets contributed by such partners to the partnership. Kommandit partners enjoy the benefits of limited liability, but they may not participate in the management of the partnership and may not represent it in commercial transactions without a special power of attorney.

Both full and kommandit partnerships are created and function on the basis of partnership agreements that need to be registered with the State Registration Chamber (or similar Russian governmental bodies in charge of corporate registrations). These partnership agreements must contain provisions regulating the size of the capital of the partnership, the amount of capital contributions of each partner, and their liability for not making such contributions. The Civil Code allows partners a great deal of flexibility in establishing procedures for managing the partnership, admitting new partners, and distributing the partnership's profits and losses. One of the few restrictive provisions contained in this section of the code prohibits an individual from being a full partner in more than one partnership.

Unlike the Anglo-American legal system, the new wave of Russian corporate legislation treats partnerships, including full partnerships, as legal entities—they need to be formally incorporated by way of registering a partnership agreement and have all other requisites of a legal entity, i.e., an existence independent from their founders, a separate balance sheet, etc. It is still not quite clear how this change in the corporate status of a full partnership will affect its status for tax purposes. Usually, profits of a full partnership are not taxed at the partnership level, but are taxed when received by the individual partners; the losses, similarly, can be written off as the investment losses of the partners.

(ii) Commercial Companies.   The Civil Code provides that companies in Russia be organized in the following forms: limited liability company, additional liability company, and joint stock company.

LIMITED LIABILITY COMPANY.   A Russian limited liability company may be described as an entity that takes its attributes from both partnerships and joint stock companies. On the one hand, the charter capital of a limited liability company, like the capital of a partnership, is divided into participatory shares (interests) of the members; and the company may not issue shares. On the other hand, liability of the participants in a limited liability company, like liability of shareholders, is limited to their capital contributions.

As a corporate form, a limited liability company is well suited for small and medium-sized businesses—the Civil Code provides that its total membership may not exceed an established maximum number. During the life of a limited-liability company, if the total of its members exceeds this number, its members must reorganize the company into a joint stock company. If within one year they fail to do so, the company may be liquidated by a court decision.

Article 88 of the Civil Code contains an additional restriction—a limited liability company "may not have as a sole member another economic company consisting of a single entity." This provision is aimed at reducing the use of a limited liability company in a parent-subsidiary structure since the parent company must have at least two shareholders or owners. The highest governing body in a limited liability company is a general meeting of members; daily matters are decided by the executive organ, which can be a collegial or one-person body.

With respect to the sale and transfer of an interest in a limited liability company, the Civil Code provides that such interest may be sold to a nonmember unless the charter of the company provides otherwise. Existing members have a right of first refusal to buy such interests in proportion to the interest in the company already owned by them. In case a member wishes to withdraw from the company and other members are not interested in purchasing this interest, the company must buy the selling member out by "paying the real value of the interest or providing [the selling member] with assets in kind, the cost of which is equal to such value" (Article 93).

Limited-liability companies as business vehicles are quite popular among Russians as well as foreign entrepreneurs. Anyone wishing to form a company of this kind in Russia should, however, keep in mind that the Civil Code contains several references to the law on limited liability companies. As of the date of this writing, this law has not yet been adopted, although several drafts of it have been circulated. It is possible that this law will be adopted in the near future. In this case, it is likely that all limited liability companies that were established prior to the adoption of this law will be required to amend and to reregister their constitutive documents, which may be a costly and burdensome procedure.

ADDITIONAL LIABILITY COMPANY.   An additional liability company is quite similar in organization and characteristics to a limited liability company, with the sole distinction being the scope of personal liability of its members. The members of an additional liability company are liable for its obligations with their personal property, but the scope of this liability is limited to the value of assets that they contributed to the company, multiplied by a certain number. This multiple must be set in the constitutive documents of the company and should be equal for all the members. In case of bankruptcy of one of the members, his or her liability is spread between the other members in proportion to their interest in the company.

JOINT STOCK COMPANY.   The new Civil Code and the Joint Stock Company Law have replaced the decree of the Council of Ministers of the Russian Soviet Federal Socialist Republic, No. 601, On Joint Stock Companies, which had been the primary source of legislation on joint stock companies. Articles 96–104 of the Civil Code establish that a joint stock company has a charter capital that is divided into a specified number of shares and that its shareholders are liable for the obligations of the company only to the extent of their share ownership.

Article 7 of the Joint Stock Company Law outlines the two different types of joint stock companies: open and closed, and they differ in the scope of the shareholders' right to transfer their shares. An *open* joint stock company has a potentially unlimited number of shareholders, who may sell their shares without the consent of the other shareholders. Shares of an open joint stock company may be sold in a public offering; they may also be distributed in a private placement, unless private placements are prohibited by the company's charter or by legislation.

In contrast, a *closed* joint stock company may have not more than fifty shareholders; its shares may only be distributed among its founders or "other previously specified group of persons." Shares of a closed joint stock company may not be offered to the general public. Shareholders of a closed joint stock company have a preferred right to purchase shares that are sold by other shareholders; thus shareholders have both preemptive rights and the right of first refusal.

The charter capital of a joint stock company is equal to the nominal value of shares issued by the company and purchased by the shareholders. By an edict of the Russian president (No. 1482) the minimum amount of the charter capital is established as 1,000 times the minimum wage, 50% of which must be paid by the founders upon registration of the company, while the balance must be paid within one year after registration. Any increase in the size of the charter capital requires an approval of the general meeting of shareholders and may be conducted by way of raising the nominal value of shares or by issuing new shares. Similarly, the charter capital may be decreased by lowering the nominal value of shares or if the company buys back some of its own shares. Before decreasing its charter capital, the company must notify all of its current creditors. The creditors may object to such a decrease or demand that the company first satisfy its obligations toward them.

For the first time in Russian corporate legislation, the Joint Stock Company Law makes a distinction between issued and authorized shares. Article 27 of this law provides that the charter of a joint stock company must establish the number of issued shares, i.e., shares that are purchased by shareholders. The charter also may set a number of authorized shares, i.e., shares that will be sold to shareholders in the future. The Joint Stock Company Law (Article 28) also provides that while the number of authorized shares may only be increased by a shareholders' vote, a decision to issue new shares within the authorized number requires only a board's approval. This change significantly simplifies the procedure of issuance of new shares, since under previous corporate laws any issuance of shares required holding a shareholders' meeting, making changes in the company's charter, and registering the amended charter.

The Joint Stock Company Law describes in detail various other types of securities that may be issued by joint stock companies, such as preferred shares, convertible shares, and several types of bonds. It is worth mentioning that joint stock companies are significantly limited by the Joint Stock Company Law in the way they can issue bonds. Unsecured bonds may only be issued by joint stock companies that (1) have existed for at least three years; (2) have at least two properly adopted annual reports, and (3) the total value of the outstanding bonds of the company may not exceed the company's paid-in charter capital. If a company cannot meet all these requirement, then the bonds must be secured by either a pledge of the company's assets or by collateral provided by a third party. Such third-party collateral may be given in the form of assets or a guarantee.

The highest managing body of a joint stock company is the general meeting of shareholders, which must be held at least once annually. A company that has more than fifty shareholders must have a board of directors, which is elected at a general meeting and provides general supervision of the company's business. The daily management is conducted by the directorate that can be a collegiatial or one-person body. The general director of the company is a member of the board of directors by law and is also the head of the directorate; only the general director may represent the company without a special power of attorney. The Joint Stock Company Law includes a number of provisions that regulate in detail procedures related to the decision-making process in the company. These provisions contain instructions on preparing for and holding a shareholders' meeting and a board of directors' meeting.

The Joint Stock Company Law takes a significant step towards securing several important rights of shareholders that guarantee their position vis-à-vis the company and its management. One, for instance, is the right of shareholders to receive accurate periodic information about the company's activities and finances, and the corresponding obligation of the company to disclose such information to its shareholders and, in some cases, to the general investing public. Under the Joint Stock Company Law, shareholders have a right to assess the shareholders' register of the company and to demand that certain items are included in the agenda of an upcoming shareholders' meeting. Another important new right introduced by the Joint Stock Company Law is the right to demand that, in certain circumstances, the company appraise and purchase shares of shareholders.

Currently, joint stock companies are the most popular corporate vehicle in Russia. One of the reasons for this is that during the course of privatization, the majority of state-owned enterprises were transformed into open joint stock companies. Another reason is that since

1990, when the first statute on joint stock companies was introduced, they remain the best legally regulated corporate vehicle in the country.

(iii) Production Cooperatives.   The Civil Code provides that a production cooperative is a legal entity that may be formed by several individuals. Other legal entities may become members of a production cooperative only if the law or the charter of the cooperative specifically allows that. The types of activities that a production cooperative can engage in are the production, processing, and sale of industrial, agricultural, or other products, and the provision of various services. The law provides that membership in a production cooperative is based not only on the contribution of assets into the capital of the cooperative, but also on the "personal labor" of its members. The concept of sweat equity is therefore clearly incorporated into the law for this form of organization.

The organization of a production cooperative is in many ways similar to a full partnership, except that the law allows its members to decide the degree of their personal liability for the obligations of the cooperative. The profits of a cooperative are distributed among its members according to their "labor participation." Members of a cooperative may decide at any time to terminate their memberships and any member may be expelled by the decision of other members. An interest in a cooperative may be transferred to a nonmember only with the permission of the cooperative.

Because production cooperatives have existed in Russia for many years and have a relatively simple legal structure they are often used by associations of goldminers, hunters and fishermen, and in the agricultural industry. It seems that this particular legal entity, because it is based on the personal labor of its members, is of little interest to a foreign investor.

(iv) State and Municipal Enterprises.   Russian bodies of federal and municipal power are prohibited by law from engaging in profit-generating business activities, but they may establish state and municipal companies that can do business and turn profits over to the state. Such companies are defined by the Civil Code as *unitary enterprises* because their capital is not subdivided into shares and is wholly owned by the federal or municipal governments. Therefore, these entities cannot be used for the purposes of foreign investment, but any foreign or jointly owned company may find itself doing business with a state or municipal enterprise. It is important to note that such enterprises are liable for their debts only to the extent of their assets and the liability does not extend to the state.

(b) Nonlegal Entities

(i) Representative Office.   The Civil Code provides that a representative office is a subdivision of a legal entity located outside its main place of business; a representative office represents and protects the interests of the main company but does not actively trade or do business. It is not a separate legal entity and does not exist separately from the main company. The main company may transfer certain assets to the representative office, but it remains the owner of such assets. The head of a representative office is appointed by the parent company and acts on the basis of a power of attorney.

For many years, representative offices were the only form of business enterprise available to foreign companies wanting to establish a presence in Russia. Representative offices are still popular in Russia's foreign business community because of their status as nonresidents for exchange-control purposes, tax benefits that they were believed to be enjoying, and their general familiarity to government officials. Russian tax authorities, however, have recently taken actions that were unfavorable and largely unfair to representative offices of foreign companies, which may make more and more foreign businesses avoid the use of this vehicle.

(ii) Branch Office.   Under the Civil Code, a branch office is very similar to a representative office, but it can conduct trade and business, as well as perform representation functions, because it has all the authority of the company of which it is a part. A branch office has a set of bylaws adopted by the parent company and must be registered in a way that is similar to a company registration.

Although a branch office as a form of business enterprise was introduced a few years prior to the adoption of the new Civil Code, many details of its status for tax and customs purposes are still unclear.

28.4 PROTECTION OF SHAREHOLDERS' RIGHTS.   As mentioned above, one of the novelties introduced by the Joint Stock Company Law and by the Securities Law is the definition and protection of several important shareholders' rights. In this respect, it is interesting to briefly review provisions of these two laws, which allow shareholders to defend their rights in the civil courts of the Russian Federation.

It is common today for Russian citizens to rely on various state, administrative, and law-enforcement agencies, such as the militia and the prosecutor's office, to monitor and defend their rights. People who feel that their rights have been violated are much more inclined to write letters to bodies of state power and law-enforcement agencies asking for help, than to turn to the courts. With respect to the shareholders rights, however, this is about to change—now, the prosecutor's office by law (in the absence of criminal violations) may not interfere with the activities of a private company. Therefore, shareholders are now forced to look to courts to defend their rights.

Under the Joint Stock Company Law, the following actions, among others, may be appealed by a shareholder in court: (1) a refusal of the company to change its shareholders' register in the case of a properly conducted transfer of shares; (2) decisions of shareholders' meetings adopted in violation of the law; (3) refusal of the board of directors to include an item proposed by a shareholder into the agenda for a shareholders' meeting; and (4) a refusal to include a candidate for a position in one of the managing bodies of the company into a voting bulletin. In these and several other instances, shareholders may also commence derivative actions against the company.

Different types of shareholders' suits must be brought to different Russian courts. If the plaintiffs are individual shareholders and the defendants are also individuals (for instance, a director of a joint stock company), such a suit must be brought to a Russian court of general jurisdiction. However, in cases where the plaintiffs are shareholders-companies, and the defendant is also a company, such actions must be brought to Russian arbitration courts. Generally, derivative actions may be brought against members of the board of directors, the General director, and other officers of the company. (The Joint-Stock Company Law, Article 71). The Civil Code allows the defendants in these actions the presumption of innocence; therefore, shareholders must prove that the defendants' actions caused them to sustain damages. Unless the shareholders are able to definitely prove that, the defendants will not be held liable for damages.

Several other laws regulating the defense of shareholders' rights are currently being drafted by the government and by the Federal Securities Commission. These laws will include a set of amendments to the Civil Code that will introduce the concept of class actions, which is currently unknown in Russia.

28.5 CONCLUSION. A review of the recently introduced second wave of Russian corporate legislation shows that it is significantly more sophisticated than previous laws. This legislation allows a wider selection of corporate forms and it regulates various types of companies. The Civil Code finally contains a complete list of all available corporate and noncorporate forms of business enterprises. The Joint Stock Company Law, although it is often criticized for containing too many imperative rules that are difficult for companies to follow, is a giant step forward, especially in the very important area of protection of shareholders' rights.

CHAPTER 29

U.S. LAWYERS IN MOSCOW

Parry Aftab

29.1 CHANGING ROLE OF LEGAL COUNSEL IN THE CIS. Notwithstanding the generalizations about Russian law (or the jokes made about the lack of it), Russia has a long and rich history of jurisprudence. In more recent history, because of the country's rapidly changing laws and the resulting confusion, many people in the West discount the Russian legal system. This can be a major and costly mistake for Western businesses and their counsel. Rather, they should recognize and take into consideration that Russian lawyers play a different role than their Western counterparts both politically and commercially.

In the United States, lawyers are an integral part of government and business. More than half of the members of the last Congress were lawyers, as well as almost two-thirds of the presidents of the United States. Like it or not, we must recognize that the United States was formed by lawyers and is still governed by lawyers. Lawyers frequently hold the keys to business in the United States, and they are essentially partners in all of their clients' business decisions. It is therefore easy to see how one can be blinded when dealing with Russian business ventures.

Russians generally do not confer with their lawyers when entering into a business venture, preferring to seek their advice on specific issues only. Russian lawyers, unlike their U.S. counterparts, do not take part in the negotiations or the structuring of business deals. Their advice is often only sought if the deal falls apart and the parties are positioned for litigation. Of course, this is often too late.

As a result, Russian businesspeople have been at a substantial disadvantage when dealing with their Western counterparts. Without the guidance of legal advisors, business transactions are often structured based on memorializations of the hand-shake deal. Russians neither understand nor care about the subtleties proffered by the other party. When an agreement is made, it is translated into Russian. If it appears to generally reflect the deal, the agreement is executed and delivered in both languages. Further, the Russians often agree to the effectiveness of the English translation of the agreement taking precedence over the Russian translation. Without a lawyer's guidance, Russians often find that in the English version of the legal document, a rose is not always a rose. The Russian businessperson has learned a costly lesson.

It should have been expected that the disparity in the role of Western and Russian lawyers would have an adverse impact on business transactions. The Russians, understandably unhappy over the fact that the deal they thought they made was not accurately reflected in the final documentation, believe that the Western businesspeople are not acting in good faith. In focusing on the written agreement rather than on the original deal, the

Western businessperson thinks that the Russian is not adhering to the agreement. Both are disappointed and believe that the other is to blame. Many deals have failed because of such differences in expectations and perspectives. Since it is unlikely that Western businesses will rely less on their legal advisors, Russian businesses need to depend more on theirs.

29.2 BUYER BEWARE.   The Russians are not the only ones who need to learn from these differing attitudes, legal systems, and expectations. Too often multinational law firms believe that they can practice law in any country, as long as the law is translated into English. Many lawyers who have set up offices and sent representatives to Moscow and elsewhere in the Commonwealth of Independent States without Russian legal training, rely on Russian lawyers to research the Russian law and translate it into English. The U.S. lawyers then read the law and interpret it for their American clients.

Aside from its arrogance, this method is dangerous for clients who believe that U.S. lawyers understand Russian law. Businesses would not take the same approach in an American interstate transaction, in which a U.S. lawyer, although familiar with multistate laws, would not dare to interpret the law of another state. In the United States, even mega-corporations would never succumb to this temptation, since it is a crime to practice law in a state jurisdiction in which a lawyer is not licensed. Typically, when a business has a matter requiring the identification and interpretation of another state's law, local counsel is retained.

Until now, international law firms in Moscow did not have a similar reason to respect the laws of Russia. This will all change. Recently, President Yeltsin issued a decree that seriously restricts services provided by international law firms operating in Russia. According to the new regulation, non-Russian law firms may not provide services to local companies and they may not render advice on Russian law. This concept is certainly not new in the legal profession, but it is changing the way business is conducted in the CIS. Russia had to regulate international law firms and other U.S. and Western law firms that were practicing in Russia unhindered by regulations. The reason for this action is illustrated by the following example.

When a well-recognized international banking organization was seeking office space in Moscow, the tenant of a local office indicating a willingness to sublet his space to the bank. The bank's U.S.-based international law firm contacted a prominent Russian lawyer, who informed it that the tenant had no right to sublet the space and the sublease was unenforceable. Rather than follow the Russian lawyer's advice, the U.S. firm allowed the bank to sign the sublease. The bank, unaware of the potential risk, took the space, believing its U.S. counsel had protected its rights with a valid lease. As it turned out, it did not have those rights, and still does not.

Often Western lawyers simply translate their form or contract into Russian, without regard to whether it complies with Russian law. If it does not, the contract is often unenforceable in Russian courts. Even a judgment obtained in accordance with international treaties may be unenforceable since the underlying contract is unenforceable as a matter of Russian law.

Unfortunately, this type of situation is common. Western businesses and lawyers believe that because Russian law is changing so rapidly, it can be completely disregarded, which is a huge mistake. The Russian authorities are cracking down on conduct outside of the law. Being from outside Russia is no excuse for failure to comply with applicable Russian law. Moreover, few U.S. lawyers can provide clients with in-depth knowledge of the law in Russia. For this, a good Russian law firm is needed.

Even lawyers who have been advising clients about the Russian market do not provide Russian legal advice. Lawyers truly familiar with Russia and the way business and legal matters are conducted there, have found Russian legal partners on whom they rely for recent legal developments. Recognizing the value of local representation, Western lawyers have become affiliated with the sole Russian equivalent of a megalaw firm and with a few small and reputable business-law firms. Most large Russian business entities maintain a captive law firm, which handles only that business's legal matters. Some of the top legal talent in Russia, familiar with Western standards, is captive and otherwise unavailable to foreign clients. The firm of Aftab and Savitt (www.aftab.com) has a Russian affiliate, comprised of over 300 lawyers in Moscow alone, that hires the top legal specialists according to the same revolving-door policy used in the United States. When an influential official leaves the government, as likely as not, the person will join the affiliate, the Moscow Legal Center. Aftab and Savitt holds the power of attorney and has been designated the exclusive U.S. affiliate of the Moscow Legal Center. Through the firm, the center is able to provide up-to-date legal advice on both the Russian and the global aspects of business.

The Russian legal system is similar to the United Kingdom's system of solicitors and barristers. In Russia, lawyers who practice specialized law, entitling them to appear in business and governmental courts are called advocates; those practicing private law, without the right to bring the cases to these courts, are called jurists. Unlike the West, where the lawyers are licensed by the state or an authority thereof, in Russia advocates are licensed only through lawyers' colleagues. Since the Russian Revolution, only one lawyer's colleague has existed in each region. Before 1993, the Moscow Lawyers' Colleague was the sole organization authorized to license advocates in Moscow. In November, 1993, the Moscow Legal Center organized the first CIS-wide colleague, the Russian Lawyers' Guild. Through this guild, over 8,000 lawyers throughout the CIS, consisting of 49 separate lawyers' colleagues, including the Moscow Legal Center, are brought together in one place.

Considering these facts and the growth of the Russian legal profession, there is no longer any excuse for large international firms to ignore the lawyers or the professional practice of law in Russia. It is hoped that these firms, to the extent that they desire to maintain a presence in Russia, will adhere to the recent changes in legislation and provide their U.S. clients with the best Russian legal advice available.

When choosing a Western legal advisor for help in the Russian market, a company should consider whether the firm is approaching this from the Russian perspective—knowing how to make the Russian system work for the company, rather than against it, which is the key to succeeding in Russia—or the U.S. perspective. Knowing how to plan, knowing the pitfalls, and providing access to the people and agencies who can get things done are the benefits that legal counsel can bring to companies that want to succeed in the burgeoning Russian market.

CHAPTER 30

JOINT STOCK COMPANIES AND LIMITED LIABILITY COMPANIES

Baker & McKenzie

30.1 INTRODUCTION. This chapter outlines the features of the two most common Russian legal entities for foreign investment: the joint stock company and the limited liability company. The chapter compares and contrasts these two legal entities in an effort to assist people in determining which vehicle will best suit their particular needs when investing in the Russian Federation.

Joint stock companies are currently regulated by the Civil Code of the Russian Federation ("Civil Code"), the law On Joint Stock Companies, which came into effect on January 1, 1996 (JSC Law), and various securities regulations. Limited liability companies are currently regulated by the Civil Code. A draft law on limited liability companies (LLC Draft) is scheduled to be considered by the Duma this spring. Where applicable, this chapter takes into consideration the provisions of the LLC Draft, although it is important to keep in mind that the final limited liability companies law may differ from this preliminary draft.

30.2 OVERVIEW OF THE LEGAL ENTITIES

(a) Joint Stock Company. The joint stock company ("aktsionernoe obshchestvo") is a Russian legal entity formed by one or more shareholders, who are liable for the debts and obligations of the company only to the extent of their investment. Joint stock companies are roughly equivalent to U.S. corporations and other similar forms of doing business in the West. Familiar variations on the joint stock company abbreviation are AO, ZAO, OAO, AOZT, and AOOT.

Joint stock companies may be either *open* or *closed.* In essence, the distinction is that an open joint stock company contemplates the issuance of stock for sale to the general public, whereas a closed joint stock company contemplates ownership by a small number of shareholders, with restrictions on transfers of stock to third parties. Open joint stock companies may have an unlimited number of shareholders, while a closed joint stock company is limited to 50 shareholders.

(i) Joint Stock Company Organization. Russian joint stock companies usually have three tiers of governing bodies: the shareholders' meeting, the board of directors (mandatory for joint stock companies with 50 or more shareholders), and the executive body. There is also an audit commission elected from among the shareholders to oversee the financial and business activities of the company.

SHAREHOLDERS' MEETING.   The shareholders' meeting is the highest authority in a joint stock company. Meetings must be held at least once a year and, in order to be valid, must be attended by shareholders holding at least one-half of the outstanding shares in the company. Shareholders may attend in person or through their legal representatives (by power of attorney). There are provisions in the JSC Law that allow for the shareholders' meeting to be conducted by mail-in ballot.

Among other items, the shareholders' meeting has exclusive competence over the following:

- Amendments to the charter of the company, including amendments to the charter capital (except that, where the charter of the company so provides, the board of directors may approve a capital increase);
- The election of directors and the auditing commission, and termination of their authority;
- The approval of the company's annual reports, balance sheets, and profit-and-loss accounts, as well as profit- and-loss distributions;
- The reorganization or liquidation of the company.

Votes in the shareholders' meeting are taken on the basis of one share being equal to one vote. In general, all decisions are made in the shareholders' meeting by a simple majority of votes by those present. However, decisions regarding changes to the charter and the reorganization or termination of the company require a three-quarters majority vote. The company charter may be drafted in such a way as to require a supermajority vote for other issues as well and, as limited by law, may also allow the delegation of certain decisions to the board of directors.

BOARD OF DIRECTORS.   Joint stock companies with more than fifty shareholders must have a board directors, while those with fifty shareholders or fewer may also have a board of directors. The company charter may, within the limits set forth by law, define the board of directors' area of authority. Where no board of directors is desired, a joint stock company having fewer than fifty shareholders may place the relevant authority in the hands of the company's executive body.

EXECUTIVE BODY.   The Civil Code and JSC Law place authority for the daily management of a joint stock company in the hands of an executive body, which may be comprised of a single person or a committee. The general director of the joint stock company chairs the executive body if it is established in the form of a committee. The executive body is accountable to the general shareholders' meeting and, if it exists, the board of directors. The executive body has authority over matters that are not under the authority of the shareholders' meeting or the board of directors. While joint stock companies are required to have an executive body, the general shareholders' meeting may choose to contract out the powers and authority of the executive body to an external commercial organization or an individual manager.

(ii) Joint Stock Company Charter Capital.   The charter capital of a joint stock company with foreign investments must be at least 1,000 times the Russian minimum monthly wage. Founder-shareholders of Russian joint stock companies are required to pay in the first 50% of their charter capital at the time of registration of the company. The remainder

of the charter capital must be paid in within one year of registration. In-kind contributions must generally be documented by means of an *act of acceptance* executed by the joint stock company's management, which is presented to registration authorities to show that the in-kind capital has been paid in. Cash contributions are evidenced by presenting a letter from a Russian bank. The charter capital of a joint stock company may be increased only after the charter capital is fully paid.

At the present time, the Russian Central Bank is asserting the position that founders wishing to fund or increase their charter capital with foreign currency must first obtain a Central Bank license. This position is based on provisions of the law On the Currency Regulation and Currency Control and Central Bank regulations. The requirements for a license have been somewhat unevenly enforced, but appear to be properly grounded in current law. In practice, this means that an additional bureaucratic step has been added to the registration process, often slowing the ultimate registration of a new company by several weeks.

As is the case with limited liability companies, a joint stock company must decrease its capital if, within two fiscal years after its registration, its net assets—as defined by Russian legislation on accounting—are less than its charter capital. The joint stock company must be liquidated if its net assets fall below the minimum level of capital set by law for joint stock companies. Furthermore, in contrast to the limited liability company, a joint stock company is prohibited from increasing its charter capital in order to cover losses to the company.

(iii) Stock and Issuance of Other Securities. All shares issued by joint stock companies must be registered with the Ministry of Finance. At the time the company is founded the shares are easily registered by means of notice to the Ministry of Finance. Registration of subsequent share issues generally involves submission of a share-issue prospectus containing detailed information about the company, the share issue, and other information to the Ministry of Finance. Due to this onerous process, it is much more time consuming and difficult to increase the capital of a joint stock company than it is to increase the capital of a limited liability company. Furthermore, registration of securities may be denied if the accounts of the joint stock company show that the company has not been making a profit, as this is deemed to be an *increase to* cover losses.

The Civil Code provides that the total number of bonds issued by a joint stock company cannot exceed the value of the charter capital of the company or any additional security for the bonds provided by third parties. Issuance of bonds also requires registration with the Ministry of Finance. Shareholders in an open joint stock company can freely sell their stock without the consent of the other shareholders. Those who own shares in closed joint stock companies, however, can only sell their stock to third parties if the other members of the company do not wish to buy it.

(b) Limited Liability Company. A limited liability company, "obshchestvo s ogranichennoi otvetstvennostiu" is a Russian legal entity established by one or more participants, who are liable for the debts and obligations of the company only to the extent of their investment in the company. The abbreviation for a limited liability company is OOO. Under previous legislation, the limited liability company was called a limited liability partnership or TOO.

(i) Limited Liability Company Organization. Due in part to the lack of developed legislation regulating their internal organization, the management structure of a Russian limited liability company is largely left up to the founders, who may establish their preferred

organizational structures in the company charter. Consequently, a limited liability company has a more flexible management structure than a joint stock company.

The Civil Code provides for a limited liability company to be governed by a participants' meeting and an executive body. While the Civil Code does not exclude the possibility of a board of directors, the LLC Draft does not include a board of directors in the management structure. Therefore, the participants' meeting will often take the role of a board of directors.

PARTICIPANTS' MEETING.   Pursuant to the Civil Code, the highest body in a limited liability company is the general meeting of its participants. The participants' meeting has exclusive authority over:

- Amendment of the company charter and changes to the size of the charter capital;
- Establishment of the company's executive bodies and their early termination;
- Approval of the company's annual statements and balance sheets as well as the distribution of profits and losses;
- Decisions to reorganize or liquidate the company;
- Election of the auditing commission.

Other duties can be exclusively delegated to the participants' meeting through the company charter.

EXECUTIVE BODY.   The Civil Code specifies that the daily governance of a limited liability company lies in the hands of an executive body that consists of one or more persons and is appointed by the participants. The Civil Code, however, does not specify or restrict the duties of the executive body. This leaves wide latitude in the structuring of management duties.

(ii) Limited Liability Company Charter Capital.   Current regulations establish that the charter capital for limited liability companies shall differ based on the presence or absence of foreign investment. Where foreign investment is involved, the minimum charter-capital requirement for a limited liability company is 1,000 times the minimum monthly wage.

The founder(s) of a limited liability company must pay in 50% of the charter capital at or before the time the company is registered. The remainder of the charter capital must be fully paid in within one year of registration. Cash contributions made in foreign currency may require a license from the Russian Central Bank. The charter capital of a limited liability company may be increased only after the charter capital is fully paid.

As is the case with joint stock companies, a limited liability company must decrease its capital if, within two fiscal years after its registration, its net assets, as defined by Russian legislation on accounting, are less than its charter capital. The limited liability company must be liquidated if its net assets fall below the minimum level of capital set by law for limited liability companies.

(iii) Participation Interests.   Ownership shares of a limited liability company are not considered securities under Russian legislation. Therefore, unlike the shares in a joint stock company, they do not need to be registered with the Ministry of Finance. This is a considerable advantage over the joint stock company, as the registration of securities is a highly bureaucratic procedure and, in certain circumstances, can limit the activities of a joint stock company.

According to provisions of the Civil Code, ownership shares in a limited liability company can be transferred, subject to the other participants' preemptive right to purchase. This preemptive right can, however, be limited by the company's charter. Finally, the participants in a limited liability company have the right to demand withdrawal of and payment for their shares by the company when the charter prohibits the sale of those shares or where the other participants decline to exercise their preemptory purchase rights.

30.3 SIMILARITIES BETWEEN JOINT STOCK COMPANIES AND LIMITED LIABILITY COMPANIES

(a) Number and Character of Founders and Participants.   There are no significant differences between joint stock companies and limited liability companies with respect to the number and character of founders or participants. Both types of companies may be created by either natural persons or legal entities, and both types may be wholly owned. The number of shareholders in a closed joint stock company is limited to 50. The LLC Draft likewise limits the number of participants in a limited liability company to 50.

(b) Wholly Owned Intermediaries.   The Civil Code provides that neither joint stock companies nor limited liability companies may be wholly owned by an entity that is, in turn, wholly owned. While the language of this provision is not completely clear, the best reading of it is that it only applies to a Russian legal entity setting up another Russian legal entity. Attorneys at the Moscow Registration Chamber are likewise taking the position that the Civil Code prohibition does not prevent a wholly owned foreign intermediary from setting up a wholly owned Russian legal entity.

(c) Capital Requirements.   Where a foreign investor is involved, there are no significant differences between the charter-capital requirements of joint stock companies and limited liability companies. Furthermore, both types of companies have nearly identical requirements for the contribution of both cash and in-kind capital to the company.

(d) Taxation, Customs, and Other Factors.   There is no difference between joint stock companies and limited liability companies under Russian law with respect to taxation, customs treatment, labor-law issues, currency regulation, accounting treatment, and similar questions. The legal and administrative costs of initially establishing each type of entity are likewise similar.

30.4 KEY DIFFERENCES: CHOOSING THE RIGHT ENTITY.   Making the choice between a joint stock company and a limited liability company nearly always turns on business, rather than purely legal, requirements. Depending on the business situation, there are several factors that may favor the formation of one legal entity over the other. In our experience, most clients consider the following four factors to be the most important in deciding between a joint stock company and a limited liability company.

(a) Stock Shares versus Participations.   Ownership shares of joint stock companies are securities and as such, the company must keep a share register and comply with Russian securities regulations. The issuance and registration of additional shares of a joint stock company is a bureaucratic and time-consuming process. These steps are avoided in the case of a limited liability company because interests in a limited liability company are not considered securities under Russian law. One advantage of issuing shares of stock is the ability to have different classes of shares and shareholders. Both preferred and common shares, and various classes of preferred shares, may be issued in a joint stock company, with different voting rights and preferences to profits. These potential advantages, however, are usually irrelevant in the case of a wholly owned company.

(b) Increasing Charter Capital.   Article 100 of the Civil Code prohibits joint stock companies from increasing their charter capital "in order to cover losses incurred." Some companies have attempted to avoid the application of Article 100 by arguing that the increase in charter capital is not made "in order to cover losses incurred." Companies wishing to pursue this approach must present a letter to the Ministry of Finance explaining in detail the purpose of the increase in charter capital and confirming that the increase will not be used to "cover losses incurred."

In any event, a joint stock company will still be required to follow the normal procedures for registration of the share increase with the Ministry of Finance. Registration of shares consists of two steps: registration of a Prospectus of Emission of Shares and registration of a Report on the Results of the Distribution of Shares. Analogous to Western practices, the Prospectus of Emission requires preparation of detailed commercial and financial information.

(c) Withdrawal Procedures and Transfers of Interest.   Where the foreign investor seeks to invest in Russia along with a Russian partner, a joint stock company may be more suitable because of Civil Code provisions that allow a limited liability company participant to withdraw from participation. Such withdrawal can, under certain circumstances, be accompanied by a demand that the assets contributed also be withdrawn. Because the Russian partner in a joint venture often contributes significant assets, such as land-use rights or buildings, the potential withdrawal of these assets in the event of a dispute between the joint venturers could seriously injure the operation of the company. This issue is less relevant in the case of a wholly owned company.

Shares in an open joint stock company may be freely traded, while shares in closed joint stock companies may not generally be transferred without the approval of the majority of the shareholders. Similar to those in a closed joint stock company, the ownership shares of a limited liability company may be transferred to third parties only if the other participants in the company decline to purchase the shares themselves. Furthermore, a limited liability company is subject to the provision that, if a participant wishes to sell but is restricted from doing so by the charter and/or if none of the other participants wishes to exercise its preemptory right of purchase, the participant may demand that the company purchase its ownership share and pay compensation in the form of cash or property. This provision is likewise less relevant in the case of a wholly owned company.

(d) Differing Legislative Basis.   As discussed previously, the legislative basis is more developed for joint stock companies than for limited liability companies. As a result, limited liability companies currently enjoy more flexibility in terms of their management structure. Conversely, it could be argued that joint stock companies enjoy more certainty in their structure. The inevitable adoption of legislation covering limited liability companies may necessitate changes to the charter or management structure of such companies. By taking into account at the initial stage the analogous principles in the JSC Law and the provisions of the LLC Draft, founders can minimize the extent of subsequent changes that may need to be made to their limited liability company following the adoption of relevant legislation.

30.5 CONCLUSION. There are advantages and disadvantages to both joint stock companies and limited liability companies. The question of which form a particular investor should adopt mainly turns on practical business considerations rather than on purely legal ones. Therefore, attention should be focused primarily on the four key differences outlined in 30.4 in order to choose the most suitable investment vehicle available in Russia.

CHAPTER 31

INTELLECTUAL PROPERTY LAW

Parry Aftab

31.1 OVERVIEW. Over the last several years, intellectual property laws and regulations in Russia have undergone radical changes. In addition to the legal changes, the scope of protection has radically changed as well. Prior to 1991, the intellectual property laws in Russia generally protected the state, rather than individuals. (This is a product of the state ownership of property under the prior Communist regime.) Over the last several years, the implementation of intellectual property laws, in multiple stages, and the establishment of regulatory frameworks for enforcement of the new laws have occupied most of the agencies and ministries charged with the enforcement of various portions of the law.

Any analysis of the Russian intellectual property law requires a twofold approach: the laws themselves and the enforcement of these laws. Currently, there is a substantial disparity between the laws as written and as enforced. This article will focus on the evolution of the intellectual property laws in Russia since the breakup of the USSR, as well as on practical enforcement issues.

31.2 POST-USSR LAWS. The post-USSR laws have been evolving since 1991, when Russia joined more than ten international conventions and agreements pertaining to intellectual property protection. Laws were adopted in 1992 providing basic patent and trademark protection, as well as laws protecting computer databases and software. In July 1993, broad copyright legislation was adopted, protecting all types of intellectual property rights, especially those related to the emerging scientific and information service industries.

In 1994 (although not taking effect until later), Russia, together with 10 other former USSR members, established the Eurasian Patent Convention. The new centralized patent registration system permitted, for the first time since the breakup of the USSR, a single application to be filed in one location (Moscow) and in one language (Russian). Once approved, the registration is effective in all member countries. The evolution was basically complete when Russia joined the Berne Convention on the Protection of Artistic and Literary Works in 1995 and the Geneva Convention on audio recordings.

Russia, as successor to the USSR, had been a party to the UNESCO Universal Copyright Convention since 1973, and the Paris Convention on Protection of Industrial Property. The accession to the Berne Convention extended copyright protection to Russian authors for works published after March 13, 1995; approximately thirty countries, in addition to those already included in the UNESCO Convention, were parties to the agreement.

The regulatory fine points of intellectual property protection have been implemented, for the most part, since 1994. Very recently, Rospatent (now a part of the Ministry of Justice) has implemented rules relating to patent assignments and administrative appeals.

31.3 OVERSIGHT OF THE INTELLECTUAL PROPERTY REGULATORY SYSTEM.
Rospatent, the commonly used name of the Committee of the Russian Federation on Patents and Trademarks formed February 12, 1993, is responsible for the protection of commercial intellectual property, as well as patent applications. The oversight of intellectual property in Russia includes a number of other agencies and ministries, including the Ministries of Justice, Foreign Economic Relations, Science and Agricultural Production, as well as the State Committee for Anti-Monopolies, the State Customs Committee, and the State Committee on Film.

In addition to the multiple ministries and agencies involved in portions of the intellectual property protection system, there are generally three juridical bodies charged with the civil enforcement of intellectual property laws in Russia: the Rospatent Appeals Board (an administrative juridical body within Rospatent), the civil court system, and the arbitration court system. (In addition, current legislation is pending for the creation of a Supreme Patent Board, which has not yet been formed.)

31.4 INTELLECTUAL PROPERTY RIGHTS FOR JOINT SCIENTIFIC DEVELOPMENT.
The International Science and Technology Center (ISTC), headquartered in Moscow, was formed in 1992 with U.S. governmental support to help match Russian and NIS scientific talent with Western scientific needs. Assuring the careful protection of intellectual property rights is a paramount objective of the ISTC.

Intellectual property rights depend on agreements reached in each transactions and, in many cases, provide greater protection for Western partners than existing patent law now available in Russia. A current weakness in Russia's patent-protection regulations is the lack of clear protection for the employer in a work-for-hire situation. In other countries, the patent rights of a person working for an employer accrue to the employer. Use of the ISTC doubly ensures work-for-hire protection of invention rights.

Although Russia is addressing many intellectual property issues, other significant ones have not yet been resolved. These include invention development, protection for inventions on a work-for-hire basis, protection against copyright infringement, criminal penalties for counterfeiting, and consistent recognition of certain previously existing Western trademarks against recent Russian claimants.

Unfortunately, enforcement is difficult at best. With all of the recent changes in commercial law, many of the amendments to the criminal code and related civil codes necessary to enforce the new intellectual property laws were not adopted. Currently enforcement responsibility is shared among many ministries and governmental departments. Furthermore, given the rapid implementation of laws and regulations, the people and departments charged with enforcement are often not sufficiently familiar with the laws. Because of the failure to enforce them with criminal penalties, infringers continue to violate trademark, patent, and copyright laws throughout Russia without fear.

31.5 CONCLUSION.
The Russian Ministry of Justice is moving quickly to educate the arbitration courts and civil court about the new intellectual property laws through seminars, with invited speakers from Russia and the West.

As the regulatory system begins to function, quirks within the system will work themselves out. The growth of industry and the need for intellectual property protection will help drive a more efficient regulatory framework. No matter how rocky the initial road to universal intellectual property rights protection might be, Russia is fully committed to their protection by the use of worldwide standards and practices.

CHAPTER 32

ANTIMONOPOLY POLICY AND SUPPORT FOR NEW ECONOMIC STRUCTURES

Leonid A. Bochin

32.1 INTRODUCTION. Formed in 1990, the State Committee of the Russian Federation for Antimonopoly Policy and Support for New Economic Structures (GKAP) is a federal branch of executive power whose mission is to implement governmental policies in the development of fair competition, restriction of monopolistic activities, and protection of consumers' rights.

GKAP's main tasks and powers were outlined by federal laws On Competition and the Restriction of Monopolistic Activities in the Commodity Market, On The Protection of Consumers' Rights, On Advertising, and On Stock Exchanges and Stock-Exchange Trade. The GKAP consists of central branches, along with regional branches in 80 subjects of the Federation. The total number of GKAP personnel is 2,700. The Chairperson of GKAP has five deputies.

The main tasks of the GKAP are:

To promote the formation of market activity on the basis of competition, demonopolization of the economy, and support for entrepreneurship;

To prevent, restrict, and discourage monopolistic activities and dishonest competition in the market;

To oversee antimonopoly laws and policy, engage in advertising to protect consumers' rights, and promote the stock exchanges.

The GKAP has a right to:

Issue obligatory provisions for enterprises concerning the cessation of violations of the antimonopoly law, the restoration of original status, and the forced division of enterprises. These provisions can force an enterprise to divest itself of a portion of its business or cancel or changes an agreement if it violates antimonopoly law;

Issue provisions that oblige executive authority to cancel or revise any of the executive authority's improper decisions, to cease any violations, and to cancel or change any agreement made by an executive authority if it contradicts antimonopoly law;

Make proposals for executive authority concerning the introduction of or ban on issuing licenses, the revision of customs duties, and the introduction of or ban on tariff quotas, tax benefits, beneficial loans, and other kinds of governmental support;

Levy fines on commercial and noncommercial organizations, impose administrative penalties on their executives or on citizens, including individual entrepreneurs, and also on executive officials for violating antimonopoly law;

Apply to the court or the arbitration court with a claim regarding violations of antimonopoly law, including the recognition of completely invalid or partially invalid agreements that contradict antimonopoly law. The GKAP may also participate in the court's proceedings in cases related to the application and violation of antimonopoly law;

Submit to the proper judicial body materials for initiating legal action on the grounds of "signs of crime" related to violations of antimonopoly law;

Declare a dominant status for the subjects of economic activity';

Provide explanations concerning the application of antimonopoly law;

Implement other powers provided by Russia's legislature.

The first version of the law Competition and Restriction of Monopolistic Activity in the Commodity Markets was adopted in early 1991. It included articles typical of countries with developed antimonopoly legislation that prohibits monopolistic activity and prevents its development.

In May 1995, amendments to the law were adopted, establishing norms of antimonopoly control, thereby restricting agreements of companies' activity and exploitation of their dominant position in the market. These amendments also strengthened norms for the obligatory coordination of those decisions concerning the establishment, reorganization, and liquidation of companies, that issue from within the antimonopoly authorities.

Acknowledging the danger of secret agreements between companies, the new version of law on competition bans some kinds of horizontal (or so-called cartel) agreements regardless of their possible beneficial effects. Other kinds of agreements, including anticompetition "vertical" agreements, may be recognized as legal if participants in the agreement can prove that the negative consequences for competition are outweighed by positive results for the economy.

According to the law, agreements between competing companies are prohibited only if the aggregate share of these companies in a particular market exceeds 35%. In the case of noncompeting companies, such an agreement is prohibited if one of the companies has a dominant position in the market, and the other is either its supplier or buyer.

A new version of the law added another clause to the article concerning the merging of commercial organizations (unions or associations). The clause stipulates that these associations are prohibited from coordinating their entrepreneurial activity if it results or may result in limiting the competition.

Article 2 of the law concerns its application to relations involving not only Russian, but also foreign legal persons or entities. This means that the antimonopoly orders contained in Article 6 are in effect for foreign organizations operating in the Russian market. Persons suffering from the monopolistic activity of import or export associations have a right to appeal to the GKAP with their complaint. Violations of the antimonopoly regulations can be sufficient grounds for the liquidation of an organization by the courts.

In the new version of the law, certain provisions in Chapter 5 were changed. These provisions restrict the GKAP from controlling the transformation of a firm's economic activity (related to changes in their organizational and judicial form) and over increasing their authorized capital, because these issues are not directly related to the restriction of competition.

During the establishment, merging, and incorporation of an enterprise, antimonopoly control does not cover the amount of authorized capital of potential monopolies (as it was outlined in the previous edition of the law), but a certain amount of the assets of the new company, through the assets a company can demonstrate its power in the market. The minimum requirement for a company's assets during the merging and incorporating stages is 100,000 times the minimum wage set by law (currently, 4 billion, 370 million rubles).

While establishing a new company, its founders are exempt from preliminary antimonopoly control. They are required, however, to inform the antimonopoly authorities about the new company within 15 days after its registration. In cases where the establishment of a new company leads to a restriction of competition, the antimonopoly authorities, after an investigation, can require the founders to restore the initial conditions of competition. If the founders are concerned about the possible anticompetitive nature of their company, they can apply to the antimonopoly authorities before registration in order to obtain proper advice. The new edition of the law significantly simplifies the registration of recently established companies.

Control over the implementation of antimonopoly legislation during the acquisition of shares of the authorized capital is outlined in Article 18 (as it was in the previous edition). Since strengthening market presence and restricting competition are possible not only by the acquisition of shares, but also by the acquisition of fixed assets, by the interweaving of boards of directors, and by other methods, Article 18 contains amendments outlining the restrictions over such means. These provisions were absent from the previous draft.

Article 19 deals with the prospect of the forced division of companies, a step that is taken only as an extreme measure. It is applied only in cases where the offending party has repeatedly taken advantage of its dominant position or if such a division can help revive competition.

It is important to note that the new version of the law can be applied not only to a company's individual judicial persons, but also to a "group of persons," that is, a group of physical and judicial persons who, by buying stocks and securities, by interweaving boards of directors, or by any other means enjoy direct or indirect control over an enterprise. Such a group of persons creates a stable unit by carrying out its coordinated policies toward competitors. According to the new version of the law, such a group is held to be a single economic entity, so the appropriate provisions of the law are to be applied to it in their full force.

One of the specific features of the law on competition is that it bans the adoption of laws and actions on the part of the authorities that are intended to restrict competition. Present practices has proved that this ban is urgently needed. As federalism grows in Russia and subjects of the Federation are getting involved in economic reform and becoming more economically independent, the number of legal cases concerning the restriction of competition on the part of authorities increased twofold since 1992.

Drastic changes have been made in the chapter concerning the responsibility of judicial persons, their supervisors, individual entrepreneurs, executive officials, and physical persons for violations of antimonopoly legislation. The new draft of the law provides serious penalties in such cases. The severity and variety of these penalties have increased significantly. The application of penalties of the antimonopoly laws varies greatly depending on the consequences of the violation and the economic status of the violator.

32.2 CESSATION OF UNFAIR COMPETITION.   The formation of market relations has required the extensive use of antimonopolistic measures toward economic entities that attempt to gain unfair advantages in business, disregard current legislation, and violate rules and customs of business etiquette, principles of honesty, reason, and justice.

Actions that qualify as forms of unfair competition are listed in Article 10 of the law on competition. In addition, the judicial branches have the opportunity to enhance this list by interpreting those actions that meet the definition of unfair competition, in the law, lead to negative consequences in the commodities market by limiting competition, or damage the interests of consumers.

An examination of the cases investigated by antimonopoly authorities reveals that the most frequently committed violations of the law on competition are the following:

Sale of a product by engaging in an illegal use of intellectual activity in the case of the product or service;

Misrepresentation to customers about the character, method, place of manufacture, consumer properties, and quality of a product;

Dissemination of false, inaccurate or distorted information likely to cause losses to another economic entity or damage its business reputation;

Obtaining, using, or disclosing of scientific, technical, production, or trade information (including commercial secrets) without the consent of its owner.

At present, Russia is swamped by piracy, that is, the illegal use of creative works of science, literature, art, music, and more. According to experts' estimates, from 60 to 95% of the records, CDs, videotapes, software, and books in Russia were produced without the consent of their copyright owners.

Currently, the active copyright laws in Russia are not effective. Copyright owners are not protected from the physical violence inflicted on them by black marketers. Also, procedures for the arrest of violators and the confiscation of counterfeit copies have not yet been judicially regulated.

Related to this problem are several especially complicated cases involving the intentional counterfeiting of famous brand-name products to hinder the entrance of the firms that produce them into the Russian market. Usually the pirates register a famous brand label (or a part of it) under their name and then try either to sell the rights to the label or to hinder market activity of the firm that had used that label without having registered it.

The investigation of such cases shows that the registration of famous brand labels is conducted formally and in accordance with the law Labels, Marks of Service and Place of Manufacture. The authorities who register labels however, do not take into account the possible negative consequences of these actions for the market. Settlement of disputes of this type requires the intervention of antimonopoly authorities and the examination of objections to the registration of labels at the Chamber of Appeal of Rospatent.

32.3 REGULATION OF ACTIVITIES OF NATURAL MONOPOLIES.

In each country there are sectors of the economy that contain natural monopolies, that is, markets in which the development of competition is either technologically impossible or economically inefficient. For natural monopolies, the task of the government is not to cease their monopolistic activity, but to create conditions for regulating their operations on a permanent basis.

The entities involved in natural monopolies include transportation of oil and petroleum products via main pipelines; transportation of gas via main pipelines; the transmission of electrical and thermal power; railroad transportation; services at transportation terminals, ports, and airports; services of general electrical utilities, and the postal service.

Natural monopolies are usually capital-intensive and require large investments for their development. In a transitional economy, funds invested by the state in these entities are frequently insufficient. Therefore, the role of private (including foreign) investments gains more importance. Natural monopolies are considered profitable industries, but the most important condition for attracting foreign investments is the stability of the regulation system, and the clarity and consistency of the decisions of regulating authorities.

According to federal legislation, the functions of regulating and controlling the activity of subjects of natural monopolies are the responsibility of specially established federal organs of executive power. The law outlines a procedure for the formation, activity, and dissolution of these organs, as well as their powers and functions. Thus, a professional and stable system of regulation has been created that is intended to promote the influx of investments into these industries and their further development.

32.4 CONTROL OVER THE IMPLEMENTATION OF THE LAW ON ADVERTISING.

The GKAP has initiated and elaborated the Russian federal law On Advertising, which went into effect in July 1995.

Since the interests of the governmental regulation of advertising are focused on providing fair competition and protecting consumers' rights, the GKAP is considered, in accordance with the law, a leading federal organ of executive power for the control of advertising activity. The procedure for governmental and public control, as outlined by the law, proved its efficiency earlier, when it was applied to the implementation of antimonopoly and consumers' laws.

The major goal of the law on advertising is protection from unfair competition in advertising and the prevention of improper advertising that can mislead consumers or bring harm to the health or reputation of citizens or judicial persons. The law regulates issues involved in the production, placement, and distribution of the advertising of goods, jobs, and services, including banking, insurance, and securities markets.

According to the law, unfair and inaccurate advertising is prohibited. Unfair advertising is defined as advertising that:

Damages the reputation of judicial and physical persons who do not use the products being advertised;

Contains incorrect comparisons of the product being advertised with the products of competitors; contains opinions and/or images damaging to the name, dignity, or reputation of a competitor;

Misleads consumers about a product being advertised through (1) imitation or copying of a general concept, written text, formulas, images, and musical or sound effects that are used in advertising other products, (2) knowingly withholding essential information about the product so as to mislead and violate the trust of the public.

Inaccurate advertising is advertising in which inaccurate information is presented with regard to the following characteristics of a product or service:

A product's nature, ingredients, components, method and date of manufacture, design, consumer properties, conditions for application, quantity, and place of manufacture;

The availability of a product on the market, including its quantities, time period, and locations for purchase;

The price of a product at the time of advertising;

The conditions covering the delivery, exchange, return, repairs, or maintenance of a product;

The use of superlative terms without available documentary proof of superiority;

Comparisons with other products and comparisons with the status of other judicial or physical persons;

The public demand for a product;

Information about the advertiser.

When the law On Advertising is violated, judicial persons and citizens are legally responsible in accordance with Russian legislation. The law is also applied to violations of the law outside Russia by Russian judicial persons or citizens that lead either to restricting competition, misleading judicial and physical persons in Russian territory, or cause other negative consequences in the Russian market.

The law also applies to foreign judicial persons, foreign citizens, and noncitizens if they are registered as individual entrepreneurs and they produce, place, and distribute advertising materials in Russian territory.

32.5 PROTECTION OF CONSUMERS' RIGHTS.

One of the priorities of GKAP activity is the protection of consumers' rights. Between 1993 and 1995, GKAP examined tens of thousands of consumers' complaints concerning violations of the law On protection of Consumers' Rights. The total cost of the reimbursements, compensation, and forfeits paid to consumers as a result of these violations are in the hundreds of millions of rubles. As a result, legislation for the protection of consumers' rights has been developed. Also, a consulting service has been provided for local authorities and consumers' associations.

The law on consumers' rights has laid a sound legal basis for securing the rights and interests of consumers. The state system for protecting consumers' rights has been formed and gone into effect on federal and regional levels. Courts have become more experienced in protecting the rights of customers. A consumers'-rights movement is growing among the people. Economic entities are becoming more aware of their responsibilities in accordance with the law. The movement to provide high-quality products, jobs, and services, as well as to protect consumer's lives and health, and the environment is strengthening.

Recently, a new law containing amendments and revisions to the law on consumers' rights went into effect. The amendments, based on an analysis of more than 30,000 cases examined by antimonopoly authorities, deal primarily with the ability of Russia's governmental and federal branches to regulate issues concerning consumers' rights and providing additional guarantees for them.

According to the new version of the law, antimonopoly authorities are empowered to issue orders for the cessation of selling the following:

Products (jobs or services) if the providers do not have a certificate of conformity;

A product with an expired date;

A product if there is no accurate and sufficient information regarding the product.

The scope of the ability of federal branches to bring a legal action to court has been specified. The federal antimonopoly branch and its territorial branches may bring legal action against manufacturers (or performers and sellers) in case of violation of the consumers' rights. These branches are also empowered to bring a legal action concerning the termination of seller's (or manufacturer's and performer's) permit for a repeated violation of the law. These branches have a right to bring legal action on behalf of the interests of an "indefinite group" of consumers, to participate in the trial proceedings at their own initiative, and to participate, at their discretion, in the trial with regard to a decision on punishment.

The maximum level penalties levied upon economic entities for their nonimplementation or tardy implementation of the court's decisions have been established in accordance with the amount of economic activity common to most economic entities. The maximum amount of the financial penalties is set at a rate divisible by the minimum wage; and it has been proposed to increase the maximum to 500 times the minimum wage. The specific penalty in each is based on the degree of guilt and the damage done.

32.6 STATE PROGRAMS FOR DEMONOPOLIZATION AND SUPPORT OF SMALL BUSINESSES. The antimonopolistic orientation of the current economic reform is reflected in the state program for the demonopolization of the economy. The program is aimed at eliminating the power of monopolistic structures from the markets. It involves executive authorities of all levels in antimonopolistic policy and has forced industries to assess themselves for possible monopolistic policies and practices. It should be noted, however, that many industries are still holding on to administrative monopolism.

Demonopolization policies have been implemented in virtually all regions of Russia. These policies affect the markets for food; the retail and wholesale trade; communications; auto transportation; and services in the construction, repair, and maintenance of roads. They also affect services in building construction, agricultural products, energy, and wood processing, to name a few more. As a main tool of demonopolization, parallel production is being practiced, including the restructuring of operating enterprises and conversion.

The destruction of institutions for the state distribution of resources has required an adequate market replacement. This is why the GKAP initiated the adoption of the law On Commodities Exchanges and Exchange Trade. One measure that has been introduced is placing state commissars at commodities exchanges. Further development of the regulation of organized commodities markets will be implemented pending the enactment of an appropriate law.

The transition from an ultramonopolistic economic system is possible only under strong state protection and the support of small business. The GKAP has initiated the establishment of a foundation for the support of entrepreneurship and the development of competition. It has also elaborated a federal law on state support for entrepreneurship that went in effect in 1995. By the GKAP's initiative, a number of regional programs for the support of entrepreneurs were launched. At the same time, fewer new small businesses in the production industries have been established, and their total share in the Russian economy (as compared to the European Union, the United States, and Japan) is insignificant. These developments demonstrate that small business has been underestimated as a factor in competition. In a balanced economy, small businesses are capable, as other countries and particularly Japan show, of providing necessary mobility and constant competition to large enterprises. Small business, however, is not only necessary and inevitable as a satellite of big corporations but also is an important autonomous element of the economy that is able, in many cases, to compete effectively with larger companies.

To such a young organization as the GKAP, it is very important to learn and creatively apply the rich experience of foreign countries in the field of antimonopolistic regulation.

In this vein, we heartily endorse cooperation with the Organization for Economic Cooperation and Development, the Commission of the European Communities, state organs, and public organizations in charge of issues of competition and protection of consumers' rights. We support entrepreneurship in Bulgaria, Slovakia, the Czech Republic, Poland, Hungary, China, Great Britain, Belgium, Japan, the United States, and other countries. We encourage mutually enriching interaction of the CIS members within the frame of the Interstate Council for Antimonopolistic Organs. Especially important is cooperation with similar organizations in central and eastern Europe. In addition, Russia belongs to the UNCTAD Committee for Restrictive Business Practice, which is a unique international body in the field of promoting competition.

The Russian Federation has chosen and secured in its Constitution the institution of a market economy. The success achieved in the first stage of economic reform has created the necessary preconditions for competition in the domestic market. In the second stage, it is necessary to strengthen the role of competition, to overcome local monopolism, to minimize disproportions in price structure, to increase competitiveness, to improve quality, and to widen the assortment of domestic products.

CHAPTER 33

ENVIRONMENTAL PROTECTION LEGISLATION AND REGULATION

Viktor I. Danilov-Danilian

33.1 OVERVIEW. The Environmental Protection Act, enacted February 1992, was meant to be fundamental in nature, so that specific principles and provisions declared in the act would be developed and defined in a system of specific laws. This is the course of action that has been undertaken consistently since enactment. The basic law has been supplemented by a series of trade laws on the use and protection of specific kinds of environmental resources (e.g., mineral, water, timber, and animal), and on the regulation of different kinds of protection activities (e.g., examination or preservation) or different spheres (e.g., environmental security or radiation protection). Simultaneously, the environmental protection system is being developed in an integrated manner by the federal authorities, their regional divisions, and Federation members authorities.

The 1993 Constitution lays the cornerstone of environmental protection legislation, declaring the people's right to a healthy environment, and the basic principles of reciprocal action and division of powers among federal authorities, Federation members, and local authorities. These constitutional provisions provide a starting point for building a system of legislation regarding environmental protection, ecological security, and regulation of the use of natural resources.

Long-term factors and current political, social, and economic considerations were taken into account during the development of the Environmental Protection Act and subsequent environmental legislation. International treaties and agreements in the field of environmental protection were also given consideration. The act was meant to promote the development of economic methods for regulating the utilization of natural resources and environmental protection.

The act requires an ecological examination of "all preplan, preproject and project material on sites and events, meant to be carried out on Russian territory, disregarding their estimated cost and proprietorship, as well as ecological substantiation of licenses and certificates" (Article 37). Article 35 stipulates that "the State Ecological Examination is held in order to check the correspondence of economic or other activities with the ecological security of society" (Article 35). The examination process and related issues are regulated by the law On Ecological Examination, of November 1995; by the provisions of the state ecological examination, approved by the Russian government; and by other acts.

33.2 STATE ECOLOGICAL EXAMINATION. The state ecological examination is carried out on one of two levels: federal and regional. The first type is implemented in cases that have national significance, for example, when the project involves attracting federal budget funds, interferes with ecological interests of more than one member of the Federation, or is connected with the fulfillment of Russia's international obligations. These cases constitute not more than 0.1% of the documents submitted for ecological examination (out of a total of over 85,000 in 1994).

The Ministry of Nature of the Russian Federation administers the examination at the federal level, and its regional bodies carry out this responsibility at the regional level. As part of the examination, a special commission of independent, competent professionals fully screens every submitted document and either approves or denies it. Approval is a necessary condition for financing a project. If the project is declined, it can be revised and resubmitted. The commission must accept or deny a proposal within three months of the date it receives a complete proposal. The law prohibits any outside pressure on experts or the whole commission. Its conclusion can be overruled only in court.

33.3 ENVIRONMENTAL LIABILITY. The Environmental Protection Act establishes the doctrine of "who pollutes—pays." The act's provisions regarding payment for pollution are supplemented by government resolutions and materials of the Ministry of Nature, which establish the method for calculating payments. The act provides for liability for any negative effects economic activities have had on the environment, but at present some types of pollution are not subject to payment requirements because of organizational, technical, and other issues that need to be resolved. Because of these exceptions, the types of pollution not yet subject to liability include carbon dioxide, nuclear waste, and various physical interferences such as, noise and electromagnetic radiation.

The economic health of an enterprise is taken into account when determining the amount of the fine: the fine must provide motivation to the firm to avoid pollution but should not cause economic ruin. If the enterprise offers a program of environmental protection measures developed in cooperation with regional authorities, part of the payment can be used to directly support these measures. Nearly all (90%) of the money collected for pollution violations goes to ecological funds, while the remainder goes to the financing of regional environmental authorities.

The law also defines other parts of the economic mechanism of environmental protection—ecological insurance, certification, and licensing. These are not yet implemented and are awaiting the necessary legislation.

The ecological inspection-and-control system determines the scale and effects of each act of pollution on the environment and can halt the operation of an enterprise or its division when they commit a gross breach of environmental norms.

33.4 ENVIRONMENTALLY PROTECTED LAND. A considerable part of environmental law in Russia is connected with national parks. Three types of especially protected natural territories exist on the federal level: About 90 Zapovedniks (nature preserves), about 30 national parks, and over 600 Zakazniks (hunting grounds where the wildlife populations are controlled). In addition, protected territories are identified at the regional level; they account for about 1.5% of the country's territory (more than 250,000 sq km). The restrictions for each type of protected territory differ. For example, any commercial or economic activity is prohibited in Zapovedniks. The law determines the corresponding restrictions, procedures for the formation of new territories, their security, financial activities, and so on.

33.5 ENVIRONMENTAL AGENCIES. The system of environmental-protection authority was started in 1988 under the former USSR; prior to that, different protection functions were implemented by hydrometeorology and sanitary-epidemiological supervision agencies. Under the Russian Federation, the existing protection system has been developed, expanded, and modernized. The most important body in this sphere—acting on specific authority from the state—is the Ministry of Environmental Protection of the Russian Federation, which coordinates all other executive bodies of power whose activities affect environmental protection issues. A considerable part of the activities involving ecological monitoring and the gathering of information is assigned to the Federal Hydrometeorological and Environmental Monitoring Service (Rosgidromet). Cartographic support of environmental protection, as well as other related activities, is the responsibility of the Federal Geodesy and Cartography Service (Roskartographii).

These three agencies are part of an ecology-resource bloc, which also consists of specially empowered agencies for different environmental resources—Water Resources Committee (Roskomvod); Land Resources and Policies Committee (Roskomzem); Mining Committee (Roskomnedra); Fishing Committee (Roskomrybolovstvo); Federal Forestry Service (Rosleskhos). The Russian Agriculture Ministry (Minselkhosprod) and one of its agencies, the Hunting Department, are authorized bodies that are involved in regulating resources in areas such as Zakazniks.

Important environmental-protection functions are also assigned to agencies that are formally not included in the bloc. These include the State Committee of Sanitary-Epidemiological Supervision of the Russian Federation (Gossanepidnadsor); Federal Mining and Industrial Supervision (Gosgortechnadsor); and Federal Nuclear and Radiation Supervision (Gosatamnadsor). The Ministry of Civil Defense, Extraordinary Situations, and Liquidation (MChS) is responsible for cleaning of the effects of technological and natural disasters that impact the environment. The State Customs Committee takes part in ecological control over transborder operations. The program of ecological education is conducted by the Ministry of Education and State Committee on Higher Education. A large number of these ministries and agencies take part in making decisions on environmental protection and ecological security within the limits of their authority.

The Government Commission on Environment and Use of Natural Resources, headed by the deputy prime minister, establishes policies for the ecology. It coordinates the environmental-protection activities of the central authorities and regional authorities, as well as the large-scale ecological programs at the federal and international levels.

CHAPTER 34

WAR ON CRIME AND CORRUPTION: THE JUDICIAL SYSTEM'S ROLE, FUNCTIONS, AND ACTIVITIES

Vladimir S. Ovchinsky, Boris S. Bolotsky, and Alexander P. Kalinin

34.1 OVERVIEW. The Constitution of the Russian Federation guarantees freedom of economic activity, the free movement of goods and services, and support for competition. All citizens are granted the right to freely use their abilities and property for business purposes and any other economic activity not prohibited by law. Everyone has a right to possess property, own it, use it, and manage it on his or her own, as well as jointly with other persons. Property rights are protected by law. The only economic activity that is not allowed is that which is aimed at monopolization and unfair competition.

Crime and corruption destabilize the social and economic environment, have a negative impact on the development of sound entrepreneurship as a foundation for economic prosperity, and deform the values of society.

The problem of criminality in the business sector is urgent even in societies with a developed market economy. In Russia, this problem has been aggravated by the active expansion of the most dangerous forms of criminal activity into the economy.

Criminal groups, including those that operate under the shield of legal economic entities, try to impose and broaden their control over the activities of commercial and private businesses, as well as over individuals engaged in legitimate business. By taking advantage of underdeveloped judicial regulations in the field of market relations and inadequate law enforcement by the state authorities, organized crime has burgeoned. The success of organized crime has harmed official, legal businesses, and generated huge uncontrolled profit for illegal enterprises. The most widespread kinds of economic crime are various financial frauds, abuses related to foreign-trade operations, privatization deals, and activities in the consumers' market.

Organized crime in the economic field is conducted primarily by organized criminal groups. This lucrative field attracts the most dangerous kinds of organized crime, such as racketeering, kidnapping, hostage taking, and contract murders, to name only a few.

While business is being penetrated by criminal elements, it also provides a favorable environment for corruption among state employees who perform administrative and managerial functions that may be of importance for business purposes. By abusing their power for their own greedy interests, such officials cultivate corruption in state bodies and involve legitimate entrepreneurs in the corrupt system.

Naturally, the burgeoning criminal environment in Russian business operations is a major cause for concern in the society. Criminality not only holds back the development of sound entrepreneurship, but also threatens the foundation of economic activity.

34.2 PROTECTION OF PROPERTY RIGHTS AND ECONOMIC ACTIVITY. This section discusses the constitutional guarantees for the protection of property rights and economic activity. These guarantees lie at the foundation of the regulation of the function and activity of judicial bodies charged with the responsibility to fight corruption and prevent crime in business.

The currently existing legislation of the Russian Federation does not define a specific list of judicial bodies. Nevertheless, the judicial system as a whole has functions that are defined by laws. Usually, judicial bodies are considered to be those responsible for inquests and preliminary trials, and include interior organs such as the tax police, federal-security service, and customs. By tradition, courts (general courts, martial courts, and arbitration courts) and prosecution organs are also considered judicial bodies.

The most extensive and diversified functions in the fight against crime and corruption in business are performed by the so-called interior organs. In accordance with a provision in the Federal Interior Ministry, their main tasks are developing and implementing measures:

- To protect human and civil rights and freedoms
- To protect material objects, regardless of their ownership
- To prevent and stop crimes and administrative abuses
- To trace, uncover, and investigate crimes

In order to accomplish these goals, the interior organs must prevent, trace, and stop crimes, search for stolen property, and fight against organized crime and corruption. Interior divisions provide protection for the property of legal entities and citizens. They also help enterprises and organizations establish measures to protect their own property and employees' personal safety. Additionally, these interior bodies issue licenses and control the training of applicants for private-detective and security agencies. This control is exercised over all enterprises and organizations, regardless of their ownership.

34.3 *MILITSIYA:* CRIMINAL POLICE. The activity of the interior organs is highly specialized. Thus, the functions of prevention, cessation, and investigation of business-related crimes are performed by different divisions of criminal police (*militsiya*), including divisions for economic crime, organized crime, and the criminal-investigation department.

According to the law establishing the *militsiya,* in cases where there is information on a violation of criminal or administrative responsibility, the *militsiya* is empowered:

- To enter buildings and offices that are occupied by enterprises and organizations regardless of their affiliation and ownership;
- To inspect, in the presence of the owner or his or her representatives, production, storage, retail, and other sites, including vehicles;
- To seize documents related to a business's material values, financial resources, credit, and other financial operations, as well as samples of raw materials and products;
- To implement any other measures, as outlined by law, that are aimed to trace, prevent, and halt crimes and violations of the law.

The powers mentioned are granted to criminal police departments responsible for the prevention of economic crimes and organized crime. Parallel to this, the organized-crime departments carry out the following functions:

- Halting the activities of organized criminal groups (organizations), including those that have interrepublic and international connections;
- Conducting intelligence and search activities in criminal environments, gathering information on activities in the criminal underworld, and uncovering the delinquent activities of leaders of criminal groups;
- Tracing and putting on trial state officials who abuse their power for the interests of criminal groups and organized crime;
- Preventing, tracing, halting, and uncovering information about robbery, kidnapping, illegal imprisonment, blackmailing, organized forms of illegal business, hostage taking, illegal purchases, and transferring, selling, storing, transporting, or carrying weapons, ammunition, explosives, or bombs;

Providing a single coordinated strategy for interior bodies in their fight against organized crime and corruption among state officials.

34.4 FEDERAL TAX POLICE.   The essential role in fighting crime and corruption in business belongs to the federal tax police. According to the law, the federal tax police are part of the economic security system in Russia. As such, they perform tasks related to tracing, preventing, and halting tax crimes and violations, and attempts to prevent corruption in taxing bodies.

Along with the functions of inquest and preliminary trial, the tax police have powers granted by law to officials of the tax service and to currency-exchange control organs. In this connection, the tax police have the right to inspect operations conducted by taxpayers on their accounts at banks and credit institutions, to impose an administrative freeze on the property of legal entities and citizens. They also have the authority to liquidate such property to pay off tax debts.

The federal security service conducts measures to trace, prevent, stop, and investigate crimes as part of its major task related to providing security for the Russian Federation. In this connection, the federal security-service fights organized crime and corruption, and legislation stipulates that it may be given other tasks related to the fight against crime.

The state enforcement of laws in the field of business, as well as in the fight against crime and corruption, is conducted by the Prosecution of the Russian Federation. To strengthen the law, protect human and civil rights and freedoms, and protect the interests of society and the state, this body supervises federal organs of executive power all over the Russian territory; legislative and executive authorities of the subjects of the Federation; other state organs and local authorities and their officials; and leaders of commercial and noncommercial enterprises and organizations.

In order to enforce the law in the fight against crime and corruption, the Prosecution also supervises organs that conduct inquests and preliminary trials, and coordinates activities of judicial departments fighting crime. Besides these responsibilities, the Prosecution conducts criminal prosecution according to the powers that are defined by the law.

The decisive role in defining the degree of responsibility for a crime and corruption belongs to the court. The Constitution of the Federation guarantees the right to legal defense. Only the court may establish whether a crime was committed and determine the punishment for it.

An important role in fighting crime and corruption in business is also played by arbitration courts. According to the legislation, the main tasks of arbitration courts in Russia are the defense of violated or disputed rights and the protection of the legal interests of enterprises, institutions, and individuals. Another task is to strengthen the law and prevent violations in business and other economic activities.

PART VII

FOREIGN TRADE AND INVESTMENT

CHAPTER 35

FOREIGN TRADE AND INVESTMENT

Oleg D. Davydov

35.1 CURRENT ECONOMIC REFORMS.   Economic reforms in Russia began in the midst of a deep crisis in the existing planned economy. The first stage of reforms in 1992 was aimed at the liberalization of the economy and designed to prepare for widespread privatization. The second stage, completed in 1995, was a struggle against both inflation and a budget deficit, as well as an effort to implement privatization. The measures of 1996 were intended to lay the foundation for investment activities and economic growth.

In 1996, the key event in Russia was the presidential election. Its result demonstrated a consistent commitment to a policy of democratic change and economic reform. The results of the presidential election were a landmark that made enormous impact on further socioeconomic developments in Russia.

The recent transformations in the Russian economy have become irreversible. The transition from a planned economy to a market economy has been completed. The most important results achieved to date are the abolishment of the centralized system of production and distribution of goods, and the introduction of the ruble's single market rate supported by the ruble's convertibility in day-to-day transactions.

The main goals of Russia's policy on prices are further liberalization of prices and improved regulation of prices for the products of natural monopolies, defense products, and products purchased for state's needs.

After the adoption of basic laws on price formation in early 1995, the share of products subject to price regulation on federal and regional levels fell from 24 to 15% of the value of the social product.

Today, the rate of decrease in production has slowed, and in some industries—such as fuel, energy, metallurgy, chemicals, and petrochemicals—a certain amount of growth has occurred. In recent years, the government's tight fiscal policy has resulted in the consistent reduction of the inflation rate, which reached virtually 0% in August 1996. Positive changes in Russia's socioeconomic development in 1996 are evident if one considers other indicators, such as the drop in state budget deficit to less than 5%. In 1997, it is expected to decline to 3.3% of the gross domestic product (GDP).

The Russian government has set the following priorities for the current stage of economic reform:

- Modernization of technology
- Further stabilization of the financial system
- Strengthening of the production infrastructure
- Expansion of the export of high-tech products

Due to the privatization of state enterprises that began in 1992, the ownership system in Russia has changed significantly. This created conditions for a drastic change in economic relations and for the development of competition in the market. Today, approximately 122,000 enterprises (constituting over 50% of all former state-owned enterprises) have changed their form of ownership. Privatized enterprises produce more than half of the gross national product (GNP).

35.2 INVESTMENT CLIMATE.   1996 was characterized by an increasing involvement of large capital and science-intensive industries in the privatization process. Among them are the fuel, energy, mechanical-engineering, transportation, and communication industries, which comprise Russia's production base.

Despite all of the mistakes made during its implementation, privatization has dramatically stimulated the development of capital markets and their infrastructure, namely banks, financial companies, and insurance companies. Though it only emerged recently, the stock market of privatized enterprises is Russia's second-leading stock market in terms of trade volume (trailing behind the stock market of state stocks and securities).

The strengthening of national capital and recent measures taken by the Russian government have created favorable conditions for the inflow of foreign investments. The total amount of accumulated foreign investment, as of mid-1996, was $9 billion and over 1.5 trillion rubles. In the first half of 1996, foreign investment increased by four times that of the first half of 1995. It is expected that foreign investments in 1996 will exceed $3–3.5 billion.

The Russian government is interested in diversifying the channels through which national and foreign capital is invested in the economy. The government strives not only to attract investments in the exploration and development of Russia's natural resources, but also to assist in commercializing Russian scientific and technological achievements. In addition, the use of free national capital for modernization and conversion, accompanied by a substantial increase in foreign investments, will promote the formation of a modern market economy in Russia and its participation in the international division of labor.

Currently, Russia can offer extensive opportunities to foreign investors. There are a number of industries that have unique technologies and substantial export potential. The integration of these industries into the world economy is the top priority of Russian economic policy. These industries can become the basis for the emergence of highly competitive financial and industrial groups that include plants, research and development institutes, trading firms, banks, and investment funds. Working together, they can provide for the manufacture of high-tech, export-oriented products.

The Russian legislature does not restrict the scope of business activities or investment opportunities for foreign investment institutions, provided they abide by the law. The current Russian laws guarantee a "national regime" to foreign investors. In certain cases, they even provide more favorable conditions than Russian firms enjoy regarding taxes on profits, value-added tax, and customs benefits.

35.3 LIBERALIZATION OF THE FOREIGN-TRADE REGIME.   The economic reforms in Russia, including first and foremost the liberalization of foreign trade, have determined the major directions of trade and economic interaction with foreign countries. In the current transformation, Russia has set priorities in its trade policy using objective and widely accepted criteria. One of the most important tasks for Russia in foreign economic activities is entry into the World Trade Organization (WTO). Russia's membership almost automatically ensures its entry into other major international economic organizations.

Europe is Russia's main trade partner with its share in Russia's trade volume exceeding 50%. In continuing to develope trade and economic relations with Europe, Russia is primarily interested in establishing a free-trade zone with the European Commonwealth. Although Russia plans to start working on this project in 1998 it will be possible only after the country's entry into the WTO. Another priority of Russian trade interests is joining the Asian Pacific Rim cooperation.

Russia's aim regarding foreign-trade policy is to become an active member in all global trade and economic processes, and also to get rid of bans on foreign trade that were imposed during the existence of the USSR.

From 1991 to 1996, Russia made a dramatic passage from the state monopoly of foreign trade to an exclusively *liberal foreign-trade regime* based on purely market principles.

Any Russian citizen or legalized person who has the status of a private entrepreneur can participate in foreign trade. As of mid-1996, 440,000 out of 2.6 million private entrepreneurs were engaged in foreign-economic activities. This compares favorably with the situation before 1991 when only about 60 governmental organizations were allowed to participate in foreign trade.

The export of goods from Russia is free from any quantitative or tariff restrictions. The system of export quotas has been repealed, and the export customs tariff has been abolished. Special restrictions apply to the export of only a few commodities (military hardware, dual-use goods, precious metals, and some other metals). Along with these, rare species of animals and plants require special licenses to be exported. There are, however, no quantitative export restrictions on them.

Export quotas are required only for goods exported to meet Russia's international obligations; Among them are some textiles, rolled steel, transformer steel, and carbide. The export quotas were set by the United States and the European Union.

The most important form of governmental regulation over exports is currency control, whereby the government oversees whether foreign-exchange earnings are brought into Russia on time and in full. Since November 1, 1996, the currency control system has covered all barter-commodities transactions, and from 1997 it will cover barter deals concerning services and intellectual property.

After the old system requiring compulsory registration of export contracts was abolished in March 1996, a new system, which is purely benevolent, was established in the following October to record foreign-trade contracts. In the new system, the record certificate granted to the requesting party is similar to a quality certificate for a foreign-trade contract.

Russia's main tool in controlling imports is *the regulation of import tariffs*. The Russian import tariff has an average rate of 14%, and a maximum rate of 30%. The exceptions apply to luxury goods and weapons, on which duties are levied at rates of 40 and 60%, respectively.

The rates are divisible by five, and the import tariffs for raw materials and semifinished products are either the lowest possible or are not levied at all. Low rates are imposed on technological and industrial equipment that is either not manufactured in Russia at all or manufactured in insufficient quantities. The average rate for consumer goods is 12–13%. However, for certain categories, such as textiles and foodstuffs produced domestically in sufficient quantities, import tariffs can reach 25 or 30%.

Regarding customs duties, basic rates apply to goods originating in countries with which Russia has agreements on mutual Most-Favored-Nation treatment. Goods from countries with which Russia has no such agreements (e.g., Estonia) are levied at a double rate. A number of developing countries have been granted preferential duties, which are levied at a rate of 75% of the basic tariffs. For members of the Commonwealth of Independent States with which Russia has free-trade agreements, and for 22 of the poorest countries in the world import duties are not levied at all.

Further development of import tariffs in Russia will result in lowering the average rate, decreasing the maximum rates, and reducing the gap within the range of rates. As it is planned by the Russian government, the average rate (using the 1996 rate as a baseline) will be reduced by 20% in 1998, and by 30% in 2000. The maximum rate will be 20% in 1998, and 15% in 2000.

The major change in import tariffs will be the reduction of rates for raw materials produced outside Russia and for semifinished products whose import will aid in reviving Russian industry. Simultaneously, rates on imported ready-made products of labor-intensive industries will be increased.

One of the key objectives of Russia's foreign economic policy is to formulate a clear and effective trade policy. In the current transitional stage, the first priority is to improve the competitiveness of domestic production by providing overall support to exporters of Russian-made goods. The relevance and consistency of these efforts are self-evident when it is noted, among other things, that Russia has made great strides toward opening its domestic market to foreign competitors. Domestic producers certainly deserve adequate protection as the Russian economy continues to open and the structural reorganization is accompanied by a significant drop in output and by intensified competition among imported goods on the domestic market.

To address these issues at close quarters, the government has set up a commission to draft protective measures, while another has been established to deal with customs tariffs. Laws are being drafted to invoke antidumping, compensatory, and special duties and tariff quotas. Protective measures will be implemented in Russia in strict accordance with the rules and regulations of the World Trade Organization. These rules mandate objective investigations with the participation of all concerned parties and nondiscriminatory protective measures, among other practices. The measures currently being developed will shield domestic producers and, simultaneously, adapt import tariffs to meet the needs of the current structural reorganization of the country's economy.

35.4 CURRENT POSITION IN THE WORLD MARKET.   The Russian policy to cultivate an open market economy was predicated, above all, on growing trade and economic relations with the West, from whom Russia's leaders wanted to obtain technologies, loans, and investments to modernize its economy. They wanted to reciprocate by exporting fuel, primary materials, and manufactured goods, including science-intensive products. This policy was at the core of the reforms and liberalization of external economic activities.

The quality of Russia's expanding and deepening cooperation in trade and economics with the West has not improved, however. The measures used in leading industrial countries to protect their domestic economies and the interests of their domestic business communities (including administrative controls) are much more rigid than anything ever used by Russia. In the meantime, the laws of these countries continue to label Russia as a nonmarket economy. The bias of this approach is evident because many countries, even those that are far behind Russia in economic change, have no problems acquiring the desired results.

This approach allows Western countries to set up, under various pretexts, roadblocks to Russian exports, even for primary materials, whenever the interests of their domestic producers are affected. In the export of high-technology goods and services, for example, Russia is pushed and shoved when it attempts to enter developing markets. Other examples of Russian exporters' interests being encroached on include the invocation of antidumping measures stemming from the discriminatory provisions of national laws; obstructions to Russian entry into high-technology goods and services markets where Russia has indisputable competitive advantages; and inadequate application of standards, technological barriers, testing, and certifying procedures that complicate, and frequently harm Russian exports.

Russia's efforts to integrate into the world economy must receive an adequate response from its international partners so that tangible progress can occur. A key role here may be played by Russia's entry into the WTO. In addition, Russia is ready to play an active part in the resolution of global economic problems, such as achieving stability and predictability of international relations in trade and economics, overhauling the international monetary system, settling the external-debt problem, and solving worldwide power, environmental, and food-security problems.

In the final analysis, Russia's full integration into the international community will become a major step toward a dramatic improvement of the mechanisms controlling the world economy, consonant with the new geopolitical realities.

35.5 EXTERNAL ECONOMIC ACTIVITY IN THE CURRENT STAGE.   From 1993 to 1996, there was distinctively dynamic growth in the volume of exports and imports and in progress toward Russia's integration into the world economy. The growth of exports and imports, under conditions of the continuing decrease of the industrial production reinforces the importance of foreign trade as an integral part of economic reform.

Between 1993 and 1995, Russia's foreign trade increased 33% from $95 billion to $127 billion. Russia's trade surplus in 1995 was $33 billion. Exports increased by 35% to $80 billion in 1995, including $14 billion to CIS-member countries. In 1995, imports reached $47 billion, growing by 29.5% over the same period. Goods imported from CIS-member countries amounted to $13.5 billion.

In the first six months of 1996, Russia's foreign-trade turnover approached $64 billion, which is 6.2% higher than during the same period of the previous year. The favorable balance during January–June 1996 was $17.4 billion. During the same period, Russia exported goods worth $40.7 billion, an increase of 4.6% over the first six months of 1995. Exports of mechanical-engineering products in January–June 1996 increased by 6.5%; their share in the overall export volume is 9.1%. Exports of natural gas increased by 3.5% to 101.8 billion cu m, while exports of oil over the same period grew by 3.1% to 61 million tons.

In the first six months of 1996, Russia's imports continued to climb, having reached $23.3 billion, 9.2% higher than the same period last year. Imports of mechanical-engineering products totaled $7.1 billion (30.4% of total imports), a growth rate of 0.7% over the previous year.

A geographical distribution of imports shows that 33.5% of imported goods were delivered from CIS-member countries, versus 23.8% in 1995. About 19% of Russia's exports were delivered to these countries, compared to 16.8% in 1995.

Currently, over 75% of Russia's foreign trade (not counting the turnover involving CIS member-countries) is produced by transactions with foreign countries. Approximately half of that 75% comes from the European Union countries, a fact that can be explained by their geographical proximity to Russia and long-standing historical ties.

Meanwhile, growing opportunities for the dynamic development of trade and economic relations between Russia and the United States are now opening. Russian-American cooperation is one of the top priorities of Russia's foreign-trade policy. In recent years, there has been consistent growth in the trade between Russia and the United States. Turnover is more than $7 billion. Especially dynamic is the trade and economic cooperation in science-intensive industries, such as space technology, the aircraft industry, nuclear energy, and ecology.

One important factor that has had a positive effect on the development of relations between the two countries was the establishment of the Russia-U.S. Commission on Economic and Technological Cooperation (Gore-Chernomyrdin Commission) in April 1993. The commission was founded in accordance with the Vancouver Declaration signed at the Vancouver Summit on April 3–4, 1993.

There are eight committees under the commission's framework:

- Intergovernmental Russian-American Committee for the Development of Business Cooperation (KRDS), which is headed by the minister of foreign economic relations of the Russian Federation and the U.S. trade secretary. (The committee was set up in June 1992 and is aimed at promoting trade relations between the two countries.);
- Committee for Energy;
- Committee for Space;
- Committee for Environment;
- Committee for Science and Technology;
- Committee for Conversion;
- Health Committee;
- Committee for Agribusiness.

The commission's co-chairs are the head of the Russian government, V. S. Chernomyrdin, and the U.S. Vice President Al Gore; the commission holds its sessions twice a year. The commission works not only on developing cooperation in the directions described, but also on solving problems in trade and economic relations between the countries. In 1996, among the problems to be solved were increasing Russia's quota for commercial launches of satellites, resuming Russia's export to the United States of sport and hunting guns, and overcoming barriers to a joint project for the creation of the IL–96M/T aircraft.

CHAPTER 36

TRADE

Mikhail Sarafanov, Valeriy Oreshkin, Yuri A. Kotlyar, Pavel Efremkin, and Sergey A. Smirnov

36.1 REFORM.* Although Russia's foreign trade has emerged almost unscathed by the deep structural crisis that has gripped the country's economy, it has failed to match the performance of the late 1980s and early 1990s. The year 1992 witnessed a slowdown in the declining rates of foreign trade in general, and exports and imports in particular; 1993 signaled a steady upturn in exports; and in 1994, imports also registered an upward trend. (See Exhibits 36.1 and 36.2.) The foreign-trade balance moved out of the red in 1991 and has since been gathering momentum.

In spite of its recovery, foreign trade has experienced a few negative developments:

- Russia's exports continue to rely heavily on primary materials, with just five commodity groups accounting for nearly 80% of export receipts: raw minerals and fuels, 45%; metals, 17%; chemical goods, 8%; timber, about 5%; and unprocessed farming produce, 3%. The export structure is being relentlessly stripped of engineering products, whose share has dropped to below 5% from 7.5% in 1994, and to less than half of the 1991 share.

- Exports have stabilized and posted a gain by virtue of sheer physical weight, selling at average contract prices that are below world prices. This trend was particularly conspicuous between 1992 and early 1994.

- The climbing export earnings from 1992 to 1994 failed to proportionally boost the state's currency revenues, which are badly needed to revive the export potential of both the processing industries and the fuel and mineral complex that produces the bulk of the hard-currency-generating export commodities.

- In imports, the share of unprocessed farming produce and foodstuffs continues to grow, having climbed by nearly a third, to more than 36%, since 1991. The level of imported foods in 1995 in the domestic consumer market reached 40%, which is considered a critical point for Russia.

- Russia's trade with the republics of the former USSR, primarily the Commonwealth of Independent States members, dropped sharply, from 60% of the total deliveries and purchases at the turn of the 1990s to 22% in late 1995. This tailspin has nearly wrecked the cooperative ties between the industries and individual enterprises in Russia and these states, contributing to the further slump in Russian manufacturing.

---

*This section was written by Mikhail Sarafanov and Valeriy Oreshkin.

Exhibit 36.1.   Comparative Volume of Russia's Foreign Trade with Foreign Countries, 1991–1995 (excluding former Soviet Republics)

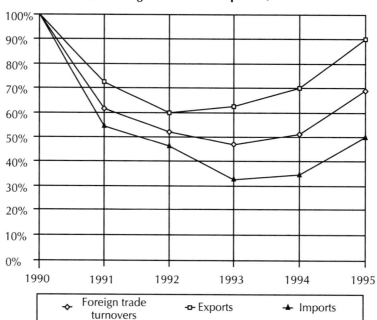

A similar impact has been produced by the shrinking trade with the countries of the former Council for Mutual Economic Assistance (CMEA).

Although Russian foreign trade grew about 25% in 1995 over the previous year, the outlook for 1996 was only 8 to 10% above the 1995 gains, including 5 to 6% for exports and 13 to 16% for imports. This slowdown forecast for foreign-trade growth rates was based on the

Exhibit 36.2.   Volume of Russia's Foreign Trade with Foreign Countries, 1990–1995 (excluding former Soviet Republics)

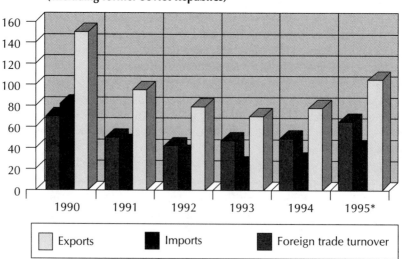

*Estimate

fact that the extensive growth potential has dried up. The key reason, however, appeared to stem naturally enough from the processes unfolding in the domestic economy.

Both favorable and unfavorable trends in Russia's foreign-trade performance derive largely from the state's foreign-trade policy. Specifically, the mechanism of tariff and non-tariff regulation of foreign trade was modified between 1992 and 1995.

(a) Exports.   Until the end of March 1995, the list of Russian export regulation tools included:

- Quotas and licenses to control the export of individual goods;
- Permits covering the export of strategically important raw materials (strategic goods);
- Export controls over the deliveries of military and dual-purpose goods (i.e., goods that can be used for both military and nonmilitary purposes);
- Mandatory registration of export contracts for basic primary goods to prevent under-pricing;
- Controls over timely remittance of foreign currency receipts from the export of all goods to Russian bank accounts;
- An export tariff.

At the end of 1995, these regulations were revamped in the course of further liberalization in export controls by the government. The result was the following:

- The requirement of licenses for export of the following goods, which in the aggregate claim nearly 10% of Russian exports: military goods, dual-purpose goods, and commodities whose export is regulated by international rules to protect the environment, maintain national security, or fulfill commitments made to curtail exports (including textile goods, some chemicals, and ferrous metals to European Union countries);
- Registration of export contracts (affecting about 50% of Russian exports);
- Foreign currency controls over the collection of receipts from all exports to the Russian territory;
- Imposition of an export tariff on limited types of raw materials and military equipment, with duty rates steadily declining over time and a decrease over time in the number of goods subject to tariff. (The weighted-average tariff rate on exports is currently around 15%.)

By contrast, in 1992 and 1993, nontariff methods were used to control almost 80% of the total exports from Russia. (See Exhibit 36.3.)

(b) Imports.   The flow of goods into Russia is controlled chiefly by the import tariff, value-added tax (VAT), and excise taxes. Quantitative restrictions apply to only about 5% of the imports (military and dual-purpose goods, drugs, poisons, psychotropic agents, and industrial waste). The imports of some consumer goods (food, household chemicals, electrical-engineering and electronic goods, and medicines) must, as a rule, be certified to verify their safety in use.

The import tariff was first introduced into the foreign-trade regulation system in the second half of 1992, and the duty rates have changed frequently ever since. (See Exhibit 36.4.)

In mid-1995, the weighted-average tariff rate for imports was about 12%. After July 1, 1995, when duty rates were raised on the imports of food, some other kinds of farming

Exhibit 36.3. Base Rates of Export Duties on Selected Russian Exports, 1992–1995 (export duty rates in European Currency Unit per ton)

Commodity	Early 1992	End of 1992	Early 1993	End of 1993	From 9/1/94	From 1/1/95	From 2/25/95	From 4/1/95	From 9/1/95	From 10/20/95
Oil	26	21	30	30	30	23	23	20	20	20
Natural gas	24	18	18	18	5	2	2	2	2	2
Engine gasoline	57	55	40	40	40	40	12[1]	12[1]	8[4]	8[4]
Diesel fuel	51	30	30	30	30	30	12[2]	12[2]	8[5]	8[5]
Fuel oil	24	52	15	8	8	8	8[3]	8[3]	6[6]	6[6]
Power coal	8	2	1	0	0	0	0	0	0	0
Coking coal	13	8	4	0	0	0	0	0	0	0
Nitrogen fertilizers	30	15	10	5	3	3	3	10[7]	2	0
Unprocessed timber	41	20	8	8	8	8	8	8	6	6
Processed timber	100	50	35	7	7	7	7	7	5	5
Pulp	69	50	30	30	10	10	10	10	7	7
Conversion pig iron	31	21	15	2	2	2	2	2	1	0
Hot-rolled steel	92	62	35	2	2	2	2	2	1	0
Primary aluminum	232	200	130	70	10	10	10	10	10	10
Refined copper	400	500	400	200	200	200	200	200	200	200
Nickel	1,600	1,500	1,200	640	640	640	640	640	640	640

1. from November to March—3 ECU

2. from October to February—4 ECU

3. from April to August—4 ECU

4. from November to March—2 ECU

5. from October to February—3 ECU

6. from April to August—3 ECU

7. effective from March 15 to August 1, 1995 (from August 1 to 31, 1995—3 ECU)

Exhibit 36.4. Comparison Table between Import Customs Duty and Tax Rates on Major Foodstuffs from Year-end 1994, to Midyear 1995 (% of taxable base)

Commodity	December 31, 1994			July 1, 1995		
	VAT & Special Tax	Duty	Total	VAT & Special Tax	Duty	Total
Meat (not including chicken)	0	8	8	11.5	15	28.23
Chicken	0	20	20	11.5	25	39.38
Sea Food	0	5	5	11.5	10	22.65
Milk and milk solids	0	2	2	11.5	10	22.65
Butter and other milk fats	0	15	15	11.5	20	33.8
Tomatoes (11/1 to 5/14)	0	0	0	11.5	15	28.23
Tomatoes (5/15 to 10/31)	0	10	10	11.5	15	28.23
Bananas	0	1	1	21.5	5	27.58
Citrus fruits	0	1	1	21.5	5	27.58
Tea	0	0	0	21.5 10, not less than 3 ECU/kg		33.65
Vegetable oils (soy & sunflower)	0	0	0	11.5	15	28.23
Olive oil	0	0	0	11.5	10	22.65
Cereals	0	1	1	21.5	1	22.72
Raw sugar	0	1	1	21.5	1	22.72
White sugar	0	20	20	11.5	25	39.38

Note: VAT is charged at two rates, 10 or 20% depending on commodity type, and the special tax is levied at a unified rate of 1.5%. The taxable base for import duties is the customs value of the imported commodity, and that of VAT and the special tax is the sum of the customs value and import duty.

produce, and pharmaceuticals, the average has jumped to 15%. With the introduction of the value-added tax and the special tax on food in late April 1995, the average amount of import-value payments has also risen, from an aggregate 11.5% to 21.5% of the taxable base. Before that date, imports in this commodity group had not been subject to either VAT or special tax. As a result, the amount of tariff and tax payments on imported foods has risen significantly since July 1, 1995.

(c) Framework for Foreign-Trade Regulation.   The framework for a foreign-trade regulation system in Russia was laid down in the last years of the former USSR, but as a form of national foreign-trade regulation it emerged in 1992. From the start, the system liberalized the former practices, with the accent shifting from administrative activities used to regulate foreign trade to economic tools, so that the key provisions of Russian foreign-trade laws could conform to the rules and norms accepted in international practice.

This is the only viable approach within the context of the market-oriented changes required in the Russian economy, including foreign trade. The liberalization of foreign trade could have brought real benefits only if its economic results could have been assessed in full. In practice, however, the liberalization turned into something of a dogma and an end in itself; as a result many excesses occurred, especially in 1992 and 1993. The system in effect at the time seriously undercut government control over foreign-trade operations, with the result that much of the nation's nonrenewable resources were wasted, many traditional markets of Russia's manufacturing industries were lost, and a great deal of foreign exchange fled the country. However, the system was mired in red tape that prevented the attempts of Russian businesses to capture their fair share of foreign markets and that led to corruption among the authorities.

The principal drawback of the existing government-run system of foreign-trade regulation is its weak legal base. There have been unjustified delays in the adoption of high-level legislative acts, while the system itself is built on a foundation of numerous institutional injunctions that are frequently at odds with one another. The harmful practice of having "too many cooks" in the form of assorted institutional bodies, each trying to lay its own imprint on the foreign-trade controls and regulations, has survived to this day. The question is still open about which methods take priority in the tariff and nontariff regulation system and how they can be consolidated into a unified control system. In fact, the institutionalized quantitative-export restrictions have been changed in name only and are unable to provide real government control over exports.

The abolition of the "special exporter" status has intensified the trend toward exports at dumping prices, and requiring the registration export contracts is a mere formality that has only a minor impact on the general problem.

(d) Foreign Currency Control.   The foreign-exchange controls introduced in 1994 have helped reduce the extent to which hard-currency receipts are squirreled away abroad. According to the Central Bank of Russia, between 50 and 70% of export earnings were not repatriated in 1992. In 1993, the figure was reduced to 30–40%; in 1994 it was slashed to 12%; and in 1995 it was pared down to 4%. However, the largest leaks opened in 1993 through import, not export, deals. Leakages were already 40% heavier in imports than in exports in 1993. In spite of this situation, the introduction of an import currency-control system was postponed until 1996.

There is yet no clear explanation about the functional purpose of customs duties and foreign-trade taxes. Under the current laws, the export tariff, which plays an adjusting role between domestic and world prices, has been scrapped. It is obvious, however, that this will not occur in practice because the tariff is one of the government's main sources of revenues.

(e) Import Tariffs. Import-tariff regulations have suffered the same drawbacks. The introduction of VAT and the special tax in the spring of 1995, and hikes in the import duties on foods in the summer of 1995 have been attributed to one of the three basic functions of the import tariff, protectionism. The new duty rates are not going to perform this function, however, as can be seen in, among other things, the year-long situation with duty rates, which were purportedly raised "in the interests" of Russian farmers.

It is axiomatic that the import tariff must be flexible enough to avoid hurting the interests of either the national producers or domestic consumers, but the economic effects of wide swings in this field must be anticipated in order to avoid rash action. Under current conditions, Russian producers (and consumers, as well) would best be protected by qualitative and technical-import regulations—those of Russia being the most liberal in the world. In particular, the goods-certification system must be applied to a much wider range of imports; and it is utterly unclear why a decision to impose it on imports from CIS members has taken so long.

(f) Gatt/World Trade Organization. Strategically, Russia needs to become a full member of GATT/WTO to meet the following goals:

Gaining nondiscriminatory access for competitive domestic goods and services to world markets;

Putting trade and economic relations with other countries on a stable legal footing;

Using the existing GATT/WTO dispute-settlement mechanism;

Improving the national legislative base.

The lifting of discriminatory barriers to trade that Russia would achieve by entry into WTO would save the country at least $1.5 billion annually.

WTO membership imposes numerous obligations on a country seeking admission and almost none on the member countries determining admission. Some of the obligations that Russia would undoubtedly be required to fulfill are the further liberalization of its trade goods and services, reduction of tariffs, removal of nontariff regulation in trade, and abolishment of licensing. Although Russia's current economic situation precludes it from meeting these requirements, it needs to join the WTO. It can do so only if it is offered preferential-entry terms, like those recently extended to Hungary, Poland, and the Republics of the Former Yugoslavia.

(g) Future Directions. The efficiency of the foreign-trade regulation system will depend on how fine-tuned its components are. Otherwise, the system could be buried in a deluge of useless ordinances that would hamper the work of all participants—exporters, importers, and government servants appointed to control them. Under such conditions, foreign trade could never be an effective tool to help restructure Russia's economy. Rather than erecting an unwieldy system to influence and control external economic activities, the nation would be better off by imitating countries whose economies and foreign-trade situations are similar to Russia's. These countries have engaged in a sensible, yet conspicuous, reconstruction of a state monopoly on the export (and import) of individual goods. The federal law on the state regulation of foreign trade, enacted in October 1995, eliminates some bottlenecks in the national legislation on external economic activities and is therefore a first step in the right direction.

36.2 PRECIOUS METALS AND PRECIOUS STONES.*

The law About Foreign Investments, enacted July 4, 1991, is the legal basis for the participation of foreign companies in the Russian economy. This law stipulates the legal and economic basis for foreign investments and is aimed at the effective use of foreign material, financial resources, technology, and administrative and management experience. The law states only general principles and does not solve the concrete problems of stimulating foreign investments. During the last few years, a number of government regulations and laws have been directed at stimulating projects funded by foreign investments. These provide taxation preferences on profits and duty-free treatment of materials, equipment, machinery, and parts brought in by foreign companies. They also have solved the accounting problems related to taxation on rate differences in the exchange of the ruble and foreign currency. These laws and regulations have general applicability and extend to all branches of the economy, including the gold-mining and diamond-mining industries.

The Russian Federation law concerning the earth's interior is the basic document that regulates the use of the earth's inner resources. This law stipulates that the interior and its minerals are government property and cannot be the object of buying, selling, donation, inheritance, investment, pledge, or alienation in any other form. According to this law, those who use such resources can be state-owned or privately owned companies, and either Russians or foreigners.

(a) Export of Gold and Diamonds.   Nevertheless, because of the special role of gold and diamonds in the economy, the activities of foreign investors in the gold- and diamond-mining industries are regulated not only by general laws and regulations, but also by special regulations.

In particular, by decree of the president of the Russian Federation, March 15, 1995, No. 273, government entities can pay joint ventures (with foreign partners) up to 50% of the gold that they mine in hard currency, on the condition that this money will be used first to pay back loans in hard currency and dividends to foreign investors (foreign partners of joint ventures). Western banks that issue loans to joint venturers investing in Russian gold and diamond mining usually require permission for the investors to export a portion of the extracted gold or diamonds. The Federation government has agreed to a compromise for several joint ventures involving foreign investors, such as that involving the Omolonsk Company and the Kamgold Company. These compromises have allowed for the realization of gold on the foreign market if it is not acquired by the state. Similar arrangements may be possible for other foreign investors involved in gold or diamond mining.

The draft of another decree of the president of the Federation, Additional Measures on Development of the Precious Metals and Precious Stones Market in the Russian Federation, has been presented to the government. The decree would provide permission to foreign investors participating in joint ventures to export precious metals obtained by foreigners based on their shares in production.

(b) Current Enterprises.   At present, six gold-mining enterprises with foreign-investor participation are registered in Russia. These are Syprus Mineral (Kubak deposit), Kinros and Grineberg Resources (Achinsk deposit), Homestake (Pokrovskoye deposit), Shreder

---

*This section was written by Yuri A. Kotlyar.

(Mnogovershinnoye deposit and Hakandga), and RTZ (Svetlinskoye deposit). The most successful foreign investment is at the Kubak deposit. About $60 million has been invested in foreign funds, and the overall project cost is $211 million; credits will total $140 million.

(c) Future Policy.   Precious metal and stones play a unique role in relation to currency values and gold-currency reserves and they play an important role in the development of technology-based industries. This makes the development of a common legal basis for their extraction, use, and circulation critical. The draft of the decree mentioned earlier attempts to create a legislative basis for such a policy. The goals of the draft decree are to stimulate the extraction and production of precious metals and stones, develop the market for these commodities, and regulate their rational and effective use in financial and production spheres.

In preparing the draft decree, all local laws and regulations were examined to take into account national interests, as well as those of the territories in which the resources are located. Under the proposed decree, extracted materials are the property of the mine operator if not otherwise stated in the license, the production agreement, or international contracts. Thus, precious metals and stones would become subject to private use, rather than being the property of the state. This change would make a significant contribution to improving the economy because it allows for the creation of a precious-metals and stones market, thus attracting private investors.

Under the proposed decree, the state monopoly would remain for refinery and assay control and state licensing and control for geological exploration, extraction, production, use, and the circulation of precious metals and stones. The state would reserve its right to purchase material from the mine owners for the creation of a state precious-metals and precious-stones fund and a gold stock under the control of the Federal Assembly. Payment would be in accordance with the prices on the world market, which would be specified in miners' contracts.

The proposed decree has been adopted by the Duma.

36.3 U.S.-RUSSIAN TRADE OF INDUSTRIAL GOODS.*   The practice and regulation of Russia's foreign trade, as an integral part of its economy, continue to experience drastic and rapid changes since the beginning of perestroika in 1987. As a result, any current analysis quickly becomes outdated and does not truly reflect today's situation in U.S.-Russian trading relations. An understanding of these relations as well as up-to date practical data, were obtained and developed by the SUPCO corporation, which specializes in the marketing of Russian industrial goods in the American market, as well as transferring successful American technologies to Russia. With this knowledge, we have formulated a few major issues that significantly impact the trading of industrial goods between the United States and Russia. These issues are considered essential to the successful operation of exporters and importers of such goods in both markets.

There are several major systematic factors that determine the specifics, opportunities, and restrictions of trade between the United States and Russia. They include:

Vast geographical differences between the two countries result in a delivery time (excluding production time), from the producer in one country to the consumer in the other, of at least 60 days. This situation does not allow companies to effectively react to

---

*This section was written by Pavel Efremkin.

rapid market changes and, hence, requires a long-term demand for the goods, as well as competitive prices and quality compared to equivalent goods from other countries.

Practical contradictions exist between the two prevailing systems regarding business relationships and behaviors of their markets. Despite the appearance of change, the major Russian industrial-goods market still continues to be controlled by monopolistic producers, who are used to consumers purchasing their goods under the terms dictated by the producer (previously, the state). The American market, on the other hand, is a buyer's market, formed in response to long-term competition between U.S. producers and numerous importers competing for their share of this massive market. As a result, strict delivery terms, absolute conformity of the quality of delivered goods to contractual specifications, convenient payment terms, etc., are recognized as minimum conditions necessary for the successful entrance of new producers and suppliers into the American market.

One of today's key problems with the Russian economy is that of nonpayments between participants in the Russian internal market, as well as these participants and the Russian state. As a result, practically all Russian industrial enterprises are in a permanent and deep financial crisis due to a lack of working capital. This problem is worsened by such things as artificially high profits and interest rates in these speculative financial markets. Because of this, Russian banks show no interest in providing credit to industrial enterprises that cannot pay interest rates at least close to current financial-market rates. Such ventures are deemed risky investments. As a result, many Russian producers have started to demand prepayments for exported market goods. This practice is absolutely unacceptable for American consumers who traditionally pay for their goods after delivery and, in many cases, enjoy deferred payments. Therefore, the possibility of building a financial bridge that would at a reasonable cost, transfer payment guarantees from American consumers into the credit facility for Russian producers, could be key for the future success of Russian producers.

There is no effective Russian legislation and relevant practical experience for protecting the interests of foreign investors, as well as ensuring strict adherence to contractual obligations. Problems arising from inefficient legislation are deepened by the lack of traditions associated with a fair and stable entrepreneurship. On the contrary, it is not unusual for Russians accept short-term benefits, a policy that prevails over long-term obligations at the expense of repeat business. In such an environment, it is recommended that U.S. companies having no prior business experience in Russia use, as a partner, an intermediary U.S. or Russian company that has a sound reputation and specializes in developing U.S.-Russian projects. Using such companies may help in avoiding common problems by defining some performance guidelines and repayment guarantees, which will be acceptable for both the American consumer and the Russian supplier. Such steps can greatly reduce the risks of doing business in Russia.

Other important factors and differences between the two markets include:

- Different systems of standards (American Society for Testing and Materials standards in the United States, and GOST standards in Russia);
- The metric system is used in Russia, and the U.S. system is used in the United States;
- Differences in such programs as safety-certification systems, employee compensation, etc.

However, an in-depth discussion of these factors goes beyond the limited format of this short chapter. These and other differences between the two markets should be thoroughly examined before beginning.

Some general recommendations can be provided to Russian exporters and producers interested in introducing their products into the American market (these also may be useful to American companies considering Russia as a new source of supply). The decision to enter the American market should be considered as a strategic investment program to achieve a long-term and consistently high-priced market for the product. Also, it must be clearly understood from the beginning that no deficit exists in the U.S. market. It is free from the harsh competitive niches usually created for Russian products. Accordingly, the implementation of such plans will require sound and, at times, substantial efforts and expenses.

The first step in such an investment decision should be a plan to conduct preliminary market research in order to evaluate the capacity of the American market for the product, as well as to compare the final costs of the product delivered to the United States with those of the average price of similar products available in the American market.

Russian and U.S. investors should know that the key point for a successful entrance into this market is to find the right strategic agent, representative, or partner. This partner-agent should be able to integrate a strong background in marketing new products in the American market with a clear understanding of the specifics and restrictions of the Russian economy in order to bridge the gap for the supplier. Such an agent-partner must also be strategically and naturally motivated to achieve the maximum volume of sales at the highest possible price.

One common error in the selection of a strategic agent-partner is choosing a representative that is already involved in the marketing and sales of the same or similar product from other producers. Of course, it is evident that such companies often possess the most complete and up-to-date information on marketing the product and, at times, are willing to help finance the marketing and other activities with the Russian producer. It is also evident, however, that the only motivation for such an agent-partner would be the prevention or delay of real sales of the competitive product in the American market. In the best scenario, the agent-partner would use the Russian producer as supplemental production source, which would be used to fulfill the extra demand for the product usually provided by their regular source of production.

Once chosen, the agent-partner should:

Conduct extensive marketing research aimed at pinpointing the potential consumers for the Russian manufacturer;

Establish direct contacts with the Russian manufacturers;

Introduce the new product to potential consumers by providing them with technical specifications and samples of the products;

Identify what grades, quantities, packing specifications, delivery terms, etc. are currently standard in the American market so that the Russian producer can adjust its production program to deliver products most in demand by American consumers.

Once regular sales to the U.S. market have been established, two additional important agent-partner's responsibilities should be undertaken. First, the agent-partner must work with U.S. banks and other financial institutions to obtain credit financing, secured by payment guarantees from U.S. consumers that will be used to finance the Russian manufacturer's production process. Second, the agent-partner must select the most effective and most cost-effective means of delivering the goods from the plant to the consumer. This may also include the establishment of consignment warehouses in the United States in order to provide fast and uninterrupted delivery of the goods. Certainly, the higher the level of accommodation to the buyer's requirements regarding delivery, payments, packing, and others the higher the selling price and, accordingly, the profit of the Russian exporter.

The introduction of Russian products to the American market requires a lot of effort from both the supplier and its agent. However, acquiring a share in this stable, capacious, and lucrative market is worth the effort. In addition, one indirect result of a successful entrance into the American market is that the acceptance of products by the American consumers will automatically open up new worldwide markets, where people are eager for successful American products.

Recent signs reveal that, despite the fact that trade between the United States and Russia is complicated by a number of difficulties and restrictions, companies of both countries are trying to develop large-scale import and export operations of industrial products. The major reason for this is that the American market is one of the largest in the world and about which it is accurate to say that "one can effectively sell almost any product if the price is right." On the other side, Russia, with its huge natural and mineral resources as well as a highly developed industrial base, will become a major supplier of industrial goods to the world markets in the upcoming decades.

36.4 CHAMBER OF COMMERCE AND INDUSTRY: ACTIVITIES WITH FOREIGN COMPANIES.* The Chamber of Commerce and Industry of the Russian Federation (CCI) has the goal of creating favorable conditions for developing of all kinds of entrepreneurship in Russia. These conditions include the modern industrial, financial, and commercial infrastructure. One of the goals of the Chamber's activities is to develop economic, trade, and scientific relations with Russian and foreign-business communities.

For this purpose, the United Information System (UIS) was created within the framework of the CCI. The UIS includes the International Information System, which is in charge of communicating with the Chamber's overseas branches, UIS foreign users, and world-information networks.

The UIS uses technical equipment and software compatible with those operated by UIS's domestic and foreign users. The UIS provides on-line services. The information available via the UIS encompasses:

Russian enterprises and organizations;

Russian branches of foreign firms;

Russian and foreign associations promoting international trade;

Import and export offers made by domestic and foreign companies.

The UIS database also contains:

Currently laws and provisions regulating business practices in Russia;

Information on Russian and international exhibition businesses;

A list of current expositions and trade shows in Russia and overseas.

The Chamber of Commerce and Industry releases the electronic publication *Weekly News of CCI RF* and publishes *Express* on a biweekly basis, which covers the latest news

---

*This section was prepared by Sergey A. Smirnov.

in the Russian legislature and in various foreign legislatures. These publications also cover the domestic real-estate market and financial and currency markets. All business information prepared by the CCI is available on magnetic tape and optical disks.

Additional information on import and export services can be obtained from the International Center for Business Information Zlaki, which is a joint-stock company operated under the auspices of the CCI. If requested, the center does research in different fields of economy, management, and market relations. Also, it gathers, processes, and disperses business information on trade, prices, and the stock market. The Center provides telecommunication access to the leading Russian and world information centers, and consulting services as well.

The joint-stock company Sovincenter, the Moscow Center for International Trade and Scientific Ties with Foreign Countries (CMT), is one of the largest business centers in the world. The CMT complex includes an office building (for foreign companies, banks, and airlines), the 600-room, luxury hotel Mezhdunarodnaya–1, a residence hotel for long-term stays, restaurants, bars, gyms, stores, a post office, a library, and other services. There is a 2000-seat conference hall equipped for simultaneous translation, along with a 500-seat concert hall and meeting rooms. The CMT helps foreign firms and their representatives in Russia organize conferences, trade shows, and press conferences. Also, the CMT provides translation, printing, and transportation services as well as those related to everyday life and leisure.

Along with the CMT, three other organizations of the Chamber provide services for foreign entrepreneurs in Moscow—the Business Center, the Service Center, and the Congress Center. The Business Center, which utilizes the United Information System, helps foreign and Russian businesspersons find business partners, conduct talks, and sign contracts. The Business Center has 40 offices, 10 hotel suites, a conference hall, meeting rooms, restaurants, and a gym. The Service Center provides foreign and Russian entrepreneurs with fully furnished offices, a conference room, and information and consulting services. The Congress Center offers a conference hall equipped for simultaneous translation, live video transmission, television systems, among other services.

The Chamber of Commerce and Industry, through its division Sojuzpatent, also provides services for patenting inventions, acquiring commercial samples, and registering trademarks if requested to do so by Russian and foreign customers. There are about 40 patent attorneys working for Sojuzpatent. It is an independent firm not controlled by government or business and it has permanent connections with patent firms in over 90 countries.

Another division of the CCI is the Foreign Trade Association Sojuzexpertiza (SOEX). One of Russia's leading control organizations, SOEX conducts quality and quantity inspections of imported and exported goods both in Russia and overseas. SOEX has branches in numerous ports, major industrial centers, and Russian border posts. It guarantees fair and objective examinations and successfully serves many foreign companies. SOEX also offers services related to compensation in kind, certification of stocks and securities, examination of their authenticity, business estimates (including estimates of property profits), intellectual property, prices and competitiveness of goods, consulting, and customs procedures.

In accordance with the law On the Chambers of Commerce and Industry in the Russian Federation, the CCI certifies and issues certificates of goods' origin and other documents for import-export transactions. The CCI is the only organization in Russia that may witness *force-majeur* circumstances in the Russian territory. Certificates are issued at the request of concerned Russian and foreign organizations.

The Russian Chamber of Commerce and Industry is the only public association of entrepreneurs in the world. Within its ranks, it has several internationally recognized institutions for solving commercial disputes, including the International Commercial Arbitration Court, the Maritime Arbitration Commission, the Court of Arbitration for Economic Disputes, and the Association of Average Adjusters.

Judicial services to foreign companies in Russia are mainly provided by Inveco, which is another division of the CCI. Inveco employs only highly qualified and experienced lawyers who prepare and examine documents, and represent companies in court. They also provide consultation to clients on judicial issues, customs and banking laws, operations with real estate, taxes, bankruptcy, and many other issues.

In accordance with the law, the CCI grants permission to various organizations to establish themselves in Russia, including representations of foreign firms and organizations, joint chambers of commerce, associations, and entrepreneurial unions. The CCI gives foreign firms operating in Russia discounts to use the United Information System and the Business Center, lists foreign firms accredited in Russia in the yellow pages, and provides different kinds of services necessary for the foreign representations' everyday activities.

One of the main activities of the CCI is organizing trade shows both in Russia and abroad. One of its divisions, Expocenter, is Russia's premier organizations for exhibitions, with a state-of-the-art exhibition center 50,000 square meters of closed exhibition space. Expocenter arranges international trade shows, provides foreign participants with visa service, rents storage space and offices for foreign firms' representatives, and helps foreign participants look for wholesale buyers, among other services.

The Chamber of Commerce and Industry also includes the following divisions:

The foreign-trade association Sojuzregion, charged with assisting Russian regions to promote their import-export transactions, and improve the regions' technical modernization based on cooperation with foreign firms;

The foreign-trade association Vnesheconomservice, which provides foreign firms with consulting, brokerage, translation, visa, and personnel services; The largest advertising agency in Russia; Sovero;

The information agency Info, providing Russian and foreign firms with consulting, information, and advertising services.

Numerous other services are provided by joint chambers of commerce, such as Bulgarian-Russian, British-Russian, Italian-Russian, Finnish-Russian, French-Russian, Polish-Russian, Greek-Russian, and Vostok, which also has representatives in Russia.

The consulting arm of the CCI also provides publishing services to Russian and foreign entrepreneurs. Among the most important CCI publications are:

The newspaper, *Torgovo-promyshlennye novosti,* which advertises the services, technologies, and goods of Russian and foreign companies;

Business Contact magazine, published in English, which offers information and advice to businesspeople on various activities and import-export opportunities in the Russian market.

CHAPTER 37

RUSSIAN-U.S. TRADE

Jan H. Kalicki, Joseph J. Grandmaison, Eileen
Cassidy, Dennis Montz, E. Vivian Spathopoulos,
Yuri V. Akremenko, Deborah A. Palmieri,
and Alexei S. Gumilevski

37.1 PROMOTING TRADE AND INVESTMENT: THE U.S. DEPARTMENT OF COMMERCE AND NEW U.S. INITIATIVES.* President Clinton said at the beginning of his first administration that helping Russia become a market democracy was one of his top foreign-policy priorities. A central element of the administration's Russia policy from the start has been to encourage economic and commercial reforms that are aimed at creating a stable and hospitable environment for private-sector development. Through increasing levels of trade and investment, the democracy and its institutions in Russia can be strengthened; and tangible benefits such as jobs, profits, technology transfer, training and enhanced consumer welfare will be realized.

The Department of Commerce formulates, coordinates, and implements U.S. commercial policy with Russia through the Joint Commission on Economic and Technological Cooperation, chaired by Vice President Gore and Prime Minister Chernomyrdin (known informally as the Gore-Chernomyrdin Commission, or GCC), on which Commerce Secretary Daley serves as vice chair. The GCC is an umbrella structure for the intragency Business Development Committee (BDC), which is cochaired by Secretary Daley with his Russian counterpart, Deputy Prime Minister Davydov. With the active participation and input of the Departments of State, Treasury and Energy, Office of the Vice President, National Security Council, Agency for International Development, and the Office of the United States Trade Representatives, as well as U.S. financing agencies such as the Export-Import Bank, Overseas Private Investment Corporation (OPIC), Small Business Administration (SBA) and Trade and Development Agency (TDA), the BDC has set the pace for high-level cooperation in improving bilateral commercial relations in such sectors as aerospace, medical equipment, oil and gas, and telecommunications. (A brief description of the operations of the Export-Import Bank, OPIC, SBA, and TDA is included in Appendix 37A at the end of this chapter.)

In addition, the counselor to the Department of Commerce was named by the White House as U.S. Ombudsman for Energy and Commercial Cooperation with the New Independent States (NIS) to troubleshoot, in coordination with ombudsmen in each of the NIS members, energy and commercial projects that could expand trade and investment quickly and pave the way for progress on a wide range of business transactions.

---

*This section was prepared by Jan H. Kalicki.

(a) Trade and Investment Trends.   Recent economic progress in Russia now provides reformers with a foundation and some latitude with which to work for more reforms. Inflation has come down markedly, and the exchange rate is relatively more stable. The country's economic decline appears close to bottoming out and, in some sectors, there is growth. Russia posted a $26.7 billion trade surplus with the rest of the world in 1995; the 1996 surplus may be even larger. This should continue to provide an important source of foreign exchange for competitive industries and the economy generally.

The April 1996, three-year, $10.2 billion International Monetary Fund (IMF) funding package recognizes Russia's progress and sets strict conditions intended to encourage its government and legislature to carry out sound economic reform policies. IMF monitoring and disbursements are on a month-to-month basis, providing further incentives for compliance with the program. Indeed, the IMF has already demonstrated it will use its monthly reviews as a tool to encourage compliance and keep Russia on a sound macroeconomic footing.

In 1995, U.S. exports to Russia grew to $2.8 billion, and expanded again by nearly 30% in the first half of 1996 compared to the same period in 1995. U.S. imports from Russia, while growing very quickly in the recent past, have now dipped. The United States imported over $4 billion from Russia in 1995. For the first half of 1995, however, U.S. imports dropped about 30% from the first half of 1995. The United States ran a $186-million trade surplus for the first six months of 1996.

U.S. firms are the leading foreign investors in Russia, with approximately $3 billion of the estimated $9 billion (direct and portfolio) invested by foreigners. According to Russian statistics, U.S. direct investment in Russia in 1995 was $800 million, or more than 30% of all foreign direct investment in the country.

During the seventh session of the Gore-Chernomyrdin Commission meetings in July 1996, Presidents Clinton and Yeltsin issued a joint statement calling on the business community to increase investment in Russia and indicating that both governments work together to encourage more U.S. direct investment. The joint statement reflects President Yeltsin's recognition that only through significant infusions of capital and technology into Russia's economy will its domestic industry develop. U.S. government support for more investment in Russia is manifest in the more than $2.2 billion of U.S. government-backed investment funds, with an additional $1.7 billion in trade credits.

Although there has been growth, actual trade and investment volumes, to date, have not come close to reaching their full potential. That potential will only be fulfilled through further economic reform, as recognized in the September 1994 joint statement of the two presidents at the Washington Summit, establishing a Partnership for Economic Progress through trade, reform, and investment. The Clinton administration, in collaboration with the private sector and through the vehicles of the GCC, the BDC, and the energy and commercial ombudsmen, is working to develop the necessary economic and other reforms for trade and investment.

(b) Business Obstacles and Initiatives to Overcome Them.

(i) Unpredictable and High Commercial Taxes.   U.S. companies have made it clear that Russia's commercial tax regime constitutes the greatest single obstacle to direct investment in Russia and, more generally, to the development of a market economy. Russian business taxes are widely regarded as unpredictable and improperly based on gross revenues, rather than on actual profits.

The U.S. government, in partnership with the U.S. private sector, has helped Russia set the stage for creation of a viable commercial tax regime. The U.S. Treasury Department has provided tax lawyers, economists, and tax administrators to assist the Russian government in reforming and updating its tax laws. The BDC's Joint Commercial Tax Dialogue and Tax Administration Working Group have produced *joint* Russian-American recommendations on commercial legislation and procedures. Some recommendations have already been implemented, or are on the way to implementation. For example, the excess-wage tax has been repealed and the State Tax Service and Finance Ministry are issuing instructions to Russian tax inspectorates removing ambiguities in the application of the value-added tax, which have often led to tax errors and unfair penalties.

U.S. government discussions with Russian government and parliamentary leaders have shown strong support for a comprehensive overhaul of Russia's tax code, which is currently before the Federal Assembly. Enactment of a new tax code, however, is likely to be a lengthy process, with some estimates that it will not be passed until 1998. In the interim, the U.S. government has been working with the Russians to identify tax measures that could be promulgated in the near term through administrative decrees such as Decree 686, issued in May 1996, that provides welcome clarification on the tax treatment for foreign and domestic businesses.

(ii) Barriers in the Energy Sector.   Despite the fact that Russia holds some of the world's largest oil and gas reserves, several factors have combined to limit investment in Russia's energy sector. Foremost among these are excessive and unpredictable energy taxes and a lack of an adequate legal basis to guarantee the sanctity of production-sharing agreements (PSAs) for large energy products.

The U.S. government's message to the Russians on energy taxes is one that has been repeated at every opportunity—an uncertain, unfair, and unstable tax regime can have a debilitating impact on domestic and foreign investment, hindering further investment by existing U.S. joint ventures (estimated at $800 million), and blocking what is estimated to be potentially $60–70 billion or more in new energy-sector projects.

The BDC's U.S.-Russian Interministerial Working Group on Oil Industry Taxation, formally established by the GCC in July 1996, is engaged in an active dialogue on energy taxes, including excise taxes and pipeline and transportation tariffs. An unprecedented interministerial initiative, the oil industry taxation working group, seeks to resolve energy-tax issues through the collaboration of the Russian Ministries of Energy, Finance, Economy and Foreign Economic Relations, and the U.S. Departments of Commerce, Energy, State and Treasury. These discussions have already resulted in a decision to reduce excise taxes on six joint ventures that had previously been granted exemptions from Russia's oil-export tax. For these joint ventures, such a reduction spells the difference between profit and loss. In the area of pipeline and transportation tariffs, the United States is working closely with the private sectors of both countries to encourage the Russian government to establish an equitable and predictable tariff structure.

Although the Russian Parliament's adoption of a law governing production-sharing agreements in the energy sector is a welcome development, important unresolved issues that will impede energy-sector investments must be addressed by administrative and legislative measures. The BDC's oil and gas working group will continue to work with the private sector to push for the passage of legislation pertaining to production sharing agreements in the near term, namely, a law listing eligible PSA fields and passing legislation that will bring related laws into conformity with the PSA legislation.

Because development of oil and gas reserves in Russia and the New Independent States is an important U.S. goal, each country is being encouraged to promote energy cooperation aimed at building a productive economic base for the region and increasing participation in international markets. In this vein, the U.S. government is pleased with the on-going dialogue with each of the energy-producing states to encourage multiple pipeline routes to transport oil from the Caspian region.

(iii) Market Access.   Although Russia has lowered its average tariff rate significantly since 1992, duties and excise taxes in several key industrial sectors such as commercial aircraft, pharmaceuticals, and semiconductors are high compared with tariffs and related taxes maintained by industrialized countries. Russia has also shown a willingness to employ trade-protection measures. For example, Russia's actions in the winter and spring of 1996 to raise tariff barriers and impose phytosanitary restrictions on poultry imports threatened to drastically reduce U.S. exports of poultry, which are a significant portion of our total exports to Russia. The U.S. government will seek to reverse any such undue burdens on U.S. exports, as was successfully done in the poultry case. The Russian government's decision to drop these restrictions is very much welcomed.

The challenge is to work closely with Russian policymakers, businesspeople, and consumers to show the benefits of increased access to both markets. For Russia, imports from the United States can contribute to Russian competitiveness by providing valuable inputs, lead to capital investments in Russian industry by American companies, provide consumers with access to a greater variety and quality of products, and help restrain inflation.

(iv) Intellectual Property Protection.   U.S. industry estimates that violations of intellectual property rights (IPRs) in Russia resulted in losses in excess of $1 billion in 1995, due in large part to inadequate enforcement of existing laws.

During the July 1996 GCC meetings, Vice President Gore and Secretary Kantor emphasized the need to make the protection of intellectual property rights the subject of even more intense discussion in bilateral commercial dialogue. Deputy Prime Minister Davydov, in turn, has made this a high priority for the Russian government and IPRs have become a higher priority for Russian law enforcement—with progress in developing a more effective judiciary and in expanding the rights of authorities to confiscate pirated goods.

However, as the United States made clear in placing Russia on the Special 301 watch list in April 1996, laws and especially enforcement must be further improved. (Special 301 is part of U.S. law aimed at protecting intellectual property rights. The watch list is a designation for countries where there are concerns regarding intellectual property rights.) Russia's own software, film, and other industries are at risk unless IPRs are strengthened. The interagency IPR working group, chaired by the Office of the U.S. Trade Representative, meets with its Russian counterparts to discuss how steps can be taken to bolster Russia's IPR regime as well as technical-assistance needs.

(v) Inefficient Customs Administration.   The Russian customs service, despite a significant expansion in staffing since 1993, has failed to keep pace with the increase in Russia's volume of international trade, particularly imports. As a result, Russian customs clearance has become a primary obstacle for U.S. companies exporting to Russia.

Following the successful model of the Business Development Committee's tax dialogue, the United States has opened talks with the State Customs Committee to cooperate in finding ways to streamline the processing of exports in Russia. U.S. and Russian customs authorities, together with the U.S. private sector, are developing a pilot project under the auspices of the BDC's U.S. West Coast-Russia Far East Working Group, for an advanced customs-notification system aimed at drastically cutting customs delays at Russian Far East ports—currently the single greatest obstacle to expanded trade and investment between the two regions.

(vi) Information Shortfall and Lack of Access to Regional Opportunities.   Aside from obstacles posed by Russian government policies, other difficulties exist, including obtaining reliable information about markets, potential business partners, laws, registration procedures and other government regulations at federal levels; these constitute a serious market barrier, especially for smaller firms. Due to infrastructure deficiencies and unfamiliarity with regional business opportunities, foreign companies are only beginning to develop business in regions beyond Moscow and St. Petersburg.

In response, the Commerce Department's Business Information Service for the New Independent States (BISNIS) serves as the clearinghouse for business information on all NIS countries, reaching over 25,000 companies through its mailings. BISNIS can be reached by telephone (202-482-4655); E-mail (bisnis@usita.gov); fax on demand (1–800–USA–TRADE); and the Internet (http://itaiep.doc.gov). The department's Special American Business Internship Training program (SABIT) has enabled over 250 companies to train nearly 800 NIS executives and scientists. In addition, the Commerce Department has established a network of Commercial Service offices and American Business Centers in 11 Russian cities. These programs—many funded by the Agency for International Development under the Freedom Support Act—provide information on the Russian market and help U.S. companies identify and develop reliable Russian business partners.

U.S. regional efforts include activities to increase and facilitate trade and investment between the West Coast of the United States and the Russian Far East under auspices of the BDC, as well as intensive advocacy efforts to advance commercial transactions and priority energy projects with U.S. participation in the Russian Far North, Sakhalin Island, and Western Siberia.

(vii) Crime Against Businesses.   Requests for bribes, extortion, and other forms of corruption, and threats of violence against businesses are an obstacle to honest business in Russia, affecting large as well as small U.S. companies and their Russian partners.

An important new initiative under the BDC is cooperation in the area of crimes against businesses, which are one of the key impediments to trade in Russia. During the July 1996 GCC meetings, a plan was signed aimed at increasing awareness and assisting business-people and law-enforcement officials in both countries to tackle criminal activities affecting businesses.

(viii) Technical Standards Barriers.   Russian standards for imported products, and the requirements that Russia imposes for certifying compliance with these standards, often differ significantly from standards and certification practices accepted in the West.

Through the BDC's Standards Working Group, the Department of Commerce has worked with Russian certifying and standards-setting agencies to clarify Russia's standard requirements, and to push for harmonization of Russian requirements with those employed in the United States and western Europe, thereby facilitating trade. Our SABIT program, in cooperation with the National Institute for Standards and Technology, is organizing internships to train standards experts in sectors with the best prospects for U.S. exports to Russia.

(c) Conclusion.   The U.S. commercial-policy dialogue with Russia is not a closed, government-to-government channel, but instead relies heavily on the participation of the United States and, increasingly, of the Russian business community. The voice of business is also becoming an important asset to those in the Russian government and Parliament who share the goals of economic reform. Private-sector participation in the Interministerial Working Group on Oil Industry Taxation and the Russian government's Foreign Investment

Advisory Council are just two examples of the business community's growing impact on Russian policymakers.

The U.S. business community has a positive role to play in helping to bring the emergent Russian business community into policy discussions. Russian industry is increasingly recognizing its interests apart from those of the state, and finding an independent voice on matters affecting its business environment. When U.S. business helps bring Russian entrepreneurs to the table, Russian government officials are more likely to be receptive to commercial concerns than if issues are perceived narrowly as American interests.

The challenge is to find common interests with Russian policymakers, businesspeople, and consumers—to show, for example, that trade and investment and private sector development can contribute to Russian competitiveness. As Presidents Clinton and Yeltsin recognized at the 1994 Washington Summit, both countries need to continue to demonstrate the link between increased trade and investment and economic reforms. U.S. investment in Russia will increase only if the commercial-tax regime is reformed, if Russia maintains its openness to external markets though low, uniform, and stable tariffs, and if it otherwise establishes an internationally competitive business climate.

In this respect, the Commerce Department will continue to focus its efforts on programs, projects, and initiatives that are intended to eliminate barriers to enhanced trade and investment, and to demonstrate ways in which the promotion of business ties and the development of a thriving private sector can serve the mutual interests of the United States and Russia.

37.2 U.S. TRADE AND DEVELOPMENT AGENCY.*   The U.S. Trade and Development Agency (TDA), an independent U.S. government agency, provides funding for American companies to conduct feasibility studies on major projects in developing and middle-income countries. By providing assistance in project planning, TDA promotes economic development, while helping U.S. companies get involved in projects that offer significant export opportunities.

TDA-funded studies determine the technical, economic, and financial feasibility of major project implementation. Historically, most TDA projects have been public-sector undertakings, planned and implemented by government ministries or agencies. Increasingly, however, developing and middle-income countries have begun to promote private-sector involvement in major infrastructure and industrial projects. Consequently, TDA now provides funding for both public and private-sector projects, including joint ventures in which U.S. companies plan to take equity.

(a) TDA in Russia.   TDA is a pioneer in providing assistance to the New Independent States (NIS), having moved quickly to establish its program in the region after the breakup of the USSR. Since signing its first grant in Russia in 1992, TDA has provided funding of about $42 million for feasibility studies on over 110 major infrastructure and industrial projects in that country, which present export opportunities of more than $4 billion for U.S. companies.

As Russia continues its transformation toward democracy and a market economy, the opportunities for U.S. exports and investment are growing. Yet, despite the tremendous long-term market potential, the uncertainties inherent in the region's social and economic transition make even the largest American companies reluctant to commit the resources needed to fully pursue these opportunities. TDA's sharing of the political and economic risks, through partial funding of project-feasibility studies, helps to allay some of these concerns.

---

*This section was prepared by Joseph J. Grandmaison.

Furthermore, because Russia cannot afford to import all of the goods and services that its economic growth demands, access to the Russian market often requires a U.S. firm to consider a joint venture, coproduction arrangement, or some other form of technological cooperation. TDA's assistance in Russia is, therefore, increasingly focused on studies that help create long-term cooperative relationships between U.S. firms and their Russian counterparts that open the door to U.S. exports. Most of TDA's feasibility studies in Russia now involve these potential joint ventures or coproduction arrangements. TDA funding in support of such projects has two benefits: it reduces the level of investment risk faced by American companies in an uncertain market like Russia; and it provides reassurance to the Russian partner that the project is backed by active U.S. government support.

In carrying out its Russian program, TDA coordinates with two other U.S. government finance agencies, the Export-Import Bank (Ex-Im Bank), which provides financing and guarantees for U.S. exports, and the Overseas Private Investment Corporation (OPIC), which provides insurance and financing for U.S. investments overseas. TDA also maintains close relations with the multilateral financing agencies that are active in Russia—the World Bank, the European Bank for Reconstruction and Development (EBRD), and the International Finance Corporation. In appropriate cases, TDA consults with U.S. government technical agencies, such as the Federal Aviation Administration and the Department of Energy. In addition, TDA works closely with the U.S. Department of Commerce, primarily through its Foreign Commercial Service.

(b) How TDA's Russia Program Operates.   To initiate TDA consideration of a project in Russia, a request for assistance must be made directly to TDA by the appropriate Russian sponsoring entity. In cases where a specific U.S. company has been identified by the Russian entity as its partner in the project, that U.S. company must also submit a detailed proposal, following a format available from TDA.

If a project appears promising, TDA hires its own technical consultant to review it and determine whether: (1) the project represents a developmental priority for Russia; (2) financing for project implementation is available if the study suggests project feasibility; (3) the potential for U.S. exports during project implementation is significant (in Russia, TDA will only consider projects with potential U.S. exports of at least $10–15 million); and (4) there is competition for the project from non-U.S. companies.

When TDA provides funding for a feasibility study, it signs a grant agreement with the relevant Russian sponsoring entity (the grantee), and it is the grantee that selects the U.S. firm to conduct the study. In many cases, the grantee already has identified that firm (typically the firm that has submitted the proposal to TDA). In other cases, a competitive selection process is undertaken by the grantee, entailing publication of a request for proposals in *Commerce Business Daily.* In either case, the selected U.S. contractor signs a contract with the grantee to conduct the study.

While the grant agreement is signed by TDA and the grantee, no funds are actually transferred to the grantee. Instead, the U.S. contractor carries out work under its contract with the grantee and submits its invoices to the grantee for approval. TDA then pays the contractor directly. While the contractor must be a U.S. company, TDA allows up to 20% of its funding to be used for Russian subcontractors.

Because of the great demand for TDA funds, in most cases TDA covers only part of the cost of the feasibility study, the remainder of the cost being borne by the U.S. firm conducting the study. TDA's contribution varies according to a number of factors. These include the size of the firm, the potential benefit from the firm as supplier to (or investor in) the project, the costs the firm has incurred in developing the project, and the risks associated with the project. In addition, TDA may require the U.S. firm conducting the study to reimburse part or all of the TDA funding if the project is implemented and the firm reaps a substantial economic benefit.

(c) TDA Gets Results.   TDA has learned from experience in other regions that the lead time between the feasibility study and implementation for major projects is typically several years. Thus, the impact of earlier TDA funding in Russia is just becoming discernible. As of October 1996, U.S. exports related to projects in Russia assisted by TDA in the 1992–94 period are over $300 million. Ex-Im Bank has issued a preliminary commitment supporting an additional $1 billion and is currently considering guarantees for several other TDA projects funded during that period. Final approval of financing for these projects would result in a multiplier of over $60 in U.S. exports for every $1 invested by TDA during that period.

In addition to promoting U.S. commercial interests, TDA's activities in Russia serve to strengthen the economic reform process under way in the region by encouraging U.S. private-sector partnerships with local entities. These partnerships, in turn, help provide the success stories needed to encourage Russia and the other NIS countries to stay the course of economic reform.

(d) Illustrative TDA Projects in Russia.   *Refinery Upgrade:* TDA provided partial funding ($300,000) for a study conducted by Lummus Crest on the modernization of the Perm Refinery. Based on the study, the refinery has purchased over $21 million in U.S. technology licenses and engineering services, and an Ex-Im Bank guarantee has been signed for an additional $96 million of U.S. goods and services.

Aircraft Coproduction: TDA provided partial funding ($1,000,000) for studies on co-production of the IL–96M aircraft, with Pratt & Whitney engines and Rockwell avionics. Ex-Im Bank has issued a preliminary commitment for a guarantee supporting $1 billion in U.S. exports for the first 20 aircraft.

Construction Equipment: TDA provided partial funding ($120,000) for a study on a construction-equipment-leasing joint venture. As a result of the study, conducted by Hoffman International, and a related visit by Russian officials to the United States, Hoffman and its Russian partner have established the joint venture; and U.S. companies have sold over $6 million in highway-construction equipment.

Air-Traffic Control: TDA provided partial funding ($1,350,000) for a study on upgrading the air-traffic-control system in the Russian Far East. Booz, Allen & Hamilton conducted the study and prepared tender documents for the procurement of equipment. The European Bank for Reconstruction and Development is expected to provide the financing, and has already released a general procurement notice for the project.

Shipyard Conversion: TDA provided partial funding ($400,000) for a study by McDermott International on converting the Komsomolsk-on-Amur shipyard from the production of nuclear submarines to the production of civilian products. As a result of the study, a joint venture established by McDermott and the shipyard has been awarded a contract (funded by the Japanese Government) for construction of a barge-mounted liquid-treatment plant to process radioactive waste from decommissioned Russian nuclear submarines. U.S. exports for this project already total about $13 million.

Fuel Cells: TDA provided partial funding ($800,000) for a study on coproduction of liquid-carbonate fuel cells. M-C Power Corporation conducted the study, and is now working with its Russian partner to begin implementation of the project.

Highway Construction: TDA provided partial funding ($229,000) for a September 1996 conference in St. Petersburg on opportunities for U.S. companies related to World Bank and EBRD highway projects in Russia and other NIS countries. The American Road and Transportation Builders Association organized the conference, in which over 50 U.S. businesspeople participated.

(e) Contact Information.   For more information on TDA programs in the NIS countries, contact: the regional director or country manager at (703) 875-4357. For information on other TDA programs, TDA publishes a quarterly newsletter, *The TDA Update,* as well as *The TDA Pipeline,* which lists TDA events and opportunities. TDA also maintains a library that is open to the public at its Rosslyn, Virginia, office. Inquiries may also be made by email at info@tda.gov. Completed feasibility studies can be viewed at TDA's library, and copies can be obtained through the National Technical Information Service (NTIS).

37.3 OPPORTUNITIES AND CHALLENGES FOR SMALL COMPANIES.*   Few people could have imagined just how far Russia would open itself up to trade in a few short years. As a result, foreign entrepreneurs were freed from having to deal with the heavy hand of Soviet governmental bureaucracies and could pursue opportunities on their own. These businesses, mostly small, flocked to Russia to determine how they could build business partnerships and prosper in Russia.

American small businesses have many reasons to conduct business in Russia. Huge pent-up demand for American products in a large and untapped market, plus a highly skilled, well-educated, and inexpensive work force, are the reasons frequently cited to enter the Russian market. It is also one of the few markets in which small and large firms can compete on an equal footing, since few firms of either size had been operating in the Soviet Union. Home Sweet Home real-estate brokers, Jack's Sandwiches delivery service, and TrenMos restaurants are only three examples of small businesses that sprouted to provide Russia's growing number of expatriates and prosperous citizens with a level of service that local providers could not.

Despite the persuasive arguments in favor of exporting to or operating in Russia, the country has many serious problems that give businesses, especially small ones, pause. All businesses, large and small, have the same complaints about Russia's taxation, bureaucracy, and cultural expectations, but small businesses face greater risks in dealing with Russia because of their smaller human and cash resources.

The U.S. Small Business Administration (SBA) and the State Committee of the Russian Federation for the Support and Development of Small Business (SCSME) founded the U.S.-Russia Small Business Working Group of the Business Development Committee of the Gore Chernomyrdin Commission (GCC) to help solve some of these issues. This working group was created in January 1995 during GCC VI, and was formalized at GCC VII in July of the same year. The American and Russian members of the working group, representing both the public and private sectors, have as their task the promotion of trade between small U.S. and Russian firms and the development of the infrastructure for small businesses in Russia. This relationship will be important in helping small U.S. businesses overcome some of the difficulties of doing business in Russia.

(a) Getting Started.   Small businesses have challenges even before they enter Russia. Basic market information is lacking or unreliable, and small businesses rarely have the research staff to verify information. The cost of business travel in Russia is one of the highest in the world. Russian businesspeople like to develop close personal relationships, so

---

*This section was written by Eileen Cassidy and Dennis Montz.

negotiations will usually take longer than expected, which adds to the cost. Small businesses may need to spend a lot of time educating their Russian partners on business basics, which many of them, although bright, lack. The goals of a small business and its Russian partner must be identical; Russian partners often have different goals and want the start-up money and possibly advice, but not interference. A small business must be prepared to spend a disproportionate amount of time monitoring the Russian business, the investment, and the political and regulatory climate. Some resources, such as the Department of Commerce's Business Information Service for the New Independent States (BISNIS) and some Russian organizations can provide a great deal of information, usually at no charge and by fax or Internet, so that businesses can know what to expect and plan for those circumstances. The SBA's counterpart in Moscow, the SCSME, can also assist businesses with information or at least refer them to organizations that can provide help.

American small business must overcome several Russian biases. A typical attitude is, "If you are so good, then why haven't I heard of you?" a point of view that reflects a bias toward the largest companies in their industries. Another attitude is, "If you are so important, why doesn't your government send a representative to this negotiation?" The respect for government support, even foreign governments, is still very high in a country where the government controlled nearly all aspects of the economy. The SBA will continue to lead groups of U.S. small-business owners to Russia, lending credibility and bringing attention to American small businesses. The SBA is also assisting the SCSME to change the Russian perception of small business.

(b) Financing. One of the biggest problems any small business faces, regardless of location or activity, is financing; and dealing with Russia complicates matters. Small businesses usually have little money for substantial international travel and communication. Another problem is that few banks provide trade financing for Russian transactions, in addition to the fact that the cost of writing a letter of credit is nearly the same for a small transaction as for a large one, but the fee is smaller. Also, if a buyer is delinquent in a payment—a chronic problem in the Russian business community—commercial laws and enforcement are inadequate, so pursuing the action may take up more time and money than it is worth.

The SBA exists to help finance small businesses. It does much of the work of the bankers to entice banks to lend to small businesses and also provides a loan guarantee to the bank of up to 90% of the loan. The SBA's Export Working Capital Program (EWCP) is designed specifically to help exporters circumvent the problems of obtaining trade finance. EWCP is a transaction-based guarantee not to exceed 12 months for either 90% of a secured loan or $750,000, whichever is less. The SBA also has an International Trade Loan program, which provides short- and long-term financing for exporters. The SBA can guarantee up to $1.25 million for a combination of fixed-asset financing and permanent working capital.

A small business can take some other steps to reduce risk and expenses. Market conditions in Russia are such that cash prepayment is the customary way to conduct business, thus reducing the possibility of delinquent payment and providing cash flow. Several investment funds, such as the Allied Capital International Small Business Fund, the New Russia Small Business Investment Fund, and The U.S.-Russia Investment Fund also offer debt and equity financing for U.S. small businesses or U.S.-Russian joint ventures. A small business may want to test the market through exporting before making a serious commitment in Russia. Russia is a better market for experienced exporters than for the new-to-export small businesses. The U.S. Export Assistant Centers, a one-stop export promotion program of the SBA, Department of Commerce, and the Export-Import Bank, can help with exporting and trade financing.

(c) Bureaucracy.   When a new Russia rose from the ashes of the Soviet Union, the antiprofit mindset was supposed to have been swept away. Yet neither the necessary legal infrastructure nor a universal promarket outlook has replaced the discarded Soviet framework. Russian and foreign businesspeople alike bemoan the high tax rates and heavy regulatory burden that affect all types of businesses.

The Russian government has taken the first step to ease the onus on small businesses by creating the SCSME and enacting laws to streamline registration and taxation, enabling small manufacturing companies to have a tax holiday in place. The SBA and the SCSME are advocating policies to improve the conditions of small businesses in Russia; they are also promoting changes in legislation and rationalizing taxation for small businesses. These changes will not occur overnight, but small businesses at least have a government agency in their corner to fight for them.

(d) Conclusion.   The opportunities and challenges facing small businesses in Russia are great. These firms, which must watch their pennies closely and are more sensitive to risk, face the same challenges as other firms, only there are more of them. In only a few markets can a small business establish a beachhead to compete against and beat its larger competitors and earn returns that equal or exceed the level of risk. Dealing with Russia requires more attention and care than one would initially estimate, but the SBA, with its SCSME partnership, is ready to help.

Note: "Contribution of this article is not an indication of the U.S. government's endorsement of the book."

For more information, contact the Office of International Trade, U.S. Small Business Administration at (202) 205-6720; (202) 205-7272 for faxes.

37.4 U.S. COMMERCIAL SERVICE AND PRIVATE INDUSTRY TEAM UP TO OPEN MARKETS IN RUSSIA AND THE NEW INDEPENDENT STATES.*   When contemplating the new markets of Russia and the New Independent States (NIS), most U.S. businesses hesitate to stray far from the relative comfort of Moscow. In doing so, however, they miss out on some of the most exciting business opportunities the region has to offer. Cities such as Nizhny Novgorod, Novosibirsk, Vladivostok, and St. Petersburg boast developed and diversified economies with sizable consumer markets and reform-oriented political climates. With the centralized economy fading into history, U.S. firms no longer need to go to Moscow to make a deal. As enterprises across Russia and the NIS privatize, the opportunities in the outlying regions will only continue to grow. Already 110,000 enterprises have privatized in whole or in part, and more than 80% of Russia's industrial workers now work in privatized firms.

As the private sector continues to grow and diversify, the demand for a wide range of American products and services promises to multiply. A large number of U.S. consumer-goods manufacturers—Coca Cola, Mars, and Procter & Gamble, for example—already have looked beyond Moscow. In addition, opportunities in oil and gas, telecommunications, health care, and aerospace are growing as the economy continues to modernize.

Along with the opportunities, however, come potentially daunting roadblocks, including ownership disputes, financial illiquidity of Russian firms, absence of a legal framework for

---

*This section was written by E. Vivian Spathopoulos.

commerce, severe infrastructure problems, frequent changes in tax and import regimes, high costs, and the general difficulty of doing business. These hurdles often suffice to keep American firms from exploring a market any further.

Fortunately, the U.S. Department of Commerce, in cooperation with the U.S. Agency for International Development and the American private sector, has established a network of offices across Russia and the NIS to provide the guidance needed to demystify these markets. The Department of Commerce, through its Commercial Service, operates six offices strategically located across Russia and the NIS. Through these offices in Moscow, St. Petersburg, Vladivostok, Kiev, Almaty, and Tashkent, the Commercial Service's experienced officers share their intimate knowledge of the language, culture, and business practices of the region, and offer numerous products and services to help move U.S. firms into these markets. Services range from export and trade-finance counseling, market research, trade contacts and partners, to trade-promotion events and programs. In cooperation with the Department of Commerce's Advocacy Center, the Commercial Service also protects and advocates for U.S. business interests in Russia and NIS markets.

Recognizing that the Commercial Service cannot cover this vast region on its own, it has established with private-sector partners a network of American Business Centers (ABCs) in 13 cities across the region. The ABCs provide a professional work environment with a full range of business services to give U.S. firms a competitive advantage. Services include international telephone, fax, and E-mail service; trade-mission, seminar, conference, and exhibit planning; office space, conference-room, and computer-equipment rental; and interpretation, translation, and secretarial services. ABCs provide U.S. firms valuable commercial and regulatory information, identify potential partners and business opportunities, and offer entree into the regional government and local business communities.

Unlike their experience in more developed markets, American businesses cannot expect to conduct their business in the region by phone and fax from the United States. U.S. firms must spend time there—especially for complicated deals—researching the markets, meeting prospective clients and partners, deepening existing partner relationships, and visiting facilities and plants. To do this effectively, companies need on-the-ground support to manage even the most basic logistical elements of their trip. When Volga River Management, Inc., won a $30 million contract from the European Bank for Reconstruction and Development to develop the Lower Volga region, including the city of Volgograd, they rented office space at the Volgograd ABC. The office carrels were fully outfitted with furniture, computers, printers, and a full range of telecommunication facilities. Volga River Management had easy access to the ABC's copying, secretarial, translation, and interpretation services whenever the need arose.

ABC services extend beyond the office walls. With the help of the Volgograd ABC, Volga River Management hired a full-time driver and located living quarters for their staff, saving them not only money but also the frustrations of hotel living as well. Joel Montgomery, director of Volga River Management, said that working through the ABC made it possible for the company to concentrate on what is really important—finding investment projects. The ABC was beneficial for relieving the burden that comes with the initial start-up of an office.

Michael Baker Corporation, a U.S. engineering and construction company involved in the oil and gas industry, used the logistical and informational support of the ABC in St. Petersburg during its initial evaluation of the northwest region. Additionally, the company used the services of the ABC to identify interpreters, transportation, lodging, and other support services in the area. The company's representative in St. Petersburg, James Taylor, concurred that the ABC was very useful during the early stages of the corporation's activities.

The company also relied on the ABC to arrange meetings with senior decision makers in the Leningrad Oblast and found the bilingual staff very helpful and enthusiastic. Until the company's new office is furnished with equipment, it will continue to use ABC services, including photocopying, telecommunications, word processing, and mailbox service.

One of the best ways to enter the Russian and CIS markets is through trade missions that enable participating U.S. companies to gain access to high-level Russian and CIS government and business officials. A U.S. Department of Commerce-sponsored medical-industry trade mission to the three ABC sites in the Russian Far East provided 16 U.S. health firms with the opportunity to develop trade and investment opportunities in Vladivostok, Yuzhno-Sakhalin and Khabarovsk. Mission activities included meetings arranged by the ABCs with key government officials, briefings, site visits to hospitals and clinics, and more than 75 one-on-one meetings with government officials and private health-company representatives.

The trade-mission results speak for themselves: 12 of the 16 participating companies together credited the mission with on-the-spot sales of $470,000, potential sales of $44 million, a contract for $1.2 million, 15 additional contracts, a letter of intent to develop a servicing and training center for medical equipment in the Sakhalin region, and contacts with six potential distributors. One firm reported prospects for a health-insurance contract that would yield annual revenues of $250,000. Shortly after the trade mission, one participant, GE Medical, established a permanent marketing presence in the region by renting office space at the Khabarovsk ABC.

In June 1996, a trade delegation sponsored by the Millers National Federation arrived in Yuzhno-Sakhalin with representatives of Fisher Mills, Inc., to promote the sale of American agricultural products. Active in sales of flour and flour products in the Russian Far East, came to Fisher Sakhalin in an effort to expand its sales in Russian. The ABC in Yuzhno-Sakhalin provided critical business services to Fisher and arranged, through its local contacts in the food industry, business meetings with individuals and companies of the region. The 10 contacts provided by the ABC led to direct sales for Fisher, along with valuable contacts for future sales in this region.

The Commercial Service and the business-friendly ABCs play an important role for Americans doing business in Russia and the NIS. By cultivating close contacts in the local business communities through outreach activities, the Commercial Service and the ABCs serve as a proactive, valuable information resource. Each office is an important link in the network, uniquely positioned to help American and Russian and NIS companies find each other easily and work together effectively. The Commercial Service and the ABCs are the partners of U.S. business in Russia and the NIS.*

37.5 TRADE AND INVESTMENT.   Russia entered the Agreement on Trade Relations with the United States in 1992 during the Russian-American summit. Under this agreement, the parties accorded each other Most-Favored-Nation (MFN) status in trade. This is remarkable because, for four previous decades, bilateral trade was repressed by the absence of such reciprocal status. Another milestone was the joint statement Partnership for Economic Progress, which was issued in 1994 by the presidents of both countries. This

---

*Appendix 37B at the end of this chapter lists the locations and other information regarding commercial services offices and ABCs in Russia.

**This section was written by Yuri V. Akhremenko.

document established principles and objectives for the development of trade, economic cooperation, and investment between Russia and the United States. The idea of an economic partnership was reconfirmed by the presidents at the 1995 Moscow Summit. In July 1996, the presidents issued a joint statement, mainly addressed to the business communities of Russia and the United States, pointing out that highly favorable conditions existed to accelerate and deepen economic cooperation between the two countries. The presidents also decided to create an intergovernmental mechanism to resolve problems and further economic and technological cooperation.

(a) Lifting of Trade Restrictions.   Since the dissolution of the Soviet Union, the United States has lifted dozens of legislative restrictions on trade and investment cooperation with Russia. In particular, it opened the way for the Export-Import Bank, Overseas Private Investment Corporation, Trade and Development Agency, Commodity Credit Corporation, and other organizations to get actively involved in developing economic relations with Russia. Government support is of great importance for American companies doing business in emerging markets such as Russia.

(b) Economic Reform.   In its turn, Russia has gone through a significant political and economic transformation and is continuing its market-oriented reforms. Russia already has a very liberalized foreign-trade system and is making further steps to improve the climate for foreign investments. Some concrete business-friendly measures were undertaken in response to the concerns of American companies. For example, foreign firms that invest more than $100 million in Russia can enjoy a 50% reduction in customs duties for their goods entering Russia. The first beneficiary of this policy was an American food company.

(c) Increase in Trade and Investment.   The new political and economic environment made it possible to double bilateral trade in three years since 1992. In 1995, the turnover exceeded seven billion dollars. This made the United States Russia's third-largest trade partner, with only Ukraine and Germany ahead. In the area of investment cooperation, American companies lead other foreign investors in the Russian economy. As of July 1996, the overall value of American investments in Russia was about $3 billion, or 30% of all foreign investments. The number of Russian-American joint ventures exceeded 1,000. More than 700 American companies, including banks, already have their offices in Moscow.

Nevertheless, if these developments are viewed in the context of the economic potential of Russia and the United States, it becomes apparent that real success is still to be achieved. American investments can grow in quantity and diversity. Priority industries for cooperation are agribusiness and food processing, aerospace, mining, medical equipment and pharmaceuticals, telecommunications, transportation, environmental equipment, housing, and defense-conversion. At present, the majority of American investments are in oil and gas. Many Russian-American joint ventures take the form of trade agencies or consulting firms.

Trade with Russia still accounts for only 0.5% of overall American foreign trade. Just 10 commodity groups comprise 80 to 90% of exports and imports. Russian exports consist mainly of raw materials and unfinished goods—aluminum, precious or semiprecious stones and metals, iron and steel, inorganic chemicals, nickel, fish, fertilizers, and petroleum products. American exports consist primarily of meat, tobacco, beverages, food and agricultural products, and several types of machinery and equipment. Trade that crosses an ocean should be more sophisticated than food, raw materials, and other commodities.

(d) Market Access. Further quantitative and qualitative development of trade depends on how successfully the two parties will resolve problems pertaining to market access. The principle of reciprocity needs to be considered. The American side conducts what it calls an aggressive trade policy to reach the Russian market, but the treatment of Russia as a trade partner in the United States does not always reflect the new political and economic realities in Russia. This may be the reason why the trade balance in most years favors the United States.

U.S. legislation still considers Russia a nonmarket economy, and thus Russian producers and exporters can be subjected to extremely tough and burdensome antidumping procedures; and the duties, if imposed, are actually prohibitive in nature. For example, the antidumping duty for ferrosilicon is 104%. For some commodities, high duties that remain in force have closed the market for a long time: titanium sponge since 1968, urea since 1987. If Russian entrepreneurs, who now are on their own, cannot make use of competitive advantages, they are faced with harder social and economic conditions and lose incentives to switch to free-market rules of play. The United States recognized Russia as an "economy in transition," but appropriate legislative measures have not yet been taken.

Despite the provisions of the 1992 trade agreement, the United States has not granted Russia MFN status—the foundation of a normal trade relationship—on an unconditional and permanent basis, even though the United States enjoys a full-value MFN status with Russia. Moreover, sometimes American companies seek conditions that are even more advantageous than those given to countries with regular MFN status.

In 1994, the Clinton administration made a positive determination that Russia is in full compliance with the Title IV criteria of the U.S. Trade Act of 1974 (the Jackson-Vanik Amendment). Nevertheless, Russia continues to be burdened by anachronistic and counterproductive legislation, with its MFN status in force only under the waiver of this amendment. Now that many other former socialist states are completely removed from the application of Title IV, unfair discrimination against Russia becomes more and more evident. The lack of permanent MFN status also creates uncertainty, which hampers bilateral trade; whereas permanent MFN status will create new business incentives in both countries.

Although Russia has become a member of the new international organization formed under the Wassenaar Agreement for export controls, the United States has kept restrictions on high-tech exports to Russia. Recently, there has been a significant relaxation of U.S. controls on exports of high-speed computers, but this did not actually end discrimination against Russia. Russia is the only member of the Wassenaar Agreement to be in the category of countries under especially strict control. The only countries that have more severe restrictions placed on them are Iraq, Iran, and Libya. Such discrimination limits the prospects for bilateral cooperation in high technology.

(e) Russian-American Commission on Economic and Technological Cooperation. The problems discussed earlier, as well as various trade and other disputes that inevitably occur between countries, are addressed by the Joint Commission on Economic and Technological Cooperation, headed by the prime minister of the Russian Federation and the vice president of the United States. Since the commission was created in 1993 by the presidents of both countries, it has expanded its responsibilities and now consists of eight committees in different fields of cooperation. The oldest is the Business Development Committee (BDC), which coordinates trade and investment issues. The most active working groups of the BDC include those for market access, standards, and oil and gas. The BDC's initiatives include the Business Development Mission to Russia in 1994, the Joint Commercial Tax Dialog, cooperation in combating crimes against businesses, cooperation in the support and development of small business, commercial cooperation between the Russian Far East and the U.S. West Coast, and Russia's Business Information Service for Trade with America (BISTA), under the umbrella of the Ministry for Foreign Economic Relations and Trade.

(f) Trade Representation of Russia. The Russian agency that promotes bilateral trade and investment cooperation is the Trade Representation of Russia in the U.S.A., which is a part of the Russian embassy. Its principal task is the observance of state interests in bilateral trade and investment cooperation. For these purposes, the agency maintains contacts with American agencies and participates in the activities of intergovernmental bodies on economic cooperation. It also participates in boosting large-scale commercial projects, for example the IL–9GM/T aircraft, or in settling problems that range from permanent MFN status to tariff and nontariff barriers. One of the agency's major functions is to provide assistance and consulting services to Russian and American private companies in searching for business partners; establishing joint ventures; signing commercial contracts; and obtaining information on legislation, taxes, exchange or customs regulations, and other rules and procedures in Russian and American markets. The bulk of the agency's work is done at its headquarters in Washington. To be closer to the centers of U.S. business activity and to be more deeply involved in regional economic cooperation, the agency also has offices in San Francisco and New York, and is considering establishment of permanent offices in Chicago, Los Angeles, and Seattle. The agency can be contacted at: Trade Representation of the Russian Federation in the U.S.A., 2001 Connecticut Ave. N.W., Washington DC 20008, U.S.A., Tel.: (202) 232-5988, fax: (202) 232-2917.

37.6 RUSSIAN-AMERICAN CHAMBER OF COMMERCE.* The Russian-American Chamber of Commerce is a transnational organization engaged in numerous aspects of promoting economic diplomacy between the United States and Russia. Its mission is to develop and facilitate U.S. trade, investment, and commerce in the Russian marketplace. The organization is dedicated to enhancing American competitive advantage in one of the most promising global markets of the twenty-first century, and to serving the American business community as an expert source on business and commercial developments in Russia. The Russian-American Chamber of Commerce is regularly engaged in transnational diplomacy—promoting activities between the two nations to enhance and build the economic and business relationship between them.

The Russian-American Chamber of Commerce has several major functions. The first is informational and educational. A significant portion of the Chamber's efforts are devoted to educating the American business community through educational conferences, seminars, and meetings. These events address an entire array of business realities, opportunities, and risks encountered by Americans in Russia. Events have been held in New York City; Boston; Washington, Missoula, Montana; Kansas City; Denver; Salt Lake City; Wichita; Los Angeles; and other cities. The topics and issues included industry-specific opportunities (telecommunications, mining, manufacturing, etc.), risks encountered in Russia (taxation, organized crime, contract enforcement, etc.), successful strategies, and regional specific issues and prospects (Siberia, the far eastern region, northwest economic region, among others).

Besides these events, the Russian-American Chamber of Commerce issues several publications, including the bi-monthly *Russian Commerce News* and a research paper series.

---

*This section was written by Deborah A. Palmieri.

The *Russian Commerce News* provides an important intelligence-briefing and business-development resource to its members. It analyzes important commercial issues and helps keep members informed about the rapidly changing, fast-paced, and complex Russian business environment. Past features include, for example, the role of the information superhighway and Russian business; learning from company experiences in Russia; tax impediments to investments; Russian real estate; the country's gold industry; the outlook on Russian foreign trade; a guide to exporting goods to Russia; the impact of political instability on its business future; Russian culture and business etiquette; Chechnhya and Russian stability; risk in the Russian marketplace; currency, conversion, and rubles; and more. The *Russian Commerce News* also offers profiles of its members, an extended guest editorial section, and a comprehensive listing of important business events in the United States and Russia.

On a day-to-day basis, the Russian-American Chamber of Commerce works to fulfill member requests for advice and information. Its staff assists in numerous other activities, including event planning and execution; gathering information from other public and private organizations on doing business with Russia; and providing a host of other support services in-house, in the community, and to members nationally. The organization also communicates with businesses and affiliates in Russia, and conducts extensive public-relations and goodwill activities to further its mission.

The second function of the Russian-American Chamber of Commerce is to enhance the degree and amount of communication between the Russian and U.S. governments and corporate players. Through this exchange and interface, governmental and nongovernmental entities can develop a greater appreciation of the problems, constraints, and issues each faces. Improved communication between the two results in a better climate to pursue business opportunities and develop appropriate and more effective commercial policies in both the United States and Russia. Towards that end, the Chamber instituted its American Advisory Council, comprised of prominent members of Congress with a special interest in Russia, and its Russian Advisory Council, headed by the current Russian ambassador to the United States. Chamber members have the opportunity to interact with these officials and their staff with the goal of expanding business operations and creating the necessary set of business and political connections to do so. These councils are complemented by American and Russian boards of directors, which are comprised mainly of companies and business leaders well known in international business circles. This liaison among key political and business decision makers of both countries makes a strong contribution to the Chamber's effectiveness and popularity.

A third function of the Chamber is to provide a host of services designed exclusively for its members. While the Chamber is not directly involved in business transactions, in its capacity as a nonprofit institution, it helps facilitate such transactions in a number of ways. It assists businesses in locating the best sources for demographic and population data and provides current listings of many governmental and nongovernmental financing sources. Members often need contacts or resources in a specific region of Russia. Through its network of contacts across Russia, the Chamber puts businesses in contact with regional officials, offices, and companies. Other members look to the organization as a resource for locating specific import or export items. The Chamber handles requests for contacts at Russian banks or companies, for information on the latest Russian ministerial officials or up-to-date business developments such as the ruble exchange rate and for materials such as telecommunications or defense conversion. Its expert experienced and staff is dedicated to fulfilling these requests backed up by an information library and database maintained in their office.

A fourth function of the Chamber is to develop a global network of contacts with other nonprofit organizations that share its mission and purpose. It provides a formal vehicle by which like-minded organizations in Russia and the United States can exchange information, advice, and recommendations to promote and expand business and trade between the two countries. These organizations include existing regional, state, and local groups, including trade associations, nonprofit organizations, research, or academic groups. The chamber's Sister Affiliate Program fosters cooperation, enhances business and networking opportunities among various regions in the United States and Russia, and encourages friendships and increased business throughout both countries. Membership is growing, and is expected to continue to grow, in the Russian Business Program, the Chamber's program to reach out to Russian businesses.

Finally, the last function of the Chamber is to support and facilitate efforts by universities and colleges to train a new generation of managers and entrepreneurs to successfully meet new business challenges. This goal is achieved in many ways, including working closely with these institutions and freely sharing their expertise and knowledge, and making their university contacts available to both countries. The Chamber is dedicated to promoting the growth of a research and policy-making framework that will increase knowledge of the Russian marketplace and of the issues, problems, and challenges involved in developing a U.S.-Russian business relationship.

There is every reason to believe that an economic relationship between the United States and Russia will be one of the most significant in the global economy of the next century. The Russian economy is already on the path to recovery, and even now, Russia enjoys a trade surplus. Its foreign trade sector is one of the strongest segments of its economy. It is especially important that the United States promotes economic diplomacy with Russia. While it now runs a trade deficit with that country, there is no reason U.S. exports cannot grow as fast as its imports, which have quadrupled since the early 1990s. What is now significant about U.S. trade with Russia is its low base due to the Cold War legacy. Currently, trade turnover with Russia amounts to only a tiny percentage of total U.S. foreign trade, about the same amount conducted with Chile, the Dominican Republic, Ireland, or Turkey. Trade with countries like Germany, England, Mexico, Japan, and Canada is 16 to 40 times greater than the present trading levels with Russia. These low levels, coupled with weak direct investment trends, suggest enormous growth potential and the need for a revitalized business strategy toward Russia. The Russian-American Chamber of Commerce is poised to contribute its expertise and resources toward that end.

37.7 DEVELOPMENT OF TRADE AND ECONOMIC COOPERATION BETWEEN REGIONS OF RUSSIA AND THE UNITED STATES.*

As part of the liberalization of foreign economic activity in Russia, all Russian regions and enterprises gained the right to directly access foreign markets, including those in the United States. While the regions can now develop direct foreign economic relationships, they do not have sufficient experience to operate independently. Consequently, to assist the regions, the Ministry of Foreign Economic Relations created a special council consisting of representatives from all 89 Russian regions. Over the last 12 months, under the supervision of the Ministry, the regions prepared nearly 500 programs and projects designed to attract foreign economic cooperation. In addition, the group is working to create a special data bank of investment projects to focus on this effort.

---

*This section was written by Alexei S. Gumilevski.

(a) Regulation through Tariffs.   Of the two major means of regulating foreign activity, administrative and economic, the Russian government has been taking full advantage of the administrative method through the use of export tariffs. Using export-tariff regulations, however, is a temporary measure. This is illustrated by the fact that the list of items that carry export tariffs has been decreasing; For example, the number of items with tariffs decreased from 90, in July 1993 to 40 the following year. Only a few items (such as oil and oil products, precious metals, and military equipment) remain on the export-tariff list.

Currently, the council is working on regulations to abolish export quotas, licenses, and tariffs for almost all strategic raw materials. Additional regulations to create economic and trade cooperation continue to be written in Russia on a regular basis.

(b) Russian-American Trade Relations.   On the Russian side, many companies have indicated a growing interest in buying high-quality American products and some high-technology items. On the American side, many companies are acting as effective intermediaries by delivering Russian products to developing countries. It seems that American companies are trying to sell their own goods and services in the Russian market, but are reluctant to export Russian products to their own market. There are U.S. companies marketing Russian mining and raw materials to such countries as Great Britain, Germany, and the Scandinavian nations, but not to America.

(c) Role of American Investors.   Research has shown that American businesspeople prefer to invest in small and medium-sized projects that require minimal capital and have the potential for quick returns. So far, they have avoided participation in long-term projects, particularly those requiring new facilities, because they view them as too risky. Also, the Americans prefer to create wholly owned companies in Russia rather than joint ventures.

(i) Where Are Americans Investing?   An analysis of 1,500 Russian-American joint ventures throughout Russia identified the most active areas for investment as Moscow, St. Petersburg, and three Russian-Pacific regions (Khabarovsk, Primorsky, and Sakhalin). Some regions have already developed strong relationships with U.S. companies. For example, in the Russian-Pacific region, the percentage of trade with U.S. companies represents approximately 10% of all foreign-economic activity. Most of the American companies act as intermediaries in trade transactions connected with the export of Russian raw materials. This is also the case with joint ventures in the Murmansk, Kamchatka, and Sakhalin regions.

(ii) What Are Americans Investing In?   U.S. businesses have established very few ventures in Russia's machinery, building, and high-tech industries. It should also be noted that a decree (No. 1,108) was signed in September 1994 to encourage foreign economic activity in Russia, which should also enhance and stimulate additional relationships.

(d) U.S. Government and Russian Military Partnership.   A very important development for Russian-American trade has been a memorandum issued jointly by the Russian Ministry of Foreign Economic Relations and the U.S. Trade and Development Agency. The memorandum calls for the United States to finance feasibility studies for select Russian projects. Also, the Ministry is preparing high-priority projects in 20 Russian regions, on which, American and Russian companies will work together.

For example, representatives of the Russian automobile union (ABBA) in the Tatar Republic are preparing a project to create two joint ventures; the first will involve General

Motors in the production of vehicles similar to American Jeeps in Elabuga auto plants. The other will result in the manufacture of small cars in the AutoVaz factory. Beyond that, several American investors are now preparing financing methods for joint projects with Russians within the lumber, paper, and pulpwood industries as well as for the timber trade.

On the same day the U.S.-Russian cooperation memorandum was signed in Washington, a second one was signed with the U.S. Department of Commerce for cooperation in developing business-information services with the Overseas Private Investment Corporation (OPIC).

According to these documents, various Russian ministries and American legislative bodies are working together to create a center for the exchange of economic expertise and information with the U.S. Department of Commerce. Additionally, the Russian-American Committee for Trade Development is creating several other business centers in Russia that will help American companies establish trade and investment relationships with Russian companies in the regions.

APPENDIX 37A
FINANCING AND INSURANCE AGENCIES
OF THE U.S. GOVERNMENT.*

The following are brief outlines of the operations of the Export-Import Bank (Ex-Im Bank), the Overseas Private Investment Corporation (OPIC), the Small Business Administration (SBA), and the Trade and Development Agency (TDA). Contact these agencies for more details.

(a) Export-Import Bank.   At present, Ex-Im Bank is willing to extend insurance, guarantees, and credits based on export-contract security arrangements, limited-recourse project risk, Russian sovereign risk, and on an exceptional basis, private-commercial-bank risk. Ex-Im Bank has specific arrangements to provide financing assistance for purchases of oil and gas equipment and forest products.

Contact: NIS Loan Officer, 202–565–3801 or 3815

(b) Overseas Private Investment Corporation.   OPIC offers a number of programs to insure U.S. investment against the risks of currency inconvertibility, expropriation, and political violence. Medium- and long-term financing for investment projects is available through loan guarantees and direct loans. Total OPIC assistance in Russia stands at $3 billion in financing and insurance, six OPIC-backed private-equity funds have a total capitalization of $1.2 billion to invest in the region.

Contact: OPIC InfoLine, 202–336–8799; for faxed information, OPIC FactsLine, 202–336–8700; E-mail address: OPIC/S=INFO@mhs.attmail.com.

(c) Small Business Administration.   The SBA has teamed up with the Russian government's State Committee for the Support and Development of Small Business to help American small businesses establish strategic alliances with partners in Russia. The SBA offers financial assistance through the Export Working Capital Program, International Trade Loans, and other loan guarantees.

Contact: Office of International Trade, 202–205–6720.

---

*This appendix was written by Jan M. Kalicki.

(d) U.S. Trade and Development Agency.   The TDA assists U.S. companies in planning for infrastructure and industrial projects by providing funding to allow U.S. firms to carry out feasibility studies. The subject project must be a Russian priority, have significant U.S. export potential, and have financing available. There also must be strong international competition for the project, and the U.S. firm must share the feasibility-study cost.

Contact: Regional Director, NIS, 703–875–4357.

APPENDIX 37B
COMMERCIAL SERVICE OFFICES
AND AMERICAN BUSINESS CENTER LOCATIONS.*

*Almaty, Kazakstan***
phone: 7 (3272) 636–618; fax: 7 (327) 581–1578
Chelyabinsk, Russia
phone: 7 (3512) 623–782; fax: 7 (3512) 623–768; E-mail: abc@ibm.urc.ac.ru
Khabarovsk, Russia
phone: 7 (4212) 332–800; fax: 7 (4212) 332–971; intl. phone: 7 (509) 014–9059; intl. fax: 7 (509) 014–9041; E-mail: abc@abc.khabarovsk.su
*Kiev, Ukraine***
phone: 380 (44) 219–1168; fax: 380 (44) 417–1419; intl. phone: 380 (44) 230–2653; intl. fax: 380 (44) 230–2659; E-mail: hmayovsk@doc.gov
Moscow, Russia (only Commercial Service office, no American Business Center)
phone: 7 (095) 255–4660; fax: 7 (095) 230–2101; intl. phone: 7 (502) 224–1105
Nizhnevartovsk, Russia
phone/fax: 7 (3466) 224–407; E-mail: allan@abcent.vartovsk.su
Nizhny Novgorod, Russia
phone/fax: 7 (8312) 372–213; E-mail: abcnn@abc.nnov.su
Novosibirsk, Russia
phone: 7 (3832) 235–569; fax: 7 (3832) 235–762; E-mail: abc@saic.nsk.su
*St. Petersburg, Russia***
phone: 7 (812) 110–6042; fax: 7 (812) 311–0794; intl. phone: 7 (512) 850–1900; intl. fax: 7 (512) 850–1901; E-mail: abcspb@sovam.com
*Tashkent, Uzbekistan***
phone: 7 (3712) 332–880; fax: 7 (3712) 330–597; intl. phone: 7 (3712) 891–705; intl. fax: 7 (3712) 891–676; E-mail: office@csabc.silk.glas.apc.org
*Vladivostok, Russia***
phone: 7 (4232) 300–093; fax: 7 (4232) 300–092; intl. fax: 7 (509) 851–1212; E-mail: abcvlad@sovam.com
Volgograd, Russia
phone: 7 (8442) 335–946; fax: 7 (8442) 362–732; E-mail: abcv@abc.tsaritsyn.su
Ekaterinburg, Russia
phone: 7 (3432) 564–623; fax: 7 (3432) 564–524; E-mail: abc_yekat@msn.com
Yuzhno-Sakhalinsk, Russia
phone/fax: 7 (4242) 223–142; intl. phone: 7 (509) 951–545; intl. fax: 7 (509) 951–540; E-mail: abc@abc.sakhalin.su

---

*This appendix was written by E. Vivian Spathopoulos.
**Indicates colocation with the Commercial Service.

For an updated list of contact numbers, call: voice mail: (202) 482–4655, option 21; FlashFax: (202) 482–3145, document #7022; homepage: http://www.itaiep.doc.gov/bisnis/abc/abc.html

Participation by the Department of Commerce in this publication does not imply endorsement by the Department of the services offered by the publisher over those of similarly situated U.S. companies or organizations.

CHAPTER 38

FOREIGN INVESTMENT

Mikhail U. Kopeykin, Andrey A. Konoplianik, Vitaliy B. Malkin, Mikhail M. Boguslavskiy, and Vladimir I. Resin

38.1 GOVERNMENT INVESTMENT POLICY.* The main objectives of the state investment policy (and the mechanisms for its realization that are aimed at the stimulation of investment) have been defined in a number of documents. These documents include various decrees and an address by the president of the Russian Federation, the state program reforms and Development of the Russian Economy in 1995–97, the Concept of State Investment Policy for 1995–97, provisions issued by the government, and other legislative acts.

The state investment policy is based on the assumption that to revive investment activity in 1997 and beyond, it is necessary to provide for the steady flow of investments of private capital, primarily in the form of capital for large national corporations. These companies have adjusted to market conditions and are capable of realizing effective profits from invested funds, increases in real income, and savings.

An important condition for the activation of the investment process is the formation of a favorable investment climate. Meeting this condition heavily depends on creating the necessary legislative basis. It should be emphasized that active market reforms have started in a legislative vacuum and without the required legal basis for investment activities.

Recently, the Russian government created a system of legislative norms and acts to regulate investment processes in a market economy. In 1996, a legislative package was prepared, including a draft of the federal law Amendments and Additions to the Law on Investment Activities in the Russian Federation. The draft integrated all existing legislative norms and is aimed at increasing investment activity in the economy.

In order to provide incentives for private investors, a presidential decree was issued in January 1996 that provided amendments and additions to the an earlier presidential decree (September 17, 1994) entitled Private Investments in the Russian Federation. Also, a governmental provision Additional Stimulation of Private Investments Russian Federation was issued of May 1, 1996. These documents stipulate three forms of state support for investment projects selected on a competitive basis:

- Providing federal funding on a reversible and paid basis;
- Securing a portion of shares of newly established joint-stock companies as state property;

---

*This section was written by Mikhail U. Kopeykin.

- Providing state guarantees for partial compensation of a lost investment in case an investment project is canceled due to reasons other than the fault of the investor.

Currently, a provision for classifying and estimating the quality of the projects submitted for the competition is in progress. Criteria for their selection are being refined.

Taking into account the importance of the amortization of fixed capital for the activation of investments, a plan for a new amortization policy is being developed, which is designed to substantially strengthen the reproductive potential of enterprises. These changes in amortization policy will be reflected in a draft of a Tax Code that is currently underway.

In order to stimulate enterprises to use their profit for investment, tax breaks on that portion of the profit that is directed to the technical development of production would be continued (the law On Amendments and Additions to Individual Laws on Taxes in the Russian Federation December 22, 1992, no. 4178; presidential decree no. 2270, Some Changes in Taxing and Relationships Between Budgets of Different Levels, December 22, 1993, no. 2270). A package of norms and legal documents has been prepared to stimulate the dynamic development of leasing activities, including a draft of the Federal Program on Leasing Development in the Russian Federation in 1996–2000. Also, the drafting of several basic bills on investments is imminent. Among these are amendments and additions to the law on foreign investments, a bill on free economic zones and, amendments to tax and customs legislation.

In 1996, the situation in the investment sphere, however, continued to be complex. Despite all of the measures that were taken, investment activities continued to decline.

According to data assembled by the Federal Committee on Statistics (Goskomstat), the total amount of investment in 1996 was 370 trillion rubles, which was lower than 1995 by 18%. In 1996, 73% of the total investments were directed to the nonstate sector, while in 1995 its share was 68%. A total of 146 trillion rubles, or 59% of the level of the previous year, was invested in the construction and reconstruction of enterprises, and 150 trillion rubles, or 41% of all investments, went to the social sector. In comparison with those of 1995, these investments declined by 18%.

The state investments that were mandated by the federal investment program in 1996 were financed in small amounts. For example, during the first 10 months of 1996 only 15.76 trillion rubles, or 54% of the estimate, were invested. The funds that were designated to be distributed on a competitive basis among commercial projects with fast returns were not provided.

The dismal investment picture is hindering the structural transformation of the economy and is aggravating production problems. In addition, the budget's capacity to finance investments is quite limited. In the meantime, private investors still cannot compensate for the lack of state funding to overcome economic stagnation.

Due to the high risk of long-term investments, the investment sphere is still not attractive to potential investors, who prefer to invest in more profitable and dependable financial assets, including state stocks and securities.

The investment situation should change drastically with the introduction of the so-called development budget, whose funds are targeted only for investment purposes and which was approved for the 1997 federal budget. The revenue part of the development budget will be based on the long-term credits given against guarantees by the Central Bank of Russia. These will include loans from the World Bank. The expenditure portion is designed for the funding of state investments in construction, the support of long-term export contracts, and for credit projects and state payments. Within the framework of the development budget, there is a list of objectives and procedures for providing state guarantees to realize investment projects in 1997. In order to accelerate the implementation of the budget, several legislative amendments will be adopted very soon. Also, it is expected that a law for regulating and managing it will be adopted.

The government has prepared a set of measures to revive the investment process in Russia, the initial results of which are expected to improve the situation. These measures include:

Enlarging the scope of centralized investment resources on a competitive basis;

Developing a mechanism for providing guarantees to investors;

Increasing the role of the state amortization policy;

Attracting foreign capital to the Russian economy;

Developing leasing activities;

Creating a mechanism for strict governmental control over state investments;

Developing a market for stocks and securities;

Attracting the population's savings into the investment sphere;

Organizing, on a commercial basis, a permanent exhibit of investment projects.

Also, further measures to attract foreign investors will be developed, and the process for the adoption of basic investment legislation by the Parliament will be accelerated. These measures are expected to reduce, by one half, import tariffs in their relation to basic tariffs, and for a term of not more than five years in cases where that the investment of a foreign investor is over $100 billion.

The adoption of the legislative acts mentioned earlier, the realization of the program for stimulating domestic and foreign investors, development budgets, and measures to stimulate the investment process in Russia should promote a favorable investment climate for domestic as well as foreign investors.

38.2 CONCESSION AND PRODUCTION-SHARING AGREEMENTS.* Under current conditions in Russia, it is especially urgent to create a proper judicial environment that will stimulate domestic and foreign businesspeople to invest their capital in the Russian economy.

There are three basic ways to attract investments:

1. Deficit financing—when a country provides a guarantee to an investor;
2. Corporate financing—when a company provides a guarantee to an investor;
3. Project financing—when parties engaged in a project provide their guarantee to an investor.

Until recently, Russia has practiced only deficit financing. Corporate and project financing have not been used because of the noncorporate structure of the Russian economy, and also because of the lack of proper laws in the country's legal code.

The privatization process has stimulated the birth of a stock market in Russia. The privatization program and its accompanying laws and provisions form the legal foundation for the transfer of state property to a nonstate investor. Thus, the judicial basis has been laid for corporate financing in the Russian economy.

---

*This section was written by Andrey A. Konoplianik.

No judicial rules exist, however, governing the transfer of that portion of state property that does not fall under privatization to a nonstate investor for temporary use. One possible solution is the introduction of agreements on concessions. Such agreements provide a non-state investor with a right to use state and municipal property (including natural resources) for a fixed term and on a compensatory basis. Also, these agreements empower a nonstate investor to carry out the kinds of economic activity that have heretofore belonged to the state monopoly.

These issues are the focus of legislative proceedings that address the laws on concession agreements and Production-Sharing Agreements. Following the adoption of these laws, investors can finally hope for a stable legislative environment that provides not only temporary benefits to investors, but also necessary long-term guarantees for returns on capital invested in the Russian economy. In return, the state gets a chance to select investors based on the criteria of available and sufficient financial resources, required technology, and the management experience needed for accomplishing the project. Such agreements not only provide a way to record the negotiated terms, but also guarantee that these terms will be maintained while the contract is in force.

The adoption of laws on concessions sets the stage for the state to discuss them openly and forthrightly with investors and come to an agreement with them. This gives greater economic flexibility to the state to efficiently run its nonprivatized property. Thus, the judicial foundation for *project financing* has been established.

(a) Law on Concession Agreements.   Russia's existing system for the legislative regulation of investments (which is related first and foremost, to the use of mineral resources) is based on *public law.* According to this legislation, relationships between a country-recipient and an investor are set by administrative acts of state. The terms of agreement follow the terms declared in those acts.

Therefore, the rules of the game for an investor are set unilaterally by the government, and only the government can change them. Since these rules are unilateral in most cases, any changes by the government do not favor investors' interests. This is why an investor lacks sufficient judicial guarantees regarding terms of the contract, with the government's actions being irrevocable. This condition results in the investor's need to incorporate an extra profit margin into the project to cover possible risks arising from the judicial instability of the agreement. Eventually, this practice damages the economy because Russia receives less profit when investors are forced to compensate for the additional expense and risk.

Under administrative regulation, when one of the parties to the contract (e.g., a state) is in a privileged position vis-à-vis the other one (e.g., an investor), this contradiction of interests can be resolved only if the rigidity of the administration is balanced with the clearly articulated legislation. Such legislation should contain clear and unambiguous procedural norms that are to be abided by and strictly followed. In this way, an investment climate, even though strict and rigid, can be made transparent and therefore predictable.

The situation in Russia today is completely the opposite: the economic and judicial environments are in the process of formation. There is no developed legislation, and the existing laws fail to secure even basic judicial principles. As they currently stand, these laws can be interpreted by government officials in many different ways—and not always to the benefit of the investor.

An influx of investments could be stimulated by the uses of *civil law.* Under an effective civil law, a country-recipient and an investor are equal parties of the agreement, which is considered valid if it is based on that principle. The judicial foundation for regulation on the basis of civil law has been partly laid by the current Russian legislature and further developed in the first section of the Civil Code adopted recently by the Duma. Judicial relations between the state and a nonstate investor, however, require additional and much more detailed regulation. This is the issue the law on Concession Agreements and Others is supposed to solve.

Russia has a history of using concessions. Foreign concessions were widespread in Russia before October 1917, as well as in the early Soviet period. Those concessions played a significant role in the country's economic development and in the restoration of the national economy after the civil war ended in the early 1920s. They were used in manufacturing, mining industries, agriculture, railroad transportation, and other sectors of the economy.

(b) Law on Agreements on Production Sharing. Recently a number of laws and provisions were adopted regulating various aspects of property-related issues, investment activities, taxation, and the use of mineral resources. Nevertheless, the current legislation is characterized by numerous contradictions and is unable to provide proper guarantees and stable conditions to an investor involved in entrepreneurial activities. This is especially true in regard to taxation, for example, returns on investments in crude oil are taxed at a rate of 65%!

Under these circumstances the most vulnerable and exposed party in the process is the nonstate investor. Elsewhere in the world, private capital is the main source (up to 80%) of total investments. The increase of entrepreneurial risk leads, on one hand, to diminishing investment offers and in the flight of capital from the country. On the other hand, this situation forces investors to increase the required level of return on investments.

Corrections are needed in the investment mechanism of the primary (especially mineral) resource industries by introducing more extensive contractual relations between investors and the state. This need arises from the relatively high capital requirements for investment projects in these industries and therefore, for their "higher" cost of risk. Additionally, the mining industry faces another kind of risk, namely, geological uncertainty. At the same time, the mining industry is most attractive to potential investors, domestic and foreign, because of the hard-currency nature of its products. Investors' participation in these projects could improve Russia's balance of primary resources, increase the influx of foreign currency, and aid in maintaining the employment rate.

Agreements on production sharing, which provide a stable long-term judicial foundation for entrepreneurial activity and are widespread in the worldwide exploitation of mineral resources, are becoming the most frequently used production contracts in the mining industry. The advantage of such agreements is their flexibility regarding the specifics of each site. However, the legal basis for agreements on production sharing is the least developed in Russia's legislation: norms that deal with production sharing are not presented at all. Again, investors have to consider that a much higher percentage of their investment is necessary to offset the risk.

This is the reason that virtually all drafts of the production sharing agreements in the oil and gas industries are still in the negotiations stage or have been frozen after the completion of negotiations. The primary law, based on principles of civil law for the regulation of relations between the state and investors, is the law on Agreements on Production Sharing.

This law refers to the agreement between two *equal* parties a concept that can be easily illustrated. One party (the state) owns natural resources, but does not have the financial resources or technologies to develop them. So, the state is interested in transferring the natural resources for temporary use to gain maximum profit (for itself). On the other side, the Russian or foreign investor has all the required financial resources and technologies, and knows how to efficiently develop the natural resources. The investor is interested in acquiring for temporary use those natural resources to gain maximum profit for itself and is ready to assume all expenses and risks.

This forms the basis for mutual cooperation between two parties. Nevertheless, a slight problem arises: the cooperation agreement will not work if it is not mutually beneficial, that is, if it does not bring profit to both the state and the investor. The agreement cannot be the result of unilateral concessions on the part of the state, whereby an investor gains benefits and the state grants them. Rather, the agreement should be based on the conditions of equivalent and fair exchange. It should be an agreement between two equal parties, each of whom is willing to make the necessary mutual concessions in order to secure mutually acceptable terms.

The mechanism for production sharing assumes a mutually acceptable compromise in each project because it is based on the lease principle, not on the taxation principle. Any taxation system is a set of *universalized* payment schedules that investors must adhere to regardless of the objective conditions of their activity. But these conditions can be very different, especially regarding the development of natural resources (e.g., geological conditions). The application of a taxation system oriented to *average* conditions inevitably leads to the undertaxation of one site and overtaxation of the other. Therefore, one investor will gain added profit, while the other will have to fight to get tax benefits so that the project can become profitable. Under any taxation system, the state cuts off those projects whose development is unprofitable unless tax benefits are granted. The result is that the state gains less than it would otherwise.

On the opposite side of the coin, lease payments, which include production sharing are strictly individualized, allowing for specific conditions on each site of mineral resources. Lease payments enable the state to obtain from an investor the optimal price for leasing its natural resources. This optimal state, however, cannot be reached the way adherents of administrative regulation propose—through the unilateral setting of the share proportions by the state—but on the basis of civil law and through negotiations.

The Russian version of production sharing is a combination of the universalized taxation system and the individualized system of lease payments. Under this hybrid system, an investor makes three kinds of payments to the state:

1. Standard profit tax
2. Standard tax on the use of mineral resources
3. Share of profitable product (in accordance with the agreement)

The last type of payment replaces all other taxes and allows the state to take the maximum share of an investor's profit while guaranteeing that he or she still receives a satisfactory return. Defining a mutually acceptable amount of payment and finding ways of establishing it are the key issues in negotiations. This payment allows the state to consider differences in the natural conditions of different sites and to take a profit from a part of the rent paid by an investor. The higher an investor's profit, the larger the share an investor pays to the state. For this purpose, each contract provides different flexible rates for sharing profit. These rates vary depending on the selected criteria, which are listed in a draft of a sample agreement that is one of the documents being prepared on the law regulating production-sharing agreements.

(c) Interests of Regions and Russian Enterprises. The production-sharing agreement is beneficial to the regions in which the sites of natural resources or the companies engaged in the project are located. These regions receive a certain amount of profit tax, payments paid by investors for the use of mineral resources, and a share of the "profitable product." The agreement also benefits those regions where plants and factories that produce equipment for projects are located. Orders for equipment are usually made on a bidding basis. Marketing research conducted by some foreign firms shows that Russian providers of goods and services have a good chance to win such bidding competitions. For example, approximately 50 to 70% of the orders by foreign companies for equipment and services in the oil and gas business are being awarded to Russian enterprises.

This process means that investments will initially and immediately flow to industrial regions, not to the oil regions (or other primary resource regions) where investors have to wait several years until the first oil is extracted and they begin paying for the use of natural resources. In the industrial regions, orders from investors for equipment and services will stimulate production capacities, and local employment will improve regional budgets and relieve social tensions.

Another positive outcome is that the state's aggregate revenues from the equipment-producing regions may equal or even exceed its revenues from the oil regions. For example, according to the development project in the Priobskoye oilfield established by the Russian company Yukos and the U.S.'s Amoco, the state's estimated oil income will be $36 billion for the entire term of the contract. In the meantime, part of the expenses incurred by both investors on orders placed at Russian equipment-producing enterprises may total $60 to 80 billion, which would be twice as much as the oil profits (see Exhibit 38.A).

It is obvious that the first regions to benefit will be those where former defense enterprises, still outfitted with advanced technologies and equipment, are located. In order to win contracts, these enterprises may need support in the event that they meet the technological requirements, but still find the economic conditions too difficult. In such cases, the Russian government could grant tax benefits to these enterprises so that they, instead of foreign competitors, receive the order. There would be two winners—Russian enterprise and the state budget.

Other mechanisms for the protection of domestic manufacturers, such as the introduction of quantitative restrictions on supplies of equipment from non-Russian sources, oppose the state interests of Russia. This protectionist measure will undermine both production and competition: an enterprise that enjoys a state guarantee for government orders will have little motivation to improve production, which will ultimately lead to a decrease in its products' competitiveness. Moreover, prices for these products will rise because they have guaranteed buyers and because mining costs will increase. Therefore, in accordance with the production-sharing agreement, the state will receive a significantly lower share of the final proceeds.

(d) Place of Both Laws in the Current Legislation. The laws entitled Concession agreements and Others and Agreements on Production Sharing belong to the civil-judicial realm and, therefore, assert several principles secured in the Civil Code. An examination of two of them follows.

(i) Interconnection with the Laws Regulating Investment Activity. Current Russian laws are based on the concept of *the national regime of investments,* which sets the same rules for both domestic and foreign investors. The formula of the national regime in Russia is as follows: the law Investment Activity in the Russian Soviet Federal Socialist Republic determines that the regime for foreign investments is defined by the proper special law; that special law (Foreign Investments in the RSFSR) sets the national regime for investors

Exhibit 38.1. Agreements on Production Sharing in the Russian Oil and Gas Industries (currently in different preparatory stages and/or the negotiation process)

Region	Investors		Starting Date of Preparing the Project	Site or Contract Territory	Current Stage of the Project
	Foreign Firms (Country)	Russian Firms			
Sakhalin Oblast	Exxon (U.S.) Sodeco (Japan)	Rosneft Sakhalin-morneftegaz	1976	Chaivo, Odoptu, and Arkutun-Daginskoye sites, shelf of Sakhalin Island (project Sakhalin–1)	Negotiations on agreement on production sharing (APS) completed in April 1995. Entering into effect as soon as the law on APS is adopted.
Sakhalin Oblast AS	Sakhalin Energy Development Co. (Former consortia 4MSH: Marathon, MacDermott (U.S.); Mitsui, Mitsubishi (Japan); Royal Dutch Shell (Great Britain/Netherlands)		1988	Piltun-Astokhskoye and Lunskoye sites, shelf of Sakhalin Island (project Sakhalin–2)	APS has been signed. In effect as soon as the law is adopted.
Sakhalin Oblast	Mobil and Texaco (U.S.)		1993	Kirinsky block, shelf of Sakhalin Island (project Sakhalin–3)	APS in preparation
Sakhalin Oblast	Exxon (U.S.)		1993	Vostochno-Odoptinsky and Ayashsky blocks, shelf of Sakhalin Island (project Sakhalin–3)	APS in preparation

Exhibit 38.1. *(cont'd)*

Nenets A.O., Arkhangel Oblast	Timan-Pechora Development Co. (Texaco, Exxon, Amoco (U.S.) Norsk Hydro (Norway))	Rosneft, Arkhangelsk-geologiya	1990	Timano-Pechorskaya oil & gas province (17.5 thousand sq km): Trebs site, Varandeyskoye site, Titov site, and others.	Negotiations on APS have been completed
Nenets A.O., Arkhangel Oblast	Totale (France)		1991	Timano-Pechorskaya oil & gas province, Kharyaginskoye site	Waiting for adoption of the law on APS
Volgograd Oblast	Elf-Neftegas (France)	Interneft	1990	Southwestern rim, Prikaspijskaya basin (6.5 thousand sq km)	Negotiations on APS completed in 1992. Due to the delayed adoption of the law on APS, Elf-Neftegas quit the project.
Khanty-Mansi A.O., Tyumen Oblast	Amoco (U.S.)	Yugansk-neftegas, Yugraneft	1992	Priobskoye site	Appraisal of technical and economical characteristics; the parties are beginning the negotiations on APS
Khanty-Mansi A.O., Tyumen Oblast	Royal Dutch Shell (Great Britain/Netherlands)	Evikhon	1992	Zapadno-Salymskoye, Verkhne-Salymskoye and Vadelupskoye sites	APS in preparation
Khanty-Mansi A.O., Tyumen Oblast	Urals-ARA (Netherlands)		1992	Khulturskoye and Slavinskoye sites	APS in preparation
Kaliningrad Oblast	RVE-DEA, Veba Oil (Germany)	Rosneft, Kaliningrad-morneftegas		Site #D-6, shelf of the Baltic Sea	APS is ready to be signed

Exhibit 38.1. *(cont'd)*

Republic of Yakutia (Sakha)	OMV (Austria)	Tact	1991	Kempendiajskaya basin (14 thousand sq km), Nepsko-Botuobinskaya Antikliza (7 thousand sq km)	Postponed
Tyumen Oblast	Norsk Hydro (Norway), Fibro Energy, Anglo-Swiss (U.S.)	Varyegan-neftegas		Zolotoi Mamont (Golden Mammoth) site	
Krasnoda Krai	Symskaya Exploration, Inc. (U.S.)	Yeniseigeofisika, Yeniseineftegasgeologia		Symskaya Square	

(with some exceptions) and thus accords foreign investors the same legal status as domestic investors. This means that instead of preparing separate laws for domestic investors and foreign investors, there is a single formula for establishing laws in which the specifics of the national regime for foreign investors may be elaborated.

The investment laws described here do not interfere with the legal relations governing concessions. None of them regulates contractual relations with investors, except for joint ventures, which do not involve the state as one of the partners. Both investment laws set general principles and establish a basic concept for investment activity in Russia. Along with the Civil Code, they can be considered as a legal basis for concessional relations. They cannot, however, replace the law on concessions itself. Moreover, the law Foreign Investments in the RSFSR strictly stipulates the adoption of the law on concession agreements.

(ii) Interconnection with the Laws Regulating the Use of Mineral Resources. One of the main spheres covered by the law on concession agreements is the use of natural resources, particularly of mineral resources. In accordance with the law on mineral resources, these resources are the state's property. As opposed to the law on concession agreements, which regulates the transfer of all kinds of state property to an investor for temporary use, the law on mineral resources sets different standards for such transfer.

In the future, the involvement of the administrative (license) system in Russia should be restricted to a few economic sectors in which—due to the interests of state security—the investor's activity is discharged on the basis of a contract. The outcome of such an approach will be the rigid regulation of the investor's activity as secured in the license. It also will be possible for the state to terminate the agreement without giving an investor any chance to file a complaint, a right based on the principle that "agreement is a part of license." Under this approach it is difficult to grant a license or to transfer the right to the license. Thus, investors in most cases have no guarantees that their investment money will be returned when there are insufficient funds to complete the project.

Given that this approach to licensing is risky for an investor, it does not provide a sound basis for attracting domestic and foreign investors to mining, which is Russia's most capital intensive industry. For example, despite the fact that, as of January 1, 1995, 9,000 licenses were issued for mining projects (including 1,711 for the exploration and development of oil and gas), the industry is still in a desperate need of investment.

It should be the contractual system that prevails in a civil society: the rules are set by laws, and bidding and negotiations are conducted according to established regulations. The system also provides that specific details are discussed by the parties during the negotiations, that the agreement is signed, and that the registering license is issued automatically, again, according to the principle that the license is a part of an agreement. Both parties are equal in the eyes of the civil court. The state gives up its right to immunity in the sphere of judicial relations, which is the essence of the laws on concession agreements and production-sharing agreements. In this way, there will be two—administrative and civil-judicial—forms of regulation simultaneously regulating the use of mineral resources in Russia.

(e) Interconnection of the Two Laws. Each of these two laws has its own sphere of application and subordination. The law on concession agreements is the basic law, while the law on production-sharing agreements is complementary. The law on concession agreements is the basic law embracing all the main issues of transferring rights for the use of state property (realty as well as natural resources) to nonstate investors, as well as covering all of the activities engaged in by the state's natural monopoly. The system of contractual relations in the sphere of mineral resources includes three main forms of production agreements between a recipient and an investor:

1. The concession itself (or agreements involving "tax + royalty")
2. Agreements on providing services (with risk and without risk)
3. Agreements on production sharing

The common ground between the two laws is:

- An agreement is made between the state and an investor;
- The laws are effective for both Russian and foreign investors;
- The nondiscriminatory character of relations with an investor is legally assured;
- A principle of "two keys" (the Russian Federation and subject of the Federation) is applied to the jointly owned mineral resources;
- A special taxation is provided, including guarantees of the taxation regime's stability during the entire term of the agreement;
- The state's relationship with an investor characterized by a contract;
- The state rejects its judicial immunity;
- Investors are permitted to transfer rights.

The differences between the two laws are: the laws differ by the *character* of their action. The law on concession agreements is a frame law that defines the rights and responsibilities of an investor who either has signed a contract with the state for the long-term exploitation of objects owned by the state, or is engaging in an activity that falls under the state's natural monopoly. This law also spells out the guarantees provided by the state to an investor. The law on production-sharing agreements is designed for the exploitation of mineral resources and it contains a mechanism for the realization of the agreement. That mechanism consists of the following steps. First, investors secure the right to develop a mineral-resources site. When the resources are found, a certain percentage of the mining revenue is paid to the state. Investors then reimburse themselves for their expenses and make a profit, which is then split with the state.

In the *sphere* of application, since the concession agreement covers primarily the manufacturing industry, transportation, and the service sector, special attention needs to be paid to the lists of concession objects, the procedure for generating these lists, and a procedure for their revision. Also, the *order of paying profits* within a budget can vary: either immediately after signing a contract (all kinds of uses, including leasing) or after obtaining the first product (under the production-sharing agreement).

Objectively speaking, the law on concession agreements has become a kind of concession code for Russia. It plays the role of the law of direct action for those economic sectors where the contractual use of private investments is possible. And the law takes on an auxiliary function for those economic sectors where a license system for the exploitation of natural resources already exists.

(f) Laws and Investment Climate.   Russia's current economic-judicial environment is unstable because a number of the laws are constantly changing. Under these circumstances, different mechanisms need to be applied to promote the stability of the country's investment climate. Temporary measures—lasting for the first three to five years—for the stabilization of investment projects need to be implemented. Stabilization clauses are of unilateral benefit to investors, but they do not provide them with legal guarantees that the terms of the project will be unchanged during its entire term. (In the mining industry, these terms sometimes are decades-long.)

Such guarantees are possible only on the basis of a civil-judicial approach, according to which any changes in the contract can only be made bilaterally. In such cases, the length of the stabilization clauses can be extended up to the entire term of the project without fear that the state can unilaterally renounce its responsibilities.

The proposed drafts of the laws presume the responsibility of the state for any violation of the contract terms and thus provide investors with the utmost guarantees for maintaining the stability of the agreements for their whole term. In particular, since the production-sharing agreement is a civil-judicial matter where both parties are equal, it becomes possible in the course of negotiations: To get an acceptable profit rate for the investor; to obtain maximum profits and economic advantages for the state, with the understanding that the realization of the project is still possible and profitable to the investor. This is why the production-sharing agreement is a tool to provide a more favorable investment climate in Russia.

In drafting the law on concession agreements as a unique concession code, its authors were striving to overcome the one-sided orientation of the current Russian legislation, along with the widespread but erroneous view that the only basic source of private investments in the Russian economy is its nonrenewable natural resources. The law can help create a huge economic potential. The state enterprises that are to be modernized can be considered as potential objects of concession as can defense-industry enterprises. There is a huge variety of potential contracts with foreign investors in many sectors, including technology, production-sharing, turnkey construction services, and the service industries.

The laws on concession agreements and production sharing agreements contain judicial mechanisms that allow for the development of contractual relations between an investor and the state. These civil-judicial, contractual relations provide equal rights and obligations to both parties. At the same time, the laws do not encroach on the prerogatives of the state as a body of public power. On one side, the state is a partner of the private investor; on the other side, it is exercising control over the investor's activity.

These laws help solve the problem of harmonizing the interests of the Russian Federation and its subjects, as well as coordinating the Federation's legislation with that of its subjects regarding concession agreements.

38.3 REGULATIONS.* According to the Russian legislature, foreign investments cover all kinds of property, including intellectual property, that are invested in by foreign investors for the purpose of entrepreneurial gain, that is, acquiring profit.

Legislation in this regard has not gone unchanged. In the first stage, specialized legislation on foreign investment prevailed because the general regulation of business activity under the new economic conditions had not been completely established. On January 1, 1995, Chapter 1 of the new Civil Code went into effect, and later that year the Russian Parliament adopted Chapter 2 and the law On Joint Stock Companies. This law established that a limited number of stockholders could form a closed corporation, and that all stocks were to be registered.

As a law of general legislation, this law is to be applied to all joint-stock companies, including those with foreign partners. Chapter 1 of the Civil Code outlines the adoption of laws On Joint Stock Companies with Limited Responsibility, Registration of Legal Persons, and others.

---

*This section was written by Mikhail M. Boguslavskiy.

The Civil Code is based on such principles as:

Freedom of agreement

Inviolability of property

Free transfer of goods, capital, and services throughout the Russian territory

The Civil Code guarantees protection of all kinds of property, as well as the rights and freedoms of entrepreneurs. Rules set by the civil legislature are applied to relations involving foreign citizens, persons without citizenship, and foreign "legal persons."

Such legislation is the reason why regulation designed exclusively for foreign investors, including foreign investors that are involved as partners, is decreasing. As for specialized legislation, in 1996 the legal status of foreign investment in Russia was still determined by the law on Foreign Investment in the RSFSR of July 4, 1991, and other laws that date from that period.

This currently active law (1991) is obviously out of date and is criticized inside Russia as well as outside. The most evident shortcomings of the law are its gaps in regulations. Even though the law declares that the purchase of shares, stocks, bonds, and securities is considered as foreign investment, in reality such activities are not regulated by the law because its focus is on establishing and actively regulating enterprises involving foreign investments.

Russia has only recently established conditions allowing greater freedom for investing. According to the law on foreign investments, all investors have the same rights to engage in investment activities.

Generally, one does not need to have a license for foreign investment. However, there are a few exceptions:

To establish an enterprise in which the volume of foreign investment is especially high, the permission of the Russian government is required;

An examination is required for large-scale construction or reconstruction activities;

Ecological, sanitary, and epidemiological examinations are required if a production operation can be hazardous to the environment;

Special rules are applied to establish a bank and carry out insurance activities;

The 1992 law on mineral resources introduced a special regulation requiring the lease of mineral resources, concessions agreements, and production-sharing agreements.

The law on foreign investments applies the national policy to foreign investors. According to it, foreign investors should be granted the same favorable conditions as those applied to domestic investors. Possibilities for exemptions from the national regime exist, but they should be in compliance with this law. Due to political and economic instability, various bills were later adopted, on both the federal and regional level, that restricted some of the rights of foreign investors and enterprises involving foreign investments. To restore stability in this area of regulation, a presidential decree was adopted in October 1993 declaring that restrictions on the activity of foreign investors in Russia can be imposed only by the laws of the Russian Federation and presidential decrees.

Russian laws concerning foreign investment provide guarantees that protect it from nationalization, confiscation, requisition, and other forced measures. The 1991 law on foreign investment declares that foreign investments in the Russian Soviet Federated Socialist Republic were not to be nationalized, requisitioned, or confiscated, except in particular instances outlined by the law when other measures are necessary to protect the public. Russian legislation and international agreements in this regard are based on the following principles:

Forced measures in the field of foreign investment should not be discriminatory;

If foreign investments are nationalized or requisitioned, a foreign investor should be reimbursed promptly, adequately, and efficiently. In other words, the Russian legislation for the first time accepted the widespread international practice of prompt and fair compensation;

Compensation must be paid in that currency in which the original foreign investment was made or in any other currency acceptable by a foreign investor.

In its turn, the Civil Code presumes that nationalization of a foreign investment must be conducted on a legal basis, and that the foreign investor be reimbursed in an amount equal to the worth of the property and other losses.

In establishing joint ventures in Russia, there is no requirement regarding the proportion between domestic and foreign investors, but this requirement is important for granting certain benefits to joint ventures. Enterprises are exempted from customs duty and from the tax on property imported by a foreign investor as an investment in the authorized capital. This exemption, however, applies only within certain time limits set by charter documents. Also, there are some tariff benefits involving oil and gas exported from Russia.

Russian legislation is inconsistent in granting benefits to foreign investors. For example, tax legislation was intended originally to grant enterprises with foreign investments an exemption from profit taxes for two years immediately following the acquisition of the declared profit (tax vacation), and to introduce other tax benefits. Later those benefits were canceled. Following that, the tax vacation was restored, but only for enterprises that involved material-production industries and registered prior to January 1, 1992.

Despite the declaration of the so-called grandfather clause by the presidential decree of September 27, 1993, it has never been introduced. If this clause is not in effect, foreign investors may receive less favorable terms if the laws change.

On January 25, 1995, the presidential decree Additional Measures to Attract Foreign Investment to the Industries of Material Production was issued. Later the decree was followed by a provision concerning the order of making and fulfilling investment agreements. Such agreements are to be made by the state and a foreign company whose contribution to the authorized capital of the Russian organization is not less than $10 million and whose direct investment to production industries is not less than $100 million. On the side of Russia, these agreements are to be signed by the Ministry of Economics.

In accordance with Russia's legislation, foreign investors and organizations with foreign participants can bring legal action at general courts that examine economic disputes (the Supreme Arbitration Court of the Russian Federation and other courts of this system). After the adoption of the Arbitration Trial Code on July 1, 1995, arbitration courts are empowered to examine disputes involving foreign investors and organizations with foreign investments, and disputes based on administrative relations (the so-called administration disputes). Before the adoption of this code, investors could bring an action against tax or customs organs at general courts only, a situation that put foreign investors in an unequal position vis-à-vis their Russian partners. Disputes may also be examined at international commercial-arbitration courts (either permanently acting or ad hoc courts). Decisions of these courts are recognized and executed in other countries because Russia was a member of the 1958 New York Convention.

Along with domestic legislation, the order for examining potential disputes between foreign investors and a country-recipient (e.g., disputes about the amount and procedures for paying compensation in case of nationalization), is outlined by various international agreements on the stimulation and protection of investments. Some agreements offer the possibility to appear at The Arbitration Institute in Sweden or an ad hoc arbitration court initiated by the regulations of the UN commission for the Right for International Trade. Some individual agreements (e.g., with Bulgaria, France, South Korea, People's Republic of China) stipulate the examination of disputes at ad hoc arbitration courts only, at the court of the country-recipient (Cuba, Greece, and Italy), or at the international center for the regulation of investment disputes. This condition applies if the 1965 Washington Convention is effective for Russia (e.g., with Romania, Slovakia, the United States).

(a) Intergovernmental Agreements. According to Russia's 1993 Constitution, generally accepted principles and norms of international law and agreements are considered as a part of the country's judicial system. The role of international legal regulation has therefore increased in recent years. If an international agreement of the Russian Federation sets rules that differ from those declared by the law, then rules of the international agreement take precedence. The approach is similar to the one used in Chapter 1 of the Civil Code. Russia has bilateral agreements on the mutual stimulation and protection of investments with the following countries: Austria, Belgium and Luxembourg, Bulgaria, Canada, Cuba, the Czech Republic, Denmark, the Federal Republic of Germany, Finland, France, Great Britain, Greece, Italy, Korea, Netherlands, the People's Republic of China, Poland, Romania, Slovakia, Switzerland, Turkey, and the United States; 14 of these were signed when the USSR still existed.

Regarding multilateral agreements for investment growth, resolutions passed at the 1985 Seoul Convention are in effect for Russia; the convention also founded the Multilateral Agency for Investment Guarantees. Russia also signed the 1965 Washington Convention order for resolving investment disputes between the state and foreign citizens, but has not ratified it yet.

All international agreements that are effective for Russia are based on the idea of the foreign-investments policy, a set of principles that applies to all of Russia's territories. This policy, however, does not exclude the possibility of more favorable terms for individual territories, and it does not permit the worsening of terms for foreign investors.

It should be noted that, in accordance with Russia's 1993 Constitution, the president is empowered to suspend the implementation of laws created by the executive authority of the subjects of the Federation if the laws contradict federal laws and the international obligations of the Russian Federation.

Thus, the a new Constitution strengthened the international legal basis for observing investors' rights and providing guarantees outlined by international agreements. When domestic legislation is unstable, defining Russia's foreign investment regime in international agreements and securing firm guarantees in it, make the regime itself and the resulting guarantees more stable.

By guaranteeing a favorable policy to foreign investors, the Russian government pledges to provide a fair and equal program for their investments and related activities. Although a proper norm of agreements is declarative, it expresses the state's intention to stimulate foreign investments and to treat foreign investors favorably and equally regarding their rights of possession, management, and termination of their investments. Such an obligation concerns granting to foreign investors Most-Favored-Nation (MFN) or the national policy.

Russia's domestic legislation and international agreements signal the beginning of national policy, which does not exclude introducing in some cases a beneficial policy and determining which industries should attract foreign capital. In those industries, foreign investors can obtain additional benefits. However, there is a possibility of setting limits, particularly by restricting or banning foreign investors from some activities. Certain kinds of activities, however, may receive more permissive treatment in order to preserve, for example, the national security and social order. According to international practice, certain activities can be declared a state monopoly and may be unavailable to foreign investors.

38.4 MOSCOW REALTY MARKET: ITS CURRENT STATE AND PROSPECTS.*
The Moscow region is one of the largest in Russia in terms of its demographic, industrial, scientific, educational, and cultural potential. It occupies a territory of 41,000 square kilometers (0.3% of Russia's territory) and is inhabited by about 16 million people (almost 11% of the country's population). More than a half of these people, 8.7 million, live in the city of Moscow, which lies in a territory of 994 square kilometers.

Such concentration of labor resources reflects the Russian lifestyle over the past few decades, the period during which Moscow was becoming an industrial center. During the transition to a market economy, the imminent, natural trends in the development of the Moscow region were in full swing. Today, it is obvious that the priority enterprises for Moscow are finance, banking, communications, hotel, travel, trade, and the general-service sector. Science and education retain their important role as well. Ecologically hazardous enterprises will soon be closed or moved out of Moscow.

The fact that an increasing number of Moscow's residents are employed in these industries affects the way of life in Moscow and impacts the real-estate market. Demand for housing remains high: apartments and houses of better quality (the so-called European class) are preferred. Private-family houses and estates are being built on a widespread scale. There is also a huge demand for office buildings, spaces for bank offices, stores, and similar enterprises.

(a) Housing Market.   As of October 1996, more than 40% of Moscow's 3.5 million apartments were privately owned (approximately 65% of the Moscow region). The market for apartments includes primary and secondary markets. The primary market consists of brand-new apartment buildings that are offered for sale either by commercial or municipal construction firms. The secondary market is represented by individual owners who sell their apartments primarily through real-estate firms.

The figures show the dynamic development of the housing market. Whereas in 1992, there were 12,000 apartments registered for sale, the next year the number increased to 65,000. In 1995, 10,000 deals were recorded monthly. The average price of an apartment in a standard apartment building went up from $312 per square meter in 1993, to $870 in 1995.

Since 1993, so-called exclusive housing has become increasingly popular. Demand for this class of housing far exceeds its supply, and price for it range between $3,500 and $4,000 per square meter. Investing in the construction of exclusive apartment buildings and houses is today the most attractive opportunity in Moscow's housing market. One-third of all municipal resources is directed to the housing sector. Nevertheless, the problem of nonbudgetary financing is still very urgent.

The local government of Moscow considers the city's housing vouchers very important and strives, therefore, to make them attractive and profitable to both buyers and the city.

*This section was written by Vladimir I. Resin.

The profitability of these vouchers is secured by governmental guarantees designed to involve a significant number of people in housing construction and the purchase of new housing. Taking into consideration the fact that three million square meters of new housing are constructed annually and that one million square meters of five-story apartment buildings are under reconstruction, the Moscow housing market retains its position as the core of the Russian real-estate market.

(b) Market for Small Privatization Objects. Today this market is the second largest, trailing only the housing market, in terms of its size and level of interest shown by Moscow buyers as well as foreigners. The market for small privatization object (commercial real estate) consists of offices, stores, hotels, service firms, among others. The demand and liquidity of these are differentiated depending on their location and function, two of the major factors also affecting the price.

The market for office space has become active since 1992 and is presently flourishing. The shortage of office space in Moscow is estimated at 300,000 square meters. As entrepreneurship has grown and more foreign firms have opened branches in Moscow, the need for office space has significantly increased. Investment in the office-construction business is a promising trend in the Moscow real-estate market.

(c) Market For Land Lots. The land-lot market is riddled with difficulties. Only after the new laws on land had been issued and auctions had been conducted by the Moscow land committee, did it become possible to organize this market and develop it in accordance with buyers' interests.

With respect to the land in Moscow, there is no property. The basis for the land policies of municipal authorities is state-land ownership. In January 1992, a land lease was introduced as the principal form of judicial relationship regarding land. The cession of rights for a long-term land lease is implemented on the basis of bidding at specialized auctions.

Prospective investors, usually through bidding, acquire the right to lease a land lot (for a term of up to 49 years) for the purpose of building on it. (See Exhibit 38.2) After construction is completed, these buildings become their property. The lease agreement provides a priority right to tenants to prolong their lease for a new term (up to another 49 years) and to purchase a leased lot in case the current laws change.

The owners of buildings are automatically given the right for a long-term lease of the occupied lots. The Moscow government guarantees and protects the rights of those land owners and land tenants who obtained their status through bidding and whose rights are confirmed by the special land committee of the Moscow government.

Exhibit 38.2. Results of Some Bids on the Sale of Land-Lease Rights in Moscow

Address	Territory (in 1,000 sq. m)	Price of a lease right (in $1,000)	Price per 100 sq. m (in $1,000)
1–7 Arbat	7.0	3385	48.4
Krylatskoye	83.0	4700	5.7
29 Novy Arbat	19.6	6100	31.1
14–16 Prospect Mira	0.3	125	41.7
33–37 Novy Arbat	8.0	5100	63.8
3 Taganskaya Street	3.0	555	18.5

(d) Market for Large Realty Projects. In March 1995, Moscow participated for the first time in the International Exhibition of Realty in Cannes, where it offered over 50 construction and reconstruction projects. The number of large realty projects that could be of interest to investors is still extensive. The following is a description of some of these potential projects.

(i) Moscow International Business Center (a.k.a. Moscow City) on Krasnaya Presnya. This is a construction site for a unique architectural complex. Several major international corporations have already reserved space for their office buildings here, and the construction of some buildings has begun. The total space occupied by these hotels and office buildings that will be erected in Moscow City, is approximately 2.5 million square meters. A transportation infrastructure connecting the International Business Center with other Moscow districts is to be built. Also, a new subway line will be laid with a stop, Mezhdunarodnaya, in the center of Moscow City.

(ii) Public Center in Nagatinskaya Poima. Construction of this center was started on a area covering approximately 100 hectares (nearly 250 acres). It will consist of an exhibition and business center, supermarket, casino, restaurants, cafes, and so on; the total space will be one million square meters. According to preliminary estimates, the total amount of investments in this project will be $1.5–1.6 billion.

(iii) Underground Moscow (Particularly, a Reconstruction of Manezhnaya Square). Construction of a two-level underground space has begun in the center of Moscow. These two levels will be sites for stores, rest areas, galleries, etc., that will cover 150,000 square meters. The estimated cost of the project is somewhere between of $500 million and $600 million. Among the parties involved in the project are Moscow and foreign investors, as well as foreign companies that provided new construction methods, technologies, and modern equipment. Construction is to be completed in 1997.

(iv) Arbat Knot on Novy Arbat. This project includes a pedestrian zone and additional spaces for stores and office buildings on Novy Arbat; it will also house an underground parking garage for 3,700 cars. Transportation routes will be transferred to the underground level at a depth of 4.5 meters. The Arbat Knot project will be implemented in two stages. In the first, a mall (with an underground infrastructure), in-ground multilevel parking, a business center, and a hotel will be erected. The second stage involves construction of an underground transportation system, which will lie under the current transportation routes, a three-story parking lot, a boulevard ramp, and the renovation of the blocks surrounding the Praga restaurant.

(v) Major Renovation and Reconstruction of the Moscow Historical District Kitaigorod. In this project, several buildings whose total space is over two million square meters are to be renovated. The reconstruction is now in progress, and, the construction of another group of buildings in that area has not been completed yet. Since they were offered for sale in April 1992, more than 130 buildings were sold to individual investors. In 1995 alone, the total amount of sales was 136.5 billion rubles.

(d) Free Economic Zones. In accordance with the presidential decree of July 6, 1993, duty-free zones have been introduced in Russia, in order to attract foreign investors. There are four free zones in Moscow today:

1. Technopolis Zelenograd
2. Sheremetyevo–2
3. Moscow Franco-Port in Vnukovo Airport
4. Franco-Port Terminal in Zapadny Rechnoi

The transformation of Moscow has just begun. Today's foreign investors consider Moscow the largest construction site in the world.

CHAPTER 39

POLITICAL AND COMMERCIAL RISK INSURANCE

Yuri S. Bugaev, Kapitolina E. Turbina, Ruth Harkin, Vladimir Krouglyak, Parry Aftab, and Georgy Urjuzhnikov

39.1 GUARANTEES OF PROTECTION OF PROPERTY INTERESTS OF FOREIGN INVESTORS*

(a) Investment. In accordance with the law Investment Activities in the RSFSR, investments are defined as financial resources, target-bank deposits, shares, stocks, securities, technologies, equipment, licenses, loans, and any other kind of property, rights for property, and intellectual property that are invested in business projects for the purpose of obtaining profit.

Defined by the law Currency Regulation and Currency Control, the concept of "exchange transactions related to the movement of capital" (investment in business projects made in foreign currency) covers the following categories:

Direct investment, that is, investment in the initial capital for establishing an enterprise or investment in an already existing enterprise, in the form of fixed and circulating assets;

Portfolio investment, that is, the acquisition of various securities;

Transfer of payment for the right of property of buildings and other real estate;

Financial loans for a term exceeding 180 days.

(b) Foreign Investment. At the same time, when establishing an enterprise with foreign investors, it is acceptable that their share in the initial capital be made in some form other than financial resources, for example, in fixed and circulating assets, intellectual property, patents, know-how, and so on.

The following categories can be considered as foreign investment:

Acquisition of stocks, securities, and shares in the initial capital of enterprises;

Fixed and circulating assets;

Funds on the enterprise's bank account;

---

*This section was written by Yuri S. Bugaev and Kapitolina E. Turbina.

Property rights;

Short- and long-term loans;

Uncompleted construction, and other investments in material values.

(c) Investment Process.   The investment process is a transfer of a part of the capital of one enterprise to another enterprise that has become an independent subject of entrepreneurial activity. Property rights and rights of investments continue to belong to an owner or a founder (in case another enterprise is established).

As an object that requires guarantees, an investment may represent a total of different individual interests that need to be protected from various risk factors. A person interested in extending these guarantees is an investor, that is, a subject-participant of the investment process.

Investment in fixed or circulating assets, uncompleted construction, and other investments in material values must be protected first of all from an actual loss or damage caused by fire, explosion, theft, and the like. These risk factors are, individually or together, traditionally considered as insurance risks whose unfavorable impact insurance agreements protect against.

An investor obtains the right to participate in managing an enterprise only after making proper adjustments in the founding documents. Until they are related to an investor's participation in the authorized capital, investments in fixed capital or liquid assets are qualified only as trade deals involving acquisition of property and equipment. Thus, the main issue concerning the insurance protection of an investment process is the protection of property interests related to property rights, the property itself, or obligations concerning loan repayment (in case the investment was made with borrowed money).

Another essential issue for an investor is estimating the value of the property to be insured and the currency of insurance. The regulation of foreign currency transactions is within the authority of the Central Bank of Russia. At present, insurance transactions concerning the kinds of insurance mentioned earlier are prohibited between residents (insurers and enterprises, including enterprises with foreign investment) in so far as these transactions involve foreign currency. Therefore, such transactions can be made only in Russian rubles.

According to the law on insurance, the amount of insured property cannot exceed its actual value, which is equal to its balance cost and is defined as the difference between the cost of its acquisition and the actual depreciation.

Short- and long-term loans given by a foreign investor to Russian enterprises may require, first of all, protection from their nonrepayment or late payment by a borrower. If loans are provided in a foreign currency, they should be repaid in the same currency, including the interest. Thus, the major risk of this kind of investment is the nonrepayment or late payment of the loan and the risk related to the limited convertibility of the ruble.

As for other forms of investments, such as stocks, shares, property rights, and intellectual property, an investor is unlikely to be interested in their physical safety. The most essential factor for an investor will be their profitability, which fluctuates depending on economic activities. The profitability of stocks and shares can only be guaranteed, if at all, by the organization and results of economic activities.

Risk for an investor in a foreign country includes situations in which the political regime changes, military actions take place, or civil mutiny occurs. In any of these, investments may be confiscated, destroyed, or damaged. Therefore, an investor should be interested in obtaining the following guarantees:

From changes in legislature;

From nationalization and requisition;

From dramatic changes in the value of currency that would affect the transfer of payments (profits, compensations, etc.) in foreign currency.

Certain contradictions exist in an investment process involving more than one country because of the differences in their general and specialized laws. In addition, a foreign investor's property right relating to property in a foreign country is regulated by the national legislation of that country. Judicial and actual persons have a right to fully possess, manage, and use this property in accordance with the requirements and rules of local legislation. This right is unconditional in regard to real property. As for nonfixed property, including the rights of demand, transportation facilities, securities, and so on, the nature of the owner's rights (including a foreign investor's rights) is determined by the local law. Therefore, the transfer of such property from one state to another changes the content of the right of property.

(d) Protection of Foreign Investment.   In accordance with Russia's current legislation, foreign investors in Russia are covered with complete and unconditional legal protection. Legislation provides guarantees from forced confiscation, illegal actions of state bodies and officials, and assumes that compensation is to be paid in the amount of the cost of damage, including lost profit.

A foreign investor's right to make investments is secured by the law, Property in the Russian Federation, which has been in effect since January 1, 1991. The law declares that foreign judicial persons have a right to own the following entities in Russian territory: enterprises, buildings, and other kinds of property for business purposes stipulated by Russia's legislature. Foreign investments can be made in any projects on Russian territory if they are not prohibited by law.

Foreign investors have a right to make investments in Russia in the forms of:

- Shares of enterprises established together with Russian judicial persons and citizens;
- Enterprises fully owned by foreign investors;
- Acquisition of rights for the use of land and other natural resources;
- Acquisition of other property rights.

The law Foreign Investments in the Russian Federation contains a thesis that states "foreign investments in the Russian Federation are not subject to nationalization and can not be requisitioned or confiscated." However, it continues to say that such measures are allowed "in exclusive cases outlined by legislation when these measures are necessary due to social interests." This judicial duality makes the status of the guarantees mentioned earlier rather vague.

At the same time, legislation provides that in case of nondiscriminatory nationalization or requisition, a foreign investor has a right to obtain compensation in the currency in which the investments were made, in the amount of the actual cost of investments prior to the moment when the official statement on nationalization or requisition was made. Current legislation, however, does not outline a mechanism to estimate the actual value of investments. Nor does it make clear whose competence it is to implement proper procedures and mandate proper repayments.

Along with proper legal norms and obligations that are set by the national legislature of the country-recipient, another efficient form of providing guarantees to foreign investors is bilateral interstate agreements for the encouragement and mutual protection of investments. The role of such agreements is determined by the priority of international law over national legislation, which is subject to rapid changes (especially during economic reform). The Russian Constitution declares that generally accepted principles and norms of international law and international agreements of the Russian Federation are a part of its legal system: "If an international agreement of the Russian Federation sets rules different from those set by the national legislature, then the rules of the international agreement are to be applied."

The goals of bilateral interstate agreements for the encouragement and protection of investments are:

Creating the most favorable conditions for the influx of foreign capital, that is, selecting regimes having Most-Favored-Nation treatment or a national regime that is favorable toward the activity of foreign interests in its territory;

Securing the acceptance by both countries of the obligations to (1) establish permanent legislation that regulates the activities of foreign investors on the territory of the country-recipient; and (2) provide guarantees of protection of rights of the foreign investor in cases of nationalization, expropriation, and other unfavorable actions toward a foreign investor.

The total number of such agreements between Russia and other countries exceeds 25, including 14 that were inherited from the USSR (see Section 38.3, "Regulations"). Some of them, however, have not been ratified by the Federal Assembly of the Russian Federation.

Because these agreements can be applied to the regimes of all investments, they regulate the influx of foreign investment and take into account the interests of a country-recipient. For example, the agreement between the governments of the Russian Federation and the United States concerning the encouragement and mutual protection of investments was signed in Washington in 1993. This agreement is currently pending ratification by Russia's Federal Assembly.

The subject of the agreement is the regulation of activities of judicial persons instituted in accordance with Russian and U.S. legislation, irrespective of capital sources, except for judicial persons who are controlled by third-party persons. The agreement also addresses organizational and judicial forms and activities, as well as situations involving citizens making investments in the Russian Federation or the United States.

Operators are treated according to the national regime, except in certain industries and activities that require the regime of Most-Favored-Nation treatment. Simultaneously, these obligations are burdened with a clause concerning nondeterioration of the regime of fixed investment.

An appendix to the agreement lists exemptions, including on the part of the Russian Federation, insurance, banking, air transportation, acquisition of state and municipal property in the course of privatization, and others. In addition, the parties retain the right to conduct expropriation or nationalization in case of social need, on a nondiscriminatory basis, with prompt repayment of adequate and efficient compensation in the amount of the market value of the investment. The agreement also contains governmental guarantees on convertibility, on market-exchange rates and conversion related to investment, including profits, compensations, returns, additional inputs into capital for supporting and enlarging production.

One of the essential parts of the agreement is the Russian government's recognition of the transfer of rights of foreign investors to the Overseas Private Investment Corporation

(OPIC) in instances that, according to the agreement and OPIC, qualify as insurance cases. Such cases carry the obligations of OPIC concerning compensation for damage to the property of U.S. investors in Russia.

After four years of OPIC's involvement with insurance guarantees for U.S. investors in Russia, it is safe to say that no insurance payments were made that changed the evaluation of Russia's investment climate. Existing data show that there has been no need to use the insurance measures against political risks relating to investment in Russia by the Multilateral Investment Guarantee Agency. Thus, the interests of foreign investors in Russia in securing their investments against political risks are protected by the Russian legislature, activities of OPIC-type national guarantee agencies, and private insurance companies such as AIG and Lloyds.

39.2 THE CHALLENGES OF INVESTING: OPIC'S ACTIVITIES AND HOW ITS PROGRAMS CAN ASSIST U.S. COMPANIES.* The Overseas Private Investment Corporation (OPIC) is an important agency for any American company thinking about establishing its own business or partnership overseas. Since its founding in 1971, OPIC has been the key U.S. government agency to encourage American private businesses to invest in emerging economies and, since 1993, in Russia. Based in Washington, D.C., the self-sustaining agency assists American investors in Russia and 140 other emerging economies by providing medium- to long-term financing and political risk insurance at market rates.

Opening new markets for U.S. businesses is central to the Clinton administration's foreign policy objectives. By helping to mitigate the risks of doing business in emerging economies, OPIC makes it possible for American companies—small, medium, and large—to pursue investment opportunities and open new markets around the globe for American goods and services.

OPIC believes that ensuring the competitiveness of American companies in emerging economies is crucial to growing the U.S. economy at home. In the 1996 fiscal year, OPIC's support leveraged $23.4 billion in American investments in emerging economies. These investments are expected to create 30,000 American jobs and generate $9.6 billion in U.S. exports. For host countries, the OPIC-supported investments will create nearly 65,000 jobs and generate $11 billion in local procurement.

American investors entering the Russian market face a whole host of obstacles not unlike the ones they face in other emerging economies. The Russian tax system, for example, has been subject to constant changes and is often discriminatory toward foreign investors. Still lacking is a single coherent set of laws governing foreign investment. Clear contract and property rights, as well as an effective dispute-resolution mechanism, also remain to be developed.

Over the years, however, the Russian government has gained a greater understanding of the needs of foreign investors, and is currently at work on resolving these critical issues. In the meantime, patient and tenacious American investors have been successfully tapping into Russia's vast investment potential in numerous industrial and service sectors.

(a) OPIC in Russia. For American private investors doing business in Russia, OPIC has provided, in the past three years, more than $3 billion in financing and political risk insurance to more than 75 U.S. private ventures. (See Appendix 39A at the end of this chapter).

OPIC's large portfolio in Russia reflects the high priority that the Clinton administration has placed on strengthening the relationship between the United States and Russia,

---

*This section was written by Ruth Harkin.

and on assisting Russia's economic development and its transition to a market economy. OPIC's involvement also reflects the wealth of investment opportunities that are available all across Russia for American private investors in a variety of sectors.

OPIC can provide up to $400 million in financing and political risk insurance to a single project created by an American private investor. The agency provides medium- to long-term, limited-recourse project financing with loan maturities ranging from 5 to 15 years, and sometimes longer for infrastructure projects. OPIC also provides direct loans to smaller ventures, ranging from $2 to $10 million, and loan guaranties of up to $200 million for a single project. Although specific rates vary from project to project, OPIC generally charges about four to five points over the U.S. Treasury-bill rate for projects in Russia.

Six OPIC-backed equity funds—which are privately owned and privately managed— are also available to make investments in Russian ventures. Together, they have a total target capitalization of $1.2 billion. Because these funds are able to leverage about nine private dollars for every one the fund invests, they are particularly effective tools for expanding the flow of private-equity capital to a region where the United States has a strong foreign policy interest.

Project sponsors can also purchase political risk insurance from OPIC to cover against risks of political violence and expropriation. In mid-1995, OPIC began offering currency-convertibility coverage on a limited basis. OPIC is now offering full currency-inconvertibility insurance coverage in Russia, a further affirmation of the stability of the Russian financial markets. OPIC encourages long-term investments by offering coverage of up to 20 years. Its premiums are generally about 1.5% of the insured amount for all three coverages combined.

Moreover, OPIC assists American investors by acting as their advocate as they conduct, or seek to conduct, business in Russia. One of the important vehicles for this has been the U.S.-Russian Joint Commission on Economic and Technological Cooperation (more popularly known as the Gore-Chernomyrdin Commission), led by Vice President Gore and Prime Minister Chernomyrdin. OPIC has been a key participant in the commission, working to expand and strengthen commercial ties for the mutual benefit of the private sector in Russia and the United States.

Since OPIC made its first loan in Russia to Polar Lights, the first new oilfield to be developed by a U.S.-Russia joint venture, its activities in Russia have grown tremendously. In 1996, OPIC was involved in 43 projects in Russia—a record year for OPIC—providing $1 billion in financing and political risk insurance. Reflecting the agency's diverse Russian portfolio, these projects were in a number of sectors, including agriculture, finance, manufacturing, oil and gas, and real estate.

Significantly, telecommunications projects, ranging from satellite communications to cellular telephone networks across Russia, constituted half of OPIC's projects in 1996. The agency is excited about these projects because, second to natural resources, telecommunications is recognized as one of Russia's most promising industries.

A number of small and medium-sized U.S. companies are successfully taking advantage of investment opportunities in Russia with OPIC support. A small Southern California-based company, for example, found a profitable niche in the Russian telecommunications market. With OPIC insurance, the company is operating a satellite earth station in Moscow, providing international telecommunications and data services from Russia to the world through its international gateway switch in New York City. The company's services enable a person in Moscow to dial anyone in the United States as if the call were being made from New York City. Launched in 1993 with just four customers, the company now claims more than 100 companies as clients and expects further growth. In 1996, it was recognized as the Small Business of the Year by the American Chamber of Commerce in Russia.

A Minnesota-based food-processing company is bringing U.S. meat-processing technology to its plant in a small town just outside of Moscow. Producing beef and pork products for the Moscow metropolitan area, the facility includes a training center, where Russian students receive training in meat-processing management.

At the fourth Gore-Chernomyrdin Commission meeting in Moscow, in December 1994, it was announced that OPIC was prepared to commit up to $500 million in resources to support U.S. companies wanting to invest in the defense-conversion sector in Russia and other countries of the Newly Independent States. OPIC has more than met its goal, with projects that include a venture by a Washington State consortium of small businesses for the operation of stevedoring and log-merchandising services at a former naval port in the Lhabarovsk region in the Russian Far East. OPIC is also providing insurance and financing support to Pratt & Whitney's joint venture to produce commercial aircraft engines in the Perm region.

OPIC also supports projects in Russia that utilize careful design and state-of-the-art technology to protect the country's environment. For example, the OPIC-insured Coca-Cola project in Moscow has completed an upgrade of its wastewater-treatment plant to reduce wastewater discharges. Also advanced process controls and state of the art waste-treatment systems used by Mars Incorporated have resulted in a significant reduction of air and water emissions.

For the first time in Russia, Western computerized environmental-monitoring equipment will be used by the Omolon gold mine in Magadan to track environmental conditions in and around the mine. These projects demonstrate that U.S. industry can provide a positive model for sustainable industrial development in Russia.

There are tremendous investment opportunities in Russia for American investors in a wide variety of sectors, including natural resources, energy, transportation, telecommunications, food processing, manufacturing, and pharmaceuticals. Moreover, these investment opportunities exist in regions all across Russia—beyond Moscow and St. Petersburg—in Siberia, the Urals, and the Russian Far East, to name a few.

(b) Conclusion. The Russian government is eager to attract greater American private investment to the country, and to be more receptive to the concerns of American investors. In addition to continue providing the services that American investors in Russia have found invaluable, OPIC will continue to engage in constructive and substantive dialogue with Russian officials to ensure that American investors can successfully engage in business in Russia.

39.3 INSURANCE MARKET.* The development of commercial insurance in Russia can be divided into several stages. The first stage, from 1988 to 1992, marks the emergence of insurance companies. During this period, the government developed procedures for licensing, and companies gained experience in operating time, conditions, and rules. Insurance companies trained personnel, developed domestic markets, and worked to create contacts with foreign insurers and reinsurers.

The second stage, in 1993 and 1994, was characterized by dangerous experiments in the insurance of bank credits. This practice was used as a vehicle to defraud clients and resulted in dozens of bankruptcies, as well as a general weakening of banks, events that created a negative attitude toward insurance as a whole. The third period, from 1994 to 1995, was marked by an increase in "reciprocal" insurance, whereby the majority of insurers

---

*This section was written by Vladimir Krouglyak.

became large cash registers for paying out earnings to workers. This practice was opposed by tax authorities, but it enabled many insurance companies to get on their feet.

The insurance industry is starting to mature in its fourth stage, which started in 1996. This stage is characterized by concentration, merging, and specialization according to types of insurance and regions. As Russia's economic and political situation stabilizes and prosperity increases, the prerequisites for the development of life insurance are gradually appearing.

(a) Obstacles Facing the Insurance Industry.   Currently, a large number of obstacles remain to prevent the dynamic growth of insurance operations. As a result, traditional types of voluntary insurance in use throughout the world, such as fire, flood, and liability insurance, do not yet occupy leading positions in Russia, although their growth is apparent.

Some operations use a form of insurance that in essence is not insurance, for instance, insurance systems for paying wages as a method of avoiding excess taxation. There is also interest in obligatory types of insurance, which are vehicles that automatically give a company guaranteed income from the government budget. Currently, many enterprises are indebted to their employees for wages, an economic condition in which insurance is a luxury, rather than a common commodity.

There is a general loss of faith in insurance in Russia and, in fact, the insurance process itself is not well understood.

(b) Insurance Companies Currently in Operation.   Before 1996, about 3,000 insurance companies were registered in Russia. The complex economic situation forced many to close their operations, so that, only about 1,700 companies remained at the beginning of 1996. The present financial position of the majority of insurers is weak. However, 10 to 20 insurance companies stand out as good performers, constantly increasing their potential and outdistancing other companies.

One Russian insurance company that is dynamically increasing the volume of its operation, especially in insurance assets, is the Ingosstrakh Insurance Company. Ingosstrakh focuses on traditional types of voluntary insurance and is experiencing success in this field, which permits the company to offer insurance services at a high international level and to retain stability.

Ingosstrakh is the largest financial insurer in Russia. The company's own capital exceeds 500 billion roubles, and the volume of its insurance reserves comprises about one-fifth of all insurance reserves of Russian insurance organizations.

(c) Insurance Union.   In 1996, all the active Russian insurers joined a unified All-Russian Union of Insurers. The All-Russian Union of Insurers has the following primary tasks:

Achievement of general goals in the sphere of legislation

Coordination of cooperation with the Federal Service of Russia for Surveillance of Insurance Activity (Rosstrakhnadzor)

Presentation of the interests of insurers to bodies in power

Creation of a consulting center for insurers

Creation of a training center that can promote, at various levels, an exchange of information among insurers and the training of qualified personnel

Analysis of the general state of the Russian insurance market and the development of types of insurance and the degree of insurance coverage

Development of valid ratings of insurance companies

Creation of subdivisions for actuarial calculation

Development of typical rules for various types of insurance to accomplish the unification of assigned insurance services

Cooperation with the insurance unions of foreign countries

Development of interaction with subdirectors of Russian insurance brokers

39.4 DEVELOPMENT OF THE INSURANCE MARKET.*   By the middle of 1996, more than 2,500 government licenses had been issued for prospective insurance businesses in the Russian Federation. According to official data, however, there are fewer than 1,900 insurance companies actually reporting any business activity. During the 1995 calendar year, the Federal Service of Russia for Surveillance of Insurance Activity (Rosstrakhnadzor) received and correlated information from 1,673 insurance company business reports.

Of the aggregate insurance premiums collected on voluntary and compulsory types of insurance in the Russian Federation, personal insurance accounts for nearly 16.7%; liability insurance 1.9%; and compulsory forms of insurance, including health insurance, 28.4%. The Russian insurance market is still very conservative, with experienced insurance and reinsurance companies being very selective about the risks being insured.

There are currently about 30 professional reinsurance companies operating in the Russian Federation reinsurance market. The largest source of premiums came from property insurance, while the remaining premiums were from personal, liability, and compulsory insurance. During the first half of 1996, the total volume of operations in the Russian reinsurance market exceeded one trillion roubles. Because of the currently high profitability of reinsurance and the insurance market generally, national insurers prefer to allocate most part of risks among each other, rather than with international professional reinsurance organizations.

In general, largely because of their conservative underwriting standards, Russian insurance companies currently have more reserves and capital than many reinsurance companies. At this time, only about 25% of the insurance underwritten in Russian is reinsured. The Russian share of this reinsurance market is approximately 40%, while the Western share is by estimated to be approximately 60%. (According to another source, there might have been more than one-and-a-half trillion rubles transferred into reinsurance abroad.)

While the size and amount of reinsurance operations are smaller than direct insurance operations, the rate of growth of reinsurance operations is much higher than those of direct insurance operations. In addition, the premiums charged for reinsurance have increased fourfold over the previous year, while the premiums for direct insurance have increased only threefold during the same period. This increase is especially apparent in property and liability insurance, where with the total growth of premiums of reinsurance is almost double that of direct insurance.

In 1995, besides continuation of some trends of the previous years, some restructuring of the insurance portfolio took place. First of all, there was a significant increase of the share of proceeds on compulsory types of insurance—from 6% in 1992 when compulsory insurance of the property of citizens and passengers first began, to 30% in 1995, 80% of which is attributed to compulsory medical insurance. The share of personal insurance has also increased considerably—from 31% of voluntary insurance in 1992, to 74% in 1995, 80% of which is attributed to life insurance.

---

*This section was written by Parry Aftab.

Life insurance, however, differs in Russian from its Western counterpart. Russian life insurance in typically has a one year or less term, which accounts for the substantially declining proportion of the entire life insurance market. The remaining market for life insurance, with terms exceeding one year, is highly dependent on market conditions and is generally linked to insurance provided by the employers.

The structure of the aggregate portfolio of premiums in the Russian insurance market shows contradictory trends, caused by significant changes in society and its laws. The instability of the latter is making the insurance industry more complicated.

The privatization of property in the Russian Federation, and the formation of modern entrepreneurial structures have not yet been accompanied by the sales of property insurance to entrepreneurs and private owners. Property insurance for legal entities is still voluntary. At the same time, insurance of leased municipal property is becoming more popular, when the lessee is obliged to insure it at its own expense. Also growing is compulsory insurance of owners of real property included in the city real property fund, as well as voluntary privileged insurance of real property owners living in coops.

An important event contributing to the development of aviation and space insurance was the creation of the Russian Association of Aviation and Space Insurers in early 1996. It incorporated 23 of the largest insurance organizations in Russia, including VSK, Rosno, Russo-Guaranty, Industrial-Insurance Company, Russia, Leksgarant, Avikos, AFES and others. Its primary task is the standardization of the rules of aviation insurance and methods of defining liability limits in aviation accidents.

The market for vehicle insurance has been rather slack. Most insurers offer vehicle insurance to only their permanent clients, because of customary high losses and frequent fraudulent claims. Also there are no unified organizational and technical methods—no infrastructure—in vehicle insurance industry. A unified code of behavior and policy in the development of vehicle insurance have to be worked out. An impetus to the development of this type of insurance may be the enactment in the near future of legislation requiring compulsory liability insurance for the owners of motor vehicles.

The recent creation of farmers' insurance companies with government financial support is becoming popular. A decree of the Russian government stipulates the participation of the federal budget in the formation of authorized capital stock of such companies. Criteria and the order of selection of the companies to which budget provisions are assigned have been approved. At the beginning of 1996, provisions from the federal budget were assigned for 18 farmers' insurance companies. Support from the budgets of the subjects of the Federation is also possible.

The market for insurance services has considerably changed over recent years. While the number of government insurance organizations is less than 3% of the total number of Russian insurers, their volume of premiums accounts for 15% of all premiums collected. Their market concentration differs substantially from region to region, however.

The most significant act regulating the insurance market is the law About Insurance of November 27, 1992, No 4015–1. On July 14, 1995, the Duma approved a law containing amendments and supplements to the earlier one, but it has not been ratified by the president and is now back in the Duma being finalized. It has to be in accordance with the second part of the Civil Code, which came into effect on March 1, 1996.

The legislative basis for compulsory insurance has been established through several laws covering such insurance for passengers of public transportation, employees of the State Insurance Service, and so. In the near future, passage of a law mandating compulsory liability insurance for owners of motor vehicles is expected. The bill About Insurance Expertise is also under discussion in the Duma.

Government licensing of insurance activity is carried out in accordance with the provisions of the licensing of insurance activity, approved by the Rosstrakhnadzor in May 1994. The current regulatory agency is struggling to determine capitalization and accounting requirements for insurance companies, and a related law recently enacted has been put on temporary hold, until the impact of the accounting rules can be determined.

The current taxation system is not as conducive to the development of the insurance industry as would be hoped and needs to be reformed. This problem will be largely resolved with the reformation of the Tax Code currently underway. In summary, the highly profitable aspects of insurance and reinsurance in Russia make it an attractive market for Russian and Western investors and insurers alike; and there are substantial opportunities for growth and development of this industry, both within and outside of Russia.

39.5 INSURANCE PROTECTION FOR FOREIGN INVESTMENTS.* Any foreign company or enterprise planning on or currently conducting business in Russia has to pay very serious attention to insurance protection for their interests there. Russia is a unique country in many respects, including the insurance business. In spite of the fact that the Russian insurance market has made great progress in recent years, it should still be considered as underdeveloped.

As an example, the number of registered insurance companies increased from 2 in 1989 to about 2,500 in 1996. In reality, not more than 1,200 companies operate on the market, and only about a dozen of these have international experience, a professional staff, and financial stability. Poor capitalization of the majority of Russian insurance companies (70% of the registered companies have authorized capital of less then $40,000, and the average capital is only $130,000) stifles the rapid growth of industrial and commercial insurance because of their lack of capacity and financial ability.

Russian industry has not been active in buying insurance protection for two reasons:

1. For 70 years, industrial property was state owned and did not have to be covered by insurance. Hence, directors and managers of Russian companies have no experience with insurance and lack the basic understanding of its necessity.

2. According to legislation, insurance costs are not considered as business expenses. Therefore, every enterprise has to pay for insurance from its net profit, an expense that few companies can afford while the Russian economy is still struggling.

Therefore, most enterprises that protect their property and liability by insurance are joint ventures with foreign capital, industrial enterprises that have local or international credit, and some private profitable companies.

With this in mind, foreign investors should understand that their investments in Russia will not be insured automatically in the same way they are in their own countries. Therefore, they have to investigate insurance programs in advance as part of their business plan.

Previously, many foreign investors in Russia were buying so-called non-admitted covers (coverage from companies *not* authorized to sell insurance in Russia) from their domestic or global insurance companies. This practice is still allowed to a certain extent, but it could create serious legal problems. The Russian insurance law adopted in 1992 considers insurance coverage as legal only if it is provided by companies licensed on the Russian insurance market. As mentioned, only a few local insurance companies can meet international standards and are reliable in a variety of ways.

---

*This section was written by Georgy Urjuzhnikov.

There is no doubt that the leading commercial insurance company on the current market is Ingosstrakh, in Moscow, which celebrates its fiftieth year in business in 1997. The company has 70 years of international insurance experience, with their first subsidiary, the Black Sea and Baltic General Insurance Company, being founded in London in 1925. With a network of subsidiary companies and representatives in Russia, the Commonwealth of Independent States (CIS), and abroad, Ingosstrakh has the unique ability to provide full insurance service of high international quality to any client.

At the end of the Cold War, trade between Russia and the United States started to grow rapidly and U.S. capital took a leading position in investments to the Russian economy. In following this trend, Ingosstrakh was the first and only Russian insurance company with a registered liaison office in New York in 1991. (The office is INGO, Inc., located at 90 Park Avenue, Suite 1600, New York, NY 10016; telephone number: 212–984–0755; fax number: 212–984–0622, which operates in both the United States and Canada.)

The mission of Ingo is to strengthen Ingosstrakh's business relations with the English-speaking North American insurance market and to provide American businesses making investments in Russia or the CIS, with an understanding of local insurance legislation, practices, and the general environment. In practice, Ingo, together with international insurance brokers and companies, prepares insurance programs for U.S. projects in Russia and the CIS according to local legislation and requirements.

Ingo pays individual attention to each project it handles, which may include ocean and marine programs, land transportation, property, all kinds of liabilities, business interruption, and so on. Such programs have to meet the requirements of foreign investors and their banks, local partners (if any), and Russian laws and traditions. Ingosstrakh in Moscow can then issue the appropriate policies and reinsure back to the North American market a part of the risks required by the client. Such programs were prepared for Conoco, Amoco, Occidential Petroleum, Andrew Corporation, Ingersoll Rand, Amerex, and many other prominent companies, for example.

Appendix 39A. OPIC's Support of Projects in Russia: A Representative Look*

U.S. Sponsor(s) (City, State)	Project Name (Description)	OPIC Support[1]	FY
Oil and Gas			
Anderman/Smith Overseas, Inc. (Denver, Colo.)	Chernogorskoye L.L.C. (Oilfield development in Chernogorskoye, Western Siberia)	$7 million insurance $40 million finance	1992 1994
Citibank, N.A. (New York, N.Y.)	JSC Neftegas (Petroleum refining)	$25 million insurance	1996
Conoco Intl. Petroleum Co. (Houston, Tex.) **E.I. Du Pont de Nemours & Co.** (Houston, Tex.)	Polar Lights Company (Oilfield development in Arkhangel, Western Siberia)	$50 million finance $200 million insurance	1993 1994
Nabors Intl, Inc. (Houston, Tex.)	Sutorminskoye (Workover services on idle oil well in Western Siberia)	$7.2 million insurance	1993
Phibro Energy Production, Inc. (Westport, Conn.)	White Nights (Oilfield development in Perm)	$20 million insurance	1994
Samson International (Tulsa, Okla.)	Ao Pechoraneftegas (Develop new oil wells and increase production at Sotcheymu oilfield)	$12 million insurance	1996
SOCO International—Snyder Oil (Forth Worth, Tex.)	Permtex (Oilfield development in Perm region)	$40 million finance	1994
Texaco Intl. Operations, Inc. (White Plains, N.Y.)	Sutorminskoye (Workover services on idle oil well in Western Siberia)	$10 million finance $13 million insurance	1993 1993
Torch Energy Advisors, Inc. (Houston, Tex.)	(Oil direct investment fund)	$100 million insurance	1996

*This appendix was prepared by Ruth Harkin.

[1]Project commitment amount as reported in OPIC annual reports.

Appendix 39A. *(cont'd)*

Natural Resources

All Alaskan Seafoods (Seattle, Wash.)	New Pollock (Crab-fishing U.S.-Russian joint venture in the Russian Far East)	$80 million finance	1996
All Alaskan Seafoods (Seattle, Wash.)	AAS-DMP Management (Crab-vessel leasing U.S.-Russian joint venture in the Russian Far East)	$13 million finance	1994
Cyprus Amax Minerals Co. (Englewood, Colo.)	Omolon Gold Mining Company (Gold mine and mill development in the Russian Far East region of Magadan)	$67 million insurance $52.5 million finance	1995 1994
Global Forestry Management Group (Portland, Ore.)	SovGavan Port (Sustainable timber harvesting in the Russian Far East)	$10 million insurance	1995
The Pioneer Group, Inc. (Boston, Mass.)	Forest Starma (Sustainable timber-harvesting project in the Russian Far East)	$9.3 million finance $52 million insurance	1995 1995

Telecommunications

Andrew Corporation (Orland Park, Ill.)	Macomnet (Fiber-optic telecommunications)	$15 million insurance	1995
Andrew Corporation (Orland Park, Ill.)	Metrocom-Russian Federation (Fiber-optic telecommunications)	$15 million insurance	1995
Andrew Corporation (Orland Park, Ill.)	RASCOM (Voice-data communications)	$46.7 million insurance	1995
Andrew Corporation (Orland Park, Ill.)	Aerocom (Telephone services)	$7.6 million insurance	1995
Chase Manhattan Bank (New York, N.Y.)	Chase Manhattan Bank International (Financing for 11 separate telecommunications	$52 million insurance	1996

Appendix 39A.   *(cont'd)*

Company (Location)	Partner (Description)	Amount	Year
Direct Net Telecommunications LLC (Newport Beach, Cali.)	Commcraft GmbH (Telecommunications services)	$2.5 million insurance	1996
Direct Net Telecommunications LLC (Newport Beach, Cali.)	Business Sviaz, Inc. (International telecommunications and data services from Russia)	$1 million insurance	1993
Global TeleSystems Inc. (SFMT) (Arlington, Va.)	SFMT-CIS, Inc. (Telecommunications project)	$60 million finance	1994
International Business Communications Systems (Sharon, Mass.)	Russtel (Satellite telecommunications project in Moscow)	$25 million insurance	1994
International Telcell, Inc. (Greenwich, Conn.)	International Telcell SPS (Cable-TV systems in four NIS capital cities, including Moscow)	$25.6 million finance $44.77 million insurance	1995 1992
Mid-Com Communications, Inc. (Seattle, Wash.)	Dial Telecom International (Wire and wireless phone service in the Russian Far East)	$38 million insurance	1994
MCT of Ekaterinburg, L.P. (Alexandria, Va.)	Uraltel (Cellular telephone services)	$5.1 million insurance	1996
MCT of Russia, L.P. (Alexandria, Va.)	SIBERINTELICOM (Cellular telephone services to Chita)	$10.3 million insurance	1996
Motorola, Inc. (Schaumburg, Ill.)	St. Petersburg Telecom (Cellular telephone network)	$42.2 million insurance	1996
Omni Capital Partners, Inc. (Schaumburg, Ill.)			
RPA Leasing, Inc. (Denver, Colo.)	Satellite Telecommunications and Information Systems (Development of a digital phone system in St. Petersburg)	$5.4 million insurance	1993
US WEST	Russian Telecommunications Development Corporation (RTDC)	$200 million finance	1995
(Englewood, Colo.)	(Telecommunications holding company that invests in and operates different telecommunications joint ventures across Russia)	$10 million insurance	1994

Appendix 39A. (cont'd)

Financial Services

Chase Manhattan Bank (New York, N.Y.)	Chase Manhattan Bank International (Revolving-credit facility in Moscow)	$200 million finance	1996
Citibank, N.A. (New York, N.Y.)	Citibank T/O (Expansion of foreign exchange activities)	$11.5 million insurance / $25 million insurance	1996 / 1994
Citibank, N.A. (New York, N.Y.)	Citibank T/O (Revolving-credit on-lending facility at Moscow branch)	$100 million finance	1995
Pioneer Omega, Inc. (Boston, Mass.)	(Privatization investment fund)	$54 million insurance	1996
Pioneer Omega, Inc. (Boston, Mass.)	(Financial services)	$3.9 million insurance	1996
Pioneer Omega, Inc. (Boston, Mass.)	(Brokerage services)	$2.1 million insurance	1996
Pioneer Omega, Inc. (Boston, Mass.)	(Securities registry)	$4.3 million insurance	1996
Pioneer Omega, Inc. (Boston, Mass.)	(Voucher fund management)	$3.3 million insurance	1996

Manufacturing

Cargill, Inc. (Minneapolis, Minn.)	Efremov Glucose-Syrup Plant (Syrup manufacturing plant)	$7.2 million insurance	1996
Continental Grain Co. (New York, N.Y.)	Finaglebex Ltd. (Egg-powder-processing facility in Moscow)	$1 million insurance	1993
Ingersoll Rand Company (Woodcliff Lake, N.J.)	Instrum Rand (Power tool manufacturing)	$12 million insurance	1992
Leathertouch Fabrics Intl. and Mel Sobel (Lafayette Hill, Pa.)	Zarya (Furniture assembly in St. Petersburg)	$4.062 million insurance	1995

Appendix 39A. *(cont'd)*

N C International Company (Seattle, Wash.)	N C International Co. (Mining equipment distribution in the Russian Far East)	$8 million insurance	1994
Paccar International (Bellevue, Wash.)	AO Novotruck (Truck parts distribution in Moscow)	$500,000 insurance	1994
VG Enterprises, Inc. (Shorewood, Minn.)	Meat Plant (Meat-processing plant in the territory of Agrofirm Chapova)	$4.35 million Insurance	1995

Consumer Goods & Services

Caterpillar, Inc (Peoria, Ill.)	(Equipment dealership and repair)	$14 million insurance	1996
Coca-Cola Export Corp. (Atlanta, Ga.)	Coca-Cola St. Petersburg Management (Regional distribution center)	$118 million insurance	1996
Coca-Cola Export Corp. (Atlanta, Ga.)	Coca-Cola Stavropolye Bottlers (Soft-drink and mineral-water bottling plant)	$32 million insurance	1996
Coca-Cola Export Corp. (Atlanta, Ga.)	Coca-Cola Refreshment Moscow (Soft-drink bottling)	$95 million insurance / $105 million insurance	1996 / 1994
Galeo Industries, Inc. (Englewood Cliffs, N.J.)	Galeo Company, Ltd (St. Petersburg fast-food restaurants)	$4.9 million insurance	1996
Great American Life Corp. (New York, N.Y.)	ROSGAL (Life-insurance underwriting company in Moscow)	$351,000 insurance	1995
Kay Khosro Hakakian (New York, N.Y.)	GUM (Department store in Moscow)	$900,000 insurance	1994
McDonald's Corporation (Oakbrook, Ill.)	McDonald's ZAO (Restaurants)	$7 million insurance	1996

Appendix 39A. *(cont'd)*

Mars, Inc. (McLean, Va.)	Master Foods A/O (Food production facility in Stupino)	$200 million insurance	1994
The Reader's Digest Assoc., Inc. (Pleasantville, N.Y.)	Publishing House Reader's Digest (Magazine publishing in Moscow)	$1.89 million insurance	1995
Defense Conversion			
EOSAT (Bethesda, Md.)	PADCO/KIBERSO (Defense-conversion project using satellite images to produce geographic-information systems, maps, and software)	$600,000 insurance	1995
Global Forestry Management Group (Portland, Ore.)	SovGavan Port (Stevedoring and log handling)	$7 million insurance	1996
Lockheed-Khrunichev-Energia Intl. (San Jose, Cali.)	M.V. Khrunichev State Research and Production Space Center (Satellite launch services)	$33.48 million Insurance	1995
PADCO, Inc. (Washington, D.C.)	PADCO/KIBERSO (Defense-conversion project using satellite images to produce geographic-information systems, maps, and software)	$253,000 insurance	1993
Pratt & Whitney (East Hartford, Conn.)	NPO Energomash (Rocket engines)	$50 million insurance	1996
Construction			
Golub & Company (Chicago, Ill.)	Nevsky Prospekt (Office development in St. Petersburg)	$13.5 million finance	1996
Robin Enterprises, Inc. (New York, N.Y.)	Robin Moscow Ltd. (Real estate development in Moscow)	$4 million insurance	1993

Appendix 39A. *(cont'd)*

OPIC-Backed Investment Funds Eligible to Make Investments in Russia

Fund	Sponsor	Target Capitalization (Status)
Agribusiness Partners International	America First Companies	$100 million (investing)
AIG Brunswick Millennium Fund	American International Group Brunswick Capital Management Ltd.	$300 million (investing)
Allied International Small Business Fund	Allied Capital Advisors	$20 million (investing)
CEENIS Property Fund	Auburndale Properties	$240 million (investing)
First NIS Regional Fund	Baring Asset Management	$200 million (investing)
Global Environment Emerging Markets Fund	Global Environment Fund Corp.	$70 million (investing)
Global Environment Emerging Markets Fund, II	Global Environment Fund Corp.	$160 million (raising capital)
New Century Capital Partners	New Century Holdings, Ind.	$250 million (investing)
Russia Partners	Siguler, Guff & Co.	$155 million (investing)

CHAPTER 40

MULTILATERAL INSTITUTIONS

Dmitri V. Tulin, Andrei E. Bugrov, and Vadim Solovyov

40.1 INTERNATIONAL MONETARY FUND.* On January 3, 1992, soon after the fall of the USSR, Russian President Boris Yeltsin sent an application to the International Monetary Fund (IMF) requesting admission of the new Russia into its international organization. After negotiations, a capital quota for Russia was established in the IMF of 2,876 million special drawing rights (SDRs), or 2.95% of the total capital of the fund. On June 1, 1993, Russia became an official member of the International Monetary Fund. The unprecedented events that led to this historic occasion will now be examined.

The first rounds of conversations with experts of the fund were held in March 1992. The Russian government and the Central Bank sent the IMF a memorandum about economic policy that laid out the basic approaches to the country's economic policy for 1993. Because Russia was not yet a member of the IMF, it could not count on the fund for credit. Correspondingly, the main goal of this document included securing not only the financial, but also the moral support of the world community for Russian reform.

The first paragraph of the March memorandum noted that for 60 years, Russia's economy, as part of the USSR, had been subject to rigid central planning. Since the mid-1990s, this system has been gradually dismantled without being effectively replaced by another coherent economic mechanism. Over the same period, enormous macroeconomic imbalances took place. As a result, by the beginning of this decade the economy was in a state of acute crisis, marked by declining output, accelerating inflation, obsolescent capital stock, pervasive distortions of the relative price structure, serious structural imbalance, and severe ecological problems. The move to a democratic form of government in 1991 created conditions in which the root causes of this problem can be addressed. The fundamental economic objectives of the Russian government, outlined in a speech by President Yeltsin on October 28, 1991, focused on achieving a transition to a market economy and macroeconomic stabilization. The memorandum set forth a summary of economic policies that occurred in early 1992 and the outline of the program that the government intended to implement in the last three quarters of the year. The Russian authorities hoped that this bold and comprehensive program would receive adequate support from the international financial community.

Immediately after the official entry of Russia into the IMF, discussions took place about the first credit installment of 719 million SDRs (25% of the quota), or approximately $1 billion at the existing rate of SDRs to the dollar. A new memorandum about economic policy was sent to the IMF in July 1992, and the session of the council of directors of the IMF

---

*This section was written by Dmitri V. Tulin

confirming the allocation of credit was held in August. It was proposed that, in the case of successful completion of the program and a successful solution of the problem of the ruble, Russia would receive a standard credit "stand-by" by the beginning of 1993.

The first paragraph of the July memorandum stated that following the move to a democratic form of government in 1991, the Russian authorities established, as their fundamental economic objectives, a transition to a market economy and macroeconomic stabilization. The memorandum referred to the March 1992 memorandum and reiterated the economic policies for attaining these objectives. The major policy initiatives included:

- The freeing of most prices;
- Gradual increases of energy prices to world levels;
- The development of effective social safety nets;
- The elimination of the budget deficit and the targeting of monetary policy (including moving to a positive real-interest rate) to achieve low single-digit monthly inflation;
- The unification of the exchange system and current account convertibility;
- Various systemic changes designed to introduce the basic institutions of a market economy.

In the July memorandum, the Russian authorities reconfirmed their commitment to these policies, which were at the core of their efforts, over the short- and long-term, to address the serious economic problems that had accumulated over the last decades, and to prevent inflationary pressures from threatening the process of economic reform. They hoped that these efforts would receive the required support from the international financial community.

Fulfillment of the program encountered significant difficulties and, even before the end of 1992, it became clear that an agreement on credit stand-by would have to be set aside. In the spring of 1993, the council of directors of the IMF confirmed a new program of credit called the Systemic Transformation Facility (STF). This program was specially designed for countries involved in system transformations, that is, countries that used a centralized planning system in the past. In May 1993, negotiations were held on the allocation of the first installment of STF credit to Russia—(1,078.275 million SDRs or approximately $1.5 billion). This comprised 25% of the new Russian quota, which, at the end of 1992, was increased to 4,313.1 million SDRs (2.98% of the total capital fund) simultaneously with an increase in the IMF capital. A memorandum on economic policy was sent to the IMF at the end of May and a meeting of the council of directors confirming allocation of credit was held on June 30, 1993.

It should be noted that by April of that year, Russia had signed its first agreement with the Paris Club about restructuring payment, taking into account servicing of the obligations of the former USSR that occurred in 1992 and 1993, which amounted to approximately $15 billion. This agreement included a provision stating that the deal could be declared void if Russia had not reached an agreement with the IMF before October 1, 1993.

The preamble to the May 1993 memorandum on economic policy noted that the fiscal and monetary policies of the government and the Central Bank were aimed at reducing the monthly rate of inflation to single-digit levels by the end of 1993, and at achieving further progress toward price stability in 1994. Other policies, including those related to external trade, the exchange-rate system, and privatization were aimed at increasing the efficiency of the Russian economy, speeding up its integration into the world economy, and expanding the role of markets while taking into account the federal structure of the state.

It was expected that the second installment of STF credit would be allocated at the end of 1993. However, difficulties with carrying out the program and political events in Russia in the fall of 1993 carried their own amendments. Eventually, talks about allocations to Russia of the second installment of STF credit of 1,078.275 million SDRs (25% of the quota), or approximately $1.5 billion, took place in February and March of 1994. A memorandum about economic policy was sent to the IMF at the beginning of April, and the meeting of the council of directors, confirming allocation of credit, was held on April 20, 1994.

The preamble to the April 1994 memorandum mentioned that the main goal of the economic policies of the government and of the Central Bank in 1994 was to create favorable conditions for overcoming the present crisis and revitalizing the Russian economy. The main effort was to be directed to gradually reducing inflation, creating the conditions for the stabilization of production, and accelerating institutional and structural changes. The principal task was to bring inflation down to the level of 7% per month by the end of 1994, and to achieve further substantial reductions during 1995.

An agreement with the IMF about the allocation of the second installment of STF credit was the basis for concluding a new agreement with the Paris Club about restructuring payment, taking into account the servicing of obligations of the former USSR existing in 1994 ($7.2 billion). An agreement with the Paris Club was signed on June 3, 1994.

Negotiations about the allocation to Russia of stand-by credit had already begun in September 1994. In October 1994, however, the abrupt drop in the ruble rate and subsequent acceleration of the rate of inflation led to an extension of the talks. Once this crises had passed, a new memorandum on economic policy was sent to the IMF in March 1995. In April, the council of directors confirmed Russia's application for credit, which comprised 4,313.1 million SDRs (100% of the quota) or $6.3 billion. Discussions with the council of directors on the course for carrying out the program resulted in specific conditions, including the division of credit into monthly transfer installments.

The preamble to the March 1995 memorandum noted that the objective of the economic policy of the government and the Central Bank in 1995 was to create conditions favorable for the recovery and growth of the Russian economy and a sustainable improvement in living standards. To this end, the government and the Central Bank intended to sharply reduce inflation and accelerate institutional and structural reforms while providing an adequate safety net for the population.

Making stand-by credit available was the basis for the next agreement with the Paris Club. Restructuring repayment was taken into consideration in the discussions of the obligations of the former USSR that were due in 1995. The allocation of three-year, extended-fund-facility credit was the basis for the agreement with the Paris Club about the long-term restructuring of the entire sum of payments due for servicing these obligations. The agreement with the Paris Club was signed on June 3, 1995.

40.2 WORLD BANK.* The Russian Federation joined the World Bank for Reconstruction and Development (WBRD) in June 1992. At the time, the bank's authorized capital was $184.1 billion, which was split into 1,840,500 shares, each with a nominal value of $100,000. As of June 30, 1995, the subscribed capital of the bank was $176.4 billion; Russia's share in the bank's capital was 44,795 shares, or 3.06%.

The degree of credit assistance rendered by the WBRD to nation-borrowers is based on the country assistance strategy, which is approved regularly for each country. This program

---

*This section was written by Andrei E. Bugrov.

relies on analyses of the current economic situations in countries interested in borrowing and on their needs for credit resources, as determined by the priorities set by their governments.

The assistance strategy for Russia (ASR) was approved by the board of directors of the WBRD on June 6, 1995. The strategy established the following priorities for the bank's assistance to Russia:

> Providing support for the development of the Russian economy, which is predicated on the private sector's assuming a leading role;

> Strengthening state institutions that promote the development of a free and competitive market and that are oriented toward the creation and development of a institutional, legislative, social, and production infrastructure;

> Reducing the negative impact of the current transitional period on unprotected social groups through support for the creation of a dependable system of social protection, social programs, and additional elements of the infrastructure; special attention should be paid to increasing the efficiency of social expenditures and to creating a more mobile labor market;

> Financing high-priority investments in the state sector, supporting the resolution of urgent social issues, and giving strategic recommendations on key economic questions.

The credit program that was adopted by the WBRD within the framework of the ASR stipulates the implementation of six or seven operations annually with a total budget of $1.5–2.0 billion. The ASR contains a number of terms that, if observed, will lead to the possible upgrading of the volume of credit programs. Among these terms are the following:

> Russian support for the WBRD's operations in the social sphere, including transformation of the system for financing social programs and targeted support for the most vulnerable social groups;

> Russian consent for the WBRD's implementation of an extended program for providing credit to the agricultural sector. The key issue is the preparation of a loan for restructuring agriculture. The main step in the preparation process is an elaboration of the basic concept of agrarian reform for Russia, which will create preconditions for the preparation of investments in agricultural projects;

> Consent on Russia's part to the use of a guarantee on the operations of the Bank. The WBRD believes that the Bank's guarantees for commercial loans will promote investment projects in the fields of energy, infrastructure, and industrial restructuring;

> Resolution of problems related to the preparation and realization of the bank's projects by Russian ministries and governmental agencies. In particular, this will involve the establishment of a single center that will be in charge of the bank's projects, creating (or consolidating, as the case may be) proper departments at ministries, and accelerating the preparation of necessary legal documents.

The volume of the WBRD's loans to Russia may approach $3.0 billion a year, which will include loans earmarked for restructuring industrial enterprises.

As of January 1, 1996, the credit portfolio of the WBRD in Russia consisted of 19 loans for a total of $4.6 billion. The distribution of loans by industry reveals that the bank's reserves ($1.2 billion, or 26% of all loans) were directed primarily to the energy industry and to conducting a market reform. These two fields were trailed by transportation ($629 million, or 14%); the municipal sector ($400 million, or 9%); agriculture ($320 million, or 7%); the financial sector ($240 million, or 5%); governmental administration ($216 million, or 5%); ecological projects ($209 million, or 5%); and industry ($200 million, or 4%).

The first restoration loan ($600 million) has been completed. It was spent for financing crucial imports to promote reform in Russia. An additional 15 of the 19 WBRD loans have gone into effect, namely:

1. A loan for the development of an employment service and a system of social protection for the population ($70 million). The loan is to be used for the purchase of equipment as well as payment for technical service. It will be used for elaborating and introducing a system for registering the unemployed and paying unemployment benefits. Also, the loan will lead to the creation of a system of controls over conditions in the labor market and of people living below the poverty line, as well as for the formation of policy and standards in the sphere of employment.

2. A loan for the support of privatization programs ($90 million). This provides assistance to the Russian government in elaborating privatization policies, and providing technical assistance and consulting to private enterprises. The project has undergone substantial changes in its support of postprivatization measures. In particular, $20 million from the loan has been redirected to financing additional costs for the transfer of kindergartens, which were serving (and under the direction of) different governmental offices, to the charge of local authorities.

3. The first restoration loan for the Russian oil industry ($610 million). The loan invests in the economic oil drilling in western Siberia and in supporting the oil-drilling enterprises connected with the project.

4. A loan for the restoration and maintenance of the country's highways ($300 million). The loan is intended to be used for a three-year program directed at main federal and regional highways, as well as for the purchase of vehicles, equipment, and materials for the Federal Department of Roads and for personnel training.

5. A loan for the support of reform in agriculture ($240 million). The loan is intended to be spent for the development of a market infrastructure, including the creation of an information and search system for 50 kinds of agricultural products and raw materials. It will also be used for the establishment of consulting services for farmers and for investments in new private enterprises in food processing and similar enterprises under reconstruction. Finally, it will be used for the development of vegetable storage facilities and farmers' markets.

6. A loan for the development of financial institutions ($200 million). The project involves improving the quality of banking services, increasing the stability of banks, and more effectively distributing bank loans in Russia. The immediate task is improving the activity of 20 private commercial banks that were selected by the WBRD to upgrade their banking services and establish a basis for a national clearing system. This process will aid in obtaining certification for Russian commercial banks as potential partners for international financial organizations.

7. A loan for the support of land reform ($80 million). The project stipulates the creation of a basis for real estate evaluation. It will also be used to develop procedures for the purchase of land, as well as for its sale, lease, and mortgage. Finally, it will create an information database for collecting land tax.

8. A second restoration loan for the Russian oil industry ($500 million). The project will restore 1,200 abandoned oil wells and reconstruct the existing infrastructure for oil sites, including 800 kilometers of pipelines. It will be used to drill 127 wells. Moreover, it will provide technical assistance in planning and organizing the production process, provide for equipment installation, and help reduce negative ecological consequences.

9. A loan for management of the environment ($110 million). This loan is aimed at improving policies and legislation in environmental protection. It is also intended to spur the development of a system of ecological epidemiology, strengthen control over the quality of water reservoirs, improve the management of hazardous industrial waste, and help establish a national fund for combatting environmental pollution.

10. A loan for housing ($400 million). The project is designed to aid in the further development of the municipal housing market through supporting the construction of private housing, and stimulating the development of municipal land and the construction of private residential housing. The project will also promote investments in the production of construction materials. This particular project consists of three parts:

    a. The development of a housing market;
    b. The development of an industry for the production of construction materials;
    c. The institutional development of administration for participating cities, commercial banks, and private construction firms.

11. A loan for the modernization of the tax service ($16.8 million). The first stage of this loan stipulates reorganizing the tax service, improving regulations, computerizing data-processing for taxes, and personnel training.

12. A loan for dealing with the consequences of the breakdown of the pipeline in the Republic of Komi ($99 million). The loan will finance works to deal with the ecological aftermath of a pipeline accident that occurred in Komi in 1995.

13. A loan for the support of enterprises ($200 million). The major goal of the project is to develop opportunities for selected Russian commercial banks to provide medium- and long-term loans for private enterprises. Such loans will be used for financing small investments.

14. A second restoration loan ($600 million) to the Russian government to fund crucial imports and programs of reform.

15. A loan for training specialists in management and finance ($40 million). The project represents the first part of a long-term program for training specialists to work in a market economy. The project has three goals:

    a. Increasing the number of well-prepared specialists in management, banking, and financial services;
    b. Establishing a national fund for the creation of a specialized organization that would mobilize and direct resources to train specialists on a commercial basis;
    c. Laying a foundation for the introduction of more extensive and modern methods for training specialists.

Along with these 15 loans, work on three more has begun; they are:

1. A loan for developing mechanisms to manage loans of international organizations ($40 million);
2. A loan for the development of urban transportation ($329 million);
3. A loan for the distribution of gas and for saving energy ($106.5 million).

From 1996 to 1998, the program of cooperation between Russia and the WBRD is mostly focused on the development of an infrastructure, as well as on support for agriculture, the social sector, and a number of depressed industries (e.g., coal mining).

In the near future, the growth of the national economy will depend on the development of a Russian private sector as its main strength. At the same time, foreign loans will also be of great importance. Correspondingly, participation of the WBRD and its members in supporting Russia's private sector (especially in the financial market and in postprivatization support for enterprises) will increase.

At present, the Russian government and the WBRD have a sufficiently clear understanding of the credit program that will be in effect for the next three years. In addition, the participation of the bank in industrial restructuring will be very important.

On the whole, reducing borrowings related to imports and increasing investments to support domestic entrepreneurs are urgent tasks for Russia, as they are for any other country in transition. This is one of the major principles informing the program of cooperation between Russia and the WBRD.

It should be noted that governmental priorities are based on a three-year program for the reform and development of the Russian economy that was adopted in March 1995.

40.3 INTERNATIONAL FINANCE CORPORATION.* The International Finance Corporation (IFC) is a member of the World Bank Group and is owned by its 147 member-countries. The IFC's mandate is to promote the growth of productive and profitable private enterprises in developing and transitional economies. Strong shareholder support and a substantial capital base make it possible for the IFC to meet client needs when conventional financing and technical resources are short.

The IFC is the world's largest source of financing for private enterprises in emerging economies. Since its founding in 1956, the IFC has provided $11 billion to more than 1,500 businesses in over 100 emerging economies. The IFC approves over $3 billion in long-term investments annually. Each year IFC participates in more than 300 financing and advisory assignments in as many as 50 countries.

The IFC supports its clients with a variety of financial and advisory services. Project financing is offered through loans, equity investments, guarantees, and other financial instruments, such as interest and currency swaps. Through loan syndication and securities underwriting, the IFC mobilizes additional financial resources from commercial banks. Finally, the IFC offers its clients in the private and public sectors advisory services and technical assistance in privatization, and infrastructure and capital-markets development, thus helping to create an enabling environment for private-sector development.

(a) Privatization and Technical Assistance. Although Russia became an IFC member in April 1993, the IFC has been active in the country since 1991 when, in coordination with the World Bank and the European Bank for Reconstruction and Development,

---

*This section was written by Vadim Solovyov.

(EBRD) the IFC initiated an extensive privatization and technical assistance effort in Russia. Using a regional approach, the IFC designed and implemented model programs to privatize the small business and transport sectors throughout the Russian Federation. The IFC subsequently assisted the government in organizing the first wave of mass privatization through the design of a system for the nationwide distribution of vouchers and the sale of over 1,100 medium and large enterprises in five provinces. The IFC is now involved in an innovative agricultural land-privatization effort in which its staff and officials in Nizhny Novgorod designed and implemented the first successful breakup and privatization of Russian state and collective farms. The land privatization effort has been endorsed by the government as the basis for a national program and has expanded to other Russian provinces.

The IFC's privatization and technical assistance efforts in Russia could not have been carried out without considerable support received from bilateral donors. The two primary donors for the IFC's work in Russia have been USAID and the British Know How Fund, with support totaling $12.8 million and $11.1 million, respectively. Other countries providing support include Canada, Sweden, Finland and Switzerland.

(i) Small-Scale Privatization.   In late 1991, the Russian government asked the IFC to design and implement a series of pilot privatizations. The IFC's objective in Russia was to create local-level privatization programs that both encouraged and required grassroots support and private initiative. A local approach was chosen in order to break with the past, Soviet top-down control, and to prevent a conservative bureaucracy from blocking reform. The intention was to complete transactions that affected ordinary Russian individuals in order to show that privatization was real and that individuals could take responsibility for their economic livelihood.

At the request of Nizhny Novgorod governor, Boris Nemtsov, the IFC started to work on privatization assistance in that region. Privatization in Russia was launched there on April 4, 1992, when 22 retail shops were sold at a public auction. The decision of Nizhny Novgorod to start privatization with the retail sector was based on the potential of private shops and service outlets to quickly change the lives of Russian consumers. The speed at which the resident team worked allowed design, testing, and implementation to occur within an eight-week period and achieve a highly visible example of reform.

To broaden and deepen the impact of small-scale privatization, the IFC resident teams assisted other cities across Russia on a partnership basis. The IFC provided direct assistance to cities that, in addition to locations in Western Russia, included many in Siberia and the Far East. Overall, more that 5,000 retail businesses were auctioned in the cities where the IFC provided direct support.

The effect of privatization of small businesses has been positive. An IFC survey of 8,000 private business owners showed that nearly all of them believed that employees were working more intensively; and the vast majority of owners reported favorably on profitability, the number of customers, and the range of goods and improvements in service.

(ii) Trucking Sector Privatization.   Using the principles and the approach developed in small-scale privatization, the IFC then successfully assisted the Nizhny Novgorod authorities in breaking up and privatizing the region's trucking monopoly. After the monopoly's 42 subdivisions were unbundled to create competing medium-sized private companies, small, private truck operations were created through open auctions based on transparent rules. Overall, in 22 auctions more than 800 trucks were transferred into private hands.

The generic nature of this program lent itself to replication in other regions of Russia. The IFC documented and distributed the detailed procedures in a manual for privatization officials and dispatched resident teams to nine other regions willing to follow the Nizhny Novgorod model. Over Russia as a whole, 70% of the regions replicated the program for demonopolizing and privatizing the trucking sector.

(iii) Large-Scale Privatization. The Russian privatization agency, GKI, in July 1992 laid out the legal framework for the privatization of Russia's medium- and large-scale state-owned enterprises. After conducting a small number of pilot voucher auctions in December 1992, the chairman of GKI, Anatoly Chubais, asked the IFC to help establish a first wave of large-scale privatization with a number of local privatization agencies to carry out locally-based voucher auctions.

IFC large-scale privatization teams were established in Nizhny Novgorod, Volgograd, Tomsk, Novosibirsk, and Yakutsk. In addition to assisting in the corporatization process and running the bid-reception and processing centers, the resident teams also undertook broad-based public relations campaigns in each region. Overall, the goal was to give the participants as much as possible so that the process was fair and open.

By June 1994, when the voucher plan ended, the IFC had assisted in the sale of 1,100 medium- and large-scale enterprises in the five regions where its teams were resident, collecting nearly six million vouchers. This resulted in the transfer of 1.5 million workers into the private sector.

(iv) Land Privatization. At the request of the governor of Nizhny Novgorod, the IFC has assisted local authorities in designing and implementing a land-privatization program in the region. The pilot program was developed by IFC agricultural experts working closely with top Russian agricultural economists.

The team designed a plan for creating new private farms and farm businesses by dividing the land and property of inefficient collective enterprises among the individual members of the farms. Land certificates were produced and distributed to each qualifying farm member defining their individual land entitlement. Each farm member received the same entitlement, which on average represented 6 hectares (nearly 15 acres). Similarly, property certificates were distributed to farm members to allow them the right to acquire the physical assets of the state farms, including machinery, buildings, fertilizers, standing crops, and seeds.

The model program used the auction system to ensure fairness during the division. Agricultural enterprises were divided into lots for auction on the basis of their existing operational division. At the auction, each lot was "sold" to the individual or group offering the highest bid. Then, at their own discretion, winners of various lots combined their shares to establish new agricultural enterprises using one of the newly introduced forms of legal entities. IFC lawyers were extensively involved in educating auction participants about the options available to them, as well as in assisting them with the paperwork and procedures.

The Nizhny Novgorod program received a great deal of nationwide publicity that demonstrated that land reform was possible. At the request of the federal authorities, the Nizhny Novgorod team drafted appropriate legislation for replicating the pilot model on a nationwide basis. On April 15, 1994, the government passed a decree recommending the model for voluntary adoption by farms in Russia; and detailed regulations were passed into law in July 1994.

The model is now being further developed in Nizhny Novgorod and replicated in Rostov, Ryazan, Orel, and a number of other cities with the help of IFC teams consisting mostly of local hires.

(v) Technical Assistance in Capital Markets Development.   The success of Russia's mass privatization program resulted in the need for assistance to improve the infrastructure and efficiency of the emerging securities markets. In particular, the IFC provided advice on the legal foundation and institutional structure for share ownership and transfer and improved corporate governance, as well as assisted in the establishment and development of the Russian Federal Securities and Capital Markets Commission. The IFC's assistance was delivered through the staff to strengthen the commission's secretariat and through the coordination of consultants paid either directly by the IFC or bilateral donors.

(b) Investment in Russia

(i) General Project Financing.   To date, the IFC's approvals in Russia total $331.4 million in 20 projects, ranging from capital markets and agribusiness transactions, to gas and oil investments. The IFC's held portfolio in Russia represents about 12% of the overall European region's portfolio. A sector analysis indicates that manufacturing approvals represent 42% of the total as against 30% in capital markets, 22% in gas and oil, 4% in agribusiness, and 2% in infrastructure.

The IFC's approach to the delivery of technical assistance has provided it with a visible identity in Russia and an association with market reforms. The IFC has also created the capability to expand its more classic project-finance operations, specifically investments in privatized enterprises both with and without foreign joint-venture partners, and the creation of new private financial institutions and services.

(ii) Selected Project Financing

MANUFACTURING: AO VOLGA.   AO Volga joint-stock company is a fully integrated newsprint mill located in Balakhna, Nizhny Novgorod. The IFC developed and structured what is the largest investment in the Russian manufacturing sector to date, a financing package to provide $150 million of corporate funding. The project is in partnership with the German paper concern Herlitz International Trading (a subsidiary of Herlitz AG). The project was designed to upgrade existing facilities, provide working capital, expand capacity, and improve quality and environmental conditions.

CAPITAL MARKETS: THE NATIONAL REGISTRY COMPANY.   In 1995, at the request of the Russian authorities, the IFC promoted the establishment of the first joint-venture share-registry company in Russia, together with The Bank of New York, NIKoil, Unexim Bank and EBRD. The National Registry Company addresses one of the key deficiencies of the Russian equity market by providing a reliable system for recording and transferring share ownership. The company, capitalized at $10 million, will provide independent registration and transfer services for privatized larger companies with the potential to attract foreign portfolio investment. This project complements the technical assistance that the IFC has been providing to the Russian authorities on the development of the country's capital markets.

OIL AND GAS: POLAR LIGHTS.   The IFC has invested $60 million in the Conoco-led joint venture, Polar Lights, with colenders EBRD ($90 million) and OPIC ($50 million). The project represents the first major oil-field development undertaken since the emergence of Russia as an independent state and one of the first nonrecourse financing packages. The project is developing the new Ardalin oil field in northern Russia in partnership with a local entity. The project has been technologically successful and is now producing oil at greater-than-planned volumes.

INFRASTRUCTURE: RUSSIAN TELECOMMUNICATIONS.   The IFC has invested $7.5 million in the equity of the Russian Telecommunications Development Corporation (RTDC), representing about 5% of the share capital. RTDC is a holding company established by U.S. West to invest in telecommunications projects in Russia. The investment will help to expand cellular networks in Russia, as well as develop landline-overlay networks, intercity switches, and digital transmission systems.

(c) How to Work with the IFC

(i) Investment Guidelines.   In order to receive funding, projects must meet a number of IFC guidelines. Whether it is the establishment of a new enterprise or the expansion of an existing one, the project must be in the private sector, be technically sound, have a good prospect of being profitable, and benefit the local economy. Another important criterion for IFC investments is that the project be environmentally sound. Thus, in addition to being financially, economically, and technically viable, the project must satisfy stringent environmental standards and conform to the host country and World Bank guidelines.

To ensure the participation of other private investors, the IFC's investment is usually limited to 25% of the total project cost. Investments in small and medium projects range from $100,000 to $1 million, and in standard-sized projects from $1 million to $100 million.

(ii) Application for IFC Financing.   There is no standard application form for IFC financing. A company or entrepreneur, foreign or domestic, seeking to establish a new venture or expand an existing enterprise, can approach the IFC directly. This can be done by requesting a meeting or submitting preliminary project or corporate information. After these initial contacts and a preliminary review, the IFC will request a detailed feasibility study or business plan to determine whether or not to appraise the project.

(iii) Appraisal and Investment Approval.   Typically, an appraisal team is composed of an investment officer with financial expertise and knowledge of the country in which the project is located, and an engineer with the relevant technical expertise. The team is responsible for fully evaluating the technical, financial, and economic aspects of the project. This process entails visits to the proposed site of the project and extensive discussions with the project sponsors.

The team then submits its recommendations to senior management. If financing of the project is approved, the IFC's legal department, with assistance from outside counsel as needed, drafts appropriate documents. After outstanding issues are negotiated with the company, government, or financial institutions involved, the project is submitted to the IFC's board of directors for approval.

(iv) Disbursement and Supervision.   Following board approval, disbursements are made under the terms of the legal documents agreed by all parties. The IFC supervises its investments closely, consults periodically with management, sends field missions to visit the enterprise, and requires quarterly progress reports, including information on factors that might materially affect the enterprise. It also requires annual financial statements audited by independent public accountants.

(v) How to Contact the IFC.   The IFC's representative office in Russia is located in Moscow; its address is Pushechnaya ul., 2, 103012 Moscow, Russia (tel. 928–53–28; fax 913–70–52). Additional information on the IFC in Russia can be obtained from its reports and publications, from which much of this article is drawn. Reports and publications are available from IFC Corporate Relations, at (202) 473–9331.

PART VIII

TAX SYSTEM

CHAPTER 41

RUSSIAN TAXATION SYSTEM

Hans J. Horn

41.1 OVERVIEW. Taxes were literally unknown in the old days of the Soviet Union because taxes have no place in a centrally governed state economy. As the state economy collapsed and a new breed of market economy developed, taxes became a necessity. Because of a lack of previous taxation, taxes were suggested and introduced more on an ad hoc basis to boost state revenues than as a part of a well-developed and planned tax system. Furthermore, the inexperience in drafting tax legislation often resulted in contradictions and confusions, as well as unintended negative consequences for the taxpayer. It is important to understand that even though the present tax regime is unsuitable for the development of a well-functioning market economy, this situation is mainly a result of a lack of understanding of how a tax regime works and inexperience in drafting tax legislation. The situation does not stem from the deliberate implementation of a repressive tax regime intended to make life miserable for all tax payers! It should be added, however, that there is still a widespread belief that the taxpayer is willing and able to cope with almost any tax burden. The situation is similar to milking a cow, slaughtering it to sell the meat, and then wondering why there is no more milk. As more and more taxpayers, and not only foreign taxpayers, get trampled under the burden of the present tax system, the tax authorities will accept changes to the tax laws to facilitate the strengthening of the Russian economy.

It is important for taxpayers to unite and come forward with constructive criticism. They should not be afraid to challenge the tax authorities in court. This is being done in all other market economies, and there is no reason why Russia should be the exception. Too often, companies seem to be afraid of tarnishing their image with Russian authorities and, as such, tolerate highly unreasonable decisions by the local or federal tax authorities rather than challenge the decisions in court. The juridical system, however, has a strong influence on the tax regime. If tax matters are never tried in court, there will never be a well-functioning tax system. There are a few tax disputes that were tried in Russian courts, but it is interesting to note that the decisions were more often than not favorable to the taxpayer. Once this is fully realized by the tax authorities, they would apply more reasonable practices than at present.

Because of the utmost importance the tax regime has in the development of business in Russia, one needs to stay current on changes in tax legislation. This is not an easy task because tax legislation seems to be subject to more frequent changes than almost any other portion of Russian legislation. The failure to stay up-to-date, however, can be extremely harmful to foreign business in Russia.

As a result, it is important to pay attention to penalties, not only to taxes. The penalties for noncompliance with Russian tax laws and procedures are extremely burdensome. Failure to declare and pay the appropriate taxes on time typically results in interest and penalty charges many times the original taxes. The effects of exorbitant penalties have brought many businesses to a halt over the last several years. Even though there is hope for drastic changes to the penalty system, it is unrealistic to assume it will happen soon. A continuous evaluation of tax compliance, as well as active tax planning, should therefore be an integral part of the risk management of any company operating in Russia.

41.2 CURRENT SYSTEM

(a) **Structure of State Power Bodies.**   The Constitution of the Russian Federation provides for the separation of state power into independent executive, legislative and judicial branches. The executive branch is represented by the president and the government of the Russian Federation. The legislative power is exercised by the Federal Assembly consisting of two chambers—the Council of the Federation and the Duma. Judicial power is exercised by the courts. It is important to keep in mind that it is the executive branch that possesses the broadest powers, including the power of the president to issue decrees that have the force of law if the relevant issue is not regulated by an existing federal law. Also, it should be noted that the judicial system has only started to evolve as an independent power.

The Russian Federation is a federal state and consists of regions, republics, territories, cities of federal importance (Moscow and St. Petersburg), and autonomous regions and areas, collectively referred to as subjects of the Federation. The state power in the subjects of the Federation is exercised by the bodies of state authority created by them. Certain powers, including the power to impose local taxes, have been given to local municipalities. The Constitution states that establishing the general principles of taxation in Russia is within the joint jurisdiction of the Federation and the subjects of the Federation; however, these principles and the tax system should be stipulated in a federal law.

The Federal Tax Service is a governmental body charged with the enforcement of tax laws. Recently its status was changed from that of a relatively independent ministry (i.e., with a status similar to that of the Ministry of Finance), to being subordinated directly to the president (i.e., with a status similar to that of the Ministries of Defense, Interior and Intelligence Services). It is yet unclear whether this change will result in the separation of functions between the Ministry of Finance and the Federal Tax Service.

The Federal Tax Service is a highly centralized federal authority consisting of a central body with the same name and state tax inspectorates supervising a particular subject of the Federation or region, for example, the city of Moscow. Every state tax inspectorate supervises local tax inspectorates within its territory. While the Federal Tax Service is a federal authority, in practice the state tax inspectorates in the subjects of the Federation administer the taxes imposed at the level of the subjects or local taxes, and interpret relevant regional or local laws.

The tax law is interpreted by the Federal Tax Service, which has broad authority to issue regulations (instructions) with the approval of the Ministry of Finance. Historically and practically, these instructions are considered to be part of law and the tax inspectors consider the instructions as a direct guidelines.

The State Customs Committee is charged with collecting import duties and certain taxes on imports. The Committee has limited powers to interpret the relevant parts of the tax law with the approval of the Ministry of Finance.

(b) **Tax Audits.**   According to the recommendations issued by the Federal Tax Service, legal entities that are engaged in business activities in Russia are supposed to be audited by the local tax inspectorates at least once every two years in order to verify all documents associated with the calculation and payment of taxes. The tax inspectors have the power to enter and inspect all production, warehouse, commercial, and other facilities of taxpayers that are used to derive income.

In practice, however, the audits are initiated more frequently. Primarily, the tax authorities pay attention to compliance with profit tax, value-added tax, and Russian currency regulations, which are the areas in which Russian taxpayers might experience significant exposure.

Another practical concern is that the authorities are very much form-oriented, rather than substance-oriented; therefore, it is of the utmost importance for taxpayers to keep all their books and records accurate and up to date. It is important to understand that any taxpayer arguments based on substance and/or good faith will do less for defending a position than proper and current documentation.

Furthermore, taxpayers should be aware of the process of issuance of documents by the tax-audit teams, which summarize results of the audit. Procedurally, there are two documents that are issued by the authorities. The first is an "*act*" of the tax audit, upon which the auditors list their findings. This document should be given to the management of the taxpayer for acknowledgment and it could be the basis for further negotiations. Even if the act mentions any penalties that are planned to be imposed, it is not the basis for any further steps (e.g., a seizure of funds from the taxpayer's bank account). Only the second document, a *decision* signed by the head of the relevant tax body, can formally impose financial sanctions.

After the act and decision have been issued, the tax authorities usually give taxpayers a 72-hour grace period to pay the deficiencies and penalties. The tax authorities are authorized under the law to prepare documents requiring that the taxpayer's bank withdraw the requested amount(s) from the taxpayer's account(s). If there are insufficient funds to meet the obligation, no amount will be transferred until adequate funds accrue within the account. During the period when such a payment order of the tax authorities is outstanding, the taxpayer cannot withdraw funds from the account.

(c) Penalty regime. Among the issues that often determine whether to make an investment or not is a risk analysis of the factors that are not controlled by the investor. One of the greatest of these risks, which both domestic and foreign investors face in Russia, is unintentional noncompliance with rapidly changing tax law. Although the difficulties that tax authorities face in a period of evolving tax laws are understandable, it is not easy, even for a highly qualified accountant, to trace the major changes that have occurred since 1991, let alone the numerous amendments.

The Russian system, however, imposes penalties of almost equal severity for unintentional accounting mistakes and for intentional concealment for the purposes of tax evasion. The Federal Tax Service has only recently allowed taxpayers in certain cases involving unintentional errors to submit amended tax computations without applying the same penalties as for intentional tax evasion.

It is the right and the duty of the authorities to punish criminals, but honest taxpayers should not be treated in the same way. Moreover, in cases where there are legitimately different interpretations of an unclear rule, a reasonable and respectful discussion between the taxpayer and the authorities would be more appropriate than the immediate application of severe sanctions. Additionally, sometimes the authorities are unable to see the difference between tax evasion and tax avoidance, the latter being a result of smart tax planning.

The following types of penalties are usually imposed by the tax authorities for violation of the tax legislation:

- For concealing income for the purposes of calculating profit tax, a recovery of the entire amount of the concealed income (not just the tax!) plus a penalty in an equal amount;
- For concealment of income for the purposes of calculating taxes other than profit tax, a recovery of the amount of the applicable tax plus a penalty in an equal amount;
- For improper accounting of the taxable base or for late filing of the returns, a 10% penalty;
- For late payment of tax, a 0.3% penalty based on the tax due, per each day of delay in payment (this amount was 0.7% before May 1996);
- For late payment of social fund contributions, a 0.3% penalty based on the contributions due, per each day of delay in payment (a 0.7% penalty rate applies to deficiencies with respect to contributions to employment fund).

Regarding the sanctions themselves, in most countries it is normal to charge the tax due and interest (the same is true if the tax was overpaid). Unfortunately, the existing Russian tax-penalty regime has not yet adopted the logic of a system, in which penalties such as amounts charged in addition to interest would not be charged where reasonable cause exists (for example, an unintentional mistake in accounting or a reasonable interpretation of a law or instruction).

It should also be noted that the compensation of local tax inspectors depends to some extent on the amount of taxes and penalties that they collect from taxpayers. This has caused numerous unreasonable and inappropriate demands being placed on taxpayers for additional taxes and penalties. It is hoped that this approach to compensating tax inspectors is not a good policy and will not continue to exist.

(d) Taxation of Businesses. Before starting the survey of Russian taxation of business it should be noted that Russia's tax system is characterized by a heavy economic and/or compliance burden of taxes other than net-income-based taxes, notably value-added tax (VAT), gross-receipts-based and payroll-based taxes. Therefore, any attempt to structure a transaction or any business arrangement cannot ignore the implications of taxes other than those based on net income.

(i) Profits Tax.

TAXPAYERS. Russia employs the commonly used mixture of residency and source-based taxation. Russian legal entities are taxed on their worldwide income.[1] Foreign legal entities[2] conducting entrepreneurial activities in Russia through permanent representations, a concept similar to but somewhat broader than that of a permanent establishment under the OECD model tax treaty, are taxed on income attributable to the permanent representation. Foreign legal entities without a permanent representation are taxed on income from Russian sources not connected with the activities conducted through a permanent representation.

---

[1]It should be noted that, under Russian Civil Code, the notion "Russian legal entity" would include a full partnership. Russian profit tax recognizes only one form of tax transparency—so called joint-activity agreement, which is an accounting entity but not a legal entity.

[2]Legal entities for this purpose includes companies, firms, or any other organizations formed under foreign-country law, which would presumably include U.S. limited-liability corporations (LLCs) and partnerships.

TAX YEAR. The tax year is always the calendar year. Enterprises established in the last quarter of a calendar year may, for audit and profit tax-filing purposes, include this period of three months or less in the subsequent calendar year's filings.

TAX RETURNS AND PAYMENTS. Russian companies, including those with foreign ownership, must submit quarterly (computed on a cumulative basis for the current calendar year) and annual returns, and financial statements to the tax and statistical authorities. Quarterly filing is due within 30 days of the end of the reporting quarter. Annual filing is due by April 1 of the year following the reporting year. Annual returns and financial statements of the following are required to be audited by an auditing firm registered in Russia:

- Open joint-stock companies;
- Enterprises with turnover exceeding 500,000 minimum monthly wages (for the purpose of threshold computation, the annual minimum wage should be computed based on the actual minimum monthly wage throughout the year; as of October 1, 1996, the minimum monthly wage is 75,900 rubles or approximately $14);
- Enterprises with assets exceeding 200,000 minimum monthly wages;
- Any other entities with foreign ownership.

Russian companies must pay their profit tax liability in rubles. Companies with foreign participation are allowed to pay either in rubles or hard currency converted at the market rate of the Central Bank on the date of payment.

Under profit-tax law, all Russian companies, except qualified small businesses, must make monthly installments by the 15th of each month. The amount of each monthly payment should be one third of the estimated tax liability for the current quarter. Any balance of tax payable on profits received in the calendar year must be paid by April 10th of the following year. If the monthly installments exceed the actual liability, a refund will be made.

For Russian-owned companies, interest is charged on the difference between the monthly installment payments actually paid and the actual tax due during the relevant quarter. The applicable interest rate is set by the Central Bank on the 15th of the second month of the quarter. The interest calculation should be filed and paid quarterly together with the profit-tax return. If the monthly installments for the quarter exceed the actual tax due for the quarter, interest is calculated and applied against future tax payments. For enterprises with foreign participation, no clear procedures exist.

COMPUTATION OF PROFITS TAX

Rates. The Federal corporate profit-tax rate is 13%. The various regions have the right to set a profit-tax rate of up to 22% for most entities and up to 30% for banks, insurance companies, brokers, and intermediaries; thus, a combined rate of 35% applies for most taxpayers. Rates up to 90% can apply to certain entertainment and gaming activities. For entities having branches, but not separate legal entities, in different regions of Russia, the requirement has been introduced to use a two-factor apportionment of taxable profits between these regions. The apportionment factors to be used are the net book value of fixed assets[3] and, at the discretion of the taxpayer, either the number of employees or the total amount of the payroll.

---

[3]The term *fixed assets* is determined in Russian statutory accounting rules and should not be assumed to be an exact equivalent to *capital assets*.

Taxable Base and Taxable Profit.   The taxable base for Russian companies is gross profit computed for accounting purposes, reduced or increased in accordance with tax regulations. For this purpose, gross profit is defined as profit from sales of goods, works, and services[4], fixed assets and other property and income from nonsale operations, less the amount of certain expenses incurred in such operations. Profit from sales of goods, works, and services is defined as sales revenue (excluding VAT) and the cost of production.

Accounting for financial purposes and accounting for tax purposes are curiously interdependent under Russian statutory accounting rules, that one might wonder whether it is possible to distinguish between the two. For example, the starting point for calculating taxable profit is the profit disclosed in the company's statutory accounts. The rules for arriving at this "balance profit" are given in the regulations on the cost of production. These Regulations combine very detailed guidance as to what can be deducted for statutory accounting purposes with certain limitations and restrictions on deductibility (e.g., ceilings on the deductibility of advertising or entertainment expenses), which in some countries are considered as tax adjustments and do not impact profits disclosed in the financial statements. At the same time, some of the adjustments to gross profits in profit-tax law include a limited allowance for a charge to a reserve fund, which one might consider an appropriate element in the computation of profits disclosed in financial statements.

Deductions are limited or denied for a number of items commonly regarded as fully deductible expenses under Western accounting rules (but not necessarily tax rules). Such items are treated as "being payable out of after-tax profits" (nondeductible and not properly chargeable to the capital account). Examples include interest on loans (with few exceptions), advertising and business-travel expenses above a certain limit, nonmandatory insurance expenses, research-and-development expenses, and training costs. By far the biggest problem with deductibility is that the existing rules do not contain a system that provides a broad allowance of necessary business expenses and denies certain types of expenses, but contains a list of long and detailed descriptions of deductible expenses. With the market economy evolving, such a structure leaves a practitioner with the sometimes impossible task of matching a particular expense with those listed in the regulations in order to justify a deduction.

Prior to January 1, 1994, separate rules applied to the taxation of the profits of banks, credit institutions, and insurance enterprises. After that date, the general profit-tax law has applied to these types of companies. Details on the application of the general rules to these specific types of companies are now available.

Nondeductibles.   In most cases, interest is both nondeductible and noncapitalizable. Interest on *bank loans* is deductible only to the extent that it does not exceed the Central Bank's refinancing rate (80%, effective August 19, 1996, but frequently revised) by more than three percentage points (i.e., 83%). Interest on bank loans connected with the purchase of capital items is neither deductible nor capitalizable. Interest on overdue loans, as well as on intercompany loans, is *not* deductible for tax purposes (see also "Discouragement of Debt Financing" later in this section on aspects of debt financing in general).

A reserve fund can be generated by certain types of legal entities in profitable years by transferring balances from accumulated profit within certain limits. Transfers to the reserve fund are deductible for profit-tax purposes, as long as the balance in the reserve fund is less than 25% of the initial paid-in capital, further limited to 50% of the current period is

---

[4]The term *goods, works, and services* is a literal translation and corresponds to *goods and services.* The word *works* usually refers to construction, design, etc.

taxable profits. The purpose of the fund is to provide stabilization in case of future losses. The reserve fund deduction currently provides the opportunity to mitigate the effect of restrictions on loss carryforwards (see the discussion of reinvestment incentives later in this section.)

It should be noted that the Ministry of Finance has been proposing the repeal of the reserve fund deduction for a number of years, and it is possible that it may be repealed at some point in the future, possibly, even in 1997.

Other Income—Investments. Russia utilizes a classical tax system, with almost no relief for the double taxation of legal entities and shareholders. Partial relief is granted to nonindividual shareholders through a reduced rate of 15% (18% when the recipient is a bank) that applies to the taxation of dividends from one resident company to another at source. Dividend income is subsequently excluded from the taxable base of the recipient, and no credit is available for tax suffered. Taking into account that the current tax system does not allow consolidated filings, this imposes a disincentive to the use of multiple-tier holding-company structures.

Other Income—Gains and Losses from Property Sales. The Russian tax law does not distinguish between capital gains and ordinary income. Gains from property sales are included in the taxable base and taxed at the applicable profit-tax rate. The gain/loss is the difference between the greater of the selling price or the fair-market value and the historical cost. Loss from sales of fixed assets is not deductible for profit-tax purposes.

Statutory revaluations of tangible fixed assets are periodically performed in accordance with prescribed limits. So far, there have been three revaluations, in June 1992, January 1994, and January 1995. See also the comments on the property-tax implications later in this section.

Tax Privileges. Since 1992, the Russian profit-tax law has offered a mixture of deductions and exemptions (i.e., those allowed in addition to the expenses deductible under-cost-of-production rules). Some of these deductions or exemptions are industry-specific and some resemble an explicit allowance for a deduction that would be considered ordinary and necessary elsewhere. Historically, these allowances have been called "tax privileges."

It should be noted that it has been a clearly stated position of the Ministry of Finance that all or almost all of these tax privileges described later in this section should be abolished. Some of the exemptions have been already repealed. It is unclear at this point whether the Ministry of Finance will be successful in removing these privileges for 1997.

Enterprises that have a minimum of 30% foreign ownership, that derive 50% or more of their turnover from material production, and that were registered before January 1, 1992, benefit from a two-year tax holiday (three years if located in the far eastern economic region); it takes effect from the moment of first receipt of a *balance profit,* which roughly corresponds to gross annual profit. Detailed listings of activities define which activities are, and which are not material production. Broadly interpreted, it is a process whereby goods are given added value.

Enterprises with a minimum of 30% foreign ownership, $10 million in foreign investment, and that were registered after January 1, 1994, and before January 1, 1996, benefit from a two-year tax holiday from the federal portion of the profit tax (13%), provided certain conditions are satisfied. In the following two years, federal profit tax will be imposed at 25% and 50% of the normal rates, respectively. The conditions are similar to those for enterprises employing small numbers of people.

For Russian legal entities having small numbers of employees (from 15 to 200 people, depending on the industry) and those carrying out construction activities, farming production or the production of consumer or medical goods, a two-year exemption from the profits tax (*both federal and local portions*) is available, provided certain conditions are met. These include a requirement that 70% of turnover comes from these types of activities. In cases where over 90% of turnover comes from these activities, the incentive is extended to reduce the profit-tax rates in the third and fourth years (25% and 50% of the normal rates, respectively).

For all Russian legal entities, taxable profits may be reduced by the amounts reinvested for specific purposes. The total reduction from this form of incentive, together with certain other reductions, may not exceed 50% of the taxable profits for the period. The most significant tax reductions are for enterprises:

- Undergoing technical re-equipping, reconstruction, expansion, or development of production facilities;
- Installing new facilities (enterprises in the oil and coal industries only);
- Carrying out a conversion of their production facilities;
- Involved in the production of medical equipment and equipment for the processing of food products;
- Involved in the production of food, medicines, and consumer goods.

Losses.   Losses may be offset against the amounts previously allocated to the reserve fund. To the extent that the fund is insufficient to absorb losses of a particular year, the unabsorbed losses may be carried forward against future profits for the next five years in equal installments (i.e., 20% each year). This ability to carry forward losses applies only to Russian legal entities and possibly some branches of foreign legal entities. It does not apply to representative offices of foreign legal entities or to branches generally.

This offset of losses against future profits is further restricted in that the total reduction of taxable profit in a given period, through the utilization of losses brought forward together with other incentives for reinvestment, is restricted to 50% of that taxable profit.

Sample Profit-Tax Computation.   Exhibit 41.1 provides a comparison of a profit-tax computation.

(ii) Value-Added Tax (VAT)

VAT DOCUMENTATION, RETURNS, AND PAYMENTS.   VAT became effective in the Russian Federation January 1, 1992. The general rate of tax is 20% on taxable supplies, which include the majority of domestic sales of goods and services. Certain food products and children's goods are subject to a 10% rate. Exported sales and services and a list of other specified supplies of goods and services are exempt from VAT (see also the discussion entitled VAT on "Export Services/Place of Supply" later in this section).

VAT on imports is collected at customs and is payable on the total value of the goods, including import duty and excise tax where applicable. Selected goods are exempt from VAT on imports. These exemptions also apply to goods imported as contributions to the initial charter capital of Russian companies. Recent changes restricted this exemption to the contribution of nonexciseable production assets and declared that VAT-recapture rules

Exhibit 41.1. Profit-Tax Computation

Type of Income/Expense	International Accounting Standards (rubles)	Russian Accounting Standards (rubles)
Revenue (cash basis)	**5 000 000**	**5 000 000**
Cost of goods including utilities	(2 000 000)	(2 000 000)
Salaries	(1 000 000)	(1 000 000)
Rent payments	(600 000)	(600 000)
Depreciation	(800 000)	(400 000)
Entertainment expenses	(225 000)	(225 000)
Travel expenses	(275 000)	(275 000)
Advertising	(210 000)	(210 000)
Charitable donations	(100 000)	0
Training expenses	(200 000)	(200 000)
Research and development	(70 000)	0
Interest expense (intercompany)	(700 000)	0
Government-bond interest income	400 000	400 000
Dividends received (plus tax credit for International Accounting Standards)	500 000	425 000
Gain on sale of assets	350 000	350 000
Gross profits before tax	**70 000**	**1 265 000**

Tax calculation

Deductions

Dividend income (taxed at source)		(425 000)
Government-bond interest income (tax-free)		(400 000)

Additions

Advertising expenses in excess of 2% of revenues		110 000
Entertainment expenses in excess of 0.5% of revenues		200 000
Training costs at unapproved establishments		200 000
Travel expenses in excess of the legally established norms		250 000
Taxable profit		**1 200 000**
Reserve fund (Note A)		(10 000)

Tax incentives and privileges

New capital investment over accumulated depreciation		(550 000)
Charitable donations of 100,000—Limited to 36,000 (Note B)		(36 000)
Loss brought forward (Note C)		(14 000)
Taxable base		**590 000**
Federal tax 13%		**76 700**
Local tax 22%		**129 800**
Total tax		**206 500**

Note A: the amount of the reserve fund cannot exceed 25% of the charter capital or 50% of the taxable profit.

Note B: charitable donations must not excced 3% (5% for certain types of charities) of the taxable profit.

Note C: the amount of tax incentives for purposes of the profit-tax computation must not exceed 50% of the taxable profit before deductions. In the example, tax losses brought forward in excess of 4,000 may not be utilized and are therefore lost. Note that the 50% limitations for the reserve fund and tax incentives are separate limitations.

will be introduced for contributed assets imported VAT-free and subsequently sold. Equipment and tools imported into Russia for production development under contracts concluded in 1992 and registered with the customs authorities before July 1, 1993, are exempt from VAT at import. Reductions in the VAT due at the time of import and deferrals at the time of payment of VAT on imports, are also available under certain customs regimes. Finally, where certain imported goods are financed by credits to Russia from foreign governments or from certain international lending agencies, then VAT will not be imposed at import.

VAT filing requirements are dependent upon the average monthly level of VAT payments to the tax authorities. For average monthly payments in excess of rubles, 10,000,000 the monthly filing requirement consists of three installment payments and one final payment every month. For average monthly payments less than rubles, 10,000,000 monthly payments are required (or quarterly if less than 3,000,000 rubles). Accredited representative offices, which are discussed later in this section, from approximately 90 designated countries (as well as accredited employees of these offices) are exempt from VAT on rental payments.

COMPUTING VAT LIABILITY. Russian VAT law utilizes the credit-invoice method with some modifications. Therefore, VAT liability is generally computed indirectly as the difference between VAT collected from the customers—the amount at an appropriate rate is charged on every invoice unless the transaction or the customer is specifically exempt—and VAT incurred—paid to the suppliers, provided that the payment can be supported by the invoice. This process is usually referred to as VAT reclaim, offset, or credit.

Under Russian law, the ability to offset VAT incurred is limited to VAT paid on the purchase of items, the net cost of which has been charged to production and distribution costs, and capital assets.

OTHER VAT CALCULATION METHODS. Certain types of activities, particularly involving the purchase and resale of goods without further processing or the receipt of income on a commission basis, can use a different type of VAT computation, usually referred to as computation at calculated or reversed rates. Under this procedure, VAT liability is computed by applying an indirect rate to the margin (or commission fee). For goods and or services subject to the 20% rate, the reversed rate is $20/120 = 16.67\%$.

Beginning in May 1995, enterprises in wholesale trade have to charge VAT on the whole amount of their sales even if they are acting as a commissioner. Prior to this date, these enterprises calculated VAT on price differences, trade margin, or commission.

Nontrade intermediaries have to calculate their VAT liability on commissions or other types of intermediary income at calculated reverse rates.

VAT REVERSE CHARGE. VAT reverse charge was introduced in Russian in April 1995. Previously, there was no mechanism for foreign companies without full tax registration in Russia to pay Russian VAT collected from their customers on sales of goods and services within the territory of the Federation. Now the law provides that all payments to the foreign legal entities not registered as Russian taxpayers are subject to withholding of VAT. Russian purchasers of goods or services have to withhold VAT from the total amount of payment and pay it directly to the Russian budget on behalf of the foreign supplier. It is still unclear whether the obligation to withhold VAT is applicable to representative offices of foreign companies. The amount of withheld VAT is recoverable by the Russian purchaser of goods and services and can be offset.

Regarding VAT reverse charge, once the relevant VAT amount has been withheld and paid to the budget on behalf of the foreign company, that company technically has the right to claim the amounts of VAT paid to customs upon import of goods, as well as on the acquisition of material resources within Russia. To obtain such a refund, however, the foreign company is required to be registered with the Russian tax authorities.

(iii) Other Business Taxes

TAXES BASED ON GROSS RECEIPTS (TURNOVER).

Road-Use Tax. In effect since January 1992, road-use tax applies to all Russian entities, including companies with foreign participation, and representative offices. The tax rate is applied to the gross sales of the company, excluding VAT and excise duties. The tax rates are 0.03% for trading companies and 0.4% for all other entities. Although it is a federal tax, its rates can be increased by local authorities. For example, Moscow has increased these rates to 0.15% and 2.5%, respectively. Taxpayers are required to pay installments before the 16th of each month, calculated on the turnover of the previous month. Taxpayers with average monthly payments of up to 2,000 rubles are allowed to pay the tax quarterly. Taxpayers complete quarterly returns, computing the sum of the tax due since the start of the year, less any monthly installments or quarterly settlements already made. The quarterly returns are remitted to the tax authorities along with any additional settlement due.

The road-use tax paid is deductible for profit-tax purposes.

Social-Infrastructure Maintenance Tax. A tax rate of 1.5% is applied to the gross sales of the company, excluding VAT and excise duties (for trading companies the same rate applies to gross margin). Taxpayers pay monthly installments before the 16th of each month, calculated on the turnover of the previous month. Taxpayers complete quarterly returns, computing the sum of the tax due since the start of the year, less any monthly installments or quarterly settlements already made. The quarterly returns are remitted to the tax authorities along with any additional settlement due.

The social-infrastructure maintenance tax paid is deductible for profit-tax purposes.

BUSINESS-PROPERTY TAX. This tax is levied on property belonging to Russian entities, including companies with foreign participation, and representative offices. The tax is based on the net book value of fixed assets, intangible assets, inventories, and deferred expenses incurred as of certain dates (basically, the average balance as of the first day of each quarter in the period). Taxpayers complete quarterly returns, computing the sum of the tax due since the start of the year, less quarterly settlements already made. The quarterly returns are remitted to the tax authorities along with any additional settlement due.

Certain assets are excluded from the tax base, namely monetary assets, social and cultural assets, environmental-protection assets, agricultural equipment, pipelines, electricity lines, and land. Prepaid rent is specifically included in the tax base. Representative offices in certain cases may use their home-country depreciation rates for the purposes of property-tax calculations. Under certain tax treaties, foreign enterprises without a permanent establishment in Russia may be exempted from this tax, at least with regard to movable property.

It is important to note that mandatory revaluations of fixed assets mentioned earlier have sometimes resulted in significant increases in the tax burden for investors who, having spent certain amounts in hard currency, had to face a doubled taxable base the next year.

The maximum rate of tax is 2%; however, specific rates can be fixed by local authorities. The rates in Moscow and St. Petersburg are 1.5% and 2%, respectively.

EXCESS WAGE TAX. This tax was in effect from January 1993 to December 1995. Prior to 1993, only amounts up to four times the minimum monthly salary were tax deductible for profit-tax purposes; excess amounts were not deductible. With the imposition of the excess-wage tax, amounts in excess of six times the minimum monthly salary were taxed at the profit-tax rate applicable to the enterprise (e.g., 35% for most Moscow-based entities).

CONTRIBUTIONS TO SOCIAL FUNDS.   Russian employers must make social-security, pension-fund, and employment-fund contributions, as well as obligatory medical-insurance contributions. The total amount payable, which is deductible for profit-tax purposes, is equal to 38.5% of each employee's gross salary, made up as follows:

Fund	Rate %
Social security	5.4
Pension	28.0
Employment	1.5
National health insurance	3.6

Although the law is not perfectly clear in requiring foreign entities doing business in Russia to pay these contributions, the social funds clearly believe that such foreign entities are liable for making social-fund contributions regarding Russian employees. Their position with respect to foreign employees is less certain, but the pension fund (covering the bulk of the contributions) has stated that it does not expect contributions regarding foreign individuals working for foreign legal entities or Russian legal entities with foreign participation.

TAXES BASED ON PAYROLL.

Transport Tax.   Effective from January 1, 1994, the transport tax is levied on all enterprises, other than state-financed ones, at the rate of 1%, based on total payroll and is included in the cost of production.

Education Needs Tax.   The education-needs tax is levied on all enterprises involved in commercial activities at the rate of 1%, based on total payroll.

ADVERTISING TAX.   Advertising tax is levied on all enterprises involved in advertising activities. The rate is 5%, based on direct and indirect advertising expenses excluding VAT.

TAX ON THE USE OF THE NAMES *RUSSIA, RUSSIAN FEDERATION,* ETC.   In accordance with Russian legislation, a 0.05% tax on the sales for trading companies and a 0.5% tax on the *turnover* of other enterprises is charged for using the words *Russia* or *Russian Federation,* or phrases that contain these words in the name of any company. There are indications that this tax—which is a rather expensive "license" fee—might be abolished in the near future.

TAX ON SECURITIES.   Tax on securities is based on their nominal value and is payable by issuing entities. The tax does not apply to a primary issue of securities or an issue of stock amounts for a revaluation of fixed assets. The tax rate is 0.8% of the nominal sum of securities.

The tax is paid by the issuer on the same date as the submission of documents for the registration of the issue with the Ministry of Finance. In cases of refusal of registration, the tax paid shall not be refunded.

EXCISE DUTIES.   Excise duties on domestic sales of certain goods produced in Russia went into effect on January 1, 1992, and excise duties on imports were implemented on February 1, 1993. The list of goods subject to duty includes alcohol, tobacco, cars, trucks with a capacity of up to 1.25 tons, carpets, jewelry, diamonds, natural leather, fur clothing, yachts, hunting guns, car tires, and gasoline. Excise rates differ for domestic products and for imports. The rates are percentages of customs value and range from 10% for engine oil, to 400% for nearly pure alcohol. In effect since 1994, imported alcohol and tobacco are cleared through customs only if they bear excise duty stamps. With some exceptions, export sales are exempt from excise duties.

It is expected that the structure of excise rates may be changed for 1997.

TAX ON VEHICLES.   There are two taxes on vehicles, one on their purchase and another on their owners. The purchase tax, which applies to legal entities but not to individuals, is defined as the percentage of the purchase price of the vehicle excluding VAT, excise and customs duties (for imported vehicles). The rates are 20% for cars, vans, and trucks, and 10% for trailers and semitrailers. The tax on vehicle owners applies to both individuals and entities and is levied at the rate of 1.3 rubles per horsepower. This tax is a federal tax, but the rates can be increased by local regions. The tax is still insignificant at about $5–50 per year for a car. (Separate VAT, and excise and customs duties also generally apply to imported vehicles.)

OIL SALES TAX.   Oil sales tax is levied on companies that carry out domestic sales of oil products. The basis for taxation is the wholesale price, excluding VAT or, in the case of entities buying and reselling oil products, the difference between the VAT exclusive sales and purchase prices. The tax rate is 25%.

(e) Taxation of Representative Offices.   This section describes in more detail taxation of a representative office—the most frequently used form of doing business in Russia without it being a Russian legal entity.

(i) Taxpayers and Tax Year.   Under domestic law, foreign legal entities conducting entrepreneurial activities in Russia are considered to have created a *permanent representation* for tax purposes. The criteria for whether an activity creates a permanent representation are somewhat more stringent than those of the OECD model treaty; for example, a construction site immediately creates a permanent representation[5]. As a practical matter, the only feasible form for the activities of a foreign legal entity in Russia is a representative office (RO), the term coming from the old USSR regulations that stipulated that the only possible presence of foreign entities was "a representation" not engaged in business activities. The tax year is the calendar year. ROs established any time in the last quarter of a calendar year may include, for audit and profit-tax purposes, this period in the subsequent calendar year's filing.

(ii) Tax Returns and Payments.   For an RO, a tax return and an annual report on the office's activities should be filed with the local tax authorities by April 15th following the end of the tax year. Before 1995, an audit of the return was necessary for all ROs. Since then, the audit is not necessary unless the RO has substantial sales or assets for the year of over 500,000 minimum monthly wages—approximately $7 million in gross income—or

---

[5]It is expected that more detailed guidance on when a permanent representation is created will be included in the procedural rules dealing with the registration of foreign legal entities for tax purposes. For example, it is likely that an activity continuing for more than 30 days would be deemed to have created a permanent representation.

200,000 minimum monthly wages—$2.8 million in assets (at the exchange rate and minimum monthly wage as of October 1996) for the year. The tax authorities, however, have said that they would like to have the previous audit requirement reinstated.

The tax payable by an RO is assessed annually after the tax return is filed and must be paid in rubles (or the hard-currency equivalent at the date of payment). Payment must be made within one month of the issue of the assessment. There are no estimated payments required during the tax year.

(iii) Deemed Method of Tax Liability Computation. Foreign legal entities operating through permanent representations in Russia are taxable on the taxable profits derived from the activities of their representations here. If a permanent representation does not have books and records sufficient for determining its taxable profits, the authorities are permitted to impute income to a permanent representation. This imputation is generally 25% of the entity's expenses incurred to run its Russian activities or, alternatively, 20% of the revenues received. There are other methods allowed, such as an apportionment of a share of the worldwide income, but this is not common practice.

(iv) Applicability of Other Taxes to Representative Offices

VALUE ADDED TAX (VAT). The Russian legislation on VAT provides that any commercial activities of representative offices of foreign legal entities bear VAT liability. Such representations are required to collect VAT from customers and clients. Commercial activities are generally understood to include the sale of goods and the provision of services within the territory of the Russian Federation.

The export of goods and services is legally stated to be exempt from VAT (see also "VAT on Export Services/Place of Supply" later in this section).

Foreign legal entities are generally subject to the same VAT regulations as Russian legal entities. However, accredited representative offices of companies resident in 90 listed countries are exempt from VAT on leased office space and living premises for their employees.

PROPERTY TAX. Under the Russian law on property tax, representative offices of foreign legal entities are subject to property tax. This includes both representative offices engaged in commercial activities and those carrying out purely auxiliary and preparatory activities. Under some treaties, including the U.S.-Russia Treaty, the latter type of representative offices should be exempt from this tax.

For purposes of property taxation, representative offices are generally treated as equals to Russian legal entities. Considering, however, that representations are foreign legal entities, they are not required to maintain a Russian balance sheet and keep their books and records in accordance with Russian accounting rules.

ROAD-USE TAX. According to Russian legislation, representative offices are required to pay the road-use tax that is intended to be used for funding the construction of roads in Russia. The taxable basis for the road-use tax is generally the gross revenues of each representative office. Representative offices became subject to the road use tax on January 1, 1993, when the relevant law was passed.

If a representative office in Moscow earned no actual income (e.g., no income from the sale of products and no fees or other charges for the performance of services), it has a zero tax base. Otherwise the representative office will have to report its road-use tax base and make tax payments monthly or quarterly, depending on the average monthly tax liability.

TRANSPORT TAX.   Transportation tax was introduced by Presidential Decree no. 2270. From the wording of the decree, it is not clear whether representative offices are subject to this tax. The position of the Federal Tax Service is, however, that representative offices are subject to it.

Under the recent amendments, however, when determining what should be included in the total payroll for representative offices, there is no distinction between the following:

Russian individuals;

Foreign individuals on the Moscow payroll of the foreign legal entity;

Foreign individuals on the home-country payroll of the foreign legal entity who work for the representative office in Moscow.

Arguably, not all salaries of foreign legal entities that are located in Moscow form the tax base; instead, only those salary costs that are recorded as salary for the purpose of the profit-tax return of the representative office are used as the basis. This should therefore include an appropriate proportion of the salary costs of employees (both Russian and foreign) of the foreign legal entities who work full or part time in the representative office. The salaries of employees of related entities not located in Moscow who are seconded to the representative office would not be included.

EDUCATION NEEDS TAX.   The state tax inspectorate for the city of Moscow has released instructions stating that representative offices of foreign legal entities that receive revenue from commercial activities are subject to the education needs tax. This means that representative offices with no actual income need not pay the tax. While the law is not completely clear on the issue, it is believed that representative offices paying profit tax on a deemed income basis (cost plus 25%) need not pay this tax. It is suggested that representative offices not paying this tax submit a quarterly letter of exemption.

SOCIAL-INFRASTRUCTURE MAINTENANCE TAX.   This tax is only due for those representative offices that carry out commercial activity. Should a representative office provide only preparatory and auxiliary services, there is no obligation to pay this tax.

(f) Taxation of Foreign Businesses with No Russian Presence

(i) Withholding-Tax Rates and Taxable Base.   Withholdings are required to be made on the repatriation of profits and other crossborder payments, including those to a foreign legal entity such as a representative office. Withholding taxes are due in the currency in which the payment was made. Russian legislation levies a general withholding tax at the rate of 15% on gross dividends and interest payments, and at the rate of 20% on other gross income from sources within the Russian Federation.

The withholding-tax regime applies only to income from sources within the Federation. Unfortunately, this concept is currently not well defined, although it is possible to infer when some types of income will be considered to be from sources within the Federation. It is clear that a payment may be subject to withholding even when it is paid by a foreign entity; that is, a payment made by a Russian permanent representation of a foreign entity may be classified as income from sources within the Federation. It appears that earlier regulations implied that the term *Russian source* referred to a payor physically located within Russia; however, the more recent guidelines attempted to use the same term to denote classes of income regardless of the location of the payor.

Income from sources within the Federation includes royalty payments for copyrights and licenses, rental payments, lease payments, payments for management services, and any other income from the use of assets or the performance of services in Russia without the existence of a permanent establishment. Such income also includes gains from the alienation of Russian assets, including securities issued by Russian companies. Starting in July 1995, certain types of "passive income" (see discussion later) paid to ROs may be exempt from withholding tax upon notifying the tax authorities that such income will be included in the profit-tax base of the RO.

The recent guidelines on Russian sources attempts to distinguish between *passive income* and *active income* (a new concept in Russian tax rules). In the absence of treaty relief, withholding must *always* be made on payments of passive income from Russian sources unless the tax authorities have been notified that this income is connected with a permanent representation and is taxable at that level. For *active income,* withholding only applies if the activity was not carried out through a permanent representation, although no specific procedure is set out to confirm this. For this purpose, passive income includes, for example, dividends from Russian legal entities; distributions of profits from Russian partnerships; other profit distributions from Russian entities; income distributions by Russian investment funds; interest (except on Russian government bonds); copyright royalties; certain other royaltylike payments; rental of Russian real estate; and other lease payments.

Active income specifically includes income from the performance of works and services rendered and/or provided in Russia, including, for example, brand-name licenses; licenses for computer programs and databases; payments for the use of know-how (technical, organizational, and commercial-information); management services; consulting; assistance and services connected with the management of scientific, industrial or commercial projects, plans, processes or joint ventures; and the transportation of freight.

(ii) Notification. A foreign entity, whether it maintains a permanent representation or not, is obliged to notify the Russian tax authorities of its Russian sources of income within one month of becoming entitled to receive the income. Presumably, a copy of the notification is also given to the source—the entity paying the income. It is not necessary for a permanent representation to give notification about sources of active business income, but it should give notification about sources of passive income that are connected with the business of a permanent representation.

(iii) Applying for Treaty Relief. Double-tax treaties, including those to which the former USSR was a party and that the Russian Federation still honors, may provide relief in the form of reduced or zero rates. When a treaty involves the reduction of any withholding tax, a form certifying the country of residence of the recipient of the income should be filed. New rules confirm that tax must always be withheld at the source and any refunds due as a result of treaty relief may be subsequently reclaimed. As an exception to the general rule, relief from the obligation to withhold may be granted for payments that are made on a regular basis and are of a similar character when applying for advanced approval. The tax authorities should review the claim within two weeks of submission. The exemption form requires residency certification by the tax authorities of the home country of the recipient. Experience suggests that this can present a hurdle to obtaining treaty benefits in an area that is coming under increasing scrutiny by the authorities.

Tax treaties to which the former USSR was party are currently honored by Russia. New treaties between Russia and Bulgaria, Hungary, Ireland, South Korea, Poland, Romania, Switzerland, Vietnam, the United States, and Uzbekistan have been established recently.

New treaties between Russia and Australia, Canada, People's Republic of China, Israel, Luxembourg, Slovakia, Sweden, and the United Kingdom have been signed, but await ratification by the parties involved.

The tax treaties of the former USSR with the following countries have not been superseded by Russian tax treaties: Austria, Belgium, Canada, Cyprus, Czech Republic, Denmark, Finland, France, Germany, India, Italy, Japan, Malaysia, Mongolia, Netherlands, Norway, Spain, Sweden, and the United Kingdom.

(iv) Double-Tax Treaty Rates. The maximum rates of withholding tax under double-tax treaties can be seen in Exhibit 41.2.

(g) Individual Taxation

(i) Taxpayers. Similarly to the use of residency- and source-based taxation of business profits, Russia taxes resident individuals on their worldwide income and nonresidents on income derived from the sources within the Russian Federation.

Exhibit 41.2. Withholding Tax under Double-Tax Treaties

Payee Resident of	Interest (%)	Dividends (%)	Royalties (%)
Austria	0	0	0
Belgium	15	15	0
Bulgaria ****	15	15	15
Canada	15	15	10
CMEA countries	0	0	0
Cyprus	0	0	0
Denmark	0	15	0
Finland	0	0	0
France	10	15	0
Germany	5	15	0
Hungary ****	15	15	15
India	15	15	20*
Ireland ****	0	10	0
Italy	0	15	0
Japan	10	15	10
Malaysia	15	15	15
Netherlands	0	15	0
Norway	0	20	0
Poland	10	10	10
Romania ****	15	15	10
Spain	0	18	5
Sweden	0	15**	0
Switzerland	0	5/15	0
United Kingdom	0	0	0
United States	0	10***	0
Uzbekistan ****	10	10	0
Vietnam ****	10	10/15	15
South Korea	0	5/10	5
Other (nontreaty)	15	15	20

* A rate of 15% applies to royalties from TV and radio.

** A rate of 5% applies where the recipient holds 100% of the payer.

*** A rate of 5% applies where the recipient holds more than 10% of the payer.

**** Effective from January 1, 1996.

A resident, for individual income tax purposes, is defined as an individual who is physically present in Russia for 183 days or more in a calendar year. Individuals not meeting this test are classified as nonresidents.

Tax on Russian-source income is normally paid by withholding tax at the source. Foreign-source income is assessed on a current-year basis.

Benefits-in-kind are taxable. The taxable benefit is the cash equivalent that is generally defined as the market value of the benefit provided. Certain exemptions apply, notably to the housing accommodations and company cars provided to foreign citizens that are residents of Russia for individual income-tax purposes.

The income of married persons is taxed separately; there is no joint filing.

(ii) Rates.   Taxable income for 1996 was taxed at the following rates:

Taxable Income (Rubles)	Tax (%)	Cumulative Tax (Rubles)
Up to 12,000,000	12	0
12,000,001–24,000,000	20	1,440,000
24,000,001–36,000,000	25	3,840,000
36,000,001–48,000,000	30	6,840,000
Over 48,000,000	35	10,440,000, plus 35% of the amount over 48,000,000

For most expatriates, none of the tax exemptions available (see later in this section) is likely to be significant, therefore the effective tax rate will be very close to the marginal rate of 35%. In previous years, however, devaluation of the ruble resulted in the effective tax rates on foreign-currency income being much lower (closer to 15% in 1994). This benefit was less significant for 1996 due to the stabilization of the exchange rate.

(iii) Social Security Contributions.   Russian nationals employed in Russia by either Russian or foreign legal entities are required to contribute 1% of gross salary to the pension fund. This amount is deducted at the source by the employer. The amount is also deductible in arriving at taxable income. Self-employed individuals have to register with the pension fund and contribute 5% of their income to it. Compulsory home-country social security contributions by foreigners are also treated as tax deductible.

(iv) Deductions and Exemptions.   All taxpayers are entitled to an individual exemption. An exemption for each child is given to each spouse. Each exemption is equal to the minimum wage; as of October 1, 1996, the minimum monthly wage is 75,900 rubles (approximately $14).

Certain donations are also exempt, as are ex-gratia payments on leaving employment. Deductions of up to 5,000 times the minimum monthly wage in any one tax year are available for expenditures incurred by individuals on purchasing or constructing their own housing.

(v) Gains.   Russian tax law does not distinguish between ordinary income and capital gains.

Prior to 1993, sales of property were not generally liable to income tax unless the sale fell within business or other profit-making activities. From 1993, the proceeds received from the sale of apartments and country houses exceeding 5,000 times the minimum monthly wage are taxable. For other property, the limit is 1,000 times the minimum monthly wage. Alternatively, an individual can elect to be taxed on a net-income basis (e.g., sales price, less substantiated expenses incurred in obtaining this income).

(vi) Investment Income. Investment income, including interest and dividends, is generally included in taxable income and is taxable at the appropriate rate.

Interest paid on deposits with Russian banks and certain other deposit-takers, as well as interest paid on Russian (and former Soviet) government bonds, is exempt from tax.

Where dividends are received by an employee of the paying company, the tax is withheld at the employee's marginal tax rate on salary. Dividends paid to other individuals are received net of the income tax withheld at a rate determined as if the gross dividend were the individual's only income for the year. Dividends that are reinvested in research and development funds are exempt from taxation.

(vii) Returns and Payments. If a taxpayer's only income is from employment that is subject to tax withholding at the source, the individual is not required to complete an income tax return. Where there is a further tax liability and the total income received during the reporting year exceeds the lowest tax bracket, a return must be completed and filed by April 1st of the year that follows the year under review. No extensions of this deadline are allowed. If the return is late, a penalty of 10% of the tax due may be charged, and criminal sanctions could also be applied.

Russian employees who receive any part of their income in hard-currency payments from outside Russia must normally file a return to pay the additional tax liability, since withholding is not generally applied to such payments. This is often a security concern that leads employers to structure payments so as to withhold tax at the source.

Foreign individuals who are residents in Russia and who receive income from abroad have to file annual returns declaring the income received in the year under review if the total income received during the reporting year exceeds the lowest tax bracket, which will usually be the case, taking into consideration the low tax brackets. In their first year of residence, foreigners should file preliminary returns estimating their income. Technically, this should be done within one month of arrival, but in practice, preliminary returns are submitted by April 1st of the first year of residence or one month after arrival, whichever is later. The preliminary return will be the basis on which the authorities seek to collect advance estimated-tax payments. In subsequent years, the installments will normally be estimated on the basis of the prior year's actual income.

(viii) Inheritance and Gift Tax. Inheritance and gift tax is charged on a specified list of items inherited by or gifted to a Russian individual. The list of items includes buildings, cars, jewelry, garages, currency values, and securities. Currently, due to the uncertainty of the law, it is believed that the tax does not apply to gifted or inherited property located outside Russia. The rates of tax are different for inherited property and gifts, but vary from 3 to 40% of the value of the property. These rates also depend on the degree of the relationships between the parties.

41.3 CURRENT PROBLEMS OF THE TAXATION SYSTEM. The Russian taxation system includes various authorities at different levels. Aside from the Federal Assembly and the president's office, which pass laws and issue decrees (and ignore the customs authorities), there are also the Ministry of Finance and the Federal Tax Service. These bodies are independent of one another, although they have some overlapping duties and authorities with respect to taxation. The Federal Tax Service is primarily responsible for enforcing the country's taxation system. It also contributes to the drafting of laws and issuing regulations and instructions on implementing existing law. Below and reporting to the Federal Tax Service are the regional and local tax inspectorates.

An unfortunate feature of the taxation system is that each body is in charge of something, but nobody is in charge of everything. The local tax authorities can exercise their rights regarding tax audits of a taxpayer's activities and impose penalties. At the same time, however, they have not been capable of making a decisions in cases where refunds of tax were involved or where a taxpayer strongly argued against imposition of the draconian penalties. In the latter case, taxpayers must appeal to the next highest level of the taxation system without being able to prevent a seizure of funds from the company's bank account (which is within the rights of the tax authorities).

Russian taxpayers do not yet enjoy a system that would allow them to defend their position in a disputed tax case before an independent judge prior to paying the alleged deficiencies and penalties. Both administrative and judicial review are possible only after the payment; in other words, the taxpayer is applying for a refund in such cases. Although a procedural rule provides the court with the discretionary power to stop such actions of tax authorities before a hearing, as a matter of practice, the courts do not exercise this power.

Unfortunately, neither existing laws nor the guidelines of the Ministry of Finance and Federal Tax Service contain concrete and clear guidance to local tax authorities and taxpayers. As a result, the tax authorities interpret the law narrowly and unfavorably for the taxpayer.

Although considerable effort has been made by various parties to prepare new and better documents and guidelines, the legislative bodies have on occasion rejected and substituted other documents because of political or other motivations. Normally, such documents are not subjected to any detailed examination or any public review process. As a result, the tax system gets another piece of vaguely worded legislation.

Formally, there are subdivisions within each taxation body; their activities are aimed at giving taxpayers advice about various compliance issues. In practice, though, these advisors are seldom able to provide guidance on significant interpretational matters. As such, there is no effective advance clearance procedure. Thus, taxpayers must take the risk and hope that what they are doing will coincide with the interpretation of the tax authorities. (One particularly difficult aspect of this is that, with the lack of business experience among the people, and the tax authorities in particular, there is little hope that many tax inspectors, either before or after a complicated transaction, will understand enough of its the economic and legal issues to properly determine or advise on its tax consequences.)

Obviously, when making business decisions, all investors consider the legal environment surrounding these decisions. Therefore, it is extremely important not to place investors in a worse position by ignoring the beneficial provisions of a preceding law or introducing unfavorable legislation and then enforcing it retroactively.

Although the Russian Constitution does not allow retroactive adoption of the laws, in practice legislation is being passed shortly before its enforcement. Some of the laws are drafted in such a way that the Federal Tax Service has to publish additional instructions to supplement the one that were issued six months earlier. Should there be any disputed interpretations of the law, the tax authorities tend to insist on their own understanding of the legislation.

Another issue pertaining to the current taxation system is a lack of coordination between tax legislation and other existing legislative acts. As an example, the Russian law concerning foreign investments provides for a creation of branches of foreign legal entities in Russia, whereas the tax laws do not clearly determine their status for tax purposes. After this fact was brought to the attention of the tax officials, they considered the adoption of new regulations to resolve the issue.

Despite the problems described, the system is capable of change, and many significant changes have taken place over the past two years.

(a) Practical Problems for Corporate Tax Payers

(i) Reinvestment Incentives. Certain expenditures are allowed to be immediately expensed for tax purposes as an incentive to encourage the reinvestment of earnings into productive assets. There is a limit imposed on the amount of the benefit, which is equal to 50% of the taxable profit of the company.

It has been suggested that a ten-year carryforward of the benefit be allowed. This would allow the incentive to be a true incentive, even to companies that are not yet profitable but expect to be in the future. In order for any carryforward not to be reduced by inflation, there are suggestions that the carryforward be adjusted annually to account for inflation. See, however, the discussion of the current Ministry of Finance position regarding tax privileges earlier in this section.

(ii) Deduction for All Business-Related Expenses. The Profit-tax law presently allows as deductible expenses those items that are included in "costs of production." Because of this reference, not all expenses that are necessary for conducting business will be deductible.

The Ministry of Finance and the Federal Tax Service are planning to propose amendments to the profit-tax law in order to provide for the deduction of all business-related expenses that are not now included in the costs of production. It is hoped that, in order to make Russian industry competitive and to encourage foreign-based multinational groups to conduct some portion of their research and development work in Russia, such costs should be included in costs of production, whereas presently they are not.

The authorities are starting to realize that businesses are the best judges of what should be spent to develop them and make them successful. Additionally, the Russian business community has alerted the authorities to the fact that in situations where certain expenditures are not deductible, some other countries might conclude that Russian tax should not be allowed as a foreign-tax credit against the tax of their countries.

In determining what expenses are "business related," the tax authorities should provide guidance to distinguish items that would not be deductible. Such guidance might cover items that are capital in nature and that must therefore be capitalized and depreciated or amortized. Also included would be items that shareholders regard as personal and that are not truly business-related expenditures of the enterprise.

(iii) Loss Carryforward Rules. The profit-tax law allows a five-year carryforward of operating losses with further restrictions on the use of the loss carryforward. Because of inflation and these restrictions, loss carryforwards are worth much less than the nominal amount of actually incurred loss.

At present, the guidelines of the Federal Tax Service concerning the profit tax of foreign legal entities do not allow the carryforward of operating losses to years following the year of the loss. It is hoped that in the future, foreign legal entities operating in Russia through a permanent representation would be allowed to carry forward any operating losses realized from the conduct of business. This would be consistent with the rules applicable to foreign taxpayers in most other countries.

(iv) Taxability of Domestic Dividends. Presently, dividends received by Russian companies from other Russian companies are taxed at a 15% rate, a situation that discourages

effective parent-subsidiary structures within corporate groups. In many countries, a distinction is made between controlled investments and portfolio investments, with dividends from the former being received tax free.

(v) Specific Aspects for Foreign Legal Entities.   It appears that foreign legal entities without any commercial presence in Russia will have some difficulty in obtaining advance clearance for treaty relief with respect to withholding tax on Russian-source income. According to double-tax treaties, many foreign legal entities are entitled to an exemption or reduction in withholding tax. However, the process of applying for advance clearance has always been difficult in practice. As a positive sign though, tax authorities have recently published recommendations that eliminate the uncertainty to some extent and provide direction to taxpayers.

The concept of Russian-source income is not defined. It is clear, however, that a payment may have a Russian source even when it is paid by a foreign legal entity; for example, a rental payment made by the foreign head office of a Russian permanent representation of a foreign legal entity for Russian office space, will have a Russian source.

Under the existing rules, withholding must always be made on payments of so called passive income, from a Russian source, unless the income is connected with a permanent representation and appropriate notification procedures regarding receipt of the rights for receipt of such income have been followed. For example, passive income includes gains from the disposal of shares, debentures, branch property, means of transportation, and connected assets, as well as other property situated in Russia. The rules, however, do not stipulate that gains on the disposal of Russian shares, securities and debentures are the only items that are classified as passive income; and there is some concern that *source* will focus on the status of the buyer. Last year, officials of the Federal Tax Service indicated that this was so. Furthermore, no decision has been made about whether the gain is calculated in rubles or in foreign currency, or what documentation is needed to establish base cost and expenses of the sale for determining the gain.

(b) Practical Problems for VAT Payers

(i) VAT on Construction Expenses.   According to the current VAT regulations, VAT on construction or installation works rendered by a contractor are capitalized and subsequently amortized by the purchaser. Should such work be performed by a subdivision within the same company, VAT should be self-imposed and accounted for as output VAT. This VAT is similarly capitalized and is subject to depreciation. Considering low statutory depreciation rates and inflation, the effective recovery of the VAT cost is negligible.

Unrecoverable VAT on construction is a clear hindrance for Russian companies willing to expand their production, as well as for foreign investors planning capital investments in Russia.

(ii) VAT on Loans.   Effective from January 1, 1994, VAT is applicable to a temporary transfer of funds if the transferring party is not a banking institution (for Russian banks a Central Bank license is required). Although illogical from a Western perspective, this regime equally applies to intercompany loans and other financial arrangements.

The latest changes in VAT law and guidelines apparently have eliminated the problem, beginning after January 1, 1996 (due to a procedural issue, the possibility of intercompany loans being subject to VAT was completely eliminated effective October 1996).

VAT on loans should be seen as an attempt to fight fictitious loans in order to reduce VAT liability, which did exist in the past. This instrument, however, did not match the internationally accepted practice of intercompany loans being used for financing start-up expenses of the subsidiaries, etc. (see also the discussion of discouraging of debt financing later in this section).

(iii) VAT on Export Services/Place of Supply. Under Russian VAT law, selected services are treated as exports, e.g., transportation of exported goods (including any part of this service rendered in Russia); transit of foreign cargoes within Russian territory; and transportation of passengers and luggage to a destination outside Russia. Partial exemption is also provided for international telecommunication services.

Certain specified services are treated as exports even if fully rendered in Russia. They include providing intellectual property; leasing of movable property subject to export; research, development, and design services; and processing imported materials into a final product with subsequent reexportation. Services are treated as outside of the scope of VAT, and as such can lead to problems, however, in the reclaiming of input VAT.

(iv) No Refund Mechanism for Foreigners. It is generally accepted that VAT systems are meant to be symmetrical, and that a company paying VAT on its inputs should be able to reclaim that VAT.

There is an exemption to this principle for foreign companies that are not engaged in a commercial activity in Russia. Such companies are not exempted from VAT on goods and services purchased on the local market. Therefore, they are charged Russian VAT as normal buyers.

Because such companies are not payers of VAT to Russia, the tax authorities do not consider them entitled to a refund of their VAT cost. As a result, input VAT is neither creditable nor refundable, but is an additional cost.

While the registration procedures imply that it is possible to register solely for the purposes of VAT, it is unclear whether such registration by itself would impose additional compliance burdens on registered entities.

(c) Discouragement of Debt Financing. The present system of debt taxation and the regulations of capital movements discourage financing Russian subsidiaries and joint ventures by means of intercompany or bank loans.

Loan interest is not deductible, unless the lender is a bank. However, interest for a deferral of payment to a supplier is deductible. This exception would not apply to normal intercompany financing of operating expenses.

Interest expense to the borrower will be deductible if the loan is arranged with a foreign bank. However, this deduction is limited to the London Interbank Offering Rate, plus three points for hard-currency loans. Interest on ruble loans is deductible within the Central Bank lending rate, plus three points.

Should the loan, however, be drawn from a foreign or Russian bank to finance a purchase of fixed assets, intangible assets, or capital construction, no deduction of interest cost is allowed. Such interest can neither be capitalized nor deducted.

CHAPTER 42

FINANCIAL LEASING

Scott C. Antel and Tatiana Orobeiko

42.1 IMPORTANCE TO THE ECONOMY.   There has been a great deal of discussion, much criticism, and little utilization of Russian financial-leasing structures to make fixed-asset (machinery, equipment, and buildings) acquisitions since the government and the Ministry of Finance issued regulations on the subject and the concept was legally recognized in Part II of the Civil Code effective March 1, 1996. This is indeed unfortunate because, despite a number of questions concerning taxation, licensing, asset registration, etc., the existing legislation sufficiently establishes leasing as the most economical way for companies operating in Russia to acquire needed fixed assets. Certainly it offers a far better alternative than an outright or financed purchase.

Why is leasing so attractive? Today a huge chasm exists between Russia's capital-investment requirements and the near-total absence of domestic medium- and long-term financing (estimates indicate that only 5% of commercial bank credits have a maturity exceeding three months). Moreover, non-Russian bank financing is similarly difficult to obtain and incurs a substantial risk premium.

Financing is further complicated by the vertical-payments crises in Russia and the severe liquidity problems of most Russian firms, and by an archaic and unstable tax regime that does not recognize the true economic cost of a taxpayer's investment. For example, depreciation allowances are extremely slow and, generally, noninflation indexed; and interest on fixed-asset acquisition borrowings is disallowed altogether (In a controlled economy no one needs to pay interest; the state advances the funds and there is no need to pay it back!) Financial leasing can avoid these difficulties by offering foreign and domestic equipment manufacturers, sellers and Russian-based potential buyers access to a economical and tax-effective form of medium-term financing.[1]

42.2 REGULATORY BASIS.   Historically, the Russian legislation has had no concept of *financial leasing* as the term is generally recognized in developed Western economies and under International Accounting Standards (IAS). Traditional Russian accounting rules have distinguished between long-term and short-term rents, with the sole distinguishing

---

[1]In the medium to long term, financial leasing may also prove to be the savior of the Russian banks. As Russia's federal budget and currency gradually stabilize, the primary business lines of Russian banks—high-yield currency speculation and Russian government-securities trading—will marginalize. Russian banks will need to replace this business with banking activities similar to those of Western banks—asset-finance lending. The financial leasing legislation provides various tax incentives to Russian banks engaging in this activity, which, combined with the benefits offered lessees, makes this a preferred financing alternative for all parties.

characteristic being the presence or absence of a purchase option in the rent contract. Thus, no matter the economic substance of the transaction (e.g., full payout, absence of residual value, a lease term approaching asset's useful life, and other indications suggesting a long-term lease or financed purchase of the asset), if the contract contains no purchase option to the lessee, it is treated as short term and accorded ordinary short-term treatment (i.e., off the lessee's balance sheet and fully deductible lease payments, etc.). While the short- and long-term lease characterizations remain in the Russian legislation, recent legislation establishing financial leasing has created a hybrid class of lease.

The first legislative mention of leasing as a general term was made in the 1990 customs legislation and in the Russian Chart of Accounts in 1991. This was followed by Presidential Decree No. 1929 of September 17, 1994, which identified and defined a financial lease as a form of "entrepreneurial activity aimed at investment of temporary or permanent financial resources in property for transfer under contractual arrangement for a determined period of time." The concept was further developed by the Governmental Provisional Regulation On Development of Leasing in Investment Activity, No. 633 of June 1995, which established detailed regulations for financial leasing; and by Ministry of Finance Order No. 105 On Accounting for Leasing Operations of September 1995, which established the requisite accounting rules. More recently, Government Resolution No. 167 of February 1996 introduced licensing requirements for leasing activity. Finally, Part II of the Civil Code, effective March 1, 1996, identified financial leasing as a separate Russian legal concept, and it is this concept that takes precedence today.

42.3 DIFFERENCES WITH WESTERN COUNTERPARTS. The practice in countries with developed leasing industries is to generally characterize leasing transactions either as short-term (operational) or long-term (financial) leases, depending on who retains "substantive economic ownership" of the asset. This depends on answers to such questions as: does legal ownership transfer to the lessee or is there a bargain-purchase option at the end of the lease term? does the lease term cover the asset's useful life? does the net present value of the sum lease payments equal or exceed the asset's purchase price? and other questions regarding a substantive transfer of the economic risks and rewards of ownership to the lessee. If most of these questions can be answered in the affirmative, the lease will normally be recognized as a financed purchase and classified as a finance lease for accounting and tax purposes. Otherwise, it will qualify as an operational lease with the lessee holding the asset off-balance sheet and expensing the lease payments related to its temporary use of the asset.

The Russian legislative definition of a financial lease differs from the traditional meaning of it in a developed market. A financial lease agreement in Russia exists where "the lessor acquires property identified by the lessee from a seller and grants the lessee temporary possession and use of this property for business purposes in return for payment." This definition suggests that there must be three participants to a financial lease: (1) a manufacturer or seller of the equipment; (2) a lessor who must purchase and lease the property; and (3) a lessee who must identify the seller and the property and lease it for business purposes from the lessor. Other notable elements of the legislation include:

- Both movable and immovable property (except land and mineral deposits) may be leased;
- The participants may be either foreign or Russian entities;
- The lease may contain a purchase option;

- Various proposed incentives such as accelerated depreciation, customs, VAT, and profit-tax exemptions for Russian lessors and Russian banks providing lease-related financing;
- Ministry of Economics licensing of financial lessors and possible Central Bank licensing of crossborder lease payments.

42.4 ATTRACTIVENESS TO RUSSIAN CAPITAL INVESTMENT. Russian financial leasing offers a hybrid of benefits in that it combines the best taxation and financial elements of both short- and long-term leasing found in Western countries. Specifically for the *lessee,* it provides:

- Off-balance-sheet financing (the assets are accounted for on the lessor's books);
- Full deductibility of the lease payments (including any finance interest element). This provides for faster and fuller recovery of the real economic cost of the asset than if purchased and amortized under the slow Russian rules with no corresponding deduction for finance interest;
- No property-tax cost as the asset remains off the lessee's balance sheet;
- Preservation of the hard currency value of the tax deductions (each rental is translated at the current rate as opposed to depreciation deductions based on an irregularly revalued asset base);
- The possibility to own the property at the end of the lease term.

For the *lessor,* financial leasing provides:

- Accelerated depreciation of the asset under a foreign lessor's home-country rules or at 300% of normal Russian rates for Russian-based lessors;
- Deductibility of any equipment-acquisition financing costs;
- Potentially favorable financing, since banks lending to financial lessors will be tax-exempt for three years on any income from such transactions;
- Retention of ownership and greater security over the asset during the lease;
- Potential VAT, customs, and profit-tax exemptions promised in future legislation;
- For foreign lessors, generally no Russian withholding tax where a treaty country is used. For nontreaty-country lessors, withholding tax is limited to its profit margin rather than the gross payment;
- A possible property-tax exemption under numerous treaties.

While the legal requirements are now in place to effectively organize and operate leasing activities in Russia, the number of Russian leasing transactions has been fairly few. The main impediment to further development, of course, remains the overall problems of the Russian economy—particularly the vertical payments crises afflicting virtually all Russian industries. The most publicized efforts at leasing to date have involved Western equipment and lease finance.

Notably, the Russian banks have not greatly pursued leasing, having found investing in currency speculation and Russian government securities far more lucrative from a yield standpoint and requiring less experience for achieving success. Moreover, the history of Russian leasing companies regarding the volume of transactions and profitability has not been good. Not surprisingly, these companies have not been overtly public about their lack of success. The few Russian leasing companies that have been able to successfully adapt their leasing activities to the present difficulties in Russia have similarly not publicized their success out of concern that it benefit or encourage potential competitors. As such, historical data on the Russian leasing industry continue to remain sketchy.

42.5 POTENTIAL PROBLEMS.   There are some potential problem areas, uncertainties, and administrative headaches associated with financial leasing of assets. At present, the main ones are the potential double-VAT charge—once when the asset is imported into Russia, and again on the lease payments—and the possible nonrecoverability of the import VAT by the lessee where the foreign lessor is not Russian tax registered. However, technical import exemptions (to the extent they are retained in the law) and other planning techniques such as limited VAT may be overcome only by tax registration.

With all of the negative commentary surrounding the uncertainties of the tax, licensing, registration, and other aspects of the existing leasing legislation, it should be noted that they are a fact of everyday business life in Russia and demand a greater level of perseverance to overcome. Given the substantial economic and tax benefits that financial leasing offers to producers and buyers of fixed assets, such perseverance should be worth the effort.

CHAPTER 43

TAXATION OF FOREIGN INVESTORS

Vladimir V. Gusev

43.1 OVERVIEW. The taxation system in Russia is in its formative stage. The foundations of a modern taxation system were laid in January 1992, and the system will continue to develop and improve along with the development of the government's economic policy and practice.

The structure of the Russian taxation system is based on the law Foundations of the Taxation System of the Russian Federation. Russian taxes contribute revenues to budgets at three levels: the federal budget, budgets of the Federation members, and local budgets.

43.2 TAXATION OF BUSINESS ENTITIES. Enterprises operating in the Russian Federation, including those with foreign investments and foreign legal entities operating through permanent representative offices, pay the following federal taxes:

- Profit tax
- Value-added tax (VAT)
- Property tax
- Transport tax
- Road-use tax

Under Russian law, local authorities may impose other taxes as well. In Moscow, for example, foreign legal entities pay advertising taxes and dues for the benefit of educational institutions.

Federal law allows foreign investments to be made in various forms, including through totally foreign-owned enterprises and interest in joint-stock companies. Foreign legal entities also may operate through representative offices and other independent units that are not legal entities under the Russian laws.

The formation of the legislative basis for foreign investment taxation in Russia is guided by two sets of principles: (1) the internal tax legislation and, (2) international tax laws.

Beginning January 1, 1992, the new taxation system in Russia has altered the previous practice of economic regulation of foreign investments. The new approach that has been applied to domestic tax legislation provides for the extension of the national format to foreign investments, including those contributed through joint ventures set up with foreign stakes.

43.3 TAX PRIVILEGES. Enterprises with foreign investments are accorded all privileges provided under the domestic tax legislation, including, in particular, the following:

1. The profit-tax base may be reduced for sums expended to:
   a. Develop the taxpayer's own manufacturing and nonmanufacturing facilities, finance manufacturing and nonmanufacturing projects through shareholder capital investment, and repay bank loans borrowed and used for these purposes;
   b. Repay investment loans contracted in foreign currency or obtained under loan agreements with international banks and credit institutions and used to:
      • Implement nature conservation projects in an amount of 30% of the expenses incurred;
      • Contribute to charitable programs an amount not to exceed 5% of the taxable profit;
      • Form reserve funds up to 25% of authorized capital.
2. The profit receives tax breaks for five years after the balance sheet shows a loss. (In combination with item 1, this privilege must not reduce the taxable sum assessed without benefits by more than 50%.)
3. Enterprises with a workforce under 200 employees (i.e., small businesses) receive the following privileges:
   • A tax holiday on the profit tax to enterprises producing and processing farm output and manufactured consumer goods, or engaged in the construction and production of building materials, provided the receipts from these activities exceed 70% of the total sales of output (work product and services);
   • An accelerated depreciation mechanism.
4. An exemption is provided from VAT when the goods (work product and services) are exported from the Commonwealth of Independent states.

Government authorities in the Russian Federation may provide extra tax incentives for enterprises, including those with foreign stakes, within the tax amounts remitted to their budgets.

43.4 TAX PAYMENTS. Enterprises with foreign interests make monthly advance payments of the profit tax throughout the year in an amount of one-twelfth of the expected annual tax. The actual tax amount is reassessed every quarter.

If an enterprise is engaged in manufacturing, has foreign investments exceeding 30%, and is registered in a lawful manner before January 1, 1992, it will continue to enjoy the profit-tax exemption over the first two years (first three years for enterprises organized in the Russian Far East) from the time its balance sheet first shows a profit. Significantly, the right to this privilege is extended only to enterprises whose revenue from manufacturing activities exceeds 50% of total revenue.

43.5 TAX EXEMPTIONS. The Russian authorities have started taking steps to stimulate the flow of foreign capital to the Russian economy. In Decree No. 1004 of May 23, 1994, the president ruled that enterprises registered after January 1, 1994, that have foreign interests engaged in manufacturing activities and whose paid-up share of foreign contributions in the authorized capital is at least 30% and is equivalent to at least $10 million, will pay a profit tax to the federal budget in the manner established for small businesses by Decree No. 2270 of December 22, 1993. Specifically, these enterprises will pay profit tax as follows:

Over the first two years of operation, these joint ventures do not pay profit tax to the federal budget if the receipts obtained in the course of manufacturing activity exceed 70% of the total receipts from the sales of output (work product and services).

In the third and fourth years of operation, they pay a profit tax to the federal budget in an amount of 25% and 50% of the base rate, respectively, if the receipts from manufacturing activity exceed 90% of their sales of output (work product and services).

If these enterprises terminate their operations before the end of the five-year term (beginning with the date of registration with a state body), the tax amount is payable to the federal budget in full for the entire period of their operations.

Circular Letter No. 143/NP–6–01–405 of October 31, 1994, from the Russian Ministry of Finance and Federal Tax Service, concerning assessment of investments attracted by privatized enterprises, clarified the rules applicable to tax exemptions for investments obtained by privatized enterprises and used for purposes specified in their investment programs.

43.6 PROFIT TAX.   Foreign entities carrying out business activities in Russia through their permanent offices pay the profit tax. The permanent office is a branch, division, bureau, office, agency, or any other permanent place of regular business concerned with the development of natural resources; involved in contract work to build a project, to install, assemble, adjust, and maintain equipment, or to sell the output from warehouses located in the Russian Federation and owned or leased by a foreign legal entity; or engaged in providing services and other activities undertaken to earn an income in the Federation or abroad. A permanent office may also be an organization or natural person authorized by foreign legal entities to exercise representative functions in the Federation.

Beginning at the time that business activities commence, each project building site is regarded as constituting a separate and permanent representative office. Tax liabilities are assessed for each separate building site.

The profit earned by the permanent offices of foreign legal entities may be assessed either by the receipts accruing from the sale of output upon shipment (completion of the jobs or provision of services) or as payment is effected for the goods shipped (completed jobs or services provided). A permanent representative office must use one of these profit assessment techniques in the course of a financial year.

The financial year is equal to 12 months, from January 1 to December 31, inclusive. The first financial year for divisions of foreign legal entities is the period from the commencement of operation to December 31 of the same year, inclusive.

The profit tax of a foreign legal entity is assessed by a tax body in the area of the Federation where business is carried out. Tax is levied on the profit of a permanent representative office, and the profit is measured as the sales of output (work product and services), minus the total of the following: value-added tax (VAT), the special tax and excise taxes, and any other revenues and expenses related directly to the operation of the foreign legal entity in the Federation, including management and general operating expenses incurred both in the Federation and abroad.

Expenses taken into account during the profit-tax assessment of a permanent representative office are determined in the same way as such expenses are determined for enterprises that are legal entities under the laws of the Federation. The expenses are defined in the Regulations Governing the Composition of Expenses Involved in the Manufacture and Sale of Output (Work Product and Services), Which Are Included in the Cost Price of the

Output (Work Product and Services), and the Procedures to Be Followed in Preparing the Financial Performance Results Considered in Profit Tax Assessment, approved by the government of the Russian Federation in Resolution No. 552 of August 5, 1992, and also in Resolution No. 661 of July 1, 1995, On Changes in and Supplements to the Regulations Related to the Composition of Costs Incurred in Manufacturing and Selling Output (Work Product and Services), Which Are Included in the Value of the Output (Work Product and Services), and to the Procedure Guiding the Preparation of Financial Performance Results, Which Are Taken into Account in Profit-Tax Assessment.

The income earned by a foreign legal entity (including rental and income from other uses) from casinos and other gambling places and businesses (e.g., automatic game machines with prizes in the form of objects or cash), video archades, and leasing of video and audio cassettes and recordings, are measured as the difference between the receipts and material expenses incurred to derive such income. The income is taxed at rates fixed by law, and the tax is transferred to the respective budgets and is not taken into account for purposes of profit-tax assessment.

Profit tax is levied only on the part of a foreign legal entity's profit that is derived from its activity in the Russian Federation. There is no tax, however, on the profit a foreign legal entity earns from foreign-trade operations carried out exclusively on its own behalf to purchase output (work product and services) in the Federation. Nor is there tax on the or profit earned from operations involving barter and the export of output (work product and services) to the Federation if the Foreign legal entity has possession, under the laws of the Federation, of the output (work product and services) before it crosses the Federation's border.

Foreign legal entities deriving income in physical form (as products or property), rather than in cash, pay the profit tax assessed on the basis of the market prices of the same or similar products or property effective at the time income is earned.

Whenever it is impossible to directly measure the profit earned by a foreign legal entity from its operation in the Russian Federation, the tax body assesses the profit tentatively on the basis of the income derived by that entity from such activity. Whenever it is impossible to determine the income earned by a foreign legal entity from operations in the Federation, it is assessed the profit tentatively on the basis of the gross income received by the entity from all sources, including its business in the Federation, and on the basis of the ratio of the staff of the representative office in the Federation to the total workforce of the entity. If it is impossible to measure the receipts obtained by a foreign legal entity from all sources, the tax body assesses the income tentatively on the basis of expenses incurred in the course of operations.

When this tentative approach is taken to the evaluation of foreign legal entities' profits, assessment is based on a profit margin of 25%. The taxable profit is calculated with the following factors:

A ratio of 0.2 is applied in assessing the taxable profit on the basis of the income gained;

A ratio of 0.25 is applied in assessing the taxable profit on the basis of losses sustained in operations carried out in the Federation.

43.7 FILING. A foreign legal entity carrying out activities in the Russian Federation through a permanent representative office must file, not later than April 15th of the year following the reporting year, a report on its activity in the Federation and an income declaration with the tax body in the registration area of the permanent representative office. If operations of the foreign legal entity are terminated before the end of the calendar year, these documents must be filed within a month of the termination date. When a foreign legal entity has several permanent representative offices registered for taxation purposes in the Federation, an income declaration is filed with each of the respective tax bodies in the area where the permanent representative office is registered.

The tax body calculates the tax payable on the profit of a foreign legal entity and draws a payment note within a month from the filing date of the income declaration. The profit tax is calculated by the tax body in rubles and must be paid by a noncash transfer or, at the taxpayer's request, in foreign currency that is bought by banks in the Federation and converted into rubles at the ruble-conversion rate quoted by the Central Bank, effective on the day of tax payment, within the time limits specified in the payment note.

43.8 SOURCE OF INCOME. Foreign legal entities that derive their income from sources within the Russian Federation are liable to tax on income at the payment source. Income at the source in the Federation include, in particular, the following kinds of income:

1. Dividends paid to Russian residents.
2. Interest paid on:
   - Promissory notes of any kinds, including sums charged by Russian banks on corresponding accounts of foreign banks, and those paid to foreign legal entities on attracted loans and deposits;
   - Premiums paid upon redemption of securities, sold previously at a discount;
   - Fines and penalty interest for defaults on contracts and debt obligations.
3. Income from copyright uses, including compensation for the use of copyright, the right to publish works of literature, art, and science, and the right to use cinematographic products, including feature films and videocassettes.
4. Income from the use of inventions, utility models, industrial designs, trademarks, brand names, service marks, and other such assets; also business reputation (good will), contacts, customers, and company staff.
5. Income from the lease of property in the Russian Federation, including income from leasing operations.
6. Income from the disposal of property, which is calculated on the basis of the excess of the property's selling amount over the acquisition price. Examples of property include:
   - Shares and other securities
   - Debt claims
   - Property in the Russian Federation.
7. Other income earned outside the area of the permanent representative office's operations, in particular, payment from jobs and services executed and provided in the Federation, including:
   - The right to use computer programs and databases;
   - The use of technical, organizational, or commercial information (know-how);
   - Managerial services;
   - Assistance provided to permit effective use of property or rights transferred;
   - Provision of assistance needed to install and operate equipment, assembly lines, and devices;

- Consultation, assistance, and services related to the management of any research, industrial, or commercial project, plan, process, or enterprise with foreign investments;
- All modes of transporting freight;
- Sales of goods imported into the Russian Federation on the basis of agreements on trade cooperation with Russian enterprises. In these cases, the income derived from a source within the Federation is the income paid to a foreign legal entity as the difference, or part of the difference, between the price quoted by it as the selling price and a more profitable price at which an intermediary sold the goods.

43.9 TAXATION RATES AND MANNER OF PAYMENT. The amount of freight income paid to foreign legal entities for sea, air, rail, road, and other kinds of international freight is taxable at a rate of 6%, dividends and interest at 15%, and any other type of income at 20% percent.

Persons who pay income to foreign legal entities are responsible for the full and timely withholding of taxes on incomes at the source within the Russian Federation. Tax on the income derived by foreign legal entities from sources within the Federation is deducted by the person who pays income to the foreign legal entity, in the currency in which the payment is effected, from the total income each time the payment is transferred. Payment also implies the reinvestment of the foreign participant's income in order to increase the participant's share in the authorized capital of a resident enterprise.

Persons who pay income to foreign legal entities submit information on the amounts of income paid out and taxes withheld to the tax body to which the person is registered for taxation purposes. Such reports are submitted every quarter within the time limits established for Russian enterprises. The reports include the income paid to foreign legal entities in the previous accounting period.

When an international treaty provides for reduced tax rates or full exemption of income taxes in the Federation, the extra tax withheld at the source is refunded upon the filing of an application requesting a tax refund.

If an entity pays income without withholding tax, the total taxes on the income of a foreign legal entity are withheld from that entity.

When international treaties duly ratified by the USSR or the Russian Federation provide for different rules, the rules of the international treaties apply.

When Russian banks perform short-term operations with foreign banks, no confirmation is required of the permanent residence of a foreign bank in a country with which Russia has a double taxation agreement if such residence is confirmed by entries in the *Bankers' Almanac* (published by the Reed Information Services the *International Bank Identifier Code* (published by SWIFT, Belgium, and the International Organization for Standardization, Switzerland).

Agreements and contracts may not include any clauses committing a legal entity or a foreign legal entity to bear tax payment expenses that are the responsibility of other taxpayers.

43.10 TAX REFUNDS. To receive a tax refund, a foreign legal entity is required to submit to the Federal Tax Service an application and an official confirmation of that entity is permanent residency in a country that currently has effective agreements with the USSR and the Russian Federation for the prevention of double taxation. Applications filed more than a year after the date of income collection are not accepted for examination.

43.11 VALUE-ADDED TAX. Under the law on Value Added Tax passed on December 6, 1991, VAT is levied on sales of goods, jobs completed, or services provided in the Russian Federation. VAT has a wide spectrum of applications, as is normal practice in other countries.

The VAT sum to be transferred to the budget is assessed as the difference between the tax sums received from customers for goods (work product and services) sold to them, and the tax sums actually paid to suppliers for material resources (work product and services), the price of which is debited as manufacturing and distribution costs.

Russian enterprises, other economic agents, and foreign legal entities engaged in manufacturing and any other commercial activity in the Federation must pay VAT. It is imposed on all services provided in Russia, including legal, auditing, consulting, and information-gathering for the benefit of Russian enterprises and those in other countries.

VAT is levied on goods brought into the Federation, in keeping with the customs laws.

Exemptions and benefits are allowed in VAT applications. In particular, reduced rates and deductions are available. A VAT exemption is allowed on exported goods and services, and on goods brought into the Federation as humanitarian aid. Leasing office space to foreign legal entities is also exempt from VAT, a benefit that is applicable to firms from 90 countries. An exemption is also available for equipment and instruments used in research, and processing equipment and parts for such equipment.

The VAT rate is 20%; on some foodstuffs and children's goods, the rate is 10%.

When goods (work product and services) are sold in the Russian Federation by foreign legal entities registered with a tax body as engaging in manufacturing or other activities, the amount of VAT to be paid to the budget is measured as the difference between the tax amounts collected from the sales of goods (work product and services) imported, produced, or acquired in Russia and sold in its territory, and tax amounts paid to customs at importation and on materials acquired for manufacturing purposes in Russian.

When goods (work product and services) are sold in Russia by foreign enterprises that are not registered with a tax body, VAT is paid in full by Russian enterprises from funds transferred to the foreign enterprises or other persons indicated by these foreign enterprises. In this case, the taxable turnover includes the total receipts obtained from the Russian purchasing enterprises. The VAT amounts paid by Russian enterprises for their foreign counterparts are not offset for these Russian enterprises.

Foreign enterprises must be registered as taxpayers to receive a refund of VAT amounts that were paid for the importation of goods into Russia, and to receive a refund for the cost of materials acquired for manufacturing purposes in Russia.

43.12 OTHER TAXES. Enterprises with foreign investments and foreign legal entities must also pay the following:

- Property tax in an amount up to 2% of the average annual value of the property (the rate is 1.5% in Moscow);
- Road-use tax at the rate (in Moscow) of 1.5% of the sales or 0.11% of the turnover;
- Tax on motor vehicle owners, which varies with the type and capacity of the vehicles;
- Tax on motor vehicle purchases at a rate of 20% for trucks, buses, and passenger cars, and 10% for trailers.

CHAPTER 44

TAX POLICE DEPARTMENT: SHARED POLICIES AND DIFFERENCES WITH WESTERN SERVICES

Sergey N. Almasov

44.1 IMPLEMENTATION OF A TOUGH TAX POLICY ENSURES FISCAL STA-BILITY.   In Russia today, the way the nation's budget is prepared and executed demands a tough policy on taxes, a policy that must be exercised to ensure a general improvement of the fiscal system. Tougher tax policing is a response to the growing strength and scope of a shadow economy, corruption among government officials, and growing tax evasion. All these are criminal threats to economic stability. It is especially important to combat income and tax-base concealment, an objective that means preventing tax-related crime and infringement of tax laws.

To control this kind of fraud, tax inquiry units, composed of criminal investigators and tax police, that have legislative law-enforcement powers, operate independently within the governmental structures (finance ministries, internal ministries, police departments, etc.) of various countries, including the United States, Great Britain, Germany, Italy, France, Switzerland, and Finland. The rationale behind the creation and structural organization of these units differs from country to country, based on the types of crimes and historical, national, and socioeconomic considerations.

During Russia's complex transition to a market economy, it was vital to deter economic crime in tax collection, which was aggravated by the uncontrolled expansion of international economic ties being created by large firms and organizations. Presidential Decree No. 262 of March 18, 1992, created a Main Tax Investigation Department within the Federal Tax Service.

As tax-related crime rates shot up rapidly, a decision was made to detach the Main Tax Investigation Department from its parent organization and establish it as an independent law enforcement authority called the Tax Police Department (TPD). The Federal Tax Police Authorities Law, passed on June 24, 1993, gave the department the status of "a law enforcement body and component of economic security maintenance forces of the Russian Federation."

Within the law-enforcement system and the tax-control system, the tax police exercise both a law-enforcement function and a fiscal function. In law enforcement, it is responsible for tracking, terminating, and preventing tax-related crimes and offenses. Its fiscal functions are ensuring that illegally concealed taxable resources are credited to the state, penalizing offenders for tax-related crimes and offenses, and supervising the flow of revenue into the budget.

44.2 STRUCTURE. In accordance with the December 1995 Federal Act, the system of Federal Tax Police bodies is comprised of two parts. The first is the Tax Police Service of the Russian Federation, which is a state committee. The second is the local Tax Police bodies in the republics of the Federation, autonomous areas, territories, regions, and the cities of Moscow and St. Petersburg.

The Tax Police Service regulates taxation and law-enforcement practices within their respective terms of reference. They are guided by the Russian Constitution, the Constitutions of the member republics of the Federation, the legislative acts of the Federation, and the legal acts of the autonomous region, autonomous areas, territories, regions, and the cities of Moscow and St. Petersburg. The Federal Tax Police Service works in cooperation with other government authorities, public associations, and private individuals, as well as with the revenue services of other states on the basis of international laws and commitments of the Federation.

Structurally, the Tax Police Service is comprised of several divisions: operations, tax audit, physical protection, and internal security. Its auxiliary and support units include office management, legal, inspection, information analysis, personnel, administration and management divisions, an external relations section, and a public relations center.

The Federal Tax Police Service has the following tasks:

Detecting, preventing, and terminating tax-related crimes and offenses (any economic crimes detected in the process must be reported by the tax police to the respective law enforcement bodies);

Ensuring security for state tax inspectors and their staff against illegal acts while performing their duties;

Preventing, detecting, and terminating corruption within the tax-collecting bodies:

44.3 POWERS. To be able to perform these tasks, the tax police have been granted the following powers by federal law:

Initiate criminal proceedings;

Carry out a full range of pre-trial investigations and pass all the information directly to the court;

Detect tax offenses;

Prosecute tax offenses;

Carry out legal-economic examinations, and review documents related to criminal activities;

Conduct field investigations within the legal framework to detect, terminate, and prevent instances of income concealment from tax collectors (inquests into which are assigned by law to the tax police), and to ensure internal security;

Exercise the rights granted to tax collection officers and currency control agents;

Conduct audits on taxpayer returns when necessary and, after they have been carried out by officers of the Federal Tax Police Service, prepare reports on the results of such audits and apply relevant sanctions;

Suspend taxpayer operations on accounts with banks and lending institutions for a period of up to one month, upon failure by the taxpayer to submit tax assessment and payment documents;

Seize the property of artificial and natural persons, followed by sale of the property in the established manner in the event that the offender defaults on tax, duty, and other mandatory payments;

Carry out urgent investigations in those instances and in the manner specified in the law on criminal procedure;

Demand that executives and officers of enterprises, institutions, and organizations, and natural persons regardless of ownership patterns terminate their violations of tax laws, and monitor compliance with the law;

Summon Russian citizens, foreign nationals, and persons without citizenship to provide explanations, clarification, and information on matters within the terms of reference of the Federal Tax Police Authorities;

Obtain any required information, free of charge, from government ministries and departments, enterprises, organizations, institutions, and natural persons regardless of ownership patterns (except in instances where the law provides for a special procedure in obtaining such information). The information obtained by the Tax Police Service is to be used exclusively for official purposes and is confidential.

CHAPTER 45

ACCOUNTING REGULATIONS

Elena Lytkina

45.1 OVERVIEW. Unlike the United States, where the accounting profession is mostly self-regulated and accounting practices are governed by the Generally Accepted Accounting Principles (GAAP) established by the American Institute of Certified Public Accountants, Russian accounting principles are passed into law by the Ministry of Finance. In 1995, the government passed into law new regulations on accounting and reporting in the Russian Federation. This ruling supersedes all prior enactments and is meant to serve as a worldwide methodological base for all organizations and business entities operating in Russia, with the exception of banking institutions.

The entire document and the manner in which it entered Russian economic reality are indicative of the state of affairs in the country. The drafters of the regulations are mostly economics, finance, and taxation experts are accounting knowledge is primarily theoretical. This explains why some sections are overly detailed while others barely touch the basics. The entire document, which attempts to lay the foundation for accounting methodologies and mandatory principles for all reporting entities, is barely four pages long. While most of the articles are clearly influenced by GAAP, the document as a whole bears unquestionable signs of Russia's growing pains. It is divided into four sections: "General Regulations," "Fundamentals of Bookkeeping," "The Place of Bookkeeping Function in the Organizational Structure," and "Financial Reporting."

The regulations establish the responsibility of the company's management for maintaining a sound system of continuous accounting, recordkeeping, and reporting. The three main accounting objectives are stated as:

1. Generating complete and reliable information necessary for the management, investors, suppliers, buyers, creditors, tax authorities, and other interested parties;
2. Providing the means of control over the assets and ensuring that company resources are used in accordance with the authorized budgets;
3. Timely prevention and identification of errors and irregularities.

The basic accounting concepts of double entry, monetary unit as the basis for measurement of business transactions, going concern, consistency, comparability, full disclosure, accounting period, cost-benefit convention, and priority of substance over the form of the transaction are all reflected in the document and carry meanings practically identical to the ones they have in Western accounting systems. The regulations place a special importance on source documents in recording business transactions. The regulations specify that to be valid, a source document must contain: the name and number of the document; date, description, and monetary value of the transaction; authorized signatures, names, and positions of the company agents or employees; and be generated simultaneously or soon after the transaction is carried out. Any corrections to the original document must be authorized by the same persons who initiated it.

Company property must be carried on the books at historical cost expressed in the national currency—rubles—unless these or other regulations adopted by the Ministry of Finance proscribe otherwise. Transactions carried out in a foreign currency are to be translated into rubles, based on the Central Bank exchange rate in effect at the time of the transaction. A company should also conduct physical inventory counts when and as often as it deems necessary. Such counts are mandatory in the following circumstances: the sale or lease of the property; the preparation of an annual financial statement unless the last inventory count was conducted no earlier than October 1st; a change of management; fraud or casualty loss; and liquidation or bankruptcy. Any discrepancies discovered during the physical inventory count must be quantified in monetary terms, investigated, and either recovered from the responsible parties or written off as a loss.

The executive team of a company has the ultimate responsibility for establishing an effective accounting system, monitoring its performance, and periodically reporting key financial data. General reporting standards are established by the Ministry of Finance. The regulations proscribe that the fiscal year for all organizations coincide with the calendar year. All errors and changes in accounting estimates have to be recorded in the period they were discovered and must be disclosed in the annual report.

The regulations provide basic guidelines for the recording of major balance-sheet and income-statement items. Property, plant, and equipment are recorded at acquisition cost and include only completed projects. Construction in progress and similar capital expenditures are classified separately. Fixed assets are depreciated using depreciation methods and useful lives recommended by the Ministry of Finance. Intangible assets are amortized over their useful life or over 10 years if useful life is not readily determinable. The terms of amortization and depreciation are identical to those in U.S. GAAP—the cumulative balance is shown on the balance sheet as a contra-asset account, and the current portion is charged off to expense. Similar to the method used in American accounting system, investments are recorded at cost or market value, whichever is lower. Russian companies are allowed to recognize monthly unrealized holding gains and losses on government securities, whereas the increase in the fair market value above the historical cost of other securities is allowed only after the securities are sold.

An American accountant will find nothing new in the Russian rules of accounting for inventory: it is recorded on the balance sheet at historical cost. Either the last-in-first-out or the first-in-first-out inventory flow conventions can be used to determine the value of the ending inventory. Finished goods in a manufacturing business can be stated at actual or at standard cost. Unfinished items (work-in-process) and raw materials must be separated from finished goods, and obsolete inventory must be written off as an expense.

Although the section on liabilities does not offer any revolutionary insights to a Western reader, it establishes an accounting concept crucial for Russian companies—reserves for uncollectable accounts, notes, and loan receivables. Many Russian companies' balance sheets are grossly inflated because they continue to carry old receivables that have no possibility of being collected. The following example helps illustrate the potential impact of these old receivables on a company's financial statements: when a Big Six CPA firm audited the books of a leading Russian bank for compliance with international accounting principles, the $10-million income figure reached by using old Russian accounting standards went down to $.3 million. This problem makes valuation of Russian companies very difficult. The regulations require that uncollectible accounts be reserved, but kept on the books, for five years after write-off or until the statue of limitations for collection expires, whichever is sooner. Other reserves and accruals, including bonuses, vacation, maintenance, and legal, are recommended but not required.

The Russian regulations touch on revenue recognition very briefly: net income is defined as the final net effect of the entity's operations for the period; the prior period's revenues received in the current year are recorded as current; and advance payments received are recognized as revenues in the future period(s). It is hoped that as more Russian companies become profitable, the Ministry of Finance will revisit this section of the regulations and elaborate on the subject. When analyzing Russian companies for profitability, a foreign investor should be aware that the risk here, unlike U.S. financials, primarily involves the understatement of earnings since tax avoidance is a major factor driving accounting and reporting irregularities.

In line with the tax enforcement crusade under way in Russia, the federal taxation authorities are first on the list of parties entitled to receive company financial statements. The annual reports must be presented no later than April 1st—three months after the year's end. Quarterly reports are to be submitted within one month after the end of the period. From the standpoint of fostering a transparent market in Russian, it is important to note that the regulations require that financial reports be made available to all interested parties (including shareholders, creditors, suppliers, buyers, etc.) at a minimal price to cover printing costs. A Westerner may not be able to appreciate this, but for Russia, where until recently any information about commercial enterprises was guarded with a zeal befitting government secrets, the concept of publicly available financial statements is an economic and psychological breakthrough. The financial reports are signed by the principal manager and the head of the accounting department (the equivalent of a controller), and must include the auditors' opinions. However, the auditors' objectivity—the underlying assumption and the cornerstone of Western-style auditing—is not mentioned anywhere in the document.

From the previous discussion it is clear that the regulations are sketchy and incomplete, but they spell out and set into law some very important concepts that businesspeople in the developed capitalist countries take for granted. Undoubtfully, the regulations will be revised and amended in the near future to reflect Russia's developing economic reality and changing regulatory priorities. This four-page collection of regulations is a skeleton of the growing body of Russian accounting standards that are based on the far more advanced American system.

PART IX

REGIONAL ECONOMIES

CHAPTER 46

LOCATION OF PRODUCTION RESOURCES

Aleko A. Adamescu, Yuri A. Kovalev, and Alexander G. Granberg

46.1 OVERVIEW. Russia is a federal state of many ethnic groups. It has an area of 17,075,400 sq km and a population of 148.0 million. The largest ethnic group in the country are Russians, of whom there are 119.9 million, or 81.5% of the country's total permanent population. After the Russians, the biggest ethnic groups are Tatars (5.5 million), Chuvashis (1.8 million), Bashkirs (1.3 million), and Mordovians (1.1 million). Another 17 ethnic groups with populations between 100,000 and 1,000,000 make up the remaining number.

On the basis of Russia's economic and natural conditions and availability of physical resources, its territory is divided into 11 economic regions. The basic economic performance figures of the regions are shown in Exhibit 46.1.

The bulk of Russia's population and most of its industrial and farming areas are concentrated in the main settlement belt stretching along the axis that runs from Moscow to Nizhny Novgorod, Ekaterinburg, Krasnoyarsk, and Khabarovsk. In the north, this belt terminates along the line extending from St. Petersburg to Berezniki and Krasnoyarsk, and in the south it reaches as far as the line from Volgograd and further east to Omsk and Abakan. East of Krasnoyarsk, the settlement belt tapers off and follows, with occasional breaks, the Trans-Siberian Railroad, ending on the Pacific coast at Vladivostok.

The European part of Russia accounts for 25% of the territory and 78% of the country's population. The settlement pattern here is made up of major industrial cities, medium-sized cities, and small towns hosting branches of enterprises headquartered in major cities and engaged in farming and produce processing. The Volga, Ural, and Volga-Vyatka regions are dominated by large industrial enterprises, with the manufacturing industry spread among a small number of cities. This industry distribution pattern raises extra problems for producers in merchandising their output and reduces employment opportunities for the population. The typical problems of these areas are low incomes, a limited number of job openings, and the need for regional programs to support industrial complexes having a large share of defense enterprises (Mordovia, Udmurtia, and Mari El republics, Penza, Vyatka and Saratov Oblasts, and elsewhere).

The Center and Central Black Earth regions are predominantly areas of small and medium-sized businesses, many of which are located in small towns and medium-sized cities, offering a moderate amount of jobs to their populations. These areas, however, have severe problems in the farming sector, which employs 20 to 30% of the economically active population. These regions seriously lack a system of marketing, telecommunications,

Exhibit 46.1.   Basic Economic Performance Indicators of the Regions in the Russian Federation (January 1996)

Economic Region	Area (thou. sq.km.)	Population (thou.)	Output (trillion roubles) Manufacturing	Farming
North	1,466.3	6,033.0	17.3	2.4
Northwest	196.5	8,092.6	12.3	2.4
Center	485.1	29,939.3	54.3	11.2
Volga-Vyatka	263.3	8,471.4	16.8	4.0
Central Black Earth	167.7	7,832.1	15.3	4.9
Volga	536.4	16,794.8	37.6	10.3
Northern Caucasus	355.2	17,396.7	14.4	8.3
Ural	824.0	20,380.4	57.9	10.7
West Siberia	2,427.2	15,148.1	45.2	7.5
East Siberia	4,122.8	9,198.1	24.7	4.7
Far East	6,215.9	7,797.6	13.4	4.8
Kaliningrad	15.1	913.0	0.9	0.4
Russian Federation	**17,075.4**	**147,997.1**	**310.2**	**71.6**

and transportation to support an interregional merchandise market. Under the prevailing conditions, the majority of businesses are geared to the needs of the local consumers and predetermined quotas of deliveries to federal food stocks. As a result, when prices rise or demand drops, these enterprises cut production because they do not have the resources to look for new markets. These regions show a trend toward consolidation of the farm produce scale and the extent of effective demand in the local market, a policy that lowers annual produce sales by 10 to 20%, which will eventually generate social and economic instability among farmers. Moreover, the Moscow metropolitan area, the country's principal food market with a population of 15.3 million, cannot be effectively supplied with the products of these areas and is thus forced to buy huge quantities of foodstuffs abroad.

The Asian part of Russia has a population of 32 million. The more thoroughly settled areas lie in the southern part of West Siberia, which has a fully developed industrial complex involved in Russia's defense and space programs, and a commercial farming zone, including the Omsk and Novosibirsk Oblasts of the Altai Krai.

East and north of Krasnoyarsk and Lake Baikal, there are numerous settled areas scattered in clusters, with cities and towns nestling around mining and lumbering enterprises, or strung out in mountain and river valleys.

46.2 NATURAL RESOURCES.   Russia's natural resources are rated among the best in the world and have great potential for sustained growth. Russia ranks among the world's richest nations in terms of coal, iron ore, potassium salt reserves, and especially timberland. It also accounts for a large share of the world's resources of oil, natural and wellhead gas, nonferrous metals, chemical minerals, and fresh water. Russia's needs for most natural resources are supplied by the Ural region and those in the Asian part of the country. Most of its oil comes from fields in the Tyumen Oblast, and the bulk of its coal is mined in the Kuznetsk coalfields in the Kemerovo Oblast. Nearby, the recently developed Kansk-Achinsk coal basin in the Krasnoyarsk Krai abounds in coal seams up to 80m thick, lying just under the top soil. In the west, the Kursk Magnetic Anomaly (KMA) in the Central Black Earth Region supplies up to 60% of Russia's needs in iron ore. In the east, the Lena, Yenisei, and Angara Rivers together represent three-quarters of the nation's water power potential. The hydroelectric dams straddling these rivers generate cheap power that is used to produce the world's least expensive nonferrous metals and chemical products. The most efficient power resources in terms of engineering and performance are found in Siberia, where a chain of five hydroelectric dams (total capacity of 22 billion kw on the Angara and Yenisei) deliver cheap power to plants manufacturing low-cost nonferrous metals and chemical products.

46.3 OIL AND GAS. Oil production in the USSR peaked at 560 million tons in 1987. Thereafter it has steadily declined, primarily because of the depletion of the richest fields and the deterioration of geological conditions, making oil extraction difficult. By 1993, industrial production had fallen, oil production had slumped to 350 million tons, and Russia stopped sending oil at internal prices to the other 14 former Soviet Republics.

More than 70% of the country's oil is produced in the Middle Ob Valley, taken up by the Khanty-Mansi and Yamal-Nenets Autonomous Okrugs and the Tomsk Oblast. All the top-quality oilfields have been depleted, and the overall plan is to extract oil from less productive fields through expensive extraction methods. The region has its hopes on developing gas fields north of the Tyumen Oblast.

Another oil-producing region, Volga-Vyatka, yields about 20% of Russia's oil. The area's potential yields include 20–25 million tons in Tatarstan, and 5–10 million tons each in the Perm and Orenburg Oblasts and the Udmurtia Republic. The predominant products are high-sulfur viscous oils, which lie at great depths. In spite of this obstacle, the production costs in some oilfields are the country's lowest because of the highly developed infrastructure, low maintenance costs, low pay rates, and the inexpensive social infrastructure. This situation explains the interest shown by growing oil companies toward the development of new, small fields in this area.

Other areas in the country that produce significant amounts of oil include the fields around the towns of Ukhta and Usinsk in the Komi Republic (up to 10 million tons) the Krasnodar and Stavropol Krais (around three million tons); Sakhalin Island (two million tons); and the Kaliningrad Oblast, the nation's westernmost enclave (one million tons).

The oil developers have been intrigued by the promise offered by the Barents Sea shelf and the Nenets Autonomous Okrug. New Reserves have been discovered on Taimyr Peninsula and in several places in the Sakha (Yakutia) Republic and the Irkutsk Oblast.

Oil from West Siberia pumped to the refining facilities in the country's European part, with most of it flowing to the refineries located between the Ural Mountains and the Volga River, where the bulk of Russia's motor fuel originates, and also to the refineries in Kstovo, Ryazan, Moscow, Yaroslavl, and Kirishi in central Russia. The oil intended for export goes to the seaports of Novorosisisk and Ventspils and is also pumped to Europe along a pipeline through Belarus.

(a) Refineries. Nearly all the oil-refining facilities in Russia are technologically outdated and deteriorating resulting in low-quality fuel caused by inefficient prerefining process. As a result, crude oil exports are more profitable than the domestic refining and exporting of oil products. Presently, many refineries are undergoing modernization, but the process is too slow because of the shortage of domestic funds; so the industry is very interested in attracting foreign investments.

(b) Natural Gas. In the long run, oil will gradually be replaced by natural gas because gas is more inexpensive and environmentally safe.

Today, natural-gas production has leveled out at about 550–600 billion cu m per year. About 90% of the country's gas is produced in the Ob Valley, including the Yamal-Nenets

Autonomous Okrug, accounting for 85% of the output, and the Khanty-Mansi Autonomous Okrug with 5%. Another 6% comes from the Orenburg Oblast, and the remaining quantities originate in the Komi Republic and the Astrakhan Oblast, with 1% each.

46.4 COAL.   The coal industry supplies about 15% of Russia's fuel resources, up to 320 million tons a year. Coal is used as the key fuel by utilities for power and heat generation in East Siberia and some areas in West Siberia. The situation will apparently remain unchanged in the foreseeable future because of the proximity of coalfields at Kuznetsk and Kansk-Achinsk. In addition, Kuznetsk has high-quality coal grades, making them suitable for preparing metallurgical coke and for firing the furnaces of power-generating plants. They are cheaper than coal from most other Russian fields and are a competitive alternative to oil and natural gas in the Volga Okrug and in Siberia now that Russian energy prices are heading toward parity with world prices. The Kuznetsk coalfields, however, have a limited export potential because of the prohibitively high transportation costs to consumers.

Coal of the Kansk-Achinsk fields is less expensive than the Kuznetsk premium coal by 25 to 30%. The quality is lower as well, with a high sulfur content and ash reaching some 40% of the gross weight. The long-distance transportation of Kansk-Achinsk coal is prohibitive, and it is too dangerous to human health to be burned near cities. These fields may become attractive some time after the year 2000, if a viable refining process is developed.

The Pechora coalfields in the Komi Republic, the lignite mines in Moscow and the Tula Oblast, and the Russian portion of the Donetsk coal basin, which is mostly in Ukraine, hold little promise for the future; so most of their mines and strip quarries are facing closure. Because miners face high costs in resettling and searching for new jobs, coal mining in these areas will not grow until perhaps 2005. Some of the modern, technologically advanced mines, capable of producing coking coals competitively, will stay in business.

46.5 NUCLEAR ENERGY.   The enterprises involved in the mining and processing of Russia's nuclear material are fully competitive in the world market. Nearly 60% of the industry's sales come from exports. The mining is primarily done in Transbaikalia, with the main processing centers located at the other end of Russia: at Sosnovy Bor in the Leningrad Oblast; Dubna in the Moscow Oblast; Obninsk in the Kaluga Oblast; Arzamas–16 in the Nizhny Novgorod Oblast; closer to the source, Sverdlovsk–45, Chelyabinsk–65, and Chelyabinsk–7 in the Urals; and still nearer, the producers at Tomsk–7, Novosibirsk (Sever production association) and Krasnoyarsk–26 in Siberia.

The power facilities supply power to all regions of the country. Some power shortages have been registered in the Northwest, in Transbaikalia, in the Far East, and in the Northern Caucasus. The shortages were made up by power from the nation's integrated power grid (operated by the Russian Integrated System Joint-Stock Company). In the long run, power-generating facilities will have to be added to the existing ones in the Rostov and Chita Oblasts and in the Khabarovsk Krai, and to complete the scheduled replacement of power units at thermal- and nuclear-power plants.

46.6 METALS.   Basic metals are essentially mined in the Ural and Kuznetsk coal-rich areas. The plants in these areas, most of which are of the integrated type, fabricate two-thirds of Russia's steel and three-quarters of its iron. The majority of the plants are technologically obsolescent, using outdated and environmentally hostile processes, such as the open-hearth. Ural-area producers specialize in the manufacture of high-quality metal, pipes, and ferroalloys. They get their coal from Kuznetsk and Karaganda, Kazakstan, and their iron ore from Kasakstan, the KMA, and local primary producers (e.g., siderites form the Baikal area or from the Kachkanar ore-dressing plant). The metal fabricating plants in Kuznetsk use the local coal, and obtain their iron ore from Mountain Shoria, Khakassia, and the Korshunovsk ore-dressing plant in the Irkutsk Region. The European part of Russia has three metal plants in Cherepovets and Lipetsk and the electrometallurgical integrated plant in Novy Oskol. All three use technologically advanced processes, which makes their products, including rolled steel for the automotive industry, competitive in the world market. These enterprises, however, will have to cut expenses for fuels and coking coal by modernizing their equipment.

Total ore production in Russia is 80 million tons per year, about 40% of which is mined in the Kursk Magnetic Anomaly, lying on both sides of the border between the Belgorod and Kursk Oblasts. Some 20% of Russia's iron ore is produced in the Ural region and the relatively young ore fields in the northwestern area, including the Murmansk Oblast and the Republic of Karelia; and 5% is produced by each the Mountain Shoria (southern Kemerovo Oblast), Khakassia, and the Irkutsk Oblast. In the long term, Russia will continue to obtain its iron ore from the KMA (reserves of 16.7 billion tons), the Kachkanar groups of ore fields in the Ural region (6.1 billion tons), and the Sokolovo-Sarbai group in Kazakstan (1.7 billion tons).

The Ural area is Russia's main producer of copper. The area abounds in metal conversion plants using concentrated feedstock from Kazakhstan. Blister copper-producing and refining plants are some distance from one another, with copper-smelting plants operating in Krasnouralsk, Kirovograd, and Mednogorsk, and copper electrolysis plants in Kyshtym and Verkhnaya Pyshma.

Russian lead and zinc producers use primary materials delivered from Sidon, in North Ossetia, Salair in the Kemerovo Oblast, the Nerchinsk deposits in Transbaikalia, and from Dalnegorsk in the Primosky Krai. Lead material is produced in Dalnegorsk, and lead concentrates in Belovo, Kemerovo Oblast. Lead and zinc conversion facilities are located in Vladikavkaz, North Ossetia, and zinc metal is produced in Chelyabinsk.

The production of Russian nickel and cobalt is centered in the city of Norilsk and the surrounding area and in Murmansk Oblast, where producers are united in the Interros financial and industrial group. The growth of the corporation is going to be curtailed for economic and environmental considerations; the Norilsk integrated plant is the chief polluter in the Arctic region, and the costs of social programs and transporting cargo along the northern sea route are overwhelming high. The industry's other center is located in the Ural towns of Verkhny Ufalei, Orsk, and Rezh.

Tin is produced in Novosibirsk Oblast, which has facilities for processing concentrates supplied from producers in East Siberia and the Far East; Sherlovogorsk, Khrustalny, Solnechny, Ese-Khai, and Deputatsky have ore beneficiation plants.

Aluminum is produced in Russia near major thermal power plants and hydroelectric plants, including Volgograd, Volkhov, Kandalaksha, Shelekhov, Novokuznetsk, Sayanogorsk, Bratsk, and Krasnoyarsk. These plants process bauxite from Tikhvin and the north Urals and nepheline from the Khibini Mountains and Kiya-Shaltyr. The best-quality materials come from the north Urals, but they lie at depths of one km or more. Short of quality primary materials, Russian aluminum plants are now processing aluminum imports from Australia, Guinea, and elsewhere. The closest integration into the world economy has so far been achieved by the Siberian aluminum plants, which use the cheap power of the dams on the Angara and Yenisei Rivers.

46.7 ENGINEERING INDUSTRY. The Russian engineering industry provides jobs to half of the workforce employed in manufacturing and produces about a quarter of the manufactured output. This industry's enterprises are organized as follows:

Engineering and metalworking enterprises constitute the economic mainstay of most larger cities in Russia, contributing the bulk of revenues to the local budgets and core incomes to the population.

The European part of Russia contains from 50 to 75% of the aggregate capacity of most engineering branches, and in Siberia major engineering centers have been established in Omsk, Novosibirsk, Krasnoyarsk, and several smaller cities in the Altai Krai and the Kemerovo Oblast.

Engineering enterprises are represented by various governmental agencies, which have established industrial centers organized around these enterprises and in one or a few regions of the country. The industrial profiles of most regions are, therefore, dominated by a group of engineering, chemical, and building enterprises whose products are related or intended to cater to a particular segment of the domestic market. The most illustrative examples are the Lipetsk Oblast (tractors and automotive equipment); the Bryansk Oblast (road-building machines); the Mordovian Republic (lighting equipment); St. Petersburg (ships, navigational equipment, power-generating units, and equipment and materials adapted for northern conditions); the Tambov Oblast (chemical engineering); Nizhny Novgorod (radar equipment, radio engineering, hovercraft building; Bashkortostan Republic (oil and gas equipment); Omsk and Novosibirsk Oblasts, and Krasnoyarsk Krai (aerospace equipment and machines for developing oilfields, woodlands, and ore resources); the Kemerovo Oblast (coal-mining equipment), and the Urals (heavy engineering and machinery for the defense industries).

It appears that over half of the engineering facilities have been set up to promote the state's strategic objectives in defense, space exploration, agriculture, metals, and equipment for Siberian development programs, and were subsidized from fuel-export revenues. Today, these facilities are operating at full capacity and are often incapable of producing competitive output for the world market. The worst situations have occurred in Udmurtia, several cities in the Urals and Central Russia, Novosibirsk, Severodvinsk, and Yoshkar-Ola, in which only a few enterprises have avoided the crisis and are still earning enough to contribute to the local budgets.

Considering its present problems, the engineering industry would benefit from attracting 30 to 50 large financial and industrial groups that would invest funds in the modernization of enterprises and the production of competitive export goods. Given the advantages Russia holds in some areas of science and engineering and the possibility of Russian enterprises joining the existing alliances of industrial countries, Western investments will be needed to deal with the problems of the Russian engineering industry.

46.8 AEROSPACE INDUSTRY. Any short-term outlooks for a competitive engineering industry in Russia are linked to the aerospace and automotive industries. The country's leading aerospace centers are located in various cities and are engaged in building various types of aircraft: Moscow (IL 96, TU 204, TU 334 and YAK 42M), Smolensk (YAK 42), Voronezh (IL 96–300), Taganrog (TU 334), Kazan (IL 42), Ulyanovsk (TU 204 and AN 124). Samara (TU 154 and AN 70), Saratov (YAK 42), Omsk (AN 74), Novosibirsk (AN 38), and Nizhny Novgorod (MIG 21 and MIG 25UB). Helicopters are being built in Moscow, Rostov-on-Don, Kazan, and Ulyanovsk. Aircraft-manufacturing prospects look fine for the former defense-industry enterprises, now producing civilian output, in Komsomolsk on Amur and Arseniev.

The space industry is centered in Moscow, Omsk, Krasnoyarsk, and Miass, which turn out orbital space stations, rockets, communications facilities, and fuel equipment. The leading enterprises include the Energia Research and Development Association, with a pilot plant in the city of Kaliningrad (Moscow region) and branches in Samara and Primorsky, Leningrad Oblast, and the Khrunichev State Research and Development Center in Moscow. The principal defense-missile-producing facilities, some of which are currently being converted to civilian output, are located in the Ural region, particularly in Udmurtia, and the Sverdlovsk and Chelyabinsk Oblasts.

46.9 AUTOMOTIVE INDUSTRY. The Russian automotive industry has 200 enterprises. The industry's biggest plants, employing over 10,000 people each, are the ZIL Joint-Stock Company in Moscow, the Gorky Motor Plant (GAZ) in Nizhny Novgorod, the Volzhsky Motor Plant in Togliatti, the Kama Motor Plant in Naberezhnie Chelny, the motor plant group in the Yaroslavl Oblast, and the Ural (Miass) and Izhevsk engineering plants.

46.10 CHEMICALS. Russia's chemical industry turns out a range of products fully competitive in the world market, and in the short run the industry will offer an attractive sector for foreign investment in Russia.

The mineral-fertilizer industry has a total capacity of 16 to 20 million tons in terms of 100% nutrients. About 40% of this quantity are nitrogen fertilizers, 30% phosphate fertilizers, 25% potassium fertilizers, and 5% compound fertilizers. Potassium-rich primary materials are mined at Solikamsk, a town in the Perm Oblast boasting the world's biggest deposits, and are converted into fertilizers in the towns of Solikamsk and Berezniki.

Nearly 75% of Russian's phosphate fertilizers is obtained from concentrated apatites mined in the Khibini Mountains (which contain about two billion tons of apatites). Other major apatite deposits are located at Egorievsk and Polpino in the central region, and the Upper Kama mines in the Kirov Oblast. Production of phosphate fertilizers is contemplated at the Beloziminskoe fields in East Siberia.

Nitrogen fertilizers are produced either at coke-using enterprises in Berezniki, Gubakha, Kemerovo, Angarsk, Dzerzhinsk, and Moscow, or from coke gas at metal-making enterprises in Magnitogorsk, Nizhny Tagil, Novokuznetsk, Lipetsk, and Cherepovets. Natural gas is processed into nitrogen fertilizers at Nevinomyssk, Novomoskovsk, Shchekino, Novgorod, and Togliatti.

The Perm Oblast has the highest concentration of fertilizer-producing facilities, manufacturing all of Russia's potassium fertilizers and also some nitrogen and phosphate fertilizers, which the producers deliver directly to consumers.

Synthetic rubber production has a bright outlook in Russia, given the stable tire and auto market, and a sizable share of the output is being exported to developing countries around the world. The industry's leading producers are located in Yaroslavl, Voronezh, Kazan, Togliatti, Nizhnekamsk, Volzhsk, Chaikovsky, Sterlitamak, Omsk, and Krasnoyarsk.

As much as 80% of Russia's chemical yarn and fibers is manufactured in its European part, particularly in the Central and Volga Regions, with the principal centers specializing in the production of rayon fibers (Tver, Shuya, Ryazan, St. Petersburg, Balakovo, and Krasnoyarsk); synthetic fibers (Kursk, Volzhsky, and Saratov); or both (Barnaul, Engels, Serphukhov, and Klin).

46.11 LUMBERING AND WOODWORKING. Russia possesses 20% of the world's wood reserves, of which 50% is ripe and overripe stock. The potential lumber output ranges from 300 to 350 million cu m a year. The most extensive lumbering operations are carried out in the North and East Siberian economic regions. In 1990, lumbering production was the highest in the Irkutsk Oblast, where 35 million cu m of lumber were produced; the Krasnoyarsk Krai, the Arkhangelsk Oblast, and the Komi Republic, with 25 million cu m each, and the Vologda, Perm, Sverdlovsk, and Tomsk Oblasts, each producing 15 million cu m. Woodworking facilities are in operation at sites where railroads meet rivers navigable by rafts (Kotlas, Omsk, Novosibirsk, and Kransnoyarsk); in cities situated in the lower reaches and estuaries of major rivers capable of floating timber (such as Arkhangelsk and Igarka); and near timber-handling railroads (including those from Murmansk to St. Petersburg, Arkhangelsk-Vologda, and Vorkuta-Kotlas).

46.12 PULP AND PAPER INDUSTRY.   The main centers of the pulp and paper industry are located in the northern region (Kondopoga, Segezha, Arkhangelsk, and Kotlas), in the Urals (Krasnokamsk, Krasnovishersk, Solikamsk, and Novaya Lialia), in the Volga-Vyatka region (Balakhna and Pravdinsk), and on Sakhalin Island. In recent years, high-capacity integrated plants have been built in Krasnoyarsk, Bratsk, Ust Ilimsk, Baikalsk, Amursk, and Kotlas.

46.13 CONSTRUCTION.   Construction and the building-materials industry are predominantly practiced in the European part of Russia and in the south of West Siberia. The Center, Volga, and Ural Regions account for nearly a third of building and assembly jobs, producing almost 50% of the total building materials. Large construction units have formed near power dams in the regions located in the Volga drainage area, in the Krasnoyarsk Krai, and in the Irkutsk Oblast. The distribution pattern of the construction industry generally overlaps with that of the manufacturing industries. Surpluses of some items are produced in the regions of Central Russia.

Specialized glass-making enterprises and corporations are located in the Nizhny Novgorod, Novgorod, Tver, and Vladimir Oblasts. Corrugated roofing plates and insulation are manufactured in the Bryansk, Kaluga, and Moscow Oblasts.

Cement is produced in all economic regions. The industry is notable for its high concentration of machinery and plants, with almost half of the total output coming from plants that each have a capacity in excess of one million tons.

Large complexes producing building materials have arisen in mining areas, such as the Belgorod, Sverdlovsk, and Perm Oblasts, where overburden material and wastes from metal-fabricating enterprises can be utilized to manufacture building materials. The Ural Region boasts the world's largest asbestos deposit, which is mined at Bazhenovo. Also, high-quality asbestos grades are mined at the Kiembai in the Orenburg Oblast and in the Tyva Republic.

46.14 TEXTILES AND LEATHER.   Textile and leather manufacturing is distributed unevenly across Russia. The country's leading area is the Central Region, which contains of the world's biggest textile centers, in the Ivanovo Oblast, with the flax industry concentrated in Vladimir Oblast. The Center accounts for 60% of all the cotton fabrics and 40% of its woolens. Large woolen-industry centers are located in the Volga region in the Ulyanovsk and Saratov Oblasts, which process raw wool shipped from the steppes of southern Russian and Kazakstan. In the 1960s and 1970s, in an effort to undercut the textile monopoly of the Central and Volga Regions, new cotton mills were built in Krasnoyarsk and Barnaul, woolen factories were set up in Krasnoyarsk and Chita, silk works in Kemerovo, Orenburg, and Chaikovsky, and a linen mill in Biisk.

Footwear industry enterprises are mostly located in Central Russia, where 85% of the country's rawhide is produced and 80% of its footwear is manufactured.

Under current market conditions, textile manufacturing capacities cannot be fully utilized because of the irrational structure of the industry. Nearly 50% of the industry's plants were created to produce nonconsumer goods, including army uniforms, parachute and technical fabrics, tarpaulins, drive belts, filters, and auto tires. After the recent cutbacks in the armed forces and reduction of arms procurements, the domestic market for these products has dwindled. Despite the comprehensive retooling of the industry in the 1980s, it cannot be directed toward export products because of their low quality and competitive level. In some good years, only 5% of the total cotton-textiles output can be exported, with the figure for knitwear even lower, at 1%. Woolens alone put in a fair showing at 13%.

The Russian producers of silk, knitted, and hosiery products have failed to meet the local demand. Within the next two or three years, the share of imports in total fabric sales is not expected to rise above 30%, with knitwear predicted to reach 50%, hosiery 30%, ready-made garments 55%, and footwear up to 70%.

Little effort is being made to replace raw material imports with domestic produce in the textile market. In 1996, flax fiber purchases in Russia went down to 48,000 tons, from 103,000 tons in 1991 and 249,000 tons in 1967.

The production of chemical yarn does not meet the textile industry's requirements. The industry is, in fact, starving for synthetic yarns and fibers, but is glutted with handmade products. The situation is especially alarming in polyurethane and niton fibers, most of which are manufactured in Belarus.

46.15 AGRICULTURE.   In 1996 agriculture generated 18% of the gross national product, and employed about 20% of the able-bodied population. In structure, the agroindustrial complex is dominated by the raising of produce. The processing industry is weak and is concentrated chiefly in major cities. Bread-baking, sugar, and fruit- and vegetable-processing enterprises are, as a general rule, equipped with outdated machinery, capable of manufacturing simple and economically limited products.

Farming is practiced across the whole of Russia. The majority of farms operate in high-risk areas, where harvests vary from year to year and subsidies have to be pumped in from the federal and local budgets. Cattle raising suffers the most, with the majority of farms ending up as net losers. Areas north of the line from Ryazan to Kazan, Chelyabinsk and on to Tomsk and Krasnoyarsk are short of food resources, and their residents are supplied with foodstuffs imported from abroad or brought in from southern Russia.

Commercial grain farming is concentrated in the steppe and forest-steppe black-earth areas in southern Siberia, the Volga Region, and the Kuban drainage area. Nearly half of the cropland is planted with wheat, much of it with strong and hard varieties. In the long run, cereal yields can be boosted by 10 to 20%, harvests stabilized, and an export-oriented sector set up within Russia's agricultural complex.

In the Central, Volga-Vyatka, and Ural Regions, wheat is rivaled by rye, oats, and barley. Grain is grown here, chiefly for cattle feed; and food wheat is purchased in other areas or imported from abroad. Among other crops, a significant share of the farmlands are occupied by buckwheat (Central Russia, Volga Region, Southern Ural Region, and Siberia); rice (Kuban); legumes (Central Black Earth, Center, and Volga Regions).

Industrial crops are predominantly cultivated in southern Russia and the Black Earth areas, where sugar beets, sunflowers and hemp are grown. Flax is planted in the Smolensk, Tver, and Yaroslavl Oblasts.

Potatoes and other vegetables are widespread in Russia, particularly on truck farms run by members of the population. On a full-time basis, potato growing is concentrated in the Bryansk Oblast, other vegetables in the Astrakhan and Volgograd Oblasts, and viticulture and tea growing are practiced in the Northern Caucasus.

Dairy and beef cattle raising have developed in the Central and Central Black Earth Regions, where the stock grazes in pastures in the summer and is kept in sheds in the winter. Dairy and beef cattle farming is practiced in the pasture-rich steppes on the east banks of the Volga and east of the Ural Range, where feeder cattle are raised.

Hog raising is concentrated in areas producing a large amount of potatoes, in particular the Central Region and some areas in the Volga-Vyatka region; poultry farming is a specialty of the grain-producing areas in the Volga Region, the Northern Cascasus, and the southern part of Siberia.

In many ethnic Russian areas, animal farming provides the bulk of the jobs for inhabitants. In particular, sheep keeping is the core of the Kalmykian Republic's economy, reindeer grazing is the mainstay of the Sakha (Yakutia) Republic and ethnic groups in the North, and reindeer are raised for their antlers in the Altai Republic.

CHAPTER **47**

NORTH REGION

Aleko A. Adamescu, Yuri A. Kovalev, and Alexander G. Granberg

47.1 REPUBLIC OF KARELIA

1. Natural Resources. Area: 172,400 sq km. Farmland: 2,140 sq km. Woodland: 98,450 sq km. Swamps: 35,900 sq km. Bodies of water: 41,800 sq km. Population: 794,200 (Jan. 1, 1996), of which 74.1% is urban and 25.9% is rural. Population is concentrated mostly in the southern part and in the narrow strip along the Murmansk-St. Petersburg railroad. Population density: 4.6 per sq km.

   The republic lies 900 km north of Moscow. Lakes—a major tourist attraction—constitute 21% of its area, and swampland another 20%. There is an average annual runoff of 56.5 cu km, which fully meets the water needs of the economy and population. Because of the presence of undesirable organic matter, 80% of the water requires treatment before it can be used for economic or domestic purposes. Water is only lightly mineralized (25mg./liter). The total timber resources are equal to 821.5 million cu m, including 738.5 million cu m of softwood. The estimated cutting area is utilized at 90% of its capacity. The commercial cutting areas have a potential of 16 million cu m.

   Mineral resources include ferruginous quartzite (at Kostomuksha and Korpagan), over 1.4 billion tons in total reserves; chromium deposits in the Pudozh District, 47 million tons (its development is inappropriate for economic considerations); compound ores (uranium-vanadium, uranium-vanadium-metals of the gold/platinum group) in the Medvezhiegorsk District; molybdenum deposits at Labesh; small fields of kyanites (aluminum-yielding primary materials) in the Louha District and nickel in the Segezha District; small gold-ore fields with a gold content of 0.5 to 12 g/ton; chemical minerals (pyrite, halleflinta, fluorite, limestone); mica; quartzite; talc; graphite; and precious and semiprecious stones (amethyst, belomorite, granite, pink quartz, agate). Kostomuksha fields, the most developed site, supply primary materials for the Cherepovets integrated metal-fabrication plant.

   The climatic conditions in the republic range from temperate-continental to marine, with the mean January temperature lying in the range of -9 to $-14°C$, and July, from 18 to 16°C. Annual rainfall is 400–600 mm., and the growing season lasts from 70 to 125 days.

2. Specialization and Sectoral Structure of the Economy (see Exhibit 47.1). Administrative division: 15 districts, 13 cities, 44 urban-type communities, and 99 village group councils.

Exhibit 47.1.   Sectoral Structure of the Economy in 1996 (% of Total)

	Industry	Farming	Transport	Construction	Other
Employment	29.4	5.5	12.0	9.6	43.5
Fixed Assets	41.4	8.0	17.4	2.2	31.0
Capital Investment	38.7	5.4	21.0	1.0	33.9

Chairman of the Council of Ministers: Tel. (81400) 722 444. Fax 74 148. Chairman of the Supreme Council: Tel. 72 435. Fax 23 770.

Principal cities: Petrozavodsk (279,700), Sortavala (22,800), Segezha (38,200), Kondopoga (37,600), and Kostomuksha (31,800).

The manufacturing structure is dominated by lumbering and woodworking (40.8%), followed by the metal industry (14.9%), power generation (13.5%), and food production (11.3%). The republic's manufacturing enterprises have been designed to process such local resources as wood, iron ore, building materials, and sea products. (See Exhibit 47.2.)

The city of Petrozavodsk is a woodworking center, manufacturing equipment for the lumber industry. Its enterprises include the Avangard JSC (furniture), an integrated timber and furniture-making plant; the Onega tractor plant; the Karellesprom JSC; and the Petrozavodskbummash JSC (equipment for the pulp and paper industry). Kondopoga is a key producer of cast stones, marble slabs (Karelian Stone JSC), and paper for duplicating equipment (Kondopoga JSC). Lumber enterprises are situated in Landenpohja (plywood plant), Pitkaranta (paper plant and pulp and paper mill), Pudozh (timber-rafting JSC), Segezha (Bumprom JSC), and Sortavala (furniture and ski-making plant). Ore-mining and processing enterprises are located in Petrozavodsk (Petromica JSC for mica, and muscovite), Kostomuksha (Karelian Pellets JSC), Chupa township (Karelsljuda mining and concentrating plant), Medvezhiegorsk (gem cutting), and Segezha (Nadvoitsi aluminum plant).

The republic exports 24% of its industrial output, including 14% of its iron ore, and 76% of its timber products.

3. Investment Opportunities. The republic has a stable social and economic climate. It is among Russia's cost-attractive areas for foreign companies, most of which are Scandinavian. The republic is building its relations with other countries on the basis of its traditionally strong cultural and economic ties with Finland, through which the flow of Russian exports has intensified in recent years.

Exhibit 47.2.   Manufacture of Principal Industrial Products

	1995	1996
Iron ore, million tons	6.1	6.1
Commercial timber, thou. cu.m.	4,065.0	3,295.0
Lumber, thou. cu.m.	652.0	420.0
Paper, thou. tons	632.0	588.0
Meat, thou. tons	6.7	4.2
Whole milk products, thou. tons.	28.3	25.5

In the entire of the Northern Region, the republic has the best business infrastructure, including transportation, communications, offices, and hotels. With the exception of outdated pulp and paper mills and an aluminum plant, not a single patch of its territory is environmentally hazardous.

Opportunities for foreign investment exist in the following areas: the tourist complex at the republic's southern fringes, including Kizhi, Kivach, Petrozavodsk, Lake Onega shores, Lake Volozero, Lake Vohtozero (motels, hotels, well-equipped recreational areas, and access roads); transportation services for local and long-distance freight traffic; production of consumer goods for the undersupplied market in Russia's northern areas; renovation of the fish canneries in Belomorsk and Petrozavodsk; development of ore deposits (Medvezhiegorsk, Belomorsk, and Segezha districts); mining and the sale of iron ore jointly with the Karelian Pellets JSC; prospecting for diamonds; modernization of wood preprocessing; woodworking operations for the Segezha Bumprom and Kondopoga JSCs; development of furniture and ski manufacturing; furniture intermediates for export to European Union countries; expansion of the airport in Petrozavodsk; development of docking facilities in Petrozavodsk and Olonets; and road building.

In 1995, the republic had 211 joint ventures in operation with $28.4 million of foreign investment accumulated in 1993–95. Private ownership embraced 3.3% of the fixed assets of enterprises and organizations, with joint stock companies (without foreign interest) owning 72.7% and the federal authorities another 7.8%. The republic also had nine operational insurance companies and seven commercial banks, including Autobank (Tel. 73 345), Agrobank (Tel. 75 734), Nordwestbank (Tel. 73 610), Petrobank (Tel 50 218), and Tekobank (Tel. 49 352).

The republic is reachable from Moscow by rail (925 km to Petrozavodsk, 15 hours from Leningrad Terminal), air (two hours from Bykovo Airport), and road (the highway from Moscow, via Tver and St. Petersburg, to Petrozavodsk, 16 to 18 hours). The republic has 34 km of hard-surfaced roads per 1,000 sq km.

47.2 KOMI REPUBLIC

1. Natural Resources. Area: 415,900 sq km. Farmland: 4,100 sq km. Woodland: 279,000 sq km. Swamps: 39,400 sq km. Reindeer-grazing grounds: 84,100 sq km. Population 1,277,900 (Jan. 1, 1996), of which 74.7% is urban and 25.3% is rural. Settlements are clustered along the Vologda-Vorkuta railroad. Population density: 3.0 persons per sq km.

The republic is situated 1,500 km from Moscow, and much of its territory is comprised of bogs and swamps. The republic's northern areas lie in the tundra zone, with its typically strong winds and wide temperature fluctuations making permanent habitation a challenge.

Woodlands contain timber resources of 2,855.5 million cu m, including 2,493.8 million cu m of softwood. The estimated cutting area in the republic is utilized at 70% capacity. The commercial woodlands have a cutting potential of 40 million cu m. The republic has vast undeveloped woodland tracts, and with the building of forest roads and floating facilities, lumbering operations could be stepped up rapidly.

The mineral resources include oil, natural gas, coal, bauxite, rock salt, gypsum, limestone, manganese, barite, titanium-bearing ores, mineralized waters, peat, and building materials.

The republic contains 94 prospective oil and natural-gas fields, with total recoverable resources of nearly 700 million tons of oil and 500 billion cu m of natural gas. Over the next five years, oil production can be raised by eight million tons as new oilfields are developed by joint ventures (Nobel Oil, Komiarcticoil, Am Komi) and more fields are made operational after 1996. The Komi Republic will continue to be the principal oil-producing area for Russia's North (with up to 12 million tons a year) until 2005. The residual natural-gas reserves in the republic are equal to 178.5 billion cu m, including 102.5 billion cu m of condensed gas at the Vuktyl fields. Gas resources can be expanded considerably, provided large investments are made in geological studies and field preparation, but expenses per unit of output will be higher even than that produced in the Stockman gas field in the Barents Sea.

The Pechora coal basin sprawls between the cities of Vorkuta and Inta. It has considerable resources for generating and coking coal, but coal mining is not economical because of the unfavorable climate and the high maintenance costs of production facilities and social services. As a result, many mines will be shut down, and others will be subsidized so they can continue operation.

A number of projects have been drawn up, and preparatory work has begun to mine and process the republic's other minerals. These include building a mine, modeled after the Middle Timan bauxite operation to produce 6.5 million tons of bauxite ore; establishing an aluminum plant in Ukhta to produce one million tons of aluminum a year; developing the Yarega field (Komititan JSC), where a mine producing 2 to 2.5 million tons of ore annually is to be built and facilities set up to produce titanium-based paints and varnishes; and mining the manganese fields at Tarnogorsk (Marganets Komi JSC).

A large part of the Komi Republic lies in an area known for its harsh climate, severe frost, and strong winds, with mean January temperatures of -20 to $-25°C$, July temperatures of $17°C$, and annual rainfall of 400 to 600 mm. The growing season is a short 30 days in the north and up to 130 days in the south, but most of the area is unsuitable for crop farming.

2. Specialization and Sectoral Structure of the Economy (see Exhibit 47.3). Administrative division: 16 districts, 10 cities, 39 urban-type communities, and 188 village group-councils.

Chairman of the Council of Ministers: Tel. (82122) 23 101. Fax 23 770).

Principal cities: Syktyvkar (242,600), Vorkuta (113,500), Ukhta (110,900), Inta (68,400), and Pechora (64,800).

The manufacturing structure is dominated by the fuel industry (50.6%), followed by lumbering and woodworking (16.6%), and power generation (16.1%). The head offices of the oil and gas enterprises are located in Vuktyl, Sosnogorsk, Usinsk, and Ukhta (Komineft JSC). Other major enterprises include the gas-processing plant in Sosnogorsk, the oil refinery in Ukhta, and the thermal power plant in Pe-

Exhibit 47.3. Sectoral Structure of the Economy in 1996 (% of Total)

	Industry	Farming	Transport	Construction	Other
Employment	28.3	5.9	11.2	12.9	32.2
Fixed Assets	42.4	3.6	28.9	2.6	18.8
Capital Investments	36.2	2.9	23.1	0.6	33.8

chora. The leading lumbering and woodworking enterprises are the Sysolales JSC, the saw mill, the woodworking group, and the furniture plant in Syktyvkar; the Pechoralesosplav JSC in Pechora; and the Pechorales JSC in Troitse-Pechorsk. (See Exhibit 47.4.)

The republic exports 11% of its industrial output, which consists mostly of crude oil, oil products (76%), and timber (23%).

3. Investment opportunities. The republic offers favorable conditions for the initiation of various projects in the oil and gas industry, ore mining, and lumbering. The principal areas of investment include geological prospecting; field development and production of oil and gas; construction of mines to extract titanium concentrate, bauxite, barite, and manganese ore; manufacture of titanium-dioxide-based paints and varnishes; modernization of the Ukhta refinery; and projects in lumbering and sawing, hunting, and tourism. Local and federal government support will be extended to projects in lumbering and sawing, hunting, and tourism, as well as to projects that provide new job openings for unneeded mine workers of the Pechora fields.

Project-risk evaluation should consider the high costs of labor, difficulties in the delivery of building materials, unreliable transportation and telecommunications, especially in the winter; and unconventional social attitudes—the area has numerous labor camps and prisons and, as a result, an above-normal proportion of people with a criminal past.

In 1995, the Komi Republic had 59 joint ventures in operation with $170.2 million of foreign investment accumulated in 1993–95. The fixed assets of enterprises and organizations were 29.9% privately owned, 16.2% owned by joint stock companies (without foreign interest), and 33.4% in federal ownership. There are 13 operating insurance companies and 16 commercial banks, including Kometabank (Tel. 36 777), Komibank (Tel. 21 548), Komiinkombank (Tel. 30 105), Sectoral Komilesbank (Tel. 24 205), and Syktyvkarbank (Tel. 20 145).

The republic is reachable from Moscow by rail (1,515 km to Syktyvkar, 26 hours from Yaroslavl Terminal) and air (two hours from Bykovo Airport).

The republic has 7.2 km of hard-surfaced roads per 1,000 sq km.

47.3 ARKHANGELSK OBLAST AND NENETS AUTONOMUS OKRUG

1. Natural Resources. Area: 587,400 sq km. Farmland: 7,600 sq km. Woodland: 226,700 sq km. Reindeer-grazing grounds: 120,800 sq km. Other land: 117,900 sq km.

Exhibit 47.4. Manufacture of Principal Industrial Products

	1995	1996
Oil, million tons	6.8	7.3
Natural Gas, bn cu.m.	3.6	3.7
Coal, million tons	22.27	21.38
Commercial timber, thou. cu.m.	6056	4784
Lumber, thou. cu.m.	800	680
Paper, thou. tons	382	302
Plywood, thou. cu.m.	52.5	48.3
Meat, thou. tons	6.1	4.8
Whole milk products, thou. tons	42.4	31

Population: 1,547,400 (Jan. 1, 1996), of which 73.3% is urban and 26.7% is rural. Population density: 2.6 per sq km, one of the lowest in central Russia. The population tends to settle along railroads and in riverside communities where there are lumbering enterprises.

The oblast lies 1,000 to 1,200 km from Moscow. A large part of its territory is water-logged or swampy, and its northern fringes open toward the White and Barents Seas.

A total of 207,600 sq km of woodlands is federally owned. The timber resources amount to 2,376.3 million cu m, including 2,194.4 million cu m of softwood. The commercial cutting potential is 40 million cu m, but the lack of a business infrastructure hinders development.

The oblast's mineral resources include oil, natural gas, bauxite, diamonds, and primary building materials.

The largest oilfields are located at Vasilievskoe, Yareiyusskoe, Layavozhskoe, Yuzhno-Shapkinskoe, and Kharyaginskoe. Bauxite is mined at Severo-Onezhskoe; limestone at Shvankinskoe and Savinskoe; and diamonds at Lomonosov. The Arkhangelsk Oblast and the Nenets Autonomus Okrug have 75 prospected oilfields (including 10 major ones) with total recoverable reserves in excess of one billion tons. Prospects for the expansion of oil and gas production are essentially associated with the Nenets area. As of January 1, 1994, the book recoverable oil reserves topped 840 million tons. Some 460 billion cu m of natural-gas reserves have been prospected, along with nearly 20 million tons of condensed gas. The oblast has coal reserves estimated at 215 million tons, including 50 million tons of coking coal. The condensed-gas deposit at Vasilkovskoe is operational at present, and great potential for more condensed gas exists through the development of deposits at Layavozhskoe (5 bil cu m/year), and Vaneivinskoe (4.3 bil cu m/year). Arkhangelsk-Geologia and the Conoco company have formed a joint venture to develop these gas fields. The Lomonosov diamond deposit, 90 km north of Arkhangelsk, consists of six pipes. The yield of jewelry-grade diamonds is estimated at 50%. The enterprise that will be established to develop the deposit will have a full annual capacity of 10 million tons of ore.

Bauxite is mined at the North Onega mine in the township of Severoonezhsk; the potential exist for raising output fivefold from the present level. The bauxite is delivered for processing to the Boksitogorsk plant in the Leningrad Oblast.

The Arkhangelsk Oblast lies in a harsh climate, with a mean January temperature ranging from −12 to −18°C, with 18°C in July. It receives an annual rainfall of 300 to 500 mm. The growing season lasts 50 days in the north and 130 days in the south.

2. Specialization and Sectoral Structure of the Economy (see Exhibit 47.5). Administrative division: 20 districts, 13 cities, 38 urban-type communities, and 240 village group-councils.

Exhibit 47.5.   Sectoral Structure of the Economy in 1996 (% of Total)

	Industry	Farming	Transport	Construction	Other
Employment	30.8	7.3	12.6	6.7	42.6
Fixed Assets	40.3	9.3	17.5	5.1	27.8
Capital Investment	35.3	2.7	17.0	0.8	44.5

Administrative head: Tel. (8182) 37 912. Fax 34 029.

Principal cities: Arkhangelsk (413,600), Severodvinsk (249,800), Kotlas (68,700), Novodvinsk (50,000), and Koryazhma (43,100).

The manufacturing structure is dominated by lumbering and woodworking (46.9%), followed by the food industry (15%), and engineering (11%). The urban and the larger rural communities in the oblast were formed around cores of one or two enterprises that employ a workforce of 1,000 or less and produce lumber; manufacture woodchips, packages, and railroad sleeping cars; export wood; and carry out rafting operations. Severodvinsk, the location of Russia's largest shipyards, builds and repairs nuclear-powered submarines. Plisetsk has a launch site for commercial satellites and other types of space vehicles that are launched into a geostationary orbit. Arkhangelsk is a large woodworking center comprised of five integrated woodworking plants, three furniture plants, a timber port at Maimak, many other smaller woodworking enterprises, and facilities for repairing and replacing equipment for the lumber industry. A large pulp and paper mill is located in Koryazhma, along with repair facilities and fish and algae-processing (agar production) enterprises. (See Exhibit 47.6.)

The Arkhangelsk Oblast exports 20% of its industrial output, including marine products (11%), timber products (86%), and satellite-launching services.

Farming and meat and milk processing in the central and northern parts of the region are only sidelines. Because of the unfavorable natural conditions, the southern areas are unsuitable for the production of high-quality, sanitary dairy products.

3. Investment Opportunities. The oblast is among the more stable areas of Russia, offering a favorable opportunity for investment in the oil and gas, lumber, and fishing industries. The socioeconomic situation is complicated by two factors: under-capacity operation of the engineering enterprise in Severodvinsk and the many areas appropriated by the Russian Defense Ministry, Interior Ministry, and Space Exploration Administration. Any investment plans should take into account the lack of building materials (cement, metalwork, heating materials, gypsum products, bricks) in the majority of the oblast's districts; shipping problems; inadequate telecommunication facilities; and the underdeveloped service industry in all but a few cities.

Investment opportunities are available for a wide range of projects in the following areas: lumbering and wood processing, oil-field and gas field development, fishing and fish processing, production of food and nonfood consumer goods (of which there is a shortage in Russia's northern areas), fee-based hunting and fishing, geological prospecting, development of the Lomonosov diamond deposits, and participation

Exhibit 47.6. Manufacture of Principal Industrial Products

	1995	1996
Oil, thousand tons	2,700	3,024
Commercial timber, thou.cu.m.	7,372	6,782
Lumber, thou.cu.m.	1,462	1,272
Paper, thou. tons	211	226
Pulp, thou. tons	1,340	938
Roofing Slate, million tiles	25.7	26.0
Fish catch, thou. tons	131	155
Meat, thou. tons	9.78	6.86
Whole milk products, thou. tons	26.4	18.8

in building the sea terminal north of the Varandei township, a project that is sponsored by a consortium consisting of Texaco, Exxon, Amoco, and Norsk Hydro.

In 1995, the Arkhangelsk Oblast had 79 joint ventures in operation with $672.6 million of foreign investment. Private owners held 7.2% of the fixed assets of the enterprises and organizations, with 23.1% owned by joint stock companies (without foreign interest), 62.3% federally owned, and 2.1% owned by companies with foreign interest. The oblast had 15 operating insurance companies and 10 commercial banks, including Agroprombank (Tel. 43 5719), Promstrojbank (Tel. 43 8189), Sevcombank (Tel. 47 3578), and Social Bank (Tel. 46 2926).

The oblast is reachable from Moscow by rail (1,133 km to Arkhangelsk, 19 hours from Yaroslavl Terminal) and air (two hours, with six flights daily from Sheremetyevo Airport).

The oblast has 9 km of hard-surfaced roads per 1,000 sq km.

47.4 MURMANSK OBLAST

1. Natural Resources. Area: 144,900 sq km. Farmland: 400 sq km. Woodland 32,900 sq km. Reindeer-grazing grounds: 74,000 sq km. Bodies of water: 12,000 sq km. Population: 1,109,400 (Jan. 1, 1996), of which 92.5% is urban and 7.5% is rural. Population density: 7.5 per sq km, one of the lowest in Russia.

   The oblast lies 1,900 km north of Moscow in the Kola Peninsula and provides Central Russia with a key outlet to sea traffic routes.

   Total timber reserves are insignificant at approximately 210.5 million cu m, including 182.7 million cu m of softwood. The estimated cutting area in use in the oblast is at 90% capacity.

   Mineral resources include kyanite, apatite-nepheline ore, copper-nickel, iron, titanium-magnesium ore, quartz, mica, rare earth metals, and various building materials. Some of the famous deposits are kyanite in the Keivin Mountains; apatite-nepheline ores at Kukisvumchor, Jukspor, and Raovumchor; copper-nickel ore at Monchegorsk and Pechenga; iron ore at Olenegorsk and Ensko-Kovdor; and mica on the riverbanks of the Ena and Streina. The oblast has the potential to become a base for the development of the oil-bearing shelf in the Barents Sea. The eight oil and condensed-gas fields discovered thus far have total book reserves in excess of 100 million tons of oil and about 3 trillion cu m of gas. The prospective reserves of oil are 275 million tons, and gas 1.7 trillion cu m. The biggest oilfield is Stockman, which contains 2.9 trillion cu m of gas and 21.8 million tons of condensed gas in recoverable reserves. A joint-stock company, Rosshelf (51% of its shares are owned by the Russian Gazprom Joint Stock Company), was established to develop the Stockman field.

   The oblast has a severe climate, with the mean temperature ranging between −5 to −11°C in January and 8 to 14°C in July. It gets 300 to 750 mm. of annual rainfall and the growing season lasts between 80 and 130 days. The climate does not support commercial farming.

2. Specialization and Sectoral Structure of the Economy (see Exhibit 47.7). Administrative division: five districts, 12 cities, 20 urban-type communities, and 20 village group-councils.

   Administration head: Tel (81500) 56 540.

   Principal cities: Murmansk (468,300), Apatit (87,300), Severomorsk (67,200), Kandalaksha (54,200), and Monchegorsk (68,200).

Exhibit 47.7. Sectoral Structure of the Economy in 1995 (% of Total)

	Industry	Farming	Transport	Construction	Other
Employment	30.7	2.2	10.4	9.7	47.0
Fixed Assets	46.1	3.1	13.5	5.9	31.4
Capital Investment	41.7	1.3	13.0	0.8	43.2

The manufacturing structure is dominated by nonferrous metallurgy (31.9%) and the food industry (22.5%), followed by power generation (19.8%), and the chemical industry (8.8%). The Murmansk Oblast is one of the more industrially developed areas of Russia's North Region, accounting for 46% of the nickel output in Russia, 11% of its refined copper, 100% of the apatite and nepheline concentrates, and a significant share of rare-earth products. The leading enterprises are the aluminum plant in Kandalaksha; the Apatite JSC in Kirov; the integrated iron-ore mining and enriching plant and the Kovdorsljuda production association in Kovdor; the Severredmet JSC in the Revda township (rare-earth metals); the Severonickel integrated plant in Monchegorsk (cobalt, blister copper, and nickel production); the integrated iron-ore mining and enriching plant in Olengorsk; the Pechenganickel integrated plant in Zapolyarny (nickel production); and the nuclear-power plant in Polyarnie Zori. Murmansk, a seaport with nine large joint-stock companies that turn out almost 20% of Russia's seafood products, has ship repair facilities and is the base for trawler and commercial fishing fleets. (see Exhibit 47.8.)

The oblast exports 16% of its manufactured output, including fish products (50%), nonferrous-metal ores and apatite concentrate (17%), and nonferrous metals (28%).

3. Investment Opportunities. The oblast holds a special political, transportation, and strategic military position in northern Russia. The Murmansk seaport is one of Russia's key transportation and fishing bases. It handles ocean-going shipments and serves as the primary point of the Northern Sea Route, which is used to deliver commodities to Russia's northern areas and to carry nickel ore from Norlisk for processing at local nickel plants. The main areas of investment include the development of the seaport and its fishing and fish-processing enterprises. Other areas attractive to investors are: the development of the Stockman gas field and the supporting infrastructure; transportation and pipeline systems; mining, including the processing and sale of ores and metals; food production, including butter, confectionery, margarine, alcoholic beverages, which are in short supply in northern markets; small-scale enterprises that manufacture colored stones, bricks, roof tiles, and other building materials for construction programs in the north; and the production of powder from

Exhibit 47.8. Manufacture of Principal Industrial Products (1994)

	1995	1996
Iron ore, million tons	7.0	6.1
Fish catch, thou. tons	357	364
Meat, thou. tons	4.6	2.1
Whole milk products, thou. tons	25.0	20.2

phlogopite and muscovite at the facilities of the Kovodorsljuda JSC. Investment plans must take into account the high risks involved in the development of gas fields on the Barents Sea shelf. These include technological problems, inexperience in Arctic commercial operations, and the unknown market.

In 1995, the Murmansk Oblast had 166 operating joint ventures with 6.7 million of foreign investment. Private owners held 2.5% of the fixed assets of enterprises and organizations; joint stock companies (without foreign interest) owned 39.3%; and the federal authorities controlled 45.5%. The oblast also had 12 insurance companies and 11 commercial banks, including Agroprombank (Tel 74 003), Articbank (Tel. 63 590), Barentsbank (Tel. 63 630), Murman (Tel. 50 787), Murmanskbank (Tel. 73 841), Murmansk Social Bank (Tel. 18 3012), Northern Marine Bank (Tel. 22 655), and Sevzapcombank (Tel. 62 153).

The oblast is reachable from Moscow by rail (1,967 km to Murmansk, 35 hours from Leningrad Terminal) and air (three hours from Sheremetyevo Airport).

The oblast has 16 km of hard-surfaced roads per 1,000 sq km.

47.5 VOLOGDA OBLAST

1. Natural Resources. Area: 145,700 sq km. Farmland: 14,600 sq km. Woodland: 104,200 sq km. Swamps: 12,400 sq km. Population: 1,355,300 (Jan. 1, 1996), of which 66.7% is urban and 33.3% is rural. Population density: 9.3 per sq km. The population is sparse despite the oblast being part of the historic core of Russia. The people tend to live near railroad lines, in lumbering communities, and on the banks of navigable rivers.

The oblast lies 500 km north of Moscow. Some of its territory is boggy and swamplike, but it has enough water for all purposes.

Woodlands include 1,335.4 million cu m in timber reserves, with 818.4 million cu m of softwood. The estimated cutting area is used at 70% of its capacity. The commercial cutting potential is 20 million cu m.

Mineral resources include peat, building materials, table salt, and quartz sands. The major mineral deposits are located at Ulom and Dedovo Pole (peat), and Petryaevskoe, Sludninskoe, and Krasnoborskoe (quartz sand).

The oblast has a temperate-continental climate with short, humid, cool summers and long, cold winters. The mean temperature is −14°C in January and 18°C in July. The annual rainfall varies from 480 to 600 mm, and the growing season lasts from 100 to 125 days.

2. Specialization and Sectoral Structure of the Economy (see Exhibit 47.9). Administrative division: 26 districts, 15 cities, 14 urban-type settlements, and 376 village group-councils.

Administration head: Tel. (81722) 20 764. Fax 51 554.

Exhibit 47.9. Sectoral Structure of the Economy in 1995 (% of Total)

	Industry	Farming	Transport	Construction	Other
Employment	31.2	12.8	7.8	10.3	37.9
Fixed Assets	42.8	15.3	10.0	5.1	26.8
Capital Investment	29.6	8.0	19.0	2.0	41.4

Principal cities: Vologda (301,400), Cherepovets (317,100), Veliky Ustyug (36,200), and Sokol (46,700).

The manufacturing structure is dominated by basic metallurgy (55.3%), the chemical industry (9.1%), and lumbering and woodworking (7.4%). Vologda has precision-engineering enterprises (an optomechanical plant, the 23rd Bearing Plant, Electrotechmash plant, and machine-tool plant); textile and leather enterprises (lace, garments decorated with northern motifs, furs, sheepskins, embroidery); food industry enterprises; and small businesses that manufacture furniture, skis, and lumbering equipment. Cherepovets, the oblast's second-largest industrial center, has the Azot production association (nitrogen fertilizers and ammonia), the Ammofos production association (sulfuric acid phosphate fertilizers), a large integrated steel plant, and a steel-rolling plant. The economic base of the oblast's small and medium-sized cities is formed by lumber, meat-packing, dairy, linen, and glass-making enterprises. The biggest of these enterprises are the Sokol and Sukhona pulp and paper mils in Sokol, the Northern Flax JSC in Veliky Ustyug, the Northern Timber JSC in Vytegra, and the glass plants in Kharovsk and Smerdomlya township. (See Exhibit 47.10.)

The oblast is one of 15 export-oriented regions exporting 41% of its industrial output, of which finished rolled stock accounts for 75%, mineral fertilizers and other chemical products for 19%, and timber products for 4%.

Most of the farm products supply local needs, but the great variety of grasses create favorable conditions for the production of meat and dairy products for sale to the oblast's adjacent areas.

3. Investment Opportunities. The oblast ranks among the most stable areas of Russia. Enterprises in lumbering, the chemical industry, and ferrous metallurgy have a solid primary base and ready markets, and provide a steady flow of revenue to the local budget. Vologda, Cherepovets, and cities situated near railroads and highways have easy access to building materials.

The principal areas of investment include the development of basic metal and chemical enterprises in Cherepovets; tourism along with recreation and hunting facilities offered by historical centers such as Vologda, the St. Cyril-St. Ferapont monastery, Belozersk, and Veliky Ustyug; production of foodstuffs for northern markets; manufacture of foodstuffs, including products made from berries and mushrooms, and confectioneries for export; small garment-making businesses (lace); and handcrafted wood carvings.

The main limitations to investment include the large distances to iron-ore suppliers (in the Murmansk Oblast) and coking-coal companies (in Vorkuta); the large

Exhibit 47.10. Manufacture of Principal Industrial Products

	1995	1996
Finished basic metal rolled stock, m. tons	6.7	7.4
Commercial timber, thou. cu.m.	4,285	4,075
Lumber, thou. cu.m.	520	416
Window panes, thou. sq. m.	3,546	2,482
Meat, thou. tons	31.24	28.74
Whole milk products, thou. tons	105	106

fluctuations in prices charged by these suppliers; the adverse environment in Cherepovets; the slow growth of the network of hard-surfaced roads; and the appropriation of the oblast's northern areas by the Interior Ministry.

In 1995, the Vologda Oblast had 62 joint ventures in operation with $27.1 million of foreign investment. Private owners held 24.1% of the fixed assets of enterprises and organizations, with 43.2% owned by joint stock companies (without foreign interest), and another 16.4% by federal authorities. It also had 11 insurance companies and 22 commercial banks, including Vaskbank in Cherepovets (Tel. 22 165), Vlogdbank (Tel. 21 610), Vologzhaniin (Tel. 50 914), Marobank (Tel. 29 282), Metallurgical Bank in Cherepovets (Tel. 73 694), Rosselkhozbank (Tel. 20 050), Servicebank (Tel. 48 128), Sovetski (Tel. 28 659), Social Development Bank (Tel. 22 596), and Cherepovetski Bank in Cherepovets (Tel. 53 310).

The oblast is reachable from Moscow by rail (497 km to Vologda, nine hours from Yaroslavl Terminal), air (two hours from Bykovo Airport), and road (the highway from Moscow, via Yaroslavl, to Vologda, 11 hours driving time).

The oblast has 71 km of hard-surfaced roads per 1,000 sq km.

CHAPTER 48

NORTHWEST REGION

Aleko A. Adamescu, Yuri A. Kovalev, and Alexander G. Granberg

48.1 ST. PETERSBURG

1. Natural Resources. Area: 600 sq km. Population: 4,883,000 (Jan. 1, 1996).

   St. Petersburg stands on the Neva River, where it empties into the Gulf of Finland, and on the islands of the Neva Delta (Vassilievsky, Krestovsky, Elagin, the Decembrists, etc., numbering 101 in all). Parts of the city are susceptible to flooding caused by strong westerly winds. The mayor has control over several cities known for their historic parks and palaces, such as Petrodvorets, Pushkino, Sestroretsk, Lomonosov, Pavlosk, Kolpino, and Kronstadt. St. Petersburg is Russia's second-largest industrial, cultural, financial, scientific, and transportation center after Moscow (see Exhibit 48.1).

   The city has a marine climate, with a mild winter and frequent thaws. The mean temperature in January is −8°C and 17°C in July. The Neva freezes over for four months.

2. Specialization and Sectoral Structure of the Economy (see Exhibit 48.1).

   The manufacturing structure is dominated by engineering (36.3%), textiles and leather (7.1%), power engineering (11.7%), power generation (13.7%), and the food industry (18.2%). The largest enterprises are the optomechanical association (LOMO), the Remote Communications Research and Development association (communications equipment), the Lenybprom industrial association, the Kalinin Plant industrial association, The Northern Plant Industrial Association, the Vector Research and Development Association, the Northern Dawn JSC (powdered articles), the Northern Shipyard JSC (shipbuilding), the Elektrosila JSC (electric machinery), the Intos JSC, the Zvezda JSC (diesel engines), the Izhora Plants JSC (equipment for nuclear-power engineering and line machines), the Position JSC (televisions), the Raduga JSC (televisions), the Svetlana JSC (electrical engineering), the Skorokhod JSC (footwear), the Aurora Plant, the turbine blade plant, the Proletarsky Plant (pumps and electrical equipment), the Kirov Plant (tractors), the Leningrad Metal Plant (hydraulic and steam turbines), the Rossia Plant (instruments), the Ferropribor Plant (acoustic systems), the Petrodvorets Watch Factory (timepieces), the LEMZ eletromechanical plant (electric meters), the Admiralty Shipyards Plant, and the Krasny Treugolnik plant (industrial-rubber products). The city's manufacturing and scientific complex has, in a large measure, been formed to help develop Russian northern areas and to expand the navy and merchant marine. It

Exhibit 48.1.   Sectoral Structure of the Economy in 1995 (% of total)

	Industry	Farming	Transport	Construction	Other
Employment	28.3	0.5	9.7	11.2	50.3
Fixed assets	26.1	0.0	22.3	2.3	49.3
Capital investment	20.8	0.1	1.7	1.3	76.1

has one of the country's largest complexes of science-intensive enterprises, producing power-generating equipment, electric machines, ships, radio electronics, radar, and instruments. (See Exhibit 48.2.)

The city exports 3.5% of its manufactured output, chiefly consisting of engineering products.

3. Investment Opportunities. St. Petersburg is a stable area with long-standing traditions of economic cooperation with European countries. It is second only to the Moscow metropolitan area in terms of the high quality of the hotel infrastructure, financial institutions, telecommunications networks, and air and sea freight facilities. St. Petersburg offers favorable conditions for locating representative and main offices and branches of firms commissioned to establish and operate dealer networks, as well as branches engaged in trading, financial, and consulting activities.

Investment prospects include science-intensive engineering; the manufacture of marine equipment, communications facilities, and telecommunications; hotel industry, tourism, and leisure facilities; modernization of port facilities; realty market operations; and programs to build an infrastructure for hosting international sports and cultural events.

In 1995, St. Petersburg had 1290 joint ventures in operation with about $280.6 dollars of foreign investment. Private owners held 12.6% of the fixed assets of enterprises, joint stock companies (without foreign interest) owned 20.5%, the federal authorities controlled 36%, and foreigners owned 6.8%. The city had 82 insurance companies and 41 commercial banks.

The city is reachable from Moscow by rail (651 km, 6–10 hours from Leningrad Terminal) and road (the highway from Moscow, via St. Petersburg, to Helsinki, 16 hours).

48.2 LENINGRAD OBLAST

1. Natural Resources. Area: 85,900 sq km. Farmland: 8,440 sq km. Woodland: 50,000 sq km. Population: 1,668,900 (Jan. 1, 1996), of which 66.1% is urban and 33.9% is rural. Population density: 76.3 per sq km, one of the highest in the country.

Exhibit 48.2.   Manufacture of Principal Industrial Products

	1995	1996
Steam turbines, thou. kW	3,225	2,000
Heating radiators, thou. kW	493	291
Televisions, thou.	4.8	0.9
Video cassette recorders, thou.	0.9	0.9
Electric vacuum cleaners, thou.	126	89.5
Meat, thou. tons	8.8	6.9
Whole milk products, thou. tons	179	190

The oblast lies 650 km north of Moscow. It is adequately provided with water and has numerous lakes. Some areas in the oblast's east are swampy and boggy, making travel and product delivery between localities that are a considerable distance from hard-surfaced roads quite difficult in the spring and fall.

The woodlands contain 790.5 million cu m of timber, including 516.1 million cu m of softwood. The oblast's estimated cutting area is used at 60% capacity. Many forests, particularly in the vicinity of St. Petersburg and on the Karelian Peninsula are used for recreation and water conservation and cannot be used for commercial purposes. The commercial cutting potential is 8 million cu m.

The oblast's scarce mineral resources include building materials and peat. It has, however, some heavily overworked deposits of strategic resources, such as bauxite at Tikhvin, phosphate at Kingisepp, and oil shale a short distance form the Estonian border. The city of Kingisepp mines 3.4 million tons of oil shale, and has an operational plant producing gas from shale and a thermal-power plant burning locally produced gas. A project has been drawn up to burn shale and generate heat and power at the new thermal-power plant in Novgorod and at a second stage of the thermal-power plant in Pskov.

The oblast's climate combines marine and temperate-continental conditions, with the mean January temperature ranging from −7 to −11°C and standing at 16°C in July. The rainfall over the oblast varies from 450 to 650 mm. The growing season lasts from 150 to 170 days.

2. Specialization and Sectoral Structure of the Economy (see Exhibit 48.3). Administrative division: 17 districts, 29 cities, 38 urban-type communities, and 212 village group-councils.

Administration Head: Telephone (812) 274–3563, Fax (812) 271–5627.

Principal cities: Gatchina (80,900), Vyborg (80,900), Tikhvin (72,000), Sosnovy Bor (57,600), and Kirishi (53,800).

The manufacturing structure is dominated by the fuel industry (35.6%), followed by lumbering and woodworking (11.8%), and nonferrous metallurgy (7.6%). The oil refinery at Kirishi is the principal supplier of motor fuels and fuel oil in the Northwest. With a full capacity of 18 million tons, it is operating at 60 to 70%. The refinery gets its oil from West Siberia and Ukhta, but its production of light products is relatively low because of its inefficient technologies. Two alumina plants in Koksitogorsk and an aluminum plant in Volkhov process local primary materials (mined at Pikalevo), materials from the North Onega mine in the Arkhangelsk Oblast, and nepheline concentrates delivered from the Kola Peninsula. These plants manufacture aluminum of extra purity for use in the aircraft industry and shipbuilding. Other products are double super phosphate, soda, and potash. The biggest woodworking enterprises include the Syask pulp and paper mill in Syasstroi, the prefabricated-housing plant in the Nevskaya Dubrovka township, the Svetlogorsk production association, the pulp and paper mill and the offset-paper

Exhibit 48.3. Sectoral Structure of the Economy in, 1995 (% of total)

	Industry	Farming	Transport	Construct	Other
Employment	29.6	13.4	6.9	8.6	41.5
Fixed assets	40.2	24.5	5.0	7.6	22.7
Capital investment	49.8	6.5	14.5	0.9	28.3

factory in Vyborg, the cigarette-paper factory in Gatchina, and the integrated furniture plant in Priozersk. (See Exhibit 48.4.)

The oblast exports 13% of its manufactured output, mainly oil products (64%).

Farming is intended to meet the needs of urban dwellers, in particular the residents of St. Petersburg. Although the oblast is short of foodstuffs, farm production is being scaled down because of its high cost to the local producers, who face several adverse conditions: a severe climate, large expenses, and low motivation on the collective farms, which continue to rely on easy-to-get loans and centralized purchases of their produce. The situation is improving in the zone adjoining St. Petersburg, where Dutch potato-growing techniques are being introduced and other moves are being made to restructure farming practices.

3. Investment Opportunities. The Leningrad Oblast is a stable area closely tied by economic links to St. Petersburg. Therefore, the biggest joint projects with St. Petersburg must be planned with an eye to their possible extension to the Leningrad Oblast, including the construction of main- and auxiliary-production space, and of warehousing and transportation facilities.

The principal areas of investment include the renovation of oil refineries and aluminum and woodworking enterprises for conversion to export operations; the construction of oil export terminals that will be connected to main oil pipelines; and development of the Leningrad tourist and recreational zone that will be linked to similar areas in Karelia and in the Novgorod, Pskov and Vologda Oblasts. In individual enterprises, investments are needed to initiate production of high-quality paints, varnishes, and household chemicals at the Morozov plant in Vsevolozsk, the Era JSC in Tikhvin and others for local and foreign markets; to boost production of phosphate fertilizers at Boksitogorsk and at the Phosphate Production Association in Kingisepp; to increase the production of artwork ceramics at Lodeinoe Pole (Dyatsk Ceramics); to help the manufacture of speedboats, yachts, and ship equipment at the Pirs Plant, the shipbuilding plant in Vyborg, Pella Mash JSC in Otradnoe, and the shipyard in the Nikolskoe township; to contribute to small-scale projects for the garment industry; and to increase production of building materials and glassware.

In 1995, the Leningrad Oblast had 49 operating joint ventures. Private owners held 29.1% of the fixed assets of enterprises, with joint stock companies owning 13.5%, the federal authorities 38.5%, and foreign and mixed interests 0.3%. The oblast had four insurance companies and five commercial banks, including Gatchinacom bank in Gatchina (Tel. 13 081) and Vyborg bank in Vyborg (Tel. 25 398).

The Leningrad Oblast can be reached from Moscow by rail (651 km to St. Petersburg, five to nine hours from Leningrad Terminal), air (1.5 hours from Shere-

Exhibit 48.4.   Manufacture of Principal Industrial Products

	1995	1996
Power, bn kWh	26.4	24.8
Primary oil products, million tons	12.1	15.2
Cement, thou. tons	1,831	1,318
Ceramic tiles, thou. sq. m.	1,025	615
Cardboard, thou. tons	120	94.8
Meat, thou. tons	21.2	12.7
Whole milk products, thou. tons	103	80.3

metyevo Airport), and the highway running from Moscow, via Tver to St. Petersburg (10–11 hours).

The amount of hard-surfaced roads is 129 km per 1,000 sq km.

48.3 NOVGOROD OBLAST

1. Natural Resources. Area: 54,500 sq km. Farmland: 8,390 sq km. Woodland: 36,120 sq km. Population: 747,400 (Jan. 1, 1996), of which 70.6% is urban and 29.4% is rural. Population density: 13.5 per sq km.

The oblast lies 600 km north of Moscow. It has sufficient water supplies, which it draws from over 1,000 big and small lakes and nearly 800 waterways. Many areas are heavily swamped or bogged. In the spring and fall, large amounts of surface water hinder the delivery of produce between localities lying more than 500 miles from hard-surfaced roads.

Woodlands contain 526.7 million cu m of timber, of which 226.2 million cu m is softwood. Coniferous trees take up 40%, and birch trees 30%, of the woodland area. The estimated cutting area is used at 50% capacity. The commercial cutting potential is 4.5 million cu m. The oblast exports lumber to many of Russia's other areas.

Available minerals include such staples as metalliferous-construction limestones, fireclay, quartz sand, mineral dyes, and others. The best-known peat fields are located at Kushaverskoe and Tesovo, and fireclay is produced at Borovichi. Building and packing sands, pebbles, and gravel are quarried all around the oblast. The Staraya Russa, Seltse, and Valdai districts are known for their mineralized-water sources.

The oblast has a temperate-continental climate, with the mean January temperature between −4 and −8°C, and the mean July temperature at 17°C. The oblast gets 600 to 650 mm of rainfall per year, and the growing season varies from 120 to 130 days.

2. Specialization and Sectoral Structure of the Economy (see Exhibit 48.5). Administrative division: 21 districts, 10 cities, 22 urban-type communities, and 275 village group-councils.

Administration head: Tel. (81600) 74 729.

Principal cities: Novgorod (235,200), Borovichi (62,500), Staraya Russa (41,600), and Valdai (19,700).

The manufacturing structure is dominated by the chemical industry (31%) and engineering (18%), followed by the food industry (11.8%), and lumbering and woodworking (12.1%). (See Exhibit 48.6.)

Engineering in the oblast is a science-intensive industry (radio electronics and equipment for the chemical industry).

The local chemical industry, with the Azot Joint Stock Company the undisputed leader, specializes in the production of nitrogen fertilizers (87% of the total output

Exhibit 48.5.   Sectoral Structure of the Economy in 1995 (% of total)

	Industry	Farming	Transport	Construction	Other
Employment	31.4	12.2	6.4	8.4	41.6
Fixed assets	33.9	20.0	7.2	15.0	23.9
Capital investment	26.1	8.9	17.0	0.6	47.4

Exhibit 48.6. Manufacture of Principal Industrial Products

	1995	1996
Mineral fertilizers (thou t)	664	744
Paper (thou t)	7.2	3.38
Plywood (thou cu m)	31.8	50.2
Televisions (thou)	16.5	1.5
Videocassette recorders (thou)	702	152
Meat (thou t)	7.2	8.0
Whole-milk products (thou t)	18.7	15.0

in the Northwest), ammonia, nitric acid, carbamide resins, caprolactam, and compound fertilizers with a high nutrient assimilation rate.

The oblast's wood-processing industry is centered around lumbering and plywood manufacture. The oblast accounts 30% of the timber exports in the Northwest and for 13% of plywood and paper output. With the current restrictions on the expansion of lumbering operations, the industry's prospects are limited to comprehensive utilization of the available stock and increased product quality.

Refractors manufactured at the integrated works at Borovichi are exported to other countries and areas. The building-materials industry meets the needs of road construction projects. The oblast exports 25% of its industrial output, primarily fertilizers and chemicals.

Farming is essentially intended to supply the local market with meat and dairy products. The agro-industrial complex has the potential to produce 240,000 to 300,000 tons of potatoes, 65,000 to 70,000 tons of other vegetables, 4,000 tons of flax fiber, and 25,000 to 30,000 tons of meat. In the medium term, the growth opportunities for cattle farming will be undercut by the industry's high share of costs, which prevent its being price competitive in the markets of the country's Northwest and Center Regions. The outlook is fairly good for flax growing once an association comprising the Kulotinskaya Manufacturer factory, the Voskhod spinning factory in Borovichi, and the Iskra Knitwear Association (which handles everything from flax growing to the production of consumer goods), is set up under the relevant Novgorod Flax program.

3. **Investment Opportunities.** The Novgorod Oblast is a thoroughly stable area. The promising areas of investment include radio electronics (14 enterprises and two research institutes), television equipment, components, and sophisticated household appliances; renovation of the refractory plant in Borovichi; the manufacture of wallpaper, furniture, lumber, and fiberboard; and development projects for railroads and roadside service facilities.

The Novgorod Oblast is one of Russia's historical centers. Its foreign-travel potential is estimated at 410,000 tour days a year, with 120,000 to 130,000 tourists driving along the road linking Moscow, St. Petersburg, and Helsinki every year. Initiatives to take advantage of this opportunity include establishing the business center in Novgorod and lodging facilities for vacationers, promoting the growth of ecologically safe produce, and generally catering to tourists.

In 1993–95, the oblast received $12.7 million of foreign investment. In 1995, it had in operation 72 joint ventures. Private owners held 20.5% of the fixed assets of its enterprises, joint stock companies (without foreign interest) owned another

16.3%, the federal authorities 28.7%, and foreign and mixed interests 12.8%. It also had six operating insurance companies and three commercial banks, including Agroprombank (Tel. 27 208), Novobank (Tel. 36 167), and Slavianbank (Tel. 36 001).

The oblast is reachable from Moscow by rail (606 km to Novgorod, nine hours from Leningrad Terminal), air (two hours from Bykovo Airport), and by the highway running from Moscow, via Tver and Novgorod, to St. Petersburg (10–11 hours).

There are 147 km of hard-surfaced roads per 1,000 sq km. of the oblast's territory.

48.4 PSKOV OBLAST

1. Natural Resources. Area: 55,300 sq km. Farmland: 15,820 sq km. Woodland: 21,890 sq km. Population: 836,600 (Jan. 1, 1996), of which 64.8% is urban and 35.2% is rural. Population density: 15 per sq km.

The oblast lies 690 km northwest of Moscow, on the main watershed of Russia's European territory. It has sufficient amounts of water. The areas bordering the Novgorod Oblast are heavily bogged, and in the fall and spring transporting farm produce more than 500 miles from hard-surfaced roads is difficult.

Woodlands contain 308 million cu m of timber, including 136.9 million cu m of softwood. The estimated cutting area is used at 50% capacity. The oblast's commercial cutting potential is equal to 2.4 million cu m a year.

The oblast has only limited natural resources. Its timber resources of 308 million cu m comprise 9.4% of Russia's total; its other resources include peat (764.4 million tons) and building stones (26 million cu m). It also has mineral-dye deposits containing 3,400 tons of the material, which are currently being developed by the St. Petersburg decorative-paints plant; a deposit of high-heat clay at Pechora; and 11 deposits of sand used in construction and the manufacture of silicate products (see Exhibit 48.7).

The oblast has a temperate-continental climate, with a mean temperature of −8°C in January and 18°C in July. The rainfall varies from 600 to 650 mm. The growing season lasts 140 days.

2. Specialization and Sectoral Structure of the Economy. Administrative division: 24 districts, 14 cities, 13 urban-type communities, and 247 village group-councils.

Administration head: Tel. (81122) 22 203.

Principal cities: Pskov (208,500), Velikie Luki (115,800), Ostrov (29,000), and Nevel (22,200).

The manufacturing structure is dominated by engineering (34.4%), the food industry (23.8%), and textiles and leather (8.5%). The biggest enterprises include the radio-engineering, cable-making, and electric-machine plants, the Elvo JSC, and

Exhibit 48.7. Sectoral Structure of the Economy in 1995 (% of total)

	Industry	Farming	Transport	Construction	Other
Employment	26.7	17.5	8.5	7.7	36.0
Fixed assets	21.3	28.2	21.5	3.5	39.9
Capital investment	20.9	5.8	10.2	0.6	62.5

Exhibit 48.8.   Manufacture of Principal Industrial Products

	1995	1996
Low power electric motors for household appliances, thou.	821	443
Ceramic facing tiles, thou. sq. m.	401	400
Tape-recorders thou.	5.2	3.2
Refrigerators, thou.	10.2	3.8
Meat, thou, tons	7.4	5.1
Whole milk products, thou. tons	21.8	17.0

Avtoelektroarmatura, which produces electrical equipment for motor vehicles. The oblast exports 3% of its industrial output, including textile products (47%), as well as metals, power cables, electric motors, and canned fish. (See Exhibit 48.8.)

The main agricultural activity is dairy farming and cattle raising. The major crops in the oblast are flax, vegetables, and potatoes. In 1992, farms under various forms of ownership raised 309,200 tons of grain, 417,500 tons of potatoes, 122,500 tons of vegetables, and 3,500 tons of flax fiber.

3. Investment Opportunities. The Pskov Oblast is a stable area. The most promising areas of investment include the building of an infrastructure in the border zone and the construction of housing for the armed forces and persons resettling from the far northern areas; fish processing; electrical engineering; and expansion of the Pskov airport.

The oblast is visited every year by 11,000 foreign tourists, who stay for an average of 1.8 days. There are no special accommodations for them, and those that are leased are below the standards of many other countries. Because only 10% of the oblast's travel potential is utilized, it is necessary to create a travel infrastructure, including hotels, campsites, and leisure homes.

In 1995, the oblast had 87 joint ventures in operation. Foreign investments in 1993–95 reached $1.1 million. Private interests held 37.5% of the fixed assets of enterprises, joint stock companies (without foreign interest) owned 20.3%, the federal authorities held 32.1%, and foreign and mixed interests held 0.4%. The oblast also had four insurance companies and 10 commercial banks, including Agroprom bank (Tel. 69 280), Pskovautodor bank (Tel. 32 904), Vesta (Tel. 39 506), and Pskovbank (Tel. 23 670).

The oblast is reachable from Moscow by rail (689 km to Pskov, 14 hours from Leningrad Terminal) and air (three hours from Bykovo Airport).

There are 151 km of hard-surfaced roads per 1,000 sq km.

CHAPTER 49

CENTER REGION

Aleko A. Adamescu, Yuri A. Kovalev, and Alexander G. Granberg

49.1 BRYANSK OBLAST

1. Natural Resources. Area: 34,900 sq km. Farmland: 19,140 sq km. Woodland: 11,340 sq km. Population: 1,471,600 (Jan. 1, 1996), of which 68.4% is urban and 31.6% is rural. Population density: 41.1 per sq km.

   The oblast lies 400 km south of Moscow. Its principal rivers are the Desna, Navlya, and Sudost, and it has numerous lakes.

   The woodlands contain 157.9 million cu m of timber resources, including 84 million cu m of softwood. The oblast's estimated cutting area is used at 85% capacity. The commercial cutting potential is 2.4 million cu m.

   The mineral resources include peat, limestone, clay, sand, and phosphorite.

   The oblast has a temperate-continental climate, with the mean January temperature equal to $-8°C$ and the mean July temperature reaching $10°C$. It receives 450 to 580 mm of annual rainfall, and the growing season varies from 180 days to 200 days.

2. Specialization and Sectoral Structure of the Economy (see Exhibit 49.1). Administrative division: 27 districts, 16 cities, 31 urban-type communities, and 413 village group-councils.

   Administration head: Tel. (08322) 42 140. Fax 13 185.

   Principal cities: Bryansk (460,600), Novozybkov (42,400), and Daytakovo (34,900).

   The manufacturing structure is dominated by engineering (31.7%) and the food industry (26.4%), followed by textiles and leather (8.2%) and building materials (12.5%). The largest enterprises include Bryansk Engineering Plant JSC, Motor Plant JSC, a road-building-equipment plant, Bryanskembel JSC (furniture producer), Portland Cement JSC, and Bryansktextile JSC. Bryansk is the oblast's major industrial center, supplying the Russian market with diesel locomotives, trucks, road graders, farm machines and spare parts, cement, glass, heating devices, paper and board, woolen fabrics, and footwear. It exports 3% of its manufactured output, of which machinery and equipment comprise 48% and transportation vehicles 30%. (See Exhibit 49.2.)

   The oblast's farms specialize in dairy and beef cattle, hogs, and sheep, as well as growing cereals, fruit, and berries. It is one of the leading suppliers of potatoes to

Exhibit 49.1.   Sectoral Structure of Economy in 1995 (% of total)

	Industry	Farming	Transportation	Construction	Other
Employment	29.9	17.0	7.5	8.6	37.0
Fixed Assets	26.9	27.8	18.2	4.8	22.3
Capital Investment	13.8	19.5	6.6	4.0	56.1

the markets of central Russia. The food industry is built around butter factories, cheese creameries, and meat-packing plants using local animals.

3. Investment Opportunities. The oblast's southern areas were severely hit by the accident at the Chernobyl nuclear-power plant in 1986. Any economic activity is limited here, and work is underway to rehabilitate the affected areas and to resettle the population from the areas with the worst contamination. The oblast's larger part, including Bryansk and its suburbs, is free from radiation. Considerable financial resources are being contributed to this rehabilitation program, and projects that create new jobs for the oblast's population are heavily promoted. The rural areas and smaller towns are faced with a motivation problem in that individuals receiving payment for damages have an income that is comparable to the wages drawn by farmers.

Promising areas of investment include the manufacture of automotive equipment, modernization of plants, construction of potato-processing facilities, and research in radiation medicine.

In 1995, the oblast had 63 joint ventures in operation, with foreign investments of $3.2 million. Private owners held 33% of the fixed assets of enterprises, joint stock companies (without foreign interest) owned another 29%, and the federal authorities controlled 24.6%. The oblast also had seven insurance companies and 10 commercial banks, including Bezhista-bank (Tel. 56 7826), Bryanskcreditbank (Tel. 61 667), Bryanskpromobank (Tel. 42 449), and Bryansksotsbank (Tel. 65 879).

The oblast can be reached from Moscow by rail (379 km to Bryansk, 10 hours from Kiev terminal) and air (1.5 hours from Vnukova Airport).

There are 193 km of hard-surfaced roads per 1,000 sq km of the oblast's territory.

49.2   IVANOVO OBLAST

1. Natural Resources. Area: 23,900 sq km. Farmland: 9,000 sq km. Woodland: 11,400 sq km. Population: 1,300,400 (Jan. 1, 1996), of which 81.6% is urban and 18.4% is rural. Population density: 54.4 per sq km.

Exhibit 49.2.   Manufacture of Principal Industrial Products

	1995	1996
Road Graders	489	445
Cement, thous. tons	2,397	1,678
Asbestos board, million tiles	23.2	11.4
Heating boilers, mW	202	151
Woolen fabrics, thous. sq.m.	4,674	1,828
Bicycles, thousands	66.5	87.8
Meat, thous. tons	20.0	16.8
Whole milk products, thous. tons	38.0	27.7

The oblast lies 330 km northeast of Moscow, and has the Volga and Klyazma as its chief waterways. Most of the oblast's territory is well supplied with water.

Woodlands include 7,600 sq km that are under federal control. Timber resources are equal to 156.9 million cu m, of which 86.9 cu m is softwood. The oblast's estimated cutting area is used at 90% capacity. The commercial potential is 2.1 million cu m.

Mineral resources include gypsum, clay, gravel, dolomite, limestone, quartz sand, marl, and phosphorite.

The climate is temperate-continental, with a mean January temperature of −12°C and 18°C in July. Rainfall varies from 550 to 600 mm annually, and the growing season is between 180 and 185 days.

2. Specialization and Sectoral Structure of the Economy (see Exhibit 49.3). Administrative divisions: 22 districts, 17 cities, 32 urban-type communities, and 216 village group-councils.

Administration head: Tel. (0932) 32 8125. Fax 37 2485.

Principal cities: Ivanovo (477,900), Kineshma (104,200), Shuya (70,200), Vichuga (49,400), and Furmanov (45,400).

The manufacturing structure is dominated by the textile and leather industry (35.6%), followed by the food industry (15.4%) and engineering (18.7%). The Ivanovo oblast, the largest textile producer in the Russian Federation, manufactures 33% of the nation's cotton fabrics. Large enterprises are located in Ivanovo, Kineshma, Shuya, Furmanov, Teikovo, and Rodniki. Linen production is centered in Privolzhsk, Kineshma, and Vichuga. In addition, the region has major woolen and knitwear factories. Engineering enterprises include the Autocrane JSC, the machine tool association, the Tochpribor JSC (precision instruments), the Ivtekmash JSC (textile machines), and the SMaTep JSC. The chemical industry is represented by enterprises producing fabric-finishing dyes and acids. (See Exhibit 49.4.)

The handicraft industries at Palekh and Kholui that produce lacquered paintings and miniature artwork are world famous. The region exports 2.3% of its manufactured output, most of it textiles (31%), and dyes and acids (57%).

Farmers specialize in raising cattle and fowl to meet local needs.

Exhibit 49.3.   Sectoral Structure of the Economy in 1995 (% of total)

	Industry	Farming	Transport	Construction	Other
Employment	38.4	9.8	6.1	7.4	38.3
Fixed assets	40.9	22.4	11.6	2.4	22.7
Capital investment	43.4	8.6	8.1	1.2	38.7

Exhibit 49.4.   Manufacture of Principal Industrial Products

	1995	1996
Crane trucks, thou	2,425	1,673
Cotton fabrics, million sq.m.	702	658
Linen fabrics, million sq.m.	17.3	12.3
Woolen fabrics, million sq.m.	5.4	3.8
Meat, thous. tons	7.75	5.42
Whole milk products, thous. tons	35.0	21.3

3. Investment Opportunities. The economic situation in the Ivanovo Oblast is, in many respects, among the worst in the country. The textile, linen, and woolen industries have problems selling their output; and technological backwardness prevents them from producing competitive large-width fabrics. Government subsidies are permanently needed to purchase imported cotton, wool, and flax and to keep a majority of enterprises in business. First priority will, therefore, be given (1) to projects capable of retaining the existing jobs at textile enterprises by renovating and converting them to the manufacture of export-bound goods, and (2) to projects aimed at creating new jobs in other industries for employees who are unneeded in the textile and woolen enterprises. Other promising areas of investment include the manufacture of cranes, road-building machines, machining centers, numerically controlled machine tools, and handicrafts.

In 1995, the oblast had 16 joint ventures in operation with foreign investments of $1.4 million. Private owners held 20.4% of the fixed assets of enterprises and organizations, joint stock companies (without foreign interest) owned another 37.9%, and the federal authorities controlled 27.4%. The oblast also had 13 insurance companies and eight commercial banks, including Agroprombank (Tel. 35 0683), Ivanovo (Tel. 23 4330), Kranbank (Tel. 32 602), and Textile (Tel. 32 623).

The oblast can be reached from Moscow by rail (381 km to Ivanovo, seven hours from Yaroslavl terminal), air (one hour from Bykovo Airport), and road (the highway from Moscow, via Vladimir, to Ivanovo, five to six hours driving time).

There are 146 km of hard-surfaced roads per 1,000 sq km of the oblast's territory.

49.3 KALUGA OBLAST

1. Natural Resources. Area: 29,900 sq km. Farmland: 14,000 sq km. Woodland: 13,700 sq km. Population 1,087,600 (Jan. 1, 1996), of which 73.5% is urban and 26.5% is rural. Population density: 36.4 per sq km, half of the average for the central economic region.

The oblast lies 200 km northeast of Moscow. Its main waterways are the Oka and its tributaries, the Zhizdra, the Ugra, and the Protva. Most of the oblast's territory is well supplied with water.

Woodlands include 6,900 sq km under federal control. The forests contain 212 million cu m of timber resources, including 64 million cu m of softwood. The oblast's estimated cutting area is used at 75% capacity. The commercial potential is 2.1 million cu m.

Mineral resources include fireclay, quartz sand, limestone, phosphorite, and low-grade sulfur-rich lignite.

The climate is temperate-continental, with a mean January temperature of $-10°C$ and 19°C in July. It gets 600 mm of annual rainfall and has a growing season of 210 days.

2. Specialization and Sectoral Structure of the Economy (see Exhibit 49.5). Administrative divisions: 24 districts, 18 cities, 14 urban-type communities, and 340 village group-councils.

Administration head: Tel. (08422) 72 357. Fax 41 636.

Principal cities: Kaluga (363,600), Obnisk (101,500), Lyudinovo (43,900), and Kirov (35,900).

The manufacturing structure is dominated by engineering (41.3%), the food industry (15.9%) and building materials (9.6%). Industrial concentration in the

Exhibit 49.5. Sectoral Structure of Economy in 1995 (% of total)

	Industry	Farming	Transportation	Construction	Other
Employment	31.5	11.7	5.2	10.3	41.3
Fixed Assets	32.2	22.5	12.9	3.7	28.7
Capital Investment	13.1	6.8	20.4	1.9	57.8

Kaluga Oblast is relatively low compared to most of the other regions of central Russia. Medium-sized and small enterprises predominate. Engineering is represented by the diesel locomotive plant in Lyudinovo, the turbine and electrical-engineering plant in Kaluga, the foundry machine undertaking in Kirov, the match and furniture enterprises in Kaluga (Gigant JSC) and Balabanovo, the paper plant in Kondrovo, and the glass plants in Kozelsk and Kaluga. The oblast exports 5% of its industrial output, chiefly metals (59%), turbines, some equipment for nuclear-power plants, and motor vehicle components. (See Exhibit 49.6.)

Farmers specialize in raising dairy cattle, hogs, and fowl. There are a few specialized flax-growing undertakings. The private truck farms run by members of the population supply potatoes, vegetables, and berries to the Moscow Oblast.

3. Investment Opportunities. The Kaluga Oblast is ranked among the more stable areas of the country. The majority of its enterprises are medium sized, so they can be easily reorganized; and the oblast has considerable territorial and labor resources to sustain development. Twenty-four former defense-industry enterprises have been converted to produce consumer goods. Science-intensive facilities can be set up in Obnisk and Kaluga to utilize the workforce currently employed by the Russian Nuclear Industry Ministry, the 12 research institutes, and the Signal plant. Plans have already been launched to begin the joint production of steam and gas units with Siemens, Germany, and the manufacture of photographic materials for Polaroid cameras. Other promising investment areas include knitted goods and linen articles, communications facilities, electrical household appliances, and development of the leisure industry and hunting facilities. Additional opportunities include the construction of enterprises to process milk, meat, and potatoes for delivery to other areas, including the Moscow Oblast.

In 1995, the oblast had 56 operating joint ventures. The foreign investments in 1993–95 totaled $77.9 million. Private owners held 25.4% of the fixed assets of enterprises and organizations; joint stock companies (without foreign interest) owned another 18.4%; and the federal authorities controlled 38%. The oblast also

Exhibit 49.6. Manufacture of Principal Industrial Products

	1995	1996
Bath tubs, thous.	153	122.4
Ceramic sanitary ware, thous.	1,027	955
Matches, thous. crates	1,597	2,044
Paper, thous. tons	30.2	24.5
Meat, thous. tons	21.2	17.6
Whole milk products, thous. tons	581	656

had 10 insurance companies and 11 commercial banks, including Agroprombank (Tel. 75 203), Invescobank (Tel. 78 520), Kaluga (Tel. 12 1886), Kaluga Innovation Bank (Tel. 23 693), Utilities Bank (Tel. 74 017), and Promstroibank (Tel. 73 259).

The oblast can be reached from Moscow by rail (188 km to Kaluga, three hours from the Kiev terminal) and road (the Moscow-Kaluga highway, 2.5 hours driving time).

The oblast has 142 km of hard-surfaced roads per 1,000 sq km of territory.

49.4 KOSTROMA OBLAST

1. Natural Resources. Area: 16,100 sq km. Farmland: 10,600 sq km. Woodland: 45,500 sq km. Population 810,200 (Jan. 1, 1996), of which 65.8% is urban and 34.2% is rural. Population density: 13.5 per sq km, one of the lowest in central Russia.

   The oblast lies 400 km northeast of Moscow. It is fully self-sufficient in water resources, and it has mineral springs, which are used in the towns of Bui, Manturovo, and Sharia for curative purposes and for balneological purposes in Kostroma and Soligalich.

   Woodlands cover 77% of the oblast's territory, with 32,800 sq km being under federal control. Forests contain 649.4 million cu m of timber, including 333.8 million cu m of softwood. The commercial potential is 10 million cu m, the biggest of the central Russian oblasts.

   Mineral resources include peat, sapropel, phosphorites, building materials such as brick clay for expanded aggregate, sand for silicate bricks, carbonate stock for cement, and construction lime. The major deposits of peat equal 283 million tons, and those of sapropel are estimated at 500 million tons, which are produced on a commercial scale at Lake Galich.

   The climate is temperate-continental, with a mean January temperature of −14°C and 18°C in July. Annual rainfall is approximately 600 mm, and the growing season lasts 160 days.

2. Specialization and Sectoral Structure of the Economy (see Exhibit 49.7). Administrative divisions: 24 districts, 11 cities, 14 urban-type communities, and 267 village group-councils.

   Administration head: Tel. (09422) 73 4762. Fax 73 395.

   Principal cities: Kastroma (282,300), Sharia (26,900), Bui (32,900), and Nerekhta (30,100).

   The manufacturing structure is dominated by electrical engineering (31.7%), mechanical engineering (14.4%), lumbering and woodworking (15%), textiles and leather (8.1%), and the food industry (12.8%). The Kostroma thermal-power station, one of the biggest hydrocarbon-fired utilities in central Russia, generates enough

Exhibit 49.7.   Sectoral Structure of Economy in 1995 (% of total)

	Industry	Farming	Transportation	Construction	Other
Employment	26.9	12.5	7.1	9.8	43.7
Fixed Assets	29.9	23.3	9.8	12.4	24.6
Capital Investment	15.8	6.9	16.9	1.9	58.5

power for the whole region. The local engineering enterprises produce digging machines, fiberglass ships, engine and crane components, heating equipment, and machine tools. The oblast's lumbering and woodworking industry delivers lumber, chipboard, and fiberboard to markets in central Russia. Large lumbering enterprises are located at Ponizovo, Bui, Manturovo, and Galich. Textile enterprises produce linen (the second largest total capacity in Russia), knitted goods, and garments. The oblast has a large-capacity printing facility specializing in calendars. It exports 5.5% of its industrial output, mostly lumber (46%), textile products (27%), and machinery (14%). (See Exhibit 49.8.)

Farmers specialize in raising beef and dairy cattle, hogs and fowl. Grain is grown to provide animal feed.

3. Investment Opportunities. Kostoma Oblast is known for its stable social climate; it is adequately provided with water and power and possesses a healthy natural environment. The best investment opportunities are in the linen industry; the manufacture of road-building machinery; instrument production; small-scale woodworking and furniture-making enterprises; the production of ecologically safe foods; processed meat and dairy products; fresh and canned berries and mushrooms, handicrafts (Krasnoe on the Volga, Kostroma, and Soligalich); the tourist and leisure industries; fee-based hunting and fishing; and the construction of hotel complexes in Kostroma, Makarievo, and Soligalich. In the long run, the oblast may revert to its former specialization in commercial meat and dairy farming and the production of butter and cheeses for export. A prospective investor should be aware of the oblast's poor network of roads (81 km of roads per 1,000 sq km) and the low level of infrastructure development in its eastern part. The most favorable conditions for construction and exporting are offered by the strips of territory on both sides of the Volga River and the Trans-Siberian Railroad.

In 1995, the oblast had 56 operating joint ventures. The foreign investments in 1993–95 were $100,000 dollars. Private owners held 31.2% of the fixed assets of enterprises and organizations, joint stock companies (without foreign interest) owned another 27.7%, and the federal authorities controlled 27.3%. The oblast also had eight insurance companies and 13 commercial banks, including Agroprombank (Tel. 57 3871), Bank for Foreign Trade (Tel. 57 7646), Kostromabank (Tel. 57 2829), and Kostromasotsbank (Tel. 55 6865).

The oblast can be reached from Moscow by rail (371 km to Kastroma, seven hours from Yaroslavl terminal), air (1.5 hours from Bykovo Airport), and road (the highway from Moscow, via Yaroslavl, to Kostroma, nine hours driving time).

There are 81 km of hard-surfaced roads per 1,000 sq km.

Exhibit 49.8.   Manufacture of Principal Industrial Products

	1995	1996
Electric power, billion kWh	10.8	10.3
Spinning machines	44	29
Wooden houses, thous. sq.m.	5.1	n/a
Linen fabrics, million sq.m.	14.4	n/a
Meat, thous. tons	6.04	5.62
Whole milk products, thous. tons	19.8	11.5

49.5 MOSCOW OBLAST

1. Natural Resources. The Moscow Oblast is the most densely populated area in the country; its 47,000 sq km supporting a population of 15,436,500, including nearly nine million in Moscow itself. Population density is 328.4 per sq km.

   The oblast is overindustrialized with over 3,500 industrial enterprises and organizations; and the density of its transportation, engineering, and pipeline networks is on a par with those of developed European countries.

   The Moscow Oblast's surface runoff is estimated at 8.2 million cu km a year. Its water needs are supplied from the reservoirs of the Moskva-Vazuza and Volga systems. In addition to this surface water, the oblast uses some 3.8 cu m of underground water daily, with its proven reserves standing at 4.7 million cu m a day. The present operating systems meet the water requirements of the oblast's industries and population, but the water quality, especially drinking water, is below standard in many areas. The prospects for increasing water consumption are also limited.

   The oblast's mineral resources include phosphorite, marl, peat, low-quality coal, and building materials.

   The availability of building materials is always critical because of the intensive industrial and housing construction. At present, over 40% of the 240 mineral deposits in the area are worked on a regular basis. The more heavily worked deposits are located in Moscow's green belt of woods and parks and in the area around its water-supply line. These deposits account for 14% of the oblast's prospected minerals and 22% of the total in operation, producing about 25% of the oblast's sand and gravel and about 45% of its clay. Preparations are under way to develop standby reserves of glass sands, gravel, broken stone, and brick components located in adjoining regions. Efforts have been stepped up to replace the traditional mineral materials with industrial wastes.

   Woodlands contain 340.4 million cu m of timber, including 176.3 million cu m of softwood. The oblast's estimated commercial potential is 2.2 million cu m.

   The climate is temperate-continental, with a mean January temperature of −10°C and 17°C in July. Annual rainfall varies from 450 to 650 mm, and the growing season lasts 175 days.

2. Specialization and Sectoral Structure of the Economy (see Exhibit 49.9). Administrative divisions: 39 districts, 73 cities, 109 urban-type communities, and 474 village group-councils.

   Administration head: Tel. (095) 20 6093. Fax 20 6862.

   Principal cities: Podolsk (206,400), Lyubertsy (163,700), Kolomna (163,300), Mytischi (153,100), Elektrostal (152,200), Serpukhov (140,100), Balashika (137,300), Kaliningrad (135,800), Orekhovo-Zuevo (135,300), Khimki (134,800), and Odintosovo (129,900).

   Nearly 15% of Moscow's regular workforce lives in the suburbs.

Exhibit 49.9.   Sectoral Structure of Economy in 1995 (% of total)

	Industry	Farming	Transportation	Construction	Other
Employment	31.1	6.8	5.7	13.0	43.4
Fixed Assets	36.3	16.9	7.9	7.7	31.2
Capital Investment	20.0	8.2	14.9	2.8	54.1

The manufacturing structure is dominated by engineering (33.8%), textiles and leather (10.9%), the food industry (9.1%), and the chemical industry (7.9%). The manufacturing industries use raw materials and fuels brought in from outside the oblast and require a highly skilled workforce. The leading enterprises include a heavy engineering plant at Kolomna, a heavy engineering association in Elektrostal, a subway-car building association in Mytishchi, a storage-battery plant in Podolsk, a farm machinery plant in Lyubertsy, a bus plant in Likino, and high-quality steel plant in Elektrostal. The chemical industry enterprises produce sulfuric acid, synthetic resins, chemical yarn and fibers (in Klin), material fertilizers (in Voskresensk), and paints and varnishes (in Sergiev Posad). The textile industry is centered in Orekhovo-Zuevo, Noginsk, Yegorievsk, Serpukhov, Naro-Fominsk, and Ivanteevka. Major construction industry enterprises are located in Voskresensk (asbestos board), Podolsk, Dmitrov, and Kolomna; and china and glazed-pottery producers have factories in Likino-Dulevo and Vertilki. The oblast is crowded with defense-industry enterprises, on the basis of which research and development complexes have been formed in Troitsk (nuclear and laser facilities); Chernogolovka (research); Kaliningrad, Khimki, Lukhovtsky (aerospace); Istra and Serpukhov (radar); Dubna (nuclear research); and Khukovsky, with an (aerodynamic center unparalleled in the world). (See Exhibit 49.10.)

Between 1993 and 1995, the automotive, aerospace, and other industries took steps to start developing competitive products. The Likino plant has been converted to the production of the LIAZ 5256 model bus, at a full capacity of 5,000 units a year. In Golitsino, facilities are being constructed to build 2,500 interurban 0303 Mercedes-Benz buses annually. The manufacture of electric trains has been launched at the Demikhovo plant near the city of Orekhovo-Zuevo. The oblast exports 4% of its industrial products, 30% of which is chemical output; metalware, machinery and equipment, instruments, fabrics, and services each account for another 10% of this output. The oblast's administration has been promoting the expansion of products intended for export to Latin America and the Middle East.

Farming is typically suburban, with vegetables (grown both in the open and in greenhouses), fruit and berries, flowers, fowl, and dairy products. The public sector, deprived of its previous generous supply allocations, is losing ground to private producers. Staple crops are experiencing one of the deepest slumps of any of the

Exhibit 49.10. Manufacture of Principal Industrial Products

	1995	1996
Sewing machines, thous.	663	n/a
Elevators	792	403
Mainline diesel locomotive, sections	12	5.2
Subway cars	144	184
Cement, thous. tons	2,658	1,887
Asbestos board, million tiles	81.82	98.18
Ceramic facing tiles, thous. sq.m.	1,665	1,149
Mineral fertilizers, thous. tons	374	340
Cotton fabrics, million sq.m.	136	108.8
Silk fabrics, million sq.m.	19.26	16.18
Meat, thous. tons	56.9	59.7
Whole milk products, thous. tons	296	272

country's economic sectors, down nearly 40% from 1991, as publicly owned farms are setting up their own sales units in order to hold on to the Moscow market against heavy competition.

Land in the Moscow Oblast trades at prices that are among the highest in the country, caused, perhaps, by the construction boom, especially by the growing number of cottage and summer-home starts.

3. **Investment Opportunities.** Many Moscow-based firms are currently expanding their operations to the suburbs because of high costs in the city. In particular, they are transferring warehousing, fuel, and lubricant storage facilities, the production of building materials and heavy structures, and food preparation for restaurants, cafes, and hotels to suburban areas. Fee-based fishing, hunting, and leisure facilities are on the rise as well (at the Ruza, Mozhaisk, and Istra reservoirs, and at the Zafidovo wildlife refuge).

The social situation is fairly calm and stable in the oblast. Most people in small towns and rural communities still live at the subsistence level and are resentful of the ongoing economic reforms because engineering and textile enterprises are operating under capacity while the farming economy remains depressed.

The Moscow Oblast offers fertile ground for investment in all economic sectors, beginning with the modernization of the metal fabrication plant in Electrostal and ending with the development of the recreation, finance, consulting, and telecommunications industries.

In the long run, the most attractive investment prospects are in the aerospace industry; research projects; science-intensive engineering; the financial, commercial, and telecommunications infrastructure; conversion of the textile industry based on the production of knitwear at factories currently specializing in yarn and fabrics; manufacture of men's and women's coats, haberdashery, and perfume; expansion of the record plant in Aprelevka, the printing plant in Mozhaisk, and the jewelry factory in Bronitsi; and the production of sophisticated household appliances at former defense enterprises. In the farming sector, investments are needed to establish a network of mechanized storage facilities close to the cropland, and to promote the sale of produce, the construction of modular processing facilities on farms, and formation of wholesale centers.

Investment and economic activities will be rigorously controlled within the 60-kilometer radius around Moscow, including the green belt and water protection zone. Additionally, restrictions will be applied to the outer zone within a 130-kilometer radius.

In 1995, the oblast had 110 operating joint ventures. The foreign investments in 1993–95 were $230 million. Private owners held 15.3% of the fixed assets of enterprises and organizations, joint stock companies (without foreign interest) owned another 17.2%, and the federal authorities controlled 46.1%. The oblast also had 67 insurance companies and 37 commercial banks, including Innovation Bank for Economic Cooperation (Lyubertsy, Tel. 553 1730), LefkoBank (Orekhovo-Zuevo, Tel. 12 3688), MDK-Bank (Khimi, Tel. 573 6077), Mytischi Bank (Mytischi, Tel 483 1727), and Suburban Bank (Ramenskoe, Tel. 32 728).

The oblast has 300 km hard-surfaced roads per 1,000 sq km.

49.6 MOSCOW CITY

1. **Natural Resources.** Area: 1,000 sq km. Population 8,793,000 (Jan. 1, 1996). The city has 150 watercourses, most of which have been diverted through underground con-

duits, and 240 open bodies of water. Because water consumption exceeds the capacity of the city's surface and underground sources, the shortfall is offset by water pumped from the Moscow Canal and the system of reservoirs in the western part of the Moscow Oblast.

2. Specialization and Sectoral Structure of the Economy. Moscow is the seat of supreme state power of the Russian Federation, the site of a number of high-tech enterprises, and of the country's leading financial, scientific, educational, and cultural institutions. Moscow is the birthplace of numerous innovative ideas and practices, which subsequently spread to the rest of Russia (see Exhibit 49.11).

The manufacturing structure is dominated by engineering (25.3%), power generation (12.5%), the food industry (24%), and textiles and leather (6.2%). The largest enterprises are the ZIL JSC and AXL JSC in the auto industry; Serog Ordjonikidze, Stankoagregat, Frezer, Kalibr, and Krasny Proletary plants (bearing, watch, and instrument plants in the machine tool industry); Dynamo and Vladimir Ilyich electrical-engineering plants; Trekhgornaya Manufaktura JSC, Krasnaya Roza JSC, and the Paris Commune textile and footwear factories; and the Khrunichev aerospace-engineering plant. (See Exhibit 49.12.)

The city's engineering complex comprises approximately 100 plants and 80 research establishments and has a total workforce of about 400,000. Of this total, 45% are employed in the auto industry; 17–20% each are employed in electrical engineering, machine tools, and instrument industries. Moscow manufactures 30 to 40% of the many types of machine tools made in Russia, along with 10 to 15% of its computers, instruments, motor vehicles, bearings, medicine, footwear, refrigerators, televisions, and watches.

More than a third of Russia's scientific community is concentrated in Moscow. The city is the seat of the Russian Academy of Sciences and hundreds of research-and-design institutes. A number of research centers have been set up in the Moscow

Exhibit 49.11.   Sectoral Structure of Economy as of January 1, 1995 (% of total)

	Industry	Farming	Transportation	Construction	Other
Employment	19.5	0.2	7.2	13.2	59.9
Fixed Assets	32.3	0.1	20.6	3.6	43.4
Capital Investment	17.2	0.2	11.0	2.0	69.0

Exhibit 49.12.   Manufacture of Principal Industrial Products

	1995	1996
Metal-cutting machine tools	1,352	473.2
Elevators	2,801	1,988.7
Trucks, thous.	2.8	1.01
Passenger cars, thous.	40.6	3.7
Cotton fabrics, million sq.m.	60.4	39.9
Silk Fabrics, million sq.m.	18.2	12.01
Televisions, thous.	332	126.2
Confectionery, thous. tons	294	255.8
Meat, thous. tons	3.4	2.01
Whole milk products, thous. tons	539	582

Oblast to work in concert with Moscow-based research institutions, including Dubna and Protvino (nuclear research); Dolgoprudny and Troitsk (physics research); Chernogolovka (chemistry); Zelenograd, Fryazino, Reutov, and Aprelevka (electrical engineering); Khimki and Kalingrad (space research); Zhukovsky (a world-class aerodynamics center); Lytkarino (optics); and Pushchino (biology).

Moscow exports 3% of its manufactured output, which mainly consists of oil products (22%), motor vehicles (14%), nonferrous metals, and services.

3. Investment Opportunities. Moscow has the following advantages that make it the most attractive center for investments in Russia: international airports with a developed ground support infrastructure; the nation's most advanced telecommunications and information exchange systems; concentration of the majority of Russia's financial institutions; a European-standard hotel, housing, and transportation infrastructure; and the possibility of recruiting skilled labor in a wide range of occupations. Moscow has become the focal point for foreign firms in Russia, which accounts for some of the country's costliest office leases, services, and goods. These costs are charged by institutions specializing in catering to foreigners and, in some instances, they are the same or higher than rates charged in New York or Paris for similar services.

The key investment areas in Moscow include financial services; trading operations; wholesale and retail trade establishments; enterprises offering consumer services to the general public and elite; telecommunications and communications facilities; information services to Russian legal entities, including information on foreign economic practices and techniques used in developing investment projects; real-estate operations; science-intensive projects; production of foodstuffs and equipment for residential homes and apartments; construction materials for luxury buildings; and programs to build housing and modernize nonresidential buildings undertaken by the Moscow government.

In 1995, the region had 6,634 operating joint ventures. The foreign investments in 1993–95 totaled 2,267 million. Private owners held 16.6% of the fixed assets of enterprises and organizations, joint stock companies (without foreign interest) owned another 12.2%, the federal authorities controlled 49.4%, and foreign nationals owned 4.1%. Moscow also had 600 insurance companies and 484 commercial banks.

49.7 OREL OBLAST

1. Natural Resources. Area: 24,700 sq km. Farmland: 20,890 sq km. Woodland: 1,900 sq km. Population: 913,200 (Jan. 1, 1996), of which 62.6% is urban and 37.4% is rural. Population density: 37 per sq km.

The oblast lies 389 km south of Moscow. Its principal rivers are the Oka (the upper reaches), the Orlik, the Tsna, and the Sosna. Restrictions apply to the construction of enterprises that use large amounts of water.

The oblast is mostly comprised of open, plowed fields. Forests grow in the river valleys and do not have any commercial value. No minerals are worked in the oblast, although deposits of sand, clay, chalk, and limestone are operated for local needs; Over 80% of the needed resources (except for farm produce) are brought in from other areas of the country.

The climate is temperate-continental, with a mean January temperature of −9°C and 20°C in July. The oblast gets 590 mm of rainfall per year, and the growing season lasts 185 days.

2. Specialization and Sectoral Structure of the Economy (see Exhibit 49.13). Administrative divisions: 24 districts, 7 cities, 15 urban-type communities, and 222 village group-councils.

   Administration head: Tel. (08600) 46 313. Fax 42 530.

   Principal cities: Orel (346,600), Livny (53,000), and Mtsensk (49,700).

   The manufacturing structure is dominated by engineering (25.4%), the food industry (22.8%), and ferrous-metal fabrication (8.9%). The biggest enterprises are the steel-rolling plant in Orel, the aluminum alloy and aluminum-casting plants in Mtsensk, the hydraulic machinery JSC in Livny, the industrial instrument JSC, and textile-engineering and machinery-handling plants in Orel. Many of the existing plants were built a relatively short time ago, so they can turn out competitive goods, including instruments, watches, loaders, rolled steel, and cast-aluminum products. The oblast exports 5.4% of its industrial output; loaders, and metal products account for 73% of the exports. (See Exhibit 49.14.)

   The Orel Oblast has a highly developed agro-industrial complex. Farmers specialize in commercial grain, sugar beets, potatoes, fruits, and berries; animal farming centers on dairy cattle, fowl, and hogs. The food industry comprises plants producing canned vegetables, butter, cheeses, sugar, and meat. Hemp-processing centers are located in Bolkhov, Novosil, and Dimtrov-Orlovsky. Because of the oblast's inadequate marketing facilities, the abandonment of the centralized allocation practice in 1992 caused a decline in food production at a rate of 10 to 20% per year.

3. Investment Opportunities. The regional administration is attempting to pull farming out of its present crisis through local self-government and the implementation—with the backing of the federal authorities—of a farm development program for central Russia. The administration is also establishing facilities to process farm produce and market the products in Moscow, St. Petersburg, and major industrial cities in the Ural Region and Siberia.

   Attractive prospects for investment are in the manufacture of sophisticated household appliances; electronics and electrical engineering; development of a

Exhibit 49.13.   Sectoral Structure of Economy in, 1995 (% of total)

	Industry	Farming	Transportation	Construction	Other
Employment	26.2	21.9	6.7	9.1	36.1
Fixed Assets	26.0	34.6	9.2	7.9	22.3
Capital Investment	14.6	12.8	16.3	1.5	54.8

Exhibit 49.14.   Manufacture of Principal Industrial Products

	1995	1996
Road graders	392	541
Hosiery, million pairs	20.0	20.1
Washing machines, thou	8.8	14.4
Vegetable oil, thous. tons	1.5	4.7
Meat, thous. tons	13.8	13.2
Whole milk products, thous. tons	31.7	31.4

steel-rolling plant; expansion of loader output; retooling of sugar- and flour-milling industries; the manufacture of ecologically safe products; and the processing of fruits and berries.

In 1995, the oblast had 43 operating joint ventures. The foreign investments in 1993–95 were $26.2 million. Private owners held 38% of the fixed assets of enterprises and organizations, joint stock companies owned another 28%, and the federal authorities controlled 20.5%. The oblast also had five insurance companies and three commercial banks, including Agroprombank (Tel. 62 920), Coopbank (Tel. 55 498), and Oka-Bank (Tel. 62 117).

The oblast can be reached from Moscow by rail (382 km to Orel, nine hours from Kursk Terminal), air (1.5 hours from Bykovo Airport), and road (the highway from Moscow, via Tula, to Orel, nine hours driving time).

Oblast has 155 km of hard-surfaced roads per 1,000 sq km.

49.8 RYAZAN OBLAST

1. Natural Resources. Area: 39,600 sq km. Farmland: 25,500 sq km. Woodland: 10,500 sq km. Population: 1,336,900 (Jan. 1, 1996), of which 67% is urban and 33% is rural. Population density: 33.8 per sq km.

The oblast lies 200 to 300 km southeast of Moscow. It is adequately provided with water, with the average river runoff totaling 257 cu km a year. Because of the heavy pollution of the Oka river, the surface sources are essentially used for industrial and farming purposes, while drinking water is increasingly being provided by high-quality underground sources.

Woodlands include 7,419 sq km under federal control. Timber resources are 137.6 million cu m, of which 66.8 cu m is softwood. The oblast's estimated cutting potential is 2.1 million cu m.

Mineral resources include low-quality lignite, phosphorite, pottery clay, glass sand, and cement stock. Most of the mineral deposits are vigorously worked, proving primary materials for the construction industry and farming. The prospected reserves of these minerals fully meet local needs. The book resources of cement limestone quarried near the city of Mikhailov for local cement plants are 446 million tons. In addition, the area yields 23 million tons of brick clay, 9.1 million tons of expanded clay, 34.5 million tons of mortar sand, 30.8 million tons of silicate-product sand, 40 million tons of carbonate, and 2.2 million tons of foundry sand. The oblast possesses considerable quantities of peat in small- and medium-sized deposits. The major peat deposits, centered around the town of Spassk, the Pilveo railroad station, and the Tuma community, are intensively worked. Because peat reserves are limited, existing deposits must be used cautiously, and the depleted areas are to be used for farming.

The climate is temperate-continental, with temperatures in January of between −10.5 and −12°, and 19°C in July. Rainfall varies from 450 to 550 mm annually, and the growing season lasts 120 days.

2. Specialization and Sectoral Structure of the Economy (see Exhibit 49.15). Administrative divisions: 25 districts, 12 cities, 27 urban-type communities, and 488 village group-councils.

Administration head: Tel. (0912) 77 4032. Fax 44 2568.

Principal cities: Ryazan (527,900), Kasimov (37,900), Sasovo (35,800), and Skopin (28,800).

Exhibit 49.15. Sectoral Structure of Economy in 1995 (% of total)

	Industry	Farming	Transportation	Construction	Other
Employment	30.2	16.8	7.0	9.3	36.7
Fixed Assets	33.4	27.5	16.6	3.5	19.0
Capital Investment	24.6	8.2	12.4	3.3	51.5

The manufacturing structure is dominated by the fuel industry (27.5%), engineering (16.1%), power generation (23.8%), the food industry (10.6%), and the building-materials industry (7.4%). The Ryazan thermal-power plant and oil refinery is the biggest enterprise in the fuel and power complex. Engineering focuses on the manufacture of machine tools, instruments and appliances (e.g., televisions, radar equipment, communications facilities, electric light bulbs, refrigeration equipment), and farm machinery. A large integrated silk plant is located in Korablino. The oblast produces tin-based alloys, chemical yarn and fibers, and building materials for delivery to the country's other regions. The majority of enterprises are in Ryazan or its immediate vicinity. The oblast exports 6.9% of its industry output, chiefly oil products. (See Exhibit 49.16.)

Farmers specialize in animal products. The oblast is also a major producer of grains and potatoes. Grain growing seeks to meet the minimum requirements of local cattle farming for feed grains. The largest productive assets are owned by the meat and dairy industry (producing 49% of the food industry's commercial output), the tea industry (7.6%), and the sugar industry (5.8%). A belt of small farms owned by individuals (specializing in vegetables—particularly cucumbers, carrots, and cabbages)—for the Moscow market has formed along the Oka River.

3. Investment Opportunities. The oblast's administration has been steadily implementing economic reforms, setting up local self-government bodies, transforming the farming enterprises on the pattern tested in Nizhny Novgorod, and establishing an infrastructure for the operation of the food market and an investment-project support system (Ikar). The Sasta machine tool JSC has launched production of machine tools competitive in the world markets for machining oil and gas pipes; the shoe factory (Ryazan West joint venture) has started production of quality footwear; and programs are underway at the Centrolit plant to turn out gas meters and specialized steel pipes to treat the discharges of the Ryazan thermal-power plant and to manufacture baking equipment. The slump has not affected the enterprises manufacturing televisions, garments, and soft roofing materials. The economic situation is, however, complicated by some differences in regional development levels. In particular, most of the oblast's eastern

Exhibit 49.16. Manufacture of Principal Industrial Products

	1995	1996
Primary oil refining products, million tons	9.6	4.7
Metal cutting machine tools	1,402	1,164
Potato harvester	96	n/a
Soft roofing materials, million sq.m.	117	108
Television, thous.	344	117
Meat, thous. tons	27.6	16.8
Whole milk products, thous. tons	38.2	34.4

and central districts are farming areas whose population has a low level of education and adheres to traditional farming practices. Another worry is the uncertain future of the oil refinery, the key contributor to the regional budget, because of its inefficient structure and deteriorating machinery.

The most promising areas of investment include oil refining (at the Ryazan refinery); and science-intensive engineering, including (laser technology; telephone and satellite communications facilities; radar equipment and navigational systems for civil aviation and marine shipping; UHV equipment; medical equipment using VHF, laser, and ultrasonic devices; and aviation equipment. Other attractive areas include garment and footwear manufacture; production of sophisticated household appliances, vacuum cleaners, televisions, and radios; retooling of the flour-milling and pasta industries; production of bread-baking equipment; modernization of the tea-packaging factory, the meat-packing plant and sugar mills; manufacture of ecologically safe products; and construction of small-scale recreational facilities in areas free of environmental hazards, including the oblast's part of the Meshchera Plain.

In 1995, the oblast had 45 operating joint ventures. The foreign investments in 1993–95 totaled $2.7 million. Private owners held 31% of the fixed assets of enterprises and organization; joint stock companies (without foreign interest) owned another 34.3%, and the federal authorities controlled 24.2%. The oblast also had nine insurance companies and 11 commercial banks, including Bank of Foreign Trade (Tel. 77 4988), Vayatch (Tel. 77 2119), Meshchera (Tel. 44 4363), and Respect-Bank (Tel. 77 4181).

The oblast can be reached from Moscow by rail (196 km to Ryazan, three hours from the Kazan terminal) and road (the highway from Moscow to Ryazan and Kuibyshev, three hours driving time).

There are 81 km of hard-surfaced roads per 1,000 sq km.

49.9 SMOLENSK OBLAST

1. Natural Resources. Area: 49,800 sq km. Farmland: 22,350 sq km. Woodland: 21,360 sq km. Population: 1,166,500 (Jan. 1, 1996), of which 69.2% is urban and 30.8% is rural. Population density: 23.4 per sq km.

The oblast lies 400 km west of Moscow. Its principal rivers are the Dnieper (the upper reaches), the Sozh, the Vazuza, and the Urga. The oblast's northern districts have numerous lakes and extensive swamps.

Woodlands include 78.4 million cu m of softwood. The oblast's estimated cutting area is used at 60% capacity. The commercial potential is 2 million cu m.

Mineral resources include peat, limestone, clay, sand, and phosphorite.

Additionally, the Smolensk Oblast has deposits of low-grade lignites (144 million tons of category A+B+C), which are worked at two mines controlled by the Safonovo mine authority and delivered to the Drogobyeh thermal-power plant. The oblast also has small-scale deposits of fireclay, phosphorite ore, and cement and glass raw materials, which have not been developed because of more effective deposits in other regions of the Center. Building-stone reserves are estimated at 91 million cu m, with 37.6 million cu m of sand and gravel mixtures. All mixtures and sand are suited for use in plastering mortar and, if properly washed, as concrete aggregate. The largest deposits are situated in the oblast's central part, near the cities of Smolensk, Drogobych, and Pochinok. In part, the oblast's requirements in sand and gravel are met by deliveries from other regions. The Smolensk Oblast's share in the book peat reserves of the Central area amounts to 16%. Its peat deposits are developed by six specialized enterprises.

The climate is temperate-continental, with a January temperature between −7 and −9°C and 18°C in July. The area gets 600 mm of rainfall annually, and its growing season is 180 days long.

2. Specialization and Sectoral Structure of the Economy (see Exhibit 49.17). Administrative divisions: 25 districts, 15 cities, 16 urban-type communities, and 413 village group-councils.

Administration head: Tel. (08100) 36 308. Fax 36 851.

Principal cities: Smolensk (351,600), Vyazma (59,900), Roslavl (60,700), Safonovo (56,400), and Yartsevo (54,600).

The manufacturing structure is dominated by engineering (19%), the food industry (12.9%), power generation (23.8%), and chemical production (8.3%). The oblast's biggest enterprises are the Analitpribor industrial association, the Iskra industrial association (computers), aircraft plants, plants manufacturing radio components, refrigeration plants, the Kristall diamond-cutting plant, the Scharm JSC (knitwear), auto component plants in Smolensk and Roslavl, the plastics plant in Safonovo, and the Dvigate plant in Yartsevo. (See Exhibit 49.18.)

Engineering is represented by enterprises producing electrical equipment, instruments, and power-generating equipment. The industry is centered in Smolensk, which manufactures road-building machines, instruments, industrial-process automation facilities, radio components, electric lightbulbs, aviation equipment, refrigerators, and cut diamonds (Kristall plant). Other major manufacturing centers are Yartsevo (looms and spinning machines), Safonovo (instruments), and Roslavl (power equipment and diamond tools).

In the chemical industry, the leading enterprises include the Mineral Fertilizer association in Dorogobuzh, which produces nitrogen fertilizers, and the plastics plants in Safonovo and Roslavl.

Exhibit 49.17.   Sectoral Structure of Economy in 1995 (% of total)

	Industry	Farming	Transportation	Construction	Other
Employment	29.4	17.4	7.2	8.7	37.3
Fixed Assets	40.7	22.6	10.5	7.8	18.4
Capital Investment	24.5	8.0	22.8	1.6	43.1

Exhibit 49.18.   Manufacture of Principal Industrial Products

	1995	1996
Electric power, bn kWh	20.5	26
Large electrical machines	1,792	1,452
Ceramic tiles, thous. sq.m.	333	n/a
Mineral fertilizers, thous. tons	368	372
Linen fabrics, million sq.m.	12.6	18.9
Hosiery, million pairs	34.7	30.9
Refrigerators, thous.	58.2	25.6
Meat, thous. tons	18.7	14.4
Whole milk products, thous. tons	38.7	38.8

The oblast's textile producers specialize in flax processing. It has 31 flax-processing plants that deliver their products to major linen plants, including the integrated plants in Smolensk and Vyazma. A large, integrated cotton plant operates in Yartsevo.

Food industry enterprises, which are adequately supplied by the local producers, specialize in making butter, cheeses, milk preserves, and meat products, with some of the dairy products sent to Moscow markets.

The focal points of the highway network are Highway M–1, which runs from Moscow to Brest, and links the Russian hinterland to European countries, and a section of Highway A–141, which connect Vitebsk to Smolensk and farther on to Orel. Five railroad lines converge on the oblast, and air travel is handled by airports in the neighboring regions. The oblast exports 23.3% of its manufactured output (cut diamonds, mineral fertilizers, electric generators, and artificial graphite and graphite-based products.)

Farmers specialize in raising beef and dairy cattle and growing long-staple flax and commercial potatoes. The oblast currently ranks among the country's surplus-producing areas for most of its farming produce, but it is short of grain and mixed feeds for its cattle farms.

3. Investment Opportunities. The Smolensk Oblast is a stable area providing a key transportation outlet for central Russia to European Union (EU) countries. Many of its facilities are controlled by federal authorities or held by Russia's defense establishment. Because Soviet armed forces formerly located in Germany and the Baltic countries are stationed in the oblast, the construction of housing and communications facilities is expanding. So far, the greatest interest in the investment area has been displayed by German investors who are drawing up a comprehensive plan for the oblast's economic development.

In 1995, the oblast had 51 operating joint ventures. The foreign investments in 1993–95 were $8.9 million. Private owners held 29% of the fixed assets of enterprises and organizations, joint stock companies (without foreign interest) owned another 5%, and the federal authorities controlled 58.2%. The oblast also had six insurance companies and 12 commercial banks, including Agroprombank (Tel. 55 6252), Kliuch (Tel. 52 0641), Titan (Tel. 96 980), Dnieper (Tel. 32 041), and SKA Bank (Tel. 30 605).

Promising areas of investment include the construction of a highway from Moscow via Minsk to Western Europe and roadside service facilities on operating highways; renovation of the mineral fertilizer plant in Drogobych; conversion of defense industry enterprises to civilian programs (Iskra association, Izmeritel, Diffuzion, and radio component plants); and small-scale recreational and fee-based hunting and fishing facilities.

The oblast can be reached from Moscow by rail (419 km to Smolensk, seven hours from the Belorussia terminal), air (1.5 hours from Vnukova Airport), and road (the highway from Moscow, via Smolensk, to Minsk, seven to nine hours driving time).

There are 107 km hard-surfaced roads per 1,000 sq km.

49.10 TULA OBLAST

1. Natural resources. Area: 25,700 sq km. Farmland: 19,800 sq km. Woodland: 3,800 sq km. Population: 1,832,300 (Jan. 1, 1996), of which 81.4% is urban and 18.6% is rural. Population density: 71.3 per sq km, one of the highest in central Russia.

The oblast lies 200 km south of Moscow. Its northern part is fully supplied with water by the Oka river, and its southern part requires the construction of small reservoirs and artesian wells.

The oblast's wooded tracts protect the supply and are used for water and recreational. About 8.0 million cu m of timber, mostly of the soft-leaf variety, is available for commercial logging. The oblast's estimated cutting area is used at 70–80% capacity. The commercial potential is 0.8 million cu m. Generally, the oblast is short of timber.

Mineral resources include lignite (book reserves of four billion tons), limestone clay, and sand. With more than four million tons of lignite mined, the oblast accounts for the bulk of the fuel extracted in the so-called Moscow Basin. This type of fuel is burned at the thermal-power plants in Cherepets and Novomoskovsk.

The climate is temperate-continental, with a mean January temperature of $-10°C$ and 19°C in July. Rainfall varies from 470 to 575 mm annually, and the growing season is between 136 and 148 days.

2. Specialization and Sectoral Structure of the Economy (see Exhibit 49.19). Administrative divisions: 23 districts, 21 cities, 50 urban-type communities, and 345 village group-councils.

Administration head: Tel. (0872) 27 8436. Fax 20 6326.

Principal cities: Tula (541,400), Novomoskovsk (145,400), Aleksin (73,700), Shchekino (68,600), and Uzlovaya (63,600).

The Tula Oblast is one of Russia's most industrialized areas. Its makeup is dominated by engineering (21.3%), the chemical industry (22%), ferrous metals (16.5%), power engineering (14.9%), and the food industry (11%). The largest enterprises include the Tulachermat ferrous-metals research and development association and a grain harvester plant in Tula, Chemical Fibers JSC in Shchekino, the household chemical JSC and Azot JSC in Novomoskovsk, and a synthetic rubber plant in Efremov. The oblast also has a large cluster of defense enterprises that produce armaments, including firearms and hunting gear. At present, 18 of the enterprises are converting to the production of civilian output. (See Exhibit 49.20.)

Exhibit 49.19.   Sectoral Structure of Economy in 1995 (% of total)

	Industry	Farming	Transportation	Construction	Other
Employment	36.6	11.2	6.1	9.2	36.9
Fixed Assets	45.6	19.1	5.9	7.9	21.5
Capital Investment	27.2	6.9	18.6	1.7	45.6

Exhibit 49.20.   Manufacture of Principal Industrial Products

	1995	1996
Coal, million tons	3.3	2.8
Electric bridge cranes	136	62.6
Mineral fertilizers, thous. tons	417	479.6
Hosiery, million pairs	4.35	10.74
Motorcycles, thous.	10.7	n/a
Meat, thous. tons	24.2	18.4
Whole milk products, thous. tons	77.8	81.7

Farmers specialize in raising beef and dairy cattle and hogs, and produce considerable quantities of grain crops. The sector's produce is primarily intended to meet local needs, with significant quantities of potatoes, vegetables, fruits, and berries supplied to Moscow. Growing environmentally safe produce is inhibited by the continuing pollution of the soil from nearby chemical enterprises and radionuclide contamination from the accident at the Chernobyl nuclear-power plant.

3. Investment Opportunities. The oblast's administration is consistently implementing economic reforms in agriculture and promoting structural changes in manufacturing. In 1995, the oblast had 40 operating joint ventures. The foreign investments in 1993–95 were $13.2 million. Private owners held 23.9% of the fixed assets of enterprises and organizations, joint stock companies (without foreign interest) owned another 35%, and the federal authorities controlled 32.8%. The oblast also had 14 insurance companies and seven commercial banks, including Agroprombank (Tel. 36 5626), Mosbusinessbank (Tel. 31 6789), Pruipskbank (Tel. 77 5573), and Tulabank (Tel. 77 2079).

Promising areas of investment include science-intensive engineering enterprises (communications facilities and waste treatment facilities); defense operations carrying out their conversion programs; manufacture of chemical products, including those for export; and processing fruits and vegetables for delivery to major cities.

The oblast can be reached from Moscow by rail (193 km to Tula, two hours from the Kursk terminal) and road (the highway from Moscow, via Tula, to Orel, 2.8 hours driving time).

There are 191 km of hard-surfaced roads per 1,000 sq km.

49.11 TVER OBLAST

1. Natural resources. Area: 84,200 sq km. Farmland: 24,630 sq km. Woodland: 46,680 sq km. Population: 1,654,500 (Jan. 1, 1996), of which 63% is urban and 37% is rural. Population density: 19.7 per sq km.

The oblast lies 150–260 km north of Moscow on the main watershed of European Russia. It has 700 watercourses with a total length of 17,500 km, more than 500 lakes, and two large reservoirs at Ivankovo and Uglich. Some of the territory is heavily water logged.

Woodlands include 20,400 sq km under federal control. The woodlands contain 663.2 million cu m of timber, of which 344.5 cu m is softwood. The forests have a water protective and regulatory, as well as, recreational role. The oblast's estimated cutting area is used at 67% capacity. The commercial potential is 6.3 million cu m.

Mineral resources are limited to a few deposits of low-quality lignite, glass sand, dolomite, and mineral dyes; there is also enough building-material deposits to supply the needs of local manufacturing and housing construction.

The climate is temperate-continental, with January temperatures ranging from −8.5 to −10.5°C and 17°C in July. Rainfall varies from 440 to 750 mm annually, and the growing season is between 120 and 133 days.

2. Specialization and Sectoral Structure of the Economy (see Exhibit 49.21). Administrative divisions: 36 districts, 23 cities, 31 urban-type communities, and 616 village group-councils.

Administration head: Tel. (08222) 31 051. Fax 37 678.

Exhibit 49.21. **Sectoral Structure of Economy in 1995 (% of total)**

	Industry	Farming	Transportation	Construction	Other
Employment	30.5	14.5	7.3	9.8	37.9
Fixed Assets	31.0	26.6	16.6	3.3	22.5
Capital Investment	23.5	5.9	15.1	1.6	54.2

Principal cities: Tver (455,600), Rzhev (70,900), Vyshny Volochek (64,300), Kimry (61,800), and Torzhok (50,600).

The manufacturing structure is dominated by engineering (25.8%), textiles and leather (9.9%), power generation (15.6%), the food industry (10.7%), and lumber and woodworking (7%). The largest enterprises include the thermal-power plant in Konakovo, an excavating-machinery plant, Tverdrev woodworking JSC, a railroad car plant, an integrated leather factory, cotton mills, a wool factory, and a printing plant. The oblast is a major supplier of foraging equipment, excavating machines, hydraulic presses, electric lightbulbs, and railroad passenger cars. The oblast's sawmills are centered in the towns of Maksatikha and Verkhnaya; papermaking is concentrated in Kuvshinovo; and prefabricated houses are manufactured in Nelidovo. The glazed-pottery plant in Konakovo is a leader in the industry, producing technical and household glass. The oblast exports 2.7% of its manufactured output; of this, 50% is leather and footwear goods, 11% woodworking production, and 11% machines and equipment. (See Exhibit 49.22.)

Farms specialize in the production of meat and dairy products to meet local demands. The oblast is a leading flax-growing area. The textile industry possesses solid production and research facilities, but has not yet produced any ready-made linen products.

The Tver Oblast has considerable potential for attracting large numbers of tourists and vacationers. Plans have been drawn up to establish a second Golden Ring (embracing Tver, Starits, Torzhok, Ostashkov, and Novgorod), develop the recreational zone in the Seliger Lakes area, and set up roadside facilities on the highway from Moscow to St. Petersburg and Helsinki.

3. Investment Opportunities. The Tver Oblast is a very stable area. In 1995, it had 43 operating joint ventures. The foreign investments in 1993–95 totaled $69.8 million. Private owners held 23.9% of the fixed assets of enterprises and organizations, joint stock companies (without foreign interest) owned another 22.6%, and the federal

Exhibit 49.22. **Manufacture of Principal Industrial Products**

	1995	1996
Digging machines	2,408	1541
Railroad passenger cars	309	194.7
Window panes, thou. sq.m.	4,293	3,606
Commercial timber, thou. cu.m.	1,120	963.2
Wood fiber board, million sq.m.	15.5	10.1
Cotton fabrics, million sq.m.	51.5	45.8
Meat, thous. tons	16.9	12.8
Whole milk products, thous. tons	40.2	33.8

authorities controlled 34.7%. The oblast also had 12 insurance companies and 17 commercial banks, including Avtovazbank (Tel. 27 471), Agroprombank (Tel. 31 513), Progressprombank (Tel. 32 563), and Tveruniversalbank (Tel. 31 243).

There are investment opportunities in science-intensive engineering projects; railroad car production; construction equipment (including excavating machinery); furniture, textiles, and garments; expansion of the hotel industry; and construction of tourist and recreational facilities.

The oblast can be reached from Moscow by rail (167 km to Tver, 2.4 hours travel time from the Leningrad terminal) and road (the highway from Moscow to St. Petersburg and Helsinki, 2.5 hours driving time).

The oblast has 120 km. of hard-surfaced roads per 1,000 sq km.

49.12 VLADIMIR OBLAST

1. Natural resources. Area: 29,100 sq km. Farmland: 10,400 sq km. Woodland: 15,600 sq km. Population: 1,648,300 (Jan. 1, 1996), of which 80% is urban and 20% is rural; the urban population is one of the highest in Russia. Population density: 56.8 per sq km.

    The oblast lies 200 km east of Moscow. It is has ample water supplies, although many bodies of water are polluted with industrial waste. Some of the oblast's terrain is heavily bogged, whereas in the drier oblasts the peat quarries are susceptible to fire.

    Woodlands include 9,470 sq km under federal control. Timber resources are equal to 209.7 million cu m, of which 137.5 cu m is softwood. The oblast's estimated cutting area is used at 90% capacity. The commercial potential is 3.5 million cu m.

    Mineral resources include limestone, clay, peat, and building materials that are used chiefly to satisfy local requirements. The quartz-sand deposits, which have given rise to a local glass industry, are known throughout Russia.

    The climate is temperate-continental, with a mean January temperature of $-11°C$ and $18°C$ in July. The annual rainfall varies from 480 to 580 mm, and the growing season is between 160 and 180 days.

2. Specialization and Sectoral Structure of the Economy (see Exhibit 49.23). Administrative divisions: 16 districts, 22 cities, 37 urban-type communities, and 222 village group-councils.

    Administration head: Tel. (09222) 25 252. Fax 26 013.

    Principal cities: Vladimir (339,500), Kovrov (161,900), Murom (126,500), Gus-Khrustalny (76,900), and Aleksandrov (68,900).

    The manufacturing structure is dominated by engineering (41.1%), textiles and leather (9.7%), and the food industry (9.5%). In cotton output, the oblast ranks third after the Ivanovo and Moscow oblasts, and its linen production is first in the coun-

Exhibit 49.23.   Sectoral Structure of Economy in 1995 (% of total)

	Industry	Farming	Transportation	Construction	Other
Employment	42.4	8.3	6.6	6.7	36.0
Fixed Assets	42.7	16.8	8.6	3.2	28.7
Capital Investment	35.4	8.4	8.0	1.6	46.6

try. Its chemical-industry enterprises produce synthetic resins and plastics, polyvinyl chloride, glass-reinforced plastics, and polymeric films. The engineering industry is centered in Vladimir (a tractor plant, aircraft instrumentation JSC, and engine plant); Kovrov (excavating-machine plant and enterprises involving the military-industrial complex); Murom (radio and diesel locomotive plants); and Aleksandrov (a radio plant). A group of glass-making enterprises, which has formed the basis of a financial-industrial group, is clustered in Gus-Khrustalny. The oblast exports 4.4% of its manufactured output, 13.2% of which is textiles, 21.7% machines and equipment, and 23.8% transportation facilities. (See Exhibit 49.24.)

Farms mostly generate meat and dairy products, which is understandable given the abundance of natural floodplains, meadows, and swamps as highly productive grazing land. These products meet 70 to 100% of the local requirements; the potential for their further expansion into the Moscow Oblast has not not been realized, however.

3. Investment Opportunities. The social climate in the oblast is fairly stable. Nevertheless, 30–80% of the manufacturing facilities stand idle in the towns of Karabanovo, Kameshkovo, Vyazniki, Strunio, Kovrov, and Murom, and in the urban communities of Butorlino and Orgutud, among others, because of the low sales for textiles and defense products. The population's income is at subsistence levels. This situation is a drag on market reforms, with the management of many enterprises seeking low-interest loans and state support.

In 1995, the oblast had 69 operating joint ventures. The foreign investments in 1993–95 were $10.9 million. Private owners held 26.1% of the fixed assets of enterprises and organizations, joint stock companies (without foreign interest) owned another 31.1%, and the federal authorities controlled 26.1%. The oblast also had 16 insurance companies and seven commercial banks, including Vladbusinessbank (Tel. 41 865), Agroprombank (Tel. 26 261), and Vladinvestbank (Tel. 38 781).

Promising investment areas include the hotel and tourist business (in Vladimir and Suzdal); renovation of the tractor plant and its ancillaries to increase production of tractors, engines, and spare parts; expanded production of road-building and handling machines, motorcycles, colored glass, cut glass, and lighting fixtures. Because of an inexpensive labor force and the desire of local and federal authorities to improve the oblast's economy, an investor can expect considerable returns for reinvigorating the textile, industry, particularly for developing knitwear, haberdashery, and linen production (including related manufacturing tools) for export. In the farming

Exhibit 49.24. **Manufacture of Principal Industrial Products**

	1995	1996
AC electric motors, 63-355 mm, thous.	152	101.2
Tractors	6,426	1,478
Window panes, thous. sq.m.	5,713	5,884
Soft roofing material, million sq. m.	38.5	25.4
Cotton fabrics, million sq.m.	97.5	62.4
Linen fabrics, million sq.m.	36.74	32.7
Televisions, thous.	46.2	12.5
Meat, thous. tons	16.06	12.04
Whole milk products, thous. tons	55.8	60.3

sector, opportunities lie in restoring the cultivation of flax and the promotion of flax-processing facilities.

The oblast can be reached from Moscow by rail (190 km to Vladimir, three hours from Yaroslavl terminal) and road (the highway from Moscow, via Vladimir, to Nizhny Novgorod, 2 to 2.5 hours driving time).

Oblast has 157 km of hard-surfaced roads per 1,000 sq km.

49.13 YAROSLAVL OBLAST

1. Natural resources. Area: 36,400 sq km. Farmland: 11,700 sq km. Woodland: 16,900 sq km. Population 1,459,800 (Jan. 1, 1996), of which 80.7% is urban and 19.3% is rural. Population density: 40.1 per sq km.

   The oblast lies 270 km northeast of Moscow. It is well supplied with water, having nearly 80 lakes (12,100 hectares), and a huge 4,550-hectare reservoir at Rybinsk that provides recreational facilities and supplies the drinking water needs of several oblasts comprising Russia's Golden Ring.

   Woodlands include 8,400 sq km under federal control. Timber resources are equal to 213.4 million cu m, of which 85.8 cu m is softwood. The oblast's estimated cutting area is used at 60% capacity. The commercial potential is 3 million cu m.

   Mineral resources include 75 deposits of building materials, 45 of which currently supply components for the production of clay and silicate bricks, sand, crushed stone, and ceramics. The bulk of the nonferrous-metal building materials is produced in the township of Petrovskoe and the Silnitsi station in the Rostov district; smaller quantities are quarried in the Volga floodplain near the cities of Yaroslavl and Rybinsk.

   The climate is temperate-continental, with a mean January temperature of −11°C and 17°C in July. The oblast receives 550 mm of rain annually, and has a growing season of 165 days.

2. Specialization and Sectoral Structure of the Economy (see Exhibit 49.25). Administrative divisions: 17 districts, 11 cities, 17 urban-type communities, and 229 village group-councils.

   Administration head: Tel. (0852) 22 0215. Fax 32 8414.

   Principal cities: Yaroslavl (636,900), Rybinsk (252,200), Pereyaslavl-Zalessky (43,400), and Tutaev (42,900).

   The manufacturing structure is dominated by engineering (31.8%), the fuel industry (24.1%), and the chemical industry (12.7%). The largest enterprises are the oil refinery in Yaroslavl; engine plants in Tutaev and Rybinsk; paint and varnish, tire and synthetic-rubber plants in Yaroslavl; the motion-picture- and photographic-materials plant in Pereyaslavl-Zalessky; and the watch plant in Uglich. Textile enterprises specialize in manufacturing cotton yarn and industrial textiles. The largest linen facilities are located in Tutaev and Gavrilov Yam. The oblast exports 8% of its

Exhibit 49.25.   Sectoral Structure of the Economy in 1996 (% of total)

	Industry	Farming	Transportation	Construction	Other
Employment	37.0	9.7	6.8	9.1	37.4
Fixed assets	43.0	14.9	14.3	4.3	25.5
Capital investment	29.3	4.5	17.1	1.0	48.1

Exhibit 49.26. **Manufacture of Principal Industrial Products**

	1995	1996
Primary oil refining (mil t)	9.6	6.8
Vehicle tires (thous)	2,741.0	2,732.7
Linen fabrics (mil sq m)	7.6	11.9
Clocks (mil)	2.5	1.55
Meat (thous t)	14.2	11.5
Whole-milk products (thous t)	59.0	42.5

manufactured output, including oil-refining products (75%), industrial rubber goods, paints and varnishes, vehicle tires, engines, and watches. (See Exhibit 49.26.)

Farmers specialize in meat and dairy products, and vegetables.

3. Investment Opportunities. Of all of the territories of Russia's Golden Ring, the Yaroslavl Oblast offers the best investment prospects. Its administration is vigorously promoting economic reforms, especially for industries manufacturing competitive products that will ensure quick returns on investments. The oblast is situated at the intersection of main railroads, waterways, and highways linking various areas in the European part of Russia.

In 1995, the oblast had 85 operating joint ventures. The foreign investments in 1993-95 were $4.1 million. Private owners held 27.3% of the fixed assets of enterprises and organizations, joint stock companies (without foreign interest) owned another 26.1%, and the federal authorities controlled 29.3%. The oblast also had 19 insurance companies and 13 commercial banks, including Agroprombank (Tel. 32 8873), Kreditprombank (Tel. 22 1742), Region (Tel. 22 6167), and Yarostsbank (Tel. 23 0496).

The most promising areas for investors include oil refining, particularly the modernization of the Yaroslavl refinery; manufacturing of engines, paints and varnishes, industrial rubber goods and vehicle tires; development of recreational areas and tourist facilities on a national and international scale (renovation of the Levtsovo airport and the hotel infrastructure within the Golden Ring in Yaroslavl, Rubinsk, Uglich, Tutaev, and Rostov; and improvement of the recreational areas on the Volga and Rybinsk reservoir); promotion of handicrafts to provide the rural population with nonfarming income sources; production of insulation and hardware, slag-cotton slabs, and gypsum-perlite walls; building refrigeration facilities for the fishing industry; creation of special facilities to produce baby food; development of enterprises to make foods for long-term storage (starch and molasses, processed potatoes, canned vegetables, butter); and construction of small-capacity brickworks and woodworking plants.

The oblast can be reached from Moscow by rail (262 km to Yaroslavl, five hours from the Yaroslavl terminal) and by road (the Moscow-Yaroslavl highway, six hours driving time).

The oblast has 163 km of hard-surfaced roads per 1,000 sq km.

CHAPTER 50

VOLGA-VYATKA REGION

Aleko A. Adamescu, Yuri A. Kovalev, and Alexander G. Granberg

50.1 CHUVASH REPUBLIC

1. Natural Resources. Area: 18,300 sq km. Farmland: 10,400 sq km. Woodland: 6,000 sq km. Population: 1,359,000 (Jan. 1, 1996), of which 60.1% is urban and 39.9% is rural. Population density: 74.3 per sq km, one of the highest in Russia.

   The republic lies 750 km east of Moscow. It stands on the Volga, which is its main waterway, straddled by a huge hydraulic-power complex at the city of Cheboksary, the republic's capital. The republic is fully provided with water. This notwithstanding, nearly 50% of its farmlands require irrigation because of the area's heavily broken terrain and shortage of woodlands. In addition, considerable investments are needed to sink artesian wells in the republic's southern districts.

   The woodlands contain 78 million cu m of timber, of which 24.2 million cu m is softwood. Although the republic's estimated cutting area is at 100% capacity, the commercial timber potential is relatively small, about 1.6 million cu m, which is not enough to meet local timber requirements.

   The republic's mineral resources are confined to phosphorite, dolomite, and locally used building materials (sand, clay, and mineral dyes).

   The republic has a temperate-continental climate, with a mean temperature of $-13°C$ in January and $19°C$ in July. The annual rainfall varies between 450 and 500 mm, and the growing season lasts 170 days.

2. Specialization and Sectoral Structure of the Economy (see Exhibit 50.1). Administrative division: 21 districts, 9 cities, 8 urban-type communities, and 349 village group-councils.

   President: Tel. (8350) 22 0764. Vice President: Tel. (8350) 22 0171.

   Principal cities: Cheboksary (441,900), Novocheboksarsk (121,000), Kanash (56,700), and Alatyr (47,700).

   The manufacturing structure is dominated by engineering (34.4%), the chemical industry (12.2%), textiles and leather (16.8%), and the food industry (15.5%). (See Exhibit 50.2.)

   The republic's engineering industry specializes in the production of tractors, automotive equipment, special-purpose motor vehicles, and electrical-measuring instruments. The biggest enterprises include the industrial-tractor plant (tractors, bulldozers, and pipe layers); the machine-unit plant; the Dieselprom JSC (diesel generators); the Kontur plant (video cassettes); the Chuvashkabel plant (aircraft

Exhibit 50.1.   Sectoral Structure of the Economy in 1995 (% of total)

	Industry	Farming	Transport	Construction	Other
Employment	31.0	19.8	5.3	8.4	35.5
Fixed assets	36.5	18.2	4.7	9.9	30.7
Capital Investment	17.5	17.2	10.8	2.8	51.7

Exhibit 50.2.   Manufacture of Principal Industrial Products

	1995	1996
Electric power, million kWh	5,800	4,930
Hosiery, million pairs	15.6	20.3
Knitted goods, million	5.3	4.98
Meat, thou. tons	21.6	14.7
Whole milk products, thou. tons	45.1	44.2

wires); the instrument-making plant; the electrical-devices plant (relays and switchgear) and the ZEIM JSC (signaling devices) in Cheboksary; the electrical-devices plant and the Elektroavtomat JSC (automatic electrical equipment) in Alatyr; the electric loader-unit plant in Kanash; the integrated auto-van plant in Kozlovka; and the integrated van plant in Shumerlya.

The giant integrated chemical plant in Novocheboksarsk produces caustic soda, pigments, plant-protection chemicals, and synthetic resins.

Enterprises producing starch, cheeses, butter, meat, mixed feeds, confectionery, oak extract, and alcohol form the economic mainstay of the republic's numerous small towns and large townships.

The republic exports 3% of its industrial output; chemical products account for 47% of this, textiles 20%, and machinery and equipment 17%.

The republic has a multisectoral agriculture, which specialized in growing grain, potatoes, and industrial crops (hemp and hops); farms in the area also raise beef and dairy cattle, and fowl.

3. Investment Opportunities. At present, the republic's enterprises are operating vastly under capacity because of low sales. In rural areas, where much of the republic's population lives, the economy is also unstable because of the underdeveloped network of marketing and processing facilities, a problem typical for all of Russia.

In 1995, the republic had 56 operating joint ventures. The foreign investments in 1993–95 totaled $2.4 million. Private owners held 27.1% of the fixed assets of enterprises and organizations, joint stock companies (without foreign interest), owned 4%, the federal authorities controlled 26%; and the republican government held 27.7%. Chuvashia had nine insurance companies and 14 commercial banks, including Agroprombank (Tel. 20 3276), Novocheboksarsk (in Novocheboksary Tel. 77 8578), Privolzhsky (Tel. 29 9003), and the Chuvahian Popular Bank (Tel. 20 6420).

The republic's administration has recently launched energetic reforms in urban and rural areas in order to expand the integrated chemical plant, increase the growing of hops and the manufacture of hop-based products; construct processing facilities in rural areas, increase the production of consumer goods, and create modern communications systems, particularly cellular communications. In the long run,

large investments will be needed to expand the manufacture of heavy-duty industrial tractors and electrical-equipment plants. Generally, the republic is a stable area,
free of overt ethnic controversies and separatist undercurrents, despite the fact that
Chuvashes make up 67% of the republic's population and Russians only 26%. The
people have had a few differences with the federal government over the siting of
chemical-weapons facilities in Novocheboksarsk.

The republic is reachable from Moscow by rail (768 km to Cheboksary, 16 hours
from Kazan Terminal), air (1.5 hours from Bykovo Airport), and highway (Moscow
to Vladimir, via Nizhny Novgorod, to Cheboksary, 15 hours driving time).

The oblast has 151 km of hard-surfaced roads per 1,000 sq km.

50.2 MARI EL REPUBLIC

1. Natural Resources. Area: 23,200 sq km. Farmland: 7,840 sq km. Woodland: 13,000 sq
km. Population: 764,700 (Jan. 1, 1996), of which 61.9% is urban and 38.1% is rural.
Population density: 33.0 per sq km.

The republic lies 850 km east of Moscow, on the Volga, which is its principal
waterway. It is fully supplied with water.

The woodlands contain 154.6 million cu m of timber, including 85.1 million cu
m of softwood. The republic's estimated cutting area is used at 80% capacity, and its
commercial logging potential is 2.7 million cu m.

The mineral resources include building stones, limestone, glass and building
sand, and mineral dyes.

The republic has a temperate-continental climate, with the mean temperature
reaching $-13°C$ in January and $19°C$ in July. The area gets 450 to 500 mm of rainfall annually and has a growing season of 170 days.

2. Specialization and Sectoral Structure of the Economy (see Exhibit 50.3). Administrative division: 14 districts, 4 cities, 19 urban-type communities, and 176 village
group-councils.

State Assembly Chairman: Tel. (83622) 56 755.

State Committee for Governance of the Mari El Republic: Tel. 56 645.

Principal cities: Yoshkar-Ola (249,200), Volzhsk (62,500), and Kosmodemyansk
(25,300).

The manufacturing structure is dominated by power generation (20.4%), engineering (25.5%), lumbering and woodworking (10.2%), and food production
(17.3%). Engineering is built around science-intensive enterprises in the electronics
and instrument industries, in particular, the Karat industrial association (transistors),
the instrument-manufacturing industrial association, the Biomatpribor JSC (chro-
matographs), the Elektroavtomatika plant, the Kristall powder metallurgy plant, the
Marikholod industrial association, and the association manufacturing refrigerators,
all based in Yoshkar-Ola. Volzhsk, the second largest industrial center in the republic,

Exhibit 50.3.   Sectoral Structure of the Economy in 1995 (% of total)

	Industry	Farming	Transport	Construction	Other
Employment	28.1	20.9	4.9	8.0	38.1
Fixed assets	27.5	24.9	3.9	12.0	31.7
Capital investment	23.0	10.1	9.3	7.2	50.4

is the site of a store equipment plant, a pulp and paper mill, and an electrical-machinery plant. The republic accounts for 75% of the refrigeration equipment (cooling units and cabinets for food storage) and 12% of the paper and board produced in the Volga-Vyatka region. (See Exhibit 50.4.)

The republic exports 2% of its manufactured output, 52% of which is comprised of chemical products and 15% is lumber.

The principal crops grown in the republic are cereals, vegetables, and staple flax, while animal farming centers on raising beef and dairy cattle and fowl.

3. **Investment Opportunities.** The investment climate is cloudy because of the continuing market crisis faced by manufacturing and farming, the republic's long distance from major financial and trading centers, and its underdeveloped telecommunications and transportation systems. There has been no threat of separatist unrest or ethnic tensions. Yet, given the closeness of Tatarstan and the nearly equal ratio of Russians and Maris (48% and 43%, respectively) living in the republic, the probability of trouble arising because of conflicts at the federal level is not to be discounted.

In 1995, the republic had 22 operating joint ventures. The foreign investments in 1993–95 totaled $100,000. Private owners held 30% of the fixed assets of enterprises and organizations, joint stock companies (without foreign interest) owned 15.7%, the federal authorities controlled 16.5%, and the republican government had 22.4%. The republic has nine insurance companies and nine commercial banks, including Akpars (Tel. 64 008), Ayar (Tel. 17 240), Lebkobank (Tel. 11 7463), Mairprombank (Tel. 25 2863), Marielektronikabank (Tel. 31 272), and San in Volzhsk (Tel. 22 615).

Short-term investment prospects include the pulp and paper mill in Volzhsk, the production of drugs and medicines (by the biopharmaceutical and industrial association, the Biomatpribor JSC, and the Maribiofarm industrial association), and the expansion of consumer goods production (garments, knitwear, and leather footwear). Considering the monopoly held by enterprises manufacturing store and refrigerating equipment, healthy returns can be expected from efforts to raise the demand for such quality goods in regional centers and small towns in Russia's European areas.

The republic is reachable from Moscow by rail (862 km to Yoshkar-Ola, 18 hours from Kazan Terminal), air (two hours from Bykovo Airport), and road (the highway from Moscow to Vladimir, via Nizhny Novgorod and Cheboksary, 20 hours driving time).

There are 107 km of hard-surfaced roads per 1,000 sq km.

50.3 MORDOVIAN REPUBLIC

1. **Natural Resources.** Area: 26,200 sq km. Farmland: 16,700 sq km. Woodland: 7,200 sq km. Population: 962,700 (Jan. 1, 1996), of which 58.3% is urban and 41.7% is rural. Population density: 36.7 per sq km.

Exhibit 50.4. Manufacture of Principal Industrial Products

	1995	1996
Electric mixers, thou.	59.5	1.2
Paper pulp, thou. tons	39.0	20.7
Meat, thou. tons	12.5	7.4
Whole milk products, thou. tons	17.1	18.5

The republic lies 610 km southeast of Moscow. Its principal watercourses are the Moksha and the Sura. The republic is adequately supplied with water. Woodlands cover 77% of the republic's territory and contain 83.8 million cu m of timber, including 31.1 million cu m of softwood. The estimated cutting area is used at 85% capacity, and the commercial logging potential of 1.5 million cu m does not meet the republic's requirements.

Mineral resources include limestone, dolomite, chalk, marl, sand, mineral dyes, phosphorite, and peat. Although the republic's mineral resources have not yet been sufficiently explored, there is very little likelihood of any strategic resources being discovered.

The republic has a temperate-continental climate, with a mean temperature in January of $-11°C$ and $19°C$ in July. The area gets 450 to 520 mm of annual rainfall, and its growing season is 137 to 145 days.

2. Specialization and Sectoral Structure of the Economy (see Exhibit 50.5). Administrative division: 22 districts, 7 cities, 19 urban-type communities, and 417 village group-councils.

Chairman of the Government: Tel. (8342) 17 6809. Fax 17 3628.

Principal cities: Saransk (3349,900), Ruzaevka (52,400), and Kovylkino (22,400).

The manufacturing structure is dominated by engineering (45.1%) and the food industry (16.3%). (See Exhibit 50.6.)

Saransk accounts for 60% of the republic's manufacturing output. Its largest enterprises are the Lisma JSC (a special-purpose lighting-fixtures plant, a miniature-lamp plant, mercury-vapor-lamp plant, a bactericidal lamp plant, and a number of smaller enterprises); the Orbita industrial association (microcircuits); an integrated biochemical plant (producing penicillin-based drugs); the Cable Plant JSC; the Instrument Plant JSC; the Electric Rectifier JSC (power converters); a dump-truck plant; the Sakeks JSC (excavating machines); the Centrolit JSC; and the Machine Plant JSC. The Lisma JSC has located some of its branches in Ardatov, Zubova Polyana township, Insar, and Ruzaevka.

Exhibit 50.5. Sectoral Structure of the Economy in 1995 (% of total)

	Industry	Farming	Transport	Construction	Other
Employment	28.8	19.6	6.7	8.1	36.8
Fixed assets	28.7	32.4	7.1	4.2	27.6
Capital investment	18.5	16.3	4.6	14.3	46.3

Exhibit 50.6. Manufacture of Principal Industrial Products

	1995	1996
Digging machines	183	272.1
Cement, thou. tons	951	789.3
Televisions, thou.	11.6	1.3
Meat, thou. tons	15.6	14.7
Whole milk products, thou. tons	13.4	11.1

Ruzaevka is the second-largest industrial center in the republic. Besides the lighting-fixture enterprise, it has a plant that manufactures automatic plate-stamping machines, a knitwear JSC (Rueteks), and a chemical-engineering plant.

The republic exports 1.6% of its manufactured output, 60% of which is chemical products and 28% machinery and equipment.

Agricultural production consists of animal farming and grain growing. A large share of the farmland is taken up by industrial crops such as hemp, sugar beets, crude tobacco, and potatoes. Animal farming mainly consists of raising beef and dairy cattle and fowl.

3. Investment Opportunities. In contrast to the prereform period, sales of products manufactured by the republic's industrial enterprises have dropped by 30 to 50%, basically because of lower domestic demand for lighting equipment, instruments, machine tools, and excavating equipment. Other factors include dwindling defense orders and difficulties in marketing the products inside and outside the country (e.g., certification problems, high advertising costs, inadequate participation in international wholesale entities, poorly made and designed merchandise). The farm crises has compounded the republic's economic woes. As a result of these problems and the republic's distance from major financial and trading centers, its economic reforms are moving slowly and foreign investments is only trickling in. Despite the economic hardships, the republic's social situation is stable, largely because of the overwhelming proportion of the Russians in the area (61%, compared to 33% Mordovians).

In 1995, the republic had six operating joint ventures. The foreign investments in 1993–95 totaled $2.1 million. Private owners held 27.8% of the fixed assets of enterprises and organizations, joint stock companies (without foreign interest) controlled 21.9%, the federal authorities 16.1%, and the republican government 22.3%. The republic had seven insurance companies and 12 commercial banks, including Agroprombank (Tel. 43 561), Aktiv-bank (Tel. 17 6749), Business Mordovia (Tel. 41 467), and Mordovpromstroibank (Tel. 17 3330).

The most attractive investment areas are science-intensive engineering, including lighting equipment, radio engineering, electronics, and cable making. In addition, there are plans to manufacture boiler tanks, process-control devices, crystal-growing modules, televisions, high-tech household equipment, lighting fixtures, and chandeliers.

The republic is reachable from Moscow by rail (642 km to Saransk, 11 hours from Kazan Terminal), air (1.5 hours from Bykovo Airport), and road (the highway from Moscow, via Ryazan and Shatsk, to Saransk, 14 hours driving time).

The republic has 138 km hard-surfaced roads per 1,000 sq km.

50.4 VYATKA OBLAST

1. Natural Resources. Area: 120,800 sq km. Farmland: 34,900 sq km. Woodland: 78,700 sq km. Population: 1,694,400 (Jan. 1, 1996), of which 70.8% is urban and 29.2% is rural. Population density: 14.0 per sq km, the lowest in the Volga-Vyatka Region.

The oblast lies 900 km northeast of Moscow. It is amply supplied with water, the total area of which is equal to 39.9 cu km; it does not require special treatment prior to use by industrial consumers. The latest estimate puts the underground water resources at 2.9 cu km.

Woodlands contain 995.7 million cu m of timber, including 608.3 million cu m of softwood. The resources accessible to logging operations equal 325 million cu m. The estimated cutting area is used at 75% capacity. The republic's commercial cutting potential of 20 million cu m is the highest of all the oblasts in the Volga-Vyatka Region. The oblast ranks fourth in Russia for logging production, and fifth in the amount of woodwork produced.

The Vyatka Oblast has one of Europe's biggest phosphorite deposits, containing two billion tons of phosphorite ore. It also has limestone, oil shale, coal, building materials, and peat.

The oblast has a temperate-continental climate, with a long winter and a short, warm summer. The mean temperature in January is −15°C and in July is 18°C. The annual rainfall is 400 mm in the south and 600 mm in the north; the growing season lasts from 155 to 170 days.

2. Specialization and Sectoral Structure of the Economy (see Exhibit 50.7). Administrative division: 39 districts, 18 cities, 57 urban-type communities, and 586 village group-councils.

Administration head: Tel. (8332) 62 9564. Fax 62 8958.

Principal cities: Kirov (492,500), Kirovo-Chepetsk (99,100), and Polyany (46,000).

The manufacturing structure is dominated by engineering (19.8%), lumbering and woodworking (12.9%), the chemical industry (14.2%), light (12%), and the food industry (25.5%). (See Exhibit 50.8.)

The engineering sector specializes in the manufacture of instruments, electrical equipment, wires, and cables. The defense complex accounts for 45% of the industry's assets and 30% of its labor force. The oblast is Russia's leading producer of air-defense systems and electrical equipment for aircraft. The biggest engineering enterprises are the Mayak plant; the Lepse JSC (producing electric motors); the measuring-devices plant (Red Instrument Maker); the New Vyatka machine plant; the Vyatka engineering enterprise (communications equipment); the cable plant in Kirov; the Molot plant and the shipbuilding plant in Vyatskie Polyany; and the plants producing instruments and electrical machines in Kirovo-Chepetsk.

Exhibit 50.7.   Sectoral Structure of the Economy in 1995 (% of total)

	Industry	Farming	Transport	Construction	Other
Employment	32.0	16.3	7.8	7.0	36.9
Fixed assets	35.1	23.9	14.3	3.4	23.3
Capital Investment	21.5	7.4	0.9	1.9	68.3

Exhibit 50.8.   Manufacture of Principal Industrial Products

	1995	1996
Commercial timber, thou. cu.m.	4,651	3,814
Lumber, thou. cu.m.	1,066	991.3
Matches, thou. crates	231	117.8
Auto tires, thou.	1,274	1,440
Washing machines, thou.	229	66.4
Meat, thou. tons	22.9	20.6
Whole milk products, th. tons	65.1	79.4

The economic backbone of the oblast's small and medium-sized towns primarily consists of enterprises producing lumber, skis, fiberboard, chipboard, furniture, meat and dairy products, peat, and linen. The largest of them—the integrated wooden-board plant, the integrated ski plant, the Kirovlesprom industrial association—and a toy factory are located in Kirov.

Chemical products are chiefly manufactured in Kirov and Kirovo-Chepetsk, which also have an auto-tire plant, biochemical plant, integrated chemical plant (producing nitrogen and phosphate fertilizers, fluoroplastics, and refrigerants), and a microbiology plant run by the Russian Defense Ministry. The oblast exports 8% of its manufactured output, chiefly lumber (18%), chemical products (62%), and machinery and equipment (5%).

The Vyatka Oblast is situated in a high-risk farming area. Cereals are grown chiefly to meet local requirements. Beef and dairy cattle farming takes advantage of the area's grazing land and has great potential because of the oblast's close proximity to the Ural Region and Siberia, which are in need of food.

3. Investment Opportunities. The Vyatka Oblast is a depressed area. Its timber and engineering industries have been hit by a product marketing crisis, and the agricultural economy in the oblast's southern areas has been hurt by low demand caused by an inadequate trading network. For these reasons, the oblast has consistently ranked 60th to 70th in the country for the ratio of the population's earnings to the prices of 19 staple products.

In 1995, the oblast had 35 operating joint ventures. The foreign investments in 1993–95 totaled $600,000. Private owners held 30.5% of the fixed assets of enterprises and organization, joint stock companies (without foreign interest) owned 20.2%, and the federal authorities controlled 30.3%. The oblast also had seven insurance companies and seven commercial banks, including Agroprombank (Tel. 62 2012), Vyatkabank (Tel. 64 0674), the Vyatka Popular Bank (Tel. 67 3711), Kirovsotsbank (Tel. 62 1304), Les (Tel. 62 4266), and the Popular Credit Bank (Tel. 64 3905).

In the near future, the most attractive areas for potential investors will be numerous timber enterprises. Considering the oblast's success with its Vyatka washing-machine enterprise, profitable returns can be expected from projects aimed at the manufacture of high-tech household appliances, garments, knitted goods, and industrial-rubber items. Other promising investment areas include the expansion of the Upper Kama phosphorite mine; the nitrogen-producing facilities at the Kirovo-Chepetsk integrated chemical plant; science-intensive engineering; measuring instruments; electrical-engineering products; electrical equipment for aircraft; laser hardware; participation in the establishment of a biotechnology center; expansion of consumer goods production; and processing produce for the industrial areas of the Ural Region and Siberia.

The oblast is reachable from Moscow by rail (896 km to Kirov, 15 hours from Yaroslavl Terminal), air (two hours from Bykovo Airport), and road (the highway from Moscow, via Vladimir, Nizhny Novgorod, and Yaransk, to Kirov, 20 to 23 hours driving time).

Oblast has 63 km of hard-surfaced roads per 1,000 sq km.

50.5   NIZHNY NOVGOROD OBLAST

1. Natural Resources. Area: 74,800 sq km. Farmland: 31,200 sq km. Woodland: 36,700 sq km. Population: 3,682,700 (Jan. 1, 1996), of which 77.7% is urban and 22.3% is rural. Population density: 49.2 per sq km.

The oblast lies 410 km east of Moscow. It is fully supplied with water.

Woodlands contain 465 million cu m of timber, including 245 million cu m of softwood. The oblast's estimated cutting area is used at 75% capacity. The commercial cutting potential is 8 million cu m.

Mineral resources are limited chiefly to peat and building materials, including brick clay, clay to make expanded materials, and sand for silica bricks.

The oblast has a temperate-continental climate, with a mean temperature of −13°C in January and 19°C in July. Annual rainfall varies from 450 to 500 mm, and the growing season lasts 165 days.

2. Specialization and Sectoral Structure of the Economy (see Exhibit 50.9). Administrative division: 47 districts, 25 cities, 70 urban-type communities, and 520 village group-councils.

Governor: Tel. (8312) 39 1012. Fax: 39 0048.

Principal cities: Nizhny Novgorod (1,440,000), Dzerzhinsk (286,600), Arzamas (112,400), and Pavlovo (72,400).

The manufacturing structure is dominated by engineering (42.7%), the fuel industry (15.5%), the chemical industry (8.9%), and the food industry (7.7%). In terms of industrial development, the oblast is among the top five leading oblasts in Russia, while the defense complex (shipbuilding, the nuclear and aerospace industries, radio engineering, radar facilities, and electronics) is one of the largest in the country. The biggest enterprises in Nizhny Novgorod include the Popov research and development association (radio equipment), the Ulyanov industrial association (electrical engineering), the Krasnoe Sormovo industrial association (shipbuilding), the Frunze industrial association (radio-measuring instruments), the GAZ Motor Plant JSC (trucks and cars), the Zefs JSC (machine tools), the Etna JSC (wire, ferrous rolled stock), the Lazur plant, the Orbita plant, the radio-measuring equipment plant, the Start plant, the Sokol aircraft plant, the Salyut Research and development enterprise, the Era plant (electrical engineering), and the Elektromash plant (radar equipment). Arzamas is a center of instrument building and research for the nuclear industry. Dzerzhinsk is home for six major chemical enterprises producing propylene, ammonia, mineral fertilizers, acetone, resins and acids, caustic soda, and household chemicals. Leather manufacturing is centered in Bogoroditsk; glass is produced in Bor; Navashino and Gorodets are shipbuilding centers; and Pavolovo has plants producing buses and tooling. Kstovo is the site of a large refinery; Kulebaki is the site of a plant manufacturing aluminum sections; Balakhna has an integrated paper plant (Volga JSC); Vyksa has a pipe plant; and Zavolzhye has an engine plant. The oblast exports 10% of its manufactured output, which includes 47% oil products, 18% chemical goods, and 10% wooden and engineering products. (See Exhibit 50.10.)

The farming sector consists mainly of cattle raising, while crop farming chiefly includes potatoes and other vegetables, and staple flax. The oblast is short of grain.

Exhibit 50.9. Sectoral Structure of the Economy in 1995 (% of total)

	Industry	Farming	Transport	Construction	Other
Employment	39.0	9.3	7.1	7.6	38.0
Fixed assets	45.1	15.1	13.8	3.3	22.7
Capital investment	28.8	6.0	16.0	2.1	46.3

Exhibit 50.10.   Manufacture of Principal Industrial Products

	1995	1996
Primary oil refining products, million tons	12.5	10.4
Trucks, thou.	62.3	59.2
Cars, thou.	119	122.6
Paper, thou. tons	492	413.3
Washing machines, thou.	201	140.7
Electric vacuum cleaners, thou.	43.2	25.1
Televisions, thou.	95.9	11.5
Meat, thou. tons	33.8	26.7
Whole milk products, thou. tons	108	97.2

3. Investment Opportunities. The Nizhny Novgorod Oblast is socially stable. It is adequately supplied with water and fuel. One of the problems it faces, unfavorable ecological situation near Nizhny Novgorod, Kstovo, and Dzerzhinsk.

In 1995, the oblast had 115 operating joint ventures. The foreign investments in 1993–95 totaled $73.6 million. Private owners held 16.7% of the fixed assets of enterprises and organization, joint stock companies (without foreign interest) owned 34.3%, and the federal authorities controlled 36%. The oblast had 34 insurance companies and 28 commercial banks, including Avtogazbank (Tel. 56 7594), Assotsiatsia (Tel. 68 6862), the Bank for Foreign Trade (Vneshtorgbank, Tel. 35 2727), Garantia (Tel. 68 3319), Incotransbank (Tel. 44 4075), Nanbank (Tel. 35 1432), Nizhegorodets (Tel. 36 8790), the Nizhny Novgorod Banking House (Tel. 34 3020), Prioksky (Tel. 66 5155), Progress (Tel. 39 0696), Promstroibank (Tel. 33 4764), Radiotechbank (Tel. 64 0691), and Khimik (in Dzerzhinsk, Tel. 55 4010).

The regional administration is attempting to introduce the latest and most efficient technologies into manufacturing and farming. To this end, it has implemented a package of institutional reforms. In manufacturing, narrowly focused major enterprises are being reorganized into multiline concerns, from which the leading-edge facilities are then detached and incorporated as independent enterprises. The Megaclass financial and industrial group (FIG) has brought under its wing a number of enterprises in the automotive and electrical-engineering industries as well as several chemical-engineering plants. The Interbank Investment House group, including the KBD-Bank, Avtovazbank, and a few other financial institutions, has been recently registered. The Vyksa metal plant has joined the Finance-Metal-Pipes FIG. Chemical enterprises in Dzerzhinsk have joined the Ruskhim FIG, which unites 11 plants, three research institutes, and six banks and commercial entities from across Russia. A petrochemical concern has been formed with the oil refinery, the Caprolactam JSC, and the Orgsteklo industrial association as its base.

To ease the problems caused by the below-capacity operation of defense-industry enterprises, individual facilities have been given the same financial privileges and rights as those available to free economic zones. The Alekseev shipbuilding concern has been split into 10 independent enterprises (including the manufacture of hydrofoils, aluminum-alloy ships and seagoing speedboats, dry-cargo ships, sailing ships, and floating pontoons). The Sokol plant and the Polyot research and development enterprise have started the manufacture of light civilian aircraft, satellite-communications systems, and aviation communications facilities. The automotive plant is switching to the production of passenger cars and 1.5-ton Gazelle trucks, now in high demand.

In agriculture, the administration has abandoned the old practice of subsidizing farming and launched the conversion of inefficient collective farms to owner-operated small farms. This approach has been approved at the federal level and has been used as an example to be followed in many other Russian regions.

Despite the lack of strategic resources and numerous defense enterprises that have lost their markets and are struggling to convert to civilian output, the Nizhny Novgorod Oblast offers the most favorable investment opportunities of any region in Russia. It has a satisfactory market infrastructure, including financial, trading, visitor, transportation, and telecommunications entities that have been incorporated into the Nizhny Nvogorod Trade Fair system and have operated on a commercial basis for a relatively long time. Westdeutsche Landesbank has been brought in to assist in the modernization of the local airport, which has the status of an international facility. The administration is trying to increase the prominence of the Nizhny Novgorod Trade Fair and use it as the basis for establishing a trade center for Russian defense industries.

The promising areas of investment include development of transportation, trading, and telecommunications facilities in conjunction with the Nizhny Novgorod Trade Fair; renovation of the oil refinery; technical assistance and consulting in the investment projects carried out jointly with the Volga-Vyatka Privatization Center; promotion of the automotive industry (the GAZ JSC and its suppliers); shipbuilding (enterprises set up on the basis of the Krasnoe Sormova JSC and the Alekseev Design Office); aerospace, radio electronics, radar, and instruments (Sokol plant, Hydromash JSC, and Polyot research and development association); chemical-industry enterprises (in Dzerzhinsk), including manufacture of polyvinyl-chloride films, acrylates, poly-isocyanates, high-purity xenon, and membrane electrolyzers; freight, transportation, including heavy freight; folk handicrafts in Voznesenskoe townships (Polkhovo-Maidan painting), Gorodets (Gorodets painting), Semenov (Semenov and Khokhloma painting), Pavlovo (artistic embroidery, accessories, knifes, and silverware).

The oblast is accessible from Moscow by rail (439 km to Nizhny Novgorod, eight hours from Yaroslavl Terminal), air (1.5 hours from Domodedovo Airport), and road (the highway from Moscow, via Vladimir, to Nizhny Novgorod, eight hours driving time).

Oblast has 108 km of hard-surfaced roads per 1,000 sq km.

CHAPTER 51

CENTRAL BLACK EARTH REGION

Aleko A. Adamescu, Yuri A. Kovalev, and Alexander G. Granberg

51.1 BELGOROD OBLAST

1. Natural Resources. Area: 27,100 sq km. Farmland: 21,600 sq km. Woodland: 2,300 sq km. Population: 1,437,600 (Jan. 1, 1996), of which 64.6% is urban and 35.4% is rural. Population density: 53.0 per sq km.

    The oblast lies 695 km south of Moscow. It is short of water, so the construction of water-consuming enterprises is restricted, and building hydroengineering facilities or sinking artesian wells is expensive. The oblast has 480 medium-sized and small watercourses, 1,100 ponds, and four small reservoirs. Its total annual water runoff is 2,692 cu km.

    The oblast's mineral resources include iron ore, bauxite, marl, clay, sand, and chalk. The area has 14 proven ferruginous-quartzite deposits containing a total of 25 billion tons of iron ore, or 73% of Russia's overall reserves. The best-known of these deposits are located at Yakovlevo, Gostishchevo, Korobkovo, Saltykovo, Lebedin, Stoileno, Pogromets, and Chernyansk. The iron-ore deposits are being developed by mining and dressing plants, which produce various building materials aside from iron-ore stock.

    The oblast has a temperate-continental climate, with a mean temperature of $-8.5°C$ in January and $20°C$ in July. The oblast receives 450 to 500 mm of annual rainfall and has a growing season of 185 to 190 days.

2. Specialization and Sectoral Structure of the Economy (see Exhibit 51.1). Administrative division: 21 districts, 9 cities, 22 urban-type communities, and 324 village group-councils.

    Administration head: Tel. (07222) 24 247. Fax 25 468.

    Principal cities: Belgorod (315,300), Stary Oskol (188,300), Gubkin (80,200), and Schebekino (45,100).

    The manufacturing structure is dominated by ferrous metallurgy (45.6%), the food industry (16.4%), and engineering (11.6%). Ferrous-metal fabrication is centered in Gubkin (the Kmaruda plant and Lebedin mining and dressing plant), Stary Oskol (Stoilenskoe mining and dressing plant, Electrometallurgy JSC, and Oskol-cement JSC), and Schebekino (Yakovlevo ore authority, a biochemical plant producing amino acids, and a chemical plant producing synthetic acids). Belgorod is the focal point of the food industry and the production of building materials (reinforced concrete and asbestos-cement items, phlogopite, steel structures, bricks,

Exhibit 51.1.   Sectoral Structure of the Economy in 1995 (% of total)

	Industry	Farming	Transport	Construction	Other
Employment	26.0	22.4	6.3	10.3	35.0
Fixed assets	44.9	25.1	10.5	3.3	16.2
Capital Investment	33.0	7.1	4.7	1.3	53.9

chalk, and cement). Two industries—engineering and biochemical production—are even stronger in Belgorod and require strong labor skills: The Sokol Industrial Association (communications facilities), the Belenergomash Industrial Association (steam boilers and equipment for nuclear-power plants), and the Belgorod Vitaminy JSC (vitamins A, B, and C, and medicaments). The economic mainstay of the majority of the oblast's small and medium-sized towns is comprised of enterprises processing farming produce and manufacturing building materials. (See Exhibit 51.2.)

The oblast exports 18.3% of its manufactured output; 36% of this iron ore, and 58% ferrous-metal rolled stock.

The oblast is a high-yield farming area enjoying the advantages of its fertile black soils. It practices commercial grain growing, sugar-beet cultivation, and production of butter and fats. Animal farming consists of beef and dairy cattle raising, in addition to hogs and fowl.

3. Investment Opportunities. The Belgorod Oblast is the most stable area in Russia's Black-Earth belt. Its iron-ore industry and the recently commissioned integrated electrometallurgical plant offer highly paid jobs for the local population and ensure a steady flow of funds into the area. However, the area has problems typical of the rest of Russia: a weak marketing infrastructure for supplying products to other areas and large, inefficient cattle farms.

Investment prospects include metal-fabrication enterprises (from geological prospecting and the mining of iron ore and bauxites, to the production of consumer goods for markets in southern Russia and neighboring Ukraine), and the possible participation in farming-development programs. Typical farming-development projects involve manufacturing units to process corn and hybrid-sunflower seeds; construction of grain dryers and silos on farms; processing of oil-bearing seeds; construction of agricultural oil mill units on farms; a modernization program for the sugar industry; modernization of major meat-packing plants to produce meats for the country's other regions (including vacuum lines for packaging meat and pre-

Exhibit 51.2.   Manufacture of Principal Industrial Products

	1995	1996
Ferrous metal rolled stock, thou. tons	1,400	1,316
Iron ore, million tons	26.1	25.3
Cement, thou. tons	3,519	2,639
Asbestos cement pipes, km.	2,680	2,439
Vegetable oil, thou. tons	37.1	92.8
Granulated sugar, thou. tons	427	474
Meat, thou. tons	44.9	40
Whole milk products, thou. tons	47.1	56

serving meats and vegetable); processing of hog and cattle hides; leather dressing; and the manufacture of footwear from local materials.

In 1995, the oblast had 135 operating joint ventures. The foreign investments in 1993–95 were $118.8 million. Private owners held 32.8% of the fixed assets of enterprises, joint stock companies (without foreign interest) owned 35.6%, and the federal authorities controlled 10.8%. The oblast also had seven insurance companies and 11 commercial banks, including Belbank (Tel. 73 595), Belgorodsotsbank (Tel. 22 208), Belekonomsotsbank (Tel. 74 204), and Credit-Service (Tel. 73 767).

The oblast is reachable from Moscow by train (695 km to Belgorod, 11 hours from Kursk Terminal), air (two hours from Bykovo Airport), and road (the highway from Moscow, via Tula and Kursk, to Belgorod, 12–13 hours).

The oblast has 160 km of hard-surface roads per 1,000 sq km.

51.2 KURSK OBLAST

1. Natural Resources. Area: 29,800 sq km. Farmland: 24,500 sq km. Woodland: 2,440 sq km. Population: 1,343,800 (Jan. 1, 1996), of which 59.7% is urban and 40.3% is rural. Population density: 45.1 per sq km.

   The oblast lies on the western slopes of the middle Russian highland, astride the roads from Russia to Ukraine. Its manufacturing and farming are adequately supplied with water, but the growth of water-consuming industries is restricted, and utilizing new water sources in the area is an expensive process.

   The oblast's principal advantages are its iron ore and rich, black-earth soil. Iron ore has been prospected at Mikhailovskoe, Dichnyanskoe, Reuteskoe, and Tim-Schigrovskoe. Mining operations are carried out at the Mikhailovskoe deposit, which has 430 million tons of iron-rich ore and 10 million tons of ferruginous quartzite. Black-earth soil occupies 60% of the oblast's area and supports high-return grain farming. The available building materials, in particular sand, clay, sapropel, and chalk, fully meet the local demands and are plentiful enough for enterprises to supply them to neighboring oblasts. In all, 40 phosphate deposits containing a total of 340 million tons have been prospected (Ukolovo, Schigrovo, and Trukhachevo), but mining operations stopped in the early 1980s due to economic considerations. Sapropel deposits are located in the river valleys of the Lgov and Fatezh districts.

   The oblast has a temperate-continental climate, with a mean temperature of −8°C in January and 19°C in July. The annual rainfall varies from 480 to 600 mm, and the growing season lasts 187 to 195 days.

2. Specialization and Sectoral Structure of the Economy (see Exhibit 51.3). Administrative division: 28 districts, 10 cities, 23 urban-type communities, and 477 village group-councils.

   Administration head: Tel. (07122) 26 262. Fax (0712) 566 573.

Exhibit 51.3.   Sectoral Structure of the Economy in 1995 (% of total)

	Industry	Farming	Transport	Construction	Other
Employment	28.0	22.6	6.4	8.2	34.8
Fixed assets	37.1	27.8	9.4	6.3	19.4
Capital Investment	38.0	10.4	7.8	1.5	42.3

Principal cities: Kursk (437,400), Zheleznogorsk (91,300), Kurchatov (46,100), and Lgov (46,100).

The manufacturing structure is dominated by the food industry (17.3%), chemical industry (9.2%), engineering (14.3%), ferrous-metal fabrication (14.2%), and power engineering (27.6%). (See Exhibit 51.4.)

The city of Kursk contains most of the oblast's enterprises, including the Accumulator JSC (producing alkaline storage batteries for motor vehicles); the Jurskchimvolokno JSC (manufacturing lavsan, polypropylene, melan, and kapron); a tractor parts plant; the Bearing Plant JSC; the Schetmash JSC (calculating machines); the Pribor Industrial Association (computers); the Elektropribor JSC (DC generators); the Elektroapparat JSC (low-voltage electrical equipment), the Mayak plant (radio-measuring devices), and the Seim JSC (knitted goods).

Kurchatov is the site of the Kurks Nuclear Power Plant. The economic framework of other districts in the oblast is based on enterprises that turn our dairy products, meat, sugar, alcohol, molasses, hemp goods, citric acid, packaging, garments, knitted goods, and building materials.

The oblast exports 7% of its manufactured output, of which iron ore represents 73%, followed by textiles and nonwoven materials.

The oblast is part of the high-yield grain and sugar-beet-farming area in southern Russia's Black-Earth belt. Potatoes and other vegetables, fruit, and berries are grown for local consumption. Lately, there has been an increasing trend among the oblast's private farmers to grow crops for markets in the Moscow Oblast. In animal farming, priority is given to beef and dairy cattle, hogs, and fowl.

3. Investment Opportunities. The situation in the oblast is stable, with no restrictions placed on power consumption, sites for new projects, recruitment of skilled and inexpensive labor (migrating from the nearby Kharkov Oblast of Ukraine), or food prices, which are among the lowest in Russia. Apart from the iron-ore mining and processing facilities, the oblast can offer little to major investors. Investment prospects include the processing of cheap local materials, including medicinal plants and apples, for the external market, and meat and milk processing to supply the domestic market. The oblast's economy hinges on farming, which is at present going through a heavy sales crisis, which accounts for the conservative mood among the oblast's people and authorities. To overcome this, assistance is urgently needed to expand the farm produce-processing facilities, and to set up a system for delivering the products to the Moscow Oblast and Russian's northern areas. The task may be facilitated by the presence of many small enterprises, most of which are privately owned.

In 1995, the oblast had 47 operating joint ventures. The foreign investments in 1993–95 were two million dollars. Private owners held 29.1% of the fixed assets of enterprises, joint stock companies (without foreign interest) owned 29.1%, and the

Exhibit 51.4.   Manufacture of Principal Industrial Products

	1995	1996
Non-woven materials, million sq. m.	2.1	2.01
Knitted goods, million	4.5	1.3
Sugar, thou. tons	254	206
Meat, thou. tons	28.9	22.8
Whole milk products, thou. tons	19.9	16.3

federal authorities controlled 25.3%. The oblast had nine insurance companies and four commercial banks, including Agroprombank (Tel. 33 3416), Kurskbank (Tel. 56 6467), and Olis (Tel. 35 4634).

The oblast is reachable from Moscow by rail (536 km to Kursk, 10 hours from Kursk Terminal), air (1.5 hours from Bykovo Airport), and road (the highway from Moscow, via Tula, to Kursk, 13 hours).

Oblast has 167 km of hard-surfaced roads per 1,000 sq km.

51.3 LIPETSK OBLAST

1. Natural Resources. Area: 24,100 sq km. Farmland: 19,500 sq km. Woodland: 2,000 sq km. Population: 1,245,800 (Jan. 1, 1996), of which 63% is urban and 37% is rural. Population density: 57.1 per sq km.

The oblast lies 300 to 400 km. southeast of Moscow in the catchment area of the upper Don. It has only limited water resources, especially in its southeastern part. The annual water consumption rate is 30.2 cu m/sec in Lipetsk (fed from the Voronezh River), 70.7 cu m/sec in Yelets (the Sosna River), 127 cu m/sec in Zadonsk (the Don River), and 0.7 cu m/sec in Usman (the Usman River). The underground water resources are equal to 2,148,800 cu m/day.

The woodlands play a role in water protection and recreation.

The oblast's resources include high-heat clay (34 million tons), fluxing limestone (254 million tons), metallurgical dolomite (737 million tons), cement stock (137 million tons), molding materials (3.5 million tons), and peat (nine million tons). The area abounds in deposits of building materials, such as brick and expanding clay, building and silicate sands, building stones, and carbonate rock. A resort called spa Lipetsk has been built at the site of waters containing chloride and sodium sulfate, and curative peat mud.

The oblast has a temperate-continental climate, with a mean temperature of −10°C in January and 20°C in July. The annual rainfall varies between 450 and 500 mm, and the growing season lasts 180 to 185 days.

2. Specialization and Sectoral Structure of the Economy (see Exhibit 51.5). Administrative division: 18 districts, 8 cities, 5 urban-type communities, and 297 village group-councils.

Administration head: Tel. (0742) 24 2526. Fax 72 2426.

Principal cities: Lipetsk (44,400), Yelets (120,500), Gryazi (47,700), and Dankov (24,800).

The manufacturing structure is dominated by ferrous-metal fabrication (63.3%), the food industry (10.7%), and engineering (7.4%). The oblast has facilities capable of producing 10 million tons of steel, seven million tons of finished rolled stock, 50,000 row-crop tractors, one million refrigerators, two million tons of cement, 2,000 metal-cutting tools, and 100,000 tons of cast-iron pipes. (See Exhibit 51.6.)

Exhibit 51.5.   Sectoral Structure of the Economy in 1995 (% of total)

	Industry	Farming	Transport	Construction	Other
Employment	29.0	18.4	7.1	9.7	35.8
Fixed assets	43.9	22.3	9.8	7.2	16.8
Capital Investment	33.2	8.0	15.0	1.5	42.3

Exhibit 51.6.   Manufacture of Principal Industrial Products

	1995	1996
Steel, million tons	7.1	7.1
Finished ferrous metal rolled stock, thou. tons	6.2	6.4
Tractors, thou.	3.4	2.8
Bathtubs, thou.	204	98
Heating radiators, thou. kW	479	244.3
Meat, thou. tons	28.2	29
Whole milk products, thou. tons	55.6	56.7

The oblast's principal enterprise, the Novolipetsk integrated metal-fabrication plant, is the biggest supplier of transformer steel and vehicle sheet steel in Russia. The economic position of this enterprise affects the oblast's investment and labor market and the flow of revenues to the local budget. The plant has been modernized in recent years (in particular, its sheet-rolling facility and the coke-over batteries), and facilities have been added to produce Stinol refrigerators, Gold Star videocassette recorders, and truck trailers. The plant is located within the city limits of Lipetsk because its environmental standards are among the lowest in the country. Efforts have also been launched to develop subsidized farming.

Another major enterprise in Lipetsk is its plant producing row-crop tractors, which gets its components from suppliers located in the oblast's smaller towns (Gryazi, Usman, Yelets, Lebedyan, and Chaplygin). Sales in the tractor industry have plunged, a crisis that occurred during the recent modernization program of its leading enterprise.

Other important enterprises include Svobodny Sokol (cast-iron pipes), the Centrolit foundry, the machine-tool plant, and the Silan JSC (manufacturing products based on organic-silicon compounds).

The oblast exports 28% of its manufactured output, with almost of all of it (98%) composed of products of the metal plants; (98%), concentrated apple juice is the other exported item.

Crop farming specializes in growing grains and sugar beets, and animal farming focuses on cattle raising and keeping hogs and fowl.

3. Investment Opportunities. Opportunities are open in ferrous-metal fabrication (including know-how and equipment that reduces power, heat, and coke consumption); modernization of the Lipetsk tractor plant (production of a new kind of general-purpose row-crop tractor, possibly under a foreign license, and tractor engines); processing of rape seeds and fruit; and production of building materials, including those from metal-fabrication wastes.

Investments in the oblast restrained by the following key limitations: an unreliable power supply, caused by a lack of major power-generating facilities; the unfavorable ecological situation in Lipetsk; and the strong influence of the performance of the Novolipetsk metal-fabrication plant and the Lipetsk tractor plant on the oblast's overall economic and social situation.

In 1995, the oblast had 53 operating joint ventures. The foreign investments in 1993–95 totaled $12.2 million. The joint projects with foreign firms include the Stinol refrigerator plant, the facilities producing disposable syringes, linoleum, and polymeric coatings, and the concentrated-juice plant. Construction is soon to be completed of a facility producing cellular concrete items using a process from a German firm. In 1993, private owners held 26% of the fixed assets of enterprises, joint stock companies (without foreign interest) held 49%, and the federal authorities controlled 12%. The oblast had 13 insurance companies and seven commercial banks, including Agroprombank (Tel. 72 2487), Lipetsk (Tel. 74 5850), Korona Bank (Tel. 77 5719), Lipetskcombank (Tel. 72 5955), and Status Bank (24 1394).

The oblast is reachable from Moscow by rail (508 km to Lipetsk, 12 hours from Paveletsky Terminal), air (1.5 hours from Bykovo Airport), and road (the highway from Moscow, via Yelets, to Lipetsk, 11 hours).

There are 200 km of hard-surfaced highways per 1,000 sq km. of the oblast's territory.

51.4 TAMBOV OBLAST

1. Natural Resources. Area: 34,300 sq km. Farmland: 27,570 sq km. Woodland: 3,680 sq km. Population: 1,314,700 (Jan. 1, 1996), of which 57.4% is urban and 42.6% is rural. Population density: 38.3 per sq km, the lowest in Russia's black-earth area.

   The oblast lies 500 km southeast of Moscow, at the watershed between the Volga and Don River systems. There are only minor restrictions on the consumption of water drawn from the Tsna and Vorona Rivers and plentiful underground water sources.

   The oblast's minerals, including building materials, phosphate, mineral dyes, and peat, are developed to meet local needs. The best-known deposits of building and sand are located at Tambov and Polkovo.

   The oblast has a temperate-continental climate, with a mean temperature of −11°C in January and 20°C in July. It gets 400 to 500 mm of annual rainfall, and its growing season varies from 180 to 185 days.

2. Specialization and Sectoral Structure of the Economy (see Exhibit 51.7). Administrative division: 23 districts, 8 cities, 13 urban-type communities, and 304 village group-councils.

   Administration head: Tel. (0752) 22 2518. Fax 22 1585.

   Principal cities: Tambov (311,500), Michurinsk (108,900), Morshansk (50,600), and Rasskazovo (50,200).

   The manufacturing structure is dominated by the food industry (25.8%), engineering (22.2%), and the chemical industry (15.9%). The oblast has a group of chemical-industry facilities and enterprises producing equipment for the chemical industry, in particular the Tambovmash industrial association (valves, pipes, and filters), Galvanotechnika Industrial Association (electroplating tanks), the Tambovpolymermash Plant (film-making equipment), a chemical engineering plant

Exhibit 51.7. Sectoral Structure of the Economy in 1995 (% of total)

	Industry	Farming	Transport	Construction	Other
Employment	24.7	23.0	7.6	7.8	36.9
Fixed assets	26.2	30.8	15.7	3.0	24.3
Capital Investment (1995)	15.2	11.5	15.3	1.3	56.7

(equipment for the petrochemical industry), and the Pigment Plant (varnishes, paints, and household chemicals) in Tambov; the Chimmash Plant (equipment from stainless steel and aluminum) in Morshansk; a chemical-engineering plant in the Pervomaisk township; and a chemical plant in Uvarovo (mineral fertilizers, acids, and powdered zinc). (See Exhibit 51.8.)

Other large enterprises are a bearing plant, asbestos products plant, the Almaz JSC, a piston ring plant, and enterprises manufacturing knitted goods, garments, and woolen fabrics (including the integrated cloth mill in Arzhensk).

The economic backbone of the oblast's small and medium-sized towns is formed by small businesses processing milk and butter, beer, sugar, vegetable oil, starch and molasses, building materials, and furniture. The oblast exports a mere 2% of its output, chiefly chemical products.

The oblast has a multisector agriculture, including high-return grain growing and a sugar industry complete with specialized farms and processing facilities. Its horticulture is recognized nationally for its highly productive facilities; its animal husbandry specializes in beef and dairy cattle raising.

3. Investment Opportunities. The Tambov Oblast is a stable area. The investment climate is complicated by the lack of a developed market infrastructure and remoteness from Russia's main financial and trading centers. For these reasons, good short-term returns may be obtained from modest projects involving the processing of cheap fruit and berries, production of ecologically safe foods, and the establishment of small-scale leisure industry enterprises. There is a great need to replace the old equipment in the sugar plants.

In view of the upturn in Russia's chemical industry, handsome return may result from investing in large-scale projects to modernize the chemical-engineering enterprises, which constitute, in many respects, monopolies in the Russian market.

In 1995, the oblast had 29 operating joint ventures. The foreign investments in 1993–95 totaled $11.7 million. Private owners held 32.3% of the fixed assets of enterprises, joint stock companies (without foreign interest) owned 23.7%, and the federal authors controlled 35.4%. The oblast had eight insurance companies and six commercial banks, including Avtotransbank (Tel. 33 5030), Agroprombank (Tel. 22 3091), Bastion (Tel. 24 1691), and Tambovsotsbank (Tel. 22 9042).

The oblast is reachable from Moscow by rail (480 km to Tambov, 11 hours from Paveletsky Terminal), air (1.5 hours from Bykovo Airport), and road (the highway from Moscow to Tambov, nine hours).

There are 132 km of hard-surfaced roads per 1,000 sq km in the oblast.

Exhibit 51.8.   Manufacture of Principal Industrial Products

	1995	1996
Mineral fertilizers, thou. tons	21.2	n/a
Woolen fabrics, million sq. m.	3.1	1.8
Tape recorders, thou.	112	30.2
Vegetable oil, thou. tons	15.3	51.3
Granulated sugar, thou. tons	178	222.5
Meat, thou. tons	18.6	14.3
Whole milk products, thou. tons	18.4	195

51.5 VORONEZH OBLAST

1. Natural Resources. Area: 52,400 sq km. Farmland: 41,150 sq km. Woodland: 4,500 sq km Population: 2,498,500 (Jan. 1, 1996), of which 61.5% is urban and 38.5% is rural. Population density: 38.3 per sq km, the lowest in Russia's Black-Earth Region.

    The oblast lies 590 km south of Moscow, along the transport routes connecting Russia's central and southern areas. The terrain is heavily broken by river valleys and gullies. The region is short of water, so water-consuming enterprises can be located only in populated areas on the Don River; such businesses must make considerable investments in the water supply systems and waste treatment facilities.

    The oblast's mineral resources include cement stock, fireclay, sand, and building stones. The more significant deposits of chalk are located at Pogorenskoe, Buturlino, Kopanishchevo, Rossosh, and Otkosino. Building materials are located at Pavlovo, Stanichnoe, and Pogorenskoe. Fireclay exists in significant quantities at Lataenskoe, and mineral dyes at Zhuravskoe and Buturlino.

    The oblast has a temperate continental climate, with a mean temperature of −10°C in January and 20°C in July. The annual rainfall varies between 440 and 560 mm, and the growing season is between 190 and 200 days.

2. Specialization and Sectoral Structure of the Economy (see Exhibit 51.9). Administrative division: 32 districts, 15 cities, 23 urban-type communities, and 491 village group-councils.

    Administration head: Tel. (0732) 55 2737. Fax 52 1015.

    Principal cities: Voronezh (903,300), Borisoglebsk (71,800), Rossosh (60,600), and Liski (55,200).

    The manufacturing structure is dominated by the food industry (22.8%), the chemical industry (11%), mechanical engineering (29%), and power engineering (18%). The oblast's major enterprises located in Voronezh include the Aircraft Industrial Association (manufacturing IL 96M aircraft equipped with Pratt & Whitney engines), the Machine Tool Plant JSC, the Upmash JSC (aircraft equipment), the Energia JSC (low-wattage electric motors), a semiconductor devices plant, radio components plant, radio manufacturing plant, the Rekord plant (diesel locomotives), the VELT state-owned enterprise (television tubes), the Synthetic Rubber JSC, the Tyazhex JSC (single-bucket shovels). Other large enterprises operating elsewhere in the oblast are an instrument plant in Borisoglebsk, the Mineral Fertilizers JSC in Rossosh, and a fireclay plant in Semiluki. (See Exhibit 51.10.)

    The oblast exports 6% of its manufactured output, of which chemical products and auto tires account for 58%, and machinery and equipment for another 38%.

    The oblast is situated in a profitable farming belt famous for its black soil. The most widespread crops cultivated here are cereals, sugar beets, sunflowers, hemp,

Exhibit 51.9. Sectoral Structure of the Economy in (% of total)

	Industry	Farming	Transport	Construction	Other
Employment	26.6	19.2	7.9	8.2	18.1
Fixed assets	31.1	26.5	12.9	3.6	25.9
Capital Investment	23.0	9.5	22.2	2.4	42.9

Exhibit 51.10.   Manufacture of Principal Industrial Products

	1995	1996
Mineral fertilizers, thou. tons	191	190
Auto tires, thou	610	1,012.6
Ceramic tiles, thou. sq.m.	3,421	2,394
Television Sets, thou.	91.2	20.1
Video cassette recorders, thou.	13.1	1.6
Vegetable oil, thou. tons	71.8	167.3
Granulated sugar, thou. tons	300	82.5
Meat, thou. Tons	44.3	33.7
Whole milk products, thou. tons	76.5	85.7

potatoes, and other vegetables. There are countless sugar beet and sunflower seed-processing enterprises, which are badly in need of new equipment and know-how. The local producers manufacture essential oils and grow coriander and anise, processing them into finished products at the essential-oils plant in Alekseevka. Animal farmers raise cattle, sheep, and bees, and engage in horse breeding (Orel trotters and Voronezh draft horses).

3. Investment Opportunities. The Voronezh Oblast is a stable area. The chief problem is the below-capacity operation of its manufacturing enterprises that produce goods for the defense industry and agriculture, and the resulting low wages of the population. The market crisis in manufacturing and farming encourages enterprises to return to the old system of distribution and the restrictions on shipping food products beyond the oblast.

The oblast has no constraints on employment, land for industrial construction, or power for small and medium-scale projects. The oblast boasts one of the most advanced communications and science-support systems in Russia's Black Earth belt.

The principal targets for investors include the aircraft industry, a particularly attractive choice, considering the experience gained under the IL 96M program; high-tech household appliances (televisions, videocassette recorders, home and office equipment, home security systems, and outboard engines) to make up for shortages in southern Russia, Ukraine, and the Middle East; modernization of the chemical facilities (mineral fertilizers, chemical reagents, paints and varnishes, and household chemicals); construction of grain-drying and storage facilities on farms; the processing of oil-bearing seeds; modernization of the sugar industry; construction of facilities to dress hog and cattle hides, and to manufacture leather and footwear from local materials.

In 1995, the oblast had 56 operating joint ventures. The foreign investments in 1993–95 were $1.3 million. Private owners held 24.4% of the fixed assets of enterprises, joint stock companies (without foreign interest) owned 22.5%, and the federal authorities controlled 39%. The oblast had 12 insurance companies and nine commercial banks, including Agroimpulse (Tel. 64 2832), Agroprombank (Tel. 55 5995), Voronezh (Tel. 55 5775), Coopbank (Tel. 16 0809), Peter the First (Tel. 55 5970), Stroitel (Tel. 57 4377), and Energia (Tel. 64 8037).

The oblast is reachable from Moscow by rail (587 km to Voronezh, 12 hours from the Kursk terminal or the Kazan terminal), air (1.5 hours from Bykovo Airport), and road (the highway from Moscow to Voronezh, 12 hours).

There are 132 km of hard-surfaced roads per 1,000 sq km.

CHAPTER 52

VOLGA REGION

Aleko A. Adamescu, Yuri A. Kovalev, and Alexander G. Granberg

52.1 REPUBLIC OF KALMYKIA

1. Natural Resources. Area: 76,100 sq km. Farmland: 59,740 sq km. Woodland: 300 sq km. Population: 320,600 (Jan. 1, 1996), of which 37% is urban and 63% is rural. Population density: 4.2 per sq km., one of the lowest in Russia.

   The republic lies in the sparsely developed arid part of the Caspian lowland (black earths) and the Sarpino lowland. Its southeastern fringe opens to the Caspian Sea. It is short of surface water, but has plenty of shallow salt lakes (Sarpisnkoe, Sostinskoe, Manych-Gudilo, and Ichgan-Khik). The principal hydroengineering facilities are the Chograi and Arshan-Egorlyk reservoirs, with irrigation systems operating at Egorlyk, Olyakai, and Black Earths.

   The republic's mineral resources include natural gas, oil, common salt, and building sand and clay. The best-known oil fields are operated at Vysokovskoe, Mezhozernoe, Komsomolskoe, and Kamyshin; natural gas is extracted at Promyslovoe, Chuvuk, Ermolinsk, Mezhevoe, and Iki-Burul; condensed gas is produced at Tengut and Oleinikovo; clay at Bashchatinsk, Tsagan-Aman, and Sarpino; and common salt is mined at Mozharskoe.

   The republic has a pronounced continental climate, with the mean temperature varying between −5 and −8°C in January and from 23 to 26°C in July. The annual rainfall is 170 to 200 mm, and the growing season lasts from 180 to 215 days. The area's climate and soils are not conducive to crop farming, but are favorable for high-yield commercial sheep grazing.

2. Specialization and Sectoral Structure of the Economy (see Exhibit 52.1). Administrative division: 13 districts, 3 cities, and 104 village group-councils.

   President: Tel. (84722) 62 741. Fax 62 880

   Principal cities: Elista (91,900), Kaspiiski (16,000), and Gorodovikovsk (11,000).

   Agriculture is the backbone of the republic's economy. This distinguishes the republic from the majority of areas employed in manufacturing or support industries. The level of farming is dictated by the available water supplies and rainfall over the year. Several irrigation systems have been built, but their further expansion is restricted by their inefficiency, salinization of the soil, and other problems hampering agricultural efficiency and growth.

   Structurally, the commercial-farming output is 70% animal produce and 30% field crops. Animal farming is dominated by raising fine-fleeced sheep, which are

Exhibit 52.1.   Sectoral Structure of the Economy in 1995 (% of total)

	Industry	Farming	Transport	Construction	Other
Employment	10.1	33.8	6.2	7.7	42.2
Fixed Assets	15.6	35.3	5.4	20.0	23.7
Capital Investment	19.0	35.8	14.5	0.4	30.3

basically the Kalmykian breed that are well adapted to pasture grazing. The merino sheep yield both fine and semifine wool. It is customary to graze sheep on distant pastures, most of which are in the western Caspian area (the so-called black earths) and are extensively used by farmers of the Stavropol, Rostov, and Volgograd areas; so the pastures are overgrazed and fall out of use. Kalmykia is a net-surplus producer of low-cost meat and wool. Due to the shortage of processing facilities, the republic's wool gets only primary treatment, with most of it being shipped to the country's other oblasts. An especially difficult problem for the republic is the marketing of its low-quality wool, which is abundant because of inadequate husbandry techniques. The poor marketing system imposes a need to reduce production and encourages the building of sheepskin-processing and meat-packing enterprises and comprehensive wool-processing facilities.

Other animal-farming sectors include horse breeding and cattle raising. Several fish-canning enterprises also operate in the republic.

In manufacturing, the food industry accounts for 30.8% of the total output, and power engineering for 33%. There is a predominance of small meat, dairy, and vehicle-repair enterprises with a workforce of 100 to 300 each. The republic exports 16% of its manufactured output (wool and food products). (See Exhibit 52.2.)

3. Investment Opportunities. The two major ethnic groups in the republic are Russians (37.7%) and Kalmyks (45.4%). The population's cultural and economic traditions are more typical of those followed on the Volga and the Don, than those of the North Caucasian groups. No major ethnic conflicts have been recorded. The republic can, therefore, be rated as a stable area despite its close proximity to the Moslem oblasts of the Caucasus.

The limited range of investment areas does not bode well for prospective investors. The most attractive prospects are those for developing oil and gas fields and producing building materials, some of which can be sold outside the republic. Due to the low cost of agricultural raw materials and the considerable surpluses of farming produce, projects for producing sheepskin items and developing meat-canning and fish-processing facilities may prove advantageous. Investments are needed to develop telecommunications and the transportation infrastructure, particularly, the construction of an airport and hard-surfaced roads.

The republic's administration is pursuing a steady policy of market reforms. In view of the extremely unfavorable economic situation and the predominance of

Exhibit 52.2.   Manufacture of Principal Industrial Products

	1995	1996
Meat, thou. tons	4.1	3.2
Whole milk products, thou. tons	3.2	2.24

low-income rural communities, outside investors have been offered numerous kinds of accommodations: an offshore zone has been set up, and the administration is helping in every way to implement construction and economic programs.

In 1995, the republic had one operating joint venture. The foreign investments in 1993–95 totaled $1.6 million. Private owners held 16.5% of the fixed assets of enterprises, joint stock companies (without foreign interest) owned 2.5%, the federal authorities controlled 35.9%, and the republican government 33.5%. The area had five insurance companies and 10 commercial banks, including Apabank (Tel. 61 312) and Aeroflot (Tel. 21 984).

The republic is reachable from Moscow by rail (1836 km to Elista, 42 hours from Paveletsky Terminal) and air (five hours from Bykovo Airport).

There are 29 km of hard-surfaced roads per 1,000 sq km.

52.2 TATARSTAN REPUBLIC

1. Natural Resources. Area: 68,000 sq km. Farmland: 45,740 sq km. Woodland: 11,870 sq km. Population: 3,743,600 (Jan. 1, 1996), of which 73.5% is urban and 26.5% is rural. Population density: 35.1 per sq km.

   The republic lies 900 km east of Moscow. It is adequately supplied with water, which is, however, heavily polluted with oil products, phenols, and heavy metals that have been discharged from the chemical, oil-mining, and oil-refining facilities in the catchment area of the Kama River.

   The woodlands contain the biggest reserves of timber in the Volga area, 144.6 million cu m, including 33.8 million cu m of softwood. The estimated cutting area is used at 100% capacity. The commercial-logging area has a potential of 3.4 million cu m.

   The republic's mineral resources include oil, natural gas, peat, bentonite clay, gypsum, gravel, and coal. The best-known fields of oil and wellhead gas are located at Romashkinskoe, Novo-Elokhovskoe, Bavlinskoe, Shungurovskoe, Bondiuzhskoe, and Aktashskoe; coal is mined in the Kama coalfields; and lime is produced at Pechishchenskoe, Chapaevskoe, and Bondiuzhskoe. About 76% of the initial recoverable oil reserves have been depleted, and today smaller fields (with less than 10 million tons) and low-yield fields are being put into production. At the present time, coal can be mined only to meet local needs and is economically inferior to oil and natural gas as fuels.

   The republic has a temperate-continental climate, with a mean temperature of −13°C in January and 19°C in July. The republic gets 450 mm of rainfall annually, and its growing season lasts 170 days.

2. Specialization and Sectoral Structure of the Economy (see Exhibit 52.3). Administrative division: 43 districts, 19 cities, 22 urban-type communities, and 848 village group-councils.

Exhibit 52.3. Sectoral Structure of the Economy in 1995 (% of total)

	Industry	Farming	Transport	Construction	Other
Employment	29.3	14.7	7.1	12.6	36.3
Fixed Assets	50.7	15.2	11.0	3.4	19.7
Capital Investment	43.6	9.6	5.9	4.5	36.4

President: Tel. (8432) 32 7001 and fax 32 7088. Prime Minister: Tel. 32 6698. Supreme Council: Tel. 32 3537.

Principal cities: Kazan (1,103,500), Naberezhnye Chelny (519,900), Nizhnekamsk (199,300), and Almetievsk (142,300).

The manufacturing structure is dominated by engineering (22.5%), the chemical industry (22.3%), the fuel industry (19.4%), power engineering (12.3%), and the food industry (10.6%). The republic's level of industrial development ranks only below that of Moscow, Sverdlovsk, Chelyabinsk, and Nizhny Novgorod Oblasts and, in some fields, the Samara Oblast as well. Kazan is one of Russia's largest centers for the aerospace and chemical industries. Its main enterprises are the Gorbunov industrial association, the Orgsintez JSC (producing ethylene and plastics), the helicopter industrial association, a research and development association manufacturing computers and automatic devices, a computer systems industrial association, the Tasma industrial association (cinemagraphic and photographic goods), a motor industrial association, the Kirov Plant industrial association, the Elekom research and development association, and the heat-control industrial association. The city also has major enterprises in virtually every industry, including producers of fur articles, equipment for the chemical and oil industries, instruments, refrigerating equipment, and pharmaceutical goods. Naberezhnye Chelny and the nearby city of Nizhnekamsk together form Russia's biggest center for producing heavy-duty trucks. In addition, Nizhnekamsk contains nine enterprises integrated into the truck-making Kamaz JSC, the Lower Kama petrochemical association (synthetic tires), the Lower Kama auto tire association, and power-generating facilities. The majority of other cities and towns in the republic grew up around farm-produce-processing enterprises or as hometowns of oil and gas production authorities, in particular, Almetievsk, Bulguma, the deep-well pump plant and the pipe-making plant in Almetievsk, the Karpov plant in Mendeleevsk (barium chloride and barium-based products). In addition, the Vostok watch factory in Chistopol produces Commander wristwatches, which are prominent in the world market. (See Exhibit 52.4.)

The republic exports 10% of its manufactured output, 45% of which is comprised of oil and oil products, and 44% trucks and chemical goods.

Farming chiefly centers on grain growing and cattle raising, and most of the farming produce is intended to meet local requirements.

3. Investment Opportunities. The republic is striving to pursue an independent economic line within the framework of the Russian Constitution. The separation of

Exhibit 52.4.   Manufacture of Principal Industrial Products

	1995	1996
Oil, million tons	25.7	25.7
Gas turbines, thou. kW	768	307.2
Trucks, thou.	8.7	7.4
Auto tires, thou.	7,845	8,473
Prefabricated reinforced concrete, thou. cu.m.	615	633.5
Refrigerators, thou.	37.3	21.6
Vegetable oil, thou. tons	n/a	n/a
Granulated sugar, thou. tons	123	116.9
Meat, thou. tons	77.3	61.8
Whole milk products, thou. tons	203	199

powers between the federal authorities and those of the republic is governed by a special agreement.

The two major ethnic groups in the republic are Russians (43.3%) and Tatars (48.5%), most of the latter living in rural areas. The republic does have certain ethnic tensions, but they are not explosive, so the area is generally stable. In the long term, investors should consider the fact that Tatarstan is one of Russia's principal Moslem centers and interethnic tensions may escalate, especially with conflicts intensifying in the Caucasian oblasts. The promising areas of investment include large-scale projects in science-intensive engineering (aerospace, the automotive industry, equipment for the chemical industry, oil and gas production, and oil refining), and the manufacture of chemical products. There is the possibility of long-term international cooperation because of the interests and financial backing of third countries (Saudi Arabia, Turkey, Egypt, and Pakistan). Several potentially profitable projects include oil production (the development of small fields and the transfer of know-how to raise bed yields); the consumer industry for the worldwide export of furs, garments, carpets, knitwear using ethnic motifs; and the development of transportation and telecommunications systems.

In 1995, the republic had 125 operating joint ventures. The foreign investments in 1993–95 totaled $190.6 million. Private owners held 9.2% of the fixed assets of enterprises, joint stock companies (without foreign interest) owned 17.8%, the federal authorities controlled 16.5%, and the republican government held 51.7%. The republic had 30 insurance companies and 37 commercial banks, including Avers (Tel. 38 6494), Avtogradbank in Naberezhnye Chelny (Tel. 42 4280), Volzhsko-Kamsky (Tel. 57 8346), Devon-Credit in Almetievsk (Tel. 28 835), Tatinvestbank (Tel. 38 0339), Tatpromstroibank (Tel. 32 6110), Tateconombank (Tel. 35 3443), and Energobank (Tel. 38 9907).

The republic is reachable from Moscow by rail (797 km to Kazan, 14 hours from Kazan Terminal), air (two hours from Domodedovo Airport), and road (the highway from Moscow, via Vladimir, Nizhny Novgorod and Cheboksary, to Kazan, 14 to 16 hours).

The republic has 149 km of hard-surfaced roads per 1,000 sq km.

52.3 ASTRAKHAN OBLAST

1. Natural Resources. Area: 44,100 sq km. Farmland: 34,370 sq km. Woodland: 1,100 sq km. Population: 1,015,400 (Jan. 1, 1996), of which 67% is urban and 33% is rural. Population density: 23.0 per sq km.

The oblast lies in the arid zone of the Caspian lowland around the delta of the Volga River as it empties into the Caspian Sea. Within the oblast, the Volga and its branch, the Akhtuba, split into numerous watercourses linked with one another by channels.

The principal hydroengineering structure here is the dam north of Astrakhan, which sends sufficient water to the Volga floodplain and delta. The river delta and the Caspian Sea are major commercial fishing grounds for sturgeon and small fish.

The oblast's minerals include natural gas, oil, limestone, marl, building sand and clay, salt, and mineral dyes. The biggest and most famous source of precipitated salt is located at Lake Baskunchak, which supplies nearly a quarter of Russia's needs of high-quality salt. Natural gas is produced at Astrakhan from the condensed-gas field that has been operating since the late 1980s, yielding 3.4 billion cu m of gas annually. The gas is comprised of 27% hydrogen sulphide, 32.7 g/cu m ethane, 224.2 g/cu m stable condensate, 0.63% nitrogen, and 14.49% carbon dioxide.

The oblast has a temperate-continental climate, with a mean temperature of -7 to $-10°C$ in January and 24°C in July. The annual rainfall varies between 175 and 240 mm, and the growing season lasts from 210 to 216 days.

2. Specialization and Sectoral Structure of the Economy (see Exhibit 52.5). Administrative division: 11 districts, 5 cities, 12 urban-type communities, and 143 village group-councils.

Administration head: Tel. (85100) 28 519.

Principal cities: Astrakhan (512,200), Akhtubinsk (50,800), and Kharabali (18,700).

The manufacturing structure is dominated by the food industry (31.1%), the fuel industry (19.4%), and engineering (14.3%). The oblast's economy rests on the fishing industry (Refrigerated Fleet Authority, the naval base, and the fishing fleet operating from the base), fish-canning plants and related enterprises for ship repair, packaging, and net making. The fish-processing plants in Astrakhan and the townships of Oranzhereinoe, Volodarsky, and Volgokaspiisky produce sturgeon and smaller fish such as carp, bream, pike, and perch, Caspian roach, and herring. Because supplies of these valuable species are dwindling increasingly large quantities of sprats are being caught. (See Exhibit 52.6.)

Natural gas is processed at the gas technology complex in Astrakhan, which has a maximum capacity of 12 billion cu m a year. So far, however, only sulfur is recovered from the gas, and the valuable hydrocarbons needed by the chemical industry are lost.

Large enterprises in other manufacturing sectors located in Astrakhan include those producing computers, machine tools, furniture, lumber, cardboard, woolen yarn, hosiery, and garments. The oblast exports 4% of its manufactured output, 13% of which is fish products and foodstuffs, and 77% are products of the gas technology complex.

Crop farming includes vegetables, tomatoes, watermelons, and rice. In animal farming, lambs are raised for their meat and wool, along with beef and dairy cattle.

Exhibit 52.5. Sectoral Structure of the Economy in 1995 (% of total)

	Industry	Farming	Transport	Construction	Other
Employment	21.5	15.0	9.8	11.0	42.7
Fixed Assets	41.8	15.6	11.5	3.9	27.2
Capital Investment	26.7	10.0	13.4	0.4	49.5

Exhibit 52.6. Manufacture of Principal Industrial Products

	1995	1996
Natural gas, billion cu.m.	4.1	3.8
Metal cutting machine tools	434	195.3
Meat, thou. tons	7.3	3.6
Whole milk products, thou. tons	17.4	13.9
Fish catch, thou. tons	87.9	78.2

Because of inadequate marketing facilities and the vegetable canneries, farms have been compelled to cut production of vegetables and melons and start producing food for the local market.

3. Investment Opportunities. In 1995, the oblast had 60 operating joint ventures. The foreign investments in 1993–95 were $2.5 million. Private owners held 26.3% of the fixed assets of enterprises, joint-stock companies (without foreign interest) owned 11.9%, and the federal authorities controlled 37.5%. The oblast had 12 insurance companies and nine commercial banks, including Agroprombank (Tel. 22 2616), Agroincombank (Tel. 24 7041), Volgo-Kaspiisky (Tel. 22 9629), Kaspryba (Tel. 22 3621), and Saksin (Tel. 22 1440).

   Good investment prospects include the fishing industry (ports facilities including piers, and warehouses, refrigerated fishing vessels, modernization of fish-processing plants and the marketing infrastructure); the transportation infrastructure (the seaport in Olya Bay, facilities providing transit services for traffic between Europe and Iran; the oilfields on the Caspian shelf); vegetable-canning facilities (tomatoes, peppers, and eggplants); recreation industry (construction of leisure facilities, fee-based hunting and fishing facilities in the unique natural delta of the Volga); and development of the gas technology complex in Astrakhan.

   The oblast is reachable from Moscow by rail (1,534 km to Astrakhan, 30 hours from Paveletsky Terminal) and air (two hours from Domodedovo Airport).

   There are 53 km of hard-surfaced roads 1,000 sq km.

52.4 PENZA OBLAST

1. Natural Resources. Area: 43,200 sq km. Farmland: 30,700 sq km. Woodland: 9,700 sq km. Population: 1,523,300 (Jan. 1, 1996), of which 63% is urban and 37% is rural. Population density: 35.3 per sq km.

   The oblast lies 700 km southeast of Moscow, on the western slopes of the Volgan upland, heavily broken by river valleys and innumerable gullies.

   Its woodlands contain 119.4 million cu m of timber, including 47.5 million cu m of softwood. The forests consist predominantly of pines and broad-leaved trees, with oak groves being widespread as well. The oblast's estimated cutting area is used at 85% capacity, and the commercial logging potential is 2.8 million cu m.

   The oblast's mineral resources include molding sand, marl, and chalk. The biggest deposits in operation are molding sand at Chaadaevskoe, and marl and chalk at Surskoe.

   The oblast has a temperate-continental climate, with a mean temperature of −11 to −13°C in January and 19 to 21°C in July. The annual rainfall is between 550 and 680 mm, and the growing season lasts from 125 to 140 days.

2. Specialization and Sectoral Structure of the Economy (see Exhibit 52.7). Administrative division: 28 districts, 10 cities, 16 urban-type communities, and 375 village group-councils.

   Administration head: Tel. (8442) 63 3575. Fax 63 6326.

   Principal cities: Penza (552,300), Kuznetsk (100,000), Serdobsk (45,300), and Kamenka (42,600).

   The manufacturing structure is dominated by engineering (33.2%), the food industry (20.8%), and power engineering (15.3%). The enterprises in Penza produce 60% of the oblast's industrial output. They specialize in the manufacture of equipment for

Exhibit 52.7.   Sectoral Structure of the Economy in 1995 (% of total)

	Industry	Farming	Transport	Construction	Other
Employment	30.3	18.9	6.5	7.1	37.2
Fixed Assets	30.6	30.4	6.2	4.0	28.8
Capital Investment	18.4	7.8	12.3	1.0	60.5

the chemical and oil and gas industries (Akonkhol JSC and the Fittings Plant JSC, which produce pipeline valves and fittings, the Compressor JSC, the Electromechanical Equipment JSC, and the chemical machinery plant); instruments and electronic systems (Start industrial association, Elektropribor electrical-instruments industrial association, a computer industrial association, computer plant, precision-instruments plant, the Era plant, an electromechanical plant, radio plant, the Rekon plant, and a watch factory); diesel engines (Penzadieselmash industrial association producing 50% of the diesel engines and diesel generators in the Volga area). Many of these enterprises fill orders for the Russian defense establishment and are currently operating under capacity. (See Exhibit 52.8.)

The Penza plants obtain components from suppliers in Kuznetsk' which include plants manufacturing instruments and capacitors, instruments, equipment for polymer manufacture, and radio components; in Serdobsk, suppliers include a watch factory, the Rhomb pump plant, and an electric-light bulb plant.

Together with the neighboring Ulyanovsk Oblast, the Penza Oblast forms a specialized wool-processing region, in which the biggest enterprises are the Sura integrated cloth plant, the textile machinery plant in Kuznetsk (scutching machines), plants in Penza producing spinning machines (Penzamash), ribbon-making machines (Penzatekstilmash), and a few enterprises making wool garments.

The oblast exports 2% of its manufactured output, 42% of which are chemical products, 18% are machines and equipment, and 17% are instruments.

The oblast's farming basically is comprised of grain growing and cattle raising. Its land is extensively plowed, with plowland occupying 85% of all its farmland. The local climate is well suited for growing sugar beets, sunflowers, onions, and potatoes. The oblast has the potential to step up the production of foodstuffs for delivery to major cities in the Volga area and Central Russia, but so far it is confined to meeting local needs because of the inadequate marketing system and processing facilities.

3. Investment Opportunities. Because of its relative distance from major cities on the Volga and in Central Russia, and given its underdeveloped marketing network, the Penza Oblast has problems selling its food products, woolen goods, and consumer durables (bicycles, electrical household appliances, watches, and wooden articles).

Exhibit 52.8.   Manufacture of Principal Industrial Products

	1995	1996
Spinning machines	89	44.5
Woolen fabrics, million sq.m.	1.3	1
Footwear, million pairs	2.5	1.5
Meat, thou. tons	13.8	7.3
Whole milk products, thou. tons	21.5	23.2

Its farms and the majority of its manufacturing enterprises have adapted themselves to filling government orders, including defense-industry contracts. As a result, the engineering plants are operating at 60% of capacity, with downtime reaching 20% because of low demand, the highest figure for the entire Volga Region.

Because of the increasing output of Russia's chemical industry, the greatest prospects for investment in the oblast today are associated with the expansion of enterprises producing chemical-engineering items and diesel engines. In a longer term, projects that could turn out to be profitable include efforts modernize the wool processing industry for the Russian market, raise ecologically safe produce, and process dehydrated milk and dried potatoes. Major projects are expected to be initiated in science-intensive engineering (electronics, illumination engineering, and manufacturing process controls) for the domestic market.

In 1995, the oblast had eight operating joint ventures. The foreign investments in 1993–95 totaled $1.2 million. Private owners held 27.7% of the fixed assets of enterprises, joint stock companies (without foreign interest) owned another 15.6%, the federal authorities controlled 31.9%, and 11.9% was under regional control. The oblast had nine insurance companies and six commercial banks, including Agroprombank (Tel. 66 1131), Penza (Tel. 63 3642), Penzacreditinvestbank (Tel. 55 9639), and Tarkhani (Tel. 46 3784).

The oblast is reachable from Moscow by rail (709 km to Penza, 14 hours travel time from Kazan Terminal), air (two hours from Bykovo Airport), and road (the highway from Moscow, via Ryazan, to Penza, 15 hours).

There are 125 km of hard-surfaced roads per 1,000 sq km.

52.5 SAMARA OBLAST

1. Natural Resources. Area: 53,600 sq km. Farmland: 40,340 sq km. Woodland: 6,100 sq km. Population: 3,332,400 (Jan. 1, 1996), of which 80.6% is urban and 19.4% is rural. Population density: 62.0 per sq km, one of the country's highest.

    The oblast lies 1,100 km southeast of Moscow. The Samara-Togliatti conurbation is one of the key industrial, cultural, and administrative centers in Russia.

    The oblast is relatively well supplied with water—there is no shortage of water for drinking and industrial needs in the belt facing the Volga, but the available water resources are heavily polluted. With 408 million cu m of waste discharged into its system in 1993, Samara is one of the Russian cities dumping the largest amounts of effluent into the water supply. Pollution is the highest in Novokuibyshevsk, where elevated concentrations of oil products and other pollutants have been recorded in the soil and underground water within a one-km radius of the local oil refineries. The steppe on the western bank of the Volga is short of water. Surface-water sources being scarce, expenditures are needed to set up artesian-water supply systems.

    The woodlands contain 80.2 million cu m of timber, including 14.8 million cu m of softwood. Wooded tracts have water protection, water regulation, and recreational functions. The oblast needs more lumber than it can produce.

    The oblast's minerals include oil, wellhead gas, oil shale, gypsum, limestone, bituminous dolomite, and native sulfur. A total of 130 oilfields have been prospected, but only 67 larger ones have been developed. About 77% of the initial recoverable oil reserves have been depleted. The biggest deposits of other minerals are at Shiryaevo, where limestone is quarried, and Vodinsk and Syreisk-Kamenodolsk, where native sulfur is mined.

The oblast has a temperate-continental climate, with the mean temperature of $-13°C$ in January and $22°C$ in July. It receives 300 to 400 mm of annual rainfall, and its growing season is 180 days.

2. Specialization and Sectoral Structure of the Economy (see Exhibit 52.9). Administrative division: 27 districts, 11 cities, 23 urban-type communities, and 309 village group-councils.

Administration head: Tel. (8462) 32 2268. Fax 32 1340.

Principal cities: Samara (1,231,800), Togliatti (677,700), Syzran (175,900), and Novokuibyshevsk (114,400).

The manufacturing structure is dominated by engineering (43.4%), the fuel industry (16.1%), and the chemical industry (12.9%). (See Exhibit 52.10.)

In engineering, the greatest potential for growth resides in automotive industry, which accounts for 40% of the commercial engineering output; bearings and electrical engineering, with 6% each; machine tools, chemical engineering, and road-building machines, 2 to 3% each. The automobile plant in Togliatti (VAZ JSC) manufactures 70% of Russia's passenger cars. The oblast is a leading oil-refining center and an oil-distribution area, supplying oil to the country's other oblasts and to foreign markets. Its chemical enterprises produce nitrogen fertilizers, organic-synthesis products, synthetic fibers, resins, and phenols. Samara is Russia's aerospace-industry center; its larger enterprises are incorporated in or technologically linked with the industry, in particular the Metallist industrial association, an aircraft plant, the Samara Metallurgical JSC (rolled-aluminum products), the Start JSC, the Progress plant, and the Ekran plant. Novokuibyshevsk, a large oil-refining center, has an integrated petrochemical plant, a synthetic alcohol plant, an insulation materials plant, an oil refinery, and a medical products factory. Besides its auto plants, Togliatti has

Exhibit 52.9.   Sectoral Structure of the Economy in 1995 (% of total)

	Industry	Farming	Transport	Construction	Other
Employment	34.2	9.6	8.9	10.6	36.7
Fixed Assets	49.8	12.4	14.2	3.1	20.5
Capital Investment	40.5	4.3	9.0	0.9	45.3

Exhibit 52.10.   Manufacture of Principal Industrial Products

	1995	1996
Primary oil processing products, million tons	16.3	16.6
Oil, million tons	9.1	8.8
Passenger cars, thou.	607	667.7
Rolling bearings, million	n/a	n/a
Mineral fertilizers, thou. tons	582	599.6
Soft roofing and insulation materials, million sq.m.	23.6	17
Knitted goods, million	1.9	0.8
Televisions, thou.	46.2	6.9
Vegetable oil, thou. tons	14.5	25.2
Confectionery, thou. tons	46.6	42
Meat, thou. tons	45.6	23.3
Whole milk products, thou. tons	144	131

chemical industry enterprises (the Sintezkauchuk industrial association and Kuiby-shevazot JSC). Chapaevsk is a major industrial center producing paints and varnishes, synthetic resins, caustic soda, and various chemical agents. In Syzran, the biggest enterprises are the oil refinery, the Tyazhmash JSC (water turbines), and the plastics industrial association (resins and film). The oblast's other cities and towns specialize in food processing or serve as sites for oil- and gas-producing authorities, with a workforce of up to 3,000 each.

The Samara oblast is Russia's biggest exporter, selling 30% of its manufactured output to other countries; 10% of this amount is comprised of oil and oil products, 65% automobiles, and 14.4% mineral fertilizers and chemical products.

Farming is basically devoted to meeting the local needs in meat, milk, and vegetables. The existing large commercial grain-growing farms prosper in a climate that favors the cultivation of valuable wheat varieties.

3. Investment Opportunities. The regional administration is carrying out economic reforms patterned on those pursued in the Moscow, Nizhny Novgorod, and Leningrad Oblasts. The Samara Oblast is faced with redundant enterprises in the engineering sector; particularly those in the defense complex; as a result, there are great differences in income between employees in the public and defense sectors, and those in the automobile and oil-refining industries, and in some chemical industry enterprises.

The more promising areas of investment include the automobile industry, in particular projects accelerating changes in car models; oil refining, especially replacement of low-capacity, primary oil-refining facilities; construction of facilities to allow more comprehensive oil refining (thermal and catalytic cracking and coking) and to improve the quality of oil products (catalytic reforming, hydrocracking, hydrodesulfurization, alklylation); prospecting and development of small-scale oilfields and techniques to raise the yield of operating fields; development of chemical industry enterprises in Togliatti, Syzran, Chapaevsk, and Samara, in order to increase their export potential; telecommunications systems and expansion of the Samara Airport; the travel and tourism infrastructure (hotels and restaurants) and recreational facilities in the Samara Bend area and the Volga riverside steppe, with its relict pine groves; aerospace industry enterprises and the manufacture of aluminum products; and consumer goods for markets in southern Russia, the lower Volga area, and the Ural Region.

In 1995, the oblast had 122 operating joint ventures. The foreign investments in 1993–95 totaled $88.7 million. Private owners held 15.5% of the fixed assets of enterprise, joint stock companies (without foreign interest) owned 41.5%, and the federal authorities controlled 34.9%. The oblast had 40 insurance companies and 24 commercial banks, including Avtovazbank (Tel. 27 1686), Adamas-Samara-Bank (Tel. 66 8790), Volgo-Kamsky (Tel. 32 1201), the Volga Social Bank (Tel. 32 8025), Inzhenerbank (Tel. 34 5383), Ladabank (Tel. 23 4598), Prima-Bank (Tel. 32 5596), Rosestbank (Tel. 26 0550), Samaraavtotransbank (Tel. 34 4531), Samaraagrobank (Tel. 36 0371), the Samara Municipal Bank (Tel. 33 0345), the Samara Exchange Bank (Tel. 38 6749), the Samara Land Bank (Tel. 32 1763), Solidarnost (Tel. 22 5838), and Togliatti-Bank in Togliatti (Tel. 24 3630).

The oblast is reachable from Moscow by rail (1,098 km to Samara, 20 hours from Kazan Terminal), air (2.5 hours from Domodedovo Airport), and road (the highway from Moscow, via Ryazan and Penza, to Samara, about 22 hours).

The oblast has 113 km hard-surfaced roads per 1,000 sq km.

52.6 SARATOV OBLAST

1. Natural Resources. Area: 100,200 sq km. Farmland: 85,490 sq km. Woodland: 5,400 sq km. Population: 2,728,400 (Jan. 1, 1996), of which 74% is urban and 26% is rural. Population density: 27.2 per sq km.

   The Saratov Oblast is situated in the steppe zone. The only area adequately provided with water stretches along the Volga River. Elsewhere in the oblast, a considerable amount of money has been spent to build artesian-water supply systems.

   The oblast's mineral resources include natural gas, oil, building materials (chalk, marl, sand, and clay), phosphorites, oil shale, and hydrogen sulfide waters. The natural-gas fields are located at Elshan, Sokolovogorsk, and Uritsk; oil shale deposits are mined at the Gorny and Ozimki townships; and chalk is produced at Volsk, Khvalynsk, and the villages of Kazandy, Zolotov, and Melovoe. The gas fields have largely been exhausted and have lost their commercial value.

   The oblast has a continental climate, with the mean temperature of −12°C in January and 22°C in July. The annual rainfall varies from 250 to 450 mm, and the growing season lasts 130 to 150 days.

2. Specialization and Sectoral Structure of the Economy (see Exhibit 52.11). Administrative division: 38 districts, 17 cities, 35 urban-type communities, and 590 village group-councils.

   Administration head: Tel. (8452) 24 5086. Fax 24 2089.

   Principal cities: Saratov (904,400), Balakovo (204,600), Engels (183,700), Balashov (97,900), and Volsk (65,000).

   The manufacturing structure is dominated by engineering (22.2%), the fuel industry (6.8%), the food industry (12.4%), the chemical industry (17.2%), and power engineering (23.5%). (See Exhibit 52.12.)

   Saratov is a major center of sophisticated and precision engineering (represented by 16 large plants and research institutes), the site of an aircraft plant and an oil refinery, and several machine tool enterprises. Diesel generators, chemical fibers,

Exhibit 52.11. Sectoral Structure of the Economy in 1995 (% of total)

	Industry	Farming	Transport	Construction	Other
Employment	24.8	22.4	8.2	7.9	36.7
Fixed Assets	33.3	22.5	13.7	3.6	26.9
Capital investment	30.9	9.9	18.3	1.1	39.8

Exhibit 52.12. Manufacture of Principal Industrial Products

	1995	1996
Electric power, bn. kWh	23.8	28.3
Trolley buses	340	132.6
Tractor trailers	1,157	532.2
Mineral fertilizers, thou. tons	274	54.8
Roofing slate, million tiles	155	142.6
Vegetable oil, thou. tons	34.5	73.5
Meat, thou. tons	28.0	22.4
Whole milk, thou. tons	50.2	40.7

mineral fertilizers, and road-building machines are manufactured in Balakovo. Engels produces trolleybuses, special-purpose vehicles, textile fibers, and tractor equipment. The majority of other cities and towns in the oblast have enterprises processing farming produce. The multi-industrial pattern of the oblast is further represented by a major printing plant, the Saratovsteklo glass factory, a jewelry case factory in Saratov, silk and mica plants in Balashov, and a cement plant in Volsk. The oblast exports 9% of its manufactured output, 17% of which is oil and oil products, 42% chemical industry products, and 25% textile goods.

Its well-developed farming puts Saratov among the five agriculture-producing oblasts in Russia. The farming sector specializes chiefly in grain growing. The area's climate is well-suited for growing high-grade hard- and strong-wheat varieties with a high protein content. The oblast is second only to the Krasnodar Krai in the amount of its commercial grain harvest, but it is first in Russia in the yield of hard wheat. Cattle farming mainly provides meat and dairy products for local needs. Farmers are forced to send their produce out of the oblast or else reduce production to match local demand. The only exception is the flour-milling and groat-making industry, which supplies many other areas of Russia; but it needs more modern equipment and an expanded product line.

3. Investment Opportunities. In 1995, the oblast had 82 operating joint ventures. The foreign investments in 1993–95 totaled $28.3 million. Private owners held 28.3% of the fixed assets of enterprises, joint stock companies (without foreign interest) owned 21.1%, and the federal authorities controlled 40.9%. The oblast had 32 insurance companies and 27 commercial banks, including Hermes-Volag (Tel. 24 5905), Complex-bank (Tel. 26 7241), Narat-bank (Tel. 24 2141), Nizhnevolzhsky (Tel. 25 0693), Radograd (Tel. 41 0031), Stemabank (Tel. 12 1637), Fia-bank (Tel. 24 7272), and Econombank (Tel. 24 0613).

The Saratov Oblast is a stable area, although its social situation is aggravated by overlapping enterprises in precision engineering and the defense industry. The oblast provides a base for the implementation of the Russian-Germans program, which attempts to secure new German investment in the area, as well as more German settlers.

Investment prospects are favorable in several sectors, including the production of consumer goods, particularly high-tech household appliances, for the markets of the Volga region and the Northern Caucasus; the growing and processing of hard wheat; participation in projects under the Russian-Germans program; expansion of the aircraft plant in Saratov, the trolleybus plant in Engels, and chemical industry enterprises in Saratov (Nitron and Binom industrial associations) and Balashov (Balashov Fibers JSC and the chemical plant of the Igriz concern); modernization of the oil refinery in Saratov; and the development of small oil and gas fields similar to the project jointly operated with the Elf Aquitaine company.

The oblast is reachable from Moscow by rail (858 km to Saratov, 20 hours from Paveletsky Terminal), air (two hours from Domodedovo Airport), and road (the highway from Moscow, via Ryazan and Penza, to Saratov, 19 hours).

There are 89 km of hard-surfaced road per 1,000 sq km.

52.7 ULYANOVSK OBLAST

1. Natural Resources. Area: 37,300 sq km. Farmland: 22,200 sq km. Woodland: 10,300 sq km. Population: 1,479,600 (Jan. 1, 1996), of which 72.4% is urban and 27.6% is rural. Population density: 39.7% per sq km.

The oblast lies 900 km east of Moscow, on the shores of the Kuibyshev Reservoir. It is abundantly supplied with water, and no restrictions are placed on the location of water-consuming enterprises.

The woodlands contain 141.4 million cu m of timber, 67.5 million cu m of which is softwood. The forest resources are chiefly used to meet local needs, and the oblast's furniture plants use timber brought in from elsewhere. The commercial logging potential is about 3 million cu m.

The oblast's mineral resources include molding sand, glass and quartz sands, and cement raw materials. The biggest deposits in production are Lukyanovsk (molding sand), Tashlino (glass and quartz sand), and Kremenskoe (cement raw materials).

The oblast has a temperate-continental climate, with a mean temperature of −13°C in January and 19°C in July. The annual rainfall ranges from 300 to 500 mm, and the growing season lasts 175 days.

2. Specialization and Sectoral Structure of the Economy (see Exhibit 52.13). Administrative division: 21 districts, 6 cities, 32 urban-type communities, and 314 village group-councils.

Administration head: Tel. (8422) 31 2078.

Principal cities: Ulyanovsk (656,400), Dmitrovgrad (128,900), Inza (24,500), and Barysh (21,300).

The manufacturing structure is dominated by engineering (55.1%) and textiles and leather (6.1%). Manufacturing specializes in motor vehicles, aircraft, electrical-engineering products, machine tools, instruments, and woolen goods. The biggest enterprises are the auto plant producing UAZ cross-country cars and buses and the Aviastar JSC, which has launched production of the TU–204–200 airliner, which was awarded an international certificate. These enterprises are technologically linked with many other major enterprises in Ulyanovsk and Dmitrovgrad, in particular the Volga Engines JSC (producing internal-combustion engines), the Itel industrial association (transistors), the Autocontact industrial association, the Ulyanovsk Machine Plant industrial association (radio equipment), a radio lamp plant, the Autodel-Service JSC, and the auto unit plant (in Dmitrovgrad). (See Exhibit 52.14.)

Exhibit 52.13.   Sectoral Structure of the Economy in 1995 (% of total)

	Industry	Farming	Transport	Construction	Other
Employment	32.6	15.5	6.9	8.9	36.1
Fixed Assets	36.9	22.8	10.0	3.1	27.2
Capital Investment	31.6	7.1	7.2	0.8	53.3

Exhibit 52.14.   Manufacture of Principal Industrial Products

	1995	1996
Trucks, thou.	8.8	8.75
Buses, thou.	25.3	20.5
Hosiery, million pairs	16.3	9.3
Vegetable oil, thou. tons	4.6	5.8
Meat, thou. tons	42.0	25.6
Whole milk products, thou. tons	100	85

The wool-processing industry is focused in Barysh and Dmitrovgrad. Barysh has four large enterprises producing yarn and woolen fabrics, in addition to enterprises making woolen garments. The enterprises process raw wool supplied from the Kalmykian Republic and the Saratov and Volgograd Oblasts. Other towns in the oblast sprang up around food industry, lumber, furniture and building-materials enterprises using local primary materials, and also around small woolen industry and engineering enterprises. The oblast exports 3% of its manufactured output, of which 63% is passenger cars and trucks.

Farming in the area specializes in grain growing and cattle raising. Large areas are farmed for potatoes and industrial crops, while beef and dairy cattle are raised, mainly to supply local needs.

3. Investment Opportunities. Promising investment areas include large-scale projects in the automotive and aircraft industries for the purpose of exporting their products to industrial countries, Latin America, and the Middle East; expansion of enterprises in the wool-processing industry in Barysh and Dmitrovgrad, including garments and knitted goods; manufacture of carpets at the Kovrotex JSC in Dmitrovgrad; and modernization of the cement enterprises in Novoulyanovsk and Sengilei.

The Ulyanovsk Oblast has a stable social climate. The administration has retained some food rationing and is effectively regulating the marketing of farm produce inside the oblast, which helps maintain existing levels of meat and milk production in rural areas.

In 1995, the oblast had 30 operating joint ventures. The foreign investments in 1993–95 totaled $2.1 million. Private owners held 20.5% of the fixed assets of enterprises, joint stock companies (without foreign interest) owned 4.7%, and the federal authorities controlled 49.4%. The oblast had 11 insurance companies and 18 commercial banks, including Avtouazbank (Tel. 36 0017), Benets (Tel. 32 6284), the Bank for Foreign Trade (Vneshtorgbank, Tel. 31 8641), Zavolzhsky (Tel. 21 3313), and Novy (Tel. 32 0682).

The oblast is reachable from Moscow by rail (893 km to Ulyanovsk, 16 hours from Kazan Terminal), air (1.5 hours from Domodedovo Airport), and road (the highway from Moscow, via Vladimir, Nizhny Novgorod and Cheboksary, to Ulyanovsk, 16 to 18 hours).

There are 120 km of hard-surfaced roads per 1,000 sq km of the oblast's territory.

52.8 VOLGOGRAD OBLAST

1. Natural Resources. Area: 113,900 sq km. Farmland: 87,800 sq km. Woodland: 5,800 sq km. Population: 2,674,300 (Jan. 1, 1996), of which 74% is urban and 26% is rural. Population density: 23.5 per sq km.

The oblast lies 1,100 km southeast of Moscow. Its southern part lies in the arid zone, and its northern part does not get sufficient water, so farming involves considerable risks.

The oblast's mineral resources include natural gas, oil, limestone, marl, building sand and clay, salt, and mineral dyes. About 85% of the initial recoverable oil reserves has been depleted. Despite this, the production costs of a ton of oil are among the lowest in the country, which makes developing small and low-yield fields attractive.

The oblast has a rigid-continental climate with a mean temperature of -8 to $-12°C$ in January and $24°$ in July. The area gets 270 to 450 mm of rainfall annually, and its growing season varies between 150 and 175 days.

2. Specialization and Sectoral Structure of the Economy (see Exhibit 52.15). Administrative division: 33 districts, 19 cities, 27 urban-type communities, and 444 village group-councils.

Administration head: Tel. (84420) 33 6688. Fax 36 4757.

Principal cities: Volgograd (1,0002,000), Volzhsky (282,800), Kamyshin (126,800), and Mikhailovka (58,700).

The manufacturing structure is dominated by power generation (14.3%), the fuel industry (10.7%), the chemical industry (16.9%), engineering (15%), ferrous metallurgy (9.4%), and the food industry (12.2%). (See Exhibit 52.16.)

The Volgograd Oblast is among the top industrial areas of Russia. The Volgograd industrial area includes the Kaustik JSC (PVC resin and soda), the Khimprom industrial association (resins, refrigerants, caustic soda), an aluminum plant essentially using toll processing, a metal fabrication plant producing rolled sections and plates, a tractor plant (producing track-laying DT–175M and DT–75D machines), and an oil refinery. The Volzhsky area includes the Orgsintez industrial association (carbon sulfide, 2MBS thiazole, and insect repellents), the Khimvolokno industrial association (chemical fibers), facilities producing bearings and steel pipes, and a synthetic-isoprene rubber plant. Kamyshin is the home of one of the largest cotton mills in Russia, a tool plant, and a forging plant. The other populated localities mainly concentrate on producing foodstuffs. The oblast exports 14% of its manufactured output, 40% of which is oil and oil products and 32% ferrous and nonferrous metals.

Farming consists of grain, vegetable, and melon growing, with 70% of the cropland planted with cereals. Vegetables, melons, and mustard are cultivated chiefly in the Volga-Akhtuba floodplain south of Volgograd, which has unparalleled conditions for the growing of tomatoes, watermelons, honeydew melons, and industrial crops. In the absence of a viable marketing system, the specialized farms are curtailing their business, producing just enough to supply the local market.

3. Investment Opportunities. Investment prospects are plentiful. The Volgograd Oblast is a stable area, in which many enterprises (chemical, oil, metal, and textile) have

Exhibit 52.15.   Sectoral Structure of the Economy in 1995 (% of total)

	Industry	Farming	Transport	Construction	Other
Employment	25.9	18.8	7.4	11.1	36.8
Fixed Assets	37.4	21.3	12.5	6.9	21.9
Capital Investment (1995)	28.2	7.4	26.3	1.1	37.0

Exhibit 52.16.   Manufacture of Principal Industrial Products

	1995	1996
Steel pipes, thou. tons	252	161.3
Tractors	3,300	4,092
Cement, thou. tons	1,655	1,224.7
Ceramic tiles, thou. sq.m.	3,222	1,901
Vegetable oil, thou. tons	39.4	54.8
Meat, thou. tons	64.8	42.1
Whole milk products, thou. tons	69.6	63.3

operated in market conditions, doing business with foreign investors. Some local experts rank the oblast among the fastest-growing areas in the Volga belt, offering a real promise to foreign investors. It must be noted, however, that the sales crisis that has engulfed the vegetable and melon growers in the Volga-Akhtuba area and the below-capacity operation of the engineering industry are souring the oblast's social climate.

Based on past experience, the most attractive areas of investment are the chemical and metal industries. Any major projects here must, however, take into account future increases in the price of power and the limited power-generating potential in the lower Volga area and southern Russia generally. Good opportunities may lie in oil production for medium-scale projects. The local oil refinery badly needs to replace its primary oil-processing equipment and building units to improve the quality of its products.

Other attractive areas of investment include consumer goods production and vegetable canning (tomato and mustard processing).

In 1995, the oblast had 157 operating joint ventures. The foreign investments in 1993–95 amounted to $25.3 million. Private owners held 29.2% of the fixed assets of enterprises, joint stock companies (without foreign interest) owned 20%, and the federal authorities controlled 41.4%. Also, the oblast had 28 insurance companies and 26 commercial banks, including Agroprombank (Tel. 93 0645), Volgoprombank (Tel. 33 5876), Zarya (Tel. 37 7264), Kazachy (Tel. 44 0634), Cooptorgbank (Tel. 36 1862), Slavyanin (Tel. 34 1101), Sotsbank (Tel. 36 3703), and Traktorobank (Tel. 77 0231).

The oblast is reachable from Moscow by rail (1,073 km to Volgograd, 22 hours from Paveletsky Terminal), air (two hours from Domodedovo Airport), and road (the highway from Moscow, via Tambov and Borisoglebsk, to Volgograd, 20 hours).

There are 68 km hard-surfaced roads per 1,000 sq km in the oblast.

CHAPTER 53

NORTHERN CAUCASUS REGION

Aleko A. Adamescu, Yuri A. Kovalev, and Alexander G. Granberg

53.1 ADYGHEI REPUBLIC

1. Natural Resources. Area: 7,600 sq km. Farmland: 3,660 sq km. Woodland: 2,850 sq km. Population: 449,000 (Jan. 1, 1996), of which 53.8% is urban and 46.2% is rural. Population density: 59.1 per sq km.

   The republic is situated in the foothills of the Northern Caucasus on the banks of the Laba and Kuban rivers. It is adequately supplied with water.

   The republic's natural resources include oil, natural gas, and mineral springs (sodium chloride and hydrogen sulfide water).

   The republic has a temperate-continental climate, with a mean temperature of $-11°C$ in January and $17°C$ in July. It gets 550 mm of annual rainfall, and its growing season is 165 days.

2. Specialization and Sectoral Structure of the Economy (see Exhibit 53.1). Administrative division: 7 districts, 2 cities, 5 urban-type communities, and 50 village group-councils.

   President: Tel. (87722) 21 900.

   Principal cities: Maikop (168,500).

   The manufacturing structure is dominated by the food industry (46.4%), engineering (13.7%), and lumbering and woodworking (15.9%). The republic's manufacturing enterprises are located in Maikop, specializing in processing farm produce and supplying the needs of local farms and consumers. The biggest plants are the Lnocord JSC (binder twine and rope), the Maikoplesprommebel JSC, with a workforce of over 5,000 employed in furniture production, and the Tochmash JSC (washing machines and mechanized warehouse equipment). The city also has several small businesses manufacturing transformers, tools, metal-cutting machine tools, and tanning extracts, and repairing motor vehicles and tractors. Large food preparation facilities are sited in Maikop and Yablonovsky township (cannery). (See Exhibit 53.2.)

   The republic exports 1% of its manufactured output, 40% of which is food products and 55% furniture.

   Farming specializes in growing cereals and melons. The area has a developed horticulture and viticulture and is expanding its rice paddies. Among industrial crops, sunflowers, essential oil-bearing crops, and tobacco are grown for shipment outside the republic. Farmers also raise sheep, cattle, hogs, fowl, and Kabardinian horses. Beekeeping, too, is an advanced commercial enterprise.

Exhibit 53.1.   Sectoral Structure of the Economy in 1995 (% of total)

	Industry	Farming	Transport	Construction	Other
Employment	28.0	15.7	7.6	6.0	42.7
Fixed assets	28.5	25.8	4.8	6.8	34.1
Capital Investment	17.8	11.1	5.4	1.4	64.3

Exhibit 53.2.   Manufacture of Principal Industrial Products

	1995	1996
Vegetable oil, thou. tons	2.3	9.3
Meat, thou. tons	5.1	4
Whole milk products, thou. tons	3.1	2

3. Investment Opportunities. The republic is situated in an unstable zone of the Northern Caucasus, but in an area (within the Krasnodar Krai) where major ethnic conflicts are unlikely.

Promising investment areas include communications; small-scale projects to produce consumer goods (clothing, furniture, household appliances, and decorating materials for private homes and apartments); geological prospecting for oil and natural gas and development of small-sized fields; production of insulin; bottling of mineral waters and pectin for deliveries to other regions of Russia; production of foodstuffs from low-priced local raw materials, in particular grapes, essential oils, sugar beets, tea, and tobacco for sale in the resort areas of the Black Sea coast and the Caucasian spas.

In 1995, the republic had 15 operating joint ventures. The foreign investments in 1993–95 totaled $200,000. Private owners held 36.3% of the fixed assets of enterprises and organizations, joint stock companies (without foreign interest) owned 9%, the federal authorities controlled 15.2%, and the republican government had control over 29.7%. The leading banks in the area include Agromprombank (Tel. 39 682), the Commercial Investment Bank (Tel. 22 462), Kommersant (Tel. 23 217), Maikopbank (Tel. 25 630), the Maikop Municipal Bank (Tel. 31 070), Nartbank (Tel. 21 472), Novatsia (Tel. 30 078), and Yug-invest Bank in Yablonovsky township (Tel. 52 7394).

The republic is reachable from Moscow by rail (3,400 km to Maikop, 33 hours from Kazan Terminal) and air (2.5 hours from Domodedovo Airport).

There are 186 km of hard-surfaced roads per 1,000 sq km in the republic.

53.2 CHECHEN AND INGUSH REPUBLICS

1. Natural Resources. Area: 19,300 sq km. Farmland: 11,900 sq km. Woodland: 4,200 sq km. Population: 1,290,000 (Jan. 1, 1996), of which 42.9% is urban and 57.1% is rural. Population density: 66.8 per sq km.

Both republics are situated on the northern slopes of the Greater Caucasus Range. Most of their territory is mountainous, with occasional plains of considerable size.

The republics' mineral resources include oil, natural gas, building materials (limestone, marl, and gypsum), and mineral springs. The biggest oil and gas fields are located at Grozny, Malgobek, and Gudermes. Building materials are quarried at Chiriyurt, and mineral springs are operated at Sernovodsk and Agaluki.

The republics have a temperate-continental climate, with a mean temperature of $-4°C$ in January and 25°C in July. The annual rainfall in the area varies from 300 to 450 mm, and the growing season lasts 230 days.

2. Specialization and Sectoral Structure of the Economy (see Exhibit 53.3). Administrative division: 15 districts, 7 cities, 4 urban-type communities, and 204 village group-councils.

President of the Ingush Republic: Tel. (87134) 23 307.

Principal cities: Grozny (401,300), Gudermes (38,900), Argun (25,900), and Nazran (20,500).

The manufacturing structure is dominated by the food and fuel industries. The largest enterprises (before October 1994) in Grozny were the Groznefteorgsintez industrial association, the Grozneft association, the Molot industrial association (chemical engineering), the Terek industrial association (low-voltage equipment), a gas-processing plant, a commercial oil-products plant, the Sheripov Oil Refinery, the Lenin Oil Refinery, a chemical industry plant (acetone, antifreeze, and propylene), and the Anisimov Oil Refinery (gasoline and hydrocarbon gas). The electrical tool plant is the biggest manufacturing enterprise in Nazran. Before the armed conflict, the Chechen Republic was the leading supplier of engine fuels in the Northern Caucasus, and some of its facilities manufactured oil products that were in short supply in Russia. (See Exhibit 53.4.)

Farming specializes in fruit, grapes, and vegetables. Some corn, sunflowers, and sugar beets are cultivated as well. Sheep raising and fowl keeping are the key activities of animal farming.

3. Investment Opportunities. It is difficult to assess the investment climate in the republics because of the continuing conflict within the Chechen Republic and the disagreements between the groups in the Ingush Republic and Northern Ossetia. Large returns can be expected from investments in trading operations. There is a potential for profits from commercial projects to develop the offshore zone in the Ingush Republic and from federal programs to rebuild the social and industrial complex in the Chechen Republic, particularly the oil refineries. In 1995, the region had no operating joint ventures and no foreign investments.

The republic has 160 km of hard-surfaced roads per 1,000 sq km.

Exhibit 53.3.   Sectoral Structure of the Economy in 1995 (% of total)

	Industry	Farming	Transport	Construction	Other
Employment	19.6	20.5	9.5	10.5	39.9
Capital Investment	44.1	13.4	1.4	0.7	40.4

Exhibit 53.4.   Manufacture of Principal Industrial Products

	1995	1996
Oil, (Ingushetia), thou. tons	739	761.2
Meat (Ingushetia), thou. tons	43.0	n/a

53.3 DAGHESTAN REPUBLIC

1. Natural Resources. Area: 50,300 sq km. Farmland: 33,600 sq km. Woodland: 4,500 sq km. Other lands: 7,800 sq km. Population: 1,953,000 (Jan. 1, 1996), of which 42.5% is urban and 57.5% is rural. Population density: 38.8 per sq km.

   The republic is situated in the eastern part of the Northern Caucasus, on the Caucasus Mountain slopes, with an outlet to the Caspian Sea. It is short of both forestland and water, although major power projects can be launched in its mountainous area.

   The republic's minerals include oil, natural gas, sulfur, chalk, quartz sand, mineral dyes, and geothermal sources. Major oil and gas fields are located on the Caspian Sea coast, and quartz sand is quarried at Karabudakhkent.

   The republic has a temperate-continental climate, with a mean temperature of 2°C in January and 24°C in July, while in the mountainous areas the temperatures are −7°C and 22°C, respectively. The annual rainfall of 250 mm in the northeast rises to 800 in the mountains. The growing season varies from 160 days in the north to 230 days in the southern areas contiguous with Azerbaijan.

2. Specialization and Sectoral Structure of the Economy (see Exhibit 53.5). Administrative division: 41 districts, 10 cities, 17 urban-type communities, and 673 village group-councils.

   Chairman of the Council of Ministers: Tel. (87200) 72 234.

   Principal cities: Makhachkala (326,500), Derbent (80,300), Khasavyurt (71,600), Kaspiisk (61,000), and Buinaksk (57,200).

   The manufacturing structure is dominated by the food industry (40.8%) and engineering (18.7%). In addition to the farm produce-processing enterprises, a traditional industry of the Northern Caucasus, the republic has a cluster of enterprises producing oil and gas equipment, pumps, vehicle parts, and low-voltage electrical equipment, including the Gajiev Plant (pumps), a glass fiber plant, and an instrumentation plant (radio-measuring devices) in Makhachkala; the Sistema research and development association (plastics), and the Elektrosignal industrial association in Derbent; the Dagdiesel and precision-engineering plants in Kaspiisk; and the Dagelektroavtomatika plant (low-voltage devices). The republic earns hard currency by developing and exporting oil through the Dagoil industrial association and manufacturing carpets. (See Exhibit 53.6.)

   The republic exports 1% of its manufactured output, which is primarily oil and oil products.

   Farming specializes in viticulture, horticulture, and sheep grazing.

3. Investment Opportunities. The republic is situated in a zone of tense territorial and ethnic relations. There are intractable problems faced by areas bordering the Chechen Republic and Azerbaijan, in which the central and republican authorities have little influence regarding the economic and political situation. Shipments of material into and out of Daghestan go though the Chechen Republic, resulting in the

Exhibit 53.5. Sectoral Structure of the Economy in 1995 (% of total)

	Industry	Farming	Transport	Construction	Other
Employment	16.1	32.2	4.8	8.6	38.3
Fixed assets	34.6	27.3	5.5	9.1	23.5
Capital Investment	35.8	13.4	7.9	8.1	34.8

Exhibit 53.6. **Manufacture of Principal Industrial Products**

	1995	1996
Diesel engines and generators	226	117.5
Meat, thou. tons	1.1	0.5
Whole milk products, thou. tons	6.8	5.5

high risk of the merchandise being partially or totally lost. In spite of this, the political situation is relatively calm and under the full control of the local authorities in the central and coastal areas of the republic.

The main areas of investment are communications equipment and systems for the North Caucasian republics, the Volga regions, Azerbaijan, Turkmenistan, and Iran; participation in projects to develop the transportation infrastructure supporting shipping in the Caspian Sea (particularly the modernization of the Makhachkala commercial port); expansion of the airport in Makhachkala; production and sales of wines and brandies; small-scale projects to promote handicrafts, woolen articles with local motifs, carpets, and decorative metalwork. Investments may be needed in the manufacture of equipment for the oil and gas industry and the construction of an oil pipeline as part of the oil development program for the Caspian Shelf.

In 1995, the republic had six operating joint ventures. The foreign investments in 1993–95 totaled $200,000. Private owners held 7.3% of the fixed assets of enterprises and organizations, joint stock companies (without foreign interest) owned 0.7%, the federal authorities controlled 19.1%, and the republic government had control over 62.6%. The republic's leading banks include Adam-International (Tel. 36 7025), Anzhi-bank (Tel. 36 8000), Garant (Tel. 36 7025), Daghestan Mountains (Tel. 36 7025), Daghestan (Tel. 36 7025), Imbank (Tel. 36 7025), Elbin (Tel. 36 7025), and Eno (Tel. 36 7025).

The republic is reachable from Moscow by rail (2,166 km to Makhachkala, 48 hours from Paveletsky Terminal) and air (2.5 hours flight time, Vnukova Airport).

There are 127 km of hard-surfaced roads per 1,000 sq km.

53.4 KABARDINO-BALKARIAN REPUBLIC

1. Natural Resources. Area: 12,500 sq km. Farmland: 7,000 sq km. Woodland: 1,900 sq km. Other lands: 2,800 sq km. Population: 785,800 (Jan. 1, 1996), of which 59.8% is urban and 40.2% is rural. Population density: 62.9 per sq km. The republic has an exceptionally high population growth rate and a high proportion of the population working on private subsidized farms.

The republic is situated on the northern slopes of the Caucasus Range. It is adequately supplied with water, and many of its mountain rivers offer suitable sites for power projects. It has 25.1 million cu m of timber, but this does not cover the local timber needs.

The republic's mineral resources include tungsten, molybdenum, and building materials. The largest deposit is at Tyrnyauz (complex ores).

The area has a temperate-continental climate, with a mean temperature of −11°C in January and 17°C in July, and −4°C and 23°C, respectively, on the flatlands. It gets 500 mm of annual rainfall (2,000 mm in mountainous areas), and the growing season is 190 days.

2. Specialization and Sectoral Structure of the Economy (see Exhibit 53.7). Administrative division: 8 districts, 3 cities, 4 urban-type communities, and 101 village group-councils.

President: Tel. (86622) 22 064. Prime Minister: Tel 22 126.

Principal cities: Nalchik (237,300), Prokhladny (57,700), and Tyrnyauz (31,200).

The manufacturing structure is dominated by the food industry (19.3%), engineering (26.6%), and nonferrous metallurgy (9.6%). Aside from farm produce processing, which is widespread in the Northern Caucasus (meat, dairy products, starch, canned vegetables, alcohol, and yeast), the republic has a number of instrument-making enterprises, in particular the Telemekhanika industrial association (producing automation facilities), the Elkor industrial association, the Sevkazekektropribor plant, and a cathode-ray tube plant in Nalchik; and the semiconductor devices plant in Prokhladny. Tungsten-molybdenum ores are mined, dressed, and processed at the integrated mining and dressing plant in Tyrnyauz and the hydrometallurgical plant in Nalchik. Major enterprises in other industries include the Druzhba integrated plant in Nalchik (manufacturing hosiery) and the chemical industry plant in Nartkala (alcohol, carbon dioxide, and oxygen). (See Exhibit 53.8.)

The republic exports 1% of its manufactured output, of which 26% is food products and 40% metals.

3. Investment Opportunities. The republic is positioned in an unstable zone of the Northern Caucasus. No major ethnic conflicts, however, have been recorded in its territory. The main ethnic groups include Kabardinians (48%), Russians (32%), and Balkarians (9%). The local population mainly engages in farming, handicrafts, and consumer goods trading. Traditions typical of Asiatic communities are present, especially in the emphasis on family farming and loyalty to fraternities. The Russians tend to settle in cities and take jobs at major industrial enterprises.

The principal limitations to business are a lack of unoccupied land, shortage of power, and the population's preference for group (family or clan) farming over individual business, a factor that is offset in part by the local residents' inclination for independent decision making and disregard of the central government or the republic's administration.

Exhibit 53.7. Sectoral Structure of the Economy in 1995 (% of total)

	Industry	Farming	Transport	Construction	Other
Employment	21.7	17.1	6.4	8.7	46.1
Fixed assets	19.8	24.8	6.5	10.2	38.7
Capital Investment	20.7	14.0	7.3	0.7	57.3

Exhibit 53.8. Manufacture of Principal Industrial Products

	1995	1996
Hosiery, million pairs	11.8	8.5
Vegetable oil, thou. tons	3,648	1,459.2
Meat, thou. tons	0.7	0.41
Whole milk products, thou. tons	8.8	8.5

There are attractive investment prospects in the production and marketing of tungsten-molybdenum concentrate; manufacture of consumer goods, including non-foods, for the local market; production of foodstuffs (canned vegetables, dried and fresh fruits, and vegetables) for export and deliveries to Russia's central and northern areas; and handicrafts. Investment opportunities may also exist in the manufacture of semiconductor devices, low-voltage electrical equipment, and chemical goods. Projects in these areas should preferably involve Russian partners from other areas of the country.

In 1995, the republic had 25 operating joint ventures. The foreign investments in 1993–95 total $10.0 million. Private owners held 16.7% of the fixed assets of enterprises and organizations, joint stock companies (without foreign interest) owned 4.7%, the federal authorities controlled 34.7%, and the republican government had 24.5% under its control. By the Russian government's Resolution No. 300 of March 22, 1995, a free economic zone was created in the republic. The republic's leading banks are Aruanbank in Nartkala (Tel. 22 374), Boom-Bank (Tel. 23 428), Kavkaz-incombank (Tel. 22 175), Nalchik (Tel. 22 688), Namys (Tel. 52 175), Nart (Tel. 54 332), Oshkhamokho (Tel. 53 011), and Cherkessia (Tel. 26 901).

The republic is reachable from Moscow by rail (1,873 km to Nalchik, 35 hours from Kursk Terminal) and air (2.5 hours Vnukova Airport).

There are 187 km of hard-surfaced roads per 1,000 sq km in the republic.

53.5 KARACHAEVO-CIRCESSIAN REPUBLIC

1. Natural Resource. Area: 14,100 sq km. Farmland: 6,770 sq km. Woodland: 4,300 sq km. Population: 434,100 (Jan. 1, 1996), of which 47.7% is urban and 52.3% is rural. Population density: 30.8 per sq km.

   The republic is situated in the mountains and foothills of the northern slopes of the Caucasus Range.

   The republic's minerals include complex ores, copper ore, coal (Elbrus, Urup, and Khumarin), and building materials, including marl, dolomite, chalk, volcanic ash, and andesite. Also quarried on a commercial scale are cement raw materials, roofing slates, quartz sand, and marble at Teberda. The republic has underground hot-water and steam resources, considerable water power, and numerous nitric, sulfite, chlorine, and chlorohydrocarbonate-sodium mineral springs, which can be used for balneological purposes.

   The republic has a temperate-continental climate, with a mean temperature of $-3°C$ in January and $22°C$ in July. Its annual rainfall ranges from 400 mm to 800 mm in mountainous areas, and its growing season is 200 days.

2. Specialization and Sectoral Structure of the Economy (see Exhibit 53.9). Administrative division: 8 districts, 4 cities, 10 urban-type communities, and 68 village group-councils.

Exhibit 53.9. Sectoral Structure of the Economy in 1995 (% of total)

	Industry	Farming	Transport	Construction	Other
Employment	27.8	18.6	5.0	10.5	38.1
Fixed assets	27.2	29.8	10.0	3.2	29.9
Capital Investment	45.0	15.4	0.0	0.0	39.6

Administration head: Tel. (87822) 24 040.

Principal cities: Karachaevsk and Cherkessk.

The manufacturing structure is dominated by the food industry (15.9%), engineering (13.2%), the chemical industry (22.4%), and the building materials industry (21%). Apart from the typical North Caucasian practice of farm produce processing, the republic has a number of manufacturing enterprises employing a workforce of 2,000 to 3,000 each, in particular the Microcomponent plant (watches) in Karachaevsk; the Mestprom industrial association (natural silk articles), the chemical industry association (resins, plastics, and sodium sulfide), the Cascade plant, a low-voltage equipment plant (1,400), a commercial rubber-product plant, and the Polyot radio plant in Cherkessk; the resistor plant at Zelenchukskaya station; and the Urup mining and dressing plant in Mednogorsky township (copper ore). (See Exhibit 53.10.)

The republic exports 5% of its manufactured output, chiefly mineral raw materials.

Crop farming is essentially focused on wheat, vegetable, and sugar beet growing. Animal farming specializes in horse breeding, beef and dairy cattle raising, sheep grazing, and primary-wool and jute processing. Horticulture is well developed in the republic.

3. Investment Opportunities. The republic is located in a socially unstable zone of the Northern Caucasus, and its rural population is largely linked by cultural and religious ties to the Moslem republics of the Caucasus. No major social conflicts, however, have occurred, despite the decision made by its Karachai population to create an independent republic, which could lead to a breakup of the republic into several ethnic entities (Cossack villages, Abazin and Nogai entities, and the Karachais themselves).

The main areas for potential investment are the production of consumer goods at local enterprises to supply the North Caucasian and Transcaucasian markets, handicrafts, and small-sized enterprises to process low-cost locally grown farming produce.

In 1995, the republic had one operating joint venture. The foreign investments in 1993–95 totaled $2.2 million. Private owners held 32.4% of the fixed assets of enterprises and organizations, joint stock companies (without foreign interest) owned 13.9%, the federal authorities controlled 20.9%, and the republican government was in control of 24.5%. The republic's leading banks are Aliger (Tel. 57 261), Aris (Tel. 51 501), Jamat (Tel. 55 888), Invest Kavkazpromstroibank (Tel. 27 027), Kavkaz-Helios (Tel. 21 124), Lakma (Tel. 42 994), Razvitie (Tel. 32 063), and Teksbank (Tel. 22 486), all in Cherkessk; and Karachaevsk-Progress in Karachaevsk (Tel. 27 277).

The republic is reachable from Moscow by rail (1,750 km to Cherkessk, 34 hours from Kursk Terminal) and air (2.5 hours from Domodedovo airport).

There are 134 km of hard-surfaced roads per 1,000 sq km in the republic.

Exhibit 53.10.   Manufacture of Principal Industrial Products

	1995	1996
Meat, thou. tons	1.1	0.3
Whole milk products, thou. tons	3.6	2.7

53.6 NORTH OSSETIAN REPUBLIC

1. Natural Resources. Area: 8,000 sq km. Farmland: 4,300 sq km. Woodland: 2,000 sq km. Other lands: 1,440 sq km. Population: 650,400 (Jan. 1, 1996), of which 70.2% is urban and 29.8% is rural. Population density: 81.3 per sq km.

   The republic is situated in the foothills and on the northern slopes of the Caucasus Range.

   The republic's mineral resources include complex ores containing lead, tungsten, molybdenum, and zinc (Sadon deposit), building materials (chalk, limestone, gravel, and stone), mineral springs, and geothermal water. Conditions exist for the construction of power-dam chains on the republic's numerous mountain rivers. So far, however, the hydropower resources are used at 7% capacity.

   The republic has a temperate-continental climate, with a mean temperature of −4°C in January and 22°C in July. The annual rainfall in the area varies widely from 400 to 800 mm, and the growing season lasts 180 to 200 days.

2. Specialization and Sectoral Structure of the Economy (see Exhibit 53.11). Administrative division: 8 districts, 6 cities, 7 urban-type communities, and 93 village group-councils.

   Chairman of the Council of Ministers: Tel. (86722) 33 644.

   Principal cities: Vladikavkaz (319,200), Mozdok (38,100), and Beslan (32,100).

   In structural terms, manufacturing is dominated by nonferrous metallurgy (19.2%), engineering (15.2%), and the food industry (22.1%). The largest enterprises mine and process local raw materials, and manufacture illumination equipment and electronic-system parts and components. They are the Binom plant (producing resistors), the Kristall plant (special-purpose processing equipment), the Pobedit plant (tungsten-based alloys), the Topaz plant (cathode-ray tube glass), the electrozinc plant (lead), the Yantar plant (lamps and VHF devices), and the electric-lightbulb plant in Vladikavkaz; the Sadon lead and zinc plant in Mizur township; and the resistor-producing plant in Alagir. (See Exhibit 53.12.)

   The republic exports 12% of its manufactured output, with metals accounting for 88% of this.

   In farming, grain and animal production is the basic activity. The crops cultivated are wheat, corn, and barley; while vegetable growing, horticulture, and viticulture are

Exhibit 53.11. Sectoral Structure of the Economy in 1995 (% of total)

	Industry	Farming	Transport	Construction	Other
Employment	27.0	12.0	5.7	10.5	44.8
Fixed assets	27.3	16.1	3.9	9.5	43.2
Capital Investment	22.6	18.2	5.6	1.0	52.6

Exhibit 53.12. Manufacture of Principal Industrial Products

	1995	1996
Vegetable oil, thou. tons	303	172.7
Meat, thou. tons	1.1	0.4
Whole milk products, thou. tons	19.5	16

widespread as well. Beef cattle, dairy cattle, and sheep are the principal animals raised.

An extensive and well-known system of therapeutic spas lies within the republic. The most popular resorts among vacationers are Kardamon at Vladikavkaz and Tamisk at Alagir.

3. **Investment Opportunities.** The republic has a common border with the Chechen and Ingush republics, which have extremely unstable social and political environments. The territory surrounding the metal fabrication facilities and in the Mizur township is unsuitable for any new economic activity because of the pollution. Restrictions have been placed on power usage because of the high concentration of power-intensive enterprises. In many other respects, however, North Ossetia offers the most favorable investment climate of all the North Caucasian republics. The majority of the republic's residents—53% Ossetians and 30% Russians—are Christians. Cooperation between the local administration and the federal authorities, is extremely close, one of the main reasons being the conflicts in the surrounding republics, the majority of whose populations are Moslems. The main highway that links Russia to Transcaucasia cuts across North Ossetia.

The republic's attractive investment areas include the mining, production, and marketing of nonferrous metals; production of goods and services for consumer markets in the Northern Caucasus and Transcaucasia; motor-transportation services; participation in programs to modernize the road network and construction of the second stage of the road across the Main Caucasus Range under the Rok Pass; participation in the program to build a chain of Zaramag power dams; and modernization of airports and telecommunications systems in the republic.

In 1995, North Ossetia had eight joint ventures in operation. The foreign investments in 1993–95 totaled $300,000. Private owners held 23.5% of the fixed assets of enterprises and organizations, joint stock companies (without foreign interest) had 5.8%, the federal authorities owned 26%, and the republican government controlled 40%. The republic's leading banks are Adamon-bank (Tel. 79 689), Art-bank (Tel. 57 348), Creditprombank (Tel. 32 604), Osbank (Tel. 43 570), Ossetia (Tel. 64 073), the North Ossetian Bank (Tel. 32 463), and Farn (Tel. 54 416).

The republic is reachable from Moscow by rail (1,923 km to Vladikavkaz, 35 hours from Kursk Terminal) and air (two hours from Vnukovo Airport).

There are 289 km of hard-surfaced roads per 1,000 sq km in the republic territory.

53.7 KRASNODAR KRAI (TERRITORY)

1. **Natural Resources.** Area: 76,000 sq km. Farmland: 47,300 sq km. Woodland: 15,500 sq km. Population: 4,939,500 (Jan. 1, 1996), of which 54.1% is urban and 45.9% is rural. Population density: 65.0 per sq km.

The krai lies 1,500 km south of Moscow. It has inadequate water supplies and has a shortage of timber. The existing woodlands play an essential water protective and recreational role.

The krai's mineral resources include oil, natural gas, building materials (gypsum, chalk, and domomite), salt, and mineral springs.

The territory has a temperate-continental climate, with a mean temperature of $-5°C$ in January and $22°C$ in July. It gets 400 to 600 mm of annual rainfall and has a growing season of 220 to 260 days. The climate on the Black Sea coast is favorable for the cultivation of tea, citruses, and other crops that thrive in the heat.

2. Specialization and Sectoral Structure of the Economy (see Exhibit 53.13). Administrative division: 38 districts, 26 cities, 24 urban-type communities, and 384 village group-councils.

Administration head: Tel. (8612) 52 5716.

Principal cities: Krasnodar (741,700), Sochi (388,300), Novorossisk (231,200), Armavir (177,900), and Maikop (168,500).

The manufacturing structure is dominated by the food industry (39.2%), the fuel industry (8.9%), and engineering (10.2%). The economic foundation of the area's towns is formed by farm produce-processing facilities. In addition, the area has medium-capacity enterprises (with a workforce of 1,000 to 2,000 each), which cater to the needs of the farming sector and the local population. The enterprises include a furniture plant, the Kavkazmebel JSC, the Yugmera JSC (instruments and automation devices), the Yugtex JSC (cotton fabrics), the Kuban Furniture JSC, a china and glazed-pottery plant, and the Alexandria JSC (clothing) in Krasnodar; the Tochmash precision-instruments industrial association, the Furniture JSC, the commercial rubber-goods plant, the Electromechanical Plant JSC (low-voltage electric motors), and a tobacco factory in Armavir; the mineral fertilizers industrial association in Belorechensk and the chemical industry plant (furfural and yeast) in Kropotkin; and the road-construction equipment plant in Tikhoretsk. The central offices of oilfield development organizations are headquartered in Krasnodar (Krasnodarneftegaz industrial association and Termneft research and development association), Apsheronsk (Khadyzhenskneft oil and gas production authority), and in Tuapse (oil refinery). (See Exhibit 53.14.)

The territory's Black Sea coast is Russia's sole seaside resort area, where 10 million people, including 200,000 foreign tourists, take their vacations every year. The hotel industry and private facilities in Greater Sochi can handle five million vacationers, with nearly one million sunseekers traveling to the coast of Anapa. Between 1992 and 1995, a number of hotel complexes on the coast were modernized to appeal to high-income tourists. Most manufacturing enterprises in this area are located

Exhibit 53.13. Sectoral Structure of the Economy in 1995 (% of total)

	Industry	Farming	Transport	Construction	Other
Employment	18.0	23.0	8.1	11.0	39.9
Fixed assets	20.5	30.7	18.7	3.3	26.8
Capital Investment	16.0	9.3	14.3	3.4	57.0

Exhibit 53.14. Manufacture of Principal Industrial Products

	1995	1996
Wood chipboard, thou. cu.m.	45.9	27.5
Cement, million tons	2.9	1.6
Soft roofing materials, million sq.m.	32.0	19.2
Cotton fabrics, million sq.m.	40.0	16.8
Vegetable oil, thou. tons	240	295.2
Granulated sugar, thou. tons	1,043	1,147.3
Meat, thou. tons	85.4	70.9
Whole milk products, thou. tons	199	217

in and near Novorossisk; they engage in fish processing, ship repair, and cement production. The biggest enterprises here are the Novorossiskrybprom industrial association, the Novorossisk cement plant, the Upper Abakan cement plant, and an engine plant (Krasny Dvigatel).

The territory exports 3.5% of its manufactured output, of which 13% is food products, and oil and oil products 16.8%.

The area's grain-farming capacity and output are among the largest in Russia, supplying Russia with the lowest-cost grain in the country. In addition, the territory is a major producer of sugar beets, sunflowers, fruit and berries, tea, grapes, and rice.

3. Investment Opportunities. The territory has a common border with several engaged in ethnic conflicts. Russians constitute 85% of its population, which is a key stabilizing factor. The main limitations on investments in the territory are shortages of power and water in the steppe area, the high price of land, and insufficient space for new construction in the coastal zone. These problems are, however, offset by the availability of low-priced farm produce, exporting facilities in the seaports (a major advantage most other areas lack), and a sizable pool of skilled, low-cost labor.

The principal investment areas are trading operations; processing of low-cost farm produce for the Russian market; concentrated juices, grapes, vegetable oil, and some varieties of wild-growing plants and fruits for export to world markets; production of consumer goods (clothing, household equipment, hiking and leisure gear, high-tech household appliances, and furniture) for the undersupplied Caucasian market; car dealerships, automotive service stations and gas stations; manufacture of polyethylene packaging for liquid and granular products; development of the hotel infrastructure on the Black Sea coast; construction of sports and hotel complexes for holding major sporting events, including world-class events and winter and summer Olympic Games; construction of highways from Sochi to Sheldok, and from Slavyansk-on-Kuban to Aguevo; port facilities and new oil-exporting terminals; and the program to build the Trans caucasus oil pipeline.

In 1995, the region had 303 operating joint ventures. The foreign investments in 1993–95 amounted to $75.8 million dollars. Private owners held 36.7% of the fixed assets of enterprises and organizations, joint stock companies (without foreign interest) owned 20.7%, the federal authorities controlled 28.8%, and foreigners held 1%. The territory's leading banks are Agrorybprombank in Novorossisk (Tel. 57 930), the Azov-Black Sea Bank (Tel. 52 8895), Vitis (Tel. 57 1276), Ekaterinodar (54 5657), Krasnodarbank (Tel. 52 2234), Kubanbank (Tel. 57 0981), Kubancoopbank (Tel. 57 0352), Kubinbank (Tel. 52 3345), Kurort (Tel. 55 5972), Novbusinessbank in Novorossisk (Tel. 50 509), Omega (Tel. 55 2076), Slavyansk in Slavyansk-on-Kuban (Tel. 23 945), Tserta (Tel. 33 1634), Yugagroinvest (Tel. 55 7919), Yugbank (Tel. 52 3920), the South Russian Bank (Tel. 52 8913), the South Black Sea Bank in Tuapse (Tel. 23 172), and Yurak (Tel. 52 3345).

The territory is reachable from Moscow by rail (1,539 km to Krasnodar, 31 hours from Kursk Terminal) and air (two hours from Vnukova Airport).

There are 131 km of hard-surfaced roads per 1,000 sq km.

53.8 STAVROPOL KRAI (TERRITORY)

1. Natural resources. Area: 66,500 sq km. Farmland: 57,900 sq km. Woodland: 1,100 sq km. Population: 2,615,100 (Jan. 1, 1996), of which 53.7% is urban and 46.3% is rural. Population density: 39.3 per sq km.

The territory is situated in the central part of the region called Cis caucasia. The area is poorly provided with water, so hydroengineering facilities are needed for developing enterprises using large amounts of water and for the farming sector.

Mineral resources include natural gas, oil, complex ores, coal, and building materials. The best-known gas fields are located at Mirnensk, Sengilevsk, and Northern Stavropol. Oil is produced at Praskoveisk, copper at Urup, and complex metals at Elbrus; and coal is mined at Khumarin. The majority of these deposits have been partially depleted or have only limited reserves. They are, however, conveniently located in a well-developed area, so the costs of transportation, labor, and heating are low.

The territory has a temperate-continental climate, with a mean temperature of −4°C in January and 22 to 25°C in July. The area receives 300 to 500 mm of annual rainfall (1,000 mm in the mountains) and has a growing season of 185 days.

2. Specialization and Sectoral Structure of the Economy (see Exhibit 53.15). Administrative division: 26 districts, 18 cities, 7 urban-type communities, and 283 village group-councils.

Administration head: Tel. (86522) 52 252. Fax 54 313.

Principal cities: Stavropol (324,600), Pyatigorsk (185,500), Nevinomyssk (122,100), Kislovodsk (120,100), and Cherkessk (115,200).

The manufacturing structure is dominated by the food industry (20.2%), the chemical industry (15.9%), engineering (9.3%), and power generation (33.8%). The largest enterprises are the Izumrud Industrial Association (producing radio equipment), the Liumino for research and development association (insecticides and bleaching agents), the Avtopritsep-Kamaz JSC (truck trailers), the Neptune plant, the Signal plant (computers), and the tractor piston-ring plant in Stavropol; the Arzil JSC (pipe valves) in Georgievsk; the Atlant plant (electrical instruments) in Izobilnoe; the Sevkavkazminvody industrial association (mineral water) in Kislovodsk; the Almaz industrial association (ammophom and mineral fertilizers) and the Mikrom plant in Lermontov; the Nevinomyssk Nitrogen industrial association (phosphate and nitrogen fertilizers, and ammonia) and the wool-processing plant in Nevinomyssk; the Stavropol Polymer JSC in Budenovsk; the Stavropol Gas industrial association in Neftekumsk; and the Impulse plant (isotope devices) and the INIKO JSC (fowl-raising equipment) in Pyatigorsk. (See Exhibit 53.16.)

The territory exports 9.6% of its manufactured output, of which chemical comprise 77%.

The Farm sector specializes in grain and sunflower growing and livestock raising, particularly fine-fleeced sheep. Horticultural and viticultural products, along with fowl, are supplied to markets outside the territory. Because of the shortage of water, major hydroengineering projects were launched in the northeastern part of

Exhibit 53.15. Sectoral Structure of the Economy in 1995 (% of total)

	Industry	Farming	Transport	Construction	Other
Employment	19.3	24.0	6.4	11.6	38.5
Fixed assets	25.2	29.0	12.2	3.5	30.1
Capital Investment	16.7	12.1	12.4	1.5	57.3

Exhibit 53.16.   Manufacture of Principal Industrial Products

	1995	1996
Woodworking machine tools	1,309	641.4
Mineral fertilizers, thou. tons	366	446.5
Electrical mixers, thou.	22.1	n/a
Vegetable oil, thou. tons	58.7	87.5
Meat, thou. tons	26.4	22.2
Whole milk products, thou. tons	73.3	67.4

the territory; and work is underway to develop new water resources north of the Kuma River, at Malkino, and on the Kuma banks, to supply water to the Caucasian Spas (Mineralnye Vody) and the arid northern areas.

The favorable physical and climatic conditions and the abundance of curative mineral springs have stimulated the establishment of a nationally prominent health-resort area in the area of the Caucasian Spas. Unlike the Black Sea coast, the area's spas have therapeutic functions. Operated at full capacity, they can accommodate between two and three million vacationers.

3. Investment Opportunities. The Stavropol Krai has a common border with the Chechen and Ingush Republics, the extremely volatile area of the Northern Caucasus. Owing to the preponderance of the Russian population (78%), short-lived and local conflicts are the worst situations that are likely to occur.

Current limitations on business opportunities include the shortage of power and water, restrictions on economic activities in the resort area and on fertile farmlands, and the inadequate transportation facilities in the krai's northeast.

Prospective investment areas include trading operations; processing of low-cost farm produce for the Russian market; manufacture of consumer goods (clothing, household equipment, hiking and leisure gear, and high-tech household appliances) for the undersupplied Caucasian region; car dealerships and service stations providing sales outlets for cars of major manufacturers, and gas stations; manufacture of polyethylene packaging for liquid and granular products; bottling and marketing of mineral water for the Russian and world markets; development of the Caucasian spas and tourist and leisure centers at Teberda, Dombai, and Arkhyz; the construction of roads, including the highway from Neftekumsk to Kizner; and modernization of the chemical industry enterprises (Liuminofor research and development association, the Stavropol Polymer JSC, the biochemical plant in Georgievsk, the Almaz industrial association, and the Nevinomyssk Nitrogen JSC).

In 1995, the region had 122 operating joint ventures. The foreign investments in 1993–95 totaled $27.6 million. Private owners held 31.1% of the fixed assets of enterprises and organizations, joint stock companies (without foreign interest) owned 16.6%, and the federal authorities controlled 35.3%. The leading banks include Agroprombank (Tel. 96 471), Apanasenkovsky (Tel. 51 310), Neftestroicombank (Tel. 29 253), Promcombank (Tel. 20 459), Pyatigorsk in Pyatigorsk (Tel. 51 306), Stavbank (Tel. 44 441), Stavinterbank (Tel. 29 977), and Stavropolye (Tel. 27 730).

The krai is reachable from Moscow by rail (1,621 km to Stavropol, 37 hours, departures from Kursk or Paveletsky Terminal) and air (two hours from Vnukovo Airport).

The krai has 107 km of hard-surfaced roads per 1,000 sq km.

53.9 ROSTOV OBLAST

1. Natural Resources. Area: 100,800 sq km. Farmland: 85,700 sq km. Woodland: 2,700 sq km. Population: 4,401,300 (Jan. 1, 1996), of which 68.0% is urban and 32.0% is rural. Population density: 43.7 per sq km.

   The oblast lies 1,210 km south of Moscow. It is insufficiently provided with water. The best-supplied areas are on the banks of the Don River.

   The forests have water protection and wind-breaking functions.

   The region's mineral resources include coal (the eastern portion of the Donetsk coalfields), quartzite, limestone, and sand. The best-known coalfields are operated at Shakhtinsk, Novoshakhtinsk, and Gukov; quartzite is quarried at Tarasovka and Meshkovo; limestone at Boguraevsk; and sand is developed at Millerovo and Karlova-Gursk. The oblast also has marl deposits containing 37 million tons of prospected reserves (a total of 300 million tons), on the basis of which a cement plant can be built. There are also indications of the presence of nickel, zirconium, and iron ore; deposits of mercury and small gas fields have also been discovered. All these deposits are not yet developed because of economic considerations.

   The region has a temperate-continental climate, with a mean temperate of −5°C in January and 23°C in July. Its southeastern area gets 400 mm of annual rainfall, and 650 mm in the northwest. The growing season lasts from 165 to 180 days.

2. Specialization and Sectoral Structure of the Economy (see Exhibit 53.17). Administrative division: 43 districts, 23 cities, 25 urban-type communities, and 441 village group-councils.

   Administration head: Tel. (8632) 66 7810. Fax: 65 6773.

   Principal cities: Rostov-on-Don (1,024,800), Taganrog (292,700), Shakhty (258,600), and Novocherkassk (201,400).

   The manufacturing structure is dominated by engineering (26.3%) and the food industry (16.5%). The region is the principal manufacturing area of the Northern Caucasus and accounts for 80 to 90% of all transit between the Caucasus, Russia, and Ukraine. Its leading enterprises, each with a workforce in excess of 3,000, are the helicopter industrial association, the Rostelmash industrial association (the key grain-harvester manufacturer in Russia), The Red Aksai industrial association (tractor attachments), the Elektroapparat industrial association, the Rostovmebel JSC, Bearing Plant 10, the Kvant plant, the Pribor plant, and the Rubin plant in Rostov; the Atommash industrial association and a chemical industry plant in Volgodonsk; coal enterprises in Gukov and Donetsk; the silo manufacturing plant in Donetsk; the Khimvolokno industrial association and the engineering plant in Kamensk-Shakhtinsky; the Shakhtugol industrial association and the metal fabrication plant in Krasny Sulin; the electric-locomotive plant, the synthetic-products plant (formalin and methanol), and the electrode plant in Novocherkassk; the Harvester Plant research and development association (field machines and rock crushers), the Krasny

Exhibit 53.17. Sectoral Structure of the Economy in 1995 (% of total)

	Industry	Farming	Transport	Construction	Other
Employment	29.5	17.6	7.6	8.9	36.4
Fixed assets	36.4	22.8	10.2	8.5	22.1
Capital Investment	32.4	8.5	11.5	1.3	46.3

Kotelshchik industrial association (steam boilers), the Bariev research and development association (hydroplanes), and the metal fabrication plant in Taganrog; and the Rostovugol industrial association and the Dontextile JSC in Shakhty. Many of the region's engineering enterprises operate as monopolies in their specific industry of fulfill orders from the Russian defense industry. (See Exhibit 53.18.)

The region exports 4.6% of its output, consisting chiefly of machines and equipment.

The Farming sector specializes in growing cereals, oil-bearing crops (sunflowers and mustard), essential oil crops, vegetables and other horicultural products. Other agricultural activities include beef and dairy cattle raising and hog keeping. The region is capable of producing 9 to 10 million tons of grain, 800,000 tons of sunflower seeds, and 100,000 to 200,000 tons of vegetables.

3. Investment Opportunities. The region is the most stable area in the entire Northern Caucasus. The social and economic problems in the area are caused not so much by the ethnic conflicts of nearby areas, as by the low level of employment and income due to the large share of the population engaged in the farming sector, and to the subsidized coal mines, defense industry enterprises, and farm machinery plants, which have lost 70 to 90% of their orders and have been incapable of producing competitive machines.

Any business plans must take into account the fact that the Rostov region is the center of the Cossack movement in Russia. The characteristics of this movement include militaristic values and personal traits, a tendency toward group management of business enterprises, including the rejection of private land ownership, and specific standards in clothing and household items.

The area's principal limitations include the shortage of water in populated areas far from the Don River, insufficient power supplies, widespread landslides, and soil that is unable to withstand heavy loads.

The promising areas of investment are hide and fur processing, production of consumer goods for markets in the Caucasus and the Volga area; manufacture of minitractors; production of road-building machines; development of port facilities and expansion of the tanker fleet; modernization of the international airport in Rostov; communications systems; construction of warehouse complexes; participation in the program to build new ports in Rostov's suburbs and on the Azov Sea coast; and the manufacture of polyethylene packaging. The federal authorities and the local administration will extend their support to projects related to the processing

Exhibit 53.18. Manufacture of Principal Industrial Products

	1995	1996
Coal, million tons	19.4	16.9
Steel pipes, thou. tons	567	544.3
Forging machines	520	132
Mainline electric locomotives	15	5
Grain harvesters	4,761	1,524
Ceramic tiles, thou. sq.m.	1,359	1,468
Vegetable oil, thou. tons	96.6	112
Meat, thou. tons	50.7	37.5
Whole milk products, thou. tons	n/a	n/a

and marketing of farm produce, production under license and leasing of uncommitted equipment at farm machinery plants and defense industry enterprises, and providing jobs to coal miners who are employed because of the closing or suspension of coal mines.

In 1995, the region had 206 operating joint ventures. The foreign investments in 1993–95 totaled $2.7 million. Private owners held 24.3% of the fixed assets of enterprises and organizations, joint stock companies (without foreign interest) owned 38.4%, and the federal authorities controlled 26.7%. The leading banks include Hermes-Don (Tel. 66 8292), Doninvestbank (Tel. 39 1892), Doncombank (Tel. 66 6223), Donkhlebbank (Tel. 66 3376), the Farmers' Bank (Tel. 34 4024), Metracombank (Tel. 65 6775), Progress–2000 (Tel. 66 3069), Promstroibank (Tel. 66 6935), Rostovsotsbank (Tel. 62 5670), Sekavbank (Tel. 34 9493), Triel (Tel. 66 3558), Tsovinar (Tel. 34 4789), Empils (Tel. 64 4510), Enabank (Tel. 64 3581), and Yugmebelbank (Tel. 53 9515).

The oblast is reachable from Moscow by rail (1,226 km to Rostov-on-Don, 23 hours from Kursk Terminal), air (1.5 hours from Vnukova Airport), and road (the highway from Moscow, via Voronezh, to Rostov-on-Don, 22–24 hours).

There are 100 km of hard-surfaced roads per 1,000 sq km of the krai.

CHAPTER 54

URAL REGION

Aleko A. Adamescu, Yuri A. Kovalev, and Alexander G. Granberg

54.1 BASHKORTOSTAN REPUBLIC

1. Natural Resources. Area: 143,600 sq km. Farmland: 73,790 sq km. Woodland: 57,700 sq km. Other lands: 3,700 sq km. Population: 4,055,300 (Jan. 1, 1996), of which 64.6% is urban, and 35.5% is rural. Population density: 28.2 per 1 sq km.

    The republic lies 1,500 km east of Moscow on the western slopes of the Ural Range and in the flatlands of the western Ural Region. Water is in adequate supply in the northern and eastern areas, but the water sources are heavily polluted with oil products, phenols, and heavy metals—in some instances, many hundredfold the maximum permissible concentrations. The water sources in the southern and southwestern areas are satisfactory, but in the dry summer months water intake may be limited, so any major projects require considerable expenses to build hydroengineering and artesian systems.

    A total of 51,700 sq km of the woodlands is controlled by the federal authorities. The forests contain 728.5 million cu m timber, including 174.1 million cu m of softwood. The republic's estimated cutting area is used at 40% capacity, and the commercial logging potential is 10 million cu m.

    The republic's natural resources include oil, natural gas (the Volga-Ural oil and gas province), iron and copper-pyrite ores, sulfur, gold, silver, cobalt, zinc, coal, and building material. Copper is chiefly mined at the Sibai and Uchaly pyrite deposits, and coal is developed at the Tyulgan mines. About 75% of the oil and gas fields has been depleted, and the undeveloped fields lie at great depths and contain insignificant reserves (about 10 million tons).

    The republic has a continental climate, with a mean temperature of $-16°C$ in January and $18°C$ in July. The annual rainfall varies from 300 to 550 mm and the growing season lasts from 120 to 135 days.

2. Specialization and Sectoral Structure of the Economy (see Exhibit 54.1). Administrative division: 54 districts, 20 cities, 41 urban-type communities, and 925 village group-councils.

    Chairman of the Council of Ministers: Tel. (3472) 23 3701.

    Principal cities: Ufa (1,094,000), Sterlitamak (249,000), Neftekamsk (108,500), Oktyabrsky (105,600), and Salavat (150,800).

    The manufacturing structure is dominated by engineering (13%), the fuel industry (30.2%), and the chemical industry (20.5%). (See Exhibit 54.2.)

Exhibit 54.1.   Sectoral Structure of the Economy in 1995 (% of total)

	Industry	Farming	Transport	Construction	Other
Employment	27.7	20.0	6.3	11.0	35.0
Fixed Assets	46.3	12.4	10.4	7.1	23.8
Capital Investment	30.8	10.0	12.9	1.4	44.9

Exhibit 54.2.   Manufacturer of Principal Industrial Products

	1995	1996
Oil, million tons	15.7	14.3
Primary oil refining products, million tons	29.9	29.9
Machines for mineral fertilizer application	26	n/a
Mineral fertilizers, thou. tons	288	325
Wood fiberboard, million sq.m.	11.1	10.3
Hosiery, million pairs	4.7	2.4
Vegetable oil, thou. tons	3.6	11.3
Granulated sugar, thou. tons	110	576.4
Meat, thou. tons	75.3	56.7
Whole milk products, thou. tons	216	205.2
Gold production, kgs	566	

The republic contains over 15% of Russia's oil-refining capacity and has a number of large petrochemical enterprises that supply engine fuels to consumers in the country's European part and to the aerospace facilities (the Bashkirian Petrochemical Plants Industrial Association, the Khimprom Industrial Association, the Bashneft Industrial Association, the Novoufimsk oil refinery JSC, the Order of Lenin Ufa Oil Refinery JSC, the Ufaneftekhim Industrial Association, the Special Chemical Plant JSC, the Salavatnefteorgsintez Industrial Association, the Soda Industrial Association, the Caustic JSC, the Kauchuk JSC, and the Mineral Fertilizers Industrial Association). These enterprises are located at Ufa, Sterlitamak, Salavat, Ishimbai, and Meleuz. Aside from engine fuels, the republic also produces synthetic resins, rubber, herbicides, soda ash, mineral fertilizers, and a range of fine chemical products.

Engineering operations are highly developed among industries supplying oil, gas, and petrochemical complex (process-control devices, equipment for extracting, refining, and transporting oil and gas, repair facilities, geological-prospecting equipment, electrical-engineering equipment, and deep-well pumps and motors). In addition to petrochemical engineering, the republic is a major producer of aerospace and automotive equipment, with the Progress Industrial Association, The Machine Unit Industrial Association, The Svet Illumination Equipment JSC, and the Engine Association in Ufa; the Avtonormal JSC in Belebei; the diesel and gas-fueled vehicle association in Neftekamsk; and the Avtopribor auto instrumentation JSC.

The republic exports 12% of its manufactured output, with oil, oil products, and metal ores accounting for 50% of that, and chemical products for 38%.

The Bashkirian farming sector is the most advanced in the entire Ural Region and is actually the economic foundation of the republic's western areas. Farming mainly consists of grain growing and livestock raising, with wheat and potatoes being the basic crops in the former, and beef and diary cattle, lambs and sheep in the latter. Also bee-keeping operations supply honey to other areas around the country and for export.

3. Investment Opportunities. The republic is noted for its stable social and economic situation. Its relations with the federal authorities are regulated by an appropriate agreement. The ethnic groups of the population include Russians (39%), Tatars (28%), and Bashkirians (22%). There are minor ethnic frictions arising over differing customs between the Tatars and the Bashkirians and Russians in the northwestern rural areas, and between the Bashkirians and Russians in the cities.

The main limitations to developing enterprises are the extremely unfavorable ecological situation in the republic's eastern areas, the relatively small share of the population in good health (40%, and even less in some populated areas), and the inadequate road system, communications network, and everyday services in the republic's western areas.

Prospective projects for investment include replacing worn-out equipment and increasing the yield of light-oil products; geological prospecting and development of small-sized oilfields; manufacture of oil and petrochemical equipment for markets in Russia, the Commonwealth of Independent States countries, and the Middle East; licensed manufacture of aircraft and auto engines; and adjusting the fuel consumption rates and environmental-safety standards of domestic projects to a competitive level. Investments in individual enterprises are needed in the production of consumer goods for markets in the Northern Caucasus, the Ural Region, and Siberia; the production of handicrafts with local ethnic motifs for export; the gathering and marketing of honey; and the modernization of metal-fabrication enterprises (the Beloretsk integrated metal plant, the copper and sulfur plant in Sibai, the copper-mining and dressing plant in Uchaly, and the Uralzoloto Industrial association at the gold mines in Mundyakino Township).

In 1995, the region had 158 operating joint ventures. Foreign investments in 1993–95 totaled $8.6 million. Private owners held 15.6% of the fixed assets of enterprises and organizations, joint stock companies (without foreign interest) owned 22.4%, the federal authorities controlled 15.9%, and the republican government had 40.4% under its control. The republic's banking system includes the following banks: Vostok (Tel. 25 1452), Ekkor-Ural (Tel. 34 2830), Bashkiria (Tel. 22 7667), and Olymp (Tel. 23 4047).

The republic is reachable from Moscow by rail (1,519 km to Ufa, 28 hours travel time Kazan Terminal), air (two hours from Bykovo Airport), and road (the highway from Moscow, via Ryazan and Samara, to Ufa, 30–35 hours driving time).

There are 111 km of hard-surfaced roads per 1,000 sq km.

54.2 UDMURTIA REPUBLIC

1. Natural Resources. Area: 42,100 sq km. Farmland: 19,100 sq km. Woodland: 20,200 sq km. Population: 1,640,700 (Jan. 1, 1996), of which 69.9% is urban and 30.1% is rural. Population density: 39.0 per sq km.

The republic lies 1,100 km east of Moscow, between the Kama and Vyatka Rivers. It is adequately supplied with water.

A total of 15,600 sq km of woodlands is under federal control. The forests contain 279.5 million cu m of timber, including 165.9 million cu m of softwood. The republic's estimated cutting area is used at 90% capacity, and the commercial logging potential is six million cu m.

The republic's mineral resources include oil, peat, quartz sand, clay, and limestone.

The area has a temperate-continental climate, with a mean temperature of $-14°C$ in January and $18°C$ in July. The annual rainfall varies from 400 to 600 mm, and the growing season is between 110 and 130 days.

2. Specialization and Sectoral Structure of the Economy (see Exhibit 54.3). Administrative division: 25 districts, 6 cities, 12 urban-type communities, and 307 village group-councils.

Chairman of the Council of Ministers: Tel. (3412) 25 4567.

Principal cities: Izhevsk (642,000), Sarapul (111,700), Glazov (105,000), and Votkinsk (104,000).

In terms of structure, manufacturing is dominated by engineering (44.3%), the fuel industry (11.1%), and the food industry (10.9%). The republic's industrial complex has been shaped by Defense Industry Enterprises and their ancillary industries. The biggest enterprises are Izhstal (quality steels and sections), the Udmurtneft Industrial Association, the Izhevsk Electromechanical Plant Industrial Association, the Bummash JSC (equipment for the pulp and paper industry), the Neftemash Industrial Association (oil and gas production equipment), Bearing Plant 13, the Izhmash (cars and trucks), a radio plant; and a mechanical plant (firearms) in Izhevsk; the radio equipment plants in Sarapul (Elekond Industrial Association and radio plant); a chemical engineering plant (Spetsatommontazh) in Glazov; and the plant manufacturing radio equipment for weapons systems (Telecom) in Votkinsk. The economic fabric of other cities and towns in the republic is formed by enterprises producing meat, milk, peat, lumber, and glass and linen items. (See Exhibit 54.4.)

The principal farming activities are beef and dairy cattle raising, sheep grazing, and fowl keeping. Crop farmers grow fodder for local livestock. The republic is self-sufficient in staple foods. With redundancies in the defense industry, the population's income is lower than in the crossborder areas of the Ural and Volga Regions, a poor incentive for increasing output on farms operating for the local market. People's hopes for an economic recovery are dependent on the special conversion pro-

Exhibit 54.3.   Sectoral Structure of the Economy in 1995 (% of total)

	Industry	Farming	Transport	Construction	Other
Employment	36.0	14.1	5.9	7.3	26.7
Fixed Assets	50.4	16.6	5.8	7.0	20.2
Capital investment	32.2	8.3	16.8	2.6	40.1

Exhibit 54.4.   Manufacturer of Principal Industrial Products

	1995	1996
Oil, million tons	8.4	8.2
Trucks, thou.	12.8	7.2
Washing machines, thou.	61.0	47.6
Tape recorders, thou.	69.3	45
Meat, thou. tons	23.7	19.6
Whole milk products, thou. tons	79.3	81.7

grams that have been launched with funding from the federal budget, and on the resurgence of flax growing in the republic.

3. Investment Opportunities. Starting in 1995, the situation in the republic's defense establishment has stabilized after decisions were made to finance the weapons programs and convert some defense industry enterprises to other industries. The availability of facilities and equipment in defense industry has opened up favorable opportunities for manufacturing science-intensive products, including those based on scientific and technological knowledge and resources that were already in place. The republic has managed to save, keep operations running, and hold onto personnel at the most valuable scientific and engineering potential enterprizes with in particular, the design outfit under Kalashnikov, the inventor of the world-famous automatic rifle.

Investment prospects can be found in small-scale projects to produce consumer goods and services and to develop communications systems and databases; joint projects with specialist teams that left major enterprises; paper manufacturing; production of oil and gas production equipment that is in short supply in Russia (Bummash JSC and Neftemash Industrial Association); hunting guns and gear; and launching production of motor vehicles for private owners. Investment plans must take into account the risks involved in joining enterprises in the closed sector of the economy.

In 1995, the region had 73 operating joint ventures. The foreign investments in 1993–95 totaled $12.4 million. Private owners held 20.9% of the fixed assets of enterprises and organizations, joint stock companies (without foreign interest) owned 9.5%, the federal authorities controlled 48.6%, and the republican government had control over 11.7%. The republic's leading banks are Aksion (Tel. 23 8450), Arkobank (Tel. 25 6684), Gerd (Tel. 78 4078), the Eurasian Bank for Economic Development (Tel. 78 0735), Igerman (Tel. 23 3404), Izhcombank (Tel. 71 4676), Izhmashbank (Tel. 71 4546), the Investment Credit Bank (Tel. 25 9613), S-bank (Tel. 25 0377), Sotskulbank (Tel. 75 1457), and Udmurtagroprombank (Tel. 42 6058).

The republic is reachable from Moscow by rail (1,129 km to Izhevsk, 22 hours from Kazan Terminal) and air (two hours from Vnukovo Airport).

There are 106 km of hard-surfaced roads per 1,000 sq km.

54.3 CHELYABINSK OBLAST

1. Natural Resources. Area: 87,900 sq km. Farmland: 51,3000 sq km. Woodland: 27,200. Population: 3,616,900 (Jan. 1, 1996), of which 80.9% is urban and 19.1% is rural. Population density: 41.1 per sq km.

The oblast lies 1,900 km east of Moscow, on the eastern slopes of the Ural Range and on the trans-Ural plains. It is poorly supplied with water, and most of its watercourses are heavily polluted with industrial effluents and unsuited for either commercial or household purposes.

A total of 22,700 sq km of the woodlands are under federal control. The forests contain 345.9 million cu m of timber, including 147.9 million cu m of softwood. The region's estimated cutting area is used at 86% capacity, and the commercial logging potential is four million cu m.

The oblast's mineral resources include lignite, iron ores, magnesite, bauxite, graphite, fireclay, quartzite, talc, gold, semiprecious and precious stones, and building materials. The largest developed mineral sources are the Chelyabinsk lignite fields (coal), Bakal siderite at Satkino, iron ore at Magnitogorsk and Zlatoust, magnesite at Satkino, graphite at Tagnisk, fireclay at Nizhneuvelesk, and gold at Plast. Most of these sources have been 50 to 80% depleted, so the region's biggest enterprises chiefly use raw materials supplied from elsewhere.

The oblast has a continental climate, with a mean temperature of −17°C in January and 18°C in July. The annual rainfall varies from 350 to 600 mm, and the growing season is between 130 and 150 days.

2. Specialization and Sectoral Structure of the Economy (see Exhibit 54.5). Administrative division: 24 districts, 27 cities, 29 urban-type communities, and 264 village group-councils.

Administration head: Tel. (3512)33-9241. Fax 33-1283.

Principal cities: Chelyabinsk (1,175,000), Magnitogorsk (443,100), Zlatoust (210,600), Miass (180,300), and Kopeisk (148,300).

The manufacturing structure is dominated by engineering (21%), ferrous metallurgy (46.2%), and power engineering (11.9%). The oblast's manufacturing complex is strung out along the railroad from Ufa, via Chelyabinsk, to Kustanai and holds a monopolistic position in Russia in the volume and variety of ordinary and special steel grades, rolled ferrous metals, heavy tractors and motor vehicles, and metal structures. The leading enterprises of the complex are the Rosspetsstal metal fabrication plant, the integrated electrometallurgical plant (ferrochromium, ferrosilicium, and ferromolybdenum), the Koliushchenko heavy-equipment plant (bulldozers and scrapers), the forging press plant (forging equipment), and the pipe-rolling plant (steel pipelines) in Chelyabinsk; the metal fabrication plant (Rosspetsstal) in Asha; the Ufaleinickel industrial association and the metal-engineering plant in Verkhny Ufalei; the engineering plant and the metal fabrication plant (Rosspetsstal concern) in Zlatoust; the integrated copper-smelting plant in Karabash; the Vishnevogorsk mining and dressing plant (niobium concentrate and feldspar) and the engineering plant (cast-iron shapes) in Kasli; the mechanical plant (refrigerators) in Yuriuzan; the engineering plant in Katav-Ivanovsk; the tramcar-building plant in Ust-Katav; the industrial stones plant (ruby stones and timepiece components) in Kusa; the Uralvermiculite Industrial Association (graphite and vermiculite) and the electrolytic copper plant (refined copper) in Kyshtym; the Ural Auto Plant (Ural trucks) in Miass; the Magnesite integrated plant (refractories) and the metal fabrication plant in Satka; the thermal-power plant and the diesel plant in Troitsk; the metal fabrication plant (forging and titanium rolled stock) in Cherbarkul; the Bakal ore authority (quartzite and iron-ore concentrate) in Bakal; and the thermal-power plant, the radio ceramics plant, and the china plant in Yuzhnouralsk. The cities of Korkino, Emanzhelinsk, and Kopeisk are centers for coal mining and refining, and the production of mining equipment. The region south of the Kustanai-Chelyabinsk-Ufa railroad line, which is used for agricultural purposes, includes a major industrial

Exhibit 54.5.   Sectoral Structure of the Economy in 1995 (% of total)

	Industry	Farming	Transport	Construction	Other
Employment	36.5	10.0	7.7	8.4	37.4
Fixed Assets	52.7	10.0	6.9	3.4	27.0
Capital investment	46.3	4.7	8.7	0.7	39.6

center, Magnitogorsk, the location of the world's largest integrated metal-producing plant for manufacturing commercial-grade rolled stock. The city is also the site of a steel products plant (grooved steel, wire, and metal cord), and a metalware plant (wire, metal net, and electrodes). Gold mining is centered in Plast. (See Exhibit 54.6.)

The oblast exports 16% of its manufactured output, most of which (93%) is metal products.

The oblast has a shortage of staple foods, a factor likely to stimulate development of its rural areas. The region's southern areas consist of fertile soils, which are farmed to grow wheat, rye, legumes, buckwheat, and millet. The livestock industry specializes in raising beef and dairy cattle, grazing sheep, and raising hogs and fowl in the generally favorable conditions of abundant fodder-producing lands. The main limitation to development here is the shortage of the water and recurring droughts.

3. Investment Opportunities. The Chelyabinsk Oblast is a stable area. The social situation is complicated by the growing gap between low-paid individuals living in rural areas or employed in the defense industry, which is under capacity, and the employees of metal, chemical, and other engineering enterprises. The problem is mitigated, however, by the overflow of labor into profitable future-oriented industries.

Some serious limitations on economic activities are imposed by the predominance of military-industrial-complex enterprises, the high level of pollution, water shortages, unsuitability of most of the industrial area for permanent residence because of the radioactive contamination caused by the Mayak plant accident, and pollution from metal-processing plants.

Investment prospects include major projects to fabricate and market ferrous metals and metalware; timepieces (at the watch plants in Chelyabinsk, Chebarkul, and Zlatoust); production of magnesite (in Satka) and ferroalloys (in Chelyabinsk); small-scale projects to manufacture clothing, furniture, footwear, and high-tech household appliances and to provide auto service facilities for the eastern Ural Region, Siberia, and the contiguous area of Kazakstan; and geological prospecting, mining, and processing of precious metals, and precious and semiprecious stones.

In 1995, the region had 219 operating joint ventures. The foreign investments in 1993–95 totaled $34 million. Private owners held 19.7% of the fixed assets of enterprises and organizations, joint stock companies (without foreign interest) owned 40.5%; and the federal authorities controlled 27.8%.

Exhibit 54.6. Manufacture of Principal Industrial Products

	1995	1996
Coal, million tons	6.1	6.6
Rolled ferrous metals, million tons	8.8	8.6
Steel pipes, thousand tons	687	666.4
Low-rated electric motors, thousand	491	358.4
Cement, thousand tons	2,166	1,992.7
Refrigerators thousand	140	43.4
Radio receivers, thousand	182	16.4
Meat, thousand tons	25.2	17.4
Whole milk products, thousand tons	112	81.8
Gold production, kgs	1,609	

So far, more than 80% of the trading enterprises in the region have been privatized. These include construction-equipment production companies, wholesale traders, and food producers. More than one third of the private dwellings are privatized. Foreign investors can participate in the privatization of enterprises.

Companies seeking foreign participation include the Bakal Mining Company, the Satka Group, and the Vishnevorogorsk Mining Company.

The Bakal Mining Company is developing mining deposits. After processing, the ore is supplied to the Chelyabinsk Metallurgical Plant. The company also is developing a deposit of metallurgical quartzite, which is being supplied to the Chelyabinsk Electrometallurgical Plant. Ore by products are used mainly in building construction. The Bakal deposits are located in an industrially developed area in the western part of the oblast. The area has a sufficient supply of labor and power.

Until 1992, the region's marble deposits had been developed by the state owned enterprise Chelabinskmramor, which was later transformed into a joint-stock company. Now the company comprises several independent plants developing marble deposits. In addition, the company produces sand and decorative broken stone, used for wall finishings and wallpaper. The company has stone-cutting factories, one to two km from railway lines, and is near a power line and water reservoirs.

The Satka Group of mineral deposits is the only source of raw material for the production of periclase refractories. It produces approximately 90% of the magnesite refractories in the CIS. The company is looking for participation in the exploration and development of magnesite deposits to increase the supply of raw materials. It is also seeking the development of new technologies to process minerals. The company is built on the Taiginka deposit of graphite, which has an annual output of 17,000 tons of graphite. The company supplies graphite to the Russian Federation, Uzbekistan and Turkmenistan.

The Vishnevorogorsk Mining Company is looking for aid in the development of a process to extract useful components from mining wastes. This is a technologically advanced enterprise for processing water and it may introduce a process that is completely waste-free.

The oblast's leading banks include the Investment Bank (Tel. 33-8444), Dorozhnik (Tel. 66-6828), Zlatcombank (in Zlatoust, Tel. 30-577), Mechel-bank (Tel. 24-6001), Miass (in Miass, Tel. 50-365), Rotor-bank (Tel. 33-5156), Sintez (Tel. 42-7319), Snezhensky (Tel. 32-591), Unikal (in Magnitogorsk, Tel. 37-433), Forum-bank (Tel. 33-5245), Chelindbank (Tel. 65-2875), and Chelyabcomzembank (Tel. 33-7851).

The oblast is reachable from Moscow by rail (1,919 km to Chelyabinsk, 40 hours from Kazan Terminal) and air (two hours from Domodedovo Airport).

There are 83 km of hard-surfaced road per 1000 sq km.

54.4 KURGAN OBLAST

1. Natural Resources. Area: 71,000 sq km. Farmland: 45,100 sq km. Woodland: 17,100 sq km. Population: 1,114,800 (Jan. 1, 1996), of which 54.7% is urban and 45.3% is rural. Population density: 15.7 per sq km.

The oblast lies 1,970 km east of Moscow, on the West Siberian Plain. The majority of its districts are adequately supplied with water, but a reservoir would have to be built on the Tobol River if any major projects are launched.

The woodlands include 9,800 sq km under federal control. The forests contain 183.3 million cu m of timber, including 63.5 million cu m of softwood. The region's estimated cutting area is used at 95% capacity, and the commercial logging area has a potential of 2.5 million cu m.

The oblast's mineral resources include building materials (clay, sand, mineral dyes, gypsum, and limestone) and peat. In its southern part, iron-ore deposits have been prospected at Glubochensk and Berezovo, but they are not developed because raw iron ore is supplied economically from the Kustanai Oblast across the border in Kazakstan.

The oblast has a continental climate, with a mean temperature of −18°C in January and 19°C in July. The area gets an annual rainfall of 400 mm, and has a growing season of about 130 days with temperatures above 10°C.

2. Specialization and Sectoral Structure of the Economy (see Exhibit 54.7). Administrative division: 24 districts, 9 cities, 6 urban-type communities, and 419 village group-councils.

Administration head: Tel. (35222) 22 534.

Principal cities: Kurgan (366,100), Shadrinsk (88,400), and Shumikha (22,000).

The manufacturing structure is dominated by engineering (45.4%), the food industry (14.1%), and power generation (21.7%). The oblast's economic complex has been shaped to supply the Ural industrial areas with food and metal products (fence and bridge structures, pipeline valves, pumps, and fire extinguishers). In addition, the oblast has a number of science-intensive auto engineering enterprises (Kurganpribor Industrial Association and the Kurgan Engineering Plant Industrial Association), the Corvette JSC, the bus plant (manufacturing Kavz small-capacity buses), a telephone plant, the Karbyshev Wheeled Prime-Mover Plant, and the Sintez integrated pharmaceutical plant (oxytetracyclin, ampicillin, and erythromycin). (See Exhibit 54.8.)

The oblast exports 2% of its manufactured output, with chemical products accounting for 66% of this amount, and machines and equipment for 11%.

Farming caters to the needs of the Chelyabinsk, Sverdlovsk, and Tyumen Oblasts. Cereals account for 60% of the crop areas and fodder for 30%. Cattle are raised for meat and dairy products. The oblast produces surplus foods, but has problems marketing produce because of a lack of processing facilities and an underdeveloped trading network.

Exhibit 54.7.   Sectoral Structure of the Economy in 1995 (% of total)

	Industry	Farming	Transport	Construction	Other
Employment	24.0	24.0	7.2	6.9	37.9
Fixed Assets	27.2	33.3	10.8	9.1	19.6
Capital Investment	22.7	12.1	18.6	1.2	45.4

Exhibit 54.8.   Manufacturer of Principal Industrial Products

	1995	1996
Buses thou.	1.2	1.3
Washing machines, thou.	13.3	2.7
Meat, thou. tons	17.5	10.5
Whole milk products, thou. tons	21.5	22.2

3. Investment Opportunities. The region is a stable area, but its economic situation is complicated by the fact that the population has a lower income than people in neighboring regions. The reasons are the proportion of rural inhabitants and the sales crisis in the basic manufacturing industries, which were previously supported by defense orders and favorable product sales. There is a good possibility that people will migrate to enterprises in the Tyumen, Chelyabinsk, and Sverdlovsk Oblasts.

The main areas of investment include trading and manufacturing facilities for processing the local farm produce and selling it in the Tyumen Oblast and other areas of the Ural Region and Siberia; manufacture of equipment and machines for the oil and gas complex in the Tyumen Oblast and metal fabrication enterprises in the Ural area (the Ikar JSC, the bus plant, the Corvette JSC, the Kurgan road-construction equipment plant, the Katai pump plant, and the Shadrinsk telephone plant); and the production of consumer goods for the Ural Region and Siberian markets.

The advantages the Kurgan Oblast has over the neighboring regions are its lower labor costs, a lower cost of living (food prices that are among the least expensive in the Ural-Siberian area, moderate rent prices, and an available labor market), a healthier environment, greater choice of building sites, railroads, and highways to the Ural Region, Siberia, and Kazakstan. All these factors should support the initiation of projects for meeting the needs of the Tyumen Oblast.

In 1995, the region had 15 operating joint ventures. The foreign investments in 1993–95 totaled $800,000. Private owners held 40.9% of the fixed assets of enterprises and organizations, joint stock companies (without foreign interest) owned 21%, and the federal authorities had 27.1% under control. The oblast's banking system included the following banks: The Trans-Ural Business (Tel. 21 613), the Investment Kurgan (Tel. 23 804), Kurgan-resurs (Tel. 29 412), Kurganinvestzembank (Tel. 23 125), Kurganprombank (Tel. 33 852), Kurgansotsbank (Tel. 78 206), and Nadezhnost (Tel. 23 552).

The oblast is reachable from Moscow by rail (1,973 km to Kurgan, 37 hours from Kazan Terminal) and air (three hours from Domodedovo Airport).

There are 71 km of hard-surfaced roads per 1,000 sq km.

54.5 ORENBURG OBLAST

1. Natural Resources. Area: 124,000 sq km. Farmland: 108,600 sq km. Woodland: 5,900 sq. km Population: 2,234,700 (Jan. 1, 1996), of which 64.6% is urban and 35.4% is rural. Population density: 18.0 per sq km.

The oblast lies 1,450 km from Moscow. It extends a considerable distance from west to east. The terrain of its western areas is similar to that of the steppe areas of the Lower Volga, and its eastern areas lie in semidesert regions beyond the Ural Range. The western areas are supplied with water from small watercourses and artesian wells, but the supplies are, as a rule, limited in the summer. In the central area, water is drawn from the Ural channel and underground sources. Water supplies in the eastern areas are very poor.

The woodlands include 4,500 sq km under federal control. The forests contain 60.1 million cu m of timber, including 10.7 million cu m of softwood. The oblast's estimated cutting area is used at 50% capacity, and the commercial logging potential is 0.5 million cu m.

The oblast's mineral resources include complex natural gas, oil, salt, shale, complex ferrous and nonferrous-metal ores, asbestos, and building materials. The main resources are contained in a group of small and greatly depleted oilfields near Buzu-luk, the condensed gas field (gas, hydrogen sulfide, ethane, propane, helium, nitrogen, and carbon dioxide) at Orenburg, common salt at Sol-Iletsk, asbestos at Kiembai, nickel at Buruktal, lignite at Tyulgan, and copper ore at Gai. In all, nearly 2,000 deposits have been discovered in the region, but only 72 are actually developed. Generally, the gas and ores have a complex makeup, which requires the use of sufficiently advanced technologies to beneficiate and process them.

The oblast has a strongly continental climate, with a mean January temperature of −14°C in the western areas and −18°C in the eastern areas, and 19°C and 22°C, respectively, in July. The annual rainfall ranges from 330 to 450 mm, and the growing season lasts 135 to 145 days.

2. Specialization and Sectoral Structure of the Economy (see Exhibit 54.9). Administrative division: 35 districts, 12 cities, 25 urban-type communities, and 577 village group-councils.

Administration head: Tel. (3532) 47 6931. Fax 47 3802.

Principal cities: Orenburg (659,500), Orsk (274,700), Novotroitsk (112,700), and Buzuluk (84,800).

The manufacturing structure is dominated by engineering (10.5%), the fuel industry (11.1%), the food industry (7.8%), and ferrous metallurgy (20.6%). The largest businesses in the oil and gas complex are the Orenburggazprom state-owned enterprise, the helium plant, the oil and lubricant plant, the Samaraneft oil and gas authority (in Buzuluk), and the Orsknefteorgsintez industrial association (in Orsk). In the metal industry, the largest enterprises are the mining and dressing plant in Gai (sulfur pyrite and copper ore), the South Ural cryolite plant in Kuvandyk, the copper-sulfur plant in Mednogorsk (refined copper, germanium concentrate, and sulfuric acid), the Orsk-Khalil integrated metal plant in Novotroitsk (rolled ferrous metals), the chromium compounds plant in Novotroitsk (sodium bichromate, chromium oxide, and sodium sulfide), and the Yuzhuralnickel integrated plant in Orsk (nickel, cobalt, and copper sulfate). In engineering, the largest businesses are the Inventor research and development association (electric machines), the Radiator JSC (tractor hydrosystems), the Electric Converter JSC in Gai (low-voltage equipment), the Uralelektro JSC in Mednogorsk (AC motors), the Mechanical Plant Industrial Association, the Uralmash Industrial Association, and the Uralmash Industrial Association in Orsk (metal fabrication equipment). (See Exhibit 54.10.)

The Orenburg Oblast is second only to Bashkortostan in the output and gross harvest of cereals. Over 50% of the commercial wheat consists of strong and hard varieties. Cattle is raised for meat and dairy products. Because of the limited fodder resources, cattle farming is confined to meeting the local needs, although it could grow by expanding into new natural fodder-yielding lands and developing mixed-feed production. In addition, sheep and fowl are kept in the region.

Exhibit 54.9. Sectoral Structure of the Economy in 1995 (% of total)

	Industry	Farming	Transport	Construction	Other
Employment	23.9	21.5	9.2	10.1	35.3
Fixed Assets	45.5	20.3	9.0	7.0	18.2
Capital Investment	36.7	8.0	6.5	1.2	47.6

Exhibit 54.10.   Manufacturer of Principal Industrial Products

	1995	1996
Oil, million tons	8.7	9
Gas, bn cu.m.	32.4	31.1
Asbestos, thou. tons	279	203.7
Vegetable oil, thou. tons	12.6	15
Meat, thou. tons	36.4	26.6
Whole milk products, thou. tons	53.3	43.7

3. Investment Opportunities. Evaluating the social situation in the region in unambiguous terms is difficult. Although serious social controversies have not appeared, the region's living standards are among the lowest in the country, despite numerous enterprises in the oil and gas complex and the metal industry, which, as a general rule, maintain high-paying jobs. The reasons may be the large amount of people working in low-income rural areas and the large number of enterprises filling defense orders and operating below capacity. Another factor is the common border with areas of Kazakstan that are predominantly populated by Russians. Presently, this is contributing to rising prices in the local market, with the prospect of more serious controversies developing in the future.

The oblast's main limitations include a shortage of water, which gets more severe as one goes from west to east; the unfavorable environment in all major and medium-sized cities and in some of the rural areas; poor transportation and telecommunications facilities in small towns and medium-sized cities. The oblast does have a number of major airports and adequate maintenance facilities for air and rail transportation.

The major projects that will require investment include enterprises in oil, gas, and metallurgy to produce and market raw materials and semifinished products; and introduction and development of techniques for comprehensive processing of raw iron ore and natural gas. Other projects include upgrading the international airport so that west-east air traffic could bypass the Moscow hub and save two hours in flight time; the manufacture of down kerchiefs for the Russian and world markets (the down kerchief factory and integrated plant); asbestos and products containing asbestos (the Uralasbest plant in Yasny); modernization of the salt industry (in Sol-Iletsk); expansion of the silk mill; and adaptation of the trade and manufacturing enterprises to produce consumer goods and services for the Orenburg Oblast, Kazakstan, and Central Asian republics.

In 1995, the region had 60 operating joint ventures. The foreign investments in 1993–95 totaled one million dollars. Private owners held 24.5% of the fixed assets of enterprises and organizations, joint stock companies (without foreign interest) owned 28.5%, and the federal authorities controlled 38.2%. The region's banking system is comprised of the following banks: Agrosoyuz (Tel. 47 6744), the Bank for Foreign Trade (Vneshtorgbank, Tel. 47 3392), Korobank (Tel. 47 9594), Nota (Novotroitsk, Tel. 23 822), Orenburzhie (Tel. 47 3046), Orenburgladabank (Tel. 41 9301), Orindbank (Tel. 47 4438), Perfectbank (Tel. 47 5014), and Stromcombank (Tel. 44 2790).

The oblast is reachable from Moscow by rail (1,478 km. to Orenburg, 28 hours from Kazan Terminal) and air (two hours from Domodedovo Airport).

There are 81 km of hard-surfaced roads per 1,000 sq km. of the region.

54.6   PERM OBLAST

1. Natural Resources. Area: 160,600 sq km. Farmland: 29,100 sq km. Woodland: 117,300 sq km. Bodies of water: 3,300 sq km. Population: 3,091,500 (Jan. 1, 1996), of which 77.1% is urban and 22.9% is rural. Population density: 19.2 per sq km.

   The oblast lies 1,360 km east of Moscow. It is adequately provided with water. The total annual river runoff is 57 cu km. Two large reservoirs have been built on the Kama River. The water quality in the Kama near the cities of Solikamsk, Berezniki, Perm, and Krasnokamsk is below the standards for water used for economic and domestic purposes.

   The woodlands include 66,300 sq km under federal control. The forests contain 1,494.1 million cu m of timber, including 1,075 million cu m of softwood. The oblast's estimated cutting area is used at 71% capacity, and the commercial logging potential is 30 million cu m. The oblast is a major supplier of lumber and logs to the Volga area.

   The local mineral resources include low-quality coal, chromium ore, gold, diamonds, quartz and citrine, uvarovite, gypsum, potassium-magnesium salts, limestone, raw material for cement, stock, and building materials. The principal oilfields are 50 to 80% depleted. The residual reserves of 422 million tons will last for 25 years at the present production level. Another 71 oilfields and three gas fields constitute a standby reserve. Aside from these, another 156 have been prepared for drilling. Chromium ore is mined in the Gornozavodsky District and is suited for the production of high-quality chrome-magnesite refractors. The chromium ore reserves amount to five million tons. Diamonds are mined in the Krasnovishersky District, but tracer gold deposits are not yet developed. The oblast is world famous for its potassium reserves in the Upper Kama area, containing a quarter of the global potassium resources (21.5 billion tons), which are developed by the Uralkaliy and Sylvinite Industrial Associations. Apart from fertilizers, potassium-bearing material is processed into products containing magnesium, rubidium, cesium, bromine, and lithium. The coalfields at Kizel and Gremyachinsk produce coal that is used for power generation and produce coke for the nonferrous-metal industry.

   The oblast has a temperate-continental climate, with a mean temperature of $-17°C$ in January and $17°C$ in July. The annual rainfall varies from 450 to 600 mm, and the growing season lasts 100 to 120 days.

2. Specialization and Sectoral Structure of the Economy (see Exhibit 54.11). Administrative division: 37 districts, 25 cities, 55 urban-type communities, 515 village group-councils.

   Administration head: Tel. (3422) 34,0790. Fax 33 5666.

   Principal cities: Perm (1,104,300), Berezniki (202,200), Solikamsk (110,200), Chaikovsky (87,300), and Lysva (77,600).

Exhibit 54.11.   Sectoral Structure of the Economy in 1995 (% of total)

	Industry	Farming	Transport	Construction	Other
Employment	31.7	9.7	7.7	9.3	41.6
Fixed Assets	46.2	8.9	20.7	2.3	21.9
Capital Investment	34.8	5.7	7.2	13.2	39.1

The manufacturing structure is dominated by engineering (12%), the fuel industry (15%), lumbering and woodworking (7.8%), the chemical industry (21.9%), and power generation (17.2%). A major chemical and engineering center of national importance has been created in Perm, which comprises the Kirov research and development association, the Velta Industrial Association (auto equipment), the Kamkabel Industrial Association (armored cable and aircraft wires), the Dzerzhinsky Engineering Plant Industrial Association, the instrument association, the Motovilikha Plant JSC, the Perm Motors industrial association, the Nefteorgsintez Industrial Association (oil refining), the Halogen Industrial Association (bromine, refrigerants, and plastics), the Sorbite Industrial Association (activated carbon and gas masks), and the Biomed Research and Development Association (immunogenic preparations). Most of these enterprises are leaders in their industries and fill defense orders. The area between Berezniki and Solikamsk is the center of the chemical and pulp and paper industries, including such major enterprises as the Azot Industrial Association (nitrogen, saltpeter, and mineral fertilizers), the Soda Industrial Association (soda ash), the Uralkaliy Industrial Association, the Avisma JSC, the Sylvinite Industrial Association, the Integrated Pulp and Paper Plant, the Timber Building Materials JSC, the Ural Plant (chemical-industry equipment), and the magnesium plant. Cement is produced in Gornozavodsky (the Gornozavodsk Cement Association); methanol and formalin are manufactured in Bugakhi (the Methanol Industrial Association), where coke is also produced at the coal-tar chemical plant; paper, board, and plywood are produced in Krasnovishersk and Krasnokamsk (the Visherabumprom JSC, the Kama pulp and paper plant, and the Gosznak paper mill); isoprene, isobutylene, synthetic rubber, and silk fabrics are produced in Chaikovsky (the synthetic-rubber plant and silk mill); transformer steel and electric machines are made in Lysva (the metal plant and the Privod Industrial Association); and spring steel is manufactured in Chusovoi (the integrated metal plant). (See Exhibit 54.12.)

The oblast exports 20.7% of its manufactured output; of this, products account for 15%, chemical products for 53.3%, lumber for 9%, and metals for 18%.

The Perm Oblast has shortages of most foodstuffs. Perm and the region's northern areas serve as markets for the produce raised in the southern rural areas, where farming activity is strong. Livestock farming specializes in raising beef and dairy cattle. Truck farming is practiced in suburban areas, where the common crops are potatoes and other vegetables. Fowl keeping is widespread.

Exhibit 54.12.   Manufacture of Principal Industrial Products

	1995	1996
Oil, million tons	9.3	8.9
Commercial timber, thou. cu.m.	3,574	3,038
Lumber, thou. cu.m.	832	665.6
Paper, thou. tons	414	318.8
Mineral fertilizers, thou. tons	2,584	2,604
Silk fabrics, million sq.m.	44.7	24.6
Hosiery, million pairs	14.7	9.9
Meat, thou. tons	45.3	38.9
Whole milk products, thou. tons	97.0	93.1
Gold, kgs	68	n/a

3. Investment Opportunities. The Perm Oblast is a stable area endowed with diverse physical resources and numerous sources of local revenue.

One of the oblast's main limitations is the high pollution levels in the atmosphere, soil, and water in the areas of Perm, Krasnokamsk and Berezniki-Solikamsk, and in the majority of the region's medium-sized cities; another drawback is the predominance of large enterprises that are not subject to privatization and work substantially under government orders.

Investment prospects include major projects in oil refining and the chemical industry (modernization of the oil refinery in Perm, and launching production of titanium-dioxide-based paints and varnishes, sulfur dyes, chemical yarn, and fibers); production and marketing of potassium fertilizers (soda ash, methanol, ammonia, reactive salts and acids, melamine, and fluoroplastics); geological prospecting and development of small oilfields; processing of precious stones and metals; research and production of superpure materials, chemical reagents, and catalysts, and expansion of aniline production from nitrobenzene; logging and shipping logs and lumber, small-scale facilities to produce lumber from deciduous wood, manufacture and marketing of newsprint (the pulp and paper mill in Solikamsk); manufacture and marketing of printing paper (Kama and Vishera pulp and paper mills); manufacture of clothes and high-tech household appliances for markets in the Ural Region and Siberia; establishment of a tourist center at the underground caves at Kungur; air and rail transportation services between Center; the Ural Region and Siberia, and between Europe and the Asia-Pacific Region.

In 1995, the area had 96 operating joint ventures. The foreign investments in 1993–95 totaled $29.7 million. Private owners held 17.9% of the fixed assets of enterprises and organizations, joint stock companies (without foreign interest) owned 28.7%, and the federal authorities controlled 44.7%. The region's banking system is comprised of the following banks: Agroprombank (Tel. 32 4384), Bis-credit (Tel. 33 5418), Dzerzhinsky (Tel. 33 8989), Zapaduralbank (Tel. 34 0370), Zarya Urala (Tel. 64 3042), Kauri (Tel. 32 4991), Credit FD (Tel. 33 1711), Motovilikhinsky (Tel. 36 3849), Musulmanbank (Tel. 64 2505), Permcombank (Tel.32 4846), Permstroicombank (Tel. 33.5011), Perm-Avers (Tel. 72 6344), Pochtobank (Tel. 34 3664), Prikamye (Tel. 33 1718), Toplivny (Tel. 44 4340), and Juventa (Tel. 66 8997).

The oblast is reachable from Moscow by rail (1,386 km to Perm, 23 hours from Yaroslavl Terminal) and air (two hours from Domodedovo Airport).

There are 39 km of hard-surfaced roads per 1,000 sq km.

54.7   SVERDLOVSK OBLAST

1. Natural Resources. Area: 194,800 sq km. Farmland: 26,120 sq km. Woodland: 135,600 sq km. Swamps: 20,600 sq km. Population: 4,666,700 (Jan. 1, 1996), of which 87.2% is urban and 12.8% is rural. Population density: 24 per sq km.

The oblast lies 1,910 km from Moscow, on the eastern slopes of the Ural Range and on the trans-Ural plains. It is adequately supplied with water. The majority of water sources in the industrial zone of Ekaterinburg and Nizhny Tagil are heavily polluted and unsuited for either economic or household needs.

The woodlands include 84,100 sq km under federal control. The local forests contain 1,758.8 million cu m of timber, 1,246.1 million cu m of which is softwood. The oblast's estimated cutting area is used at 70% capacity. The commercial logging areas have a potential of 30 million cu m.

The oblast's mineral resources include iron ore, chromium, manganese, copper ore, bauxite, nickel, coal, asbestos, kaolin, aggregates, limestone, dolomite, fire-clay, raw materials for cement and glass, gold, platinum, and precious and semi-precious stones. The 10 registered iron-ore deposits contain a total of 4.2 billion tons, including 3.4 billion tons of lean, easily concentrated titanium-magnetite ore in the Gusinogorsk fields near the town of Kachkanar. The chromium deposits at East Tagil, Klyuchevskoe, and the Alapaevsk deposit are not developed because high-quality raw material is available in the Saranovsk deposit group in the Perm Oblast. A total of 18 copper-ore deposits have been registered, some of which are developed and processed at the local plants. Bauxite is mined in the northern Urals mineral-rich area, which is near the town of Severouralsk and which is the main source of high-quality bauxite in Russia. The beds lying close to the surface have been depleted, and production at the current rate can be maintained only at a depth of more than one km, which is not cost-effective. Nickel has been registered in four deposits (Serov, Porovskoe, Kungur, and Parushinskoe); but apart from the Serovo deposit, development is unlikely at this time because of the competition from the Norilsk-Murmansk group of nickel-industry enterprises. There are coalfields in the Serovo and Alapaevsk districts, which produce low-quality coal used only on a limited scale for local needs. The asbestos deposit at Bazhenov, with 2,751 million tons of ore reserves, is the largest in the world and has kept the highly profitable asbestos industry in business for 100 years. The oblast is one of Russia's key centers for mining and processing precious stones. Gold and platinum are chiefly mined in the Berezovsky province.

The oblast has a continental climate, with a mean temperature of $-18°C$ in January and $16°C$ in July. Its annual rainfall averages between 350 to 600 mm, and the growing season lasts 130 days.

2. Specialization and Sectoral Structure of the Economy (see Exhibit 54.13). Administrative division: 30 districts, 45 cities, 97 urban-type communities, and 429 village group-councils.

Administration head: Tel. (3432) 51 1365. Fax 58 1502.

Principal cities: Ekaterinburg (1,414,400), Nizhny Tagil (439,600), Kamensk-Uralsky (210,200), and Pervouralsk (175,400).

The manufacturing structure in the oblast is dominated by engineering (20.7%), ferrous metallurgy (27.1%), nonferrous metallurgy (17.1%), and power generation (11.4%). The manufacturing industries are comprised of 3,300 enterprises, 60% of which are located in the strip stretching from Ekaterinburg to Nizhny Tagil. Many of these are monopolistic producers, taking orders from the defense establishment. Ferrous metallurgy includes 49 enterprises manufacturing such items as electric steel, reinforcement and transformer steel, rolled shapes, commercial-steel grades, beams, channel bars, and rails. Many enterprises manufacture and process nonfer-

Exhibit 54.13.   Sectoral Structure of the Economy as of January 1, 1995 (% of total)

	Industry	Farming	Transport	Construction	Other
Employment	36.6	6.2	7.2	8.6	41.4
Fixed Assets	54.4	7.0	12.0	6.6	20.0
Capital Investment	32.8	2.3	20.3	2.9	41.7

rous metals (aluminum, nickel, cobalt, and copper). The biggest of them are the Upper Isetsk metal fabrication plant in Ekaterinburg; the Nizhny Tagil integrated metal plant and the Vysogorsk mining and dressing plant in Nizhny Tagil; the integrated metal plant in Alapaevsk; the Uralelektromed integrated plant in Verkhnaya Pyshma; the Sinar pipe plant and the aluminum plant in Kamensk-Uralsky; the Kachkanar mining and dressing plant (raw iron ore); the integrated copper-smelting plant and the hard-alloy plant in Kirovograd; the Bogoslov aluminum plant and the Svyatogor JSC in Krasnouralsk; the pipe plant and the Khrompik JSC in Pervouralsk; the Seversk pipe plant in Polevskoi; the metalware and metal plant and the Middle Ural integrated copper plant in Revda; the nickel plant in Rezh; the North Urals Bauxite Mine industrial association in Severouralsk; the Serov integrated metal plant and the ferroalloy plant in Serov; and the Mikhailovsky Plant JSC (nonferrous metal processing) in Nizhny Sergi. (See Exhibit 54.14.)

The engineering industry consists mainly of heavy-power and transportation engineering. The largest enterprises, which employ a workforce of 5,000 to 40,000 each, are the Turbine Engine Plant JSC, the Uralkhimmash JSC, the Ural Auto Engine Plant JSC, the Kalinin Plant, a precision mechanics plant, the Uraltransmash plant, the Uralelektrotyazhmash, and the Ural heavy engineering plant in Ekaterinburg; the Motorcycle Plant JSC and the instrument plant in Irbit; and the Ural Carriage Plant (the key military tank-building center in Russia).

The economic framework of some of the oblast's cities is supplemented with large forest industry enterprises, including the lumber plant in Lobva, the pulp and paper mill and the woodworking plant in Novaya Lyalya, the lumber plant in Vostochny township, the plywood plant and hydrolysis plant in Tavda, the match factory and the pulp and paper mill in Turinsk; asbestos enterprises (the Uralasbest integrated plant of the Malyshev ore authority), and cement enterprises (the Sukhoi Log Cement industrial association, a cement plant, and an integrated asbestos-cement plant in Sukhoi Log).

The oblast exports 11% of its manufactured output, which consists chiefly of metal products (84%).

Because the oblast has scarce food supplies, it gets its perishables from the Kurgan Oblast, and buys its other products from other areas of Russia and by importing 30 to 40% of them from other countries. Local farmers specialize in raising beef and dairy cattle, keeping fowl, and growing potatoes and other vegetables. The returns are not high, however, because of the unfavorable soil and climate.

Exhibit 54.14. Manufacturer of Principal Industrial Products

	1995	1996
Rolled ferrous metals, million tons	4.6	4.8
Freight cars	2,740	2,493.4
Fodder harvesters	282	451.2
Lumber, thou. cu.m.	1,229	1,044.7
Cement, thou. tons	2,728	1,827.8
Auto tires, thou.	1,111	799.9
Washing machines, thou.	80.6	32.2
Meat, thou. tons	74.9	74.9
Whole milk products, thou. tons	191	180
Gold, kgs.	3,267	

3. Investment Opportunities. The Sverdlovsk Oblast is one of the country's largest industrial and administrative centers. Many of its enterprises fill defense orders and will maintain this status for a long time. The economic foundation of most medium-sized cities and small towns in the belt extending from Ekaterinburg to Nizhny Tagil and on the Serov consists, as a rule, of metal, engineering, and chemical-industry enterprises. This industrialization sets the oblast apart from the majority of its neighbors areas in the Urals and Siberia and must be taken into account by prospective joint-venture projects.

The region's main limitations are the environment, which has been irreversibly polluted by metal and chemical-industry wastes, and restricted access to many enterprises and populated centers across the oblast.

The oblast is open to investments in virtually every economic activity, including geological prospecting, manufacture and marketing of ferrous and nonferrous metals, auto servicing, clothing production, and manufacture of wood and plastic items. The greatest yields may come from investments in the manufacture and marketing of ferrous and nonferrous metals; production of equipment for the oil and gas industry in the Tyumen Oblast and the Middle East; joint research and pilot projects in high-tech metalworking, manufacture of specialized metals, and biotechnologies. Profitable joint ventures may be established with the group of plants processing precious and semiprecious stones (the Russian Gems industrial association, the Uralmramor industrial association, and the Ural Jewelers JSC), and with enterprises that process complex polymetal deposits containing 20 million tons.

In 1995, the region had 152 operating joint ventures. The foreign investments in 1993–95 totaled $9.3 million. Private owners held 12.9% of the fixed assets of enterprises and organizations, joint stock companies (without foreign interest) owned 29.4%, the federal authorities controlled 20.3%, and the municipal authorities had 37.2% under their control. The oblast's leading banks are Agros-bank (Tel. 55 9013), the White Tower (Tel. 449539), Brig-bank (Tel. 25 2712), Viz-bank (Tel. 51 7013), Gracombank (Tel. 25 0572), Zavodskoi (Tel. 22 5202), Gold-Platinum Bank (Tel. 22 7775), Kub-bank (Tel. 22 8286), Fifei (Tel.55 2244), Sverdlsotsbank (Tel. 51 2740), SKB-bank (Tel. 22 7700), Sreduralbank (Tel. 55 9497), Uktussky (Tel. 25 2420), the Ural Foreign Trade Bank, Uralvneshtorgbank (Tel 25 2420), the Uralcombank (Tel 55 4347), Uralpromstroibank (Tel. 51 2188), Uraltransbank (Tel 63 0390), and Uraleksobank (Tel. 22 7080).

The oblast is reachable from Moscow by rail (1,923 km to Ekaterinburg, 33 hours from Yaroslavl Terminal) and air (2.5 hours from Domodedovo Airport).

There are 46 km of hard-surfaced roads per 1,000 sq km.

CHAPTER 55

WEST SIBERIA REGION

Aleko A. Adamescu, Yuri A. Kovalev, and Alexander G. Granberg

55.1 ALTAI REPUBLIC

1. Natural Resources. Area: 92,600 sq km. Farmland: 17,600 sq km. Woodland: 42,700 sq km. Population: 198,300 (Jan. 1, 1996), of which 26.3% is urban and 73.7% is rural. Population density: 2.1 per sq km.

   The republic lies in the upper reaches of the Ob River and its tributaries, the Biya and the Katun. It is adequately provided with water.

   The republic's mineral resources include lignite, marble (at the Orotai deposit), mercury (at Aktash), and gold (in the Choi District).

   The area has a strongly continental climate, with a mean temperature of −20°C in January and 20°C in July. The annual rainfall ranges widely from 800 to 1,500 mm, and the growing season is 160 days.

2. Specialization and Sectoral Structure of the Economy (see Exhibit 55.1). Administrative division: 10 districts, 1 city, 2 urban-type communities, and 86 village group-councils.

   Principal city: Gornoaltaisk.

   The manufacturing structure is dominated by textiles and leather (15%) and the food industry (41%). Manufacturing enterprises with a workforce of 100 to 500 are the footwear, curtain, and textile mills, and the small meat-packing and dairy enterprises located in Gornoaltaisk; the integrated mining and metal fabrication plant in the Aktash township (mercury); and the gold mine in the Setka township. (See Exhibit 55.2.)

   The republic exports 14% of its manufactured output, chiefly crops.

   The republic is a fringe area with a sparse population and predominance of farming. Animal farming forms the core of its economy. Most of the livestock are sheep, goats, and cattle, while other livestock specialties are the Altai breed of horses, yaks, Siberian stags, and spotted deer, in mountain steppe areas. Fur farming and bee-keeping are also practiced.

   Aside from animal farming, the rural population is employed at logging enterprises, centered in the republic's northeastern area, within reach of the Biya River. In addition to logs and lumber, the republic produces turpentine, rosin, and fir oil. Spotted deer and Siberian stags are grazed in the area. Favorable conditions exist for the wide-scale production of environmentally safe items.

Exhibit 55.1. Sectoral Structure of the Economy in 1996 (% of total)

	Industry	Farming	Transportation	Construction	Other
Employment	9.2	32.6	4.7	7.1	46.4
Fixed assets	7.0	19.8	5.3	25.5	42.4
Capital investment	5.5	21.1	4.8	0.1	68.5

Exhibit 55.2. Manufacture of Principal Industrial Products

	1995	1996
Meat (thou t)	2.1	1.01
Whole-milk products (thou. t)	1.0	6
Gold	259	

3. Investment Opportunities. Any assessment of investment opportunities in the republic is difficult. Initiating any high-return manufacturing projects is difficult because of the area's remoteness from the markets, limited transportation and telecommunications systems, and lack of an infrastructure and laborforce. Projects in agriculture would face problems as well, ranging from the production and processing of produce to marketing it. More likely investment opportunities are geological prospecting for and production of nonferrous and precious metals; small-scale projects to process rare kinds of vegetables and animal materials, including medicinal plants, honey, velvet antlers, and fresh and canned deer meat; construction of recreational facilities and a tourist infrastructure, provided a recreational and tourist center is established in region; and telecommunications systems.

In 1995, the region had 10 operating joint ventures. The foreign investments in 1993–95 totaled five thousand dollars. Private owners held 40.3% of the fixed assets of enterprises and organizations, joint stock companies (without foreign interest) had 9.2%, the federal authorities controlled 25.2%, and the republican government owned 17.7%. The republic's leading banks are Altaienergobank (Tel. 32 365), Gornoaltaibank (Tel. 31 949), Irbisbank (Tel. 31 990), Noosphere (Tel. 3 265), and Ulalubank (Tel. 5 765).

The republic is reachable from Moscow by rail (3,419 km to Barnaul, 63 hours from Kazan Terminal) and air (four hours from Domodedovo Airport, and then by the highway from Barnaul, via Biysk, to Gornoaltaisk).

There are 23 km of hard-surfaced roads per 1,000 sq km.

55.2 ALTAI KRAI (TERRITORY)

1. Natural Resources. Area: 169,100 sq km. Farmland: 110,400 sq km. Woodland: 37,700 sq km. Population: 2,686,400 (Jan. 1, 1996), of which 52.2% is urban and 47.8% is rural. Population density: 15.9 per sq km.

The krai lies 3,400 km from Moscow, in the drainage area of the Ob River and its tributaries, the Biya and the Katun. It is adequately provided with water. Its surface runoff is 53.5 cu km, and its total estimated commercial underground water resources are 39,600 cu km. per day. Nevertheless, the western areas of the Kulunda steppe are poorly supplied with surface water, and some areas have virtually no underground water for drinking.

The woodlands include 55,400 sq km. under federal control. The local forests contain 1,063.3 million cu m of timber, 810.6 million cu m of which is softwood. The krai's estimated cutting area is used at 49% capacity, and the commercial logging potential is 7 million cu m.

The area's mineral resources include iron ore, nonferrous and rare metals, common salt and Glauber's salt, soda, semiprecious stones, and building materials. The officially registered iron-ore reserves at the Beloretsk and Intinsk deposits are equal to 298 and 163 million tons, respectively, and prospects are good for the Kharlov and Kholzun deposits, which contain about five billion tons between them. More than 20 deposits of complex ores and mercury have been prepared for commercial development. Nearly 200 deposits of building materials are in operation, and no limitations exist on the expansion of building-material production. Chemical raw materials are produced on the salt lakes of Kuchuk, Great Yarovoe, and Burlin in the Kulunda steppe. The local radon springs (at Belokurikha) and curative muds (at Zavyalovo) are suitable for therapeutic purposes.

The krai has a strongly continental climate, with a mean temperature of −19°C in January and 19°C in July. The annual rainfall ranges from 50 to 25 mm (between 1,500 and 3,000 mm in mountainous areas), and the growing season lasts from 160 to 170 days.

2. Specialization and Sectoral Structure of the Economy (see Exhibit 55.3). Administrative division: 60 districts, 12 cities, 14 urban-type communities, and 719 village group-councils.

Administration Head: Tel. (3852) 22 6814. Fax: 22 8542.

Principal cities: Barnaul (661,400), Biysk (240,200), Rubtsovsk (172,200), and Novoaltaisk (67,800).

The manufacturing structure is dominated by engineering (26%), the chemical industry (11.3%), the food industry (18.1%), and power engineering (15.8%). The krai's manufacturing complex was formed largely to mine and process local resources and to meet the needs of the agricultural complex, the heat-supply programs, and consumer needs in the virgin lands of Siberia and Kazakstan. The biggest enterprises in Barnaul are the Khimvolokno industrial association (viscose and Kapron nylon fibers), the transport engineering industrial association (diesel engines), the Sibenergomash industrial association (steam boilers), the Altai Diesel JSC (diesel engines), the commercial rubber-goods plant, the tire plant, and the Altaimebel association; in Biysk, the largest manufacturers are the Sibpribor industrial association, the Biyskenergomash industrial association, and an oleum plant (cleansing agents, paints and varnishes, acetone, and perfumes); the Altaikoks JSC in Zarinski; the Altaivagon (railroad freight cars) in Novoaltaisk; the Altai Tractor Plant industrial association, the Engineering Plant industrial association, the tractor equipment plant, and the tractor spare-parts plant in Rubtsovsk; and the Altaikhimprom industrial association (enamels, organosilicon compounds, refrigerants, and

Exhibit 55.3. Sectoral Structure of the Economy in 1996 (% of total)

	Industry	Farming	Transportation	Construction	Other
Employment	25.5	22.8	6.9	6.6	38.2
Fixed assets	28.9	27.2	8.0	8.5	27.4
Capital investment	21.0	11.7	11.0	1.4	54.9

potassium perchlorate), and a radio equipment plant in Slavgorod. (See Exhibit 55.4.)

Some communities sprang up near the site of mineral source development, such as Stepnoe Ozero township, with the Kuchuksulfate industrial association (sodium sulfide, sodium bisulfate, cleansing agents) as its core; Zmeinogorsk, where complex ores are mined; the Kolyvan village, the site of a stone-cutting plant; and Gorniak, the hometown of the Altai integrated mining and dressing plant (lead, copper, and barite concentrates).

The krai exports 3% of its manufactured output.

The Altai Krai is one of the main food-producing regions in Siberia. The area encompassed by its farmlands and the volume of its harvested crops rank among Russia's top five agricultural regions. It is third or fourth in the gross output of farming produce, second or third in the production of cereals, including strong and hard wheat, first in milk output, and fifth in meat production. The krai also produces potatoes and other vegetables, sugar beets, sunflowers, and crown flax.

3. Investment Opportunities. The economy of the Altai Krai is experiencing problems typical of agro-industrial areas in Russia, in particular the lack of know-how in marketing farm produce, and the low output by major of machinery producers and consumer goods for rural areas, above all the tractor complex in Rubtsovsk. Added to these is the marketing crisis at major defense industry enterprises. Unlike the farming regions in the European part of Russia, the Altai Krai is close to areas with food shortages, a situation that improves its prospects for a rapid economic recovery. Accordingly, it may pay, in the long term, to invest in the processing marketing and delivery of farm produce to Siberia, and the Far East and Far North.

Other investment areas include small-scale projects to manufacture clothing, apartment furnishings, and auto services for the local market and for Siberian industrial cities; manufacture of ecologically clean products, medicines, and honey; construction of a recreational area and tourist center in the mountainous areas, including facilities for handling large numbers of foreign tourists; and communications systems and airport services in Barnaul.

Investment plans should allow for the inadequate transportation network, consumer service establishments, and the leisure industry. A further limitation is the low-level radioactive contamination from nuclear testing at the Semipalatinsk test site and at test sites in China.

In 1995, the region had 100 operating joint ventures. The foreign investments in 1993–95 totaled $28.9 million. Private owners held 35.9% of the fixed assets of en-

Exhibit 55.4.   Manufacture of Principal Industrial Products

	1995	1996
Railroad freight cars	1,314	1,629.4
Auto tires (thou)	763	1,495.3
Soft roofing materials (mil sq m)	27.5	16.8
Cotton fabrics (mil sq m)	17.9	12
Washing machines (thou)	32.3	17.1
Meat (thou t)	56.5	45.2
Whole-milk products (thou t)	94.6	99
Gold (kg)	44	

terprises and organizations, joint-stock companies (without foreign interest) owned 16.8%, and the federal authorities controlled 32.3%. The krai's leading banks are Agroprombank (Tel. 24 2495), Altaicreditprombank (Tel. 22 2390), Barnaul-bank (Tel. 24 4517), Biysk-bank (Biysk, Tel. 23 0496), Krips (Tel. 24 0960), and the Siberian Social Bank (Tel. 24 1321).

The krai is reachable from Moscow by rail (3,419 km to Barnaul, 63 hours from Kazan Terminal) and air (four hours from Domodedovo Airport).

There are 51 km of hard-surfaced roads per 1,000 sq km.

55.3 KEMEROVO OBLAST

1. Natural Resources. Area: 95,500 sq km. Farmland: 26,600 sq km. Woodland: 59,800 sq km. Population: 3,157,900 (Jan. 1, 1996), of which 87.2% is urban and 12.8% is rural. Population density: 33.1 per sq km.

   The oblast lies 3,200 km from Moscow. It is adequately supplied with water.

   The federal authorities control 48,000 sq km of the woodlands. The forests contain 597.7 million cu m of timber, including 358.6 million cu m of softwood. The oblast's estimated cutting area is used at 33% capacity, and the commercial logging potential is nine million cu m.

   The oblast's mineral resources include coal and lignite, iron ore, complex ores, nepheline, phosphate, and building materials. Coal reserves are concentrated in one of the world's largest fields, the Kuznetsk coal fields. Power and coking coals from Kuznetsk are delivered economically to nearly every corner of the country. In principle, it is possible to raise coal production by 50 to 100% from the present level.

   The oblast has a continental climate, with the mean temperature of $-20°C$ in January and $20°C$ in July. It's annual rainfall is 300 to 500 mm (900 mm in the mountains), and its growing season lasts from 137 to 160 days.

2. Specialization and Sectoral Structure of the Economy (see Exhibit 55.5). Administrative division: 19 districts, 20 cities, 47 urban-type communities, and 235 village group-councils.

   Administration Head: Tel. (3842) 26 4333. Fax: 25 5372.

   Principal cities: Kemerovo (560,800), Novokuznetsk (615,400), Prokopievsk (275,100), Belovo (174,400), and Leninsk-Kuznetsky (173,300).

   The manufacturing structure is dominated by the fuel industry (29.5%), the chemical industry (6.7%), and ferrous metallurgy (27.5%). The oblast's manufacturing complex is comprised of major coal-mining enterprises, metal fabrication plants, chemical-industry units, and related engineering enterprises that provide repair and maintenance services and manufacture mining equipment. Coal is mined at the following centers: Kemerovo (three mines, two strip mines, and the Oblkemerovougol complex), Anzhero-Sudzhensk (four mines), Belovo (six strip mines and seven mines), Berezovsky (one strip mine and four mines), Kisilevsk (two strip

Exhibit 55.5. Sectoral Structure of the Economy in 1996 (% of total)

	Industry	Farming	Transportation	Construction	Other
Employment	38.0	6.9	8.6	10.9	35.6
Fixed assets	57.5	9.8	13.0	2.9	16.8
Capital investment	51.8	3.4	8.0	2.2	34.6

mines and 10 mines), Leninsk-Kuznetsky (six mines), Mezhdurechensk (three strip mines and five mines), Novokuznetsk (four strip mines and 11 mines), Polysaevo (four mines), and Prokopievsk (two strip mines and 14 mines). The biggest metal fabrication enterprises are the coal-tar chemical plant in Kemerovo; the Kurako plant (rolled sections) in Gurievsk; the West Siberian integrated metal plant, the Kuznetsk integrated metal plant, the NKAZ JSC (aluminum), the Sibruda JSC, and the ferroalloy (ferrosilicium) plant in Novokuznetsk; iron-ore enterprises in Tashtagol; and a zinc plant in Belovo. The biggest chemical-industry enterprises are the Progress Industrial Association (nitro-enamels, solvents, and ether), the Azot Industrial Association (mineral fertilizers, caprolactam, and carbamide), the Khimprom Industrial Association (caustic soda and chlorozinc), the Khimvolokno JSC (polyamide and cord fabric), and the Tokem JSC (phenol-formaldehyde resins and fabric-based laminate) in Kemerovo; and a chemical pharmaceutical firm (aspirin, and levomycin) in Novokuznetsk. (See Exhibit 55.6.)

Large enterprises in other manufacturing industries include the engineering plant (mining equipment) in Anzhero-Sudzhensk; the Kuzbassradio plant (switching systems) in Belovo; the Chernykh engineering plant (railroad cars) in Kisilevsk; the worsted-cloth plant in Leninsk-Kuznetsky; the mining-equipment plant in Novokuznetsk; the Elektroshina JSC (DC machines), the china plant and the bearing plant in Prokopievsk; and the Engineering Plant industrial association (cranes and loaders) and the abrasive materials plant in Yurga.

The oblast exports 19.6% of its manufactured output, of which coal and ore account for 14%, chemical products for 6.6%, and metals for 7.9%.

The oblast lacks sufficient foodstuffs. Agriculture consists of truck farming, with a predominance of beef and dairy cattle raising and fowl keeping. The principal crops are cereals, potatoes, and other vegetables.

3. Investment Opportunities. Because the oblast is a monopolistic producer of power-generating and coking coals in Russia, it relies on steady sources of income to finance joint-venture projects. The marketing of coals and coke in areas west of the Volga River and their export are limited because of high transportation costs. This condition may be expected to improve only after the numerous mines operating at a loss in the Komi Republic and in the Perm, Chelyabinsk, Rostov, and Tula Oblasts have been closed; domestic fuel prices have been increased to match world levels. So far, however, these factors have been a drag on the profitability of coal mining and marketing, pushing investors toward to other industries.

Exhibit 55.6.   Manufacture of Principal Industrial Products

	1995	1996
Coal (mil t)	99.0	97
Rolled ferrous metals (mil t)	6.5	6
Wheeled cranes	184	90.2
Cement (thou t)	1,520	1,231.2
Heating radiators (thou kW)	230	172.5
Commercial timber (thou cu m)	504	443.5
Silk fabrics (mil sq m)	17.0	8.2
Meat (thou t)	13.4	8.3
Whole-milk products (thou t)	87.5	67.4
Gold (kg)	873	

The promising areas of investment include the modernization of coal-mining equipment to reduce production costs; coal preparation and transportation; major projects to develop small-capacity chemical industry facilities and the modernization of metal fabrication enterprises; production and marketing of nonferrous metals; the zinc plant in Belovo, the Salair mining and dressing plant (lead and zinc), the Barit strip mine in the Ursk township, and the Altai gold mine in the Spassk township; geological prospecting for complex-metal deposits, gold, and platinum; small-scale projects to produce consumer goods for the markets in Siberia (clothing, auto services, communications systems, apartment furnishings, and ferrous- and nonferrous-metal articles); recreational and amusement facilities for employees of the coal, metal, and chemical industries.

In 1995, the region had 96 operating joint ventures. The foreign investments in 1993–95 totaled $13.4 million. Private owners held 8% of the fixed assets of enterprises and organizations, joint stock companies (without foreign interest) owned 30.5%, and the federal authorities controlled 51.5%. The oblast's leading banks are Agroprombank (Tel. 26 5833), Vector (Kisilevsk, Tel. 62 333), Kuzbass (Tel. 23 6766), Kuzbassotsbank (Tel. 53 9577), Kuzbaprombank (Tel. 26 6243), Kuzbassugolbank (Tel. 52 3859), Kuzbasskhimbank (Tel. 25 7592), Loskus (Tel. 26 3293), and Nadezhda (Novokuznetsk, Tel. 44 6965).

The oblast is reachable from Moscow by rail (3,482 km to Kemerovo, 62 hours from Yaroslavl Terminal) and air (four hours from Vnukovo Airport).

There are 49 km of hard-surfaced roads per 1,000 sq km.

55.4 NOVOSIBIRSK OBLAST

1. Natural Resources. Area: 178,200 sq km. Farmland: 84,500 sq km. Woodland: 47,300 sq km. Swamps: 31,000 sq km. Population: 2,792,100 (Jan. 1, 1996), of which 74.3% is urban and 25.7% is rural. Population density: 15.7 per sq km.

   The oblast lies 3,100 km from Moscow in the eastern part of the West Siberian Plain. It is adequately provided with water resources.

   The woodlands include 25,500 sq km under federal control. They contain 434.6 million cu m of timber, including 117.3 million cu m of softwood. The oblast's estimated cutting area is at 72% capacity, and commercial logging operations have a potential of 3 million cu m.

   The oblast has only limited mineral resources, most of which are used locally, such as peat, coal, and building materials.

   The oblast has a strongly continental climate, with a mean temperature of −20°C in January and 20°C in July. Its annual rainfall ranges from 300 to 450 mm, and its growing season is between 144 and 163 days.

2. Specialization and Sectoral Structure of the Economy (see Exhibit 55.7). Administrative division: 30 districts, 14 cities, 19 urban-type communities, and 420 village group-councils.

   Administration Head: Tel. (3852) 23 2995. Fax: 23 5700.

   Principal cities: Novosibirsk (1,471,900), Iskitim (68,200), and Berdsk (80,400).

   The manufacturing structure is dominated by engineering (36.3%), nonferrous metallurgy (3.2%), power engineering (18.3%), and the food industry (16.3%). The Novosibirsk Oblast is one of the chief industrial and scientific centers in Siberia. It has 43 institutes of the Siberian branch of the Russian Academy of Sciences and the Russian Academy of Medical Sciences, more than 100 sectoral-research institutes,

Exhibit 55.7.   Sectoral Structure of the Economy in 1996 (% of total)

	Industry	Farming	Transportation	Construction	Other
Employment	25.2	13.0	9.2	11.3	41.3
Fixed assets	30.4	22.9	16.9	4.3	25.5
Capital investment	31.2	6.0	21.0	1.0	40.8

and many design and technology institutes. The oblast's manufacturing complex is based on the science-intensive sectors of the aerospace, electrical-engineering, electronics, and radio-engineering industries, which are largely based in Novosibirsk. The largest enterprises, with a workforce of 3,000 to more than 5,000 each, are the Aviation Industrial Association (producing AN–38 class aircraft), the Sibstanokelektroprivod Research and Development Association, the Kometa Industrial Association (microwave equipment), the Luch Industrial Association (radio engineering), the Sever Industrial Association, the Sibivt JSC (electric drives and computer technologies), the Aurora JSC (radio engineering), the Elektrosignal JSC (electronic units and radio stations), the Elektroagregat JSC (mobile-power plants), the Komintern plant (electronics), the high-voltage equipment plant (magnetic starters), the radio component plant (capacitors), the Ekran plant (picture tubes and Geiger counters), the capacitor plant (silver-zinc capacitors), the precision-engineering plant (radio electronics), the semiconductor plant, and the electronic-devices plant (cathode-ray and voltage-stabilizing tubes and microcircuits). Quality metal for engineering enterprises is supplied by Russia's largest integrated tin plant in Novosibirsk and the Kuzmin metal plant of the Spetsstal concern. Novosibirsk is also home to the Sibtextilemash plant (looms), the Farmatsia industrial association (pharmaceuticals), and the chemical-concentrates plant (lithium chloride, carbon dioxide, and chemical reagents). (See Exhibit 55.8.)

The enterprises located in other cities of the oblast are the Vega Industrial Association (radio industry), the electromechanical plant (display stations), and the biological preparation plant in Berdsk; the Ob Industrial Association, the Inskitimcement Industrial Association, and the electrode plant in Iskitim; and the chemical plant in Kuibyshev (sodium percarbonate, hydrogen peroxide, and acetone). The cities of Barabinsk, Bolotnoe, Kargat, Kupino, Tatarsk, Toguchin, and Cherepanovo are farm produce-processing centers.

The oblast exports 2% of its manufactured output, of which nonferrous-metal products account for 12%, chemical products for 33%, and machinery and equipment for 18%.

Farming consists of producing grain, potatoes and other vegetables, flax, and meat and dairy products.

Exhibit 55.8.   Manufacture of Principal Industrial Products

	1995	1996
Looms	750	330
Radio receivers (thou)	61.0	2.5
Meat (thou t)	48.0	47.9
Whole-milk products (thou t)	109	127.5

3. Investment Opportunities. The economic situation in the Novosibirsk Oblast is among the most complex in Russia. Unlike most other areas in Siberia, the oblast has virtually no mining enterprises, oil refineries, or chemical or woodworking facilities. Its economic power is based on one of the country's largest science-intensive engineering complexes, which has lost nearly 50% of its previous customers. This interferes with fund-raising, compelling the enterprises and the regional authorities to look for outside investors and federal subsidies. The oblast has for years been among Russia's worst performers in terms of the ratio of the population's income and the prices of the 19 food and consumer goods basket, a condition that undercuts the possibility of investment resources coming from the population's earnings.

It is unlikely that this situation will attract commercial investments. Because, it may remain unchanged for a considerable period of time, social tensions could increase and lead to a partial loss of the scientific and technological potential in the engineering industry.

Under current conditions, the oblast can probably absorb various programs financed by the federal budget and secure outside investors against loss. Most likely, such programs will be targeted at modernizing the existing engineering enterprises in order to continue to manufacture technological products.

Investment opportunities include projects to manufacture science-intensive products and communications services, including those involving small enterprises that have split off from larger organizations; expansion of the Novosibirsk airport and the city's communications system; manufacture of clothing, footwear, and foodstuffs for markets in Siberia and the Ural Region; manufacture of equipment for the oil and gas, mining, and timber industries; and production of tin-based metals. Support will be given to projects providing jobs for employees of defense enterprises that are converted to civilian output.

In 1995, the region had 186 operating joint ventures. The foreign investments in 1993–95 totaled $75.6 million. Private owners held 19.8% of the fixed assets of enterprises and organizations, joint stock companies (without foreign interest) held 16.2%, and the federal authorities controlled 41.3%. The oblast's leading banks are Agroprobank (Tel. 29 7739), Accept (Tel. 66 3861), Alemar (Tel. 21 4561), Aurum (Tel. 29 8762), Belonfinbank (Tel. 22 1237), Zapsibtransbank (Tel. 29 5820), Levoberezhny (Tel. 43 7457), the Novosibirsk Bank for Foreign Trade (Novosibirskvneshtorgbank, Tel. 22 0809), Prokom (Tel. 41 2911), the Russian Popular Bank (Tel. 77 3062), Sibakadembank (Tel. 39 7270), the Siberian Bank (Tel. 22 4646), the Siberian Trading Bank (Tel. 98 0200), the Siberian Accord (Tel. 66 1282), Sibholdingbank (Tel. 40 9647), Sibekobank (Tel. 76 3302), and Sikom (Tel. 66 3955).

The oblast is reachable from Moscow by rail (3,191 km to Novosibirsk, 63 hours from Yaroslavl Terminal) and air (three hours from Domodedovo Airport).

There are 46 km of hard-surfaced roads per 1,000 sq km.

55.5 OMSK OBLAST

1. Natural Resources. Area: 139,700 sq km. Farmland: 68,100 sq km. Woodland: 45,700 sq km. Swamps: 20,600 sq km. Population: 2,172,600 (Jan. 1, 1996), of which 67.5% is urban and 32.5% is rural. Population density: 15.6 per sq km.

The oblast lies 2,500 km from Moscow on the West Siberian Plain. It is adequately supplied with water.

The woodlands have an area of 43,800 sq km, 26,200 sq km of which are under federal control. The forests have 513.6 million cu m of timber, including 120.2 million cu m of softwood. The oblast's estimated cutting area is used at 26% capacity, and the commercial logging potential eight million cu m.

The oblast has only very limited mineral resources, which are chiefly building materials and peat.

The oblast has a continental climate, with a mean temperature of −20°C in January and 20°C in July. It has 300 to 400 mm of annual rainfall, and its growing season lasts from 153 to 162 days.

2. Specialization and Sectoral Structure of the Economy (see Exhibit 55.9). Administrative division: 32 districts, 6 cities, 24 urban-type communities, and 360 village group-councils.

Administration Head: Tel. (3812) 24 1415. Fax: 24 2372.

Principal cities: Omsk (1,182,500), Tara (26,400), and Isilkul (26,300).

The manufacturing structure is dominated by engineering (12.1%), the fuel industry (40.5%), food (11.1%), the chemical industry (10%), and electrical engineering (12.5%). All major and medium-sized manufacturing enterprises are located in Omsk. The city was established as a refining center to process oil produced in the Tyumen Oblast and as a support facility for aerospace programs, including those at Baikonur. The biggest oil-refining and petrochemical enterprises, each with a workforce of 3,000 to 5,000 or more, are the Omskshina industrial association, the Nefteorgsintez industrial association, the Omskkhimprom JSC (polystyrene, phthalic anhydride, and ethylene glycol), and the synthetic-rubber plant. In the engineering sector, the largest producers are the Irtysh industrial association, the Polyot industrial association (light-class rockets, AN-series aircraft, and commercial satellites), the Relero JSC (radio relay equipment), the Siberian instruments plant, the Kozitsky instrument plant, the Revolution Fighters Siberian Plant (tractor equipment), the Baranov engine Plant, and the Sibcryotekhnika Research and Development Enterprise (equipment to produce nitrogen and inert gases). (See Exhibit 55.10.)

Exhibit 55.9.   Sectoral Structure of the Economy in 1996 (% of total)

	Industry	Farming	Transportation	Construction	Other
Employment	22.7	18.9	8.0	8.4	42.0
Fixed assets	31.3	29.0	15.3	3.4	21.0
Capital investment	27.3	10.0	16.0	1.2	45.5

Exhibit 55.10.   Manufacture of Principal Industrial Products

	1995	1996
Primary oil refining products, million tons	16.4	15.4
Auto tires, thou.	933	1,072.9
Soft roofing materials, million sq. m.	23.8	23.8
Washing machines, thou.	133	93.1
Meat, thou. tons	64.1	57
Whole milk products, thou. tons	70.6	65

The oblast exports 10% of its manufacturing output, of which oil and oil products account for 28%, chemical products for 68%.

The Omsk Oblast produces a surplus of foodstuffs and has the potential to supply a farm produce to the northern areas of the Tyumen Oblast and the Krasnoyarsk Krai. The farming specialties are beef and dairy cattle raising, along with growing cereals, industrial crops, potatoes, and other vegetables. Fine-fleeced sheep are grazed in the oblast's southern areas. The rural population engages in fur trapping (squirrels, muskrats, and ermine).

3. Investment Opportunities. The oblast's economic situation has been worsened by the crisis at its defense-industry enterprises, which are largely operating below capacity and putting their workforce on a part-time basis. This fact limits the amount of investment that could have been provided by revenues collected from local oil-refining, chemical, and forest enterprises. In view of the reduction of the Russian space program and the limited growth opportunities of the export-oriented industries, this investment crisis may take a long time to resolve. Accordingly, investment capital will be needed in engineering enterprises to maintain their valuable potential and to maintain available scientific and engineering skills, knowledge and potential contracts. To these ends, investments can be made in major programs involving the Gazprom JSC and the vertically integrated oil companies and aluminum-industry associations. These outlays can also be utilized to produce licensed products for the oil and gas, power, and aluminum complexes in Siberia and to sell technologically based products in Latin America and the Middle East.

Other investment prospects include small-scale projects to produce foodstuffs and other consumer goods for Siberia's northern areas; development of telecommunications systems and airport infrastructures; and involvement in programs to modernize oil refinery and chemical-industry enterprises.

In 1995, the region had 110 operating joint ventures. The foreign investments in 1993–95 totaled $2.8 million. Private owners held 34% of the fixed assets of enterprises and organizations, joint stock companies (without foreign interest) owned 24.7%, and the federal authorities controlled 26.1%. The oblast's leading banks are Agroprombank (Tel. 23 1965), Investro (Tel. 25 5597), Omskcreditbank (Tel. 33 9531), Omsk-bank (Tel. 25 1496), Omtorbank (Tel. 31 5888), Promstroibank (Tel. 23 1603), Siberia (Tel. 25 17036), Sibes (Tel. 23 3466), and the Compatriots (Tel. 25 4757).

The oblast is reachable from Moscow by rail (2,555 km to Omsk, 42 hours from Yaroslavl Terminal) and air (3.5 hours from Domodedovo Airport).

There are 50 km of hard-surfaced roads per 1,000 sq km.

55.6 TOMSK OBLAST

1. Natural Resources. Area: 316,900 sq km. Farmland: 13,700 sq km. Woodland: 199,900 sq km. Swamps: 92,000 sq km. Population: 1,000,600 (Jan. 1, 1996), of which 62.1% is urban and 37.9% is rural. Population density: 3.2 per sq km.

The oblast lies 3,300 km from Moscow in the southeastern part of the West Siberian Plain. It is fully provided with water.

The oblast's woodlands occupy an area of 188,800 sq km, including 176,200 sq km under federal control. The forests contain 2,765.1 million cu m of timber, 1,578.4 million cu m of which is softwood. The estimated cutting area is used at 20% of capacity, and the commercial logging potential is 25 million cu m.

The area's mineral resources include oil, natural gas, and building materials.

The oblast has a continental climate, with a mean temperature of $-20°C$ in January and $17°C$ in July. The annual rainfall varies from 400 to 500 mm, and the growing season is 135 to 140 days.

2. Specialization and Sectoral Structure of the Economy (see Exhibit 55.11). Administrative division: 16 districts, 5 cities, 2 urban-type communities, and 217 village group-councils.

Administration Head: Tel. (3822) 22 3686. Fax: 22 4884.

Principal cities: Tomsk (506,500), Strezhevoi (44,100), Asino (33,400), and Kolpashevo (31,500).

The manufacturing structure is dominated by engineering (10.1%), the fuel industry (29.5%), lumbering and woodworking (3.9%), and the food industry (7.7%). The engineering industries are centered in Tomsk, in which the major enterprises are the Sibelektromotor industrial association (electric motors), the Kontur industrial association (computers), Bearing Plant 5 JSC, and an electrical-engineering plant, as well as smaller enterprises, with a workforce of about 1,000 each, producing drills, cables, winding wire, noise meters, and electric lightbulbs. Oil is chiefly produced at Strezhevoi. The potential volume of the local oilfields is between 10 and 12 million tons, provided adequate investments are made in geological prospecting and equipment. The oblast contains a number of chemical and petrochemical enterprises (the Tomsk petrochemical plant and a large rubber-footwear plant). The economic life of the majority of the oblast's towns is built around the forest industry, including the Tomsklesprom industrial association in Tomsk, the Askom JSC in Asino, the Kargas integrated timber plant in the Kangasok township, the Togur timber plant in Kolpashevo, and the timber plant in the Mogochino township. A pulp and paper mill is under construction in Asino. (See Exhibit 55.12.)

The oblast exports 14.6% of its manufactured output, most of which is oil and oil products (35%) and chemicals (58%).

The oblast is short of foodstuffs. Local farming specializes in beef and dairy cattle and has limited possibility for expansion because of the area's physical and cli-

Exhibit 55.11.   Sectoral Structure of the Economy in 1995 (% of total)

	Industry	Farming	Transport	Construction	Other
Employment	25.1	9.5	9.5	13.1	42.8
Fixed Assets	49.6	8.4	9.9	3.7	28.4
Capital Investment	45.7	4.2	10.1	0.5	39.5

Exhibit 55.12.   Manufacture of Principal Industrial Products

	1995	1996
Oil, million tons	6.7	6.7
Lumber, thou. cu. m.	1,286	1,131.7
Wood fiberboard, million s.q.m.	408	306
Tape records, thou.	2.7	0.19
Meat, thou. tons	5.7	1.3
Whole milk products, thou. tons	8.2	4.6
Commercial timber, thou. cu. m.	36.1	32.9

matic conditions. Other specialties include fur trapping (squirrel, ermine, and sable) and fur farming.

3. Investment Opportunities. The administration, the oil and gas producers, and the petrochemical and woodworking enterprises have reliable sources of local revenue that can be invested in joint ventures with foreign firms. The key prospects for investment are geological prospecting and equipment for oil and gas fields in the oblast's northern areas; modernization of petrochemical enterprises; construction of new facilities and modernization of enterprises engaged in logging and processing of timber into lumber, paper, cardboard, furfural, and yeast; small-size enterprises producing clothing, wallpaper, and insulation; and production and repair of equipment for the forest industry and motor vehicles.

In 1995, the region had 95 operating joint ventures. The foreign investments in 1993–95 totaled $126 million. Private owners held 11.1% of the fixed assets of enterprises and organizations, joint stock companies (without foreign interest) owned 40.5%, federal authorities controlled 32.3%, and foreign firms held 1.1%. The oblast's leading banks are the Popular Joint-Stock Bank (Tel. 23 2591), Geolbank (Kolpashevo, Tel. 63 6420), Dvizhenie (Tel. 44 3126), Roscommunbank (Tel. 23 1772), Tomsksotsbank (Tel. 22 2674), and Tom (Tel. 75 1575).

The oblast is reachable from Moscow by rail (3,500 km to Tomsk, 57 hours travel time from Yaroslavl Terminal) and air (four hours from Domodedovo Airport).

There are 8.6 km of hard-surfaced roads per 1,000 sq km in the oblast.

55.7 TYUMEN OBLAST, KHANTY-MANSI, AND YAMAL-NENETS AUTONOMOUS OKRUGS (AREAS)

1. Natural Resources. Area: 1,435,200 sq km. Farmland: 41,100 sq km. Woodland: 401,000 sq km. Swamps: 256,000 sq km. Bodies of water: 170,000 sq km. Population: 3,130,200 (Jan. 1, 1996), of which 76.1% are urban and 23.9% are rural. Population density: 2.2 per sq km.

The region lies on the West Siberian Plain and stretches from south to north. Its southern areas are in the forest-steppe zone; the Khanty-Mansi Autonomous Okrug occupies the central portion with vast areas of taiga; and the Yamal-Nenets Autonomous Okrug is lies within the forest-tundra area, which looks on to the Kara Sea. No restrictions are placed on water use in the entire region.

The federal authorities control 505,900 sq km of woodlands. The forests contain 5,422.8 million cu m of timber, including 4,236.3 million cu m of softwood. The region's estimated cutting area is used at 30% of capacity, and the commercial logging potential is 45 million cu m.

The local mineral resources include oil, natural gas, lignite, iron ore, building materials, dolomite, sand, and mineral springs. The region contains one of the world's richest concentrations of oil and gas. The largest oilfields are located at Samotlor, Ust-Balyk, Fedorov, Pravdinsk, Mamontovo, Solkino, Agansk, Variegan, Pokachevo, Kholmogorskoe, Povkhovskoe, and Em-Egovskoe; the best-known gas fields are at Urengoi, Medvezhie, Yamburg, Vyngapur, Kharasavel, and Bovanenkovo. The region produces 70% of Russia's oil and 90% of its gas.

The region has a continental climate, with a mean temperature of $-30°C$ ($-18°C$ in its southern parts) in January, and 4°C (19°C in the south) in July. The annual rainfall varies between 220 and 580 mm, and the growing season is from 155 to 160 days (115 days in the Khanty-Mansi Autonomous Okrug).

2. Specialization and Sectoral Structure of the Economy (see Exhibit 55.13). Administrative division: 38 districts, 26 cities, 44 urban-type communities, and 424 village group-councils.

Administration Head: Tel. (3452) 26 5180.

Principal cities: Tyumen (540,100), Nizhnevartovsk (246,000), Tobolsk (113,700), Nefteyugansk (95,300), Ishim (66,400), and Surgut (222,800).

The manufacturing structure is dominated by the fuel industry (78.8%). The key oil- and gas-producing centers are strung along the Ob River in the region's north, at the towns of Kogalym, Nefteyugansk, Pyt-Yakh, Langepas, Megion, Nyagan, Raduzhny, Surgut, Urai, Nadym, Novy Urengoi, and Noyabrsky, and at the Gubkinsky township. The towns also serve as headquarters for the oil and gas authorities, and as sites of gas-processing plants, oil-producing enterprises with foreign participation, the Surgut thermal-power plant, and small businesses producing fish, meat, dairy products, and building materials for consumers and the economic infrastructure. Tyumen has several enterprises employing about 1,000 employees each supplying the region's enterprises with oil- and gas-producing equipment, repair services, metal structures, and temporary houses. Tyumen also produces machinery for southern Siberia's farming areas through such enterprises as the engine-manufacturing association, a storage battery plant, and an automotive equipment plant. A major integrated petrochemical plant is located in Tobolsk. (See Exhibit 55.14.)

The region exports 14% of its output, mainly oil and natural gas. The actual figure may be much bigger, as some export activities are conducted by companies registered elsewhere.

Farming is concentrated in the region's southern part, which specializes in beef and dairy cattle raising. In the north, reindeer farms are run by members of the northern ethnic minority groups, and there are fishing operations as well. The population here also engages in fur trapping and farming.

Exhibit 55.13.   Sectoral Structure of the Economy in 1995 (% of total)

	Industry	Farming	Transport	Construction	Other
Employment	17.3	8.7	14.3	19.8	39.9
Fixed Assets	63.4	1.8	23.5	2.6	8.7
Capital Investment	66.7	1.1	9.2	1.4	21.6

Exhibit 55.14.   Manufacture of Principal Industrial Products

	Tyumen Oblast		Khanty-Mansi Okrug		Yamal Nenets Okrug	
	1995	1996	1995	1996	1995	1996
Oil, million tons	202	196	166	161	35.3	33.5
Natural gas, bn cu.m.	545	550	17.4	17.7	527	532
Power, bn kWh	61.5	60.9	51.5	51.3	0.15	0.16
Commercial timber, thou. cu.m.	2,647	2,038	2,300	1,794	15.7	11.3
Lumber, thou. cu. m.	635	931	486	403	14.7	11.6
Meat, thou. tons	37.8	38.2	n/a	n/a	2.0	2.6
Whole milk products, thou. tons	102	101.3	32.3	30.3	13.0	12.8

3. Investment Opportunities. The oil and gas fields in the Tyumen Oblast supply the bulk of Russia's hard-currency revenues, which allow domestic relative fuel prices to be kept low and subsidies to be issued to the majority of the country's areas. Because the causes behind the poor performance of a significant part of Russia's economy are not likely to be resolved, the gap between domestic and world fuel prices is very likely to persist for a long time. This makes the region's oil and gas industries particularly attractive to foreign investors seeking a foothold in Russia. The main areas of investment in the oil and gas industries are geological prospecting, renovation of closed wells, increase of oil-bed yields, and development of new fields. At present, between 12,000 and 15,000 oil wells are idle in northern West Siberia. So far, the Russian government has earmarked hard currency to recondition only 3,500 idle wells, leaving the remainder to willing foreign investors. It is possible to recover an additional 20 to 30 million tons of oil over a five-year period by applying the latest bed-treatment techniques. No discoveries of major oil-rich fields are expected, and only medium-sized and small deposits will be drawn into production. The biggest projects with possible foreign involvement include the oil and gas fields at Surgut, Megion, Vakh, Salyn, and elsewhere.

The best prospects in gas production are associated with the Yamal-Nenets Autonomous Okrug, which contains 36 trillion cm m of natural gas, or 70% of Russia's total gas wealth. The principal gas-producing areas are located at Nadym-Pur-Taz (18 trillion cu m), Yamal (nine trillion cu m), and Gydan. These gas fields are developed by the Surgutgazprom (Vyngapur), Nadymgazprom (Medvezhie and Yubileinoe), and Yamburggazdobycha (Yamburg) authorities. Depending on the world market situation and government decisions about the structure of the country's fuel and power balance, gas production may reach 680 to 770 billion cu m by the year 2000. As expected, a credit of $8.7 billion will be used to develop the gas industry on the Yamal Peninsula. The amount will be allocated as follows: $2.1 billion for the development of new fields on Yamal and in the Nadym-Pur-Taz area; $4.1 billion for the construction of a pipeline to export the gas; and $1 billion for the modernization and replacement of equipment for Russia's Integrated Gas Supply System.

To process crude oil and gas, participation is invited in the programs to modernize the petrochemical complex in Tobolsk, specifically the utilization of wellhead gas that is currently burned in flares, and to construct small, modular oil-refining units in the oil- and gas-producing areas of the Ob region.

Because enterprises of the Tyumen Oblast's oil and gas complex will, in the short term, be key partners willing to contribute to major joint ventures, investment plans should consider the possibility of such ventures being launched with these enterprises in Russia and abroad.

Smaller projects include producing consumer goods for the Siberian market, manufacturing equipment, and performing repair and building services for enterprises of the oil and gas complex.

In 1995, the region had 140 operating joint ventures. The foreign investments in 1993–95 totaled $273.4 million. Private owners held 10.1% of the fixed assets of enterprises and organizations, joint-stock companies (without foreign interest) owned 48.8%, and the federal authorities controlled 33.2%. The region's leading banks are Avantazh (Tel. 22 8923), Agroprombank (Tel. 26 1196), Akkobank (Surgut, Tel. 24 8312), Alliance (Nizhnevartovsk, Tel. 22 1758), the Yamal Bank (Nadym, Tel. 42 446), the Revival and Development of Northern Peoples (Khanty-Mansi, Tel. 40 067), the East European Siberian Bank (Nizhnevartovsk, Tel. 23

0366), Druzhba (Tel. 26 1662), Zapsibcombank (Tel. 24 0984), Kapital (Nizhnevartovsk, Tel. 23 5248), Kogalym (Kogalym, Tel. 22 590), Langepas (Langepas, Tel. 31 410), Lukoilsibbank (Tel. 24 3859), Monolir (Nizhnevartovsk, Tel. 27 3225), Nkib (Nizhnevartovsk, Tel. 22 0449), Noyabrsky (Noyabrsk, Tel. 42 076), Priobye (Nizhnevartovsk, Tel. 27 1531), Pripolyarny (Novy Urengoi, Tel. 32 135), Severcombank (Tel. 22 8352), the Siberian Oil Bank (Tel. 24 2998), Surgutneftegazbank (Surgut, Tel. 33 4938), Tura (Tel. 26 2997), the Tyumen Credit Bank (Tel. 24 5950), Tyumen-Hermes (Tel. 26 4085), Tyumenprofbank (Tel. 26 1336), Yuganskneftebank (Nefteyugansk, Tel. 23 034), and Yamal-bank (Labytnangi, Tel. 31 056).

The region is reachable from Moscow by rail (2,144 km to Tyumen, 34 hours from Yaroslavl Terminal) and air (3.5 hours from Domodedovo Airport).

There are 3.2 km of hard-surfaced roads in the region per 1,000 sq km.

CHAPTER 56

EAST SIBERIA REGION

Aleko A. Adamescu, Yuri A. Kovalev,
and Alexander G. Granberg

56.1 BURYAT REPUBLIC

1. Natural Resources. Area: 351,300 sq km. Farmland: 31,500 sq km. Woodland: 232,000 sq km. Bodies of water: 27,000 sq km. Population: 1,052,800 (Jan. 1, 1996), of which 59.2% is urban and 40.8% is rural. Population density: 3 per sq km.

   The republic lies in the southern part of East Siberia. It is adequately supplied with water. Some of its areas, however, do not have underground water that is sufficient for the area, and the uses of surface water are restricted to protect waters in the drainage area of Lake Baikal.

   The woodlands include 215,000 sq km under federal control. The local forests contain 2,141.1 million cu m of timber, including 1,946.8 million cu m of softwood. The republic's estimated cutting area is used at 45% of capacity, and the commercial logging potential is 12 million cu m.

   The mineral resources include tungsten, molybdenum, gold, complex metals, coal, lignite, asbestos, apatite, and quartz sandstone. The major deposits are Judinskoe (tungsten and molybdenum), Ozernoe and Kholodninskoe (complex metals), Oshchurkovskoe (apatite), Molodezhnoe (asbestos), and Cheremshanskoe (quartz sand).

   The republic has a strongly continental climate, with a mean temperature of $-25°C$ in January and $18°C$ in July. The annual rainfall ranges from 250 to 300 mm (450 mm in the mountains), and the growing season lasts from 120 to 160 days.

2. Specialization and Sectoral Structure of the Economy (see Exhibit 56.1). Administrative division: 21 districts, 6 cities, 29 urban-type communities, and 219 village group-councils.

   Administration Head: Tel. (30122) 24 563. Fax 20 251.

   Principal cities: Ulan-Ude (359,000), Gusinoozersk (30,200), and Severobaikalsk (29,500).

   The manufacturing structure is dominated by engineering (17.3%), lumbering and woodworking (7.5%), the food industry (13.8%), and power engineering (32.1%). The Buryat Republic and Federation members east of it have undergone recent economic development particularly the establishment of operations for mining ores, diamonds, and gold. The settlement pattern here is, therefore, formed by communities and small townships clustered around mines and enterprises strung along mountain valleys. The largest populated center is Ulan-Ude, whose economic

Exhibit 56.1.   Sectoral Structure of the Economy in 1995 (% of total)

	Industry	Farming	Transport	Construction	Other
Employment	21.8	16.7	9.0	9.1	43.4
Fixed Assets	22.9	10.3	44.3	3.4	19.1
Capital Investment	31.4	4.8	22.8	0.5	40.5

framework is based on enterprises of the food industry, textiles and leather, and construction, all of which supply the needs of the republic's population. Another important part of the economy is a number of engineering plants employing a workforce exceeding 1,000 each, in particular the Termopribor JSC, the Ulan-Udestalmost JSC, the Elektromashina JSC (electric motors), the locomotive and railroad-car repair plant, and the glass plant. Minerals are mined at the Malovsk-Uskaninsk township (gold), the Osokino Kliuchi village (coal strip mine), Znamensk, the site of the Jidokombinat plant (tungsten), the Sagan-Nur township (Tugnui strip coal mine), the Khoronkhoi township (Kyakhta fluorospar plant), and Gusinoozersk, the site of the Kholboljin strip mine supplying coal to the republic's largest thermal-power plant. Major logging enterprises are headquartered in the townships of Onkhoi, Novoilyinsk, and Chelutai; and a pulp and board mill, and enterprises manufacturing cement and asbestos-cement products are located in the city of Selenginsk. (See Exhibit 56.2.)

The republic exports 6% of its manufacturing output, with raw materials accounting for 24% of this, lumber for 39%, and metals for 13%.

The area is short of foodstuffs, with the rural population engaged in labor-intensive operations at mines, logging projects, and ancillary operations. Farming specializes in meeting local demands for meat, dairy products, potatoes, keeping sheep and goats, and breeding horses.

3. Investment Opportunities. The republic is a Buddhist area, a factor that gives local enterprises favorable exporting opportunities in the Asia-Pacific region. The situation in the area is further stabilized by the fact that Russians comprise 70% of the population (Buriats comprise 25%).

High-return projects can be initiated in the following areas: geological prospecting for and mining of minerals, including the program to develop the Ozerny ore deposit and the Molodezhny asbestos deposit; expansion of coal mining at the Gusinoozersk and Tugnui strip mines, modernization and expansion of the Jidin plant and the Kyakhta mine; production of consumer goods for markets in Transbaikalia,

Exhibit 56.2.   Manufacture of Principal Industrial Products

	1995	1996
Tractor trailers	620	n/a
Asbestos board, million standard tiles	50.6	46.6
Commercial timber, thou. cu. m.	623	616.8
Electric teapots, thou.	40.2	25.3
Meat, thou. tons	6.9	4
Whole milk products, thou. tons	10.4	11.3
Gold, kgs	4,293	

Siberia, and the Far East, and manufacture of goods with local ethnic motifs for export; reequipment of saw mills and increased production of output for Asian countries (China, Mongolia, and Kazakstaan); telecommunications systems; and modernization of the Ulan-Ude airport.

Investment plans should take into account the growing restrictions on economic activities in the Lake Baikal area, in particular the transfer of logging operations to areas beyond the lake's drainage area, the inadequate transportation network and the domestic and telecommunications service infrastructures, and the shortage of building materials and difficulties of transporting them to many areas in the republic.

In 1995, the region had 62 operating joint ventures. The foreign investments in 1993–95 totaled $2.3 million. Private owners held 11.9% of the fixed assets of enterprises and organizations; joint stock companies (without foreign interest) owned 18.5%, the federal authorities controlled 50.5%, and the republican government had 12.3% under its control. The leading banks in the area are Agroprombank (Tel. 25 260), Baikalbank (Tel. 26 495), Bicombank (Tel. 42 025), Buriataviabank (Tel. 31 507), the Buriatian Bank (Tel. 29 513), and Oktyabrsky (Tel. 31 790).

The republic is reachable from Moscow by rail (5,532 km to Ulan-Ude, 100 hours from Yaroslavl Terminal) and air (seven hours from Domodedovo Airport).

There are 17 km of hard-surfaced roads per 1,000 sq km.

56.2 KHAKASSIAN REPUBLIC

1. **Natural Resources.** Area: 61,900 sq km. Farmland: 19,100 sq km. Woodland: 33,100 sq km. Other lands: 6,900 sq km. Population: 584,000 (Jan. 1, 1996), of which 72.3% is urban and 27.7% is rural. Population density: 9.4 per sq km.

   The republic lies in the extreme south of East Siberia and is adequately supplied with water.

   The mineral resources in Khakassia are coal (at Chernogorsk), nonferrous metals (copper and molybdenum), and iron ore.

   The republic has a strongly continental climate, with a mean temperature of −20°C January and 21°C in July. It gets 400 to 800 mm of annual rainfall and has a growing season of 150 to 170 days.

2. **Specialization and Sectoral Structure of the Economy** (see Exhibit 56.3). Administrative division: 8 districts, 5 cities, 17 urban-type communities, and 73 village group-councils.

   Chairman of the Council of Ministers: Tel. 63 322. Fax: 65 096.

   Principal cities: Abakan (156,600), Sayanogorsk, and Chernogorsk.

   The manufacturing structure is dominated by nonferrous metallurgy (45.3%) and power engineering (17.2%). The republic's enterprises are concentrated in the manufacturing complex of the Krasnoyarsk Krai. The Sayany Aluminum Plant produces internationally competitive product, taking advantage of the inexpensive

Exhibit 56.3.   Sectoral Structure of the Economy in 1995

	Industry	Farming	Transport	Construction	Other
Employment	29.7	13.4	8.2	10.9	37.8
Fixed Assets	57.5	12.8	9.4	7.3	13.0
Capital Investment	53.0	5.3	5.4	1.1	35.2

power generated by the Sayany-Shushenskaya power dam at Sayanogorsk. Raw materials are mined in the Bely Yar village and the city of Chernogorsk (coal), Vershina Tei township and the town of Abaza (iron ore), Sayanogorsk (marble), Sorsk (molybdenum and copper), and the Shira township (gold and silver). (See Exhibit 56.4.)

The republic exports 19% of its manufactured output, most of which (84%) is aluminum products.

The republic is short of foodstuffs. It has fertile fields and livestock-grazing pastures, where long-term commercial farming operations can be launched, but it lacks food-processing facilities.

3. Investment Opportunities. The principal investment areas include geological prospecting, mining, and production of nonferrous metals (molybdenum, gold, silver, and copper) and aluminum (at the Sayany aluminum plant); production of consumer goods for markets in Siberia, the Far East, and Kazakstan at existing textile and leather facilities, including the Sayany footwear factory and the textile plant in Abakan, and the integrated artificial-leather plant, the Syntex JSC, and the wool-preprocessing plant in Chernogorsk; and manufacture of equipment for woodworking and logging operations at the Lesmash pilot-machinery plant in Abakan.

In 1995, the region had eight operating joint ventures. The foreign investments in 1993–95 totaled $1.3 million. Private owners held 27.9% of the fixed assets of enterprises and organizations, joint-stock companies (without foreign interest) owned 46.8%, the federal authorities controlled 10.7%, and the republican government had 11.4% under its control. The leading banks include Abakaninvestbank (Tel. 54 898), Agroprombank (Tel. 62 250), Monolitbank (Tel. 91 448), Sayany (Tel. 62 598), and Solbank (Tel. 91 839).

The republic is reachable from Moscow by rail (4,050 km to Abakan, 80 hours from Yaroslavl Terminal) and air (five hours from Domodedovo Airport).

There are 30 km of hard-surfaced roads per 1,000 sq km.

56.3 TYVA REPUBLIC

1. Natural Resources. Area: 170,500 sq km. Farmland: 39,800 sq km. Woodland: 83,200 sq km. Other lands: 22,600 sq km. Population: 306,300 (Jan. 1, 1996), of which 48% is urban and 52% is rural. Population density: 1.8 per sq km.

The Tyva Republic lies in the extreme south of East Siberia. It has a mountainous terrain, in which extensive valleys alternate with towering ranges.

The woodlands contain 1,115.7 million cu m of timber, including 1,085.5 million cu m of softwood. The republic's estimated cutting area is used at 15% of capacity, and the commercial logging potential is two million cu m.

Exhibit 56.4.   Manufacture of Principal Industrial Products

	1995	1996
Coal, thou. tons	7,000	6,090
Woolen fabrics, thou. sq. m.	2,294	1,652
Meat, thou. tons	13.1	9.6
Whole milk products, thou. tons	13.6	15.6
Gold, kgs	1,343	n/a

The area's mineral resources include nonferrous metals, asbestos, coal, and chemical raw materials. The biggest deposits are at Bayankol, Ulug Tenzek, and Khovu-Aksy (coal), Ak-Dovuzak (asbestos), Kaa-Khem, Chadan, and Mezheregei (coal), and Khairek (chemical raw materials).

The republic has a strongly continental climate, with a mean temperature of $-30°C$ in January and 25°C in July. The annual rainfall varies between 160 and 180 mm (500 to 800 mm in the mountains), and the growing season is between 160 and 180 days.

2. Specialization and Sectoral Structure of the Economy (see Exhibit 56.5). Administrative division: 16 districts, 5 cities, 3 urban-type communities, and 96 village group-councils. Chairman of the Supreme Council: Tel. (39422) 37 300. Fax: 20 251.

President: Tel. 37 300. Fax: 36 948.

Principal cities: Kyzyl (87,500), Ak-Dovurak (15,400), and Shagonar (10,300).

The manufacturing structure is dominated by nonferrous metallurgy (17.7%), the building materials industry (6.7%), and the food industry (25.8%). The leading enterprises are the Tyvazoloto gold-mining enterprise and small businesses in the food, garment, and construction industries in Kyzyl, the Tyvaasbest integrated plant in Ak-Dovurak, the strip coal mine in the Kaa-Khem township, and the Tyvacobalt integrated plant in the Khovu-Aksy township. (See Exhibit 56.6.)

The republic exports 7% of its manufactured output, mainly asbestos and leather goods.

Farming is the main activity of the rural population, particularly raising goats, horses, and yaks, a situation that is typical of Asian steppe regions. Cereals and fodder crops are grown as well. Farming produce is processed in limited quantities. Most sheep wool, goat down, mutton, hides, and strong and hard wheats are processed outside the republic.

3. Investment Opportunities. The republic is populated mostly by native Tyvinians, who account for 64.3% of the total, with Russians comprising 32%. In 1992 and 1993, ethnic tensions in Tyva were running high, and even today some of the clauses of the local constitution are at variance with the Russian Constitution. Generally, however, the situation has stabilized.

Exhibit 56.5.   Sectoral Structure of the Economy in 1995 (% of total)

	Industry	Farming	Transport	Construction	Other
Employment	8.9	26.9	5.0	6.2	53.0
Fixed Assets	16.1	22.0	23.1	2.1	36.7
Capital Investment	20.4	18.2	9.2	2.1	50.1

Exhibit 56.6.   Manufacture of Principal Industrial Products

	1995	1996
Asbestos (Groups 0–6), thou. tons	12.4	n/a
Meat, thou. tons	1.4	0.85
Whole milk products, thou. tons	3.2	1.6
Gold, kgs	775	n/a

Assessing the investment climate in the republic is difficult. Possible areas for capital input are geological prospecting, mining of asbestos and complex ores, small-scale projects to process local produce, hides, and goat down. These projects would, however, require major outlays for shipping products out of the republic, developing the infrastructure, and recruiting skilled labor.

In 1995, the region had no operating joint ventures. The foreign investments in 1993–95 totaled $700,000. Private owners held 4.8% of the fixed assets of enterprises and organizations, joint stock companies (without foreign interest) owned 3.4%, the federal authorities controlled 26%, and the republican government had control over 41.2%. The leading banks in the area are Agroprombank (Tel. 24 063), the Siberian Credit Bank (Tel. 37 114), Tyvacredit (Tel. 21 650), and Tyvasotsbank (Tel. 33 779).

The republic cannot be reached from Moscow by rail (4,668 km to Kyzyl), but there is air service to its main city (eight hours from Domodedovo Airport).

There are 16 km of hard-surfaced roads per 1,000 sq km.

56.4 KRASNOYARSK KRAI (TERRITORY)

1. Natural Resources. Area: 2,339,700 sq km. Farmland: 55,300 sq km. Woodland: 1,150,900 sq km. Bodies of water: 79,500 sq km. Swamps: 86,00 sq km. Reindeer-grazing lands: 417,000 sq km. Other lands: 588,600 sq km. Population: 3,028,500 (Jan. 1, 1996), of which 72.3% is urban and 27.7% is rural. Population density: 1.3 per sq km.

   The Krasnoyarsk Krai lies in the central part of Siberia. Its southern borders extend close to the steppes of Mongolia, and its northern areas are covered by forest tundra, opening to the Arctic seas. The krai is adequately provided with water resources and has enough water power for a chain of major power dams to be built.

   The woodlands contain 14,370.1 million cu m of timber, including 12,557.7 million cu m of softwood. The krai's estimated cutting area is used at 30% of capacity, and the commercial logging potential is 66 million cu m.

   The area's mineral resources include coal, oil and natural gas, iron ore, nonferrous and rare metals, common salt, and phosphorite. The largest fields and deposits are Kansk-Achinsk, Minusinsk, and Taimyr (coal); Tei and Irbinsk (iron ore); Norilsk (copper, nickel, and cobalt), and Gorevsk (lead and zinc). The Kansk-Achinsk coal and lignite basin is famous for its coal beds extending from near the surface to a depth of 90 m. The basin is Russia's chief standby source of coal. At present, the strip mine at Borodino is the only one in operation here. Programs are progressing to develop the Gorevsk-complex ore mine and to prospect for oil and gas in the Evenki Autonomous Okrug.

   The krai has a strongly continental climate, with a mean temperature of $-30°C$ in the north and $-18°C$ in the south in January, and 13°C and 20°C, respectively, in July. The annual rainfall varies from 200 to 500 mm, and the growing season lasts 140 to 150 days (in the southern areas).

2. Specialization and Sectoral Structure of the Economy (see Exhibit 56.7). Administrative division: 48 districts, 23 cities, 43 urban-type communities, and 510 village group-councils.

   Administration Head: Tel. (3912) 22 2263. Fax: 22 1178.

   Principal cities: Krasnoyarsk (921,900), Norilsk (267,300), Abakan (156,600), Achinsk (12,300), Kansk (109,500), and Lesosibirsk (82,800).

Exhibit 56.7. Sectoral Structure of the Economy in 1995 (% of total)

	Industry	Farming	Transport	Construction	Other
Employment	29.8	9.7	8.2	10.7	41.6
Fixed Assets	56.3	8.7	8.5	8.4	18.1
Capital Investment	43.7	4.7	8.9	2.9	39.8

The manufacturing structure is dominated by nonferrous metallurgy (46.9%), engineering (8.5%), the fuel industry (6.7%), and power generation (9.5%). The krai has two well-defined economic sectors, whose enterprises are competitive in the world market despite the high costs of shipping raw materials and finished products. Its power dams at Krasnoyarsk and Sayany-Shushenskoe and thermal-power plants at Nazarovo and Berezovo generate the world's cheapest power, which can be used to manufacture aluminum and chemical products for the world market. At present, this possibility is being made a reality by a group of aluminum plants in the krai (the aluminum and metal fabrication plants in Krasnoyarsk and the aluminum plant in Achinsk), which process imported aluminum under toll agreements. Krasnoyarsk has a forward-looking group of chemical industry facilities, in particular the Khimvolokno Industrial Association (chemical fibers and cord fabric), the Sibvolokno Industrial Association (chemical fibers), the commercial-rubber goods plant, and the tire plant. An oil refinery is located in Achinsk.

The krai's forest complex can supply the world market with low-cost products from extensive tracts of high-quality coniferous timber. The leading enterprises are the pulp and paper mill in Krasnoyarsk, the Krasnoyarskkhimles Association at the Boguchany station, the Yeniseiskles JSC in Yeniseisk, the Kansk Forest Association in Kansk, and four saw-milling and woodworking plants in Lesosibirsk.

A third powerful economic sector is composed of science-intensive, operations, most of which are engineering oriented. Such enterprises, each with a workforce of 3,000 to 5,000 or more, include the Grain Harvesters Industrial Association, the Iskra Industrial Association (transformers), the Radio Engineering Industrial Association, the Siberian Heavy Engineering Plant (overhead cranes and mining equipment), the integrated mining and chemical plant, the Yenisei chemical plant, the refrigerator plant (producing Biriusa refrigerators), and the Sibelektrostal plant in Krasnoyarsk; the low-voltage equipment plant in Divnogorsk; and the Elektrocomplex plant (low-voltage equipment) and the Spetstekhonologia JSC in Minusinsk. (See Exhibit 56.8.)

The manufacturing industry is concentrated primarily in the krai's southern part, along the Trans-Siberian railroad. The Zaveniagin Integrated Mining and Metal Fabrication Plant, the world's largest full-cycle nonferrous-metal complex, is located in the krai's north. It is the leading enterprise of the Norilsk Nickel JSC, which also includes the machine plant in Olenegorsk, the nonferrous metal fabrication plant in Krasnoyarsk, and the Severnickel and Pechnganickel integrated plants in Murmansk.

The krai exports 19% of its manufactured output, 80% of which is nonferrous metals and 8.7% is lumber.

The krai is short of foodstuffs, especially in its northern areas. The southern districts have extensive areas of fertile farmland and livestock pastures, which can, in the long term, benefited from commercial farming enterprises.

Exhibit 56.8.   Manufacture of Principal Industrial Products

	1995	1996
Power, bn kWh	45.4	51.3
Coal, million tons	32.1	38.2
Commercial timber, thou. cu. m.	6,359	5,914
Lumber, thou. tons	2,015	1,672
Fiber board, million sq. m.	37.4	37.4
Cardboard, thou. tons	79.8	56.7
Cement, thou. tons	1,700	1,360
Chemical yarn and fibers, thou. tons	29.8	20.9
Auto tires, thou.	380	673
Televisions, thou.	15.8	12.5
Meat, thou. tons	43.4	35.6
Whole milk products, thou. tons	75.9	63
Gold, kgs	7,047	n/a

3. Investment Opportunities. The Krasnoyarsk Krai is one of the areas in Russia where major projects can be initiated to manufacture products for the world market. The main areas of investment here are geological prospecting, mining and production of nonferrous metals, including nickel and molybdenum (Norilsk Nickel JSC), aluminum (a group of enterprises in the Krasnoyarsk Krai and the neighboring Irkutsk Oblast), complex metals (Gorevsk integrated mining and metal fabrication plant), precious stones and quartz (Artemovsk, and Razdolinsk, Severo-Yeniseisk, and Tura townships); involvement in programs to develop the various resources of the Evenki Autonomous Okrug (logging operations with a total capacity of 1 to 1.3 million cu m of timber, the Yurubchensk and Sobinovsk hydrocarbon deposits, feldspar deposits, and fur trapping); participation in the state program to develop the lower Angara area; modernization of the Achinsk refinery; involvement in the program to develop the Kansk-Achinsk coal basin; communications systems; and small-scale projects to produce consumer goods for markets in Siberia and Russia's northern areas.

In 1995, the region had 46 operating joint ventures. The foreign investments in 1993–95 totaled $416.4 million. Private owners held 15.1% of the fixed assets of enterprises and organizations, joint stock companies (without foreign interest) owned 9.4%, and the federal authorities controlled 62.6%. The leading banks in the area are Angara (Tel. 22 790), Agro-Bank (Tel. 27 3933), Biner (Tel. 21 6965), Vostok-Sib-Business (Tel. 21 8889), Yenisei (Tel. 23 2518), Kedr (Tel. 23 7443), Krasinvestbank (Tel. 21 6014), Petabank (Tel. 27 8894), Sibinter (Tel. 33 1739), Sintobank (Tel. 22 6617), Stromcombank (Tel. 23 7384), and Yarbank (Tel. 43 0752).

The krai is reachable from Moscow by rail (3,955 km to Krasnoyarsk, 65 hours from Yaroslavl Terminal) and air (4.5 hours from Demodedovo Airport).

There are 3.8 km of hard-surfaced roads per 1,000 sq km.

56.5 CHITA OBLAST

1. Natural Resources. Area: 431,500 sq km. Farmland: 78,000 sq km. Woodland: 299,400 sq km. Swamps: 12,600 sq km. Other lands: 33,200 sq km. Population: 1,368,200 (Jan. 1, 1996), of which 64.8% is urban and 35.2% is rural. Population density: 3.2 per sq km.

The oblast lies in eastern Transbaikalia. Although it is adequately provided with water resources, some areas do not have enough underground water. The mean annual river runoff is 65.4 cu km, and the river network density is 0.7 km/sq km.

The woodlands contain 2,555.8 million cu m of timber, including 2,222.2 million cu m of softwood. The oblast's estimated cutting area is used at 30% of capacity, and the commercial logging potential is 15 million cu m.

The local mineral resources include nonferrous metals (lead, tin, and copper), placer vein gold, uranium, fluorspar, iron ore, coal, building materials, and mineral springs. The major deposits include Novoshirokino (complex metals), Udokan (copper), Kruchinino (titanium-magnetite ores), and Kharanor (coal). The oblast mines the bulk of Russian is uranium. The majority of its uranium-thorium deposits contain radon water, and its gold and molybdenum ores contain substantial impurities of arsenic. There are also rich fluorine-bearing provinces. The ores also contain significant amounts of tantalum, niobium, lithium, germanium, beryllium, bismuth, and cadmium. These are, however, not enriched and are lost in the mining process because of poor technology. In addition, 75 deposits of polymetals have been formed through the development of 31 ore deposits.

The oblast has a strongly continental climate, a mean temperature of $-26°C$ in January and $19°C$ in July. The annual rainfall ranges from 240 to 400 mm, and the growing season lasts 120 to 160 days.

2. Specialization and Sectoral Structure of the Economy (see Exhibit 56.9). Administrative division: 31 districts, 10 cities, 45 urban-type communities, and 363 village group-councils.

Administration Head: Tel. (30222) 33 443. Fax: 63 319.

Principal cities: Chita (373,000), Krasnokamensk (71,000), and Borzya (36,600).

The manufacturing structure is dominated by nonferrous metallurgy (28.8%), power engineering (22%), and the food industry (13.5%). The oblast's settlement pattern is composed of townships and small towns built near mines and enterprises stretching chainlike in mountain valleys. The biggest city, Chita, is the site of a worsted-cloth mill, a locomotive repair plant, a compressor plant, and nearly 50 smaller enterprises (with a workforce of 100 to 500 each) in the woodworking, food, garment, and construction industries, and in repair operations. Metal fabrication is centered in Petrovsk-Zabaikalsky, which is the site of Transbaikalia's only metal conversion plant. Raw minerals are mined at the Novoorlovsk township (tungsten), the Sherlovaya Gora township (tin concentrate), the Kalanchui township (fluorspar), the Novopavlovka and Vostochny townships (coal), the Klichka township (lead and zinc concentrate), the Zhireken township (molybdenum), and the Pervomaisky township (rare metals). (See Exhibit 56.10.)

The oblast exports 3% of its manufactured output, of which chemical products account for 7% and nonferrous metals for 67%.

Exhibit 56.9. Sectoral Structure of the Economy in 1995 (% of total)

	Industry	Farming	Transport	Construction	Other
Employment	20.3	15.5	12.7	8.4	43.1
Fixed Assets	31.4	11.2	36.4	2.3	18.7
Capital Investment	27.7	5.2	24.2	1.3	41.6

Exhibit 56.10.   Manufacture of Principal Industrial Products

	1995	1996
Coal, million tons	12.5	11.8
Finished rolled stock, thou. tons	84.4	54
Woolen fabrics, million sq. m.	0.4	n/a
Meat, thou. tons	4.3	1.2
Whole milk products, thou. tons	11.9	10.8
Gold, kgs	7,228	n/a

The oblast is short of foodstuffs, although the Dauria area in the oblast's southeast has favorable climate conditions for intensive crop farming. Livestock farming produces three-quarters of the oblast's agricultural output.

3. Investment Opportunities. The social situation in the oblast is complicated by the closure of some unprofitable mines and by the large number of people employed in other industries, a situation that places an added burden on the local budget.

The limitations to investments include deficient supplies of underground water and high seismic activity in some areas, inaccessibility of some areas by surface transportation, underdeveloped transportation and telecommunications networks, and power shortages.

Promising investment areas include geological prospecting for and mining of mineral resources, including the program to develop the Udokan copper deposit; small-scale projects to produce consumer goods for markets in Trans-Baikalia and the Far East; woodworking products for Mongolia, China, and Asian-Pacific countries; processing of hides and sheepskins and boot manufacturing; telecommunications systems; and modernization of the airport in Chita.

In 1995, the region had 45 operating joint ventures. The foreign investments in 1993–95 totaled $3.9 million. Private owners held 18.6% of the fixed assets of enterprises and organizations, joint stock companies (without foreign interest) owned 15.2%, and the federal authorities controlled 59.3%. The oblast's leading banks include Zabaikalzoloto (Tel. 30 037), Zabailkalsky (Tel. 33 823), Kadalinsky (Tel. 42 772), Chitacompromstroibank (Tel. 35 628), and Chitinsky (Tel. 25 941).

The oblast is reachable from Moscow by rail (6,074 km to Chita, 115 hours from Yaroslavl Terminal) and air (eight hours from Domodedovo Airport.)

There are 21 km of hard-surfaced roads per 1,000 sq km.

56.6 IRKUTSK OBLAST

1. Natural Resources. Area: 767,900 sq km. Farmland: 27,500 sq km. Woodland: 653,500 sq km. Bodies of water: 25,400 sq km. Other lands: 46,600 sq km. Population: 2,860,900 (Jan. 1, 1996), of which 79.7% is urban and 20.3% is rural. Population density: 3.7 per sq km.

The oblast lies in the southeastern part of the Siberian upland, much of it is heavily exposed to earthquakes. There are no restrictions on water use, except for the Lake Baikal area, where construction of water-intensive facilities is not allowed.

The woodlands contain 9,131.8 million cu m of timber, including 8,123.9 million cu m of softwood. The oblast's estimated cutting area is used at 50% of capacity, and the commercial logging potential is 70 million cu m.

The local mineral resources include iron ores, gold, rare metals, coal, chemical raw materials (common salt, pure limestone, apatite, and phosphorite), mica, building materials, and oil. The largest deposits are in Korshunovskoe, Rudnogorskoe, Neryundinskoe, and Kapaevskoe (iron ores); Migunskoe, Ishideiskoe, and Azeiskoe (coal); Usolskoe, Tyreiskoe, and Ziminskoe (common salt); Beloziminskoe (apatite); Maisko-Chuiskoe (muscovite); Slyudiansoe (phlogopite); and the Neisk District (sylvanite ores).

The oblast has a strongly continental climate, with a mean temperature of −30°C in January and 19°C in July. The area receives 350 to 450 mm of annual rainfall, and its growing season lasts from 115 to 127 days.

2. Specialization and Sectoral Structure of the Economy (see Exhibit 56.11). Administrative division: 33 districts, 22 cities, 60 urban-type communities, and 380 village group-councils.

Administration Head: Tel. (3952) 34 1385. Fax: 33 3340.

Principal cities: Irkutsk (637,500), Bratsk (286,100), Angarsk (274,400), Ust-Ilimsk (111,000), and Usolie-Sibirskoe (106,700).

The manufacturing structure is dominated by the fuel industry (25.6%), lumbering and woodworking (17.8%), and nonferrous metallurgy (16.4%). The oblast's industrial complex is composed of enterprises manufacturing products that are competitive in the world market, in particular lumber, aluminum, chemicals, precious metals, mica, and items made from them. The leading producers include the Irkutskhimless association in Irkutsk; the Kitoiles JSC and the Angarsknefteorgsintez in Angarsk; an aluminum plant, a lumbering and woodworking complex, and the Bratskles association in Bratsk; the Nizhneudinskles industrial association in Nizhneudinsk; the Sayanskkhimprom JSC (mercury caustic soda, polyvinyl chloride, and dichloroethane) in Sayansk; a pulp and paper mill in Baikalsk; the Zheleznogorskles association in Zheleznogorsk Ilimsky; the Yurtinskles JSC in Taishet; the hydrolysis plants in Tulun and Biriusinsk; the Khimprom industrial association (caustic soda, chlorine, argon, and enamels), a plywood and match plant, and the Khaitinsky China JSC in Usolie Sibirskoe; an integrated lumbering and woodworking plant, a pulp and paper mill, the Ilimskles association, and timber-handling facilities in Ust-Ilimsk; and the Irkutsk aluminum plant in Shelekhov. These facilities can take advantage of low processing costs, and high-quality production conditions, along with cheap power generated by the Bratsk power dam and the Ust-Ilimsk thermal-power plant. (See Exhibit 56.12.)

The oblast exports 12.6% of its manufactured output, of which mineral products account for 31%, chemical products for 23%, lumber for 36%, and nonferrous metals for 7.5%.

The Irkutsk Oblast is deficient in foodstuffs. Its farming sector specializes in beef and dairy cattle, sheep, hogs, and fowl. Cereals, potatoes, and other vegetables are grown as well.

Exhibit 56.11. Sectoral Structure of the Economy in 1995 (% of total)

	Industry	Farming	Transport	Construction	Other
Employment	30.0	8.6	9.6	10.4	41.4
Fixed Assets	48.3	8.0	14.1	7.1	22.5
Capital Investment	31.0	6.1	19.1	1.9	41.9

Exhibit 56.12.   Manufacture of Principal Industrial Products

	1995	1996
Power, bn kWh	59.2	53.9
Primary oil processing products, million tons	16.6	14.3
Coal, million tons	15.0	13.8
Commercial timber, thou. cu. m.	9,997	8,198
Lumber, thou. tons	1,472	1,207
Chipboard, million cu. m.	154	63.1
Cardboard, thou. tons	141	88.8
Heating boilers, MW	378	223
Meat, thou. tons	23.4	23.2
Whole milk products, thou. tons	92.3	78.5
Gold, kgs	11,646	n/a

3. Investment Opportunities. The oblast's local enterprises and administration have their own reliable sources of finance that they can commit to fund projects launched jointly with foreign firms. There are practically no limitations on water and power, but problems may arise in recruiting skilled labor for large-scale projects. The oblast's construction industry has a potential for surplus, which is at present being diverted to carry out building projects beyond the region.

The Irkutsk Oblast is an area where major projects can be initiated to produce output for the world market. The principal areas of investment are logging operations, manufacture and marketing of lumber, paper, and plywood, construction of facilities to produce furniture, chipboard, and fiberboard for export, and modernization of woodworking enterprises; a program to develop forest resources in the Kireinsk district; production and marketing of aluminum products including those obtained by processing imported aluminum; mica products at the Irkutskslyuda JSC, the Vostok industrial association, the Mamslyuda mining and dressing plant in the Mama township, the Sever–2 JSC, and the Cheremkhovo mica factory; geological prospecting for and mining of gold and nonferrous and precious metals at Bodaibo, the Belozimsky mine (ferroniobium master alloy), and the new Lena integrated plant; mining and processing vein-gold ore in the Bodaibo district; the Kharanut mine in the Ust-Ordynsky township; the program to develop the Kovytkino gas fields and the Verkhnerechensk, Yaratinsk, and Dulisminsky oilfields; geological prospecting for potassium salts, oil, and natural gas in the drainage areas of the lower Tunguska and Vilyui Rivers; and modernization of the chemical enterprises and the oil refinery in Angarsk to produce output for markets in the far eastern oblasts.

In 1995, the region had 103 operating joint ventures. The foreign investments in 1993–95 totaled $89.5 million. Private owners held 11.3% of the fixed assets of enterprises and organizations; joint stock companies (without foreign interest) owned 44.7%, and the federal authorities controlled 31.8%. The oblast's leading banks include Baikalsky (Tel. 42 1162), Bratsky (in Bratsk, Tel. 41 371), the East Siberian Bank (Tel. 33 4148), Irkutsksnabbank (Tel. 24 2132), the Russian-Asian Bank (Tel. 27 4662), the Social Development Bank (Tel. 34 9593), and Trustcombank (Tel. 34 8209).

The Irkutsk Oblast is reachable from Moscow by rail (5,042 km to Irkutsk, 79 hours travel from Yaroslavl Terminal) and air (seven hours from Domodedovo Airport).

There are 14 km of hard-surfaced roads per 1,000 sq km.

CHAPTER **57**

FAR EAST REGION

Aleko A. Adamescu, Yuri A. Kovalev, and Alexander G. Granberg

57.1 SAKHA (YAKUTIA) REPUBLIC

1. Natural Resources. Area: 3,103,200 sq km. Farmland: 18,300 sq km. Woodland: 1,441,700 sq km. Swamps: 139,100 sq km. Bodies of water: 126,500 sq km. Reindeer-grazing grounds: 945,800 sq km. Other lands: 406,000 sq km. Population: 1,060,700 (Jan. 1, 1996), of which 65.2% is urban and 34.8% is rural. Population density: 0.3 per sq km, one of the lowest in Russia.

   The republic is situated in Russia's northeast and is one of its biggest and least developed territories.

   The woodlands cover an area of 1,474,900 sq km and contain 9,413 million cu m of timber, including 9,136.6 million cu m of softwood. The republic's estimated cutting area is used at 15% of capacity, and the commercial logging potential is 20 million cu m.

   The area's mineral resources included diamonds, gold, phlogopite, coal, lignite, iron ore, natural gas, tin, tungsten, complex ores, piezoelectric quartz, antimony, mercury, and apatite. The major deposits are located in the area of the Vilyui and Olenek Rivers and in the Alkhal-Udachny area (diamonds); the Aldan, Jugjur, and Indigirka Rivers (gold); at Deputatskoe, Tenkeli, Ilin-Tas, Alys-Khaya, and Burgogan (tin); Septagan and Syrylakh (antimony); Agylkin (copper and tungsten); Sardan (lead and zinc); the Middle Vilyui, Middle Butuobinsk, and Mastakh (natural gas); Timpton, Elkon, and Emeljik (phlogopite); Chulman, Neryungri, and Mastakh (coal); Pionerskoe, Sivaglinskoe, and Tayezhnoe (iron ore); and Seligdar (apatite). The republic is one of the world's richest diamond-bearing areas.

   The republic has a strongly continental climate, with a mean temperature of −6°C in the south and −50°C in the northern mountainous areas in January, and 10 and 20°C, respectively, in July. The annual rainfall varies from 140 to 280 mm (400 to 600 mm in the south), and the growing season lasts from 120 to 130 days.

2. Specialization and Sectoral Structure of the Economy (see Exhibit 57.1). Administrative division: 33 districts, 11 cities, 68 urban-type communities, and 354 village group-councils.

   Administration Head: Tel. (41122) 23 627.

   Principal cities: Yakutsk (222,300), Neryungri (119,600), Mirny (39,500), Lensk (30,900), and Aldan (27,500).

Exhibit 57.1. Sectoral Structure of the Economy in 1995 (% of total)

	Industry	Farming	Transport	Construction	Other
Employment	17.5	12.8	11.1	8.9	49.7
Fixed Assets	43.6	4.9	18.7	6.5	26.3
Capital Investment	37.1	5.4	12.5	1.0	44.0

The manufacturing structure is dominated by nonferrous metallurgy (58.4%), the fuel industry (12%), and power engineering (12%). The republic's settlement pattern is based on townships and small towns located on the sites of mines and enterprises, which extend chainlike along mountain lowlands. The area's biggest city is Yakutsk, which is the site of administrative offices and authorities, such as the Sakhmebel Industrial Association, the Yakutgazprom Industrial Association, the Yakutenergo Industrial Association, the Yakutia Building Materials Industrial Association, the Yakutian Gold Industrial Association, the Yakutles JSC, the thermal-power plant, the cogeneration plant, and nearly 25 small-scale enterprises in the food, timber, garment, leather, footwear, and building materials industries. Minerals are mined at the Kanchalassy, Ugoiny, Bangar, and Jebariki townships, and the town of Neryungri (coal); the Nizhny Kuranakh township and the town of Tommot in the Aldan District (gold); the Kyzyl-Syrt township and the town of Lensk (natural gas); the Mirny, Alkhal, and Udachny townships in the Mirny District (diamonds); the Kempedyai township in the Middle Olyma District (salt); the Ust-Nera township in the Oimyakon District and the Ust-Maisky District (gold); the Deputatsky township in the Ust-Yana District (gold and tin); and the Severny township (gold). Of all these communities, the largest industrial centers are the towns of Mirny (three diamond mines, the Yakutalmaz Research and Development Association, the Russian Sakha Diamonds JSC, and the Vilyui power dam) and Neryungri, which is the major point of the railroad branch running to the Baikal-Amur mainline and is the site of the Chulman thermal-power plant, the Yakutugol Industrial Association, an enrichment factory, and a coal strip mine. The republic is substantially a producer and supplier of primary materials, but lacks any significant secondary industries. (See Exhibit 57.2.)

The republic exports 3.8% of its manufactured output, which consists chiefly of uncut diamonds and coal.

Farming is carried out in clusters, of activity specializing in fur trapping and farming, raising beef and dairy cattle, and growing potatoes and other vegetables. Reindeer grazing, fur farming, and fur trapping are widely practiced in the north. The southern areas have suitable conditions for crop farming and food depots to supply grains, vegetables, milk, and meat to the republic's northern territories.

Exhibit 57.2. Manufacture of Principal Industrial Products

	1995	1996
Natural gas, bn cu. m.	1.7	1.68
Coal, million tons	11.8	10.9
Meat, thou. tons	9.3	7.8
Whole milk products, thou. tons	36.5	36.5
Gold, kgs	28,759	n/a

3. Investment Opportunities. There is friction between Russians and Yakuts in those areas having a majority of Yakuts. The friction is rooted in customs and traditions, some of them going back as far as the 1930s, when the local population was encouraged to apprehend prisoners escaping from labor camps on the Kolyma and in local area. In the entire republic, Russians account for 50% and Yakuts for 35%.

The principal limitations for investors are the undeveloped transportation network, the telecommunications, social, and housing infrastructure; and the high costs of construction work and delivery of building materials; and the shipping of output from most of the republic's areas. The republic's southern areas around Neryungri, which has a railroad and highways leading to the southern part of the Russian Far East and to China, are better developed in these respects.

The best investment prospects are in the geological prospecting, mining, and marketing of diamonds, gold, and tin, including the construction of underground mines on diamond "pipe" deposits and the development of new placer deposits in the gold industry; construction of small-scale processing enterprises to cut diamonds and make jewelry and diamond-tipped tools; mining of coal (at Neryungri) for the markets of the Asia-Pacific region; development of new gas fields and, possibly, construction of a gas pipeline from western Yakutia to China and South Korea; participation in road-building programs, including the delivery of road-building machines and establishment of facilities on the highways connecting the southern and northern areas of the Far East, railroad outlets from Yakutia and the Magadan Oblast to the Baikal-Amur mainline (the railroad from Berkakit to Yakutsk), the highway from Yakutsk to the Kolyma highway, and modernization of the Amur-Yakutsk highway; and small-scale projects to produce articles with ethnic motifs from furs, bone, and leather.

In 1995, the region had 34 operating joint ventures. The foreign investments in 1993–95 totaled $19.3 million. Private owners held 7.7% of the fixed assets of enterprises and organizations, joint stock companies (without foreign interest) owned another 15.4%, the federal authorities controlled 6.2%, and the republican government possessed 57.5%. The republic's leading banks include Agroprombank (Tel. 22 475), Aldanzoloto (Aldan, Tel. 21 662), Vilcombank (Vilyui, Tel. 21 869), Grandbank (Tel. 50 237), Infrobank (Tel. 23 205), Makbank (Mirny, Tel. 20 882), Sakhabank (Tel. 23 031), Sakhabiliibank (Tel. 26 573), Sakhacreditbank (Tel. 36 254), Sakhatransbank (Tel. 50 658), Sir (Tel. 41 227), Ergien (Tel. 22 261), Yakut-zolotocombank (Tel. 40 533), and Yakutia (Tel. 40 991).

The republic cannot be reached from Moscow by rail (8,468 km to Yakutsk); air services operate from Domodedovo Airport (seven hours flight time).

There are 1.5 km of hard-surfaced roads in the republic per 1,000 sq km.

57.2 KHABAROVSK KRAI (TERRITORY)
INCLUDING JEWISH AUTONOMOUS REGION

1. Natural Resources. Area: 788,600 sq km. Farmland: 11,000 sq km. Woodland: 437,500 sq km. Swamps: 91,300 sq km. Bodies of water: 11,500 sq km. Reindeer-grazing grounds: 20,150 sq km. Population: 1,608,200 (Jan. 1, 1996), of which 80.6% is urban and 19.4% is rural. Population density: 2 per sq km.

The Khabarovsk Krai lies in the center of the Russian Far East. It is fully supplied with water.

The woodlands contain 5,378.5 million cu m of timber, including 4,617.2 million cu m of softwood. The krai's estimated cutting area is at 35% capacity, and its commercial logging potential is 30 million cu m.

The krai's mineral resources include tin, mercury, gold, iron ore, coal, lignite, graphite, brucite, manganese, feldspar, phosphorite, alunite, building materials, and peat.

The krai has a monsoon climate, with a mean temperature of $-20°C$ in the south and $-40°C$ in the north in January, and $20°C$ in July. It has 600 to 800 mm of annual rainfall, and its growing season lasts between 170 and 180 days.

2. Specialization and Sectoral Structure of the Economy (see Exhibit 57.3). Administrative division: 17 districts, 7 cities, 31 urban-type communities, and 183 village group-councils.

Administration Head: Tel. (4212) 33 5540. Fax: 33 8756.

Principal cities: Khabarovsk (618,600), Komsomolsk on Amur (318,400), Birobijan (85,300), and Amursk (59,000).

The manufacturing structure is dominated by engineering (15.3%), the fuel industry (16.6%), lumbering and woodworking (8.5%), the food industry (12.7%), and power generation (20.3%). The Khabarovsk Krai is the key engineering area of the Russian Far East. The industry's biggest enterprises are the Dalenergomash JSC (turbines and compressors), the Splav plant (integrated circuits), the aluminum alloy plant, the Daldiesel plant, the heating equipment plant (radiators and convectors), and the cable plant in Khabarovsk; the Amurlitmash (foundry equipment), the electrical-engineering plant (storage batteries), the aviation plant, the Amurstal metal plant (rolled steel), and the handling equipment plant (overhead cranes) in Komsomolsk on Amur; ship repair and shipbuilding plants in Gavan and other cities on the Amur River; and the Dalselmash industrial association (harvesters) and the power-transformer plant in Birobijan. The krai has two oil refineries (in Khabarovsk and Komsomolsk on Amur), which supply engine fuels to the entire far eastern area. The timber industry enterprises include the Amurskbumprom industrial association and the furniture and plywood plants in Amursk; the Kopninsky logging and woodworking JSC in Oktyabrsky and the woodworking plant in the Vanino township; three woodworking enterprises and a hydrolysis plant in the Lazo District (Suiktai, Mukhen, and Khor townships); and the Lazarevles JSC in Nikolaevsk-on-Amur. (See Exhibit 57.4.)

Raw materials are mined at the Chekdomyn township (Urgal coal development), the Solnechny township (copper, tungsten, lead, and tin), the Khingansk township (tin), and the Izvestkovy township (brucite). The main organization of the gold-mining enterprises, the Primorzoloto Gold-Mining Industrial Association, has its headquarters in Khabarovsk.

The krai exports 25% of its manufactured output, with oil and oil products accounting for 17% of this, lumber for 70%, and metals for 10%.

The krai is deficient in foodstuffs. Farm crops include wheat, barley, soybeans, potatoes, fruits, and berries. Beef and dairy cattle raising is the main livestock activity.

Exhibit 57.3.   Sectoral Structure of the Economy in 1995 (% of total)

	Industry	Farming	Transport	Construction	Other
Employment	28.0	4.1	11.9	11.4	44.6
Fixed Assets	36.6	6.0	19.7	7.2	30.5
Capital Investment	31.2	2.3	15.8	1.1	49.6

Exhibit 57.4.   Manufacture of Principal Industrial Products

	Khabarovsk Krai		Jewish AO	
	1995	1996	1995	1996
Primary oil processing products, million tons	3.4	3.1	n/a	n/a
Electric overhead cranes	96	50	n/a	n/a
Commercial timber, thou. cu. m.	2,627	2,285	9.6	5.8
Lumber, thou. cu. m.	213	156	n/a	n/a
Radiators and convectors, thou. kW	180	131.4	n/a	n/a
Washing machines, thou.	0.6	n/a	n/a	n/a
Fish and processed sea products, thou. tons	213	114	n/a	n/a
Meat, thou. tons	6.0	3.5	0.44	0.09
Whole milk products, thou. tons	31.0	26.7	2.3	1.5
Gold, kgs	8,358	n/a	n/a	n/a

3. Investment Opportunities. Air and rail transportation in the krai link far eastern enterprises (except for those in Yakutia and the Amur Oblast) with those in other areas in Russia. The local administration is more loyal toward the federal government than its counterparts in Yakutia and Primorsky Krai. This is explained, in part, by the krai's need for federal subsidies for defense industry enterprises in Komsomolsk-on-Amur, Khabarovsk, and Nikolaesk, which have an insufficient volume of orders and payroll problems.

Investment opportunities are open in the prospecting and development of non-ferrous- and precious-metal deposits; modernization of the oil refineries; renovation of the infrastructure conveying oil from Sakhalin Island and West Siberia, including the possible construction of a pipeline from Achinsk to Khabarovsk; modernization of the bridge across the Amur River at Khabarovsk and the railroad from Khabarovsk to Bikin; modernization of the Khabarovsk airport; construction of transportation terminals in the Vanino commercial port, including facilities for receiving raw materials for Siberia's aluminum plants and for exporting seven to eight million tons of Yakutsk coals and lumber; participation in the program to develop the Urgal coal deposits and construction of a complex of three thermal-power plants; involvement in conversion programs, if a favorable resolution is adopted by the appropriate authorities; and processing of metal scrap and production of recycled aluminum. In view of the krai's central position in the far eastern region and the availability of manufacturing facilities and skilled labor, would-be investors are advised to carefully assess the local opportunities if they decide to take part in the following programs: licensed production of equipment for woodworking, logging, farming, the food industry, fisheries, mining, warehousing, and seaport facilities; and production of consumer goods.

In 1995, the region had 22 operating joint ventures. The foreign investments in 1993–95 totaled $247 million. Private owners held 21.7% of the fixed assets of enterprises and organizations, joint stock companies (without foreign interest), owned 23.5%, and the federal authorities controlled 43.9%. The area's leading banks are Bison-capital (Tel. 33 4518), Gavancombank (Gavan, Tel. 33 527), Grad-bank (Tel. 33 0966), Dakobank (Tel. 34 3585), Dalcombank (Tel. 33 0380), Dallesbank (Tel. 33 7993), Dalprogress (Komsomolsk, Tel. 43 598), Dalstroibank (Tel. 33 7631), Zolotostarbank (Tel. 33 4644), Kafcombank (Tel. 35 2011), Nakbank (Komsomolsk,

Tel. 34 317), Ofibank (Tel. 33 4954), Promstroibank (Tel. 33 0115), Regionbank (Komsomolsk, Tel. 43 636), Ussuri (Tel. 55 2858), Khakobank (Tel. 33 8263), and Expa (Tel. 34 8855).

The krai is reachable from Moscow by rail (8,533 km to Khabarovsk, 157 hours from Yaroslavl Terminal) and air (10 hours from Domodedovo Airport).

There are 4.2 km of hard-surfaced roads per 1,000 sq km.

57.3 JEWISH AUTONOMOUS OBLAST (REGION)

1. Natural resources. Area: 36.0 thou. sq. km., population: 211.9 thou. (January 1, 1996). It is fully supplied with water.

The oblast's mineral resources include brown coal, graphite, brucite, feldspar, phosphorites, building materials, and peat.

The region has a monsoon climate, with a mean temperature of −23°C in January and 20°C in July. It has 600 mm of annual rainfall, and its growing season is between 170 and 180 days.

The manufacturing structure is dominated by engineering (27.1%), building materials industry (15.7%), the food industry (14.2%), and power generation (20.4%). (See Exhibit 57.6.)

The oblast exports 4% of its manufactured output, with metals accounting for 77% of this.

Investment Opportunities. In the near future, the region will have to solve a few social and economic problems, among them:

Building living facilities (at the Birobijan power station and the water collection facilities in Bira and Budukan);

Developing telecommunications systems (a digital-telephone station in Obluchie, a local television station, cable lines);

Strengthening the support for health care, education, and culture (including the Jewish Culture Center in Birobijan, maternity homes, the Birobijan Pedagogical Institute);

Establishment of a flood protection program;

Creation of the Bastak national park;

Exhibit 57.5.   Sectoral Structure of the Economy in 1995 (% of total)

	Industry	Farming	Transport	Construction	Other
Employment	22.7	16.5	10.2	6.5	44.1
Fixed Assets	26.0	24.1	2.8	15.5	31.6
Capital Investment	12.2	14.5	28.7	0.3	44.3

Exhibit 57.6.   Manufacture of Principal Industrial Products

	1995	1996
Commercial timber, thou. cu. m.	9.6	5.8
Bricks, mio.	20.3	7.3
Cement, thou tons	272	204
Meat, thou. tons	437	91.8
Whole milk products, thou. tons	31.0	20.5
Bread and baked goods, thou. tons	14.4	11.4

Prospecting and developing the region's mineral resources, including the Ushum coal reserve, and increasing the production of mines to 1.5 million tons annually.

New investments should be directed at developing mineral reserves, modernizing the engineering industry, processing farm produce for the regional market, organizing the pharmaceutical industry, and modernizing the Birobijan airport. In addition to increasing coal production, attractive projects involve the Khingalovo metal plant (tin) and the plant in Kuldur producing brucite. Another investment opportunity lies in the production of lumber and furniture for the local market and for export to China.

In 1995, the region had 22 operating joint ventures. The foreign investments in 1993–95 totaled $173 million.

57.4 PRIMOSKY KRAI (TERRITORY)

1. **Natural Resources.** Area: 165,900 sq km. Farmland: 16,200 sq km. Woodland: 131,000 sq km. Population: 2,286,900 (Jan. 1, 1996), of which 77.6% is urban and 22.4% is rural. Population density: 13.8 per sq km., the highest in the Far East.

   The krai lies in the southern part of Russian Far East and has the most favorable conditions for living and economic activity of all the areas in the region.

   The woodlands contain 1,988.1 million cu m of timber, including 1,335.1 million cu m of softwood. The krai's estimated cutting area is used at 30% of capacity, and the commercial logging potential is 10 million cu m.

   The area's mineral resources include tin, lead, complex metals, gold, fluorite, coal, and building materials. The major deposits are those of tin in the Kavalerovsky area, tungsten at Vostok–2, complex metals at Nikolaevsk, fluorite at Voznesensk, and coal at Lipovets, Rettikhovsk, Pavlovsk, and Bitkin.

   The region has a monsoon climate, with a mean temperature of $-12°C$ on the coast and $-27°C$ further inland in January, and 14 and 21°C, respectively, in July. The annual rainfall varies from 600 to 900 mm, and the growing season lasts between 160 and 200 days.

2. **Specialization and Sectoral Structure of the Economy** (see Exhibit 57.7). Administrative division: 25 districts, 11 cities, 46 urban-type communities, and 222 village group-councils.

   Administration Head: Tel. (4232) 22 3800.

   Principal cities: Vladivostok (669,500), Nakhodka (189,700), Ussuriisk (159,200), and Arseniev (70,600).

   The manufacturing structure is dominated by the food industry (49.5%) and engineering (13.9%). Vladivostok is a center of the fishing and ship repair industries, in which the major enterprises are the Dalmoreprodukty industrial association, the Primorrybprom JSC, the trawler and refrigerator fleet base, the Pacific Commercial

Exhibit 57.7. Sectoral Structure of the Economy in 1995 (% of total)

	Industry	Farming	Transport	Construction	Other
Employment	24.9	9.0	12.6	11.3	42.2
Fixed Assets	37.8	9.0	23.5	3.2	26.5
Capital Investment	27.0	2.7	20.4	0.5	49.4

Fishery Tracking Center, three fish-processing plants, and three ship repair plants. The city also has approximately 40 small-scale food industry, construction, furniture, and pharmaceutical enterprises. Minerals are mined and processed at Dalnegorsk (lead and tin), the Kavalerovo township (tin), the Vostok township (copper and tungsten), the Vostretsova township (gold), the Yaroslavsky township (fluorspar), the Lipovets township (coal), and the Svetlogorsk township (tungsten). Fishing industry activities are centered in the Kamenka township (a fish-processing plant), the Preobrazhnie township (trawler-fleet base), Nakhodka (three large ship repair facilities, a sea fishery base, and a fishing gear factory), the village of Astrakhanka, the Slavianka township, the town of Bolshoi Kamen, and the Yuzhno-Morskoi township (seiner fleet base). The chemical industry is focused in Dalnegorsk (boric acid, chemical compounds of boron, and sodium peroxyborate); the timber industry, in Lesozavodsk (furniture and woodworking plants and a biochemical plant), in the Plastun township (Terneiles JSC), in Ussuriisk (cardboard plant), and in Dalnerechensk (a saw mill and woodworking plant); building materials, in Artem (chinaware plant), in Spassk (asbestos-cement products plant), the Spasskcement JSC, a foundry machinery plant producing heating radiators; and the defense industry, in Arseniev and Bolshoi Kamen. (See Exhibit 57.8.)

The krai exports 26% of its manufactured output, of which fish, crabs, caviar, and canned seafood account for 66%, and lumber 14%.

The krai is deficient in most consumer goods except for seafood and some wool articles and garments. Farming specializes in beef and dairy cattle; some rice, buckwheat, soy beans, wheat, and potatoes are grown as well. Other agricultural activities include fur farming (mink and silver fox) and bee-keeping.

3. Investment Opportunities. In its climate level of manufacturing and domestic-service infrastructure, and availability of skilled labor, Primorie Krai has an advantage over the majority of Russian far eastern and Siberian areas.

The krai's main limitations on economic activity are high levels of pollution in ore-mining and processing areas; the shortage of water resources and land suitable for economic activity in maritime cities; the underdeveloped transportation, telecommunications, and domestic-service infrastructures in inland areas (Sikhote-Alin Range, and northern mountainous and coastal areas).

Attractive investment prospects include geological prospecting, mining, and marketing of nonferrous metals; expansion of the trawler, seiner, and refrigerator fleets; renovation of equipment in fish-processing plants; and processing of seafood for sale in the world market; development of port facilities, including involvement in projects to build general-purpose terminals on the shores of Peter the Great Bay near Vladivostok and expansion of the commercial seaport in the Zarubino township; produc-

Exhibit 57.8.   Manufacture of Principal Industrial Products

	1995	1996
Coal, million tons	10.8	10.3
Washing machines, thou.	2.7	1.4
Fish and sea food, million tons	1.3	1.3
Meat, thou. tons	9.2	10.8
Whole milk products, thou. tons	37.3	33.2
Gold, kgs	421	n/a

tion of consumer goods at local enterprises for the Far East and Siberia; production of paints and varnishes; construction of multipurpose transportation and warehousing facilities; research in oceanology making use of sea resources, and developing relevant technology; and establishment of mutual-trade holding companies.

In 1989, the Association for Free Economic Zone Development was set up at Nakhodka. Compared to similar attempts elsewhere, the Nakhodka FEZ was successful and consideration was duly given to creating a similar facility in Posyet. The revocation of most customs privileges in 1995, however, reduced the possibility of establishing profitable trading operations and any other projects being launched jointly with Nakhodka FEZ participants. At present, the Nakhodka seaport handles about 20% of Russia's exported cargoes. The privatization campaign in the FEZ was completed in 1992, and today all major and medium-sized enterprises have long-term development programs, which are 20 to 40% complete. Plans have been drawn up to convert the military airfield in the Golden Valley into a civilian airport, to modernize railroad facilities, and to build a technological, a communications system, and an oil pipeline between Angarsk and Nakhodka. Water consumption is at present limited in Nakhodka, and the coastal roads are choked with traffic, so a new highway and new water supply system are to be built by 1997.

In 1993, the Primorsky Krai had 288 joint ventures in operation. The foreign investments in 1993–95 totaled $83.9 million. Private owners held 15.3% of the fixed assets of enterprises and organizations, joint stock companies (without foreign interest) owned 27.1%, the federal authorities controlled 43.4%, and foreign firms held 1.1%. The krai's leading banks are Vladivostok (Tel. 25 4631), Dalcombank (Tel. 22 8005), Lesozavodskbank (Lesozavodsk, Tel. 93 258), Nakhodka (Nakhodka, Tel. 20 128), Primorsotsbank (Tel. 31 9939), the Bank of Trade and Industry (Nakhodka, Tel. 59 634), and the Transnational Bank for Foreign Trade (Tel. 22 1715).

The krai is reachable from Moscow by rail (9,302 km to Vladivostok, 187 hours from Yaroslavl Terminal) and air (11 hours from Domodedovo Airport).

There are 41 km of hard-surfaced roads per 1,000 sq km.

57.5 AMUR OBLAST

1. Natural Resources. Area: 363,700 sq km. Farmland: 27,200 sq km. Woodland: 234,200 sq km. Swamps: 48,500 sq km. Bodies of water: 11,100 sq km. Reindeer-grazing grounds: 26,900 sq km. Population: 1,056,700 (Jan. 1, 1996), of which 65.4% is urban and 34.6% is rural. Population density: 2.9 per sq km.

The oblast lies in the southwestern part of the Russian Far East. It is adequately supplied with water.

The woodlands contain 2,033.2 million cu m of timber, including 1,644.7 million cu m of softwood. The oblast's estimated cutting area is used at 55% of capacity, and the commercial logging potential is 12 million cu m.

The local mineral resources include gold, lignite, coal, quartz sand, kaolin, limestone, fireclay, tufa, and mineral springs. The largest deposits of gold are located in the upper reaches of the Zeya and Selemzha Rivers, those of coal and lignite at Raichikhinsk, Erkovo, and Svobodnoe, kaolin at Chalgan, and limestone at Chagoyan.

The oblast has a continental climate, with a mean temperature of -25 to -32°C in January and 18 to 21°C in July. The annual rainfall varies from 460 to 800 mm, and the growing season lasts from 126 to 170 days.

2. Specialization and Sectoral Structure of the Economy (see Exhibit 57.9). Administrative division: 20 districts, 9 cities, 28 urban-type communities, and 281 village group-councils.

Administration Head: Tel. (41 622) 40 322. Fax: 46 201.

Principal cities: Blagoveshchensk (211,400), Svobodny (80,900), Belogorsk (74,500), and Tynda (63,500).

The manufacturing structure is dominated by nonferrous metallurgy (17.6%), power engineering (29.9%), the food industry (13.7%), and lumbering and woodworking (6.7%). Apart from its gold-mining enterprises, the oblast has small-scale manufacturing facilities catering to the local economy's needs for machines and equipment, including electric-measuring instruments, beneficiation equipment, river craft and railroad car repairs, road-building machines, industrial glass, and overhead cranes. In addition, a number of major enterprises have been built to meet the demands of the far eastern area, in particular the Amurselmash JSC (cattle-farming equipment and heating boilers) and the Avtozapchast plant, which provides auto repair services to far eastern enterprises. Local natural resources are used by the 1,290 kW Zeya power dam, the Dalvostokugol association (in Raichikhinsk), the Amurlesprom JSC, the Iskra match factory (in Blagoveshchensk), and large-scale lumbering and saw-milling operations in the Zeya township and in the towns of Skovorodino, Tynda, and Shimanovsk. (See Exhibit 57.10.)

The oblast exports 6% of its manufactured output, with transportation vehicles accounting for 13% of this, metals 28%, and lumber 36%.

The majority of farming operations are concentrated in the Zeya-Bureya flatland, which contains nearly half of the far eastern area's farm land, producing a third of the milk and meat, 80% of the soy beans, and 50% of the cereals grown in the area. The local bioclimatic conditions are ideal for establishing a livestock industry to supply the needs of the majority of Federation members in the Far East. At present, however, the oblast's agriculture is going through a crisis despite its proximity to markets with scarce food supplies and a significant pent-up demand.

3. Investment Opportunities. Facilities in the oblast's construction complex have become idle upon the completion of the Baikal-Amur railroad project. The oblast has

Exhibit 57.9.   Sectoral Structure of the Economy in 1995 (% of total)

	Industry	Farming	Transport	Construction	Other
Employment	17.4	15.2	15.7	11.7	40.0
Fixed Assets	15.4	12.2	34.1	3.4	34.9
Capital Investment	27.6	7.1	25.0	0.8	34.9

Exhibit 57.10.   Manufacture of Principal Industrial Products

	1995	1996
Power, bn kWh	6.8	5.8
Coal, million tons	4.7	4.5
Electric overhead cranes	67	77.7
Meat, thou. tons	4.7	2.6
Whole milk products, thou. tons	16.1	9.5
Gold, kgs	12,418	n/a

significant investment potential because a considerable amount of Russian exports to China flow through the oblast. Also, there are no restrictions imposed on lands suitable for industrial, housing, and recreational projects, and the oblast is provided with more power, water, and unskilled labor than any of the other far eastern areas. The oblast's most serious problem is the undeveloped transportation and domestic-service infrastructure, shortage of skilled labor, and a large transient population that tends to leave after several years of working in the oblast.

Prospective investment areas include geological prospecting for and mining of nonferrous metals, gold in particular; programs to develop power engineering, including the construction of power dams at the Bureya River and in its lower reaches; development of the Garin iron-ore deposit, construction of an integrated mining and dressing plant and a metal plant to manufacture high-quality steels for markets in the Asia-Pacific region; participation in the program to establish a space launch site near Svobodny and provide it with production and ancillary infrastructures; manufacture of equipment for mining and woodworking enterprises in Siberia and the Far East; production of consumer goods under license; and an infrastructure for trading operations and freight shipments between Russia and China.

In 1995, the Amur Oblast had 52 joint ventures in operation. The foreign investments in 1993–1995 totaled $78.8 million. Private owners held 12.5% of the fixed assets of enterprises and organizations, joint stock companies (without foreign interest) owned 29.9%, the federal authorities controlled 24.4%, and foreign companies held 3.6%. The oblast's leading banks include Asia-trust (Tel. 44 877), Amurbank (Tel. 40 465), Amurbusinessbank (Tel. 52 343), Amurzolotobank (Tel. 27 612), Amurpromstroibank (Tel. 25 818), Bamcredit (Tynda, Tel. 31 211), and Superbank (Tel. 25 656).

Pursuant to the Russian president's order regarding an agreement between Russia and China to establish an international economic-cooperation and development zone between Blagoveshchensk and Heihe, China, the Amur Oblast's administration and the Heihe government have set up a preparatory committee. The telephone numbers of the appropriate Russian authorities are (8–4162) 42 2404 and 44 3962.

The oblast is reachable from Moscow by rail (7,985 km to Blagoveshchensk, 147 hours from Yaroslavl Terminal) and air (10 hours from Domodedovo Airport).

There are 17 km of hard-surfaced roads per 1,000 sq km.

57.6 KAMCHATKA OBLAST AND KORYAK AUTONOMOUS AREA

1. Natural Resources. Area: 472,300 sq km. Farmland: 3,400 sq km. Woodland: 138,800 sq km. Swamps: 28,600 sq km. Reindeer-grazing grounds: 171,000 sq km. Other lands: 89,900 sq km. Population: 439,400 (Jan. 1, 1996), of which 81.7% is urban and 18.3% is rural. Population density: 0.9 per sq km.

The oblast lies at the eastern-most end of Russia on the Kamchatka Peninsula and the Komandorskie Islands.

The oblast's woodlands contain 1,230.4 million cu m of timber, including 146.9 million cu m of softwood. The local cutting area is used at 33% of capacity, and its commercial logging potential is 1 million cu m.

The mineral resources in the oblast include coal, gold, mercury, complex metals, sulfur, and building materials. The oblast is Russia's only area with active volcanoes and geothermal springs such as geysers, mud volcanoes, and warm lakes of balneological significance.

The oblast has a maritime, monsoon-type climate, with a mean temperature of
$-15°C$ in the north to $0°C$ in the south in January, and $14°C$ in July. The area receives 500 mm of annual rainfall and 1,200 mm in coastal areas on the islands. Its
growing season lasts from 65 to 110 days.

2. Specialization and Sectoral Structure of the Economy (see Exhibit 57.11). Adminis-
    trative division: 11 districts, 3 cities, 11 urban-type communities, and 50 village
    group-councils.
    Administration Head: Tel. (41 500) 22 091. Fax: 24 712.
    Principal cities: Petropavlovsk-Kamchatsky (283,400), Elizovo (47,800), and
    Kliuchi (11,300).
    The manufacturing structure is dominated by the food industry (64.9%) and
    power engineering (18.1%). The oblast's economy includes enterprises playing a
    primary or secondary role in the processing of rich biological resources obtained in
    the adjoining waters (fish, crabs, and molluscs). Petropavlovsk-Kamchatsky is the
    home port of the refrigerator fleet (Rybkholodflot); the site of a shipyard, the Nevod
    JSC (fishing gear), and the Sea Products JSC; and the headquarters of the trawler-
    fleet authority. Fish-canning enterprises are located in the townships of Kruto-
    gorovo, Ozernovsky, Oktyabrsky, and Ust-Kamchatka. Fish-processing enterprises
    within the Koryak Autonomous Area are located in the townships of Osora, Ilpyn-
    sky, Ivashka, Korf, and Ust-Khairiuzovo. (See Exhibit 57.12.)
    All other enterprises in the oblast have a local significance. The largest of them
    are the 11,000 kW Pauzhetsk geothermal-cogeneration plant and two thermal-
    cogeneration plants in the oblast's center.
    The oblast exports 22.8% of its manufactured output, most of which is fish and
    seafood.

3. Investment Opportunities. The key investment prospects are development of the
    marine resources of the Okhotsk and Bering Seas, modernization of fish-processing
    plants, construction of fish farms, and development of nonferrous-metal deposits
    and geothermal resources, including tourist and recreational projects. Realistic proj-

Exhibit 57.11.   Sectoral Structure of the Economy in 1995 (% of total)

	Industry	Farming	Transport	Construction	Other
Employment	27.1	7.3	9.8	8.1	47.7
Fixed Assets	33.8	8.4	8.9	6.7	42.2
Capital Investment	62.2	2.2	5.3	0.6	29.7

Exhibit 57.12.   Manufacture of Principal Industrial Products

	Kamchatka Oblast		Koryak AD	
	1995	1996	1995	1996
Fish and other sea products, thou. tons	752	n/a	17	38.6
Meat, thou. tons	2.2	0.64	n/a	n/a
Whole milk products, thou. tons	8.8	3.7	0.7	0.3
Gold, kgs	n/a	n/a	421	n/a

ects include the construction of a chain of small-capacity power dams on the Bystraya and Tolmacheva Rivers; expansion of the dry-cargo fleet; renovation of the tarmac at the Elizovo airport; extension of the runway, and modernization of the terminal at the Petropavlovsk-Kamchatsky airport; modernization of the passenger terminal and construction of a new terminal at the Petropavlovsk-Kamchatsky port facilities; establishment of an alpine-skiing center; expansion of the tanker fleet; joint development of the telephone service with the Daltelecom concern and satellite-television systems; renovation of the fishing and processing fleet, and the equipment of on-shore processing enterprises, including the Kamchatimpex external economic association, the Oktyabrsky JSC, the Fleet Base JSC, and the fishing port in Mokhovaya Bay; manufacture of articles from cast basalt; and enrichment of perlite from the Naginiksk deposit.

Investment plans have to take into account the hazards of marine shipping (frequent storms, permanent fog, and complex ice conditions) and restrictions imposed on economic activities in view of the Defense Ministry's facilities on the peninsula.

In 1995, the Kamchatka Oblast had 62 joint ventures in operation. The foreign investments in 1993–95 totaled $45.1 million. Private owners held 1.2% of the fixed assets of enterprises and organizations, joint stock companies (without foreign interest) owned 55.4%, and the federal authorities controlled 35.2%. The oblast's leading banks are Yedinenie (Tel. 36 945), Kamchatbusinessbank (Tel. 21 917), Kamchatinbank (Tel. 26 936), Kamchatcomagrobank (Tel. 31 643), Kamchatkobank (Tel. 23 015), Kamchatprombank (Tel. 24 341), Kamchatrybbank (Tel. 23 618), Kamchatsotsbank (Tel. 21 871), the Far North (Tel. 31 762), and Piko-bank (Tel. 59 943).

The oblast cannot be reached from Moscow by rail. Air service is available to the peninsula (nine hours from Domodedovo Airport).

There are 2.5 km of hard-surfaced roads per 1,000 sq km.

57.7 MAGADAN OBLAST AND CHUKOTKA AUTONOMOUS AREA

1. Natural Resources. Area: 1,199.1 sq km. Farmland: 1,500 sq km. Woodland: 207,200 sq km. Swamps: 14,000 sq km. Reindeer-grazing grounds: 616,300 sq km. Other lands: 303,900 sq km. Bodies of water: 29,400 sq km. Population: 306,900 (Jan. 1, 1996), of which 85.9% is urban and 14.1% is rural. Population density: 0.7 per sq km.

The area lies in the extreme northeastern corner of Russia.

The woodlands cover an area of 227,800 sq km. and contain 574.9 million cu m of timber, including 383.6 million cu m of softwood. The oblast's estimated cutting area is used at 45% of capacity, and its commercial logging potential is 0.7 million cu m.

The oblast's mineral resources include gold, tin, tungsten, coal, mercury, and building materials. The best-known deposits are at Dukat and Karamken (gold), Vilkument and Zapadno-Polyanskoe (tin), and Anadyr, Arkagala, and Bering (coal). The Magadan Oblast is Russia's principal gold-mining area. Most deposits rich in placer gold have been worked out, however, and the mines are gradually switching to more costly vein-gold development.

The oblast has a strongly continental climate, with a mean temperature of −19°C in January and 14°C in July. The annual rainfall varies between 300 and 350 mm in Okhotsk (between 500 and 700 mm on the Bering Sea coast), and the growing season is between 100 and 150 days.

2. Specialization and Sectoral Structure of the Economy (see Exhibit 57.13). Administrative division: 8 districts, 2 cities, 32 urban-type communities, and 33 village group-councils.

Administration Head: Tel. (41300) 23 134. Fax: 23115.

Principal cities: Magadan (165,900) and Susuman (16,400).

The manufacturing structure is dominated by nonferrous metallurgy (46.6%), the food industry (8.7%), and power generation (31.8%). The oblast's settlement pattern is made up of communities built at the sites of mines, which extend in a chain-like manner along the mountain valleys. The area's largest city is Magadan, which is the seat of administrative authorities and the site of the main offices of gold- and coal-mining enterprises. The city contains a port, an airport, small-scale food, garment, and construction enterprises, auto and mining-equipment repair facilities, and fish-processing plants. Minerals are mined in the townships of Ust-Srednekansk, Shiroky, Susuman, Ust-Omchug, Matrosova, Karamken, Orotukan, and Yagodnoe (gold, tin, and tungsten); and Galimy, Arkagala, and Kadykchai (coal). Within the Chukotka Autonomous Area, precious metals are mined in the townships of Bilibino, Komsomolsky, and Polyarny; and coal is produced in the townships of Shakhtersky, Ugolnie Kopi, and Nagorny. (See Exhibit 57.14.)

The oblast exports only 1% of its manufactured output, of which 70% is seafood and 10% is metals.

3. Investment Opportunities. The Magadan Oblast does not have a railroad outlet to the rest of Russia, and is reachable by air and river transportation. The level of domestic services and the transportation and telecommunications infrastructure is below modern standards, and the majority of the oblast's population resides here temporarily, attracted by the high wages in the gold-mining industry. The social structure is complicated by the disproportionate share of subsidized organizations and institutions located in the oblast during the decades of Soviet rule. Some of the employees of these institutions and of the closed mines, as well as elderly pensioners, have to be resettled elsewhere in Russia. Investment plans should also take into account that after a year or two of working in the oblast, people born in other areas tend to leave.

Exhibit 57.13.   Sectoral Structure of the Economy 1995 (% of total)

	Industry	Farming	Transport	Construction	Other
Employment	24.6	6.6	12.4	10.1	46.3
Fixed Assets	20.0	9.2	14.7	7.7	48.4
Capital Investment	64.1	1.6	17.6	0.5	16.2

Exhibit 57.14.   Manufacture of Principal Industrial Products

	Magadan Oblast		Chukotka AD	
	1995	1996	1995	1996
Fish and other sea foods, thou. tons	67.5	43.9	n/a	n/a
Meat, thou. tons	1.5	0.9	0.7	1.1
Whole milk products, thou. tons	10.4	8.3	1.1	0.95
Golg, kgs	22,343	n/a	9,790	n/a

Promising investment areas include geological prospecting for and development of precious and nonferrous metal deposits on the mainland and on the shelf, including the Kubaka and Evenskoe gold-ore deposits, construction of a dressing plant to handle 400,000 tons of ore per year at the Lunny gold and silver deposit, and a second stage of the dressing facility at the Dukat mining and dressing plant; development of the gold and silver deposits at Valuninskoe, Dvoinoe, Tumannoe, Maiskoe, Pyrkai, and Iultinskoe in the Chukotka Autonomous Area; renovation of equipment in fish-processing plants and marketing of fish products; small-scale projects in fur farming, fur trapping, and manufacture of fur clothing and bone articles for the world market; the airport infrastructure, communications, and port facilities, particularly in the Bering Strait area (at Pevek, Providenia, Egvekinot, Anadyr, Beringovsky, and Nechaevo); joint establishment of the Beringia national park with the U.S. state of Alaska; and international sports-fishing and hunting projects. In addition to major projects in the gold mining industry, substantial profits may be gained by developing small deposits of placer gold, relying persons with property rights and a lot of experience in gold-digging teams and in other gold-mining activities.

In 1995, the Magadan Oblast had 34 joint ventures in operation. The foreign investments in 1993–95 totaled 74.2 million. Private owners held 3.5% of the fixed assets of enterprises and organizations, joint stock companies (without foreign interest) owned 24.8%, and the federal authorities controlled 53.9%. The leading banks in the oblast include Agroprombank (Tel. 29 253), Kolymabank (Tel. 28 041), Kolymsky (Palatka township, Tel. 93 152), Magadantorgbank (Tel. 35 791), Maksotsbank (Tel. 28 873), Svak-bank (Tel. 26 645), and the Territorial Security Bank (Tel. 21 065).

The Magadan Oblast cannot be reached from Moscow by rail (7,110 km to Magadan). Air service is available from Domodedovo Airport (seven hours).

There are 5.7 km of hard-surfaced roads per 1,000 sq km.

57.8 SAKHALIN OBLAST

1. Natural Resources. Area: 87,100 sq km. Farmland: 1,900 sq km. Woodland: 55,300 sq km. Reindeer-grazing grounds: 11,900 sq km. Population: 698,600 (Jan. 1, 1996), of which 84.7% is urban and 15.3% is rural. Population density: 8 per sq km.

The oblast is the easternmost area of Russia, lying on Sakhalin Island and the Kurile Islands.

The oblast's woodlands cover an area of 56,300 sq km and contain 689.7 million cu m of timber, including 597.6 million cu m of softwood. The estimated cutting area is used at 50% of capacity, and the commercial logging potential is 6 million cu m.

The area's mineral resources include coal, oil, natural gas, native sulfur, and ilmenite-magnesite sand. The largest deposits of power-generating coal are at Gornozavodskoe, Vakhrushevskoe, and Solntsevskoe; those of coking coal, at Lesogorskoe and Uglegorskoe; oil at Mongi, Dagi, Ust-Tomi, Katangli, Yubileinoe, and Okruzhnoe; natural gas at Vostochno-Lugovskoe; oil and condensed gas at Odontu, Chaivo, and Lunskoe; and sulfur at Novoe and Iturup Island.

The total oil reserves on the northeastern shelf of the Sakhalin Island amount to 290 million tons, and the overall natural-gas resources exceed 420 billion cu m. At present, feasibility studies have been initiated in preparation for developing a number of oil and gas fields on Sakhalin jointly with foreign firms, in particular Sakhalin–1 and Sakhalin–2 projects, which will develop the Lunskoe fields. In the first project, the participants' royalties and product shares have been estimated; and in the second project, a concern, 4M & SH, has been created. The costs of developing the Lunskoe fields are put at $11.3 billion. The financial agreement between the parties is based on the "production shelling" arrangement, under which the concern receives 90% of the output at the initial stage, with a profit margin of or under 10%; subsequently, with the margin rising above 10%, Russia's share will rise to 70% and that of the concern will go down to 30%. The project provides for the construction of a pipeline running to the oblast's southern tip, where liquefied gas will be shipped to consumers. Under these circumstances, however, the prime cost of liquefied gas is estimated at $531 a ton, compared with $333 per ton produced in Alaska.

A tender has been announced for a project to develop the Kirinskoe and South Lunskoe deposits of the Sakhalin shelf (20 million tons of oil and 130 billion cu m of natural gas).

The oblast has a monsoon climate, with a mean temperature of −6°C in the south and −24°C in the north in January, and 19 and 10°C, respectively, in July. It gets 400 to 750 mm of annual rainfall.

2. Specialization and Sectoral Structure of the Economy (see Exhibit 57.15). Administrative division: 17 districts, 18 cities, 34 urban-type communities, and 65 village group-councils.

Administration Head: Tel. (42400) 31 402. Fax: 33 741.

Principal cities: Yuzhno-Sakhalinsk (170,900), Kholmsk (51,400), Korsakov (44,700), and Okha (36,400).

The oblast's manufacturing structure is dominated by the food industry (33.1%), the fuel industry (17.2%), and lumbering and woodworking (8.9%). These three industries are represented by collective fisheries, fish-canning plants, and ship repair facilities; oil- and gas-processing authorities, coal mines, and strip mines; and enterprises producing lumber, paper, wallpaper, and cardboard. No engineering enterprises or large enterprises in other industries have ever been located on the island. Oil and gas production is centered in the Okha area in Sakhalin's north; and coal is mined in Alexandrov-Sakhalinsky, Dolinsk, and Uglegorsk. Pulp and paper mills operate in Makarov, Poronaisk, Krasnogorsk, Uglegorsk, and Kholmsk, and sawmilling facilities are located in Poronaisk. Fishing-industry facilities are found in Korsakov (fish-processing plant), Nevelsk (two ship repair plants and a collective fishery), Chekhov (two collective fisheries), and Kholmsk (fishing port, the Sakhmorprodukt JSC, the Sakhalin fish and seafood-processing facility, a can-making plant, and a collective fishery). Fishing operations also are located in Dolinsk, the Redovo village on the Kurile Islands, Okha, Poronaisk, and the Yuzhno-Kurilsk township. (See Exhibit 57.16.)

The oblast exports 16% of its manufactured output, 54.6% of which is fish, seafood, and canned food, and 27.5% lumber.

Exhibit 57.15.   Sectoral Structure of the Economy in 1995 (% of total)

	Industry	Farming	Transport	Construction	Other
Employment	27.6	4.9	12.3	12.2	43.0
Fixed Assets	33.3	6.0	15.8	10.7	34.2
Capital Investment	30.8	2.9	22.7	0.8	42.8

Exhibit 57.16. **Manufacture of Principal Industrial Products**

	1995	1996
Oil, million tons	1.7	1.6
Coal, million tons	2.79	2.7
Commercial timber, thou. cu. m.	1,063	829
Paper, thou. tons	14	8.1
Fish and sea food, thou. tons	357	300
Meat, thou. tons	3.1	3.1
Whole milk products, thou. tons	7.8	8.3

3. Investment Opportunities. The Sakhalin Oblast's limitations, typical for the Russian Far East, are inaccessibility, and undeveloped domestic services, and inadequate transportation and telecommunications infrastructures. These are mitigated by its insular position, the railroad between Yuzhno-Sakhalinsk and Nogliki, and sufficiently favorable living conditions in the island's central and southern parts. The towns, townships, and port facilities were built, to a large extent, by the Japanese (before 1945) and Koreans.

The area's actual limitations include occasionally intense seismic activity; a shortage of skilled labor; a high proportion of people who arrive on temporary work contracts and leave after a few years; the hostility in some areas toward Defense Ministry authorities; and the need for large amounts of building materials, foodstuffs, equipment, and metal products to be shipped from Russia's other areas or from other countries.

The main investment areas are geological prospecting, production, and marketing of oil and natural gas; expansion of the fishing fleet and renovation of fish-processing enterprises; and modernization of the port facilities and the airport in Yuzhno-Sakhalinsk. Projects in the timber industry require careful assessment because of inadequate raw materials; forests in the island's southern part were completely destroyed by the Japanese and have not been restored.

In 1995, the Sakhalin Oblast had 104 joint ventures in operation. The foreign investments in 1993–95 totaled $67.6 million. Private owners held 23.2% of the fixed assets of enterprises and organizations, joint stock companies (without foreign interest) owned 13.5%, the federal authorities controlled 42.7%, and foreign firms owned 1.7%. The oblast's leading banks include Akobank (Korsakov, Tel. 24 301), Aksbank (Tel. 38 077), Dikebank (Tel. 36 249), Dom (Tel. 22 937), Iturup (Tel. 22 937), Manas (Tel. 22 831), Okhabank (Okha, Tel. 2 680), Satobank (Tel. 22 938), Sakhagro (Tel. 21 703), Sakhalin (Kholmsk, Tel. 46 015), Sakhalin-vest (Tel. 37 426), Sakhsotsbank (Tel. 21 851), Sintesksbank (Tel. 36 709), and Flagman-bank (Tel. 36 665).

The oblast is reachable from Moscow by air (10,417 km to Yuzhno-Sakhalinsk, ten hours from Domodedovo Airport).

There are 21 km of hard-surfaced roads per 1,000 sq km.

CHAPTER 58

KALININGRAD OBLAST

Aleko A. Adamescu, Yuri A. Kovalev, and Alexander G. Granberg

1. Natural Resources. Area: 15,100 sq km. Farmland: 8,090 sq km. Woodland: 2,800 sq km. Bodies of water: 2,000 sq km. Population: 913,100 (Jan. 1, 1996), of which 78.2% is urban and 21.8% is rural. Population density: 60.5 per sq km.

   The oblast lies 1,300 km west of Moscow on the Baltic Sea coast. It is situated between Poland and Lithuania and has no shared borders with Russia.

   The woodlands contain 39.4 million cu m of timber, including 14.3 million cu m of softwood. The forest tracts have water conservation, water protective, and recreational functions. The estimated cutting area is used at 86% of capacity and has a commercial logging potential of 0.4 million cu m. Other areas supply the oblast with the lumber it needs, including the wood processed into paper by the local pulp and paper mills.

   The oblast's minerals include building materials, oil, and peat. It contains the world's most active amber quarry, where amber is mined at a rate of 1,000 tons per year. The amber reserves here amount to hundreds of thousands of tons, or almost 90% of the world's total.

   The oblast has a temperate-continental climate, with a mean temperature of −2.5 to −4.5°C in January, and 16°C in July. The annual rainfall varies from 650 to 700 mm, and the growing season lasts 160 to 180 days.

2. Specialization and Sectoral Structure of the Economy (see Exhibit 58.1). Administrative division: 13 districts, 22 cities, 5 urban-type communities, and 96 village group-councils.

   Administrative Head: Tel. (0112) 464231, 467545. Fax: 463862.

   Principal cities: Kaliningrad (405,800), Svetlogorsk (33,600), and Baltiisk (27,400).

   The manufacturing structure is dominated by the food industry (42.7%), engineering (11.2%), and the pulp and paper industry (13.7%). The biggest enterprises are the trawler-fleet authority, the Reftransflot JSC, the Yantar plant (ship repair), the Quartz plant (processors), and the Sistema JSC (temperature sensors) in Kaliningrad; the oceanic fishing-fleet base in Pionersky; the lighting fixtures plant in Gusev; the pulp and paper mills in Neman, Kaliningrad, and Sovetsk; and the amber factory in Svetlogorsk.

   The oblast exports 28% of its manufactured output, with fish products accounting for 37% of this, and the products of five pulp and paper manufacturers for 6%. (See Exhibit 58.2.)

Exhibit 58.1.   Sectoral Structure of the Economy in 1995 (% of total)

	Industry	Farming	Transport	Construction	Other
Employment	25.0	12.0	8.7	8.7	45.6
Fixed Assets	24.8	14.0	9.8	10.9	40.5
Capital Investment	26.1	6.8	12.2	0.5	54.4

Exhibit 58.2.   Manufacture of Principal Industrial Products

	1995	1996
Paper, thou. tons	48.1	53.4
Hosiery, million pairs	1,678	973.2
Fish, thou. tons	206	245.1
Meat, thou. tons	10.9	9.9
Whole milk products, thou. tons	26.1	28.7

The oblast has a port complex capable of handling 10 to 15% of Russia's exports and imports. The commercial seaport is situated in the drainage area of the Pregel River and is approachable via a sea channel 40 km long. The maximum draft is 8m and displacement 12,000 tons, which makes the port accessible to most ship classes operated today by shipping companies of the Baltic countries. The port's facilities, with a total capacity of eight million tons, specialize in bulk and general cargoes. The port has a container-handling and ferry terminal.

A fishing port complex adjoins the commercial port and has refrigerated-warehouse facilities capable of storing 16,000 tons of products at a time. A branch of this port is located in Pionersky. Baltiisk is the site of a naval base (including four harbors), whose port facilities are used by commercial enterprises to ship cargoes and receive passenger liners.

In the early 1990s, the oblast's port complex handled 10 to 13 million tons of freight a year, 90% of which were exports and imports. Deterioration of the economic situation in Russia led to a decline of exports and imports passing through the oblast, and the downturn was intensified by problems of rail and vehicular passage through the Lithuanian Republic. To deal with these, a free economic zone, called Yantar, was established in the oblast. The legal entities in the zone were given the right to decide independently on forming joint ventures with foreign investors. Enterprises registered with the Yantar FEZ Development Committee and operating within the manufacturing sector are given a tax credit on their profits from the time it is announced. Depending on the activity of the enterprise, credit is given for four to five years. The part of the profit that is reinvested in the development of the oblast's social programs is fully exempt from taxes. The profit-tax rate for manufacturing enterprises is reduced by 50% if the share of the export-bound products in the total output is 50% or more. Foreign investors are guaranteed the right to transfer their after-tax profits to other countries. They also have an unrestricted right to the transfer, assignment, pledge, export, and termination of their investment.

At present, the oblast has about 1,000 enterprises with foreign involvement, including over 200 enterprises with 100% foreign interest. Of the enterprises with foreign involvement, Poland accounts for 37% and Germany for 22%, the remainder being distributed among the United States, Lithuania, Latvia, and a few other countries.

3. Investment Opportunities. The Kaliningrad Oblast offers preferential treatment to foreign investors. Incentives offered by the local and federal authorities to foreign investors will vary from tax breaks to a system of steps leading to the formation of special economic zones. The principle of special economic management in the Kaliningrad Oblast, which offers foreign investors an opportunity to operate at high-profit margins, will remain unchanged, however.

In 1995, the oblast had 352 joint ventures in operation. The foreign investments in 1993–95 totaled $22.9 million. Private owners held 20.5% of the fixed assets of enterprises and organizations, joint stock companies (without foreign interest) owned 32.1%, the federal authorities controlled 35.1%, and enterprises with foreign involvement were in control of 2%. The oblast's leading banks are Agroprombank (Tel. 21 4921), Alt-Koenigsbergbank (Tel. 21 7271), Atlantbank (Tel. 45 1578), Baltvneshtorgbank for foreign trade (Tel. 47 2701), Baltika (Tel. 21 7898), Baltkonversbank (Tel. 45 0737), Bam-Bank (Tel. 27 6891), the Western Baltic Bank (Tel. 43 6204), Investbank (Tel. 43 4662), Quartz (Tel. 23 6000), the Monskoy Bank (Tel. 44 2355), Rosvestbank (Tel. 21 2504), the Russian-Baltic Bank (Tel. 45 3966), Hopebank (Tel. 43 6488), Embakoenigbank (Tel. 44 5502), Energotransbank (Tel. 45 1519), and Yantar (Tel. 22 9781).

Investment prospects include trading operations, the transportation infrastructure, export-oriented manufacturing facilities, and modernization of pulp and paper enterprises. Current projects include modernization of bleached pulp facilities in the Tsepruss JSC (Kaliningrad pulp and paper plant), Tel. (0112) 27 4063; modernization of sea-container manufacturing facilities in the Yantar JSC, Tel. (0112) 44 8581; development of the Khrabrovo Airport, Tel. (0112) 46 0828; construction of a highway from Dorozhnoe to Gosgranitsa, 40.3 km, 50% of the project completed, Tel. (0112) 21 5950; construction of a cargo and passenger complex in Svetly (port structures, trade and amusement facilities, and restaurants), Tel. (0112) 44 0436; customs-warehouse complex in the Mamonovo township, Tel. (0112) 930 9693; completion of the mineral-water bottling plant, Tel. (0112) 46 4229; and manufacture of electric motors for household appliances, Tel. (0112) 27 3349.

The oblast is reachable from Moscow by rail (1,300 km, 30 hours to Kaliningrad from Belorussia Terminal) and road (the highway from Moscow, via Smolensk, Minsk and Vilnius, 33 hours).

There are 306 km of hard-surfaced roads per 1,000 sq km.

CHAPTER **59**

FREE ECONOMIC ZONES

Aleko A. Adamescu, Yuri A. Kovalev, and Alexander G. Granberg

59.1 OVERVIEW. By early 1995, 19 free economic zones (FEZs) had been officially registered in Russia. FEZs are being created, with varying degrees of progress, through the efforts of the authorities in the Kemerovo, Novgorod, Chita, Sakhalin, Leningrad, Moscow, and Kaliningrad Oblasts, the Primorsky, Krasnodar, and Khabarovsk Krais, and the Republics of Kabardino-Balkaria and Ingushetia.

The majority of FEZs in Russia have been established for purposes different from those accepted in international practice, and today they are not effective economic and legal entities in the true sense of the term. Initially, FEZs were planned as an arm of the state's external economic activity, ensuring distribution of privileges and subsidies among the administrative territorial units. Guided by criteria obscure to specialists, the government parceled out privileges to administrative territorial entities. Not infrequently, the local authorities announced at their own discretion the adoption of a FEZ status and lobbied for its approval at the federal level. Occasionally, special zones were announced in territories that were larger in size than either Greece or Ireland.

59.2 REGULATION OF EXTERNAL ECONOMIC ACTIVITIES. In 1992, the Russian Federation adopted a legislative package to regulate external economic activities and implement new tax laws that did not propose any exemptions for the FEZs already in operation. Although the statutory regulations in force in the zones have not been repealed officially, the federal-revenue service bodies interpreted them to be null and void, thereby abolishing a large proportion of the early privileges.

Federal and local authorities frequently indulged in the practice of obtaining unilateral advantages by announcing the territory of an administrative unit FEZ, such as at the Yantar FEZ in the Kaliningrad Oblast and the Sadko FEZ in the Novgorod Oblast, the offshore zones in Ingushetia, in the Northern Caucasus, and in some other areas of the Russian Federation.

In 1994, the Russian government was swayed toward closing "free zones" created within the territorial boundaries of administrative units. The draft law on FEZs that was prepared accordingly provides for the establishment of two predominant types of microzones: free customs zones and export-oriented output zones. The law abolished the numerous export and import benefits, including tax breaks in the zones. The freedom to establish new customs and export-output zones was not, however, endorsed by the legislature.

The following trends emerged in the government's attitude toward this issue:

- The area of special zones was limited to between one and two square kilometers, and a ban was placed on FEZs that were identical in size to the area of the respective administrative territories.

- Documents, conceptions, economic feasibility reports, and particular decisions concerning special zones were now prepared with an eye to international practice, but without giving a clear-cut picture of development prospects or allowing for the specific Russian environment.

- Regulation of economic activity in the zones now involved the federal authorities, among others, meaning that special zones can no longer be established at the will of the local authorities.

59.3 BARRIERS TO ADOPTION OF INTERNATIONAL PRACTICES.   The adoption of international practices in FEZs in Russia is complicated by a number of factors. High inflation, the lack of a legislatively guaranteed private-land ownership right, and the country's sociopolitical instability preclude any possibility of long-term investment, which is the purpose of special zones. The stereotyped idea of zones as a way for a Federation member to gain unilateral financial and economic advantages by shedding federal taxes and customs duties is still very much alive. Significantly, contrary to its declared policy toward new local zones, the federal government continues to hand out privileges to administrative territories, such as the Kaliningrad Oblast (in foreign trade), the city of Nakhodka in the Sakhalin Oblast, and to the Jewish Autonomous Oblast (both financial benefits). The government has also established an economic most-favored zone in Ingushetia, where, in fact, some individuals are availing themselves of the chance to line their pockets by shortchanging the federal revenues.

Quite a few spokespersons for the regions and the federal authorities still regard the creation of special zones as a factor "contributing to Russia's economic, scientific, technological, ecological, and social development." What the country needs, however, are partnerships and mutually beneficial cooperation between foreign firms and their Russian counterparts, of the kind that helps each party to achieve its economic and social ends.

Differences in the understanding of the objectives and operating principle of special zones by the Russians and foreigners have not been smoothed out as yet and must be taken into account in plans for any joint activities.

59.4 NAKHODKA FEZ.   Among the FEZs now registered, the Nakhodka FEZ, the special customs zones in the Moscow Region, and, to some extent, the Yantar FEZ are closest to world standards in terms of their organizational structure and development patterns. The Nakhodka FEZ was created in 1990 on the initiative of the managing directors of major enterprises in that city. The FEZ operates on the basis of the zone is Regulation and the Russian government's resolutions, including Resolution No. 1033, September 8, 1994, On Measures to Promote the Free Economic Zone in Nakhodka. Pursuant to these regulations, enterprises in the Nakhodka FEZ in which a foreign partner has an interest of at least 30% have been granted the following privileges:

- The federal tax on the profit share transferred abroad is equal to 7%, and the respective local tax must not exceed 5%.

- The profit, or part thereof, that is transferred abroad is completely exempt from tax for five years (starting with the reporting of regular profits).

- Part of the profit reinvested in production development or plowed back into social programs within the FEZ is exempt from taxes.

All issues relating to economic regulation and supervision in the Nakhodka FEZ are decided upon by the Administrative Council, which was formed by a resolution of the authorities of Nakhodka and the Partizan District, Primorsky Krai. The Administrative Council acts on the basis of the regulations on the FEZ in the Nakhodka area, Primorie, which were approved by the Council of Ministers of the RSFSR in Resolution No. 540, November 23, 1990.

The Administrative Council is an executive body of the Nakhodka administration. It adheres to the following policies in its strategy to develop the FEZ:

- Building infrastructure facilities (water, heat, and energy, roads, housing, hotels, etc.);
- Providing the FEZ with goods and services;
- Using in a comprehensive manner the labor, natural, and other resources available within the FEZ area.

Early in 1995, the Nakhodka FEZ had 15 banks. Some of them had general licenses to engage in foreign-exchange operations and were hooked up to the SWIFT interbank information-exchange system. The Finance Stock Co. and the Investment Co., representing the interests of Nakhodka enterprises, have been active on the Russian stock market since August 1992. Six companies are offering insurance services. Nakhodka's biggest enterprises have joined the Primorie financial and industrial group, which was instituted by the territory's authorities to promote external economic links.

In the area of customs regulation, in 1994 and 1995 the Administrative Council set up free customs territories, in particular free customs zones (FCZ) and free warehousing rules. The council's investment project division and the Progressor firm have been drawing up rules to govern FCZs and free warehouse activities. Their efforts are aimed at transportation and seaport services, the fish-processing industry, primary-material processing, and ship repairs. For all practical purposes, they have decided to institute a free customs regime at the can-making plant, in the Dalinterm JSC (ship dismantling), the Epsi firm (assembly of computer printers), and Yuzhmorflot (fishing).

The Russian government has opened a credit line of $40 million a year for the Nakhodka Administration until the year 2000. The loan will be spent to develop infrastructure facilities, including construction of a cogeneration plant and a water supply system, modernization of the Golden Valley airport, and construction of additional cargo-handling facilities at the seaport.

Investment prospects in the Nakhodka FEZ include:

- Expanding the Vostochny port to enable it to handle export and import freight, including the construction of a complex to receive five million tons of grain, complete with a 300,000-ton silo;
- Modernizing the Nakhodka port, including the construction of new forest-product-handling facilities;
- Modernizing oil-product storage and distribution facilities in Nakhodka and populated localities of the Partizan District;

- Construction of a complex in the Vostochny port to export three million tons of mineral fertilizers;
- Construction of a 250-MW cogeneration plant;
- Construction of a reservoir on the Olga River, with a daily intake of 38,000 to 52,000 cu m, and a reservoir on the Vodopadnaya River, with a daily intake of 70,000 cu m.;

Two technological parks have been established in the Nakhodka FEZ by South Korean and U.S. interests. The Russian-Korean technopark, with an area of 330 hectares, is equipped on the inside by the Korean group, while the Russians will provide the outside infrastructure (water, heat, and power supply lines). It is expected to accommodate about 100 consumer-goods-producing enterprises. The Russian-American Pacific Industrial technopark, with an area of 200 hectares, is organized as a closed joint stock company. The company holds a renewable 50-year lease, and has the right to sublease plots within the area for a term of 70 years and to use the land and all improvements made on it as security. The leaseholders will get customs and distribution warehouses, which will enable them to establish businesses and workshops to assemble high-tech and office equipment.

59.5   SHERIZONE.   Efforts have been underway since 1995 to set up a special economic zone, Sherizone, near the Sheremetyevo International Airport, Moscow Oblast. The project has been contracted to the Sherizone open joint stock company. The 140-hectare project will cost an estimated $300 million. A general conception for the establishment and operation of the SEZ has been drawn up, a series of predesign and design jobs has been completed, and approval has been obtained on all engineering issues. An access road, with a bridge across the Klyazma River, has been built; and work has begun to expand the waste treatment facilities and build other infrastructure elements. In fact, the groundwork has virtually been laid for the development and operation of the SEZ.

It is expected that after the zone is fully outfitted, the Sherizone JSC will start to sort out the tenders, including those already submitted, for the construction of customs terminals, vegetable- and fruit-processing enterprises, and enterprises to make packaging for small items and food products; and the establishment of export-oriented assembly facilities. Other enterprises to be set up are workshops to assemble airport and aircraft equipment and electronic-radio devices, multipurpose warehouses and storage, a wholesale market, and other facilities, with a total area of 500,000 sq m. Priority, however, will be given to the construction of warehousing facilities to handle containerized cargoes.

The administration in the Solnechnogorsk District of the Moscow Oblast has passed a resolution to give exemptions from local taxes to enterprises that will start putting up facilities in Sherizone. Federal authorities are considering giving privileges to entrepreneurs operating within the zone. It appears, however, that Sherizone will become the first special zone in Russia to benefit from its proximity to an international airport and, generally, to Moscow, Russia's financial and scientific center, and from the preferential treatment the local authorities will give its economic activities.

59.6   MOSCOW'S WESTERN ADMINISTRATIVE DISTRICT.   Pursuant to the Russian president's Decree No. 847, June 3, 1993, On the Free Customs Zones, the Moscow government has adopted a resolution to begin a phased establishment of a free customs zone in Moscow's Western Administrative District. A joint-stock company, Terminal AT, has been set up to implement the project and has been named the general customer. The project provides for the construction of a tunnel to connect the western river port to the Moscow City International Business Center in downtown Moscow; a comprehensive modernization of the western river port and promotion of international container traffic; creation of a free customs zone in the port; and negotiations with carrier companies on the inclusion of the western river port in the international shipping system.

59.7 YANTAR FEZ. The Yantar FEZ was established in the Kaliningrad Oblast on the initiative of the regional authorities. On January 1, 1994, the oblast's registers showed 791 enterprises with foreign capital, including 565 businesses with foreign interest, and 206 companies that were 100% foreign owned. For a considerable time after its creation, the region enjoyed privileges in external economic operations, a situation that was advantageously used by the regional authorities to attract partners from European Union countries to implement joint projects. In particular, EU experts handpicked seven comprehensive projects for development by Western consulting companies. These projects include:

- A comprehensive program to develop a management system for the Kaliningrad Oblast operating as an FEZ;
- Restructuring of the region's manufacturing industry and establishment of a business promotion center;
- Development of a transportation system in Kaliningrad;
- A comprehensive power supply program;
- Technological support for the modernization of the region's fish-processing complex.

In addition to these, attractive investment areas tentatively include modernization of the Khrabrovo Airport, construction of additional port facilities to handle 12 million tons of freight (first stage) and 20 tons of freight (second stage), production of large-capacity containers, expansion and modernization of the road network, and modernization of the bleached-pulp-manufacturing facilities.

59.8 OTHER FEZS. The performance of other officially registered zones in Russia is not easily assessed because their operation is chiefly directed by the regional authorities at obtaining privileges from the federal government, which has restricted this practice. Besides, these zones in no way meet the international requirements for units of this type.

There is a great deal of hope for other new projects, including:

- The Tumagan SEZ in Primorie, where the borders of Russia, China, and North Korea converge;
- The Taman-Kerch SEZ, on which tentative agreement has been reached between the Russian and Ukrainian governments;
- A project to create FEZs at science-intensive engineering plants in Nizhny Novgorod;
- Projects patterned on the Sherizone idea in Russia's regional centers, which have major international airports and science-intensive industries.

CHAPTER **60**

OFFSHORE ZONES

Aleko A. Adamescu, Yuri A. Kovalev, and Alexander G. Granberg

60.1 OVERVIEW.   Russia does not have offshore zones that meet international standards for such facilities. The ruble's limited convertibility, the undeveloped banking system, and the fluid economic situation in the country hamper, for the time being, the creation of zones trading on the Eurocurrency market alongside such recognized centers as the Isle of Man, Malta, and the Bahamas. The term *offshore zone* is typically applied in Russia to the free economic zone in Ingushetia and, more rarely, to the Kalmykian Republic.

60.2 REPUBLIC OF KALMYKIA.   In his Decree No. 59, March 14, 1994, Kalmykia's president, K.N. Ilyumzhinov, set a preferential tax rate on the profit transferred to the republic's budget by enterprises and organizations that do not use local primary and financial resources in their operations and invest funds on Kalmykia's soil. The total profit-tax rate for these enterprises (nonresident firms) is 18%, including a mandatory 13% to the federal budget and 5% to the Kalmykian Republic.

The next step was the abolition of taxes paid by nonresidents for the upkeep of housing and sociocultural facilities (equal to 1.5% of total sales in 1994). The majority of nonresident firms pay the road user tax at a preferential rate (0.27%). Aside from manufacturing enterprises, the legal entities entitled to these privileges are banks, insurance companies, and enterprises fully owned by foreigners.

These steps have resulted in the creation of an offshore zone model in Kalmykia and the promotion of businesses with foreign involvement. The Agency for Development and Cooperation (ADAC), which has been based in Moscow since April 1994, was created under the Kalmykian president to coordinate the process of granting tax breaks. The republic's government plans to introduce other measures to stimulate business and attract investors, including firms to set up a telecommunications network in the republic and build an international-class airport; the government also wants these measures to serve in the longer term as a basis for special zones that comply with international standards. The ADAC telephone in Moscow is (095) 291 4812, and the fax is (095) 291 9105.

60.3 INGUSHETIA.   In Ingushetia, an offshore zone was established by the Russian government's Resolution No. 740, June 19, 1994, under which Ingushetia was assigned a budget loan of 950 billion rubles, which was equal to the tax revenue and mandatory transfers to the federal budget in 1994 and 1995. To register in the zone, an offshore company must pay a fee of $3,935. The authorized capital of a closed joint stock company and a single-owner private business has been set at 25 and 2.5 million rubles, respectively. The

Exhibit 60.1. Comparison of Ingushetia FEZ Tax Rates to Regular Tax Rates

Taxes	Rate in Russia, %	Rate in Ingushetia Zone, %
Value-added tax (VAT)	20; 10	10; 5
Special tax	3	2
Profit tax	38	13
Maximum pay excess tax	38	0
Property tax	2	0
Motor road user tax	0.8; 0.6	0
Housing maintenance tax	1.5	0
Transport tax	1	0
Education tax	1	0
Sales tax on fuels and lubricants	25	5
Securities trading tax	0.3	0.1

number of offshore firms permitted to operate in Ingushetia has been limited to 15,000. Tax privileges are in effect for not more than one year and are extended to newly created or newly registered enterprises for the duration of the favored economic zone, from July 1, 1994 to July 1, 1995. The favored status has not been extended as yet. Privileges for Russia's southern republics will, however, be applied in varying degrees as is evidenced, among other things, by the formation of an FEZ in neighboring Kabardino-Balkaria under the Russian Federation's Resolution No. 300, March 22, 1995.

The preferential tax rates applied to offshore companies registered in Ingushetia have slashed tax payments by 80%. Enterprises in this zone were exempted from all taxes and payments to the Federation members' budget (Resolution No. 153, August 19, 1994, of the Ingush Republic's Council of Ministers) (see Exhibit 60.1). In addition, enterprises were exempted from advertising taxes and target duties for the maintenance of the police force and area improvement.

Enterprises manufacturing and selling excisable goods pay 50% of the tax rate.

Enterprises are entitled to a 50% reimbursement of the customs expenses (in and out duties, value-added tax (VAT), and excises).

The Russian State Customs Committee has established a special customs-clearance procedure for goods and vehicles. The offshore enterprises in the Ingushetia FEZ are allowed to use their actual address, instead of the firm's legal address, for customs clearance of their freight. The obvious advantages of securing registration in this zone for Russian and foreign entrepreneurs may be accompanied by additional advantages, such as relevant legal security, extension of the zone life, changes in rules concerning the mandatory assignment of a firm to a single resident bank, and a lower amount of the required authorized capital at the registration stage.

PART **X**

INFRASTRUCTURE

CHAPTER 61

TRANSPORTATION SYSTEM: PERSPECTIVES FOR INTERNATIONAL COOPERATION

Vitali B. Yefimov

61.1 OVERVIEW. Russian entrepreneurs are increasing their business activity, including their interest in developing international cooperation. Likewise, foreign investors are recognizing the attractiveness of the Russian market. The transportation complex plays a dual role in the nation: it is both a means for economic links, facilitating Russia's integration into the global economic system, and a field of active cooperation.

Today's Russian transportation system comprises 160,000 km of railways, 750,000 km of roads, 7,000 km of tram and trolley lines, 101,000 km of inner waterways, and 203,000 km of pipelines. Air transportation routes cover 1 million km, sea routes 600,000 nautical miles, and bus routes 1 million km. Russian transportation companies transfer more than 13 million tons of cargo and nearly 130 million passengers daily.

61.2 ECONOMIC FACTORS. The transportation industry currently employs more than 4.5 million people. Assets rose by the beginning of 1994 to 245 trillion rubles, which equals 21.9% of assets of material industries. Transportation accounts for 9% of total profit of the Russian economy. The industry has been one of the most dynamic sectors of Russia's economy which has seen profound structural changes in the last several years.

The transportation field has undergone a rapid process of privatization—60% to 80% of the value of assets are transferred to share capital or privatized in different types of transportation. The monopoly of large state structures has been fully eliminated. In all forms of water transportation, and in air transportation, hundreds of independent companies are active; and about one million people are using commercial vehicles. Only railway transportation remains state controlled.

61.3 MANAGEMENT. In a short time, the system of vertical state management of transportation has been abolished. The new management system is built on legal regulations, licensing, certification, and state support of critical transportation activities and priority start-up projects.

The main authoritative body is the Ministry of Transportation, created in 1990, which formulates state transportation policies, develops legislation, implements special state programs and oversees their fulfillment, and coordinates the growth of different types of transportation. The ministry represents Russia's interests in international transportation organizations, enters into treaties and agreements on international conveyance, and coordinates international cooperation both in developing the transportation system in Russia and in negotiating international transportation issues.

The ministry does not have absolute authority over businesses. Instead, it works with foreign partners to support their investment projects, and it also conducts joint research. The ministry's task is to give both sides maximum information about general conditions and legal provisions that may affect a project, help them choose a partner, and suggest the most effective types of activity. Of course, the larger and more important transportation projects with foreign participation receive state support.

61.4 DEVELOPING THE TRANSPORTATION COMPLEX. The most important tasks of developing the Russian transportation complex are:

- Creating a new legal foundation for transportation;
- Developing a modern transportation infrastructure;
- Reengineering transportation facilities;
- Modernizing the system of international communications and integrating Russia's transportation complex into the world transportation system;
- Educating the new generation of personnel and reeducating the current one.

The most important tasks of developing the transportation complex are decided within a framework of special long-term state programs, among them air transportation development, revival of the trade fleet, building automobile routes, and converting military industries to benefit the transportation complex.

The Ministry of Transport gives most of its attention to the financial support of the programs, including those involving foreign capital. Independent Russian transportation enterprises are not strong enough, financially, and the loan practices of the country's banks are still not well suited to the transportation industry. Thus, the acquisition of new passenger planes and vessels and the development of terminals without state support looks doubtful.

The ministry constantly works on raising the efficiency of investment activities in the field of transportation. Recently, a new contract system for interactions between partners took effect for all federal programs and investment projects, which has resulted in positive changes.

The globally accepted system of preparation, analysis, examination, and management of investment projects is being developed for implementation in Russia. This will not only raise the overall level of financial activities and investment, but will also let Russian transportation authorities better understand their colleagues abroad.

61.5 WORKING WITH FOREIGN PARTNERS. A number of the problems encountered working with foreign partners have been solved. The most pressing problem is the insufficient development and inadequate technological condition of transportation facilities. For many years, money has been invested in developing a great amount of transportation equipment, while at the same time the development of the road system, sea and river terminals, and airports lagged behind. This is why the Terminal program has been implemented as one of the first of its kind for developing the transportation infrastructure. As a result, when completed by the year 2000, the program will have built or renovated a total of 3,000 terminals, warehouse complexes, container-system elements, and other facilities.

Recently, a good deal of work has been done to reconstruct sea and river ports, airports, and roads. A whole group of projects has been carried out with foreign participation, for example, a World Bank loan of $300 million for road reconstruction. Agreements to receive similar loans for repairing road bridges and reconstructing seaports are about to be finalized.

Nevertheless, the investment potential of Russia's transportation system is not being fully utilized, and many projects are awaiting interested investors, including the following:

- Plans to modernize Moscow's air transportation complex, including four airports, which represent $800 million investments;
- Modernized or new port complexes on the Baltic and Black Seas and in the Russian Far East;
- Plans for a north-south transportation corridor with a modern cargo system supported by an effective infrastructure and communications system.

The second problem encountered by foreign investors is the need for modern transportation equipment. The problem touches on the vital interests of many branches of the economy and is solved, first of all, through the state's military conversion program. Production of new passenger jets (TU–204, IL–96, and IL–114) is already under way. Various types of ships are being built at converted facilities, as well as modern city buses, road maintenance vehicles, and modern communication and management systems.

It is very difficult to create a new generation of transportation facilities without the scientific and technical assistance of developed countries. That is why the Ministry of Transportation constantly studies possibilities for mutually beneficial cooperation.

One example is the special government program for improving air-traffic management. The United States is participating, and the participation of the European Bank for Reconstruction and Development (EBRD) is expected. Loans associated with the program total $350 million. The financial success of the project will be affected by the unique geographical position of Russia, over whose territory a large number of international flights are conducted. In addition, Russia has active transcontinental routes, and new regular flights are being added to connect Russia with other countries. In 1994, 20 additional routes were opened, and eight airports became international (including those at Astrakhan, Chelyabinsk, Vladivostok, Belgorod, Pskov, and Ufa). The overall number of international airports has doubled since 1992 to 48. These programs result in airfare increases, some of which is allocated to cover the costs of modernizing air-traffic management systems.

Another large international program is the IBRD-assisted City Transport project. The $329 million loan is going toward purchasing 1,800 transportation vehicles for 14 Russian cities.

61.6 GROUNDWORK.   Stable development of the transportation system is impossible without a corresponding legal basis. Transportation legislation is being developed based on principles that are compatible with those generally accepted in developed countries. An invitation has been extended to foreign experts to participate in the preparation of these legal documents, which is a very promising development. A World Bank project currently in its initial stage will bring together a group of Russian and foreign experts to work to improve the legal groundwork for transportation management.

Another area of international cooperation involves the training of personnel for the complex. A new generation of transportation workers will need to be educated with a modern professional and market mentality. Hundreds of specialists have already been trained in Europe, and the European Union is participating in the creation of five educational centers for such training.

Foreign investors are participating actively in developing the transportation system. Examples include the expansion of the Tuapse port, development of Baltic seaports, and improvement of air-traffic management in the Far East. Some Russian enterprises are working to directly attract foreign investment. For example, Russian freight companies have gotten about $650 million in foreign loans to assemble sea-going vessels. Another opportunity for foreign partners is participation in creating a new international system of transportation communications, based on a concept of integrated transportation corridors and intermodal transportation.

CHAPTER 62

INFORMATION AND TELECOMMUNICATION SYSTEMS

Arkadiy S. Golubkov, Vladimir B. Bulgak, Yuri A. Nisnevich, Anne Grey, Barbara Ristau and Yuri D. Poroykov

62.1 INFORMATION SYSTEMS.* The creation and maintenance of information systems and data management in Russia involves more than 10,000 enterprises and organizations nationwide. Approximately 2.5 million computers are in use in Russia, and computer use is growing as more and more companies transfer information to electronic media. Systems are being switched to international standards and operating systems (OSI, EDI, SWIFT). The share of nonstate informational systems and resources is growing constantly.

(a) Current and Developing Applications. State information systems are used by the president, the Duma and the Council of Federation, the Russian government, and other public organizations in getting and receiving information. Electronic information includes databases on the activities of the committees and commissions of the Chambers of the Federal Assembly and on domestic and foreign legislation. Currently these systems are being expanded and made more interactive to widen the user base and the services offered.

Ministries and agencies are creating and developing branch and interbranch information systems in areas such as population and property censuses, ecological monitoring and response, domestic and foreign trade, archive services, cultural activities, welfare, employment, and taxation.

Regional bodies are using information systems to manage data on the industrial and scientific potential of the region and its natural and land resources. Moscow, St. Petersburg, Ekaterinburg, Tomsk, Nizhny Novgorod all have developed information systems. The heaviest use by regional bodies involves real estate, population censuses, and welfare. A system of informational centers for entrepreneurship support is also being developed.

An information infrastructure now exists in Russia for business activities. Exchange information, exchange rates, and credit rates are provided by the Economic News Agency (AEN), Russian Exchange Brokers Company, RSIFT Argonaft, MASTAK Info, and Informational Bank of *Business World* (IDM). Financial and commercial information on the Russian market is provided by the International Financial Information Agency (MAFI),

---

*This section was written by Arkadiy S. Golubkov.

KOMINFO, PAL-Inform, Reuters, and Information Agency MOBILE. Information on Russian banks can be found on IDM, Mosvneshinform, and East-Service. Other business systems that are being developed offer analytical information on specific problems and markets. Other information is available to businesses through the state agencies ITAR-TASS and RIA-Novosti, and a few independent services, including AEN, KOMINFO, MIR, and ISTOK.

Economic and demographic statistical information is mainly provided by State Statistics Committee organizations, which offer services based on more than 300 databases.

The Russian Federation accounts for a large part of the global flow of scientific and technical information from 30 leading information centers, institutes, and libraries in Russia (including VINITI, VNITCentre, INION, GPNTB, NPO "Poisk," and UNIIKI) which have databases for all leading fields of science. In addition, an information network of Russian educational and scientific centers is being created.

Legal information tends to be the most widespread information service in Russia. The leading providers include NCPI of the Justice Ministry, NTC "Systema" FAPSI, and independent companies such as Garant-Servis, Delo & Pravo, Infra-M, Rusika, Justisinform, and VMI.

Several specialized information centers have information on available electronic databases: Informregistr, DIZ, and MBIT. Access to foreign databases can be obtained through the databases IAS, MCITI, and VINITI.

Geological-information systems include VNITS "Forestry" (forest cartographics), MNTK "Geos" (geology, geophysics, geochemistry data processing), and State Center "Nature" (cartography using space technology). A database of digital geographic and mining information is also available.

The volume of services provided by electronic transactions and trade systems is increasing. The most developed system for commercial information is the system of business cooperation of the Chamber of Commerce and Industry, which has offices in the regions and uses telecommunications to exchange information.

(b) Production of Hardware and Software.   Most information systems in Russia use imported hardware. Its hardware market, which represents all major international producers, is highly competitive and demands high-quality products. Domestic companies in this field mainly operate assembly lines for producing personal computers (IVK, Kami, Stins-Coman), but in the future will create and produce their own products. For software, especially information-system-user software, the share of domestic producers is considerably higher. Russian developers have demonstrated clear success in system integration, especially for financial and banking activities.

(c) Policy.   The formation and implementation of state policies regarding information technology and systems are provided by state bodies and include: the Duma (Information Policies and Communications Committee), Committee on Information Policies under the president (Roskominform), Federal Agency of Government Communications and Information (FAPSI) under the president, Information and Document Support Department of the Administration, State-Legal Department under the president, Russian government (Science and Education Department), Ministry of Science and Technical Policies, and the State Committee on Defense Industries.

Decisions on creating federal information networks and databases at the state's expense are based on expert reports provided by Roskominform; and if special or protected systems are involved, the reports are obtained from FAPSI. Roskominform is the official state contractor for federal information systems.

Roskominform coordinates the development of federal programs, together with the Ministry of Science, in the field of information; provides, with Gosstandard, services for the standardization of information systems in cooperation with other countries (working with the Ministry of Foreign Affairs); and develops proposals on regulating the information services market.

State policies are directed at supporting the prospective information technologies, creating competitive conditions in the market, forming conditions for entrepreneurship, stimulating investment, and creating a favorable climate for investment activities. To promote industrial development, special attention has been given to the following information technologies:

- Speech synthesis and legibility, as well as text and pictures
- Modeling of complex dynamic processes
- Parallel calculations
- Creating high-reliability projection software
- Integration of technologies into function-oriented complexes
- Working with large bodies of information
- Intellectual systems using virtual reality technology

(d) Investment Opportunities.   Opportunities for investment exist in the following fields:

- Geoinformation systems, including systems processing cartographic information
- Automation of banking, financial, credit, and insurance operations
- Office and word-processing systems
- Transportation management systems
- Information services
- Electronic-trade systems
- Medical-information systems

Development of these fields was hampered because of insufficient hardware development. In this context, projects focused on the following areas of interest:

- Creating prospective hardware (optical computers, transputers, neurocomputers)
- Creating state-of-the-art processors

Steps are being taken to develop cooperation between domestic and foreign companies. The most important task here is the development of an international information exchange to solve international intellectual-property issues. Although some software and databases are being promoted in foreign markets, the current volume of exports is insignificant.

(e) Taxation and Legislation.   Special tax treatment is not available for computer hardware or software in Russia. Information legislation is being developed, however. The federal law of February 20, 1995, On Information, Informatization, and Information Protection, which regulates creation and use of documented information, information technology, and information security, has been adopted. Another law in effect is the September 23, 1992 law, On Legal Protection for Software and Databases.

62.2 TELECOMMUNICATIONS.* The rapid development of communications in Russia in recent years has been achieved by the policy mapped out in the national communications program. The program contains guidelines for a structural and technological overhaul of the industry and is being implemented in stages. To carry it out, Russia needs to attract a stream of investments into the communications industry in the shortest possible time.

(a) Structural Reorganization. The groundwork laid in 1992 and 1993 for a steady advance of the industry was further solidified during 1994 through 1996 by a major structural overhaul, which included dividing the multiline state-owned communications business into three independent operations:

1. Telecommunications
2. Postal service
3. Radio, television, and continued privatization of the telecommunications services

The majority of enterprises in the industry have been converted into open joint-stock companies, which are in the final stage of reorganization. Of the 137 telecommunications enterprises slated for privatization, 121 have been registered as open joint-stock companies, with a total authorized capital in excess of $5 billion. The sale of shares floated by the these joint-stock companies at specialized voucher and cash auctions and by investment tender has confirmed their investment attractiveness for Russian and foreign investors. Foreign investors have acquired 21.3% of the shares sold in the open market, which amounts to 5% of the total authorized capital of the private enterprises.

The first privatization stage did not aim exclusively at attracting major investment amounts. Its purpose was to achieve a qualitative change in the property relations in the industry. This perhaps explains why specialized investment tenders were held in five joint stock companies only. These five, however, included such giants as Moscow Long-Distance and International Telephone Service and the Moscow City Telephone Network. Tenders arranged by these joint stock companies to sell blocks of shares to investors have attracted more than $150 million in investments. The proportion of foreign investments that rose to 41% of the total in Russian telecommunications in 1994 is generally focused on high-yielding projects in the long-distance and international communications services, mobile communications services, and data transmission. (The share of foreign capital was 16% in 1993 and 4% in 1992.) The influx of foreign capital allowed major projects in long-distance and international communications to be completed on the basis of the latest technologies and modern communication modes that were introduced in 1993 and 1994.

The Communications Ministry has appreciated the need to look for completely new ways of attracting investments. Foreign investment, which is flowing at an annual rate of $400 to $500 million, must be at least ten times as large.

(b) Sviazinvest: New Opportunities for Foreign Investors. The Sviazinvest joint stock company was created pursuant to the Russian president's decree to that effect. Its authorized capital consists of state-held stocks of the privatized telecommunications enterprises. Amounting to 38% (until August 1997) of their authorized capital, these stocks are owned by the federal authorities and kept at the central depository of the Russian State Property Com-

---

*This section was written by Vladimir B. Bulgak

mittee. The blocks of shares consolidated in Sviazinvest are valued at more than $2 billion. The Russian government has decided to sell 49% (in 1997) of its common stock through a commercial tender on investment terms and to retain 51% federal ownership.

The purpose of this move is to accumulate funds to finance modern telecommunications networks, integrate local intrazonal and interurban networks into a single digital network, and make effective capital investments in the communications infrastructure. The shares of the Sviazinvest joint-stock company are to be sold through the Russian Federal Property Foundation. The bidders will include domestic and foreign investors.

The establishment of Sviazinvest will help sort out and implement the growth priorities of the public-access telecommunications network. In turn, this will allow its individual components to develop harmoniously. An equally important objective is setting up a competitive local, long-distance, and international communication operator that is competent to enter international communication-service markets.

What opportunities are open to foreign investors with the creation of the Sviazinvest joint-stock company? First, purchasing Sviazinvest shares is a profitable proposition, with high returns on investment, considering the current demand for communications services in Russia. Second, Sviazinvest shareholders are entitled, in practical terms, to a role in the management of communications services in Russia. A shareholder has the right to vote at decision-making meetings regardless of the number of shares held.

The Rostelecom joint-stock company, the key long-distance and international telephone operator, does not have influence over all communications development issues. Sviazinvest will help considerably to expand the investment market based on an integrated policy.

In addition, the emergence of yet another operator, armed with a license in all telecommunications fields, will give rise to a healthy competition that will benefit Russian customers greatly.

(c) Shares of Joint-Stock Companies. The shares of privatized enterprises in the telecommunications industry are among the most attractive segments of the securities market in Russia. According to independent analysts, the industry's stock-market indicators surpass the aggregate stock-market figures. Yet, many joint-stock companies have not availed themselves of the opportunity to raise investment funds through specialized cash auctions. Through the end of 1995, the 12 regional telecommunications operators were sold at specialized auctions and investment tenders, a process that will gather momentum in the future.

Foreign investors are among the most active purchasers of shares offered by regional telecommunications joint-stock companies. So far, foremost among these investors have been Cable & Wireless, C.S. First Boston, VLM Enterprises, and Kunto Ltd.

Because of the underdeveloped secondary market, sale/purchase transactions involving shares of privatized communications enterprises have been rare; but here, too, there are indisputable leaders like Rostelecom, Moscow City Telephone Network, St. Petersburg Telephone Network, and the Novosibirsk Telephone Network joint stock companies.

Interest in the shares of other regional operations is just beginning to grow. For the most part, these are securities of telephone companies operating in major industrial centers. The shares of the Rostelecom joint stock company are at present the most reliable and fastest-growing asset on the stock market, enjoying a high demand among foreign investors. By early 1995, their proportion of authorized capital had grown to 33.4%, having doubled within a single year. Rostelecom plans to float its securities in foreign capital markets, a move that will help attract a few hundred million U.S. dollars in the short term.

(d) Regulation of Investment Activity.   Reforms and quality improvement in the communications industry have the backing of Russian legislators and tax-policy enforcers.

The principal legal act regulating operations in the communications industry is the Federal Communications Law, which defines the powers of the government authorities, the legal entities, and the people involved. In particular, the law provides guidelines for investment activities in the communications industry and outlines moves to attract foreign investors. Recently, the Russian government adopted a general program to stimulate the flow of domestic and foreign investments into the Russian economy; and a new version of the Law on Foreign Investments and amendments to the Law on the Fundamentals of the Taxation System in the Russian Federation are being prepared.

A number of tax benefits and exemptions are applied to the communications industry. In particular, the Taxation Law exempts from tax that part of the profit enterprises plow back into business as an investment.

Under the Law on the Value-Added Tax:

- Exemptions from the value-added tax are allowed on securities circulation operations.

- Exemptions are available (for one year from the date of registration) from the value-added tax, the special tax, and the customs duties on equipment brought in from abroad as part of the unauthorized capital of joint ventures.

Certain benefits apply to purchases by the Communications Ministry of communications equipment that is not manufactured by Russian enterprises. In addition, although the import-customs policy has been tightened, attempts to secure preferential treatment are being met with understanding and cooperation.

(e) Promising Projects and International Cooperation.   The Communications Ministry has drawn up and is implementing additional plans to technologically upgrade and modernize Russian telecommunications by using digital systems and introducing new and modern communications services. This work runs along two lines. The first is completion of international projects involving foreign investors that will allow Russia to join the world telecommunications network. The program implementation has largely been assigned to the Rostelecom joint-stock company. In 1993 and 1994, Russia completed a number of major projects with foreign participation. These include two international communications projects, the north (Russian-Denmark) and the east (Russia-Japan-South Korea), at a total cost of nearly $260 million, with construction of international switching centers in Moscow, St. Petersburg, and Khabarovsk.

In addition to these projects, work is proceeding on the construction of a digital radio-relay line between Moscow and Khabarovsk, at a cost of $235 million, and a south international complex (Italy-Turkey-Russia-Ukraine) at a cost of $120 million, including erection of four international switching centers. When work is completed, the number of international telephone channels will reach 48,000, and automatic telephone links will be available to 168 countries. Next in line are projects to develop the networks of fiber-optic communication lines from Moscow to St. Petersburg, Samara, and Khabarovsk. The plan is to involve foreign investors in the implementation of the Samara-Khabarovsk project. The south project and the fiber-optic line from Moscow to St. Petersburg are paid for in part by foreign loans.

The second line of the modernization program involves projects developed by regional operators, which include projects to set up cellular, local, and long-distance communications networks. For example, the Moscow City Telephone Network joint stock company is working on three strategic projects: one covered by its own funds; another, called Gold Bullet, carried out jointly with AT&T, the Rostelecom joint stock company, and the Telmos joint stock company, and paid for with American loans; and a third, called Golden Goose, implemented jointly with the Comstar limited partners and financed by British loans. Once completed, these projects will allow Moscow's telecommunications networks to be thoroughly overhauled.

Strapped for cash, the Russian regional operators are ready to cooperate with Western investors. Most have designs and business plans for network improvements available, but some of these are below international standards. Western partners will be able to help Russian regional operators a great deal in preparing business plans attractive to Western investors. The regional investors are just starting to formulate their intentions to conform with commonly accepted world standards. A major problem with the regional projects is their long payback periods. The experience of some joint stock companies in the telecommunications business shows that ways can be found to improve the profit-earning power of these projects or work out terms and conditions that will make them attractive to foreign and domestic investors. Participation in regional projects may take various forms, such as through investment loans or establishment of joint ventures to build and operate the communications networks.

Russian operators, working with their foreign partners, have acquired extensive experience. Ground rules have been worked out based on international standards and Russian specifics and are gradually being assimilated by the regional operators. The industry has a portfolio of projects, both major undertakings and local ventures, that are attractive to foreign investors. The completed projects are already paying for themselves faster than projected by their business plans. For example, the fiber-optic project between Moscow and Copenhagen is a year ahead of the repayment schedule.

Foreign capital is involved in various ways in Russia's telecommunications development. Attractive prospects are opening in response to the stability of the shares issued by the telecommunications joint stock companies and other operators in the stock market, as well as the establishment of the Sviazinvest joint-stock company. Foreign investments in telecommunications enjoy preferential treatment that is regularly enhanced by Russian regulators. Undoubtedly, Russia will have a modern digital-telecommunications network that will raise it to the level of the world's leading telecommunications systems.

62.3 LAW ON TELECOMMUNICATIONS.* The Federal Communications Law came into force on February 22, 1995. During the process of developing it, legislators were trying to take into account dynamic situations, foresee possible changes, and learn from and utilize information based on foreign legislation.

The importance of the communications field for the government was a fact understood early in this century by the Russian Empire, and it would not be an exaggeration to claim that, in many cases, current government communications agencies took into consideration legislation from this period. The telecommunications boom in pre-Revolutionary Russia was supported by a dynamic and effective legislation process in combination with a flexible investment policy.

After 1917, the communications industry was militarized, and its activities were determined by communications laws, the last of which was established in 1971 by a Resolution of the Council of Ministers of the USSR and amended in 1978. This resolution appointed a government-owned, centralized, and strictly controlled system of field operations.

---

*This section was written by Yuri A. Nisnevich.

In 1991, the Supreme Soviet of the Russian Federation and other branches of communications experienced problems because of changes in the economic, social, and political environment. This situation pointed out the need to develop new legislation in the communications field that would serve to define the area, its purposes, and problems, as well as providing general rules for regulating the activities of communications agencies and the postal service.

The first regulation was the 1993 law Regarding the Federal Branches in Government Communication and Information. This law helped to establish a legislative base for providing government agencies and other organizations with special communications and information systems. The law established a common system of federal agencies for government communications and information under the direct authority of the president.

The next significant piece of legislation in the communications field, approved by the Russian Duma, became effective in 1994. Based on the law About Federal Communication by Courier, which regulates a specific system of postal communications used by the government and defense, the president made the postal system an organ of the federal government.

(a) Integration into a Global Information System. Creation of global information system requires compatible communication networks, the key to which is the use of modern technologies and a common set of standards. The recognized international leader in the telecommunications field is the International Telecommunications Union (ITU), and the leader in the postal field is the Worldwide Postal Union (WPU). Russia's recent ratification of conventions related to these organizations provides a basis for the integration of Russia into global telecommunications.

(b) Basic Principles. The basic law, Regarding Communications, which recently went into effect, is based on the following principles:

- Competition and limitation of monopolistic activities on the commodities markets
- Protection of consumers' rights
- Certification of production operations and services
- Promotion of investment activities
- Privatization of state and municipal enterprises

This is the first law in Russia that establishes the legal foundation for activities in the communications field under the legislation of the Russian Federation. The law determines the level of government authority in regulating these activities, and also the rights and responsibilities of persons and judicial entities participating in these activities and using communications services. The development and guarantee of stable and qualified communications play a crucial role in the activities of government and society as a whole.

The law establishes the following:

Equal rights of persons and judicial entities to participate in telecommunications activities and use the results of such activities;

Balancing the interests of the Russian Federation and its subjects;

Freedom in the transmission of communications, freedom of the postal service and the transit of mail within the entire Russian Federation;

Considering the interests of users of communications;

Development of entrepreneurial activities and limitation of monopolistic activities;

Guaranteeing reliable and well-managed communications in compliance with the standards of the ITU and the WPU

Introduction of new communications technologies;

Attraction of foreign investment and the use of foreign technologies and managerial experience;

Expansion of global cooperation;

Liberalization of the federal organs of the executive authority.

(c) Participants in Telecommunications.   Individuals and judicial entities have equal rights to participate in telecommunications activities and to use their results. Specific communications enterprises may be established by any person or judicial entity, including foreign investors; and they must obtain a license.

Federal authorities in the defense field and police authorities have the right to use communications for commercial purposes. They must obtain a license to offer communications services. In addition, private postal services must obtain a license.

Foreign organizations and citizens practicing communications activities in the Russian Federation are subject to the same regulations as persons and judicial entities of the Federation.

The Federation government and federal bodies of executive authority in the communications field are responsible for the general regulation of communications. The Federal bodies manage and are responsible for maintaining and developing all branches of communications. Their authority includes:

Development of proposals for government policy

Coordinating branches of communications

Supervision and government control

Development of proposals to develop and use radio frequencies

Development of postal communications

The law also specifies procedures for consumers presenting complaints, filing lawsuits, and resolving disagreements.

(d) Financing and Investment.   The Financing of communications activities using federal funds is based on state programs for the development of communications. Entities participating in the development of communications projects may receive guarantees, favorable credit terms, tax exemptions, and other benefits. Foreign investments in communications may receive guarantees in accordance with legislation regarding the foreign investment.

(e) Freedom of Information.   All communication users within the federation are guaranteed equal rights regarding the transmission of information using telecommunications and postal-service networks. No users can be refused access to the general communications networks.

All communications operators are obliged to respect communications secrecy. Parties are permitted to listen to telephone conversations, divulge telecommunications information, or review and remove postal material and official correspondence only with the permission of a court.

(f) Tariffs. Tariffs for communications services are established by contract. Some groups of citizens and official persons can receive easements and favorable rates.

62.4 BISNIS: THE BUSINESS INFORMATION SERVICE FOR THE NEWLY INDEPENDENT STATES*

(a) Overview. For forward-looking U.S. companies, markets in the Newly Independent States (NIS) are simply too important to ignore. That is why so many U.S. companies are turning to BISNIS, the Business Information Service for the Newly Independent States at the U.S. Department of Commerce. BISNIS is the U.S. government's clearinghouse of information on doing business in the countries of the former Soviet Union. Reliable, time-sensitive commercial information is critical for U.S. companies to stay ahead of their competition—particularly when the business climate is as unpredictable as it is in the NIS. Through timely dissemination of business information to U.S. companies, BISNIS helps strengthen the U.S. export position in a highly competitive global environment.

Numerous small and medium-sized U.S. firms are doing business in the NIS, exporting record volumes of processed foods to Russia's burgeoning consumer markets, establishing telecommunications networks in remote areas of Central Asia, and supplying capital goods to key NIS industries. More than 650 American companies of all sizes now have offices in Moscow and St. Petersburg; while more than 170 have offices in Kiev, 80 each in Almaty, Kazakstan and Tashkent, Uzbekistan, and 70 in Baku, Azerbaijan.

Despite much negative media commentary, U.S. companies active in Russia are now beginning to see a substantial return on their investments:

- Kodak sales went up 1000% in the last three years, and the firm now has 50% of the market in Russia with an investment of $40 million;
- Russia is Polaroid's largest overseas market;
- GE's sales in Russia reached $500 million in 1996;
- Hewlett Packard's sales hit $210 million in 1996;
- Xerox's sales up 50% in 1996;
- IBM will boost sales in Russia by 30% in 1997.

(b) BISNIS Services. As the NIS countries move forward with market-oriented reforms, BISNIS will continue to provide U.S. companies with the best commercial information possible, as it has since opening in 1992. BISNIS draws its data from a wide network of contacts at U.S. embassies and consulates throughout the NIS, from other U.S. government agencies, and from many nongovernmental programs working in the NIS. BISNIS also maintains its own overseas network of 14 representatives in Russia, Ukraine, Moldova, Armenia, Azerbaijan, Kazakstan, Tajikistan, Uzbekistan, Kyrgyzstan and Georgia. To date, BISNIS has assisted U.S. companies in generating over $1.6 billion in trade and investment transactions in the NIS.

BISNIS's U.S.-based trade specialists, who together cover all 12 NIS countries and many important industry sectors, provide one-on-one counseling and basic business information and referrals to U.S. companies of all sizes doing business in the NIS. Together with BISNIS's overseas network, they provide U.S. companies with time-sensitive trade leads, the latest information on export and project finance, and insights into developing long-term strategies for NIS markets.

---

*This section was written by Anne Grey and Barbara Ristau.

BISNIS makes the latest commercial information about the NIS available to U.S. companies through a variety of channels:

(i) BISNIS Online. BISNIS's own Internet home page, BISNIS Online, is internationally recognized for its substantive information on the NIS and is rated among the top 5% world wide web sites. BISNIS Online is the backbone of BISNIS's information distribution service, disseminating cable communications from BISNIS overseas network, trade leads, and publications. On average, U.S. companies download 3000 documents per day from BISNIS Online. Companies seeking venture capital can turn to its "Sources of Finance" for project finance offered in the NIS by the U.S. government, and bilateral and multilateral agencies, such as the World Bank, the European Bank for Reconstruction and Development, and the Asian Development Bank. Information on exchange rates and legislation is just a mouse-click away, as well as lists of U.S. companies in the NIS, including law firms, shipping companies and freight forwarders, and the latest on upcoming trade events.

(ii) BISNIS E-mail Broadcast Service. The BISNIS E-mail broadcast service covers topics of general interest to the business community. U.S. companies are invited to identify areas that interest them, so that they can receive more specific data on NIS countries and/or industries directly. As of January 1997, 3800 U.S. companies interested in receiving the latest trade leads, opportunities, and late-breaking developments in the NIS had requested this service.

(iii) BISNIS Fax Retrieval. Companies that prefer to use fax technology can turn to the BISNIS fax retrieval system 24 hours a day. This system disseminates nearly 400 documents on trade leads, sources of finance, and other commercial information on the NIS and fills 1000 requests for documents each month. The system is updated weekly.

(iv) Publications. BISNIS produces a number of highly regarded publications. The monthly *BISNIS Bulletin* reports on timely, practical NIS-business information—for U.S. companies. The bulletin emphasizes in-depth coverage of major issues (legal and regulatory issues, trade and project finance, major product markets), as well as the latest on U.S. government trade-promotion programs and activities. The "Tricks of the Trade" column provides expert advice on topics such as product certification, wholesale and retail product distribution, shipping and customs procedures, taxation, and advertising. The "Regional Corner" feature alerts readers to opportunity-rich areas less-well known to U.S. firms, such as Samara in Russia, Petropavlovsk in Kazakstan, and Gekharkunik Province in Armenia.

Search For Partners, BISNIS's monthly, matchmaking publication, disseminates time-sensitive information on NIS enterprises and businesses looking to establish long-term business relationships with U.S. partners. Created to help U.S. companies find "bankable" opportunities, *Search for Partners* identifies NIS enterprises looking for U.S. partners in a variety of business endeavors including investments, licensing, and distribution. *Search for Partners* is now available biweekly in electronic form.

Another electronic publication, *BISNIS Trades & Tenders,* publicizes trade leads and tenders from local NIS sources, as well as from traditional sources in multilateral financial institutions. It publicizes sales opportunities financed directly by NIS enterprises, as well as numerous procurement opportunities funded by U.S.AID, the World Bank, the European Bank for Reconstruction and Development, and other bilateral and multilateral funding sources open to U.S. companies. *Trades and Tenders* is available via the BISNIS fax retrieval system, E-mail, and BISNIS Online.

Contact Information:
Business Information Service for the Newly Independent States
U.S. Department of Commerce International Trade Administration
Room 7413
Washington, DC 20230
Tel.: (202) 482-4655
Fax: (202) 482-2293
Fax Retrieval
System: (202) 482-3145
E-mail: bisnis@usita.gov
BISNIS Online: http://www.iep.doc.gov/bisnis/bisnis.html

62.5 INFORMATION MARKET IN RUSSIA.*   The activities of the Russian press
are based on national legislation, presidential decrees, and governmental provisions. The
key legislative act governing these activities is the law On Mass Media of December 27,
1991. This law grants freedom to the mass media and constitutes a general rejection of
censorship. At the same time, the law prohibits the use of the mass media to promote
crime, advocate the overthrow of the constitutional order, or promote war, ethnic, class, social, or religious intolerance.

Other important legislative acts are the federal law on the Procedure for the Publication
and Elucidation of Policies by State Authority and Publicized by State Mass Media (January 13, 1995), presidential decrees On Protection of the Freedom of Mass Media (March
20 and December 5, 1993) and On Improvement of State Regulation Concerning Mass
Media (December 22, 1993).

In accordance with the latter decree, central bodies of executive power have been
formed—the Federal Service for Television and Radio Broadcasting (FSTV & RBC) and
the State Committee on the Press. The new position of vice premier in charge of the mass
media was introduced into Russia's government. At present, this position is held by Vitaly
Ignatenko, Director General of the ITAR-TASS News Agency.

The main tasks of the FSTV & RBC are the coordination of activities of Russian and regional television and radio organizations; the implementation of a single state policy in
production, technical, and financial issues; and registration and licensing of state and nonstate television and radio organizations.

At present, there are three federal television and radio broadcast companies in Russia.
According to the Presidential decree On Improvement of Television and Radio Broadcasting & RBC in the Russian Federation (October 6, 1995), the status of "all-russian" television and radio companies was granted to Russian Public TV. This company, ORT, is a
closed stock corporation, with 51% of its shares owned by the state. This same status was
granted to All-Russian State Television and Radio Broadcasting company (VGTRK a.k.a.,
Russian Television), and to Petersburg-Channel 5.

Along with these, there are 90 regional state television and radio companies. The rest of
the 950 licenses issued by FSTV & RBC as of November 1995 were received by nonstate
companies, including 530 broadcast and cable television companies.

The state television and radio companies are financed from the state budget, although
this source of income recently accounted for only 47% of the required amount. The re-
minder had to be covered by profits from advertising. Nonstate companies, naturally, are
financed by their founders. For example, the most popular and influential among nonstate

---

*This section was written by Yuri D. Poroykov.

television and radio companies is MOST. The group also owns the daily newspaper *Segodnya* and the weekly *Itogi*.

According to data gathered by FSTV & RBC, the state television and radio companies cover the entire territory of Russia and most of the essential parts of former Soviet republics. More exact numbers are not available because some of these new independent states have created electronic barriers preventing the reception of Russian programs in their territories. Others are just not able to pay for these programs. The average 24-hour volume of television broadcasting by state companies in 56 languages to the nationalities living in Russia is 162 hours, while the volume for radio broadcasting 318 hours.

The State Committee on the Press is responsible for the implementation of state policy concerning periodical publications, book publishing, printing, and book distribution. As the presidential decree has defined it, one of the main aims of the committee is "the protection of freedom of expression and of the independence of the press." Among the committee's functions are the registration and reregistration of periodical publications, the licensing of publishing and printing activities, the enforcement of measures created by Russia's legislation to prevent the abuse of freedom of mass media, and preventing censorship on the part of state officials and the state.

In recent years, most Russian newspapers and magazines have experienced a financial crisis. Thus, it is extremely important that for the last five years financing has been provided to the press via Roskompechat. As a result of these state subsidies, about 600 publications have managed to survive. Among these 600 were governmental publications such as *Rossijskaya gazeta* and *Rossijskiye vesti,* and magazines such as *Rodina* and *Rossijskaya Federatsiya.* These publications received approximately 40 billion rubles from the federal budget in 1994. Financial assistance has also been provided to a number of publications of different, sometimes opposing ideological orientations. For example, in 1994 subsidies were granted to *Pravda* and *Sovetskaya Rossija,* publications of the pro-Communist opposition.

In late 1995, the new law On State Support for Mass Media and Book Publishing in the Russian Federation was adopted. The law declares that state subsidies are to be replaced by tax exemptions, favorable customs treatment, and other benefits. The law also defines a new procedure for the privatization of printing presses that allows their employees to become co-owners of these plants. At a meeting with editors-in-chief of leading mass-media publications, Russia's Prime Minister Victor Chernomyrdin stated that journalists must become "inspectors," thereby assuming the responsibility for controlling the implementation of this law.

In 1994, the total number of newspapers published in Russia was 4,526, and their annual circulation exceeded eight billion copies. These included 230 all-Russian newspapers. The total number of magazines was 1,454, with an annual circulation of approximately 185 billion copies. The average number of newspapers and magazines per 100 persons was 58 and 23, respectively. Also, over 30,000 books with a total circulation of 600 million copies were published.

At present, there are 17 federal and regional newspapers published in Moscow alone, with a total daily circulation of 10.5 million copies; and there are about 110 weekly publications. In the outlying regions, on average, 5 to 20 local newspapers and magazines are published in each region.

In 1994, major Russian publications had 18.1 million subscribers, 3% higher than in the preceding year. About 25.2 million Russians subscribed to local publications whose growth rate was 10% over the same period. In the opinion of experts, these figures demonstrate a trend of increasing public interest in local news versus news coming from central information sources. According to the latest poll conducted by Russia's Association of Journalists, 36% of all Russians read local town newspapers, 30% read regional newspapers, and 23% read county newspapers. As for central or nationally circulated newspapers, the numbers were much lower: 4–6% for such newspapers as *Trud, Rossijskaya gazeta, Selskaya zhizn, Semja, Pravda,* and *Izvestija.* About 7% of the respondents said they do not read newspapers at all. In terms of circulation the major Russian newspapers are the weekly *Argumenty i Fakty,* and the dailies *Trud, Komsomolskaya pravda, Rossijskaya gazeta, Izvestiya,* and *Rossijskiye Vesti.* The leaders are trailed by newspapers such as *Segodnia, Moskovskiye novosti, Pravda, Literaturnaya gazeta, Krasnaya zvezda,* and *Obshchaya gazeta.*

The largest economic publication is the weekly *Ekonomika i zhizn.* Quite popular also are newspapers and magazines of the Kommersant publishing house.

As for magazines, they generally enjoy less popularity than newspapers. According to a poll conducted in 1995 by sociologists from the Moscow State University, even in Moscow three-quarters of the respondents do not read magazines. Even the leading magazines had less than 5% of both permanent and occasional readers. It is noteworthy that first place in the poll held by a magazine, *Den'gi* (*Money*), which is published by Kommersant and which commanded a market share of 2.4% of permanent readers and 1% of occasional readers. Among the leaders was the Russian edition of the American women's magazine *Cosmopolitan* (rating 4th, with 1.8% of permanent readers and 0.8% of occasional readers). From these data, researchers have concluded that the interests of a growing affluent stratum of "new Russians" have begun to shape the publications market. The least-read publications (with 0.2 to 0.7% of all readers) were literary journals, which traditionally had enjoyed high reputation and popularity. Today they are experiencing great financial difficulties.

Approximately 300 domestic news agencies are presently engaged in gathering news inside Russia and about Russia. However, only 120 of them produce information on a regular basis. Two agencies (ITAR-TASS and RIA) have the status of state news agencies, but only ITAR-TASS is a central news agency in the Russian Federation. It has become the legal descendant of TASS, which had been rated by UNESCO as one of five major news agencies in the world.

Among nonstate news agencies, the most famous are Interfax, Postfactum, IMA-Press, PAL-Inform, News & Information Agency, RAU-Press, and Modus Vivendi.

ITAR-TASS, which is financed partly by the state, is today the most powerful information structure in Russia. It has 75 offices in Russia and the CIS countries, and 65 offices in 62 countries abroad. Relying on its own satellite system of communications, the news agency broadcasts 24 hours a day the latest news in six languages (Russian, English, French, Spanish, German, and Arabic). ITAR-TASS distributes special-information products, including packages of economic and business news, texts of laws, and legislative acts. It provides an electronic database, telecommunications, advertising, and marketing services to its customers. Among the first concerns of its type in Russia, ITAR-TASS has begun to produce digital graphic and photo information, as well as thematic CD-ROMs.

ITAR-TASS is the founder of the magazine *Ekho planety,* which specializes in social and political issues. The news agency also participates in publishing business magazines in Great Britain, Greece, and Turkey. In the United States, the agency has a branch, ITAR-TASS, USA, which publishes the Russian newspaper *ITAR-TASS Express* and is involved in different kinds of information businesses and consulting.

As mentioned earlier, advertising today is vitally important for the survival of the Russian mass media. In 1992–93 the amount of advertising increased more than twice in print media, fourfold in television, and five-fold in radio. Advertising via the six basic channels of Russian TV in 1994 totaled more than 250,000 segments, with a total length of 1,830 hours. Their total cost was about $400 million. Advertising on radio is also developing quickly.

A number of specialized advertising publications have appeared, such as *Optovik, Iz ruk v ruki, Extra,* and *Vas-bank.*

Though Russia's advertising market is predominantly concentrated in Moscow, there is a trend for its decentralization. In 1990–91 the Moscow share of the market exceeded 90%, but in 1995 it was only about 80%.

Advertising rates are quite high. For example, the cost per column in the weekly *Argumenty i Fakty* runs $55,000. At the ORT TV company, a minute of air time during rush-hour is estimated to cost between $20,500 and $30,000. At the leading commercial radio broadcasting companies, 30 seconds of air time cost from $100 to $230.

Until recently, advertising activities in Russia were regulated by laws and legislative acts that were not related directly to advertising. On July 16, 1995, the special law On Advertising went into effect. The law outlined a number of restrictions, including the requirement that the amount of advertising in publications (except specialized advertising publications) cannot exceed 40% of their total volume. The functions of state control of advertising were granted to the State Committee for Anti-Monopoly Policy.

Some observers (e.g., the American research organization Freedom House) believe that the Russian mass media cannot be considered free in the full sense because they (especially television) still depend financially on the state. Such a problem does exist in the relationship between state power and the press. Indeed, it is unavoidable in the current situation. There are a number of other problems too, including, for example, the fact that Russia is among three countries in the world where the profession of journalist is considered highly dangerous. According to Freedom House data, between January 1994 and mid-April 1995, fourteen Russian journalists died while carrying out a professional mission. Despite all the difficulties, however, Russia is following the road toward a civilized information market.

APPENDIX

Resources

The resources listed in this appendix are currently available in Russia.*

INDUSTRIAL ENTERPRISES

Aerosyemka Research and Development Enterprise
Workforce: 41
Annual turnover: $85,700
Business lines: produces cartographic and photographic documents relating to the environment (thematic maps, photo plans, and aerospace photographs for land use, topography, forest management, oil production, and environmental projects). Develops and operates territorial-land-use, nature conservation and environmental-information systems. Carries out practical and experimental air surveys and air photography projects.
Manufactures photographic products based on data provided by aerospace photographs. Operates an airfreight service.
Address: 7 Bolshoi Predtechensky Lane, Moscow 123242
Telephone: (095) 205 3921
Fax: (095) 200 4210

ARTI Plant, a joint stock company
Workforce: 2,100
Annual turnover: $10 million
Business lines: manufactures molded-rubber articles, hoses, gas masks; asbestos-braking and friction articles, and rubberized asbestos fabric.
Address: 19A Morshanskoe Highway, Tambov 392683, Russia
Telephone: (0752) 33 4516
Fax: (0752) 35 2473

Astratex Open Joint Stock Company
Workforce: 4,397

---

*The companies listed in this appendix have not received the endorsement of either the publisher, editor, or contributors of this volume. If legal advise or other expert assistance is required, the services of a competent professional should be sought.

Annual turnover: 30 billion rubles (in 1993 prices)
Business lines: manufactures outer knitted goods and yarns from in-house designs, and carries out import and export operations.
Address: 40 Vokzalnaya Street, Astrakhan 414041, Russia
Telephone: (851–0) 22 7076 and 24 5971
Fax: (851–0) 22 6787

Beloretsk Integrated Metal Plant, a joint stock company
Workforce: 16,330
Annual turnover: $93.8 million
Business lines: fabricates metal (steel) and metal products (rolled wire, drawn wire, wire ropes, bands, and metal cord).
Address: 1 Bluecher Street, Beloretsk 453500, Bashkortostan, Russia
Telephone: (34792) 4 0405 and 4 5599
Fax: (34792) 4 0464, 4 4042 and 5 1880

Bouest Closed Joint Stock Company
Workforce: 63
Business lines: designs, builds, and operates projects and provides services in telecommunications and communication facilities. Designs, introduces, assembles, and maintains computer networks, and provides training programs and consulting services for specialists in computer network planning and maintenance. Supplies foodstuffs and everyday staples on a wholesale basis.
Address: 2 Chistoprudny Boulevard, Apt. 47, Moscow 101000
Telephone: (095) 923 4947 and 923 4798
Fax: (095) 928 5360

Burevestnik Research and Development Enterprise
Workforce: 1,050
Sales: 7,757 million rubles (1994)
Business lines: develops and manufactures X-ray diffractometers and spectrometers, X-ray luminescent separators, X-ray radiation deflectors, and electrochemical devices; and provides relevant methodological support facilities.
Address: 68 Malookhtinsky Avenue, St. Petersburg 195272
Telephone: (812) 528 7272
Fax: (812) 6633

Camneft Joint Engineering Company
Workforce: 16
Annual turnover: $230,000
Business lines: designs and organizes oil production operations and the manufacture of machinery for the oil industry. Provides consulting services in privatization and incorporation of oil and gas production and oil-refining enterprises; and it offers services relating to foreign trade.
The company's foreign partner is CAT GmbH, Germany.
Address: 38/3 Narodnogo Opolchenia Street, Moscow 123298
Telephone: (095) 192 8057
Fax: (095) 943 0044

Chernogorneft Open Joint Stock Company
Workforce: 3,396

Annual turnover: $171.8 million
Business lines: develops, produces, conveys, stores, processes, and sells oil, gas, and oil products.
Address: 15 Mendeleev Street, Nizhnevartovsk 626440, Tyumen, Russia
Telephone: (3466) 27 4893
Fax: (3466) 23 8804

Elektrougli Kudinovsky Plant
Workforce: 870
Annual turnover: $2.3 million
Business lines: produces all kinds and types of brushes for electrical machines; element-welding and searchlight electrodes and spectral carbons; carbon rods for various applications; and semifinished products for making electric brushes.
The plant has convenient access roads, and spare floor space and facilities to set up joint operations (not necessarily in its core business).
Address: 97 Tsentralnaya Street, Elektrougli 142490, Moscow Region, Russia
Telephone/Fax: (095) 917 2090
Telex: 411700

Flaximpex Closed Joint Stock Company
Workforce: 20
Annual turnover: $5 million
Business lines: produces and markets linen goods for industrial and technical applications; manufactures, purchases, sells, and processes farming produce; carries on foreign trade; produces and markets linen and cotton textiles; and provides intermediary, information and consulting services.
Address: 26 Shabolovka Street, Moscow 113162
Telephone: (095) 237 1819
Fax: (095) 237 0421

Glinozem Association, Pikalevo, an open joint stock company
Workforce: 6,000
Annual turnover: $46.1 million
Business lines: produces alumina, aluminum hydroxide, soda ash, potassium carbonate, and cement.
Address: 1 Spriamlennoe Highway, Pikalevo 187600, Leningrad Region, Russia
Telephone: (812–66) 4 5118 and 4 1511
Fax: (812–66) 4 5002

Gus Khrustalny Textile Mill, an open joint stock company
Workforce: 1,750
Annual turnover: $600,560
Business lines: manufactures cotton and mixed fabrics, coarse fabrics, and jersey cloth.
Address: 3 Rudnitskaya Street, Gus Khrustalny 601550, Vladimir, Russia
Telephone: (09241) 2 4843
Fax: (09241) 2 4442 and 2 0339

Irkutsk Road Building Machine Plant, a joint stock company
Workforce: 150
Annual turnover: $1 million

Business lines: produces machinery for building and repairing automobile highways (asphalt spreaders, bitumen tanks, tank trailers).
Address: 44 Petrov Street, Irkutsk 664035, Russia
Telephone: (3952) 33 4500
Fax: (3952) 33 4502

Izhevsk Radio Plant, an open joint stock company
Workforce: 7,615
Annual turnover: $15.7 million
Business lines: manufactures equipment for digital radio-relay communication, digital multichannel-communication systems, commercial satellite-communication systems, portable, personal radio-communication units, telemetric systems and safety systems for mobile objects. Produces mechanical devices and tools. Provides maintenance services. Engages in commercial operations.
Address: 19 Bazisnaya Street, Izhevsk 426034, Udmurtia, Russia
Telephone: (341–2) 22 8639
Fax: (341–2) 75 6555

Izhstal Industrial Association
Workforce: 17,245
Annual turnover: $57 million
Business lines: fabricates bars, cold-rolled strip, wire, bright-polished carbon-tool steel, high-precision steel sections, reinforcement steel rods, angles, flat strips, and forged and stamped products.
Address: Novo Akimova Street, Izhevsk 426006, Udmurtia, Russia
Telephone: (3412) 78 7066
Fax: (3412) 78 7283 and 71 1058

Kolchugino Nonferrous Metalworking Plant, an open joint stock company
Workforce: 9,200
Annual turnover: $45.5 million
Business lines: manufactures nonferrous metal products (rods, piping, wire, strips, bands); silver- and gold-plated tableware; and silver-, chromium-, and nickel-plated dishware.
Address: 25 Karl Marx Street, Kolchugino 601744, Vladimir, Russia
Telephone: (09245) 2 2441
Fax: (09245) 2 3157

Krasnodar ZIP Joint Stock Company
Workforce: 2,560
Annual turnover: $2.3 million
Business lines: develops and manufactures electrical measuring instruments and consumer goods.
Address: 5 Zipovskaya Street, Krasnodar 350010, Russia
Telephone: (8612) 54 0643 and 54 0455
Fax: (8612) 54 0470

Kromy Rural Construction Plant, a closed joint stock company
Workforce: 230
Annual turnover: 5 billion rubles

Business lines: manufactures cottages, paneled structures, round logs, bathhouses, modular houses, solid doors, and window frames. Builds cottages and industrial facilities.
Address: Kromy 30200, Orel, Russia
Telephone: (08600) 4 8224 and 9 6731
Fax: (08600) 9 8806

KRONTIF Joint Stock Company, Sukreml Iron Casting Plant
Workforce: 2,000
Annual turnover: $7.9 million
Business lines: produces cast-iron articles for internal-plumbing sewage pipes, cast-iron sewage hatches; and grinds iron spheres for ore-dressing plants.
Address: 1A Shcherbakov Street, Liudinovo 249400, Kaluga, Russia
Telephone: (08444) 2 3345
Fax: (08444) 2 2874

Kropotkin Chemical Plant, an open joint stock company
Workforce: 1,100
Annual turnover: $2.3 million
Business lines: produces chemical output: furfural, furfural alcohol, tetrahydrofuran, polyfurite, and casting binders (hydrofuran-aldehyde resins).
Address: 5 Zavodskaya Street, Kropotkin 352130, Krasnodar, Russia
Telephone: (86138) 4 4451
Fax: (86138) 4 4294

Kursk Integrated Medication Plant, an open joint stock company
Workforce: 1,200
Annual turnover: $10 million
Business lines: produces medications in substance and ready-to-use forms, dialyzers, and blood-supply lines (artificial kidneys).
Address: 1A/18, 2nd Agregatnaya Street, Kursk 305909, Russia
Telephone: (07122) 6 1465
Fax: (07122) 6 0211

Lebedin Integrated Mining and Ore Dressing Plant, a joint stock company
Workforce: 17,500
Annual turnover: $400 million
Business lines: produces and exports Europe's best raw materials for the metal industry, along with metal articles, building materials, finely dispersed chalk, and foodstuffs.
Address: Gubkin 309510, Belgorod, Russia
Telephone: (07241) 2 4455 and 2 5472
Fax: (095) 936 2076

Liksar State Enterprise, Saratov
Workforce: 500
Annual turnover: $13 million
Business lines: produces vodka, liqueurs, mineral water, and carbonic acid.
Address: 110 Chernishevsky Street, Saratov 410028, Russia
Telephone/Fax: (8452) 25 0944

LUKOIL Oil Company, a joint stock company
Workforce: 82,900
Annual turnover: $3.9 billion (1994)
Business lines: prospects for and produces oil. Processes and sells crude oil. Exports oil and oil products. Provides services in oil production, major well repairs, renovation, and construction of oil depots and gasoline-filling stations. Develops and manufactures oil-prospecting, drilling, and other equipment. Implements high-yielding commercial projects in diversified fields. Develops and tests methods and techniques of oil recovery and yield improvement. Develops new drilling techniques and deep oil-refining complexes. Carries out environmental-protection measures.
Address: 11 Srevensky Boulevard, Moscow 101000
Telephone: (095) 928 9841
Fax: (095) 916 0020 and 916 3339

Lysva Metal Plant, a joint stock company
Workforce: 8,912
Annual turnover: $12.7 million
Business lines: manufactures coating for thin-rolled-metal sheets, nonstandard equipment, household electric ranges, enamelled utencils; applies enamel to various articles, zinc-plated utencils, aluminum flasks, and other consumer goods.
Address: 1 Metallistov Street, Lysva 618960, Perm, Russia
Telephone: (34249) 2 6122
Fax: (34249) 2 7172

Magnitogorsk Sizing Plant, an open joint stock company
Workforce: 6,980
Annual turnover: $687.5 million
Business lines: manufactures sized rolled products, cold-rolled strip, engineering and railroad fasteners, steel wire and ropes, metal cord, metal lines, netting, and consumer goods.
Address: 3 May 9 Street, Magnitogorsk 455015, Chelyabinsk, Russia
Telephone: (351–1) 33 2829 and 33 7550
Fax: (351–1) 37 0541 and (095) 291 5732

Meson Plant, an open joint stock company
Workforce: 770
Annual turnover: 1.3 billion rubles
Business lines: manufactures (1) tantalum-oxide semiconductor capacitors, series KB3 (Cnom. up to microF; Unom. up to 60 V); foreign analogs: types TDC, TAC, Mallory (U.S.), T421, Union Carbide (U.S.) 935D, Sprague (U.S.); (2) electric-pulse capacitors with combined dielectric series K75 (Cnom. up to 100 microF, Unom. up to 5,000 V); foreign analogs: type 282P, Sprague (U.S.); (3) ionisters, superhigh capacity capacitors, series KB8 (Cnom. up to 3.3 F, Unom.=2.5 V; Unom.=6.3 V); foreign analogs: series DC, DX, DB, Elna (Japan); (4) heat safety fuses TP 130 C–2A, 250 V; foreign analogs: ELCUT, Uchihashi Metal Industrial (Japan); (5) nickel-lanthanum NLZ–0.9 storage cells (Cnom.=0.9 A/hr, Unom.=1.2 V); foreign analogs: type TH–1000 AA, Toshiba (Japan). Offers electronic-equipment-assembly services.
Address: 28 Bolshoi Samsonievsky Avenue, St. Petersburg 194175
Telephone: (812) 542 0298
Fax: (812) 542 5041

Metako Metal Structure Plant, a closed joint stock company, Domodedovo
Workforce: 356
Annual turnover: 17.6 billion rubles
Business lines: produces bolted pylons for power-transmission lines and 35 to 1,500 kV substations, zinc-plated for rust protection.
Manufactures metal fences to act as road barriers, zinc-plated for rust protection.
Address: 10 Kashirskoe Highway, Domodedovo 142040, Moscow
Telephone: (095) 546 5558
Fax: (09679) 3 4813

Murmanservice Open Joint Stock Company
Workforce: 250
Annual turnover: $20 million
Business lines: provides consumer services, produces consumer goods, offers catering facilities, and engages in trading operations.
Address: 62 Poliarnie Zori Street, Murmansk 183782, Russia
Telephone: (81500) 54 4251
Fax: (81500) 54 6704

Novorossiisk Rail Car Repair Plant
Workforce: 1,900
Annual turnover: $5.6 million
Business lines: repairs railroad passenger cars and refrigeration units; assembles and repairs railroad-car wheels; manufactures spare parts for the rolling stock.
Address: 1 Mikhailov Street, Novorossiisk 353906, Krasnodar, Russia
Telephone: (861–34) 5 2021
Fax: (861–34) 2 4396

Omsk Vodka and Liqueur Enterprise, an open joint stock company
Workforce: 230
Annual turnover: $7 million
Business lines: produces vodka, liqueurs, fruit liqueurs, punches, dessert drinks, gin, balsams, and aperitifs, which are manufactured from natural raw materials. Ten of them have been developed by the house specialists. In the year 2002, the enterprise will be 100 years old.
Address: 51B, 22nd Partsyezda Street, Omsk 644105, Russia
Telephone: (3812) 21 0821
Fax: (3812) 21 5405

Paints and Varnishes Plant, a joint stock company
Workforce: 340
Annual turnover: $706,000
Business lines: manufactures paints and varnishes, household chemicals, wrapping paper, and articles from sheet iron and nonstandard paper.
Address: 134 Boevaya Street, Astrakhan 414021, Russia
Telephone: (8510) 33 0572
Telex: (8510) 33 0588

Partner Joint Stock Company
Workforce: 145
Annual turnover: $625,000

Business lines: the company is a multidisciplinary research and development enterprise committed to science-intensive technologies, including those in the defense industry that are converting to civilian applications; develops and manufactures biological products for medical and veterinary applications and bacterial biomasses. Organizes output of dairy products enriched with living bifidobacteria. Develops processes and equipment for producing protective gaseous media. Contracts formerly defense-oriented enterprises to manufacture machines, assemblies, and units from steel and alloys with special properties. Develops and supplies devices for controlling manufacturing processes and assessing quality in the building-materials, and construction industry.
Address: 30/15 Ryazansky Avenue, Moscow 109428
Telephone: (095) 928 0384
Fax: (095) 923 0163

Penza Branch of the State Antibiotics Research Center
Workforce: 110
Annual turnover: $200,000
Business lines: carries out research, and technological and design projects in the production of antibiotics, and develops specifications for their manufacture. Turns out cephalexin and semifinished products for synthesizing cephalosporin antibiotics; reactor filters; and coarse and fine (sterile) process air-cleaning filters. Licenses the manufacturing techniques for cephalosporin antibiotics and semifinished products. Leases land, facilities, and equipment for launching the joint production of medications.
Address: 6 Druzhby Street, Penza 440033, Russia
Telephone: (841–2) 66 8335 and 57 7278
Fax: (841–2) 57 7290

Polytrade International, Ltd., a closed joint stock company
Workforce: 15
Business lines: the company is an official distributor of the firm Glory, Japan, for bank equipment. Provides equipment maintenance; manufactures and sells specialized bank furniture; leases out equipment; and operates a showroom.
Address: 8 Gorokhovsky Lane, Moscow 103064
Telephone: (095) 237 5752 and 237 5934
Fax: (095) 237 5843

Priboi Collective Fishery
Workforce: 725
Annual turnover: 162.5 billion rubles (1994)
Business lines: Catches and processes fish and other seafood; exports fish and seafood products; repairs fishing boats; builds and repairs fishing gear.
Address: 2 Rechnaya Street, Pravdy Township, Holm District 694710, Sakhalin, Russia
Telephone: 2 3027

Severodvinsk Road Building Machine Plant (Dortechstroi), an open joint stock company
Workforce: 1,200
Annual turnover: $60 million

Business lines: manufactures road-building and snow-removal equipment. The company is the biggest supplier of municipal and specialized machinery to the Commonwealth of Independent States countries.
Address of the Moscow Branch: 4 Spartakovskaya Street, Moscow 107066
Telephone: (095) 261 1079 and 261 6435
Fax: (095) 267 3507

Sevkavroentgen Joint Stock Company
Workforce: 652
Annual turnover: $1 million
Business lines: manufactures X-ray diagnostic and therapeutic equipment, and provides equipment maintenance services.
Address: 167 May 9 Street, Maisky 361100, Kabardino-Balkaria, Russia
Telephone: (866–33) 4 1745
Fax: (866–33) 4 1911

Shtamp Cooperative
Workforce: 45
Annual turnover: $420,000
Business lines: manufactures stamping units for the automotive industry and produces stamped products in small batches.
Address: 74 Mira Avenue, Apt. 224, Naberezhnie Chelny 423818, Tatarstan, Russia
Telephone: (8439) 54 0802 and 57 9558
Fax: (8439) 59 2098

Smichka Engineering Plant, Plavsk, an open joint stock company
Workforce: 1,275
Annual turnover: $2.1 million
Business lines: manufactures liquid separators for the dairy, brewing, yeast, starch, wine-making, butter and fat, meat-packing, medical, and other industries; and produces miniplants and units for deep milk processing.
Address: 27 Kommunarov Street, Plavsk 301050, Tula, Russia
Telephone: (08752) 2 1065
Telephone/Fax: (08752) 2 2132 and 2 2847

Smolensk Bread and Confectionery Open Joint Stock Company
Workforce: 556
Annual turnover: 25–30 billion rubles
Business lines: produces confectionery, bread, and other baked products. Markets food products and fufills special orders from customers.
Address: 17 Krasninskoe Highway, Smolensk 214030, Russia
Telephone: (081–00) 6 4470 and 6 3889
Fax: (081–00) 6 2655

Stalkonstruktsia Holding Company
Workforce: 27,000
Annual turnover: $115 million
Business lines: manufactures and assembles all types of metal structures for various industries; designs facilities and production techniques; and assembles structures on site.

Address: 8–12 Sadovo-Kudrinskaya Street, Moscow 103001
Telephone: (095) 209 9560
Fax: (095) 975 2217

Syktyvkar Timber Industry Complex, an open joint stock company
Workforce: 9,500
Annual turnover: $90.2 million
Business lines: produces printing paper, cardboard for packing liquid and loose products, toilet paper, wallpaper, feed yeast, chipboard, plywood, heat and electric power. Has a representative office in Moscow ($1/13$ Tikhvinskaya Street, Building 2) and in St. Petersburg (6 Kutozov Embankment).
Address: 2 Bumazhnikov Drive, Syktyvkar 167026, Russia
Telephone: (82122) 1 4709 and 1 4760
Fax: (82122) 6 5698

TAOPIN Beer and Beverage Joint Stock Company, Tula
Workforce: 845
Annual turnover: $10.9 million
Business lines: produces beer, nonalcoholic beverages, malt, vodka, liqueurs, dry autolysate of beer yeast, and mixed feeds from beer-making wastes; offers cargo transportation services.
Address: 85 Shosseinaya Street, Tula 300036, Russia
Telephone/Fax: (0872) 39 7577

Tver Integrated Bread Plant, an open joint stock company
Workforce: 540
Annual turnover: $19 million
Business lines: produces wheat flour of all varieties, semolina, hulled rye flour, and mixed feeds; packs flour and groats; and bakes bread and related products.
Address: 1 Vokzalnaya Street, Tver 170630, Russia
Telephone: (08222) 3 2462 and 3 1287
Fax: (096) 902 1570

Uralneftechim Joint Stock Company
Workforce: 5,000
Annual turnover: $28 million
Business lines: produces isoprene (facilities in renovation), liquefied gases, synthetic rubber goods, chemical equipment, and furniture; and operates new butadiene-producing facilities.
Address: Chaikovsky 617740, Perm, Russia
Telephone: (34241) 6 2428, 7 1761 and (095) 928 8169
Fax: (34241) 7 1170 and (095) 298 3144

Vertiazin Open Joint Stock Company
Workforce: 123
Annual turnover: $480,000
Business lines: produces equipment and spare parts for fowl farming; manufactures nonstandardized equipment. Makes work outfits. Manufactures custom-made articles from hardwood and stone.
Address: Gorodnia on Volga 171331, Konakovo District, Tver, Russia
Telephone/Fax: (095) 539 2702

Vneshtruboprovodstroi External Economic Association
Workforce: 23
Annual turnover: $1.25 million
Business lines: designs and builds oil- and gas-industry facilities in Russia and abroad; carries out export and import operations; purchases and leases furniture, equipment, and real estate.
Address: 14 Zhitnaya Street, Moscow 117970
Telephone: (095) 238 7510
Fax: (095) 238 6934

Yarpolymermash Joint Stock Company
Workforce: 1,385
Annual turnover: $1.9 million
Business lines: develops and manufactures equipment and machine attachments (assembly drums and curing molds) for the tire-making, tire-repair and synthetic-rubber industry, and for producing plastics and processing rubber-industry wastes.
Address: Polushkina Roshcha, Yaroslavl 150040, Russia
Telephone: (0852) 25 1593
Fax: (0852) 25 3483

Zavolzhskoe Prefabricated Panel Housing Enterprise, an open joint stock company
Workforce: 950
Annual turnover: $15 million
Business lines: produces prefabricated and reinforced concrete components for housing construction and industrial, public, social, cultural, and agricultural projects; manufactures consumer goods (garden huts, garages, fences, household appliances, and hardware); carries out design, assembly, building, repair, and restoration jobs.
Address: Upper Terrace, Ulyanovsk 432046, Russia
Telephone: (8422) 20 6337
Fax: (8422) 20 6345

FINANCIAL, INVESTMENT, AND INSURANCE COMPANIES

ALFA CAPITAL
Staff: 150
Annual turnover: Over $300 million (1994)
Business lines: provides all kinds of services in the Russian stock market; makes portfolio investments; packages information; makes strategic investments; and offers analytical and consulting services.
Address: 11 Masha Poryvaeva Street, Moscow 107078
Telephone: (095) 204 7300 and 208 8484
Fax: (095) 208 1350

ALTEI Medical Insurance Company
Staff: 45
Annual turnover: $700,000
Business lines: provides group, individual, and family medical-insurance services (voluntary and compulsory).

Address: 6 Vinnitskaya Street, P.O. Box 24, Moscow 117192
Telephone: (095) 952 3428
Fax: (095) 932 6780

ATOMIC Independent Management Firm, a closed joint stock company
Staff: 20
Annual turnover: $496,192 (1994)
Business lines: manages assets of investment and pension funds; keeps registers of shareholding companies; provides brokerage services in the securities market; and offers consultation on licensing of operations in the Russian securities market.
Address: 5/10 Karetny Riad Street, Moscow 103006
Telephone: (095) 299 1165
Fax: (095) 299 6581

CenterInvest Group
Staff: Over 70
Annual turnover: $30 million
Business lines: an independent firm offering strategic consulting and management services and information technologies. Specializes in corporate finance; provides information, legal consulting, and day-to-day and management consulting. Provides assistance for the equity market (research, analysis, sale, Sirius system); custody/deposits/registration.
The firm's clients are oil companies, leading banks, consulting firms, and research institutes.
Address: 12 Wrubel Street, Moscow 125080
Telephone: (095) 564 8290 and (502) 222 8290
Fax: (095) 564 8299 and (502) 222 8299

East European Insurance Company Plc, a joint stock company
Staff: 253
Insurance reserves (April 1, 1995): 42 billion rubles ($8.4 million)
Business lines: insures property, cargoes, overland, air and water transportation facilities, and construction and assembly projects. Sells cumulative-life insurance, accident insurance, and voluntary medical insurance. Offers various kinds of civil and professional liability insurance.
Address: 9A Tverskaya Street, Building 4, Moscow 103009
Telephone: (095) 229 8062, 229 7327, 229 1163, and 229 7861

Energia Ltd., an insurance company
Staff: 74
Annual turnover: 32.4 billion rubles (1994)
Business lines: carries all kinds of personal and property insurance, liability insurance, and all kinds of reinsurance; develops and offers software for insurance companies.
Foreign partners: Wills Faber Ltd., Zurich Re Ltd., and Gerling Konzern Aviation.
Address: 16 Bersenevskaya Embankment, Moscow 109072
Telephone/Fax: (095) 233 1651
The company holds License No. 1879 of April 15, 1994, from the Russian Federal Service for Supervision over Insurance Business.

Grant Financial Group, a closed joint stock company
Staff: 100
Annual turnover: $200 million
Business lines: purchases and sells securities and manages assets.
Address: 9, 2nd Verkhne-Mikhailovsky Drive, Moscow 117419
Telephone: (095) 955 7181 and 958 5011
Fax: (095) 958 5838

Index XX, Ltd., a closed joint stock company
Staff: 22
Annual turnover: $30 million (1994)
Business lines: allocates uncommitted capital in the stock market; forms and manages investment portfolios; provides brokerage services in the stock-exchange and over-the-counter markets; transacts in the futures-contracts markets; makes investments in privatized enterprises and government securities; provides investment consulting and registration services.
Address; 14/2 Bolshaya Nikitskaya Street, Moscow 103009
Telephone: (095) 201 6383
Fax: (095) 229 6646

Inkorn Investment Company, an open joint stock company
Staff: 21
Business lines: selects high-technology investment projects of the Ministry for Science and Technological Policy and develops business plans to implement these projects; forms pools of Russian and foreign investors; manages investment projects; provides legal and accounting services to protect investors; offers consulting services in securities issues and circulation, and trust services in the financial and stock markets.
Address: 28 Malaya Trubetskaya Street, Moscow 119868
Telephone: (095) 242 9933 and 242 9985
Fax: (095) 331 6854 and 242 9933

Interbank Financial House, Ltd.
Staff: 144
Own capital: $2 million
Business lines: carries out clearing services; handles dealer and stock operations in the interbank market; provides financial information on the markets of Russia and the CIS countries in real-time format through computer networks; trains and upgrades bank personnel; develops and maintains public relations; and supports the operation of the arbitral tribunals.
Chairman of the Board of Directors: Tosunian, Garegin Ashotovich
Legal address: 5/7 Sredne-Tishinsky Lane, Moscow 123557
Telephone: (095) 252 1550
Fax: (095) 252 5102
The firm holds License No. 3-r of November 19, 1993, from the Central Bank of the Russian Federation to perform clearing operations without the predeposition of funds in the clearing participants' accounts with a clearing institution.

Intrust Ltd., a closed joint stock company
Staff: 37
Annual turnover: 97 billion rubles (1994)

Business lines: performs operations with the Russian government and corporate securities; manages its clients' investment portfolios; performs investment planning; and invests in timber production.
Address: 56 Trifonovskaya Street, Moscow 129110
Telephone: (095) 132 6944 and 132 6945
Fax: (095) 132 6946
The company holds Investment Institute License No. 238 of December 1993, issued by the Finance Department of the Moscow Government.

OLMA Investment Firm, an open joint stock company
Staff: 66
Annual turnover: $792.7 million (1994)
Business lines: performs information analysis and brokerage operations in the government and corporate securities market; provides depository and investment consulting services; manages securities portfolios; and floats new issues.
Address: 7 Maly Karetny Lane, Building 1, Moscow 103051
Telephone: (095) 209 2637
Fax: (095) 299 4062
The firm holds License No. 7 of December 18, 1992, from the Finance Department of the Moscow Government.

Rinako Depository Closed Joint Stock Company
Staff: 32
Annual turnover: $550,000 (in 1994)
Business lines: keeps a register of securities owners; provides custody and keeps records of securities; offers nominal holder services; provides services in altering securities ownership rights in more than 200 shareholders' registers. Performs representation functions: legalizes transactions with its clients' securities; receives and transfers dividends; and provides consulting services.
Address: P.O. Box 343, Central Post Office, Moscow 101000
Telephone: (095) 923 1652 and 924 9533
Fax: (095) 923 1652

RINAKO Plus Brokerage Company
Staff: 50
Annual turnover: $250 million
Business lines: deals in shares of Russian enterprises, Russian (government and private) debt instruments, and derivative financial instruments; and analyzes company performance.
Address: 3/4 Novaya Square, Entrance 4, Moscow 101000
Telephone: (095) 262 4860 and (501) 921 8457
Fax: (501) 928 5241
The company holds License No. 49 of March 16, 1993, from the Finance Department of the Moscow Government.

Rombotex, LLC
Business lines: investment, development, and construction; Moscow, New York, Berlin.
Address: 350 5th Avenue, Suite 1232, New York, NY 10118
Telephone: (212) 629-7951
Fax: (212) 629-4265
Executives: Lenard Percy, Valeriy Korotkov, Yevgeny Ardemassov, and Ken Percy.

Russian Exchange Closed Joint Stock Company
Staff: 211
Annual turnover: 1.65 trillion rubles
Business lines: carries out stock exchange operations and operations in the futures and commodities markets.
Address: 15 Schmidtovsky Drive, Moscow 101000
Telephone: (095) 262 8080 and 262 2352
Fax: (095) 262 5757

SINCo Group, Insurance Brokers and Consultants, a closed joint stock company
Staff: 15
Annual turnover: $250,000 (1994)
Business lines: acts as insurance brokers; provides information and insurance-consulting services, and risk-management-consulting services.
Address: 9 2nd Drive of Perovo Pole, Moscow 111141
Telephone/Fax: (095) 956 4710

Sistema Joint Stock Financial Corporation
Staff: 30,000
Annual turnover: $400 million
Business lines: carries out financial operations; finances construction projects; promotes innovations, trade, telecommunications and tourism; and participates in regional cooperation projects.
Address: 29 Ryleev Street, Moscow 119034
Telephone: (095) 241 7633
Fax: (095) 241 7392

Small and Medium-Sized Business Development Foundation, a closed joint stock company
Annual turnover: 12 billion rubles
Business lines: makes investments and issues loans; promotes export operations; engages in wholesale trade; organizes production; participates in tourist and private business; searches out and promotes new technologies.
Address: 16 Krasin Lane, Moscow 123056
Telephone: (095) 254 7524
Fax: (095) 254 7727

SOZIDANIE Voucher Investment Fund
38,500 shareholders
Annual turnover: $6.5 million (1994)
Business lines: invests in securities; forms round lots of shares in privatized enterprises from its own funds and sells them to interested investors.
Address: 5/10 Karetny Riad Street, Moscow 103006
Telephone: (095) 299 2707
Telephone/Fax: (095) 299 3485

TRANSINVEST Financial and Investment Company
Core staff: 8
Annual turnover: 0.5 billion rubles
Business lines: assists in providing information for financial and investment operations; provides consulting and brokerage services in the money, securities and

precious-metals markets, and insurance services; arranges investment portfolios; provides assistance in entering international capital and commodity markets; and supports commercial and investment projects.

The company is always prepared to undertake: (1) the development of a project-financing schedule, and the negotiation of terms and conditions with potential participants; (2) assistance in obtaining loans for project implementation, development of a schedule for accumulation of main security stocks for a project, and distribution of written agreements in Russia and abroad.

The company maintains contacts with leading Russian and foreign banks (in Switzerland, Austria, Germany, Hungary and Poland).

Address: 23 Vorontsovskaya Street, Moscow 109147
Telephone: (095) 270 4792
Fax: (095) 200 3937
The company holds License No. 30 of April 15, 1994, from the Ministry of Finance.

BANKS AND BANKING INSTITUTIONS

Aeroflot Bank

Staff: Approximately 1,000
Annual turnover: over 100 trillion rubles (first half of 1995)
Business lines: issues loans; attracts and places deposits, including short-term deposits; opens and maintains accounts; provides cash services; purchases and sells currency; performs operations with securities; issues guarantees and sureties for third persons; and provides safety-deposit boxes.

The Bank has 12 branches in Russia and Ukraine.
Address: 21 Novy Arbat Street, Moscow 121996
Telephone: (095) 232 3903
Fax: (095) 230 2593
The bank holds General License No. 36 of January 20, 1992, from the Central Bank of the Russian Federation and a license to perform operations with precious metals.

AMIK, Interregional Investment Commercial Bank

Staff: 50
Annual turnover: $43 million
Business lines: opens settlement accounts for legal entities; provides cash services; accepts monetary resources from legal entities and private persons on deposits; issues loans to legal entities and private persons; operates in the short-money and securities markets; and performs overdraft operations, bill business, leasing, trust, and factoring operations. Maintains correspondent relations with 15 banks.

Branches: Liublino and Yugo-Zapadnoe in Moscow; Ingushsky in Nazran and Prokhladnoe in the Kabardino-Balkarian Republic
Address:8 Svobodny Avenue, Moscow 111558
Telephone: (095) 918 9408
Fax: (095) 918 9408 and 918 5309
The bank holds License No. 2795 of April 19, 1994, from the Central Bank of the Russian Federation to perform banking operations.

ASKO Bank, Joint Stock Commercial Bank

Staff: 60
Business lines: performs all kinds of banking operations.

Address: 6A Basmanny Blind Alley, Moscow 103064
Telephone/Fax: (095) 971 5640, 913 2016/17 and 261 1714/8083
The bank holds License No. 2558 of July 19, 1994, from the Central Bank of the Russian Federation to perform banking operations in foreign currency.

Bank for the Promotion of Business, a joint stock bank
Staff: 250
Assets: 250 billion rubles
Business lines: performs all kinds of banking operations; opens correspondent accounts in rubles, hard currencies, and limited convertibility currencies.
Legal address: 14 Goncharnaya Street, Moscow 109240
Telephone: (095) 915 0906
Fax: (095) 915 1009
The bank holds General License No. 2836 of May 16, 1994, from the Central Bank of the Russian Federation.

Bank for Trade, Export, Industry, Credits and Services, a joint stock commercial bank (Tepkobank)
Staff: 223
Annual turnover: over 4 trillion rubles (in 1994)
Business lines: carries out all kinds of banking operations, and is a member of the SWIFT system and a direct-settlement participant.
The bank has four branches.
Its correspondent banks for foreign-currency settlements include ABN-AMRO Bank AG, Vienna; Dresdner Bank AG and GB Ausland, Frankfurt; and the Republic National Bank of New York.
Address: 66 Varshavskoe Highway, Block 2, Moscow 113556
Telephone: (095) 113 5030/9752
Fax: (095) 113 8810 and 316 8771
The bank holds General License No. 290 of November 14, 1990, from the Central Bank of the Russian Federation.

Business Joint Stock Commercial Bank
Staff: 440
Annual turnover: 38 trillion rubles
Business lines: performs all kinds of banking operations.
Address: 3 Protopopovsky Lane, Moscow 129010
Telephone: (095) 288 4056 and 280 5265
Fax: (095) 288 4056 and 288 3892
The bank holds General License No. 486 of March 21, 1995, from the Central Bank of the Russian Federation.

DialogBank, Joint Stock Commercial Bank
Staff: 450 in Moscow divisions and 150 in Nizhny Novgorod divisions
Annual turnover: 55.5 trillion rubles (1994)
Business lines: performs the full range of banking operations accepted in international banking practice.
Was one of the first Russian banks to join the SWIFT system. Cooperates with the American Express company; active in the EuroCard/MasterCard and Visa card market; and has introduced DialogBank's own credit card within the framework of the Cirrus/Maestro international system.
Address: 4 Staropansky Lane, Moscow 103012

Telephone: (095) 244 8960/65 and (501) 882 4231 (international)
Fax: (095) 244 8959/29
The bank holds General License No. 207 of August 19, 1992, from the Central Bank of the Russian Federation.

Doris Bank Ltd., Trust, Equality and Cooperation Commercial Bank
Staff: 27
Annual turnover: $600 million (1994)
Business lines: opens and maintains accounts in rubles and foreign currencies for legal entities and private persons; opens and maintains ruble accounts for nonresidents; carries out settlements relating to its clients' export and import operations in foreign currencies; provides foreign-currency services to legal entities and private persons; and attracts and invests funds in rubles and foreign currencies.
Address: 1 Georgievsky Lane, Moscow 103050
Telephone: (095) 292 7984
Fax: (095) 292 0476
The bank holds Extended License No. 1679 of July 19, 1994, from the Central Bank of the Russian Federation to perform banking operations in rubles and foreign currency.

East-West Investment Bank
Staff: 172
Annual turnover: $15.1 billion (in 1994).
Business lines: specializes in international-settlement services; and performs banking operations related to keeping accounts for and providing other forms of banking services to legal entities, including purchasing and selling currency for rubles or other freely convertible currencies and performing operations with securities; financing export and import operations; performing leasing operations; exercising currency control; collecting checks; issuing and servicing credit cards.
Has a branch in Kaliningrad.
Address: 8 Bolshaya Sadovaya Street, Moscow 103379
Telephone: (095) 232 1441/42
Fax: (095) 232 1444
The bank holds General License No. 1930 of June 17, 1992, from the Central Bank of the Russian Federation.

Econatbank, National Joint Stock Bank for Environmental Protection
Staff: 50
Balance-sheet currency: $3.7 million
Business lines: opens and maintains accounts for legal entities and private persons (both residents and nonresidents) in rubles and foreign currency; issues loans; attracts funds from enterprises and individuals into savings deposits and deposits; issues guarantees and sureties; performs operations with securities; and provides brokerage and consulting services.
Address: 8 Kedrov Street, Block 1, Moscow 117874
Fax/Telephone: (095) 125 4201
Telephone: (095) 125 7344
The bank holds License No. 2765 of March 28, 1994, from the Central Bank of the Russian Federation.

Economics of Fisheries and Construction Investment Joint-Stock Commercial Bank (ERSI Bank)
Staff: 120

Turnover: $128 million
Business lines: provides all kinds of banking services and performs operations in the stock market.
Address: 41 Vernadsky Avenue, Moscow 117947
Telephone: (095) 431 5766 and 432 5751
Fax: (095) 434 8711
The bank holds Extended License No. 2393 of July 23, 1993, from the Central Bank of the Russian Federation.

ELBIM Bank, commercial
Staff: 1,000
Annual turnover: 100 trillion rubles
Business lines: carries out a full range of banking services in rubles and foreign currency and has its own international multicurrency debit checks issued at fixed and nonfixed par values. These cheques were patented in Germany, Ireland, Japan, Spain, and Russia. The bank has 12 divisions in Moscow and Novorossisk.
Legal address: 12 Krasnopresnenskaya Embankment, Moscow 123610
Telephone: (095) 232 1143; 9670684
Fax: (095) 2321138
The bank holds General License No. 250 of August 18, 1992, from the Central Bank of the Russian Federation.

Ergobank, Commercial Bank
Staff: over 60
Annual turnover: over 300 billion rubles (May 17, 1995)
Business lines: provides all kinds of banking services offered in the Russian financial market; issues and handles STB-Cards; active in the market of government and corporate securities and in the interbank-credit market; issues commercial loans and makes investments.
Legal address: 15 Osipenko Street, Moscow 113035
Telephone: (095) 220 3217
Fax: (095) 230 5656
The bank holds License No. 2856 of May 17, 1994, from the Central Bank of the Russian Federation to perform banking operations.

First Professional Bank
Staff: 240
Annual turnover: 1.5 trillion rubles
Business lines: opens and maintains ruble and foreign-currency settlement (current) accounts; carries out international settlements (transfers, collections, and letters of credit); issues rubles and foreign currency and loans; issues ruble and foreign-currency bills of exchange and certificates; performs conversion operations; extends interbank credits and places deposits; active in the futures and forward markets; provides individual and corporate Union Card, STB-Card, Golden Crown, and VISA card services; has a Bank-Client system; and provides consulting services.
The bank has a division in Moscow and a branch in Yaroslavl.
Legal address: Russian Army Central House (Right Wing), 2 Suvoroskaya Square, Moscow 127157
Telephone: (095) 974 1031
Fax: (095) 974 1030

The bank holds General License No. 1986 of August 26, 1994, from the Central Bank of the Russian Federation (including precious-metals operations).

First Russian Bank
Staff: 350
Annual turnover: $6 billion
Business lines: opens and maintains ruble and foreign-currency accounts; and provides all kinds of banking services.
Address: 2 Dmitrovskoe Highway, Moscow 127434
Telephone: (095) 210 7200/8000
Fax: (095) 210 8666
The bank holds General License No. 1965 of February 16, 1993, from the Central Bank of the Russian Federation.

Fundament Bank, a commercial bank
Staff: 150
Annual turnover: 2.6 trillion rubles (1994)
Business lines: provides cash services in rubles and foreign currency; carries out lending and deposit operations in rubles and foreign currency, and a variety of foreign-currency and international settlements accepted in foreign practice; and provides all kinds of banking services to the public.
Its correspondent banks include joint-stock commercial banks in Moscow, Dnepropetrovsk, Kiev, Minsk, and Tallinn; The Bank of New York; The National Westminster Bank Plc; and Kommerzbank AG.
Legal address: 100A Profsoyuznaya Street, Moscow 117485
Telephone: (095) 330 3271
Fax: (095) 330 2500
The bank holds General License No. 2118 of November 25, 1992, from the Central Bank of the Russian Federation.

IBEC, International Bank for Economic Cooperation
Staff: 160
Business lines: performs operations in freely convertible currency and other currencies; conducts documentary operations; keeps and settles clients' accounts; issues guarantees; places deposits; carries out conversion operations; and provides banking consulting services.
The bank is an international organization, members of which include, apart from the Russian Federation, such countries as Bulgaria, Cuba, the Czech Republic, Mongolia, Poland, Romania, Slovakia, and Vietnam.
Address: 11 Masha Poryvavaeva Street, Moscow 107815
Telephone: (095) 204 7220 and 975 3851
Fax: (095) 975 2202
Satellite fax: 501–204 2033
The Bank Establishment Agreement was registered by the United Nations Secretariat in August 1964.

ICFI Joint Stock Commercial Bank (International Company for Finance and Investments)
Staff: 400
Assets: $1.6 billion (January 1, 1995)
Business lines: attracts and places deposits and loans; opens and maintains current and deposit accounts for clients in rubles and foreign currency; carries out settle-

ments for export and import operations; operates with securities; performs factoring and forfeiting operations; issues short-term loans for foreign trade operations; transfers clients' funds for resource management and performs various kinds of fiduciary operations; finances projects; and carries out leasing and trust operations.

Postal address: P.O. Box 208, Moscow 107078
Legal address: 11 Masha Poryvaeva Street, Moscow 107078
Telephone: (095) 975 1564
Fax: (095) 208 7975
The bank holds General License No. 2864 of May 25, 1994, from the Central Bank of the Russian Federation.

Kupavinsky Commercial Bank

Staff: 36
Annual turnover: 300 billion rubles
Business lines: provides services to enterprises under all forms of ownership; attracts funds from private persons on personal and time deposits and on savings deposits in rubles and foreign currency; floats its own bills of exchange; carries out stock operations; finances export-import transactions; performs trust operations and operations with real-estate, industrial, and corporate property; provides assistance in conducting expert examination in the development and implementation of investment programs and foreign-capital projects in Russia.

The bank has a branch near the Baikonur Space Complex.
Address: 34 Verkhnaya Street, Bldg. 1, Moscow 125040
Telephone: (095) 257 1923
Fax: (095) 257 7852
The bank holds License No. 3189 of December 27, 1994, from the Central Bank of the Russian Federation.

Lefco Bank, a joint stock commercial bank

Staff: 350
Annual turnover: over 5 trillion rubles (1994)
Business lines: performs all kinds of banking operations.

Has two branches (Taganskoe and Turgenevskoe) in Moscow and four branches in the towns of Stupino and Balashikha, Moscow Region, and in the cities of Kaluga and Chelyabinsk.

Address: 19A Lefortovsky Val Street, Moscow 112250
Head Office address: 38 Vavilov Street, Block 6, Moscow 117942
Telephone: (095) 132 6160
Fax: (095) 135 7150
The bank holds Foreign Currency License No. 1605 of November 24, 1992, from the Central Bank of the Russian Federation.

Metropol Commercial Bank

Staff: 200
Annual turnover: 55 trillion rubles (1994 and 1995)
Business lines: performs the full range of banking operations within the scope of its license.

Branch: Smolenskoe Division.

Maintains correspondent relations abroad with The Bank of New York, the United States; Berliner Bank AG, Germany; CENTRO Internationale, Austria; National

Westminster Bank, United Kingdom; Eesti-Krediidipank, Estonia; Privatbank JSC, Ukraine; and Dresdner Bank, Germany.
Address: 7 Donskaya Street, Bldg. 3, Apt. 2, Moscow 117049
Telephone: (095) 230 0237 and 230 0037
Fax: (095) 230 0926
The bank holds General License No. 1639 of November 14, 1994, from the Central Bank of the Russian Federation.

Mezheconomsberbank, International Joint Stock Bank of Savings Banks
Staff: 703
Business lines: offers a full range of banking services; opens and maintains foreign-currency and ruble accounts for legal entities, banks' correspondent accounts, and deposit and current accounts for private individuals.
Address: 17 Skakovaya Street, Moscow 125040
Telephone: (095) 945 2105
Fax: (095) 945 5731 and 945 1683
The Bank holds General License No. 1716 of December 31, 1992, from the Central Bank of the Russian Federation.

Mezhkombank
Staff: 700
Annual turnover: $71.6 billion (1994)
Business lines: carries out all kinds of banking operations.
Maintains relations with such correspondent banks as Midland Bank plc, London; Bankers Trust Company, New York; Societe Generale SA, Paris; Deutsche Bank AG, Frankfurt; Union Bank of Finland Ltd, Helsinki; State Export-Import Bank of Ukraine, Kiev; the National Bank of Ukraine, Kiev; Belpromstroi, Minsk; and the National Bank of the Republic of Uzbekistan for External Economic Activities, Tashkent.
Address: 12 Wrubel Street, Moscow 125180
Telephone: (095) 752 7000/01/02/03/04
Fax: (095) 752 7005
The bank holds General License No. 306 of June 8, 1993, from the Central Bank of the Russian Federation.

Mortgage Joint Stock Bank (MJSB)
Staff: 141
Annual turnover: $191.8 million
Business lines: performs all kinds of banking operations; opens housing, accumulating, time, and demand accounts in rubles and freely convertible currency; issues mortgage loans to the public and finances housing construction.
The bank is a member of the Russian Mortage Bank Association and the Mortgage Bankers Association of America. It has branches in several cities, including Yaroslavl, Briansk, Stary Oskol, Ulan Ude, and Chita.
Address: 13/14 Vorontsovskaya Street, Moscow 109004
Telephone: (095) 912 0149, 912 1345 and 912 1468
Fax: (095) 271 1032
The bank holds General license No. 2201 of December 26, 1994, from the Central Bank of the Russian Federation.

Moscow Center Joint Stock Commercial Bank
Staff: 70
Annual turnover: 155 billion rubles

Business lines: active in international currency settlement by providing all kinds of traditional services to clients; operates a wide correspondent network; is connected to the SWIFT and Reuters systems; acts as a dealer in the stock market; and handles all the major credit cards.

Legal address: 1 Suvorovskaya Square, Moscow 103473

Telephone: (095) 971 7704 and 973 2510

Fax: (095) 971 7607

The bank holds Extended Foreign Currency License No. 2464 of February 17, 1995, from the Central Bank of the Russian Federation.

Moscow Industrial Bank

Staff: 2,857

Turnover: 160 trillion rubles (first half of 1995)

Business lines: provides all kinds of banking services; maintains correspondent relations with 18 of the largest banks in the world; is a member of the international SWIFT and Reuters systems; and has 20 branches in Moscow and nine in other regions of Russia.

Address: 5 Orjonikidze Street, Moscow 117419

Telephone: (095) 952 7408

Fax: (095) 952 6927

The bank holds General License No. 912 of October 20, 1993, from the Central Bank of the Russian Federation.

Moseximbank, Moscow Export-Import Bank

Staff: 220

Balance currency: 420 billion rubles (August 10, 1995)

Business lines: carries out all kinds of banking operations, including providing free settlement services in rubles and foreign currency; performs all international settlements; issues loans and accepts deposits in rubles and foreign currency; operates in the interbank market; performs operations with securities and Visa and Union cards. Holds membership in SWIFT (SWIFT, BIC, META, RU, MM).

Address: 17 Raketny Boulevard, Moscow 129301

Telephone: (095) 208 0615/4445

Fax: (095) 207 3083

The bank holds General License No. 1945 of June 17, 1994, from the Central Bank of the Russian Federation.

Mytishchi Commercial Bank (MCB), JSC

Staff: 956

Business lines: (1) for legal entities: provides comprehensive cash services; handles settlement accounts in rubles and foreign currency; makes noncash transfers in one day; performs collection operations; issues loans; invests free funds in deposits, state short-term bonds, bills of exchange, and other financial instruments; sells corporate MCB credit cards; provides consulting services; and finances projects; (2) for private persons; accepts deposits (in rubles and hard currencies); purchases and sells foreign currencies; handles international Visa, EuroCard/MasterCard, and its own credit cards; performs operations with commercial checks; and provides safety-deposit boxes.

The bank is a member of the Moscow Central Stock Exchange and the SWIFT, Reuters and Europay International systems.

Address: 30/1 Novomytishchinsky Avenue, Mytishchi 141002, Moscow Region, Russia

Telephone: (095) 586 8686/7843
Fax: (095) 581 4412
The bank holds General License No. 722 of February 25, 1993, from the Central Bank of the Russian Federation.

New Moscow Joint Stock Commercial Investment Bank
Staff: 125
Turnover: 4.2 trillion rubles (first half of 1995)
Business lines: provides the full range of modern banking services; performs lending and cash services, trust operations, and settlements of export and import transactions; operates a Client-Bank system; carries out several programs for the construction and renovation of real-estate projects in Moscow and St. Petersburg, and for shipbuilding (Baltic Plant); it has also participated in setting up the following enterprises which are presently in operation: an insurance company, nonstate pension fund, specialized-leasing firm, and realty firm.
Address: 4 Bolotnaya Square, Bldg. 1, Moscow 109072
Telephone: (095) 247 9003
Fax: (095) 247 9001
The bank holds General License No. 2209 of December 15, 1992, from the Central Bank of the Russian Federation to perform banking operations in rubles and foreign currency.

Optimum Commercial Bank
Staff: 350
Paid-up authorized capital: 18 billion rubles (July 1, 1995)
Business lines: provides services to its clients (including VIPs); performs foreign-currency operations, lending and collection operations, and operations with securities; carries out international settlements; and handles credit cards (Visa, American Express, STB, Optimum) and checks.
Over 10,000 private individuals, organizations, and enterprises are clients of the bank, including the Federal Employment Service of the Russian Federation, Rostest, Spetspozhstroi JSC, Conafor Finance AG, Zurich, Ekonika LP, etc.
The bank has branches in Moscow, Samara, Tula, and Novosibirsk.
Address: 10 Krymsky Val Street, Moscow 117049
Telephone/Fax: (095) 238 0000 and 129 2200
The bank was registered with the Central Bank of the Russian Federation in Moscow on May 16, 1989, and it holds General License No. 94 of April 28, 1993, from the Central Bank of the Russian Federation.

Petrokommerz Commercial Bank
Staff: 107
Business lines: carries out international business.
Has the following correspondents abroad: ABN-ARMO Bank AG, Vienna; Deutsche Bank AG, Frankfurt; Midland Bank PLC, London; The Bank of New York; The Cyprus Popular Bank Ltd., Nicosia; and Latvijas Privatbank JSCB, Latvia.
Address: 24 Petrovka Street, Moscow 103051
Telephone: (095) 200 7550
Fax: (095) 923 3607
The bank holds General License No. 1776 of September 6, 1993, from the Central Bank of the Russian Federation.

Promradtechbank
Staff: 697
Annual turnover: $10 billion (1994)
Business lines: provides banking services.
Address: 35 Miasnitskaya Street, Moscow 101959
Telephone; (095) 204 1871
Fax: (095) 207 9836
The bank holds General License No. 228 of January 16, 1995, from the Central Bank
of the Russian Federation.

Rosexportbank, Republican United Commercial Bank for the Promotion of Export Trade and Investments
Staff: 100
Business lines: (1) for legal entities: provides cash services; performs operations with securities; manages clients' funds in the government short-term bonds market; buys and sells short-term bonds; offers factoring services; restores accounting; plans tax policies; and analyzes the financial performance of enterprises; (2) for private persons: accepts deposits, bills of exchange, and housing certificates; and issues individual loans against security.
Legal address: 45 Liublinskaya Street, Moscow 109390
Postal address: 15 Butlerov Street, Moscow 117342
Telephone: (095) 333 4404 and 336 2930
Fax: (095) 913 3109
The bank holds License No. 2434 of July 26, 1993, from the Central Bank of the
Russian Federation.

Russian Acceptance Bank
Staff: 200
Annual turnover: $2.5 billion (1994)
Business lines: provides services to over 500 legal entities, including the fishing port in Astrakhan, the Caspian Joint Stock Fishing Company, ship repair plants, several realty firms, and over 1,650 private persons; opened 20 accounts in freely convertible currency; performs clearing operations for over 100 regional banks; is a member of the Moscow Interbank Currency Exchange, and the SWIFT and Reuters systems; maintains correspondent relations with Russian and foreign banks; has branches in Astrakhan and Petropavlovsk-Kamchatsky.
Address: 15A Kalanchevskaya Street, Moscow 107078
Telephone: (095) 975 5321
Fax: (095) 975 5403
The bank holds General License No. 1678 of October 4, 1993, from the Central
Bank of the Russian Federation.

Russian Credit Commercial Bank
Staff: 2,090
Assets: 10.2 trillion rubles (June 1, 1995)
Business lines: provides cash services; issues loans to enterprises, organizations, and companies; carries out all kinds of operations with CIS currencies and a variety of international settlements; performs operations in various segments of the financial market, including interbank lending, operations with securities in the Russian and foreign markets, and precious metals and other valuables; implements investment

programs in the electronic, chemical, ferrous and nonferrous metallurgical, mechanical-engineering industries, among others; maintains correspondent relations with 200 banks abroad and has 48 branches and divisions in the Russian Federation.
Address: 7 Seventh Peschanaya Street, Moscow 125252
Telephone: (095) 943 5101
Fax: (095) 943 7533
The bank holds General License No. 324 of December 2, 1992, from the Central Bank of the Russian Federation.

Russian Insurance Bank
Staff: 300
Business lines: a universal commercial bank that specializes in international foreign-currency settlements; has its own VSAT system, TES-TM satellite-communication ground station; and is a member of the SWIFT system.
Its correspondent banks include: Credit Suisse, Switzerland; Bankers Trust Company, United States; Barclay's Bank, Great Britain; Lloyd's Bank, Great Britain; Dresdener Bank, Germany; and Cariplo, Italy.
Address: 14 Ostashkovskaya Street, Moscow 129345
Telephone: (095) 475 5570/7156/8971 and 474 9383
Fax: (095) 475 6867
The bank holds Extended License No. 1427 of March 28, 1991, from the Central Bank of the Russian Federation.

Russobank, Russian Coal and Raw Materials Joint Bank
Staff: 221
Business lines: keeps settlement (current) accounts in rubles and current accounts in foreign currencies; attracts deposits in rubles and foreign currencies; performs conversion operations; issues loans; issues and handles international and Russian credit cards; carries out stock operations; purchases and sells government securities, and draws up investment plans.
Address: 10 Pliushchikha Street, Moscow 119121
Telephone: (095) 241 3231
Fax: (095) 241 3245
The bank holds License No. 2313 of April 23, 1993, from the Central Bank of the Russian Federation.

Slaviansky Bank, a joint-stock commercial bank
Staff: 130
Annual turnover: 742.2 billion rubles
Business lines: Carries out all kinds of banking services.
Address: 26 Volgogradsky Avenue, Moscow 109315
Telephone: (095) 270 6805
Fax: (095) 270 0800
The bank holds Extended License No. 383 of August 3, 1994, from the Central Bank of the Russian Federation.

Sovinkom Commercial Bank
Staff: 87
Annual turnover: 10 trillion rubles
Business lines: Provides all kinds of banking services.
Address: 4B Atarbekov Street, Moscow 107076

Telephone: (095) 964 3574
Fax: (095) 964 4910
The bank holds Extended License No. 2302 of July 29, 1994, from the Central Bank of the Russian Federation to perform operations in foreign currency.

Stolichny Savings Bank, a joint stock commercial bank

Staff: approximately 1,500
Business lines: provides all kinds of banking services.
Has branches in Moscow, Aleksandrov, Chelyabinsk, Elista, Krasnoyarsk, Kursk, Minusinsk, Omsk, St. Petersburg, Tyumen and Vyborg, and a subsidiary Stolichny Bank International in Amsterdam.
Address: 70 Piatnitskaya Street, Moscow 113095
Telephone: (095) 233 3916 and 231 4560
Fax: (095) 956 3927
The bank holds General License No. 61 of October 20, 1993, from the Central Bank of the Russian Federation

Suprimexbank, a commercial bank

Staff: Over 200
Turnover: 38.3 billion rubles (Jan.-July 1995)
Business lines: carries out all kinds of banking operations in rubles and foreign currency; specializes in operations with legal entities; opens and maintains ruble and foreign-currency accounts; issues credits and loans; converts foreign currency and ruble funds; opens letters of credit; carries out collection operations and money transfers to partners in the former Soviet republics and foreign countries; and handles Visa cards and Suprimexbank Union cards.
The bank is a member of the SWIFT system and has correspondent relations with the largest banks in Russia, the former Soviet republics, and the world.
Address: 10 Mozhaiskoe Highway, Moscow 121374
Telephone: (095) 444 2774 and 444 2001
Fax: (095) 440 2354
The bank holds General License No. 1438 of August 25, 1994, from the Central Bank of the Russian Federation.

Taler Bank, a joint stock commercial bank

Staff: 85
Annual turnover: 9 trillion rubles
Business lines: provides a full range of banking services; has modern banking technologies and automated facilities; effects payments promptly and responsibly on the day-to-day principle; provides high-quality services and safe monetary operations; opens and handles ruble and foreign currency accounts free of charge; purchases and sells noncash currency; performs cash-currency operations and operations in the soft-currency market; handles Visa, EuroCard/MasterCard, and American Express cards; active in the securities market; calculates interest on account balances; performs all kinds of cash services; pursues active credit and investment policies; is active in the short-money market; conducts legal audits and provides financial consulting services; provides assistance in drawing up balance sheets and tax assessments, and in executing transaction registration certificates.
Address: 6 Khamovnichesky Val Street, Moscow 119270
Telephone: (095) 201 0640

Telephone/Fax: (095) 248 1672
The bank holds Internal Foreign Currency License No. 2349 of October 19, 1994.

Technopolis Innovation Bank
Staff: 48
Annual turnover: 2.5 trillion rubles (1994)
Business lines: carries out all kinds of banking operations; participates actively in the stock market; and its location in the town of Zelenograd, the leading center of the Russian microelectronics industry, is favorable for investment.
Address: Block 317A, Zelenograd, Moscow 103482
Telephone: (095) 534 1449
Fax: (095) 536 3755
The bank holds License No. 316 of December 9, 1992, from the Central Bank of the Russian Federation to perform foreign-currency operations.

TEMBR Bank, Interregional Fuel and Power Bank for Reconstruction and Development
Staff: Approximately 100
Turnover: 1,600 billion rubles (Jan-June 1995)
Business lines: opens and maintains accounts in rubles and foreign currencies and NOSTRO and LORO correspondent accounts; provides lending services; performs stock and trust operations; carries out all kinds of deposit operations; fulfills clients' orders in the securities market; uses the Bank-Client system; and handles Union Cards, STB-Cards, and Visa cards.
The bank has a branch in Blagoveshchensk, Amor.
Address: 8 First Volkonsky Lane, Moscow 103473
Telephone/Fax: (095) 299 5476
The bank holds Extended License No. 2764 of December 22, 1994, to perform operations in foreign currencies.

United Export-Import Bank
Staff: 350
Assets: $2.01 billion (January 1, 1995)
Business lines: attracts and places deposits and allocates loans; opens and maintains its clients' current and deposit accounts in rubles and foreign currencies; performs settlements of export-import operations, securities operations, and factoring and forfeiting operations; issues short-term loans to finance foreign-trade operations; places clients' resources in fund management projects and conducts various trust operations; finances projects; and carries out operations with precious metals, leasing, and trusts.
Postal address: P.O. Box 207, Moscow 107078
Legal address: 11 Masha Poryvaeva Street, Moscow 107078
Telephone: (095) 204 9780/7695
Fax: (095) 275 2205
The bank holds General License No. 2301 of April 20, 1993, from the Central Bank of the Russian Federation.

Unity Co-opbank, a joint stock consumer cooperative bank
Staff: 211
Annual turnover: 3.8 trillion rubles
Business lines: provides all kinds of banking services in rubles and foreign currency, including cash services for its clients; short-term and long-term lending services; for-

eign currency purchase/sale and conversion; international settlements relating to export and import operations; lending in foreign currency; purchase/sale of foreign currency at the stock exchange; purchase/sale of shares and certificates of deposit, government short-term bonds (GSB), and other securities; and consulting services.
Legal address: 15 Bolshoi Cherkassky Lane, Moscow 103626
Central Office address: 11 V. Radishchevskaya Street, Building 1, Moscow 109004
Telephone: (095) 915 3456
Fax: (095) 915 5001
The bank holds General License No. 56 of December 29, 1992, from the Central Bank of the Russian Federation.

Urengoibank, a joint stock commercial bank
Staff: 85
Annual turnover: 1.7 trillion rubles
Business lines: attracts and places money deposits, deposits, and credits under agreements with borrowers; opens and maintains accounts for its clients and correspondent banks, including foreign banks, and nostro accounts with correspondent banks, including foreign banks; finances capital investments from its own funds; issues, purchases, sells, and safeguards payment documents and securities; issues surities, guarantees, and other pecuniary obligations for third persons; and provides brokerage and consulting services.
Its main domestic correspondent banks are Vneshtorgbank, Eurofinance CB, Tokobank CB, Russian Stock Exchange Bank CB, and Tveruniversalbank; its main foreign correspondent banks are Raifeizen Zentralbank AG, Midland Bank, Credit Lyonnais, Internationale Nederlanden Bank, The Bank of New York, and Kommerzbank AG International.
Address: 47 Leninsky Avenue, Moscow 117913
Telephone: (095) 282 5865/6895
Fax: (095) 956 4855
The bank holds General License No. 2725 of March 1, 1994, from the Central Bank of the Russian Federation.

Zauralsky Business Joint Stock Commercial Bank
Staff: 380
Annual turnover: over $600 million
Business lines: carries out all kinds of banking services.
Address: 35 Kuibyshev Street, Kurgan, 640000, Russia
Telephone: (352 22) 2 1613
Fax: (352 22) 2 2025 and 2 3281
The bank holds License No. 1707 of January 27, 1995, from the Central Bank of the Russian Federation to perform foreign currency operations, with an additional permit of February 28, 1995, to perform operations with precious metals (gold and silver).

JOINT VENTURES AND FOREIGN FIRMS IN RUSSIA

Americom Moscow
Staff: approximately 200
Services: leasing and other business services, including a business center, printing and copying service, and computer center.

Address: 2 Berezhkovskaya Embankment, Moscow 121059 (Radison-Slavyanskaya Hotel)

Leasing services: telephone, (095) 941 8200/8815/8427; fax, (095) 941 8963/8376; international fax, (502) 224 1107

Business services: telephone, (095) 941 8427, 941 8739, and 941 8701; fax, (095) 240 6915 and 956 9894.

ASTELITE Telecommunications Services Joint Venture, a joint stock company (Telecom, Italy, and Astra, Russia)

Staff: 60

Business lines: provides telecommunications services in Moscow, St. Petersburg, and other areas across Russia: international and domestic telephones and faxes, international and domestic communication lines, data transmission, WSAT systems, multi-fax, and video conferencing.

Commercial Director: Mr. Esilo Mancuso

Address: 19 Khlebnikov, Floor 5, Moscow 121069

Telephone: (095) 292 0925, 928 4040 and (505) 214509

Fax: (095) 291 0832 and (505) 214510

Booz-Allen & Hamilton Inc.

Staff: 12

Business lines: provides consulting services in technologies and management; transportation systems; modernization of air-traffic-control systems; privatization and structural adaptation; corporate reengineering; information, financial, and banking systems; personnel management; and environmental problems.

Address: 15/500 Bolshoi Cherkassky Lane, Moscow 103626

Telephone: (095) 924 9778 and 927 0657

Telephone/Fax: (095) 923 6814

Clifford Chance Law Firm

Staff: 60, including 21 lawyers, five translators, three researchers (two with legal training) and four paralegals

Business lines: provides legal advice on foreign investments, bank deposits, securities, main markets, commercial laws, company laws, foreign trade, property, taxes, employment, intellectual property, litigations, and clientele.

Address: 24/27 Sadovaya-Samotechnaya Street, Floor 2, Moscow 103051

Telephone: (095) 258 5050

Fax: (095) 258 5051

Eastern Eagle International, Inc. (United States), Moscow representative office

Staff: 10

Annual turnover: $9 million

Business lines: provides consulting and intermediary services to Russian and foreign firms in attracting and allocating investments in Russian investment projects and in launching and expanding businesses in Russia.

Address: 113/1 Leninsky Avenue, Office E–302, Moscow 117198

Telephone: (095) 956 5915

Fax: (095) 956 5157

HFT Corporation, an east European finance and trade company, Moscow representative office

Business lines: operates in the fields of finance, trade and assistance, bank deposits, and industrial know-how, including power, agribusiness, and the environment.

Head office in New York: 654 Fifth Avenue, Olympic Tower Building, New York, N.Y. 10022

Telephone: (212) 759 8100

Fax: (212) 759 9758

Moscow office: 24 Povarskaya (Vorovsky) Street, Rooms 13–17, Moscow 121069

Telephone: (095) 202 7585 and 290 2844

Fax: (095) 230 2802

Paterson, Belknap, Webb and Tyler LLP Law Firm, Russian representative office in Moscow

Staff: 25 lawyers from the United States and CIS, working in CIS

Business lines: offers assistance to customers in day-to-day planning and analysis of country risk (in Russia, the Caucasus, and central Asia); carries out international projects with private partners; prepares and launches joint ventures and other investment projects; analyzes taxes and organizes tax-free days; purchases insurance for property confiscation, currency convertibility, civil disputes, and contract breaches; plans financial projects; handles bankruptcies and reschedules debt repayment; provides advice on laws relating to freight carriage, export controls, intellectual property (patents, copyright, and technology transfer), and labor laws; analyzes and provides advice on absolute immunity; resolves disputes through litigation, arbitral tribunals, mediation, and negotiations.

Address: 26 Koniushkovskaya Street, Moscow 123242

Telephone: (095) 253 9607

Telephone/Fax: (095) 564 8063 and (502) 221 1857

New York office: 1133 Avenue of the Americas, New York, N.Y. 110036–6710

Telephone: (212) 336 2000

Fax: (212) 336 2222

Radoslav Russian-American Joint Venture

Annual turnover: 8 billion rubles

Business lines: manufactures light-weight, heat-structured components for residential, public, and industrial buildings; foamed polystyrene heat insulation; and packaging materials. Designs facilities from own concepts.

Address: 5 Pereyaslavl-Zalessky, P.O. Box 106, Yaroslavl, 152140, Russia

Telephone/Fax: (08–535) 2 0277

Foreign partner: Radwa Corporation, U.S.

Rosgal Russian-American Insurance Company

Staff: 36

Annual turnover: 2.8 billion rubles

Business lines: offers all traditional types of insurance, including the ecological variety; Engages in stock market investment operations; Provides legal support for foreign investors in Russia, and for Russian securities floated in international markets.

Address: 36 Krasnovorotsky Drive, Moscow 107078

Telephone: (095) 975 1320

Fax: (095) 975 4637

Founder: Great America Life, U.S.

Rosintex Closed Joint Stock Company, a Russian-Portuguese joint venture
Staff: 60
Annual turnover: $6.5 million (1994)
Business lines: exports yarn, fabrics, and textile fibers; imports fabrics, garments for men and women, and textile equipment; manufactures women's clothing.
Address: 10 Savvinskaya Street, Zheleznodorozhny 143980, Moscow Region, Russia
Telephone: (095) 912 0779, 912 0666, 912 6983, and 272 3173
Fax: (095) 911 3378 and 911 1787

RussCon AG Moscow, a closed joint stock company
Staff: 14
Annual turnover: $160,000
Business lines: provides consulting and marketing services in promoting business in Russia; registers representative offices; conducts marketing research; provides information services; and handpicks staff for foreign firms.
Address: 20–1 Nagornaya Street, Offices 306 and 308, Moscow 113185
Telephone: (095) 127 4926
Fax: (095) 436 0396
Founder: RussCon AG, Biel, Switzerland

Russian-Italian Insurance Company
Staff: 10
Business lines: provides life, property, and liability insurance.
Address: 3 Nastasyinsky Lane, Block 2, Moscow 103006
Telephone: (095) 299 8032
Fax: (095) 299 7990
Founders: Rosgosstrakh JSC, Russia, and National Insurance Institute, Italy

Sawyer & Co.
A Russian closed joint stock company with 90% American capital.
Business lines: offers assistance in the lease, sale, and purchase of office, trade, and warehousing space; invests in real estate; provides services in real estate development and in construction and repairs.

Sekretan Troyanov & Partners, Moscow representative office of the Geneva law office
Staff: 9
Business lines: provides legal services; performs financial and banking operations; establishes companies; and attends to the legal execution of contracts.
Address: 35 Usachev Street, Moscow 119048
Telephone: (095) 245 5203
Fax: (095) 244 1663

Spencer Company Formations, Ltd., an offshore company
Staff: 42
Business lines and services: a leading offshore company with a registration firm and managed by qualified British lawyers, it has tax-free companies in Ireland, the United States, Switzerland, and other offshore jurisdictions; keeps bank accounts in

Switzerland, Ireland, the United Kingdom, and Latvia; handles Visa, EuroCard/MasterCard, and American Express credit cards; draws up individual offshore mechanisms; guarantees complete secrecy.

Also has offshore insurance companies, banks, British and Russian companies, and representative offices in Russia.

Address: 27–7 Krasnoarmeiskaya Street, Moscow 125319
Telephone: (095) 151 1882 and 151 1583
Fax: (095) 151 1882

CONSULTING, LEGAL, AND AUDITING FIRMS

A&A Closed Joint Stock Company

Staff: 20
Business lines: provides all types of legal and consulting services, including financial and banking business; developing projects in any business area; registering enterprises, including representative offices and enterprises with foreign interest; representing business interests in courts of law, courts of arbitration, and arbitral tribunals.
Address: 5/6 Volkhonka Street, Building 9A, Entrance 3, Floor 3, Moscow 121019
Telephone: (095) 203 9408
Fax: (095) 203 3398

ACEM, Russian Association for Consulting in Economics and Management

Staff: 2,000
Annual turnover: $36 million
Business lines: provides management consulting; auditing services; training; business information; a database on the latest Russian technologies and consulting support for their export; advice on export and import operations; technical programs of assistance to Russia; and training to Western businesspeople under the Doing Business in Russia program.
ACEM is an associate member of the European Federation of Economics and Management Consulting Associations.
Address: 20/12 Podsosensky Lane, Moscow 103062
Telephone: (095) 928 2616
Fax: (095) 917 5454 and 200 4452

ALRud Closed Joint Stock Company, a joint venture

Business lines: provides legal, consulting, and auditing services to Russian and foreign companies, organizations, and private customers, in particular information and advice on incorporation, international trade and other legal services; accounts and audits; general and private taxes, including tax assessments for employees of representative offices of foreign companies and representation of their interests to taxation bodies; multinational court proceedings and arbitral tribunals.
The company has partners in the United States, Great Britain, Switzerland, Spain, France, Portugal, and Cyprus.
Address: 10 Mansurovskaya Line, Building 1, Moscow 119034
Telephone: (095) 201 3595
Fax/Telephone (095) 201 3962

ARNI Audit Consulting Company, a closed joint stock company
Staff: 128
Business lines: provides auditing and accounting services that adhere to Russian and international standards in audits of banks, insurance companies, and enterprises; consulting services for bookkeeping and accounting operations; financial analysis; advice on tax policies, tax planning, and taxation of foreign nationals; management consulting, including assessment of business operations, market reviews and assessment of investment strategies, development of business plans, reorganization, and optimization of corporate businesses.
Address: 62 Usachev Street, Moscow 119048
Telephone: (095) 245 5517
Telephone/Fax: (095) 245 4961

Audit Felix, an auditing firm
Staff: 37
Annual turnover: $260,000
Business lines: conducts audits on open joint stock companies and other corporate bodies and insurance companies; restores and keeps accounts; draws up quarterly and annual statements; offers consulting services in accounting, including subscription services; and develops business plans.
Legal address: 12 Yaroslavskoe Highway, Block 1, Moscow 129348
Contact: 23, 1st Shchipovsky Lane, Office 37, Moscow 113054
Telephone/Fax: 236 4100

Consulting Joint Stock Company
Staff: 50
Business lines: provides consulting services in corporate finance; develops financial plans to optimize taxes; handles capital patriation and repatriation; develops and examines investment projects and manages investments; provides consulting services in international law; conducts legal examination of and support in controversial situations involving state authorities and government bodies, courts, and arbitration bodies; sets up and registers enterprises, including banks and insurance companies in Russia and abroad; issues bank guarantees for various operations.
Address: 29, 1st Tverskaya-Yamskaya Street, Moscow 125047
Telephone: (095) 204 1281 and 251 0105
Fax: (095) 207 6046
The company holds License No. 66 of July 13, 1995, from the Russian Ministry of Justice.

Gladyshev & Associates
Staff: 10
Business lines: provides legal and consulting services regarding foreign investments in Russia, taxes, real estate, and international commerce; insures foreign deposits; represents the interests of foreign companies to Russian government and legislative bodies, at courts, including Russian commercial arbitral tribunals. The firm's top priority is providing legal and consulting services for investments in Siberian projects.
Its foreign partners include De Diego, Benalal and Partners, Spain, 4 JZDA 54, Alcala, Madrid, Telephone: 522 2410; Raffine, Raffine-Curb, Goffard and Partners, France, 77 rue Boisier, Paris

Telephone: 44–17–48–00; and Properties of Mayfair, U.K. 54 Shepherd Market, Mayfair, London, Telephone: 0171–355–1156.

Guild of Russian Lawyers
Staff: Over 6,000
Business lines: the lawyers and economists of the guild's more-than 40 bars provide legal advice on such issues as defense of the rights, liberties, and legitimate interests of legal entities and private persons; privatization; external economic business; mortgage, lease, and land tenure. They check the reliability and solvency of partners and customers; prepare documents for state registration of legal entities, including those with foreign nationals on their staff and foreign interest in their capital; carry out economic and legal analysis and provide legal support for audits; and offer advice on notarial services.
Address: 3/5 Maly Poluyaroslavsky Lane, Moscow 107120
Telephone: (095) 916 2273 and 916 1248
Fax: (095) 975 2416

Intelservice Ltd.
Staff: 15
Business lines: offers notarial translation and legalization of documents with Russian official services; notarial services to foreign nationals and firms; registration of enterprises of all types and accreditation of foreign firms and representative offices in Moscow; executes licenses on trademarks and business activities in Russia; provides consulting and visa services.
Address of head office: 34–2 Bolshaya Molchanovka Street, Moscow 121069
Telephone: (095) 202 4872
Telephone/Fax: (095) 230 7724
Branch Office: 1 Kaluzhskaya Square, Moscow 117936
Telephone: (095) 230 3336

International Law Consulting Center on Corporate and Personal Income Taxes, a closed joint stock company
Staff: 204
Annual turnover: 6.2 billion rubles (1994)
Business lines: conducts audits; restores accounts; offers consultations on taxes and accounts; provides computerized accounting services and information software.
General Director: Vinokurov, Mikhail Dmitrievich
Address: 6/2 Kalanchevskaya Street, Moscow 107078
Telephone: (095) 975 1892
Fax: (095) 262 2004

Jurinflot International Law Office
Staff: 18
Business lines: provides legal services in Russia, CIS countries, and abroad for businesses, corporations, foreign investment, joint ventures, commercial projects, commercial contracts, loans and securities, maritime law, commercial legal proceedings, and arbitral courts; specializes in commercial law. It has nine partners, three of whom are associates.
Address: 30 Leningradsky Lane, Floor 4, P.O. Box 44, Moscow 125124
Telephone: (095) 214 6058, 214 0552, 214 2192, and (505) 211–301
Fax: (095) 212 8074 and (505) 211-306

Juris International Consultants
Staff: 25
Business lines: offers legal, tax-related, and accounting consultations and services; and provides audits. The firm's clients include Bestel Energy Resources, Parmalat, Mannesmann AG, Man Takraf, SKF, Rowenta, Tefal, Steilmann, and Schwarzkopf.
Address: 3/4 2nd Smolensky Lane, Moscow 121099
Telephone: (095) 241 9301
Fax: (095) 241 0044

JUS T Ltd. Law Firm, Moscow
Staff: 25 lawyers (15 in Moscow and 10 in St. Petersburg)
Business lines: offering all legal services regarding business matters in Russia and abroad, the firm's practice extends to international trade and investment, joint ventures and other types of business, defense of intellectual rights, technology transfers and issue of licenses, dissemination and acquisition of voting rights, money deposition in banks, trusteeship, taxation, labor issues, insurance, Russian privatization, property projects, construction contracts and other commercial deals, legal proceedings, arbitral court in Russia and abroad, and enforcement. The firm has a division in St. Petersburg and collaborates with Fromm Harnischeger-Ksoll, Dolce & Wenner, which has offices in Munich, Frankfurt, Dusseldorf, Paris, Berlin, Zurich, Budapest, and Shanghai.
Address: 43 Sivtsev Vrazhek Lane, Moscow 121002
Telephone: (095) 241 4459 and 241 4479
Fax: (095) 241 1948

Klishin & Partners, Attorneys at Law
Staff: Over 30 lawyers
Business lines: Provides legal support for state-owned and municipal enterprises being privatized in Russia; offers legal advice on taxes, duties, draft laws, bank deposits and insurance, foreign-currency and circulation-means regulation; offers legal support for investments, including mineral-resource development projects; and defends the interests of its clients in courts of law and arbitral tribunals.
Postal address: P.O. Box 315, Moscow 101000
Legal Address: 5/2 Antonov-Ovseenko Street, Moscow 123317
Telephone: (095) 925 0761, 925 0247, 925 0995, and 925 0834
Fax: (095) 924 9371

MaTEC-Juris Law Firm
Staff: 25
Annual turnover: $372,233
Business lines: provides consulting services in finance, establishment of banks and other lending institutions, defense of foreign investments, legal support for investment projects, arbitral tribunal proceedings, and notarial and other legal services.
Address: 16/16 Pokrovka Street, Building 1, Moscow 101000
Telephone: (095) 917 4216 and 917 4733
Fax: (095) 921 0016

MaTEC. Yakovlev & Partners Law Firm
Staff: 15
Annual turnover: 121.3 million rubles (1994)

Business lines: provides legal consultations on proceedings in courts of law, arbitration, and arbitral tribunals; tax planning; registration of entities of any legal organizational form; immigration consulting and legal support in all European countries and in Canada. The firm is a member of the Lawspan International network of legal firms.
Address: 10 Novaya Basmannaya Street, P.O. Box 32, Moscow 107078
Telephone: (095) 956 2992
Telephone/Fax: (095) 267 5148
Fax: (095) 956 2993

Prema-Invest Closed Joint Stock Company
Staff: 83
Annual turnover: $14 million
Business lines: provides investment consulting and finance brokering; carries out investment projects; purchases shares of major privatized enterprises from the population and resells them to major investors, including foreign investors; provides services in allocating direct investments (the purchase of controlling stakes in small and medium-sized privatized enterprises on behalf of investors).
Address: 26 Miasnitskaya Street, P.O. Box 2120, Moscow 101000
Telephone: (095) 925 9103
Fax: (095) 924 0464

Prist Consulting Firm, a closed joint stock company
Staff: 12
Annual turnover: $35,000
Business lines: Provides personnel consulting; evaluates personnel through unique testing systems; organizes and restructures work groups; and selects skilled personnel according to the employer's needs and criteria.
Address: 31 Staromonetny Lane, Moscow 109017
Telephone: (095) 231 1487 and 201 2127

Russian Financial Corporation
Staff: over 100
Annual turnover: $23,000
Business lines: examines, develops, and finances investment projects; carries on securities operations; provides financial consulting services; conducts banking operations; and sponsors conferences on financial and investment subjects.
Address: 1 Georgievsky Lane, Moscow 103009
Telephone: (095) 292 7482 and 292 8543
Fax: (095) 292 9107

SEKO Enterprise
Staff: 22
Annual turnover: $5.2 million (1994)
Business lines: provides consultations on property and land purchases; carries out investment projects in properties, organic chemistry, and telecommunications; distributes medical equipment and available trade items.
Address: 23/1 Novaya Bashmachnaya Street, P.O. Box 45, Moscow 107078
Telephone: (095) 216 0824 and 267 7843
Fax: (095) 420 2525 and 261 0824 (night)

Sobolev Consulting Agency
Staff: 20
Business lines: provides consultation regarding the financial market, the government bond and corporate securities markets, the structuring of investment portfolios, and the legal aspects of the financial market.
The agency carries out comprehensive analyses of enterprises and prepares new investment projects according to UNIDO standards.
Address: 3 Raspletin Street, Moscow 123060
Telephone: (095) 946 8756, 192 7931, and 192 9872
Fax: (095) 192 8857 and 946 9891

Success Technology Firm
Staff: 15
Annual turnover: $70,000
Business lines: represents the interests of foreign investors in Russia, deals in technologies, and handles finance and real estate.
Address: 2 Kozitsky Street, Office 51, Nizhny Novgorod 603122, Russia
Telephone/Fax: (831–2) 67 7617

Trian Audit Consulting Firm
Staff: 10
Business lines: conducts audits to confirm the authenticity of financial statements of commercial banks, insurance companies, joint ventures, foreign firms and their representative offices, and other enterprises and organizations; provides a full range of consulting services in taxation and accounting, and in the organization, keeping, and restoration of accounting; and draws up split and liquidation balance sheets.
Address: 144 Leninsky Avenue, Block 2, Moscow 117526
Telephone/Fax: 433 9895

Validata, affiliate of Yankelovich Partners International
Staff: 12 employees and 300 interviewers
Business lines: conducts market-research and public-opinion studies, based on the operations of over 40 branches in the former Soviet Union. Techniques used include quantitative approaches: (1) core groups, interviews, route studies of advertisement-type radio broadcasts; (2) key areas: studies of advertising and communications, attitude to and use of knowledge, studies of quality impression, customer satisfaction, concept research; (3) new products: development and testing, position studies, strategic market segments, political and social processes.
President: Masha M. Volkenstein, ESOMAR member
Address: 13/2 Orjonikidze Street, Moscow 117071
Telephone: (095) 945 9895
Fax: (095) 954 9896

Victoria International Law Firm
Staff: 15
Annual turnover: $50,000
Business lines: offers legal services in television, radio, film, and show business (establishment, registration, licensing, and legal backing of television and radio companies, defense of their copyrights, and related rights); provides insurance, offshore services, bank account handling, and real estate operations abroad.
Address: 13 Miasnitskaya, Building 4, Moscow 101941

Telephone: (095) 927 2319
Fax: (095) 975 2610

MISCELLANEOUS ENTERPRISES

Abris Closed Joint Stock Company
Staff: 10
Annual turnover: $300,000–350,000
Business lines: develops software for automating the preparatory stages in the garment industry; supplies equipment and software for designing and making applied advertisements; packaging samples; and automation of preparatory operations in the garment industry.
Its foreign partners are: SVENTA AG and ZUEND Systemtechnik AG, Switzerland; Arden Software Ltd., United Kingdom; and SCANVEC Co., Israel.
Legal address: 24/1 Chasovaya Street, Moscow 125315
Telephone: (095) 155 4574
Telephone/Fax: (095) 155 8682

Academy of Innovation Management (AIM), Russia's Foreign Policy Foundation
Staff: 60
Annual turnover: $25,000
Business lines: provides a world-class higher education in economics, in particular auditing (general, insurance, finance), finance management, securities, bank-lending services, certification of products and services, and law; arranges for classroom and field training in Russia and elsewhere; and issues certificates confirming adherence of graduation requirements to UNESCO system standards.
Address: 16A Novaya Basmannaya Street, Moscow 107078
Telephone: (095) 263 9481
Fax: (095) 267 8695

Agency WPS
WPS USA, Inc. in New York
Staff: 120 (6 in WPS USA)
Business lines: provides electronic media monitoring, a newspaper-clipping service; a Russian-to-English translation service, electronic reference-book publishing, transcripts and recordings of television and radio broadcasts.
Address: 128–1 Varshavskoe Highway, Moscow 113587
Telephone: (095) 955 2950 and 955 2708
Fax: (095) 952 3022
WPS USA: 330 East 38th Street, No. 10M, New York, N.Y., 10016
Telephone/Fax: (212) 599 2305 and (212) 949 7571

AMITI small business
Staff: 6
Annual turnover: $150,000
Business lines: provides services for the promotion of goods to the Russian market; offers exhibition services; conducts market-research studies; and provides advertising.

Address: P.O. Box 15, Moscow 123458
Telephone/Fax: (095) 942 2379

Analytical and Marketing Research Consulting Company
Staff: 80
Annual turnover: $120,000
Business lines: develops, designs, monitors, and presents investment projects that adhere to world standards; draws up regional investment projects; drafts stock-issue prospectuses for privatized enterprises and housing certificates; and promotes practices public relations.
Address: 11 Novinsky Boulevard, Moscow 121099
Telephone: (095) 255 4036, 255 4366, and 255 4881
Fax: (095) 255 4607 and 253 7982

APR-MEDIA Joint-Stock Company
Staff: 200
Annual turnover: $54 million
Business lines: electronic, print, and outdoor advertising; and media planning and buying,
Address: 3 Tsvetnoi Boulevard, Moscow 103051
Telephone: (095) 200 4594
Fax: (095) 923 4958

Aspect Press Joint Stock Company
Staff: 15
Annual turnover: $500,000
Business lines: publishes Russian and foreign-language textbooks for high school, colleges, and institutes in the disciplines of history, economics, political science, religion, the environment, literature, philosophy, and culture. Under a separate program, the company is putting out a 33-volume Russian biographical dictionary. A total of 50 titles were published in 1995.
Address: 23 Plekhanov Street, Block 3, Moscow 111398
Telephone: (095) 309 4015
Fax: (095) 309 1166 and 200 3937

Avrora Advertising Agency
Staff: 90
Annual turnover: $111 million
Business lines: provides marketing services and a complete package of advertising services; does media planning; produces advertising materials for all the mass media; and analyzes the efficiency of advertising campaigns.
Address: 21 Bolshaya Molchanovka Street, Building 1, Moscow 121069
Telephone: (095) 202 5959
Fax: (095) 956 9215

Baltic Communications Ltd. (BCL)
Annual turnover: $6 million
Business lines: provides international communication services, including international direct telephone lines: leasing of office space to international tenants; telephone installation in Moscow; the sale, installation, and maintenance of PABX equipment in hotels and offices; BCL public telephones.

The company's biggest stockholder is Cable & Wireless Plc, United Kingdom.
Address: 4 Konnogvardeisky Boulevard, St. Petersburg 190000, Russia
Telephone: (812) 315 0073
Fax: (812) 314 8660

BANKOS Closed Joint Stock Company (Banking Equipment and Maintenance)
Staff: 21
Annual turnover: $2 million
Business lines: provides computer maintenance services under warranty and post-warranty arrangements, and intermediary services in the marketing of computers, printers, components, bank office equipment, and computer accessories.
Address: 46 Novocheremushkinskaya Street, Moscow 117418
Telephone: (095) 128 9022, 128 9171, and 128 7738
Fax: (095) 128 9133

Biology Research Institute, Irkutsk State University
Staff: 120
Annual turnover: $200,000
Business lines: conducts basic research into the ecosystems of Lake Baikal and adjacent areas; sponsors environment-friendly exploratory, educational, and scientific tours on Lake Baikal and the Angara River.
Address: 3 Lenin Street, P.O. Box 24, Irkutsk 664003, Russia
Telephone: (395 2) 34 4277
Fax: (395 2) 34 5207

Chrysanthemum Firm
Staff: 25
Annual turnover: $2 million
Business lines: carries on operations involving artificial furs and primary materials for producing them, and offers dealer services.
Address: 3A, 15th Parkovaya Street, Moscow 105203
Telephone: (095) 465 5262, 465 2349, and 965 3965
Fax: (095) 465 0245

Dialogue Closed Holding Company (joint stock company and joint venture)
Staff: 6,000
Annual turnover: over $300 million
Business lines: assembles and sells computers; provides system integration; distributes copying equipment, office telephone stations, cash registers, office equipment, and engineering products; carries on financial and trading operations; provides legal, architectural, construction, advertising, medical, warehousing, and transportation services. The company's foreign partner is Management Partners Int., United States.
Address: 13 Spartakovskaya Street, Moscow 107066
Telephone: (095) 261 4407 and 261 4417
Fax: (095) 265 5714

DialogueScience Inc.
Staff: 22 full-time and 17 part-time employees
Annual turnover: $300,000
Business lines: produces the DialogueScience Antivirus Kit, the most popular computer-virus-fighting software in Russia, capable of detecting and removing over

3,000 viruses; disk scanning at the BIOS level is used to detect all new and unknown viruses, reliably neutralizing 97% of file viruses and 100% of boot viruses. Its U.S. stockholder is MPI Inc., Chicago.
Address: 13 Spartakovskaya Street, Moscow 107066
Telephone/Fax: (095) 938 2855 and 938 2970

Eurikom-Kuzbass Firm
Staff: 20
Annual turnover: $450,000
Business lines: provides design, installation and maintenance, services for computer networks, and electronic security systems for banks and offices; and supplies and services personal computers.
Address: 4 Festivalnaya Street, Novokuznetsk 654005, Russia
Telephone: (3843) 44 4671
Fax: (3843) 46 0792

Favorite Advertising Agency
Staff: 45
Business lines: designs and places advertisements on Moscow trolleybuses, trams, and buses.
Address: 31 Michurinsky Avenue, Block 1, Moscow 117607
Telephone/Fax: (095) 932 3243

Force R&D Innovation Enterprise
Staff: 120
Annual turnover: $2.8 million
Business lines: provides system integration, banking automation, licensed installation of Oracle products with full support services (installation, telephone hot-line maintenance, consultations, training facilities) and development of applied systems in distributed media.
Address: 15 Chayanov Street, Block 5, Floor 9, Moscow 125267
Telephone: (095) 973 4066 and 973 4067
Fax: (095) 251 1073

Garant Service R&D Enterprise
Staff: 100
Annual turnover: $1 million
Business lines: compiles databases on Russian legislative acts in Russian and English for IBM-compatible computers and through on-line networks.
Address: Physics Department, Moscow University, Lebedev Street, Moscow 119899
Telephone: (095) 939 1888, 939 1605, and 939 0806
Fax: (095) 938 2873 and 939 0071

Garant International, St. Petersburg Branch
Staff: 30
Annual turnover: $150,000
Business lines: Compiles databases on Russian legislative acts in Russian and English for IBM-compatible computers and through on-line networks.
Address: 22 Malaya Posadskaya Street, St. Petersburg 197046

Telephone: (812) 119 6322
Fax: (812) 119 6399

Giatcint Closed Joint Stock Company

Staff: 12
Business lines: provides scientific and technological developments in physics and materials science (structure and properties of materials at hardening, solidification, growth, and extrusion), including composites; offers industrial-design services, printing and stamp making, and legal services.
Address: 1 First Kolobovsky Lane, Moscow 103051
Telephone: (095) 487 3754
Telephone/Fax: (095) 299 1984

Greatis Joint Stock Company

Staff: 105
Annual turnover: $9.8 million
Business lines: advertising of all types.
Address: 23 Vorontsovskaya Street, Moscow 109147
Telephone/Fax: (095) 127 0536 and 127 5980

Hinocon Ltd., Moscow

Staff: 15
Annual turnover: $5 million
Business lines: Hinocon Foods supplies food products. Hinocon Ligistica provides customs and transportation services, while Hinocon Exports watches, decorations, and other manufactured goods.
Address: 11 Eighth Tekstilshchikov Street, Block 3, Moscow 109120
Telephone: (095) 235 0935, 235 1350, and 235 9106
Fax: (095) 235 8746

Intermicro Open Joint Stock Company

Staff: 120
Annual turnover: approximately $10 million (1994)
Business lines: supplies computerized publishing systems and printing complexes with turnkey operations; distributes equipment from prominent computer companies; provides warranty services and post-sale maintenance; and conducts training for its staff. The company has a developed infrastructure, with several branches in Russia and the CIS countries.
Address: 39A Nizhnaya Krasnoselskaya Street, Moscow 107066
Telephone: (095) 261 3047 and 261 0447
Fax: (095) 267 3400

International Business Academy

Staff: 25
Annual turnover: $380,000
Business lines: provides training programs for short-term postgraduate still improvement in a variety of business areas; and engages in consulting, scientific, methodological, and publishing activities.
Address: 2 Kolskaya Street, Moscow 129329
Telephone: (095) 189 1525
Fax: (095) 189 2544 and 180 0530

Lenfintorg Foreign Trade Association
Staff: 120
Annual turnover: approximately $200 million
Business lines: carries on export, import, reexport, and barter operations in a wide range of goods; undertakes investment operations in Russia and elsewhere; and provides consulting services in foreign-trade organization and marketing-research services for a wide variety of goods.
Address: 20 Chaikovsky Street, St. Petersburg 191123
Telephone: (812) 275 9102
Fax: (812) 275 9108

Menatep-Impex Concern
Staff: 140
Annual turnover: $350 million
Business lines: engages in trade and investment projects; exports oil and ferrous and nonferrous metals; and imports and processes raw sugar.
Address: 20 Shchipok Street, Moscow 113054
Telephone: (095) 956 6163 and 956 6164
Fax: (095) 956 6329

Mezhdunarodnaya Kniga Association
Staff: 340
Business lines: exports and imports books, albums, periodicals, postage stamps, audio and video media, works of art, and handicrafts; publishes books and produces CD-ROMs; assigns copyrights; and provides advertising, printing, and consulting services.
Address: 39 Bolshaya Yakimanka Street, Moscow 117049
Telephone: (095) 238 4600
Fax: (095) 230 2117

Mosexpo Joint Stock Company
Staff: 250
Annual turnover: $6.9 million
Business lines: carries on wholesale trade in jewelry; exports nonferrous metals; imports consumer goods; conducts financial and investment operations; and provides customs and warehousing services.
Address: 10 Nametkin Street, Moscow 117420
Telephone: (095) 120 9009
Fax: (095) 310 7092 and 330 2674

Nefteyugansk United Air Unit, an open joint stock company
Staff: 800
Annual turnover: $5.31 million
Business lines: arranges and sells charter flights on passenger airliners; uses helicopters in economic applications; provides airliner and helicopter maintenance services, including airport services.
Address: Airport, Nefteyugansk 626430, Tyumen, Russia
Telephone: 2 3790
Fax: 2 9759

PC Magazine/Russian Edition, PC Week/Russian Edition
Staff: 150
Business lines: publishes the Russian editions of *PC Magazine* and *PC Week,* and *Who's Who in the Russian Computer Market;* prepares advertising and printing products, and designs advertising campaigns, for computer companies; conducts marketing research on the Russian computer market.
Address: SK Press, Moscow University Press, 5/7 Bolshaya Nikitskaya Street, Moscow 103009
Telephone: (095) 203 1485, 203 1338, 203 0434, and 229 5969
Fax: (095) 229 6013

Pelican Closed Joint Stock Company
Staff: 63
Annual turnover: $235 million
Business lines: undertakes investment projects in real estate construction and renovation; carries on wholesale trade in sugar, cocoa, and other foodstuffs; trades on the stock market.
Address: 12 First Kadashevsky Lane, Building 1, Moscow 113035
Telephone: (095) 231 0309
Fax: (095) 233 4933

Renaissance Hotel, Moscow
Address: 18/1 Olympiisky Avenue, Moscow 129110
Telephone: (095) 93 9000 and 931 9833
Fax: (095) 931 9076 and 931 9876
Satellite telephone: (7–502) 223 9000
Satellite fax: (7–502) 223 9076

Russian Gallery Closed Joint Stock Company
Staff: 35
Business lines: arranges and holds major festivals and exhibitions in Russia and abroad; designs and decorates interior settings for these events; develops corporate graphic images and applies corporate logos to works of art and souvenirs; revives handicraft traditions; and produces copies and authors' originals from bronze, china, and glass.
Address: 5 Vozdvizhenka Street, Moscow 121019
Telephone: (095) 298 6563
Telephone/Fax: (095) 202 3979

Russian Information Center for Science and Engineering
Staff: 300
Annual turnover: $400,000
Business lines: builds and maintains a national stock and database of reports on research and development projects, experimental designs, and dissertations; publishes informational material; conducts thematic inquiries and searches in the database; performs copying and printing tasks; distributes information via magnetic tape and CD-ROMs; and develops software products.
Address: 14 Smolnaya Street, Moscow 125493
Telephone: (095) 456 7681
Fax: (095) 456 7521

Russian Public Relations Group, Ltd.
Staff: 60
Business lines: monitors television, radio, print, and outdoor advertising in Moscow and other major Russian cities; analyzes, records, and provides television and press materials; offers clipping services; conducts market research; and promotes public relations.
Address: 10 Geroev Panfilovtsev Street, Offices 808–809, Moscow 123363
Telephone: (095) 496 9070 and 495 1313
Fax/Telephone: (095) 494 0455

SCAN Firm, a repair and construction design enterprise
Business lines: conducts engineering evaluations of buildings, including engineering studies, examination of building structures, preparation of design documents regarding major repairs, carrying out architectural and construction projects; and utilizes injection techniques to reinforce deformed structures; develops software programs and databases.
Address: 4 Yakimanskaya Embankment, Moscow 109180
Telephone: (095) 238 0234
Telephone/Fax: (095) 230 7842

Sporting and Leisure Goods Joint Stock Company
Staff: 415
Annual turnover: $10.5 million
Business lines: sells leisure and sporting goods, including cars, on a retail and limited wholesale basis, and goods on commission.
Address: 21 Lenin Street, P.O. Box 273, Kazan 420111, Tatar
Telephone/Fax: (8432) 32 0160

St. Petersburg Telephone Network, an open joint stock company
Staff: 6,300
Annual turnover: $42.5 million
Business lines: provides urban telephone services.
Address: 24 Bolshaya Morskaya Street, St. Petersburg 191186
Telephone: (812) 315 4105
Fax: (812) 315 4636

SYMCO Association (Official Consular Service of the Confederation of Russian Business Unions)
Staff: 14
Annual turnover: $21,000
Business lines: provides program planning, organization, and support for cooperative projects between Russian and foreign business partners in the private, public, and government sectors; organizes and conducts symposiums, conferences, trade and arts exhibitions, and research exhibitions; provides various services, including consular (passports, entry and exit visas), protocol, transportation, interpretation and translation, hotel reservations; and carries out cultural programs.
The association has business partners in Russia (including the TEKO firm, the Small Business Support Foundation, and the Russian Foreign Trade Academy) and abroad the National Democratic Institute, the Center for International Private Enterprise, and The Heritage Foundation, United States, and the Netherlands Measurement Institute.
Address: 19 Novy Arbat Street, Room 309, Moscow 103025
Telephone: (095) 203 2340
Telephone/Fax: (095) 203 8517 and 425 3195

INDEX